WEBSTER'S
NEW
DICTIONARY

COMPACT EDITION

© Geddes & Grosset Ltd., New Lanark, Scotland 1990

Published by Russell, Geddes & Grosset, Windsor Court,
New York, N.Y. U.S.A.

Printed in the U.S.A.

This book is not published by the original publishers of
WEBSTER'S DICTIONARY or by their successors.

Pronunciation guide

Accented syllables are marked thus ', e.g. *ban'dit, as-ton'ish-ing*

Vowels and diphthongs in accented syllables

Sound		Examples	Pronunciation
as in	(1) fate	name, aid, rein	*nām, ād, rān*
	(2) bare	tare, wear, hair, heir	*tār, wār, hār, ār*
as in	(1) father	grass, path	*gräss, päth*
	(2) far	harm, heart, palm	*härm, härt, päm*
as in	sat	bad, have	*bad, hav*
as in	(1) me	lean, keel, chief, sieze	*lēn, kēl, chēf, sēz*
	(2) fear	gear, sheer, here, bier	*gēr, shēr, hēr, bēr*
as in	pet	red, thread, said, bury	*red, thred, sed, ber'i*
as in	(1) mine	side, shy, dye, height	*sīd, shī, dī, hīt*
	(2) sire	hire, byre	*hīr, bīr*
as in	bid	pin, busy, hymn	*pin, biz'i, him*
as in	(1) mote	bone, road, foe, dough	*bōn, rōd, fō, dō*
	(2) more	fore, soar, floor	*fōr, sōr, flōr*
as in	got	shot, shone	*shot, shon*
as in	(1) all	haul, lawn, fall, bought	*höl, lön, föl, böt*
	(2) for	swarm, horn	*swörm, hörn*
as in	(1) moon	fool, sou	*fōōl, sōō*
	(2) poor	boor, tour	*bōōr, tōōr*
as in	foot	good, full, would	*good, fool, wood*
as in	(1) mute	tune, due, newt, view	*tūn, dū, nūt, vū*
	(2) pure	endure	*en-dūr'*
as in	bud	run, love	*run, luv*
as in	her	heard, bird, world, absurd	*hûrd, bûrd, wûrld, absûrd'*
as in	(1) house	mount, frown	*mownt, frown*
	(2) hour	sour	*sowr*
as in	boy	toy, buoy, soil	*toi, boi, soil*

Certain acceptable variations in pronunciation of vowels before *r* are not allowed for in the table above. For instance, the *o* in *port* is often pronounced *ŏ*.

Vowels of Unaccented Syllables

Sound		Examples	Pronunciation
as in	(1) signal	mental, infant, desperate	*men'tàl, in'fànt, des'per-àt*
	(2) beggar	altar	*ölt'àr*
as in	(1) moment	potent	*pōtènt*
	(2) silver	never	*nev'èr*
as in	perish	merit, minute, mountain, silly	*mer'it, min'it, mownt'in, sil'i*
as in	(1) abbot	faggot, bishop	*fag'òt, bish'òp*
	(2) doctor	sailor, rigor	*sāl'òr, rig'òr*
as in	(1) circus	nimbus, bulbous	*nim'bùs, bul'bùs*
	(2) figure	treasure	*trezh'ùr*
	(3) tenure	adventure	*ad-ven'tyùr*
			(or *ad-ven'chùr* see below)

Consonants

Sound		Examples	Pronunciation
ch	as in cheap	church, feature, match	*chúrch, fē'chùr* (or *fē'tyùr*), *mach*
f	as in fate	fell, phone, laugh	*fel, fōn, lāf*
g	as in good	game, mitigate, guard, ghastly	*gām, mit'i-gāt, gärd, gäst'li*
gw	as in penguin	linguist	*ling'gwist*
gz	as in example	exist	*egz-ist'*
H	as in loch	pibroch, leprechaun	*pē'broH, lep'rè-Hôn*
hw	as in where	what	*hwot*
j	as in just	jade, gentle, midge, rigid, region	*jād, jen'tl, mij, rij'id, rē'jòn*
k	as in keel	kite, cold, chorus	*kīt, kōld, kō'rus* (or *kò'rus*)
ks	as in axe	explain	*eks-plān'*
kw	as in queen	quite, choir, coiffeur	*kwīt, kwīr, kwäf-ær'*
ng	as in sing	rang, rank, longer	*rang, rangk, long'gèr*
s	as in see	sole, cede, scent, mass	*sōl, sēd, sent, mas*
sh	as in shine	shape, machine, sugar, pressure, precious, mention	*shāp, ma-shēn, shoog'àr, presh'ùr, presh'ùs, men'sh(ò)n*
th	as in thin	theme, health	*thēm, helth*
TH	as in then	though, bathe	*THō, bāTH*
y	as in yet	young, super, feature	*yung, s(y)ōō'pèr, fē'tyùr* (or *fē'chùr*)
z	as in zone	zero, maze, muse, xylem, roads	*zē'rò, māz, mūz, zīlem, rōdz*
zh	as in azure	measure, vision, rouge	*mezh'ùr, vizh'(ò)n, rōozh*

Additional sounds in foreign words

Sound		Examples	Pronunciation
e	as in père	maître	*metr'*
ø	as in deux	douloureux	*dōo-lōo-rø*
œ	as in œuvre	fauteuil, fleur	*fō-tœ-y', flœr*
ü	as in Führer		*fü'rèr*

Nasalised vowels

ã	as in blanc	outrance, mélange	*ōō-trãs, mā-lãzh*
ɛ̃	as in vin	poussin, timbre	*pōos-ɛ̃, tẽbr'*
ɔ̃	as in mon	accompli, convenance	*a-kɔ̃-plē, kɔ̃'ve-nãs*
œ̃	as in lundi	un	*œ̃*

An apostrophe is used to mark such pronunciations as t'h
(where the sound is two separate consonants. It is also used in such words as timbre (*tẽbr'*).

Abbreviations used in the dictionary

bbrev	abbreviation	E	East
bl	ablative	econ	economics
cc	accusative	e.g	(L. *exempli gratia*)
dj(s)	adjective(s)		for example
dv(s)	adverb(s)	elect	electricity
ero	aeronautics	erron	erroneous(ly)
lg	algebra	esp	especially
nat	anatomy	ety	etymology
nc	ancient(ly)		
nthrop	anthropology	facet	facetiously
or	aorist	fem	feminine
pp	apparently	fig	figuratively
pprox	approximately	foll	followed
rch	archaic		following
rcheol	archeology	freq	frequently
rchit	architecture	fut	future
rith	arithmetic		
strol	astrology	gen	genitive
stron	astronomy	geog	geography
t no or	atomic number	geol	geology
t numb		geom	geometry
		gram	grammar
B	Bible (Authorised Version)		
iol	biology	her	heraldry
ook-k	book-keeping	hist	history
ot	botany		
	(L. *circa*) about	i.e	(L. *id est*)
ap	capital		that is
ent	century	imit	imitative
f	(L. *confer*) compare	imper	imperative
hem	chemistry	impers	impersonal(ly)
og	cognate	incl	including
oll	colloquial(ly)	indic	indicative
omp	comparative	infin	infinitive
onj	conjunction	inten	intensive
onn	connected	interj	interjection
	connection	interrog	interrogative(ly)
ontr	contracted	intrans	intransitive
	contraction		
ook	cookery	lit	literal(ly)
orr	corruption		
	corresponding	mach	machinery
at	dative	masc	masculine
emons	demonstrative	math	mathematics
er	derived	mech	mechanics
	derivation	med	medicine
erog	derogatory	mil	military
	derogatorily	min	mineralogy
ial	dialectal	mod	modern
Dict	Dictionary	mus	music
im	diminutive	myth	mythology
ub	dubious, doubtful		

N	North	*pron(s)*	pronoun(s)
n(s)	noun(s)	*pron*	pronounced
naut	nautical		pronunciation
neg	negative	*pros*	prosody
neut	neuter	*psych*	psychology
nom	nominative		
n pl	noun plural		
n sing	noun singular	*q v*	(L. *quod vide*)
N T	New Testament		which see
	(Authorised Version)		
		R C	Roman Catholic
obs	obsolete	*reflex*	reflexive
opp	opposed	*rel*	related, relative
orig	original(ly)		
	origin		
O T	Old Testament	*S*	South
	(Authorised Version)	*Shak*	Shakespeare
		sing	singular
		subj	subjunctive
p	participle	*suffx*	suffix
p adj	participial adjective	*superl*	superlative
pa p	past participle		
part	participle		
pass	passive	*theat*	theatre
pa t	past tense	*theol*	theology
perf	perfect	*trans*	transitive
perh	perhaps		translation
pers	person(al)	*trig*	trigonometry
pfx	prefix	*TV*	television
phil(os)	philosophy		
phonet	phonetics		
phot	photography	*ult*	ultimately
phys	physics	*usu*	usually
pl	plural		
poet	poetical		
pop	popular(ly)	*vb(s)*	verbs
poss	possessive	*v(s) i*	verb(s) intransitive
	possibly	*voc*	vocative
Pr Bk	Book of Common	*v(s) t*	verb(s) transitive
	Prayer	*vulg*	vulgar(ly)
pr p	present participle		
prep	preposition		
pres	present	*W*	West
print	printing		
priv	privative		
prob	probably	*zool*	zoology

The Dictionary

A

a [a] (when emphatic sometimes ā), *adj* the indefinite article, a broken-down form of **an**, used before words beginning with the sound of a consonant; one; any.

A-bomb [ā'bomb] *n* atomic bomb.

aardvark [ärd'värk] *n* an edentate (*Orycteropus afer*) of Africa.

aback [a-bak'] *adv* (*naut*) (of sails) pressed backward against the mast by the wind—**taken aback**, taken by surprise.

abacus [ab'a-kus] *n* a frame with sliding beads for doing arithmetic.

abaft [a-bäft'] *prep* behind.

abandon [a-ban'don] *vt* to give up; to desert; to yield (oneself) without restraint (to).—*n* **aban'don**, careless freedom of action.—*adj* **aban'doned**, deserted; very wicked, unrestrained.—*n* **aban'donment**.

abase [a-bās'] *vt* to humble;—*n* **abase'ment**.

abash [a-bash'] *vt* to disconcert, mortify.—*n* **abash'ment**, confusion from shame.

abate [a-bāt'] *vti* to make or become less; (*law*) to end.—*n* **abate'ment**, the act of abating; the sum or quantity abated.

abattoir [ab'a-twär] *n* a slaughter house.

abbacy [ab'a-si] *n* the office, tenure, etc.— of an abbot; *adj* **abbatial** [ab-ā'shál].

abbess [ab'es] *n* the head of a convent of nuns.

abbey [ab'i] *n* a convent or monastery; the church attached to it;—*pl* **abb'eys**.

abbot [ab'ot] *n* the head of a monestery.

abbreviate [a-brē'vi-āt] *vt* to make shorter, esp to shorten (a word) by omitting letters.—*n* **abbrevā'tion**, an act of shortening; a shortened form.

abdicate [ab'di-kāt] *vti* formally to renounce or give up (office or dignity).—*n* **abdicā'tion**.

abdomen [ab'dó-mén, ab-dō'men] *n* the belly.

abduct [ab-dukt'] *vt* to take away by force.—*ns* **abduc'tion**, **abduc'tor**.

abeam [a-bēm'] *adv* (*naut*) on a line at right angles to a ship's keel.

aberrant [ab-er'ánt] *adj* deviating from what is usual, normal, or right.—*n* **aberrā'tion**.

abet [a-bet'] *vt* to encourage or aid;—*pr p* **abett'ing**; *pt p* **abbett'ed**.—*n* **abett'er**, **abett'or**.

abeyance [a-bā'áns] *n* a state of suspension; temporary inactivity.

abhor [ab-hör'] *vt* to shrink from with horror; to detest, loathe;—*pr p* **abhorr'ing**; *pt p* **abhorred'**.—*n* **abhorr'ence** [-hor'], extreme loathing.—*adj* **abhorr'ent**, detestable.

abide [a-bīd'] *vt* to endure; to tolerate.—*vi* to remain in a place; (*arch*) to reside.—*pt* and *pt p* **abode'**.

ability [a-bil'i-ti] *n* being able; power to do; talent; skill.—*pl* **abil'ities**.

abject [ab'jekt] *adj* miserable; wretched; degraded.—*n* **abjec'-tion**.—*adv* **ab'jectly**.

abjure [ab-jōōr'] *vt* to renounce on oath; to renounce.—*n* **abjurā'tion**.

ablative [ab'lat-iv] *adj* (*gram*) in or belonging to a case which in Latin, etc. denotes direction from a place, time and source, agent, instrument, etc.—*n* the ablative case.

ablaze [a-blāz'] *adj* flaming; greatly excited.—*adv* on fire.

able [ā'bl] *adj* having enough strength, power or means (to do a thing); talented; skilled; (*law*) competent.—*adv* **a'bly**.—*adj* **a'ble-bod'ied**, strong.

ablution [á-blōō'sh(ó)n] *n* the washing of one's body, or part of it.

abnegate [ab'ni-gāt] *vt* to deny and refuse; to renounce.—*n* **abnegā'tion**.

abnormal [ab-nör'mál] *adj* not normal, average, or typical; irregular.—*n* **abnormal'ity**—*adv* **abnor'mally**.

aboard [a-börd', -börd] *adv*, *prep* on or in (a ship, a train, etc.); alongside.

abode¹ [a-bōd'] *n* a home, residence.

abode² [a-bōd'] *pt p, pt p* of **abide**

abolish [ab-ol'ish] *vt* to put an end to; to annul.—*ns* **aboli'tion**, the act of abolishing; **Abolition**, the abolishing of slavery in the US; **aboli'tionist**.

abominate [ab-om'in-āt] *vt* to abhor, to detest extremely.—*adj*

abom'inable, hateful, detestable.—*n* **abom'inableness**.—*adv* **abom'inably**.

aborigine [ab-o-rij'in-ē] *n* any of the first known inhabitants of a region.—*adj* **aborig'inal**.

abort [ab-ört'] *vi* to miscarry in birth; to come to nothing.—*vt* to cause to abort; to terminate prematurely.—*n* the premature termination of the flight of an aircraft, —*adj* **abort'ed**.—*n* **abor'tion**, —*adj* **abort'ive**.

abound [ab-ownd'] *vi* to overflow, be in great plenty; to teem.

about [a-bowt'] *prep* on all sides of; near to; with; on the point of; concerning.—*adv* all around; near.

above [a-buv'] *prep* over, on top of; better or more than.

abrade [ab-rād'] *vt* to scrape away, to rub off.—*n* **abrasion** [ab-rā'zh(ó)n], the act of rubbing off; an abraded place.—*adj* **abrā'sive** [-ziv, -siv].

abreast [a-brest'] *adv* side by side; informed (of); aware.

abridge [a-brij'] *vt* to shorten, lessen, curtail; to shorten by using fewer words but keeping the substance.—*n* **abridg'-ment**, **abridge'ment**.

abroad [a-bröd'] *adv* over a wide area; out of doors; in circulation, current; at large; in or to another country.

abrogate [ab'ro-gāt] *vt* to abolish; to repeal; to annul.—*n* **abrogā'tion**.

abrupt [ab-rupt'] *adj* sudden; unexpected; brusque; very steep; disconnected, as some writing.—*adv* **abrupt'ly**.—*n* **abrupt'ness**.

abscess [ab'ses] *n* an inflamed area, containing pus localized in some tissue of the body.

abscond [ab-skond'] *vi* to hide, or get out of the way, esp in order to escape a legal process.

abseil [ap'zīl, ab-sīl'] *vi* to lower oneself down a rock face using a double rope attached to a higher point.—*n* **abseiling**.

absent [ab'sènt] *adj* away, not present; not existing; inattentive.—*adv* **ab'sently**, in an inattentive manner.—*vt* **absent'**, to keep (oneself) away.—*n* **ab'sence**, the state of being away, the time of this; a lack, **absentēē**, one who is absent, as from work.

absolute [ab'sól-(y)ōōt] *adj* free from limits or conditions; complete; certain, positive; perfect, pure; not relative (*inf*) utter, out-and-out *an absolute shame*.—*adv* **ab'solutely**.—*ns* **ab'soluteness**; **ab'solutism**.

absolution [ab-sol-(y)ōō'sh(ó)n] *n* forgiveness; remission of sin or its penalty.

absolve [ab-zolv', or -solv'] *vt* to set free from guilt, a duty, etc.; to give religious absolution to.

absorb [ab-sörb'] *vt* to suck up; to take in; to swallow up; to incorporate; to pay for (costs, etc.); to take in (a shock) without recoil; to engage wholly.—*adj* **absorb'able**.—*n* **absorbabil'ity**.—*advs* **absorb'edly**; **absorb'ingly**.

abstain [ab-stān'] *vi* to keep oneself from some indulgence, esp from drinking alcohol; to refrain from using one's vote.—*ns* **abstain'er**, drinks; **absten'tion**.

abstemious [ab-stēm'i-us] *adj* temperate; sparing in food, drink or enjoyments.—*adv* **abstem'iously**.—*n* **abstem'iousness**.

abstinent [ab'stin-ént] *adj* abstaining from.—*ns* **ab'stinence**, **ab'stinency**, an abstaining or refraining, esp from food and drink.

abstract [ab-strakt'] *vt* to remove; to summarize in writing.—*adj* **abstract'ed**, not paying attention.—*adv* **abstract'edly**,—*ns* **abstract'edness**; **abstraction**.—*adj* **abstract** [ab'strakt], art.

abstruse [ab-strōōs'] *adj* difficult to understand.—*adv* **abstruse'ly**.—*n* **abstruse'ness**.

absurd [ab-sûrd'] *adj* obviously unreasonable, ridiculous.—*ns* **absurd'ness**; **absurd'ity**,—*adv* **absurd'ly**.

abundance [ab-und'áns] *n* ample sufficiency; great plenty.—*adj* **abund'ant**, plentiful; rich (in).—*adv* **abund'antly**.

abuse [ab-ūz'] *vt* to use wrongly; to maltreat; to revile; to violate.—*n* **abuse** [ab-ūs'], ill use; misapplication; an unjust or corrupt usage; vituperation.—*adj* **abusive**[-ūs-]—*adv* **abus'ively**.—*n* **abus'iveness**.

abut [a-but'] *vi* to end or lean (on, upon, against).—*n* **abut'-ment** a part supporting a bridge, an arch, etc.

abyss [a-bis'] *n* a bottomless depth; anything too deep to measure (*an abyss of shame*).

academy [a-kad'em-i] *n* a private secondary school; a school for specialized training, a society of scholars, writers, scientists, etc.—*adj* academ'ic.—*adv* academ'ically.—*n* academician

acanthus [a-kan'thus] *n* a genus (*Acanthus*) of prickly-leaved plants; (*archit*) an ornament resembling their leaves used in the capitals of the Corinthian order.

accede [ak-sēd'] *vi* to come into some office or dignity; to agree or assent (*with to*).

accelerate [ak-sel'ėr-āt] *vt* to increase the speed of; to hasten the progress or occurrence of.—*vi* to move faster.—*n* accelerā'tion, the act of hastening.—*adj* accel'erative.—*n* accel'erator, one who or that which accelerates.

accent [ak'sėnt] *n* stress on a syllable or word; a mark used to direct this stress; any mode of utterance characteristic of a region, a class, or an individual; .—*vt* ac'cent or accent', to mark the accent; to emphasize.—*vt* accent'uate, to accent; to emphasize.—*n* accentuā'tion.

accept [ak-sept'] *vt* to receive, esp willingly; to approve; to agree to; to believe in; to agree to pay; to treat as welcome.—*adj* acceptable.—*ns* accept'ableness, acceptabil'ity.—*adv* accept'ably.—*ns* accept'ance, act of accepting or state of being accepted.—*ns* accept'er; accept'or.

access [ak'ses] *n* approach; or means of approach; the right to enter, use, etc.; an outburst.—*adj* access'ible, able to be reached; open (to).—*n* accessibil'ity.—*adv* access'ibly.

accession [ak-sesh-(ȯ)n] *n* act of reaching a rank or position; an addition as to a collection.

accessory, accessary [ak-ses'ȯr-i] *adj* additional; contributory; aiding; (*law*) participating in a crime; adventitious.—*adj* accessor'ial.

accidence [ak'si-dėns] *n* (*gram*) the inflectional changes of words to denote changes in number, tense, etc. of the same word.

accident [ak'si-dėnt] *n* an unforeseen or unexpected event; a mishap or disaster; chance.—*adj* accident'al.—*adv* accident'ally.

acclaim [a-klām'] *vt* to applaud; to hail.—*vi* to shout applause.—*n* a shout of applause or assent;—*n* acclamā'tion, acclaim .—*adj* acclam'atory.

acclimatize [a-klīm'a-tīz] *vt* to adapt to a new climate or environment. Also acclim'ate.—*n* acclimatizā'tion.

accolade [ak-ol-ād', -ād'] *n* a light touch on each shoulder with the flat of a sword conferring knighthood; praise, approval; an award.

accommodate [a-kom'od-āt] *vt* to adapt; to oblige; to lodge.—*adj* accommo'dating, obliging;—*n* accommodā'tion, adjustment; willingness to do favors; a help; (*pl*) lodgings; (*pl*) traveling space, as on a train.—*adj* accomm'odative.

accompany [a-kum'pan-i] *vt* to go with; to supplement (with something).—*ns* accom'paniment, that which accompanies; an instrumental part supporting a solo instrument, a voice, or a choir, accom'panist, one who performs an accompaniment.

accomplice [a-kom'plis, or -kum'-] *n* an associate, esp in crime.

accomplish [a-kum'plish] *vt* to complete; to effect, fulfill;—*adjs* accom'plishable, that may be accomplished; accom'plished, done; completed; skilled; expert; polished.—*n* accom'plishment.

accord [a-kȯrd'] *vi* to agree; to harmonize (with).—*vt* to make agree; to grant.—*n* agreement; harmony.—*n* accordance, agreement; conformity.—*adj* accordant, agreeing; harmonious.—*adv* accord'antly.—*adj* accord'ing, in accordance; agreeing.—*adv* accord'ingly, consequently.

accost [a-kost'] *vt* to approach and speak to.

account [a-kownt'] *vt* to probe into; to think of as, consider.—*vi* to give a financial reckoning (to).—*adj* account'able, liable; to account, responsible; explicable.—*ns* account'ableness, accountabil'ity—*adv* account'ably.—*ns* account'ant, one whose work is accounting, account'ancy, the profession or practice of an accountant.

accredit [a-kred'it] *vt* to authorize; to certify; to believe in; to attribute; to furnish with credentials.—*adj* accred'ited, certified officially; accepted as valid; certified as being of a prescribed quality.—*n* accredītā'tion.

accretion [a-krē'sh(ȯ)n] *n* process of growing or increase by means of gradual additions; accumulated matter; a growing together of parts.

accrue [a-krōō'] *vi* to grow as a natural result; to accumulate or be added periodically.

accumulate [a-kūm'ūl-āt] *vti* to pile up, to amass.—*n* accumulā'tion,—*adj* accum'ulative.

accurate [ak'ūr-åt] *adj* done with care, exact.—*n* acc'uracy, correctness;—*adv* acc'urately.—*n* acc'urateness.

accursed [a-kûrs'id, -kûrst] *adj* under a curse; damnable.—Also accurst'.

accuse [a-kūz']*vt* to bring a charge against; to blame.—*n* accusā'tion, the act of accusing; the charge brought against anyone.—*adj* accus'atory, containing accusation.—*adj* accused [a-kūzd'], charged with a crime.—*n* accus'er.

accustom [a-kus'tȯm] *vt* to make familiar by habit, use, or custom.—*adj* accus'tomed.

ace [ās] *n* the one in dice, cards, dominoes, etc., a point won by a single stroke, as in tennis; an expert.

acerbity [a-sûr'bi-ti] *n* sharpness of speech or manner.

acetic [a-sēt'ik, a-set'ik] *adj* of vinegar.—*n* ac'etate, a salt or ester of acetic acid; a fabric made of an acetate of cellulose.

acetone [as'ė-tōn] *n* a fragrant flammable liquid C_3H_6O used as a solvent and found in abnormal quantities in diabetic urine.

acetylene [a-set'i-lēn] *n* a gas formed by the action of water on carbide of calcium which burns with oxygen in a hot flame used for welding etc.

ache [āk] *n* a dull, continuous pain—*vi* to suffer a dull, continuous mental or physical pain; (*inf*) to yearn.—*pr p* āch'ing; *pt p* āched.—*adj* ach'ing.

achieve [a-chēv'] *vt* to perform, accomplish; to gain, win.—*adj* achiev'able.—*n* achieve'ment, a thing achieved; an exploit.

achromatic [a-krōm-at'ik] *adj* refracting light without dispersing it into its constituent colors.—*n* achrom'atism, the state of being achromatic.

acid [as'id] *adj* sharp, tart, sour; of an acid; looking or sounding bitter; rich in silica.—*n* a sour substance; (*slang*) LSD—*vti* acid'ify, to make or become acid; to convert into an acid.—*vi* to become acid.—*pr p* acid'ifying; *pt p* acid'ified.—*ns* acidificā'tion; acid'ity, being acid.—*vt* acid'ulate, make acid or slightly acid.—*adj* acid'ulous.

acknowledge [ak-nol'ij] *vt* to admit that something is true and valid ; to show that one has noticed or recognized.—*n* acknow'ledgment.

acme [ak'mē, -mi] *n* the top or highest point; the culimination or perfection.

acne [ak'nē, -ni] *n* inflammation of sebaceous glands producing pimples.

acolyte [ak'o-līt] *n* an altar boy; an attendant or assistant.

acorn [ā'kȯrn] *n* the nut of the oak.

acoustic [a-kōōs'tik] *adj* of the sense of hearing; of sounds; of acoustics.—*n pl* acous'tics, properties (eg of a room or hall) determining how clearly sounds can be heard in it.

acquaint [a-kwänt'] *vt* to make (oneself) familiar (with); to inform.—*ns* acquaint'ance, knowledge from personal experience; a person known slightly; acquaint'anceship, slight knowledge.—*adj* acquaint'ed (*with*), having personal knowledge of .

acquiesce [ak-wi-es'] *vi* to rest satisfied with, or make no opposition to (*with* in).—*n* acquiesc'ence, acceptance; assent.—*adj* acquiesc'ent.

acquire [a-kwīr'] *vt* to gain by one's efforts; to get as one's own.—*adj* acquir'able, that may be acquired.—*n* acquisi'tion, the act of acquiring; that which is acquired; something worth acquiring, a useful gain.—*adj* acquis'itive, directed towards, acquiring (possessions); grasping.—*n* acquis'itiveness. acquired immunodeficiency syndrome, AIDS.

acquit [a-kwit'] *vt* to free from an obligation; to behave or conduct (oneself); to declare innocent;—*pr p* acquitt'ing; *pt p* acquitt'ed—*ns* acquitt'al.

acre [ā'kėr] *n* a measure of land containing 4840 sq yards.—*n* acreage [ā'ker-ij] the number of acres in a piece of land.

acrid [ak'rid] *adj* sharp and bitter to the taste, and smell; sharp in speech, etc.—*ns* acrid'ity, ac'ridness.

acrimony [ak'ri-môn-i] *n* bitterness of feeling or language.—*adj* acrimō'nious.

acrobat [ak'ro-bat] *n* one who performs spectacular gymnastic feats.—*adj* acrobat'ic.—*n pl* acrobat'ics, an acrobat's tricks.

acronym [ak'rŏ-nim] *n* a word formed from the initial letters of other words (as *radar*).

acrophobia [ak-rŏ-fŏ'bi-à] *n* fear of heights.

across [a-kros'] *prep* from one side to the other of; on at an angle; on the other side of; into contact by chance.

acrostic [a-kros'tik] *n* a poem or puzzle in which certain letters of each line, spell a word, motto, etc. or a sentence.

act [akt] *vi* to exert force or influence; to produce an effect; to conduct oneself; to perform as on the stage; to function. — *vt* to perform. — *n* something done, a deed; an exploit; the process of doing something; a law; a main division of a play or opera; **Acts** (*Bible*), 5th book of the New Testament. — *n* **act'ing**, the art of an actor. — *n* **act'or**, one who does something; one who acts in plays, movies, etc.; **ac'tress**, a female performer.

action [ak'sh(ŏ)n] *n* a state of acting; a deed operation; a gesture; a battle; a lawsuit; the sequence of events in a drama, novel, etc. — *adj* **ac'tionable**, liable to a lawsuit. — **action painting**, abstract expressionism.

active [akt'iv] *adj* that acts; working; energetic; busy; nimble; effective; (*gram*) of that voice in which the subject of the verb represents the doer of the action. — *adv* **act'ively**. — *ns* **act'iveness; ac'tivism, activist, activ'ity**() — **act'ivate**.

actual [ak'tū-àl, ak'chŏŏ-àl] *adj* real; existing in fact and now. — *vt* **act'ualize**, to realize in action; to represent realistically. — *n* **actual'ity**. — *adv* **act'ually**.

actuary [ak'tū-ar-i] *n* one who figures insurance risks, premiums, etc. — *adj* **actuā'rial**.

actuate [ak'tū-āt] *vt* to put in motion; to incite to action.

acuity [a-kū'i-ti] *n* sharpness of thought or vision.

acumen [a-kū'men, a'-] *n* sharpness, of perception, penetration.

acute [a-kūt'] *adj* sharp-pointed; keen; sensitive (*acute hearing*); severe, as pain; very serious; less than 90° (*acute angles*); (of a disease) severe but not long lasting. — *adv* **acute'ly**. — *n* **acute'ness**.

adage [ad'ij] *n* an old saying, a proverb.

adagio [à-dä'j(y)ŏ] *adv* (*mus*) slowly. — *n* a slow movement; a slow ballet dance.

adamant [ad'a-mánt] *n* a very hard substance. — *adj* inflexible, unyielding.

Adam's apple [ad'amz-ap'l] *n* the hard projection in front of the throat, esp of a man.

adapt [a-dapt'] *vt* to make apt or fit; to adjust (oneself) to new circumstances. — *adj* **adapt'able**. — *ns* **adaptabil'ity; adaptā'tion**.

add [ad] *vt* to join (one thing to another) as an increase or supplement; to put numbers or amounts together to get a total; to say in continuation, to remark further. — *vi* to increase (*with* to); to find a sum. — *n* **addi'tion**, an adding of numbers to get a sum . — *adj* **addi'tional**, added; more; extra. — **in addition** (to), besides.

addendum [a-den'dum] *n* a thing to be added. — *pl* **adden'da**.

adder[1] [ad'èr] *n* the venomous viper (*Vipera berus*) of Europe; any of several harmless No American snakes, esp puff adder.

adder[2] [ad'èr] *n* one that adds, esp a device in a computer that performs addition.

addict [a-dikt'] *vt* to give (oneself) up (to a strong habit); to cause (a person) to become dependent upon a drug. — *n* [ad'ikt] one who is addicted (as to a drug). — *adj* **addict'ed**. — *n* **addic'tion**.

additive [ad'i-tiv] *adj* characterized by addition; produced by addition. — *n* something added.

addle [ad'l] *vti* to make, to make or become rotten; to make or become confused.

address [a-dres'] *vt* to direct words (to); to speak or write to; to direct in writing; to turn one's skill or energies (to); (*computer*) to indicate or find (the location of a piece of stored information). — *n* a formal communication in writing; a speech; manner, deportment; the place to which a letter is directed [also ad'res] a place of residence. — *adj* **address'able**. — *n* **addresséé'**, the person to whom a letter is addressed.

ad'enoids [ad'en-oidz] *n pl* enlarged masses of tissue in the throat behind the nose.

adept [ad-ept', ad'ept] *adj* highly skilled. — *n* an expert. [L *adeptus* (*artem*), having attained (an art), pt p of *adipisci* — *ad*, to, *apisci*, to reach, obtain.]

adequate [ad'e-kwàt] *adj* sufficient; equal to requirement. — *adv* **ad'equately**. — *ns* **ad'equateness, adequacy**.

adhere [ad-hēr'] *vi* to stick; to remain attached, to give allegiance or support (to). — *n* **adhēr'ence**, state of adhering; steady attachment. — *adj* **adhēr'ent**, sticking (to) — *n* a follower, a partisan.

adhesion' [ad-hē'zh(ò)n] *n, n* the act of adhering or sticking; steady attachment (to). — *adj* **adhēs'ive**, sticky; apt to, or intended to, adhere. — *n* an adhesive substance. — *adv* **adhes'ively**. — *n* **adhes'iveness**.

ad hoc [ad hok] *adj* (of a committee or other body) constituted for this purpose. [L, to this.]

ad infinitum [ad in-fin-īt'um, -ēt ŏŏm] to infinity.

ad interim [ad int'ē-rim] for the meantime.

adjacent [a-jās'ént] *adj* near (to); adjoining. — *n* **adjac'ency**. — *adv* **adjac'ently**.

adjective [aj'ek-tiv] *n* a word added to a noun or other substantive to qualify it or to limit it. — *adj* **adjectīv'al**. — *advs* **adjectīv'ally, ad'jectively**.

adjoin [a-join'] *vt* to be next to. — *vi* to be in contact. — *adj* **adjoin'ing**.

adjourn [a-jûrn'] *vt* to discontinue (a meeting) in order to resume it at another time or place. — *vi* to suspend proceedings for a time; (*inf*) to retire (to another room, etc.) — *n* **adjourn'ment**.

adjudge [a-juj'] *vt* to decide by law; to declare, order, or award by law.

adjudicate [a-jŏŏ'di-kāt] *vt* to (*Law*) to hear and decide (a case). — *vi* to serve as a judge (in or on). — *ns* **adjū'dicator; adjudicā'tion**.

adjunct [a'jungkt] *adj* joined or added; attached in a temporary or subordinate position to the staff of an institution, as a university. — *n* a thing joined or added.

adjure [a-jŏŏr'] *vt* to charge on oath or solemnly. — *n* **adjurā'tion**.

adjust [a-just'] *vt* to arrange properly; to regulate, to settle rightly; to decide the amount to be paid in settling (an insurance claim). — *vi* to adapt oneself. — *adj* **adjust'able**. — *n* **adjust'ment**.

adjutant [a'jŏŏ-tânt] *n* an assistant; a military staff officer who assists the commanding officer. — *ns* **ad'jutancy**, the office or rank of an adjutant.

administer [ad-min'is-tèr] *vt* to manage, direct; to give out as punishment; to apply (medicine, etc.); to tender (an oath, etc.) — *n* **administrā'tion**, management; **Administration**, the executive officials of a government, their policies, and term of office. — *adj* **admin'istrative**, that administers. — *n* **admin'istrātor**, one who manages or directs; (*law*) one appointed to settle an estate.

admiral [ad'mir-àl] *n* the commanding officer of a fleet; a naval officer of the highest rank.

admire [ad-mīr'] *vt* to regard with wonder or surprise; to esteem, often in a somewhat impersonal manner; to regard with enthusiastic approval. — *adj* **admirable** [ad'-mir-à-bl] worthy of being admired. — *adv* **ad'mirably**. — *n* **admirā'tion**. — *n* **admiŕ'er**. — *adv* **admiŕ'ingly**.

admit [ad-mit'] *vt* to allow to enter or use; to concede; to acknowledge; to be capable of; to leave room for. — *vi* to allow (with of) — *pr p* **admitt'ing**; *pt p* **admitt'ed**. — *adj* **admiss'ible**, that may be admitted or allowed. — *ns* **admissibil'ity; admitt'ance**, the act of admitting; **admiss'ion**, an admitting or being admitted; an entrance fee; a conceding, confessing, etc.; a thing conceded, confessed, etc. — *adv* **admitt'edly**.

admixture [ad-miks'chûr] *n* a mixture; a thing added in mixing.

admonish [ad-mon'ish] *vt* to warn; to reprove mildly.

admonition [ad-mon-ish'(ò)n] *n* gentle or friendly reproof; warning or counsel against fault or oversight. — *adj* **admon'itory**, containing admonition.

ad nauseam [ad nŏ'shi-am, now'si] to a sickening degree. [L]

ado [a-dŏŏ'] *n* trouble, fuss.

adobe [a-dŏ'bi] *n* a sun-dried brick; clay for making this brick; a house made of such bricks.

adolescent [ad-o-les'ént] *adj* of or in adolescence. — Also *n* — *n* **adolesc'ence**, the period of youth, between childhood and maturity.

adopt [a-dopt'] *vt* to take legally into one's family and raise as one's own child; to take as one's own; **adop'tion**, the act of adopting; the state of being adopted.—*adj* **adopt'ive**, that adopts or is adopted.

adore [a-dōr', -dör'] *vt* to worship; to love intensely.—*adj* **ador'able**, worthy of being adored; extremely charming.—*n* **ador'ableness**.—*adv* **ador'ably**.—*ns* **adŏrā'tion**, worship, homage; profound regard; **ador'er**,—*adv* **ador'ingly**.

adorn [a-dörn'] *vt* to deck or dress; to embellish.—*n* **adorn'ment**, ornament; decoration.

adrenal [ad-rē'nàl] *adj* near the kidneys.

adrift [a-drift'] *adj*, *adv* floating without mooring.

adroit [a-droit'] *adj* skillful and clever.—*adv* **adroit'ly**.—*n* **adroit'ness**.

adscititious [ad-si-tish'ùs] *adj* derived or acquired from something extrinsic.

adsorb [ad-sörb'] *vt* of a solid, to take up a liquid or vapor on its surface.—*n* **adsorption**.

adulation [ad-ū-lā'sh(ó)n] *n* fawning; flattery.—*adj* **adulatory** [ad'ū-la-tör-i].

adult [ad'ult, ad-ult'] *adj* grown; mature; euphemism for dealing in pornography, etc.—*n* a mature person, animal, or plant.

adulterate [a-dul'tèr-āt] *vt* to make impure, inferior, etc. by adding an improper substance.—*adj* [-āt] spurious.—*n* **adul'terant**, a substance used to adulterate—Also *adj*; **adulterā'tion**.

adultery [a-dul'tèr-i] *n* sexual intercourse between a married man and a woman not his wife, or between a married woman and man not her husband.—*ns* **adul'terer**, a man guilty of adultery; **adul'teress**, a woman who commits adultery.—*adj* **adul'terine**, resulting from adultery.

ad valorem [ad va-lō'rem, -lö'-] *adj* imposed at a percentage of the value.

advance [ad-väns'] *vt* to bring forward; to promote; to raise the rate of; to lend.—*vi* to go forward; to make progress; to rise in rank, price, etc.—*n* progress; improvement; a rise in value; payment beforehand; (*pl*) approaches to get favor;—*adj* in front (*advance guard*); beforehand.—*adj* **advanced'**, in front; old; ahead or higher in progress, price, etc.

advantage [ad-vänt'ij] *n* superiority over another; gain or benefit; (*lawn tennis*) first point gained after deuce—*vt* to be a benefit to, profit—*adj* **advantā'geous**, of advantage; useful—*adv* **advantā'geously**.—*n* **advanta'geousness**.—**take advantage of**, to use for one's own benefit; to impose upon.

Advent [ad'vent] *n* the period including four Sundays before Christmas; **advent**, a coming.

adventitious [ad-ven-tish'ùs] *adj* coming from outside; added by chance; (*bot*) developed out of the usual order or place.—*adv* **adventi'tiously**.

adventure [ad-ven'chùr] *n* a strange or exciting undertaking; an unusual, stirring, often romantic experience.—*vti* to risk; venture.—*n* **adven'turer**, one who engages in hazardous enterprises.—*adjs* **adven'turous**, **adven'turesome**, enterprising; ready to incur risk.—*adv* **adven'turously**.—*n* **adven'turousness**.

adverb [ad'vèrb] *n* a word which modifies a verb, adjective, or other adverb—*adj* **adver'bial**.—*adv* **adver'bially**.

adversary [ad'vèr-sàr-i] *n* an opponent

adverse [ad'vèrs] *adj* hostile; opposed; unfavorable.—*adv* **ad'versely**.—*ns* **ad'verseness**; **advers'ity**, adverse circumstances; affliction, misfortune.—*adj* **advers'ative**, denoting opposition or antithesis.

advert [ad-vûrt'] *vi* to call attention (to).

advertise [ad'vèr-tīz, or -tīz'] *vt* to call public attention to, esp in order to sell something, by buying space or time in the media, etc.—*vi* to call public attention to things for sale; to ask (for) by public notice.—*ns* **advert'isement** [-iz, -is-], the act of advertising; a public notice usu. paid for; **adverti'ser**, one who advertises; a paper carrying advertisements; **ad'vertising**, the business of preparing advertisements.

advice [ad-vīs'] *n* counsel; recommendation with regard to a course of action; (usu. *pl*) information or notice given.

advise [ad-vīz'] *vt* to give advice or counsel to; to recommend; to inform.—*vi* to give advice; to take counsel.—*pr p* **advīs'ing**; *pt p* **advised** [-vīzd']—*adj* **advīs'able**, prudent, expedient.—*ns* **advisabil'ity**, **advis'ableness**.—*adv* **advis'ably**.—

adjs **advis'ory**, giving advice; **advised'**, thought out (as in *well-advised* and *ill-advised*).—*adv* **advis'edly**, after consideration.—*n* **advis'er**, **advisor**, one who advises.

advocacy [ad'vo-kà-si] *n* the function of an advocate; a pleading in support (of).

advocate [ad'vo-kàt] *n* one who pleads the cause of another, esp in a court of law or before a tribunal; a supporter.—*vt* [-āt] to plead in favor of.

adz, adze [adz] *n* a carpenter's tool consisting of a thin arched blade with its edge at right angles to the handle.

aerate [ā'èr-āt] *vt* to supply (blood) with oxygen by respiration; to supply or impregnate with air; to combine or charge with gas.—*n* **aerā'tion**.

aerial [ā-ē'ri-àl] *adj* belonging to the air; existing in the air; of aircraft or flying.—*n* a radio or TV antenna.

aerie [ā'ri, also ē'ri, ī'ri] *n* the nest of any bird of prey, esp an eagle.—Also **aery, eyrie, eyry**.

aerobatics [ā-èr-ō-bat'iks] *n* stunts done while flying an aircraft.

aerobic [ā-erōb'ik] *adj* living only in the presence of oxygen; of exercise that conditions the heart and lungs by increasing efficient intake of oxygen by the body.

aerodynamics [ā-èr-ō-di-nam'iks] *n* the branch of dynamics with forces exerted by air or other gases in motion.—*adj* **aerodynam'ic**.

aerolite [ā'èr-o-līt] *n* a stony meteorite.

aeronaut [ā'èr-o-nöt] *n* one who operates or travels in a balloon or airship.—*n* **aeronaut'ics**, the science dealing with the operation of aircraft; the art or science of flight.

aerophobe [ā'èr-ō-fōb] *n* a person with an abnormal fear of flying.—*n* **aerophob'ia** (*biol*) movement of organism or part of organism away from air.

aerosol [ā'èr-ō-sol] *n* a liquid in a container under pressure, with a device for releasing it in a fine spray; the container.

aerospace [ā'èr-ō-spās] *n* the earth's atmosphere together with space beyond.—*adj* of missiles, etc. for flight in aerospace.

aesthetics [es-thet'iks, or ēs-thet'iks] *n* the philosophy of art and beauty—*n* **aesthete** [es'thēt], one who is or pretends to be highly sensitive to art and beauty.—*adj* **aesthet'ic**.—*adv* **aesthet'ically**.—*n* **aesthet'icism**, the doctrine that the principles of beauty are basic to other. Also **esthetics, esthete**, etc.

afar [a-fär] *adv* (*arch, poetic*) at or to a distance.

affable [af'a-bl] *adj* easy to speak to; approachable;—*ns* **affability, affableness**.—*adv* aff'ably.

affair [a-fār'] *n* a thing done or to be done; (*pl*) public or private business; (*inf*) an event; (*inf*) a thing, a temporary romantic or sexual relationship.

affect[1] [a-fekt'] *vt* to act upon; to produce a change in; to move the feelings of.—*n* **affectabil'ity**.—*adjs* **affect'able**, **affect'ed**, touched with feeling.—*adv* **affect'edly**.—*adj* **affect'ing**, having power to move the feelings.—*adv* **affect'ingly**.

affect[2] [a-fekt'] *vt* to make a show or pretence of; to have, show a preference for.—*n* **affectā'tion**, a striving after, or an attempt to assume, what is not natural or real; pretence.—*adj* **affect'ed**, assumed artificially.—*n* **affec'tedness**.

affection [a-fek'sh(ó)n] *n* fond or tender feeling; liking; a disease or diseased condition.—*adjs* **affec'tionate**, full of affection, loving **affec'tionless**.—*adv* **affec'tionately**.

affiance [a-fī'àns] *vt* to betroth.

affidavit [af-i-dā'vit] *n* a written declaration on oath.

affiliate [a-fil'i-āt] *vt* to connect as a subordinate member or branch; to associate (oneself with).—*vi* to join.—*n* an affiliated person club, etc.—*n* **affiliā'tion**.

affinity [a-fin'i-ti] *n* relationship by marriage; nearness of kin; structural resemblance; similarity, likeness; attraction, liking.

affirm [a-fûrm'] *vt* to assert confidently or possitively; (*law*) to make a formal declaration or affirmation, without an oath; to ratify (a judgment).—*adj* **affirm'able**.—*n* **affirmā'tion**, firming; that which is affirmed.—*adj* and *n* **affirm'ative**, that affirms or asserts; the side upholding the proposition in a debate.—*adv* **affirm'atively**.

affix [a-fiks'] *vt* to fasten; to add; to attach.—*n* **aff'ix**, a prefix or a suffix.

afflict [a-flikt'] *vt* to cause pain, distress, or grief to.—*n* **afflic'tion**, pain; suffering; state or cause of distress;—*adj* **afflict'ive**.

affluent [af'lōō-ènt] *adj* abounding; wealthy; rich.—*n* a tributary stream, a rich person.—*n* **aff'luence**, abundance; wealth.

afford [a-förd', -förd'] *vt* to spare (money, time, etc.) without much inconvenience; to yield, produce.

affray [a-frā'] *n* a noisy brawl.

affright [a-frīt'] *vt* to frighten.—*n* sudden terror.

affront [a-frunt'] *vt* to insult openly.—*n* an open insult.

affusion [a-fū'zh(ó)n] *n* the act of pouring liquid upon, as in baptism.

Afghan [af'gan] *n* native or inhabitant of Afghanistan; Pashto, **afghan**, a knitted or crocheted blanket.

aficionado [å-fish'i-nä'dō] *n* a devotee of some sport, art, etc.

afield [a-fēld'] *adv* far away from home; to or at a distance; astray.

afire [a-fīr'] *adj, adv* on fire.

aflame [a-flām'] *adj, adv* in flames, burning.

afloat [a-flōt'] *adv, adj* floating; at sea; flooded.

aforementioned [a-för'men-shond] *adj* mentioned before.

aforesaid [a-för-sed] *adj* spoken of before.

aforethought [a-för'thöt] *adj* thought out beforehand; premeditated.

afraid [a-frād'] *adj* frightened (of, that, or to); admit with regret.

afresh [a-fresh'] *adv* anew; beginning again.

African [af'rik-àn] *adj* of Africa, its peoples, or languages.—*n* a native or inhabitant of Africa, esp a dark-skinned person.

Afrikaans [af-ri-käns'] *n* one of the two official languages of So Africa; developed from Dutch.

aft [äft] *adv* at, near, or toward the stern of a ship or rear of an aircraft.

Afro [af'rō] *adj* of or denoting a full, bouffant hair style, as worn by some blacks.—Also *n* **Af'ro-**, in composition, Africa; African.—*adj* **Afro-American**, of black Americans, their culture, etc.

after [äft'èr] *prep* and *adv* behind in place; later, later than; following in search of; in imitation of.—*adj* behind in place.

again [a-gen'] *adv* back into a former condition; once more; besides; on the other hand.—**again and again**, often; as much **again**, twice as much.

against [a-genst'] *prep* in opposition to; in contact or in collision with; in preparation for; as a charge on.

agape¹ [ag'a-pē] *n* a love-feast, held by the early Christians in connection with the Lord's Supper.

agape² [a-gāp'] *adj, adv* with the mouth wide open.

agate [ag'åt] *n* a chalcedony with striped or clouded coloring used as a gemstone; a playing marble made of or like this.

age [āj] *n* the time during which a person or thing has lived or existed; a stage of life; later years of life; a period of time; any great division of geology or history; (*inf*) a long time (often *pl*).—*vti* to grow or make old, ripe, mature, etc.—*pr p* **aging** [aj'ing] *pt p* **aged** [äjd].—*adj* **aged** [āj'id] advanced in age; [äjd] of the age of..—*n* **ageism** [āj'izm], discrimination on grounds of age against the old.—*adjs* **age'ist**, **age'-ist**; **age'less**, never growing old; **age'-old**, ancient.—**the ag'ed**, old people.

agenda [a-jen'da] *n* a list of things to be done, as items of business to be considered at a meeting.

agent [ā'jènt] *n* a person or thing that acts or exerts power; any natural force acting on matter; one authorized to transact business for another; a representative of a government agency; a spy.—*n* **ag'ency**, action; power; means; a firm, etc. empowered to act for another; an administrative government division.

agglomerate [a-glom'ér-āt] *vti* to gather into a mass or a ball.—Also *adj*.—*ns* **agglom'erate** [-āt] something consisting of irregular fragments; **agglomera'tion**.

agglutinate [a-glōōt'in-āt] *vti* to stick together, as with glue.—*n* **agglutina'tion**, sticking or fusing together.—*adj* **agglut'i-native**.

aggrandize [ag'rand-īz] *vt* to make greater in power, rank, wealth, etc.; —*n* **aggrandizement** [a-gran'diz-ment].

aggravate [ag'ra-vāt] *vt* to make worse. (*inf*) to provoke, irritate.—*adj* **aggr'avated** (*law*), denoting a grave form of a specified offense.—*n* **aggrava'tion**.

aggregate [ag're-gāt] *vt* to collect into a mass; to total.—*adj* [-åt] formed of parts collected in a mass; taking all units as a whole.; (*geol*) a mass of distinct things gathered into a whole.

aggress [a-gres'] *vi* to act aggressively.—*adj* **aggress'ive**, boldly hostile; quarrelsome; self-assertive, enterprising.—*ns* **aggression** [a-gresh'(ó)n], the act of making an unprovoked attack; a hostile action or behavior; **aggress'iveness**; **aggress'or**, a person or country that attacks first.

aggrieve [a-grēv'] *vt* to cause grief or injury to; to offend; to slight; to treat unfairly.

aghast [a-gäst'] *adj* stupefied with horror.

agile [aj'īl, aj'il] *adj* active, nimble.—*n* **agility** [a-jil'i-ti], quickness of motion, nimbleness.

agitate [aj'i-tāt] *vt* to shake, set in motion; to stir violently; to disturb, excite—*vi* to keep up the discussion of, esp with a view to reform.—*ns* **agita'tion**, **ag'itator**, one who stirs or keeps up a public agitation; **agitprop** [aj'it-prop], propaganda.

aglet [ag'let] *n* the tag or point of a lace or point; any ornamental stud, pin or cord worn in clothing.

aglow [a-glō'] *adj* radiant with warmth or excitement.

agnate [ag'nāt] *adj* related on the father's side.—Also *n*.

agnostic [ag-nos'tik] *n* one who holds that we know nothing of God, or of an unseen world beyond material phenomena.—*n* **agnos'ticism**.

ago [a-gō] *adv* in the past.—*adj* gone by; past.

agog [a-gog'] *adj* eager; expectant.

agony [ag'o-ni] *n* extreme mental or physical suffering; death pangs. *vt* **ag'onize**, to torture.—*vi* to struggle; to be in agony.—*adj* **ag'onizing**.—*adv* **ag'onizingly**.

agoraphobia [ag'or-åfō'bi-a] *n* morbid fear of crossing open places.

agrarian [ag-rā'ri-àn] *adj* relating to land, or its management.—*n* **agra'rianism**, a social or political movement advocating land reform and improvement of the economic status of the farmer.

agree [a-grē'] *vi* to get on with one another; to come to an understanding; to consent (to); to assent (to).—*vt* to grant. *pr p* **agree'ing**; *pt p* **agreed'**.—*adj* **agree'able**, pleasant; pleasing; willing to consent; conformable.—*n* **agree'ableness**.—*adv* **agree'ably**.—*n* **agree'ment**, concord; conformity.

agriculture [ag'ri-kul-chùr] *n* art or practice of producing crops and raising livestock; farming;—*adj* **agricult'ural**—*n* **agricult'urist**, **agricult'uralist**, one skilled in agriculture.

aground [a-grownd'] *adj, adv* on to or onto the shore, a reef, etc.

ah [ä, ö] *interj* an exclamation of pain, delight, surprise, etc.

aha [ä-hä'] *interj* an exclamation of satisfaction, triumph, etc.

ahead [a-hed'] *adj, adv* in or to the front; forward; onward; in advance; winning or profiting.—**get ahead**, to advance financially etc.

ahoy [a-hoi'] *interj* a nautical call used in hailing.

aid [ād] *vti* to help, assist.—*n* help; anything that helps; a helper;—*n* **aid'er**,—*adj*.

AIDS [ādz] *n* a condition of deficiency in certain leukocytes leading to cancer, pneumonia, etc.

aigrette [ā'gret] *n* a spray of feathers for the hair; a plume composed of feathers, or of gems, like a heron's crest.

ail [āl] *vi* to be in poor health.—*vt* to cause pain and trouble to.—*n* **ail'ment**, pain; indisposition; disease.

aileron [ā'lèr-on, el'è-rō] *n* a hinged section at the trailing edge of an airplane wing, used to control its rolling.

aim [ām] *vti* to point or direct towards a mark so as to hit; to direct (one's efforts;) to intend—*n* the action or manner of aiming; the mark aimed at; design, intention.—*adj* **aim'less**, without purpose or object.—*adv* **aim'lessly**.

air [år] *n* the mixture of gases we breathe; the atmosphere; any special condition of atmosphere; a breeze; outward appearance, manner, look; (*mus*) a melody; (*pl*) affectation.—*adj* of aviation.—*vt* to expose to the air; to bring to public notice; **air base**, a base for military aircraft .—*adj* **air'borne**, carried by or through the air; aloft or flying; **air'bus'**, an extremely large passenger aircraft, esp for short trips; **air conditioning**, regulation of air humidity and temperature in buildings, etc.—*vt* **air-condition**.—*n* **air-conditioner**.—*adj* **air-cooled**, cooled by having air passed over, into, or through it.—*ns* **air'craft'**, any machine for traveling through air;—*pl* **air'craft'**; **aircraft carrier**, a warship with a large flat deck, for carrying aircraft;—Also *vt*—*ns* **air'field**, a field where aircraft can take off and land; **air'foil**, a wing, rudder, etc. of an aircraft; **air force**, the aviation branch of a country's armed forces; **air'ing**, exposure to open air for drying or freshening; exercise in open air; exposure to public view; a radio or television broadcast; **air lane**, a route for travel by air; airway; .—*n* **air'line**, a system or company for transportation by aircraft.—*adj* of, or on an airline.—*ns* **air'lin'er**, a large passenger aircraft operated by an airline; **air'mail'**, mail transported by aircraft.—*vt* to send by airmail.—*ns* **air'man**, an aviator; an enlisted person in the US Air Force ranking above airman basic and below airman first class; **air'plane**, a fixed-wing motor-driven or jet-propelled aircraft kept aloft by the forces of air upon its wings; **air'play**, the playing of a recording over radio or TV; **air'port**, a place where aircraft can land and take off, usu. with facilities for repair, etc.; **air'ship**, a self-propelled steerable aircraft that is lighter than air.—*ns* **air'space**, the space above a nation over which it maintains jurisdiction.—*adj* **air'tight**, too tight for air or gas to enter or escape; invulnerable (*an airtight alibi*)..—*adj* **air'worthy**, fit for operation in the air.—*n* **air'worthiness**.—*adj* **airy**, of air; open to the air; breezy; light as air, graceful; lighthearted; flippant; (*inf*) putting on airs.—**in the air**, prevalent; (**on** or **off**) **the air**, that is (or not) broadcasting; **up in the air**, not settled; (*slang*) angry, excited, etc.

aisle [īl] *n* a passageway, as between rows of seats; a side part of a church.

aitchbone [āch'bōn] *n* the bone of the rump; the cut of beef over this bone.

ajar [a-jär'] *adv* partly open, as a door.

akimbo [a-kim'bō] *adv, adj* with hands on hip and elbows bent outward.

akin [a-kin'] *adj* related by blood; having similar characteristics.

alabaster [al'a-bäs-tèr, or -bäs'-] *n* a semi-transparent gypsum.—Also *adj*.

alacrity [a-lak'ri-ti] *n* briskness, cheerful readiness.

alarm [a-lärm'] *n* notice of danger; sudden surprise with fear; vivid apprehension; a mechanical contrivance to arouse from sleep or to attract attention.—*vt* to give notice of danger; to fill with dread.—*adj* **alarm'ing**, frightening.—*n* **alarm'ist**, one who excites alarm.

alas [a-läs'] *interj* expressive of grief.

albatross [al'ba-tros] *n* any of several large web-footed seabirds (family Diomediadae) of the Pacific Ocean; a heavy burden, as of debt, guilt, etc.

albino [al-bē'no] *n* a person, animal, or plant lacking normal coloration. Human albinos have white skin, whitish hair, and pink eyes.—*pl* **albi'nos**.

album [al'bum] *n* a blank book for the insertion of portraits, autographs, etc. a single long-playing record or tape recording.

alburnum [al-bûr'num] *n* sapwood.

alchemy [al'ki-mi] *n* the forerunner of modern chemistry, its chief aims being to transmute base metals into gold and to discover the elixir of life.—*n* **al'chemist**.

alcohol [al'kō-hol] *n* a liquid generated by the fermentation of sugar or other carbohydrates, and forming the intoxicating element of wine, beer, and spirits; the name for the class of chemical compounds to which common alcohol (ethanol) belongs.—*adj* **alcohol'ic**, of alcohol; suffering from alcoholism.—*n* one addicted to excessive drinking of alcohol.—*n* **al'coholism**, condition of an alcoholic; a resulting diseased condition.

Alcoran [al-ko-rän'] *n* (*arch*) the Koran.

alcove [al'kōv, al-kōv'] *n* a recess in a room, as a breakfast nook.

alderman [öl'dèr-man] *n* in some cities, a municipal officer representing a certain district or ward.

ale [āl] *n* a beverage made from malt by fermentation, similar to beer.

aleatory [ā'lē-a-tor-ē] *adj* depending on chance or luck; (*mus*) of elements chosen at random.—Also **aleatoric**.

alee [a-lē'] *adv* on or toward the lee.

alert [a-lûrt'] *adj* watchful; brisk.—*n* a danger warning.—*vt* to forewarn, put on the alert.—*adv* **alert'ly**.—*n* **alert'ness**.—**on the alert**, vigilant.

alexia [a-leks'i-a] *n* impaired ability to read.

Alfa [al'fa] communication code word for the letter *a*.

alfalfa [al-fal'fa] *n* a deep-rooted leguminous plant (Medicago sativa) grown widely for hay and forage.

alfresco [al-fres'ko] *adv, adj* in the open air.

alga [al'ga] *n* any of a group (Algae) of chiefly aquatic lower plants classified according to color; —*pl* **algae** [-je], **algas**.—*n* **algol'ogist**, a specialist in the study of algae.

algebra [al'je-bra] *n* the branch of mathematics dealing with the properties and relations of numbers; the generalization and extension of arithmetic.—*adjs* **algebra'ic**, **-al**.—*n* **algebra'ist**.

ALGOL, Algol [al'gäl, -gōl] *n* an algebraic computer programming language designed for mathematical and scientific uses.

algorithm [al'go-ridhm] *n* (*math*) any method or procedure for computation.

alias [ā'li-as] *adv* otherwise named.—*n* an assumed name;—*pl* **a'liases**.

alibi [al'i-bī] *n* (*law*) the plea that a person charged with a crime was elsewhere when it was committed; (*inf*) any excuse.—*vi* (*inf*) to offer an excuse.

alien [āl'yen, or ā'lē-en] *adj* foreign; strange.—*n* one belonging to another country; one of foreign birth who is not naturalized; a hypothetical being from outer space.

alienate [āl'yèn-āt, ā'li-en-āt] *vt* to transfer (property) to another; to estrange; to divert affection (from).—*adj* **āl'ienable**, capable of being transferred to another.—*ns* **alienabil'ity**; **alienā'tion**.

alienist [al'yen-ist, ā'li-en-ist] *n* a psychiatrist, esp one dealing in the legal aspects of psychiatry.

alight [a-līt] *vi* to come down, as from a horse; to descend after a flight.

align [a-līn'] *vt* to arrange in a straight line, to bring into agreement, etc.—*vi* to line up.

alike [a-līk'] *adj* like one another.—*adv* equally; similarly.

aliment [al'i-mènt] *n* nourishment food.—*adj* **aliment'ary**, pertaining to aliment.—*ns* **alimentā'tion**, the act or state of nourishing or of being nourished; **al'imony**, an allowance for support made to a wife when legally separated from her husband.

aliquant [al'i-kwant] *adj* (*math*) of a quantity or number that is not an exact divisor of a given quantity or number.

aliquot [al'i-kwot] *adj* (*math*) of a part which is contained in the whole an exact number of times.

alive [a-līv'] *adj* in life; alert; in existence, operation, etc.—**alive to**, aware of; **alive with**, teeming with.

aliyah, aliya [a-lē'ya] *n* the immigration of Jews to Israel.

alkali [al'ka-li, or -lī] *n* (*chem*) a substance that dissolves in water to form a strongly basic solution, esp the hydroxides of sodium and potasium; **alkalies, alkalis**.—*adj* **alkaline** [al'ka-lin, or lïn].—*n* **alkalinity** [-lin'].—*vt* **al'kalize**.—*adj* **al'kaloid**.

all [öl] *adj* the whole of; every one of.—*adv* wholly; completely; entirely.—*n* the whole; everyone; everything.

Allah ä'la] *n* the Muslim name of God.

allay [a-lā'] *vt* to lighten, relieve; to make quiet or calm.

allege [a-lej'] *vt* to assert or declare, esp without proof; to offer as an excuse.—*n* **allegation** [al-e-gā'sh(ò)n], an assertion, esp without proof.—*adj* **alleged**, declared, but without proof.

allegiance [a-lē'j(y)àns] *n* the duty of being loyal to one's country, etc.; devotion, as to a cause.

allegory [al'e-gor-i] *n* a description of one thing under the image of another as in a fable.—*adjs* **allegor'ical**.—*adv* **allegor'ically**.—*vt* **all'egorize**, to put in form of an allegory.—*vi* to use allegory.

allegro [a-le'grō, or -lā'-] *adv, adj* (*mus*) fast.—*adv, adj* **allegrett'o**, moderately fast.

allergy [al'ér-ji] *n* an altered or acquired state of sensitivity; abnormal reaction of the body to substances normally harmless; antipathy.—*n* **all'ergen**, a substance inducing an allergic reaction.—*adj* **aller'gic**, *n* **all'ergist**, a doctor who specializes in treating allergies.

alleviate [a-lē'vi-āt] *vt* to lessen or relieve (pain); to mitigate.—*ns* **alleviā'tion**, *adv* **allevi'iātor**.

alley [al'i] *n* a narrow street between or behind buildings; a bowling lane;—*pl* **all'eys**.—*n* **all'eyway**, an alley between buildings.

All Fools' Day [öl fōōlz' dā] *n* April 1, April Fool's Day.

all hail [ŏl-hāl'] *interj* used to express greeting, welcome, or acclamation.

All-hallows [ŏl-hal'ŏz] *n* All Saints' Day.

alliance [a-lī'áns] *n* union by marriage or treaty; any union for a common purpose; an agreement for this; the countries, groups, etc. in such an association.

alligator [al'i-gā-tŏr] *n* a large reptile (genus *Alligator*) of the US similar to the crocodile but having a short, blunt snout.

alliteration [a-lit-ĕr-ā'sh(ó)n] *n* the recurrence of the same *sound* at the beginning of two or more words in a phrase, etc.—*vi* allit'erate, to begin with the same sound.

allocate [al'o-kāt] *vt* to distribute or allot; to set apart for a specific purpose.—*n* alloca'tion.

allocution [al-o-kū'sh(ó)n] *n* a formal speech, esp a hortatory address.

allot [a-lot'] *vt* to divide as by lot, to assign as one's share;—*pr p* allott'ing; *pt p* allott'ed.—*n* allot'ment, the act of allotting; part of share allotted.

allow [a-low'] *vt* to permit; to acknowledge, admit, concede; to give, grant (sum of money at regular intervals); to add or deduct in estimating.—*vi* to admit (of).—*adj* allow'able, not forbidden; permissible.—*n* allow'ance, that which is allowed.

alloy [a-loi'] *vt* to make into an alloy.—*n* [a'loi] a mixture of two or more metals; something that debases another thing when mixed with it.

all-round [ŏl-rownd'] *see* all-around.

allspice [ŏl'spīs] *n* the berry of a West Indian tree (*Pimenta dioica*); the tree; an aromatic spice combining the flavor of cinnamon, nutmeg, and clove prepared from allspice berries.

all-star [ŏl'star] *adj* made up entirely of outstanding performers.

all-time [ŏl tīm] *adj* unsurpassed until now.

allude [a-l(y)ōōd'] *vi* to refer indirectly to.—*n* allu'sion, an indirect reference.—*adj* allus'ive, containing an allusion; or many allusions.—*adv* allus'ively.

allure [a-l(y)ōōr'] *vt* to draw on as by a lure to entice.—*n* fascination; charm.—*n* allure'ment.—*adj* allur'ing.—*adv* allur'ingly.

alluvium [a-l(y)ōō'vi-um] *n* earth, sand, gravel, etc. deposited by moving water;—*pl* allū'via.—*adj* allū'vial.

ally [a-lī'] *vti* to join or unite for a specific purpose; to relate by similarity of structure, etc.—*pt p*, *adj* allied'.—*n* ally [a-lī', or a'lī],—*pl* all'ies [-īz] a country or person joined with another for a common purpose.

alma mater [al'ma mā'ter] *n* one's university or school; the song or hymn of a school, college, or university.

almanac [al', ŏl', ma-nak] *n* a calender with astronomical data, weather forecasts, etc.

almighty [ŏl-mīt'i] *adj* all-powerful.—*adv* almight'ily.—*n* almight'iness.—**the Almighty**, God.

almond [ä'mónd] *n* edible kernel of the fruit of a tree (genus *Prunus*) of the rose family; the tree bearing this fruit.—*adj* oval and pointed at one or both ends.

almost [ŏl'mōst] *adv* all but, very nearly. **[all + most** (adv).]

alms [ämz] *n* (*sing* and *pl*) relief given out of pity to the poor.

aloft [a-loft'] *adv* in the air, flying; at a great height; (*naut*) high above the deck.

aloha [ä-lō'a, ä-lō'hä] *interj* a word used in greeting and farewell.

alone [a-lōn'] *adj* by oneself; solitary; unique.—*adv* singly, by oneself.

along [a-long'] *adv* in the direction of the length; together with one; forward.—*prep* by the side of; near.—*prep*, *adv* along'side, beside; side by side.

aloof [a-lōōf'] *adv* at a distance but in view; apart.—*adj* cool and reserved.—*n* aloof'ness.

aloud [a-lowd'] *adv* with a normal voice; loudly.

alp [alp] *n* a high mountain.—*adj* al'pīne, of the Alps; of high mountains.—*n* a mountain plant, esp a small herb.—**the Alps**, the high mountain range in south central Europe.

alpaca [al-pak'a] *n* a Peruvian llama, having long silken wool; cloth made of its wool.

alpha [al'fa] *n* the first letter of the Greek alphabet.—*adj* (*chem*) involving helium nuclei; (*chem*) denoting isomeric or allotropic form of a substance.

alphabet [al'fa-bet] *n* the letters used in writing a language

arranged in conventional order.—*adjs* alphabet'ical.—*adv* alphabet'ically.

alphanumeric [al-fa-nōō-mer'ik] *adj* having both alphabetical and numerical symbols.

already [ŏ-red'i] *adv* previously or before the time specified.

also [ŏl'sō] *adv* in addition.—*ns* als'o-ran', (*inf*) a defeated contestant in a race, an election, etc; also-runner, an also-ran.

altar [ŏlt'är] *n* an elevated place or structure, on which sacrifices are offered; a table, etc. for sacred purposes in a place of worship.

alter [ŏl'tĕr] *vti* to make different; to change.—*adj* al'terable, that may be altered.—*adv* al'terably.—*n* alterā'tion, change.-*adj* al'terative, having power to alter.—*n* a medicine that alters favorably the course of an ailment.

altercate [ŏl'tĕr-kāt] *vi* to dispute or wrangle.—*n* altercā'tion, an angry or heated quarrel.

alter ego [al'tĕr eg'o, ŏl'tĕr ēg'ō] *n* one's other self; a constant companion.

alternate [ŏl'tĕr-nāt] *vt* to do or use by turns.—*vi* to act, happen, etc. by turns; to take turns regularly.—*adj* al'ternáte [-nát], (of two things) coming or following by turns; (of leaves) placed singly with change of side at each node.—*n* a substitute.—*adv* alter'nately.—*n* alternā'tion.—*adj* alter'native, offering a choice of two things.—*adv* alter'natively.—*n* alt'ernator, a generator of alternating current.

although [ŏl-THŌ'] *conj* admitting that; notwithstanding that.

altimeter [al-tim'e-tèr] *n* an instrument for measuring altitude.

altitude [al'ti-tūd] *n* height, esp above sea level, a high point or position; angle of elevation above horizon.

alto [ält'o] *n* the range of the lowest female voice; a singer with this range.—*adj* of, for or in the alto.

altogether [ŏl-tōō-geTH'èr] *adv* in all; on the whole; completely.

alto-relievo [al'tō-re-lē'vō] *n* high relief; a sculpture in high relief.

altruism [al'trōō-izm] *n* the principle of living and acting for the interest of others; animal behavior that seems analogous to human altruism.—*adj* altruist'ic.

aluminum [a-lōō-min'-um] *n* a silvery metallic element (Symbol Al; at wt 27.0; at no 13) remarkable for its lightness.

alumna [al-um'nà] *n* a girl (or woman) who has attended or been graduated from a particular school, college or university.

alumnus [al-um'nus] a male alumna.—*pl* alum'ni.

always [ŏl'wāz] *adv* at all times; continually; in any case.

Alzheimer's disease [älts'hīm-èrz] *n* a degenerative brain disease.

am [am] the 1st pers sing pres indic of the verb to be.

amalgam [a-mal'gam] *n* a mixture of metals in which one is mercury; a mixture.—*vt* al'gamate, to combine, unite.—*n* amalgamā'tion, the blending of different things; consolidation; a close union.

amanuensis [a-man-ū-en'sis] *n* one who writes to dictation; a copyist; a secretary;—*pl* amanuen'ses [-sēz].

amaranth [am'är-anth] *n* any of a large genus (*Amaranthus*) of coarse herbs, some cultivated as food crops, others for their large showy flowers.

amass [a-mas'] *vt* to gather in large quantity; to accumulate.—*vi* to come together.

amateur [am'a-chûr', or am-a-tûr'] *n* one who cultivates a particular activity for the love of it, and not for professional gain.—*adj* of or done by amateurs.—*adj* amateur'ish, lacking professional skill.

amatory [am'a-tòr-i] *adj* of or showing sexual love.

amaze [a-māz'] *vt* to confound with surprise or wonder, astonish—*n* amaze'ment,—*adj* amaz'ing,—*adv* amaz'ingly.

Amazon [am'a-zón] *n* in Greek myth, a race of female warriors; a tall strong masculine woman;—*adj* Amazō'nian.

ambassador [am-bas'a-dór] *n* the highest-ranking diplomatic representative from one country to another; an authorized messenger; an unofficial representative.—*adj* ambassadō'rial.

amber [am'bèr] *n* a yellowish fossil resin, used for ornaments, etc.—*adj* made of amber; amber-colored.

ambergris [am'bèr-grēs] *n* a waxy substance found floating in or on the shores of warm seas, believed to originate in the intestines of the sperm whale and used as a fixative for perfume.

ambient [am′bi-ènt] *adj* surrounding;—*ns* **am′biance, ambience;** surrounding influence, atmosphere.

ambiguous [am-big′ū-us] *adj* admitting of more than one meaning, equivocal; not clear; vague.—**ambigū′ity,** an ambiguous expression.—*adv* **ambig′uously.**

ambit [am′bit] *n* a circuit; space included; scope.

ambition [am-bish(ó)n] *n* desire for power, honor, fame, excellence.—*adj* **ambi′tious,** full of ambition; showing ambition.—*adv* **ambi′tiously.**—*n* **ambi′tiousness.**

ambivalence [am-biv′à-lèns] *n* (*psych*) the coexistence in one person of opposing emotional attitudes (eg love and hate) toward the same object.—*adj* **ambiv′alent,** characterized by ambivalence.

amble [am′bl] *vi* (of a horse) to move at an easy gait; to walk in a leisurely way.—*n* a horse's ambling gait; a leisurely walking pace.—*n* **am′bler.**

ambrosia [am-brō′z(h)i-a] *n* (*Greek and Roman myth*) food of the gods; anything that tastes or smells delicious.—*adj* **ambrō′sial,** fragrant; divine.

ambulance [am′būl-àns] *n* a special vehicle for the sick or injured.—Also *adj*—*adjs* **am′bulant,** moving from place to place; **am′bulatory,** having the power of walking.

ambuscade [am′bus-kād] *vti* ambush.

ambush [am′bŏŏsh] *n* a concealment of assailants to make a surprise attack; the bushes or other cover in which they are hidden.—*vti* to attack from ambush.

ameer [a-mēr′] *n see* emir.

ameliorate [a-mēl′yór-āt] *vti* to make or become better.—*n* **ameliorā′tion.**

amen [ä′men′, or ä′men′] *interj* may it be so!

amenable [a-mēn′a-bl, a-men′a-bl] *adj* easy to lead, tractable.—*ns* **amenabil′ity, amen′ableness.**—*adv* **amen′ably.**

amend [a-mend′] *vt* to correct; to improve; to alter in detail.—*vi* to improve one's conduct.—*adj* **amend′able.**—*n* **amend′ment,** correction.

amenity [a-mēn′i-ti] *n* pleasantness, as regards situation, climate, manners, or convenience; (*pl*) courteous acts.—**amenity horticulture,** the growing of ornamental plants.

amenorrhoea [a-, ä-men-ō-rē′a] *n* abnormal absence of menstruation.

amerce [a-mûrs′] *vt* to punish by a fine.—*n* **amerce′ment.**

American [a-mer′i-kán] *adj* of the American continent or the US.—*n* a native or inhabitant of America.—*npl* **Amer′ican′a,** artifacts typical of American civilization; American culture.

Amerindian [a-mer-ind′i-àn] *n* member of any of the aboriginal peoples of the Western Hemisphere.—Also **Amerind′, American Indian.**

amethyst [am′e-thist] *n* a purple or violet quartz or corundum used as a gemstone; purple or violet; a bluish-violet variety of quartz.—*adj* **amethyst′ine.**

amiable [ām′i-abl] *adj* lovable; likable.—*ns* **amiabil′ity, am′iableness,** quality, or instance, of being good-natured, obliging.—*adv* **am′iably.**

amicable [am′i-ka-bl] *adj* friendly; peaceable.—*ns* **amicabil′ity, am′icableness.**—*adv* **am′icably.**

amice [am′is] *n* a liturgical vestment made of white linen worn about the neck and shoulders.

amid [a-mid′], **amidst** [a-midst′] *prep* in the middle of; among.—*adv* **amid′ships, amid′ship,** in or toward the middle of a ship.

amigo [à-mē′gō] *n* a friend.—*pl* **amigos.** [Sp]

amir [a-mēr′] *n see* emir.

amiss [a-mis′] *adj* wrong; improper; faulty.—*adv* in a faulty manner, astray.

amity [am′i-ti] *n* friendship; goodwill.

ammeter [am′e-tèr] an instrument for measuring electric current in amperes.

ammonia [a-mō′ni-a] *n* a pungent gas, a compound of nitrogen and hydrogen NH_3 very soluble in water; (loosely) a solution of ammonia in water.—*adj* **ammon′iac,** pertaining to, or having the properties of, ammonia.—*adj* **ammōn′iated,** containing ammonia.

ammunition [a-mū-nish′(ó)n] *n* bullets, gunpowder, bombs, grenades, rockets, etc.; any means of attack or defense; facts and reasoning used to prove a point in an argument.

amnesia [am-nē′zh(y)a, or -si-a] *n* partial or total loss of memory.

amnesty [am′nest-i] *n* a general pardon, esp of political offenders.

amoeba [a-mē′ba] *n* any of a genus (*Amoeba*) of one-celled microorganisms found in water, damp soil, and digestive tracts of animals;—*pl* **amoeb′ae.**

amok [a-mok′] *adv* in a frenzy; to kill.—Also **amuck.**

among [a-mung′], **amongst** [a-mungst′], *prep* of the number of; amidst; to or for each or several of.

amoral [ā-mor′àl] *adj* neither moral nor immoral; without moral sense.

amorous [am′or-us] *adj* fond of making love; full of love; of sexual love.—*adv* **am′orously.**—*n* **am′orousness.**

amorphous [a-mör′fus] *adj* without definite shape, shapeless; (*chem*) not crystalline.

amortize [a-mört′īz] *vt* to put money aside at intervals for gradual payment of (a debt, etc.); to wipe out (as a debt).—*n* **amortizā′tion.**

amount [a-mownt′] *vi* to come in total (to); to be equivalent in substance (to).—*n* the whole sum; the whole value or effect; a quantity.

amour [am-ōōr′] *n* a usu. illicit love affair.—**amour propre,** self-esteem.

ampere [am′pār, am′pēr] *n* the standard unit by which an electric current is measured equal to one coulomb per second.

ampersand [am′pèr-sand] *n* a sign (&) meaning 'and'.

amphetamine [am-fet′á-mēn, -min] *n* a drug used esp as a stimulant, and to suppress appetite.

amphibian [am-fib′i-an] *n* any of a class (Amphibia) of cold-blooded egg-laying vertebrates with soft skin, gills at tadpole stage when aquatic, replaced by lungs as land-living adults (eg frogs, salamanders, toads); vehicle able to travel on land or water; aircraft that can alight on land or water.—*adj* **amphib′ious.**

amphitheater [am′fi-thē′a-tèr] *n* an oval or circular edifice having rising rows of seats around an open space.

amphora [am′fo-ra] *n* an ancient Greek two-handled jar with a large oval body and a narrow neck.

amphoteric [am-fo-ter′ik] *adj* partly one and partly the other, specifically, capable of reacting chemically either as an acid or as a base.

ample [am′pl] *adj* large in size, scope, etc.; large enough; copious.—*n* **am′pleness.**—*adv* **am′ply.**

amplify [am′pli-fī] *vt* to express more fully; to strengthen (electrical signals) etc.—*n* **amplificā′tion.**—*adj* **amplificā′tory.**—*n* **am′plifier,** a device that increases electric voltage, current, or power, or the loudness of sound.

amplitude [am′pli-tūd] *n* largeness; breadth; abundance; range from mean to extreme, as of an alternating current.—**amplitude modulation,** the changing of the amplitude of the transmitting radio wave in accordance with the signal being broadcast.

ampoule [am-pōōl′] *n* a small, sealed, glass capsule for one dose of a hypodermic medicine; a vial resembling this.—Also **ampule, ampal.**

ampulla [am-pul′a] *n* a small two-handled flask used in ancient Rome.

amputate [am′pū-tāt] *vt* to cut off, esp by surgery.—*n* **amputā′tion.**

Amtrak [am′trak′] *n* a nationwide system of passenger railroad service.

amuck [a-muk′] *see* amok.

amulet [am′ū-let] *n* something worn as a charm against evil.

amuse [a-mūz′] *vt* to occupy or entertain pleasantly; to divert; to excite mirth in.—*n* **amuse′-ment.**—*adj* **amusing,**—*adv* **amus′ingly.**

an [an] *adj* one; the indefinite article, used before words beginning with the sound of a vowel.

-an [en, in, 'n] *suffix* meaning of belonging to (*diocesan*); born in, living in (*Chicagoan*); believing in (*Christian*).

Anabaptist [an-a-bapt′ist] *n* one who holds that baptism ought to be administered only to adults, and therefore that those baptized in infancy ought to be baptized again.

anabolism [an-ab′ol-izm] *n* the constructive part of metabolism in which complex molecules are synthesized from simpler ones in the living organism.—*adj* **anabol′ic.**

anachronism [an-a′kron-izm] *n* an error in chronology, whereby a thing is assigned to a period to which it does not belong;

the representation of this; a person, custom, or idea regarded as out of date. —*adj* **anachronist'ic.**

anacoluthon [an-a-ko-lū'thon] *n* want of sequence in the construction of a sentence, when the latter part does not correspond grammatically with the former.

anaconda [an-a-kon'da] *n* a large S American semiaquatic snake (*Eunectus murinus*) that kills its prey by constriction.

anaemia, anae'mic *see* anemia, anemic.

anaesthesia, anaesthetic *see* anesthesia, anesthetic.

anaglyph [an'a-glif] *n* an ornament carved in low relief, a stereoscopic still or motion picture. —*adj* **anaglypt'ic.**

anagram [an'a-gram] *n* a word or sentence formed by rewriting in a different order the letters of another word or sentence; as, 'live' for 'evil', 'Flit on, cheering angel' for 'Florence Nightingale'. —*adjs* **anagrammat'ic, anagrammat'ical.**

anal [ān'ál] *adj* pertaining to or near the anus.

analects [an'a-lekts] *n pl* selected miscellaneous written passages. —Also **analec'ta.**

analgesia [an-al-jē'zi-a] *n* insensibility to pain without loss of consciousness. —*n* **analgē'sic,** a pain-relieving drug. —*adj* that dispels pain.

analogy [an-al'o-ji] *n* an agreement or correspondence in certain respects between things otherwise different; the inference that certain resemblances imply further similarity. —*adj* **analog'ical.** —*adv* **analog'ically.** —*vti* **anal'ogize,** to use, or explain, by analogy. —*adj* **anal'ogous,** similar in certain respects (to). —*n* **an'alogue, an'alog,** a word or thing bearing analogy to, another.

analysis [an-al'i-sis] *n* a resolving or separating a whole into its elements or component parts; a statement of the results of this process. —*pl* **anal'yses.** *n* **analysand',** a person undergoing psychoanalysis. —*vt* **an'alyse** [-īz], to resolve (a whole) into elements; to separate into component parts to psychoanalyze. —*adj* **analyz'able.** —*n* **an'alyst** [-ist], one who analyzes; a psychoanalyst. —*adjs* **analytic** [-it'ik], **-al,** pertaining to analysis; —*adv* **analyt'ically.** —**analytical geometry,** technique of using algebra to deal with geometry; coordinate geometry.

anarchy [an'ärk-i] *n* the absence of government; political confusion. —*adjs* **anarch'ic,** —*ns* **an'archism,** the theory that all government is unneccessary; **an'archist,** one who strives to create anarchy, esp by violence.

anathema [an-ath'em-a] *n* anything greatly detested; any strong curse; a solemn ecclesiastical curse or denunciation; any person or thing anathematized. —*vt* **anath'ematize,** to pronounce accursed.

anatomy [an-a'tom-i] *n* the dissection of an organism to study its structure; the science of the structure of plants and animals; the structure of an organism; the analysis of anything; —*adjs* **anatom'ic, -al,** relating to anatomy. —*adv* **anatom'ically.** —*vti* **anat'omize,** to disect; to study structure; to analyze. —*n* **anat'omist.**

ancestor [an'ses-tór] *n* one from whom a person is descended, a forefather. —*adj* **ances'tral.** —*n* **an'cestry,** all one's ancestors; lineage.

anchor [ang'kór] *n* a hooked implement that sticks into the bed of a sea or river and thus holds a ship in position; anything that gives stability; a newscaster who coordinates the various reports. —*vt* to fix by an anchor; to be the final contestant (on a relay team, etc.). —*ns* **anch'orage,** a place for anchoring. —**an'chorman; anchorwoman.**

anchorite, anchoret, [ang'kór-īt, ang'kór-et] *n* one who has withdrawn from the world, usu. for religious reasons. —*n* **anch'oress,** a female anchorite.

anchovy [an'chō-vi, also an'chó'vi] *n* a small Mediterranean fish (*Engraulis encrasicholus*) used for pickling, and for making sauce, paste, etc.

ancient [ān'shént] *adj* very old; belonging to times long past, —*n* an aged person. —*adv* **an'ciently,** in ancient times. —*n* **an'cientness.** —*n pl* the **an'cients,** those who lived in remote times.

ancillary [an'si-lár-ē] *adj* subordinate (to); auxiliary.

and [and] *conj* signifies addition, repetition, contrast or consequence, and is used to connect words, phrases, clauses, and sentences; informally, as a substitute for *to* (*try and get it*)

andante [an-dan'tā] *adv, adj, n* (*mus*) moderately slow.

andiron [and'ī-érn] *n* either of a pair of metal supports for logs in a fireplace; a firedog.

androgen [an'drō-jén] *n* a male sex hormone that can give rise to masculine characteristics.

androgynous an-droj'i-nus] *adj* not distinguishable as to sex in appearance, behaviour, etc.; having roles characteristic of both sexes.

android [an'droid] *n* in science fiction, an automaton made to look like a man.

anecdote [an'ek-dōt] *n* a brief entertaining account of any curious or interesting incident. —*adj* **an'ecdotal.**

anemia [a-nē'mi-a] *n* a condition in which the blood is low in red cells or in hemoglobin, resulting in paleness, weakness, etc. —*adj* **ane'emic.**

anemometer [an-e-mom'it-ér] *n* an instrument for measuring the force or speed of the wind; wind gauge.

anemone [a-nem'ó-ne] *n* a genus (*Anemone*) of the buttercup family, a sea anemone.

anent [a-nent'] *prep* concerning, about.

aneroid barometer [an'é-roid] *n* a barometer for working by the bending of a thin metal plate instead of by the rise and fall of mercury.

anesthetic [an-es-thet'ik] *n* a drug, gas, etc. used to produce anesthesia, as before surgery. —*adj* of or producing anesthesia. —*ns* **anesthē'sia,** a partial or total loss of the sense of pain, touch, etc.; **anesthēsiológist,** a doctor who specializes in giving anesthetics; **an'esthēsiol'ogy; anēs'thetist,** a person trained to give anesthetics. —*vt* **anēs'thetize,** to cause anesthesia in.

aneurysm, aneurism [an'ūr-izm] *n* the permanent abnormal dilation of an artery.

anew [a-nū'] *adv* afresh; again, once more; in a new way or form.

anfractuous [an-frakt'ū-us] *adj* full of windings; tortuous. —*n* **anfractuos'ity.**

angel [ān'jél] *n* a messenger of God; an image of a human figure with wings and a halo; a person of extraordinary beauty or virtue; (*slang*) financial backer as for a play. —*adjs* **angel'ic, [an-], angel'ical.** —*adv* **angel'ically.** —**angel dust,** (*slang*) an illicit hallucinogenic drug; **angel food cake,** a light sponge cake made only with egg whites, flour, and sugar.

angelica [an-jel'i-kà] *n* any of a genus (*Angelica*) of herbs of the carrot family used in cookery and medicine.

angelus [an'ji-lus] *n* a short devotional exercise in honor of the Incarnation; the bell rung at morning, noon, and sunset, the times for this exercise.

anger [ang'gér] *n* hot displeasure, often because of opposition, a hurt, etc. —*vti* to make or become angry; —*adj* **ang'ry,** excited with anger; inflamed; of sullen aspect (eg of the sky). —*n* an angry young man. —*adv* **ang'rily.** —*n* **ang'riness.**

angina [an-ji'na] *n* angina pectoris; a spasmodic gripping sensation of pain. —**angina pec'toris,** a disease of the heart marked by paroxysms of intense pain.

angle[1] [ang'gl]*n* a corner; the point from which lines or surfaces diverge... —*adj* **ang'ūlar,** having an angle or angles; forming an angle; measured by an angle; stiff and awkward in manner.

angle[2] [ang'gl] *vi* to fish with a hook and line; to use tricks to get something. —*ns* **ang'ler; ang'ling.**

Anglican [ang'glik-án] *adj* belonging to or of the Church of England.

Anglo- [ang'glo] *pfx* English—as in *Anglo*-Saxon, etc. —*n* (and *adj*) **Ang'lo-Catholic,** (member) of a High Church movement in Anglicanism fostering continuity with the RC church by use of RC liturgy, etc.

Anglo [ang'glō] *n* (among Hispanics and Amerindians) a person of Caucasian descent; an English-speaking Canadian.

anglophil(e) [ang'glō-fil] *n,* and *adj* (one) who admires England and things English.

anglophobe [ang'glō-fōb] *n, adj* (one) fearing or disliking England. —*n* **anglophobia,** [ang-glōfō'bi-a;] dislike of England and things English.

Angora [ang-gō', -gō', ra] *n* a breed of goat with long white silky hair; mohair; a breed cat or a breed rabbit with long silky hair.

angry *see* anger.

angst [angst] *n* a feeling of apprehension, fear, or anxiety.

angström [ang'strom] *n* one hundred-millionth of a centimeter, a unit used in measuring the length of light waves.— Also **angstrom unit.**

anguish [ang′gwish] *n* excessive pain of body or mind, agony.—*vti* to make or feel anguish.

anhydrous [an-hī′drus] *adj* free from water and esp water and crystallization.

anile [an′īl, ān′īl] *adj* of or resembling a senile old woman.

animadvert [an-im-ad-vûrt′] *vi* (*with* **on** or **upon**) to express criticism of usu. to censure.—*n* **animadver′sion**, criticism.

animal [an′im-ál] *n* any living organism except a plant or bacterium, typically able to move about; a lower animal as distinguished from man, esp mammals; a brutish or bestial person.—*adj* of or like an animal; bestial; sensual.—*n* **an′imalism,** sensualism.

animalcule, animalculum [an-im-al′kūl, -um] *n* a small animal; that cannot be seen by the naked eye;—*pl* **animal′cules, animal′cula.**

animate [an′im-āt] *vt* to give life to; to enliven; to actuate.—*adj* [-át] living.—*adj* **an′imated,** lively; full of spirit; endowed with life; moving as if alive.—*n* **anima′tion,** liveliness; vigor.—**animated cartoon,** a film made by photographing a series of drawings, giving the illusion of movement.

animism [an′im-izm] *n* the belief that all life is produced by a spiritual force, or that natural objects and phenomena have souls.

animosity [an-im-os′i-ti] *n* strong dislike; enmity.

animus [an′im-us] *n* animosity; feeling of like or dislike; ill-will.

anise [an′is] *n* an umbelliferous plant (*Pimpinella anisum*) whose aromatic seeds are used in flavoring.—Also **an′iseed.**

ankh [angk] *n* a cross with a loop for its upper vertical arm, an emblem of life.

ankle [angk′l] *n* the joint connecting the foot and leg, the part of the leg between the foot and calf.—*n* **ank′let,** an ornament for the ankle.

annals [an′álz] *n pl* a written account of events year by year; historical records generally.—*n* **ann′alist,** a writer of annals.

anneal [an-ēl′] *vt* to subject (glass or metals) to heat and gradual cooling to prevent brittleness; to heat in order to fix colors on (eg glass).

annex [a-neks′] *vt* to attach esp to something larger; to incorporate into a state the territory of (another state).—*n* [an′eks] something annexed, esp an addition to a building.—*ns* **annexā′tion;**

annihilate [an-nī′hil-āt] *vt* to reduce to nothing; to put out of existence.—*ns* **annihilā′tion.**

anniversary [an-i-vûrs′ár-i] *n* the yearly return of the date of some event.—*adj* of an anniversary.

anno Domini [an′ō dom′in-ī, -ē] in the year of our Lord.

annotate [an′ō-tāt] *vti* to provide with explanatory notes.—*ns* **annota′tion; ann′otator.**

announce [a-nowns′] *vt* to give public notice of; to make known the arrival of; to be an announcer for.—*vi* to serve as an announcer.—*ns* **announce′ment; announc′er,** one who announces.

annoy [a-noi′] *vt* to vex, tease, irritate, as by a repeated action.—*pr p* **annoy′ing;** *pt p* **annoyed′.**—*n* **annoy′ance,** that which annoys; state of being annoyed.

annual [an′ū-ál] *adj* of or measured by a year; yearly; coming every year; living only one year or season.—*n* a plant that lives only one year; a periodical published once a year.—*adv* **ann′ually.**

annuity [a-nū′i-ti] *n* an investment yielding fixed payments esp yearly; such a payment.—*n* **annū′itant,** one who receives an annuity.

annul [a-nul′] *vt* to do away with; to deprive of legal force, nullify.—*pr p* **annull′ing;** *pt p* **annulled′.**—*n* **annul′ment.**

annular [an′ūl-ár] *adj* like or forming a ring.—*adj* **ann′ulate,** formed with rings.—*n* **ann′ulus** (*biol*), a ring-shaped structure.—**annular eclipse,** an eclipse of the sun during which a ring-shaped part of its surface encircles the portion obscured by the moon.

Annunciation [a-nun-si-ā′sh(ó)n] *n* the angel Gabriel's announcement to Mary that she would bear Jesus; the church festival commemorating this; **annunciation,** an announcing.

anode [an′ōd] *n* the positive electrode by which an electric current enters an electrolytic cell, gas discharge tube, or thermionic valve; the electrode to which electrons flow.

anodyne [an′ō-dīn] *n* anything that relieves pain or or soothes.

anoint [an-oint′] *vt* to consecrate with oil.—*n* **anoint′ment.**

anomaly [a-nom′á-li] *n* abnormality; anything anomalous.—*adj* **anom′alous,** abnormal; inconsistent or odd.

anon [an-on′] *adv* soon; at another time.

anon [a-non′] a contr of **anonymous.**

anonymous [a-non′im-us] *adj* lacking a name; without the name of the author; lacking individuality.—*n* **anonym′ity,** the quality or state of being anonymous.—*adv* **anon′ymously.**

anorexia [an-ór-ek′si-a] *n* loss of appetite, esp the pathological condition **anorexia nervosa.**—*adj* **anorex′ic.**

another [an-uᴛн′ér] *adj* a different or distinct (thing or person); one more of the same kind; any other.—Also *pron.*

anserine [an′sèr-in, or -in] *adj* relating to the goose.

answer [än′sèr] *n* a reply or response; retaliation; the solution of a problem.—*vt* to reply or respond; to satisfy (eg one's requirements) or to correspond to (eg a description); to comply with or obey; to defend oneself against (a charge).—*vi* to reply; to act in response (to); to be accountable (for); to conform (to).—*adj* **an′swerable,** capable of being refuted.

ant [ant] *n* any of a family (Formicidae) of small, generally wingless insects of many species, all of which form and live in highly organized groups. **ant bear,** a large anteater (*Myrmecophaga jubata*) of S America; **ant cow,** an aphid from which ants obtain honeydew; **ant′eater,** any of several mammals that feed largely or entirely on termites and ants; echidna; aardvark; **ant′hill,** a mound thrown up by ants or termites in digging their nests.

antacid [ant-as′id] *n* a substance that counteracts acidity.

antagonist [ant-ag′on-ist] *n* an adversary; one who strives against another; an opponent;—*vt* **antag′onize,** to arouse opposition in.—*n* **antag′onism,** opposition; hostility; an opposing force, principle, etc. *adj* **antagonist′ic.**—*adv* **antagonist′ically.**

antarctic [ant-ärk′tik] *adj* of, near, or relating to, the South Pole or to south polar regions.—*n* **the Antarctic,** land are about the South Pole.

ante- [an-ti] *pfx* meaning; in front of (*anteroom*); earlier than (*antediliviam*).

ante [ant′ē] *n* a player's stake in poker.—*vi* to place an ante; to pass.

antebellum [ant-ē-bel′um] *adj* existing before a war, esp the American Civil War.

antecedent [an-ti-sēd′ént] *adj* going before in time; prior(to).—*n* that which precedes in time.

antechamber [an′ti-chām-bèr] *n* an anteroom.

antedate [an′ti-dāt] *vt* to put a date on that is earlier than the actual date; to come before in time.

antediluvian [an-ti-di-l(y)ōō′vi-àn] *adj* existing or happening before the Biblical Flood; antiquated.—Also *n.*

antelope [an′ti-lōp] *n* any of an old world family (Bovidae) of swift and graceful ruminant quadrupeds, resembling the deer; pronghorn; leather from an antelope hide.

ante meridian [an-ti-me-ri′di-àn] *adj* being before noon.

antenatal [an-ti-nā′tàl] *adj* prenatal.

antenna [an-ten′a] *n* either of a pair of feelers on the head of an insect, crab, etc.;—*pl* **antennae** [-nē]; an arrangement of rods and wires, etc. used in sending and receiving the electromagnetic waves in broadcasting;—**antennas.**

antepenult [an-ti-pen-ult′] *n* the third syllable before the end of a word.

anterior [antē′ri-ór] *adj* at or toward the front; earlier, previous.

anteroom [an′ti-rōōm] *n* a room leading into a larger or main room.

anthelmintic [an-thel-mint′ik] *adj, n* (a drug) destroying or expelling worms.

anthem [an′thêm] *n* a religious choral song; a song of praise or devotion, as to a nation.

anther [an′thér] *n* that part of the stamen in a flower which contains the pollen.

anthology [an-thol′oj-i] *n* a collection of poetry or prose.—*n* **anthol′ogist.**

anthracite [an′thra-sīt] *n* a hard coal which give much heat and little smoke.

anthrax [an'thraks] *n* a contagious, bacterial disease of cattle and sheep, etc. that can be transmitted to people.

anthropocentric [an-thrō-pō-sent'rik] *adj* regarding man as the center of the universe.

anthropoid [an'throp-oid, or -thrōp'-] *adj* manlike; applied esp to the great apes, ie chimpanzee, gorilla, orangutan, or gibbon.—*n* an anthropoid ape.

anthropology [an-thrō-pol'oj-i] *n* the scientific study of human beings, their origins, distribution, physical attributes, and culture; the aspect of Christian teaching dealing with the origin, nature, and destiny of human beings.—*adj* **anthropolog'ical**. *n* **anthropol'ogist**.

anthropomorphism [an-thrōp-o-mörf'izm] *n* the ascription of human characteristics to other beings or to things.—*adj* **anthropomorph'ic**.

anthropophagy [an-thrō-pof'a-ji] *n* cannibalism.—*n* **anthropoph'agi**, cannibals.—*adj* **anthrophoph'agous** [-a-gus].

anti- [ant'i-] *pfx* meaning against, in opposition to; rival; prevents, cures.

anti [an'tī or -tē] *n* (*inf*) a person opposed to something.—*adj* (*inf*) opposed.

antibiotic [an-ti-bī-ot'ik] *n* any of various chemical, fungal or synthetic substances used against bacterial or fungal infections.—Also *adj*.

antibody [an'ti-bod-i] *n* a defensive substance produced in an organism in response to the action of a foreign body such as the toxin of a parasite.

antic [ant'ik] *adj* grotesque.—*n* a fantastic figure; (*arch*) a buffoon; (usu in *pl*) a fantastic action or trick, a caper.—*vi* to cut capers.

Antichrist [an'ti-krīst] *n* (*Bible*) the antagonist of Christ; an enemy of Christ, or His teachings.—*adj* **antichristian** [-krist'-].

anticipate [an-tis'ip-āt] *vt* to be beforehand with (another person or thing), to forestall; to use, spend, deal with, in advance; to foresee; to count upon as certain, to expect.—*vi* to speak, act, before the appropriate time.—*n* **anticipā'tion**.—*adj* **anti-cipātory**.

anticlerical [an-ti-kler'i-kál] *adj* opposed to the clergy or their power in secular matters.

anticlimax [an-ti-klī'maks] *n* a sudden drop from the important to the trivial; an ineffective or disappointing ending to a story or series of events.

anticoagulant [an-ti-kō-ag'ū-lánt] *n* a substance that hinders clotting of blood.

anticyclone [an-ti-sīklōn] *n* a rotatory outflow of air from an area of high atmospheric pressure.

antidote [an'ti-dōt] *n* that which is given to counteract poison; anything that prevents evil.—*adj* **an'tidotal**.

antifreeze. [an'ti-frēz] *n* a substance used, as in an automobile radiator, to prevent freezing up.

antihistamine [an-ti-hist'á-mēn] *n* any of a group of drugs that prevent the action of histamines in allergic conditions.

antimony [an'ti-món-i] *n* a brittle, bluish-white metallic element (symbol Sb); at wt 121.8; at no 51 used in alloys, drugs, and dyes.

antinomy [an-tin'ō-mi] *n* the opposition of one law to another; (*philos*) contradiction between two conclusions correctly derived from two laws both assumed to be correct.

antipathy [an-tip'ath-i] *n* rooted dislike; aversion; an object of this.—*adjs* **antipathet'ic, -al**.

antipersonnel [an'ti-pér-só-el'] *adj* intended to destroy persons rather than objects.

antiphon [an'tif-on] *n* a form of church music sung by two groups, each responding to the other—also **antiph'ony**.—*adj* **antiph'onal**, pertaining to antiphony.—*n* a book of antiphons or of anthems.

antipodes [an-tip'od-ēz] *n pl* two places on the earth's surface opposite each other.—*adj* **antip'odal**.

antipope [an'ti-pōp] *n* a pope in opposition to one who is held to be canonically chosen.

antipyretic [an-ti-pī-ret'ik] *adj* counteracting fever.—*n* an agent that reduces fever.

antiquary [an'ti-kwàr-i] *n* one who studies or collects monuments and relics of the past.—*adj* **antiquār'ian**, connected with the study of antiquities.—*n* an antiquary.—*n* **anti-**

quār'ianism, study of, or devotion to the study of, antiquities.

antique [an-tēk'] *adj* ancient; old-fashioned; after the manner of the ancients.—*n* anything very old; a piece of furniture etc. made at an earlier period and according to customs laws at least 100 years old.—*adj* **an'tiquated**, grown old, or out of fashion; obsolete.—*ns* **antiq'uity**, ancient times.

anti-Semite [an'ti-sem'ī̇t, or -sēm'ī̇t] *n* one who is hostile toward or discriminates against Jews as a religious or racial group. *adj* **anti-Semit'ic**.—*n* **anti-Sem'itism**.

antiseptic. [an-ti-sept'ik] *n* a substance that destroys or prevents the growth of disease-producing microorganisms.—Also *adj*—*adv* **antisept'ically**.—*n* **antisep'sis**, antiseptic treatment.

antisocial [an-ti-sō'shàl] *adj* avoiding the company of other people, unsocial; contrary to the interests of society in general.

antithesis [an-tith'i-sis] *n* a contrast or opposition, as of ideas; the exact opposite;—*pl* **antith'esēs** [-sēz]—*adjs* **antithetical** [-thet'-].—*adv* **antithet'ically**.

antitoxin [an-ti-tok'sin] *n* a substance formed in the body that acts against a specific toxin; a serum containing an antitoxin, injected into a person to prevent disease.—*adj* **antitox'ic**.

antler [ant'lér] *n* a bony outgrowth from the frontal bone of a deer.—*adj* **ant'lered**.

antonym [ant'ō-nim] *n* either of two words that have opposite meanings, as 'long' and 'short'.

antrum [an'trúm] *n* (*anat*) a cavity esp a sinus, in the upper jaw.

anus [ān'us] the lower orifice of the alimentary canal.

anvil [an'vil] *n* an iron block on which metal objects are hammered into shape.

anxious [angk'shùs] *adj* worried; uneasy; eagerly wishing; causing anxiety.—*n* **anxiety** [ang-zī'i-ti], state of being anxious; state of chronic apprehension as a symptom of mental disorder.—*adv* **an'xiously**.—*n* **an'xiousness**.

any [en'i] *adj* one out of many, some.—*pron* **an'ybody**, any person; an important person.—*advs* **an'yhow**, in any way whatever; in any case; **an'ymore**, now; nowadays.—*pron* **an'yone**, any person; anybody.—*adv* **an'yplace**, anywhere.—*pron* **an'ything**, any object, event, fact, etc.—*n* a thing, no matter of what kind.—*adv* in any way.—*advs* **an'yway**, in any manner; at any rate; haphazardly; **an'ywhere**, in, at, or to any place.

aorist [ā'ór-ist] *n* a tense, expressing past action where time is indefinite or unimportant.

aorta [ā-ör'ta] *n* the great artery that carries blood from the heart to be distributed by branch through the body.—*adj* **aort'ic**, arteries.

apace [a-pās'] *adv* at a quick pace; swiftly.

apart [a-pärt'] *adv* separately; aside; asunder.—**apart from**, leaving out of consideration; **set apart**, to separate, consecrate.

apartheid [á-pärt'hāt, -pär'tid] *n* official government policy of racial segregation, esp in South Africa.

apartment [a-pärt'ment] *n* room or rooms, furnished with housekeeping equipment and usu. rented.—**apartment building**, **apartment house**, building containing separate apartments; **apartment hotel**, hotel containing apartments as well as accommodation for transients.

apathy [ap'ath-i] *n* lack of feeling; absence of passion; indifference.—*adj* **apathet'ic**.—*adv* **apathet'ically**.

ape [āp] *n* a chimpanzee, gorilla, orangutan, or gibbon; any monkey; a mimic; a gross, clumsy man.—*vt* to imitate.

apeak [a-pēk'] *adv*, *adj* being in a vertical position.

aperient [a-pē'ri-ént] *adj* laxative.—Also *n*

apéritif [á-pār-i-tēf] *n* an alcoholic drink taken before a meal.

aperture [a'pér-tyúr, -chúr] *n* an opening; a hole.

apex [ā'peks] *n* the summit; climax; culminating point; the vertex of a triangle;—*pl* **ā'pexes, apices**

aphaeresis, apheresis [a-fēr'i-sis] *n* (*gram*) the taking away of a letter or syllable at the beginning of a word, as in *coon* for *raccoon*.

aphasia [a-fā'zi-a] *n* loss of power to use or to understand words. [Gr *a-*, priv, *phasis*, speech.]

apheresis *see* **aphaeresis**.

aphesis [af'es-is] *n* aphaeresis, in which an unaccented vowel at the beginning of a word is lost, as in *lone* for *alone*.—*adj* **aphet′ic**.

aphis [af′is, ā′fis] **aphid**, *ns* a plant-louse or greenfly, any of a large number of small insects that suck the juice of plants.—*pl* **aphides** [af′i-dēz, āf′i-dēz].

aphorism [af′ōr-izm] *n* a brief, pithy saying, an adage.—*adj* **aphoris′tic**.

aphrodisiac [af-rō-diz′-i-ák] *adj* exciting sexually.

apiary [āp′i-ár-i] *n* a place where bees are kept.—*n* **ap′iarist**, one who keeps bees.

apices *pl* of apex.

apiculture [ā′pi-cul-tyúr, -chùr] *n* beekeeping.

apiece [a-pēs′] *adv* to or for each one. [a, indefinite article, + piece.]

apish [āp′ish] *adj* apelike. [ape.]

aplomb [a-plɔ′] *n* poise; self-possession.

Apocalypse [a-pok′al-ips] *n* (*Bible*) the book of Revelation in the Douay Version of the New Testament; **apocalypse**, prophetic revelation, of Jewish and Christian writing of 200 BC to 150 AD; a cataclysmic event, the end of the world.

apocope [a-pok′o-pe] *n* the loss of the last letter or syllable of a word as *th′* for *the*, *I* for OE *ic*

Apocrypha [a-pok′rif-a] *n* fourteen books of the Septugint rejected in Protestantism and Judaism; eleven are in the Roman Catholic Bible; **apocrypha**, any writings of dubious authenticity.—*ads* **Apocryphal**, of the Apocrypha;—*adj* **apoc′ryphal**, untrue; invented.

apodosis [a-pod′o-sis] *n* (*gram*) the main clause of a conditional sentence.

apogee [ap′o-jē] *n* the greatest distance of the orbit of the moon, or any satellite from the earth, the sun's apogee corresponding to the earth's aphelion, and the moon's being the point of its orbit farthest from the earth.

apolitical [ā-pol-iti′k-ál] *adj* indifferent to political affairs; uninvolved in politics.—*n* **apol′iticism**.

apologetic, -al [a-pol-o-jet′ik, -ál] *adj* excusing; penitently acknowledging; said or written in defence.—*adv* **apologet′ically**.—*n* **apologet′ics**, the defensive argument, esp the defence of Christianity.

apologue [ap′o-log] *n* an allegorical tale intended to convey a moral.

apology [a-pol′oj-i] *n* a defence or justification; an expression of penitence; a poor substitute (*with* for).—*vi* **apol′ogize**, to make excuse; to express regret for a fault.—*n* **apol′ogist**, one who makes an apology.

apoplexy [a′po-pleks-i] *n* sudden loss of sensation and of motion, generally the result of a broken or blocked blood vessel in the brain.—*adjs* **apoplec′tic**, pertaining to or causing apoplexy.

apostasy [a-pos′ta-si] *n* abandonment, or desertion of one's religion, principles, or political party.—*n* **apost′ate**, one guilty of apostasy;—Also *adj*—*vi* **apost′atize**.

a posteriori [ā-pos-te-ri-ō′rī, -ō′rī] *adj* applied to reasoning from effect to cause.

Apostle [a-pos′l] *n* one of the twelve disciples of Christ: **apostle**, the principal champion or supporter of a new system or cause.—*adjs* **apostol′ic** [ap-os-tol′ik, -á].—*n* **apostolic′ity** [-is′i-ti].—**Apostles′ Creed**, the oldest form of Christian creed that exists, early ascribed to the apostles.

apostrophe¹ [a-pos′trof-e], *n* (*rhetoric*) a sudden turning away from the ordinary course of a speech to address some absent person or personified object.—*vt* **apos′trophize**, to address by apostrophe; to make use of apostrophe.

apostrophe² [a-pos′trof-e] *n* a mark (′) showing the omission of a letter or letters in a word; also a sign of the possessive case.

apothecary [a-poth′ek-ár-i] *n* (*arch*) one who dispenses drugs and medicines; (*obs*) a medical practitioner.—**apothecaries′ weight**, the system of weights used by pharmacists in which the pound equals 12 ounces.

apothegm [a-po-thém] *n* a startling or paradoxical aphorism.

apotheosis [a-po-the-ō′sis] *n* the deification of a principle or person.

appall, appal [a-pöl′] *vt* to terrify, dismay;—*pr p* **appall′ing**; *pt p* **appalled′**—*adj* **appall′ing**, *adv* **appall′ingly**.

apparatus [ap-ar-ā′tus, -a′tus] *n* things prepared or provided for a specific use; any complex machine, device, or system.

apparel [a-par′él] *n* covering for the body, dress.—*vt* to dress; to clothe.

apparent [a-pār′ent, a-par′ênt] *adj* that may be seen; evident; seeming.—*adv* **appar′ently**.

apparition [a-par-ish′(ó)n] *n* an appearance or manifestation; a visionary appearance, a ghost.—*adj* **appari′tional**.

appeal [a-pēl′] *vi* to call, make application, have recourse (*with* to); to refer (to a witness or superior authority); to make earnest request; to be pleasing (*with* to).

appear [a-pēr′] *vi* to become visible; to come into view; to be published; to present oneself formally; to be manifest; to seem.—*n* **appear′ance**, the act of appearing; that which appears; form, aspect.

appease [a-pēz′] *vt* to pacify, esp by granting demands; to propitiate; to allay.—*n* **appease′ment**, the action of appeasing; the state of being appeased.

appellant [a-pel′ánt] *n* one who makes an appeal from a lower court to a higher.—*adj* **appell′ate court** [-it], a court that can review appeals and reverse the decision of lower courts.

appellation [ap-el-ā′sh(ó)n] *n* that by which anything is called; a name or title.—*n* **appell′ative**, (*obs*) a common noun.—*adj* of the hearer of a language; of the giving of names.

append [a-pend′] *vt* to hang (one thing) to another; to add.—*n* **append′age**, something appended; an external organ or part, as a tail.—*ns* **appendec′tomy**, surgical removal of vermiform appendix; **appendicī′tis**, inflammation of the vermiform appendix; **append′ix**, something appended or added. **append′ixes, append′ices**.

apperception [ap-er-sep′sh(ó)n] *n* the mind's perception of itself as a conscious agent.

appertain [ap-ér-tān′] *vi* to be the property or attribute of.—*adj* **appertain′ing**, proper, appropriate (to).

appetency [ap′et-ens-i] *n* appetite; desire; a natural affinity.—Also **app′etence**.

appetite [ap′et-īt] *n* sensation of physical need and desire; natural desire; desire for food; craving (*with* for).—*n* **appetiz′er**, a food that whets the appetite.—*adj* **app′etizing**, stimulating the appetite.

applaud [a-plöd′] *vt* to praise by clapping the hands; to praise loudly; to extol.—*n* **applause′**, praise loudly expressed, esp by clapping; acclamation.

apple [ap′l] *n* a round, firm, fleshy, edible fruit; the tree (genus *Malus*) bearing this fruit; (*slang*) derogatory name for Amerindian who is part of or cooperates with the white establishment.—*ns* **apple butter**, jam made from applesauce; **app′lejack**, liquor distilled from fermented cider.—*adj* **applepie**, having or showing American values and traits.

appliqué [a-plē′kā] *n* ornamental fabric work applied to another fabric.—*vt* to ornament thus.

apply [a-plī′] *vt* to set, place, bring close (to); to bring to bear on; to devote (oneself, to a pursuit).—*vi* to make a request; to be relevant;—*pr p* **apply′ing**; *pt p* **applied** [-plīd′].—*n* **appli′ance**, a device or machine, esp for household use.—*adj* **app′licable**, that may be applied; appropriate, relevant (to).—*adv* **app′licably**.—*ns* **applicability** [ap-li-ka-bil′iti],—*ns* **app′licant**, a person who applies, esp for a job; **applicā′tion**, the act of applying, as the administration of a remedy; diligent effort.

appoggiatura [a-pod-jä-tōō′ra] *n* (*mus*) an embellishing note, usu. written in a smaller size in front of the melodic note.

appoint [a-point′] *vt* to fix; to prescribe; to assign; to select for an office.—*adj* **appoint′ed**, fixed; furnished (as in *well-appointed*).—*n* **appoint′ment**, engagement, rendezvous; a position filled by appointing. (*pl*) furniture.

apportion [a-pōr′, -pör′, sh(ó)n] *vt* to portion out; to divide in shares.—*n* **appor′tionment**.

apposite [ap′oz-it] *adj* suitable, appropriate.—*adv* **app′ositely**.—*ns* **app′ositeness; apposi′tion**, state of being placed beside or against.

appraise [a-prāz′] *vt* to set a price on; to value, esp with a view to sale; to estimate the amount and quality of (anything).—*ns* **apprais′al, apprais′ement**, a valuation, estimation of quality; **apprais′er**.

appreciate [a-prē′shi-āt] *vt* to esteem highly; to recognize gratefully; to be sensitively aware of.—*vi* to rise in value.—*adj* **apprē′ciable**, capable of being estimated; perceptible.—*adv* **apprē′ciably**.—*n* **apprecia′tion**, appraisement; generous esteem; a sympathetic literary essay; increase in value.—*adj* **apprē'ciative.**—*n* **apprē'ciatory.**

apprehend [ap-re-hend'] *vt* to capture or arrest; to perceive by the senses; to grasp by the intellect; to understand; to fear.—*adj* **apprehen'sible**—*n* **apprehen'sion.**—*adj* **apprehens'ive,** uneasy; anxious.—*n* **apprehens'iveness.**

apprentice [a-prent'is] *n* one being taught a trade or craft, usu as a member of a labor union; a novice.—*vt* to place or accept as an apprentice.—*n* **apprent'iceship.**

apprise [a-prīz'] *vt* to give notice to, to inform.

apprize [a-prīz] *vt* to value; to appreciate.

approach [a-prōch] *vi* to draw nearer; to make an approach in golf.—*vt* to come near to.—*adj* **approach'able.**

approbation [ap-rob-ā'sh(ò)n] *n* formal sanction; approval.

appropriate [a-prō'pri-āt] *vt* to take as one's own; to set apart for a purpose.—*adj* [-àt] set apart for a particular purpose; peculiar (to); suitable. *adj* **apprō'priately.**—*ns* **apprō'priateness; appropriā'tion.**

approve [a-prōōv'] *vt* to sanction or ratify; to commend.—*vi* to be satisfied with (*with of*).—*n* **approv'al,** the act of approving; approbation.—*adj* **approv'ingly.**

approximate [a-proks'im-àt] *adj* nearest or next; approaching correctness.—*vt* to come near to; to be almost the same as.—*vi* to come close.—*adv* **approx'imately.**—*n* **approximā'tion,** a close estimate; a near likeness.

appurtenance [a-pûr'ten-àns] *n* that which appertains (to something else) as an appendage or accessory.

apricot [ā', or a'pri-kot] *n* a small, oval orange-pink fruit resembling the plum and peach; the tree (*Prunus armeniaca*) bearing this fruit; the color of an apricot.

April [ā'pril] *n* the fourth month of the year, having 30 days.—*n* **A'pril-fool,** the victim of a hoax on April 1, **All Fools' Day.**

a priori [ā prē-ōr'ē, ä prī-ōr-ī] *adj* from cause to effect, based on theory instead of experience.

apron [ā'prön] *n* a cloth or piece of leather, etc. worn before one to protect the dress; a short cassock, part of the official dress of a bishop, etc.; applied to a number of things resembling an apron in shape or use, as a paved area where a driveway meets the road.

apropos [a-pro-pō'] *adv* at the right time; opportunely; appropriately.—*adj* to the purpose, apt.

apse [aps] *n* a domed or vaulted recess, esp at the east end of the choir of a church.—*adj* **ap'sidal.**

apsis [ap'sis] *n* one of the two extreme points in the orbit of a planet or a satellite.—*pl* **apsides** [ap'si-dēz].—*adj* **ap'sidal.**

apt [apt] *adj* liable, ready, or prone; suitable, appropriate; quick to learn.—*n* **apt'itude,** fitness; readiness; capacity; talent.—*adv* **apt'ly.**—*n* **apt'ness**

apterous [ap'tèr-us] *adj* without wings.

aquamarine [a-kwa-ma-rēn' (or ā-)] *n* a variety of beryl used as a gemstone.—*adj* bluish-green, sea-colored.

aquaplane [ak'wa-plān] *n* a board on which one stands and is towed behind a motorboat.—*vi* to ride on an aquaplane; (of automobile) to be in contact with water on a road, not with the road surface.

aquarium [a-kwä'ri-um] *n* a tank or series of tanks for keeping aquatic animals or plants; a building in which such tanks are exhibited;—*pl* **aquā'riums, aquā'ria.**

Aquarius [a-kwä'ri-us] *n* the water carrier, 11th sign of the zodiac; in astrology, operative January 20 to February 18.

aquatic [a-kwat'ik] *adj* relating to water; living or growing in water.—*n pl* **aquat'ics,** water sports.

aquatint [a'kwa-tint or, ā'] *n* a mode of etching in imitation of drawing.

aqueduct [ak'we-dukt] *n* a large pipe or conduit for conveying water; from a distant point; an elevated structure supporting this.

aqueous [ā'kwe-us] *adj* watery; of, like, or formed by water.

aquiline [ak'wil-in, or -īn] *adj* relating to or like the eagle; curved or hooked, like an eagle's beak.

Arab [ar'ab] *n* a native or inhabitant of Arabia; general term for inhabitants of Middle Eastern countries; an Arabian horse, a small breed used for riding.—*adj* of or belonging to Arabia.—*adj* **Arāb'ian,** relating to Arabia.—*n* a native of Arabia.—*adj* **Ar'abic,** relating to Arabia, or to its language.—*n* language of Arabia.

arabesque [ar'ab-esk] *adj* after the manner of Arabian designs.—*n* a fantastic style of decoration.

arable [ar'a-bl] *adj* fit for plowing or planting crops.

arachnid [à-rak'nid] *n* any of a class of land-living arthropods with four pairs of legs, as Scorpions, spiders, mites, and ticks.

arbiter [är'bit-ėr] *n* a judge; an umpire; anyone having absolute power of decision or absolute control.—*n* **arbit'rament,** decision by an arbiter.—*vi* **ar'bitrate,** to act as an arbiter.—*vt* submit to an arbiter; to act as an arbiter upon.—*ns* **arbiträ'tion; ar'bitrātor,** arbiter.

arbitrary [är'bi-tràr-i] *adj* not bound by rules; despotic, absolute; capricious, unreasonable.—*adv* **ar'bitrarily.**—*n* **ar'bitrariness.**

arboreal [är-bōr', -bör'i-àl] *adj* living in trees; of or like a tree.—*vi* **arboresc'ent,** growing or formed like a tree.—*ns* **arboresc'ence,** tree-like growth; **arborē'tum,** a place in which specimens of trees and shrubs are cultivated;—*pl* **arborē'ta.**

arbor [är'bòr] *n* a place shaded by trees, plants, etc.; a bower.

arborvitae [är-bòr-vīt'ē] *n* any of various scale-leaved evergreen trees (genus *Thuja*), esp *T. occidentalis,* the white cedar.

arbutus [är'būt-us] *n* a trailing woody vine of the heath family (*Epigaea repens*) of temperate N America.

arc [ärk] *n* a part of the circumference of a circle or other curve; angular measurement (eg 60 *seconds of arc*); (*elect*) a luminous discharge of electricity across a gap between two conductors or terminals.—*vi* to form an electric arc.

arcade [ärk-ād'] *n* a walk arched over; a covered passageway lined with shops.

arcanum [ärk-ān'um] *n* mysterious knowledge known only to the initiate;—*pl* **arcan'a.**—*adj* **arcane',** secret or esoteric.

arch¹ [ärch] *n* a curved structure so built that the stones or other component parts support each other by mutual pressure and can sustain a load; of the foot, the part from heel to toes.—*vti* to cover with an arch; to curve, raise in an arch.—*n* **arch'way,** an arched or vaulted passage, esp that leading into a castle.

arch² [ärch] *adj* clever, sly; mischievous, roguish.—*adv* **arch'ly.**—*n* **arch'ness.**

arch- [ärch] *prefix* meaning chief, principle (archbishop, archenemy).

-arch [ärk] *suffix* meaning ruler (*matriarch oligarch*).

archaeology, archeology [ärk-e-ol'oj-i] *n* a knowledge of ancient art, customs, etc.; the science that studies the extant relics of ancient times.—*adj* **archaeolog'ical.**—*adv* **archaeolog'ically.**—*n* **archaeol'ogist.**

archaic [ärk-ā'ik] *adj* ancient; old-fashioned, no longer in common use, esp of language.—*n* **arch'āism,** an archaic word or phrase.

archangel [ärk-ān'jèl] *n* an angel of the highest order.—*adj* **archangel'ic.**

archbishop [ärch-bish'óp] *n* a bishop of the highest rank.—*n* **archbish'opric.**

archdeacon [ärch-dē'kòn] *n* the ecclesiastical dignitary next under a bishop.—*ns* **archdeac'onate; archdeac'onry,** the jurisdiction, or residence of an archdeacon; **archdeac'onship,** the office of an archdeacon.

archdiocese [ärch-dī'o-sēz] *n* the diocese of an archbishop.

Archeozoic [är-kē-ō-zō'ik] *adj* of the earliest era of geologic history; relating to the system of rocks of this era.

archer [ärch'ėr] *n* one who shoots with a bow and arrows.—*n* **arch'ery,** the art of shooting with the bow.

archetype [ärk'e-tīp] *n* the original pattern or model, a prototype.—*adj* **achetyp'al.**

archimandrite [är-ki-man'drīt] *n* in the Eastern Catholic Church, the dignitary ranking below a bishop; the superior of a monastery or a group of monasteries.

archipelago [ärk-i-pel'a-gō] *n* a sea abounding in small islands; a group of such islands;—*pl* **archipel'agoes, -s.**

architect [ärk'i-tekt] *n* one qualified to design buildings and superintend their erection.—*n* **architectonics** [ärk-i-tek-ton'iks], the science of architecture; structural design, as of a symphony.—*adj* **architectonic.**—*n* **architec'ture.**

architrave [ärk'i-trāv] *n* (*archit.*) the lowest division of the entablature; ornamental band surrounding a door or window.

archives [ärk'īvz] *n pl* the place in which public records are kept; public records kept in such a place.—*n* **arch′ivist** [-iv-], a keeper of archives.

archon [ärk′on] *n* a chief magistrate of ancient Athens a presiding officer.

arctic [ärk′tik] *adj* of, near, or relating to the North Pole or to north polar regions; extremely cold.—**Arctic Circle**, an imaginary circle parallel to the equator, 66°33′ north of it.—**the Arctic**, the region around the North Pole.

ardent [ärd′ént] *adj* burning; fiery; passionate.—*adv* **ard′ently**.—*n* **ard′or**, warmth of passion or feeling; eagerness.—*Also* **ard′ency**.

arduous [ärd′ū-us] *adj* steep; difficult to accomplish; laborious.—*adv* **ard′uously**.—*n* **arduousness**.

are[1] [är] *n* a unit of measure, equals 100 sq meters.

are[2] [är] the plural of the present indicative of the verb *to be*. [Old Northumbrian *aron* of Scand origin. This form ousted the older, OE *sind, sindon*. Both are cog with Gr *eisin*, L *sunt*, etc.]

area [ā′re-a] *n* an expanse of land; a total outside surface, measured in square units; a part of a house, district, etc.; scope or extent; (*geom*) region on a plane enclosed by bounding lines or the measure of the surface of a geometric solid.

arena [a-rē′na] *n* the center of the Roman amphitheater used for the combats of gladiators and wild beasts; a place or sphere of contest or struggle.

argent [ärj′ent] *adj* and *n* silver, or like silver, silvery-white, esp in heraldry.

argil [är′jil] *n* clay, esp potter′s.—*adj* **argillaceous** [är-jil-ā′shùs].

argol [är′gol] *n* crude tartar deposits in wine casks during the aging process.

argon [är′gon] *n* an inert gaseous element (symbol A; at wt 39.944; at no 18).

argot [är′got] *n* the special vocabulary of any set of persons, as of tramps, criminals, etc.

argue [ärg′ū] *vt* to prove, or to maintain, by reasoning; to debate, dispute; to persuade (into, out of);—*vi* to offer reasons; to dispute;—*pr p* **arg′ūing**; *pt p* **arg′ūed**.—*adj* **arg′ūable**.—*n* **arg′ument**, a quarrel *n* **argumentā′tion**, an arguing or reasoning.—*adj* **argument′ative**, controversial.—*adv* **argument′atively**.—*n* **argument′ativeness**.

aria [ä′ri-a] *n* a song, in a cantata, oratorio, or opera, for one voice supported by instruments.

arid [ar′id] *adj* dry, parched; uninteresting; dull.—*ns* **arid′ity**, **ar′idness**.

Aries [ā′ri-ēz] *n* the Ram, the 1st sign of the zodiac; in astrology, operative March 21 to April 21.

aright [a-rīt′] *adv* correctly.

arise [a-rīz′] *vi* to get up, as from bed; to rise, ascend; to come into being, to result (from).—*pt* **arose′**; *pt p* **arisen** [a-riz′n].

aristocracy [ar-is-tok′ras-i] *n* government by a privileged minority class; a country with such a government; the nobility, the upper class.—*n* **aristocrat**, [aris′-to-krat or ar′-is-], one who belongs to, or has the characteristics of, or favors, an aristocracy.—*adj* **aristocrat′ic**,—*adv* **aristocrat′ically**.

arithmetic [ar-ith′met-ik] *n* the science of numbers; the art of reckoning by figures.—*adj* **arithmet′ical**.—*adv* **arithmet′ically**.—*n* **arithmetician**, [-ish′án]— **arithmetic mean**, average.

ark [ärk] *n* (*Bible*) the boat in which Noah and his family and two of every kind of creature survived the flood; an enclosure in a synagogue for the scrolls of the Torah.—**ark of the covenant** (*Bible*) the chest containing the two stone tablets inscribed with the Ten Commandments.

arm[1] [ärm] *n* the limb extending from the shoulder to the hand; anything projecting from the main body, as an inlet of the sea, a rail or support on a chair; a sleeve.—*n* **arm′chair**, a chair with arms.—*adj* (of a critic, etc.) without practical knowledge, doctrinaire.—*ns* **arm′ful**, as much as the arms can hold; **armhole**, the hole in a garment through which the arm is put.—*adj* **arm′less**.

arm[2] [ärm] *n* a weapon; a branch of the military service;— (*pl*) weapons; heraldic bearings.—*vt* to furnish with weapons etc.—*vi* to prepare for war or any struggle; take arms.—*adj* **armed**.—**arms race**, competition among nations in building up armaments.—**under arms**, ready for war; **up in arms**, armed for combat; indignant.

armada [är-mä′da, är-mā′da] *n* a fleet of warships; a fleet of warplanes.

armadillo [ärm-a-dil′ō] *n* a family (Daspypodidae) of small tropical American quadrupeds, having the body armed with bony plates;—*pl* **armadill′os**.

Armageddon [är-ma-ged′ón] *n* (*Bible*) the site of the last decisive battle between good and evil; any great, decisive battle. [Heb.—(*H*)*ar* (of doubtful meaning), and *Megiddo*, a famous battlefield]

armament [ärm′a-mént] *n* (often *pl*) all the military forces and equipment of a nation; all the military equipment of a warship, etc.; an arming or being armed for war.

armature [är′ma-tyùr] *n* any protective covering; the iron core wound with wire, in which electromotive force is produced in a generator or motor; the rigid framework used by a sculptor as a foundation for a moldable substance.

armistice [ärm′ist-is] *n* a truce; preliminary to a peace treaty.—**Armistice Day** November 11, anniversary of the signing of armistice that ended World War I; Veteran′s Day.

armor [ärm′ór] *n* any defensive or protective covering.—*vti* to put armor on.—*adjs* **arm′ored**; **armō′rial**, of coats of arms; heraldic.—*ns* **armored car**, a vehicle covered with armor plate, as a truck for carrying money to or from a bank; **arm′ory**, an arsenal; an armaments factory; a military drill hall.

army [ärm′i] *n* a large organized body of soldiers for waging war, esp on land; any large number of persons, animals, etc.

aroma [a-rō′ma] *n* a pleasant smell; fragrance.—*adj* **aromat′ic**, fragant; spicy; (*chem*) of the class of cyclic organic compounds derived from or having similar properties to benzene.—*vt* **arom′atize**.

arose [a-rōz′] *pt* of **arise**.

around [a-rownd′] *prep* on all sides of; on the border of; in various places in or on.—*adv* in a circle; in every direction; in circumference; to the opposite direction.

arouse [a-rowz′] *vt* to wake from sleep; to stir, as to action; to evoke (to arouse pity).

arpeggio [är-pej-(y)ō] *n* (*mus*) a chord whose notes are played in rapid succession.

arquebus *see* **harquebus**.

arrack [ar′ak] *n* a coarse spirit distilled from rice, etc.

arraign [a-rān] *vt* to call (one) to account; to put (a prisoner) on trial; to accuse publicly.—*n* **arraign′ment**.

arrange [a-rānj′] *vt* to set in a rank or row; to put in order; to settle; (*mus*) to adapt (a composition) for performance by instruments or voices other than those for which it was originally written.—*vi* to come to an agreement (with a person); to make preparations.—*n* **arrange′ment**, act of arranging.

arrant [ar′ánt] *adj* downright, notorious (used in a bad sense).

arras [ar′as] *n* an elaborate kind of tapestry; a wall hanging, esp of tapestry.

array [a-rā′] *n* an orderly grouping, esp of troops; an impressive display; fine clothes.—*vt* to put in order, to arrange; to dress in finery.

arrears [a-rēr′z′] *n pl* overdue debts.—**in arrears**, behind in paying a debt, doing one′s work, etc.

arrest [a-rest′] *vt* to stop; to seize; to catch the attention of; to apprehend by legal authority.—*n* an arresting or being arrested.—*adj* **arrest′ing**, attracting attention; interesting.—**under arrest**, in legal custody.

arrière pensée [ar-yer′ pä′sā′] *n* mental reservation.

arrive [a-rīv′] *vi* to reach any place; to come (*the time has arrived*); to achieve success, recognition.—*n* **arriv′al**, the act of arriving; a person or thing that arrives—**arrive at**, to reach by thinking, etc.

arriviste [a-rē-vēst′] *n* a person who is a new and uncertain arrival.

arrogate [ar′og-āt] *vt* to claim without right.—*ns* **arr′ogance**, undue assumption of importance.—*adj* **arr′ogant**, haughty; overbearing.—*adv* **arr′ogantly**.

arrondissement [a-rŏ-dēs′mä] *n* the largest division of a French department; an administrative district of some large French cities.

arrow [ar′ō] *n* a straight, pointed weapon, made to be shot from a bow; a sign used to indicate direction.(→).—*n* **arr′owhead**, the head or pointed part of an arrow; any triangular shape.—*adj* **arr′owy**, consisting of arrows; swiftly moving.

arroyo [à-roi'ō] *n* a dry gully; a rivulet or stream.

arsenal [är'se-nàl] *n* a magazine or manufactory for weapons and ammunition; a storehouse.

arsenic [ärs'(e-)nik] *n* a metalloid element (symbol As; at wt 74.9; atomic no 33), highly poisonous. — *adj* **arsen'ical**.

arson [ärs'ón] *n* the crime of wilfully setting fire to a building.

art' [ärt] (*arch*) 2d pers sing of the present tense of the verb *to be* used with thou.

art² [ärt] *n* human creativity; skill, acquired by study and practice; any craft and its principles; making of things that have form and beauty; any branch of this, as painting, sculpture, etc.; drawings, paintings, statues, etc.; (*pl*) sly trick, wile. — *adj* **art'ful**, cunning; skillful; clever; crafty. — *adv* **art'fully**. — *n* **art'fulness**. — *ns* **art'ist**, one who practices fine art, esp painting; one who does anything very well; **artiste** [-tēst], a professional, usu. musical or theatrical, entertainer. — *adj* **artist'ic**, of art or artists; done skillfully; sensitive to beauty. — *n* **art'istry**, artistic quality, ability, work, etc. — *adj* **art'less**, simple, guileless. — *adv* **art'lessly**. — *n* **art'lessness**. — *adj* **art'y** (*inf*), affectedly artistic. — *n* **art form**, an accepted form of artistic expression. — *adj* **art'sy-craft'sy**, art'y-craft'y, arty.

artery [är'tèr-i] *n* a tube that conveys blood from the heart; any main channel of communication. — *adj* **artēr'ial**.

artesian [är-tē'zhàn, -zi-àn] *adj* pertaining to a type of well in which water rises of itself by internal pressure.

arthritis [är-thrī'tis] *n* inflammation of a joint. — *adj* **arthritic** [-thrit'ik].

arthropod [är'thropod] *n* any of a member of a phylum (Arthropoda) of invertebrate animals, with bodies consisting of segments bearing jointed appendages — including crustaceans, spiders, insects, etc.

artichoke [är'ti-chōk] *n* a thistlelike plant (*Cynara scolymus*) with large scaly heads, parts of which are succulent and edible. — **Jerusalem artichoke**, a perennial American sunflower (*Helianthus tuberosus*) with edible tubers.

article [ärt'i-kl] *n* a section of any document; a literary composition in a newspaper, magazine, encyclopaedia, etc., dealing with a particular subject; a separate item (*an article of luggage*); (*gram*) the name given to the adjectives the (definite article) and *a* or *an* (indefinite article).

articulate [är-tik'ūl-àt] *adj* jointed; capable of speech, or of expressing one's thoughts clearly; distinct, clear, intelligible. — *vt* [-āt] to form into distinct sounds; to put together in a connected way; to express clearly. — *adj* **artic'ular**, of joints or structural components in a joint. — *adv* **artic'ulately**. — *ns* **artic'ulateness; articula'tion**.

artifact [är'ti-fakt] *n* any product of human workmanship.

artifice [ärt'i-fis] *n* a contrivance; a trick; contrivance; trickery. — *n* **artificer** [ar-tif'is-èr], a skilled craftsman; an inventor. — *adj* **artificial** [ärt-i-fish'àl], made by art; not natural. — *n* **artificial'ity**. — *adv* **artific'ially**. — *ns* **artificial intelligence**, the means by which computers, robots, etc. perform tasks which normally require human intelligence.

artillery [är-til'ér-i] *n* mounted guns, esp cannon; the science of guns; gunnery. — *n* **artill'eryman**, a soldier of the artillery. — **the artillery**, the branch of an army using heavy mounted guns.

Aryan [ā'ri-àn, är'ri-àn] *adj* relating to the Indo European family of languages; non-Jewish and Caucasian, esp Nordic; the language of Iran; the language of India. — *n* member of descendant of prehistoric people who spoke Indo-European; (in Nazi doctrine) non-Jewish Caucasian, esp of Nordic stock.

as [az] *adv* equally; for instance ; when related in a certain way. — *conj* in the same way that; while ; because. — *prep* in the role or function of. — **as for** (or **to**), concerning; **as is** (or **though**), as it (or one) would if; **as is** (*inf*), just as it is; **as it were**, as if it were so.

asbestos [az-best'os] *n* an incombustible siliceous mineral, of a fine fibrous texture, and capable of being woven.

ascend [a-send'] *vti* to go up; to succeed to a (throne). — *adj* **ascend'ant, -ent**. — *n* the part of the ecliptic rising above the eastern horizon at any moment. — *ns* **ascend'ancy**, controlling influence — also **ascend'ency; ascen'sion**, a rising or going up.

ascertain [as-èr-tān'] *vt* to obtain certain knowledge of. — *adj* **ascertain'able**. — *n* **ascertain'ment**.

ascetic [a-set'ik] *n* one who trains himself to endure severe bodily hardship as a religious discipline; any extremely abstemious person. — *adjs* **ascet'ic**, austere. — *n* **ascet'icism**.

ascribe [a-skrīb'] *vt* to attribute; to assign. — *adj* **ascrib'able**. — *n* **ascrip'tion**, act of ascribing; any expression of ascribing, esp arbitrary placement (as at birth) in a particular social class.

asepsis [a-sep'sis] *n* condition of being aseptic. — *adj* **asep'tic**, free from disease-producing germs.

asexual [a-seks'ū-àl] *adj* without sex or sexual organs; of reproduction without the union of male and female germ cells.

ash' [ash] *n* any of a genus (*Fraxinus*) of widely distributed N American tree grown for shade and for its tough, elastic timber.

ash² [ash] *n* powdery remains of anything burnt; fine, volcanic lava; the gray color of wood ash; (*pl*) the substance remaining after a thing has been burned; the remains of the human body when burnt. — *adjs* **ash'en**, like ashes, esp in color; pale.

ashamed [a-shāmd'] *adj* affected with shame.

ashlar [ash'lár'] *n* hewn stone; a thin facing of squared stones to cover brick or rubble walls.

ashore [a-shōr', shör] *adv, adj* to or on the shore; to or on land.

aside [a-sīd'] *adv* on or to one side; in reserve (*put one ticket aside*); notwithstanding (*joking aside*). — *n* words spoken by an actor which the other persons on the stage are supposed not to hear. — **aside from** with the exception of; apart from.

asinine [as'in-īn] *adj* like an ass; silly; stupid. — *n* **asinity** [-in'i-ti].

ask [äsk] *vt* to request, beg; inquire; inquire of; invite. — *vi* to make request (for) or inquiry (about). — *n* **ask'er**.

askance [a-skans'], **askant** [a-skant'], *adv* with a sideways glance; with suspicion.

askew [a-skū'] *adv* to one side; awry. — *adj* on one side, awry.

aslant [a-slänt'] *adv* on a slant. — *prep* slantingly across. — *adj* slanting.

asleep [a-slēp'] *adj* sleeping; inactive; numb; dead. — *adv* into a sleeping condition.

aslope [a-slōp'] *adv, adj* being in a sloping or slanting position or direction.

asocial [ā-sō'shàl] *adj* avoiding contact with others; selfish.

asp [äsp] *n* a small venomous snake of Egypt.

asparagus [as-par'a-gus] *n* a genus (*Asparagus*) of plants one species (*A officinalis*) of which is cultivated for its young shoots, esteemed as a table delicacy.

aspect [as'pekt] *n* look; view; appearance of a thing or idea from a specific viewpoint; position in relation to the points of the compass.

asperity [as-per'i-ti] *n* roughness; harshness; sharpness of temper.

asperse [as-pûrs'] *vt* to slander. — *n* **asper'sion**, calumny, slander.

asphalt [as'-fölt] *n* a dark, hard bituminous substance, used for paving and to waterproof cement. — **asphalt jungle**, a big city or a specified part of a big city.

asphyxia [as-fik'si-a] *n* unconsciousness due to deficiency of oxygen or excess of carbon dioxide in the blood. — *vt* **asphyx'iāte**, to cause to suffer asphyxia, to suffocate. — *n* **asphyxiā'tion**.

aspic [as'pik] *n* a jelly used to coat fish, game, hard-boiled eggs, etc.

aspidistra [as-pid-ist'ra] *n* an Asian plant (*Aspidistra lurida*) with large leaves, often grown in pots.

aspirant [as'pir-ànt, or as-pīr'ànt] *n* one who aspires; — *adj* aspiring.

aspirate [as'pir-āt] *vt* to pronounce with a full breathing, as *h* in *house*.

aspire [as-pīr'] *vi* to desire eagerly; to aim at high things. — *n* **aspiration**, [as-pir-ā'sh(ò)n], eager desire, ambition. — *adj* **aspīr'ing**. — *adv* **aspīr'ingly**.

aspirin [as'pir-in] *n* a sedative drug used for relieving pain and fever.

ass [as] *n* any of several species of quadrupeds of the same genus (*Equus*) as the horse; a silly, stupid person; (*slang*) the buttocks; the anus.

assagai *see* **assegai**.

assail [a-sāl'] *vt* to attack suddenly or repeated either physically or with arguments. — *n* **assail'ant**, attacker, esp physical.

assassin [as-as'in] *n* one who takes the life of another, esp a politically important person by treacherous violence.—*vt* **assass'inate**.—*n* **assassinā'tion**.

assault [a-sölt'] *n* a violent attack, euphemism for rape; (*law*) an unlawful threat or attempt to harm another physically.—*vti* to make an assault (upon).

assay [a-sā'] *vt* to make an assay of; to test.—*vi* to be shown by assay to have a specified proportion of something.—*n* the determination of the quantity of metal in an ore or alloy; a test;—*n* **assay'er**.

assemble [a-sem'bl] *vti* to gather together; to collect; to put together the parts of.—*ns* **assem'blage**, a collection of persons or things; (*art*) things assembled in a sculptural collage; **Assembly**, the lower house of some state legislatures; **assem'bly**, the act of assembling; the company so assembled; a gathering of persons for a particular purpose; a fitting together of parts to make a whole.

assent [a-sent'] *vt* to agree in thought; to indicate agreement.—*n* consent or agreement.

assert [a-sûrt'] *vt* to maintain or defend (eg rights); to declare, affirm.—*n* **asser'tion**, the act of asserting; affirmation.—*adj* **assert'ive**, persistently positive or confident.—*adv* **assert'ively**.—*n* **assert'iveness**.

assess [a-ses'] *vt* to fix the amount of, as a tax; to tax or fine; to value, for taxation; to estimate; to judge the worth, importance, etc. of—*adj* **assess'able**.—*ns* **assess'ment**; **assess'or**.

asset [as'et] *n* anything owned that has value; a desirable thing (*charm is an asset*); (*pl*) all the property, accounts receivable, etc. of a person or business; (*pl*) (*law*) property usable to pay debts.

asseverate [a-sev'ėr-āt] *vt* to state positively.—*n* **asseverā'tion**.

assid'uous [as-id'ū-us] *adj*, constant or unwearied in application; diligent.—*adv* **assid'uously**.—*n* **assid'uousness**.

assign [a-sīn'] *vt* to designate; to allot; to appoint; to ascribe; (*law*), to transfer (a right, property, etc.).—*n* one to whom any property or right is made over.—*adj* **assign'able**, that may be assigned.—*ns* **assignation** [as-ig-nā'sh(ò)n], an appointment to meet, esp one made secretly by lovers; **assignee** [as-in-ē', or -sīn-], one to whom a right or property is assigned; **assign'ment** [-sīn-], act of assigning.

assimilate [a-sim'il-āt] *vt* to take in as nourishment; to take into the mind and thoroughly absorb; to make similar; to alter by assimilation; to absorb yinto the cultural tradition of a group or population.—*vi* to become assimilated.—*adj* **assim'ilable**.—*ns* **assimilabil'ity**; **assimila'tion**.—*adj* **assim'ilative**, having the power or tendency to assimilate.

assist [a-sist'] *vti* to help.—*n* **assist'ance**, help; aid.—*adj* **assist'ant**, helping or hending aid.—*n* one who assists; a helper.—**assistant professor**, member of a college or university faculty ranking above instructor and below associate professor.

assizes [a-sīz'-is] *n pl* the sessions or sittings of a court held periodically in English counties; the time or place of these.

associate [a-sō'shi-āt] *vt* to join in friendship of partnership, to bring together; to unite in the same body; to connect in thought.—*vi* to keep company (with); to combine or unite.—*adj* [-āt], allied or connected; having secondary status or privileges.—*n* one joined or connected with another. *n* **associā'tion** [-si-], act of associating; union or combination; a society of persons joined together to promote some object; a connection between ideas, etc.—*adj* **assō'ciative**, tending to association.

assonance [as'on-àns] *n* a correspondence in sound; a kind of rhyme, consisting in the coincidence of the vowels of the corresponding syllables, without regard to the consonants as in *mate* and *shape*, *feel* and *need*.—*adj*, *n* **ass'onant**, resembling in sound.

assort [a-sört'] *vt* to separate into classes according to kind.—*vi* to agree in kind; to keep company.—*adj* **assort'ed**, arranged in sorts; miscellaneous.—*n* **assort'ment**, act of assorting; that which is assorted; a variety.

assuage [a-swäj'] *vt* to soften, mitigate, or allay.—*n* **assuage'ment**, abatement; mitigation.—*adj* **assuä'sive**, soothing, calming.

assume [a-sūm', or -sōōm'] *vt* to take on; to seize, usurp; to take upon oneself; to take for granted; to pretend to possess.—*adjs* **assumptive** [as-um(p)'tiv], taken as one's own; making undue claims; **assumed'**, appropriated, usurped; pretended; taken as the basis of argument; **assum'ing**, presumptuous, arrogant.

assure [å-shōōr'] *vt* to make sure or certain; to give confidence; to tell positively; to guarantee.—*n* **assur'ance**, feeling of certainty; self-confidence; promise.—*adj* **assured'**, certain; without doubt; self-confident.—*adv* **assur'edly** [-id-li].—*n* **assur'edness**.

astatic [ā-stat'ik] *adj* (*Physics*) having no tendency to take a fixed position.

asterisk [as'tėr-isk] *n* a star-shaped mark, used in printing to mark footnotes, omission of words, etc., thus*.

astern [a-stûrn'] *adv* behind a ship or aircraft; at or toward the rear of a ship, etc.; backward.

asteroid [as'tėr-oid] *n* any of the small planets between Mars and Jupiter.—*adj* **asteroid'al**.

asthma [az'ma] *n* a chronic disorder of the organs of respiration, characterized by paroxysms in which the sufferer gasps painfully for breath.—*adjs* **asthmat'ic**.—*adv* **asthmat'ically**.

astigmatism [a-stig'ma-tizm] *n* a defective condition of the eye, in which rays proceeding to the eye from one point are not correctly brought to a focus at one point.—*adj* **astigmat'ic**.

astir [a-stûr] *adv* on the move; out of bed.

astonish [as-ton'ish] *vt* to impress with sudden surprise, to amaze.—*adj* **aston'ishing**.—*adv* **aston'ishingly**.—*n* **aston'ishment**.

astound [as-townd'] *vt* to astonish greatly.—*pt p* **astound'ed**; *pr p* **astound'ing**.—*adv* **astound'ing**.

astraddle [a-strad'l] *adv* sitting astride.

astragal [as'tra-gal] *n* a narrow half-round modelling; a projecting strip on the edge of a folding door.

astrakhan [as-tra-kan'] *n* lambskin with a curled wool; a fabric made in imitation of it.

astral [as'tràl] *adj* belonging to the stars; in theosophy, descriptive of an impalpable essence supposed to pervade all space and enter into all bodies.

astray [a-strā'] *adv* off the right path; into error.

astride [a-strīd'] *adv* with a leg on either side.—*prep* with a leg on either side of; extending over and across.

astringent [as-trin'jènt] *adj* that contracts body tissues; harsh; biting.—*n* an astringent substance.—*n* **astrin'gency**.—*adv* **astrin'gently**.

astro- [as'tro] prefix meaning of a star or stars (*astrophysics*).

astrolabe [as'trō-lāb] *n* an instrument formerly used for calculating the positions of the sun or stars.

astrology [as-trol'o-ji] *n* the study of the positions and motions of the heavenly bodies (out of which grew astronomy) to determine their supposed influence on human affairs.—*n* **astrol'oger**, one versed in astrology.—*adjs* **astrolog'ic**, -al.—*adv* **astrolog'ically**.

astronaut [as'trō-nöt] *n* one trained to make flights in outer space.—*adj* **astronaut'ical**—*n* **astronaut'ics**, the science of travel in space, navigation in space beyond the earth's atmosphere.

astronomy [as-tron'óm-i] *n* the science of the stars and other heavenly bodies.—*n* **astron'omer**, one versed in astronomy.—*adj* **astronom'ical**, **astronomic**, of, or pertaining to, astronomy; (of numbers) very large.—*adv* **astronom'ically**.

astrophysics [as-trō-fiz'iks] *n* that branch of astronomy which deals with the physical properties and chemical constitution of the stars.

astute [ast-ūt'] *adj* crafty, cunning; shrewd.—*adv* **astute'ly**.—*n* **astute'ness**.

asunder [a-sun'dèr] *adv* apart; in direction or position; into pieces.

asylum [a-sīl'um] *n* a place of safety, a refuge; an earlier name for an institution for the blind, the mentally ill; orphans, etc.

asymmetry [ā-sim'ė-tri] *n* lack of symmetry; (*chem*) condition of not being superimposable on a mirror image.—*adj* **asymmetric**, -al.

asymptote [a'sim-tōt] *n* (*math*) a line that continually approaches nearer to some curve without ever meeting it.—*adjs* **asymptot'ic**.

at [at] *prep* on; in; near; by; to or toward; from; attending; busy with; in the state or manner of; because of; with reference to; in the amount of, etc.

atavism [at'av-izm] *n* appearance of remotely ancestral, characteristics; reversion to a more primitive type. — *adj* **atavis'tic**.

ate [et, or āt] *pt p* of **eat**.

atelier [at-èl-yā'] *n* studio workshop as of an artist or couturier.

atheism [ā'the-izm] *n* disbelief in the existence of God. — *n* **a'theist**. — *adjs* **atheist'ic, -al**.. — *adv* **atheist'ically**.

athenaeum, atheneum [ath-e-nē'um] *n* a building or room where books, periodicals, and newspapers are kept for use; a literary or scientific association.

athirst [a-thûrst'] *adj* (*arch*) thirsty; eager (for).

athlete [ath'lēt] *n* a person trained in games or exercises requiring skill, strength, stamina, etc. — *adj* **athlet'ic**, relating to athletics; strong, vigorous. — *n pl* **athlet'ics**, athletic sports, games, etc. — **athlete's foot**, ringworm of the feet.

athwart [a-thwört'] *prep* across; against. — *adv* crosswise.

atlas [at'las] *n* a book of maps; a bound collection of tables, charts, or plates. [Gr *Atlas*, the Titan condemned to bear the sky on his shoulders, whose figure used to be shown on the title-page of atlases.]

atmosphere [at'mos-fēr] *n* the gaseous envelope that surrounds the earth or any of the heavenly bodies; a unit of pressure equal to 14.69 lb per sq in; any surrounding influence. — *adjs* **atmospher'ic**, of or depending on the atmosphere. — *n pl* **atmospher'ics**, in radio reception, interfering or disturbing signals due to atmospheric conditions.

atoll [a-tol', or āt'ol] *n* a coral island formed by a circular belt or coral enclosing a central lagoon.

atom [at'òm] *n* the smallest particle of an element that can take part in a chemical reaction; anything very small. — *adjs* **atom'ic**, arising from the atom; — *ns* **atomic'ity** [-is-], number of atoms contained in the molecule of an element; the combining power of an atom; **atomiza'tion**, the reduction of liquids to the form of spray. — *vt* **at'omize**, to reduce to a fine spray or minute particles; to destroy by bombing. — *ns* **atomi'zer**, a device for discharging liquids in a fine spray; **at'omy**, a tiny particle; **atom(ic) bomb**, a bomb whose immense power derives from nuclear fission or fusion; **atomic energy**, nuclear energy.

atonal [a-tōn'ál] *adj* (*mus*) avoiding traditional tonality; not referred to any scale or tonic. — *n* **atōnal'ity** — *adj* **atōn'ic**, uttered without accent or stress.

atone [at-ōn'] *vi* to give satisfaction or make reparation; to make up (for deficiencies). — *n* **atone'ment**, the act of atoning; expiation; reparation; esp (*theol*) the redemption of man by means of the incarnation and death of Christ.

atrium [ā'tri-um] *n* the open central court in Greek and Roman dwellings; an auricle of the heart. — *pl* **a'tria**.

atrocious [a-trō'shùs] *adj* extremely cruel or wicked; abominable; (*inf*) very bad; offensive. — *adv* **atrō'ciously**. — *ns* **atrō'ciousness**, gross cruelty; **atrocity** [a-tros'it-i], atrociousness; an atrocious act; (*inf*) a very displeasing thing.

atrophy [at'rof-i] *n* a wasting away or failure to grow of an organ of the body. — *vt* to cause atrophy in. — *vi* to undergo atrophy.

atropine [at'ro-pin] *n* a poisonous alkaloid obtained from deadly nightshade; used medicinally; main ingredient of belladonna.

attach [a-tach'] *vt* to bind or fasten (to something); to append; to join (oneself); to associate as an adjunct (eg *to attach a condition*); to attribute (eg importance); to affix (a signature, etc.); to connect by ties of affection, etc.; to seize (property, etc.) by legal process. — *vi* to become attached; to adhere. — *adj* **attach'able**. — *adj* **attached'**, fastened, fixed; joined by taste or affection, devoted (to). — *n* **attach'ment**, act or means of fastening; something attached.

attaché [a-tash'ā] *n* a technical expert on a diplomatic staff (*commercial attaché*); (*Brit*) a junior member of an ambassador's staff. — *n* **attach'é case**, a briefcase.

attack [a-tak'] *vt* to fall upon violently, to assault; to assail in speech or writing; to begin to affect (of a disease). — *vi* to make an assault. — *n* an assault; onset of illness; severe criticism; a beginning of performance, task, undertaking, etc.

attain [a-tān'] *vt* to reach or gain by effort; to arrive at. — *vi* to come to or arrive at by growth or effort. — *adj* **attain'able**. — *ns* **attain'ableness, attainabil'ity; attain'ment**, act of attaining; the thing attained; accomplishment.

attainder [a-tān'dèr] *n* (*law*) loss of civil rights and property, usu. through conviction for high treason. — *vt* **attaint'**, to punish by attainder.

attar [at'ár] *n* a fragrant essential oil, esp from rose petals; fragrance.

attempt [a-tempt'] *vt* to try; to try to do, get, etc. — *n* a try, endeavor, or effort; an attack (eg *an attempt on one's life*).

attend [a-tend'] *vt* to take care of; to accompany; to be present at; to wait for. — *vi* to give heed; to act as an attendant; to wait (on or upon); to apply oneself (to). — *n* **attend'ance**, act of attending; presence; the number of person attending. — *adj* **attend'ant**, giving attendance.

attention [a-ten'sh(ò)n] *n* act or faculty of taking notice or of giving heed; notice, heed; steady application of the mind; care; (usu. *pl*) an act of courtesy; the erect posture of soldiers standing rigidly erect with hands by the sides and heels together. — *adj* **attent'ive**, full of attention; courteous. — *adv* **attent'ively**. — *n* **attent'iveness**.

attenuate [a-ten'ū-āt] *vt* to make thin; to dilute; to lessen or weaken. — *vi* to become thin or fine. — *adj* **attenuated** [a-ten'ū-àt-id]. — *n* **attenuā'tion**.

attest [a-test'] *vt* to testify, to certify, as by oath; to give proof of, manifest. — *vi* to bear witness (to). — *n* **attestā'tion**. — *adj* **attest'ed**.

attic [at'ik] *n* the room or space just under the roof; a garret.

attire [a-tīr'] *vt* to clothe; to dress up. — *n* dress, clothing.

attitude [at'i-tūd] *n* posture; position; state of thought or feeling. — *vi* **attitud'inize**, to assume affected attitudes.

attorney [a-tûr'ni] *n* one authorized to act for another, esp a lawyer. — (*pl*) **attor'neys**. — *ns* **attor'ney-gen'eral**, the chief law officer of a government. **attor'neyship** — (*pl*) **attorneys general, attorney generals**. — **attorney at law**, a lawyer.

attract [a-trakt'] *vt* to draw (to); to cause to approach; to allure; to get the admiration, attention, etc. of. — *vi* to be attractive. — *adj* **attract'able**. — *ns* **attractabil'ity; attract'ant**, something that attracts; **attrac'tion**, act of attracting; power of attracting, esp charm; (*physics*) the mutual action by which bodies tend to be drawn together. — *adj* **attract'ive**. — *adv* **attract'ively**. — *n* **attract'iveness**.

attribute [a-trib'ūt] *vt* to consider as belonging (to); to ascribe, impute (to). — *adj* **attrib'utable**. — *ns* **att'ribute**, that which is attributed; a quality or property inseparable from anything; that which can be predicated of anything; **attribū'tion**, act of attributing; that which is attributed. — *adj* **attrib'utive**, expressing an attribute; (of an adjective) standing before the qualified noun (eg a *loud* noise).

attrition [a-tri'sh(ò)n] *n* a wearing away by or as by friction.

attune [a-tūn'] *vt* to put (an instrument) in tune; to harmonize with.

aubade [ō-bäd'] *n* a sunrise song.

auburn [ö'bûrn] *adj* reddish brown.

auction [ök'sh(ò)n] *n* a public sale of items to the highest bidder. — *vt* to sell by auction. — *n* **auctioneer'**, one who is licensed to sell by auction.

audacious [ö-dā'shùs] *adj* daring, bold; too bold; insolent; brazen. — *adv* **audā'ciously**. — *ns* **audā'ciousness, audacity** [ö-das'i-ti].

audible [öd'i-bl] *adj* able to be heard. — *ns* **aud'ibleness, audibil'ity**. — *adv* **aud'ibly**. — *n* **aud'ience**, those gathered to hear and see something; all those reached by a broadcast, book, movie, etc.; a hearing, esp a formal interview. — *n* **aud'it**, a formal checking of financial records. — *vti* to check (accounts, energy levels, etc.); to attend (a college class) to listen without credits. — *n* **audi'tion**, a hearing to test a performer — *vti* to try out in an audition. — **aud'itor**, a hearer; one who audits accounts; one who audits classes. — **auditōr'ium**, space allotted to the audience in a building; a building or hall for speeches, concerts, etc. *adj* **aud'itory**, relating to the sense of hearing. — **audit trail**, (*computer*) a record of the passage of data in a computer or data processing machine.

audio [öd'i-ō] *adj* of frequencies corresponding to audible sound waves; of the sound phase of television. — *n* sound; the part of television or motion-picture equipment dealing with sound; the reproduction, transmission or reception of sound.

auger [ö'gèr] *n* a carpenter's tool used for boring holes in wood.

aught [öt] *n* anything; whatever; a zero. — *adv* in any way; part.

augment [ög-ment'] *vti* to increase. — *adj* **augment'ative**, having the quality or power of augmenting.—*ns* (*gram*) a word formed from another by adding an augmentative suffix; **augmentative suffix**, a suffix added to a word, usu. a noun, to convey the idea of bigness.—*n* **augmentā′tion**.—*adj* **aug-ment′ed**, (*mus*), of an interval, greater by a semitone than the perfect or the major.

augur [ö′gŭr] *n* a prophet.—*vti* to prophesy; to be an omen (of).—*n* **augury**, [ö′gū-ri] divination from omens; a portent; an omen.

august [ö-gust′] *adj* venerable; imposing; majestic.—*adv* **augus-st′ly**.—*n* **august′ness**.

August [ö′gust] *n* the eighth month of the year, having 31 days.—*adj* **Augus′tan**, pertaining to the Roman Emperor Augustus, or to his reign (31 BC-AD 14); classic, as applied to a period of 18-century English literature.

aunt [änt] *n* a father's or mother's sister; an uncle's wife.— **Aunt Tom**, (*slang; derogatory*) a black woman with a servile attitude toward whites; a woman who does not support the cause of woman's liberation.

aura [ör′a] *n* an invisible emanation; a particular quality sur-rounding a person or thing.—*pl* **aur′ae** [-ē].

aural [ör′ál] *adj* pertaining to the ear or the sense of hearing.— *adv* **aur′ally**.

aureole [ör′i-ōl], **aureola**, [ör-ē′o-la] *n* a halo; a sun's corona.—*adj* **aur′eoled**, encircled with an aureole.

auricle [ör′i-kl] *n* the external ear; either of the two upper chambers of the heart an earlike part.—*adj* **auric′ular**, per-taining to the ear; known by hearing; told in the ear (ie privately).

auriferous [ör-if′ér-us] *adj* bearing or yielding gold.

aurochs [ör′oks] *n* the extinct urus of wild ox; (*Bos primo-genius*) of the German forests; a nisent.

Aurora [ö-rö′, -rö′, ra] *n* the Roman goddess of dawn; **aurora**, the dawn; -*pl* **-ras -rae**, [rē]; either of the luminous bands seen in the night sky **aurora borealis**, [bō-re-ā′lis] in the northern hemisphere; **aurora australis**, [ös-tra′lis] in the southern hemisphere.—*pl* **auro′ras, -rae** [-rē].

auscultation [ös-kult-ā′sh(ö)n] *n* a listening, often with a stethoscope, to sounds in the chest, abdomen, etc. that indi-cate the patient's condition.—*vti* **aus′cultate**.—*adj* **auscul-t′atory**.

auspice [ö′spis] *n* an omen; good augury; (*pl*) sponsorship; patronage—*adj* **auspi′cious**,—*adv* **auspi′ciously**.—*n* **auspi′ciousness**.

austere [ös-tēr′] *adj* harsh; stern; strictly upright; severely simple.—*adv* **austere′ly**,—*ns* **austere′ness, austēr′ity**, stern-ness; (*pl*) an austere practice; a tightened economy.

austral ös′trál] *adj* southern.

autarchy [öt′är-ki] *n* absolute sovereignty.

autarky [öt′är-ki] *n* (of a political unit) policy of economic self-sufficiency.

authentic [ö-thent′ik] *adj* not spurious or counterfeit; genuine, original; certified by valid evidence; unquestionably true.— *adv* **authent′ically**.—*vt* **authent′icate**, to prove authentic; to make valid; to verify.—*ns* **authenticā′tion**, act of authenticat-ing; confirmation; **authentic′ity**, [-is-], quality of being auth-entic.

author [öth′ór] *n* one who brings anything into being; the writer of a book, article, etc.—*vt* to be the author of.—*vt* **auth′orize**, to give official approval to; to give authority to; to justify.—*ns* **authorizā′tion**; **auth′orship**, state of being an author.—**Authorized Version**, the revised English transla-tion of the Bible, published in 1611, authorized by King James I.

authority [öth-or′i-ti] *n* legal power of right to command; (*pl*) officials with this power; influence resulting from knowledge, prestige, etc.; a person, writing, etc. cited to support an opinion; an export.—*pl*) **author′ities**.—*adj* **authoritärian**.

autism [öt′izm] *n* (*psych*) a mental state marked by disregard of external reality—*adj* **autist′ic**.

auto-, **aut-**, **auth-** [ötö-, öt-, öth-] in composition pertaining to oneself, for oneself, by oneself, independently.

auto- [ö′tö] *prefix* meaning; self; by oneself or itself.

auto [ö′tö] *n* an automobile.

autobiography [ö-to-bī-og′raf-i] *n* the biography or life of a person written by himself.—*n* **autobiog′rapher**.—*adjs* **autobiograph′ic**. **-al**.

autocrat [ö′to-krat] *n* an absolute sovereign; any domineering

person.—*n* **autoc′racy**, government by one man, with absol-ute power.—*adj* **autocrat′ic**.—*adv* **autocrat′ically**.

autocross [ö-tö-kros′] *n* an automobile gymkhana.

autograph [ö′to-gräf] *n* one's own handwriting; a signature;— *vt* to write one's signature in or on.—*adj* **autograph′ic**.

automaton [ö-tom′a-ton] *n* any automatic device, esp a robot; a human being who acts like a robot.—*pl* **autom′atons**, **autom′ata**.—*vt* **au′tomate**, to apply automation to.—*adjs* **auto-mat′ic**, acting like an automaton, self-acting; done unthink-ingly, as by habit or by reflex; using automatic equipment.—*n* an automatic pistol or rifle.—*adv* **automat′ically**.—*n* **auto-mation**.

automobile [ö-to-mō-bēl′ or ö′-] *n* a self-propelling (usu. by internal-combustion engine) vehicle for passenger transpor-tation on streets and roadways.

autonomy [ö-ton′om-i] *n* the power or right of self-govern-ment.—*adjs* **autonom′ic**, of or controlled by that part of the nervous system that regulates the motor functions of the heart, lungs, etc. and operates independently of the will; **auton′omous**.

autopsy [ö′top-si or -top′-] *n* a post-mortem examination to determine the cause of death; a critical analysis.

autosuggestion [ö′to-su-jes′ch(ö)n] *n* a mental process (toward health, etc.) originating in the subject's own mind.

autumn [ö′tum] *n* the season between summer and winter fall.—*adj* **autum′nal**.

auxiliary [ög-zil′yär-i] *adj* helping; subsidiary; supple-mentary.—*n* a helper; an assistant—**auxiliary verb**, a verb that helps form tenses, moods, voices, etc. of other verbs, as *have, be, may, shall,* etc.

avail [a-vāl′] *vti* to be of value, use, or service to,—*n* benefit use or help.—*adj* **avail′able**, that can be obtained or used; accessible.—*ns* **avail′ableness, availabil′ity**,—*adv* **avail′ably**.

avalanche [av′al-änsh -önsh] *n* a mass of snow, ice, and rock sliding down from a mountain; an overwhelming influx.

avarice [av′ar-is] *n* greedy, desire for wealth,—*adj* **avaricious** [av-àr-i′shùs],—*adv* **avari′ciously**.—*n* **avari′ciousness**.

avast [a-väst′] *interj* (*naut*) hold fast! stop!

avatar [a-va-tär′] *n* the descent of a Hindu deity in a visible form.

avaunt [a-vönt′] *adv* away, hence.

Ave Maria [ävä Ma-rē′a] (*R C Church*) 'Hail Mary', the first words of a prayer; this prayer (Luke i 28).

avenge [a-venj′, -venzh′] *vt* to get revenge for (an injury) to exact due penalty on behalf of (a person).—*n* **aveng′er**.

avenue [av′én-ū] *n* a street; drive, etc. esp when broad; means of access.

aver [a-vûr′] *vt* to declare to be true; to assert;—*pr p* **averr′ing**; *pt p* **averred′**.—*n* **aver′ment**.

average [av′ér-ij] *n* the result of dividing the sum of two or more quantities by number of quantities; the usual kind amount, etc.

averse [a-vûrs′] *adj* unwilling; opposed (to).—*ns* **averse′ness** **aver′sion**, dislike, hatred;—*vt* **avert′**, to turn from or aside (eg eyes, thoughts); to prevent, ward off.—*adj* **avert′ible**.

aviary [ā′vi-ár-i] *n* a building or large cage for keeping many birds.

aviation [ā-vi-ā′sh(ö)n] *n* the science of flying airplanes; the field of airplane design, construction, etc.—*n* **avia′tor**, an airplane pilot.

avidity [a-vid′i-ti] *n* eagerness; greediness.—*adj* **av′id**,—*adv* **av′idly**.

avionics [ā′vē-än-iks] *npl* electronics as applied in aviation and astronautics.

avitaminosis [ā-vīt-à-min-ō′ s or -vit-] *n* disease (as scurvy) resulting from a deficiency of vitamins.

avocado [av′ó-kä′dö or äv-] *n* a tropical tree (genus Persea); its thick-skinned, pear-shaped fruit with yellow buttery flesh.— Also **alligator pear, avocado pear**.

avocation [a-vo-kā′sh(ö)n] *n* occupation in addition to one's regular employment; hobby.

avoid [a-void′] *vt* to escape, keep clear of; to shun;—*n* **avoid′able**.—*n* **avoid′ance**.

avoirdupois [av′ér-dé-poiz′] *n* a system of weights in which the lb equals 16oz; (*inf*) weight, esp of a person.

avouch [a-vowch′] *vt* to vouch for; to affirm.

avow [a-vow′] *vt* to declare openly; to acknowledge.—*n*

avowed, [-vowd'].—*adv* **avow'edly,** [-id-li].—*adj* **avow'-able.**—*n* avow'al.

avuncular [a-vung'kū-lár] *adj* pertaining to an uncle.

await [a-wāt'] *vti* to wait for; to be in store for.

awake [a-wāk'] *vti* to rouse from sleep; to rouse from inaction;—*pt* awoke', awaked'; *pt p* awaked', or awoke'.—*adj* not asleep; active; vigilant.—*vti* awak'en, to awake; to rouse into interest or attention.—*n* awak'ening, ceasing to sleep; an arousing from indifference.

award [a-wörd'] *vt* to give, as by a legal decision; to give (a prize, etc.); to grant.—*n* a decision, as by a judge; a prize.

aware [a-wār'] *adj* realizing; informed; conscious.—*n* aware'-ness.

awash [a-wosh'] *adj* on a level with the surface of the water; filled or overflowing with water.

away [a-wā'] *adv* from a place; in another place or direction; off, aside; far; from one's possession; at once; continuously.—*adj* absent; at a distance.—*interj* be gone!—away with, go, come, or take away; do away with, get rid of or kill.

awe [ö] *n* a mixed feeling of reverential fear, wonder and dread.—*vt* to fill with awe.—*adjs* awe'some, full of awe; inspiring awe; awe'struck, struck or affected with awe; aw'ful, inspiring awe; terrifying; (*inf*) very bad.—*adv* (*inf*) very.—*n* aw'fulness.

awhile [a-hwīl'] *adv* for a short time.

awkward [ök'wård] *adj* clumsy; ungraceful; embarrassing; embarrassed; unwieldy; difficult to deal with.—*adv* awk'-wardly.—*n* awk'wardness.

awl [öl] *n* a pointed instrument for boring small holes in leather, wood etc.

awn [ön] *n* the bristles on a head of oats, barley, etc.—*adjs* awned; awn'less.

awning [ön'ing] *n* a structure, as of canvas extended above or in front of a window, door, etc. to afford shelter from the sun or weather.

awoke [a-wōk'] (*Brit*) *pt, pt p* of awake.

awry [a-rī'] *adj* twisted to one side; crooked.—*adv* crookedly, obliquely; perversely.

ax, axe [aks] *n* a tool with a long handle and bladed head, for chopping wood, etc.—*pl* ax'es.—*vt* to trim, split, etc. with an ax.—get the ax, (*inf*) to be discharged from one's job; have an ax to grind, (*inf*) to have an object of one's own to gain or promote.

axiom [aks'i-ôm, aks'yóm] *n* a self-evident truth; an established principle in an art or science.—*adjs* axiomat'ic,—*adv* axiomat'ically.

axis [aks'is] *n* a real or imaginary straight line about which a body rotates; a central line about which the parts of a figure, body or system are symmetrically arranged; (*math*) a fixed line along which distances are measured or to which positions are referred.—the Axis, Germany, Italy, and Japan, in World War II.—*pl* axes, [aks'ēz].—*adj* ax'ial.

axle [aks'l] *n* a rod on or with which a wheel turns; a bar connecting two opposite wheels, as of an automobile; the spindle at each end of such a bar.—*n* axle-tree, an axle of a wagon, carriage, etc.

ayatollah [ī'ä-tō'lä] *n* a Shiite Muslim leader; a title of respect.

aye,[1] *adv* [ī] *adv* yes;—*n* aye, [ī], a vote in the affirmative; (*pl*) those who vote in the affirmative.

aye,[1] *adv* [ā] *adv* (*poet*) ever; always; for ever.

azalea [a-zā'li-a] *n* gardening term for a genus (*Azalea*) of rhododendron.

azimuth [az'im-uth] *n* the arc of the horizon between the meridian of a place and a vertical circle passing through any celestial body; angular distance of this from meridian.—*adj* az'imuthal.

azure [azh'yūr] *adj* sky-blue.—*n* the blue color of the clear sky; the unclouded sky.

B

baa [bä] *n* the cry of a sheep.—*vi* to cry or bleat as a sheep.

babble [bab'l] *vi* to speak like a baby; to talk incessantly or incoherently; to murmur, as a brook.—*vt* to prate; to utter.—

ns **babb'le,** idle senseless talk, prattle; a murmuring sound; babb'ler.

babe [bāb] *n* a baby; a naive person; (*slang*) a girl or young woman.—babe in the woods, a naive person.

Babel [bā'bél] *n* (*Bible*) city thwarted in building a tower to heaven when God created a confusion of tongues.—*n* babel, a confused combination of sounds; a scene of confusion.

baby [bā'bi] *n* an infant or child; one who acts like an infant; a very young animal; the youngest or smallest of a group; (*slang*) a girl or young woman; (*slang*) any person or thing.—Also *adj.*—*vt* to pamper.—*n* bā'byhood.—*adj* bā'byish.

baccalaureate [bak-a-lö're-āt] *n* the university degree of bachelor; a commencement address.

baccarat [bak'är-ä] *n* gambling card game in which object is to hold a combination of cards totaling 9, differing from chemin de fer in that players bet against the house.

bacchanal [bak'a-nál] *n* one who indulges in drunken revels.—*adj* relating to drinking or drunken revels—also **baccha-nā'lian.**—*ns pl* **bacchanā'lia, bacch'anals,** drunken revels.

bachelor [bach'el-ór] *n* (*hist*) a young knight who followed the banner of another; an unmarried man; one who has completed a four-year course leading to a degree in the humanities (or science, etc.) at a college or a university.—*n* bach'elorhood.

bacillus [ba-sil'us] *n* any of a genus of a rod-shaped bacteria; (*loosely*) any bacterium;—*pl* bacill'i.

back [bak] *n* the rear surface of the human body from neck to hip; the corresponding part in animals; a part that supports or fits the back; the part or surface of an object that is less used or less important, the part furthest from the front; (*sports*) a player or position behind the front line.—*adj* at the rear (*back teeth*); remote or inferior (*back streets*); of or for the past (*back pay*); backward.—*adv* at or toward the rear; to or toward a former condition, time, etc. (*pay him back*); in reserve or concealment.—*vt* to move backward; to support; to bet on; to provide or be a back for.—*vi* to go backward.—*n* back'ache, an ache or pain in the back.—*ns* back'drop, a curtain, often scenic, at the back of a stage; background; back'er, a patron; one who bets on a contestant; back'field, (*football*) the players behind the line, esp the offensive unit; —*adj* back-to-back, (*inf*) one right after another.—*vi* back'track, to return by the same path; to retreat or recant.—*adj* back'up, back-up, standing by as an alternate or auxiliary; supporting.—*n* a backing up, esp an accumulation of support and help.—*adv* backward, backwards, toward the back; with the back foremost; in a way opposite the usual; into the past.—*adj* backward, turned toward the rear or opposite way; shy; slow or retarded.—back and forth, backward and forward; back down, to withdraw from a position or claim; back off (*or away,* etc.), to move back (or away, etc.); back out (of), to withdraw from an enterprise; to evade keeping a promise, etc.; back up, to support; to move backward; to accumulate because of restricted movement; go back on, (*inf*) to be disloyal to; to betray; to fail to keep (one's word, etc.); turn one's back on, to turn away from, as in contempt; to abandon.

backgammon [bak-gam'ón] *n* a game played by two persons on a board with dice and fifteen men or pieces each.

bacon [bā'kón] *n* salted and smoked meat from the back or sides of a hog.—to bring home the bacon, (*inf*) to achieve an object; provide material support.

bacteria [bak-tē'ri-a] *n pl* miscroscopic unicellular organisms;—*sing* bactēr'ium.—*ns* bacterēm'ia, invasion of blood by bacteria without giving rise to symptoms of disease, but resulting in boils or sore throats; bacter'icide, an agent that destroys bacteria; bacteriol'ogy, the study of bacteria.

bad [bad] *adj* not good; not as it should be; inadequate or unfit; unfavorable; rotten or spoiled; incorrect or faulty; wicked; immoral; mischievous; harmful; severe; ill; sorry; distressed.

bade [bad] *pt* of bid.

badge [baj] *n* a distinguishing mark or emblem.

badger [baj'ér] *na* burrowing hibernating animal (genera *Meles* and *Taxidea*) of the weasel family; the pelt or fur of the badger; Badger, nickname for a resident or inhabitant of Wisconsin.—*vt* to pester or annoy persistently.

badinage [bad'in-äzh] *n* light playful talk, banter.

badminton [bad'min-ton] *n* a court game for two or four players played with light rackets and a shuttlecock volleyed over a net.

baffle [baf′l] *vt* to check or make ineffectual; to bewilder.—*n* **baffle plate**, a device for regulating the flow of liquids, gas, etc.

bag [bag] *n* a usu. flexible container of paper, plastic, etc. that can be closed at the top; a satchel, suitcase, etc.; a purse; game taken in hunting; a baglike shape or part.

bagatelle [bag-a-tel′] *n* a trifle; a game played on a board with nine balls and a cue.

bagel [bā′gl] *n* a ring-shaped bread roll, hard and glazed on the outside, soft in the center.

baggage [bag′ij] *n* traveler's luggage; a worthless or saucy woman; things that get in the way.

bagpipe [bag′pīp] *n* (often in *pl*) a wind instrument, consisting of a bag fitted with pipes.—*n* **bag′piper**.

bail¹ [bāl] *n* one who procures the release of an accused person by becoming security for his appearing in court; the security given; such a release.—*vt* to set a person free by giving security for him; to help out of financial or other difficulty.

bail² [bāl] *vti* to dip out (water) from (a boat) (*usu. with* out).—*n* a bucket for dipping up water from a boat.—**bail out** to parachute from an aircraft.

Bailey bridge [bā′li-brij] a bridge prefabricated for rapid erection.

bailiff [bāl′if] *n* a minor official in some US courts, usu. a messenger or usher.

bait [bāt] *n* food put on a hook to allure fish or make them bite; any allurement.—*vt* to set food as a lure; to set dogs on (a bear, badger, etc.); to worry, persecute, harass, esp by verbal attacks; to lure, to tempt; to entice.

baize [bāz] *n* a coarse woolen cloth.

bake [bāk] *vt* to dry and harden pottery by the heat of the sun or of fire; to cook food by dry heat, esp in an oven.—*vi* to work as a baker; to become firm through heat;—*pt p* **baked** [bākt]; *pr p* **bāk′ing**.—*ns* **bak′er**, one who bakes bread, etc.

baksheesh [bak′shēsh] *n* a present of money as a bribe or tip to expedite service.

balance [bal′áns] *n* an instrument for weighing, usu. formed of two dishes or scales hanging from a beam supported in the middle; act of weighing; equality of weight or power (as *the balance of power*); state of mental or emotional equilibrium; a remainder.

balata [bal′a-ta] *n* the dried juice of a tree (*Manilkara bidentata*) of tropical America, used as a substitute for rubber and gutta-percha; the tree yielding this.

balcony [balk′on-i] *n* a platform projecting from an upper story and enclosed by a railing; an upper floor of seats in a theater, etc. often projecting over the main floor.

bald [böld] *adj* lacking a natural or usual covering (as of hair, vegetation, or nap); having little or no tread; plain or blunt; marked with white; bare, unadorned. **bald eagle**, the common eagle (*Haliaeetus leucocephalus*) of the US, the national bird.—*adv* **bald′ly**.—*n* **bald′ness**.

balderdash [böl′dér-dash] *n* nonsense.

baldric [böld′rik] *n* a warrior's belt worn over the shoulder to support a sword, etc.

bale¹ [bāl] *n* a large bundle, esp a standardized quantity of goods, as raw cotton compressed and bound.—*vt* to make into bales.

bale² [bāl] *n* great evil; woe.—*adj* **bale′ful**, full of evil; malignant; deadly; ominous.—*adv* **bale′fully**.—*n* **balefulness**.

baleen [ba-lēn′] *n* whalebone.

balk [bök] *n* an unploughed ridge of turf; hindrance, obstruction; blunder, error; (*baseball*) an illegal motion by the pitcher entitling base runners to advance one base.—*vt* to obstruct or foil.—*vi* to stop and refuse to move and act.

ball¹ [böl] *n* anything spherical or nearly so; a globular or egg-shaped object to play with in tennis, football, etc.; any of several such games, esp baseball; a throw or pitch of a ball; a missile for a cannon, rifle, etc.; (*pl*) testicles; any rounded protuberant part of the body.

ball² [böl] *n* a formal social dance; (*slang*) a good time.—*n* **ball′room**.

ballad [bal′ád] *n* narrative poem or song usu. anonymous, with simple words, short stanzas, and a refrain; a slow, sentimental, 'popular' song.

ballade [bä-läd′] *n* a medieval form of music or a poem of one or more triplets of stanzas, each of seven or eight lines, including a refrain.

ballast [bal′ást] *n* heavy matter placed in a ship or vehicle to keep it steady when it has no cargo; crushed rock or gravel, etc. used in railroad beds.

ballerina [bal-ler-ēn′á] *n* a female ballet-dancer;—*pl* **baller-in′as, balleri′ne**.

ballet [bal′ā] *n* a theatrical exhibition of dancing and panto-mimic action; the troupe that performs it.—*adj* **ballet′ic**.—*ns* **balletomane** [-et′ō-mān] ballet enthusiast; **balletomā′nia**.

ballista [bä-lis′tá] *n* a Roman military engine, in the form of a crossbow, which propelled large and heavy missiles.—*adj* **ballistic**, of or pertaining to forcible throwing of missiles; relating to projectiles *n* **ballis′tics**, the science of projectiles.

balloon [ba-lōōn′] *n* a large airtight bag, that ascends when filled with a gas lighter than air; an airship with such a bag; a toy of similar form; balloon-shaped drawing enclosing words spoken in a strip cartoon.—*vt* to inflate.—*vi* to swell; to expand.

ballot [bal′ót] *n* a ticket or paper used in voting; act or right of voting, as by ballots; the total number of votes cast.—*vi* to vote;—*pr p* **ball′oting**; *pt p* **ball′oted**.—*n* **ball′ot box**, a box to receive ballots.

ballyhoo [bal-i-hōō′ (or bal′-)] *n* noisy talk, sensational advertising, etc.

ballrag [bal′i-rag] *see* **bullyrag**.

balm [bäm] *n* a fragrant and healing ointment; anything that heals or soothes pain.—*adj* **balm′y**, fragrant; soothing; bearing balm.

balogna [bä-lōn′ē] *n* a large sausage made of pork, veal, porksuet, etc. sold ready for eating cold.

baloney [bá-lōn′ē] *n* (*inf*) foolish talk; nonsense.

balsa [bäl′sa, böl′sa] *n* a tropical American tree (*Ochroma lagopus*) with very light porous wood; its wood.

balsam [böl′sam] *n* a preparation having a balsamic odor and used esp in medicine;—*ns* **balsam fir**, an American evergreen tree.

Baltic [böl′tik] *adj* denoting the Baltic Sea or the nations bordering it; of the group of Indo-European languages comprising Lithuanian and Latvian.

baluster [bal′us-tèr] *n* any of the small posts of a railing, as on a staircase.—*adj* **bal′ustered**.—*n* **bal′ustrade**, a row of balusters joined by a rail.

bambino [bam-bē′no] *n* a representation of the infant Jesus.

bamboo [bam-bōō′] *n* any of various often tropical woody grasses.

bamboozle [bam-bōō′zl] *vt* to deceive.

ban [ban] *n* a condemnation, an official prohibition; a strong public condemnation.—*vt* to forbid or prohibit, esp officially.

banal [bān′ál, ban′ál, ban-äl′] *adj* commonplace, trivial.—*n* **banality** [ban-al′-i-ti].

banana [bá-nä′ná] *n* a herbaceous plant (genus *Musa*) bearing its fruit in compact, hanging bunches.

banana republic, (*inf*) a small country, esp in Central America, that is dominated by foreign interests; —**go bananas**, (*slang*) go crazy.

band¹ [band] *n* a strip of cloth, etc., to bind round anything; a stripe crossing a surface, distinguished by its color or appearance; (*radio*) a group of wavelengths.—*n* **band′age**, a strip to bind up a wound or fracture, etc.—*vt* to bind with such.

band² [band] *n* a number of persons bound together for any common purpose; a troop of conspirators, etc.

bandanna, bandana [ban-dän′á] *n* a large colored handkerchief.

bandeau [ban-dō′] *n* a narrow ribbon; a narrow brassiere.—*pl* **bandeaux** [ban-dōz′].

banderole, banderol [ban′de-rōl] *n* a long, narrow forked flag or streamer.

bandit [ban′dit] *n* an outlaw; a brigand;—*pl* **band′its**.

bandolier, bandoleer [ban-do-lēr′] *n* a belt worn over the chest, esp for holding cartridges.

bandy¹ [ban′di] *n* a game similar to hockey and believed to be its forerunner.

bandy² [ban′di] *vt* to bat (as a tennis ball) to and fro; to pass (rumours, etc.) freely; to exchange words, esp angrily);—*pt*, *pt p* **ban′died**.—*n* **ban′dying**.

bandy³ [ban'di] *adj* (of legs) bent outward at the knee.—*adj* **ban'dy-legged'**.

bane [bān] *n* destruction, mischief, woe; poison; source or cause of evil.—*adj* **bane'ful**, destructive.—*adv* **bane'fully**.—*n* **bane'fulness**.

bang¹ [bang] *n* a heavy blow; a sudden loud noise; (*inf*) a burst of vigor; (*slang*) a thrill.—*vt* to beat; to strike violently; to slam.—*vi* to make a loud noise; to hit noisily or sharply.—*vt* **bang up**, to damage.—*adj* **bang-up**, (*inf*) very good, excellent.

bang² [bang] *vt* to cut hair short and straight.—*n* (usu. *pl*) banged hair over the forehead.

bangle [bang'gl] *n* a bracelet worn on arms or legs.

banish [ban'ish] *vt* to condemn to exile; to drive away; to get rid of.—*n* **ban'ishment**, exile.

banister, bannister [ban'istėr] *n* the railing or supporting balusters in a staircase.

banjo [ban'jō] a stringed musical instrument with a body like a shallow drum, long fretted neck, and usu. six strings that are plucked.

bank¹ [bangk] *n* a mound or ridge; the margin of a river; rising ground in a lake or the sea; the lateral, slanting turn of an aircraft.—*vt* to pile up; to cover (a fire) so as to lessen the rate of combustion; to make (an aircraft) slant laterally on a turn; to make (a billiard ball) recoil from a cushion.

bank² [bangk] *n* a row of oars; a row or tier, as of keys in a keyboard.—*vt* to arrange in a row or tier.

bank³ [bangk] *n* a place where money or other valuable material, eg blood, data (**blood, data bank**) is deposited until required; an institution for the keeping, lending, exchanging etc., of money.—*vti* to deposit in a bank.

bankrupt [bangk'rupt] *n* a person, etc. legally declared unable to pay his debts; one who becomes insolvent; one lacking a particular thing (*a moral bankrupt*).—*vt* to reduce to bankruptcy.—Also *adj*.—*n* **bank'ruptcy**, the state of being, or act of becoming, bankrupt.

banner [ban'ėr] *n* a flag or ensign; a headline running across a newspaper page; a strip of cloth bearing a slogan or emblem carried between poles in a parade or stretched between lampposts across a street.

bannerol, banner roll [ban'ėr-ōl] *n* a banderol.

bannock [ban'ok] *n* a usu. unleavened biscuit made with oatmeal or barley meal.

banns [banz] *n pl* a proclamation of intention, esp in church, to marry.

banquet [bangk'wet, -wit] *n* a feast; an elaborate and sometimes ceremonial dinner, in honor of a person or occasion.—*vt* to give a feast to.

banquette [bang-kėt'] *n* a raised gunner's platform behind a parapet; an upholstered bench.

banshee [ban'shē] *n* a female fairy in Irish folklore who wails and shrieks before a death in the family.

bantam [ban'tàm] *n* any of several dwarf breeds of domestic fowl; a small, aggressive person.—*adj* like a bantam.

banter [bant'ėr] *vt* assail with good-humored raillery.

bantling [bant'ling] *n* a very young child.

Bantu [ban'tōō] *n* member of a group of Negroid peoples in equatorial and southern Africa.

banyan [ban'yàn] *n* an Indian fig tree (*Ficus benglensis*) with vast rooting branches.

baobab [bā'o-bab] *n* a broad-trunked tropical tree of Africa and India (*Adonsonia digitata*) marked by angular branches and edible gourdlike fruit.

baptize [bap-tīz'] *vt* to administer baptism to.—*n* **bap'tism**, immersion in, or sprinkling with, water as a rite of admitting a person to a Christian church; an initiating experience.—*adj* **baptis'mal**.—*adv* **baptis'mally**.—*ns* **Bap'tist**, member of Protestant Christian denomination holding that the true church is of believers only, who are all equal, that the only authority is the Bible, and that adult baptism by immersion is necessary; **bap'tistery**, a place where baptism is administered.

bar¹ [bär] *n* a rod of any solid substance; a counter across which alcoholic drinks are served; a place with such a counter; an oblong piece, as of soap; anything that obstructs or hinders; a band or strip; a law court, esp that part where the lawyers sit; lawyers collectively; the legal profession; (*mus*) a vertical line dividing a staff into measures; (*mus*) a measure.—*vt* to fasten or secure, as with a bar; to hinder or exclude; to oppose;—*pr p*

barr'ing; *pt p* **barred**.—*prep* excluding, excepting (eg *bar none*).

bar² [bar] *n* a unit of pressure equal to one million dynes per square centimeter.

barb¹ [bärb] *n* a beardlike growth; the jag near the point of a fishhook, etc.; a wounding or pointed remark.—*vt* to provide with a barb.—*adj* **barbed**.—*n* **barbed wire, barb'wire'**, wire with barbs at close intervals.

barb² [bärb] *n* a swift kind of horse of No Africa, related to Arabians.

barb³ [bärb] *n* (*slang*) barbiturate.

barbarous [bär'bàr-us] *adj* uncivilized; primitive; brutal.—*adj* **barbār'ian**.—*n* an uncivilized savage, primitive man; a cruel, brutal man.—*adj* **barbär'ic**.—*vti* **bar'barize**, to make or become barbarous.—*ns* **bar'barism**, word or expression that is not standard; the state of being primitive or uncivilized; a barbarous act or custom; **barbär'ity**, cruelty.—*adv* **bar'barously**.—*n* **bar'barousness**.

Barbary ape [bär'bär-i āp] *n* the small tailless ape (*Macaca sylvana*) found in N Africa and Gibraltar.

barbecue [bärb'e-kū] *vt* to roast or broil over an open fire (as a pit, a special container, etc.) a party.

barber [bärb'er] *n* one who shaves faces and cuts hair.—*vti* to cut the hair (of), shave, etc.

barberry [bär'bėr-i] *n* a genus (*Berberis*) of thorny shrubs with yellow flowers and red berries.

barbican [bär'bi-kàn] *n* a tower at the gate of a fortress, esp the outwork defending the drawbridge.

barbital [bär'bi-tàl] *n* a white, crystalline, addictive hypnotic.—*n* **barbiturate**, a salt or ester of an organic acid (**barbituric acid**), esp. one used as a sedative, hypnotic or antispasmodic.

bard [bärd] *n* a poet and singer among the ancient Celts; a poet.—*adj* **bard'ic**.

bare [bär] *adj* uncovered; naked; open to view; poor, scanty; unadorned; without furnishings; mere or by itself.—*vt* to strip or uncover.—*adj* **bare'back**, on a horse with no saddle.—Also *adv*.—*adj* **bare'faced**, with the face uncovered; shameless.—*adv* **bare'facedly**.—*n* **bare'facedness**.—*adjs* **bare'foot, -ed**, having the feet bare; **bare'hand'ed**, with hands uncovered; without weapons, etc.

bare [bär] old *pt* of **bear**.

bargain [bär'g(i)n] *n* a contract or agreement; an agreement with regard to its worth (*a bad bargain*); something sold at a price favorable to the buyer.

barge [bärj] *n* flat-bottomed freight boat, used on rivers and canals; a large pleasure or state boat.—*vi* to move clumsily; to enter rudely or abruptly (in or into).

baritone [bar'i-tōn] *n* a male voice between bass and tenor; a singer with such a voice; a brass or woodwind instrument having a range between tenor and bass.

barium [bä'ri-ùm] a metallic element (symbol Ba; at wt 137.3; at no 56).

bark¹ [bärk] *n* the abrupt cry of a dog, wolf, etc.; any similar sound.—*vi* to yelp like a dog; to speak sharply.— to **bark up the wrong tree**, to direct one's attack, energy, etc. in the wrong direction.

bark², barque [bärk] *n* a three-masted vessel whose mizzenmast is fore-and-aft rigged; any boat propelled by sails or oars.

bark³ [bärk] *n* the outside covering of a woody stem.—*vt* to strip or peel the bark from; (*inf*) to scrape; to skin (the knees, etc.)

barley [bär'li] *n* a hardy grain used for food and for making malt liquors and spirits.

barm [bärm] *n* the yeast formed on fermenting malt drinks.

Barmecide [bär'me-sīd] *adj* providing only the illusion of abundance.—*adj* **Barmecī'dal**.

bar mitzvah [bär mitz'va] *n* (*Judaism*) the ceremony marking the 13th birthday of a boy, who then assumes full religious obligations; the boy himself.

barn [bän] *n* a farm building in which grain, hay, etc., are stored.—*n* **barn dance**, a social dance featuring several dance forms (as square dancing).—*ns* and *adjs* **barn'-door, barn'-yard**.

barnacle [bär'na-kl] *n* any of numerous marine shellfish that, in the adult stage, adhere to rocks and ship bottoms; a European goose (*Branta leucopsus*) that breeds in the Arctic, also **bar'nacle goose**.

barometer [bar-om'et-ĕr] *n* an instrument by which the pressure of the atmosphere is measured, and changes of weather indicated; anything that marks change. — *adj* **baromet'ric**. — *adv* **barometrically**

baron [bar'on] *n* a title of rank, the lowest in the British peerage; a powerful businessman; the indeterminate rank of a European nobleman.

baronet [bar'on-et] *n* the lowest British hereditary title.

baroque [bar-ōk'] *adj* grotesque, extravagant, whimsical; extravagantly ornamented, esp in architecture and decorative art.

barouche [ba-rōōsh'] *n* a double-seated four-wheeled carriage with a folding top.

barque *see* **bark** (2).

barrack [bar'ăk] *n* (usu. *pl*) a building for soldiers; a huge bare building.

barracuda [bar-a-kōō'dà] *n* a fierce, food fish (*Sphyraena barracuda*) of eastern Atlantic waters.

barrage [bar-äzh'] *n* an artificial dam across a river; heavy artillery fire; continuous and heavy delivery.

barratry [bar'à-tri] *n* the fraudulent breach of duty by the master of a ship; the stirring up of law suits.

barrel [bar'él] *n* a round wooden vessel made of curved staves bound with hoops; the quantity which such a vessel contains; anything long and hollow, as the barrel of a gun. — *vt* to put in a barrel. — *adj* **barr'elled**, having a barrel or barrels; placed in a barrel.

barren [bar'èn] *adj* incapable of bearing offspring; unfruitful; dull, stupid; unprofitable. — *adv* **barr'enly**. — *n* **barr'enness**.

barrette [bar-et'] *n* a bar or clasp for holding a girl's hair in place.

barricade [bar'ik-ād] *n* a temporary fortification raised to block a street; an obstruction. — *vt* to block with a barricade.

barrier [bar'i-èr] *n* a fence or other structure to bar passage, prevent access, control crowds, etc. — *n* **barr'ier reef**, a coral reef fringing a coast with a navigable channel inside.

barrister [bar'is-tèr] *n* one who is qualified to plead at the bar in an English or Irish law-court.

barrow¹ [bar'ō] *n* a small hand-cart used to bear or convey a load.

barrow² [bar'ō] *n* a burial mound.

barter [bär'tèr] *vt* to give (one thing) in exchange (for another); to give (away for some unworthy gain). — *vi* to traffic by exchanging. — *n* traffic by exchange of commodities.

bartizan [bär'ti-zan] *n* a parapet or battlement.

baryta [bä-rī'ta] *n* barium oxide, barium hydroxide. — *n* **barytes** [bä-rī'tēz], barium sulfate.

basalt [bas'ölt, bas-ölt'] *n* hard, compact, dark-colored igneous rock. — *adj* **basalt'ic**.

base¹ [bās] *n* that on which a thing rests; bottom, foundation, support; the chief or essential ingredient; a place from which operations are conducted; a fixed goal in games such as baseball; — *vt* to found (on); — *pr p* **bas'ing**; *pt p* **based** [bāst]. — *adj* **bäs'al**. *adj* **base'less**, without a base; unfounded. — *adj* **bäs'ic**, fundamental; (*chem*) alkaline. — *n* a basic principle, factor, etc.

base² [bās] *adj* low in place, value, estimation or principle; mean, vile, worthless; menial. — *adj* **base'born**, illegitimate. — *adv* **base'ly**. — *n* **base'ness**. — **base metal**, any metal other than the precious metals.

baseball [bās'böl] *see* **base** (1).

bash [bash] *vt* (*inf*) to hit hard. — *n* (*slang*) a party.

bashful [bash'fōōl, -fl] *adj* easily embarrassed, shy. — *adv* **bash'fully**. — *n* **bash'fulness**.

BASIC [bās'ik] *n* a simple language for programming and interacting with a computer. [Beginners' All-purpose Symbolic Instruction Code.]

basil [baz'il] *n* a genus (*Ocimum*) of aromatic plants, the leaves of which are used to season food.

basilica [baz'il'ik-a] *n* a church with a broad nave, side aisles, and an apse; (*RC Church*) a church with special ceremonial rites. — *adj* **basil'ican**.

basilisk [baz'il-isk] *n* a fabulous creature with fiery death-dealing eyes; any of several crested tropical American lizards

(genus *Basiliscus*) noted for their ability to run on their hind legs.

basin [bās'n] *n* a wide shallow container for liquid; its contents; a sink; any large hollow, often with water in it; the area drained by a river and its tributaries.

basinet [bas'i-net] *n* a light helmet worn with a visor.

basis [bās'is] *n* a base or foundation; a principal constituent; a fundamental principle or theory. — *pl* **bas'es** [bās'ēz].

bask [bäsk] *vi* to lie in warmth or sunshine. — Also *fig*.

basket [bäs'kèt] *n* a receptacle made of interwoven cane, wood strips, etc.; (*basketball*) the goal, a round, open hanging net; a scoring toss of the ball through it. — *ns* **bas'ketball**, a team game in which goals are scored by throwing a ball into a basket; this ball.

Basque [bask] *n* one of a people inhabiting the western Pyrenees, in Spain or France, or their language which is a relic of a non-Indo-European language; a continuation of the bodice a little below the waist. — *adj* relating to the Basques or their language or country.

bas-relief [bä'-re-lēf'] *n* sculptures in which the figures do not stand far out from the ground on which they are formed.

bass¹ [bās] *n* the range of the lowest male voice; a singer or instrument with this range; a double-bass; a low, deep sound. — *adj* of, for, or in the range of a bass. — **bass clef**, clef that places the F below middle C on the fourth line of the staff.

bass² [bas] *n* any of numerous freshwater food and game fishes of N America (esp families Centrarchidae and Serranidae).

bassinet [bas'i-net] *n* a kind of basket with a hood, used as a cradle.

basso [bäs'sō] *n* a bass singer, esp one singing opera.

bassoon [ba-sōōn'] *n* an orchestral woodwind instrument of the oboe family pitched two octaves below the oboe with a tube bent back on account of its great length. — *ns* **bassoon'-ist; double bassoon**, sounds an octave lower.

bass viol [bās-vī'ol] *n* viola da gamba; double bass.

bast [bast] *n* phloem; bast fiber. [OE bæst; Ger *bast*.]

bastard [bas'tàrd] *n* a child born of parents not married; (*inf*) person (*lucky bastard*); something of dubious origin. — *adj* born out of wedlock; not genuine; false. — *vt* **bas'tardize**, to prove or declare to be a bastard; to reduce to a lower state or condition. — *n* **bas'tardy**, the state of being a bastard.

baste¹ [bāst] *vt* to beat severely. — *n* **bast'ing**.

baste² [bāst] *vt* to drop fat over (roasting meat, etc.).

baste³ [bāst] *vt* to sew with long loose stitches as a temporary seam.

bastion [bast'yòn] *n* a kind of tower at the angle of a fortification; any strong defense. — *adj* **bast'ioned**.

bat¹ [bat] *n* a heavy stick; a club for baseball, etc.; a turn at batting (*at bat*); (*inf*) a blow; a paddle used in various games (as table tennis). — *vt* to hit as with a bat; to advance (a base runner) by batting; to consider or discuss in detail. — *pr p* **batt'ing**; *pt p* **batt'ed**. — *ns* **bat'ter**, one who wields the bat at baseball, etc.

bat² [bat] *n* any of an order (Chiroptera) of nocturnal, mouse-like, flying mammals with forelimbs modified to form wings. — *adj* **batt'y**, bat-like; bat-infested; (*inf*) crazy.

bat³ [bat] *vt* to wink. — **not to bat an eyelid**, to show no emotion.

batch [bach] *n* the quantity of bread etc. baked at one time; one set, group, etc.; an amount of work for processing by a computer in a single run.

bath [bäth] *n* water for immersing the body; a bathing; a receptacle or a house for bathing.

bathe [bāTH] *vt* to moisten with any liquid. — *vi* to take a bath; to go swimming; to become immersed. — *ns* **bath'er**.

bathometer [bath-om'et-èr] *n* an instrument for ascertaining the depth of water.

bathos [bä'thos] *n* a ludicrous descent from the elevated to the ordinary in writing or speech. — *adj* **bathetic** [ba-thet'ik].

bathysphere [bath'i-sfēr] *n* a strongly built steel diving sphere for deep-sea observation.

batik [bat'ik] *n* a method of producing designs on cloth by covering with wax, for each successive dipping, those parts that are to be protected from the dye.

bating [bāt'ing] *prep* excepting.

batiste [ba-tēst′] *n* a fine sheer fabric of linen and cotton; an imitation made from rayon or wool.

batman [bat′, bä′, or bö′man] *n* a British officer's servant.

baton [bat′ón] *n* a staff serving as a symbol of office; a hollow cylinder carried by each member of a relay team in succession.

batrachian [ba-trā′ki-an] *n* any vertebrate amphibian, esp frog or toad.—Also *adj*.

battalion [bat-al′yón] *n* a US Army Unit consisting of four or more companies usu. commanded by a lieutenant colonel; a large group.

batten¹ [bat′n] *vti* to fatten, thrive.

batten² [bat′n] *n* a sawed strip of wood; a strip of wood put over a seam between boards.—*vt* to fasten or supply with battens.

batten³ [bat′n] *n* in a loom, the frame moved to press the woof threads into place.

batter¹ [bat′ér] *vt* to beat with successive blows; to wear with beating or by use.—*vi* to strike heavily and repeatedly.—*n* a mixture of flour, egg, and milk or water thin enough to pour or drop from a spoon.

batter² [bat′ér] *n* a receding upward slope of a structure.—*vt* to give a receding upward slope to (as a wall).

battery [bat′ér-i] *n* a set of heavy guns; the place on which cannon are mounted; the unit of artillery or its personnel; a series of two or more electric cells arranged to produce a current.

battle [bat′l] *n* a contest between opposing armies; armed fighting, a fight or encounter.—*vti* to fight. **batt′lefield**, the place on which a battle is fought; **battle group**, a military unit normally made up of five companies; **battle royal**, a free-for-all; a heated dispute; **batt′leship**, a heavily armed, heavily armored warship.—**to join, do battle**, to fight.

battlement [bat′l-mènt] *n* a wall or parapet with embrasures, from which to shoot; an indented parapet.

battue [bä-tōō′ or tü′] *n* a method of hunting in which animals are driven into some place for the convenience of the hunters; a hunt in which this method is used.

bauble [bö′bl] *n* a trifling piece of finery; a fool's scepter.

bauxite [bök′sĭt, -zit, bō′zĭt] *n* the most important aluminum ore.

bawd [böd] *n* a woman who keeps a house of prostitution.—*adj* **bawd′y**, obscene, unchaste.

bawl [böl] *vti* to shout; to weep loudly.—*n* a loud cry; a noisy weeping.—*ns* **bawl′er, bawl′ing.—bawl out**, (*slang*) to reprimand.

bay¹ [bā] *adj* reddish brown.—*n* a horse of this color.

bay² [bā] *n* a wide inlet of a sea or lake, along the shore.

bay³ [bā] *n* a principal compartment in a building; a main division in a structure; any of various sections or compartments used for a special purpose as in an airplane, automobile, filling station, etc.

bay⁴ [bā] *n* the European laurel (*Laura nobilis*); any of various shrubs (genera *Magnolia, Myrica*, and *Gordonia*) resembling the laurel; (*pl*) honor, fame.—*ns* **bay leaf**, dried leaf of European laurel used as a flavoring agent; **bay rum**, an aromatic liquid used in cosmetics and medicine prepared from leaves of the West Indian bayberry.

bay⁵ [bā] *vi* to bark or howl in long, deep tones.—*vt* to bark at; to bring to bay; to utter in deep, long tones.—*n* the position of one forced to turn and fight; the position of one checked; a baying of dogs.—**at bay**, cornered; held off; **bring to bay, to corner**.

bayonet [bā′on-et] *n* a stabbing instrument of steel fixed to the muzzle of a musket or rifle.—*vt* to stab with a bayonet.

bayou [bī′ōō] *n* in the Southern US the marshy offshoot of a lake or river.

bazaar [ba-zär′] *n* an Eastern market-place; a benefit sale for a church, etc.

bazooka [ba-zōō′ka] *n* a portable weapon, used chiefly against tanks, consisting of a long tube that launches a projectile with an explosive head.

be [bē] *vi* to live; to exist; to have a specified state or quality;—*pr p* **bē′ing**; *pt p* **been.—be off**, go away.

beach [bēch] *n* the sandy shore of the sea or of a lake.—*vti* to drive or haul (a boat) up on the beach.—*ns* **beach′head**, a position on a seashore in enemy territory seized by an advance force and held to cover the main landing.

beacon [bē′kón] *n* a light for warning or guiding; a radio transmitter sending guiding signals to aircraft; a source of light or inspiration.—*vt* to furnish with a beacon.—*vi* to shine as a beacon.

bead [bēd] *n* a little ball pierced for stringing; (*pl*) a string of beads; (*pl*)) a rosary; a bubble or drop of liquid; the small knob of metal forming the front sight of a rifle; a projecting rim, band, or molding.—*vt* to furnish with beads or a beading.—*vi* to form into a bead.—*adj* **bead′ed**, having beads or a bead; in beadlike form; **bead′y**, small and bright (of eyes); covered with beads or bubbles.—*ns* **bead′ing**, beadwork; an openwork trimming.

beadle [bēd′l] *n* a minor official who keeps order in certain churches.

beagle [bē′gl] *n* a breed of small hound with short legs and drooping ears.

beak [bēk] *n* the bill of a bird; anything pointed or projecting; the nose; the projecting mouth parts of various insects, fishes, etc.—*adj* **beaked** [bēkt].

beaker [bēk′ér] *n* a large drinking cup, or its contents; a cylindrical vessel with a pouring lip used by chemists and pharmacists.

beam [bēm] *n* a large and straight piece of timber or metal; the crossbar of a balance; a ship's breadth at its widest point; a slender shaft of light, etc.; a radiant look, smile, etc.; a steady radio or radar signal for guiding aircraft or ships.—*vt* to send forth (light) in a beam; to direct (a radio signal, etc.).—*vi* to shine; to smile radiantly.—*adj* **beam′y**, emitting beams of light; broad in the beam.

bean [bēn] *n* a leguminous plant bearing kidney-shaped seeds; a seed or pod of such a plant; any beanlike seed (*coffee beans*); (*slang*) the head or brain.—*vt* (*slang*) to hit on the head.—*ns* **bean′ery**, (*inf*) a restaurant.

bear¹ [bār] *vt* to carry; to support; to endure; to admit of (eg an interpretation); to behave or conduct (oneself); to bring forth or produce; to need; to give.—*vi* to be patient; to have reference to (*with* **upon**); to be productive; to be situated;—*pr p* **bear′ing**; *pt* **bōre**; *pt p* **borne** [börn, börn], **born** [börn]—the latter referring to something brought forth.—*adj* **bear′able**, that may be endured.—*adv* **bear′ably**.—*ns* **bear′er**, one who or that which bears.

bear′ing, demeanor; a compass direction; relation to, a machine part on which another part slides, revolves, etc.; **bear down**, to press down by weight; overwhelm; **bear out**, to corroborate; **bear up**, to keep up one's courage.

bear² [bār] *n* any of a family (Ursidae) of massive mammals with coarse fur, short legs, plantigrade feet and feeding mainly on fruit and insects; any of various other bearlike animals (eg ant bear, Koala bear); **Bear**, either of two constellations in the northern hemisphere, Great Bear (Ursa Major) and Little Bear (Ursa Minor); a rough or ill-bred fellow; one who sells stocks anticipating a fall in price so that he may buy them back at a lower price.

beard [bērd] *n* the hair that grows on the chin and cheeks of a man; any beardlike part; an awn.—*vt* to oppose to the face; to provide with a beard.—*adjs* **beard′ed, beard′less**.

beast [bēst] *n* a large four-footed animal; a brutal gross person.—*n* **beast′ie**, a wild or strange beast.—*adj* **beast′ly**, like a beast in actions or behavior; coarse; (*coll*) disagreeable, irksome.—*n* **beast′liness.—beast of burden**, any animal used to carry things; **beast of prey**, any animal that hunts and kills for food.

beat [bēt] *vt* to strike repeatedly; to thrash; to overcome; to be too difficult for; to mark (time) with a baton, etc.; to mix (eggs, etc.) by hard stirring; to move (esp wings) up and down; to form (a path, way, etc.) by repeated treading or riding; to keep walking on; (*inf*) to puzzle; (*inf*) to cheat; (*slang*) to escape the penalties of.—*vi* to hit, dash, etc. repeatedly; to throb;—*pr p* **beat′ing**; *pt* **beat**; *pt p* **beat′en.**—*adj* **beat′en**, made smooth or hard by beating or treading; worn by use; shaped by hammering; exhausted; defeated.—*ns* **beat′er**, an implement for beating (as an eggbeater or the blade of an electric mixer); **beat′ing**, the act of striking; the damage resulting; thrashing; pulsation or throbbing.

beatify [bē-at′i-fī] *vt* to make blissfully happy; (*RC Church*) to declare one who has died to be among the blessed in heaven.—*adj* **beatif′ic**, making blessed; expressing and communicating happiness.—*n* **beatificā′tion**, act of beatifying.

beatitude [bē-at'i-tūd] *n* perfect blessedness or happiness.—
the Beatitudes, the pronouncements of Jesus in the Sermon
on the Mount.

beau [bō] *n* a woman's suitor or sweetheart.—*pl* **beaux**
[bōz].—*ns* **beau geste**, a graceful or magnanimous gesture.

Beaufort scale [bō'fört] *n* system of indicating wind strength
(from 0, calm, to 12, hurricane).

beauty [bū'ti] *n* a pleasing combination of qualities in a person
or object; a particular grace or excellence; a beautiful person,
esp a woman; good looks.—*adj* **beauteous** [-ti-ùs, -tyùs]
(*poet*) full of beauty, fair.—*adv* **beau'teously**.—*n* **beau'teous-
ness.**—*adj* **beau'tiful**, having beauty.—*adv* **beau'tifully**.—*vti*
beau'tify, to make or become beautiful.—*ns* **beautician** [bū-
tish'an] one who works in a beauty shop; **beautificā'tion**;
beau'tifier.

beaver[1] [bēv'ėr] *n* either of two large semiaquatic rodents
(genus *Castor*) valuable for their fur and castoreum; the fur of
the beaver; a hat with a plush finish; a man's high silk hat;
(*slang*) a beard; (*offensive*) female genitals.

beaver[2] [bēv'ėr] *n* in medieval armor, the covering for the
lower part of the face; a helmet visor.

bebop [bē'bop] *n* a style of jazz of the early 1940's characterized by improvised solo performances in dissonant and complex patterns.

becalm [bi-käm'] *vt* to make calm; to make (a ship) motionless
from lack of wind.—*adj* **becalmed'.**

became [bi-kām'] *pt* of **become**.

because [bi-koz', bi-köz'] *conj* for the reason that.—**because
of,** on account of.

béchamel sauce [bā-shà-mel'] *n* a thick, rich white sauce.

beck [bek] *n* a sign with the finger or head.—**at someone's
beck,** subject to someone's slightest whim.

beckon [bek'ón] *vti* to summon by a sign.

becloud [bi-klowd'] *vt* to obscure by clouds; to muddle.

become [bi-kum'] *vi* to come or grow to be.—*vt* to suit or
befit;—*pt* **became'**; *pt p* **become'.**—*adj* **becom'ing**, appropriate; seemly; suitable to the wearer.—*adv* **becom'ingly**.

bed [bed] *n* a piece of furniture for sleeping on; a plot of soil
where plants are raised; the bottom of a river, lake, etc.; any
flat surface used as a foundation; a stratum.—*vt* to put to bed;
to embed; to plant in a bed of earth; to arrange in layers.—*vi*
to go to bed, rest, sleep; to stratify.

bedaub [bi-döb'] *vt* to daub over or smear.

bedeck [bi-dek'] *vt* to deck or ornament.

bedevil [bi-dev'l] *vt* to plague or bewilder.—*n* **bedev'ilment**.

bedew [bi-dū'] *vt* to moisten gently, as with dew.

Bedford cord [bed'förd] *n* a very strong fabric with a prominent rib weave made of cotton, wool, or rayon.

bedim [bi-dim'] *vt* make (the eyes or vision) dim;—*pa p*
bedimmed'.

bedizen [bi-dīz'n, bi-diz'n] *vt* to dress gaudily.

bedlam [bed'làm] *n* an asylum for lunatics; a place of uproar.—*adj* fit for a madhouse.—*n* **bed'lamite**, a madman.

bedouin, beduin [bed'ōō-in] *n* a nomadic Arab of the north
African deserts.

bedraggle [bi-drag'l] *vt* to soil by dragging in the wet or dirt.

bee[1] [bē] *n* a social colonial four-winged insect (*Apis melifera*)
that is often kept in hives to make honey; any of numerous
insects (superfamily Apoidea) that also feed on pollen and
nectar and are related to wasps; an eccentric notion.—*ns*
bee'hive, a container for keeping honeybees; a scene of
crowded activity; a woman's hairdo resembling a conical beehive; **bee'keep'er**, one who keeps bees for producing honey;
bee'keep'ing; **bee'line**, the most direct course from one point
to another.

bee[2] [bē] *n* a meeting of people to work together or to compete.

beech [bēch] *n* a genus (*Fagus*) of trees with smooth silvery
bark and small edible nuts; its wood.—*adj* **beech'en.**—*n*
beech'nut, the small, three-cornered nut of the beech tree.

beef [bēf] *n* a full-grown ox, cow, bull, or steer, esp one bred
for meat; these animals collectively; their meat; (*inf*) brawn;
(*slang*) a complaint;—*pl* **beefs, beeves.**—*vt* to add weight,
strength, or power to (*with* **up**).—*vi* (*slang*) to complain.—
ns **beef'cake'**, (*slang*) photographic display of the muscular
development of a nude, or nearly nude man; —*adj* **beef'y**.

been [bin] *pt p* of **be**.

beep [bēp] *n* the brief, high pitched sound of a horn or electronic signal.—*vti* to make or cause to make this sound.

beer [bēr] *n* an alcoholic beverage made by slow fermentation,
from malted barley and hops; a soft drink made from extracts
of roots, etc. (*root beer, birch beer, etc.*).—*adj* **beer'y**, smelling
or tasting of beer; of, or affected by, beer.—*n* **beer'iness**.

beestings [bēst'ingz] *n* the first milk drawn from a cow after
calving.

beet [bēt] *n* a genus (*Beta*) of plants with a succulent root used
as food and as a source of sugar.

beetle[1] [bē'tl] *n* any of an order (Coleoptera) of insects having
hard front wings that cover the membraneous back wings
when these are folded.

beetle[2] [bē'tl] *n* a heavy wooden mallet used for driving
wedges, or the like; a wooden pestle.

beetle[3] [bē'tl] *adj* overhanging.—*vi* to overhang.—**beetle-
browed**, having bushy eyebrows; frowning.

beeves [bēvz] plural of **beef**.

befall [bi-föl'] *vti* to happen or occur to;—*pr p* **befall'ing**; *pt*
befell'; *pt p* **befall'en**.

befit [bi-fit'] *vt* to be suitable to; to be right for;—*pr p* **befit-
t'ing**; *pt p* **befitt'ed**.—*adj* **befitt'ing.**—*adv* **befitt'ingly**.

befog [bi-fog'] *vt* to envelop in fog; to obscure.

before [bi-fōr', -för'] *prep* in front of; in the presence or sight
of; previous to; in preference to.—*adv* in front; earlier; until
now.—*conj* previous to the time that; rather than.—*adj, adv*
before'hand, ahead of time; in anticipation.

befoul [bi-fowl'] *vt* to make foul; to soil; to cast aspersions on.

befriend [bi-frend'] *vt* to act as a friend to, to favor.

beg [beg] *vti* to ask for alms; to ask earnestly; to beseech;—*pr p*
begg'ing; *pt p* **begged.**—*n* **beggar** [beg'àr] one who begs; one
who lives by begging; a pauper.—*vt* to impoverish; to make
(description, etc.) seem inadequate.—*adj* **begg'arly**, poor;
inadequate; worthless.—*ns* **begg'arliness; begg'ary**, extreme
poverty, the occupation or practice of begging.

began [bi-gan'] *pt* of **begin**.

beget [bi-get'] *vt* to become the father of; to cause;—*pr p*
begett'ing; *pt* **begot'** (*arch* **begat'**);—*pt p* **begott'en** (*arch*
begot').—*n* **begett'er**, one who begets; a father.

begin [bi-gin'] *vti* to start doing, acting, etc.; to originate;—*pr
p* **beginn'ing**; *pt* **began'**; *pt p* **begun'**.—*ns* **beginn'er**, one who
is beginning to learn or do something; a novice.—**beginn'ing**,
origin or commencement.

begird [bi-gûrd'] *vt* to surround or encompass (with);—*pt*
begirt', **begird'ed**; *pt p* **begirt'.**

begone [bi-gon'] *interj* lit be gone! be off! get away!—For
woe'-begone', *see* **woe**.

begonia [bi-gōn'ya] *n* a genus (*Begonia*) of tropical plants with
showy flowers and remarkable unequal sided and often colored leaves.

begot [bi-got'] *pt, pt, p,* **begotten** [bi-got'n], *pt p* of **beget**.

begrime [bi-grīm'] *vt* to grime or soil deeply.

begrudge [bi-gruj'] *n* to grudge, envy (eg *to begrudge him his
success*).

beguile [bi-gīl'] *vt* to mislead; to divert attention from.—*ns*
beguile'ment; beguil'er.—*adv* **beguil'ingly**.

beguine [bé-gēn'] *n* a dance of French West Indian origin or its
music, resembling the rhumba.

begum [bē'gum] *n* a Muslim princess or lady of rank; a defer-
ential title given to any lady.

begun [bi-gun'] *pt p* (sometimes *pt*) of **begin**.

behalf [bi-häf'] *n* support.—**in, on behalf of,** in the interest of;
for.

behave [bi-hāv'] *vti* to conduct (oneself) in a specified way; to
conduct (oneself) properly;—*pt, pt p* **behaved'.**—*n* **behavior**
[bi-hāv'yòr], way of behaving; conduct or action.

behead [bi-hed'] *vt* to cut off the head of.—*n* **behead'ing**, the
act of cutting off the head.

beheld [bi-held'] *pt, pt p* of **behold**.

behemoth [bi-hē'moth] *n* an animal described in the Book of
Job; a great beast.

behest [bi-hest'] *n* a command, charge.

behind [bi-hīnd'] *prep* at the back of; concealed by; later than;
supporting.—*adv* in the rear; slow; late.—*adv, adj* **behind'-
hand**, behind, as in progress, time, etc.

behold [bi-hōld'] *vt* to see, observe; to contemplate.—*vi* to
look;—*pt, pt p* **beheld'.**—*imper* or *interj* see! lo! observe!—*adj*

behold'en, bound in gratitude, obliged. — *n* behold'er, one who beholds; an onlooker.

behoof [bi-ōōf'] *n* benefit, convenience.

behoove, behove [bi-hōōv'] *vt* to be incumbent upon or proper for. [OE *behōfian*, to be fit.]

beige [bāzh] *n* grayish tan wool. — *Also adj.*

being [bē'ing] *n* existence; any person or thing existing; substance, essence. — *adj* bē'ing, existing, present. — being as, being that (*inf*) since; because; for the time being, for now.

bel [bel] *n* ten decibels.

belabor [bi-lā'bòr] *vt* to beat soundly; to attack verbally; (*inf*) to labor (a point, etc.).

belated [bi-lā't'èd] *adj* tardy. — *adv* belat'edly.

belay [bi-lā'] *vti* to secure (a rope) by coiling it round a cleat, etc.; to secure by a rope.

bel canto [bel cän'tō] *n* a style of singing with brilliant vocal display and purity of tone.

belch [belch, belsh] *vti* to emit gas from the stomach by the mouth; to eject violently. — *n* eructation.

beldam, beldame [bel'dam] *n* an old woman, esp an ugly one.

beleaguer [bi-lēg'èr] *vt* to lay siege to.

belfry [bel'fri] *n* the part of a steeple or tower in which bells are hung.

Belgian [bel'ji-ân, -jàn] *adj* belonging to *Belgium*, a country of Europe. — *n* a native or citizen of Belgium; any of a breed of usu. roan or chestnut Belgian draft horses.

Belial [bēl'yal] *n* the devil.

belie [bi-lī'] *vt* to give the lie to; fail to justify or act up to (hope, promise); to present in a false character; — *pr p* bely'ing; *pt p* belied'.

believe [bi-lēv'] *vt* to regard as true; to accept as true what is said by (a person); to think or suppose. — *vi* to have faith in. — *n* belief', persuasion of the truth of anything; religious faith; the opinion or doctrine believed. — *adj* believ'able, that may be believed. — *n* believ'er. — *adj* believ'ing, trustful.

belittle [bi-lit'l] *vt* to make small; to represent as small, to depreciate.

bell[1] [bel] *n* a hollow vessel of metal which rings when struck; anything bell-shaped; the sound of a bell; (*naut*) a bell rung to mark the periods of the watch. — *vt* to furnish with a bell. — *vi* to become bell-shaped.

bell[2] [bel] *vi* to bellow, roar; to utter loudly. — *n* bellow.

belladonna [bel-a-don'a] *n* the deadly nightshade (*Atropa belladonna*), all parts of which are narcotic and poisonous from the presence of atropine; atropine.

belle [bel] *n* a pretty woman or girl.

belles-lettres [bel-let'r] *n pl* nontechnical literature, including poetry, fiction, criticism, etc.

bellicose [bel'ik-ōs] *adj* contentious, warlike.

belligerent [bel-ij'ér-ènt] *adj* at war; of war; warlike; ready to fight or quarrel. — *n* a belligerent person, group, or nation. — *n* bellig'erency.

bellow [bel'ō] *vi* to roar like a bull; to make any violent outcry. — *vt* to utter very loudly. — *n* the roar of a bull; any deep sound or cry.

bellows [bel'ōz] *n pl* (often treated as *sing*) a device for producing and directing a current of air by compression of its collapsible sides; anything collapsible like a bellows.

Bell's palsy [belz] *n* paralysis of one side of the face produced by degeneration of the nerve that supplies the muscles of the face.

belly [bel'i] *n* the part of the body between the chest and the thighs; the abdomen; the stomach; the underside of an animal's body; the deep interior, as of a ship. — *vti* to swell or bulge out.

belong [bi-long'] *vi* to have a proper place; to be related (to); to be a member (with to); to be owned (with to). — *n pl* belong'ings, possessions.

beloved [bi-luv'id, bi-luvd'] *adj* dearly loved, much loved, very dear. — *n* one who is much loved.

below [bi-lō'] *prep* lower than; not worthy of. — *adj*, *adv* in or to a lower place; beneath; later (in a book, etc.); in or to hell; on earth; under in rank, amount, etc.

belt [belt] *n* a band of leather, etc. worn around the waist; any similar encircling thing; a continuous moving strap passing over pulleys and so driving machinery; a distinctive region or strip; (*slang*) a hard blow; (*slang*) a gulp of liquor; (*slang*) a thrill.

belvedere [bel've-dēr] *n* a structure (as a cupola) designed to command a view; a shrubby herbaceous perennial (*Kochia trychophylla*) grown for its foliage. — *Also* summer cypress.

bemoan [bi-mōn] *vt* to lament.

bemuse [bi-mūz'] *vt* to muddle; to preoccupy. — *adj* bemused'.

ben [ben] *n* (*Scottish*) a mountain peak.

bench [bench, -sh] *n* a long hard seat for two or more persons; a long worktable (*laboratory bench*); the place where judges sit in a court of law; the status of a judge; judges collectively. — *vt* (*sports*) to take (a player) out of a game.

bend [bend] *vt* to curve or make crooked; to subdue; to turn, esp from a straight line; to adapt to one's purpose, distort; (*naut*) to tie. — *vi* to turn, esp from a straight line; to yield from pressure to form a curve; to curve the body (*with over or down*); to give in; — *pt*, *pt p* bent, also bend'ed (in *bended knee*). — *n* a bending or being bent; a bent part; any of various knots for tying rope; (*pl*) (*inf*) caisson disease. — *ns* bend'er, a spree. — around the bend, crazy, mad. *See* bent.

beneath [bi'nēth'] *prep* underneath; below; unworthy. — *adj*, *adv* in a lower place; underneath.

benedict [ben-i-dikt] *n* a newly married man, esp one who has long disdained marriage — from *Benedick* in Shakespeare's *Much Ado*.

Benedictine [ben-i-dik'tin] *adj* pertaining to St Benedict or his monastic rule. — *n* a monk or nun of the order founded by St *Benedict* (480–543).

benediction [ben-i-dik'sh(ò)n] *n* a blessing; a solemn invocation of a blessing esp at the end of a church service. — *adj* benedict'ory.

benefaction [ben-i-fak'sh(ō)n] *n* the act of doing good; a good deed done or benefit conferred; the money or help given. — *n* ben'efactor, one who confers a benefit.

benefice [ben'i-fis] *n* an endowed church office. — *vt* ben'efice.

beneficence [ben-nef'i-sêns] *n* active goodness, kindness, charity; a gift, benefaction. — *adj* benef'icent. — *adv* benef'icently.

beneficial [ben-i-fish'àl] *adj* useful, advantageous. — *adv* benefic'ially. — *n* benefic'iary, one receiving or who will be receiving benefit, as from a will, an insurance policy, etc.

benefit [ben'i-fit] *n* advantage; anything contributing to improvement; (often *pl*) payments made by an insurance company, public agency, etc. as during sickness or retirement or for death; a public performance, bazaar, etc. the proceeds of which are to help some person or cause. — *vt* to help. — *vi* to receive advantage. — *pr p* ben'efiting; *pt*, *pt p* ben'efited.

benevolence [ben-ev'o-êns] *n* disposition to do good; an act of kindness; generosity. — *adj* benev'olent. — *adv* benev'olently.

benighted [bi-nīt'id] *adj* surrounded by darkness; ignorant.

benign [bin-īn'] *adj* favorable; gracious; kindly; (*med*) of a tumor, not malignant. — *adv* benign'ly. — *adj* benignant [bi-nig'nànt], kind; gracious. — *n* benig'nancy. — *adv* benig'nantly. — *n* benig'nity, goodness of disposition; kindness and graciousness.

benison [ben'izn] *n* a blessing.

benny [ben'ē] *n* (*slang*) an amphetamine pill, esp Benzedrine.

bent [bent] *pt*, *pt p* of bend. — *n* a tendency; natural inclination of the mind. — *adj* curved or crooked; strongly determined (*with on*).

bent grass [bent] *n* any of a genus (*Agrostis*) of low-growing perennial grasses which spread by rhizomes and is used widely as a fine lawn grass.

benumb [bi-num'] *vt* to make numb, to deaden the mind, will, etc. of. — *adj* benumbed'.

benzine [benzēn, ben-zēn'] *n* a mixture of hydrocarbons from petroleum; gasoline.

benzoin [ben'zō-in, -zoin] *n* the aromatic resin from trees (genus *Styrax*) of southeastern Asia used in medicine, as a perfume fixative and incense. — *adj* benzo'ic.

bequeath [bi-kwēth'] *vt* to leave (property, etc.) by will; to transmit to posterity.

bequest [bi-kwest'] *n* act of bequeathing; that which is bequeathed, a legacy.

bereave [bi-rēv'] *vt* to deprive (of); to leave desolate; — *pt*, *pt p*

bereaved'—the latter also **bereft'**.—*adj* **bereaved'**, robbed by death.—*n* **bereave'ment**.

beret [ber'ā] *n* a flat, round, soft cap.

berg [bûrg] *n* an iceberg.

bergamot [bûr'ga-mot] *n* a pear-shaped orange (*Citrus bergamia*) whose aromatic rind yields oil used in perfumery; any of several mints (genus *Monarda*).

beriberi [ber'i-ber'i] *n* a disease, due to lack of vitamin B.

berm, berme [bûrm] *n* a ledge or shoulder as along the edge of a paved road.

berry [ber'i] *n* any small succulent, stoneless fruit; (*bot*) fruit in which seeds are imbedded in pulp (eg tomato, melon, orange, grape); a coffee-bean; the egg of a lobster or crayfish.—*adj* **berr'ied**, bearing berries.

berserk, berserker [bêr-sûrk'(êr), -zûrk'(êr)] *n* a Norse warrior filled with a frenzied and resistless fury; one whose actions are recklessly defiant.—*adj, adv* in a violent frenzy.

berth [bûrth] *n* a ship's station at anchor or in port; a built-in bed, as in a ship or train; a situation or place of employment.—*vt* to put into or furnish with a berth, to moor a ship at a berth.—*vi* to occupy a berth.—**give a wide berth to**, to keep well away from.

bertha [bûr'tha] *n* a wide round collar covering the shoulders.

beseech [bi-sēch'] *vt* to entreat, to implore; to beg, pray earnestly for;—*pt, pt p* **besought'**.—*adv* **beseech'ingly**.

beseem [bi-sēm'] *vi* to be seemly or fit for, to suit.

beset [bi-set'] *vt* to surround or hem in; to attack from all sides; to harass.—*pr p* **besett'ing**; *pt, pt p* **beset'**.—*adj* **beset'ting** constantly harassing one.

beside [bi-sīd'] *prep* at, by the side of, near; in comparison with; in addition to; aside from.—**be beside oneself**, to be distraught with anxiety, fear, or anger.

besides [bi-sīdz'] *prep* other than; in addition to.—*adv* in addition; except for that mentioned; moreover.

besiege [bi-sēj'] *vt* to hem in with armed forces; to close in on; to overwhelm, harrass, etc.—*n* **besieg'er**.

besmear [bi-smēr'] *vt* to smear over.

besmirch [bi-smûrch'] *vt* to soil; to sully.

besom [bē'zòm] *n* a bunch of twigs for sweeping, a broom.

besot [bi-sot'] *vt* to make dull, or stupid; esp to muddle with drunkenness or infatuation.—*pr p* **besott'ing**; *pt p* **besott'ed**.

bespatter [bi-spat'êr] *vt* to spatter with mud; to defame.

bespeak [bi-spēk'] *vt* to speak for or engage beforehand;—*pt* **bespoke'**; *pt p* **bespōke'**, **bespōk'en**.

bespoke, bespoken [bi-spōk(-n)] *adj* custom-made; dealing in such articles; (*inf*) engaged to be married.

besprinkle [bi-spring'kl] *vt* to sprinkle.

best [best] *adj* (*superlative* of **good**) most excellent; most suitable, desirable, etc; largest, good in the highest degree, first, highest, most excellent.—*n* one's utmost endeavour; the highest perfection;—*vt* to defeat or outdo.—**best man**, the principal attendant of the bridegroom at a wedding; **best part**, greater part; **best-seller**, a book or other product that has had one of the biggest sales of the season; the writer of such a book.

bestial [best'i-ál] *adj* like a beast; brutally sensual.—*n* **bestial'ity**.

bestiary [best'i-àr-i] *n* a medieval book with fables about real or mythical animals.

bestir [bi-stûr'] *vt* to put into lively action; to rouse (oneself).

bestow [bi-stō'] *vt* to present as a gift.—*n* **bestow'al**, a disposal; act or fact of conferring as a gift.

bestrew [bi-strōō'] *vt* to strew or scatter about.—*pt p* **bestrewed'**, **bestrown'**, **bestrewn'** (followed by **with**).

bestride [bi-strīd'] *vt* to sit, mount, or stand astride.—*pt* **bestrid'**, **bestrode'**; *pt p* **bestrid'**, **bestridd'en**.

bet [bet] *n* a wager, something staked to be lost or won on an uncertain issue; the thing or sum staked; a person or thing likely to bring about a desired result.—*vti* to declare as in a bet; to stake (money, etc.) in a bet (with someone).—*pr p* **bett'ing**; *pt, pt p* **bet** or **bett'ed**.—*ns* **bett'er, bett'or**, one who bets; **bett'ing**, act of betting or proposing a wager.

beta [bēta] *n* the second letter of the Greek alphabet; second in a group or series.—*n* **beta particle**, an electron or positron ejected from the nucleus of an atom during radioactive disintegration.

betake [bi-tāk'] *vt* (*arch*) to cause (oneself), to go.

bête noir [bet nwär] pet aversion.

bethel [beth'el] *n* a hallowed spot; a place of worship for Nonconformists or seamen.

bethink [bi-thingk'] *vt* to remember or call to mind;—*pt, pt p* **bethought** [bi-thöt'].

betide [bi-tīd'] *vti* to befall, to happen to.

betimes [bi-tīmz'] *adv* in good time; early.

betoken [bi-tō'kn] *vt* to show by a sign, signify; to presage.

betray [bi-trā'] *vt* to reveal disloyalty to an enemy; to expose treacherously; to fail to uphold; to deceive, esp to seduce and fail to marry; to reveal unknowingly.—*ns* **betray'al**, **betray'er**.

betroth [bi-trōTH', -troth'] *vt* to promise in marriage,—*n* **betrōth'al**.—*n, adj* **betrōthed**.

better [bet'êr] *adj* (comparative of **good**) good in a greater degree; preferable; improved; stronger in health; larger.—*adv* (comparative of **well**) in a more excellent manner; in a higher degree; more.—*n* a person superior in position, etc.; a more excellent thing, condition, etc.—*vt* to improve; to surpass.—*n* **bett'erment**, a bettering; an improvement. **be better off**, to be in more desirable circumstances; **get the better of**, to defeat; to outwit.

between [bi-twēn'] *prep* the space time, etc. separating (two things).

betwixt [bi-twikst'] *prep, adv* between.—**betwixt and between**, not altogether one nor altogether the other.

bevel [bev'l] *n* an instrument for measuring angles; an angle other than a right angle; angled part or surface.—*adj* having the form of a bevel; slanting.—*vt* to cut to an angle other than a right angle.—*vi* to slope at an angle.—*pr p* **bev'elling**; *pt p* **bev'elled**.—*n* **bev'el gear**, a gearwheel meshing with another at an angle.

beverage [bev'êr-ij] *n* any liquid for drinking, esp one other than water.

bevy [bev'i] *n* a group, esp of girls or women; a flock of birds, esp of quails.

bewail [bi-wāl'] *vi* to lament; to mourn.

beware [bi-wār'] *vi* and *vti* to be wary or careful (of).

bewilder [bi-wil'dêr] *vt* to perplex; to confuse hopelesssly.—*n* **bewil'derment**.

bewitch [bi-wich'] *vt* to cast a spell over; to fascinate or charm.—*ns* **bewitch'ery**, **bewitch'ment**.—*adj* **bewitch'ing**, charming, enchanting.—*adv* **bewitch'ingly**.

beyond [bi-yond'] *prep* farther on than; past; later than; outside the reach of (*beyond help*); more than.—*adv* farther away.—**the (great) beyond**, whatever follows death.

bezel [bez'él] *n* the oblique side or face of a cut gem; the grooved rim in which a gem or watch crystal is set; the slope at the edge of a chisel or plane.

biannual [bī-an'ū-ál] *adj* occurring twice a year.

bias [bī'as] *n* a slanting or diagonal line, cut or sewn across the grain in cloth; partiality; prejudice.—*vt* to prejudice.—*pt, pt p* **bī'ased** or **bī'assed**.—*adj* slanting; diagonal.

biathlon [bī-ath'lon] *n* an athletic event comprising skiing and rifle shooting.

bib [bib] *n* a cloth or plastic cover tied under a child's chin at meals; the upper part of an apron.

Bible [bī'bl] *n* the sacred writings of the Christian Church, consisting of the Old and New Testaments; the Holy Scriptures of Judaism, the Old Testament; any authoritative book.—*adj* **biblical** [bib'li-kl] of or relating to the Bible; scriptural.—*adv* **bib'lically**.

bibliography [bib-li-og'raf-i] *n* a list of writings on a given subject or by a given author.—*n* **bibliog'rapher**.—*adjs* **bibliograph'ic**, **bibliograph''** al.

bibliolatry [bib-li-ol'at-ri] *n* an excessive reverence for a book, esp the Bible.—*n* **bibliol'ater**.—*adj* **bibliol'atrous**.

bibliomania [bib-li-ō-mān'i-a] *n* a mania for collecting books.—*n* **bibliomān'iac**.

bibliophile [bib'li-ō-fil] *n* a lover or collector of books.

bibliopole [bib'i-ō-pōl] *n* a dealer, esp in rare or curious books.—Also *ñ*bibliŏp'olist.—*n* **bibliop'oly**.

bibulous [bib'(-lus] *adj* addicted to or fond of alcoholic liquor.

bicameral [bī-kam'êr-ál] *adj* having two legislative chambers.

bicarbonate [bī-kär'bon-át] *n* sodium bicarbonate.

bicentenary [bī-sen-ten'à-i, -tēn'-] *adj* pertaining to two hundred years.—*n* the two hundredeth anniversary.

centennial [bī-sen-ten'i-ǎl] *adj* pertaining to two hundred years. —*n* a two hundredth anniversary or its celebration.

ceps [bī'seps] *n* the muscle with two points of origin, esp the large muscle in the front of the upper arm.

cker [bik'ěr] *vi* to squabble, quarrel. —Also *n*.

cuspid [bī-kus'pid] *adj* having two points. —*n* any of the eight adult teeth with two pointed crowns.

cycle [bī'si-kl] *n* a vehicle consisting of a metal frame on two wheels, and having handlebars and a seat. —*vti* to ride or travel on a bicycle. —*n* bī'cyclist.

d [bid] *vt* to command or ask; to offer (an amount) as the price one will pay or accept; to express (to bid farewell); (cards) to state (a number of tricks) and declare (trumps). —*vi* to make a bid.

ddy [bid'ē] *n* a hen; (slang) an old woman who is eccentric, gossipy, etc.

de [bīd] *vi* (arch, dial) to wait; to dwell. —*vt* (arch, dial) to endure. —*adj* bided. —bide one's time, to wait patiently for an opportunity.

det [bi-dā] *n* a low, bowl-shaped bathroom fixture with running water for bathing the crotch.

ennial [bī-en'i-al] *adj* lasting two years; happening once in two years. —*n* a plant that flowers and fructifies only in its second year, then dies. —*adv* bienn'ially.

er [bēr] *n* a portable framework on which a coffin is put.

f [bif] *n* (slang) to strike, hit. —Also *n*.

focal [bī-fō'kǎl] *adj* having two foci, used of eyeglasses for near, or for distant, vision. —*n pl* bi'focals.

g [big] *adj* large or great; pregnant; important; pompous (esp to talk big, to look big). —*adj* bigg'ish, rather big. —*ns* big'ness, bulk, size.

gamy [big'àm-i] *n* the crime of marrying a second time when one is already legally married. —*n* big'amist. —*adj* big'amous. —*adv* big'amously.

ght [bīt] *n* a wide bay; a bend or coil of a rope.

got [big'ót] *n* one blindly and obstinately devoted to a particular creed or party. —*adj* big'oted. —*n* big'otry.

jou [bē'zhōō] *n* a trinket; a jewel. —*pl* bijoux [bē'zhōō]. —*adj* small and elegant.

ke [bīk] *n* (inf) a bicycle; a motorcycle.

kini [bi-kē'nē] *n* a very scanty form of two-piece bathing suit for women.

labiate [bī-lā'bi-ât] *adj* having two lips, as some corollas.

lateral [bī-lat'ėr-ǎl] *adj* having two sides; affecting two parties reciprocally. —*adv* bilat'erally.

lberry [bil'ber-i] *n* any of several plants (genus Vaccinium) that differ from typical blueberries in having their flowers rising singly; its dark blue berry.

lbo[1], **bilboa** [bil'bō] *n* a rapier or sword.

lbo[2] [bil'bō] *n* a long bar of iron used to confine the feet of prisoners, esp on shipboard.

le [bil] *n* a gall, a thick bitter fluid secreted by the liver; bad temper. —*adj* bilious [bil'-yù per-taining to or affected by bile. —*n* bil'iousness.

lge [bilj] *n* the bulging part of a cask; the broadest part of a ship's bottom; filth such as collects there; (slang) nonsense. —bilge' wat'er, the foul water in a ship's bilge.

lharzia [bil-här'zi-ä] *n* schisto somiasis.

lingual [bī-ling'gwǎl] *adj* expressed in two languages; speaking two languages (eg English and Welsh).

lk [bilk] *vt* to cheat, swindle. —*n* bilk'er.

l[1] [bil] *n* a weapon used formerly, a long staff ending in a hook-shaped blade; a billhook. —*n* bill'hook, a cutting or pruning tool with a hooked blade.

l[2] [bil] *n* the beak of a bird; a beaklike mouth part, as of a turtle. —*vi* to touch bills together. —bill and coo, to kiss, talk softly, etc. in a loving way.

l[3] [bil] *n* a statement for goods supplied or services rendered; a list, as a menu or theater program; a poster or handbill; a draft of a proposed law, to be discussed by a legislature; a bill of exchange; a piece of paper money; (law) a written declaration of charges and complaints filed. —*vt* to make out a bill of (items); to present a statement of charges to; to advertise by bills; to book (a performer). **bill'ing**, the order in which actors' names are listed. —bill of exchange, a written order to pay a certain sum of money to the person named; bill of fare, a program. bill of lading, a receipt issued to a shipper

by a carrier, listing the goods received for shipment; **Bill of Rights**, the first ten amendments to the US Constitution, which guarantees civil rights; **bill of sale**, a written statement transferring ownership by sale.

billabong [bil'a-bong] *n* (Austr) an effluent from a river; a waterhole, pond, or small lake.

billet[1] [bil'ét] *n* a written order to provide lodging for military personnel; the lodging; a position or job. —*vt* to assign to lodging by billet. —*pr p* bill'eting; *pt p* bill'eted.

billet[2] [bil'ét] *n* a chunky piece of wood (as for firewood); a bar of metal.

billet-doux [bil'e-dōō] *n* a love letter. —*pl* billets-doux [bil'e-dōōz].

billiards [bil'yårdz] *n* a game played with three hard balls driven by a cue on a felt-covered table with raised, cushioned edges. —*adj* bill'iard.

billion [bil'yón] *n* a thousand millions, the numeral 1 followed by 9 zeros; in France, Germany and the United Kingdom, a million millions, the numeral 1 followed by 12 zeros.

billow [bil'ō] *n* a large wave; any large swelling mass or surge, as of smoke. —*vi* to surge or swell in a billow. —*adjs* bill'owed, bill'owy.

billy [bil'i] *n* a club, esp a policeman's heavy stick. —*pl* bill'ies.

billy goat [bil'i] *n* (inf) a male goat.

biltong [bil'tong] *n* (S Africa) jerked meat.

bimbo [bim'bō] *n* a generalized disparaging term for a man or a woman; a prostitute.

bimetallism [bī-met'ál-izm] *n* the use of two metals, esp gold and silver, as the monetary standard, with fixed values in relation to each other. —*adj* bimetall'ic. —*n* bimet'allist.

bimonthly [bī-munth'li] *adj* once in two months; loosely twice a month.

bin [bin] *n* a box or crib etc. for storing grain, coal, etc.

binary [bī'når-i] *adj* made up of two parts; double; denoting or of a number system in which the base is two, each number being expressed by using only two digits, specifically 0 and 1.

bind [bīnd] *vt* to tie together, as with rope; to hold or restrain; to encircle with a belt, etc.; to bandage (often with up); to constipate; to reinforce or ornament the edges of by a band, as of tape; to fasten together the pages of (a book) and protect with a cover; to obligate by duty, love, etc.; to compel, as by oath or legal restraint. —*vi* to become tight or stiff; to stick together; to be obligatory. —*n* anything that binds; (inf) a difficult situation. —*pt, pt p* bound. —*n* bind'er, one who binds, as books.

bingo [bing'gō] *n* a game of chance played by covering on a card each number called.

binnacle [bin'á-kl] *n* (naut) the box in which a ship's compass is kept.

binocular [bīn-ok'ūl-år] *adj* having two eyes; suitable for two eyes. —*n* (pl) a field glass having two tubes, one for each eye.

binomial [bī-nōm'i-ál] *adj, n* (denoting) a mathematical expression consisting of two terms connected by a plus sign or a minus sign.

bio- [bī-ō] in composition, life; of living things.

bioavailability [bī-ō-a-vāl-a-bil'it-i] *n* the rate at which a drug, etc. enters the bloodstream and circulates, as to organs.

biochemistry [bīō-kem'is-tri] *n* a science concerned with the chemistry of plants and animals. —*adj* biochem'ical. —*n* biochem'ist.

biocide [bī'ō-sīd] *n* a chemical agent that can kill living organisms.

bioclean [bī'ō-klīn] *adj* as free as possible from microorganisms; aseptic.

biodegradable [bī-ō-dė-grā'di-bl] readily decomposed by bacterial action.

biogenesis [bī-ō-jen'es-is] *n* the theory that life can come only from living things; biosynthesis.

biography [bī-og'raf-i] *n* an account of a person's life written by another; biographical writings in general; account of the chronology of something (as an animal, a coin, a building). —*n* biog'rapher. —*adjs* biograph'ic, -al. —*adv* biograph'ically.

biology [bī-ol'oj-i] *n* the science that treats of living organisms. —*adj* biolog'ical. —*adv* biolog'ically. —*n* biol'ogist.

biomass [bī'ō-mas] *n* the amount of living material (animals, plants, etc.) in a unit of area; fuel from plant materials and animal waste.

bionics [bī-on′iks] *n* the science of designing instruments or systems modeled after living organisms.—*adj* **bion′ic**, of bionics.

biophysics [bī-o-fiz′iks] *n* the application of physics to the study of living things.

biopsy [bī′op-si] *n* the removal of bits of living tissue for diagnosis of disease; such examination.

biorhythm [bī′ō-riŦH′m] *n* an inherent rhythm that seems to control or initiate biological processes.

biosynthesis [bī-ō-sin′the-sis] *n* the formation of chemical compounds by living organisms.

biotin [bī′ō-tin] *n* a factor of the Vitamin B group.

bipartisan [bī-pär′ti-zn] *adj* of, representing, or supported by two political parties.

bipartite [bī-pärt′īt] *adj* having two parts, involving two.

biped [bī′ped] *n* an animal with two feet.—*adj*.

biplane [bī′plān] *n* an airplane with two sets of wings, one above the other.

birch [bûrch] *n* a genus (*Betula*) of trees having many forms and sizes; a rod for punishment, consisting of a birch twig or twigs.—*vt* to flog.—*adjs* **birch, birch′en**.

bird [bûrd] *n* any of a class (Aves) of warm-blood egg-laying vertebrates with a feathered body, scaly legs, and forelimbs modified to form wings; a game bird; a shuttlecock; (*inf*) a fellow, esp a peculiar person; anything resembling a bird esp by flying or being aloft.—*vi* to observe or identify birds in their wild environment. **bird of prey**, a carnivorous bird that lives on meat taken by hunting or on carrion; **for the birds** (*slang*) not to be taken seriously, of little value; **get the bird** (*slang*), be rejected.

bireme [bī′rēm] *n* an ancient vessel with two tiers of oars.

biretta [bir-et′a] *n* a square cap with three projections worn by Roman Catholic clergy.

birth [bûrth] *n* the act of bearing or bringing forth; coming into the world; the offspring born; lineage; dignity of family; beginning or origin.

bis [bis] *adv* twice; (*mus*) a direction for repetition.

biscuit [bis′kit] *n* a quick bread baked in small pieces; pottery that has undergone the first firing before being glazed.—*adj* pale brown in color.

bisect [bī-sekt′] *vt* to cut into two equal parts; (*geom*) to divide into two equal parts.—*ns* **bisec′tion; bisec′tor,** a line that bisects.

bisexual [bī-seks′ū-ål] *adj* attracted sexually to both sexes.—Also *n*.

bishop [bish′óp] *n* a high-ranking Christian clergyman governing a diocese or church district; a chessman that can move in a diagonal direction.—*n* **bish′opric,** the office and jurisdiction of a bishop; a diocese.

bismuth [biz′muth, or bis′-] *n* a metallic element (symbol Bi; at wt 209.0; no 83).

bison [bī′son] *n* a large wild ox (genus *Bison*), wisent; the buffalo.

bisque[1] [bisk] *n* unglazed white porcelain.

bisque[2] [bisk] *n* a handicap whereby the recipient chooses the time at which to claim the concession allowed.

bisque[3] [bisk] *n* a thick cream soup made of shellfish, game, or pureed vegetables; an ice cream containing ground nuts or powdered macaroons.

bister, bistre [bis′tér] *n* a warm brown pigment used in art.

bit[1] [bit] *n* a bite, a morsel (of food); a small piece; (*inf*) a coin in former use (12½ cents); the smallest degree; a brief space of time; a small part in a theatrical performance; the aggregation of identifying characteristics of a situation, condition, activity, etc.—*adj* **bitt′y,** small, tiny; made up of scraps of something.—**a bit,** rather, somewhat; **a bit much,** a little more than one is willing to tolerate; **bit by bit,** gradually; **do one's bit,** to do one's share.

bit[2] [bit] *n* a metal mouthpiece in a bridle, used as a control; a drilling or boring tool for use in a brace, drill press, etc.; something bit and held between the teeth, as the stem of a pipe or cigar holder.—*vt* to put the bit in the mouth; to curb or restrain; **take the bit between one's teeth,** to be beyond restraint.

bit[3] [bit] *n* a unit of information in computers equivalent to on, off or yes, no; the physical representation of this (as in a computer tape or memory).

bit[4] *ptp* of bite.

bitch [bich] *n* the female of the dog, wolf and other carnivorou animals; (*slang*) a spiteful woman.

bite [bīt] *vti* to seize or tear with the teeth; to puncture with th mouth parts, as an insect; to eat into chemically; to cause t smart; to wound by a sharp weapon;—*vi* to press or snap the teeth (into, at etc.);—*pt* **bit**; *pt p* **bit** or **bitt′en**.—*n* a grasp b the teeth; a puncture by an insect; (*inf*) a sum deducted, as b tax.—*n* **bit′er.**—*adj* **bit′ing.**

bitt [bit] *n* a post on a ship's deck for fastening cables (usu. i *pl*).—*vt* to fasten round the bitts.

bitter [bit′ér] *adj* biting or acrid to the taste; sharp; sorrowfu painful; acrimonious; harsh; resentful; cynical.—*adj* bit t′erly.—*n* **bitt′erness.**—*n pl* **bitt′ers,** a liquor containin bitter herbs etc. used in some cocktails.

bitumen [bi-tū′men, or bit′-] *n* any of several substance obtained as residue in the distillation of coal tar, petroleum etc. or occurring naturally as asphalt.

bivalent [bī-vā′lént, or biv′a-lént] *adj* (*chem*) having a valenc of two; pertaining to one of a pair of homologuous chromo somes (also *n*).—*ns* **bivalence, bivalency.**

bivalve [bī′valv] *n* any mollusk having two valves or shell hinged together, as a clam.

bivouac [biv′ōō-ak] *n* a temporary camp, esp one without ten or other cover.—*vi* to pass the night in a bivouac.—*pr biv′ouacking; *pt p* **biv′ouacked.**

biweekly [bī′wēk′li] *adj* occurring once in two weeks, or twic a week.—*n* a periodical issued twice a week.

bizarre [bi-zär′] *adj* odd, fantastic, extravagant.

blab [blab] *vti* to reveal (a secret); to gossip.—*pr p* **blabb′ing;** *p* **blabbed**—*n* gossip.—*n* **blabb′er.**

black [blak] *adj* of the darkest color, like coal or soot; havin dark-colored skin and hair, esp Negro; without light; dirty evil, wicked; sad, dismal; sullen.—*n* black color; or pigmen absence of color; a Negro; black clothes, esp when worn i mourning.—*vti* to make or become black.

bladder [blad′ér] *n* a sac that fills with fluid, esp one that hol urine flowing from the kidneys; a thing resembling this (esp football bladder).—*ns* **bladd′ernut,** a shrub or small tree (*St phylea trifolia*) of temperate N America grown as an orn mental.

blade [blād] *n* the flat part of a leaf or petal, esp a leaf of gras the cutting part of a knife, sword, etc; the flat part of an oar o paddle; the free outer part of the tongue; a sword or sword man; the runner of an ice skate; a dashing fellow.—*a* **blad′ed.**

blain [blān] *n* an inflamed swelling or sore.

blame [blām] *vt* to censure; to attribute the responsibility to.- *n* imputation of a fault; censure.—*adjs* **blam′able, blame′fu** deserving of blame or censure;—*adv* **blame′fully.**—*adj* **bl me′less,** without blame; innocent.—*adv* **blame′lessly.**— **blame′lessness.**—*adj* **blame′worthy,** worthy of blame.— **blame′worthiness.**

blanch [blānch or -sh] *vt* to whiten or bleach; to make pale; scald (vegetables, almonds, etc.);—*vi* to turn pale.

blancmange [blåman(g)zh′] *n* a dessert made from gelatino or starchy ingredients (as cornstarch) and milk.

bland [bland] *adj* smooth; gentle; mild; insipid.*a* **bland′ly.**—*n* **bland′ness.**

blandish [bland′ish] *vti* to flatter and coax; to cajole.— **bland′ishment.**

blank [blangk] *adj* of paper, without writing or marks; empt vacant; empty of thought (*a blank mind*); utter, complete.— *blank denial*.—*n* an empty space; esp one to be filled out on printed form; such a printed form; an empty place or tim a powder-filled cartridge without a bullet.—*vt* to hold (opponent) scoreless.—*adv* **blank′ly.**—*n* **blank′ness, bla verse,** unrhymed verse, usually written in iambic pentamete

blanket [blang′ket] *n* a large, soft piece of cloth used f warmth, esp as a bed cover; a covering generally.—*adj* appl ing generally or covering all cases.—*vt* to cover.—**blank stitch,** a reinforcing hand stitch used on blankets on oth thick fabrics to prevent wear.

blare [blār] *vti* to sound loudly.—*n* a loud, harsh sound.

blarney [blär′ni] *n* flattery.—*vti* to flatter or coax.

blasé [blä-zā] *adj* satiated and bored.

blaspheme [blas-fēm′] *vt* to speak impiously of, (God).—*vi*

utter blasphemy. — n blasphem′er. — adj blasphemous [blas′-emus], profane; impious. — adv blas′phemously. — n blas′-phemy, profane speaking; contempt or indignity offered to God.

last [bläst] n a blowing or gust of wind; a forcible stream of air; the sound of a horn; an explosion or detonation; an outburst of criticism. — vt to blight; to blow up, explode; to criticize sharply. — vi to make a loud, harsh sound; to set off explosives, etc. — adj blast′ed, blighted.

atant [blāt′ant] adj noisy, obtrusive, glaring; boldly conspicuous. — adv blat′antly.

ather [blaTH′er] vi to chatter foolishly. — n foolish chatter. — blath′erskite, a loquacious fool.

aze¹ [blāz] n a rush of light or flame; an active display, outburst; intense light. — vi to burn with a strong flame; to throw out a brilliant light; to be excited, as with anger. — n blaz′er, a light sports jacket of bright color.

aze² [blāz] n a white mark on a beast's face; a mark made on a tree by chipping the bark. — vt to mark a tree with a blaze; to indicate a forest track by trees so marked.

aze³ [blāz] vt to proclaim.

azon [blā′zn] vt to make public; to adorn; to describe (heraldic or armorial bearings) in technical terms. — n the science or rules of coats of arms; a heraldic shield.

each [blēch] vti to make or become white or colorless. — n a substance for bleaching.

eachers [blēch′ers] n pl outdoor uncovered plank seats for spectators at sporting events.

eak [blēk] adj cold, unsheltered, bare; harsh; gloomy; not hopeful. — adv bleak′ly. — n bleak′ness.

ear [blēr] adj dim with water or tears; obscure to the view of imagination. — Also vt — adj blears.

eat [blēt] vi to cry as sheep, goat, or calf. — n a bleating cry or sound.

ed [bled] pt, pt p of bleed.

eed [blēd] vi to lose blood; to ooze sap; to be filled with grief or sympathy. — vt to draw blood or sap from; (inf) to extort money from; — pt, pt p bled. — ns bleed′er, one who is liable to bleed, esp hemophiliac; bleed′ing, a discharge of blood; the operation of letting blood.

eep [blēp] vi to give out a high sound or radio signal, beep.

emish [blem′ish] n a flaw or defect, as a spot. — vt to mar; to spoil.

ench¹ [blench] vti to bleach (something); to blanch.

ench² [blench] vi to shrink back, to flinch.

end [blend] vt to mix or mingle (varieties of tea, etc.); to mix so that the elements cannot be distinguished. — vi to mix; merge; to shade gradually into each other, as colors; to harmonize; — pt p blend′ed. — n a mixture. — ns blend′er, one that blends.

ende [blend] n a zinc ore; any of several sulfide ones.

enheim [blen′em] n a variety of English toy spaniel with rich chestnut markings on a pearly whitecoat.

ess [bles] vt to consecrate; to praise; to invoke divine favor upon; to make happy; to make the sign of the cross over; — pt blessed [blest], or blest. — adj bless′ed [-id], holy, sacred; fortunate; blissful; beatified. — adv bless′edly. — ns bless′ed-ness; bless′ing, a wish or prayer for happiness or success; any cause of happiness; good wishes or approval; a grace said before or after eating.

est [blest] pt p of bless.

ew [blō] pt p of blow.

ight [blīt] n any insect, disease, etc. that destroys plants; anything that injures or destroys. — vt to affect with blight; to blast; to frustrate.

imp [blimp] n (inf) a non rigid airship; Colonel Blimp.

nd [blīnd] adj without sight; ignorant or undiscerning; not directed, or affording no possibility of being directed; by sight or by reason concealed; closed at one end; (aeronautics) by the use of instruments. — n something to mislead; a window-screen, a shade. — vt to make sightless; to deprive of insight; to dazzle; to deceive; — pt, pt p blīnd′ed. — n anything that obscures sight or keeps out light, as a shade for the window or eyes; a place of concealment; a decoy. — adj blind′ing, tending to make blind. — pr p making blind. — adv blind′ly. — n blind′-ness, want of sight; failure or inability to perceive and understand. blind to, unaware of, unable to appreciate.

blink [blingk] vi to twinkle, or wink; flash on and off; to ignore (with at). — vi to shut out of sight, to avoid or evade. — n a glimpse, glance; a momentary gleam. — n pl blink′er, a flashing warning light; a cloth hood with projecting sidepieces at the eye openings used in skittish racecourses. — on the blink (slang), out of order.

blip [blip] n a luminous image on an oscilloscope.

bliss [blis] n the highest happiness; spiritual joy. — adj bliss′-ful. — adv bliss′fully. — n bliss′fulness.

blister [blis′tèr] n a raised patch on the skin, containing watery matter, as caused as by burning or rubbing; a similar raised spot on any other surface. — vt to raise a blister; to lash with words. — vi to form blisters. — adj blis′tering, (of criticism) savage, cruel. — n blister beetle, various beetles (family Meloidae) used for blistering.

blithe [blīTH] adj happy, gay, sprightly. — adv blithe′ly. — n blithe′ness. — adj blithe′some, joyous. — adv blithe′somely. — n blithe′someness.

blitz [blits] n any sudden destructive attack. — vt to subject to a blitz.

blizzard [bliz′ärd] n a blinding storm of wind and snow.

bloat [blōt] vti to swell as with water or air; puff up, as with pride. — adj bloat′ed. — n bloat′er, a common cisco (Coregonus hoyi) of the Great Lakes; a lightly salted and briefly smoked herring or mackerel.

blob [blob] n a drop of liquid; a round spot; zero. — vti to splash with blobs.

bloc [blok] n a combination of parties, nations, etc. to achieve a common purpose.

block [blok] n a solid piece of wood or stone, etc.; a piece of wood; an auctioneer's platform, used as a support (for chopping, etc.), or as a mold (for hats), or for printing (illustrations), or as a toy (for building); a city square; a group or row of buildings; a number of things as a unit; a pulley with its framework; an obstruction. — vt to enclose or shut up; to obstruct; to shape; to sketch roughly (often with out). — vi to block an opponent in sports. — ns blockade′, the isolation of a place by blocking every approach by land or sea (vt to isolate by blockade); any strategic barrier; block′age, act or instance of obstructing or state of being obstructed. — block and tackle, pulley blocks and ropes, used for lifting heavy objects.

blond, blonde [blond] adj having light-colored hair and skin; light-colored. — n a blond(e) person.

blood [blud] n the red fluid in the arteries and veins of animals; the sap of a plant; the essence of life; life; kinship; descent; temper, anger; bloodshed; (among blacks) an Afro-American. — adjs blood′ed, having a specific kind of blood (hot-blooded); of fine breed; blood′y, stained with blood; blood thirsty; (Brit slang) murderous, cruel; (Brit slang) vulgarly, as an expletive or intensive (adj or adv). — vt to make bloody. — adv blood′ily. bad blood, anger, hatred; in cold blood, with cruelty; deliberately.

bloom [blōōm] n a blossom or flower; the state of being in flower; a period of most health, vigor, etc.; a youthful, healthy glow; the powdery coating on some fruit and leaves. — vi to blossom; to be at one's prime; to glow with health, etc. — adj bloom′ing.

blooper [blōōp-èr] n (slang) a stupid mistake; (baseball) a fly that falls just beyond the infield for a hit.

blossom [blos′óm] n a flower, esp one that precedes edible fruit; a state or time of flowering. — vi to put forth blossoms or flowers; to begin to flourish.

blot [blot] n a spot or stain, esp of ink; a stain in reputation. — vt to spot or stain; to obliterate; to disgrace; to dry with blotting paper. — pr p blott′ing; pt p blott′ed. — ns blott′er, a piece of blotting paper.

blotch [bloch] n an irregular discoloration on the skin; any large blot or stain. — vt to mark or cover with blotches. — adjs blotched, blotch′y.

blouse [blowz] n a shirtlike garment worn by women and children; a uniform coat worn by soldiers, etc. — vti to gather in and drape at the waistline.

blow¹ [blō] n a hard hit, as with the fist; a sudden attack; a sudden misfortune or calamity. — come to blows, to fight.

blow² [blō] vi to bloom or blossom. — pr p blōw′ing; pt blew [blōō]; pt p blown [blōn].

blow³ [blō] vi to produce a current of air; to drive air; to move, as air or the wind; to burst suddenly (*often with out*); to breathe hard or with difficulty; to spout, as whales; to emit a sound produced by a current of air; (*inf*) to brag; (*slang*) to leave. —*vt* to drive by a current of air; to sound by blowing; to drive air into; to burst by an explosion (*often with up*); to melt (a fuse, etc.); (*inf*) to spend (money) freely; (*slang*) to leave; (*slang*) to bungle. —*pt* **blew** [blōō]; *pt p* **blown** [blōn]. —*n* **blow′er**, one that blows; a braggart; a device for producing astream of gas or air. —*adj* **blown**, swollen or bloated; having fly excrement deposited; being out of breath. —*n* **blowout** (*inf*), a festive social event; a bursting of a container (as a tire) by pressure on a weak spot; an uncontrolled eruption of a gas or oil well. —*vi* **blow out**, to become extinguished by a gust of air; (of a gas or oil well) to erupt out of control. —*vt* to extinguish by a gust; (of a storm) to dissipate (itself) by blowing. **blow′up**, an explosion; an enlarged photograph; (*slang*) an angry outburst. —*adj* **blow′y**, windy. —**blow off** (*inf*), to release emotions, as by shouting; **blow over**, to pass over or pass by; **blow up** (*inf*), to lose one's temper.

blubber [blub′ẻr] *n* the fat of whales and other large sea animals; excessive fat on the body; the action of blubbering. —*adj* puffed out; thick. —*vi* to weep effusively.

blucher [blōōch′ẻr or blōōk′-] *n* a kind of shoe in which the vamp and tongue are made in one piece.

bludgeon [bluj′ôn] *n* a short stick with a heavy end for striking. —*vti* to strike with a bludgeon; to bully or coerce.

blue [blōō] *adj* of the color of the clear sky; (of the skin) livid; dismal; depressed; (of a story) indecent; puritanical (*blue laws*). —*n* the color of the spectrum lying between green and violet; any blue pigment; (*pl*) (*inf*) a depressed feeling (*with the*); (*pl*) a style of vocal and instrumental jazz having usu. slower tempo than ragtime in a 12-measure pattern; clothing, esp of a police force. —(**out of**) **the blue**, without warning, as a thunderbolt from a clear sky; **once in a blue moon**, exceedingly seldom; **the blue**, the sky; the sea.

bluff[1] [bluf] *adj* rough and hearty in manner; outspoken; ascending steeply with a flat front. —*n* a high steep bank or cliff. —*n* **bluff′ness**.

bluff[2] [bluf] *vti* to mislead or frighten by a false, bold front. —*n* a bluffing; one who bluffs. —*n* **bluff′er**. —**call someone's bluff**, to expose or challenge someone's bluff.

blunder [blun′dẻr] *vi* to make a foolish mistake; to flounder about. —*n* a foolish mistake.

blunt [blunt] *adj* having a dull edge or point; rough, outspoken. —*vti* to make or become dull. —*adv* **blunt′ly**. —*n* **blunt′ness**.

blur [blûr] *n* a smudge, smear; a confused impression. —*vti* to blot; to make or become indistinct in shape, etc.; to dim. —*n* **blurr′iness**. —*adj* **blurr′y**. —*pr p* **blurr′ing**; *pt p* **blurred**. [blear.]

blurb [blûrb] *n* (*inf*) a publisher's descriptive notice of a book; an exaggerated advertisement.

blurt [blûrt] *vt* to utter impulsively (*with out*).

blush [blush] *n* a red glow on the skin caused by embarrassment; any rosy color. —*vi* to show shame, confusion, joy, etc., by blushing (*with for or at*); to become rosy. —*n* **blush′er**, a cosmetic that gives color to the face; a person who blushes readily. —*adv* **blush′ingly**. —**at the first blush**, at the first glance or appearance; off-hand.

bluster [blus′tẻr] *vi* to make a noise like a blast of wind; to bully or swagger. —*n* a blast or roaring as of the wind; bullying or boastful language. —*adv* **blus′teringly**.

boar [bōr, bör] *n* an uncastrated male pig, the wild hog (*sus scrofa*) of Europe from which most domestic swine derive.

board [bōrd, börd] *n* a table to put food on; meals, esp when provided regularly for pay; a long, flat piece of sawed wood; a flat piece of wood, etc. for some special use; pasteboard; a council; a body of persons who direct or supervise; the side of a ship (*overboard*) —*vt* to supply with board and fixed terms; come onto the deck of (a ship); to get on (a train, bus, etc.). —*vi* to receive meals or room and meals, regularly for pay. —*ns* **board′er**, one who received board; **boardroom**, a room designated for meetings of a board; **boardwalk**, a walk made of thick boards, esp one along a beach. —**board up**, to cover with boards; **on board**, on a ship, aircraft, etc.; **the boards**, the stage (of a theater).

boast [bōst] *vi* to talk vaingloriously; to brag. —*vt* to brag of,

speak proudly of; to possess with pride. —*n* a bragging; subject of pride, a cause of boasting. —*n* **boast′er**. —*ad* **boast′ful**. —*adv* **boast′fully**. —*n* **boast′fulness**.

boat [bot] *n* a small open craft; a ship; a dish shaped like boat. —*vt* to place in or bring into a boat. —*vi* to go about in boat. —*ns* **boat′er**, a flat straw hat with a brim; **boat′ hook**, a iron hook fixed to a pole used for pulling or pushing a boat into position; **boat′ing**, rowing, sailing, etc.; **boat′man**, man who works on, deals in, or operates boats; **boat peop**l refugees fleeing by boat. —**in the same boat**, in the sam plight.

boatswain [bō′sn] *n* a ship's officer in charge of hull maintenance and related work; a petty officer on a merchant ship; naval warrant officer in the US Navy.

bob [bob] *vi* to move quickly up and down; to curtsey; to fis with a bob. —*vt* to move in short jerks; to cut (hair, etc short; —*pr p* **bobb′ing**; *pt p* **bobbed**. —*n* a short jerkin motion; the weight on a pendulum, plumbline, etc.; a woma or girl's short haircut. —*n* **bob′sled**, a long racing sled. —*vi* t ride or race on a bobsled.

bobbin [bob′in] *n* a reel or spool for winding yarn, wire, etc.

bobby pin [bob′ē] *n* a small metal hairpin with the prong pressing close together.

bobby socks, bobby sox [bob′ē] *n* (*inf*) girls' ankle-lengt socks. —**bobby-soxer**, an adolescent girl.

bobcat [bob′kat] *n* a medium-sized feline (*Lynx rufus*) of eas ern N America with a black-spotted reddish-brown coat. —Also **wildcat**.

bobeche [bō-besh′, -bāsh′] *n* a usu. glass collar on a candle stick to catch drippings.

bobolink [bob′ō-lingk] *n* a N American songbird (*Dolichony oryzivorus*).

bobstay [bob′stā] *n pl* (*naut*) stay for holding the bowspr down.

bobtail [bob′tāl] *n* a short or cut tail; a horse, dog, or cat with very short tail; something abbreviated.

bobwhite [bob′hwīt] *n* any of a genus (*Colinus*) of quail, esp th favorite game bird (*C. virgianus*) of the eastern and centra US.

bode [bōd] *vt* to portend; to prophesy. —*vt* to be an omen of. —**bode ill** (or **well**) to be a bad (or good) omen.

bodega [bo-dē′ga] *n* a wineshop; a store specializing i Hispanic groceries.

bodice [bod′is] *n* the upper part of a dress.

bodkin [bod′kin] *n* a small dagger; a small instrument fo pricking holes in cloth; a large blunt needle.

body [bod′i] *n* the whole physical substance of a man, anima or plant; the trunk of a man or animal; a corpse; the main pa of anything; a distinct mass (*a body of water*); substance o consistency, as of liquid; a richness of flavor; a person; distinct group; —*pl* **bod′ies**. —*vt* to give form to; t embody; —*pr p* **bod′ying**; *pt p* **bod′ied**. —*adjs* **bod′iles bod′ily**, physical; relating to the body. —*adv* in the flesh; as whole; altogether. —*ns* **bod′ybuild′er**, person who exercise and diets in preparation for competitive exhibition of phy ique; **bodybuilding**; **bod′yguard**, person or persons assigne to guard someone; **body language**, gestures, unconsciou bodily movements, etc. which function as a means of con munication.

Boer [bōōr] *n* a South African of Dutch or Huguene descent. —Also *adj*.

bog [bog] *n* soft spongy ground, a small marsh. —*vti* sink in in a bog. —*adj* **bogg′y**. —*n* **bog asphodel**, a herb (*Nartheciu americanum*) of the lily family.

bogey [bō′gi] *n* (*golf*) one stroke more than par on a hole. — Also **bogie**.

boggle [bog′l] *vi* to start back in fear or agitation; to hesitat (at). —*vt* to confuse (the imagination, mind, etc.).

bogie, bogey [bō′gi] *n* a low strongly built cart; a small su porting or aligning wheel.

bogus [bō′gus] *adj* counterfeit, spurious.

bogy, bogie [bō′gi] *n* a goblin; a bugbear or special object dread. —*n* **bo′gyman**.

bohea [bō-hē′] *n* a black tea.

Bohemian [bō-hē′mi-ân] *n* a Czech; a gipsy; one who defi social conventions. —Also *adj*.

boil[1] [boil] *vi* to pass rapidly from the liquid state into vapor;

seethe like boiling liquid; to cook in boiling liquid; to be excited, esp with anger. — *vt* to heat to a boiling state; to cook by boiling. — *ns* boil′er, a container in which to boil things; a tank in which water is heated and stored, or steam is generated; boil′ersuit, a coverall; boil′ing point, the temperature at which a liquid boils; the point at which a person loses his temper; the point of crisis. — boil down, to reduce by boiling; to condense; boil over, to bubble over the sides of the containing vessel; to burst into passion.

boil² [boil] *n* an inflamed, pus-filled, painful swelling on the skin.

boisterous [bois′tėr-us] *adj* wild, noisy, turbulent; loud and exuberant. — *adv* bois′terously. — *n* bois′terousness.

bok choy [bŏk choi] *n* a cabbage (*Brassica Chinensis*) forming an open head with long white stalks and dark green leaves.

bola, bolas [bō′la, bō′las] *a* weapon used for hunting consisting of weights joined by cords or things; — *pl* bo′las.

bold [bōld] *adj* daring or courageous; forward, impudent, presumptuous; executed with spirit; striking to the sight. — *adj* bold′faced, impudent. — *adv* bold′ly. — *n* bold′ness. — make bold, to take the liberty (to).

bole [bōl] *n* a tree trunk.

bolero [bo-lā′ro, or bo-lē′ro] *n* a Spanish dance; the music to which it is danced; a short open vest.

boll [bōl] *n* the pod of a plant, esp of cotton or flax. — *ns* boll′wee′vil, a weevil (*Anthonomus grandis*) that feeds on cotton bolls as a larvae and as an adult; boll′worm, the corn earworm; any of several moth caterpillars that destroys cotton bolls.

bollard [bol′ärd] *n* a short post on a wharf or ship round which ropes are secured; one of a line of short posts barring the passage of motor vehicles.

bologna [ba-lōn′ä] *n* a baloney sausage.

Bolshevik [bol′shė-vik, bŏl-] *n* (*pl* bol′sheviks, bolshev′iki), a member of the majority faction that came into power in Russia in 1917; a Communist, esp of the Soviet Union. — *vt* bol′shevize, to make Bolshevist. — *ns* Bol′shevism; Bol′shevist, a Bolshevik; a revolutionary communist (of any country).

bolster [bōl′stėr] *n* a long narrow pillow; any bolsterlike object or support. — *vt* to support as with a bolster, (*often with up*).

bolt¹ [bōlt] *n* a bar used to fasten a door, etc.; an arrow, esp for a crossbow; a flash of lightening; a threaded metal rod used with a nut to hold parts together; a roll (of cloth, paper, etc.); a sudden dash. — *vt* to fasten with a bolt; to swallow hastily; to say suddenly; blurt (out); to abandon (a party, group, etc.). — *vi* to rush away (like a bolt from a bow); to withdraw support from one's party, etc. — *adv* erectly upright.

bolt² [bōlt] *vt* to sift (as flour) usu. through a fine-meshed cloth. — *n* bolt′er, a machine for bolting flour; the operator of such a machine.

bolus [bō′lus] *n* a small, round lump; a large pill.

bomb [bom] *n* a hollow case containing explosives, incendiary, or chemicals thrown, dropped, or otherwise reaching its target; a small container with compressed gas in it; (*slang*) a complete failure. — *vt* to attack with bombs. — *vi* (*slang*) to be unsuccessful, to flop. — *vt* bombard′, to attack with artillery or bombs; to assail (as with questions); (*phys*) to subject, as the atom, to a stream of particles at high speed. — *ns* bombardier [-bär-dēr], one who releases the bombs in a bomber; bombard′ment; bomber [bom′er], one who bombs; an airplane designed for bombing.

bombazine [bom′ba-zēn′] *n* a twilled or corded fabric of silk and worsted, or of cotton and worsted.

bombast [bom′-bast] *n* pompous language. — *adj* bombas′tic. — *adv* bombas′tically.

bombe [bŏb] *a* dessert, usu. ice cream, frozen in a round mould.

bon mot [b′ŏn mō] *a* witty saying; — *pl* bons mots [bŏ mō]; bon ton [bän tän], good style, the fashionable world; bon vivant [bän vē-vänt], one who lives well or luxuriously.

bona fide [bō′na fīd, bän′ä, bō′nė fī′dē, -fīd′e] *adj* in good faith; genuine.

bonanza [bon-an′zä] *n* a rich vein of ore; any source of wealth.

bonbon [[bän bän] *n* a small piece of candy.

bond¹ [bond] *n* anything that binds, fastens, or unites; (*pl*) shackles; an obligation imposed by a contract, promise, etc.; the status of goods in a warehouse until taxes are paid; an interest-bearing certificate issued by the government or business, redeemable on a specified date; surety against theft, absconding, etc.; an amount paid as surety or bail; a systematic lapping of bricks in a wall. — *vt* to join, bind, or otherwise unite; to provide a bond for; to place or hold (goods) in bond. — *vi* to hold together by means of a bond. — *ns* bond′hold′er, one who holds a government or corporation bond; bond′man, a slave or serf; bonds′man; one who assumes the responsibility of a bond; bond paper, a durable paper orig intended for bonds.

bond² [bond] *adj* (*arch*) in a state of servitude. — *n* bond′age, captivity, slavery; subjugation to a person or force.

bone [bōn] *n* a hard substance forming the skeleton of higher animals; a piece of the skeleton; a bonelike substance or thing; (*slang*) dice. — *vt* to take the bones out of, as meat. — *vi* (*slang*) to study hard (usu. with up). — *adjs* boned, having the bones removed; bon′y, full of, or consisting of, or like, bones; having large bones or little flesh. — *ns* bone′ash, the remains when bones are burnt in an open furnace; bone′black, the remains when bones are heated in a close vessel. — *adj* bone′dry′, absolutely dry. — *ns* bone china, translucent china made with bone ash as a constituent; — *adj* bone′less. — *ns* bone meal, fertilizer or feed made of crushed or ground bone; boner (*slang*), a blunder; bone′sett′er, one who treats broken or displaced bones without being a licensed physician.

bonfire [bon′fīr] *n* an outdoor fire. [bone, fire.]

bongo, bongo drum [bong′ō] *n* either of a pair of small drums of different pitch struck with the fingers.

bonhomie [bon′o-mē] *n* easy good natured.

bonito [bō-nēt′ō] *n* any of various medium-sized tunas (esp genera *Sarda* and *Euthynnus*) important as food fishes.

bonne [bon] *n* a French maidservant, nursemaid.

bonnet [bon′ėt] *n* a hat with a chin ribbon, worn by women and children.

bonus [bŏn′us] *n* a voluntary addition to the sum due as interest, dividend, or wages.

bonze [bonz] *n* a Buddhist monk.

boo [bŏŏ] *interj* expressive of disapprobation or contempt. — *vti* to utter 'boo!', to hoot. — *vt* boo′-hoo′, to weep noisily.

boob [bŏŏb] *n* a stupid awkward person; a boor; a Philistine; (*slang*) a woman's breast. — boob tube, television or a TV set.

booby [bŏŏ′bi] *n* a simpleton; any of several small gannets (genus *Sula*) of tropical seas. — *ns* boo′by prize, a prize for the lowest score; boo′by trap, a device for playing a practical joke on a guileless victim; an apparently harmless mechanical contrivance which, if touched, automatically injures the finder.

boogie-woogie [bŏŏg′i-wŏŏg′i] *n* a style of fast jazz for the piano, with a persistent rhythm in the bass.

book [bŏŏk] *n* a collection of sheets of paper bound together, either printed, written on, or blank; a literary composition; a division of such; a libretto; a record of bets; six tricks gained by a side at bridge; any source of information; (*pl*) formal records of financial transactions. — *vt* to note in a book; to engage in advance; of police, to take the name of, for an alleged offence. — *vi* to make a reservation. — in one's book, in one's own opinion; in one's good books, in favor with one; one for the book, an act or occurrence worth noting; on the books, on the records.

boom¹ [bŏŏm] *n* a pole by which a sail is stretched; a chain or bar stretched across a harbor.

boom² [bŏŏm] *vi* to make a hollow sound or roar. — *n* a hollow sound, as of the sea; the cry of the bittern.

boom³ [bŏŏm] *vi* to become suddenly active or prosperous. — *vt* to push into sudden prominence. — *n* a sudden increase of activity in business, or the like; a sudden rise in price or value. — boom town, a town that booms and enjoys abnormal economic prosperity.

boomerang [bŏŏm′e-rang] *n* a curved hardwood missile used by the natives of Australia, so balanced that, when thrown to a distance, it returns towards the thrower; an act that recoils on the agent.

boon¹ [bŏŏn] *n* a petition; a gift, favor.

boon² [bŏŏn] *adj* (*arch*) gay, merry, congenial (of a companion); kind (eg *boon nature*).

boondoggle [bŏŏn′dog-l] *n* an article of simple handcraft; work of little or no practical value.

boor [bōōr] *n* a peasant; a coarse or awkward person. — *adj* **boor'ish.** — *adv* **boor'ishly.** — *n* **boor'ishness.**

boost [bōōst] *vt* to help forward; to raise; to advertize fervently; to supplement voltage of; to increase supply of air to, or pressure. — *n* a push. — *n* **boost'er,** any device which increases the effect of another mechanism; an auxiliary motor in a rocket, usu. breaking away after delivery of its impulse; a substance that increases the effectiveness of medication; (*slang*) a shop lifter.

boot[1] [bōōt] *n* a covering for the foot and lower part of the leg, generally made of leather; an instrument for torturing the leg; (*slang*) unceremonious dismissal, (*with* **the**); a navy or marine corp recruit undergoing basic training. — *vt* to put boots on; to kick; to bring a computer program from a disc into computer memory. — *ns* **boot'black,** one who shines shoes; **boot'legger,** one who deals illicitly in alcoholic liquor.

boot[2] [bōō] (*arch, poetic*) *vt* to profit or advantage. — *n* advantage, profit. — *adj* **boot'less** (of an action) useless. — *adv* **boot'lessly.** — *n* **boot'lessness. — to boot,** in addition.

bootee, bootie [bōōt-ē'] *n* an ankle-length boot, slipper or sock, esp a knitted or crocheted one for an infant.

booth [bōōTH, or -th] *n* a stall for selling goods; a small enclosure.

booty [bōōt'i] *n* spoil, plunder; a prize.

booze [bōōz] *vi* to drink deeply or excessively. — *n* intoxicating liquor esp hard liquor.

bop [bop] *n* a style of jazz in the 1950s, the earliest form of 'cool' jazz, a development of *bebop.*

Bordeaux [bōr-dō'] *n* any of several red, white, or rosé wines produced around Bordeaux in southwest France.

border [bōrd'èr] *n* the edge or margin of anything; a dividing line between two countries; a narrow strip along an edge; (*slang*) the US—Mexican border. — *vi* to come near, to adjoin (*with* **on, upon**). — *vt* to adorn with a border; to adjoin; to be a border to.

bore[1] [bōr, bör] *vt* to pierce so as to form a hole; to weary, to fail to interest. — *n* a hole made by boring; the size of the cavity of a gun; a tiresome person or thing. — *n* **bore'dom,** tedium.

bore[2] [bōr, bör] *pt* of **bear.**

bore[3] [bōr, bör] *n* a tidal flood which rushes violently up the estuaries of certain rivers.

boreas [bō're-as] *n* the north wind personified.

boric *see* **boracic acid.**

born [börn] *pt p* of **bear,** to bring forth — **born-again,** of a person having undergone a revival of a personal faith or conviction or of a former activity; **not born yesterday,** difficult to deceive.

borne [börn, bōrn] *pt p* of **bear,** to carry.

borough [bur'ō] *n* a self-governing, incorporated town; any of the five administrative units of New York City.

borrow [bor'ō] *vt* to obtain or loan or trust; to adopt (an idea, etc.) as one's own. — *n* **borr'ower.**

borscht, borsch [börsh(t)] *n* Russian soup made with beetroot, etc. Also **bortsch—borscht belt, borscht circuit,** the theaters and nightclubs in the Jewish summer resorts in the Catskills in New York State.

borzoi [bör'zoi] *n* breed of tall hound with long, silky coat and narrow head; the Russian wolfhound.

boscage [bosk'ij] *n* a thicket; woodland.

bosh [bosh] *n* (*inf*) nonsense. — Also *interj.*

bosky [bosk'i] *adj* woody or bushy.

bosom [bōōz'-, bōōz'óm] *n* the breast of a human being, or the part of the dress that covers it; the seat of the passions and feelings, the heart; the interior. — *adj* confidential; intimate.

boson [bō'son] *n* any of a class of subatomic particles whose spin is zero or an integral number.

boss[1] [bos] *n* a knob or stud; a raised ornament. — *vt* to ornament with bosses.

boss[2] [bos] *n* the master, manager, or foreman; the person who pulls the wires in political intrigue. — *vt* to manage; (*inf*) to keep in subjection. — *adj* (*slang*) excellent.

bot, bott [bott] *n* the maggot of the bot'fly, esp one infesting the horse.

botany[1] [bot'án-i] *n* the science of plants. — *adjs* **botan'ic,** - **ical.** — *n* **botan'ical,** a vegetable drug, esp in the crude state. — *adv* **botan'ically.** — *vi* **bot'anize,** to study plants, esp on a field trip. — *n* **bot'anist,** one skilled in botany.

botany[2] [bot'án-i] *adj* a fine grade of wool from the merino sheep.

botch [boch] *n* a swelling on the skin; a clumsy patch; ill-finished work. — *vt* to patch or mend clumsily; to put together unsuitably or unskilfully.

botfly [bot'flī] *n* any of various stout two-winged flies (group Oestroidea) with larvae parasite in tissues of various mammals including man.

both [bōth] *adj* and *pron* the two; the one and the other. — *conj* (or *adv*) as well, equally.

bother [boTH'èr] *vt* to perplex or tease. — *ns* **both'er, bother-ā'tion.** — *adj* **both'ersome.**

bo tree [bō'-trē] *n* the sacred fig tree (*Ficus religiosa*) planted close to Buddhist temples in Ceylon.

botryoidal [botrioid'al] *adj* resembling a bunch of grapes.

bottle [bot'l] *n* a hollow narrow-necked vessel for holding liquids; the contents of such a vessel. — *vt* to enclose in bottles; to confine as if in a bottle. — *adj* **bott'led,** enclosed in bottles; shaped like a bottle; kept in restraint. **bott'leneck,** a narrow section of a road where traffic is apt to be congested; any stage of a process at which facilities for progress are inadequate. — **bottle up,** to confine repress.

bottom [bot'óm] *n* the lowest part of anything; that on which anything rests or is founded; the sitting part of the body; the seat of a chair; the hull of a ship lying below the water; the bed of the sea, etc.; the basis of anything. — *vt* to found or rest upon; to bring to the bottom, to get to the bottom of. — *vi* to become based; to reach the bottom. — *adj* **bott'omless.** — *ns* **bott'omland,** low-lying land along a watercourse; **bottom line,** the crux; the line at the bottom of a financial report that shows the net profit or loss; the final result.

botulism [bot'yōōl-izm] *n* food poisoning caused by contamination by anerobic soil bacillus.

bouclé [bōō'klā] *n* a yarn having the threads looped to give a bulky effect; a textile fabric of bouclé yarn.

boudoir [bōōd'wär] *n* a lady's private room.

bouffant [bōōf'ã] *adj* puffed out.

bough [bow] *n* a branch of a tree.

bought [böt] *pt, pt p* of **buy.**

bouillon [bool-yän'] *n* a strong broth, a clear seasoned soup made from lean beef. — **bouillon cube,** a cube of evaporated seasoned meat extract.

boulder [bōld'èr] *n* a large stone or mass of rock rounded by the action of water, weathering, etc. — *adj* containing boulders.

boulevard [bool'e-vär] *n* a broad road, often lined by trees.

bounce [bowns] *vi* to jump or spring suddenly; to rebound like a ball; (*slang*) (of a worthless check) to be returned; to boast, to exaggerate. — *vt* to cause a ball to bounce; (*slang*) to put (a person) out by force; (*slang*) to fire from a job. — *n* a thud; a leap or spring; capacity for bouncing; (*inf*) energy, dash, etc. — *n* **bounc'er,** (*slang*) a man hired to remove disorderly people from nightclubs, etc. — *adj* **bounc'ing,** big, healthy, etc.

bound[1] [bownd] *pt, pt p* of **bind.** — In composition, restricted to or by, as *housebound, stormbound.* — **bound to,** obliged to; sure to.

bound[2] [bownd] *n* the limit of a definite area; (*pl*) the area so defined; (*pl*) the limits (of what is reasonable or what is permitted). — *vt* to set bounds to; to limit, restrain, or surround; to name the boundaries of. — *n* **bound'ary,** the line by which an area is defined. — *adj* **bound'less,** having no limit; vast. — **out of bounds,** beyond the boundaries; forbidden.

bound[3] [bownd] *vi* to spring or leap. — *n* a spring or leap.

bound[4] [bownd] predicative *adj* ready to go to, on the way to (eg *bound for the North, outward bound*).

bounden [bownd'n] *adj* obligatory (*bounden duty*).

bounty [bown'ti] *n* liberality in bestowing gifts; the gifts bestowed; a reward or premium. — *adjs* **bounteous, boun'tiful,** liberal in giving; generous. — *advs* **boun'teously, boun'tifully.**

bouquet [bōōk'-ā, or -ā'] *n* a bunch of flowers, a nosegay; the perfume exhaled by wine. — **bouquet garni,** [gär'nē], a bunch of herbs used in cooking, removed before serving.

bourbon [bûr′bón, bŏŏr-] *n* a whiskey distilled from corn mash.

bourgeois [bŏŏrzh′wä] *n* one of the **bourgeoisie** [bŏŏrzh′wä-zē or -zē′], the social class between the very wealthy and the middle class.—*adj* smug, respectable, conventional; humdrum.

bourgeon *See* **burgeon**.

bourn¹, bourne [bôrn, bŏŏrn] *n* (*arch*) a boundary, a limit, a goal.

bourn², bourne [bŏŏrn] *n* a stream, a brook.

bourse [bŏŏrs] *n* a European stock exchange.

bout [bowt] *n* a turn, spell a period spent in some activity; a contest or struggle.

boutique [bŏŏ-tēk′] *n* a small shop, or department in a shop, selling one type of goods, esp clothing.

bovine [bō′vīn] *adj* pertaining to cattle; dull, unemotional. *n* an ox, cow, etc.

bow¹ [bow] *vi* to bend the neck, body, in saluting a person, etc.; to submit.—*vt* to bend, incline downwards; to weigh down, crush; to usher with a bow; to express by a bow.—*n* a bending of the neck or body in salutation.—**take a bow**, to acknowledge applause, etc.

bow² [bō] *n* anything in the shape of an arch, as the rainbow; a tough, flexible curved rod by which arrows are shot from a string; the instrument by which the strings of a violin or the like are sounded; a looped knot of ribbon, etc.—*vti* to bend, curve; to play (a violin, etc.) with a bow.—*n* **bow′leg**, a leg bowed outward at or below the knee.—*adj* **bow′legged**.—*ns* **bow′man**, an archer; a boatman, oarsman, or paddler stationed at the front of the boat.

bow³ [bow] *n* the forward part of a ship.—*ns* **bow′er**, an anchor carried at the bow of a ship.

bowdlerize [bowd′lér-īz] *vt* to expurgate (a book) by altering or omitting indelicate expressions, esp to do so unnecessarily.

bowel [bow′él] *n* an interior part of the body; (in *pl*) the entrails, the intestines; (*pl*) the deep and remote part of anything; (*pl arch*) the heart, pity, tenderness.—**move one's bowels**, to defecate.

bower [bow′ér] *n* an arbor; a lady's private apartment in a medieval castle; a shelter (as in a garden made with entwined vines and tree boughs.)

bowie knife [bō′i-nīf] *n* a stout hunting knife with a sharp curved, concave back edge sharpened at the point.

bowl¹ [bōl] *n* a wooden ball used for rolling along the ground; (*pl*) a game played on a smooth lawn with bowls having a bias.—*vti* to play at bowls; to speed smoothly (along) like a bowl.—*ns* **bowl′er**, one who bowls; **bowling**, a game in which a heavy ball is bowled along a bowling alley at ten wooden pins; **bowl′ing all′ey**, a long narrow wooden lane, usu. one of several in a building designed for them; **bowl′ing green**, a smooth grassy plot for bowls.—**bowl over**, to knock over; (*inf*) to astonish.

bowl² [bōl] *n* a deep, rounded dish; a large drinking cup; an amphitheater, stadium; the contents of a bowl.

bowler [bō′ler] *n* a derby hat.

bowline [bō′lin] *n* a rope to keep a sail close to the wind; a knot used to tie a bowline so that it will not slip or jam.

box¹ [boks] *n* a genus (*Buxus*) of evergreen shrubs and small trees with very compact habit of growth and hard, strong, heavy wood; a case or receptacle for holding anything; the contents of a box; a boxlike thing or space; in a theater, a group of enclosed seats; the driver's seat on a carriage; a television set; (*slang*) a guitar; (*baseball*) any of six areas on a baseball diamond designated for the batter, pitcher, catcher, etc.—*vt* to put into a box; to enclose.

box² [boks] *n* a blow on the head or ear with the hand.—*vt* to strike with the hand or fist.—*vi* to fight with the fists.—*ns* **box′er**, one who boxes; **box′ing**, the skill or sport of fighting with the fists.

boy [boi] *n* a male child; a lad; a servant.—*n* **boy′hood**, time, or state, of being a boy.—*adj* **boy′ish**.—*adv* **boy′ishly**.—*n* **boy′ishness**.—*ns* **boy′friend**, a male friend with whom a person is romantically or sexually involved.

boycott [boi′kot] *vt* to shut out from all social and commercial intercourse in order to punish or coerce.

bra [brä] *n* short for **brassière**.

brace [brās] *n* anything that draws together and holds tightly; a rod or bar connecting two parts of a structure for stiffening purposes; an instrument for turning a bit; in printing, a mark connecting two or more words or items to be considered together ({}); a pair, couple; (*pl*) (*Brit*) straps for supporting the trousers; ropes for turning the yards of a ship; a dental appliance for straightening the teeth.—*vt* to tighten or to strengthen.—*adj* **brac′ing**, invigorating.

bracelet [brās′lét] *n* an ornament for the wrist.

bracero [brä-sèr′-ō] *n* a Mexican laborer admitted to the US esp for seasonal contract work in agriculture.

brachial [brāk′-, or brak′i-ál] *adj* belonging to the arm.

bracken [brak′én] *n* a large, coarse fern, esp the brake (*Pteridium aquilinum latiuscalum*) whose young shoots are edible, found in eastern and central N America; a growth of brakes.

bracket [brak′ét] *n* a support for a shelf, etc., projecting from a wall; people classified according to income (eg *in the lower, middle, upper income bracket*); (*pl*) in printing and writing, the marks [] used to enclose one or more words.—*vt* to support by brackets; to enclose by brackets; to classify together.

brackish [brak′ish] *adj* somewhat salty; nauseating.—*n* **brack′ishness**.

bract [brakt] *n* a modified leaf growing at the base of a flower.—*adj* **brac′teal** [-ti-ál].

brad [brad] *vt* a small nail having a slight projection at the top on one side instead of a head; a thin wire nail having a barrel-shaped head.—*vt* to fasten with brads.—*n* **brad′awl**, an awl to pierce holes.

brag [brag] *vti* to boast.—*pr p* **bragg′ing**; *pt p* **bragged**.—*n* a boast or boasting.

braggadocio [brag-a-dō′shi-ō] *n* a braggart or boaster; empty boasting.—Also *adj*.

braggart [brag′árt] *adj* boastful.—*n* a loud, arrogant boaster.

braid [brād] *vt* to interweave three or more strands (of hair, straw, etc.); to make by such interweaving.—*n* a narrow band made by such interweaving used to bind or decorate clothing; a strip, as of hair, formed by braiding.

braille [brāl] *n* printing for the blind, using a system of dots in relief.—Also *adj*.

brain [brān] *n* the part of the central nervous system which is contained within the skull of vertebrates; the intellect; a person of exceptional intelligence; (often *pl*), the chief planner of an organization or enterprise.—*vt* to dash out the brains of; to hit on the head.—*adj* **brain′y** (*inf*), having a good mind; intelligent.

braise [brāz] *vt* to stew in a closed vessel.

brake¹ [brāk] obsolete *pt* of **break** (1).

brake² [brāk] *n* a fern, esp any of the genus *Pteridium*; bracken.

brake³ [brāk] *n* rough or marshy land overgrown usu. with one kind of plant.—*adj* **brak′y**.

brake⁴ [brāk] *n* an instrument to break flax or hemp; a harrow; a contrivance for retarding the motion of a wheel by friction; a kind of vehicle.—*vt* to retard or stop by a brake.—*vi* to apply the brake on a vehicle; to become checked by a brake.

bramble [bram′bl] *n* any rough prickly shrub or vine of the genus *Rubus*, esp raspberries and blackberries.

bran [bran] *n* the husks of cereal grain sifted from the flour.

branch [bränch or -sh] *n* an armlike extension of a tree; any offshoot from a parent stem; a separately located department of a business or enterprise; the tributary of a river; a subdivision, section of a subject.—*vi* to spread out as a branch, or in branches to come out (from the main part) as a branch.—*vt* to ornament with designs of branches; to divide up.—**branch off**, to separate into branches; to diverge; **branch out**, to extend one's interests, activities, etc.

brand [brand] *n* a piece of wood burning or partly burned; a mark stamped with a hot iron; such a mark inflicted on the person as a sign of guilt or disgrace, now used to identify cattle; particular make (of goods); a trademark.—*vt* to mark with a hot iron; to fix a mark of infamy upon.—*ns* **bra̅nd′er**; **brand name**, the name by which a certain make of commodity is known.—Also *adj*.—*adj* **brand′-new**, entirely new and unused.

brandish [brand′ish] *vt* to wave or flourish as a brand or weapon.—*n* a waving or flourish.

brandy [brand′i] *n* an alcoholic liquor distilled from wine or from fermented fruit juice.

brant [brant] *n* any of several wild geese (genus *Branta*) esp the

American brant (*B bernicla*) which has a black head, neck, and breast and is prized for its flesh. —(*pl*) **brant, brants.**

brash [brash] *adj* impetuous; bumptious; bold.

brass [bräs] *n* an alloy of copper and zinc; (*inf*) effrontery; (often *pl*) the brass instruments of an orchestra or band; (*slang*) officers or officials of high rank. **brass tacks,** (*inf*) basic facts.

brassard [bras'ärd] *n* a cloth worn around the upper arm usu. with an identifying symbol.

brassière [bras'i-er] *n* a woman's undergarment supporting the breasts.

brat [brat] *n* an ill-mannered, annoying child. —*n* **bratt'iness.**

brattice [brat'is] *n* a wooden partition or lining, esp to control ventilation in a mine. —*vt* to furnish with a brattice.

bratwurst [brat'wûrst] *n* a highly spiced fresh pork sausage for cooking.

braunschweiger [brown'shwī-gèr] *n* smoked liver sausage.

bravado [brav-ä'dō, brav-ä'dō] *n* pretended bravery; a boastful threat. —*pl* **brava'do(e)s.**

brave [brāv] *adj* courageous; noble; finely dressed, handsome. —*vt* to meet boldly; to defy; to face (it out). —*n* any brave man; a N American Indian warrior. —*adv* **brave'ly.** —*n* **brav'ery,** heroism; finery. —**brave new world,** a future society characterized by totalitarianism and technological advance.

Bravo communication word for the letter *B.*

bravo¹ [brä'vō] *n* a daring villain; a hired assassin. —*pl* **bra-vo(e)s** [bräv'ōz].

bravo² [bräv'ō] *interj* well done! excellent!

bravura [bräv-öōr'a] *n* bold daring; dash; (*mus*) bold and spirited execution; a passage requiring such execution.

brawl [bröl] *n* a noisy quarrel. —*vi* to quarrel noisily.

brawn [brön] *n* strong, well-developed muscles; muscular strength. —*adj* **brawn'y,** muscular.

bray¹ [brā] *vt* to break, pound, or grind small.

bray² [brā] *n* the cry of the donkey; any harsh sound. —*vi* to utter such sounds.

brayer [brā'ér] *n* a printer's hand inking roller.

braze [brāz] *vt* (*arch*) to harden. —*adjs* **brā'zen,** of or belonging to brass; impudent; **brazen-faced,** marked by bold disrespect. —*vt* to face (a situation) with impudence (as in *to brazen it out*). —*n* **brazier** [brāzh'(y)ér], a worker in brass.

braze [brāz] *vt* to solder with a metal having a high melting point. —*n* **brazier,** [brāz'yèr, brāzh'(y)èr] a pan for hot coals.

Brazil'ian [bra-zil'yän] *n* a native of Brazil, in South America. —*adj* belonging to Brazil. —*ns* **Brazil' nut,** a tall S American tree (*Bertholletia excelsa*) that bears an edible, three-sided seed; its nut; **brazil'wood,** the heavy wood of various tropical leguminous trees (esp genus *Caesalpina* used as dyewood and in cabinet work.

breach [brēch] *n* an act of breaking; a break ôr gap, as in the walls of a fortress; a breaking of law, contract, covenant, promise, etc.; a break in friendship. —*vt* to make a breach or opening in. —**breach of promise,** breach of a promise of a marriage.

bread [bred] *n* food made of flour or meal baked; livelihood (also **bread-and-butt'er,**); food; (*slang*) money; **bread'winner,** one who earns a living for a family; **breadline,** a line of people waiting to receive free food (as from a welfare agency or charity.)

breadth [bredth] *n* extent from side to side; width; liberality (eg of mind); in art, subordination of details to the harmony of the whole.

break [brāk] *vt* to sever forcibly; to divide; to shatter; to crush; to tame; to violate; to fail to fulfil; to check, as a fall; to interrupt (eg silence); to discontinue; to cure (of a habit); to make poor, ill, bankrupt etc.; to impart (news); to surpass; to decipher or solve. —*vi* to fall asunder; to pass suddenly (into a condition or action); to force a passage; to dawn or come into view; to become bankrupt; to crack (as the voice); to sever a connection; to stop activity temporarily; to suffer a collapse, as of spirit; (of news, etc.) suddenly and sensationally to become public; —*pt* **brōke,** (*arch*) **brāke;** *pt p* **brok'en,** —*n* state of being broken; an opening; a pause or interruption; a sudden change; an escape; (*slang*) a stroke of luck. —*adj* **break'able.** —Also *n* in *pl* —*ns* **break'age,** the action of breaking, or its consequences.

breakfast [brek'fâst] *n* a break or breaking of a fast—the first meal of the day. —*vi* to take breakfast.

bream [brēm] *n* a small freshwater fish (*Lepomus gibbosus*) common in streams and ponds with sand and mud bottoms throughout eastern and central US. —Also **sunfish, pumpkin seed**; any of various European or Australian marine food fishes.

breast [brest] *n* the forepart of the human body between the neck and the belly; one of the two mammary glands; the corresponding part of any vertebrate; conscience, disposition, affections. —*vt* to bear the breast against; to oppose; to mount.

breath [breth] *n* the air drawn into and then expelled from the lungs; power of breathing; life; a single act of breathing; a very slight breeze; an exhalation. —*adjs* **breath'less,** out of breath; panting; gasping; unable to breathe easily because of emotion; **breath'taking,** very exciting. —*n* **breath'lessness.**

breathe [brēTH] *vi* to draw in and expel breath or air from the lungs; to take breath, to rest or pause; to live; to speak or sing softly; to whisper. —*vt* to draw in or expel from the lungs, as air; to infuse (into); to give out as breath; to whisper; to exercise; to let (a horse) recover breath. —*ns* **breath'er** a spell of exercise; (*inf*) a rest to recover breath; **breathing,** the act of breathing; respite; one or other of two signs used in Greek to signify presence or absence of the aspirate; **breath'ing space,** **breathing spell, breathing room,** time in which to recover, get organized or get going. —**breathe again,** to have a feeling of relief.

breccia [brech'yä] *n* a rock composed of angular fragments.

bred [bred] *pt, pt p* of **breed.**]

breech [brēch] *n* the lower part of the body behind; the hinder part of a gun; the bottom part of a pulley block. —*n pl* **breeches** [brich'ez], a garment for the lower limbs of the body coming just below the knee.

breed [brēd] *vt* to generate or bring forth; to train or bring up; to propagate, raise (eg *he breeds horses*); to cause or occasion. —*vi* to be with young; to produce offspring; to be produced (eg *trouble breeds there*). —*pt, pt p* **bred.** —*n* progeny or offspring; race or type. —*ns* **breed'er; breed'ing,** act of producing; education and training; good manners resulting from good training. —**breeder reactor,** a nuclear reactor capable of creating more fissile material than it consumes in maintaining the chain reaction.

breeze¹ [brēz] *n* a light gentle wind; a wind from 4 to 31 miles an hour; (*inf*) a thing easy to do. —*adj* **breez'y,** fanned with or subject to breezes; airy; nonchalant; bright, lively. —*n* **breezeway,** a covered passageway, as between a house and garage.

breeze² [brēz] *n* furnace refuse from coal or coke.

brethren [breTH'ren] *pl* of **brother.**

breviary [brēv'i-âr-i also brev'-] *n* book containing the daily service of the RC Church.

brevity [brev'it-i] *n* shortness; conciseness.

brew [brōō] *vt* to make (beer, ale, etc.) from malt and hops by boiling and fermenting; to steep (tea, etc.); to plot, scheme. —*vi* to perform, or undergo, the operation of brewing; to be in preparation. —*n* something brewed. —*ns* **brew'er,** one who brews; **brew'ery,** a place for brewing beer, etc.

briar See **brier** (1).

briar [brī'ér] *n* a tobacco pipe made from the root of a brier.

bribe [brīb] *n* something offered to influence the judgment unduly or corrupt the conduct, esp to do something illegally. —*vt* to offer or give a bribe to. —*n* **brib'ery,** the act of giving or taking bribes.

bric-a-brac [brik'a-brak] *n* curios, treasured odds and ends.

brick [brik] *n* a block of baked clay for building; a similar block of other material. —*vt* to lay or pave with brick. —*ns* **brick'bat,** a piece of brick, esp as a missile; an unfavorable remark; **brick'layer,** one who lays bricks; **brick'work,** work of bricks or a structure formed of bricks; —**drop a brick,** to make a blunder.

bridal [brīd'àl] *n* a wedding. —*adj* belonging to a bride or a wedding, nuptial.

bride [brīd] *n* a woman about to be married or newly married. —*ns* **bride'groom,** a man about to be married; a man newly married; **bride-price,** a payment (as of money, cattle, etc.) given by a prospective husband to the bride's family in many cultures; **bridesmaid**, a young woman attending the bride during a wedding.

bridewell [brīd′wel] *n* a prison.

bridge[1] [brij] *n* a structure by which traffic is conveyed over a river or intervening space; the narrow raised platform whence the captain of a ship gives directions; the bony part of the nose; an arch to raise the strings of a violin, etc.; a mounting for false teeth; anything that connects across a gap.

bridge[2] [brij] *n* any of various card games for four players in two partnerships that bid for the right to name a trump suit, score points for tricks above six, and played with the declarer's hand exposed, esp contract bridge.

bridle [brī′dl] *n* the headgear to which a horse's reins are attached; any restraint. — *vt* to put a bridle on; to manage by a bridle; to restrain. — *vi* to draw one's head back as an expression of anger, scorn, etc. — *ns* **bri′dle path**, a trail suitable for horseback riding.

brief [brēf] *n* a short account of a client's case for the instruction of counsel in a trial at law; an outline of an argument, esp that setting out the main contentions; (*pl*) snug, legless underpants. — *vt* to furnish with precise, final instructions. — *adj* short; concise. — *adv* **brief′ly**. — *n* **brief′ness**. — *adj* **brief′less**, having no legal clients. **in brief**, in a few words.

brier[1] [brī′ėr] *n* a plant (as of the genera *Rosa*, *Rubus* and *Smilax*) with a thorny or prickly woody stem; a mass of these.

brier[2] [brī′ėr] *n* a heath (*Erica arborea*) of southern Europe from whose root tobacco-pipes are made. — *n* **brier′root**, the root of the brier.

brig [brig] *n* a two-masted, square-rigged vessel.

brigade [brig′ād′] *n* a US army unit consisting of three or more battalions and usu. commanded by a colonel; a group of people organized to function as a unit in some work.

brigand [brig′ånd] *n* a bandit, usu. one of a roving gang. — *n* **brig′andage**, plundering.

brigantine [brig′ån-tēn] *n* a brig without a square mainsail.

bright [brīt] *adj* shining; clear; (*arch*) beautiful; cheerful; brilliant in color or sound; favorable or hopeful; clever; illustrious. — *adv* brightly; clearly. — *vti* **bright′en**, to make or become bright or brighter. — *adv* **bright′ly**. — *n* **bright′ness**.

brilliant [bril′yånt] *adj* sparkling; splendid; talented. — *n* a gem (as a diamond) cut in a particular form with from 80 to 88 facets giving it a special brilliance. — *adv* **brill′iantly**. — *ns* **brill′iance**, **brill′iancy**, brightness; splendor; great cleverness;

brim [brim] *n* the upper edge of a hollow vessel; the rim of a hat. — *vti* to fill or be full to the brim. — *pr p* **brimm′ing**; *pt p* **brimmed**. — *adj* **brim′ful**, full to the brim; completely full. — **brim over**, to overflow.

brimstone [brim′stōn] *n* sulfur.

brindled, **brindle** [brin′dld, brin′dl] *adj* brownish or gray, marked with darker spots or streaks.

brine [brīn] *n* water saturated with common salt; a strong saline solution (as of calcium chloride); the water of a sea or salt lake. — *vt* to treat (as by steeping) with brine. — *adj* **brin′y**, pertaining to brine or to the sea; salt.

bring [bring] *vt* to fetch; to lead or carry 'here' or to the place where the speaker will be; to cause to come (eg rain, relief), to result in; to lead to an action or belief; to sell for. — *pt*, *pt p* **brought** [brawt]. — *n* **bringer**. — **bring about**, to bring to pass, to effect; **bring around**, to restore to consciousness; **bring down**, to cause to fall by or as if by shooting.

brink [bringk] *n* the edge or border of a steep place or of a river; the point of onset; the threshhold of danger.

brioche [brē-osh′] *n* a light, rich roll made with eggs, flour, yeast, etc.

briquette, **briquet** [bri-ket′] *n* a brick-shaped block of usu. fine compressed material.

brisk [brisk] *adj* full of life and spirit; active, energetic; pleasingly tangy; sharp in tone. — *adv* **brisk′ly**. — *n* **brisk′ness**.

brisket [brisk′ėt] *n* meat from the breast of an animal.

brisling, **bristling** [bris′ling] *n* a small herring (*Clupea sprattus*) resembling, and processed like, a sardine.

bristle [bris′l] *n* a short, stiff hair. — *vi* to stand erect, as bristles; to have the bristles erect; to show anger or desire to resist; to be thickly covered (with). — *pr p* **brist′ling**; *pt p* **brist′led**. — *adj* **brist′ly**, set with bristles; rough. — **bristle with**, to be full of, beset with.

bristol board [bris′tól bōrd, -bȯrd] *n* a smooth pasteboard, paperboard, esp for artwork. — Also called **bristol**.

Britannia [brit-an′i-a] *n* Britain; female figure personifying it. — *adj* **Britann′ic**.

British [brit′ish] *adj* pertaining to Great Britain or the British Commonwealth; relating to the English language as spoken in Britain. — *n* natives or inhabitants of Britain; the Celtic language of the ancient Britons, Welsh.

Briton [brit′ón] *n* one of the Brythonic inhabitants of Britain, or one of their descendants; a native or citizen of Great Britain.

brittle [brit′l] *adj* easily broken; frail. — *n* **britt′leness**.

broad [brȯd] *adj* of large extent from side to side; wide; large, free or open; obvious; coarse, indelicate; strongly marked in pronunciation or dialect; tolerant; giving prominence to main elements, or harmony of the whole, without insisting on detail. — *n* (*slang*) a woman. — *advs* **broad**, **broad′ly**. — *adj* **broad′cast**, scattered or sown by hand; widespread.

broccoli [brok′o-li] *n* a kind of cauliflower (*Brassica oleracea*) with loose heads of tiny green buds.

brochette [brō-shet′] *n* a skewer for broiling chunks of meat, etc.; food broiled on a brochette.

brochure [bro-shōōr′] *n* a pamphlet.

brock [brok] *n* a badger.

brogan [brō′gn] *n* a heavy work shoe, fitting high on the ankle.

brogue [brōg] *n* a stout shoe; a manner of pronunciation, esp that of English by the Irish (perh a different word).

broider [broid′ėr], **broidery** [broid′ėr-i] *See* **embroider**, **embroidery**

broil[1] [broil] *n* a noisy quarrel; a confused disturbance. — Also *vti*.

broil[2] [broil] *vti* to cook by exposure to direct heat. — *n* **broil′er**, a pan, grill, etc. for broiling; a bird fit for broiling esp a young chicken of up to 2½ pounds dressed weight.

broke [brōk] *pt*, old *pt p* of **break**, surviving as *pt p* chiefly in the informal sense of hard up.

broken [brō′kn] *pt p* of **break**. — *adj* splintered, fractured; violated; ruined; tamed; incomplete, interrupted; intermittent; irregular; imperfect — *adv* **brok′enly**. — *adjs* **brok′en-down**, extremely infirm; worn out.

broker [brōk′ėr] *n* an agent who arranges marriages; an agent who negotiates contracts of purchase and sale (as of real estate, commodities, or securities); a power broker. — *n* **brok′erage**, the business of a broker; the commission charged by a broker.

bromine [brō′mēn] *n* a nonmetallic element (symbol Br; at wt 79.9; at no 35), named from its pungent fumes. — *n* **brō′mide**, a compound of bromine and another element or radical, esp those used as medicinal sedatives; (*slang*) an old joke; a trite saying; a dull person. — **bromide paper**, in photography, paper with a highly sensitive surface containing bromide of silver, used in printing from a negative.

bronchus [brongk′us] *n* either of the main forks of the windpipe. — *pl* **bronch′i**. — *adjs* **bronch′ial**; **bronchit′ic**, pertaining to bronchitis. — *n* one suffering from bronchitis. — *n* **bronchitis** [brongk-ī′tis] inflammation of the lining of the bronchial tubes.

bronco [brong′ko] *n* a wild or half-tamed horse or pony of the western US. — *n* **bron′co buster** (*inf*), a tamer of broncos.

brontosaurus [bron-to-sȯ′rus] *n* a genus (*Apatosaurus*) of dinosaurs, found fossil in the US.

bronze [bronz] *n* an alloy of copper and tin and sometimes other elements; a copper alloy without tin; anything cast in bronze; a reddish-brown color. — *adj* made of, or like, bronze. — *n* bronzing, a bronze coloring or discoloration (as of leaves). — **Bronze Age**, the prehistoric period that began between 4000 and 3000BC in which tools and weapons were made from bronze.

brooch [brōch] *n* an ornament held by a pin or a clasp and usu. worn near the neck.

brood [brōōd] *vi* to sit as a hen on eggs; to hang or hover (over); to meditate silently (on, over); to think anxiously for some time. — *n* a group having a common nature or origin, esp the children in a family; the number hatched at once. — *adj* kept for breeding, as in **brood mare**, etc. — *n* **brood′er**, one that broods; a heated shelter for raising fowl. — *adj* **brood′y**, inclined to sit or incubate; contemplative, moody.

brook[1] [brŏŏk] *n* a small stream.—*ns* **brook'let**, a little brook; **brook trout**, a mottled stream trout (*Salvelinus fontinalis*) of N America.

brook[2] [brŏŏk] *vt* to bear or endure.

broom [brŏŏm] *n* any of various evergreen shrubs (genera *Cytisus, Genista*) of the pea family with yellow flowers; a bundle of fibers or twigs attached to a long handle used for sweeping.—*n* **broom'stick**, the handle of a broom.

broth [broth] *n* a thin soup made by boiling meat, etc. in water; a fluid culture medium.

brothel [broth'-, brŏTH'ĕl] *n* a house of prostitution.

brother [bruTH'ĕr] *n* the name applied to a male child by the other children of his parents; a friend who is like a brother; a fellow member of any group or association; a lay member of a men's religious order;—*pl* **broth'ers**, used chiefly in formal address or in referring to the members of a society or sect. *adj* **broth'erly**, like a brother; kind; affectionate.—*n* **broth'erliness**.

brougham [brŏŏ'ăm, brŏŏm] *n* a closed carriage (or automobile) with the driver's seat outside.

brought [brŏt] *pt, pt p* of **bring**.

brouhaha [brŏŏ'hä-hä] *n* fuss, clamor.

brow [brow] *n* the eyebrow, the ridge over the eyes; the forehead; the edge of a cliff.—*vt* **brow'beat**, to cow by stern looks or speech, to bully.

brown [brown] *adj* having the color of chocolate, a mixture of red, black, and yellow; tanned.—*n* a brown color.—*vti* to make or become brown.—*adj* **brown'ish; brown'y**.—*n*— **brown study**, a reverie, orig a gloomy one; **brown sugar**, refined or partially refined sugar.

browse [browz] *vti* to feed on the rough shoots or leaves of plants; to read desultorily.

brucellosis [brŏŏ-sĕl-ō'sis] *n* a bacterial disease occurring in goats, cattle, hogs, and man.—Also **undulant fever**.

bruin [brŏŏ'in] *n* a bear.

bruise [brŏŏz] *vt* to injure and discolor (body tissue) without breaking the skin; to dent the surface (of wood); to break down (as leaves and berries) by pounding; to inflict psychological pain on.—*vi* to inflict a bruise; to undergo bruising.—*n* discoloration of the skin; a similar injury to plant tissue; an abrasion, scratch on furniture; an injury, esp to the feelings.—*n* **bruis'er**, a strong, pugnacious man.

bruit [brŏŏt] *vt* to noise abroad.

brummagem [brum'a-jem] *adj* showy but worthless.

brunch [brunch] *n* breakfast and lunch combined.

brunette [brŏŏn'et'] *n* a woman with black or dark-brown hair, often with dark eyes and complexion.—Also *adj*.

brunt [brunt] *n* the shock of an onset, the force of a blow; the chief shock or strain of anything (*bear the brunt of*); the hardest part.

brush [brush] *n* an instrument set with bristles or the like for cleansing or for applying friction or a coating of some material; a painter's hair pencil; a bushy tail; a grazing contact.—*vt* to pass a brush over; to remove by a sweeping motion.—*vi* to pass with light contact.—*ns* **brush'off**, a curt dismissal.

brusque, brusk [brusk] *adj* blunt and abrupt in manner.—*adv* **brusque'ly**.—*ns* **brusque'ness**

brut [brŏŏt] *adj* (of champagne) the driest made by the producer.

brute [brŏŏt] *adj* belonging to, or as if belonging to, the lower animals; soulless; irrational; stupid; cruel; material, without consciousness.—*n* one of the lower animals; a brutal man.—*adj* **brut'al**, like a brute; unfeeling; inhuman.—*vt* **brut'alize**, to make like a brute, to degrade.—*n* **brutal'ity**.—*adv* **brut'ally**.—*adj* **brut'ish**, brutal; stupid.—*adv* **brut'ishly**.—*n* **brut'ishness**.—**brute force**, sheer strength.

bryony [brī'o-ni] *n* any of a genus (*Bryonia*) of climbing vines of the gourd family with large leaves and red or black fruit.

bryophyllum [brī-o-fil'um] *n* a succulent kalanchoe (*Kalanchoe pinnata*) grown as a foliage plant.

bryophyte [brī'o-fīt] *n* a plant phyllum comprising mosses and liverworts.

Brython [brith'on] *n* a Celt of the group to which Welsh, Cornish and Bretons belong.—*adj* **Brython'ic**.

bubble [bub'l] *n* a film of liquid forming a ball around air or gas; a tiny ball of gas or air in a liquid or a solid; a transparent dome; an unsound or fraudulent scheme; to boil; to make a gurgling sound;—*pr p* **bubb'ling**; *pt p* **bubb'led**.—*adj* **bubb'ly**.—*n* **bubb'le chamber**, device for showing the path of a charged particle by the string of bubbles left in its track.

bubo [bū'bo] *n* an inflammatory swelling of the glands in the groin or armpit.—*adj* **bubon'ic**, accompanied by buboes— **bubonic plague**, an epidemic caused by a bacterium (*Yersinia pestis*) and marked by buboes and fever, transmitted from rats to man through fleas.

buccaneer [buk'ăn-ēr'] *n* one of the freebooters in the West Indies during the seventeenth century; a pirate; an unscrupulous adventurer, esp in politics or business.—*vi* to act as a buccaneer.

buck [buk] *n* the male of the antelope deer, goat, hare, rabbit, and rat; a dashing fellow; (*slang*) a dollar.—*vi* (of a horse) to rear upward quickly; (*inf*) to resist.—*vt* (*football*) to charge against; to throw by bucking; (*inf*) to resist stubbornly.—*adj* of the lowest grade within a military rank.—*ns* **buck'passer** (*inf*), one who regularly shifts blame or responsibility to someone else; **buck'shot**, a large kind of shot, used in shooting deer; **buck'skin**, a soft leather made of deerskin or sheepskin; (*pl*) breeches or suit of buckskin.—*adj* made of or like the skin of a buck.—*n* **buck'tooth**, a projecting front tooth.—**buck for** (*slang*), to work eagerly for (a promotion, raise, etc.); **buck up** (*inf*) to cheer up.

buckboard [buk'bŏrd, -bŏrd] *n* a four-wheeled wagon with a springy platform.

bucket [buk'ĕt] *n* a container with a handle for drawing or holding liquid or substances in small pieces; —**kick the bucket**, to die.

buckle [buk'l] *n* a fastening for a strap or band; a bend or bulge.—*vti* to connect with a buckle; to bend or crumple under pressure, etc.—*n* **buck'ler**, a small shield used for parrying; **buckle down**, to apply oneself.

buckram [buk'răm] *n* a coarse fabric of jute, cotton, or linen, stiffened with size.—*adj* made of buckram; stiff; precise.

buckthorn [buk'thorn] *n* a tall thorny shrub (*Rhamnus cathartica*) widely used as a hedge plant in N America.

buckwheat [buk'hwēt] *n* any of a genus (Fagopyrum) esp two plants (*F esculentum* and *F tartaricum*) cultivated for their edible seeds; the seed used as cereal grain.

bucolic [bū-kol'ik] *adj* pertaining to the tending of sheep; pastoral; rustic.—*n* **bucol'ic**, a pastoral poem.

bud [bud] *n* an embryo shoot, flower, or flower cluster of a plant; an early stage of development.—*vi* to put forth buds; to begin to grow.—*vt* to produce or develop from buds; to cause (as a plant) to bud; to graft by inserting a bud under the bark of another tree;—*pr p* **budd'ing**; *pt p* **budd'ed**.—*n* **budd'ing**, being in an early stage of development.—**in the bud**, in a budding condition; in an early stage.

Buddah [bŏŏd'ä] *n* the state of perfect enlightenment; an image of Siddharta Gautama (about 563–483 BC), founder of Buddhism.—*ns* **Buddhism**, a system of ethics and philosophy based on the belief that the purpose of life is to attain enlightenment, manifested in many forms such as Lamaism, Zen, etc.; **Buddhist**, a believer in Buddhism.

buddy [bud'ē] *n* (*inf*) a friend; a term of informal address.— **buddy system**, an arrangement on which two persons are paired, usu. for mutual safety.

budge [buj] *vti* to move or stir.

budgerigar [buj-er-i-gär'] *n* a small Australian parrot (*Melopsittacus undulatus*) usu. light green in the wild, but bred in many colors.—Also (*coll*) **budgie**.

budget [buj-ĕt] *n* a collection stock; any plan of expenditure.— *vi* to prepare a budget or plan of revenue and expenditure; to allow (for) in a budget.—*vt* to put on a budget; to plan (*budget your time*).

buff [buf] *n* a heavy, soft, brownish-yellow leather; a military coat made from this; a dull brownish yellow; (*inf*)a devotee, fan.—*adj* made of buff; of a buff color.—*vt* to clean or shine with leather or a leather-covered wheel.—*n* **buffer**.—**in the buff**, naked.

buffalo [buf'a-lō] *n* any of various wild oxen, any of a genus (*Bison*), esp the large shaggy-maned N American wild Ox (*B bison*); a freshwater fish (*Ictiobus cyprinellus*) related to the carp;—*pl* **buff'alo, buff'aloes**.—*ns* **buffalow bug**, carpet beetle; **buff'alo robe,** the hide of an American buffalo lined with fabric and used as a coverlet.

buffer [buf'ẽr] *n* anything that lessens shock, as of collision; something that serves as a protective barrier; a temporary storage area in a computer.—*vt* to treat or supply with a buffer.

buffet[1] [buf'ẽt] *n* a blow with the fist, a slap.—*vt* to strike with the hand or fist; to contend against.—*vi* to make one's way esp under difficult conditions.—*n* **buffet'ing,** repeated blows.

buffet[2] [bûfã'] *n* a sideboard or table at which guests serve themselves food; a meal served thus.

buffoon [buf-ōōn'] *n* one who amuses by jests, grimaces, etc.; a clown; a fool.—*n* **buffoon'ery,** ludicrous or vulgar jesting.

bug[1] [bug] *n* an object of terror.—*ns* **bug'aboo,** a bogy; **bug'-bear,** an object of terror (generally imaginary) or of abhorrence; a continuing source of irritation.

bug[2] [bug] *n* an insect with sucking mouth parts; any insect; (*inf*) a germ or virus; (*slang*) a defect, as in a machine; (*slang*) a hidden microphone.—*vt* (*slang*) to plant a concealed listening device in; (*slang*) to annoy, anger, etc.—*adj* **bug'eyed** (*slang*), with bulging eyes.

bugger [bug'ẽr] *n* a sodomite; a rascal; a fellow, chap.—*vt* to commit buggery with.—*n* **bugg'ery,** sodomy.

buggy [bug'i] *n* a light four-wheeled, one-horse carriage with one seat; a small carriage for a baby.

bugle[1] [bū'gl] *n* valveless brass instrument like a small trumpet used esp for military calls.—*vti* to signal by blowing a bugle.—*n* **bū'gler.**

bugle[2] [bū'gl] *n* any of a genus (*Ajuga*) of low-growing plants with spikes of blue flowers with basal rosettes.

bugle[3] [bū'gl] *n* a small cylindrical bead used for trimming, esp on women's clothing.

build [bild] *vt* to erect; to form or construct, to establish, base; to create or develop (*often with* up).—*vi* to put up buildings; to grow or intensify (*often with* up).—*pt p* **built** (*arch* **build'ed**).—*n* the way a thing is built or shaped.—*ns* **build'er; build'ing,** —*adjs* **built'-in,** formed as part of a main structure, present as part of one's genetic inheritance (as *built-in aptitude*); firmly fixed; **built'-up,** made higher, stronger, etc. with added parts; having many buildings on it, **build up,** to develop gradually by increments.

bulb [bulb] *n* a subterranean bud with swollen leaf bases in which reserve materials are stored, as in onions, narcissi, etc.; any similar protuberance; the globe of an electric light.—*adjs* **bulbed, bul'bous.**

bulbul [bŏŏl'bŏŏl] *n* the 'Persian nightingale'; any of several birds (family Pycnonotidae) of Asia and Africa.

bulge [bulj] *n* a swelling; a rounded projecting part;—*vti* to swell or bend outward.—*adj* **bul'gy.**

bulgur [bul'gur] *n* parched cracked wheat.

bulk [bulk] *n* magnitude or size; great size; large quantity; the greater part;—*vi* to have, or increase in size or importance.—*adj* total, aggregate; not packaged.—*adj* **bulk'y,** having bulk; unwieldy.*adj* **bulk'iness.**

bulkhead [bulk'hed] *n* a watertight, fireproof, etc. partition separating one part of a ship's interior from another; a retaining wall, a boxlike structure over an opening.

bull[1] [bŏŏl] *n* the male of bovine and certain other animals, as the whale, walrus, elephant, moose; one who seeks to raise the price of stocks and speculates on a rise; a bull's-eye; (*slang*) nonsense;—*adj* male; rising in price.—*n* **bull'bait'ing,** the sport of baiting or exciting bulls with dogs; **bull'-head'ed,** impetuous and obstinate.—*ns* **bull'horn,** a portable electronic voice amplifier; **bull'ock,** a castrated bull; young bull; **bull'-pen,** a temporary detention room in a jail; (*baseball*) a practice area for relief pitchers; **bull'ring,** the enclosure in which a bullfight takes place; **bull's-eye,** the center of a target, of a different color from the rest, and usually round; a direct hit.

bull[2] [bŏŏl] *n* an edict of the pope which has his seal affixed.

bull[3] [bŏŏl] *n* a ludicrous blunder in speech.

bulldoze [bŏŏl'dōz] *vt* (*inf*) to intimidate; to clear by bulldozer.—*n* **bull'dozer,** tractor with horizontal ram for clearing and leveling.

bullet [bŏŏl'ẽt] *n* the ball fired from any kind of small-arm.—*adj* **bull'etproof,** proof against bullets.

bulletin [bŏŏl'e-tin] *n* an official report of public news, or of a patient's progress.

bullion [bŏŏl'yón] *n* gold and silver in the mass and uncoined; dress trimming of gold and silver threads.

bullock *See* **bull** (1)

bully[1] [bŏŏl'i] *n* a cruel and boastful oppressor of the weak.—*adj* blustering; brisk; (*inf*) excellent.—*vt* to treat with persistent petty cruelty; to domineer over; to coerce (into).—*pr p* **bull'ying;** *pt p* **bull'ied.**—*vt* **bull'y-rag** (*inf*), to overawe by threats and taunts.

bully[2] [bŏŏl'i] *ns* canned or pickled beef.

bulrush, bullrush [bŏŏl'rush] *n* any of a genus (*Scirpus*) of annual or perennial sedges with a bristly spikelet of flowers.

bulwark [bŏŏl'wãrk] *n* a fortification or rampart; the side of a ship projecting above the deck; any means of defence or security.—*vt* to defend; to fortify.

bum [bum] *n* (*inf*) a tramp; a devotee, as of skiing or tennis.

bumble [bum'(b)l] *vi* to utter indistinctly; to bungle.—*n* **bum'blebee,** a large wild loud-humming bee (genus *Bombus*).

bumboat [bum'bōt] *n* a boat bringing provisions for sale to ships.

bump [bump] *vi* to knock dully; to jolt.—*vt* to strike against or on; to jolt.—*n* a dull, heavy blow, a thump; a lump or swelling; one of the protuberances on the surface of the skull supposed to indicate certain mental characteristics.—**bump'er,** a bar on a motorcar to lessen the shock of collision; a cup or glass filled to the brim; anything large or generous in measure.—Also *adj*—**bump off** (*slang*), to murder.

bumpkin [bump'kin] *n* an awkward clumsy rustic; a clown.

bumptious [bump'shùs] *adj* offensively self-assertive.—*adv* **bump'tiously.**—*n* **bump'tiousness.**

bun [bun] *n* a kind of sweet cake; a rounded mass of hair.

Buna [bōō'na] *n* one form of synthetic rubber.

bunch [bunch or -sh] *n* a lump (*rare*); a number of things fastened together; a cluster; something in the form of a tuft or knot; (*inf*) a group of people.—*vi* to cluster.—*vt* to make a bunch of, to concentrate.

bundle [bun'dl] *n* a number of things bound together; a loose package; (*biol*) a strand of conducting vessels, fibers, etc.—*vt* to make into bundles; to put, push hastily or unceremoniously.—*vi* to go hurriedly or in confusion (away, off, out).—**bundle up,** to dress warmly.

bung [bung] *n* the stopper of the hole in a barrel; a large cork.—*vt* to stop up with a bung.—*n* **bung'hole,** a hole for a bung.

bungalow [bung'ga-lō] *n* a lightly built house of one story occupied by Europeans in India; any similar house of one story.

bungle [bung'gl] *n* anything clumsily done; a gross blunder.—*vi* to act in a clumsy awkward manner.—*vt* to make or mend clumsily; to manage awkwardly.—*n* **bung'ler.**

bunion [bun'yón] *n* a lump or inflamed swelling on the first joint of the great toe.

bunk [bungk] *n* a box or recess in a ship's cabin; a sleeping berth anywhere.—*n* **bunk'er,** a large bin or chest, esp for stowing coal on a ship; an obstacle on a golf course.—*vti* to fuel.—*adj* **bunk'ered.**—*n* **bunk'ering,** loading fuel into a ship.

bunkum, buncombe [bung'kùm] *n* (*inf*) shallow pretentious oratory, humbug; pretentious nonsense—also **bunk.**

bunny [bun'i] *n* child's word for a rabbit.

Bunsen burner [bun'sen] *n* a gas burner in which air mingles with the gas and produces a smokeless flame of great heating power.

bunt[1] [bunt] *vti* (*baseball*) to bat (a pitch) lightly so that it does not go beyond the infield.—*n* a bunted ball.

bunt[2] [bunt] *n* a disease of wheat or the fungus that causes it.

bunting[1] [bunt'ing] *n* a thin worsted stuff for ships' colors; flags, cloth decorations.

bunting[2] [bunt'ing] *n* a genus (*Emberiza*) of finches nearly allied to the crossbills.

bunting[3] [bunt'ing] an infant's hooded sleeping bag made from thickly napped fabric.

buntline [bunt'lin] *n* a rope passing from the foot of a square sail, led up to the masthead and thence on deck, to help in hauling up the sail.

buoy [boi] *n* a floating secured mark, serving as a guide or as a warning for navigation, or as a mooring point.—*vt* to fix buoys or marks to; to keep afloat, or sustain; to raise the spirits of—

in last two meanings usu. with **up**.—*n* **buoy'ancy**, capacity for floating lightly on water or in the air; cheerfulness, elasticity of spirit.—*adj* **buoy'ant**, tending to float; cheerful.

bur *See* **burr** (1).

burble [bûr'bl] *vi* to talk incoherently, esp from excitement; to gurgle.—*n* **burb'ling**, the breaking up of a streamline flow of air about a body (as an airplane).

burbot [bûr'bot] *n* a fish (*Lota lota*) having a longish beard on its lower jaw, the only freshwater species of the cod family.

burden[1] *n* a load; cargo; tonnage (of a ship); that which is oppressive or difficult to bear; responsibility.—*vt* to load; to oppress; to encumber.—*adj* **bur'densome**, heavy, oppressive.

burden[2] [bûrd'n] *n* part of a song repeated at the end of every stanza, a refrain; the leading idea (of anything).

bureau [bū'rō, bū'rō] *n* a chest of drawers; a branch of a newspaper, magazine, or wire service in an important news center; a government department.—*pl* **bureaus**, **bureaux** [-öz].

bureaucracy [bū-rok'ra-si or -rōk'-] *n* a system of government by officials, responsible only to their chiefs.—*n* **bur'eaucrat**, one who practises or favors bureaucracy.—*adj* **bureaucrat'ic**.

burette, **buret** [bū-ret'] *n* graduated glass tube, usu. with a tap, for measuring the volume of liquids.

burgeon [bûr'jon] *n*, *vi* to put forth buds, etc.; to grow or develop rapidly.

burgess [bûr'jes] *n* a freeman or citizen of a borough.

burgh [bur'ö] *n* another spelling of **borough**, used for Scottish burghs.—*ns* **burg** (same as **borough**); **burgher** [bûrg'ér], an inhabitant of a borough; a citizen or freeman.

burglar [bûrg'lär] *n* one who enters a building to commit a felony, eg to steal.—*adj* **burglär'ious**.—*adv* **burglär'iously**.—*vt* **burg'le** (a back-formation).—*n* **burg'lary**.

burgomaster [bûr'gö-mäs-tér] *n* the chief magistrate of a Dutch, Flemish, or German town.

burgundy [bûr'gun-di] *n* a French wine, so called from *Burgundy*, the district where it is made; a blended red wine produced elsewhere.

burial [ber'i-ál] *n* the act of burying.

burin [bûr'in] *n* a chisel used in copper engraving.

burke [bûrk] *vt* to stifle, to suppress.

burlesque [bûr-lesk'] *n* a ludicrous and exaggerated imitation.—*adj* of the nature of burlesque.—*vt* to mock by burlesque.

burly [bûr'li] *adj* big and sturdy.—*n* **bur'liness**.

Burmese [bur'mēz, -mēz'] *adj* relating to *Burma* or its Sino-Tibetan language.—*n* a native of Burma, or the language of Burma.

burn [bûrn] *vt* to consume or injure by fire; to expose to great heat.—*vi* to be on fire; to consume through fire; to feel excess of heat; to be inflamed with passion.—*pt*, *pt p* **burned**, **burnt**.—*n* a hurt or mark caused by fire.—*n* **burn'ing**, conflagration.—Also *adj*.—*ns* **burn'er**, in a lamp or stove, the part from which the flame arises.

burnish [bûrn'ish] *vt* to make bright by rubbing.—*n* polish; luster.

burnous [bûr-nöös'] *n* a mantle with a hood much worn by the Arabs.

burnt *pt*, *pt p* of **burn**.

burp [bûrp] *vi* (*slang*) to belch.—*vt* to pat a baby's back to cause it to belch.—Also *n*.

burr, **bur**[1] [bûr] *n* the prickly adhesive seed-case or head of certain plants; rough edge to a line on a dry-point plate.—*n* **bur'dock**, a plant (genus *Arctium*) with a bur or prickly head and docklike leaves.

burr[2] [bûr] the rough sound of *r* pronounced in the throat, as in Northumberland, England.

burro [bûr'ö] *n* a donkey. [Sp.]

burrow [bûr'ö] *n* a hole excavated by certain animals for shelter.—*vi* to make, live in, holes underground, as rabbits; to dwell in a concealed place.—*vti* to tunnel.

bursa [bûr'sä] *n* a sac or cavity with a lubricating fluid, as between a tendon and a bone.—*n* **bursīt'is**, inflammation of a bursa.

bursar [bûrs'ár] *n* a treasurer.

burst [bûrst] *vt* to break into pieces; to break open suddenly or by violence.—*vi* to fly open or break in pieces; to break forth or away; to force one's way (into); to break (into—some

sudden expression of feeling, condition, or activity).—*pt*, *pt p* **burst**.—*n* a sudden outbreak; a spurt; a volley of shots.

bury [ber'i] *vt* to hide in the ground; to cover; to consign to the grave, the sea, etc., as a dead body; to hide or blot out of remembrance.—*pr p* **bur'ying**; *pt p* **bur'ied**.—**bury the hatchet**, to renounce enmity.

bus [bus] *n* an omnibus; (*slang*) a car.—*pl* **buses**, **busses**.—*vt* to transport by bus.—*vi* to go by bus; to do the work of a busboy.—*ns* **bus'boy**, a waiter's assistant who cleans tables, brings water, etc.; **bus'ing**, **buss'ing**, the transporting by bus of children from one district to school in another, esp to achieve a more even racial balance.

busby [buz'bi] *n* a tall, fur hat, esp one worn by a guardsman.

bush[1] [böösh] *n* a shrub thick with branches; anything of bushy tuft-like shape; forest; wild uncultivated country.—*vi* to grow thickly.—*adj* **bush'y**, full of bushes; thick and spreading.—*ns* **bush'iness**; **bush'man**, one who lives in the Australian bush; one of an almost extinct aboriginal race in southern Africa; a Khoisian language of the Bushmen; **bush'rang'er** [-rănj'-], in Australia, one who leads a lawless life in the bush.—**bush league** (*slang*) (*baseball*), a small or second-rate minor league; **bush'master**, to tropical American viper (*Lachesis mutis*) that is the largest New World venomous snake; **bush shirt**, **jacket**, a garment, often of cotton, with four patch pockets and a belt; **bush telegraph**, the obscure and rapid transmission of news through a country or population.—**beat about the bush**, to talk without coming to the point.

bush[2] [böösh] *n* the metal box or lining of any cylinder in which an axle works.

bushel [böösh'l] *n* a dry measure equal to 4 pecks or 32 quarts.

business [biz'nis] *n* trade, profession, or occupation; one's concern or affair; one's duty; a matter or affair; (*theat*) the details of action, as distinguished from dialogue, that make up a part.—*adj* bus'inesslike, methodical, systematic, practical.

buskin [busk'in] *n* a half-boot, esp one with thick soles worn in ancient times by actors of tragedy—hence, the tragic drama as distinguished from comedy.—*adj* **busk'ined**, tragic; dignified.

buss [bus] *n* a kiss.—Also *vti*.

bust[1] *n* a sculpture representing the head and breast of a person; the upper front part of the human body, esp a woman's.

bust[2] [bust] *vti* (*slang*) to burst or break; to make or become bankrupt or demoted; to hit; to arrest.—*n* (*slang*) a failure; financial collapse; a punch; a spree; an arrest.—*n* and *v*.

bustle[1] [bus'l] *vi* to busy oneself noisily or fussily.—*n* hurried activity, stir, tumult.

bustle[2] [bus'l] *n* a frame or pad for causing a skirt to hang back from the hips.

busy [biz'i] *adj* fully employed; active; diligent; meddling; of a design or picture, having too much detail; (of a telephone in use).—*vt* to make busy; to occupy (esp oneself).—*pr p* **busying** [biz'i-ing]; *pt p* **busied** [biz'id].—*adv* **bus'ily**.—*ns* **bus'yness**, state of being busy; **bus'ybody**, a meddling person.

but [but] *prep* only; except.—*conj* on the other hånd; in contrast; nevertheless; except that (merging in *prep*.—eg *they had all left but he*, *him*); that not (developing into negative rel pron.—eg *there is none of them but thinks*).—*adv* only; merely; just.—*pron* who . . . not; which . . . not.—**but for**, if it were not for.

butane [bū'tän] *n* a hydrocarbon used as a fuel, in organic synthesis, etc.

butch [bööch] *n* (*slang*) a very short haircut; (*slang*) the 'male' parter in a lesbian relationship.

butcher [bööch'ér] *n* one whose business is to kill cattle for food, or who deals in their flesh; one who delights in slaughter.—*vt* to kill for food; to put to a bloody death, to kill cruelly; to spoil by bad acting, reading, etc.—*ns* **butch'erbird**, any of various strikes; **butch'ery**, the preparation of meat for sale; a butching; great or cruel slaughter.

butler [but'lér] *n* a manservant, usu. the head servant of a household, etc.

butt[1] [but] *vti* to strike with the head, as a goat, etc.—*n* a push with the head.—**butt in**, to intervene; to intrude.

butt[2] [but] *n* a large cask for wine and beer.

butt[3] [but] *n* a mound behind targets; a victim of ridicule; (*pl*) a shooting range.

butt[4] [but] *n* the thick and heavy end; the stump; (*slang*) a cigarette.—*vi* to join end to end.

butte [byōōt] *n* a steep hill standing alone on a plain.

butter [but′ér] *n* an oily substance obtained from cream by churning.—*vt* to spread over with butter; (*inf*) to flatter (*with* **up**).

butt′erfly, an insect (order Lepidoptera) with a slender body and four usu. brightly colored wings; a gay flighty person; a swimming stroke executed in a prone position by moving both arms simultaneously in a circular motion while kicking the legs simultaneously.—*pl* **butt′erflies**.

—*adj* **butt′ery**, like, containing, or with, butter; offensively flattering.

buttery [but′ér-i] *n* a storeroom for liquors. [Fr *bouteillerie*, lit 'place for bottles'.]

buttock [but′ók] *n* either half of the rump or protuberant part of the body behind.

button [but′n] *n* a knob or disk of metal, bone, etc., used as a fastening, ornament, or badge; any similar knob or disk.—*vti* to fasten by a button or buttons.—*n* **butt′onhole**, the hole or slit into which a button is passed; a flower of flowers therein.—*vt* to work with a stitch (*buttonhole stitch*) suitable for defence of edges; to detain in talk.

buttress [but′res] *n* a projecting support built on to the outside of a wall; any support or prop.—*vt* to prop or support.

Butyl[1] [bū′tïl] *n* trade name for any of various synthetic rubbers.

butyl[2] [bū′tïl] *n* an alcohol radical C₄H₉. [should be C_4H_9]

buxom [buks′óm] *adj* yielding, elastic; plump and comely.

buy [bï] *vt* to purchase (for money); to bribe; to obtain in exchange for something not necessarily concrete; (*inf*) to accept, believe.—*pr p* **buy′ing**, *pt*, *pt p* **bought** [bawt].—Also *n*—*n* **buy′er**.—**buyer's market**, one in which, because the supply exceeds the demand, the buyers control the price.

buzz [buz] *vi* to make a noise like that of an insects' wings; to murmur; to hover (about).—*vt* to whisper or spread secretly; (*aero*) to fly very low over or very close to; to interfere with in flight by flying very close to.—*n* the noise of bees and flies; a whispered report.—*n* **buzz′er**, an electrical or other apparatus producing a buzzing sound.—**buzz word**, a hackneyed, almost meaningless word used as part of the jargon of a particular subject.

buzzard [buz′àrd] *n* any of various large birds of prey, as the turkey buzzard; a contemptible or rapacious person.

by [bï] *prep* at the side of; near to; along a route passing through, via; past; through denoting the agent, cause, means, etc.; to the extent of (eg *short by three inches*); measured in terms of (eg *by the yard, by this standard*); of time, at or before; during, or under specified conditions (*by day, by candlelight*).—*adv* near; in reserve; past; aside. **by′pass**, a side track to avoid an obstruction or a congested area; a channel carrying a fluid around a part and back to the main stream; **by′-pro′duct**, a product formed in the process of making something else; **by′road**, byway; **by′stander**, a chance spectator; **by′way**, a private and obscure way; **by′word**, a common saying;—**by and large**, on the whole; **by the way**, incidentally.

bye [bï] *n* the state of one who has not drawn an opponent and passes without contest to the next round; in golf, the holes played after the match is won.—*adj* and *prefix* subsidiary. [**by.**]

bylaw, byelaw [bï′lö] *n* a law adopted by an organization or assembly for its own meetings or affairs.

byte [bït] *n* in computers a set of usually eight bits treated as a unit.

C

cab [kab] *n* a taxicab; the place where the driver sits in a truck, crane, etc.—*ns* **cabb′ie, cabb′y** (*inf*) one who drives a cab for hire; **cab′driver**.

cabal [ka-bal′] *n* a small party united for some secret design; a conspiracy.

cabala, cabbala, caballah [käb′ä-la] *n* a secret system of the Jewish rabbis for the interpretation of the hidden sense of Scripture.—*n* **cab′alist**, one versed in the cabbala.—*adj* **cabalist′ic**.

caballero [kab-â-ler′ō, -ä-yer′ō] *n* a Spanish gentleman; (*southwest US*) a horseman or a lady's escort.

cabaret [kab′a-rä] *n* a restaurant with musical entertainment; an entertainment of the type given in such a restaurant.

cabbage [kab′ij] *n* a garden plant with thick leaves formed usu into a round compact head, used as a vegetable.

cabin [kab′in] *n* a hut or cottage; a small room, esp in a ship; a compartment for passengers in an aircraft.—*vt* to shut up in a cabin.

cabinet [kab′in-et] *n* a case with drawers or shelves; a case holding a TV, radio, etc.; a body of official advisers to a chief executive.

cable [kā′bl] *n* a strong rope often of wire strands for hauling or tying anything; a wire for carrying electric current; a cablegram.—*vt* and *vi* to telegraph by cable.—*ns* **cable car**, a car drawn by a moving cable, as up a steep incline; **cable television**, the transmission of TV programmes by cable to individual subscribers.

caboose [ka-bōōs′] *n* the trainman's car at the rear of a freight train.

cabriolet [kab-ri-ō-lā′] *n* a light carriage with two wheels; a former style of convertible coupé; a cab.

cacao [ka-kä′o, or ka-kā′o] *n* the tropical American tree from whose seeds cocoa and chocolate are made.

cachalot [kash′a-lot, -lö] *n* sperm whale.

cache [kash] *n* a hiding-place for treasure stores, etc.; treasure, stores, etc., hidden.—*n* **cachepot, cache pot**, a decorated jar for holding potted plants.

cachet [kash′ā] *n* a seal; any distinctive stamp, esp something showing or conferring prestige.

cachinnate [kak′in-āt] *vi* to laugh loudly.

cachou [kash′ōō] *n* a pill or pastille used to perfume the breath.

cacique [ka-sēk′] *n* a native Indian chief in areas dominated by Spanish culture.

cackle [kak′l] *n* the sound made by a hen; talk or laughter of similar sound.—*vti* to make such a sound.—**cut the cackle**, to stop the useless talk.

cacophony [ka-kof′o-ni] *n* a disagreeable sound; discord of sounds.—*adj* **cacoph′onous**.

cactus [kak′tus] *n* any one of a family of prickly plants whose stems store water and do the work of leaves;—*pl* **cac′tï** or **cac′tuses**.

cad [kad] *n* one who lacks the instincts of a gentleman.—*adj* **cadd′ish**.

cadaverous [ka-dav′ér-us] *adj* gaunt, haggard; pallid, livid.—*n* **cadav′er**, a dead body intended for dissection.

caddie, caddy [kad′i] *n* one who carries clubs for a golfer.—Also *vt*

caddy [kad′i] *n* a small box for holding tea.

cadence [kā′dens] *n* the fall of the voice; rhythm; measured movements as on marching.

cadet [ka-det′] *n* a student at an armed forces academy; any trainee, as a practice teacher.—*n* **cadet′ship**.

cadge [kaj] *vti* to beg or get by begging.—*n* **cadg′er**.

cadmium [kad′mi-ùm] *n* a metallic element.

cadre [kad′r] *n* a nucleus, framework, esp the officers of a political or military unit.

caducous [ka-dū′kus] *adj* falling early, as leaves.

caecum [sē′kum] *n* *See* cecum.

caesura [se-zū′rä] *n* (*pros*) division of a foot between two words; a pause in a line of verse (generally near the middle).—*adj* **caesū′ral**.

café, cafe [kaf′ā] *n* a small restaurant, a barroom, a nightclub, etc.

cafeteria [ka-fe-tēr′i-a] *n* a self-service restaurant.

caffeine [kaf′-ēn] *n* an alkaloid present in coffee, tea and kola.

caftan [kaf′tan] *n* a long-sleeved Persian or Turkish garment.

cage [kāj] *n* a box made of wire and wood for holding captive birds or animals; any similar structure.—*vt* to imprison in a cage.—*n* **cager** (*slang*), a basketball player.

cagey, cagy [kāj′i] *adj* (*coll*) wary, not frank.

caiman, cayman [kā′màn] *n* any of several tropical American crocodiles related to the alligator. [Sp.]

caisson [kās′ón] *n* an ammunition chest or wagon; a strong case for keeping out the water while the foundations of a bridge are being built; an apparatus for lifting a vessel out of the water for repairs or inspection.

caitiff [kāˈtif] *n* a mean despicable fellow.—*adj* mean, base.

cajole [ka-jōlˈ] *vti* to coax by flattery.

Cajun, Cajan [kāˈjùn] *n* inhabitant of Louisiana descended from 18th-century French-Canadian immigrants; the dialect spoken by Cajuns.

cake [kāk] *n* a mass of fried dough, batter, hashed food etc.; a mixture of flour, eggs, sugar, etc. baked in small flat shapes or a loaf; a small block of compacked or congealed matter.—*vti* to form into a cake or hard mass.—**take the cake** (*slang*) to win the prize.

calamary [kalˈá-mâr-i] *n* squid.

calamine [kalˈa-mīn, -min] *n* a zinc oxide powder used in skin lotions, etc.

calamity [kal-amˈi-ti] *n* a great misfortune; affliction.—*adj* **calamˈitous**, disastrous.—*adv* **calamˈitously**.

calamus [kalˈa-mus] *n* the traditional name of the sweet flag, an aromatic plant; the reed pen used by the ancients;—*pl* **calamī**.

calcareous [kal-kāˈre-us] *adj* like or containing limestone, chalk or lime.

calcium [kalˈsi-úm] *n* the metal (symbol Ca; at wt 40.1; at no 20) present in chalk and lime.

calculate [kalˈkū-lāt] *vt* to count or reckon; to think out, esp mathematically; to plan, think, purpose, suppose.—*vi* to make a calculation; to rely, base one's plans or forecasts (on).—*adj* **calˈculable**.—*adjs* **calˈculated**, fitted (to), likely (to); deliberate; **calˈculating**, given to forethought; selfish and scheming.—*n* **calculāˈtion**, the art or process of calculating; estimate; forecast.—*n* **calˈculātor**, a machine for doing arithmetic rapidly; one who calculates.

calculus [kalˈkū-lus] *n* an abnormal stony mass in the body (*pl* **calˈculi**); (*math*) the study of the changes of a continuously varying function (*pl* **calˈculuses**).

caldron, cauldron [kölˈdrόn] *n* a large kettle or boiler; a state of violent agitation.

calefactory [kal-e-fakˈtόr-i] *n* a room in which monks warmed themselves.

calendar [kalˈen-dàr] *n* a system of determining the length and divisions of a year; an almanac or table of months, days, and seasons.

calender [kalˈen-dèr] *n* a press with rollers for finishing the surface of cloth, paper, etc.—*vt* to press in a calender.

calenture [kalˈen-tyùr] *n* tropical fever caused by exposure to heat.

calf¹ [käf] *n* the young of the cow, elephant, whale, and certain other mammals; calfskin leather;—*pl* **calves** [kävz].

calf² [käf] *n* the fleshy back part of the leg below the knee.—*pl* **calves** [kävz].

caliber, calibre [kalˈi-bèr] *n* the size of the bore of a tube; diameter; (*fig*—of a person) degree of excellence or importance.—*vt* **calˈibrāte**.

calico [kalˈi-kō] *n* a cotton cloth first brought from *Calicut* in India.

californium [kal-i-förˈ-ni-úm] *n* a transuranic element.

caliper, calliper [kalˈi-pèrz] *n* measuring instrument with legs suitable for measuring the inside or outside diameter of bodies.

caliph, calif [kalˈif, or kāˈlif] *n* the name assumed by the successors of Mohammed.—*n* **calˈiphate**, the office, rank, or government of a caliph.

calisthenics [kal-is-thenˈiks] *n pl* exercises for promoting gracefulness and strength of body.—*adj* **calisthenˈic**.

calk [kök] *n* a spike in a horseshoe to prevent slipping; a similar device worn on the sole of a shoe.—*vt* to provide or wound with a calk.

call [köl] *vi* to cry aloud; to make a short visit; to telephone.—*vt* to name; to summon; to describe as specified; to awaken; to give orders for; to stop (a game); to demand payment of;—*n* a summons or invitation; a sense of vocation; a demand; a short visit; a telephone connection or conversation or a request for one; a cry, as of an animal or a bird; need, or demand, as for a product.—*ns* **callˈboy**, a bellhop; a page; **callˈer**, one who pays a short visit; **call girl**, a prostitute who is called by telephone to assignations; **callˈing**, vocation, trade, profession; **on call**, ready to answer summons.

calligraphy [kal-igˈra-fi] *n* handwriting, esp fine penmanship.

callous [kalˈus] *adj* hardened; unfeeling.—*ns* **callosˈity**, a hard thickening of the skin; **callˈus**, a hardened, thickened place on the skin.—*adv* **callˈously**.—*n* **callˈousness**.

callow [kalˈō] *adj* inexperienced, immature.

calm [käm] *adj* still or quiet, serene, tranquil.—*n* absence of wind; repose; serenity.—*vti* to become or make calm; to quiet.—*adv* **calmˈly**.—*n* **calmˈness**.

calomel [kalˈō-mel] *n* a white tasteless powder $Hg_2 Cl_2$ used in medicine, esp as a purgative and fungicide.

calorie, calory [kalˈor-i] *n* the amount of heat needed to raise the temperature of a gram of water from 15°C to 16°C, equal to 4.186 joules, a heat unit 1000 times as great as this (also kilogram calorie or large calorie), used in measuring the energy-producing value of food.—*adjs* **calorˈic**, of heat; of calories; **calorifˈic**, causing heat.

caltrop, calthrop [kalˈtrop, kölˈtrop, kalˈthrop, köl´] *n* an instrument armed with four spikes so arranged that one always stands upright, used to obstruct the progress of an enemy.

calumny [kalˈum-ni] *n* false accusation; slander.—*vt* **calumˈniāte**, to accuse falsely; to slander.—*vi* to spread evil reports.—*ns* **calumˈniātion**; **calumˈniātor**.—*adj* **calumˈnious**.—*adv* **calumˈniously**.

calvary [kalˈva-ri] *n* an open-air representation of Christ's crucifixion; an experience of intense mental suffering.

calve [käv] *vt* and *vi* to bring forth (a *calf*).

Calvinism [kalˈvin-izm] *n* the doctrines of the great Genevan religious reformer, John *Calvin* (1509–64). The distinguishing doctrine of his system is predestination, coupled with the irresistibility of God's grace.—*n* **Calˈvinist**.—*adjs* **Calvinistˈic, -al**.

calypso [kà-lipˈsō] *n* folk song, usu a commentary on a current happening, made up as the singer goes along, originally from Trinidad.

calyx [kalˈiks, or kāˈliks] *n* the outer green covering or cup of a flower, consisting of sepals.—*pl* **calyces**, or **calyxes**.

cam [kam] *n* a device to change rotary to reciprocating motion.—*n* **camˈshaft**, the rotating shaft to which cams are fitted to lift valves in motors.

camaraderie [kam-a-rädˈèr-ē] *n* the spirit of comradeship.

camarilla [kam-ar-ilˈä] *n* a body of secret unofficial advisers; a cabal.

camber [kamˈbèr] *n* a slight convexity upon an upper surface, as of a road surface.—*vti* to arch slightly.

cambium [kamˈbi-úm] *n* the layer of cells between the wood and the bark of a stem from which new wood and bark grow.

cambric [kāmˈbrik] *n* a fine white linen or cotton cloth.

camel [kamˈèl] *n* an animal with one or two humps on its back, used as a beast of burden and for riding.

camellia [ka-mēlˈya, -melˈ] *n* a genus (*Camellia*) of evergreen shrubs of the tea family, natives of eastern Asia, grown for the singular beauty of their flowers.

camelopard [kam-elˈō-pärd] *n* early name for the giraffe.

cameo [kamˈē-ō] *n* an engraved gem in which the figure or subject is carved in relief; an outstanding bit role, esp in a motion picture; a bit of fine writing.—*pl* **camˈeos**.

camera [kamˈer-a] *n* a vaulted room; a judge's private chamber (**in camera**, of a case, tried in secret); the apparatus in which a photographer exposes a sensitive plate or film.

camisole [kamˈis-ōl] *n* a woman's loose underbodice without sleeves.

camouflage [kaˈmŏŏ-fläzh] *n* any device (esp deceptive coloring) for deceiving an adversary.

camp¹ [kamp] *n* the ground on which tents are pitched; a recreational place in the country for vacationers, esp children; the supporters of a particular cause.—*vi* to encamp or pitch tents.—*ns* **campˈer**.

camp² [kamp] *adj* (*slang*) theatrical, affected, exaggerated; homosexual. Also *n*.—*adj* **camˈpy**.

campaign [cam-pānˈ] *n* a series of military operations with a particular objective; organized action in support of a cause.—*n* **campaignˈer**.

campanile [kam-pan-ēˈlä] *n* a bell tower, esp one detached from the church; (*pl*) **campaniles** [ēˈlez]

campanology [kam-pan-olˈo-ji] *n* the art of bell ringing.

campestral [kam-pesˈtràl] *adj* growing in, or pertaining to, fields or open country; rural.

camphor [kam'för] *n* a solid essential oil, obtainable from the camphor tree of the laurel family, having a peculiar aromatic taste and smell used to repel insects, as a stimulant in medicine, etc. — *adj* **cam'phorated**.

campus [kam'pús] *n* the grounds, and sometimes buildings of a school, college, or university. — Also *adj*.

can[1] [kan] *vt* to be able, to have sufficient power. — *pt* **could**.

can[2] [kan] *n* a container, usu metal, with a separate cover; a vessel of tinplate in which meat, fruit, etc., are hermetically sealed; a jar for packing and preserving fruits and vegetables; (*slang*) a jail; (*slang*) a toilet; (*slang*) an ounce of marijuana. — *adj* **canned**.

Canadian [ka-nā'di-án] *adj* and *n* pertaining to *Canada*; a native of Canada.

canal [kan-al'] *n* an artificial watercourse for navigation or irrigation; a duct in the body for conveying fluids. — *vt* to construct a canal through or across.

canard [ka-när(d)'] *n* a false rumor.

canary [ka-nā'ri] *n* a small finch (*Serinus canarius*) found in the Canary islands that is usu greenish to yellow and kept as a cage bird and singer; (*slang*) an informer. — *adj* canary-coloured.

cancel [kan'sel] *vt* to strike out by crossing with lines as used; to annul or suppress; to countermand. — *n* a printed page, etc., canceled, or substituted for one canceled. — *n* **cancel-lā'tion**.

Cancer [kan'sèr] *n* the crab, the 4th sign of the zodiac; in astrology, operative June 21 to July 21; **cancer**, the abnormal and uncontrollable growth of the cells of living organisms, esp a malignant tumor. — *adj* **canc'erous**.

candelabrum [kan-de-lā'brum] *n* a branched and ornamented candlestick or lampstand; — *pl* **candelā'bra**.

candid [kan'did] *adj* frank, ingenuous; free from prejudice, impartial. — *adv* **can'didly**. — *n* **can'didness**.

candidate [kan'di-dåt] *n* one who has nomination for an office or qualification for membership or award; a student taking examinations for a degree. — **can'didacy**.

candle [kan'dl] *n* a cylinder of wax, tallow, or like substance surrounding a wick; a light.

candor [kan'dór] *n* freedom from prejudice; sincerity, frankness.

candy [kan'di] *n* a solid confection of sugar or syrup with flavoring, fruit, nuts, etc.

cane [kān] *n* the slender, jointed stem of certain plants, as bamboo; a plant with such a stem, as sugar cane; a walking stick.

canine [kan'īn, kān'īn, kan-īn'] *adj* like or pertaining to a dog; of the family of animals that includes wolves, dogs, and foxes.

canister [kan'ist-tèr] *n* a small box or can for holding tea, coffee, flour, etc.

canker [kang'kèr] *n* an erosive or spreading sore; an area of necrosis in a plant; a plant disease marked by cankers; anything that corrupts or consumes. — *adj* **cank'erous**.

cannabis [kan'ábis] *n* a narcotic drug variously known as hashish, bhang, marijuana, etc.; (*cap*) the hemp genus.

cannel coal [kan'él] *n* a bituminous coal that burns with a bright flame.

cannibal [kan'i-bål] *n* an eater of the flesh of his own species. — *adj* relating to, or indulging in, cannibalism. — *vti* **cann'ibalize**, to strip (old equipment) of parts for use in other units.

cannon [kan'ón] *n* a large mounted piece of artillery; an automatic gun on an aircraft. — *vi* to discharge cannon. — *vt* cannonade. — *n* **cannonade'**, an attack with cannon.

cannot [kan'ot] am, is, or are, unable to.

canoe [ka-nōō'] *n* a narrow, light boat propelled by paddles. — Also *vi*. — *n* **canoe'ist**.

canon [kan'ón] *n* a law or rule, esp in ecclesiastical matters; a standard; the books of the Bible accepted by the Christian Church; the recognized genuine works of any author; a clerical dignitary belonging to a cathedral; (*mus*) a round.

canopy [kan'o-pi] *n* a covering hung over a throne, bed or person; a rooflike projection. — *vt* to cover as with a canopy.

cant[1] [kant] *vi* to talk in an affectedly solemn or hypocritical way. — *n* a hypocritical or affected style of speech; the language peculiar to a class (eg to thieves); conventional talk of any kind.

cant[2] [kant] *n* an inclination from the level; a sloping or tilted position. — *vti* to slant; to tilt.

can't [kant, känt] contraction for **cannot**.

cantankerous [kan-tang'kèr-us] *adj* perverse in temper, quarrelsome. — *adv* **cantan'kerously**. — *n* **cantan'kerousness**.

cantata [kan-tä'tä] *n* a choral composition for a story.

canteen [kan-tēn'] *n* a recreation center for servicemen, teenagers, etc.; a flask for carrying water.

canter [kan'tèr] *n* a horse's 3-beat gait resembling a slow, smooth gallop.

canticle [kan'ti-kl] *n* a song, particularly one of several liturgical songs (as the Magnificat) taken from the Bible.

cantilever [kan'ti-lēv-èr] *n* a bracket or block projecting as a support, esp a projecting structure anchored at one end only. — *vt* to support by means of cantilevers.

cantle [kan'tl] *n* a corner, edge, or slice of anything; the upward, projecting rear part of a saddle.

canto [kan'tō] *n* a division of certain long poems. — *pl* **can'tos**.

cantor [kan'tór] *n* a singer of liturgical solos in a synogogue; the leader of singing in a church choir.

Canuck, Kanuck [kan-uk'] *n* a Canadian-American; a French Canadian.

canvas [kan'vás] *n* a coarse cloth made of hemp or other material, used for sails, tents, etc., and for painting on; the sails of a ship; a tent; an oil painting on canvas.

canvass [kan'vås] *vti* to go through (places) or among (people) asking for votes, opinions, orders, etc.

canyon [kan'yon] *n* a long, narrow valley between high cliffs.

cap [kap] *n* any closefitting head covering, visored or brimless; a caplike thing; a cover; a top. — *vt* to cover with a cap; to cover (the end of); to equal or excel.

capable [kāp'a-bl] *adj* having ability or skill to do (*often with of*); competent; susceptible (of); suitable for, adapted to. — *n* **capabil'ity**.

capacity [kap-as'i-ti] *n* power of holding; containing, absorbing, or grasping; volume; ability; power of mind; character; legal competence; maximum possible content, or output. — *adj* **capā'cious**, roomy, wide.

caparison [ka-par'is-ón] *n* the covering of a horse; a rich cloth laid over a warhorse.

cape[1] [kāp] *n* a sleeveless garment fastened at the neck and hanging over the back and shoulders.

cape[2] [kāp] *n* a head or point of land running into the water.

caper[1] [kā'pér] *n* any of a genus (*Capparis*) of a low prickly Mediterranean shrub.

caper[2] [kā'pèr] *vi* to leap or skip like a goat; to dance in a frolicsome manner. — *n* a leap; a prank.

capercaillie, capercailzie [kā-pér-kāl'yi] *n* the largest Old World grouse (Tetroa urogallus).

capillary [ka-pil'år-i, kap'il-år-i] *adj* as fine or minute as a hair; having a very small bore, as a tube.

capital [kap'it-ål] *adj* relating to the head; involving the loss of life; chief, principal; of, or being the seat of government; of capital or wealth; excellent. — *n* a city that is the seat of government; a large letter; capitalists collectively; the stock or money for carrying on any business; a city preeminent in some special activity. — *vt* **cap'italize**, *ns* **capitalizā'tion**; **cap'italism, cap'italist**, — *adv* **cap'itally**, excellently.

capital [kap'it-ål] *n* the head or top part of a column, etc.

capitation [kap-it-ā'sh(ó)nl] *n* a direct uniform tax imposed on each head or person, a poll tax.

Capitol Hill [kap'it-ol] *n* the legislative branch of the US government.

capitulate [kap-it'ūl-āt] *vi* to yield or surrender on certain conditions; to stop resisting. — *n* **capitulā'tion**.

capon [kā'pón] *n* a castrated cock fattened for eating.

capote [[ka-pōt'] *n* a long hooded cloak or mantle.

caprice [ka-prēs'] *n* a change of humor or opinion without reason. — *adj* **capri'cious** [-ri'-shùs]. — *adv* **capri'ciously**. — *n* **capri'ciousness**.

Capricorn [kap'ri-körn] *n* the goat, the 10th sign of the zodiac; in astrology, operative December 21 to January 19.

capsize [kap-sīz'] *vt* to upset. — *vi* to be upset.

capstan [kap'stan] *n* an upright drum, around which cables are wound to haul them in.

capsule [kap'sūl] *n* a dry, dehiscent seedpod consisting of two or more carpels; a fibrous or membraneous covering; a gelatin case for holding a dose of medicine; a metal or other container.

captain [kap'tin] *n* a chief, leader; the master of a ship; the leader of a team, as in sports. —*n* **cap'taincy**.

caption [kap'sh(ó)n] *n* a newspaper heading, or a note accompanying an illustration.

captivate [kap'tiv-āt] *vt* to charm; to engage the affections of.

captive [kap'tiv] *n* a prisoner; one kept in confinement. —*ns* **captiv'ity**; **cap'tor**, one who takes a captive or a prize; **cap'ture**, the act of taking; the thing taken; an arrest.

car [kär] *n* a vehicle moved on wheels, as an automobile, etc.; a vehicle moved on rails; an elevator cage.

caracal [kar'a-kal] *n* a long-legged reddish-brown nocturnal cat (*Felis caracal*) of savannas in Africa.

carafe [ka-räf'] *n* a bottle holding water or wine.

caramel [kar'a-mél] *n* a dark-brown substance produced by heating sugar above its melting-point. —*vti* **car'amelize**, to burn sugar.

carat [kar'ât] *n* a measure of weight for precious stones equal to 200 milligrams.

caravan [kar'a-van] *n* a company traveling together for security, esp in crossing the desert; a train of pack animals; a van. —*n* **caravansary** [kar-a-van'ser-ē], **caravanserai** [kar-a-van'ser-ī], a kind of unfurnished inn or extensive enclosed court where caravans stop in eastern countries; a hotel, inn.

caraway [kar'a-wā] *n* a biennial plant (*Carum carvi*) with aromatic seeds, used as a tonic and flavoring.

carbide [kär'bīd] *n* a compound of carbon with another element; calcium carbide.

carbine [kär'bīn] *n* a short-barreled rifle; a light, semiautomatic or automatic .30-caliber rifle.

carbohydrate [kär-bō-hī'drāt] *n* a compound of carbon, hydrogen, and oxygen, the last two being in the same proportion as in water, esp in sugars and starches as components of food.

carbolic acid [kar-bol'ik as'id] *n* phenol.

carbon [kär'bon] *n* a nonmetallic element a constituent of all organic matter. —*adj* **carbona'ceous**, pertaining to, or composed of, carbon. —*n* **car'bonate**, a salt of carbonic acid. —*adj* **carbonif'erous**, producing carbon or coal. —*vt* **car'bonize**, to convert into carbon or a carbon residue. —*n* **carboniza'tion**; **carbon black**, a fine carbon used in the manufacture of pigments and inks; **carbon copy**, a duplicate of writing made by means of **carbon paper**, a paper coated with a black, waxy pigment; etc.; **carbonic acid**, a weak acid formed by the solution in water of **carbon dioxide**, a gas evolved by respiration and combustion; **carbon monoxide**, a colorless, odorless, highly poisonous gas.

carboy [kär'boi] *n* an often cushioned container of glass, plastic, or metal.

carbuncle [kaï'bung-kl] *n* a fiery red gemstone (a garnet); an inflamed ulcer. —*adj* **carbun'cular**.

carburetor [kär'bū-ret-ór] *n* part of an internal-combustion engine in which air is mixed with gasoline spray to make an explosive mixture.

carcass [kär'kás] *n* the dead body of an animal; a framework or shell.

carcinoma [kär-si-nō'ma] *n* any of several kinds of epithelial cancer. —*n* **carcin'ogen**, a substance that produces cancer. —*adj* **carcinogen'ic**.

card¹ [kärd] *n* a small piece of pasteboard; one with figures for playing a game, with a person's name and address, with a greeting, invitation, message, etc. —*n* **card'board**, a stiff, finely finished pasteboard.

card² [kärd] *n* an instrument for combing fibers of cotton, wool and flax. —*vt* to comb (wool, etc.).

cardiac [kär'di-ak] *adj* belonging to the heart. —*ns* **car'diograph**, an instrument for recording movements of the heart; **car'diogram**, a tracing obtained from a cardiograph; **cardiol'ogy**, the branch of medicine concerned with diseases of the heart. —*adj* **cardiovas'cular**.

cardigan [kär'di-gan] *n* a knitted woolen sweater.

cardinal [kär'din-âl] *adj* denoting that on which a thing hinges or depends, fundamental. —*n* an official appointed by the Pope to his council; bright red. —*ns* **car'dinalate**, **car'dinalship**, the office or dignity of a cardinal. —**cardinal numbers**, numbers expressing how many (1,2,3, etc.); **cardinal points**,

the four chief points of the compass—north, south, east, and west.

care [kār] *n* affliction; anxiety; heedfulness; charge, keeping; the cause or object of anxiety. —*adjs* **care'free'**, lighthearted; **care'ful**, full of care; heedful. —*adv* **care'fully**. —*n* **care'fulness**. —*adj* **care'less**, without care; heedless, unconcerned. —*adv* **care'lessly**. —*ns* **care'lessness**; **care'tak'er**.

careen [ka-rēn'] *vti* to lean or cause to lean sideways; tip; tilt; lurch.

career [ka-rēr'] *n* a race; a rush; progress through life, esp advancement in calling or profession. —*adj* having a professional career; dedicated to a career. —*vi* to move or run rapidly.

caress [kä-res'] *vt* to touch endearingly, to fondle. —*n* an endearing touch.

caret [kar'ét] *n* a mark, △, to show where to insert something omitted.

cargo [kär'gō] *n* the load carried by a ship, truck, aircraft, etc.; freight. —*pl* **car'goes, cargos**.

caribou [kar'i-bōō'] *n* a large deer (*Rangifer caribou*).

caricature [kar'i-kä-chûr] *n* a likeness or imitation so exaggerated or distorted as to appear ridiculous.

caries [kä'ri-ēz] *n* decay of bones or esp of teeth.

carillon [kar'il-on] *n* a set of bells usu hung from a tower and played by means of a keyboard or other mechanism.

carl, carle [kärl] *n* a man; a fellow.

carminative [kär-min'ä-tiv] *n* a medicine to relieve flatulence. —Also *adj*.

carmine [kär'mīn, -min] *n* the red coloring prepared from cochineal.

carnage [kär'nij] *n* slaughter.

carnal [kär'nál] *adj* fleshy; sensual; worldly. —*n* **carnal'ity**, state of being carnal. —*adv* **car'nally**. —**carnal knowledge** (*law*), sexual intercourse.

carnation [kär-nä'sh(ó)n] *n* the color of human flesh; a garden flower developed in many forms from the Old World pink (*Dianthus caryophyllus*).

carnival [kär'ni-vál] *n* a feast observed by Roman Catholics just before the fast of Lent; any revelry or indulgence; an entertainment with sideshows.

carnivora [kär-niv'ō-ra] *n pl* carnivorous mammals. —*adj* **carniv'erous**, flesh-eating. —*adv* **carniv'orously**. —*ns* **carniv'orousness; car'nivore**.

carob [kar'ob] *n* a leguminous Mediterranean tree.

carol [kar'ol] *n* a song of joy or praise. —*vi* to sing a carol; to sing or warble. —*pr p* **car'olling**.

carouse [kar-owz'] *n* a noisy drinking party. —*n* **carous'al**, a carouse.

carousel *See* **carrousel**.

carp¹ [kärp] *vi* to catch at small faults or errors. —*n* **car'per**.

carp² [kärp] *n* a freshwater fish (*Cyprinus carpio*).

carpenter [kär'pent-èr] *n* a worker in timber as used in building houses, etc. —*n* **car'pentry**.

carpet [kär'pêt] *n* the woven or felted covering of floors, stairs, etc. —*pr p* **car'peting**; *pt p* **car'peted**. —*ns* **car'petbag**, a traveling-bag made of carpeting; **car'petbagg'er**, an outsider, esp a nonresident who meddles in politics.

carriage [kar'ij] *n* act, or cost, of carrying; a vehicle for carrying; behavior, bearing.

carrion [kar'i-ôn] *n* the dead and putrid flesh of any animal.

carrot [kar'ót] *n* a biennial herb (*Daucus carota*) grown for its edible, fleshy, orange root; the root; an inducement, often illusory. —*adj* **carr'oty**, carrot-colored.

carrousel, carousel [kar-ōō-sel', -zel] *n* a tournament; a merry-go-round; a rotating conveyor, eg for luggage at an airport.

carry [kar'i] *vt* to convey or transport; to bear; to support, sustain; to bear (oneself); to extend; to take by force; to gain. —*pr p* **car'rying**; *pt p* **car'ried**—*ns* **car'rier**, one who carries, esp for hire; a receptacle or other device for carrying; one who transmits an infectious disease without himself suffering from it.

cart [kärt] *n* a small wagon. —*vti* to carry in a cart, truck, etc.; to transport. —*ns* **cart'age; car'ter**.

cartel [kär-tel'] *n* a written agreement between belligerent nations; an association of business in an international monopoly.

cartilage [kär'ti-lij] *n* in vertebrate animals, a firm elastic substance, lacking blood vessels and nerves; gristle.—*adj* **cartilaginous** [-laj'-].

cartography [kär-tog'ra-fi] *n* map-making.—*ns* **cartog'rapher.**

carton [kär'tòn] *n* a cardboard box or container.

cartoon [kär-tōōn'] *n* any large sketch or design on paper; a comic or satirical drawing; a comic strip; an animated cartoon.

cartridge [kär'trij] *n* a case containing the charge for a gun.

carve [kärv] *vt* to cut into forms, devices, etc., to make or shape by cutting; to cut up (meat) into slices or pieces.—*adj* **carv'en,** carved.—*ns* **carv'er,** carving, **carve up,** to subdivide, apportion.

caryatid [ka-i-at'id] *n* a column carved in the shape of a draped female figure used to support an entablature;—*pl* **caryat'ides** [-id-ēz].

cascade [kas-kād'] *n* a small, steep waterfall; a shower, as of sparks, etc.—*vti* to fall in cascades.

cascara [kas-kä'ra] *n* cascara buckthorn; cascara sagrada.—*ns* **cascara buckthorn,** a tree (*Rhamnus purshiana*) of the U.S. Pacific coast yielding cascara sagrada; **cascara sagrada,** the dried bark of cascara buckthorn used as a laxative.

case[1] [kās] *n* a covering, box, or sheath; the boards and back of a book; *vt* **case' hard'en,** to harden on the surface; *adj* **case-hardened.**

case[2] [käs] *n* that which falls or happens, event; state or condition; subject of question or inquiry; a person under medical treatment; a legal statement of facts.—*ns* **case'** law, law as decided in previous cases.

casein [kāsē-in] *n* a protein, the principal albuminous constituent of milk or cheese.—*adj* **cā'sēous.**

casemate [käs'māt] *n* a heavily protected chamber or compartment.

cash [kash] *n* coin or money; ready money; money, a check, etc. paid at the time of purchase.—*vt* to exchange for money.—*ns* **cashier',** one who has charge of the receiving and paying of money; **cash' reg'ister,** a device, that automatically and visibly records the amount put in.

cashier [kash-ēr'] *vt* to dismiss from a post in disgrace; to discard or put away.

cashmere [kash'mēr] *n* a fine, carded wool from goats of northern India, Tibet, and China; the yarn spun from this wool.

casino [ka-sē'no] *n* a room or building for gambling, dancing, etc.

cask [käsk] *n* a barrel of any size, esp one for liquids; its contents.

casket [käsk'et] *n* a small box or chest for holding jewels, etc.; a coffin.

cassava [ka-sä'vä] *n* a tropical plant (genus *Manihot*) with starchy roots; used in tapioca.

casserole [kas'e-rōl] *n* a vessel in which food is both cooked and served; the food itself.

cassette [kas-et'] *n* a case with magnetic tape or film in it, for loading in a tape recorder or camera.

cassock [kas'ók] *n* a long black robe worn by clergymen.

cast [käst] *vt* to throw or fling; to shed, drop; to reckon; to direct; to mold or shape.—*vi* to throw, hurl.—*pt, pt p* **cast.**— *n* act of casting; a throw; a plaster form for immobilizing a limb; a mold; the form received from a mold; type or quality; a tinge; the assignment of the various parts of a play to the several actors; the company of actors playing roles.— *n* **cast'away,** a person or thing cast off.—*adj* **cast' down,** dejected.—*ns* **cast'ing, cast'ing-vote.**—*adj* **cast'-off,** laid aside or rejected.—

caste [käst] *n* a hereditary Hindu social class in India; any exclusive social class.

caster [käst'ėr] *n* a small wheel on the legs of furniture; a small vessel with perforated top for pepper, sugar, etc.

castigate [kas'tig-āt] *vt* to chastise; to criticise severely.—*ns* **castigā'tion; cas'tigātor.**

castle [käs'l] *n* a fortified house or fortress; anything built in the likeness of such.—*adj* **cas'tellated,** having turrets and battlements like a castle.

castor [käs'tór] *n* the beaver; a hat made of its fur.

castor oil [käs'tór-oil] *n* a medicinal and lubricating oil obtained from a tropical plant (*Ricinus communis*).

castrate [kas'trāt] *vt* to deprive of the power of generation by

removing the testicles, to geld; to deprive of the ovaries, to spay.—*n* **castrā'tion.**

casual [kaz(h)'ū-àl] *adj* accidental; unforeseen; occasional; careless; unceremonious.—*adv* **cas'ually.**—*n* **cas'ualty,** a person injured or killed in an accident.

casuistry [kaz'ū-is-tri] (or kazh'-) *n* a method of solving conflicts of obligation by applying general principles of ethics and moral theology to particular case of human conduct.—*n* **cas'uist.**—*adjs* **casuist'ic, -al.**

cat [kat] *n* a wild or domesticated animal of genus *Felis*; a spiteful woman; short for the **cat-o'-nine-tails,** a whip with nine lashes; **cat'gut,** a kind of cord made from the intestines of sheep; **cat'kin,** a spike or tuft of small flowers, as in the willow, hazel, etc.—*adj* **cat'-like,** noiseless, stealthy.—*ns* **cat's'-eye,** a variety of quartz showing opalescent reflections; a playing marble with eyelike concentric circles.—*adj* **catt'y,** like a cat; spiteful.

catabolism [kat-ab'ol-izm] *n* the breaking down of complex molecules in the living organism to release energy; destructive metabolism.

cataclysm [kat'a-klizm] *n* a flood of water; any sudden violent change.—*adj* **cataclys'mic.**

catacomb [kat'a-kōm] *n* a subterranean burial-place.

catafalque [kat'a-falk] *n* a temporary structure representing a tomb placed over the coffin during a lying in state.

catalectic [kat-a-lek'tik] *adj* incomplete—applied to a verse wanting one syllable at the end.

catalepsy [kat'a-lep-si] *n* a state of temporary insensibility with bodily rigidity, as in epilepsy.—*adj* **catalep'tic.**

catalog, catalogue [kat'a-log] *n* a classified list of names, books, etc.—*vti* to put in a catalog; to make a catalog of;—*pr p* **cat'aloguing;** *pt p* **cat'alogued.**

catalysis [ka-tal'i-sis] *n* the acceleration or retardation of a chemical reaction by a substance which itself undergoes no permanent chemical change.—*n* **cat'alỹst** (or **catalyt'ic agent).**

catamaran [kat-a-mär-an'] *n* a raft of logs lashed together, a boat with two hulls.

catapult [kat'a-pult] *n* anciently an engine of war for throwing stones, arrows, etc.; any similar device.

cataract [kat'a-rakt] *n* a waterfall; an opaque condition of the lens of the eye causing blindness.

catarrh [kat-är'] *n* (*old fashioned*) a discharge of fluid due to the inflammation of a mucous membrane, esp of the nose; a cold.—*adj* **catarrh'al.**

catastrophe [kat-as'trō-fe] *n* a sudden, violent change in a feature of the earth; utter failure; a calamity.—*adj* **catastroph'ic.**

catch [kach] *vt* to take hold of, esp a thing in motion; to seize after pursuit; to trap or ensnare; to be in time for; to surprise, detect; to become infected with (a disease); (*inf*) to see, hear, etc.; to grasp (eg a meaning).—*vi* to be contagious; to be entangled or fastened;—*pt, pt p* **caught** [köt].—*n* **catch'er.**— *adj* **catch'ing,** infectious; captivating, attractive.—**catch'-phrase,** a phrase that becomes popular and is much repeated; a slogan; **catch'word,** a guide word.—*adj* **catch'y,** attractive; deceptive; readily caught up, as a tune, etc.

catechize [kat'e-kīz] *vt* to instruct by question and answer; to question, examine searchingly.—*adjs* **catechis'mal, catechis'tic,** relating to a catechism or to oral instruction.—*adv* **catechet'ically.**—*ns* **cat'echizer; cat'echĭsm,** oral instruction.

catechumen [kat-e-kū'men] *n* one who is being taught the rudiments of Christianity.

category [kat'e-gor-i] *n* a class or division in a scheme of classification.—*adj* **categor'ical,** (of a statement) positive; absolute, without exception; of, as, or in a category.—*adv* **categor'ically.**

cater [kā'tėr] *vi* to provide food and service, as for parties (*with* for).—*n* **cā'terer.**

caterpillar [kat'ėr-pil-àr] *n* the wormlike larvae of a butterfly or moth; extended to other larvae; a tractor made for use on rough or soft ground running on endless articulated tracks.

cathedral [kath-ēd'rál] *n* the principal church of a diocese.— *adj* belonging to a cathedral.

cathode [kath'ōd] *n* the negative terminal of an electrolytic cell at which positively charged ions are discharged into the exterior electric circuit.—*adjs* **cath′odal; cathod′ic.—cathode rays,** streams of negatively charged particles (electrons).

catholic [kath′ol-ik] *adj* universal; general, embracing the whole body of Christians; liberal, the opposite of exclusive; relating to the Roman Catholic Church.—*n* **Catholic,** an adherent of the RC Church.—*ns* **Cathol′icism.**

cattle [kat′l] *n pl* oxen, bulls, and cows, held as property or raised for use.

caucus [kö′kus] *n* private meeting of leaders of a political party or faction, usu to plan strategy.

caudal [kö′dál] *adj* pertaining to the tail.—*adj* **cau′dāte,** tailed.

caul [köl] *n* the membrane covering the head of some infants at their birth.

cauldron *See* **caldron.**

cauliflower [kol′i-flow(è)r] *n* a variety of cabbage (*Brassica oleracea botrytis*) whose inflorescence is eaten.

caulk [kök] *vt* to render (a boat) watertight by pressing oakum, etc., into the seams.—*n* **caulk′er.**

cause [köz] *n* that which produces an effect; ground, motive, justification; a legal action; the aim proposed, or the opinions advocated, by an individual or party.—*vt* to produce; to bring about.—*adj* **caus′al.**—*adj* **caus′ative.**—*adv* **caus′atively.**

causerie [köz′èr-ē] *n* a talk or gossip; a short and informal essay.

causeway [köz′wä] *n* a pathway raised and paved with stone as across wet ground or water.

caustic [kös′-, kos′tik] *adj* burning tissue by chemical action; corrosive; sarcastic, cutting.—*n* a substance that burns or wastes away the skin and flesh.—*adv* **caus′tically.**—*n* **caustic′ity.**

cauterize [kö′tèr-īz] *vt* to burn with caustic or a hot iron so as to destroy dead tissue, etc.; to deaden.—*ns* **cau′tery, cauterizā′tion.**

caution [kö′sh(ó)n] *n* heedfulness; warning.—*vt* to warn.—*adj* **cau′tionary,** containing caution; **cau′tious,** possessing or using caution; watchful; prudent.—*adv* **cau′tiously.**—*n* **cau′tiousness.**

cavalcade [kav-ál-kād′] *n* a procession of persons on horseback; a dramatic sequence or procession.

cavalier [kav-ál-ēr′] *n* a knight; a swaggering fellow; a gallant gentleman, esp a lady's escort.—*adv* **cavalier′ly.**

cavalry [kav′ál-ri] *n* combat troops originally mounted on horseback.

cave [kāv] *n* a hollow place inside the earth open to the surface.—*vti* to collapse or make collapse (*with* **in**).

caveat [kā′ve-at] *n* a notice or warning; a notice to stay proceedings in a court of law.

cavern [kav′èrn] *n* a cave, esp a large cave.

caviar, caviare [kav′i-är] *n* salted roe of the sturgeon.

cavil [kav′il] *vi* to make empty, trifling objections.—*pr p* **cav′illing;** *pt p* **cav′illed.**—*n* **cav′iller.**

cavity [kav′it-i] *n* a hollow; a hollow place.

cavort [kav-ört′] *vi* to curvet, frolic, bound.

caw [kö] *vi* to cry as a crow.—*n* the cry of a crow.

cayenne [kā-en′] *n* a very pungent red pepper (*Capsicum frutescens*).—**cayenne pepper.**

cease [sēs] *vt* and *vi* to give over, to stop.—*vi* to be at an end.—*adj* **cease′less,** without ceasing; incessant.—*adv* **cease′lessly.**

cedar [sē′dár] *n* any of a genus (*Cedrus*) of large coniferous evergreen trees.—*adj* made of cedar.

cede [sēd] *vt* to yield or give up to another, esp by treaty; to assign or transfer the title of.

ceil [sēl] *vt* to furnish (as a wooden ship) with a lining.—*n* **ceil′ing,** the inner roof of a room; the upper limit of visibility.

celandine [sel′an-dīn] *n* a variety of poppy (*Chelidonium majus*) with yellow flowers.

celebrate [sel′e-brāt] *vt* to make famous; to honor with solemn ceremonies; to perform with proper rites and ceremonies.—*n* **cel′ebrant.**—*adj* **cel′ebrated.**—*ns* **celebrā′tion, celeb′rity,** fame; a notable person.

celerity [sel-er′it-i] *n* quickness, rapidity of motion.

celery [sel′èr-i] *n* a kitchen vegetable with long succulent stalks.

celestial [sel-est′yál] *adj* heavenly; dwelling in heaven; in the visible heavens.

celibacy [sel′i-bas-i] *n* the unmarried state; complete sexual abstinence.—*adj* **cel′ibate.**

cell [sel] *n* a small room in a prison, etc.; a small cavity, as in a honeycomb; a part of the atmosphere that behaves as a unit.—*n* **cell′ule,** a little cell.—*adj* **cell′ūlar.**—*ns* **celluloid,** a motion-picture film; **cell′ulose,** the chief component of cell membrane of plants, used in making paper, textiles, etc.

cellar [sel′ár] *n* a basement; a covered excavation; a stock of wines.—*ns* **cell′arage,** cellar space, esp for storage; **cell′aret,** a case for holding bottles of wine or liquor.

cello [chel′ō] *n* an instrument of the violin family.—*n* **cellist.**

cellophane [sel′ō-fān] *n* a tough transparent wrapping material made from cellulose.

Celt [kelt, selt] *n* a Gaul; extended to include members of other Celtic-speaking peoples.—*adj* **Celt′ic,** pertaining to the Celts.—*n* a branch of the Indo-European family of languages, including Breton, Welsh, Cornish, Irish, Gaelic, Manx.

cement [se-ment′] *n* a powdered substance of lime and clay, mixed with water, etc. to make mortar or concrete, which hardens upon drying.—*n* **cementā′tion.**

cemetery [sem′e-tèr-i (or -tri)] *n* a place for the burial of the dead.

cenotaph [sen′ō-täf] *n* a sepulchral monument to one who is buried elsewhere.

censer [sens′ér] *n* a pan in which incense is burned.

censor [sen′sór] *n* an official with the power to examine literature, mail, etc. and remove or prohibit anything considered obscene, objectionable, etc.—*adjs* **censo′rial,** belonging to a censor; **censo′rious,** expressing censure; fault-finding.—*adv* **censo′riously.**—*ns* **censo′riousness; cen′sorship.**

censure [sen′shùr] *n* an unfavorable judgment, blame, reproof.—*vt* to blame; to condemn as wrong.—*adj* **cen′surable.**

census [sen′sus] *n* an official enumeration of inhabitants and recording of age, sex, etc.

cent [sent] *n* a coin = the hundredth part of a dollar; a penny.

centaur [sen′tör] *n* a fabulous monster, half man, half horse.

centenary [sen-ten′ár-i or sen′tin-] *n* a century or hundred years; a hundredth anniversary.

centennial [sen-ten′i-ál] *adj* happening once in a hundred years.—*n* a hundredth anniversary or its celebration.

center [sen′tèr] *n* the middle point of a circle or sphere; the approximate middle point or part of anything, a pivot.—*pr p* **cen′tering;** *pt p* **cen′tered.**—*adj* **central.**—*n* **centralizā′tion,** the tendency to administer affairs by a central rather than a local authority.—*vt* **cen′tralize,** to draw to a center.—*adv* **cen′trally.**

centigrade [sen′ti-grād] *adj* divided into a hundred degrees, as the *centigrade thermometer.*

centigram [sen′ti-gram] *n* a unit of weight, the hundredth part of a gram.

centiliter [sen′ti-lē-tèr] *n* a unit of volume, the hundredth part of a liter, 10 cubic centimeters.

centimeter [sen′ti-mē-tèr] *n* a unit of measure, the hundredth part of a meter.

centipede [sen′ti-pēd] *n* any of a class (Chilopoda) of long flattened arthropods with a pair of legs for each body segment.

centrifugal [sen-trif′ū-gál] *adj* tending away from the center of rotation, as in *centrifugal force.*—*n* **centrifuge.**

century [sen′tū-ri] *n* a period of a hundred years; unit of one hundred .—*n* **centū′rion,** the commander of a hundred Roman soldiers.

cephalic [se-fal′ik] *adj* belonging to the head.—*adj* **ceph′alous,** having a head.

cephalopod [sef′-al-opod] *n* any of a class (Cephalopoda) of marine mollusks characterized by a well-developed head and eyes and a ring of sucker-bearing tentacles.

ceramic [se-ram′ik] *adj* of earthenware, porcelain, or brick, or any product manufactured by the firing at a high temperature of a nonmetalic mineral.

cere [sēr] *vt* (*obs*) to cover with wax; to wrap in or as if in a cerecloth.—*adj* **cērā′ceous** [-shùs], of or like wax.—*ns* **cere′cloth; cere′ment,** a shroud.

cerebrum [ser′e-brum] *n* the front and larger part of the brain of vertebrates; the dominant part of the brain in man, associated with intellectual function; the brain as a whole.—*n* **cerebell′um.**—*adj* **cer′ebral,** pertaining to the cerebrum.—*n* cerebra'tion, thinking.—*adjs* cer'ebrospīn'al, cer'ebrova-s'cular.

ceremony [ser'e-mo-ni] *n* a sacred rite; behavior that follows rigid etiquette; pomp or state.—*adj* ceremō'nial, relating to ceremony.—*n* outward form; a system of ceremonies.—*adv* ceremō'nially.—*adj* ceremō'nious, full of ceremony; precise.—*adv* ceremō'niously.

cerise [ser-ēz, also -ēs'] *n, adj* a light and clear red.

certain [sûr'tin, -tn] *adj* sure, convinced; unerring; sure to happen; regular, inevitable; sure (to do); indisputable; some; one.—*adv* cer'tainly.—*ns* cer'tainty, cer'titude.

certificate [sêr-tif'i-kât] *n* a written declaration of some fact; a testimonial of character.—*vt* to give a certificate to.—*n* certifica'tion.—*vt* cer'tify;—*pr p* cer'tifying; *pt p* cer'tified.

cerulean [si-rōō'li-ân] *adj* sky blue.

cervical [sûr'vi-kâl, sêr-vī'kâl] *adj* belonging to the neck; belonging to the neck of the womb.

cesarean, cesarian section [sē-zar'i-an] *n* the delivery of a child by cutting through the walls of the abdomen.

cesium, caesium [sēz'i-ùm] *n* a metallic element (symbol Cs; at wt 132.9, at no 55).

cessation [ses-ā'sh(ó)n] *n* a ceasing or stopping; a pause.

cession [sesh'(ó)n] *n* a yielding up, a surrender.

cesspool [ses'pōōl] *n* a pool or pit for collecting filthy water.

cestus [ses'tus] *n* a girdle, esp one worn by a bride.

cetacean [se-tā'shi-an] *adj* of an order (Cetacea) of aquatic mammals, mostly marine, including the whales, dolphins, porpoises, etc.—*n* cetā'cean.—*adj* cetā'ceous.

chafe [chāf] *vt* to make hot by rubbing; to fret or wear by rubbing; to cause to fret or rage.—*vt* to fret or rage.—*n* heat; anger.—*n* chaf'ing dish.

chafer [chāf'êr] *n* any of various large beetles.

chaff [chāf] *n* the husks of grain as threshed or winnowed; cut hay and straw; worthless matter.

chaffer [chaf'êr] *vi* to bargain; to haggle about the price.—*n* chaff'erer.

chaffinch [chaf'inch, -sh] *n* a European songbird (*Fringilla coelebs*) of the finch family.

chagrin [shâ-grin'] *n* that which wears or gnaws the mind; vexation; annoyance.—*vt* to vex or annoy.

chain [chān] *n* a series of links or rings passing through one another; any continuous series; anything that binds; a measure of 100 links used in surveying; a group of stores, etc. owned by a company; chain' stitch, an ornamental stitch resembling the links of a chain.

chair [chār] *n* a moveable seat for one, with a back to it; the seat or office of one in authority; a chairman.—*ns* chair' lift, a set of seats suspended from overhead wires for taking sightseers or skiers up a hill; chair'man, -woman, -person, one who takes the chair, or presides at a meeting; chair'manship.

chalcedony [kal-sed'ó-ni, or kal'-] *n* a kind of quartz with the luster of wax, generally pale blue or gray in color.

chalet [shal'ā] *n* a summer hut used by Swiss herdsmen in the Alps; any similar building.

chalice [chal'is] *n* a cup or bowl; a communion cup.

chalk [chök] *n* a soft limestone, composed of calcium carbonate; a substitute for this used for writing on a blackboard.—*adj* chalk'y.—*n* chalk'iness.—chalk up, to score, get

challenge [chal'enj] *vt* to summon to a combat or contest; to defy; to accuse (of—*with* with); to object to; to claim (as due).—*n* a demand for identification; a calling of anyone or anything in question.—*n* chall'enger.

chalybeate [ka-lib'e-āt] *adj* containing iron.—*n* a water or medicine containing iron.

chamber [chām'bêr] *n* a room, esp a bedroom; the place where an assembly meets; a compartment.—*adj* cham'bered; cham'ber mu'sic, music for performance by a small group, as a string quartet.—chamber of commerce, an association formed in a town or district to promote the interests of local commerce.

chamberlain [chām'bêr-lin] *n* an officer in charge of the private apartments of a king or nobleman; (*Brit*) the treasurer of a corporation.

chameleon [ka-mēl'yòn, or ē-ón] *n* any of various American lizards (genus *Anolis*) capable of changing their color; an inconstant person.

chamfer [cham'fêr, or sham'] *n* a bevel or slope; a groove, channel, or furrow.—*vt* to groove or bevel.

chamois [sham'wä] *n* a small Alpine antelope (*Rupicapra rupicapra*) of Europe and the Caucasus; chamm'y, shamm'y [sham'i] a soft pliable leather made from its skin; any material resembling this.

champ [champ] *vti* to make a snapping noise with the jaws in chewing.

champagne [sham'pān'] *n* a white sparkling wine from *Champagne* in France.

champion [cham'pi-ón] *n* one who fights in single combat for himself or for another; one who defends a cause; in games, a competitor who has excelled all others.—*adj* firstclass.—*vt* to defend, to support.—*n* cham'pionship.

chance [chäns] *n* that which falls out or happens without assignable cause; an unexpected event; risk; opportunity; possibility; probability; a ticket in a lottery.—*vt* to risk.—*vi* to happen.—*adj* happening accidentally, without assignable cause, without design.—*adj* chanc'y.

chancel [chän'sl] *n* the part of the church around the altar, for the clergy and the choir.

chancellery, chancellory [chän'sê-lê-ri] *n* office attached to embassy; the office or staff of an embassy or consulate;—*pl* -ies.

chancellor [chän'sel-ór] *n* a high government official, as, in certain countries, a prime minister; in some universities, the president or other executive officer; a chief judge of a court of chancery or equity in some States; any of several church officials.—*n* chan'cellorship.

chancery [chän'sêr-i] *n* a court of equity; an office of public archives; a chancellery.

chandelier [shan-dê-lêr'] *n* a frame with branches for holding lights.—*n* chandler [chand'lêr] a candle maker; a dealer in candles; a dealer retailing supplies of a specified kind (a *yacht chandler*).

change [chānj] *vt* to alter or make different; to make to pass from one state (into another); to put, give, take, put on, in place of another or others; to exchange; to give or get smaller coin for.—*adj* change'able .—*adv* change'ably.—*ns* change-abili'ity, change'ableness.—*adj* change'ful—*adv* change'fully.—*n* change'fulness.—*adj* change'less.—*n* change'ling, a child secretly left in place of another.

channel [chan'l] *n* the bed or the deeper part of a river, harbor, etc.; a body of water joining two larger ones; a navigable passage; (*pl*) an official means of communication.

chant [chänt] *vti* to sing; to celebrate in song; to recite in a singing manner.—*n* song.—*ns* chant'er; chant'ry, an endowment, or chapel, for the chanting of masses.

Chanuka, Channuka or Hanuka [hā'nu-kà] *n* (*Judaism*) the Feast of Lights, an eight-day holiday in December memorializing the successful rebellion against Greco-Syrian despots.

chaos [kā'os] *n* disorder; the state of matter before it was reduced to order by the Creator.—*adj* chaot'ic, confused.—*adv* chaot'ically.

chap¹ [chap] *vti* to crack open, split, roughen, the skin in cold weather.—*n* a chapped place in the skin.

chap² [chap] *n* (*inf*) a fellow.

chap³ [chap] *n* (*pl*) the mouth and lower cheeks.—*adj* chap'-fall'en, having the lower jaw hanging loosely; depressed.

chapbook [chap'book] *n* a small book containing poems, stories, tales, etc.

chapel [chap'êl] *n* a building for Christian worship, not so large as a church; a subordinate or private place of worship; an association of printers in a printing office.

chaperon, chaperone [shap'e-rōn] *n* a lady under whose care a girl appears in society.

chaplain [chap'lin] *n* a clergyman serving in a religious capacity with the armed forces, or in a prison, hospital, etc.—*n* chap'laincy.

chaplet [chap'let] *n* a garland or wreath for the head.

chaps [chaps] *npl* leather trousers without a seat, worn over ordinary trousers by cowboys.

chapter [chap'têr] *n* a main division of a book; a subject or category generally; an organized branch of some society or fraternity.—*n* chap'ter house.

char¹ [chär] *n* any of a genus (*Salvelinus*) of small trouts.

char[char] *vt* to reduce to charcoal or carbon by burning.—*vti* to scorch;—*pr p* **charr'ing.**

character [kar'ak-tèr] *n* a letter or distinctive mark; writing generally, handwriting; a secret cipher; any essential feature or peculiarity; a formal statement of such qualities; a person of remarkable individuality; a personality as created in a play or novel.—*vt* **char'acterize.**—*ns* **characteriza'tion; characteris'tic.**—*adj* **characteris'tic.**—*adv* **characteris'tically.**

charade [shar-ād'] *n* an acted riddle in which the syllables of the word proposed.

charcoal [chär'kōl] *n* the carbonaceous residue from the partial combustion of wood or animal matter.

charge [chärj] *vt* to load, to fill (with); to burden; to lay a task, trust upon (one); to exhort; to accuse; to ask as the price; to attack at a rush.—*vi* to make an onset; an accumulation of electricity; command; exhortation; accusation; attack or onset; (*pl*) expenses.—*adj* **charge'able.**—*n* **charg'er.**

chariot [char'i-ôt] *n* a pleasure or state carriage; a car used in ancient warfare or racing.—*n* **charioteer'.**

charisma [kar-is'må] *n* a spiritual power given by God; personal quality that enables an individual to influence his fellows.—*adj* **charismat'ic.**

charity [char'i-ti] *n* (*NT*) universal love; benevolence; a benevolent fund or institution.—*adj* **char'itable.**—*n* **char'itableness.**—*adv* **char'itably.**

charlatan [shär'la-tàn] *n* a quack.—*n* **char'latanry.**

charlock [chär'lok] *n* wild mustard (*Brassica kaber*).

charlotte [shär'lot] *n* a molded dessert consisting of fruit, whipped cream or custard enclosed by strips of bread, ladyfingers, or biscuits.

charm [chärm] *n* a spell; something thought to possess occult power, attractiveness.—*vt* to influence by a charm; to enchant; to delight.—*adj* **charmed.**—*n* **charm'er.**—*adv* **charm'ingly.**

charnel [chär'nèl] *n* a place where the bones thrown up by gravediggers are put.—Also **charnel house.**

chart [chärt] *n* a map, esp for use in navigation; an information sheet with tables, graphs, etc.; a table, graph, etc.

charter [chärt'èr] *n* any formal writing conferring or confirming titles, rights, or privileges, or the like.—*vt* to establish by charter; to let or hire, as a ship, on contract.

chary [chär'i] *adj* sparing (of, in); unwilling to risk (*with of*); cautious.—*adv* **char'ily.**—*n* **char'iness.**

chase[chās] *vt* to pursue; to hunt; to drive away.—*n* pursuit; a hunting; that which is hunted; an unenclosed game preserve.—*n* **chas'er.**

chase[chās] *vt* to decorate (metal) with engraving.—*n* **chas'er.**

chasm [kazm] *n* a yawning or gaping hollow.

chassé [shas'ā] *n* a gliding step in dancing.

chassis [chas'ē, shas'ē] *n* the frame of an automobile or airplane; a frame, as for the parts of a TV set; the assembled frame and parts;—*pl* **chassis**

chaste [chāst] *adj* modest; virtuous; virgin; pure in taste and style.—*adv* **chaste'ly.**—*ns* **chaste'ness; chäs'tity.**

chasten [chās'n] *vt* to free from faults by punishing—hence, to punish or correct.

chastise [chas'tīz'] *vt* to punish for the purpose of correction; to reduce to order or to obedience.—*n* **chas'tisement.**

chat [chat] *vi* to talk easily or familiarly;—*pr p* **chatt'ing;** *pt p* **chatt'ed.**—*adj* **chatty.**

chattel [chat'èl] *n* any kind of property that is not freehold.

chatter [chat'èr] *vi* to talk idly or rapidly; to sound as the teeth when one shivers.—*n* idle talk.—*ns* **chatt'erbox, chatt'erer.**

chauffeur [shō'fèr, shō-feer'] *n* one employed to drive a private automobile for someone else.

chauvinism [shō'vin-izm] *n* excessive national pride and contempt for other countries; excessive attachment to any group, cause, etc.—*n* **chau'vinist.**—*adj* **chauvinist'ic.**—See also **male chauvinist pig.**

chaw [chö] *vt* (*dial*) to chew, as tobacco.

cheap [chēp] *adj* low in price; of small value; paltry; inferior.—*vti* **cheap'en.**—*adv* **cheap'ly.**—*ns* **cheap'ness.**

cheat [chēt] *vt* to deceive; to defraud.—*vi* to practice deceit.—*n* a fraud; one who cheats.—*n* **cheat'er.**

check[chek] *vt* to bring to a stand; to restrain or hinder; to rebuke; to scrutinize; to verify.—*n* in chess, a threat to the king; repulse; a mark put against items in a list; a token or counter; a pattern of small squares.—*ns* **check'er, check'mate,** in chess, a position from which the king cannot escape; **check'out,** the desk at a self-service store, etc., where one pays for goods.

check[chek] *n* a money order to a bank.—*n* **checkbook,** a book containing blank checks to be drawn on a bank.

checker [chek'èr] (*arch*) chessboard.

checkers [chek'èrz] *n pl* a board game for two.

cheddar [ched'är] *n* a kind of cheese first made at *Cheddar* in Somersetshire, England.

cheek [chēk] *n* the side of the face below the eye; (*inf*) effrontery, impudence.—*adj* **cheek'y.**

cheer [chēr] *n* disposition, frame of mind; joy; a shout of approval or welcome; entertainment; fare, food.—*vt* to comfort; to encourage; to applaud.—*vi* to cheer up.—*adj* **cheer'ful, cheer'y.**—*advs* **cheer'fully; cheer'ily.**—*ns* **cheer'fulness; cheer'iness.**—*adj* **cheer'less.**—*n* **cheer'lessness.**

cheese [chēz] *n* the curd of milk coagulated and often pressed into a hard mass.; **cheese'par'ing,** miserly economy.—*adj* miserly, niggardly.—*adj* **chees'y,** having the consistency or odor of cheese; containing cheese.

cheetah [chē'tä] *n* a large spotted cat.

chef [shef] *n* a master cook.

chemise [she-mēz'] *n* a woman's short, one-piece undergarment.

chemistry [kem'is-tri] *n* the science that treats of the properties of substances both elementary and compound, and of the laws of their combination and action one upon another.—*adjs* **chem'ical.**—*adv* **chem'ically.** *n pl* **chem'icals.**—*n* **chem'ist.**

chenille [she-nēl'] *n* a wool, cotton, silk, or rayon yarn with a protruding pile.

cherish [cher'ish] *vt* to protect and treat with affection.

cheroot [she-rōōt'] *n* a cigar cut square at each end.

cherry [cher'i] *n* any of several species of trees of the same genus (*Prunus*) as the plum; the small fruit, which they bear.

cherub [cher'ub] *n* a winged creature with human face;—*pl* **cher'ubs, cher'ubim** [(-y)ōō-bim], **cher'ubims.**—*adjs* **cheru'bic** [-ōō'bik], **-al.**

chess [ches] *n* a game played by two persons with figures or 'men', which are moved on a checkerboard;—*n pl* **chess'men,** pieces used in chess.

chest [chest] *n* a large strong box; a treasury; the part of the body between the neck and the abdomen, the thorax.

chesterfield [chest'èr-fēld] *n* a long overcoat; a heavily padded sofa.

chestnut [ches'nut] *n* any of a genus (*Castanea*) of trees or shrubs of the beech family, the edible nut of a chestnut; (*slang*) a stale joke.—*adj* of chestnut color, grayish to reddish brown.

chevalier [shev-a-lēr'] *n* a cavalier; a knight; a gallant.

cheviot [shev'ē-ot] *n* a breed of hardy sheep that are a source of quality mutton; a cloth made from their wool.

chevron [shev'rón] *n* a rafter; the V-shaped bar on the sleeve of a uniform, showing rank.

chew [choo] *vt* to bruise and grind with the teeth.—*n* **chew'ing gum.**

chiaroscuro [kyär-o-skōō'rō] *n* management of light and shade in a picture.

chic [shēk] *n* style, fashion.—*adj* stylish.

chicane [shi-kān'] *vi* to use shifts and tricks.—*vt* to deceive.—*n* (also **chicā'nery**), trickery or artifice.

Chicano [chi-kän'ō] *n* a US citizen or inhabitant of Mexican descent;—*pl*—**nos.**

chick [chik] *n* the young of a fowl..—*adj* **chick'enheart'ed.**—*ns* **chick'enpox,** a contagious febrile disease.

chicle [chik'l, chick'li] *n* the gum of the sapodilla tree.

chicory, chickory [chik'o-ri] *n* a salad plant; its dried, ground, roasted root used to flavor coffee.

chide [chīd] *vt* to scold, rebuke.

chief [chēf] *adj* head; principal, most important.—*n* the head of a clan or tribe; a leader.—*adv* **chief'ly.**—*ns* **chief'tain,** [-tin], the head of a clan; a leader.

chiffon [shē'fõ, shif'on] *n* a thin gauzy material.—*n* **chiffonier,** [shif-on-ēr], *n* a high bureau or chest of drawers.

chignon [shē'nyõ] *n* a fold or roll of hair worn on the back of the head and neck.

chilblain [chil'blān] *n* a painful red swelling, esp on hands and feet, in cold weather.

child [chīld] *n* a very young person; a son or daughter;—*pl* **chil'dren.**—*ns* **child'bear'ing, child'bed,** the state of a woman brought to bed with child; **child'birth, child'hood.**—*adj* **child'ish.**—*adv* **child'ishly.**—*n* **child'ishness.**—*adjs* **child'less, child'like.**

chill [chil] *n* coldness; a cold that causes shivering; anything that damps or disheartens.—*adj* shivering with cold; slightly cold.—*vti* to make or become cold;—*adj* **chill'y.**—*ns* **chill'iness.**

chili, chille, chilli [chil'i] *n* the pod of some of the capsicums, pungent and stimulant.

chime [chīm] *n* a set of bells or metal tubes, etc. tuned in a scale; the ringing of such bells; accord; harmony.—*vi* to sound in harmony; to accord or agree.—*vt* to strike, or cause to sound in harmony. —**chime in,** to break into a conversation or discussion.

chimera, chimaera [kī-mir-á or ki-] *n* in Greek mythology, a fire-breathing she-monster made up of the parts of various animals; **chimera, chimaera,** an impossible fancy.—*adjs* **chimer'ic, chimer'ical.**

chimney [chim'ni] *n* a passage for the escape of fumes, smoke, or heated air; **chim'ney sweep, chim'ney sweep'er,** one who sweeps or cleans chimneys.

chimpanzee [chim-pan'zē also shim-] *n* an anthropoid ape of equatorial Africa.

chin [chin] *n* the face below the mouth.

china [chīn'á] *n* porcelain originally made in China; any earthenware.

chinchilla [chin-chil'a] *n* a small rodent of S America; its soft gray fur.

chine [chīn] *n* the spine or backbone; a ridge, crest.

chink[1] [chingk] *n* a cleft, a narrow opening.

chink[2] [chingk] *n* the clink, as of coins.

Chinook [chin-ook'] *n* member of an Amerindian people of Oregon; -*pl* **-nook, -s; chinook,** a warm moist wind that blows down the eastern side of the Rocky Mountains.

chintz [chints] *n* glazed cotton printed in several colors.

chip [chip] *vt* to strike small pieces from the surface of;—*pr p* **chipp'ing;** *pt p* **chipped.**—*n* a small piece chipped off; a thin slice of food; a games counter; a minute piece of semiconducting material on which microcircuits can be printed.

chipmunk [chip'mungk] *n* any of various small striped semiterrestial American squirrels.

Chippendale [chip'ěn-dāl] *adj* applied to a style of furniture made in England in the 18th century.

chiropodist [kī-rop'o-dist] *n* one who practices chiropody; a podiatrist.—*n* **chirop'ody,** the care and treatment of minor ailments of the feet.

chiropractic [kī'rō-prak-tik] *n* method or practice of curing diseases by manipulating joints, esp of the spine;—*n* **chi'ropractor**

chirp [chûrp] *n* the sharp, thin sound of certain birds.—*vi* to make such a sound.—*adj* **chirp'y.**

chisel [chiz'ěl] *n* tool with the end beveled to a cutting edge.—*vt* to cut, carve, etc., with a chisel.

chit[1] [chit] *n* a voucher or a sum owed for drink, food, etc.; a brief note; an order or pass.—*Also* **chitt'y.**

chit[2] [chit] *n* a child (*slightingly*) a girl.

chitin [kī'tin] *n* the substance that forms most of the hard parts of crustaceans, insects, and spiders.

chivalry [shiv'ál-ri] *n* the usages and qualifications of chevaliers or feudal knights; bravery and courtesy.—*adjs* **chival'ric, chiv'alrous.**—*adv* **chiv'alrously.**

chlorine [klō'rēn, -rin, rīn] *n* a yellow green gas used in bleaching, disinfecting, and in industry. **chlō'rate,** a salt containing the group Cl0₃.—*n* **chlō'ride.**—*vt* **chlō'rinate.**—*ns* **chloroform,** [klor'ō-förm² or ¹klō'rō-förm], a colorless, volatile liquid used to induce insensibility (also *vt*); **chlō'rophyll,** the ordinary green photosynthetic coloring matter of vegetation.

chock [chok] *vt* to fasten as with a wedge.

chocolate [chok'ō-lât] *n* a paste made of the roasted pounded cacao bean; beverage made by dissolving this paste in boiling water; a small candy with a center (as fondant, etc.) and chocolate coating.—*adj* **chocolate-colored,** dark reddish brown.

choice [chois] *n* act or power of choosing; the thing chosen; alternative; preference; the best (part.—*adj* worthy of being chosen; select.

choir [kwīr] *n* a chorus or band of singers, esp those belonging to a church; the part of a church appropriated to the singers.

choke [chōk] *vt* to throttle; to suffocate; to stop or obstruct.—*vi* to be choked.—*n* the action of choking; the sound of choking; the valve that chokes a carburetor. **chok'er,** one who chokes; a high collar; a high tight necklace.

choler [kol'ěr] *n* the bile; anger.—*adj* **chol'eric.**

cholera [kol'ěr-a] *n* any of several severe, infectious intestinal diseases of man and domestic animals.

choose [chōōz] *vt* to take (one thing) in preference to another.—*vi* to will or determine, to think, fit;—*pt* **chose;** *ptp* **chos'en.**—*adj* **choos'(e)y.**

chop[1] [chop] *vt* to cut with a sudden blow; to cut into small pieces.—*n* a cut of meat and bone from the rib, loin, or shoulder; a sharp downward blow.—*ns* **chop'-house** ; **chop'p'er,** one that chops.

chop[2] [chop] *vi* to change direction.—*pr p* **chopp'ing;** *pt p* **chopped.**

chop[3] [chop] *n* the chap or jaw.

chord[1] [körd] *n* (*mus*) three or more notes played together.

chord[2] [körd] *n* (*poet*) a string of a musical instrument.

chore [chōr, chôr] *n* a household task; an unenjoyable task.

choreography [kor-i-og'ra-fi] *n* dancing; the art of arranging dances.—*adj* **choreograph'ic.**—*n* **choreog'rapher.**

chortle [chört'l] *vi* to utter a low deep laugh.—Also *n*.

chorus [kō'rus, kō'] *n* a band of singers and dancers performing together; a refrain; a combined utterance.—*vt* to sing or say together.—*adj* **chōr'al.**—*n* **chôrale', chôrral'.**—*adv* **chôr'ally.**—*adj* **cho'ric.**—*n* **chôr'ister.**

chose, chosen *See* **choose.**

chow [chow] *n* (*inf*), food.

chow chow [chow chow] *n* a breed of dog from China.—Also **chow.**

chrism [krizm] *n* consecrated or holy oil, confirmation, and ordination.

Christ [krīst] *n* the Anointed, the Messiah.—*vt* **christen** [kris'n], to baptize in the name of Christ; to give a name to.—*ns* **Christendom** [kris'n-], the part of the world in which Christianity prevails; **Chris'tian** (chán), a follower of Christ.—*adj* relating to Christ or His religion.—*vt* **chris'tianize.**—*n* **Christian'ity,** the religion of Christ; **Christian name,** a given name at baptism; loosely, a forename; **Christian Science,** a religion—founded in 1866 by Mary Baker Eddy.

Christmas [kris'mas] *n* an annual festival, in memory of the birth of Christ.—*adj* **Christ'massy, Christmassy, Christ'mas tree,** a tree, usu. an evergreen, decorated at Christmas.

Christology [kris-tol'o-ji] *n* that branch of theology which treats of the nature and person of Christ.

chromatic [krō-mat'ik] *adj* relating to color or colors; (*mus*) proceeding by half tones;—*ns* **chromatic'ity; chrōme,** chromium; something plated with an alloy of chromium.—*vt* to treat with a chromium compound (as in dying). **chrō'mium,** metallic element.—*adj* **chrōm'ic, chrō'mosome,** any of the microscopic rod-shaped bodies bearing genes.

chronic [kron'ik, -âl] *adj* lasting a long time.

chronicle [kron'i-kl] *n* a record of events in order of time; a history.—*vt* to record.—*n* **chron'icler.**

chronograph [kron'o-gräf] *n* an instrument for taking exact measurements of time.

chronology [kron-ol'o-ji] *n* the science of computing time and of dating events; a scheme of time; order in time.—*ns* **chronol'oger, chronol'ogist.**—*adjs* **chronolog'ic, -al.**—*adv* **chronolog'ically.**

chronometer [kron-om'é-tér] *n* a very accurate form of timekeeper.

chrysalis [kris'a-lis], **chrysalid** [kris'a-lid], *n* the pupa of a butterfly, enclosed in a cocoon; the cocoon.—*adj* **chrys'alid.**

chrysanthemum [kris-an'thè-mum] *n* a genus (*Chrysanthemum*) of composite plants; the flower head of a garden form.

chub [chub] *n* a small freshwater fish..—*adj* **chubb'y,** plump.—*n* **chubb'iness.**

chuck [chuk] *n* a gentle blow (under the chin).—*vt* to pat gently (under the chin); to toss; to pitch.

chuckle [chuk′l] *n* a quiet laugh; the cry of a hen.

chum [chum] *n* (*inf*) a close companion. — *vi* (*inf*) to be a chum. — *adj* **chumm′y**.

chump [chump] *n* (*inf*) a stupid person; a fool.

chunk [chungk] *n* a short, thick piece of anything, as wood, bread, etc. — *adj* **chunk′y**.

Church [chûrch] *n* all Christians; a particular Christian denomination; **church**, a building for public worship, esp Christian worship; the clerical profession; a religious service. — *vt* to bring to a church service on a special occasion. — *ns* **church′man, church′war′den**, a lay officer who looks after certain secular interests of a church; **church′yard**, the yard around a church often used as a burial ground.

churl [chûrl] *n* a rustic; an ill-bred, surly fellow — *adj* **churl′ish**. — *adv* **churl′ishly**. — *n* **churl′ishness**.

churn [chûrn] *n* a container for the production of butter. — *vt* to agitate so as to obtain butter; to shake or beat violently.

chute [shōōt] *n* a waterfall, rapid; an inclined trough or a passage for sending down water, logs, rubbish etc.

chutney [chut′ni] *n* a relish of fruits, spices, and herbs.

cicada [si-kā′da], **cicala** [si-kä′la] *ns* any of a family of large flylike insects with transparent wings, the male producing a loud, shrill sound.

cicatrix [sik′a-triks] *n* a scar over a wound that is healed; — *pl* **cicatrices** [si-kat′ri-sēz]. — *vt* **cic′atrize**.

cicerone [chich-er-ō′nā] *n* a guide.

cider [sī′der] *n* a drink made from apples.

cigar [si′gär] *n* a compact roll of tobacco leaves for smoking. — *ns* **cigarette′**, finely cut tobacco rolled in thin paper. **cigarill′o**, a small, thin cigar.

cinch [sinch] *n* saddle or pack girth; (*coll*) something easy to do. — *vt* to tighten a girth on.

cincture [singk′tyúr] *n* a girdle or belt. — *vt* to gird, encompass.

cinder [sin′dėr] *n* a tiny piece of partly burned wood, etc.; (*pl*) ashes from wood or coal.

cine- [sin′i-] in composition, motion picture as **cinecamera**, a camera for taking motion pictures; **cinefilm**, film for a **cinecamera**.

cinematography [sin-i-mat-o′gräf-i] *n* the art or science of motion-picture photography. — *n* **cinematog′rapher**.

cinnamon [sin′a-mòn] *n* the spicy bark of any of several trees of the laurel family; the tree, a light yellowish-brown. — Also *adj*.

cipher [sī′fėr] *n* (*arith*) the symbol O; any of the Arabic numerals; anything of little value; a nonentity; a secret mode of writing.

circle [sûr′kl] *n* a plane figure bounded by one line every point of which is equally distant from a certain point called the center; the line which bounds the figure; a ring; a company or group (of people); extent, scope, as of influence.

circuit [sûr′kit] *n* the way or path round; the path of an electric current; area, extent; a round made in the exercise of a calling; a chain or association. — *adj* **circū′itous**. — *adv* **circū′itously**.

circular [sûr′kū-lár] *adj* round; ending in itself; circuitous. — *n* an advertisement, etc. sent to a number of person. — *n* **circular′ity**. — *vy* **cir′cularize**.

circulate [sûr′ku-lāt] *vt* to make or go round as in a circle; to spread. — *vi* to move around; to be spread about. — *n* **circulā′tion**. — *adj* **cir′culatory**.

circumcise [sûr′kum-sīz] *vt* to cut off the foreskin of (a male) or the clitoris of (a female). — *n* **circumci′sion**.

circumference [sûr-kum′fėr-ėns] *n* the boundary line of a circle, a ball, etc.; the length of this line. — *adj* **circumferen′tial**.

circumflex [sûr′kum-fleks] *n* an accent ( ) originally denoting a rising and falling of the voice on a vowel or syllable. — Also *adj*.

circumlocution [sûr-kum-lō-kū′sh(ò)n] *n* roundabout and evasive speech.

circumnavigate [sûr-kum-nav′i-gāt] *vt* to sail or fly around — *ns* **circumnavigā′tion; circumnav′igator**.

circumscribe [sûr-kum-skrīb′] *vt* to draw a line round ; to confine within limits, restrict. — *n* **circumscrip′tion**.

circumspect [sûr′kum-spekt] *adj* looking round on all sides watchfully, cautious, prudent. — *n* **circumspec′tion**. — *adv* **cir′cumspectly**. — *n* **cir′cumspectness**.

circumstance [sûr′kum-stáns] *n* a fact or event; a detail; the state of one's affairs.. — *adj* **circumstantial**. — *adv* **circumstan′tially**. — *vt* **circumstan′tiate**, [-shi-] to prove by circumstances.

circumvent [sûr-kum-vent′] *vt* to surround so as to intercept or capture; to outwit (a person). — *n* **circumven′tion**.

circus [sûr′kus] *n* a large arena for the exhibition of games, feats of horsemanship etc.; a traveling show consisting of exhibitions of horsemanship, acrobatics, performances by animals, etc.

cirrus [sir′us] *n* thin, wispy, feathery clouds formed of ice crystals; — *pl* **cirri**, [sir′ī]. — *adjs* **cirr′ous**.

cistern [sis′tėrn] *n* an artificial reservoir or tank for storing water.

citadel [sit′a-dèl] *n* a fortress in or near a city.

cite [sīt] *vt* to call or summon; to summon to appear in court; to quote; to adduce. — *n* **citā′tion**.

citizen [sit′i-zėn] *n* a member of a state or nation. — *n* **cit′izenship**.

citron [sit′ròn] *n* a fruit resembling a lemon; the tree bearing this fruit. — *n* **cit′rus**, a genus including the citron, lemon, lime, orange, etc. — **citric acid**, the acid to which lemons and certain other fruits owe their sourness.

city [sit′i] *n* a large town; the people of a city.

civic [siv′ik] *adj* pertaining to a city or citizen. — *n* **civics**, the science of citizenship.

civil [siv′il] *adj* pertaining to the community or to a citizen; having the refinement of city-bred people; polite; pertaining to ordinary, as opposed to military or ecclesiastical, life; (*law*) relating to actions other than criminal. — *ns* **civil′ian, civil′ity**, politeness. — *adv* **civ′illy**.

civilize [siv′il-īz] *vt* to reclaim from barbarism; to instruct in arts and refinements. — *n* **civilizā′tion**. — *adj* **civ′ilized**.

clack [klak] *vi* to make a noise as by striking wood with wood; to talk noisily.

clad [klad] *pt*, *pt p* of **clothe**. — *adj* clothed or covered. — *n* **cladd′ing**.

claim [klām] *vt* to call for; to demand as a right. — *n* a demand for something supposed due; right; the thing claimed. — *adj* **claim′able**. — *n* **claim′ant**, one who makes a claim.

clairvoyance [klär-voi′áns] *n* the alleged power of seeing things not present to the senses. — *n* and *adj* **clairvoy′ant**.

clam [klam] *n* an edible marine bivalve molusk; a freshwater mussel.

clammy [klam′ē] *adj* moist and sticky. — *n* **clamm′iness**.

clamant [klam′ánt, klām′ánt] *adj* calling loudly, insistently.

clamber [klam′bėr] *vi* to climb with difficulty, grasping with the hands and feet. — *n* **clamb′erer**.

clamor [klam′ór] *n* a loud continuous outcry; uproar. — *adj* **clam′orous**. — *adv* **clam′orously**. — *n* **clam′orousness**.

clamp [klamp] *n* a piece of timber, iron, etc. used to fasten things together or to strengthen any framework. — *vt* to bind with a clamp.

clan [klan] *n* a tribe or collection of families subject to a single chieftain, and supposed to have a common ancestor; a clique, sect or group. — *adj* **clann′ish**. — *adv* **clann′ishly**. — *ns* **clann′ishness**.

clandestine [klan-des′-tin] *adj* concealed or hidden, private, sly. — *adv* **clandes′tinely**.

clang [klang] *vi* to produce a loud, deep ringing sound. — *vt* to cause to do so. — *n* a ringing sound. — *n* **clang′or**. — *adj* **clang′orous**. — *adv* **clang′orously**.

clank [klangk] *n* a sound, less prolonged than a clang.

clap[1] [klap] *n* a sudden blow or stroke; the noise made by the sudden striking together of two things, as the hands; a burst of sound. — *vt* to strike together so as to make a noise; to applaud with the hands; to put suddenly. — *vi* to strike together with noise; to applaud; — *pr p* **clapped** — *ns* **clapp′er**, **clap-trap**, empty words.

claret [klar′et] *n* a dry dark red wine of Bordeaux.

clarify [klar′i-fī] *vt* to make clear or pure. — *pr p* **clar′ifying**; *pt p* **clar′ified**. — *ns* **clarificā′tion; clar′ifier**.

clarinet [klar-in-et′] *n* an orchestral woodwind instrument.

clarion [klar′i-òn] *n* a kind of trumpet whose note is clear and shrill; a thrilling note.

clarity [klar′i-ti] *n* clearness.

clash [klash] *n* a loud noise, such as is caused by the striking together of weapons; contradiction. — *vi* to dash noisily (against, into); to meet in opposition; to disagree. — *vt* to strike noisily together.

clasp [kläsp] *n* a hinged fastening; an embrace. — *vt* to fasten with a clasp; to grasp in the hand; to hold in the arms, embrace. — *n* **clasp'knife.**

class [kläs] *n* a rank or order of persons or things; high rank or social standing; a number of students or scholars who are taught together; a group of things alike in some respect. — *vt* to form into a class or classes; **class'ic,** any standard writer or work; (*pl*) Greek and Latin studies. — *adjs* **class'ic, -al,** of the highest class or rank, esp in literature; of the best Greek and Roman writers; of music conforming to certain standards of form, complexity, etc. traditional; authoritative. — *adv* **class'ically.** — *ns* **class'icism, class'icist.** — *adj* **class'y.**

classify [klas'i-fī] *vt* to arrange in classes; to make secret for security reasons; — *pr p* **class'ifying;** *pt p* **class'ified** — *n* **classification.** — *adj* **class'ified.**

clatter [klat'èr] *n* a repeated rattling noise; noisy talk.

clause [klöz] *n* a sentence; part of a sentence with subject and predicate; an article or part of a contract, will, etc.

claustrophobia [klö-strö-fö'bi-a] *n* a morbid dread of confined places.

clavichord [klav'i-körd] *n* a stringed musical instrument with a keyboard, predecessor of the piano.

clavicle [klav'i-kl] *n* the collarbone. — *adj* **clavic'ular.**

claw [klö] *n* the hooked nail of an animal or bird; the leg of a crab, insect, etc. or its pointed end or pincer; anything like a claw. — *vti* to scratch or tear as with the claws or nails.

clay [klā] *n* a tenacious ductile earthy material; earth in general; the human body. — *adj* **clay'ey.**

claymore [klā-mōr', -mōr'] *n* a large sword formerly used by the Scottish Highlanders.

clean [klēn] *adj* free from dirt or defilement; pure; guiltless; neat; complete. — *adv* quite; entirely; smoothly, neatly. — *vti* to make or to be clean or free from dirt. — *ns* **clean'er, cleanness** [klēn'ne+s]. — *adj* **cleanly** [klen'li]. — *adv* [klēn'li]. — *n* **cleanliness** [klen'li-nes].

cleanse [klenz] *vt* to make clean or pure. — *n* **cleans'er.**

clear [klēr] *adj* pure, bright, undimmed; transparent; free from obstruction or difficulty; plain, distinct, obvious; without blemish. — *adv* plainly; wholly; apart from. — *vt* to make clear; to empty; to free from obscurity or obstruction; to free from suspicion; acquit or vindicate; to leap, or pass by or over. — *vi* to become clear; to go away. — *adv* **clear'ly.** — *ns* **clear'ness, clear'ance,** act of clearing. — *ns* **clear'ing, clear'inghouse,** an office in which banks adjust their mutual claims.

cleat [klē] *n* a wedge; a piece of wood nailed across a structure to keep it firm; a projection to which ropes are made fast.

cleave [klēv] *vti* to divide by a blow; split; sever. — *pr p* **cleav'ing;** *pt* **clōve** or **cleft;** *pt p* **cleaved** or **clov'en** or **cleft.** — *ns* **cleav'age, cleav'er.**

cleave [klēv] *vi* to stick or adhere. — *prp* **cleaving** *pt* **cleaved** or **clove** or **clave;** *pt p* **cleaved.**

clef [klef] *n* a sign placed on a musical staff by which the pitch of notes is fixed.

cleft [kleft] *n* an opening made by cleaving or splitting; a crack, fissure, or chink.

clematis [klem'a-tis] *n* a vine or herb of the buttercup family having three leaflets on each leaf and showy flowers.

clement [klem'ènt] *adj* (of weather) mild; kind, merciful. — *n* **clem'ency.** — *adv* **clem'ently.**

clench [klench] *vt* to close (the teeth or fist) tightly; to grasp; to clinch. — *n* a firm grip.

clerestory [klēr-stō'ri] *n* an outside wall with windows that rises above a roofed section of a building. — Also **clearstory.**

clergy [klûr'ji] *n* ministers, priests, rabbis, etc. collectively; the ministers of the Christian religion. — *n* **cler'gyman.** — *adjs* **cler'ic, -al** [kler'ik, -àl]. — *ns* **cler'ic.**

clerk [klûrk] *n* a layman with minor duties in a church; an office worker who types, files, etc.; a public official who keeps the records of a court, town, etc. — *adj* **cler'ical.**

clever [klev'èr] *adj* able or dexterous; ingenious; intelligent; skilful. — *n* **clev'erness.** — *adv* **clev'erly.**

clew, clue [klōō] *n* a ball of thread, or the thread in it; anything that points to the solution of a mystery.

cliché [klē-shā] *n* a hackneyed phrase; something that has become commonplace.

click [klik] *n* a short, sharp ticking sound. — *vi* to make a light, sharp sound.

client [klī'ènt] *n* one who employs a lawyer, accountant, or consultant; one using the services of a social agency; a customer. — *ns* **clientele** [klī'en-těl], **clientèle** [klē-ä-tel'].

cliff [klif] *n* a high steep rock; the steep side of a mountain.

climacteric [klī-mak'tèr-ik or klī-mak-ter'ik] *n* a critical period in human life. — *adj* **climacter'ical.**

climate [klī'màt] *n* the average weather conditions of a region.

climax [klī'maks] *n* the arrangement of a series of ideas, or of words or phrases, in ascending order of emphasis; the last term of the arrangement, a culmination. — *vti* to reach, or bring to a climax.

climb [klīm] *vti* to ascend or mount by clutching with the hands and feet; to ascend with effort. — *n* an ascent. — *ns* **climb'er.**

clime [klīm] *n* climate.

clinch [klinch] to settle or confirm.

cling [kling] *vi* to adhere or stick close; to adhere in interest or affection. — *pr p* **clinging;** *p t, pt p* **clung.**

clinic [klin'ik] *n* the teaching of medicine by treating patients in the presence of students; a place where medical specialists practice as a group. — *adj* **clin'ical.** — *adv* **clin'ically.**

clink [klingk] *n* a ringing sound made by striking metal, glass, etc. — *vti* to make or cause to make a ringing sound.

clip [klip] *vt* to cut with shears; to trim. — *vi* to move rapidly. — *pr p* **clipp'ing;** *pt p* **clipped.** — *n* the thing clipped off; **clipp'er,** one that clips; a sailing vessel; **clipp'ing,** an item cut out from a publication.

clip [klip] *vt* to hold firmly; to fasten with a clip. — *n* any device that grips, clasps, or hooks.

clique [klēk] *n* an exclusive group of persons in union for a purpose; a faction. — *adj* **cliqu'ish.**

clitoris [klit'ör-is] *n* a small sensitive organ of the vulva.

cloak [klök] *n* a loose outer garment; a covering; that which conceals, a disguise, pretext. — *vt* to put a cloak on; to cover; to conceal. — *n* **cloak'room,** a room for keeping coats and hats.

clock [klok] *n* a device for measuring and indicating time.

clock [klok] *n* an ornament on a sock or stocking.

clod [klod] *n* a thick round mass or lump that sticks together, esp of earth or turf; the ground; a stupid fellow.

clog [klog] *n* a block of wood; an impediment; a shoe with a wooden sole. — *vt* to accumulate in a mass and cause stoppage in; to obstruct; to encumber.

cloister [klois'tèr] *n* a covered arcade forming part of a monastery; a place of religious retirement; an enclosed place. — *vt* to confine in a cloister; to confine within walls. — *adjs* **clois'tral, claus'tral** [klös'trál].

close [klös] *adj* shut up; with no opening; hot and airless; stifling; narrow, confined; stingy; near, in time or place; intimate; compact, dense (eg of texture); hidden; reserved, secretive; strict, careful; nearly alike; nearly even or equal; nearly; densely. — *n* an enclosed place. — *adv* **close'ly.** — *ns* **close'ness.** — *ns* **close-up,** a photograph taken near at hand and thus detailed and big in scale.

close [klöz] *vt* to make close; to stop up (an opening); to draw together and unite; to shut, to end. — *vi* to come together; to grapple (with); to agree (with); to come to an end. — *n* the manner or time of closing; a pause or stop; the end. — *n* **clos'ure; closed shop,** an establishment in which the employer by agreement hires only union members in good standing.

closet [kloz'èt] *n* a small room or cupboard for clothes, supplies, etc.; a small private room; a toilet or toilet bowl. — *vt* to shut up in a private room for a confidential talk. — *pr p* **clos'eting;** *pt p* **clos'eted.**

clot [klot] *n* a thickened mass or soft lump, as blood. — *vti* to form into clots, to coagulate. — *pr p,* **clott'ing;** *pt p* **clott'ed.**

cloth [kloth] *n* woven, knitted, or pressed material from which garments, coverings, etc. are made; a piece of such material. — *pl* **cloths** [kloths]. — *vt* **clothe** [klōTH] to cover with a garment; to provide with clothes; to cover; *pr p* **clōth'ing** [TH]; *pt pt p* **clōthed** [TH], **clad.** — *n pl* **clothes** [klōz, klōTHz] garments or articles of dress; **clothier** [klōTH'i-èr] one who makes or sells clothes; **clothing** [klōTH'ing] clothes, garments.

cloud [klowd] *n* a mass of fog, consisting of minute particles of water, often in a frozen state, floating in the atmosphere; a great number or multitude; anything gloomy or ominous.—*vt* to darken or obscure as with clouds.—*adj* **cloud′ed**.—*adj* **cloud′y**.—*adv* **cloud′ily**.—*n* **cloud′iness**.—*adj* **cloud′less**.

clout [klowt] *n* a blow.

clove [klōv] *n* the dried flower bud of a tropical tree, as a spice.—*n* **clove′ pink**, a variety of pink smelling of cloves.

cloven [klōv′ėn] *adj* split; divided.—*adjs* **clov′en-foot′ed**, **clov′en-hoofed**, having the hoof divided, as the ox or sheep.—**the cloven hoof**, a symbol of devilish agency or of evil character.

clover [klōv′ėr] *n* a genus of three-leaved plants, growing among grass and affording rich pasturage.

clown [klown] *n* a clumsy or boorish person; one who entertains, as in a circus, by antics, jokes, etc.—*vi* to act the clown.—*adj* **clown′ish**.—*adv* **clown′ishly**.—*n* **clown′ishness**.

cloy [kloi] *vt* to sate by too much that is rich, sweet, etc.—*pr p* **cloy′ing**; *pt p* **cloyed**.—Also *vi*.

club [klub] *n* a heavy tapering stick, a cudgel; an implement for striking a ball as in golf; an association of persons for social, political, athletic, or other ends; any of one of the four suits of cards.—*adj* **club(b)′able**, sociable.

cluck [kluk] *n* the call of a hen.—*vi* to make such a sound.

clue [klōō] *See* **clew**

clump [klump] a cluster (eg of trees or shrubs); the sound of heavy footsteps.

clumsy [klum′zi] *adj* shapeless; ill-made; unwieldy; awkward in movement.—*adj* **clum′sily**.—*n* **clum′siness**.

clung [klung] *p t, pt p* of **cling**.

cluster [klus′tėr] *n* a bunch; a group or crowd.—*vti* to grow or gather into clusters.

clutch[1] [kluch] *vt* to seize or grasp; a grasp; a device by which two shafts or rotating members of a machine may be connected or disconnected.

clutch[2] [kluch] *n* a nest of eggs; a brood of chicks.

clutter [klut′ėr] *n* confusion; stir; noise.—*vt* to jumble, put into disorder (*often with* up).

coach [kōch] *n* a large, closed, four-wheeled carriage; a railroad passenger car; a bus; the lowest-price class of airline accommodations; an instructor or trainer, as of athletes, actors, singers, etc.; **coach′man**, the driver of a coach.

coadjutor [kō-aj′ū-tôr *or* kō′á-jōō′ter] *n* a helper or assistant, esp to a bishop.

coagulate [kō-ag′ū-lāt] *vt* to clot; to make to curdle or congeal.—*vi* to curdle or congeal.—*adj* **coag′ulable**.—*ns* **coag′ūlant**, **coagulā′tion**.—*adj* **coag′ulātive**.—*n* **coag′ulum**.

coal [kōl] *n* a solid, black, combustible mineral, derived from vegetable matter, used for fuel; an ember.

coalesce [kō-al-es′] *vi* to grow together or unite.—*n* **coales′cence**.—*adj* **coales′cent**.—*ns* **coali′tion**.

coarse [kōrs, körs] *adj* common, base, or inferior; rough; rude; gross; consisting of rather large particles.—*adv* **coarse′ly**.—*n* **coarse′ness**.—*vti* **coars′en**.

coast [kōst] *n* border of land next to the sea; the seashore.—*vi* to sail along or near a coast.—*vt* to sail along the shore of.—*adj* **coast′al**.—*ns* **coast′er**.

coat [kōt] *n* outer garment; the natural covering of a plant or animal; a membrane or layer.—**coat of arms**, heraldic bearings.—*vt* to provide with a coat.

coati [kō-ä′ti *or* kō′ä-ti] *n* an American mammal allied to the raccoons.

coax [kōks] *vt* to persuade by fondling or flattery; to humor or soothe.—*adv* **coax′ingly**.

cob [kob] *n* a corncob; a short-legged strong riding horse; a male swan.

cobalt [kō′bölt] *n* metallic element; blue pigment prepared from it.

cobble[1], **cobblestone** [kob′l-stōn] *ns* a rounded stone used in paving.—*vt* to pave with such.

cobble[2] [kob′l] *vt* to repair, to make (shoes); to put together roughly or hastily.—*n* **cobbler**.

COBOL, cobol [kō-böl] *n* a standardized business language for programming a computer.

cobra [kō′bra] *n* a poisonous snake which dilates its neck so as to resemble a hood.

cobweb [kob′web] *n* the spider's web.

coca [kō′ka] *n* any of several S American shrubs with leaves resembling tea; dried leaves of this coca.—*n* **cocaine** [kō-kān] an alkaloid obtained from coca leaves, used as a local anesthetic and as an intoxicant.

cochineal [koch′i-nēl] *n* a red dye consisting of the dried bodies of female cochineal insects.—*n* **cochineal insect**.

cock[1] [kok] *n* the adult male of the domestic fowl; male of other birds; a faucet or valve; the hammer of a gun; its position, drawn back.—*vt* to set erect or upright; to set up; to draw back the cock of a gun.—*ns* **cock′chafer**, a large European beetle destructive to vegetation; **cock′pit**, enclosed space where gamecocks fought; a compartment in the fuselage of an aircraft for pilot or passenger.—*adj* **cock′sure**, very sure; over-confident.—*n* **cock′tail**, a mixture of spirituous or other liquors.

cock[2] [kok] *n* a small pile of hay.

cockade [kok-ād′] *n* a rosette worn on the hat as a badge.

cockatoo [kok-a-tōō′] *n* any of numerous crested parrots.

cockatrice [kok′a-trīs, -tris] *n* a fabulous monster supposedly able to kill by a look.

cockboat [kok′bōt] *n* a small boat.

cockle [kok′l] *n* a bivalve mollusk.

cockney [kok′ni] *n* one born in London.

cockroach [kok′rōch] *n* any of an order (Blattaria) of chiefly nocturnal insects, including the common household pest.

coco [kō′kō] *n* the coconut palm.—*ns* **co′conut**, the fruit of the coconut palm.

cocoa [kō′kō] *n* a powder made from roasted cacao seeds; a drink made from the powder.

cocoon [ko-kōōn′] *n* the sheath spun by many insect larvae in passing into the pupa stage.

cod [kod] *ns* a food fish of northern seas.

coda [kō′da] *n* (*mus*) a passage forming the conclusion of a piece.

coddle [kod′l] *vt* to pamper, treat as an invalid.

code [kōd] *n* a collection of laws; a standard of behavior; a system of symbols.—*vt* **cod′ify**, [kod′-, kōd′-].—*pr p* **cod′ifying**; *pt p* **cod′ified**.—*n* **codificā′tion**.

codex [kō′deks] *n* a manuscript volume esp of the Scriptures.—*pl* **codices**, [kōd′isēz].

codicil [kod′i-sil] *n* an addition to a will.

coeducation [kō-ed-ū-kā′sh(ó)n] *n* education of pupils of each sex in the same school.

coefficient [kō-ef-ish′ent] *n* that which acts together with another thing to produce an effect.

coerce [kō-ûrs′] *vt* to compel; to enforce.—*adj* **coer′cible**.—*n* **coer′cion**, [-sh(ó)n]].—*adj* **coer′cive**.—*adv* **coer′cively**.

coeval [kō-ē′vál] *adj* of the same age.

coexist [kō-egz-ist′] *vi* to exist at the same time.—*n* **co-exis′tence**.—*adj* **co-exist′ent**.

coffee [kof′i] *n* a drink made from the seeds of the coffee tree; the seeds, or the shrub.

coffer [kof′ėr] *n* a chest for holding money or treasure.

coffin [kof′in] *n* a coffer or chest for a dead body.—*vt* to place within a coffin.

cog [kog] *n* a catch or tooth on a wheel.

cogent [kō′jėnt] *adj* powerful, convincing.—*n* **cō′gency**.—*adv* **cō′gently**.

cogitate [koj′i-tāt] *vi* meditate, ponder.—*n* **cogitā′tion**.—*adj* **cog′itātive**.

cognac [kon′yak] *n* a French brandy.

cognate [kog′nāt] *adj* related; of the same kind, nature, or origin.

cognition [kog-nish′(ó)n] *n* knowledge; the mental processes by which knowledge is apprehended.—*adj* **cog′nizable**.—*n* **cog′nizance**.—*adj* **cog′nizant**.—*adj* **cog′nitive**.

cognomen [kog-nō′men] *n* a surname; a nickname.

cohabit [kō-hab′it] *vi* to dwell together as, or as if, husband or wife.—*n* **cohabitā′tion**.

cohere [kō-hēr′] *vi* to stick together; to be consistent.—*ns* **cohēr′ence**.—*adj* **coher′ent**.—*adv* **coher′ently**.—*n* **cohē′sion**.—*adv* **cohē′sive**.—*adv* **cohē′sively**.—*n* **cohē′siveness**.

cohort [kō′hört] *n* a tenth part of a Roman legion; any band of warriors.

coif [koif] *n* a covering for the head; a close-fitting cap.—*ns* **coiff′eur**, [kwäf-œr′] a hairdressing; a head-dress.

coign of vantage [koin] *n* a commanding position.

coil [koil] *vt* to wind (flexible material) in concentric rings. — *vi* to wind in rings. — *n* a length (of flexible material) coiled in rings; one of these rings.

coil [koil] *n* tumult; fuss.

coin [koin] *n* a piece of metal legally stamped and current as money. — *vt* to convert a piece of metal into money; to stamp; to invent (a word, phrase). — *ns* coin′age.

coincide [kō-in-sīd′] *vi* to occupy the same space or time; to be identical; to agree, correspond (*often with* with). — *n* coin′cidence. — *adj* coin′cident. — *adv* coin′cidently.

coir [koir] *n* the strong fiber from the outer husk of the coconut.

coitus [kō′it-us] *n* sexual intercourse. — Also **coition** [kō-ish′ón].

coke [kōk] *n* a fuel obtained by distilling coal; residue when any substance is carbonized.

cola [kō′la] *n* a carbonated soft drink flavored with extracts. from the Kola nut and coca leaves.

colander [kul′end-ér, or kol′-] *n* a strainer.

cold [kōld] *adj* the opposite of hot; chilly, without passion or zeal; indifferent; unfriendly; without application of heat. — *n* lack of heat; the feeling or sensation caused by the absence of heat; a virus infection of the respiratory tract. — *adv* cold′ly. — *n* cold′ness. — *adj* cold feet, lack of courage; cold storage, storage and preservation of goods in refrigerating chambers.

coleopteran [kol-e-op′ter-an] an order of insects having two pairs of wings; the beetles.

colic [kol′ik] *n* severe pain in the abdomen.

colitis *See* colon (2).

collaborate [kol-ab′ór-āt] *vi* to work in association; to work with, help, an enemy of one's country, etc. — *ns* collabor-ā′tion; collab′orator.

collage [kol-äzh] *n* an art form made up from scraps of paper and other odds and ends pasted down.

collapse [kol-aps′] *n* a falling away or breaking down. — *vi* to fall or break down; to go to ruin. — *adj* collaps′ible.

collar [kol′ár] *n* something worn round the neck. — *vt* to put a collar on; to seize.

collate [kol-āt′] *vt* to examine and compare, to place in, appoint to, a benefice. — *ns* collā′tion.

collateral [kol-at′ár-ál] *adj* running parallel or together; descended from the same ancestor, but not in direct line. — *n* a collateral kinsman; a collateral security. — *adv* collat′erally.

colleague [kol′ēg] *n* one associated with another in a profession or occupation.

collect [kol-ekt′] *vt* to assemble or bring together; to gather (payments or contributions); to put (one's thoughts) in order; to regain control of (oneself). — *vi* to accumulate. — *adj* collect′ed, composed, cool. — *adv* collect′edly. — *ns* collect′edness, collec′tion. — *adj* collect′ively. — *ns* collect′ivism, the theory advocating collective control, esp over production and distribution. — *n* collect′or.

colleen [kol′ēn] *n* an Irish girl.

college [kol′ij] *n* a group of individuals with certain powers and duties (*the electoral college*); an institution of higher learning; any of the schools of a university. — *adj* collē′gial, collē′gian, a college student. — *adj* collē′giate.

collide [kol-īd′] *vi* to dash together; to clash. — *adjs* collid′ed, collid′ing. — *n* colli′sion.

collie [kol′i] *n* a breed of sheepdog originating in Scotland.

collier [kol′yér] *n*; one who works in a coal mine; a ship that carries coal. — *n* coll′iery, a coal mine and its connected buildings.

collinear [ko-lin′e-ár] *adj* in the same straight line.

collodion [kol-ō′di-on] *n* a gluey solution of cellulose nitrates in alcohol and ether, used in surgery and photography.

colloid [kol′oid] *n* a substance in a state in which it can be suspended in a liquid, but is not able to pass through a semipermeable membrane. — *adj* colloid′al.

collop [kol′op] *n* a small piece or slice of meat.

colloquy [kol′o-kwi] *n* conversation. — *adj* collō′quial. — *ns* collō′quialism. — *adv* collō′quially.

collude [kol-(y)ōōd′] *vi* to act in concert, esp in a fraud. — *n* collu′sion. — *adj* collu′sive. — *adv* collu′sively.

colon¹ [kō′lon] *n* a punctuation mark (:) used esp to indicate a distinct member or clause of a sentence.

colon² [kō′lon] *n* the greater portion of the large intestine; **colic**, acute abdominal pain.

colonel [kûr′nél] *n* (*US mil*) a commissioned officer ranking just above a lieutenant colonel and below a brigadier general; col′onelcy, office or rank, of a colonel.

colonnade [kol-én-ād′] *n* a range of columns placed at regular intervals; a similar row, as of trees.

colony [kol′on-i] *n* a body of persons under the laws of their native land who form a fixed settlement in another country. — *adj* colon′ial. — *ns* colon′ialism, colon′ialist. — *vt* col′onize, — *ns* colonizā′tion; col′onist.

colophon [kol′o-fon] *n* a publisher's imprint or device.

color [kul′ór] *n* a sensation induced in the eye by light of certain wavelengths — particular color being determined by the wavelength; color of the face or skin; pigment; dye; paint; (*pl*) a flag. — *vt* put color on, stain, paint; to misrepresent. — *vi* to show color; to blush. — *ns* colorā′tion; col′or bar′, social discrimination between white and other races. — *adj* col′or blind, unable to distinguish certain colors. — *n* col′or blind′ness. — *adjs* col′ored, having color; belonging to a dark-complexioned race; col′orful, full of color; vivid. — *ns* col′oring, any substance used to give color; manner of applying colors; specious appearance. — *adj* col′orless.

Colorado potato beetle [kol-ó-rā′dō] a black-and-yellow striped beetle that feeds on the leaves of potatoes.

colossus [kol-os′us] *n* a gigantic statue. — *adj* coloss′al.

colporteur [kol′pór′tûr, -pör, or kol-pört-ér′] *n* a peddler, esp one selling tracts and religious books. — *n* col′portāge [or kol′pôr′täzh].

colt [kōlt] *n* a young male horse. — *adj* colt′ish, — *n* colts′foot, any of various plants with yellow flowers appearing before the leaves.

columbine [kol′um-bīn] *n* any of a genus of plants with showy spurred flowers.

column [kol′um] *n* a long, round body, used to support or adorn a building; a body of troops; a perpendicular row of figures etc.; a perpendicular section of a page of print, etc.; a feature article appearing regularly in a newspaper, etc. — *adj* column′nar

colza [kol′za] *n* cole seed, yielding oil.

coma [kō′ma] *n* deep prolonged unconsciousness. — *adj* com′atose.

Comanche [kó-man′ché] *n* member of an Amerindian people ranging from Wyoming and Nebraska into New Mexico and Texas; — *pl* -che, -s; the Uto-Aztecan language of the Comanche.

comb [kōm] *n* a toothed instrument for separating and cleaning hair, wool, flax, etc.; the fleshy crest of some birds; an aggregation of cells for honey. — *vt* to separate, arrange, or clean by means of a comb; to search thoroughly. — *n* comb′er.

combat [kumbat′, or kom′bat] *vi* to contend or struggle. — *vt* to contend against, oppose. — *n* [kom′bat′] a struggle; a fight. — *adj* com′batant, — *n* one who is fighting. — *adj* com′bative, — *n* com′bativeness..

combine [kom′bīn′] *vt* to join together; to unite closely. — *vi* to come into close union. — *n* [kom′bīn], an association formed for commercial or political, purposes; a machine for harvesting and threshing grain. — *n* combinā′tion. — *adj* com′binative.

combustible [kom-bust′ibl] *adj* liable to take fire and burn; excitable. — *n* anything that will take fire and burn. — *ns* combustibil′ity; combustion [kombus′ch(ó)n], burning.

come [kum] *vi* to move towards; to draw near; to extend (to); to issue; to arrive at (a certain state or condition — *with* to); to amount (to); to become (eg *to come loose*); to happen; to occur in a certain order; to be derived or descended; to be caused; to result; to be available; — *pr p* com′ing; *pt* came; *pt p* come. — *n* com′er.

comedy [kom′e-di] *n* a play with a pleasant or humorous character; an amusing event. — *n* comē′dian.

comely [kum′li] *adj* pleasing, graceful, handsome. — *n* come′liness.

comestible [kom-est′ibl] *adj* edible. — Also *n* (usu. *pl*) food.

comet [kom′ét] *n* a heavenly body, having a definite nucleus and commonly a luminous tail. — *adj* com′etary.

comfit [kum′fit] *n* a candy that has a center of a piece of fruit, a nut, etc. coated and preserved with sugar.

comfort [kum'fôrt] *vt* to relieve from pain or distress; to cheer, revive.—*n* relief; encouragement; ease; quiet enjoyment; freedom from annoyance; any source of ease, enjoyment, etc.—*adj* com'fortable,—*adv* com'fortably.—*n* com'forter.

comic [kom'ik] *adj* pertaining to comedy; raising mirth; droll.—*n* (*inf*) an amusing person; an actor of droll parts, a comedian; a comic book; a comic strip; (*pl*) a section of comic strips.—*adj* com'ical,—*n* comical'ity.—*adv* com'ically.—*ns* comic book, a magazine containing comic stories told in pictures like those of a comic strip; comic strip, a strip of small pictures showing consecutive stages in an adventure.

comity [kom'i-ti] *n* courtesy, civility.

comma [kom'a] *n* in punctuation, the point (,) which marks a slight separation in a sentence.

command [kom'änd'] *vt* to order; to bid; to exercise supreme authority over; to have within sight, influence, or control; to deserve and get.—*vi* to have authority, to govern.—*n* an order; authority; control; the thing commanded.—*n* commandant', an officer who has the command of a place or of a body of troops.—*vt* commandeer', to seize for military use.—*ns* command'er.—*adj* command'ing.—*adv* command'ingly.—*ns* command'ment.

commemorate [ko-mem'o-rāt] *vt* to call to remembrance, esp by a solemn or public act; to celebrate; to serve as a memorial of.—*n* commemorā'tion.—*adj* commem'orative.

commence [kom-ens'] *vi* and *vt* to begin; to originate.—*n* commence'ment, act, instance, or time of commencing; the day or ceremonies for conferring diplomas or degrees.

commend [kom-end'] *vt* to commit as a charge (to); to recommend as worthy; to praise.—*adj* commend'able.—*n* commend'ableness.—*adv* commend'ably.—*n* commendā'tion.—*adj* commend'atory.

commensalism [ko-men'sàl-izm] *n* the association of two kinds of organisms in which one obtains food or other benefits from the other without damaging it or benefitting it.—*adj, n* commen'sal.

commensurable [ko-men'sū-ra-bl] *adj* having a common standard of measurement.—*adv* commen'surably.—*adj* commen'surate (equal in measure or extent; in due proportion (with, to).—*adv* commen'surately.

comment [kom'ent] *n* a note conveying an illustration or explanation; a remark, observation, criticism; talk, gossip.—*vi* to make critical or explanatory notes.—*ns* comm'entary, a series of explanatory notes or remarks; comm'entator, one who reports and analyzes events, trends, etc. as on television.

commerce [kom'ėrs] *n* interchange of merchandise on a large scale between nations or individuals; social intercourse.—*adj* commer'cial.—*n* commer'cialism.—*adv* commer'cially.—*vt* commer'cialize.

commination [kom'in-ā-shòn] *n* denunciation.—*adj* comm'inatory, threatening punishment.

comminute [kom'in-ūt] *vt* pulverize.—*n* comminū'tion.

commiserate [kom-iz'ē-āt] *vt* pity.—*vi* condole (with).—*n* commiserā'tion.

commissary [kom'is-ár-i] *n* formerly, an army officer in charge of supplies; a store, as in an army camp, where food and supplies are sold.—*ns* commissar [-àr], formerly, in USSR the head of a government department; commissā'riat, the department charged with the furnishing of provisions, as for an army.

commission [kom-ish'(ò)n] *n* act of committing; that which is committed; a document conferring authority, or the authority itself; something to be done by one person on behalf of another; the fee paid to an agent for transacting business; a body of persons appointed to perform certain duties.—*vt* to give a commission to or for; to empower.—*ns* commiss'ioner.

commit [kom-it'] *vt* to give in charge or trust; to consign; to become guilty of, perpetrate; to compromise, involve; to pledge (oneself);—*pr p* committ'ing; *pt p* committ'ed.—*ns* commit'ment, committ'al.—*adj* committ'ed.—*n* committ'ee, a number of persons, selected from a more numerous body, to whom some special business is committed.

commodious [kom-ō'di-ùs] *adj* convenient; spacious; comfortable.—*n* commode', a chest of drawers; a movable washstand; a toilet.—*adv* commō'diously.—*ns* commō'diousness; commŏdity, convenience; an article of traffic; (*pl*) goods, produce.

commodore [kom'o-dōr] *n* a naval officer intermediate between a rear admiral and a captain; the senior captain in a fleet of merchantmen; the chief officer of a yacht club or boating association.

common [kom'ón] *adj* belonging equally to more than one; public; general; widespread; familiar; usual; frequent; easy to be had; of little value; vulgar; denoting a noun (as a book) that refers to any of a group.—*n* a tract of open land, used in common by the inhabitants of a town, etc.—*ns* comm'onalty, the general body of the people; comm'oner.—*adv* comm'only.—*ns* comm'onplace, a common topic; a platitude;—*adj* lacking distinction; hackneyed.—*ns* common law, law based on custom, usage, and judicial decisions.

commonwealth [kom'ón-welth] *n* the people of a nation or state; a democracy or republic; a federation of states.

commotion [kom-ō'sh(ò)n] *n* a violent motion or moving; excited or tumultuous action, physical or mental; agitation; tumult.

commune¹ [kom'ūn] *n* a group of people living together and sharing possessions.—*adj* commū'nal.

commune² [kom-ūn'] *vi* to converse together spiritually or confidentially.

communicate [kom-ū'ni-kāt] *vt* to make known; to give.—*vi* to have mutual access; to exchange information by letter, etc.; to partake of Holy Communion; to succeed in conveying one's meaning to others.—*adj* commū'nicable.—*ns* commū'nicant, one who receives the Holy Communion; communicā'tion, act, or means, of communicating; information given; a letter, message; (in *pl*) routes and means of transport; (in *pl*) means of giving information, as the press, radio, and television.—*adj* commū'nicative.—*n* commū'nicativeness.—*adj* commū'nicatory.—*n* communiqué [kom-ū'ni-kā], official announcement.

communion [kom-ūn'yon] *n* fellowship; common possession; union in religious service.

communism [kom'ū-nizm] *n* a social order under which private property is abolished, and all things held in common.—*n* comm'unist.—*adj* communist'ic.

community [kom-ūn'i-ti] *n* common possession or enjoyment; agreement; a society of people having common rights, etc.; any group having work, interests, etc. in common.

commute [kom-ūt'] *vt* to exchange; to exchange (a punishment) for one less severe.—*vi* to travel regularly between two places, esp between suburban home and place of work in a city.—*adj* commut'able.—*ns* commutabil'ity; commuta'tion.—*adj* commu'tative.—*ns* comm'utātor, commut'er.

compact¹ [kom-pakt'] *adj* closely placed or fitted together; firm; brief.—*vt* to press closely together; to consolidate.—*n* [kom'pakt] a small cosmetic case, usu. containing face powder and a mirror.—*n* compac'tor, compact disc, a small plastic optical disc usu. containing recorded music.—*adv* compact'ly.—*n* compact'ness.

compact² [kom'pakt] *n* a mutual bargain or agreement; a league, treaty, or union.

companion¹ [kom-pan'yòn] *n* one who keeps company or frequently associates with another, including one who is paid for doing so; an associate or partner; one of a pair or set.—*adj* of the nature of a companion; accompanying.—*adj* compan'ionable.—*adv* compan'ionably.—*adj* compan'ionless.—*n* compan'ionship.

companion² [kom-pan'yòn], *n* a hood covering at the top of a companionway; a companionway.

company [kum'pa-ni] *n* any assembly of persons; a number of persons associated together for trade, etc.; a society; a military unit; the crew of a ship; fellowship; society.

compare [kom-pār] *vt* to set (things) together to ascertain how far they agree or disagree; to set (one thing) beside another for such a purpose (*with* with); to liken or represent as similar (to).—*vt* to stand in comparison; to reflect or modify (an adjective or adverb) according to the degree of comparison.—*vi* to make comparisons; to be equal or alike.—*adj* com'pārable,—*n* com'parableness.—*adv* com'parably.—*adj* compār'ative.—*adv* compar'atively.—*n* compār'ison.

compartment [kom-pärt'mènt] *n* a separate part or division of any enclosed space; a separate section or category.—*compartment'alize*, to divide into categories or into units.

compass [kum'pás] *n* a circuit or circle; space; limit, bounds;

an instrument consisting of a magnetized needle, used to find directions; (often *pl*) an instrument consisting of two movable legs, for describing circles, etc. —*vt* to pass or go around; to surround or enclose; to besiege; to bring about or obtain; to contrive or plot.

compassion [kom-pash´(ó)n] *n* fellow feeling, or sorrow for the sufferings of another; pity. —*adj* **compassionate** [-sh(ó)n-àt] —*adv* **compass´ionately.** —*n* **compass´ionateness.**

compatible [kom-pat´ibl] *adj* consistent; consistent (with); able to coexist. —*n* **compatibil´ity.** —*adv* **compat´ibly.**

compatriot [kom-pā´tri-ót or -pat´-] *n* a fellow countryman. —Also *adj*.

compeer [kom-pēr´] *n* one who is equal; a companion.

compel [kom-pel´] *vt* to drive or urge on forcibly; to oblige; to force. —*pr p* **compell´ing;** *pt p* **compelled.** —*adjs* **compell´able; compell´ing.**

compendium [kom-pen´di-ùm] *n* a shortening or abridgment; a summary; a collection. —*pl* **compendiums, -dia.** —*adj* **compen´dious.** —*adv* **compen´diously.** —*n* **compen´diousness.**

compensate [kom´pen-sāt] *vt* to recompense; to counterbalance. —*vi* to make up (for). —*n* **compensā´tion, compen´satory.**

compete [kom-pēt´] *vi* strive; contend. —*n* **competition** [-pet-i´-]. —*adj* **compet´itive.** —*n* **compet´itor.**

competent [kom´pe-tènt] *adj* suitable; sufficient; capable; legally qualified. —*ns* **com´petence, com´petency.** —*adv* **com´petently.**

compile [kom-pī´] *vt* to write or compose by collecting the materials from other books; to draw up or collect. —*ns* **compilā´tion, compil´er.**

complacent [kom-plā´sènt] *adj* showing satisfaction; self-satisfied. —*ns* **complā´cence, complā´cency.** —*adv* **complā´cently.**

complain [kom-plān´] *vi* to express grief, pain, sense of injury; to state a grievance or make a charge; to find fault. —*ns* **complain´ant** (*law*) a plaintiff; **complain´er, complaint´,** an expression of grief, distress, or dissatisfaction; the thing complained of.

complaisant [kom-plā´zànt] *adj* desirous of pleasing, obliging; lenient. —*n* **complai´sance** [or kom-plāz´-áns]. —*adv* **complai´santly.**

complement [kom´pli-mènt] *n* that which completes or fills up; full number or quantity. —*adjs* **complement´al, complement´ary.**

complete [kom-plēt´] *adj* perfect; entire; finished. —*vt* to finish; to make perfect or entire. —*adv* **complete´ly.** —*ns* **complete´ness, complē´tion.**

complex [kom´pleks] *adj* not simple, intricate, difficult. —*n* a complex whole; a collection of interrelated buildings or units. —*n* **complex´ity.** —*adv* **com´plexly.**

complexion [kom-plek´sh(ó)n] *n* color or look of the skin. —*adj* **complex´ioned.**

compliance [kom-plī´áns] *n* action in obedience to another's wish. —*adj* **compli´ant.** —*adv* **compli´antly.**

complicate [kom´pli-kāt] *vt* to entangle; to render complex, intricate, difficult. —*adj* **com´plicated.** —*ns* **com´plicacy, complicā´tion, complicity** [kom-plis´i-ti] partnership in wrongdoing.

compliment [kom´pli-mènt] *n* an expression of regard or praise; (*pl*) respects. —*vt* **compliment´,** to pay a compliment to; to congratulate (on). —*adj* **com´plimentary.**

compline [kom´plin] *n* the seventh and last of the canonical hours.

comply [kom-plī´] *vi* to act in accordance (with the wishes or command of another, or with conditions laid down, etc.). —*pr p* **comply´ing;** *pt, pt p* **complied´.**

component [kom-pō´nènt] *adj* making up; forming one of the elements of a compound whole. —*n* one of the elements of a compound; one of the parts of which anything is made up.

comport [kom´pört´] *vi* to agree, suit (with). —*vt* to bear, behave (oneself).

compose [kom-pōz´] *vt* to form by putting together or being together; to set in order or at rest; to settle; to create (esp in literature or music). —*vi* to create musical works, etc. —*adj* **composed´,** calm. —*adv* **compos´edly.** —*ns* **compos´edness; compos´er,** a writer, an author, esp of a piece of music. —*adj* **com´posite,** made up of two or more distinct parts. —*adv*

com´positely. —*ns* **com´positeness; composi´tion; compos´itor,** one who puts together, or sets up, type for printing; **com´post,** a mixture of decomposed organic matter for fertilizing soil. —*n* **compō´sure,** calmness.

compos mentis [kom´pos ment´is] of sound mind, sane.

compote [kom´pōt] *n* fruit stewed in syrup.

compound¹ [kom-pownd´] *vt* to mix or combine; to make by combining parts; to intensify by adding new elements; to settle or adjust by agreement. —*vi* to become joined in a compound; to come to terms of agreement. —*adj* **com´pound,** mixed or composed of a number of parts; not simple. —*n* [kom´pownd] a mass made up of a number of parts. —*ns* **compound´er.**

compound² [kom´pownd] *n* an enclosure around a building or buildings.

comprehend [kom-prè-hend´] *vt* to seize or take up with the mind, to understand; to comprise or include. —*adj* **comprehen´sible.** —*adv* **comprehen´sibly.** —*ns* **comprehensibil´ity, comprehen´sibleness.** —*n* **comprehen´sion.** —*adj* **comprehen´sive.** —*adv* **comprehen´sively.** —*n* **comprehen´siveness.**

compress [kom-pres´] *vt* to press together; to force into a narrower space; to condense. —*n* **com´press,** a pad used in surgery to apply pressure to any part. —*adj* **compress´ible.** —*ns* **compress´ibleness, compressibil´ity, compress´ion.** —*adj* **compress´ive.** —*n* **compress´or.**

comprise [kom-prīz´] *vt* contain, include.

compromise [kom´prō-mīz] *n* a settlement of differences by mutual concession; anything of intermediate or mixed kind. —*vti* to adjust by compromise; to lay open to suspicion, disrepute, etc. —*adj* **com´promised,** exposed to discredit.

compulsion [kom-pul´sh(ó)n] *n* the act of compelling. —*adj* **compul´sive.** —*adv* **compul´sively.** —*adj* **compul´sory.** —*adv* **compul´sorily.**

compunction [kom-pungk´sh(ó)n] *n* uneasiness of conscience; remorse tinged with guilt. —*adj* **compunc´tious.** —*adv* **compunc´tiously.**

compute [kom-pūt´] *vt* to determine; to calculate by means of a computer. —*vi* to reckon; to use a computer. —*adj* **comput´able.** —*n* **computā´tion, comput´er,** a mechanical, electric or electronic device that stores numerical or other information and provides logical answers at high speed. —*vt* **comput´erize,** to store in a computer; to put in a form that a computer can use; to equip with computers; to bring computer(s) into use to control (an operation).

comrade [kom´rād] *n* a close companion, intimate associate. —*n* **com´radeship.**

con¹ [kon] a contraction of L *contrā,* against, as in **pro and con,** for and against.

con² [kon] *vt* to study carefully. —*pr p* **conn´ing;** *pa p* **conned.**

con³ [kon] *adj* abbrev for **confidence** as in **con man** (*slang*) a swindler. —*vt* (*slang*) to swindle, trick.

con⁴ [kon] *n* (*slang*) a convict.

concatenate [kon-kat´e-nāt] *vt* to link together, to connect in a series. —*n* **concatenā´tion.**

concave [kon´kāv] *adj* curved inward. —*n* a concave line or surface. —*n* **concāv´ity.**

conceal [kon´sēl] *vt* to hide; to keep secret. —*n* **conceal´ment.**

concede [kon-sēd´] *vt* admit; grant; yield.

conceit [kon-sēt´] *n* overweening self-esteem; vanity; a witty thought. —*adj* **conceit´ed.** —*adv* **conceit´edly.** —*ns* **conceit´edness.**

conceive [kon-sēv´] *vt* become pregnant; to form in the mind; to imagine or think; to understand. —*vi* become pregnant; form an idea of. —*adj* **conceiv´able.** —*adv* **conceiv´ably.** —*ns* **conceivabil´ity, conceiv´ableness.**

concentrate [kon´sen-trāt] *vt* to bring towards a common center; to focus; to direct with a single purpose or intention; to condense. —*vi* to draw towards a common center; to direct one's energies to a single aim. —*n* a product of concentration, esp a food reduced in bulk by eliminating fluid; foodstuff relatively high in nutrients. —*n* **concentrā´tion.** —*adj* **concen´trative, concentration camp,** a camp where persons (as prisoners of war, political prisoners, and refugees) are detained or confined.

concentric [kon-sent´rik] *adj* having a common center.

concept [kon´sept] *n* a thing conceived, a general notion. —*n*

concep'tion, the act of conceiving; the thing conceived; the formation in the mind of an image or idea; a concept.—*adj* **concep'tual.**

concern [kon-sûrn'] *vt* to relate or belong to; to affect or interest; to make uneasy.—*n* that which concerns or belongs to one; interest in or regard for a person or thing; anxiety; a business, or those connected with it.—*adj* **concerned'.**—*adv* **concern'edly.**—*prep* **concern'ing.**

concert [kon'sèrt] *n* union or agreement in any undertaking; harmony; a musical entertainment.—*vt* **concert'**, to frame or devise together; to arrange, plan.—*vi* to act in harmony or conjunction.—*ns* **concertina** [kon-sèr-tē'na] a musical instrument the sounds of which are produced by free vibrating reeds of metal, as in the accordion; **concerto** [kon-chèr'to] a composition for solo instrument(s), with orchestral accompaniment.

concession [kon-sesh'(ô)n] *n* the act of conceding; the thing conceded.—*adj* **concess'ive.**

concierge [kô-si-erzh'] *n* a resident doorkeeper, janitor, landlord's representative, esp in France.

conciliate [kon-sil'i-āt] *vt* to gain or win over; to appease.—*ns* **concilia'tion, concil'iator.**—*adj* **concil'iatory.**

concise [kon-sīs'] *adj* cut short; brief, using, or expressed in, few words.—*adv* **concise'ly.**—*ns* **concise'ness; concision** [-sizh'-].

conclave [kon'klāv] *n* a private meeting, esp of Roman Catholic cardinals secluded continuously while choosing a pope.

conclude [kon-klōōd'] *vt* to end; to decide; to infer.—*vi* to end; to form a final judgment.—*n* **conclusion** [-clōō'zh(ô)n].—*adj* **conclusive** [clōō'siv].—*adv* **conclus'ively.**—*n* **conclus'iveness.**

concoct [kon-kokt'] *vt* to make by combining ingredients; to devise, to plan; to fabricate (eg a story).—*n* **concoc'tion.**

concomitant [kon-kom'i-tànt] *adj* accompanying.

concord [kon'kôrd or kong'-] *n* agreement; a treaty; grammatical agreement.—*n* **concord'ance,** agreement.

concourse [kon'-, kong'-kōrs] *n* a moving or flowing together of persons; an open space where crowds gather.

concrete [kon-krēt'] *adj* having a material existence; denoting a thing, not a quality or state; particular, not general; made of concrete.—*n* [kon'krēt] anything concrete; a mixture of lime, sand, pebbles, etc., bonded together with cement, used in building.—*vti* **concrēte'**, to form into a solid mass; to cover with concrete.—*adv* **concrēte'ly.**—*ns* **concrēte'ness; con-crē'tion.**

concubine [kong'kū-bīn] *n* a woman living in a socially recognized state of concubinage; a mistress.—*n* **concū'binage.**

concupiscence [kon-kū'pis-èns] *n* lust.—*adj* **concū'piscent.**

concur [kon-kûr'] *vi* (*obs*) to run together; to act together; to agree in opinion (with).—*pr p* **concurr'ing;** *pt p* **concurred'.**—*n* **concurr'ence.**—*adj* **concurr'ent.**—*adv* **concurr'ently.**

concuss [kon-kus'] *vt* to affect with concussion.—*n* **concussion** [-kush'-], a violent shock caused by sudden impact.—*adj* **concuss'ive.**

condemn [kon-dem'] *vt* to pronounce guilty; to censure or blame; to pronounce unfit for use.—*adj* **condem'nable** [-dem'nà-bl].—*n* **condemnation.**—*adj* **condem'natory.**

condense [kon-dens'] *vt* to render more dense or compact; to express in fewer words; to change to a denser form.—*vi* to become condensed.—*adj* **condens'able.**—*ns* **condensabil'ity; condensā'tion, condens'er,** an apparatus in which gas or vapor is condensed.

condescend [kon'di-send'] *vi* to act graciously or patronizingly to inferiors; to deign; to stoop.—*adj* **condescend'ing.**—*adv* **condescend'ingly.**—*n* **condescen'sion.**

condign [kon-dīn'] *adj* well merited; adequate.—*adv* **condign'ly.**—*n* **condign'ness.**

condiment [kon'di-mènt] *n* a seasoning or relish.

condition [kon-dish'(ô)n] *n* anything required for the performance, completion, or existence of something else; (*pl*) attendant circumstances; rank, standing; a prerequisite.—*vt* to agree upon; to limit, determine, control; to put into the required state; to prepare, train for a certain activity or for certain conditions of living; to make accustomed (to).—*adj* **condi'tional,** expressing condition; depending on conditions;

not absolute.—*adv* **condi'tionally.**—*adj* **condi'tioned.**—*ns* **condi'tioner, condi'tioning.**

condole [kon-dōl'] *vi* to grieve (with another); to express sympathy.—*n* **condol'ence.**

condom [kon'-dòm, kän'-] *n* a sheath, for the penis.

condominium [kon-dō-min'i-um] *n* an apartment in an apartment building owned by an individual; joint sovereignty.

condone [kon-dōn'] *vt* to pass over without blame, to excuse.—*n* **condonā'tion.**

condor [kon'dôr] *n* a large vulture of S America.

conduce [kon-dūs'] *vi* to tend, to contribute (to some end).—*adj* **conduc'ive.**—*n* **conduc'iveness.**

conduct [kon-dukt'] *vti* to lead; to convey; to direct; to manage; to behave (oneself).—*ns* **con'duct,** management; behavior.—*adj* **conduct'ible.**—*ns* **conductibil'ity; conduc'tion.**—*adj* **conduct'ive.**—*ns* **conductiv'ity,** a power that bodies have of transmitting heat and electricity; **conduct'or.**

conduit [kun'dit, or kon'-] *n* a channel or pipe to convey water, etc.

cone [kōn] *n* a solid figure with a circular or elliptical base tapering to a point; any cone-shaped object; the scaly fruit, more or less conical, as that of the pine, fir, etc.; **cō'nic.**—*adj* **conical.**

coney, cony [kō'nē] *n* a rabbit or its fur.

confabulate [kon-fab'ū-lāt] *vi* to chat.—*n* **confabulā'tion; con'fab** (*inf*) an informal talk.

confection [kon-fek'sh(ô)n] *n* a candy, ice cream, preserve, etc.; a medicine prepared with sugar, syrup, or honey; a piece of fine craftsmanship.—*ns* **confec'tionary, confec'tioner, confec'tionery.**

confederate [kon-fed'èr-àt] *adj* leagued together, allied.—*vti* [-āt] to league together or join in a league.—*ns* **confed'eracy, confederā'tion.**

confer [kon-fûr'] *vt* to give or bestow; to compare views or take counsel; to consult;—*pr p* **conferr'ing;** *pt p* **conferred'.**—*n* **con'ference.**

confess [kon-fes'] *vt* to acknowledge fully; to own or admit; to make known, as sins to a priest; to hear confession from, as a priest.—*vi* to make confession; to hear a confession.—*ns* **confes'sion, confess'ional,** an enclosure in a church where a priest hears confessions.—*adj* pertaining to confession or to a creed.—*n* **confess'or,** a priest who hears confessions; one who confesses.—*adj* **confessed'.**—*adv* **confessedly.**

confetti [kon-fet'tē] *n pl* bits of colored paper thrown about at celebrations, esp weddings.

confide [kon-fīd'] *vt* to trust; to impart secrets with trust.—*vt* to entrust; to impart with reliance upon secrecy.—*ns* **confi-dant',** one to whom secrets are confided; **con'fidence,** firm trust, belief, or expectation; belief in one's own abilities.—*adj* **con'fident.**—*adv* **con'fidently.**—*adj* **confiden'tial.**—*adv* **confiden'tially.**

configuration [kon-fig-ū-rā'sh(ô)n] *n* shape, outline; aspect.

confine [kon'fīn] *n* border, boundary, or limit—generally in *pl*—*vt* [kon-fīn'] to restrict, to keep within limits; to keep shut up, as in prison, a sickbed, etc. limit; to imprison.—*adj* **confin'able.**—*n* **confine'ment.**

confirm [kon-fûrm'] *vt* to strengthen, to establish more firmly; to ratify; to corroborate; to verify; to admit to full church membership.—*n* **confirmā'tion,** a making firm or sure; convincing proof, the rite by which persons are admitted to full church membership.—*adjs* **confirm'ative, confirm'atory, confirmed'.**

confiscate [kon'fis-kāt] *vt* to seize by authority.—*adj* forfeited to the state.—*adjs* **confis'cable, confis'catory** [or kon'-].—*ns* **confiscā'tion, con'fiscator.**

conflagration [kon-fla-grāsh'(ô)n] *n* a great fire.

conflict [kon'flikt] *n* violent collision; a struggle or contest; emotional disturbance.—*vi* [kon-flikt'] to fight, contend; to be in opposition; to clash.—*adj* **conflict'ing.**

confluence [kon'flōō-èns] *n* a flowing together; the place of meeting; a concourse.—*adj* **con'fluent.**—*adv* **con'fluently.**—*n* **con'flux.**

conform [kon-fôrm'] *vi* to be or become of the same form; to comply with; to act in accordance with.—*vt* to make like; to adapt.—*adj* **conform'able.**—*adv* **conform'ably.**—*ns* **conformā'tion,** particular form, shape, or structure; **conform'er, conform'ist, conform'ity.**

confound [kon-fownd'] *vt* to confuse; to throw into disorder; to discomfit; to perplex.—*adj* **confound'ed.**—*adv* **confound'edly.**

confraternity [kon-fra-tûr'ni-ti] *n* a brotherhood; a religious society, usu. of laymen.

confront [kon-frunt'] *vt* to face in a hostile manner; to oppose; to encounter.—*n* **confrontā'tion.**

confucianism [con-fū'shyán-izm] *n* ethical system of Confucius, the Chinese philosopher.—*adj* **confu'cian.**

confuse [kon-fūz'] *vt* to throw into disorder; to perplex; to fail to distinguish.—*adj* **confused'.**—*adv* **confus'edly.**—*n* **confū'sion.**

confute [kon-fūt'] *vt* to prove to be false to refute.—*adj* **confūt'able.**—*n* **confutā'tion.**

congeal [kon-jēl'] *vt* to jell; to solidify, as by cold.—*adj* **congeal'able.**—*ns* **congeal'ment, congelā'tion.**

congener [kon'je-nèr] *n* a plant or animal of the same genus; a person or thing of the same kind.

congenial [kon-jē'niál] *adj* of the same nature; in accordance with one's tastes; agreeable (to).—*n* **congēnial'ity.**—*adv* **congē'nially.**

congenital [kon-jen'i-tàl] *adj* begotten or born with a person.—*adv* **congen'itally.**

conger eel [kong'gèr] *n* a strictly marine eel.

congest [kon-jest'] *vt* to pack closely.—*vi* to accumulate excessively.—*adj* **congest'ed,**—*n* **congest'ion,** an accumulation of blood in any part of the body; an overcrowded condition; an accumulation causing obstruction.

conglomerate [kon-glom'èr-àt] *adj* gathered into a rounded mass.—*vt* to gather into a ball.—*n* a large corporation made up of companies which often have diverse and unrelated interests.—*n* **conglomerā'tion.**

congratulate [kon-grat'ū-lāt] *vt* to express pleasure in sympathy with, to felicitate; to deem happy.—*n* **congratulā'tion.**—*adj* **congrat'ulatory.**

congregate [kong'grē-gāt] *vt* to gather together, to assemble.—*vi* to flock together.—*n* **congregā'tion,** an assemblage of persons or things; a body of people united to worship in a particular church.—*adj* **congregā'tional,**—*ns* **Congregā'tionalism,** a form of church government in which each congregation is independent in the management of its own affairs.

congress [kong'gres] *n* an association or society; an assembly or conference, esp for discussion and usu. action on some question; a meeting; **Congress,** the legislature of the US, comprising the Senate and the House of Representatives.—*adj* **congressional** [kon-gresh'-ôn-ál].

congruence [kong'grōō-éns] *n* quality or state of agreeing, coinciding or being congruent.—*adj* **cong'ruent,** agreeing; harmonious.—*n* **congru'ity.**—*adj* **cong'ruous.**—*adv* **cong'ruously.**—*n* **cong'ruousness.**

conic, conical *See* **cone.**

conifer [kon'i-fèr] *n* any evergreen trees and shrubs with true cones (as pines) and others (as yews).—*adj* **conif'erous.**

conjecture [kon-jek'tyùr] *n* a guess.—*vt* to guess.—*adj* **conjec'tural.**—*adv* **conjec'turally.**

conjugal [kon'jŏŏ-gàl] *adj* pertaining to marriage.—*adv* **con'jugally.**

conjugate [kon'jŏŏ-gāt] *vt* (*gram*) to give the various inflections or parts of a verb; to couple, unite.—*adj* [-àt] joined, connected.—*n* a word agreeing in derivation with another word.—*n* **conjugā'tion.**

conjunct [kon-junkt'] *adj* conjoined.—*ns* **conjunc'tion,** connection, union; (*gram*) a word that connects sentences, clauses, and words; **conjuctī'va,** the modified epidermis of the front of the eyeball; **conjunctivītis,** inflammation of the conjunctiva.—*adj* **conjunc'tive.**—*adv* **conjunc'tively.**—*n* **conjunc'ture,** combination of circumstances.

conjure [kon'jè] *vt* to practice magical arts.—*vt* [kon-jōōr'] to invoke by a sacred name or in a solemn manner; to compel (a spirit) by incantation; to implore earnestly; to call before the imagination; to effect by magic or jugglery;—*pr p* **con'juring;** *pt p* **con'jured.**—*ns* **conjurā'tion, con'jurer, -or.**

connate [kon'āt] *adj* inborn, innate.

connect [kon-ekt'] *vt* to tie or fasten together; to establish a relation between; to associate in the mind.—*vi* to join.—*adj* **connect'ed.**—*adv* **connect'edly.**—*n* **connec'tion.**—*adj* **connect'ive.**

connive [kon-īv'] *vi* to wink (at a fault); to give tacit consent; to be an accomplice.—*n* **conniv'ance.**

connoisseur [kon'-es-ûr'] *n* an expert critic of art, music, etc.—*n* **connoisseur'ship.**

connote [kon-ōt'] *vt* to signify secondarily; to imply as inherent attributes; to include.—*vt* **conn'otāte,** —*n* **connotā'tion.**—*adj* **conn'otātive** [or -nōt'a-tiv].

connubial [kon-ū'bi-ál] *adv* pertaining to marriage.—*adv* **connū'bially.**

conquer [kong'kèr] *vt* to gain by force; to overcome or vanquish.—*vi* to be victor.—*adj* **con'querable.**—*ns* **con'queror, conquest** [kong'-kwest].

consanguine [kon-sang'gwin] *adj* related by blood, of the same family or descent—also **consanguin'eous.**—*n* **consanguin'ity.**

conscience [kon'shèns] *n* the knowledge, or the consciousness, of our own acts and feelings as right or wrong with a compulsion to do right.—*adj* **conscientious** [-shi-ensh'-].—*adv* **conscien'tiously.**—*ns* **conscien'tiousness; conscientious objector,** one who objects on grounds moral or religious to bearing arms or to military service.

conscious [kon'shùs] *adj* having awareness or knowledge (of); aware (that); unduly aware; awake mentally; deliberate, intentional.—*adv* **con'sciously.**—*n* **con'sciousness.**

conscript [kon'skript] *adj* enrolled into service by compulsion; drafted.—*n* a conscripted person (as a military recruit.)—*vt* [kon-script'] to enlist compulsorily.—*n* **conscrip'tion.**

consecrate [kon'se-krāt] *vt* to set apart for a holy use; to devote.—*n* **consecrā'tion.**

consecution [kon-se-kū'sh(ò)n] *n* a series of things that follow one another.—*adj* **consec'utive.**—*adv* **consec'utively.**—*n* **consec'utiveness.**

consensus [kon-sen'sus] *n* an opinion held by all or most; general agreement, esp in opinion.

consent [kon-sent'] *vi* to agree; to give assent (to).—*n* agreement, permission; concurrence.—*adjs* **consentā'neous.**

consequence [kon'si-kwéns] *n* that which follows or comes after as a result, or as an inference; importance; social standing.—*adj* **consequent.**—*adv* **con'sequently.**—*adj* **consequen'tial** [-shàl], self-important.—*adv* **consequen'tially.**

conserve [kon-sûrv'] *vt* to keep entire; to keep from damage or loss; to maintain (a quantity) constant during change. *adj* **conser'vable.**—*ns* **conser'vancy, conservā'tion,** planned management in conserving (flora and fauna, environment); **conservā'tionist,** —*adj* **conser'vatism.**—*adj* **conser'vative.**—*ns* **conser'vativeness; conser'vatory,** a greenhouse in which exotic plants are kept.

consider [kon-sid'èr] *vt* to look at carefully; to think or deliberate on; to weigh advantages and disadvantages, with a view to action; to take into account; to show regard or consideration for; to believe, think.—*vi* to think seriously or carefully, to deliberate.—*adj* **consid'erable.**—*adv* **consid'erably.**—*adj* **consid'erāte.**—*adv* **consid'erately.**—*ns* **consid'erateness, considerā'tion.**

consign [kon-sīn'] *vt* (*obs*) to sign or seal; to entrust; to commit (to); to transmit; send or deliver goods.—*ns* **consignee', consign'er; consign'ment.**

consist [kon-sist'] *vi* (*arch*) to exist; to be composed (of); to be comprised (in), or to be essentially; to agree, be consistent (with).—*ns* **consist'ence, consist'ency,** degree of density; agreement.—*adj* **consist'ent.**—*adv* **consist'ently.**—*n* **con'sistory** [or kon-sist'-], an assembly or council.

console [kon-sōl'] *vt* to give solace or comfort to.—*adj* **consol'able.**—*ns* **consolā'tion.**—*adj* **consol'atory.**—*n* **consol'er.**

console [kon'sōl] *n* a bracket to support cornices; the desklike frame containing the keys, stops, etc. of an organ; control unit of an electrical, electronic, or mechanical system.

consolidate [kon-sol'i-dāt] *vt* to make solid; to strengthen; to merge, combine.—*vi* to grow solid or firm; to unite.—*n* **consolidā'tion.**

consommé [k5-som-ā'] *n* a kind of clear soup made from well-seasoned stock.

consonant [kon'son-ànt] *adj* consistent (with, to); harmonious.—*n* an articulation that can be sounded only with a vowel;

a letter of the alphabet representing such a sound.—ns con'-
sonance, con'sonancy.—adj consonant'al.—adv con'son-
antly.

consort[1] [kon'sört] n a partner, companion; a wife or husband,
esp of a reigning queen or king; an accompanying ship.—vti
consort', to associate.—n consortium [kon-sör'tium, or -shi-
um], an international banking or financial combination.

consort[2] [kon'sört] n group; assembly.

conspectus [kon-spek'tus] n a comprehensive survey; a synopsis.

conspicuous [kon-spik'ū-us] adj catching the eye, noticeable.—n conspic'uousness.—adv conspic'uously.

conspire [kon-spīr'] vi to plot or scheme together; to cooperate
(towards one end).—vt to plot.—ns conspir'acy, conspirator,
conspiratō'rial.

constable [kon'sta-bl] n a public officer responsible for keeping
the peace (Brit); a policeman.—n constab'ulary.

constant [kon'stänt] adj fixed; unchangeable; faithful; continual.—n con'stancy.—adv con'stantly.

constellation [kon-stel-ā'sh(ó)n] n any of 88 groups of fixed
stars; an assemblage of brilliant persons.

consternation [kon-stėr-nā'sh(ó)n] n fear; shock; dismay;
panic.

constipate [kon'stip-āt] vt to cause constipation in.—n consti-
pā'tion, infrequent and difficult movement of the bowels.

constitute [kon'stit-ūt] vt to establish; to set up in a legal
form; to appoint; to form, to make up, be equivalent to.—
n constit'uency, the voters in a district.—adj constit'uent,
constituting or forming.—n an essential part; a voter in a
district.—n constitū'tion, the natural condition of body or
mind; disposition; structure; the system of basic laws and
principles of a government, society, etc.; a document stating
these specifically.—adj constitū'tional, inherent in the natural frame, natural; agreeable to the constitution or frame of
government, legal.—n a walk for the sake of one's health.—ns
constitū'tionalism, constitū'tionalist.—adv constitū'tionally.—adj con'stitutive.

constrain [kon-strān'] vt to force, compel; to confine,
imprison.—adj constrained'.—n constraint', compulsion;
confinement; a reserved or embarrassed manner.

constrict [kon-strikt'] vt to press together, to cramp; to cause
to contract.—n constric'tion.—adj constric'tive.—n constrict'or.

construct [kon-strukt'] vt to build up; to put together the parts
of.—ns construct'or; construc'tion.—adj construc'tional.—
adj construc'tive.—adv construct'ively.

construe –[kon-strōō'] vti to elucidate grammatically; to translate literally; to interpret.

consuetude [kon'swe-tūd] n custom; social usage.—adj con-
suetū'dinary, customary.—adj a ritual of customary devo-
tions.

consul [kon'sul] n one of the two chief magistrates in the
Roman republic; a government official appointed to live in a
foreign city to attend to the interests of his country's citizens
and business there.—adj con'sular.—ns con'sulate, con'-
sulship.

consult [kon-sult'] vt to ask advice or information of; to act in
accordance with.—vi to consider in company; to take counsel;
to give professional advice.—ns consult'ant, one who consults
another; one who gives technical or professional advice; con-
sultā'tion.—adj consult'ative.

consume [kon'sūm'] vt to destroy by wasting, fire, etc.; to
devour; to waste or spend.—vi to waste away; to utilize economic goods.—adj consum'able.—ns consum'er.

consummate [kon'sum-āt] vt to complete or finish.—adj consumm'ate [-āt].—adv consumm'ately.—n consummā'tion.

consumption [kon-sum'sh(ó)n] n the act or process of con-
suming.

contact [kon'takt] n touch; meeting; association; a person
through whom one can get in touch with an individual or
group, esp with disreputable or criminal person(s); an influential acquaintance.—vti to bring or come into touch, connection, with.—adj contact'ual, contact lens, a tiny, thin cor-
rectional lens placed in the fluid over the cornea of the eye.

contagion [kon-tā'jòn] n (transmission of a disease by) direct
contact; the spreading of an emotion, idea, etc.—adj contā'gious.—adv contā'giously.—n contā'giousness.

contain [kon-tān] vt to have within, enclose; to comprise,
include; to restrain; to hold back or restrain within fixed
limits.—adj contain'able.—n contain'er.

contaminate [kon-tam'i-nāt] vt to defile; to pollute, corrupt,
infect.—ns contaminā'tion, contam'inent.

contemn [kon-tem'] vt to express contempt.—n contem'ner.

contemplate [kon'tem-plāt] vt to consider or look at attentively; to meditate on or study; to intend.—vi to muse.—n
contemplā'tion.—adj con'templātive [or -tem'-plā-].—adv
con'templatively.

contemporaneous [kon-tem-po-rā'ne-us] adj living, happening, or being at the same time.—adv contemporā'neously.—
n contemporā'neousness.—adj con'temporary, contemporaneous; of about the same age; present day.—n one who lives
at the same time.

contempt [kon-tempt'] n the feeling one has toward someone
or something considered low, worthless, etc.; the condition of
being despised.—adj contempt'ible.—adv contempt'ibly.—
adv contempt'uous.—adv contempt'uously.—n
contempt'uousness.

contend [kon-tend'] vi to strive; to struggle; to dispute or
debate.—vt to assert.—ns contend'er, conten'tion [-
sh(ó)n].—adj conten'tious [-shùs].—adv conten'tiously.—n
conten'tiousness.

content[1] [kon'tent] n (usu. pl) what is in a container; (usu pl)
what is in a book; substance or meaning.

content[2] [kon-tent'] adj satisfied; willing; assenting.—n satisfaction.—vt to make content; to satisfy.—adj content'ed.—
adv content'edly.—ns content'edness, content'ment.

conterminous [kon-tèr'min-us] adj having a common boundary; coextensive (with).

contest [kon-test'] vt to call in question or make the subject of
dispute; to contend for.—n con'test, a struggle for superiority; strife; debate.—adj contest'able.—n contest'ant.

context [kon'tekst] n the parts of a discourse or treatise that
precede and follow a passage; associated surroundings, setting.—n contex'ture, the interweaving of parts into a whole.

contiguous [kon-tig'ū-us] adj touching, adjoining; near.—ns
contigū'ity, contig'uousness.—adv contig'uously.

continent [kon'ti-nènt] n a large extent of land not broken up
by seas; one of the six or seven great divisions of the land
surface of the globe.—adj restraining the indulgence of pleasure, esp sexual.—n con'tinence, the restraint imposed by a
person upon his desires, esp total abstinence; the ability to
retain a bodily discharge voluntarily.—adj continent'al.—the
Continent, the mainland of Europe.

contingent [kon-tin'jènt] adj dependent (on something else);
liable but not certain to happen; accidental.—n a quota or
group, esp of soldiers.—ns contin'gence, contin'gency.—
adv contin'gently.

continue [kon-tin'ū] vt to draw out or prolong; to extend; to go
on with; to resume.—vi to remain in the same place or state;
to last or endure; to preserve.—adj contin'ual.—adv con-
tin'ually.—ns contin'uance, continuā'tion.—adj contin'uāt-
ive.—n contin'uātor.—adj contin'ued.—ns continū'ity.—
adj contin'uous.—adv contin'uously.

contort [kon-tört'] vti to twist or turn violently, distort.—ns
contor'tion.

contour [kon'tōōr or kon-tōōr'] n the outline of a figure, land,
etc.; the line representing this outline; contour line, a line
drawn on a map through all points at the same height above
sea level.

contra[1] [kon'tra] prep against.

contra[2] [kon'tra] n one of a rebel group trying to overthrow the
Nicaraguan government established in 1979.

contraband [kon'tra-band] adj illegal to import or export.—n
smuggled goods.

contraception [kon-tra-sep'sh(ó)n] n the deliberate prevention
of conception.—n contracep'tive.—Also adj.

contract [kon-trakt'] vt to draw together; to lessen; to undertake by agreement; to incur; to shorten.—vi to shrink, to
become less; to make a contract.—n con'tract, an agreement,
esp a written one enforceable by law.—adjs contract'ed, contract'ible, contract'īle [or -īl].—ns contractīl'ity; contrac'-
tion, ;—n contract'or, one of the parties to a bargain or
agreement; one who engages to execute work or furnish supplies on a large scale.

contradict [kon-tra-dikt'] vt to deny; to accuse of a misstatement; to be contrary to.—n contradic'tion.—adjs contradic'tive, contradict'ory.—n a proposition so related to another that if either of the two is true the other must be false and if either is false the other must be true.

contradistinction [kon-tra-dis-tingk'sh(ò)n] n distinction by contrast.—adj contradistinct'ive.

contralto [kon-tral'tō] n a singing voice having a range between tenor and mezzo-soprano; a person having this voice; the part sung by a contralto.

contraption [kon-trap'sh(ò)n] n (inf) a contrivance.

contrapuntal See counterpoint

contrary [kon'tra-ri] adj opposed; opposite in nature; [kon-trā'ri] perverse.—n a thing that has opposite qualities.—n contrari'ety.—adv contrarily [kon'- or -trā'-].—n contrariness [kon'- or -trā'-].—adv con'trariwise, on the other hand; vice versa.

contrast [kon-träst'] vt to show marked difference from.—vt to compare so as to point out the differences.—n [kon'träst] opposition or unlikeness in things compared; exhibition of differences.

contravene [kon-tra-vēn'] vt to go against; to oppose in argument; to infringe.—n contraven'tion.

contretemps [kän-trè-tän'] n a confusing, embarrassing or awkward occurrence.

contribute [kon-trib'ūt] vti to give, for a common purpose; to write as for a magazine; to furnish ideas, etc.—n contribū'tion.—adjs contrib'utive, contrib'utory.—n contrib'utor.

contrite [kon'trīt] adj brokenhearted for sin.—adv con'tritely.—ns con'triteness, contri'tion.

contrive [kon-trīv'] vt to plan; to invent; to manage.—n contriv'ance.—adj contrived.-n contriv'er.

control [kon-trōl'] n restraint; authority, command; .—vt to verify (an experiment) by comparison; to° restrain; to govern.—pr p controll'ing; pt p controlled'.—adj controll'-able.—n controll'er.

controvert [kon'tro-vûrt] vt to dispute or oppose by reasoning.—vi to engage in controversy.—adj controvert'ible.—adv controvert'ibly.—n con'troversy, a discussion of opposing views; contention; strife.—adj controver'sial [-shàl].—n controver'sialist.—adv controver'sially.

contumacious [kon-tū-mā'shùs] adj obstinately disobedient; rebellious.—adv contuma'ciously.—ns contumā'ciousness, con'tumacy.

contumely [kon'tūm'li, kèn-, kon'tū-mē-lē] n humiliating treatment or scornful insult; an instance of such language or treatment.—adj contumē'lious.—adv contumē'liously.

atuse [kon-tūz'] vt to bruise.—n contū'sion.

conundrum [kon-un'drum] n a riddle turning on a play on words; any puzzling question.

conurbation [kon-ûr-bā'sh(ò)n] n a vast urban area around and including a large city.

convalesce [kon-val-es'] vi to regain health and strength; to get better.—adj convales'cent.—n one recovering health.—n convales'cence.

convection [kon-vek'sh(ò)n] n transmission, esp that of heat through fluid.

convene [kon-vēn'] vti to assemble for a meeting.—n conven'er, conven'or.

convenient [kon-vēn'yènt] adj suitable; handy; occasioning little or no trouble.—n conven'ience.—adv conven'iently.

convent [kon'vent] n a house of a religious order or congregation, esp an establishment of nuns.

conventicle [kon-vent'i-kl] n an illegal gathering; an assembly for religious worship.

convention [kon-ven'sh(ò)n] n the act of convening; an assembly, of representatives for some common object; established usage.—adj conven'tional.—n conventional'ity.—adv conven'tionally.

converge [kon-vûrj'] vti to come or bring together.—ns conver'gence, conver'gency.—adj conver'gent.

conversazione [kon-vèr-sat-se-ō'ne] n a meeting for conversation, particularly on literary subjects;—pl conversaziō'nes or conversaziō'ni [-nē].

converse [kon-vûrs'] vi to talk familiarly.—n con'verse, adjs convers'able, con'versant.—n conversā'tion.—adj conversā'tional.—n conversā'tionalist.

convert [kon-vûrt'] vt to change or turn from one thing, to another; to alter; to apply; to exchange for an equivalent, to misappropriate.—n con'vert, a converted person.—adj con'verse, reversed in order of relation.—n that which is the opposite of another.—adv converse'ly.—ns conver'sion [-sh(ò)n].—adj convert'ible.—n anything convertible.—adv convert'ibly.—n convertibil'ity.

convex [kon'veks, kon-veks'] adj curving outward like the surface of a sphere.—n convex'ity.—adv con'vexly [or -veks'].

convey [kon-vā'] vt to carry; to transmit; to impart, communicate; to make over in law.—ns convey'er, -or (also adj); convey'ance, act of conveying; (law) the act of transferring property; convey'ancer, one who effects transference of property; convey'ancing.

convict [kon-vikt'] vt to prove guilty; to pronounce guilty.—n [kon'vikt] a convicted person serving a prison sentence.—n convic'tion, act of convincing or convicting; strong belief; consciousness (of sin).

convince [kon-vins'] vt to persuade by argument or evidence; to satisfy (as to truth or error).—adj convinc'ible.—adv convinc'ingly.—n conviction.

convivial [kon-viv'i-àl] adj pertaining to a feast; social, jovial.—n convivial'ity.—adv conviv'ially.

convoke [kon-vōk'] vt to call together, to assemble.—n convocā'tion, act of convoking; the ceremonial assembly of members of a college or university.

convolve [kon-volv'] vt to roll together, or one part on another.—adj con'voluted.—n convolū'tion.

convolvulus [kon-vol'vū-lus] n any of a genus of twining, trailing or erect herbs and shrubs.

convoy [kon-voi'] vt to accompany for protection.—n [kon'voi] the act of convoying; protection.

convulse [kon-vuls'] vt to agitate violently; to shake with irregular spasms.—n convul'sion, any involuntary contraction of the muscles by which the body is thrown into violent spasms; any violent disturbance.—adj convuls'ive—adv convuls'ively.—n convuls'iveness.

cony See coney.

coo [kōō] vi to make a sound as a dove or pigeon.

cook [kōōk] vt to prepare (food); (inf) to manipulate for any purpose, or falsify, as accounts, etc.; to subject to the action of heat or fire.—vi to be a cook; to undergo cooking.—n one who cooks; one whose business is to cook.—ns cook' book, a book of recipes.

cookie, cooky [kōōk'i] n a small, sweet flat cake.

cool [kōōl] adj slightly cold; tending to reduce the effects of heat; free from excitement, calm; not zealous, ardent, or cordial; indifferent; impudent.—vti to make or become cool;—n that which is cool; coolness n cool'er, a place for keeping things cool.—n cool'ness.

coolie [kōōl'i] n formerly, an Indian or Chinese hired laborer.

coop [kōōp] n a small pen for poultry; a small building for housing poultry.—vt to confine as in a coop.

cooper [kōōp'ér] n one who makes and repairs barrels, etc.—n coop'erage.

cooperate [kō-op'ér-āt] vi to work together.—ns co'-op, a cooperative; cooperā'tion, coop'erative, an organization or enterprise owned by and operated for the benefit of those using its services.—n coop'erātor.

co-opt [kō-opt'] vt to elect or chose as a member; to assimilate.—ns co-optā'tion, co-op'tion.—adj co-op'tative.

coordinate [kō-ör'di-nàt] adj holding the same order or rank.—vt [-āt] to make coordinate.—n an equal thing or person; any of a series of numbers which, in a given frame of reference, locate a point in space.—adv coor'dinately.—n coordinā'tion.

coot [kōōt] n of birds of the rail family resembling ducks.

cop [kop] vt (slang) to catch.—n (slang) policeman.

copal [kō'pal] n hard resin from many tropical trees.

cope[1] [kōp] n an ecclesiastical vestment consisting of a long semicircular cloak, a coping.—vt to cover with a cope, or with coping.—ns cope'stone, the stone that tops a wall; a finishing touch; cop'ing, the covering course of a wall, usu. with a sloping top.

cope[2] [kōp] *vi* to contend; to deal with successfully.

coping *See* cope (1).

copious [kō'pi-us] *adj* plentiful, overflowing. — *adv* cō'piously. — *n* cō'piousness.

copper [kop'ėr] *n* a reddish metallic element; money made of copper. — *adj* made of copper; copper-colored. — *vt* to cover with copper. — *ns* copp'erplate, a plate of polished copper on which something has been engraved; an impression taken from the plate; copp'ersmith, a smith who works in copper.

copperas [kop'ėr-as] *n* sulphate or iron, used in making ink and pigments.

coppice [kop'is], **copse** [kops] *n* a thicket of small trees and shrubs.

copra [kop'ra] *n* the dried coconut meat yielding coconut oil.

copse *See* coppice.

copula [kop'ū-la] *n* that which joins together, a bond or tie. — *vi* cop'ulāte, to unite in sexual intercourse. — *n* copulā'tion. — *adj* cop'ulative.

copy [kop'i] *n* an imitation; a reproduction; an individual specimen of a book; a model for imitation; matter for printing; material for a newspaper writer; text for an advertisement. — *vt* to write, paint, etc., after an original; to imitate. — *pt p* cop'ied. — *ns* cop'yholder, a device for holding copy, esp for a typesetter; one who reads copy for a proofreader; copy'right, the exclusive legal right to the publication and sale of a literary, dramatic, musical, or artistic work in any form.

coquet, coquette [ko-ket'] *vi* to deal with something playfully rather than seriously. — *ns* cō'quetry.

coracle [kor'a-kl] *n* a small oval rowboat made of skins.

coral [kor'ál] *n* the hard skeleton secreted by certain marine polyps. — *adj* made of or like coral. — *ns* cor'alline, a family of calcareous red algae. — *adj* of, or resembling coral or coralline. — *n* cor'al reef, a reef formed by the growth and deposit of coral.

corbel [kor'bel] *n* (*archit*) a projection from the face of a wall, supporting a cornice, arch, etc.

cord [kord] *n* a small rope or thick string; anything that binds or restrains; a rib on the surface of a fabric; a slender electric cable. — *vt* to bind with a cord. — *ns* cord'age, cord'ite, a smokeless explosive.

cordial [kor'di-ál] *adj* hearty, sincere; affectionate. — *n* an invigorating medicine or drink. — *n* cor-dial'ity. — *adv* cor'dially.

cordillera [kor-dil-yä'rä or -dil'ėr-á] *n* a system or chain of mountains.

cordon [kor'don, -dón] *n* a cord or ribbon bestowed as an award; a line of sentries or policemen to prevent access to an area.

corduroy [kor-du-roi'] *n* a thick cotton fabric, corded or ribbed; (*pl*) trousers made of corduroy; a road laid transversely with logs.

core [kōr, kör] *n* the heart; the inner part of anything, esp of fruit.

correspondent [kö-rè-spond'ėnt] (*law*) a person named as having committed adultery with the husband or wife from whom a divorce is sought.

Corinthian [kor-inth'i-án] *adj* of *Corinth*, Greece, or an ornate style of Greek architecture; profligate. — *n* man of fashion.

cork [kork] *n* the outer bark of the cork oak used esp for stoppers and insulation; a stopper made of cork; any stopper. — *adj* made of cork. — *vt* to stop with a cork; to plug. — *ns* cork oak, an oak that produces the cork of commerce; cork'screw, a screw for drawing corks from bottles.

corm [korm] *n* a compact thickened underground stem.

cormorant [kor'mó-ránt] *n* any of various web-footed seabirds of great voracity.

corn[1] [korn] *n* a small hard seed, esp of a cereal plant; the plants themselves; maize. — *vt* to pickle (meat, etc.) in brine. — *ns* corn'ball, an unsophisticated person; corn'cob, the elongated woody center of the ear of maize; corn ear-worm, a moth (*Heliothis zea*) whose yellow-headed larva is destructive to maize, tomatoes, and cotton bolls; corn'flower, corn cockle; corn oil, a yellow oil got from the germ of maize kernels corn starch, starch made from maize.

corn[2] [korn] *n* a small hard growth on the foot.

cornea [kor'ne-a] *n* the transparent membrane that forms the front covering of the eyeball.

cornelian [kor-nē'li-án] *n* a fine chalcedony generally translucent and red. — Also carnē'lian.

corner [kor'nėr] *n* the point where two lines meet; a secret or confined place; an operation by which a few speculators gain control of the whole available supply of a commodity. — *vt* to put in a corner; to gain control of the supplies of (a commodity). — *vi* to turn a corner; to meet at a corner or angle.

cornet [kor-net'] *n* a valved musical instrument of brass, more tapering than the trumpet.

cornice [kor'nis] *n* (*classical archit*) the highest molded projection of a wall or column; plaster molding round a ceiling.

cornucopia [kor-nū-kō'pi-a] *n* a horn-shaped container overflowing with fruits, flowers, etc. emblematic of abundance, an inexhaustible store.

corny [kor'ni] *adj* (*inf*) old-fashioned, out-of-date.

corolla [kor-ol'a] *n* the inner covering of a flower composed of one or more leaves called petals.

corollary [kor-ol-á-ri] *n* an obvious inference; a consequence or result.

corona [ko-rō'na] *n* a colored ring round the sun or moon; the halo seen around the sun during a total eclipse; the upper portion of a bodily part. — *n* cor'onal; cor'onary, pertaining to a crown. — *n* coronā'tion, the act of crowning a sovereign.

coroner [kor'o-nèr] *n* a public officer who holds inquests into the causes of accidental or suspicious deaths.

coronet [kor'o-net] *n* a small crown.

corporal[1] [kor'po-rál] *n* the lowest rank of non-commissioned officer, just below a sergeant.

corporal[2] [kor'po-rál] *adj* belonging or relating to the body; having a body; not spiritual. — *adv* cor'porally. — *adj* por'ate, legally united into a body so as to act as an individual belonging to a corporation; united. — *adv* cor'porately. — *n* corpora'tion, a group of people organized as to operate business, under a charter granting them as a body some of the legal rights, etc. of an individual. — *adj* corpō'real, having body or substance, material.

corps [kōr] *n* an organized subdivision of the military establishment; a tactical unit usu. consisting of two divisions or more and auxiliary arms and services.

corpse [kōrps, or körs] *n* a dead body esp of a human being.

corpus [kor'pus] *n* a corpse; a body of laws, etc. — *n* cor'pora. — *ns* cor'pulence, cor'pulency, fleshiness of body; excessive fatness. — *adj* cor'pulent. — *adv* cor'pulently. — cor'puscle [or -pus'l], a minute particle; a cell not in continuous contact with others — also corpus'cule [-kūl]. — *adj* corpus'cular [-kū-].

corral [kor-al'] *n* an enclosure for cattle, etc.; a defensive enclosure. — *vt* to form, or put in, a corral.

correct [kor-ekt'] *vt* to remove faults from; to mark faults in; to set right; to punish; to counteract, neutralize. — *adj* free from faults; true; in accordance with the accepted standard. — *adv* correct'ly. — *n* correc'tion. — *adjs* correc'tional, corrective; correct'ive, correct'ness.

correlate [kor'e-lāt] *vt* to be related to one another. — *vt* bring into relation with each other. — *n* correlā'tion. — *adj* correl'ative.

correspond [kor-e-spond'] *vi* to suit, to agree; to be analogous (to) in function, position or other respect; to hold intercourse esp by letter. — *n* correspond'ence, correspond'ency. — *n* correspond'ent. — *adv* correspond'ingly.

corridor [kor'i-dör] *n* a passageway into which compartments or rooms open.

corrie [kor'i] *n* a semicircular recess in a mountain.

corrigendum [kor-i-jen'dum] *n* an error in a printed work. — corrigen'da.

corrigible [kor'ij-ibl] *adj* that may be corrected. — *n* corrigibil'ity.

corroborate [kor-ob'o-rāt] *vt* to confirm, esp by evidence. — corrob'orative. — *n* corroborā'tion.

corrode [kor-ōd'] *vti* to eat into or wear away by degrees as rust, chemicals, etc. — *n* corro'sion. — *adj* corros'ive. — *n* corros'ively. — *n* corros'iveness.

corrugate [kor'(y)ōō-gāt] *vt* to form into parallel ridges and grooves. — *n* corrugā'tion.

corrupt [kor-upt'] *vti* to make or become corrupt. — *adj* putri

depraved; defiled; not genuine; full of errors; venal; taking bribes; dishonest. —*adv* corrupt'ly. —*ns* corrupt'ness; corrupt'er; corrup'tion. —*adjs* corrupt'ive, corrupt'ible. —*n* corruptibil'ity.

corsage [kör'sij, kör-säzh'] *n* the bodice or waist of a woman's dress; a bouquet to be worn.

corsair [kör'sär] *n* a pirate ship or pirate.

corset [kör'et] *n* a closefitting undergarment worn, to support the torso.

corslet, corselet [körs'let] *n* (*hist*) a defensive covering for the body, chiefly of leather; a form of corset.

cortege, cortège [kör-tezh'] *n* a train of courtiers; a procession, esp a funeral procession.

cortex [kör'teks] *n* the outer layer of plant tissue; (*zool*) the outer layer of an organ; —*pl* cortices [kör'tisēz]. —*n* cortisone [kör'ti-sōn] the hormone used esp in the treatment of rheumatoid arthritis.

corundum [ko-run'dum] *n* a mineral consisting of alumina, second in hardness only to the diamond.

coruscate [kor'us-kät] *vi* to sparkle. —*adj* corus'cant. —*n* corusca'tion.

corvette [kör-vet'] *n* an escort vessel, specially designed for protecting convoys against submarine attack.

corvine [kör'vīn] *adj* pertaining to the crow.

cosignatory [kō-sig'na-to-ri] *adj* uniting with others in signing. —*n* cosign'er.

cosmetic [koz-met'ik] *adj* beautifying or correcting faults in the face, hair, etc. —*n* a preparation to enhance beauty. —*adv* cosmet'ically.

cosmic *see* cosmos (1).

cosmogony [koz-mog'o-ni] *n* theory, or a myth, of the origin of the universe. —*n* cosmog'onist.

cosmography [koz-mog'ra-fi] *n* a description of the world. —*n* cosmog'rapher. —*adjs* cosmograph'ic, -al

cosmology [koz-mol'o-ji] *n* a branch of philosophy that deals with the nature of the universe. —*adj* cosmolog'ical. —*n* cosmol'ogist.

cosmonaut [koz'mō-nöt] *n* a Russian astronaut.

cosmopolitan [koz-mo-pol'i-tàn], cosmopolite [koz-mop'ō-līt] *n* a citizen of the world; one free from local or national prejudices. —*adj* belonging to all parts of the world; having international tastes; unprejudiced. —*n* cosmopol'itanism.

cosmos [koz'mos] *n* the universe as an orderly or systematic whole; any orderly system. —*adjs* cos'mic, of, or relating to, the cosmos; vast in extent, intensity, or comprehensiveness; cos'mical. —*adv* cos'mically. —cosmic rays, streams of highly penetrating charged particles bombarding the earth from outer space.

cossack [kos'ak] *n* one of a people in southeastern Russia, famous as horsemen.

cosset [kos'et] *n* a pet lamb. —*vt* to pamper.

cost [kost] *vt* to bring, or be valued at; to require, involve (in suffering, or loss); to estimate the cost of production of; —*pt, pt p* cost. —*n* what is paid or suffered to obtain anything; (*pl*) expenses of a lawsuit. —*adj* cost'ly. —*n* cost'liness.

costive [kos'tiv] *adj* constipating; constipated.

costume [kos'tūm, kos-tūm'] *n* a manner of dressing; dress; a woman's outer dress. —*adj* costumed'. —*n* costum'er.

cosy *see* cozy.

cot¹ [kot] *n* a small dwelling, a cottage.

cot² [kot] *n* a narrow collapsible bed.

cote [kōt] *n* a cot; a small shelter for fowl, sheep, etc.

coterie [kō'te-rē] *n* a social, literary, or other exclusive circle.

cotillion [ko-til'yón], cotillon [ko-tē'yə] *n* an intricate, formal group dance; a formal ball.

cottage [kot'ij] *n* a small house. —*n* cott'ager.

cotton [kot'n] *n* a soft fibrous substance; the hairs covering the seeds of a tropical plant of the mallow family; such a plant, esp one grown to produce cotton; thread; yarn or cloth made of cotton. —*adj* made of cotton. —*vi* to agree (with); to become attached (to).

cotyledon [kot-i-lē'don] *n* (*bot*) the first leaf developed by the embryo of some plants. —*adj* cotylē'donary.

couch [kowch] *vt* to lay down on a bed, etc.; to express (in words). —*vi* to lie down for the purpose of sleep, concealment, etc. —*n* any place for rest or sleep; a bed.

cougar [kōō'gär] *n* a large tawny cat formerly found through-

out the Americas. —Also catamount, mountain lion, painter, puma.

cough [kof] *vi* to expel air with a sudden opening of the glottis and a harsh sound. —*n* the act or sound of coughing.

could [kŏd] *pt* of can.

coulee [kŏō-lā', kŏō'li] *n* a small stream; a gully.

coulomb [kŏō-lom'] *n* a unit of electric charge.

coulter [kōl'tèr] *n* the cutting tool attached to the beam of a plow.

council [kown'sil] *n* an elected or appointed legislative or advisory body; a central body uniting a group of organizations; an executive body whose members are equal in power and authority. —*ns* coun'cilman, coun'cilor, coun'cilwoman.

counsel [kown'sel] *n* consultation, deliberation; advice; plan, purpose; one who gives counsel, a lawyer or a group of lawyers, a consultant. —*vt* to advise; to recommend. —*vt* to give or take advice. —*pr p* coun'seling; *pt p* coun'seled. —*ns* coun'selee', one receiving counsel; coun'seling, professional guidance for an individual or a couple from a qualified person; coun'selor, one who counsels; a lawyer.

count¹ [kownt] *n* a European noble equal in rank to a British earl; count'ess, a woman of this rank; the wife, ex-wife, or widow of a count or earl. —*n* coun'ty, the domain of a count; the largest territorial division for local government in a state of the US. —Also *adj*.

count² [kownt] *vt* to number, sum up; to ascribe; to esteem, consider; to call aloud (beats or time units); to include or exclude by counting. —*vi* to name numbers or add up items in order; to have a (specified) value; to be of account; to be reckoned; to depend (*with* on). —*n* act of numbering; the number counted; a particular charge in an indictment. —*ns* count'er, he, who, or that which, counts; that which indicates a number; a token used in reckoning; a table on which money is counted or goods laid; count'inghouse, the premises in which a merchant keeps his accounts and transacts business. —*adj* count'less, innumerable.

countenance [kown'ten-àns] *n* the face; the expression of the face; appearance; goodwill, support.

counter¹ *see* count (2).

counter² [kown'tèr] *adv* in the opposite direction; in opposition. —*adj* contrary; opposite. —*n* that which is counter or opposite; (*naut*) the curved part of a ship's hull *vt* to contradict, combat; to meet or answer by a stroke or move. —*vi* to meet attacks or arguments with defensive or retaliatory measures. —*vt* counteract', to act in opposition to, to hinder or defeat; to neutralize. —*n* counterac'tion. —*adj* counterac'tive. —*n* coun'terattack, an attack in reply to an attack. —*vt* counterbal'ance, to balance by weight on the opposite side; to act against. —*ns* coun'terbalance, an equal weight, power, or agency working in opposition; coun'terclaim, an opposing claim, esp in law. coun'terirr'itant, an irritant used to relieve another irritation. —*vi* coun'termarch, to march back or in a contrary direction. —*n* coun'termine, any means of counteraction. *ns* coun'terpart, (*law*) one of two corresponding parts of a legal instrument; part that answers to another part; that which fits into or completes another; a duplicate, double; coun'terplot. —*ns* Count'er-Reformation, (*hist*) a reform movement within the Roman Catholic Church, following the Reformation; coun'terrevolu'tion. —*vt* countersign', to sign in addition to another, to attest the authenticity of a document. —*ns* coun'tersign, a military private sign or word, which must be given in order to pass a sentry; (also coun'tersig'nature) a name countersigned to a writing.

counterfeit [kown'tèr-fit] *vt* to imitate; to copy without authority, to forge. —*n* something false or copied that pretends to be genuine. —Also *adj*.

countermand [kown-tèr-mänd'] *vt* to recall or to stop; to revoke, cancel (a command, an order). —*n* a revocation of a former order. —*adj* countermand'able.

counterpane [kown'tèr-pän] *n* a bedspread.

counterpoint [kown'tèr-point] *n* (*mus*) a melody added as accompaniment to another. —*adj* contrapunt'al.

country [kun'tri] *n* a rural, as distinct from an urban, region; the land in which one was born, or in which one resides; the territory of a nation; a nation. —*adj* belonging to the country;

of farm supplies and procedures; relating to country music.—
adj **coun'trified, coun'tryfied**, rustic, unsophisticated; **country music**, rural folk music, esp of the Southern US; **coun'tryside**, a district or part of the country.

county see **count** (1).

coup [kōō] n a blow, stroke; a successful stroke or stratagem.

coupé [kōō-pā], **coupe** [kōōp] n a closed, two-door automobile.

couple [kup'l] n that which joins two things together; two of a kind joined together, or connected; two; a pair.—vt to join together.—ns **coup'let**, two consecutive lines of verse that rhyme with each other; **coup'ling**, a joining together.

coupon [kōō'pon(g)] n a detachable certificate on a bond, presented for payment of interest; a certificate entitling one to a discount, gift, etc.

courage [kur'ij] n bravery; spirit.—adj **coura'geous**.—adv **coura'geously**.—n **coura'geousness**.

courier [kōō'ri-èr] n a messenger, a runner of contraband; a member of the armed services responsible for carrying mail, information, or supplies; a person hired to take care of hotel accommodation, etc. for a traveler.

course [kōrs, kōrs] n act of running; path in which anything moves; a channel for water; the direction pursued; the ground over which a race is run, golf is played, etc.; a race; regular progress; method of procedure; conduct; a prescribed series of studies; any of the studies; each of the successive divisions of a meal; a range of bricks or stones on the same level in building.—vt to run, chase, or hunt after.—vi to move with speed along an indicated path.—ns **cours'er**, a runner; a swift horse; one who courses or hunts; **cours'ing**, hunting with hounds.

court [kōrt, kört] n an uncovered space surrounded by buildings or walls; a short street; a playing space, as for tennis, etc.; the palace of a sovereign; the body of persons who form his suite or council; attention designed to procure favor, affection, etc., as 'to pay court'; (law) the hall of justice; the judges and officials who preside there.—vt to pay attention to; to woo; to solicit, to seek.—vi to carry on a courtship; **court'ier**, one in attendance at a royal court.—ns **court'liness**; **court'-mar'tial** [-shäl], a court held by officers of the armed forces to try offences against service discipline; **court'ship**, the act of wooing; **court'yard**, a court or enclosed ground adjoining or in a large building.

courteous [kûr'tē-us] adj polite.—adv **court'eously.**—ns **court'eousness; courtesy** [kûrt'e-si], courteous behavior; an act of civility or respect.

cousin [kuz'n] n a kinsman generally, esp one descended from a remote ancestor in a different line; the son or daughter of an uncle or aunt.

cove [kōv] n a small bay or inlet in a body of water.

covenant [kuv'è-nánt] n a mutual agreement, the writing containing the agreement.—vt to promise by a covenant.—vi to enter into an agreement.—adj **cov'enanted**.

cover [kuv'èr] vt to overspread; to clothe, be a covering to; to hide; to screen, protect; to extend over; to comprise; to be sufficient for; to traverse; to command with a weapon; to report for a newspaper.—vi to spread over, as a liquid does; to provide an excuse (for).—n that which covers or protects; undergrowth, thicket, concealing game, etc; a tablecloth and setting; something used to hide one's real actions, etc.—ns **cov'erage, cov'ering**.—adj **cov'ert**, covered; secret, concealed.—adv **cov'ertly**.

coverlet [kuv'èr-let] n a bedspread.

covet [kuv'et] vt to desire or wish for eagerly; to wish for (what belongs to another).

covey [kuv'i] n a mature bird or pair of birds with a brood of young; a small flock of birds, esp partridge or quail.

cow[1] [kow] n the mature female of domestic cattle; the mature female of certain other animals, as the elk, elephant, whale, etc.—ns **cow'boy**, one who tends cattle or horses; **cow'catch'er**, an apparatus on the front of a locomotive to throw off obstacles.

cow[2] [kow] vt to subdue, intimidate.

coward [kow'árd] n, one without courage; one who is afraid.—adjs **cow'ard, cow'ardly**.—ns **cow'ardice, cow'ardliness**.

cower [kow'èr] vi to sink down through fear, etc.; to crouch timidly.

cowl [kowl] n a cap or hood; a monk's hood; a cover for a chimney, etc.

cowrie, cowry [kow'ri] n a marine gastropod having glossy often brightly-coloured shells.

cowslip [kow'slip] n a common British primrose with fragrant yellow flowers.

coxcomb [koks'kōm] a fool; a fop.

coxswain [kok'sn, or kok'swän] n one who steers a boat or racing shell.—Often contr **cox**.

coy [koy] adj modest; coquettishly bashful.—adv **coy'ly.**—n **coy'ness**.

coyote [kī'ōt, or kī-ōt'ē] n a small wolf.

cozen [kuz'n] vt to cheat.—ns **coz'enage**, deceit; **coz'ener**.

cozy, cosy [kō'zi] adj warm and comfortable, snug.

crab[1] [krab] n any of numerous chiefly marine broadly built crustaceans.

crab[2] [krab] n a sour-tempered person.

crab' apple [krab] n a small, wild sour apple.

crack [krak] vt to make a sharp sudden sound; to split; to break partially or suddenly and sharply; (slang) to make (a joke); (inf) to break open (as a safe); to solve the mystery of (a code).—vi to make a sharp explosive sound; (inf) to lose control under pressure; to shift erratically in vocal tone.—n a sudden sharp splitting sound; a chink; a flaw.—adj (inf) excellent.—ns **crack'er**.

crackle [krak'l] vi to give out slight but frequent cracks.—n the sound of such cracks.—n **crack'ling**, (usu. pl) the rind of roast pork.—adj **crack'ly**, brittle.—n **crack'nel**, a light, brittle biscuit.

cradle [krā'dl] n a small bed, usu. on rockers, in which a child is rocked; a place where anything is nurtured in the earliest period of its existence; a supporting framework.—vt to lay or rock in a cradle; to nurture.

craft [kräft] n cunning; dexterity; an art, skilled trade; the members of a skilled trade; (pl **craft**) a boat, ship, or aircraft.—ns **crafts'man, crafts'manship**.—adj **craf'ty**, having skill; cunning, wily.—adv **craft'ily**.—n **craft'iness**.

crag [krag] n a rough steep cliff.—adjs **cragg'ed, cragg'y**.—ns **cragg'iness; crags'man**, one skilled in climbing rocks.

cram [kram] vt to press close; to stuff, to fill to superfluity; (inf) to stuff the memory with (information required for an examination).—vi to eat greedily; to learn by cramming;—pr p **cramm'ing**; pt p **crammed**.—n a crush.

cramp [kramp] n a spasmodic contraction of the muscles; (pl) abdominal spasms and pain; a clamp.—vt to affect with spasms; to confine narrowly; to restrict, restrain unduly.—vi to suffer from cramps.

cranberry [kran'bèr-i] n the red acid berry of a genus of small evergreen shrubs.

crane [krān] n any of a family of large wading birds, with long legs, neck, and bill; a machine for raising, shifting, and lowering heavy weights.—vt to raise with a crane.—vi to stretch out (the neck).

cranium [krā'ni-um] n the skull.—adj **crā'nial**.

crank[1] [krangk] n a conceit in speech; a whim; (inf) an eccentric person; a handle bent at right angles.—vt to move or seek to move by turning a crank.—adj **crank'y**, crooked; shaky; cross.

crank[2] [krangk] adj (of a boat) liable to be upset by an external force.—n **crank'ness**.

cranny [kran'i] n a fissure, chink; a secret place.

crape [krāp] n crêpe; a band of crêpe worn as a sign of mourning.

crap'ulous [krap'yù-lès] adj characterized by intemperance.

crash[1] [krash] n a noise as of things breaking or being crushed by falling; a collision; a sudden failure, as of a business; a collapse, as of the financial market.—adj involving suddenness or speed or great effort; planned to deal with an emergency speedily; intended to lessen effects of a crash.—vi to fall to pieces with a loud noise; to be violently impelled (against, into); to land in such a way as to be seriously damaged, or destroyed.

crash[2] [krash] n a coarse strong linen cloth.

crasis [krā'sis] n (gram) the mingling or contraction of two vowels into one.

crass [kras] adj thick; coarse; stupid.

crate [krāt] n an open box of wood slats, for shipping.

crater [krāt'ėr] *n* a bowl-shaped mouth of a volcano; a hole made in the ground by the explosion of a shell, mine, bomb, etc.

cravat [kra-vat'] *n* a kind of necktie worn chiefly by men.

crave [krāv] *vt* to beg earnestly, to beseech; to long for; to require.—*n* crav'ing.

craven [krāv'n] *n* a coward, a spiritless fellow.—*adj* cowardly, spiritless.

craw [krö] *n* the crop of a bird or insect.

crawfish [krö'fish'] *n* a crayfish; the spiny lobster.

crawl [kröl] *vi* to move as a worm; to behave abjectly; to move slowly or stealthily; to be covered with crawling things.—*n* the act of crawling; a slow pace; an alternate overhand swimming stroke.—*n* crawl'er.

crayfish [krā'fish] *n* any of numerous freshwater crustaceans.

crayon [krā'on] *n* a stick made of wax or chalk, variously colored, a drawing in crayons.

craze [krāz] *vt* to weaken; to derange (of the intellect).—*n* a foolish enthusiasm, fashion, hobby.—*adj* craz'y, frail; demented; fantastically composed of irregular pieces (as a quilt).—*n* craz'iness.

creak [krēk] *vi* to make a sharp, grating sound.—*n* a noise of this kind.—*adj* creak'y.

cream [krēm] *n* the oily part of milk; the best part of anything; a yellowish white.—*vt* to add cream to; to beat into a soft, smooth consistency.—*vi* to gather or form cream; to break into a creamy froth.—*n* cream'ery, an establishment where butter and cheese are made.—*adjs* cream'y.—*n* cream'iness.

crease [krēs] *n* a mark made by folding.—*vt* to make creases.—*vi* to become creased.

create [krē-āt'] *vt* to bring into being; to produce, as any work of imagination; to act for the first time (a character in a new play); to make (eg an impression).—*vi* to make something new.—*n* crea'tion.—*adj* crea'tive.—*adv* crea'tively.—*ns* crea'tiveness; creativ'ity; crea'tor; creature [krē'-chúr], what has been created, esp an animated being, an animal, a person; a dependent or puppet.

creature *See* create.

crèche [kresh] *n* a display of the stable scene of Jesus's birth.

credence [krē'dėns] *n* belief esp in the reports or testimony of another; small table beside the altar on which the bread and wine are placed before being consecrated.—*adj* crēden'tial, giving a title to belief or credit; written evidence of trustworthiness or authority.—*adj* credible [kred'-] that may be believed.—*ns* credibil'ity.—*adv* cred'ibly.—*n* cred'it, belief; honor; reputation; influence derived from good reputation; a source of honor; sale on trust; time allowed for payment; the side of an account on which payments received are entered; a sum placed at a person's disposal in a bank.—*vt* to believe; to enter on the credit side of an account; to attribute to.—*adj* cred'itable.—*n* cred'itableness.—*adv* cred'itably.—*n* cred'itor, one to whom a debt is due.—*adj* cred'ulous, apt to believe without sufficient evidence; unsuspecting.—*adv* cred'ulously.—*ns* cred'ulousness, credū'lity.—credit card, a card issued by a credit card company which enables the holder to have purchases debited to an account kept by the company.

creed [krēd] *n* a summary of articles of religious belief.

creek [krēk] *n* a natural stream of water smaller than a river.

creel [krēl] *n* an angler's fishing basket.

creep [krēp] *vi* to move on or near the ground; to move slowly or stealthily; to grow along the ground or on supports, as a vine; to fawn or cringe; to shudder;—*pt, pt p* crept.—*n* a crawl; a narrow passage.—*n* creep'er, a creeping plant.—*adj* creep'y, creeping; causing creeps, weird.

cremation [krem-ā'sh(ó)n] *n* act of burning, esp of the dead.—*vt* cremate'.—*n* crematōr'ium, a place where cremation is done.

crenellated [kre'nel-āt-id] *adj* furnished with battlements; indented.

Creole [krē'ōl] *n* a person descended from the original French settlers of Louisiana; a person of mixed Creole and Negro descent.

creosote [krē'ō-sōt] *n* an oily liquid obtained by the destructive distillation of wood tar or coal tar.—*vt* to treat with creosote as a preservative.

crêpe [krāp] *n* a thin, crinkled cloth of silk, rayon, wool, etc.; thin paper like crêpe; a thin pancake.—*vt* to frizz, as hair.—*n* crêpe-de-chine [dė shēn], a soft, fine, sheer clothing crêpe, esp of silk.

crepitate [krep'i-tāt] *vi* to crackle, snap.—*n* crepitā'tion.

crept [krept] *pt, pt p* of creep.

crepuscular [kre-pus'kū-lär] *adj* of or pertaining to twilight

crescendo [kresh-en'dō] *adv* (*mus*) gradually increasing in force or loudness.—*n* increasing loudness or intensity.

crescent [kres'ėnt] *adj* increasing; shaped like the new or old moon.—*n* the moon as it increases towards half-moon.

cress [kres] *n* any of numerous crucifers with pungent leaves used in salad.

cresset [kres'et] *n* an iron basket, for combustibles, placed on a beacon, lighthouse, etc.

crest [krest] *n* the comb or tuft on the head of a bird; the summit of anything; a plume of feathers or other ornament on the top of a helmet; a badge or emblem.—*vt* to furnish with, or serve for, a crest; to surmount.—*vi* to rise to a crest.—*adjs* crest'fallen, dejected, dispirited.

cretaceous [krē-tā'shùs] *adj* composed of or like chalk.

cretin [krē'tin (or kre'-)] *n* one affected with cretinism.—*n* crē'tinism [or kre'-], a state of mental defect, associated with bodily deformity or arrested growth.-*adj* cre'tinous.

cretonne [kret-on', or kret'on] *n* a strong printed linen or cotton fabric.

crevasse [krėv-as'] *n* a crack or split, esp applied to a cleft in a glacier.—*n* crevice [krev'is].

crew [krōō] *n* a group of people working together.—*vi* to act as a member of the crew of a ship, etc.

crewel [krōō'ėl] *n* a loosely twisted worsted yarn used for embroidery and tapestry.

crib [krib] *n* a manger or fodder receptacle; a child's bed with high sides; an enclosure for storing grain.—*vt* to put in a crib, confine; to furnish with a crib; (*inf*) to plagiarize;—*pr p* crib'bing; *pt p* cribbed.—*n* cribbage [krib'ij], a card game.

crick [krik] *n* a spasm or cramp of the muscles, esp of the neck or back.

cricket¹ [krik'et] *n* a leaping orthopteran insect

cricket² [krik'et] *n* an outdoor game played with bats, a ball, and wickets, between two sides of eleven each.—*n* crick'eter.

cried [krīd] *pt, pt p* of cry.

crime [krīm] *n* an act punishable by law; such acts collectively; an offense, sin.—*adj* criminal [krim'-], relating to crime; guilty of crime; of the nature of crime.—*n* one guilty of crime.—*n* criminal'ity.—*adv* crim'inally criminol'ogy, the scientific study of crime and criminals. criminol'ogist

crimp [krimp] *adj* made crisp or brittle.—*vt* to press into folds or pleats.

crimson [krim'zn] *n* a deep-red color.—*adj* deep-red.

cringe [krinj] *vi* to bend or crouch with servility or fear; to behave obsequiously.

crinkle [kring'kl] *vt* to twist, wrinkle, crimp.—*vi* to wrinkle up, curl.—*n* a wrinkle.—*adj* crink'ly.

crinoline [krin'o-lin] *n* a petticoat distended by hoops.

cripple [krip'l] *n* a lame or otherwise disabled person.—*adj* lame.—*vt* to lame; to disable.

crisis [krī'sis] *n* point or time for deciding anything; the decisive moment or turning point;—*pl*.

crisp [krisp] *adj* curling closely; having a wavy surface; dry and brittle; fresh and bracing; firm, decided (eg style).—*vt* to curl or twist; to make crisp or wavy.

criterion [krī-tē'ri-on] *n* a means or standard of judging;—*pl* crité'ria.

critic [krit'ik] *n* one who appraises literary or artistic work; a faultfinder.—*adj* crit'ical, relating to criticism; discriminating; captious; decisive.—*adv* crit'ically.—*n* crit'icalness.—*vt* crit'icize.—*ns* crit'icism, critique [kri-tēk'] a review.

croak [krōk] *vi* to utter a low hoarse sound, as a frog.—*n* the sound of a frog.—*n* croak'er.—*adj* croak'y.

crochet [krō'shā] *n* needlework done by means of a small hook.—*vti* to do, or to make in, such work.

crock¹ [krok] *n* a pot or jar.—*n* crock'ery, earthenware, vessels of baked clay.

crock² [krok] *n* a decrepit person.

crocodile [krok'o-dīl] *n* large amphibious reptiles.—*n* crocodilian.—Also *adj.*—crocodile tears, affected tears, hypocritical grief.

crocus [krō′kus] *n* a bulbous plant with brilliant yellow, purple, or white flowers.

cromlech [krom′lek] *n* a stone circle; formerly applied to a dolmen.

crone [krōn] *n* an ugly, withered old woman.

crony [krōn′i] *n* a close companion.

crook [krŏŏk] *n* a bend; anything bent; a staff bent at the end, as a shepherd's or bishop's; a trick; a swindler. —*vt* to bend or form into a hook. —*vi* to bend or be bent. —*adj* crook′ed [-id], not straight; dishonest.

croon [krōōn] *vti* to sing or hum in an undertone; to sing quietly in an extravagantly sentimental manner. —Also *n.* —*n* croon′er.

crop [krop] *n* a hunting whip; mode of cutting or wearing short hair; the total quantity of any agricultural product cut or harvested; total growth of produce *vt* to cut short; to raise crops on; to cut the hair of; —*pr p* cropp′ing; *pt p* cropped. —*adj* crop′-eared, having ears cropped, or hair cropped to show the ears.

cropper [krop′ér] *n* a fall; a failure.

croquet [krŏ′kā] *n* a game in which wooden balls are driven by long-handled mallets through a series of arches set in the ground.

croquette [krok′et′] *n* a deep-fried ball or cake of minced meat or fish.

crosier, crozier [krō′zhyèr] *n* the pastoral staff of a bishop.

cross [kros] *n* a gibbet on which the Romans exposed malefactors; the gibbet on which Christ suffered; (the symbol of) the Christian religion; the sufferings of Christ; anything that crosses or thwarts. —*vti* to mark with a cross, or to make the sign of the cross over; to set something across; to draw a line across; to place crosswise; to pass, or cause to pass, from one side to the other of; to thwart; to interbreed. —*adj* lying across, transverse; oblique; adverse; ill-tempered; reciprocal; hybrid. —*adv* cross′ly. —*n* cross′bill, a genus of finches with the mandibles of the bill crossing each other. —*ns* cross′bow, a weapon for shooting arrows formed by a bow placed crosswise on a stock or wooden bar. —*adjs* cross′-country, denoting cross-country racing or skiing. —*vt* cross′-exam′ine, to test the evidence of a witness by subjecting him to an examination by the opposite party; to question searchingly. —*n* cross′-examinā′tion. —*adj* cross′-eyed, having a squint. —*ns* cross′ing, act of going across; the place where a road etc., may be crossed; thwarting; crossbreeding. —*adj* cross′-legged, having the legs crossed. —*ns* cross′-pur′pose, a contrary purpose; cross′road, a road crossing the principal road; (*pl*) the place of crossing of two roads; cross′ section, a transverse section; a comprehensive representation (eg of the people of a locality, of their opinions). —*n* cross′wind′, a wind blowing across the path of. —*adv* cross′wise, in the form of a cross; across. —*ns* cross′word, a puzzle in which a square with blank spaces is to be filled with letters which, read across or down, will make words corresponding to given clues.

crotchet [kroch′ét] *na* perverse whim or stubborn notion. —*adj* crotch′ety.

croton [krō′ton] *n* a genus of tropical plants, producing a brownish-yellow oil.

crouch [krowch] *vi* to squat or lie close to the ground; to cringe, to fawn.

croup¹ [krōōp] *n* inflammation of the larynx and trachea.

croup² [krōōp] *n* the rump of a horse.

croupier [krōō′pi-ér] *n* an employee of a gambling casino who watches the cards and collects the money at the gambling tables.

crow [krō] *n* any of various usu. large entirely glossy black birds; uttering a cawing cry, the cry of a cock; a child's inarticulate cry of joy. —*vi* to croak; to cry as a cock; to boast, swagger; —*pt* crew [krōō] or crowed; *pt p* crowed. —*ns* crow′bar, a large iron lever bent at the end like the beak of a crow.

crowd [krowd] *n* a number of persons or things closely pressed together, without order; the rabble, multitude; (*inf*) a set; a clique. —*vt* to fill by pressing or driving together; to fill excessively full; to compress (*with* into). —*vi* to press on; to press together in numbers, to swarm. —*adj* crowd′ed.

crown [krown] *n* a wreath worn on the head, esp as a mark of honor; reward; completion or consummation; the head covering of a monarch; kingship; the sovereign; governing power in a monarchy; the top of anything, as a head, hat, tree, hill; the part of a tooth projecting above the gum line. —*vt* to cover or invest with a crown; to invest with royal dignity; to adorn; to dignify; to complete happily; *n pl* crown′ jew′els, jewels pertaining to the crown or sovereign.

crozier *See* crosier.

crucial [krōō′shál] *adj* testing or decisive; severe; critical.

crucible [krōō′si-bl] *n* a heat-resistant container for melting ores, metals, etc.; severe trial.

crucifer [krōō′sif′ér] *n* any of a family of plants with four petals arranged in the form of a cross. —*adj* crucif′erous.

crucify [krōō′si-fī] *vt* to put to death on a cross. —*pt p* cru′cified. —*ns* cru′cifix, a figure or picture of Christ fixed to the cross; Crucifix′ion, death on the cross, of Christ.

crude [krōōd] *adj* raw, unprepared; not reduced to order or form, unfinished, undigested; immature; unrefined. —*adv* crude′ly. —*ns* crude′ness; crud′ity,

cruel [krōō′el] *adj* disposed to inflict pain, or pleased at suffering; void of pity, merciless, savage. —*adv* cru′elly. —*n* cru′elty.

cruet [krōō′et] *n* a small glass bottle for vinegar and oil, etc. for the table.

cruise [krōōz] *vi* to sail, fly, drive, or wander to and fro. —*vt* to cruise over or about. —*n* a voyage from place to place for pleasure or on a naval commission. —*ns* cruis′er, one who cruises; fast warship smaller than a battleship.

crumb [krum] *n* a small bit or morsel of bread; any small particle.

crumble [krum′bl] *vt* to break into crumbs. —*vi* to fall into small pieces; to decay. —*adj* crum′bly.

crumpet [krump′et] *n* a batter cake.

crumple [krump′l] *vti* to twist or crush into wrinkles; to crease; to collapse. —*n* a wrinkle or crease made by crumpling. —*adj* crump′ly.

crunch [krunch] *vt* to crush with the teeth or underfoot; to chew hard, and so make a noise. —*n* the act or sound of crunching.

crupper [krup′ér] *n* a strap of leather fastened to the saddle and passing under the horse's tail.

crusade [krōō-sād′] *n* any of the Christian military expeditions to recover the Holy Land from the Muslims; concerted action to further a cause. —*vi* to go on a crusade. —*n* crusad′er.

cruse [krōōz] *n* a small pot or jar for holding liquid.

crush [krush] *vt* to break, bruise, or crumple; to squeeze together; to beat down or overwhelm, to subdue. —*vi* to become crushed. —*n* a violent squeezing; a throng; (*slang*) an infatuation.

crust [krust] *n* the hard rind or outside coating of anything; the outer part of bread. —*vti* to cover or become covered with a crust. —*adj* crust′y. —*adv* crust′ily. —*n* crust′iness.

crustacean [krus-tā′s(h)i-an] *n* any aquatic arthropods including crabs, lobsters, shrimps, and barnacles. —Also *adj.* —*adj* crustā′ceous.

crutch [kruch] *n* a staff with a cross-piece at the head to place under the arm of a lame person; any prop or support.

crux [kruks] *n* a difficult problem; the essential or deciding point.

cry [krī] *vi* to utter a shrill loud sound, esp one of pain or grief; to shed tears, weep. —*vt* to utter loudly, to exclaim; to proclaim or make public.

crypt [kript] *n* an underground vault, esp one under a church, used for burial. —*adj* cryp′tic, hidden, secret; enigmatic.

cryptogram [krip′tō-gram] *n* a message in code or cipher.

crystal [krist′l] *n* anything clear, as a covering over a watch face; very clear, brilliant glass; articles of such glass, as goblets. —*adjs* crys′tal, crys′talline, etc. —*vti* crys′tallize, to become or cause to become crystalline; crystalliz̄ā′tion.

cub [kub] *n* a young carnivorous mammal; a young shark; a young person. —*n* Cub Scout, a member of the scouting program of the Boy Scouts.

cube [kūb] *n* a solid body having six equal square faces, a solid square; the third power of a quantity. —*vt* to raise to the third power; to cut into cubes. —*adjs* cū′bic, of the third power or degree; three-dimensional; cū′bical, shaped like a cube; *adv* cū′bically. —*adjs* cū′boid, cuboid′al.

cubicle [kū-bi-kl] *n* a small place (esp for sleeping) partitioned off from a larger room.

cubit [kū'bit] *n* a measure employed by the ancients, from 18 to 22 inches.

cuckold [kuk'old] *n* a man whose wife has proved unfaithful.

cuckoo [kŏŏ'kŏŏ] *n* a grayish brown European bird remarkable for depositing its eggs in the nests of other birds. — *ns* **cuck'oo clock,** a clock in which the hours are told by a cuckoo call; **cuck'ooflow'er,** a bitter cress **cuck'oopint** [-pint], a European arum **cuck'oospit,** a froth secreted on plants by the nymphs of spittle insects; a spittle insect.

cucumber [kūkum-bèr] *n* a creeping plant with large elongated fruit used as a vegetable.

cud [kud] *n* the food brought from the first stomach of a ruminating animal back into the mouth and chewed again.

cuddle [kud'l] *vt* to hug, to embrace, to fondle. — *vi* to lie close and snug together. — *n* a close embrace.

cuddy [kud'i] *n* a small cabin formerly under the poopdeck.

cudgel [kuj'l] *n* a heavy staff; a short thick club. — *vt* to beat with a cudgel.

cue[1] [kū] *n* the last word of an actor's speech serving as a hint to the next speaker; any signal to do something; a hint. — *vt* to give a cue to.

cue[2] [kū] *n* a rod used in playing billiards and pool to strike the cue ball.

cuff[1] [kuf] *n* a stroke with the open hand. — *vt* to strike with the open hand.

cuff[2] [kuf] *n* the end of the sleeve near the wrist; a covering for the wrist.

cuirass [kwi-ras' or kū-] *n* a defensive covering for the breast and back, esp one of leather or iron. — *n* **cuirassier,** [-ēr']

cuisine [kwi-zēn'] *n* a style of cooking or preparing food; the food prepared.

cul-de-sac [kū(l)-dè-sak] *n* a blind pouch; a blind alley.

culinary [kū'lin-àr-i] *adj* of or relating to cooking.

cull [kul] *vt* to select; to pick out, gather.

culm[1] [kulm] *n* refuse coal screenings.

culm[2] [kulm] *n* a monocotyledonous stem.

culminate [kul'min-āt] *vi* to reach the highest point. — *vt* to bring to a head or the highest point. — *n* **culminā'tion.**

culpable [kul'pa-bl] *adj* deserving of blame. — *ns* **culpabil'ity, cul'pableness,** *adv* **cul'pably.**

culprit [kul'prit] *n* a person accused, or found guilty, of a crime.

cult [kult] *n* a system of religious belief; devoted attachment to a person, principle, etc., a religion regarded as unorthodox or spurious; its body of adherents. — Also **cult'us.**

cultivate [kul'ti-vāt] *vt* to till or prepare for crops; to produce by tillage; to devote attention to; to civilize or refine. — *ns* **cultivā'tion, cul'tivator.**

culture [kul'chùr] *n* cultivation of the soil; a growth of bacteria, etc. in a prepared substance; improvement of the mind, manners, etc.; the skills, arts, etc. of a given people in a given period; the customary beliefs, social forms, and material traits of a religious, social, or racial group. — *vt* to cultivate; to improve. — *adj* **cul'tural.** — *adj* **cul'tured.**

culverin [kul'vèr-in] *n* an early form of cannon.

culvert [kul'vèrt] *n* a drain or conduit under a road.

cumber [kum'bèr] *vt* to impede, to get in the way of; to burden uselessly. — *adjs* **cum'bersome, cum'brous.**

cumin [kum'in] *n* a plant cultivated for its seeds which are used as a spice.

cum laude [kumlowd'ē] *adj, adv* with distinction.

cummerbund [kum'èr-bund] *n* a sash worn as a waistband, esp with a man's tuxedo.

cumulate [kūm'ū-lāt] *vt* to heap together; to combine into one; to build up by adding new material. — *adj* **cum'ulative.** — *adv* **cum'ulatively.**

cumulus [kū'mū-lus] *n* a heap; a cloud form having a flat base and rounded outlines.

cuneate [kū'ni-āt, or àt] *adj* of the form of a wedge. — *adj* **cuneiform,** [kū-nē'i-förm, kū'n(ē)i-förm] wedge-shaped; written in wedge-shaped characters. — *n* the wedge-shaped syllabary written by being impressed in wet clay.

cunning [kun'ing] *adj* (*arch*) knowing; sly; crafty; pretty; cute. — *n* slyness, craftiness.

cup [kup] *n* a small, bowl-shaped container for liquids, usu.

with a handle; the liquid contained in a cup; an ornamental vessel used as a prize; anything shaped like a cup. — *vt* to take or place as in a cup; to curve into the shape of a cup; to treat by cupping; — *pr p* **cupp'ing;** *pt p* **cupped.** — *ns* **cupboard,** [kub'órd] a closet or cabinet with shelves for cups, plates, utensils, food, etc. **cup'ful,** as much as fills a cup.

Cupid [kū'pid] *n* the Roman god of love.

cupola [kū'po-la] *n* a dome, esp a small one.

cupri-, cupro- [kū'pri, -ō] (in composition) of or containing copper [L *cuprum,* copper]; — *eg* **cupri'ferous,** of rocks, yielding copper; **cup'ronick'el,** an alloy of copper and nickel).

cur [kur] *n* a worthless dog, of low breed; a churlish fellow. — *adj* **cur'ish.**

curaçao, curaçoa [kū'ra-sō, kū-ra-sow, sä-o] *n* a liqueur flavored with the dried peel of the sour orange.

curare [kū-rä'ri] *n* extract of a vine used in arrow poisons by S American Indians. — *n* **curarine,** [kū-rä'rēn] alkaloids from curare.

curate [kūr'àt] *n* a clergyman in charge of a parish; a clergyman assisting a rector or vicar.

curator [kūr-ā'tòr] *n* a superintendent, esp. of a museum, zoo, or other place of exhibit. — *n* **curā'torship.**

curb [kûrb] *n* a chain or strap attached to the bit for restraining a horse; a check or restraint; a stone or concrete edging along a street. — *vt* to restrain or control. — *n* **curb'stone,** the stone or stones making up a curb.

curd [kûrd] *n* coagulated milk. — *vti* **curd'le,** to turn into curd; to coagulate.

cure [kūr] *n* act of healing; that which heals; a method of medical treatment. — *vt* to heal; to rid of; to preserve, as by drying, salting, etc.; to process as by drying or aging; — *pr p* **cur'ing;** *pt p* **cured.** — *adj* **cūr'able.** — *n* **cūrabil'ity.** — *adjs* **cur'ative,** tending to cure.

curé [kū'rā] *n* a parish priest in France.

curfew [kûr'fū] *n* in feudal times the ringing of a bell as a signal to put out all fires and lights; a prohibition against being abroad in the streets after a specified hour.

curious [kū'ri-ùs] *adj* anxious to learn; inquisitive; singular, rare; odd. — *n* **curios'ity,** state or quality of being curious; inquisitiveness; anything rare or unusual. — *adv* **cū'riously.** — *ns* **cū'riousness.**

curium [kū'ri-ùm] *n* a transuranic element.

curl [kûrl] *vt* to twist into ringlets, to coil; to furnish with curls. — *vi* to grow into coils; to move in curves; to play at the game of curling. — *n* a ringlet of hair, or anything like it; a wave, bending, or twist. — *ns* **curl'er, curl'ing,** a game in which two teams of four persons each slide curling stones over a stretch of ice toward a target circle. — *adj* **curl'y,** having curls; full of curls. — *n* **curl'iness.**

curlew [kûr'l(y)ōō] *n* birds having long curved bill and long legs.

curmudgeon [kûr-muj'ón] *n* a churlish, ill-natured fellow; a miser. — *adj* **curmudge'only.**

currant [kur'ànt] *n* a small kind of black raisin or dried seedless grape; the fruit of several garden shrubs; a plant bearing currants.

current [kur'ènt] *adj* running or flowing; generally received; now passing; present. — *n* a running stream; a body of water or air moving in a certain direction; a flow of electricity; course (*eg* of events). — *n* **curr'ency,** circulation; that which circulates, as the money of a country; prevalence; general acceptance. — *adv* **curr'ently.**

curricle [kur'i-kl] *n* a two-wheeled open carriage, drawn by two horses abreast. — *n* **curric'ulum,** a course of study at a school or university. — **curriculum vitae,** [kū-rik'ū-lum vē'tī] (biographical sketch of) the course of one's life.

curry[1] [kur'i] *n* a food or dish seasoned with curry powder; curry powder. — *vt* to cook with curry powder or a curry sauce.

curry[2] [kur'i] *vt* to dress (leather); to rub down and dress (a horse); to drub; — *pr p* **curr'ying;** *pt p* **curr'ied.** — *ns* **cur'r'ier.** — **curry favor,** to seek to gain favor by flattery or attention.

curse [kûrs] *vt* to invoke or wish evil upon; to consign to perdition; to vex or torment. — *vi* to utter imprecations; to swear. — *n* invocation or wishing of evil or harm; evil invoked on another; any great evil.—*adj* **curs′ed** [also kûrst].—*adv* **curs′edly.**—*n* **curs′er.**

cursive [kûr′siv] *adj* (of handwriting) written with a running hand flowing.—*adv* **cur′sively.**

cursory [kûr′sòr-i] *adj* running quickly over, hasty, superficial.—*adv* **cur′sorily.**

curt [kûrt] *adj* short; concise; discourteously brief.—*adv* **curt′ly.**—*n* **curt′ness.** [L *curtus*, shortened.]

curtail [kûr-tāl′] *vt* to cut short; to deprive of a part (of); to abridge.—*n* **curtail′ment.**

curtain [kûr′t(i)n] *n* the hanging drapery at a window, around a bed, etc.; the movable screen separating the stage from the auditorium.—*vt* to enclose, or to furnish, with curtains.—*n* **cur′tain rais′er,** a short play preceding the main performance in a theater.

curtsy, curtsey [kûrt′si] *n* an obeisance, made by bending the knees, proper to women and children.—*vi* to make a curtsy.

curve [kûrv] *n* a bend in a direction continuously deviating from a straight line; anything so bent.—*vti* to bend, or to be bent, in a curve; to move in a curve.—*n* **cur′vature,** a curving or bending; the continual bending or the amount of bending from a straight line.

curvilinear [kûr-vi-lin′i-ár] *adj* bounded by curved lines; represented by a curved line.

cushion [kŏŏsh′òn] *n* a case filled with some soft, elastic stuff, for resting on; a pillow; any elastic pad or lining; anything that serves to deaden a blow.—*vt* to seat on, or furnish with, a cushion; to serve as a cushion for or against.

cushy [kŏŏsh′i] *adj* easy and comfortable.

cusp [kusp] *n* an apex; a prominence on a tooth; the point or horn of the moon, etc.—*adjs* **cus′pidate.**

cuspidor [kus′-pi-dōr, dōr] *n* a spittoon.

cuss [kus] *n* (*inf*) a curse; a fellow.—*adj* **cuss′ed.**—*n* **cuss′edness.**

custard [kus′tàrd] *n* a mixture of milk, eggs, etc.

custody [kus′to-di] *n* a watching or guarding; care; imprisonment.—*adj* **custo′dial.**—*n* **custo′dian.**

custom [kus′tòm] *n* what one is wont to do; usage; frequent repetition of the same act; regular trade or business; a tax on goods; (*pl*) taxes or duties imposed on imports.—*adj* **cus′tomary.**—*adv* **cus′tomarily.**—*n* **cus′tomer,** one who buys from one, esp one who buys regularly.

cut [kut] *vt* to make an incision in; to cleave or pass through; to sever a piece, pieces of, from a larger portion; to fell, hew, mow, trim; to carve, hew, or fashion by cutting; to strike sharply; to reduce or curtail; to divide (a pack of cards) into two portions, or to draw (a card) from the pack; (*inf*) to refuse ostentatiously to recognize (an acquaintance); to intersect (a line); (*inf*) to absent oneself from (a school, class, etc.); to execute (as *to cut a caper*); to strike (a ball) obliquely to the off side by a sharp movement; to impart spin to (a ball).—*vi* to make an incision; to intersect; to change direction suddenly; to swing a bat, etc. (at a ball); to take cutting; (in motion pictures) to cease photographing;—*pr p* **cutt′ing;** *pt, pt p* **cut.**—*n* a cleaving or dividing; a stroke or blow; a passage or channel cut out; an incision or wound; a piece cut off, as of meat; manner of cutting, or fashion; type, kind; a degree, grade; a stroke that cuts a ball; spin imparted by such a stroke; (*slang*) a share, as of profits.—*ns* **cutt′er,** the person or thing that cuts; a small swift vessel with one mast and sharp prow, fore-and-aft rigged; a light sleigh; **cutt′ing,** a dividing or lopping off; an incision; a piece cut out or off; a piece of plant cut off for propagation; editing of film or recording; a recording.

cutaneous *see* **cutis.**

cute [kūt] *adj* (*inf*) acute, shrewd; pretty or attractive, esp in a dainty way.

cutis [kū′tis] *n* the vascular layer of the skin.—*adj* **cūtān′eous.**—*n* **cū′ticle,** the outermost layer of the skin.

cutlass [kut′las] *n* a short, broad sword, with one cutting edge, formerly used in the navy.

cutler [kut′lèr] *n* one who makes or sells knives.—*n* **cut′lery,** the business of a cutler; edged or cutting instruments in general, often implements for eating food.

cutlet [kut′let] *n* a small slice of meat cut off from the ribs or leg.

cuttlebone [kut′l-bōn] *n* the shell of cuttlefishes.—*n* **cuttlefish,**

any of a family of 10-armed marine mollusks having a calcified internal shell.

cyanide [sī′àn-īd] *n* a chemical compound containing the group CN, HCN, and metal cyanides.—*adj* **cyan′ic.**—*ns* **cy′an,** one of the primary colors in color printing and photography; a greenish blue color; **cy′anide,** a direct compound of cyanogen with a metal; **cy′anine,** any of a group of dyes used in photography; **cyanō′sis,** blueness of the skin.

cyclamen [sik′la-men] *n* a genus of the same family as the primrose.

cycle [sī′kl] *n* a period of time in which events happen in a certain order, and which constantly repeats itself; an age; a recurring series of changes; centering around a figure or event; a bicycle, motorcycle, or tricycle.—*vi* to move in cycles; to recur in cycles; to ride a bicycle or tricycle.—*vt* to cause to pass through a cycle of operations or events.—*adjs* **cy′clic, -al.**—*n* **cy′clist,** one who rides a bicycle.

cyclone [sī′klōn] *n* a storm blowing spirally inwards toward a center of low pressure.—*adj* **cyclon′ic.**

cyclopedia [sī-klō-pē′di-a] *See* **encyclopedia.**

cygnet [sig′net] *n* a young swan.

cylinder [sil′in-dèr] *n* a figure generated by a straight line remaining parallel to a fixed axis and moving round a closed curve; a roller-shaped object; applied to many parts of machinery of cylindrical shape, esp the turning part of a revolver and the piston chamber of an engine.—*adjs* **cylin′drical, cylin′dric.**

cymbal [sim′bàl] *n* (*mus*) one of a pair of two brass plates struck together to produce a ringing or clashing sound in a symphony orchestra.

cynic, -al [sin′ik- -àl] *adj* sneering; disinclined to recognize goodness or selflessness as a motive for behavior.—*ns* **cyn′ic,** one who takes a low view of human character and conduct; **cynicism.**—*adv* **cyn′ically.**

cynosure [sīn′ō-shōōr, or sī′-] *n* a center of attraction or admiration.

cypress [sī′pres] *n* a genus of mostly evergreen trees with overlapping leaves resembling scales; any of several other coniferous trees; the wood of a cypress; a symbol of mourning.

cyst [sist] *n* a closed sac developing abnormally in the structure of plants or animals.—*adj* **cyst′ic.**

czar [zär] *n* the title of any of the former emperors of Russia; an autocrat.—*ns* **czar′evitch,** an heir apparent of a czar; **czarina** [zär-ēnà] the wife of a czar.—Also **tsar, tsarina.**

Czech [chek] *n* a native or inhabitant of Czechoslovakia, esp of the western provinces of Bohemia, Moravia, or Silesia; the Slavic language of the Czechs.—*adjs* **Czechoslō′vak, Czechoslovak′ian.**

D

dab¹ [dab] *vt* to strike gently with something soft or moist; to peck;—*pr p* **dabb′ing;** *pt p* **dabbed.**—*n* a gentle blow; a small lump of anything soft or moist; (*usu. in pl; slang*) fingerprint.—*n* **dab′chick** the pied-billed grebe of America; the little grebe of Europe.

dab² a species of flounder of light-brown color.

dab³ [dab] *n* (*inf*) an expert person—*also* **dab-hand.**

dabble [dab′l] *vi* to do anything in a superficial or dilettante way.—*n* **dabb′ler.**

da capo [dä kä′pō] a term in music, indicating 'return to the beginning'—*usu. written* **DC.**

dace [dās] *n* any small fresh-water fish of the carp family.

dachshund [däks′hŏŏnt] *n* a breed of short-legged, long-bodied hound.

dacoit [da-koit′] *n* in India and Burma, one of a gang of robbers or brigands.—*n* **dacoit′y,** brigandage.

Dacron [dak′ron] *n* trade name for polyester fiber.

dactyl [dak′til] *n* in poetry, a word or word-group consisting of one heavily-stressed syllable followed by two lightly-stressed syllables.

dad [dad], **daddy** [dad′i] *n* (*inf*) father.—*n* **dadd′y-long-legs** (*inf*) any of various spiders or insects with long slender legs.

dado [dā′dō] *n* the lower part of the walls of a room when

paneled or painted separately; the part of the pedestal in a classical column below the surbase and above the base.

daffodil [daf′o-dil] *n* a yellow-flowered narcissus. Also **lent-lily**.

daft [däft] *adj* silly; insane. — *adv* **daftly**

dagger [dag′er] *n* a short sword for stabbing; a mark of reference (†).

daguerreotype [dä-ger′-ō-tīp] *n* an early method of photography on a copper plate.

dahlia [dāl′yä] *n* a genus (*Dahlia*) of half-hardy tuberous perennials of the aster family grown for its range of colors and flower forms.

daily [dā′li] *adj, adv* every day. — *n* a daily paper.

dainty [dān′ti] *adj* delicate; tasteful; fastidious. — *n* a delicacy. — *adv* **dain′tily**. — *n* **dain′tiness**.

dairy [dā′ri] *n* the place where milk is kept, and butter and cheese made; an establishment for the supply of milk. — **dai′ry farm**. — **dairy cattle**, cows raised mainly for production of milk; **dairy products**, milk, butter, cheese, yogurt, etc.

dais [dā′is, dās] *n* a raised floor at the end of a hall.

daisy [dā′zi] *n* any of various composite plants having heads with white or pink rays and a yellow disk, esp English daisy; **daisy-wheel**, flat wheel-shaped printing device with characters at the ends of spokes.

dakoit *see* **dacoit**.

dale [dāl] *n* the low ground between hills.

dally [dal′i] *vi* to lose time by idleness or trifling; to play (with); to exchange caresses; — *pr p* **dally′ing**; *pt p* **dall′ied**. — *n* **dall′iance**

Daltonism [döl′ton-izm] *n* congenital, usu. red-green color blindness.

dam[1] [dam] *n* a barrier to restrain water; the water thus confined.

dam[2] [dam] *n* a mother of a four-footed animal.

damage [dam′ij] *n* injury; loss; the value of what is lost; (*inf*) cost; (*pl*) payment due for loss or injury sustained by one person through the fault of another. — *vt* to harm. — *adj* **damageable**, fragile.

damask [dam′ask] *n* reversible, figured, woven fabric esp linen; Damascus steel or its surface pattern. — *adj* of a red color, like that of a damask rose. — *n* **damascene** [dam′a-sēn], (*cap*) a native of Damascus; a Damascus sword; inlay of metal on steel. — *vt* to decorate metal (esp steel) by inlaying; to ornament with the wavy appearance of Damascus steel; **dam′ask-rose**, a hardy, large, fragrant, pink rose (*Rosa damascena*).

dame [dām] *n* title of a woman having the same rank as a knight; (*slang*) a woman.

damn [dam] *vt* to censure or condemn; to sentence to eternal punishment. — *n* an oath, a curse. — *adj* **dam′nable**, deserving damnation; hateful, pernicious; (*inf*) very annoying. — *adv* **dam′nably**. — *n* **damnā′tion, dam′natory**.

Damocles, Sword of [dam′-ō-klēs] *n* a symbol of insecurity. — *adj* **Damoclean** (*dam-ō-clē′an*).

damp [damp] *n* humidity; in mines, any gas other than air. — *vt* to moisten; to discourage. — *adj* moist, *n* **damper**; a depressive influence; a metal plate in a flue for controlling combustion; (*mus*) device for stopping vibration of stringed instruments; unleavened bread made with flour and water — (*Australia*) *n* **damp′ness**.

damsel [dam′zèl] *n* a young unmarried woman; a girl.

damson [dam′z(ó)n, -sòn] *n* a small dark-purple oval-fruited variety of plum.

dance [däns] *vi* to move with the rhythm of sound, esp to music; to move lightly and gaily. — *vt* to make to dance or to move up and down; to perform (a dance). — *n* a dance performance of an artistic nature; a social function at which dancing is the chief entertainment; a tune to which dancing is performed. — **dan′cer**.

dandelion [dan′di-liön] *n* a common composite (*Taraxacum officinale*) with jagged-tooth leaves, (edible) yellow flower and fluffy seed head.

dander [dan′dèr] *n* (*inf*) anger, passion.

dandle [dan′dl] *vt* to fondle or toss in the arms, as a baby.

dandruff [dand′rùf] *n* a scaly scurf on the scalp.

dandy [dan′di] *n* a man who pays too much attention to dress. — *adj* (*inf*) excellent, fine — *vt* **dan′dify**, to dress up. — *n* **dandification**.

Dane [dān] *n* a native of *Denmark*; *adj* **Dan′ish**, belonging to Denmark. — *n* the language of the Danes.

danger [dān′jėr] *n* a state or circumstances involving injury or risk; a source of harm or risk. — *adj* **dan′gerous**. — *adv* **dan′gerously**.

dangle [dang′gl] *vi* to hang loosely; to follow (after someone), to hang (about, around someone).

Daniel [dan′yel] *n* the 27th book of the Old Testament written by the prophet Daniel describing Jerusalem under Gentile control.

dank [dangk] *adj* unpleasantly moist.

dap [dap] *vi* to drop (bait) gently into the water.

dapper [dap′ėr] *adj* quick; little and active; spruce.

dapple [dap′l] *adj* marked with spots. — *vt* to variegate with spots. — *adj* **dapple-gray**, mottled with darker gray.

dare [dār] *vti* to be bold enough; to venture; — *3rd pers sing* **dare(s)**. — *vt* to challenge; to defy. — *n* **daredev′il**, a rash, venturesome person. — *adj* **daring**, bold; courageous.

dark [därk] *adj* having little or no light; of a shade of color closer to black than white; (of a person) having brown or black skin or hair; gloomy; (*inf*) secret, unknown; mysterious. — *n* absence of light; obscurity; a state of ignorance. — *vt* **dark′en**. — *adj* **dark′ish**. — *adv*, *adj* **dark′ling**, in the dark. — *adv* **dark′ly**. — *n* **dark′ness**. — *n* **dark′y**, **dark′ey** *offensive*, a Negro; **darkroom**, a room protected from actinic light for processing film.

darling [där′ling] *n* one dearly loved; a favourite.

darn[1] [därn] *vt* to replace or reinforce broken or worn threads in a fabric. — *n* the place darned. — *n*

darn[2] [därn] *vti n, adj; interj* form of **damn** as a mild oath.

dart [därt] *n* a small pointed missile; anything that pierces; a tapering fold sewn on fabric; (*in pl*) a game in which darts are thrown at a board. — *vti* to move rapidly; **dar′ter**, any of several small fresh-water fishes allied to the perch.

Darwinism [där′win-izm] *n* the theory that new species of plants and animals originate from those descendents of parent forms which are naturally selected through survival of the fittest, propounded by Charles *Darwin* (1809–82).

dash [däsh] *vt* to throw, thrust, or drive violently; to bespatter; to frustrate (hopes); to depress, confound (eg one's spirits); to write quickly. — *vi* to rush violently. — *n* a short race; a violent striking; a rush; a small amount of something added to food; a blow; a punctuation mark (—); verve; display.

dastard [das′tard] *n* a mean, sneaky coward — *adj, adv* **das′-tardly**. — *n* **das′tardliness**.

data [dā′ta] *n pl* (now often with sing verb) facts, statistics, or information either historical or derived by calculation or experimentation. — *sing* **dātum**. — **dat′a bank, dat′abase**, a large body of information stored in a computer for analysis or use. — **data processing**, analysis of information stored on a computer by using strictly defined systems of procedure.

date[1] [dāt] *n* day of month; a statement of time of writing, sending, executing, as on a letter, book, document; the time of an event; period to which something belongs; an appointment or engagement. — *vt* to affix a date to; to ascertain or suggest the date of; (*inf*) to make a date with; (*inf*) to go out regularly esp with a member of the opposite sex. — *vi* to reckon from a point in time; to show signs of belonging to a particular period. — *adj* **dāt′able**. — *adj* **dāte′less**, undated; having unknown beginning; immemorial.

date[2] [dāt] *n* the sweet, oblong fruit of a palm.

dative [dāt′iv] *adj* (*gram*) expressing an indirect object. — *n* the dative case.

datum [dā′tum] *n* singular of data; (*engineering and surveying*) **datums**; *pl* **data**.

daub [döb] *vt* to smear; to paint coarsely. — *n* a coarse painting. — *n* **daub′er**.

daughter [dö′tėr] *n* a female child; a female descendant; a female personification (*the US is the daughter of the original British colonies*). — *n* **daugh′ter-in-law**, a son's wife.

daunt [dönt] *or* **dänt**, *vt* to frighten; to discourage. — *adj* **daunt′less**, not to be daunted. — *adv* **daunt′lessly**. — *n* **daunt′-lessness**.

dauphin [dö′fin] *n* the eldest son of a king of France. — *n* **dau′phine**, his wife.

davenport [dav′èn-pört, -port *n* a large, upholstered couch or settee often convertible to a bed; a small desk with drawers and lift-up top.

davit [dav´it] *n* one of a pair of pieces of timber or iron to raise a boat over a ship's side or stern.

daw [döw] *n* a jackdaw.

dawdle [dö´dl] *vi* to waste time by acting or moving slowly.—*n* **daw´dler**.

dawn [dön] *vi* to become day; to begin to grow light; to begin to appear.—*n* **daybreak**; beginning.—Also **dawn´ing**.

day [dā] *n* twenty-four hours, the time the earth takes to make a revolution on her axis; the time of light, from sunrise to sunset; a day set apart for a purpose; a successful period of vogue, or influence;—**day´book**, a diary; book-keeper's daily ledger; **day´break**, dawn; **daycare center**, place where young children of working parent(s) stay; **daydream**, a dreaming or musing while awake (also *vi*).—*n* **daylight saving time**, the creation of daylight by advancing the clock during summer months.

daze [dāz] *vt* to stun, to stupefy.—*n* bewilderment.—*adj* **dazed** (*dāzd*).—*adv* **dazedly** (*dāz´id-li*).

dazzle [daz´l] *vt* to daze or overpower with a strong light; to confound by brilliancy, beauty, or cleverness.—*n* **dazz´ler**.

de- [dē- di-] down; away from; completely.

deacon [dē´kon] *n* in certain churches, a member of the clergy under priests; an elected or appointed church officer; the lowest grade in the Mormon priesthood;—*fem* **dea´coness**, in some Protestant churches a woman officer who helps the minister;—**dea´conry, dea´conship**.

dead [ded] *adj* without life; death-like; without vegetation; extinguished (*eg of fire*); numb (*eg of a limb*); spiritually or emotionally insensitive; dull (*of color, sound, etc.*); without motion; out of play (*of a ball*); obsolete; unsaleable; complete; absolutely accurate; unerring;—*adv* in a dead manner; absolutely; utterly.—*n* one who is dead; the time of greatest stillness, as 'the dead of night'; **the dead**, those who are dead; **dead´-beat**, (*inf*) quite overcome, exhausted;—*vt* **dead´en**; to lessen (*a sensation, as pain*).—**dead-end**, a pipe, passage, etc. closed at one end; (*lit and fig*) a cul-de-sac; **dead heat**, a race in which two or more competitors are equal at the end; **dead language**, one no longer spoken; **dead´-lett´er**, a law or rule which has been made but is not enforced; a letter undelivered and unclaimed at the post-office; **dead´line**, the date by which something must be done; a line drawn in a military prison, by going beyond which a prisoner makes himself liable to be shot instantly; **dead´lock**, a complete standstill, also *vt.*—*adj* **dead´ly**, causing death; fatal; death-like; implacable; intense; **dead´ march**, a solemn march played at funerals;—**dead´ness**; deadpan an expressionless face; one having such;—esp when the situation implies feeling of some kind, eg amusement.—**dead reck´oning**, an estimation of a ship's place by the logbook and compass

deaf [def] *adj* dull of hearing; unable to hear; not willing to hear;—*vt* **deaf´en**, to make deaf; to stun; to render impervious to sound; **deaf´ness**.

deal¹ [dēl] *n* a portion, amount (a great, good, deal); (*inf*) a large amount; the act of dividing playing cards; a business transaction, esp a favorable one.—*vt* to divide, to distribute; to deliver (*eg a blow*).—*vi* to transact business (with); to trade (in); —*pt, p p* **dealt** [delt].—**deal´er**, a trader; in cards, one whose turn it is to deal or who has dealt the hand in play.—**deal with**, to tackle and dispose of (any problem or task).

deal² [dēl] *n* fir or pine wood.—*adj* of deal.

dean [dēn] *n* a dignitary in cathedral and collegiate churches who presides over the canons; the head of a faculty in a university or college; high school administrator in charge of discipline; **dean´ery**, group of parishes presided over by a dean; a dean's house; **dean´ship**.

dear [dēr] *adj* high in price, costly; highly valued; beloved; a conventional form of address used in letter-writing.—*n* one who is beloved.—*adv* at a high price.—*adv* **dear´ly**.—**dear´ness; dearth** [*dûrth*], scarcity; famine.

death [deth] *n* the end of life; manner or cause of dying; state of being dead; the destruction of something.—**death´blow**, a blow that causes death; a mortal blow; —*adj* **death´less**, never dying; everlasting.—*n* **death´lessness**.—*adj* **deathly**, deadly; deathlike.—**death march**, a forced trek on which many will die of exhaustion; **death´mask**, a plaster-cast taken from the face after death; **death´rate** the proportion of deaths to the population; **deathtrap**, an unsafe structure or place; **death´watch beetle** (family **Anobiidae**) name for several insects that produce a ticking noise; **death´-wish**, conscious or unconscious wish for death for oneself or for another.

debacle [dā-bäk´l, di-bak´l] *n* a breaking up of ice on a river; a complete break-up or collapse.

debar [di-bär´] *vt* to bar out (from); to exclude.

debark [di-bärk´] *vt* to disembark.—*n* **dēbarkā´tion**.

debase [di-bās´] *vt* to lower; to make mean or of less value, to degrade; to adulterate, as the coinage.

debate [di-bāt´] *n* a contention in words; a formal argument; a (parliamentary) discussion.—*vt* to argue about.—*vi* to deliberate; to join in debate.—*adj* **debāt´able**, liable to be disputed.—*n* **debāt´er**.

debauch [di-böch´] *vt* to corrupt; to seduce; to lead away from duty or allegiance.—*vi* to over-indulge.—*n* a fit of intemperance or debauchery.—*p adj* **debauched´**, corrupt; profligate.—*n* **debauch´ery**, indulgence in harmful or immoral sensual behavior.

debenture [di-ben´tyür, -chür] *n* a written acknowledgment of a debt; a security issued by a company for borrowed money.

debilitate [di-bil´i-tāt] *vt* to make weak, to impair the strength of.—**debilitā´tion; debil´ity**.

debit [deb´it] *n* an entry in a ledger of a debt.—*vt* to charge (a person, with a debt); to enter on the debit side of an account.

debonair [deb-o-nār´] *adj* having a carefree manner; courteous, gracious, charming.

debouch [di-bowch´, di-böösh´] *vi* to come out from a narrow pass or confined place.—*n* **debouchure´**, the mouth of a river or strait.

debrief [dē-brēf´] *vt* to gather information from (a soldier, astronaut, etc.) on his return from a mission.

debris [deb´rē] *n* remains of wreckage, (*geol*) a mass of rocky fragments.

debt [det] *n* something one person owes to another; liability to pay or to do something; a state of obligation or of indebtedness.—*n* **debt´or**, one who owes money to another.

debunk [de-bungk´] *vt* to show up (a claim or theory as false.

début [dā-bü´] *n* a beginning or first attempt; a first appearance before the public or in society.

decade [dek´ād, -ād´, dek´ad] *n* a group of ten, esp a series of ten years (*eg the 80s*).

decadence [dek´a-dens] *or* **de-kā´-, dec´adency** (*or de-kā´-*), *n* state of decay; deterioration in standard,—*adj* **dec´adent** (*or de-kā´-*).

decaffeinated [dēkaf´ināted] *adj* (of coffee or tea) with caffeine reduced or removed.

decagon [dek´a-gon] *n* a plane figure of ten angles and sides, a ten-sided polygon—*adj* **decag´onal**.

decahedron [dek-a-hē´dron] *n* a solid figure having ten faces.—*adj* **decahē´dral**.

decameter *see* **dekameter**.

decamp [di-kamp´] *vi* to leave suddenly or secretly.—*n* **decamp´ment**.

decant [di-kant´] *vt* to pour off, leaving sediment; to pour from one vessel to another.—**decantā´tion; decant´er**, an ornamental bottle for holding decanted liquid.

decapitate [di-kap´i-tāt] *vt* to behead.—*n* **decapitā´tion**.

decarbonize [dē-kär´bon-īz] *vt* to remove carbon from. Also **decarburize**.—*n* **decarbonizā´ation**.

decasyllable [dek-a-sil´a-bl] *n* a verse line, or a word, with ten syllables.—*adj* **decasyllab´ic**.

decathlon [dek-ath´lon] *n* a track-and-field contest consisting of ten events.

decay [di-kā´] *vi* to fall away from a state of health or excellence; to waste away; to rot.—*vt* to cause to decompose or rot.—*n* a falling into a worse state; a wearing away; (*chem, phys*) disintegration of a radioactive substance.—*p adj* **decayed´**, (*fig*) reduced in circumstances.

decease [di-sēs´] *n* death.—*vi* to die.—*adj* **deceased´**, dead.—*n* the dead person previously referred to.

deceit [di-sēt´] *n* act of deceiving; anything intended to mislead; fraud; falseness.—*adj* **deceit´ful**, disposed or tending to deceive; insincere.—*adv* **deceit´fully**.—*n* **deceit´fulness**.—*vt* **deceive** (di-sēv´), to mislead; to cheat; to disappoint.

decelerate [dē-sel´er-āt] *vti* to slow down.

December [di-sem'bėr] *n* the twelfth and last month of the year with 31 days.

decennial [de-sen'yål] *adj* of period of ten years.

decent [dē'sėnt] *adj* respectable, proper; moderate; not obscene; (*inf*) quite good; kind, generous—*n* **dē'cency.**—*adv* **dē'cently.**

decentralize [dē-sen'trål-īz] *vt* to transfer functions from central government, organization or head to local centers.—*n* **decentraliza'tion.**

deception [di-sep'sh(ò)n] *n* act of deceiving; state of being deceived; means of deceiving or misleading; trick; illusion.—*adj* **decep'tive, decep'tively.**—*n* **decep'tiveness.**

decide [di-sīd'] *vt* to determine, to end, to settle; to resolve.—*vi* to make up one's mind.—*adj* **decid'ed,** determined, settled; clear, unmistakable; resolute.—*adv* **decid'edly.**

deciduous [di-sid'ū-us] *adj* liable to be shed at a certain period; shedding (teeth, leaves, antlers, etc.).

decimal *adj* of tenths, of numbers written to the base 10.—**decimalize,** to express as a decimal or to convert to a decimal system.—*adv* **dec'imally.**—**decimal number system,** the ordinary number system which denotes real numbers according to place values for multiples of ten; **decimal point,** a dot written before the numerator in a decimal fraction, thus 0.5 = ½.

decimate [des'i-māt] *vt* to reduce greatly in number, as by slaughter or disease; to punish by killing every tenth man.—*n* **decimā'tion.**

decipher [di-sī'fėr] *vt* to read or transliterate from secret writing; to make out what is unknown or difficult.—*adj* **deci'pherable.**

decision [di-sizh'(ò)n] *n* the act of deciding; a settlement; a judgment; firmness (eg *to act with decision*); the quality of being decided in character.—*adj* **deci'sive.**—*adv* **deci'sively.**

deck [dek] *vt* to cover; to adorn.—*n* the floor on a ship, airplane, bus, or bridge; an extension to a dwelling made of planks; a pack of playing cards; the turntable of a phonograph; the playing mechanism of a tape recorder; (*slang*) the ground, the floor; a portion of narcotics.—**deck'chair,** folding chair made of canvas suspended in a frame. Also **steamer chair.**—**deck'hand,** (*inf*) a stagehand.

deckle [dek'l] *n* in paper-making a frame for fixing the width of a sheet.—*n* **deck'le-edge,** the rough edge of hand-made paper, or imitation of it.

declaim [di-klām'] *vti* to make a rhetorical speech; to recite.—*n* **declamation,** [de-kla-māsh'(ò)n].—*adj* **declăm'ătory.**

declare [di-klār'] *vt* to make known; to assert; to make a full statement of, as of goods at a custom-house.—*vi* (*law*) to make a statement; (*with* **for, against**) to announce one's decision or sympathies.—*adj* **declār'able.**—**declaration,** a written affirmation.—*adj* **declared'.**

declassify [dē-klas'i-fī] *vt* to take off the secret list.

decline [di-klīn'] *vi* to deviate; to move down; to deteriorate; to fail; to draw to an end; to refuse.—*vt* to turn away from, to refuse; (*gram*) to give the various cases of a declension.—*n* a falling off; a down-slope; decay; a gradual sinking of the bodily faculties.—*n* **declinā'tion** act of declining; a sloping downward; (*astron*) angular distance from the celestial equator.

declivity [di-kliv'i-ti] *n* a place that slopes downward.

decoct [di-kokt'] *vt* to prepare or extract by boiling.—*n* **decoc'tion.**

decode [dē-kōd'] *vt* to translate from a code.

décolleté [dā-kol-tā] *adj* cut low at the neckline.

decolorize [dē-kul'ór-īz] *vt* to deprive of color.

decompose [dē-kom-pōz'] *vt* to separate the component parts of; to resolve into elements.—*vi* to decay.—*adj* **decompos'-able.**—*n* **decomposi'tion.**

decompress [dē-kom-pres'] *vt* to decrease the pressure on, esp gradually.—*n* **decompression.**

decontaminate [dē-kon-tam'in-āt] *vt* to free from contamination.—*n* **decontaminā'tion.**

decontrol [dē-kon-trōl'] *vt* to remove (esp) official control.

décor [dā-kór] *n* scenery and stage embellishments; disposition of ornament; general decorative effect, eg of a room.

decorate [dek'o-rāt] *vt* to ornament; to honour with a badge or medal.—*adj* **dec'orated,**—*n* **decorā'tion,** ornament; badge of

an order.—*adj* **dec'orātive,** ornamental.—*n* **dec'orātor,** one who decorates, esp houses.

decorous [dek'o-rus] or [de-kō'rus] *adj* becoming, proper, decent; showing propriety and dignity.—*adv* **decō'rously** [or **dek'o-rus-li**].—*ns* **decō'rousness** [or **dek'o-**]; **decō'rum,** what is becoming in outward appearance, propriety of conduct, decency.

decorticate [dē-kōr'ti-kāt] *vt* to deprive of the bark, husk, or peel.—*n* **decorticā'tion.**

decoy [di-koy'] *vt* to lure into a trap.—*n* anything intended to allure into a snare; a trap for wild ducks.

decrease [di-krēs'] *vi* to become less.—*vt* to make less.—*n* (*dē'krēs*) a growing less; the amount of diminution.—*adj* **decreas'ingly.**

decree [di-krē'] *n* an order, edict or law; a judicial decision; a predetermined purpose (of God).—*vt* to decide by sentence in law; to appoint.

decrement [dek're-mėnt] *n* the act or state of decreasing; the quantity lost by decrease.

decrepit [di-krep'it] *adj* worn out by the infirmities of old age; in the last stage of decay.—*ns* **decrep'itness, decrep'itude.**

decretal [di-kre+'tal] *n* a decree, esp of the Pope; a book containing decrees.

decry [di-krī'] *vt* to cry down, to censure as worthless;—*pt p* **decried'.**—*ns* **decrī'al, decrī'er.**

decumbent [di-kum'bėnt] *adj* reclining on the ground.

dedicate [ded'i-kāt] *vt* to consecrate (to some sacred purpose); to devote wholly or chiefly; to inscribe (to someone).—*ns* **dedicā'tion, ded'icātor.**—*adj* **ded'icātory.**

deduce [di-dūs'] *vt* to derive; to infer from what precedes or from premises.—*adj* **deduc'ible** [-dūs'-].—*vt* **deduct'**, to take (from); to subtract.—*adj* **deduct'ible.**—*n* **deduc'tion.**

deed [dēd] *n* an act; an exploit; a legal document recording a transaction.

deem [dēm] *vt* or *vi* to judge; to think, to believe.

deep [dēp] *adj* extending or placed far down or far from the outside; far involved (in eg difficulties); engrossed (in, eg study); profound, intense (eg learning, sleep, distress, sin), heartfelt (eg thankfulness), penetrating (eg understanding); difficult to understand; secret; cunning; sunk low; low in pitch; (of a color) of high saturation and low brilliance.—*adv* in a deep manner; far in, into (eg *deep in the forest, in the night*).—*n* that which is deep; the sea.—**deep'en,** to make deeper in any sense; to increase.—*vi* to become deeper.—*adv* **deep'ly.**—*n* **deep'ness.**

deer [dēr] *n* any animal of the *Cervidae,* a family characterised by the possession of antlers, by the males at least, including stag, reindeer, etc.;—*pl* **deer.**—*ns* **deer'-for'est,** wild tract (not necessarily woodland) reserved for deer; **deer'-stalk'er,** one who stalks deer; a sportsman's cap peaked at back and front.

deface [di-fās',] *vt* to disfigure; to obliterate.—*n* **deface'ment.**

defalcate [dē'-] or [de'fal-kāt] or [di-fal'kāt] *vi* to embezzle.—*ns* **defalcā'tion, def'alcātor.**

defame [di-fām'] *vt* to destroy the good reputation of; to speak evil of.—*n* **defamā'tion,** slander.—*adj* **defam'atory.**

default [di-fölt'] *n* a fault or failure; neglect to do what duty or law requires; failure to fulfil a financial obligation.—*vi* to fail in one's duty (as honoring a financial obligation, or appearing in court).—*n* **default'er,** one who defaults.—**in default of,** in the absence of; for lack of.

defeasible [di-fēz'ibl] *adj* that may be defeated or annulled.

defeat [di-fēt'] *vt* to frustrate; to win a victory over.—*n* a frustration of plans; overthrow, as of an army in battle; loss of a game, race, etc.—*ns* **defeat'ism,** disposition to accept defeat; **defeat'ist**—also *adj.*

defecate [def'e-kāt, dēf'-] *vt* to clear from impurities or extraneous matter.—*n* **defecā'tion.**

defect [di-fekt, dē'fekt] *n* a deficiency; a blemish, fault.—*vi* (*di-fekt'*), to desert one's country or a cause, transferring one's allegiance (to another).—*ns* **defec'tion,** failure; a falling away from duty or allegiance; **defec'tionist.**—*adj* **defec'tive,** having a defect; faulty; incomplete; (*gram*) not having all the inflections.—*n* a person defective in physical or mental powers.

defence [di-fens'] *n* a defending; capability or means of resisting an attack; protection; vindication; (*law*) a defendant's plea; the defending party in legal proceedings.

defend [di-fend'] *vt* (*arch*) to prohibit; to guard or protect; to maintain against attack (*law*) to resist, as a claim; to contest (a suit).—*adj* **defend'able**, that may be defended.—*ns* **defend'ant**, a defender; (*law*) a person accused or sued; **defnd'er**; **defense**, American spelling of **defence**.—*adj* **defens'ible**.—*n* **defnsibil'ity**.—*adj* **defens'ive**, serving to defend; in a state or posture of defence.

defer [di-fûr'] I*vt* to put off to another time; to delay;—*pr p* **deferr'ing**; *pa p* **deferred'**.—*n* **defer'ment**; **deferred payment**, payment by instalments.

defer [di-fûr'] *vi* to yield (to wishes or opinions of another, or to authority);—*pr p* **deferr'ing**; *pa p* **deferred'**.—*n* **deference** (def'-ér-èns), a deferring or yielding in judgment or opinion.—*adj* **deferen'tial**, expressing deference or respect.—*adv* **deferen'tially**.

defiance [di-fi'áns] *n* the act of defying; a challenge to combat; contempt of opposition.—*adj* **defi'ant**.—*adv* **def'antly**.

deficient [di-fish'ént] *adj* wanting, lacking.—*ns* **defic'iency**, defect; lack; **def'icit**, deficiency, esp of revenue, as compared with expenditure.

defile [di-fil'] *vi* to march off in file or line, or file by file.—*n* (*dē'fīl*), di-fil') a long narrow pass or way, in which troops can march only in file or with a narrow front.—*n* **defile'ment**.

defile [di-fil'] *vt* (*lit* and *fig*) to pollute or corrupt; (*arch*) to ravish.

define [di-fīn'] *vt* to fix the bounds or limits of; to mark the limits or outline of clearly; to describe accurately; to fix the meaning of.—*adjs* **defin'able**, that may be defined; **def'inite**, defined; having distinct limits; fixed; exact; clear—*adv* **def'initely**.—*ns* **def'initeness**; **defini'tion**, a defining; a description of a thing by its properties; an explanation of the exact meaning of a word, term, or phrase; sharpness of outline.—*adj* **defin'itive**, defining or limiting; decisive, final—*n* (*gram*) an adjective used to limit the signification of a noun.—*adv* **defin'itively**.

deflate [dē-flāt'] *vt* to undo or reverse the process of inflation.—*n* **deflā'tion**.

deflect [di-flekt'] *vti* to turn aside; to swerve or deviate from a right line or proper course.—**deflec'tion**, **deflec'tor**.

deflower [di-flow'(è)r] *vt* to deprive of virginity.—*n* **defloration**.

deforest [dē-for'est] *vt* to clear of forests.—*n* **deforestā'tion**.

deform [di-förm'] *vt* to spoil the natural form of; to put out of shape.—**deformā'tion**; **deform'ity**, a deformed part of the body, depravity.

defraud [di-fröd'] *vt* to deprive by cheating or deceiving.

defray [di-frā'] *vt* to pay (the expenses of).

defrost [dē-frost'] *vt* to thaw out; to remove frost or ice from;—also *vi*.

deft [deft] *adj* adroit, skilful, quick and neat in action.—*adv* **deft'ly**.—*n* **deft'ness**.

defunct [di-fungkt'] *adj* no longer being in existence or functioning or in use.

defuse [de'fūz'] *vt* to remove the fuse from (a bomb or mine).

defy [di-fi'] *vt* to challenge; to brave, to flout, or to resist (eg convention, order, person);—*pr p* **defy'ing**; *pt p* **defied'**.

degauss [dē-gows'] *vt* to demagnetize.

degenerate [di-jen'ér-åt] *adj* having declined in physical or moral qualities; sexually deviant.—Also *n*—*vi* become or grow worse; (*biol*) to return to a simpler state.—**degen'eracy**, **degenerā'tion**.

degrade [di-grād'] *vt* to lower in grade or rank; to deprive of office or dignity; to debase; to disgrace.—**degradation**.

degree [di-grē'] *n* a step in an ascending or descending series; a stage in intensity; the relative quantity in intensity; a unit of measurement in a scale; an academic title awarded as of right or as an honor; the classification of a crime; a point on the earth's surface as measured by degrees latitude or longitude.—**by degrees**, gradually.

dehumanize [dē-hū'man-īz] *vt* to deprive of human qualities, to brutalize.

dehumidify [dē-hūmid'ifī] *vt* to remove moisture from air—*n* **dehumid'ifier**, an electrical appliance for removing moisture from the air.

dehydrate [dē-hī-drāt'] *vt* to deprive of water chemically; to

dry (foodstuffs); (*fig*) to deprive of strength, interest, etc.—*n* **dehydrā'tion**, loss of moisture; (*med*) excessive loss of water from the tissues of the body.

dē-ice [de-īs] *vt* to remove ice.

deify [dē'i-fī] *vt* to exalt to the rank of a god; to worship as a deity;—*pr p* **dē'ifying**; *pt p* **dē'ified**.

deign [dān] *vi* to condescend.—*vt* to condescend to give.

deist [dē'ist] *n* one who believes in the existence of God, but not in revealed religion.—*n* **dē'ism**.—*adjs* **deist'ic**, **-al**.

deity [dē'i-ti] *n* divinity; godhead; a god or goddess; **Deity**, the Supreme Being.

déjà vu [dā-zhā vū] *n* an illusion of having experienced something that is really being experienced for the first time.

deject [di-jekt'] *vt* to cast down the spirits of.—*adj* **deject'ed**, **dejec'tion**.

delay [di-lā'] *vt* to put off to another time, to postpone; to hinder, retard.—*vi* to pause, linger, or put off time;—*pr p* **delay'ing**; *pt p* **delayed'**.—*n*.

delectable [di-lekt'a-bl] *adj* delightful, pleasing.—*n.* **delect'ableness**.—*adv.* **delect'ably**.—*n* **delectā'tion**.

delegate [del'e-gāt] *vt* to send as a representative; to entrust power, task or responsibility to (an agent or assembly).—*n* [-gåt] a deputy or an elected representative.—*n* **delegā'tion**.

delete [di-lēt'] *vt* to blot out, to erase.—*n* **delē'tion**.

deleterious [del-e-tē'ri-us] *adj* hurtful or destructive.

delft [delf(t)] *n*, a kind of tin-glazed earthenware originally made at *Delft*, Holland.

deliberate [di-lib'ér-åt] *vt* to weigh in the mind.—*vi* to discuss or debate thoroughly; to consider.—*adj* [-åt] well considered; intentional; considering carefully; cautious; quiet, unflurried.—*adv* **delib'erately**.—**delib'erateness**; **deliberā'tion**.—*adj* **delib'erative**, proceeding or acting by deliberation.

delicate [del'i-kåt] *adj* fine in texture; fragile, not robust; requiring tactful handling; of exquisite workmanship; requiring skill in techniques.—*n* **del'icacy**, a luxurious food; sensibility or behaviour.—*adv* **del'icately**.—*n* **del'icateness**.

delicatessen [del-i-kà-tes'n] *n* a store selling prepared foods, esp meat. Also **deli**.

delicious [di-lish'us] *adj* highly pleasing to the senses, esp taste; giving exquisite pleasure.—*adv* **deli'ciously**, delightfully;—*n* **deli'ciousness**.

delight [di-līt'] *vt* to please highly.—*vi* to have or take great pleasure.—*n* a high degree of pleasure; that which gives great pleasure.—*adjs* **delight'ful**.

delimit [di-lim'it] *vt* to fix or mark the limit of.—*n* **delimitā'tion**.

delineate [di-lin'e-åt] *vt* to describe accurately in pictures or words.—*ns* **delineā'tion**, **delin'eator**.

delinquent [di-ling'kwènt] *adj* failing in duty; guilty of an offense; (of a bill) overdue.—*n* a person guilty of misdeed, esp young person who breaks the law.—*n* **delin'quency**.

delirious [di-lir'i-us] *adj* wandering in mind, light-headed; wildly excited.—*adv* **delir'iously**;—*ns* **delir'iousness**.

deliver [de-liv'ér] *vt* to transport (goods) to their destination; to distribute regularly; to liberate, to rescue; to give birth; to assist at a birth; to launch (a blow); to pitch (a baseball); to utter (a speech).—*adj* **deliv'erable**.—**deliv'erance**, act of delivering or freeing; **deliv'erer**; **deliv'ery**.

dell [del] *n* a little hollow, usu. with trees.

Delphic utterance [del'fik] a statement open to more than one interpretation.

delta [del'ta] *n* the fourth letter of the Greek alphabet, Δ; a tract of land of like shape formed at the mouth of a river; word used in communication for the letter *d*.

delude [di-l(y)ōōd'] *vt* to deceive.

deluge [del'ūj] *n* a flood, esp that in the days of Noah; (*fig*) anything happening in a heavy rush.—*vt* to inundate (*lit*, *fig*).

delusion [di-l(y)ōō'zh(ó)n] *n* a false belief; a persistent false belief that is a symptom of mental illness.

de luxe [dè lūks', di lŏŏks', luks'] adj sumptuous, luxurious.

delve [delv] *vti* to search deeply; (*literary*) to dig.

demagnetize [dē-mag'net-īz] *vt* to remove magnetic power from.

demagogue [dem'a-gog] *n* a political orator who appeals to the passions and prejudices of the people.—*adjs* **demagogic**, **-al** [-gog'- or -goj'-].—*n* **demagogy** [-goj'-].

demand [di-mänd'] *vt* to ask for in an imperious manner.—*n* the asking for what is due; an asking for with authority; an urgent claim; desire shown by consumers.—*n* **demand′ant**; a plaintiff—**in demand**, sought after.

demarcation [dē-märk-ā′sh(ó)n] *n* the act of marking off or setting bounds to;—*vt* **dē′marcate**.

demean[1] [di-mēn′] *vt* to behave.—*n* **demeanor**, conduct; bearing.

demean[2] [di-mēn′] *vt* to lower in dignity.

dement [di-ment′] *vt* to deprive of reason.— *adj* **dement′ed**, out of one's mind; insane.—*n* **dementia** [de-men′shi-a], the failure or loss of mental powers.—*n* **dementia praecox** [pre′-kaks] schizophrenia.

demerit [dē-mer′it] *n* a defect, a fault.

demesne [di-mān′, -mēn′] *n* a mansion, with lands adjacent to it not let out to tenants; any estate in land.

demi- [dem′i] half.

demigod [dem′i-god] *n* the offspring of a god and a mortal.

demi-john [dem′i-jon] *n* a glass bottle with a full body and narrow neck holding from one to ten gallons.

demilitarize [dē-mil′itäriz] *vt* to remove armed forces, installations, etc. from; to replace military with civilian government.—*n* **demilitariza′tion.—demilitarized zone**.

demimonde [dem′i-mond] *n* a class of women of dubious reputation.

demise [di-mīz′] *n* death, esp of a distinguished person.—*vt* to bequeath to a successor.

demission [di-mish′(ó)n] *n* relinquishment (of).

demobilize [dē- or di-mōb′il-īz, or -mob′-] *vt* to take out of mobilization, to disband; (*inf*) to discharge from the armed forces.—*n* **demobiliza′tion**.

democracy [di-mok′ra-si] *n* a form of government in which the supreme power is retained by the people collectively and exercised directly or indirectly through their representatives; a state or society characterized by recognition of equality of rights and privileges; political, social or legal equality;—*n* **dem′ocrat**, one free from snobbery; one who adheres to or promotes democracy as a principle; a member of the Democratic party.—*adjs* **democrat′ic,**—*adv* **democrat′ically.**—*vt* **democratize′**.

demography [di-mog′ra-fi] *n* the study of population statistics concerning birth, marriage, death and disease.

demolish [di-mol′ish] *vt* to pull down or knock down (a building); to destroy (an argument); (*inf*) to eat up.—*n* **demoli′tion** [dem-].

demon [dē′mon] *n* an evil spirit, a devil; an energetic and skillful person.—*adjs* **demoniac** [di-mōn′i-ak], **demoniacal** [dē-mo-nī′a-kl].—*n* **demon′iac**, one possessed by a demon or evil spirit.—*adv* **demonī′acally.—demonology**, the study of demons.

demonstrate [de′mon-strāt or di-mon′strät] *vt* to show or point out clearly; to prove with certainty.—*vi* to exhibit one's feelings.—*adj* **demon′strable** [or dem′-],—*n* **demon′strability.**— *adv* **demon′strably** (or *dem′-*).—*n* **demonstrā′tion**, a pointing out; proof by evidence; a practical display or exhibition; a display of emotion; a public manifestation of opinion, as by a rally or parade etc. (*Also* **demo**); a display of armed force.— *adj* **demon′strative**, showing one's feelings; making evident; proving with certainty; of the nature of proof.

demoralize [dē-mor′al-īz] *vt* to corrupt in morals; to lower the *morale* of—that is, to deprive of spirit and confidence or to throw into confusion.—*n* **demoraliza′tion**.

demote [dē-mōt′] *vt* to reduce in rank.

demulcent [di-mul′sènt] *adj* soothing.

demur [di-mûr′] *vi* to raise objections—*pr p* **demurr′ing**; *pt p* **demurred′**.—*n* a hesitation; an objection.

demure [di-mūr′] *adj* sober, staid, modest; affectedly modest; making a show of gravity.—*adv* **demure′ly**.

den [den] *n* a cave or lair of a wild beast; a place where people gather for illegal activities, esp gambling or smoking opium; a room in a house for relaxation or study.

denationalize [dē-nash′on-àl-īz] *vt* to transfer from government to private ownership.

denaturalize [dē-nat′ûr-àl-īz] *vt* to make unnatural; to deprive of citizenship.

denazify [dē-not′sifī] *vt* to obliterate Nazi influence from.

dendroid [den′droid] *adj* having the form of a tree.

dendrology [den-drol′o-ji] *n* the natural history of trees. [Gr *dendron*, a tree, and *logos*, a discourse.]

dengue [deng′gē, -gā] *n* disease of tropical and subtropical regions transmitted by the mosquito. Also **breakbone fever**.

denial [di-nī′al] *n* act of denying or saying no; contradiction; refusal (of request, claim, etc.); disavowal, rejection.—*adj* **denī′able**, that may be denied.

denigrate [den′i-grāt] *vt* to sully the character of; to belittle.— *n* **denigrā′tion**.

denim [den′im] *n* a durable twilled cotton cloth; used for jeans, overalls, etc.

denizen [den′i-zn] *n* an inhabitant, esp any animal or plant indigenous to a different region.

denominate [di-nom′in-āt] *vt* to name; to designate.—*n* **denominā′tion**, the act of naming; a name or title; a religious group comprising many local churches, larger than a sect; one of a series of related units, esp monetary.—*adj* **denomina′-tional.**—*n* **denominā′tionalism.**—*adj* **denom′inative**, giving or having a name.—*adv* **denom′inatively.**—*n* **denom′inator**, (*arith*) the part of a fractional expression written below the fraction line.

denote [di-nōt′] *vt* to note, mark; to indicate, be the sign of; to mean; (*logic*) to name.—*n* **denotā′-tion**.

dénouement [dā-nōō′mä] *n* the unraveling of a plot or story; the issue, event, or outcome.

denounce [di-nowns′] *vt* to inform against publicly; to give information against; to notify formally the ending of (treaties, etc.).—*n* **denounce′ment** (same as **denunciation**).

dense [dens] *adj* difficult to see through; massed closely together; dull-witted.—*adv* **dense′ly.—dense′ness**; **dens′ity**, the ratio of mass to volume.

dent [dent] *n* a small hollow made by the pressure or blow of a harder body on a softer.

dental [den′tàl] *adj* of, or for, the teeth; produced by the aid of the teeth.—*n* a sound produced by applying the tongue to the teeth.

denticle [den′ti-kl] *n* a small tooth or toothlike part.—*adjs* **dentic′ulate, -d**, having notches.

dentiform [den′ti-fòrm] *adj* having the form of a tooth; of teeth.

dentifrice [den′ti-fris] *n* a substance used in cleaning the teeth.

dentine, dentin [den′tin] *n* the hard bonelike part of teeth.

dentist [den′tist] *n* licensed practitioner who treats diseases of the teeth and gums or inserts artificial teeth.—*n* **den′tistry**, the profession of a dentist.

dentition [den-tish′(ó)n] *n* the cutting or growing of teeth; the conformation, number, and arrangement of the teeth; a set of teeth (eg the *milk dentition*).

denture [den′tyùr, -chùr] *n* a set of artificial teeth.

denude [di-nūd′] *vt* to make naked; to deprive, strip.—*n* **dēnu-dā′tion**, a making bare; (*geol*) laying bare by erosion.

denunciate [di-nun′s(h)i-āt] *vt* same as **denounce**.—*n* **denunciation** (*-shi-ā′-*, or *-si-ā′-*), act of denouncing; an arraignment (of);—*adj* **denun′ciatory**, containing, or of the nature of, a denunciation.

deny [di-nī′] *vt* to declare not to be true; to reject; to refuse; to disown;—*pr p* **deny′ing**; *pt p* **denied′**.

deodar [dē-o-där′] *n* a Himalayan cedar (*Cedrus deodara*).

deodorize [dē-ō′dor-īz] *vt* to take the odor or smell from.— **deō′dorant, deō′dorizer**.

depart [di-pärt′] *vi* to go away; to leave, start; to deviate, diverge (from).—*n* **depart′ure**.

department [di-pärt′ment] *n* a unit of specialized functions into which an organization or business is divided; a province.—*adj* **departmental** [dē-pärt-ment′al].—*adv* **department′ally**.

depend [di-pend′] *vi* to hang down; to be based on or connected with anything; to be contingent (on); to rely (on).—*adj* **depend′able**, that may be relied on.—*n* **depend′ent** (also **-ant**), one who depends on, or is supported by, another.—*adj* **depend′ent** (also **-ant**), depending, relying on, contingent; (*gram*) subordinate.—**depend′ence (-ance), depend′ency**, a territory dependent on a distant country.

depict [di-pikt′] *vt* to draw a likeness of: to describe minutely.

depilatory [di-pil′a-tòr-i] *adj* taking hair off.—*n* a substance for removing superfluous hair.

deplete [di-plēt'] *vt* to use up a large quantity of.—*n* **deplē'tion**, the act of emptying or exhausting.

deplore [di-plōr', -plôr'] *vt* to regret deeply; to complain of; to deprecate.—*adj* **deplor'able**.—*adv* **deplor'ably**.

deploy [di-ploi'] *vt* to spread out and place strategically (any forces).—*vi* to open; to extend from column into line, as a body of troops.—*n* **deploy'ment**.

depone [di-pōn'] *vt* to testify upon oath.—*adj* **depōn'ent**.

depopulate [di-pop'ū-lāt (or dē-)] *vt* to reduce the population of.—**depopulā'tion**.

deport [di-, dē-pōrt', -pôrt',] *vt* to expel from a country.—*n* **deportā'tion**.

deport [di-pōrt', -pôrt'] *vt* to behave (*reflexive*).—*n* **deport'ment**, bearing, manners; behavior.

depose [di-pōz'], *vt* to remove from power; to attest.—*adj* **depos'able**.—*n* **depos'al**.

deposit [di-poz'it] *vt* to put or set down; to entrust for safekeeping; to let fall, leave.—*n* that which is deposited; something entrusted to another's care, esp money put in a bank; money given in part payment or security; matter let fall or left in a layer.—**depos'itary**, the one receiving a deposit; a depositary; **depos'itor**; **depos'itory**, a place where anything is deposited.

depot [dep'ō, dē'pō] *n* a storehouse; a bus station, a railroad station.

deprave [di-prāv'] *vt* to make bad or worse; to corrupt.—*n.* **depravā'tion**, act of depraving; state of being depraved, depravity.—**deprav'ity**, a vitiated or corrupt state of moral character; extreme wickedness; corruption.

deprecate [dep'ri-kāt] *vt* to express disapproval of; to seek to avert, esp by prayer.—*n* **deprecā'tion**, **dep'recatory**, apologetic, trying to avert evil by prayer.

depreciate [di-prē'shi-āt] *vt* to lower the worth of; to disparage.—*vi* to fall in value.—*n* **depreciā'tion**.—*adjs* **deprē'ciative**.

depredate [dep'ri-dāt] *vt* to lay waste; to plunder or ravage;—**depredā'tion**, **dep'redator**.

depress [di-pres'] *vt* to press down; to lower; to make less active; to make sad;—*adj* **depressed'**, pressed down; dejected, dispirited.—*adj* **depress'ing**.—*adv* **depress'ingly**.—*n* **depress'ion**, a falling in or sinking; an area of law; atmospheric pressure; a hollow; (*med*) an abnormal state of inactivity; a phase of the business cycle characterized by stagnation, widespread unemployment, etc.

deprive [di-prīv'] *vt* to take a thing away from; to prevent from using or enjoying.—*n* **deprivā'tion**.—*adj* **deprived**.

depth [depth] *n* deepness; the degree of deepness down or inwards; an abyss; the intensity of color; the intensity of emotion or feeling; the profundity of thought; the mid-time of night or of winter; the lowness of sound or pitch; the quality of being deep.—*n* **depth'-charge**, a bomb that explodes under water. **in depth**, intensively and extensively (investigated).

depute [di-pūt'] *vt* to appoint as a substitute; to delegate.—*n* **depūtā'tion**, act of deputing; the person or persons deputed or appointed to transact business for another.—*vi* **dep'utize**, to act as deputy.—*n* **dep'ūty**, a delegate or representative, or substitute.

derail [dē-rāl'] *vt* to cause to leave the rails.—*vi* (of a streetcar, subway train, etc.)—*n* **derail'ment**.

derange [di-rānj'] *vt* to throw into confusion; to make insane.—*adj* **deranged'**, disordered; insane.—*n* **derange'ment**.

der'by contest of any kind open to all; stiff felt hat with dome-like crown.

derelict [der'e-likt] *adj* abandoned; falling in ruins.—*n* a person abandoned by society; a wrecked vehicle.—*n* **derelic'tion**, neglect (of duty).

deride [di-rīd'] *vt* to laugh at, to mock.—*n* **derid'er**.—*adj* **derid'ingly**.

derision [di-rizh'(ó)n] *n* act of ridiculing; mockery; a laughing-stock.—*adjs* **deri'sive**, **deris'ory**.

derive [di-rīv'] *vt* to take from a source or origin; to infer, deduce (from); to trace (a word) to its root.—*vi* to descend or issue (from).—*adj* **deriv'able**.—*n* **derivation** [dèr-iv-ā'sh(ó)n], the tracing of a word to its root; source; descent.—*adj* **deriv'ative**, derived or taken from something else; not radical or original.—*n* that which is derived; a word formed from another word.—*adv* **deriv'atively**.

der'mis[dûr'mis] the fine skin below the epidermis containing blood vessels.—*adj* **der'mal**.—*n* **dermatol'ogy**, the science of skin.

derogate [der'o-gāt] *vi* (*with* from) to detract.—*n* **derogā'tion**, a taking from, detraction, depreciation.—*adj* **derog'atory**, contemptuous; disparaging, deprecating.

derrick [der'ik] *n* any apparatus using a tackle at the end of a beam; a tower-like structure over a drilled hole, esp an oil well.

derring-do [der'ing-dōō] *n* (*false archaic*) daring action.

derringer [der'in-jer] *n* a pocket pistol with a large bore.

dervish [dûr'vish] *n* a member of any Muslim religious order vowing chastity and poverty, noted for frenzied, whirling dancing.

desalinate [dēsal'ināt] or **desalinize** [-īze] *vt* to remove salt from (esp sea water).

descant [des'kant] *n* an accompaniment higher than and harmonizing with the main melody.

descend [di-send'] *vi* to climb down; to pass from a higher to a lower place or condition; to incline downward; to invade (*with* on, upon); to be derived.—*vt* to go down.—*n* **descendant**, one who descends, as offspring from an ancestor.—*adjs* **descend'ent**, **descend'ible**.—*n* **descent'**.

describe [di-skrīb'] *vt* to give an account of; to trace out or delineate.—*adj* **describ'able**.

description [di-skrip'sh(ó)n] *n* act of describing; an account of anything in words; sort, class, or kind.—*adj* **descrip'tive**, serving to describe; containing description.—*adv.*

descry [di-skrī'] *vt* to catch sight of;—*pr p.*

desecrate [des'i-krāt] *vt* to profane; to divert from a sacred purpose;—*n* **desecration**, profanation; act of desecrating.

desert[1] [di-zûrt'] *n* that which is deserved; claim to reward; merit.

desert[2] [di-zûrt'] *vt* to leave; to forsake.—*vi* to run away; to leave the armed forces without permission.—**desert'er**; **deser'tion**.

desert[3] [dez'èrt] *n* a barren place; a waste; a solitude.—*adj* desolate; uninhabited; uncultivated; barren.

deserve [di-zûrv'] *vt* to earn by service; to merit.—*vi* to be worthy of reward.—*adj* **deserv'ing**, worthy.—*advs* **deserv'ingly**, **deserv'edly** [-id], according to desert, justly.

desiccate [des'i-kāt] *vt* to dry up; to preserve by drying;—*vi* to grow dry.

desiderate [di-sid'er-āt] *vt* to wish for or want.—*adj* **desid'erative**, implying desire.—*n* **desiderā'tum**, something desired or much wanted;—*pl* **desiderā'ta**.

design [di-zīn'] *vt* to make working drawings for; to contrive; to intend—*n* a working drawing; a plan or scheme formed in the mind; intention; relation of parts to the whole, disposition of forms and colors; pattern.—*adj* **design'able**.—*adv* **design'edly** [-id-li], intentionally.—*adj* **design'ing**, artful, scheming.—*vt* **des'ignate** [-ig-nāt], to mark out, specify, make known; to name; to be a name for; to appoint or nominate.—*adj* [-āt] appointed to office but not yet installed (*placed after noun*).—*n* **designā'tion**, a pointing out; name; title.

desire [di-zīr'] *vt* to long for, wish for; request, ask.—*n* an earnest longing or wish; a prayer or request; the object desired; lust.—*adj* **desir'able**, worthy of desire; pleasing, agreeable.—**desir'ableness**, **desirabil'ity**.—*adv* **desir'ably**.—*adj* **desir'ous**, full of desire.

desist [di-zist', -sist'] *vi* to stop.

desk [desk] *n* a table for writing or reading; a counter; the specialized section of an organization such as a newspaper or the Department of State; position in an orchestra.

desolate [des'o-lāt] *vt* to make joyless, wretched; to deprive of inhabitants; to lay waste.—*adj* [des'o-lāt] solitary; joyless; destitute of inhabitants; laid waste.—*adv* **des'olately**.—**des'olateness**; **desolā'tion**, waste, destruction; a place desolated; sorrow without hope.

despair [di-spār'] *vi* to be without hope; to despond.—*n* hopelessness; that which causes despair.—*adv* **despair'ingly**.

despatch *see* **dispatch**.

desperate [des'pér-àt] *adj* in a state of despair; hopeless; despairingly reckless; frantic; (of a remedy) extreme.—*adv*

des'perately.—des'perateness, desperā'tion, state of despair; disregard of danger, recklessness.

despicable [des'pi-ka-bl, -pik'] adj deserving to be despised, contemptible, worthless.

despise [di-spīz'] vt to look down upon with contempt; to scorn.

despite [di-spīt'] n a looking down upon with contempt; violent malice or hatred.—prep in spite of, notwithstanding.—adj despite'ful.—adv despite'fully.—n despite'fulness.

despoil [di-spoil'] vt to spoil or strip completely (eg of possessions); to rob.—despoil'er; despōliā'tion.

despond [di-spond'] vi to be wanting in hope, to be dejected.—despond'ence, despond'ency, dejection.—adj despond'ent, desponding.—advs despond'ently; despond'ingly.

despot [des'pot] n one invested with absolute power; a tyrant.—adjs despot'ic, -al.—adv.—n des'potism.

desquamate [des'kwa-māt] vi to scale off.—n desquamā'tion.

dessert [diz-ûrt'] n the sweet course at the end of a meal.

destine [des'tin] vt to predetermine; (in passive) to be fated; to doom (to good or evil).—destinā'tion, the place to which one, anything, is going; des'tiny, the purpose or end to which any person or thing is appointed; unavoidable fate.

destitute [des'ti-tūt] adj in utter want; (with of) entirely lacking in.—n destitū'tion, poverty.

destroy [di-stroi'] vi to pull down, demolish; to ruin, to put an end to; to do away with, to kill;—pr p destroy'ing; pt p destroyed'.—n destroy'er, a person or thing that destroys; a fast small warship.

destruction [di-struk'sh(ó)n] n act, or means, of destroying; ruin.—vt destruct', (inf) to destroy (a rocket or missile) in flight.—adj destruc'tible, able, or liable, to be destroyed.—n destructibil'ity.—adj destruc'tive.

desuetude [des'wi-tūd] n passing into disuse.

desultory [des'ûl-tòr-i] adj going aimlessly from one thing to another, unmethodical.—adv des'ultorily.—n des'ultoriness.

detach [di-tach'] vt to release; to separate, disengage; (mil) to send off on special service.—vi to separate.—adj detach'able.—p adj detached', unconnected; separate; aloof; free from emotion.—n detach'ment, that which is detached, as a body of troops.

detail [di-tāl'] vt to relate minutely; to enumerate; (mil) to set apart for a particular duty.—n (dē'tāl, or di-tāl') a small part; an item; an account that goes into particulars; intricate decoration.—adj detailed', giving full particulars; exhaustive.

detain [di-tān'] vt to delay, stop; to keep in custody.—detainee (di-tān'ē), one who is held in custody; detain'er, one who detains; detain'ment.

detect [di-tekt'] vt to discover; to find out; to discern.—adj detect'able, detect'ible.—n detec'tion.—adj detect'ive, of detection or detectives.—n a person, usually a police-officer employed to find evidence of crimes.—n detec'tor, one who detects; a device for detecting the presence of something.

détente [dā-tāt'] n relaxation of strained relations between countries.

deter [di-tûr'] vt to frighten, hinder, or prevent (from);—pt p deterr'ing; pt p deterred'.—adj deterrent.

detergent [dē-tûr'jent] n a cleaning agent. Also adj.

deteriorate [di-tē'ri-ò-rāt] vt to make worse.—vi to grow worse.—n detēriorā'tion.

determine [di-tûr'min] vt to limit; to fix or settle; to find out; to put an end to; to regulate; to impel.—vi to come to a decision; to come to an end.—adj deter'minable.—adj deter'minant, serving to determine.—n that which serves to determine; (math) an algebraic term expressing the sum of certain products of numbers represented by arranging the terms in a square or matrix.—adj deter'minate.—adv deter'minately.—n determinā'tion, that which is determined or resolved on; direction to a certain end; resolution; fixed purpose; decision of character. deter'mined, firm in purpose, resolute; fixed.—adv deter'minedly.—n deter'minism, the doctrine that all things, including the will, are determined by causes.

detest [di-test'] vt to dislike intensely.—adj detest'able, worthy of being detested, extremely hateful, abominable.—adv detest'ably.—n dētestā'tion, extreme hatred.

dethrone [di-thrōn'] vt to remove from a throne; depose.—n dethrone'ment.

detonate [det'o-nāt, dē'to-nāt] vi to explode rapidly and violently.—vt to cause so to explode.—detonā'tion, det'onātor, a device that initiates an explosion.

detour [dē'tōōr, di-tōōr'] n a deviation from an intended course, esp one temporarily replacing a more direct route.

detract [di-trakt'] vt to take away.—vi to take away (from), lessen, esp reputation or worth.—detrac'ter, detrac'tor; detrac'tion, slander.

detrain [dē-trān'] vi to come out of a train.

detriment [det'ri-mènt] n damage, injury.—adj, n detriment'al.

detritus [di-trī'tus] n fragments formed by the rubbing away from a larger mass, any waste, esp of rock.

deuce[1] [dūs] n a card or die with two spots; a two-dollar bill; the sum of two dollars; (lawn tennis); the score of forty all in a game or five all in a set.

deuce[2] [dūs] n the devil—in exclamatory phrases.

deuterogamy [dū-ter-og'a-mi] n second marriage.

devalue [dē-val'ū] vt to reduce the value of.—vt deval'uate.—n devaluā'tion [de-+value.]

devastate [dev'as-tāt] vt to lay waste; to plunder—vi to be overwhelmed.—n devastā'tion, havoc.

develop -e [di-vel'op] vt to lay open by degrees; to evolve; to bring to maturity; to show, reveal the symptoms of (eg a habit, a disease); to elaborate (eg a plan); to treat photographic film or plate to reveal image; to improve the value of.—vi to grow (into); to become apparent.—devel'oper; a reagent for developing photographs; an apparatus for developing muscles; devel'opment.

deviate [dē'vi-āt] vi to turn aside (from a course, topic, principle, etc.); to diverge, differ, from a standard, norm, etc.; to vary from type.—dē'viant, that which deviates from an accepted norm.—also adj; deviā'tion.

device [di-vīs'] n a contrivance; an invention; a scheme, a plot; a heraldic or emblamatic figure or design.

devil [dev'l] n (Devil) supreme spirit of evil, Satan; any evil spirit; a very wicked person; (inf) a reckless, lively person; (inf) someone or something difficult to deal with; an expletive; an apprentice; a highly seasoned dish.—vt to season highly.—vi to drudge for another;—pr p dev'illing; pt p dev'illed.—adj dev'ilish, fiendish, malignant.—adv (inf) very, exceedingly.—adv devilishly.—adj dev'il-may-care, reckless, audacious. devil's advocate, one who advocates opposing cause, esp for the sake of argument; in RC Church, an official appointed to present arguments against beatification or canonization.

devious [dē'vi-us] adj indirect; not straightforward; underhand.—adv dē'viously.—n dē'viousness.

devise [di-vīz'] vt to invent, contrive; to plan; to leave real estate by will.—ns devīs'er, one who contrives; devīs'or, one who bequeaths.

devitalize [dē-vī'ta-līz] vt to deprive of life or vitality.—n devitalizā'tion.

devitrification [de-vitri-fica'shun] n loss of glassy or vitreous condition.

devoid [di-void'] adj (with of) lacking; free from.

devolution [dev-] or [dēv-ol-ū'sh(ó)n] n a transference from one person to another; (biol) degeneration.

devolve [di-volv'] vt to hand on to a successor or deputy; to deliver over.

devote [di-vōt'] vt to set apart; to dedicate by solemn act; to give or use for a particular activity or purpose.—adj devōt'ed, zealous; strongly attached;—adv devōt'edly.—ns devotee [-tē' or dev'-], one wholly or superstitiously devoted (with of or to); a fanatic; devō'tion, consecration; given to the worship of God; piety; strong affection, or attachment (to); ardor; (pl) prayers.

devour [di-vowr'] vt to swallow greedily; to eat up; to consume or waste; to take in eagerly by the senses or mind.—n devour'er.

devout [di-vowt'] adj given up to religious thoughts and exercises, pious.—adv devout'ly.

dew [dū] n air moisture, deposited on a cool surface, esp at night; any beaded moisture.—vt to wet with dew; to moisten.—ns dew'drop; dew'point, the temperature at which dew begins to form; the temperature at which a vapor begins to condense.—*adj* **dew'y**.

dewlap [dū'lap] *n* the pendulous skin under the throat etc.—*adj* **dew'lapped**.

dexter [deks'ter] *adj* (of a heraldic shield) on the right-hand side; right.—*n* **dexter'ity** right-handedness; readiness and skill, adroitness.—*adjs* **dex'terous**, **dex'trous**, right-handed; adroit, clever.—*adj* **dex'tral**, right, as opposed to left.

dex'trose [deks'trōs] *n* glucose.

dhow [dow] *n* a lateen-sailed Arab vessel of the Indian Ocean.

diabetes [dī-a-bē'tēz] *n* a disorder marked by the persistent and excessive discharge of urine.—*n, adj* **diabet'ic**, (of) a person who suffers from diabetes.—**diabetis insipidus**, a condition whereby large quantities of dilute urine are discharged.—**diabetes mellitus** [meli'tes], a disorder marked by inability of the body to use carbohydrates due to the failure of the pancreas to secrete insulin.

diablerie [dē-äb'lè-rē] *n* black magic, sorcery.

diabolic, **-al** [dī-a-bol'ik, -al] *adjs* devilish.—*adv* **diabol'ically**.

diaconate [dī-ak'o-nàt] *n* the office of a deacon; an official body of deacons.—*adj* **diac'onal**, a deacon or deaconess.

diadem [dī'a-dem] *n* a crown; royalty.

diagnosis [dī-ag-nō'sis] *n* the identification of a disease by means of its symptons; the analysis of the nature or cause of a problem.—*pl* **diagnō'ses**.—*vt* **diagnose** [-nōz', -nōs'].

diagonal [dī-ag'o-nàl] *adj* stretching from one corner to an opposite corner of a figure with four or more sides; slantwise.—*n* a straight line so drawn.—*adv* **diag'onally**.

diagram [dī'a-gram] *n* a figure or plan drawn in outline to illustrate any statement.—*adj* **diagramma'tic**.

dial [dī'àl] *n* an instrument for showing the time of day by the sun's shadow; the face of a watch or clock; a circular plate with a moveable index used for various purposes.—*vt* to measure or indicate by dial; to make a telephone connection by using a dial.

dialect [dī'a-lekt] *n* a variety or form of language peculiar to a district or class.

dialec'tic [dī-alek'tik] *n* branch of logic which teaches the art of arriving at the truth by logical discussion, in matters of opinion;—*adv* **dialec'tically**.—*n* **dialecti'cian** [-shàn], one skilled in dialectic, a logician.

dialogue, dialog [dī'a-log] *n* conversation between two or more persons, esp in a play or novel; an exchange of views in the hope of ultimately reaching agreement.

dialysis [dī-al'i-sis] *n* the separation of a colloid from a true solution by diffusing it through a membrane; dissolution;—*pl* **dial'yses** [-sēz].—*vt* **dialyze** [dī'à-līz], to separate by dialysis.—*adj* **dialy'tiç**.

diameter [dī-am'e-ter] *n* a straight line passing through the center of a circle; the length of this line.—*adjs* **diamet'ric, -al**, like the opposite ends of the diameter (as in *diametrical opposition*).—*adv* **diamet'rically**.

diamond [dī'a-mónd] *n* a valuable gem, a crystallized form of pure carbon, and the hardest of all minerals; (*baseball*) the playing field, esp the infield; a suit of playing cards denoted by a red lozenge.

diapason [dī-a-pā'zòn] *n* (*mus*) an interval of an octave; a full volume of various sounds in concord; the compass of a voice or instrument; a tuning fork; one of two organ stops (**open** and **stopped diapason**).

diaper [dīa-pèr] *n* absorbent material worn by an infant to retain bodily waste; woven fabric or design in diamond pattern.

diaphanous [dī-af'a-nus] *adj* allowing to shine or appear through, transparent; clear;

diaphoretic [dī-a-for-ret'ik] *adj* promoting perspiration.—*n* a medicine that increases perspiration.

diaphragm [dī'a-fram] *n* a thin partition or dividing membrane; the midriff, a structure separating the chest from the abdomen; device for regulating aperture of a camera lens; contraceptive cap covering cervix.

diarchy [dīär-ki] *n* a form of government in which two persons, states, or bodies are jointly vested with supreme power.

diarrhea, diarrhoea [dī-a-rē'a] *n* excessive looseness of the bowels.—*adjs* **diarrheic**, **diarrhoet'ic**.

diary [dī'à-ri] *n* a daily record.—*n* **dī'arist**, one who keeps a diary.

diastase [dī'as-tās] *n* any enzyme having the power of converting starch into sugar.

diastole [dī-as'to-lē] *n* the dilation of the chambers of the heart during which they fill with blood.

diathermy [dī-a-thûr'mi] *n* the generation of heat in body tissues by the passage of an electric current through them for medical or surgical purposes.

diatonic [dī-a-ton'ik] *adj* of major and minor scales as opposed to chromatic scale.—*adv* **diaton'ically**.

diatribe [dī'a-trīb] *n* an abusive harangue.

dibble [dib'l] *n* a pointed tool used for making holes to put seeds or plants in.

dice [dīs] Plural of **die**.

dicephalous [dī-sef'a-lus] *adj* two-headed.

dichotomy [dī-kot'o-mi] *n* a division into two parts.—*adj* **dichot'omous**.

dickey, dicky [dik'i] *n* a false shirt front; an apron; a seat at the back of an automobile.

Dictaphone [dik'ta-fōn] *n* trade name for an apparatus that records and plays back dictation.

dictate [dik-tāt'] *vt* to say or read for another to write; to lay down with authority; to command, require.—*vi* to give orders (to).—*n* [dik'tāt] an order, rule, direction, impulse.— **dicta'tion**, act of dictating; overbearing command; something dictated; **dicta'tor**, one invested with absolute authority.—*adj* **dictāto'rial**, like a dictator; absolute; overbearing.—*adv* **dictāto'rially**.—*n* **dicta'torship**.

diction [dik'sh(ó)n] *n* manner of speaking, enunciation; choice of words, style.

dictionary [dik'sh(ó)n-â-ri] *n* a book containing the words of a language alphabetically arranged, with their meanings, etc., a lexicon; a work containing information on any department of knowledge, alphabetically arranged.

dictum [dik'tum] *n* an authoritative saying;—*pl* **dic'ta**.

didactic, -al [di-dak'tik, -à (or dī-)] *adjs* fitted, or intended, to teach; instructive.—*adv* **didac'tically**.

die¹ [dī] *vi* to cease existence; to become extinct;—*pr p* **dy'ing**; *pt, and pt p* **died** (*dīd*).—*n* **diehard**, one who prolongs vain resistance; usu. an extreme conservative.

die² [dī] *n* a small cube with one to six spots on each face; a stamp for impressing coin, etc.;—*pl* (playing games and the like) **dice** (*dīs*); (stamping) **dies** (*dīz*).—*vt* **dice**, to play with dice (*inf*) to take a risk; *vt* to cut into small cubes.—*pr p* **dic'ing**; *pt p* **diced** (*dīst*).

dielectric [dī-e-lek'trik] *adj* of non-conducting material;—*n* any substance which insulates against electricity.

diesel [dēz'l] *n* a vehicle driven by a diesel engine.—**diesel engine**, an oil-burning engine in which ignition is produced by the heat of highly-compressed air.

diet¹ [dī'et] *n* mode of living, with special reference to food; food selected to adjust weight, to control illness, etc.—*vt* to put on a diet.—*vi* to take food according to rule.—*adjs* **dietet'ic**, pertaining to diet.—**dietet'ics**, application of the principles of nutrition.

diet² [di'et] *n* a formal assembly; the English name for various legislative bodies.

differ [dif'èr] *vi* to be unlike (*used by itself, or followed by* from); to disagree with (*with* with, from); to quarrel, be at variance (with);—*pr p* **diff'ering**; *pt p* **diff'ered**.—*n* **diff'erence**, that which distinguishes one thing from another; the amount or manner of being different.—*adj* **diff'erent**, distinct, separate; unlike, not the same (*with* than); novel.—*adj* **differen'tial**, of, or showing a difference.—*vt* **differen'tiāte**, to make different; to become specialized; to note differences.—*n* **differentiā́tion**.—*adv* **diff'erently**; differential gear, a gear permitting relative rotation of two shafts driven by a third.

difficult, [dif'i-kult] *adj* hard to understand; hard to make, do, or carry out; hard to please.—*n* **difficulty**, thing that is hard to understand; obstacle; hard work; trouble.

diffident [dif'i-dènt] *adj* shy, lacking self-confidence, not assertive.—*n* **diff'idence**.—*adv* **diff'idently**.

diffraction [di-frak'sh(ò)n] *n* the breaking up of a ray of light into colored bands of the spectrum or into a series of light and dark bands.

diffuse [di-fūz'] *vt* to spread in all directions.—*vti* (*of gases, fluids or small particles*) to intermingle.—*adj* **diffūsed'**, spread widely, not concentrated.—*adj* **diffuse** (*di-fūs*), diffused, widely spread; wordy, not concise.—*adv* **diffuse'ly.**—*n* **diffuse'ness.**—*adj* **diffūs'ible,** that may be diffused.—**diffūsibil'ity, diffū'sion.**—*adj* **diffus'ive,** extending; spreading widely.—*adv* **diffus'ively.**

dig [dig] *vt* to use a tool or hands, claws etc. in making a hole in the ground; to unearth by digging; to excavate; to thrust; to nudge; (*slang*) to understand, approve.—*pr p* **digg'ing;** *pt, pt p* **dug.**—*n* (*slang*) a thrust; an archaeological excavation.—*n* **digger,** one who or that which digs.

digest [di-jest'] *vt* to convert (food) into assimilable form; to reduce (facts, laws etc.) to convenient form by classifying or summarizing; to form clear view of (a situation) by reflection.—*vi* to undergo digestion; **digestion** [di-jes'ch(ŏ)n].

digest [dī'jest] *n* an orderly summary of any written matter; a periodical synopsis of published or broadcasted material.

digit [dij'it] *n* any of the basic counting units of a number system, including zero; a human finger or toe; a beast's toe.—*adj* **dig'ital,** of or using digits; *n* **digitā'lis,** a powerful heart stimulant obtained from the foxglove. **digitā'tion.**—*adj* **dig'itigrade,** walking on the toes.—*n* an animal that walks on its toes, not touching the ground with heel.—*vt* **dig'itize,** to put (data) into digital form for use in a digital computer.

dignify [dig'ni-fī] *vt* to invest with honor; to exalt;—*pr p* **dig'nifying;** *pt p* **dig'nified.**—*adj* **dig'nified.**

dignity [dig'ni-ti] *n* the state of being dignified; the claim(s) to respect, worthiness.—*n* **dig'nitary,** one in a high position or rank, esp in the church.

digress [di-gres', dī-gres'] *vi* to turn aside from the main subject in speaking or writing.—*n* **digress'ion.**—*adjs* **digress'ional, digress'ive.**

dike [dīk] *n* a ditch; a causeway; (*geol*) a wall-like mass of igneous rock. Also **dyke.**

delapidate [di-lap'i-dāt] *vt* to bring (a building) to ruin.—Also *vi*—*adj* **dilap'idated,** in structural disrepair.—**dilapidā'tion,** state of damage or disrepair.

dilate [di-lāt', dī-lāt'] *vt* to enlarge;—*vi* to widen; to be enlarged, esp pupil of eye.—**dilātā'tion, dilā'tion,** expansion; **dilāt'or.**

dilatory [dil'a-tór-i] *adj* tardy; causing or intending to delay.—*adv* **dil'atorily.**—*n* **dil'atoriness.**

dilemma [di-lem'a] *n* a situation where each of two alternative courses (or of all the feasible courses) is eminently undesirable.

dilettante [dil-et-an'ti] *n* a person who dabbles in a subject for amusement.—*pl* **dilettan'ti** [-tē].—*n* **dilettan'tism.**

diligent [dil'i-jênt] *adj* industrious.—*n* **dil'igence,** hard work, industry; a public stagecoach [also pronounced dē-lē-zhōs].—*adv* **dil'igently.**

dill [dil] *n* an edible hardy annual herb (*Anethium graveolens*) of the carrot family.—**dill pickle,** a cucumber pickled in dill water.

dillydally [dil'i-dal'i] *vi* to loiter, trifle.

dilute [di-l(y)ŏŏt', dī-l(y)ŏŏt'] *vt* to diminish the strength etc., of, by mixing, esp with water.—*adj* [also dī'l(y)ŏŏt], diminished in strength by mixing.—*n* **dilution.**

dilū'vial, dilū'vian [dil-(y)ŏŏ'vi-al, -en] *adj* of a flood.

dim [dim] *adj* faintly lit, not seeing, hearing, understanding, etc. clearly.—*vt* to make dark;—*vi* to become dim—*adv* **dim'ly; dim'ness;**

dime [dīm] *n* the tenth part of a US or Canadian dollar, 10 cents.

dimension [di-, dīmen'sh(ó)n] *n* any linear measurement of width, length, or thickness; extent; size.—*adj* **dimen'sional,**

diminish [di-min'ish] *vti* to make or become smaller in size, amount, or importance.—*p adj* **dimin'ished** (*mus*), of an interval, less by a semitone than the perfect or the minor of the same name.—*adj* **dimin'ishable.**

diminuendo [di-min-ū-en'dō] *adv* (*mus*) gradually becoming quieter.

diminution [dim-in-ū'sh(ó)n] *n* act or process of being made smaller.—*adj* **dimin'utive,** very small; expressing diminution (eg of a suffix).—*n* a word formed by a suffix (as -ette, -kin, -ling), by clippings (Nan for Nancy), or by altering (Jack for John) to express small size, familiarity, etc.—*adv* **dimin'utively.**—*n* **dimin'utiveness.**

dimity [dim'i-ti] *n* a fine, thin, corded cotton fabric.

dimple [dim'pl] *n* a small hollow, usu on the cheek or chin.

din [din] *n* a loud continued noise.—*vt* to repeat loudly and persistently;—*pr p* **dinn'ing;** *pt p* **dinned.**

dinar [din-är'] *n* the unit of money of Iraq, Jordan, Libya, and Yugoslavia.

dine [dīn] *vi* to eat dinner.—*vt* to give a dinner.—**din'er,** one who dines. **dining car,** a restaurant car on a railroad train; **din'ing room,** a room used for meals.

ding dong [ding dong'] *n* the sound made by bells.

dinghy [ding'gi]*n* a small open boat propelled by oars or sails.

dingle [ding'gl] *n* a dell.

dingo [ding'gō] *n* the wild dog of mainland Australia;—*pl* **ding'oes** (-ōz).

dingy [din'ji] *adj* dirty-looking, shabby.—*n* **din'giness.**

dinner [din'ér] *n* the main meal of the day; a formal meal in honor of a person or occasion.

dinosaur [dī'no-sör] *n* any of an order of extinct (Mesozoic) reptiles.

dint [dint] *n* the mark of a blow; force (as in *by dint of*).—*vt* to make a dint in.

diocese [di'o-sēs, -sis] *n* the district over which a bishop has authority.—*adj* **diocesan** (*dī-os'esn,-ezn*), of a diocese.—*n* a bishop having jurisdiction.

diopter [dī-op'ter] *n* a unit for measuring the reflective power of light.—*n pl* (*with sing v*) **diop'tics,** the science of the refraction of light.

diorama [dī-o-rä'ma] *n* a miniature three-dimensional scene, esp a museum exhibit; device for producing changing effects by manipulating light on a partly translucent picture.—*adj* **dioram'ic.**

dioxide [dī-oks'īd] *n* an oxide with two molecules of oxygen to one molecule of the other constituents.

dip [dip] *vt* to put (something) under the surface (as of a liquid) and lift quickly out again; to immerse (as a hog) in an antiseptic solution; to lower and raise again.—*vi* to go into water and come out quickly; to suddenly drop down or sink out of sight; to read superficially; to incline downward from the plane of the horizon.—*pr p* **dipping;** *pt p* **dipped.**

diphtheria [dif-thē'ri-a] *n* an infectious throat disease.—*adjs* **diphther'ial, diphtherit'ic.**

diphthong [dif'thong] *n* two vowel-sounds (represented by one letter or by two) pronounced as one syllable, as in *my* [ma'i], roam [rō'um] and other so-called 'long vowels'.

diploma [di-plōma] *n* a certificate given by a school, college or university to its graduating students.

diplomacy [di-plō'ma-si] *n* the management of relations between nations; skill in handling affairs without arousing hostility.—*adj* **diplomat'ic,** of diplomacy; employing tact and conciliation.—*adv* **diplomat'ically.**—**diplō'matist, dip'lomat,** one employed or skilled in diplomacy.

diplopia [dip-lap'ēa] *n* double vision.—*adj* **diplop'ic.**

dipper [dip'ér] *n* something used for dipping articles; any of several birds (as a water ouzel) skilled in diving; the seven principal stars in the constellation Ursa Major called **Big Dipper;** the seven principal stars in Ursa Minor, with the handle pointing to the North Star, called **Little Dipper.**—*n* **dipperful.**

dipsomania [dip-sō-mā'ni-a] *n* the abnormal craving for alcoholic beverages.—*n* **dipsoma'niac.**

diptych [dip'tik] *n* a pair of paintings or carvings on two panels hinged together.

dire [dīr] *adj* dreadful; desperately urgent.—*adv* **dire'ly.**—*n* **dire'ness.**

direct [di-rekt', dī'rekt] *adj* straight; in an unbroken line; frank; truthful.—*vt* to manage, to control; to tell or show the way; to point to, to aim at; to address (a letter or package); to carry out the organizing and supervising of; to train and lead performances.—*vi* to determine a course; to act as director.—*n.* **direc'tion,** management, control; order, command; knowing or telling what to do, where to go, etc.; a name and address on a letter or package; onward movement; tendency; any way in which one may face or point.—*adj* **direc'tional,** relating to direction in space; **direc'tive,** *n* an order as to procedure.—*adv* **direct'ly,**—*n* **direct'ness; direct'or,** a person who directs, esp the production of a show for stage or screen; one of the persons directing the affairs of a company or an institution; **direct'orate directorship, direct'ory,**—*n* a book or collection of rules, ordinances, etc.; an alphabetical or classified list (as of names and telephone numbers etc. in an organization).

dirge [dûrj] *n* a funeral song or hymn; a slow, mournful piece of music.

dirigible [dir'i-ji-bl] *adj* that can be steered. — *n* an airship.

dirk [dûrk] *n* a dagger. — *vt* to stab with a dirk.

dirt [dûrt] *n* matter in the wrong place, esp filth; loose earth; obscenity; spiteful gossip. — **dirt farmer**, a farmer who earns his own living by farming his own land, esp one without hired labor; — *adj* **dirt'y**, foul, filthy; unclean; despicable; mean. — *vt* to soil with dirt. — *adv* **dirt'ily**. — *n* **dirt'iness**.

dis- [dis-] opposite of (**discontent**); reverse of (**disentangle**); exclude or expel (**disbar**); negative (**disagreeable**).

disable [dis-ā'bl] *vt* to make useless; to cripple. — *ns* **disability**.

disabuse [dis-a-būz'] *vt* to undeceive or set right.

disaffect [dis-a-fekt'] *vt* to make discontented or unfriendly. — *adj* **disaffect'ed**, ill-disposed, disloyal. — *n* **disaffec'tion**.

disallow [dis-a-low'] *vt* to refuse to sanction; to deny the truth or value of; to reject.

disappoint [dis-a-point'] *vt* to frustrate, fall short of, the hopes of (a person); to defeat the fulfilment of (eg hopes). — *adjs* **disappointed**; **disappointing**. — *adv* **disappointingly**. — *n* **disappoint'ment**, the defeat of one's hopes; frustration; vexation due to failure.

disarm [dis-ärm'] *vt* to deprive of weapons; to render defenseless or harmless; (*fig*) to conciliate. — *vi* to reduce national armaments. — *n* **disarm'ament** — *adj* **disarm'ing**, (*fig*) conciliating, instantly gaining good will or favor.

disarray [dis-a-rā'] *vt* to throw into disorder; to strip of array or dress. — *n* want of array or order; undress.

disaster [diz-äs'tèr] *n* an adverse or unfortunate event; great and sudden misfortune, calamity. — *adj* **disas'trous**.

disavow [dis-a-vow'] *vt* to disclaim, to disown, to deny. — *n* **disavow'al**.

disband [dis-band'] *vt* to disperse, break up (esp an army).

disburse [dis-bûrs'] *vt* to pay out. — *n* **disburse'ment**.

disc *see* **disk**; abbrev of discount.

discard [dis-kärd'] *vti* to throw away (a card) as useless; to cast off, get rid of.

discern [dis-sûrn', di-zûrn'] *vt* to perceive; to see clearly. — *adj* **discern'ible**, **discernable**. — *adv* **discern'ibly**. — *adj* **discern'ing**, discriminating, acute; having insight and understanding. — *n* **discern'ment**.

discharge [dis-chärj'] *vt* to unload, as a cargo; to set free; to acquit; to dismiss; to fire, as a gun; to let out, emit; to perform, as duties; to pay, as a debt. — *vi* to unload; to be released from a charged state. — *n* act or process of discharging; that which is discharged; release; dismissal; acquittal; payment. — *n* **discharg'er**.

disciple [dis-ī'pl] *n* one who follows or believes in the doctrine of another; one of the twelve apostles of Christ. — *n* **disci'pleship**.

discipline [dis'i-plin] *n* instruction; a branch of learning; branch of sport; training, or mode of life in accordance with rules; subjection to control; order maintained by control; penance. — *vt* to subject to discipline; to train; to bring under control; to chastise. — *n* **disciplinā'rian**, — *adj* **dis'ciplinary**.

disclaim [dis-klām'] *vi* to deny connection with; to renounce all legal claim to. — *n* **disclaim'er**, a denial of legal claim; a writing embodying this.

disclose [dis-klōz'] *vt* to lay open, bring to light, to reveal. — *n* **disclō'sure**.

discobolus [dis-kob'o-lus] *n* a discus thrower.

discolor [dis-kul'ór] *vt* to change or to spoil the color of; to stain. — Also *vi* — *n* **discolorā'tion**.

discombobulate [dis-kumbob'èlāt] *vt* to disconcert, upset, confuse. — *n* **discombobulation**.

discomfit [dis-kum'fit] *vt* to defeat the plans or hopes of; to frustrate; — *pr p* **discom'fitting**; *pt p* **discom'fited**. — *n* **discom'fiture**.

disconcert [dis-kon-sûrt'] *vt* to confuse; to upset.

disconnect [dis-kon-ekt'] *vt* to separate or disjoin. — *adj* **disconnect'ed**, separated; incoherent. — *n* **disconnec'tion**.

disconsolate [dis-kon'so-làt] *adj* forlorn; dejected. — *adv* **discon'solately**.

discontent [dis-kon-tent'] *adj* not content. — *n* want of content-

ment; dissatisfaction; ill-humor. — *vt* to deprive of content. — *p adj* **discontent'ed**, **discontent'ment**.

discontinue [dis-kon-tin'ū] *vt* to stop; to give up. — *vi* to cease. — **discontin'uance**, **discontinuā'tion**, a breaking off or ceasing;

discord [dis'körd] *n* disagreement, strife; (*mus*) a lack of harmony; harsh clashing sounds.

discount [dis'kownt] *n* a deduction from the amount or cost; the percentage charged for doing this. — *vt* **discount'**, to deduct from the amount a cost; to allow for exaggeration; to disregard; to make less effective by anticipation. — *vi* to make and give discounts. — *adj* **discount'able**.

discourage [dis-kur'ij] *vt* to take away the courage of; to try to prevent; to hinder. — **discour'ager**, **discour'agement**.

discourse [dis-kōrs', -kórs', or dis'-] *n* a formal speech or writing; conversation. — *vi* to talk.

discover [dis-kuv'èr] *vt* to see, find or learn of for the first time. — *adj* **discov'erable**. — **discov'erer**; **discov'ery**.

discredit [dis-kred'it] *n* doubt; disgrace. — *vt* to cast doubt on; to refuse belief in; — *adj* **discred'itable**, not creditable, disgraceful. — *adv* **discred'itably**.

discreet [dis-krēt'] *adj* wisely cautious, prudent. — *adv* **discreet'ly**. — *n* **discreet'ness**.

discrepancy [dis-krep'än-si, or dis'-] *n* difference; disagreement. — *adj* **discrep'ant**, contrary, disagreeing.

discrete [dis'krēt, dis-krēt'] *adj* separate; consisting of distinct parts; not mathematically continuous. — *adv* **discrete'ly**. — *n* **discrete'ness**.

discretion [dis-kresh'(ó)n] *n* the freedom to judge or to choose; good judgment. — *adj* **discre'tionary**, left to discretion; unrestricted.

discriminate [dis-krim'i-nāt] *vi* to make a difference or distinction; (*with* in favor of, **against**) to treat favorably or unfavorably in comparison with others. — *adj* **discrim'inating**, making a distinction; gifted with judgment and penetration. — *n* **discriminā'tion**. — *adj* **discrim'inative**, — *adv* **discrim'inatively**.

discursive [dis-kûr'siv] *adj* wandering from one subject to another; rambling.

discus [dis'kus] *n* a heavy, circular plate of stone or metal used for throwing by atheletes; — *pl* **discuses**.

discuss [dis-kus'] *vt* to talk over; to investigate by reasoning or argument. — **discuss'ion**, debate.

disdain [dis-dān'] *vt* to scorn, reject. — *n* scornful aversion; haughtiness. — *adj* **disdain'ful**. — *adv* **disdain'fully**.

disease [diz-ēz'] *n* sickness; illness, ailment; any particular illness. — *adj* **diseased'**.

disembody [dis-èm-bod'i] *vt* to separate (a soul, spirit etc.) from the body.

disembogue [dis-èm-bōg'] *vti* to discharge at the mouth, as a stream. — *n* **disembogue'ment**.

disembowel [dis-èm-bow'el] *vt* to remove the entrails of; to remove the substance of.

disenchant [dis-èn-chänt'] *vt* to free from a magic spell or illusion. — *n* **disenchant'ment**.

disencumber [dis-èn-kum'ber] *vt* to free from a burden. — *n* **disencum'brance**.

disenfranchise [dis-en-fran'chīz] *vt* take the rights of citizenship away from. — *n* **disenfranchisement**. Also **disfranchise**, **disfranchisement**.

disengage [dis-èn-gāj'] *vt* to separate or free from being engaged; to separate; to release. — *n* **disengage'ment**.

disentangle [dis-èn-tang'gl] *vt* to free from complications. — *n* **disentang'lement**.

disenthrall, **disenthral** [dis-èn-thröl'] *vt* to release from enchantment.

disentomb [dis-èn-tōōm'] *vt* to remove from a tomb.

disequilibrium [dis-ē-kwil-i'brium] loss or lack of equilibrium.

disestablish [dis-es-tab'lish] *vt* to deprive of an established position. — *n* **disestab'lishment**.

disfavor [dis-fāvór] *n* dislike; condition of being out of favor. — *vt* to withhold favor from, to disapprove.

disfigure [dis-fig'ùr] *vt* to spoil the beauty or excellence of, to deface. — *n* **disfig'urement**.

disgorge [dis-görj'] *vt* to discharge from the throat, to vomit; to give up (what one has wrongfully seized).

disgrace [dis-grās'] *n* loss of trust, favor, or honor; something that disgraces.—*vt* to put out of favor; to bring disgrace or shame upon.—*adj* disgrace'ful.—*adv* disgrace'fully.

disgruntle [dis-grun'tl] *vt* to make ill-humored and dissatisfied.—*adjs* disgruntling, disgruntled.

disguise [dis-gīz'] *vt* to hide what one is by appearing as something else; to hide what (a thing) really is.—*n* the use of a changed appearance to conceal the identity of the wearer; a false appearance.

disgust [dis-gust'] *n* sickening dislike.—*vt* to excite disgust in.—*adjs* disgust'ed; disgust'ing.—*adv* disgust'ingly.

dish [dish] *n* anything to serve food in; the amount of food served in a dish; the food served; any of various shallow concave vessels; a directional microwave antenna having a concave reflector; the state of being concave; an attractive woman.

disharmony [dis-här'mo-ni] *n* lack of harmony; discord; incongruity.

dishearten [dis-härt'n] *vt* to discourage.

dishevel [di-shev'el] *vt* to throw into disorder;—pr p dishev'e-ling; pt p *adj* dishev'eled, rumpled.

dishonor [dis-on'ör] *n* disgrace; shame.—*vt* to deprive of honor; to bring shame on, to disgrace; to refuse the payment of, as a check.—*adj* dishon'orable.

disillusion [dis-i-l(y)ōō'zh(ó)n] *n* act of setting free from illusion; state of being freed from illusion.—disillusioned.

disinfect [dis-in-fekt'] *vt* to destroy germs.—*n* disinfect'ant, any chemical agent that inhibits the growth of or destroys germs.—Also *adj*—*n* disinfec'tion.

disinformation [dis-informa'shun] *n* false information given out by intelligence agencies to mislead foreign spies.

disintegrate [dis-in'ti-grāt] *vti* to separate into parts; to crumble.—*ns* disintegrā'tion.

disinterested [dis-in'tėr-est-ed] *adj* impartial; uninterested.

disk, disc [disk] *n* any flat thin circular body; the circular figure presented by a spherical body, as the sun; a cylindrical elastic pad made of fibrocartilage between vertebrae; a phonograph record; a storage device in a computer; see floppy disk (under flop) and hard disk (under hard).—diskectomy, the surgical removal of a portion of an intervertebral disk.—disk' jockey one who provides a commentary on a program of recorded music.—floppy disk *see* floppy.

dislocate [dis'lo-kāt] *vt* to put out of joint; to disturb—*n* dislocā'tion.

dislodge [dis-loj'] *vt* to drive from a place of rest, or of hiding, or of defense; to force, or to knock accidentally, out from its place.—*n* dislodg'ment.

dismal [diz'màl] *adj* gloomy, dreary, cheerless.—*adv* dis'-mally.

dismantle [dis-man'tl] *vt* to strip of guns, covering, etc.; to pull down; to take apart.

dismay [dis-mā'] *vt* to make afraid.—*n* loss of courage through fear.

dismember [dis-mem'ber] *vt* to cut or tear the limbs from.—*n* dismem'berment.

dismiss [dis-mis'] *vt* to send away; to remove from office or employment; to stop thinking about; (*law*) to put out of court.—dismiss'al, dismiss'ion.

disorder [dis-ör'der] *n* confusion; riot; an illness in which symptoms are produced without the intervention of germs.—*vt* to disarrange; to upset the health of.—*adj* disor'dered, *adj* disor'derly, out of order, in confusion;—*n* disor'derliness.

disorient [dis-orē'ent] *vt* to cause the loss of sense of time, place, or identity; to confuse.—*n* dis-orientation. Also disorientate [-āt].

disparage [dis-par'ij] *vt* to belittle.—dispar'agement, dispar'-ager.—*adv* dispar'agingly.

disparate [dis'pàr-àt] *adj* unequal, incapable of being compared.

disparity [dis-par'i-ti] *n* essential difference; the quality of being unlike.

dispassion [dis-pash'(ó)n,] *n* freedom from passion; calm state of mind.—*adj* dispass'ionate

dispatch [dis-pach'] *vt* to send off to some place; to perform speedily; to kill.—*n* a sending off (of a letter, a messenger etc); rapid performance; haste; a written message, esp of news. Also despatch.

dispel [dis-pel'] *vt* to drive away and scatter;—pr p dispell'ing; pt p dispelled'.

dispensable [dis-pens'à-bl] *adj* which can be done without.

dispensary [dis-pens'àr-i] *n* a place where medicines are made up and dispensed.

dispensation [dis-pen-sā'sh(ó)n] *n* the act of distributing or dealing out; licence or permission to neglect a rule.—*adjs* dispens'ătional, dispens'atory, granting permission.—*vt* dispense, to deal out in portions; to distribute; to administer.

disperse [dis-pûrs'] *vt* to scatter; to send in different directions; to cause to evaporate or vanish.—*vi* to separate; to spread; to vanish.—dispers'al.

dispersion [dis-pûr'sh(ó)n] *n* a scattering, or state of being scattered; the separation of light into colors by diffraction or refraction.

dispirit [dis-pir'it] *vt* to depress.—*adj* dispir'ited, dejected.—*adv* dispir'itedly.

display [dis-plā'] *vt* to show; to exhibit; to set out ostentatiously.—*n* a displaying; exhibition; ostentatious show;—*n* display'er.

disport [dis-pōrt, -pört'] *vt* to divert, amuse; (*reflexive*) to amuse oneself.

dispose [dis-pōz'] *vt* to arrange; to influence—*vi* to settle a matter finally.—*adj* dispos'able, intended to be thrown away or destroyed after use.—*n* dispos'al, disposed', inclined.

disposition [dis-po-zish'(ó)n] *n* natural way of behaving toward others; tendency; arrangement.

disproportion [dis-pro-pōr'sh(ó)n] *n* lack of symmetry.—*vt* to make out of proportion.—*adj* dispropor'tional.

dispute [dis-pūt'] *vt* to make a subject of argument; to oppose by argument; to call in question; to resist; to contend for.—*vi* to argue; to debate.—*n* an argument; a quarrel.—*adj* disput'-able [also dis-].—*adv* dis'putably.—*ns* dis'putant, disputā'tion.

disquiet *dis-kwī'et*, *n*. uneasiness, restlessness: anxiety.—*v.t.* to make uneasy.—disquietude, state of disquiet.

disquisition [dis-kwi-zish'(ó)n] *n* a careful inquiry into any matter by speech or writing.

disrepute [dis-ri-pūt'] *n* disgrace.

disrupt [dis-rupt'] *vti* to break up.—*n* disrup'tion.—*adj* disrup'tive.

dissect [di-sekt'] *vt* to cut apart (a plant, an animal, etc.) in order to determine the structure of; to analyze and interpret minutely.—*adj* dissect'ed.—dissec'tion.

dissemble [di-sem'bl] *vt* to pretend.—*vi* to assume a false appearance; to play the hypocrite.—*n* dissem'bler.

disseminate [di-sem'i-nāt] *vt* to sow or scatter (*usually fig*), to spread (knowledge etc.).—*n* disseminā'tion.—*n* dissem'i-nator.

dissent [di-sent'] *vi* to disagree; to withhold assent.—*n* difference of opinion; religious nonconformity; a justice's nonconcurrence with a majority decision.—dissen'sion, dissention, dissent'er,.—*adj* dissen'tient [-shent].

dissertate [dis'ėr-tāt] *vi* to discourse.—*n* dissertā'tion, a treatise.

dissever [di-sev'ėr] *vt* to sever; to separate, disunite.—*vi* to come apart.—*n* dissev'erance.

dissident [dis'i-dėnt] *adj* dissenting, disagreeing, esp with the views of a government.—*n* a dissenter.—*n* diss'idence, disagreement.

dissimulate [di-sim'u-lāt] *vt* to conceal or disguise, dissemble.—*vi* to practise dissimulation.—*n* dissimulā'tion, hypocrisy.

dissipate [dis'i-pāt] *vt* to scatter; to cause to spread thinly; to dissolve; to lose (heat or electricity) irrecoverably; to squander.—*vi* to separate and disappear; to be extravagant in the pursuit of pleasure.—*adjs* diss'ipated, dissolute, esp addicted to drinking, dissipative; of dissipation, esp of heat.—*n* dissi-pā'tion.

dissociate [di-sō'shi-āt] *vt* to think of apart (from), separate in thought; (*reflexive*) to repudiate connection with; to separate (*also vi*).—*n* dissociā'tion (-sō-si).

dissolve [di-zolv'] *vt* to cause to pass into solution; to disperse (as an assembly); to break up (as a partnership or marriage) legally.—*vi* to become liquid; to be overcome by emotion.—*adj* dissol'vent, having power to dissolve.—*n* that which can dissolve.—*adj* dissoluble [dis'ol-(y)ōō-bl, or disol'ū-bl], capable of being dissolved.—n **dissolubil'ity**.—adj **diss'olute**, loose, esp in morals, lewd, licentious.—adv **diss'olutely**.— **diss'oluteness; dissolū'tion**.

dissonant [dis'-o-nånt] adj not agreeing or harmonizing in sound, etc.; discordant.—n **diss'onance**.

dissuade [di-swād'] vt to prevent or deter by advice or persuasion.—n **dissuā'sion**.—adj **dissuā'sive**.

distaff [dis'täf] n the stick that holds the bunch of flax, tow, or wool in spinning.—**distaff side**, the female part of a family.

distance [dis'tåns] n a space or interval (between); a distant place or point (eg in the distance); remoteness; reserve of manner.—vt to place at a distance; to leave at a distance behind.

distaste [dis-tāst'] n disrelish, dislike.—adj **distaste'ful**, unpleasant to the taste.

distemper¹ [dis-tem'pėr] n a paint made by mixing the color with eggs or glue instead of oil.

distemper² [dis-tem'pėr] n an infectious often fatal disease of dogs and other animals; sickness of the mind or body.

distend [dis-tend'] vt to stretch; to swell, esp from internal pressure.—vi to swell.

distich [dis'tik] n a couple of lines or verses making complete sense, a couplet.

distill, distil [dis-til'] vi to fall in drops; to use a still.—vt to let or cause to fall in drops; to convert a liquid into vapor by heat, and then to condense it again; to extract the spirit or essential oil from anything by evaporation and condensation;—pr p **distill'ing**; pt p **distilled'; distill'er**, one who or that which distills; **distill'ery**, a place where distilling esp of alcoholic liquor is carried on.

distinct [dis-tingkt'] adj separate; different; well-defined; clear.—adj **distinct'ive**, marking or expressing difference; characteristic.—adv **distinct'ly**.—n **distinct'ness**.

distinction [dis-tingksh(ô)n] n separation or division; excellence, superiority; a mark of honor.

distinguish [dis-ting'gwish] vt to tell apart; to see or hear clearly; to confer distinction on; to make eminent or known.—vi to perceive a difference.—adj **disting'uishable** adjs **disting'uished**, illustrious; distingué; **disting'uishing**, characteristic.

distort [dis-tört'] vt to twist out of shape; to misrepresent.—n **distor'tion**.

distract [dis-trakt'] vt to draw away, esp of the mind or attention; to confuse.—adjs **distract'ed, distractible**.—adv **distract'edly**.—n **distrac'tion**, state of being distracted; perplexity; agitation.

distrait [dis-trā'] adj absent-minded; inattentive because worried or harassed.

distraught [dis-tröt'] adj distracted, wildly perplexed; crazed.

distress [dis-tres'] n suffering; that which causes suffering; calamity; condition of being in danger and requiring help.—vt to afflict with pain or suffering; to harass; to grieve.—adj **distress'ful**.—adv **distress'fully**.—adj **distress'ing**.—adv **distressingly**.

distribute [dis-trib'ūt] vt to divide and share out; to spread; to divide into parts; to arrange; to transport goods to retail outlets.—n **distrib'utary**, a river branch flowing away from the main stream.—**distrib'utor**, an agent who sells goods, esp wholesale; a device for distributing current to the spark plugs in an engine.—**distribū'tion, distrib'utively**.

district [dis'trikt] n a portion of territory defined for political, judicial, educational, or other purposes; a region or area with a distinguishing character.—vt to divide into districts.

disturb [dis-tûrb'] vt to interrupt; to throw into confusion; to disquiet.—adj **disturbed**, showing symptoms of emotional illness.—ns **disturb'ance, disturb'er**.

ditch [dich] n any long narrow depression dug in the ground.— vt to dig a ditch in or around; to drive (a car) into a ditch; to make a forced landing of (an airplane) on water; to get rid of.

dither [dith'er] vi to tremble, quake; to waver.

dithyramb [dith'i-ram(b)] n (derog) any extravagantly emotional passage of prose or verse.—adj **dithyram'bic**, wildly enthusiastic.

dittany [dit'à-ni] n gas plant; any of various plants of the mint family.

ditto [dit'ō] n that which has been said; the same thing rep-

resented by two turned commas. **ditto marks**, in lists or tables to avoid repetition.

ditty [dit'i] n a song; a little poem to be sung.

ditty-bag [dit'i-bag] n a sailor's bag for needles, thread, etc.— Also **ditty-box**.

diuretic [dī-ū-ret'ik] adj promoting the discharge of urine.—n a substance causing this discharge.

diurnal [dī-ûr'nål] adj daily; of the daytime; having a daily cycle.—adv **diur'nally**.

diva [dē-va] n a great woman singer.

divagate [dī'va-gāt] vi to wander about; to digress.—n **dīvagā'tion**.

divan [di-van'] n a large couch without back or sides often used as a bed; an Oriental council of state; a court of justice; a council chamber with cushioned seats; an Eastern couch; a smoking room.

divaricate [dī-var'i-kāt] vt to spread apart; to branch off; to diverge.—adj widely divergent, spreading apart.—n **divaricā'tion**, a divergence of opinion.

dive [dīv] vi to plunge headfirst into water or down through the air; to plunge (the body, hand, or mind) suddenly into anything.—pr p **diving**; pt p **dove, dived**.—n a plunge; a swoop; (slang) a disreputable public place, a speakeasy; in prizefighting, a pre-arranged feigned knockout.—n **div'er**.

diverge [di- or dī-vûrj'] vi to branch off; to differ, deviate (from a standard). adj **diverg'ent**.

diverse [dīvėrs, or dī-vûrs'] adj different, unlike; multiform, various.—adv **dī'versely** (or diverse'ly).—n **diver'sity**.

diversify [di-vûr'si-fī] vt to make (investments) in securities of different types so as to lessen risk of loss; to engage in production of a variety of (manufactures, crops).

diversion [di-vûr'sh(ô)n] n amusement, recreation; act of diverting or turning aside; that which diverts; a tactical move to take an enemy's attention off a more important operation.

divert [di-vûrt'] vt to turn aside; to amuse.—adj **divert'ing**.— adv **divert'ingly**.

divertissement [dē-ver-tēs'mō] n a diversion, amusement; a short ballet, primarily for presentation between longer ballets; a short light-hearted piece of music; a musical pot-pourri.

divest [di- or dī-vest'] vt to strip or deprive (of anything).

divide [di-vīd'] vt to break up, or mark off, into parts, actually or in imagination; to separate into equal parts; to keep apart; (math) to ascertain how many times one quantity contains another.—vi to separate; to fall apart.—n a watershed.— adv **divid'edly**.—n **divid'er**, furniture, plants, etc. used to separate functions in a room; one who or that which divides.—adj **divid'ing**, separating.

dividend [div'i-dend] n a number or quantity which is to be divided by another number or quantity; the money earned by a company and divided by the owners of the company.

divine [di-vīn'] adj of, from, or like God or a god; excellent in the highest degree.—n a minister of the gospel; a theologian.—vt to discover intuitively; to dowse.—vi to profess or practise divination; to prophecy.—ns **divinā'tion**, the act or practice of foretelling the future or of finding a hidden thing by supernatural means; intuitive perception; **divin'er**, one who divines or professes divination.—adv **divine'ly**.

divinity [di-vin'i-ti] n any god; theology; the quality of being God or a god.

divorce [di-vörs', -vörs'] n the legal dissolution of marriage; separation.—vt to dissolve the marriage of; to become divorced from; to separate.—ns **divorcee**, a divorced person; **divorce'ment**.

divot [div'öt] n a piece of turf dug from a golf course while making a shot.

divulge [di-vulj'] vt to tell; or reveal.

dixie [dik'sē] n (inf) cooking utensil or mess tin.—**Dixie**, southern states of the US.

dizzy [diz'i] adj not steady; confused; causing dizziness; (slang) silly; foolish.—vt to make dizzy; to confuse.—adv **dizz'ily**.— n **dizz'iness**, giddiness.

do¹ [dŏŏ] vt to perform; to work; to end, to complete; to make.—vi to act or behave; to be satisfactory; pt **did**; pr p **do'ing**; pt p **done** [dun]. Do has special uses where it has no definite meaning, as in asking questions (Do you like milk?), emphasizing a verb (I do want to go), and standing for a verb

already used (*My dog goes where I do*).—*adj* **do'ing,** active.—
doings, things done; actions.

dobbin [dob'in] *n* a workhorse.

docile [dō'sil or dos'il] *adj* teachable; easily managed.—*n*
docil'ity.

dock¹ [dok] *n* (*Rumex*) a pernicious weed.

dock² [dok] *vt* to cut short; to curtail; to clip.—*n* the part of a
tail left after clipping.

dock³ [dok] *n* a wharf; an artificial basin for the reception of
ships.—*vt* to join (spacecraft) together in space.—Also to
enter a dock.—**dock'er,** one who works at the docks; **dock'-
yard,** an establishment with storage, and facilities for repairing and refitting ships.

docket [dok'et] *n* a list of lawsuits to be tried by a court.—*vt* to
enter on a docket.

doctor [dok'tor] *n* person qualified to treat diseases or physical
disorders; the highest academic degree; the holder of such a
degree. Also **doc.**—*vt* to treat medically; to patch up (machinery, etc.); to tamper with, falsify; (*inf*) to castrate or spay.—*n*
doc'torate, the degree of doctor given by a university.—*adj*
doctoral.

doctrinaire [dok-tri-nār'] *n* one whose opinions are formed by
theory rather than by experience.

doctrine [dok'trin] *n* a thing taught; a principle of belief.—*adj*
doc'trinal.

document [dok'ū-ment] *n* a paper containing information, or
proof or evidence of anything.—*vt* [dok'ū-ment, or -ment'] to
furnish with documents; to support or prove by documents.—*adj* **document'ary, documentā'tion.**

dodder² [dod'er] *vi* to tremble or shake as a result of old age or
weakness; to progress unsteadily.

dodeca- [dō-deka-] having twelve (Gr *dōdeka,* twelve).—
dodec'agon, a plane figure having twelve angles and sides (Gr
gonia, an angle); **dodecahe'dron,** a solid figure having twelve
plane faces.—**dodecasyll'able,** etc.

dodge [doj] *vi* evade an obligation by trickery; to move quickly
in an irregular course.—*vt* to avoid by a sudden movement or
shift of place; to trick.—*n* a trick.—*n* **dodg'er.**

dodo [dō'dō] *n* a large clumsy bird, now completely extinct; a
stupid person.—*pl* **do'does.**

doe [dō] *n* a female deer, rabbit, or hare.

doer [dōōer] *n* one who does, or habitually does, anything; an
agent.

does [duz] 3rd pers sing pres indic of **do.**

doff [dof] *vt* to take off, remove (esp one's hat).

dog [dog] *n* a domestic carnivorous mammal closely related to
the wolf with great differences in form; the male of wolf, fox,
etc.; a worthless person; any of various usu. simple mechanical devices for holding, gripping or fastening by a spike, rod
or bar; andiron.—*adj* **dog-like.**—*pr p* **dogging;** *pt p* **dogged.**—
adv extremely, utterly.—**dogcart,** a two-wheeled carriage
with crosswise seats set back to back; **dog collar,** a collar for a
dog; (*slang*) a clerical collar; a wide, snug-fitting necklace; **dog
days,** a period of inactivity or stagnation; **dog-ear,** the turned
down corner of a page, esp of a book.—**dogged,** tenacious.—
adv **doggedly.**—*n* **doggedness.**—*adj.*—*adv* **doggishly.**—*n*
doggishness. dogfight, (*loosely*) a fiercely disputed contest; a
fight between two fighter planes esp at close quarters; **dogfish,**
a bowfin; any of various small sharks; **dogleg,** something
having a sharp angle or a sharp bend.—*adj* crooked like a
dog's hind leg.—*vt* **dognap,** to steal (a dog).—**dog paddle,** an
elementary form of swimming in which the arms paddle in the
water.—**dogtooth,** canine, eyetooth; an architectural ornament consisting of four leaves radiating from a raised point in
the center; **dogtrot,** a quick easy gait like that of a dog.—*vi* to
move at a dogtrot; **dogwatch,** either of two half watches on
shipboard between 4–6 pm or 6–8 pm.

doge [dōj or dō'jā] *n* the chief magistrate in republican Venice
and Genoa.

doggerel [dog'ėr-ėl] *n* worthless verse.

dogma [dog'ma] *n* a belief taught or held as true, esp by a
church; a doctrine; a belief.—*adjs* **dogmăt'ic, -al,** pertaining
to a dogma; asserting a thing as if it were a dogma; asserting
positively; overbearing.—*adv* **dogmat'ically.**—*n* **dogmat'ics,**
branch of theology that tries to interpret the dogmas of
religious faith.—*vi* **dog'matīze,** to state one's opinion dog-

matically or arrogantly.—**dog'matizer;** dog'matism, dogmatic or positive assertion of opinion; **dog'matist.**

doily [doi'li] *n* a small ornamented mat, often laid on or under
dishes.

doldrums [dol'drumz] *n pl* those parts of the ocean about the
equator where calms and light baffling winds prevail; low
spirits.

dole¹ [dōl] *n* something given in charity; a small portion.—*vt* to
deal (out) in small portions.

dole² [dōl] *n* (*arch*) grief; heaviness at heart.—*adj* **dole'ful,** full
of dole or grief, melancholy.—*adv* **dole'fully.**

doll [dol] *n* a toy in human form; a pretty woman without
personality; a woman.—*n* **doll'y,** a child's name for a doll; a
low platform on wheels for moving heavy objects.

dollar [dol'ár] *n* the unit of money in the US, Canada, Australia
and many other countries.

dolly See **doll.**

dolman [dol'mán] *adj* of a sleeve on a woman's garment that is
wide at the armhole and tapers to fit the wrist.—*n* a woman's
coat with cape-like flaps instead of sleeves.

dolmen [dol'men] *n* a prehistoric structure of two or more
erect unhewn stones, supporting a large flattish stone, found
esp in Britain and France.

dolor [dol'ór, dōl'ór] *n* pain, grief, anguish.—*adj.*

dolphin [dol'fin] *n* any of various whales (family *Delphinidae*)
with a beak-like snout; either of two large food fishes (genus
Coryphaena) of tropical and temperate seas.—**dolphinarium,** a
pool or aquarium where dolphins are displayed.

dolt [dōlt] *n* a dull or stupid fellow.

domain [do-mān'] *n* territory under the control of one ruler or
government; field of thought, action, etc. (*math.*) the set on
which a function is defined.

dome [dōm] *n* a large, rounded roof; something high and
rounded.—*adj* **domed,** having a dome.

domestic [do-mes'tik] *adj* belonging to the house; fond of
home; private; tame; not foreign.—*n* a servant in the house.—
vt **domes'ticāte,** to make domestic; to tame;—**domestic-
ā'tion; domestic'ity** (-*tis*'-).

domicile [dom'i-sil, -sīl] *n* a house, home; a person's legal place
of residence.—*adj* **domicil'iary,** pertaining to the domicile.

dominant [dom'in-ánt] *adj* prevailing, predominant; overtop-
ping others.—*n* (*mus*) the fifth note above the tonic.—*n*
dom'inance, ascendancy.—*adv* **dom'inantly.**

dominate [dom'in-āt] *vt* to control or rule by strength; to hold
a commanding position over.—*n* **dominā'tion,** control; rule.

domineer [dom-in-ēr'] *vi* to exercise arrogant mastery; *vt* to
tyrannize over.

dominical [do-min'ik-ál] *adj* belonging to the Lord, as the
Lord's Prayer, the Lord's Day.

dominion [do-min'yón] *n* a domain or territory with one ruler,
owner, or government; control; (*in pl*) one of the orders of
angels.

domino [dom'i-nō] *n* one of the oblong pieces, with two
compartments each blank or marked with from one to six
spots, with which the game of **dom'inoes** [-nōz] is played; a
half-mask worn with a masquerade costume.

don [don] *vt* to put on (clothing, etc.).

Doña [don'ya] *n* a Spanish title, corresponding to Mrs or
Madam; a Spanish lady.

donation [do-nā'sh(o)n] *n* a contributing; a contribution.—*vt*
donāte', to give as a gift; to contribute, esp to a charity; to
give off or transfer (as electrons).—**dōnee',** the person to
whom a gift is made; **dō'nor,** a giver; one used as a source of
blood, semen, tissue, or organs.

done [dun] *pt p* of **do.**

dong [dong] *n* the unit of money in Vietnam.

donjon [dun'jón] *n* a strong central tower in ancient castles.

donkey [dong'ki] *n* a small animal resembling a horse, an ass; a
stupid person.—**don'key-en'gine,** a portable auxiliary
engine; a small locomotive used for switching.

don't [dōnt] for **do not.**—*n,* don't know respondent to an
opinion poll who does not reveal his position on an issue.

doodle [dōōd'l] *vi* to scrawl, scribble meaninglessly.

doom [dōōm] *n* destiny; ruin; final judgment.—*vt* to pronounce judgment on; to condemn, destine (often in *pass,* eg
it was doomed to failure);—*pr p* **dōōm'ing;** *pt p* **dōōmed.**—

dooms'day the day of God's final judgment of mankind; **doomsayer, doomster** a person who predicts calamity.

door [dōr, dör] *n* a movable barrier to close an opening in a wall; a similar part of a piece of furniture; a doorway.—**doormat,** a mat placed in front of or inside a doorway for wiping dirt from shoes; a person who submits without protest to indignities or abuse; **doorstop,** a device (as a wedge or weight) for holding a door open; **doorway,** the opening in a wall that a door closes; a means of gaining access, as knowledge is the doorway to success.

dope [dōp] *n* a thick pasty material; lubricating grease; airplane varnish; opium; a drug, narcotic or stimulative; anything calculated to dull mental and moral energy; a stupid person; information.—*vt* to drug (*lit* and *fig*).

Doric [dor'ik] *adj* denoting the simplest of the Greek orders of architecture.—*n* a dialect of ancient Greek.

dormant [dor'mant] *adj* sleeping; quiet, as if asleep; inactive; (*heraldic*) in a sleeping posture.—*n* **dor'mancy.**

dormer [dör'mer] *n* an upright window that projects from a sloping roof.

dormitory [dör'mi-tôr-i] *n* a building with many sleeping rooms; a large sleeping room with many beds.

dormouse [dör'mows] *n* any of several Old World rodents (family *Gliridae*) that resembles a squirrel;—*pl* **dor'mice.**

dormy, dormie [dör'mi] *adj* (*golf*) said of a player when he is as many holes 'up' or ahead as there are holes still to play.

dorsal [dör'sàl] *adj* of, on, or near the back.

dory [dör'ē] *n* a small rowing boat with a flat bottom.

dose [dōs] *n* the quantity of medicine, X-rays, etc. administered at one time; a part of an experience; a gonorrheal infection.—*ns* **dōs'age.**

dossier [dos'i-èr, do-syā] *n* a collection of documents about some subject or person.

dost [dust] 2nd pers sing pres indic of **do.**

dot[1] [dot] *n* a small spot, a point; a centered point used as a multiplication sign; (*mus*) a point indicating augmentation of a note or rest or one that is to be played staccato; a precise point in time; the short element in the Morse code.

dot[2] [dot] *n* a marriage portion.—*adj* **dō'tal,** pertaining to dowry.

dote [dōt] *vi* to be weak-minded because of old age; to show weak or excessive affection (*with on or upon*).—**dōt'age,** childishness of old age; **dōt'ard,** one showing the weakness of old age.

doth [duth] 3rd pers sing pres indic of **do.**

dotterel [dot'èr-el] *n* an old world plover (*Chardrius morinellus*).

double [dub'l] *adj* twice as large, as strong, etc.; for two; made of two like parts; having two meanings, characters, etc.; (*bot*) flowers with more than the normal number of petals.—*adv* twice.—*n* number or amount that is twice as much; person or thing just like another; a sharp turn.—*vt* to make twice as much or as many; to fold, to bend; to bend sharply backward; to go around.—*vi* become twice as much or as many.—*ns* **double agent,** a spy secretly acting for two governments at the same time; **double-barrel,** a double-barreled gun.—*adj* **double-blind,** of an experimental procedure in which neither the subjects nor the experimenters know the makeup of the test and control groups during the course of the experiment; **double cross,** an act of winning a fight or match after agreeing to lose it; the betrayal of an associate; a cross between first-generation hybrids of four separate inbred lines.

doublet [dub'lèt] *n* (formerly) a man's close-fitting jacket; one of a pair, eg *balm, balsam.*

doubloon [dub-lōōn'] *n* an old gold coin of Spain and Spanish America.

doubt [dowt] *vi* to be undecided.—*vt* to hold in doubt; to distrust; to suspect.—*n* uncertainty of mind; suspicion; fear.—*n* **doubt'er.**—*adj* **doubt'ful,** full of doubt; not confident; suspicious; undetermined, uncertain; not clear.—*adv* **doubt'fully.**—*n* **doubt'fulness.**—*advs.* **doubt'less.**

douche [dōōsh] *n* a jet of water directed on or into the body.

dough [dō] *n* a mixture of flour and other ingredients stiff enough to knead or roll; something resembling dough, esp in consistency.

doughty [dow'ti] *adj* able, strong; brave.—*adv* **dough'tily.**

dour [dōōr] *adj* obstinate; sullen; grim.

douse [dows] *vt* to plunge into water; to strike or lower, as a sail; to put out, quench.

dove [duv] *n* a small bird of the same family (*Columbidae*) as the pigeon; an advocate of peace or a peaceful policy, emblem of innocence, gentleness; **dove'cote,** a box or building in which pigeons breed; **dove'tail,** a mode of fastening boards together by fitting pieces shaped like a wedge or a dove's tail spread out (*tenons*) into like cavities (*mortises*).—*vt* to fit (one thing exactly into another).—Also *vi.*

dowager [dow'à-jèr] *n* a widow with a dower or jointure; a dignified elderly woman.

dowdy [dow'di] *adj* poorly dressed, not stylish.

dower *n* [dow'èr] a widow's life share in her husband's estate. [OFr *douaire*—Low L *dōtārium*— L *dōtāre*, to endow.]

down[1] [down] *n* soft feathers; a covering of fluffy hairs.—*adj* **down'y,** covered with, or made of, down or the like; soft.

down[2] [down] *adv* toward or in a lower physical position; to a lying or sitting position; toward or to the ground, floor, or bottom; in a direction opposite of up; to or in a lower status or worse condition; from a past time.—*adj* occupying a low position, esp lying on the ground; directed or going downward; being at a lower level; depressed, dejected; *prep* in a descending direction in, on, along, or through; to or toward the lower end or bottom of.—*n* a low period (as in activity, emotional life, or fortunes); one of a series of attempts to advance a football.—*ns* **downbeat,** (*mus*) the downward stroke of a conductor indicating the accented note; the first beat of a measure; a decline in prosperity; **downer,** a depressant drug esp barbiturate; a depressing experience or situation; **downfall,** a sudden fall (as from high rank or power); a sudden or heavy fall of rain or snow; **downtown,** the main business district of a town or city.

dowry [dow'ri] *n* the property which a woman brings to her husband at marriage.

dowse [dowz] *vi* to use a divining-rod.—*vt* to find by dowsing.—*n* **dowser,** a rod used for dowsing; a person who uses such.

doxology [doks-ol'o-ji] *n* a hymn or statement praising God.

doyen [doi'èn, dwä-yä] *n* a senior member of a group; an expert in a field; the oldest example of a category.

doze [dōz] *vi* to sleep lightly; to be half-asleep or in a stupefied state.

dozen [duz'n] *n* a set of twelve.

drab [drab] *adj* dull, monotonous, uninteresting.—*n* **drab'ness.**

drachm [dram] *n* a drachma; a dram.—*n* **drachma** [drak'ma]) the unit, money in Greece.

draft [dräft] *n* anything drawn; a smaller body (of men, animals, things) selected from a larger; conscription; an order for the payment of money; a demand (on resources, credulity, etc.); a plan; a preliminary sketch.—*n* **drafts'-man,** one who draws up documents, plans, designs, etc.

drag [drag] *vt* to draw by force; to draw slowly; to pull roughly and violently; to explore (a river-bed) with a drag-net or hook.—*vi* to hang so as to trail on the ground; to move slowly and heavily;—*pr p* **dragg'ing;** *pt p* **dragged.**

draggle [drag'l] *vt* to make or become wet and dirty as by dragging along the ground.

dragoman [drag'o-màn] *n* an interpreter or guide in the Middle East.—*pl* **drag'omans.**

dragon [drag'ón] *n* a fabulous winged reptile; the constellation Draco; a fierce person; **drag'onfly,** any of a suborder [Anisoptera] of large harmless four-winged insects.

dragoon [dra-gōōn'] *n* a soldier who fights on horseback—*vt* to harass or compel by bullying commands.

drain [drān] *vt* to draw (off or away) by degrees; to clear of water by drains; to make dry; to exhaust.—*vi* to flow off gradually; to lose moisture by its flowing or trickling away.—*n* watercourse; ditch; sewer; exhausting expenditure.—**drain'age.**

drake [drāk] *n* the male of the duck.

dram [dram]; a small portion of something to drink.

drama [drä'mä] *n* a story of life and action for representation by actors; a composition intended to be represented on the stage; dramatic literature; a dramatic situation or a series of deeply interesting events—*adjs* **dramatic** [drámat'ik], **-al,** vivid, striking, often with an element of unexpectedness.—

adv **dramat′ically.** — *vt* **dram′atize.** to compose in, or turn into, the form of a drama or play; to exaggerate the importance or emotional nature of. — *n* **dram′atist.** a writer of plays; **dram′atis persōnae [ē]** the characters of a drama or play.

dramaturgy [dram′a-tûr-ji] *n* the principles of dramatic composition; theatrical art.

drape [drāp] *vt* to cover with cloth; to hang cloth in folds about. — *n* a hanging or curtain. — *ns* **drāp′ery,** hangings.

drastic [dras′tik] *adj* acting with force and violence.

drat [drat] *vt* a mild oath.

draw [drö] *vti* to haul, to drag; to cause to go in a certain direction (*drew her aside*); to pull out (as a hand from a pocket); to attract; to delineate, to sketch; to extract the essence (as of tea); to require (a specified depth) to float in; to accumulate; to gain; to receive (as a salary); to bend (a bow) by pulling back the string; to leave (a contest) undecided; to write up, to draft (a will); to elongate (metal) by pulling through dies; to produce or allow a current of air. — **drawback,** a hindrance, handicap; **drawbridge,** a bridge made to be drawn up, down, or aside; **drawer,** one that draws; a sliding boxlike compartment (as in a table, chest, or desk); *pl* an undergarment for the lower part of the body; **drawing,** the act or art of making a figure, plan, or sketch by using lines.

drawl [dröl] *vt* to speak or utter in a slow, lengthened tone. — *n* a slow, lengthened utterance.

dray [drā] *n* a low strong cart for heavy goods.

dread [dred] *n* great fear; awe; an object of fear or awe. — *adj* dreaded, inspiring great fear or awe. — *vt* to fear greatly; to reverence. — *adj* **dreadful.** — *n* **dread′nought** a type of warship, both swift and heavily armoured, esp of the early 20th century.

dream [drēm] *n* a sequence of thoughts and fancies, or a vision during sleep; a state of abstraction, a reverie; an unrealised ambition; something only imaginary. — *vi* to fancy things during sleep; to think idly. — *vt* to see in, or as in, a dream. — *adj* **dreamy,** full of dreams, languid; addicted to dreaming, abstracted, unpractical.

dreary [drēr′i] *adj* gloomy; cheerless. — *adv* **drear′ily.** — *n* **drear′iness.**

dredge¹ [drej] *n* a bag-net for dragging along the ocean or river bottom to take specimens of plants and animals, mud, etc.; apparatus for deepening a harbor or channel by removing mud from the bottom, or for raising alluvial deposits containing minerals. *n* **dredg′er,** a vessel fitted with dredging apparatus.

dredge² [drej] *vt* to coat (food) by sprinkling. — *n* **dred′ger,** container with perforated lid for sprinkling.

dregs [dregz] *n pl* impurities in liquid that fall to the bottom; the most worthless part of anything.

drench [drench or -sh] *vt* to wet thoroughly, to soak; to saturate. — *n* a dose of medicine forced down the throat of an animal. — *n* **drench′ing,** a soaking.

dress [dres] *vt* to straighten; to set in order; to prepare; to draw (fowl); to trim; to treat, bandage; to tend; to clothe; to adorn. — *vi* to come into line; to put on clothes. — *adj* **dress′y,** showy; too fond of dress or adornment. — **dress′ cir′cle;** **dress′er,** one who dresses; a person who assists an actor to dress; a kind of kitchen sideboard; **dress′ing,** dress or clothes; any application used in a preparation process (as manure applied to land, sauce or stuffing added to food); the bandage, etc. applied to a wound. — **dress down,** to scold severely.

drew [drōō] *pt* of draw.

dribble [drib′l] *vi* to fall in small drips; to allow saliva to trickle from the mouth. — *vt* to spend in small amounts; (*football*) to kick (the ball) along little by little. — *n* **drib′let** a drop, trickle, small quantity.

dried [drīd] *pt* and *pt p* of dry.

drift [drift] *n* a heap of matter driven together, as snow; the direction in which a thing is driven; natural course, tendency; the general sense or intention (of what is said). — *vt* to carry by drift. — *vi* to be floated or blown along; to be driven into heaps; to wander around without any definite aim. — *ns* **drifter,** a person who or thing which drifts; a fisherman or a fishing-boat that uses a drift-net.

drill¹ [dril] *vt* to bore, pierce, as with a drill; to exercise (soldiers, pupils, etc.). — *n* an implement that bores; the exercising of soldiers, etc.; exercise, practice; correct procedure or routine; a furrow with seed or growing plants in it.

drill² [dril] *n* a kind of strong twilled cloth.

drink [dringk] *vt* to swallow, as a liquid; to take in through the senses. — *vi* to swallow a liquid; to take intoxicating liquors to excess; — *pr p* **drinking;** *pt* **drank;** *pt p* **drunk.** — *n* something to be drunk; intoxicating liquor. — *n* **drink′er,** a tippler.

drip [drip] *vi* to fall in drops; to let fall drops; — *pr p* **dripping;** *pt p* **dripped.** — *n* a falling in drops; that which falls in drops; the edge of a roof; a device for passing a fluid slowly and continuously, esp into a vein of the body; the material so passed. — Also *vi*, *vt* — *ns* **dripp′ing,** that which falls in drops, as fat from meat in roasting; **drip′stone,** a projecting molding over doorways, etc., serving to throw off the rain.

drive [driv] *vt* to urge, push or force onward; to direct the movement or course of; to convey in a vehicle; to set or keep in motion or operation; impress forcefully (*drove the lesson home*); to propel an object of play (as a ball or shuttlecock) by a hard blow. — *p* **driven.** — *n* a trip in an automobile; a driving together of animals (as for capture or slaughter).

drivel [driv′l] *vi* to slaver; to speak like an idiot; — *pr p* **driv′e-ling;** *pt p* **driv′eled.** — *n* slaver; nonsense.

drizzle [driz′l] *vi* to rain in small drops. — *n* a small, light rain. — *adj* **drizz′ly.**

drogue [drog] *n* a sea anchor; a small parachute for slowing down or stabilizing something (as an astronaut's capsule); a funnel-shaped device enabling an airplane to be refueled from a tanker airplane while in flight.

droll [dröl] *adj* odd; amusing. — *n* a jester. — *n* **droll′ery.**

dromedary [drom′i-dár-i̯, or drum′-] *n* a swift camel; a one-humped Arabian camel.

drone [drōn] *n* the male of the honey-bee; one who lives on the labor of others, like the drone-bee — a lazy, idle fellow; a deep humming sound; a bass-pipe of a bagpipe; a monotonous tiresome speaker or speech; an aircraft piloted by remote control.

droop [drōōp] *vi* to sink or hang down; to grow weak or faint; to decline.

drop [drop] *n* a small amount of liquid in a roundish shape; a sudden fall; the distance down. — *vi* to fall in drops; to fall suddenly; to go lower, to sink; to stop, to end; to come (in); to let go; to dismiss; to leave out, to omit. — *vt* to let fall, to cause to fall; to lower or cause to descend; to set down from a ship or vehicle; to cause (the voice) to be less loud; to bring down; to give up (as an idea); to leave incomplete; to lose; to kill. — *pr p* **dropping;** *pt p* **dropped; droplet,** a tiny drop (as of liquid).

dropsy [drop′si] *n* edema. — *adj* **drop′sical.**

dross [dros] *n* the scum of melting metals; waste matter; refuse.

drought [drowt], drouth [drowth] *n* dryness; want of rain or of water. — *adjs* **drought′y, drouth′y.**

drove [drōv] *pt* of drive. — *n* a number of cattle, or sheep, driven. — *n* **drov′er,** one whose occupation is to drive cattle.

drown [drown] *vi* to die of suffocation in liquid. — *vt* to submerge; to flood; to overwhelm.

drowse [drowz] *vi* to be heavy with sleep. — *adj* **drows′y,** sleepy. — *adv* **drows′ily.** — *n* **drows′iness.**

drub [drub] *vt* to beat or thrash; — *pr p* **drubb′ing;** *pt p* **drubbed.** — *n* **drubbing,** a beating.

drudge [druj] *vi* to do dull, laborious, or very menial work. — *n* one who does such work — a hack, or a menial servant. — *n* **drudg′ery.**

drug [drug] *n* any substance used in the composition of medicine; a substance used to stupefy or poison or self-indulgence; an article that cannot be sold, generally owing to overproduction. — *vt* to mix or season with drugs. — *vi* (*inf*) to be addicted to taking drugs; **drugg′ist,** a pharmacist. — **drug-store,** a retail store selling medicines and other miscellaneous articles such as cosmetics, film, etc.

druid [drōō′id] *n* (also **Druid**) a priest among the ancient Celts of Britain, Gaul, and Germany; an Eisteddfod official. — *adjs* **druid′ic, -al.** — *n* **dru′idism.**

drum [drum] *n* an instrument of percussion, stretched on a frame (usu. cylindrical or hemispherical in shape); anything shaped like a drum, as a container for liquids; the tympanum of the ear; (*archit*) the upright part of a cupola. — *vi* to beat a drum; to beat or tap rhythmically; to thump continuously. —

vt to expel with beat of drum (*with* **out, down**); to summon as by drum (*with* **up**); **drummer**, one who plays a drum; a traveling salesman.

drunk [drungk] *pt p of* **drink**. — *adj* intoxicated. — *n* a drunk person. — *n* **drunk'**, one who frequently drinks to excess. — *adj* **drunk'en**. — *n* **drunk'enness**.

drupe [drōōp] *n* a fleshy fruit containing a stone, as the plum, etc. — *adj* **drupa'ceous**.

dry [drī] *adj* free or freed from water or liquid; (of land) not being in or under water; thirsty; characterized by the absence of alcoholic beverages; not giving milk; (of a cough) lacking natural lubrication; austere; marked by a matter-of-fact, ironic, or terse manner of expression; uninteresting, wearisome; (of wine) not sweet. — *adv* dryly; **dry dock**, a dock that can be kept dry during ship construction and repair; **dry goods**, textiles, ready-to-wear clothing and notions; **dry ice**, solidified carbon dioxide used chiefly as a refrigerant; **drypoint**, an engraving made with a steel or jeweled point without the use of acid; **dry rot**, the decay of wood caused by fungi.

dryad drī'ad] *n* a wood nymph; — *pls* **dry'ads, -adēs.**

dual [dū'ăl] *adj* twofold; consisting of two. — *n* **dū'alism** (*philos*) any of various theories which admit of two independent and mutually irreducible substances in any given domain; **dū'alist**, a believer in dualism; **dual'ity**, doubleness, state of being double.

dub [dub] *vt* to confer knighthood upon, by touching each shoulder with a sword; to confer any dignity upon; to nickname, style; — *pr p* **dubb'ing**; *pt p* **dubbed**. — *n* **dubb'ing**, the accolade; (or **dubb'in**) a preparation of grease for softening leather.

dub [dub] *vt* to give (a film) a new sound-track, eg one in a different language; to add sound effects or music to (a film, etc.). — *n* **dubb'ing**.

dubious [dū'bi-us] *adj* doubtful (about, of); uncertain as to the result (eg *a dubious contest*); equivocal (eg *dubious reply*); of questionable nature. — *adv* **dūbiously.**

ducal [dū'kal] *adj* of a duke.

duchy [duch'i] *n* the territory of a duke, a dukedom. — **duch'-ess** [duch'es] the wife or widow of a duke; a woman of the same rank as a duke in her own right.

duck¹ [duk] *n* coarse cloth for small sails, sacking, etc.; (*pl*) garments made of such.

duck² [duk] *vt* to dip for a moment in water; (*coll*) to avoid. — *vi* to dip or dive; to lower the head suddenly. — *n* a quick lowering of the head or body. — *n* **duck'ing-stool.**

duck³ [duk] *n* any of a family (Anatinae) of water birds related to geese and swans; the female of this bird.

duck⁴ [duk] *n* an amphibious truck.

duct [dukt] *n* a tube or pipe for fluids, electric cable, etc. — **ductless gland**, an endocrine gland.

ductile [duk'-til] — *adj.* easily led; yielding; capable of being drawn out into threads. — *n.* **ductil'ity.**

dud [dud] *n* anything worthless. — Also *adj.*

dude [dūd] *n* fop, dandy.

dudgeon [duj'ŏn] *n* resentment; angry feeling.

due [dū] *adj* owed; that ought to be paid or done to another; proper; expected to arrive, be ready, be paid, etc. — *adv* directly (eg *due east*). — *n* what is owed; perquisite.

duel [dū'ĕl] *n* combat, under fixed conditions, between two persons over a matter of honor, etc; (*fig*) single combat of any kind (eg *a verbal duel*). — *vi* to fight in a duel. — **dū'elist.**

duenna [dū-en'a] *n* an elderly lady who acts as guardian to a younger.

duet [dū-et'] *n* a composition in music for two performers; the performance of such. — *n* **duett'ist.**

duffel [duf'l] *n* a thick, coarse woolen cloth with a thick nap. Also **duffle.** — **duffelbag.**

duffer [duf'ĕr] *n* an ineffectual or clumsy man.

dug [dug] *pt* and *pt p* of **dig.** — *n* **dug'out**, a boat made by hollowing out the trunk of a tree; a rough dwelling or shelter.

dugong [doo'gong] *n* a genus (*Dugong*) of large herbivorous mammals of tropical seas related to the manatee. Also **sea cow.**

duiker [dī'kĕr, di'ker] *n* any of several small African antelopes (*Cephalophus*) or related species.

duke [dūk] *n* the highest order of British nobility; a title of European nobility. — *n* **duke'dom.**

dulcet [duls'et] *adj* sweet to the taste, or to the ear; melodious, harmonious.

dulcimer [dul'si-mèr] *n* a musical instrument played by striking the strings with two hammers.

dull [dul] *adj* not sharp or pointed; not bright or clear; stupid; boring; not active.

dulse [duls] *n* an edible red seaweed.

duly [dū'li] *adv* properly; fitly; at the proper time.

dumb [dum] *adj* not able to speak; silent; stupid. — *n* **dumb'-ness.** — **dumb'bell**, a short bar with heavy disks or round ends used to exercise the muscles. — *vti* **dum(b)found'**, -er, to confound briefly, usu. with astonishment.

dumdum [dum'dum] *n* a soft-nosed expanding bullet.

dummy [dum'ē] figure of a person used to display clothes; a stupid person; an imitation; (*bridge*) the exposed cards of the declarer's partner; the declarer's partner.

dump [dump] *vt* to unload; to discard, as on a rubbish heap; to sell goods abroad at a price lower than the market price abroad. — *n* a place for refuse or other unwanted material; a dirty, dilapidated place.

dumpling [dump'ling] *n* a rounded piece of dough cooked by boiling or steaming; a short, fat person.

dumpy [dump'i] *adj* short and thick.

dumps [dump] *n* gloominess, low spirits.

dun¹ [dun] *adj* greyish-brown in color. — *n* a dun horse.

dun² [dun] *vt* to importune for payment; — *pr p* **dunn'ing**; *pt p* **dunned.**

dunce [duns] *n* one slow at learning; a stupid person.

dunderhead [dun'dèr-hed] *n* a stupid person.

dune [dūn] *n* a hill of sand piled up by the wind.

dung [dung] *n* excrement; manure. — *vt* to manure with dung; **dung'hill**, a heap of dung; a situation that is repulsive.

dungaree [dung-gă-rē' or dung'-] *n* a kind of coarse cotton cloth, trousers, often bibbed, made from this. (*pl*).

dungeon [dun'jón] *n* a close, dark prison, esp a cell underground.

dunlin [dun'lin] *n* the red-backed sandpiper.

duo [dū'ō] *n* a duet; two persons associated in some way.

duodecimo [dū-ō-des'i-mō] *n* size of book in which each sheet is folded into 12 leaves; a book of this size. — *adj* of this size.

duodenum [dū-o-dēnum] *n* the first part of the small intestine. — *adj* **duo-dē'nal.**

duologue [dū'ō-log] *n* a piece spoken between two.

dupe [dūp] *n* one who is cheated. — *vt* to deceive; to trick. — *n* **dū'pery**, the art of deceiving others.

duplex [dū'pleks] *adj* twofold, double. — *n* an apartment on two floors; a two-family house. — **duplicity** (dū-plis'i-ti), contradictory, doubleness; treachery.

duplicate [dū'pli-kāt] *adj* double; twofold; exactly like. — *n* another thing of the same kind. — **duplica'tion; dū'plicātor,** a copying apparatus.

durable [dūr'a-bl] *adj* able to last or endure; resisting wear, etc. — **dur'ableness, durabil'ity.** — **dur'ance** imprisonment; **duration,** continuing in time; the time in which an event persists.

duralumin [dūr-al'-ūm-in] *n* an aluminum-based alloy.

durbar [dûr'bar] *n* a reception or levee, esp of Indian princes.

duress [dūr'es or dūr-es'] *n* unlawful constraint; imprisonment.

durian [dōōr'ian] *n* a large, oval, tasty but foul-smelling fruit with a prickly rind; the tree of SE Asia bearing this fruit.

during [dū'ring] *prep* throughout the time of; in the course of.

durra [dōō'ra] *n* any of several grain sorghums grown widely in warm dry regions. — Also **dura.**

durst [dûrst] *pt of* **dare**, to venture.

dusk [dusk] *adj* dark brown. — *n* twilight; partial darkness. — *adj* **dusk'y**, having dark skin. — *n* **dusk'iness.**

dust [dust] *n* fine particles of solid matter; earth; the grave. — *vt* to free from dust; to sprinkle with flour, sugar, or the like. — *adj* **dust'y**, covered with, containing, or characterized by dust. — **dust bowl,** a drought area subject to duststorms; **dustjacket,** a paper cover for a book.

Dutch [duch] *adj* pertaining to Holland, its people, or its language; (*obs*) German.

duty [dūti] *n* that which one is bound by any obligation to do; one's business, occupation, functions, etc. (eg *on duty, the duties of this post*); service; respect; tax on goods, etc. — *adjs*

dū′teous, devoted to duty; obedient; **dū′tiable**, liable to be taxed; **dū′tiful**, attentive to duty; respectful; **dū′ty-free**, free from tax or duty.

dwarf [dwörf] *n* an animal or plant much below normal size; a star (as the sun) of ordinary or low luminosity and relatively small mass and size.—*vt* to hinder from growing; to make to appear small.—*adj* **dwarf′ish**, like a dwarf; very small.

dwell [dwel] *vi* to abide (in a place); to remain, to continue long; (*with* on) to rest the attention on, to talk at length about;—*pr p* **dwell′ing**; *pt* and *pt p* **dwelt** or **dwelled**.—*ns* **dwell′er**; **dwell′ing**, the place where one dwells, habitation.

dwindle [dwin′dl] *vi* to grow less; to grow feeble; to become degenerate.

dye [dī] *vt* to stain; to give a new color to;—*pr p* **dye′ing**; *pt p* **dyed**.—*n* color; tinge; a coloring material, esp in solution.—*ns* **dy′er**, one whose trade is to dye cloth, etc.; **dye′stuff**, material used in dyeing.

dying [dī′ing] *pr p* of **die**.—*adj* occurring immediately before death, as *dying words*; pertaining to death; declining, becoming extinct.—*n* death.

dyke *see* **dike**.

dynam-, dynamo- [din′am(-ō) or dī′] [Gr *dynamis*, power—*dynasthai*, to be able.]—*adjs* **dynam′ic, -al**, relating to force; causal; forceful, very energetic.—*adv* **dynam′ically**.—*ns* **dynam′ic**, a moving or driving force; **dynamics** (*pl* as sing), the science which treats of matter and motion, or mechanics, sometimes restricted to kinetics; **dyn′amite**, a powerful explosive agent (nitroglycerine and kieselguhr); **dyn′amītard**, **dyn′amīter**, user of dynamite, esp for political purposes; **dynamo**, contr for **dynamo-electric machine**, a machine which generates electric currents by means of the relative movement of conductors and magnets;—*pl* **dyn′amos**; **dyna-mom′eter**, an instrument for measuring force or power.

dynast [din′ast or dīn′-] *n* a ruler.—*n* **dyn′asty**, a succession of hereditary rulers or of members of any powerful family or connected group.—*adj* **dynas′tic**.

dysentery [dis′en-tri] *n* painful inflammation of the large intestine with associated diarrhea.—*adj* **dysenter′ic**.

dyslexia [dis-leks′i-á] *n* impaired ability in learning to read or spell.—*adjs* **dyslec′tic, dyslex′ic**.

dyspepsia [dis-pep′si-á] *n* indigestion—also **dyspep′sy**.—*n* **dyspep′tic**, a person afflicted with dyspepsia.

E

each [ēch] *adj* every one, separately considered, in any number.

eager [ē′gėr] *adj* excited by desire (to do, or for); earnest, keen, enthusiastic.—*adv* **ea′gerly**.—*n* **ea′gerness**.

eagle [ē′gl] *n* various birds of prey with feathered legs, keen eyes, and powerful wings; (golf) score of two strokes under par.—*adj* **ea′gle-eyed**.—*n* **ea′glet**, a young eagle.

ear [ēr] *n* a spike, as of corn.—*vi* to put forth ears.

ear [ēr] *n* the organ of hearing, or the external part merely; the sense of hearing; the faculty of distinguishing sounds, esp of different pitch; attention; anything shaped like an ear.—*ns* **ear′drum**, the tympanic membrane; **ear′mark**, an owner's mark set on the ears of sheep; a distinctive mark.—*vt* to put an earmark on; to set aside.—*adj* **ear′splitting**, shrill, screaming.—*ns* **earring**, an ornament for the earlobe or rim of the ear; **earwig**, any of numerous insects (order Dermaptera) with slender many-jointed antennae and appendages like forceps.

earl [ûrl] *n* a nobleman ranking between a marquis and a viscount.—*fem* **count′ess**.—*n* **earl′dom**, the dominion or dignity of an earl.

early [ûr′li] *adj* belonging to or happening in the first part (of a time, period, series); happening in the remote past or near future.—*adv* near the beginning; soon; in good time; before the appointed time.—*n* **ear′liness**.

earn [ûrn] *vt* to gain by work or service; to acquire; to deserve.—*n pl* **earn′ings**, something earned.

earnest [ûr′nest] *adj* intent; sincere; serious.—*n* seriousness.—*adv* **ear′nestly**.—*n* **ear′nestness**.

earnest [ûr′nest] *n* money given in token of a bargain made; a pledge.

earth [ûrth] *n* the third planet in order from the sun; the world; the inhabitants of the world; the matter on the surface of the globe; soil; dry land, as opposed to sea; dirt; dead matter; the human body; a burrow.—*vt* to hide or cause to hide in the earth or in a hole.—*adj* **earth′en**.—*ns* **earth′enware**, ceramic ware made of coarse clay.—*adj* **earth′ly**.—*n* **earth′liness**.—**earth′quake**, a shaking of the earth's crust caused by changes far beneath the surface.—*adj* **earth′y**, consisting of, relating to, or resembling earth or soil; gross; crude.—*n* **earth′iness**.

ease [ēz] *n* freedom from pain or disturbance; rest from work; quiet; freedom from difficulty; naturalness.—*vt* to free from pain, trouble, or anxiety; to relieve (the mind); to relax, slacken, release (pressure, tension); to moderate; to facilitate; to move slowly and carefully.—*vi* to become less intense (also **ease off**); to become less in demand.—*n* **ease′ment**, the right held by one person in land owned by another.—*adj* **eas′y**, at ease; free from pain, trouble, anxiety, difficulty; unconstrained (eg of manner); not tight; not strict; equally pleased with either alternative.—*adv* **eas′ily**.—*n* **eas′iness**.—*adjs* **eas′ygō′ing** indolent; placid. **easy street**, a situation of no financial worries.

easel [ēz′l] *n* the frame on which painters support their pictures while painting.

east [ēst] *n* the direction of the sunrise; the direction toward the right of one facing north; the compass point opposite west.—*adj, adv* **eastward**; *adv* **eastwards**; *adj, adv* **easterly**, situated toward or belonging to the east, coming from the east.—*n* a wind from the east.—*adjs* **Eastern**, of a region designated East; **eastern, easternmost**, lying toward the east; coming from the east.

Easter [ēstėr] *n* a church feast observed on a Sunday in March or April in commemoration of the resurrection of Christ.

eat [ēt] *vt* to chew and swallow, or to swallow; to consume; (*also with* into) to waste away, to corrode.—*vi* to take food;—*pr p* **eat′ting**; *pt* **ate** (*āt*); *pt p* **eaten** (*ētn*).—*adj* **eat′able**, fit to be eaten.—*n* anything used as food; *pl* food.

eaves [ēvz] *n pl* the projecting edge of a roof.—*vi* **eaves′drop**, to listen secretly to private conversation.—*n* **eaves′dropper**.

ebb [eb] *n* the fall of the tide; a decline.—*vi* to flow back; to sink, to decline.

ebony [eb′ón-i] *n* a hard heavy wood.—*n* **eb′onite**, vulcanized rubber.

ebullient [e-bul′yėnt] *adj* exuberant, enthusiastic; boiling up or over.—*n* **ebulli′tion**, outburst (of feeling, etc.); act of boiling (also **ebull′ience**).

eccentric [ek-sen′trik] *adj* deviating from a usual or accepted pattern; deviating from a circular path; set-up axis or off-center; support; being off-center.—*n* **eccen′tric** an eccentric person.—*adv* **eccen′trically**.—*n* **eccentric′ity** [-tris′-].

ecclesias′tic [e-klēzi-as′tik] *n* a priest, a clergyman.—*adjs* **ecclēsias′tic, -al**, of, belonging to, the church.—*ns* **ecclesi-ol′ogy**, the study of building and decorating churches.

echelon [esh′e-lon, āsh′e-lō] *n* a stepwise arrangement of troops, ships, or airplanes; a level (of authority) in a hierarchy.

echidna [ek-id′nä] *n* a genus of Australian toothless, spiny, egg-laying, burrowing nocturnal mammals.

echo [ek′ō] *n* the repetition of a sound caused by a sound-wave being reflected; imitation; the reflection of a radar signal by an object.—*vi* to reflect sound; to be sounded back.—*vt* to send back the sound of; to repeat; to imitate.—*pr p* **ech′oing**; *pt p* **ech′ōed**.

éclair [ā-klär′] *n* a usu. chocolate-frosted small oblong shell of choux pastry with cream or custard filling.

éclat [ā-klä′] *n* a striking effect; fame; striking success; applause.

eclectic [ek-lek′tik] *adj* selecting or borrowing; choosing the best out of everything.

eclipse [e-klips′] *n* the total or partial disappearance of a heavenly body by the interposition of another between it and the spectator, or by its passing into the shadow of another; temporary failure; loss of brilliancy; darkness.—*vt* to hide wholly or in part; to darken; to throw into the shade, surpass.—*n* **eclip′tic**, the line in which eclipses take place.

eclogue [ek′log] *n* a short pastoral poem.

ecology [ē-kol'o-ji] n the study of organisms in relation to environment; human ecology.

economy [ek- or ēk-on'o-mi] n the thrifty and judicious use of money or goods; an instance of this; the economic system of a country. —adjs econom'ic, -al, pertaining to economy; (usu. economic) considered from the point of view of supplying man's needs; capable of yielding a profit; (usu. economical) thrifty. —adv econom'ically. —n econom'ics, a social science concerned with the production, consumption, and distribution of goods and services. —vti econ'omize, to spend money carefully; to save; to use prudently. —n econ'omist.

ecru [ā'krōō] adj beige.

ecstasy [ek'stá-si] n excessive joy; poetic frenzy; any exalted feeling. —adj ecstat'ic. —adv ecstat'ically.

ecumenical [ek-ū-men'ik -al] adj of the whole Christian world; worldwide; universal; of relations between religions.

eczema [ek'si-ma] n inflammation of the skin.

eddy [ed'i] n a whirlpool or whirlwind. —vi to move round and round. —pr p edd'ying; pt p edd'ied.

edelweiss [ā'dèl-vīs] n a small white-flowered alpine perennial herb.

Eden [ē'dn] n the garden where Adam and Eve lived; a paradise.

edentate [e-den'tāt] adj toothless.

edge [ej] n the border of anything; the brink; the cutting side of an instrument; something that wounds or cuts; sharpness (eg of mind, appetite), keenness. —vt to put an edge on; to border; to move by little and little; to insinuate. —vi to move sideways. —adjs edged; edge'less. —advs edge'ways, edge'-wise. —adj edg'y, with edges, sharp, hard in outline; irritable. —ns edg'iness, edg'ing, any border or fringe round a garment, etc.; a border of box, etc. round a flowerbed. —on edge, nervous, anxious.

edible [ed'i-bl] adj fit or safe to eat. —n something for food. —ns edibil'ity, ed'ibleness.

edict [ē'dikt] n a decree.

edifice [ed'i-fis] n a large building or house.

edify [ed'i-fī] vt to build up the faith of; to comfort; to improve the mind of. —pr p ed'ifying; pt p ed'ified. —n edificā'-tion.

edit [ed'it] vt to prepare for publication, broadcasting, etc; to make up the final version of a motion picture by selection, rearrangement, etc; of material photographed previously. —ns edi'tion, number of copies of a book, etc., printed at a time; form in which a book is issued (eg the annual edition of the yearbook, a limited edition); ed'itor, adj editō'rial. —n an article in a newspaper or periodical expressing the opinions of the publishers or editors.

educate [ed'ū-kāt] vt to provide schooling according to an accepted standard. —adj ed'ucable. —educabil'ity; educā'tion. —adj educā'tional. —adv educā'tionally. —adj ed'ucative.

educe [e-dūs'] vt to draw out; to infer. —adj educ'ible.

EEC Abbrev for European Economic Community.

eel [ēl] n a snakelike fish.

eerie [ē'ri] adj exciting fear, weird; affected with fear, timorous. —adv ee'rily. —n ee'riness.

efface [e-fās'] vt to destroy the surface of a thing; to rub out; (fig) to obliterate, wear away; to eclipse; to treat (oneself) as insignificant, to shun notice. —adj efface'able. —n efface'-ment.

effect [e-fekt'] n the result, consequence, outcome; impression produced; (pl) goods, property; vt to produce; to accomplish. —adjs effec'tive, having power to produce a specified effect; powerful; serviceable (eg fighting force); not merely nominal; striking (eg illustration, speech). —n one capable of service. —adv effec'tively. —n effec'tiveness. —adjs effec'tual. —n effectual'ity. —adv effec'tually.

effeminate [e-fem'in-àt] adj womanish; unmanly; n effem'inacy.

effendi [e-fen'di] n a man of property, authority, or education in an eastern Mediterranean country.

efferent [ef'è-rènt] adj conveying outward or away.

effervesce [ef-èr-ves'] vi to emit bubbles of gas; to be exhilarated. —n efferves'cence. —adj efferves'cent.

effete [e-fēt'] adj decadent; effeminate.

efficacious [ef-i-kā'shus] adj producing the result intended. —adv efficā'ciously. —n eff'icacy.

efficient [e-fish'ént] adj capable of doing what may be required (of a person or other agent or of an action). —n efficiency [e-fish'n-si]. —adv effi'ciently.

effigy [ef'i-ji] n a crude figure of a hated person; the head on a coin.

effloresce [ef-lo-res'] vi to blossom forth. —n efflores'cence. —adj efflores'cent.

effluent [effiōō-ènt] adj flowing out. —n a stream that flows out of another stream or a lake; that which flows out. —eff'lu-ence, a flowing out.

effluvium [e-flōō'vi-um] n disagreeable vapors. —pl efflu'via. —adj efflu'vial.

effort [ef'òrt] n exertion; attempt; struggle. —adj eff'ortless.

effrontery [e-frunt'èr-i] n impudence; insolence.

effulgence [e-fulj'èns] n radiant splendor; brilliance. —adj efflulg'ent.

effuse [e-fūz'] vt to pour out; to pour forth (as words). —n efflū'sion. —adj efflu'sive. —adv effusively. —n efflū'siveness.

eft [eft] n a newt.

egg[1] [eg] n a round or oval body laid by birds, reptiles, and fishes from which the young is hatched; an ovum: anything resembling an egg; egghead, an intellectual; eggplant, a widely-cultivated perennial herb of the nightshade family; the smooth dark purple egg-shaped fruit of this plant; egg'shell, the hard outer covering of an egg.

egg[2] [eg] vt (followed by on) to incite (a person to do something).

eglantine [eg'lan-tīn] n the sweetbrier.

ego [e'gō, ē'gō] n the 'I', or self—that which is conscious and thinks. —n egocen'tric, self-centered. —n e'gōist; one who thinks and speaks too much of himself. —adjs egōist'ic, -al. —n e'gotism, speaking much of oneself, self-exaltation. —n e'gotist. —adjs. egotist'ic, -al.

egrēgious [e-grē'jyus] adj glaringly bad; outrageous; notorious. —adv egrē'giously. —n egrē'giousness.

egress [ē'gres] n act of going out; the way out.

egret [ē'gret] any of various herons.

eider [īdèr] n the eider-duck, any of several northern sea ducks. —n ei'derdown, the soft down of the eider; a comforter stuffed with eiderdown.

eight [āt] adj n one more than seven; the symbol for this. —n eighth, (mus) an octave; the last of eight.

eighteen [āt-ēn] adj one more than seventeen; the symbol for this. Also n—adj eighteenth, the last of eighteen. —Also n.

eighty [ā'te] adj, n eight times ten; symbol for this. —pl eighties (80s); the numbers from 80 to 89; the same numbers in a life or a century. —adj eightieth, the last of eighty. Also n.

eisteddfod [ī-stéTH'vod] n a Welsh competitive festival of the arts, esp singing.

either [ī'THèr, or ē'THèr] adj, pron the one or the other; one of two; each of two. —conj correlative to or.

ejaculate [e-jak'u-lāt] vt to eject a fluid (as semen); to exclaim. Also vi—n ejaculā'tion. —adj ejac'ulatory.

eject [e-jekt'] vt to cast out; to emit; to turn out, to expel. —vi to cause oneself to be ejected from an aircraft or spacecraft. —n ejec'tion. —adj ejec'tive. —ns eject'ment, expulsion; (law) an action for recovery of the possession of land, etc.; eject'or, one who ejects; any mechanical apparatus for ejecting.

eke [ēk] vt to add to, to lengthen. —eke out, to supplement (with); to use sparingly so as to make suffice.

elaborate [e-lab'ór-āt] vt to work out in detail; to improve by successive operations. —Also vi (often with on, upon). —adj [-àt] worked out with fullness and exactness; highly detailed. —elaborā'tion.

élan [ā-lã'] n verve, spirit characterized by poise.

eland [ē'land] n either of two large African antelopes.

elapse [e-laps'] vi to slip or glide away; to pass silently, as time. —n passing.

elastic [e-las'tik] adj having the ability to recover the original form, when forces that changed that form are removed; springy; able to recover quickly a former state or condition after a shock. —n fabric, tape, etc., woven partly of elastic thread. —adv elas'tically. —adj elast'icized. —elasticity, [tis'-], tendency of a body to return to its original size or shape, after having been stretched, compressed, or deformed.

elate [e-lāt'] vt to make exultant or proud. —adv elat'edly. —n ela'tion.

elbow [el'bō] *n* the joint of the arm; any sharp turn or bend.— *vt* to push with the elbow; to jostle.

elder[1] [eld'ėr] *n* any of a genus of trees or shrubs of the honeysuckle family with flat clusters of white or pink flowers.— **el'derberry**, the edible black or red berry borne by the elder.

elder[2] [eld'ėr] *adj* older.— *n* one who is older; an ancestor; one of a class of office-bearers in Presbyterian churches.— *adj* **eld'erly**, somewhat old; bordering on old age.— *adj.* **eld'est**, oldest.

El Dorado [el dō-rä'dō] the golden land of imagination of the Spanish conquerors of America.

elect [e-lekt'] *vt* to choose by voting; to make a selection of; to decide on.— *vi* to make a selection.— *adj* chosen; chosen for an office but not yet in it.— *n* any group of persons set apart by excellence.— *pl* **elect**.— *n* **elec'tion**, the act of electing; the public choice of a person for office; predestination to eternal life.— *vi* **electioneer'**, to work to secure the election of a candidate.— *adj* **elec'tive**, pertaining to, dependent on, or exerting the power of, choice.— *n* an elective course or subject.— *n* **elect'or**, one who has a vote at an election; a member of the US electoral college.— *adj* **elect'oral**, pertaining to elections or to electors.— *n* **elect'orate**, the body of electors.

electrical, -al [e-lek'trik -àl] *adj* of electricity; charged with electricity; producing electricity; run by electricity; exciting, thrilling.— *adv* **elec'trically**.— *ns* **electrician** [e-lek-trish'àn], person whose work is installing or repairing electric wires, motors, lights etc.; **electricity** [tris'-], a form of energy that can produce light, heat, magnetism, and chemical changes; an electric current; a feeling of excitement.— *vt* **elec'trify**, to charge with electricity, to equip for the use of electric power; to excite suddenly; to astonish.— *pt p* **elec'trified**.— *n* **electrification**.

electro- [e-lek'trō-] of, associated with, accomplished by, electricity.— *vt* **elec'trocute**, to kill by electricity.— *ns* **electrocū'tion**.— *vt* **elec'trolyze**, [-īz], to subject to electrolysis.— *ns* **electrol'ysis** [-isis], the decomposition of a chemical compound by electricity.— *ns* **elec'tromagnet**, a piece of iron rendered magnetic by a current of electricity passing through a coil of wire wound round it.— *adj* **elec'tromagneti'c**.— *vt* **elec'troplate**, to plate or cover with metal by electrolysis.— *n* articles covered with silver in this way.— *ns* **elec'troplating**.

electrode [el-ek'trōd] *n* a conductor through which a current of electricity enters or leaves an electrolytic cell, gas discharge tube, or thermionic valve.

electron [el-ek'tron] *n* a negatively charged elementary particle that forms the part of the atom outside the nucleus.— *adj* **electronic**.— *n* **electronics**, the physics of electrons and their use.— *n*.

eleemosynary [el-i-ē-moz'i-nar-i or -mos'-] *adj* of a nonprofit organization; given in charity.

elegant [el'e-gànt] *adj* expensive and in good taste; graceful; refined.— *n* **el'egance**.

elegy [el'e-ji] *n* a slow plaintive song; a poem praising and mourning a specific dead person.— *adj* **elegi'ac, -al** belonging to elegy.

element [el'e-mėnt] *n* the natural environment; a constituent part; the simplest principles, rudiments; a substance not separable by ordinary chemical means into substances different from itself; any of the four substances (earth, air, fire, water) in ancient and medieval thought believed to constitute the universe.— *pl* weather conditions, esp severe weather.— *adjs* **element'al**, pertaining to elements, or produced by elements; **element'ary**, primary; pertaining to the elements; treating of first principles.

elephant [el'e-fànt] *n* any of a family of huge heavy mammals with a long trunk, thick skin, and ivory tusks.— *n* **elephantī'asis**, a disease in which the limbs or the scrotum become greatly enlarged.— *adj* **elephant'ine**, very large and clumsy.— *n* **elephant seal**, a nearly extinct large seal.

elevate [el'e-vāt] *vt* to lift up; to raise in rank, to improve in mind or morals; to elate. **eleva'tion**, a raised place; the height above the earth's surface or above sea level; the act of elevating or raising; a drawing that shows how the front, rear, or side of something looks from the outside; exaltation.— **el'evator**, a cage or platform for moving something from one level to another; a building for storing grain.

eleven [e-lev'n] *adj, n* one more than ten.— *ns* the symbol for this.— *adj* **elev'enth**, the last of eleven; being one of eleven equal parts.

elf [elf] *n* a mischievous fairy.— *pl* **elves**.— *adjs* **elf'in, elf'ish, elv'ish**.— *adv* **elfishly**.

elicit [e-lis'it] *vt* to draw forth.— *n* **elicitā'tion**.

elide [e-līd'] *vt* to omit or slur over in pronunciation.— *n* **eli'sion**.

eligible [el'i-ji-bl] *adj* fit or worthy to be chosen; legally qualified; desirable.— **eligibil'ity**.

eliminate [e-lim'in-āt] *vt* to thrust out, expel; to remove, to exclude; to ignore, leave out of consideration; to get rid of.— *adj* **elim'inative**.— *n* **eliminā'tion**.

elite [ā-lēt'] *n* the choice part; a superior group.

elixir [e-liks'ėr] *n* a substance supposed to have the power of indefinitely prolonging life.

elk [elk] *n* the largest existing deer of Europe and Asia.

ell [el] *n* an old measure of length.

ellipse [el-ips'] *n* (geom) an oval; having both ends alike.— *n* **ellip'sis**, the omission of a word or words needed to complete the grammatical construction of a sentence; the marks (. . .) used to show an omission in writing or printing.— *pl* **ellip'sēs**.— *adjs* **ellipsoi'dal**; **ellip'tic, -al**— *adv* **ellip'tically**.

elm [elm] *n* a tall deciduous shade tree with spreading branches and broad top; its hard heavy wood.

elocution [el-o-kū'sh(ò)n] *n* the art of public speaking.— *adj* **elocū'tionary**.— *n* **elocu'-tionist**.

elongate [ē'long-gāt] *vt* to make longer, to extend.— *adj* **e'longāted**.— *n* **elongā'tion**.

elope [e-lōp'] *vi* to run away esp with a lover; **elope'ment; elop'er.

eloquence [el'o-kwèns] *n* flow of speech that has grace and force; the power to persuade by speaking.— *adj* **el'oquent**.— *adv* **el'oquently**.

else [els] *adv* otherwise; besides, except that mentioned.— *adv* **else'where** in or to another place.

elucidate [e-l(y)ŏŏ'si-dāt] *vt* to make clear; to explain.— *n* **elucidā'tion**.— *adjs* **elu'cidative, elu'cidatory**.— *n* **elu'cidator**.

elude [e-l(y)ŏŏd'] *vt* to slip away from; to baffle.— *adj* **elu'sive**.— *adv* **elu'sively**.— *n* **elu'siveness**.

elves, elvish *see* **elf**.

Elysium [e-liz(h)'i-um] *n* the abode of the blessed after death; any delightful place.— *n* **elys'ian fields** Elysium; exceedingly delightful.

em [em] *n* (*printing*) the square of the body of any type.— *Also* **em quad**.

emaciate [e-mā'sh-āt, 'si-āt] *vt* to make unnaturally thin.— *vi* to become lean, to waste away.— *adjs* **emā'ciate (-àt), -d**.— *n* **emaci-ā'tion**.

emanate [em'a-nāt] *vi* to come forth from a source.— *n* **emanā'tion**.

emancipate [e-man'si-pāt] *vt* to set free, esp from bondage or slavery.— *ns* **emancipā'tion; eman'cipātor**.

emasculate [e-mas'kū-lāt] *vt* to castrate; to deprive of strength.— *adj* [-lat], deprived of vigor or strength; **emascu-lā'tion**.— *adj* **emas'culātor**.

embalm [em-bäm'] *vt* to preserve (a dead body) with drugs, chemicals, etc.; to perfume; to preserve with care and affection.

embank [em-bangk'] *vt* to enclose or confine with a bank or dike.— *n* **embank'ment**, the act of embanking; a bank, mound, or ridge, made to hold back water or to carry a roadway.

embargo [em-bär'gō] *n* an order of a government forbidding ships to enter or leave its ports; any restriction put on commerce by law; a prohibition, ban.

embark [em-bärk'] *vt* to put on board a ship or airplane.— *vi* to board a boat or airplane for transportation; to make a start in an activity or enterprise.— *n* **embarkā'tion**.

embarrass [em-bar'as] *vt* to impede; to involve in difficulty; to perplex; to put out of countenance, disconcert.— *a adj* **embarr'assed**.— *n* **embarr'assment**.

embassy [em'bas-i] *n* a person or group officially sent as ambassadors; an ambassador's official residence.

embattle [em-bat'l] *vt* to arrange in order of battle; prepare for battle.— *n adj* **embatt'led**.

embed [em-bed'] *vt* to fix in a mass of matter; to lay, as in a bed.—Also **imbed**.

embellish [em-bel'ish] *vt* to decorate, to adorn.—**embell'isher**; **embell'ishment**.

ember [em'bėr] *n* a piece of live coal or wood; (*pl*) smouldering remains of a fire (*lit* and *fig*).

emberday [em'bėr-dā] *n* any of appointed days of fasting and prayer in Western churches.

embezzle [em-bez'l] *vt* to steal (money, securities, etc. entrusted to one's care).—*ns* **embezz'lement**, fraudulent appropriation of property entrusted; **embezz'ler**.

embitter [em-bit'ėr] *vt* to make bitter.—*adj* **embitt'ered**, soured.—Also **imbitter**.

emblazon [em-blā'zón] *vt* to adorn with heraldic devices, etc.; to make bright with color; to celebrate, extol.

emblem [em'blem] *n* a symbol; a figure adopted and used as an identifying mark; a heraldic device, a badge.—*adjs* **emblemat'ic**, **-al**.—*adv* **emblemat'ically**.

embody [em-bod'i] *vt* to express in definite form; to bring together and include in a single book, law, system, etc.—*adj* **embod'ied**.—*n* **embod'iment**.

embolden [em-bōld'n] *vt* to inspire with courage.

embolism [em'bo-lizm] *n* the obstruction of a blood vessel by a foreign or abnormal particle (as an air bubble or blood clot) during life.

embonpoint [ã-bɔ̃-pwē] *n* plumpness of person.

emboss [em-bos'] *vt* to raise bosses on, to ornament with raised-work; to mould or carve in relief.

embrace [em-brās'] *vt* to take in the arms; to press to the bosom with affection; to take eagerly (eg an opportunity); to adopt or receive (eg Christianity); to comprise.—*vi* to join in an embrace.—Also *n*.

embrasure [em-brā'zhúr] *n* a recess of a door or window; an opening in a wall for cannon.

embrocate [em'brō-kāt] *vt* to moisten and rub, as with a lotion.—*n* **embroca'tion**, act of embrocating; the lotion used.

embroider [em-broid'ėr] *vt* to ornament with stitches; to elaborate in florid detail.—*ns* **embroid'erer**; **embroid'ery**.

embroil [em-broil'] *vt* to involve in a quarrel; to bring into a state of discord; to throw into confusion.—*n* **embroil'ment**.

embryo [em'bri-ō] *n* an animal during the period of its growth from the fertilized egg to the eighth week of life; a thing in a rudimentary state.—*pl* em'bryos.—*ns* embryol'ogy, embryol'ogist.—*adj* embryon'ic, immature, undeveloped.

emend [ē-mend', e-mend'] *vt* to correct errors in a text.—Also em'endate.—*ns* emenda'tion, e'mendātor.

emerald [em'ėr-áld] *n* a rich green gemstone; any of various gemstones resembling this.—*ns* emerald green, brightly or richly green.

emerge [e-mûrj'] *vi* to rise out of; to come forth, come into view; (*fig*) to come out as a result of enquiry.—*ns* emer'gence, emer'gency, an unexpected occurrence or situation demanding immediate action.—*adj* emer'gent.

emeritus [e-mer'i-tus] *adj* and *n* retired from active service, but still holding one's rank and title.

emery [em'ėr-i] *n* a hard granular mineral used for grinding and polishing; a hard abrasive powder.

emetic [e-met'ik] *adj* causing vomiting.—*n* a medicine that causes vomiting.

emigrate [em'i-grāt] to leave one's country in order to settle in another.—*adj* em'igrant, *n* emigrā'tion.

eminent [em'i-nėnt] *adj* rising above others; conspicuous; distinguished; exalted in rank or office.—*adv* em'inently.—*ns* em'inence, em'inency, a rising ground, hill; (*lit* and *fig*) height; distinction; a title of honor.—*n* eminence, high rank or position; a person of high rank or attainments; a high place; Eminence, the title for a cardinal of the RC church.

emir [ām-ēr', or ē'mir] *n* a native ruler in parts of Africa and Asia.

emit [e-mit'] *vt* to give out; to put into circulation; to express, to utter.—*pr p* emitt'ing; *pt p* emitt'ed.—*ns* em'issary, one sent out on a secret mission; emiss'ion, the act of emitting; that which is issued at one time.—*adj* emiss'ive.

emmet [em'et] *n* (*dial*) the ant.

emollient [e-mol'yėnt] *adj* softening; making supple; soothing.—*n* something that softens and soothes.

emolument [e-mol'ū-mėnt] *n* the product of an employment.

emotion [e-mō'sh(ó)n] *n* a strong feeling of any kind.—*adj* emō'tional, of the emotions; liable to emotion.—*adv* emō'tionally.—*adj* emō'tive,.

empathy [em'pa-thi] *n* capacity for participating in the feelings or ideas of another.—*vi* em'pathize.

emperor [em'pėr-ór] *n* the sovereign ruler of an empire.—*fem* em'press.

emphasis [em'fa-sis] *n* particular stress or prominence given.—*pl* em'phases [-sēz].—*vt* em'phasize, to lay stress on.—*adjs* emphat'ic, -al, expressed, or expressing, with emphasis; forcible.—*adv* emphat'ically.

empire [em'pīr] *n* a large state or group of states under a single sovereign, usu. an emperor.

empiric, empirical [em-pir'ik, -ál] *adj* resting on trial or experiment; known by experience only.—*n* empir'ic, one who makes trials or experiments; one whose knowledge is got from experience only.—*adv* empir'ically.—*n* empir'icism.

emplacement [em-plās'mėnt] *n* the act of placing; (*mil*) a gun platform.

emplane [em-plān'] *see* enplane.

employ [em-ploi'] *vt* to give work and pay to; to make use of.—*n* employment.—*p* *adj* employed'.—*ns* employ'ēē; employ'er; employ'ment.

emporium [em-pō'ri-um, -pō'] *n* a large store carrying many different things.

empower [em-pow'ėr] *vt* to authorize.

empty [emp'ti] *adj* containing nothing; not occupied; lacking reality, substance, or value; hungry; *vt* to make empty; to transfer by emptying.—*vi* to become empty; to discharge its contents.—*n* emp'tiness, state of being empty.

empyema [em-pī-ē'ma] *n* the presence of pus in a bodily cavity.—*pl* empye'mata, empye'mas.

empyreal [em-pir-ē'ál', em-pir'i-ál] *adj* pertaining to the highest and purest region of heaven; sublime.—*adj* empyrē'an [or -pir'-], empyreal.—*n* the highest heaven; the region of pure light.

emu [ē'mū] *n* a fast-running Australian bird, related to the ostrich.

emulate [em'ū-lāt] *vt* to strive to equal or excel; to rival; (*loosely*) to imitate.—*n* emulā'tion, act of emulating; rivalry, competition.—*adj* em'ulative.—*n* em'ulator.—*adj* em'ulatory.

emulsion [e-mul'sh(ó)n] *n* a mixture of mutually insoluble liquids in which one is dispersed in droplets throughout the other; a light-sensitive coating on photographic paper or film.—*vt* emul'sify.—*adjs* emulsible, emul'sive.

en- [en-] used to form verbs, meaning: (1) to put into, eg encage; (2) to bring into the condition of, eg enslave; (3) to make, eg endear. Before *b*, *p*, and sometimes *m*, *en*- becomes *em*-, eg embed, emplane, emmesh for enmesh.

enable [en-ā'bl] *vt* to make able, by supplying the means; to give legal power or authority to.

enact [en-akt'] *vt* to establish by law; to act.

enamel [en-am'el] *n* a glasslike substance used to coat the surface of metal or pottery; the hard outer layer of a tooth; a usu. glossy paint that forms a hard coat.—*vt* to coat with or paint in enamel; to form a glossy surface upon, like enamel.

enamor [en-am'ór] *vt* to inflame with love.

encamp [en-kamp'] *vt* to settle in a camp.—*vi* to make a stay in a camp.—*n* encamp'ment.

encaustic [en-kōs'tik] *n* a paint fixed by heat after application; the method of using encaustic.—*adj* prepared by heat; burnt in.

enceinte[1] [ã-sɔ̃t'] *n* (*fort*) an enclosure, generally the whole area of a fortified place.

enceinte[2] [ã-sɔ̃t'] *adj* pregnant, being with child.

encephal(o)- [en-sef'al-(ó)-, -kef'] of the brain.—*ns* encephali'tis, inflammation of the brain.

enchant [en-chãnt'] *vt* to bewitch, to charm.—*n* enchant'er.—*fem* enchant'ress.—*n* enchant'ment.

encircle [en-sûrk'l] *vt* to surround (with); to go or pass round.

enclave [en'klāv], also en-klāv', or ã-klãv'] *n* a piece of territory entirely enclosed within foreign territory.

enclitic [en-klit'ik] *n* (*gram*) a word or particle without accent which always follows another word and usually modifies the accentuation of the word it follows (eg Gr *te*, L *-que*, *-ne*).—Also *adj*.

enclose [en-klōz'] *vt* to shut up or in; to surround.—*n* **enclos'ure**.

encomium [en-kō'mi-um], also **encōm'ion**, *n* high commendation; a formal expression of praise.

encompass [en-kum'pàs] *vt* to surround or enclose.—*n* **encom'passment**.

encore [ong-kōr'] *interj* again!—*n* [also ong'-] a call for the repetition of a performance; repetition in response to a call.—*vt* to call for a repetition of, or a further performance by.

encounter [en-kown'tèr] *vt* to meet, esp hostilely or unexpectedly.—*n* a meeting; a fight, passage of arms (*lit* and *fig*).

encourage [en-kur'ij] *vt* to put courage in; to inspire with spirit or hope; to incite.—*n* **encour'agement**.

encroach [en-krōch'] *vi* to extend into (territory, sphere, etc. of others—*with* on), to seize on the rights of others.—*n* **encroach'er**.—*n* **encroach'ment**.

encrust [en-krust'] *vt* to cover with a crust or hard coating; to form a crust on the surface of.—*vi* to form a crust.

encumber [en-kum'bèr] *vt* to weigh down; to hinder the function or activity of.—*n* **encum'brance**.

encyclical [en-sīk'lik-ál, or -sik'-] *adj* sent round to many persons or places.—*n* a letter addressed by the pope to all his bishops.

encyclopedia, -paedia [en-sī-klo-pē'di-a] *n* a work containing information on all branches of knowledge or treating comprehensively a particular branch of knowledge usu. in alphabetical order.—*adj* **encyclope'dic**, **encyclopae'dic**.—*ns* **encyclope'dist**.

end [end] *n* the last part; the place where a thing stops; purpose; result, outcome.—*vt* to bring to an end; to destroy.—*vi* to come to an end; to result (in).—*adj* final; ultimate.—*adj* **end'ed**.—*n* **end'ing**.—*adj* **end'less**.

endanger [en-dān'jèr] *vt* to place in danger.

endear [en-dēr'] *vt* to make dear or more dear.—*adv* **endear'ingly**.—*n* **endear'ment**.

endeavor [en-dev'ôr] *vi* to strive or attempt (to).

endemic [en-dem'ik] locally prevalent (*an endemic disease, endemic plants*).—*adv* **endem'ically**.

endive [en'dīv'] *n* an annual or biennial herb widely cultivated as a salad plant.

endocardium [en-dōkär'di-um] *n* the lining membrane of the heart.

endocrine [en'do-krin] *adj* secreting internally, specifically producing secretions that are distributed in the body by the bloodstream.—*ns* **endocrinologist, endocrinology**.

endogamy [en-dag'am-ē] *n* marriage within a specific group as required by custom or law.

endogenous [en-daj'en-is], **endogenic** [-ik] *adj* growing from or on the inside.

endorse [en-dōrs'] *vt* to write one's name, comment, etc. on the back of to approve; to support.—*n* **endorse'ment**.

endow [en-dow'] *vt* to give money or property to provide an income for; to enrich.—*n* **endow'ment**.

endue [en-dū'] *vt* to provide with a quality or power.

endure [en-dūr'] *vt* to bear with patience; to undergo; to tolerate.—*vi* to remain firm; to last.—*adj* **endur'able**.—*adv* **endur'ably**.—*n* **endur'ance**, state, or the power, of enduring or bearing; continuance.

enema [en'e-ma, or e-nē'ma] *n* liquid injected into the rectum; the material injected.

enemy [en'e-mi] *n* one who hates or dislikes and wishes to injure another, a foe, esp a military opponent; something harmful or deadly.

energy [en'èr-ji] *n* capacity of acting or being active; vigorous activity; capacity to do work; vigor; forcefulness.—*pl* **energies**.—*adj* **energet'ic**.—*adv* **energet'ically**.—*vt* **en'ergize**.

enervate [en'èr-vàt] *vt* to lessen the strength or vigor of; to weaken in mind and body.

enfeeble [en-fē'bl] *vt* to weaken.—*n* **enfee'blement**.

enfilade [en-fi-lād'] *n* gunfire that rakes a line of troops, or a position, from end to end.—*vt* to rake with shot through the whole length of a line.

enfold [en-fōld'] *vt* to wrap up (in, with); to embrace.—Also **infold**.

enforce [en-fōrs', -fôrs'] *vt* to compel obedience by threat; to execute with vigor.—*n* **enforce'ment**.

enfranchise [en-fran'chīz] *vt* to set free; to admit to citizenship; to grant the vote to.—*n* **enfran'chisement**.

engage [en-gāj'] *vt* to pledge as security; to promise to marry; to keep busy; to hire; to attract and hold, esp attention or sympathy; to cause to participate; to bring or enter into conflict; to begin or take part in a venture; to connect or interlock, to mesh.—*adj* **engaged'**.—*n* **engage'ment**.—*adj* **engag'ing**, winning, attractive (eg of manner).—*adv* **engag'ingly**.

engender [en-jen'dèr] *vt* to bring into being, to produce; to cause to develop.

engine [en'jin] *n* a machine by which physical power is applied to produce a physical effect; a locomotive; a mechanical device, esp a machine used in war.—*ns* **engineer**, a member of a military group devoted to engineering work; a designer or builder of engines; one trained in engineering; one that operates an engine; etc.—*vt* to arrange, contrive.—*n* **engineer'ing**.

English [ing'glish] *adj* of, relating to, or characteristic of England, the English people, or the English language.—*n* the language of the English people, the US and many areas now or formerly under British control; English language and literature as a subject of study.

engraft en-gräft'] *vt* to graft; to insert.

engrave [en-grāv'] *vt* to produce by incising a surface; to incise to produce a representation that may be printed from; to impress deeply.—*ns* **engrav'er; engrav'ing**.

engross [en-grōs'] *vt* to occupy fully; to copy in a large hand; to prepare the final text of.—*adv* **engrossingly**.—**engross'er; engross'ment**.

engulf [en-gulf'] *vt* to swallow up; to flow over and enclose.—*n* **engulf'ment**.

enhance [en-häns'] *vt* to heighten or intensify; to raise in value or in importance; to add to, increase.—*n* **enhance'ment**.

enigma [en-ig'ma] *n* a statement with a hidden meaning to be guessed, a riddle; a puzzling person or thing.—*adjs* **enigmat'ic, -al**.—*adv* **enigmat'ically**.

enjambment, enjambement [en-jamb'mènt, ä-zhäb'mä] *n* the continuation of the sense without a pause beyond the end of a line of verse.

enjoin [en-join'] *vt* to order or direct with authority; to forbid, to prohibit.

enjoy [en-joi'] *vt* to take pleasure or satisfaction in; to possess or use; to experience.—*adj* **enjoy'able**.—**enjoy'ableness; enjoy'ment**.

enlarge [en-lärg'] *vti* to make or grow larger; to expand or increase the capacity of; to exaggerate; to be diffuse in speaking or writing.—*adj* **enlarged'**.—*n* **enlarge'ment**.

enlighten [en-līt'n] *vt* to instruct; to inform.—*p ad.* **enlight'ened**, free from prejudice or superstition; informed.—*n* **enlight'enment**.

enlist [en-list'] *vt* to engage for service in the armed forces; to secure the aid or support of.—*vi* to register for services; to enter heartily into a cause.—*n* **enlist'ment**.

enliven [en-līv'n] *vt* to excite or make active; to make sprightly or cheerful.

enmesh [en-mesh'] *vt* to catch, entangle, as in a mesh or net.—Also **immesh'**.—*n* **enmesh'ment**.

enmity [en'mi-ti] *n* ill-will, esp mutual hatred.

ennoble [e-nō'bl], *vt* to dignify; to exalt, to raise to the nobility.—*n* **ennō'blement**.

ennui [on-wē'] *n* boredom.—*adj* **ennuyé** [-yä].

enormous [e-nōr'mus] *adj* very large.—*n* **enor'mity**, a great crime; great wickedness; huge size.

enough [e-nuf'] *adj* sufficient.—*adv* sufficiently.—*n* a sufficient number, quantity or amount.

enow [e-now'] *adj adv* (*arch*) = **enough**.

enquire *See* **inquire**.

enrage [en-rāj'] *vt* to make angry.—*adj* **enraged'**.

enrapture [en-rap'tyùr, -chùr] *vt* to transport with pleasure or delight.

enrich [en-rich'] *vt* to make rich or richer; to adorn; to increase the proportion of some valuable substance to.—*n* **enrich'ment**.

enroll, enrol [en-rōl'] *vti* to enter or register on a roll or list.—*pr p* **enroll'ing**; *pt p* **enrolled**.—*ns* **enrollee; enrollment**.

ensconce [en-skons'] *vt* to establish in a safe, secure, or comfortable place.

ensemble [äsäbl'] n all the parts of a thing taken together; the general effect; the performance of the full number of musicians, dancers, etc.; a complete harmonious costume.

enshrine [en-shrīn'] vt to enclose in or as if in a shrine; to cherish as sacred.

ensign [en'sīn, en'sin] n a flag; a mark or badge; a commissioned officer in the navy.

ensilage [en'sil-ij] n silage.—vt **ensile**, to prepare and store (fodder) for silage.

enslave [en-slāv'] vt to reduce to slavery; to subject to a dominating influence.—**enslave'ment; enslav'er.**

ensue [en-sū'] vi to follow as a consequence or in time.—pr p **ensū'ing**; pt p **ensūed'.**

ensure [en-shŏŏr'] vt to make sure, certain, or safe. See insure.

entablature [en-tab'la-tyûr] n the part of a building resting on the top of columns.

entail [en-tāl'] vt to settle on a series of heirs, so that the immediate possessor may not dispose of the estate; to bring on as an inevitable consequence; to necessitate.—n an estate entailed; the rule of descent of an estate.

entangle [en-tang'gl] vt to twist into a tangle; to involve in complications or difficulties; to ensnare.—n **entang'lement.**

entente [ä-tät'] n an understanding; a friendly agreement or relationship between states.

enter [en'tèr] vi to go or come in or into; to become a member of; to put down one's name (with for).—vt to come or go into; to penetrate; to join or engage in; to begin; to put into; to enroll or record.

enter- [en'tèr-] between, among.

enteric, enteral [en-ter'ik, en'-ter-al] adj intestinal.

enterprise [en'tèr-prīz] n a bold or dangerous undertaking; a business project; willingness to engage in undertakings of risk.—adj **en'terprising**, forward in undertaking projects; adventurous.

entertain [en-tèr-tan'] vt to receive and treat as a guest; to hold in mind; to amuse; to consider.—n **entertain'er.**—p adj **entertain'ing.**—adv **entertain'ingly.**—n **entertain'ment.**

enthrall [en-thröl'] vt to enslave; to hold spellbound.

enthrone [en-thrōn'] vt to place on a throne; to install as a king or bishop.—n **enthrōne'ment.**

enthusiasm [en-thū'zi-azm] n intense interest; passionate zeal.—n **enthūsiast.**—adjs **enthūsias'tic.**—adv **enthūsias'tically.**—vti **enthūse'**, to make, be, become, or appear enthusiastic.

entice [en-tīs'] vt to attract by offering some pleasure or reward; to lead astray.—n **entice'ment.**

entire [en-tīr'] adj whole; complete; unimpaired, unbroken, unmingled.—adv **entire'ly.**—ns **entire'ness, entire'ty**, completeness; the whole.

entitle [en-tī'tl] vt to give the title of, to style; to give a claim (to).

entity [en'ti-ti] n a real substance; a thing that exists.

entomology [en-to-mol'o-ji] n the branch of zoology that deals with insects.—adj **entomolog'ical.**—n **entomol'ogist.**

entourage [ä-tōō-räzh'] n retinue, group of attendants.

entr'acte [ä-trakt'] n the interval between acts in a play; a piece of music or other performance between acts.

entrails [en'trālz] n pl the internal parts of an animal's body, the bowels.

entrain [en-trān'] vti to put (troops) into or to go into a railroad car.

entrance[1] [en'trans] n act of entering; power or right to enter; a place of entering; a door.—n **en'trant.**

entrance[2] [en-träns'] vt to put into a trance; to fill with rapturous delight.—n **entrance'ment.**

entrap [en-trap'] vt to catch, as in a trap; to ensnare; to entangle.—n **entrap'ment.**

entreat [en-trēt'] vt to ask earnestly; to beg for.—Also **intreat.**—n **entreat'y.**

entrée, entree [ä'trä] n the right or privilege of admission; the principal dish of the meal in the US.

entrench [en-trench', -sh] vt to dig a trench around; to establish in a strong position.—vi to encroach (upon).—n **entrench'ment.**

entrepôt [ä'trè-pō] n an intermediate center of trade and transshipment.

entrepreneur [ä-trè-prè-nœr'] n one who undertakes a business enterprise, esp one involving risk.

entrust [en-trust'] vt to commit as a trust (to); to commit to another with confidence.—Also **intrust.**

entry [en'tri] n act of entering; entrance; writing in a record; the thing so written; the person or thing that takes part in a contest.

entwine [en-twīn'] vt to twine together or around.

entwist [en-twist'] vt to entwine.

enumerate [e-nū'mer-āt] vt to count the number of; to list.—n **enumerā'tion.**

enunciate [e-nun-s(h)i-āt] vt to state definitely; to pronounce distinctly.—n **enunciation** [e-nun-s(h)i-ā'sh(ó)n].—n **enun'ciator.**

envelop [en-vel'op] vt to enclose completely with or as if with a covering.—ns **envelope** [en'vèl-ōp, on'-], that which envelops, wraps, or covers; a paper container for a letter; the bag containing the gas in a balloon or airship; **envel'opment**, a wrapping or covering on all sides.

envenom [en-ven'óm] vt to make poisonous; to embitter.—n **envenomization.**

environ [en-vī'ròn] vt to surround, to encircle.—n **envī'ronment**, surroundings.—n pl **environs** [en-vī'rónz or en'vi-], the outskirts of a place; neighborhood.—adj **environmen'tal.**—n **environmentalist.**

envisage [en-viz'ij] vt to have a mental picture of.

envoy [en'voi] n a diplomatic agent; a representative.

envy [en'vi] n ill-will or discontent at another's well-being or success; an object of envy.—vt to feel envy towards; to feel envy on account of, to grudge.—adjs **en'viable, en'vious**, feeling envy; directed by envy.

enzyme [en'zīm] n a complex substance produced by living cells, which induces or speeds chemical reactions in plants and animals without itself undergoing any alteration. Cf catalyst.

eolian [ē-ōlien] adj borne, deposited, produced or eroded by the wind.

eolith [ē'ō-lith] n a very crudely-chipped flint.

epaulet [ep'öl-et] n a shoulder ornament, esp on a uniform.

epergne [e-pûrn'] n a branched ornamental centerpiece for the dinner table.

ephemeral [ef-em'èrèl] adj existing only for a day; short-lived.

epic [ep'ik] n a long poem in elevated language narrating the deeds of a hero.

epicene [ep'i-sēn] adj common to both sexes; having characteristics of both sexes.

epicenter [ep'i-sen-tèr] n the earth's surface directly above the focus of an earthquake.

epicure [ep'i-kyûr] n a person of refined and fastidious taste, esp in food and wine.—adj **Epicurē'an**; given to luxury.—n a follower of Epicurus; one given to the luxuries of the table.—ns **epicurē'anism, ep'icurism.**

epicycle [ep'i'-sīkl] n a circle having its center on the circumference of a greater circle on which it moves.

epidemic [ep-i-dem'ik, -âl] adj affecting many persons at one time.—n **epidem'ic**, an epidemic outbreak, esp of disease.

epidermis [ep-i-dûr'mis] n an outer layer, esp of skin.

epiglottis [ep-i-glot'is] n a cartilaginous flap over the glottis.

epigram [ep'i-gram] n a short witty poem or saying.—adjs **epigrammat'ic, -al.**—adv **epigrammat'ically.**—vt **epigramm'atize.**—n **epigramm'atist.**

epigraph [ep'i-gräf] n an inscription, esp on a building.

epilepsy [ep'i-lep-si] n a nervous disorder marked typically by convulsive attacks and loss of consciousness.—adj, n **epilep'tic.**

epilogue [ep'i-log] n a speech or short poem at the end of a play; the concluding section of a book.

Epiphany [e-pif'àn-i] n a church festival in commemoration of the coming of the Magi to Jesus.

episcopacy [e-pis'ko-pàs-i] n the government of the church by bishops; the office of bishop; a bishop's period of office; the bishops, as a class.—adj **epis'copal.**—adj **episcopā'lian.**—ns **episcopā'lianism, epis'copate.**

episode [ep'i-sōd] n a unit of action in a dramatic or literary work; an incident in a sequence of events.—adj **episōd'ic(al).**

epistemology [ep-is-te-mol'oj-i] n the theory of knowledge.

epistle [e-pis'l] n a letter; **Epistle**, a letter written by one of

Christ's Apostles to various churches and individuals.—*adj* **epis′tolary**.

epitaph [ep′i-tåf] *n* an inscription in memory of a dead person, usu. on a tombstone.

epithalamium [ep-i-tha-lā′mi-um] *n* a song or poem in celebration of a marriage.

epithet [ep′i-thet] *n* a characterizing and often abusive word or phrase.—*adj* **epithet′ic(al)**.

epitome [e-pit′o-mē] *n* a condensed account; something that represents or typifies another on a small scale.—*vt* **epit′omize**.

epoch [ēp′ok, ep′ok] *n* a point of time fixed or made remarkable by some great event from which dates are reckoned; an age in history.—*adj* **ep′ochal**.

epode [ep′ōd] *n* a lyric poem in which a long line is followed by a shorter one; the last part of a lyric ode, sung after the strophe and antistrophe.

eponym [ep′o-nim] *n* one who gives his name to something.—*adj* **epon′ymous**.

equable [ek′wå-bl or ēk′-] *adj* uniform; free from extremes; of even temper, not easily annoyed or agitated.—*n* **equa-bil′ity**.—*adv* **e′quably**.

equal [ē′kwal] *adj* the same in amount, size, number, or value; (*with* to) strong enough for; impartial, regarding or affecting all objects in the same way; tranquil of mind; capable of meeting a task or situation.—*n* one that is equal.—*vt* to be equal to, esp to be identical in value; to make or do something equal to.—*vt* **equalize**.—*n* **equalization**.—**equality**, sameness in size, number, value, rank, etc.—*adv* **equally**.—*vt* **equate**, to make, treat, or regard as comparable.—*vi* to correspond as equal.—*n* **equation**, an act of equaling; the state of being equal; a usu. formal statement of equivalence (as in logical and mathematical expressions) with the relations denoted by the sign =; an expression representing a chemical reaction by means of chemical symbols.

equanimity [ē-kwa-nim′i-ti, e-] *n* composure.

equator [e-kwā′tôr] *n* (*geog*) an imaginary circle passing round the globe, equidistant from N and S poles.—*adj* **equatō′rial**.

equerry [ek′swe-ri] *n* an officer in charge of the horses of a prince or nobleman; a personal attendant of a male member of the British royal family.

equestrian [e-kwes′tri-ån] *adj* pertaining to horsemanship; on horseback.—*n* one who rides on horseback.—*fem* (*sham Fr*) **equestrienne′**.

equi—[ē′kwi-] equal.

equilibrium [ēk-wi-lib′ri-um] *n* balance; a state of even balance.—*pl* **-riums** or **-ria**.—**equil′ibrist** [or -lib′-, or -lĭb′-].

equine, equinal [e′kwīn, e-kwīn′ål] *adj* of a horse.

equinox [ek′wi-noks, ēk′wi-noks] *n* the time when the sun crosses the equator, making the night equal in length to the day.—*adj* **equinoc′tial** [-shål].

equip [e-kwip′] *vt* to supply with everything needed.—*pr p* **equipp′ing**; *pt p* **equipped′**.—*ns* **e′quipáge**, a horse-drawn carriage and attendants; **equip′ment**.

equity [ek′wi-ti] *n* fairness; a legal system developed into a body of rules supplementing the common law; the value of a property or of an interest in it in excess of the claims against it.—*adj* **e′quitable**, fair; pertaining to equity in the legal sense.—*n* **eq′uitable-ness**.—*adv* **eq′uitably**.

equivalent [e-kwiv′å-lènt] *adj* equal in value, power, meaning, etc.; virtually identical, esp in effect or function.—*n* a thing equivalent.—*n* **equiv′alence**.—*adv* **equiv′alently**.

equivocal [e-kwiv′o-kål] *adj* ambiguous; uncertain; suspicious; questionable.—*adv* **equiv′ocally**.—*n* **equiv′ocalness**.—*vi* **equiv′ocāte**, to use equivocal words in order to mislead.—*ecjuivocā′tion; equiv′ocātor**.

era [ē′ra] *n* a period typified by some special feature; a chronological order or system of notation reckoned from a given date as basis.

eradicate [e-rad′i-kāt, or ē] *vt* to pull up by the roots; to extirpate.—*adjs* **erad′icable, eradicative**.—*ns* **erad′icā′tion; eradicator**.

erase [e-rāz′, e-rās′] *vt* to rub or scratch out.—**erā′ser, erā′s-ure** [-zhúr, -zhūr], a rubbing out.

erbium [ûr′bi-úm] *n* a metallic element of the rare-earth group.

ere [ār] *prep* and *conj*, before.

erect [e-rekt′] *adj* upright; not leaning or lying down.—*vt* to build; to set upright.—*n* **erec′tion, erect′ly**.—*n* **erect′ness**.

eremite [er′e-mīt] *n* a hermit.

erg [ûrg] *n* the unit for measuring work.

ergo [ûr′gō] *adv* therefore.

ergonomics [ėr-go-nom′iks] *n* biotechnology.

ergot [ûr′got] *n* a disease of rye and other cereals caused by a fungus; this fungus; a medicine derived from an ergot fungus.—*n* **er′gotism**, toxic condition caused by ergot fungus or chronic excessive use of an ergot drug.

ermine [ûr′min] *n* the weasel in its winter coat; the white fur of the winter coat; a rank or office whose official robe is edged with ermine.

erne [ûrn] *n* the eagle, esp the white-tailed sea eagle.

erode [e-rōd′] *vt* to eat or wear away gradually.—*n* **erō′sion** [e-rō′zh(ó)n], the action or process of eroding.—*adj* **erō′sive**.

erotic [e-rot′ik] *adj* of sexual love.

err [ûr] *vi* to be or do wrong.—*adjs* **errat′ic, -al**, capricious; irregular; eccentric, odd.—*adv* **errat′ically**.—*ns* **errat′ic**, a stone or boulder transported by ice and deposited far from its original source; **errā′tum**, an error in writing or printing.—*pl* **errā′ta**, a page bearing list of corrigenda.—*adj* **errō′neous**, wrong; mistaken.—*adv* **errō′neously**.—*ns* **errō′neousness**; **err′or**, (*arch*) wandering; a blunder or mistake; wrong-doing.

errand [er′ånd] *n* a short journey on which one is sent to say or do something on behalf of another; the object of this journey.

errant [er′ánt] *adj* wandering; going astray, esp doing wrong; moving aimlessly.—*n* **err′antry**, a wandering state, esp in search of chivalrous adventure.

ersatz [er-zäts′] *adj* substitute; synthetic.

Erse [ers, ûrs] *n* Scottish Gaelic; Irish Gaelic.

erst [ûrst] *adv* at first; formerly.—*adv* **erst′while**, formerly.—*adj* former.

erubescent [er-(y)ŏŏ-bes′ėnt] *adj* growing red; blushing.—*n* **erubes′cence**.

eruct [e-rukt′, -āt] *vt* to belch.—*n* **eructā′tion** (*ė-*).

erudite [er′(y)ŏŏ-dīt] *adj* learned.—*adv* **er′uditely**.—*n* **erudĭ′-tion**, knowledge gained by study.

erupt [e-rupt′] *vi* to burst forth; to break out into a rash.—*n* **erup′tion**, a breaking or bursting forth; that which bursts forth; a breaking out of spots on the skin.—*adj* **erupt′ive**.

erysipelas [er-i-sip′e-lås] *n* an acute bacterial disease, marked by a fever and skin inflammation.

escalade [es-ka-lād′] *n* the scaling of the walls of a fortress by means of ladders.—*vt* to scale; to mount and enter by means of ladders.

es′calate, to ascend, descend on an escalator; to increase rapidly in scale or intensity.—Also *vt*.—**escalā′tion; es′calātor**, a power-driven set of stairs arranged to ascend or descend continuously.

escallop [es-kal′óp] *n see* scallop.

escape [es-kāp′] *vt* to get clear away from; to evade; to go unnoticed; to elude the memory; of words or sounds, to issue inadvertently from.—*vi* to emerge into or gain freedom; to flee; to leak.—*n* act of escaping; a means of escaping; flight; a leakage; flight from reality.—*ns* **escapāde′**, a mischievous adventure; **escāpe′ment**, a device in a timepiece by which the motions of the wheels and of the pendulum wheel are accommodated to each other; **escāp′ism**, desire or tendency to escape from reality into fantasy; **escāp′ist**, one who seeks escape, esp from reality (also *adj*).

escargot [es-kar-gō′] *n* a snail prepared for food.

escarp [es-kärp′] *n* a steep slope or scarp; (*fort*) the side of the ditch next the rampart.—*vt* to make into an escarp.—*n* **escarp′ment**.

eschatology [es-ka-tol′o-ji] *n* the doctrine of the last or final things, as death, judgement, the state after death.

escheat [es-chēt′] *n* property that falls to the state for want of an heir, or by forfeiture.—*vi* to fall to the state.

eschew [es-chōō′] *vt* to shun on moral grounds.

eschscholzia, eschscholtzia [e-sholt′zē-a] *n* a genus of herbs of the poppy family with bright showy flowers; the California poppy.

escort [es′kört] *n* a person or persons, ship or ships, etc. accompanying for protection, guidance, custody, or merely courtesy.—*vt* **escort′**, to attend as escort.

escritoire [es-kri-twär′] *n* a writing-desk.

esculent [es′kū-lènt] *adj* fit to be used for food by man.—*n* something that is eatable.

escutcheon [es'kuch'ón] *n* a shield on which a coat of arms is represented.

Eskimo [es'ki-mō] *n* a group of peoples of northern Canada, Greenland, Alaska, and eastern Siberia; a member of this group; their language.—Also *adj.*—*pl* **Eskimo** or **Eskimos**.

esoteric [es-o-ter'ik] *adj* understood by a select few; secret; private.

espadrille [es'pa-dril] *n* a flat shoe usu. having a fabric upper and rope soles.

espalier [es-pal'yèr] *n* a plant (as a fruit tree) trained to grow flat against a support.

esparto [es-pär'tō] *n* either of two Spanish and Algerian grasses used esp to make cordage, shoes, and paper.

especial [es-pesh'(à)l] *adj* particular; special.—*adv* **espec'ially**.

Esperanto [es-pèr-an'tō] *n* an auxiliary international language.

espionage [es'pyon-äzh, es'pi-ó-nij, es-pī'ó-nij] *n* spying; use of spies.

esplanade [es-pla-näd'] *n* any level space for walking or driving, esp along a shore.

espouse [es-powz'] *vt* to give or take in marriage; to support or embrace, as a cause.—*n* **espous'al**.

espresso [es-pres'ō] *n* coffee brewed by forcing steam through finely-ground darkly roasted coffee beans.

espy [es-pī'] *vt* to catch sight of.

esquire [es-kwīr', sometimes es'-] *n* a general title of respect in addressing letters. Abbrev **Esq**.

essay [es'ā] *n* a trial; an attempt; a written composition usu. dealing with a subject from a limited or personal point of view.—*vt* **essay'**, to try, to attempt.—*pr p* **essay'ing**; *pt p* **essayed'**.—*n* **ess'ayist**, a writer of essays.

essence [es'ėns] *n* that which makes a thing what it is; a substance distilled or extracted from another substance and having the special qualities of the original substance; a perfume.—*adj* **essen'tial** [-shàl], relating to, constituting, or containing the essence; indispensable, important in the highest degree.—*n* an absolutely necessary element or quality.—**essential'ity.**—*n* **essentialness.**—*adv* **essen'tially.**

establish [es-tab'lish] *vt* to set up permanently; to settle; get generally accepted; place beyond dispute as of a custom, belief; to prove as a fact.—*n* **establishment**, act of establishing; a fixed state; that which is established.

estate [es-tāt'] *n* condition or rank; total possessions; property, esp landed property; a social or political class.

esteem [es-tēm'] *vt* to set a high value on; to consider or think.—*n* high estimation, favorable opinion.—*vt* **es'timate**, to judge the worth of; to calculate.—*n* judgement or opinion of the worth or size of a preliminary calculation of cost.—*n* **estimā'tion**, a reckoning; judgment; esteem, honor.

estrange [es-trānj'] *vt* to alienate the affections or confidence of.—*adj* **estranged'.**—*n* **estrange'ment.**

estrogen [es'trė-jen] *n* a substance (as a hormone) that stimulates the development of female characteristics and promotes estrus.—*adjs* **estrogen'ic.**—*n* **es'trus** or **es'trum**, a regularly occurring state of sexual excitability during which the female of most mammals is capable of conceiving and will accept the male.

estuary [es'tū-àr-i] *n* an arm of the sea at the mouth of a river.—*adjs* **estuarial**, **es'tūarine**.

et cetera [et set'ėr-a] and so forth; usually written etc. or &c.

etch [ech] *vti* to make lines on (as metal or glass) usu. by the action of acid; to produce (as a design) by etching; to delineate clearly.—*n* **etch'ing**, the act, art or process of etching; the design produced on or print made from an etched plate.

eternal [e- or ē-tûr'nàl] *adj* without beginning or end; everlasting; unchangeable; seemingly endless..—*adv* **eter'nally.**—*n* **eter'nity.**—**the Eternal**, God.

ethane [ē-thän'] *n* a colorless odorless gaseous hydrocarbon found in natural gas and used esp as fuel.

ethanol [eth'a-nl] *n* alcohol.—Also **ethyl alcohol**.

ether [ēthèr] *n* (*chem*) a light flammable liquid used as an anesthetic or solvent; the upper regions of space; the invisible elastic substance supposed to be distributed evenly through all space.—*vt* **etherize.**—*adj* **ethe'real**, consisting of ether; heavenly; airy; spirit-like.

ethics [eth'iks] *n sing or pl* study of standards of right and wrong; system of conduct or behavior, moral principles.—*adj* **eth'ical.**—*adv* **eth'ically.**

ethnic, -al [eth'nik, -àl] *adj* of races or large groups of people classed according to common traits and customs.—*n* **ethnography**, ethnology, esp descriptive anthropology.—*adj* **ethnograph'ic(al).**—*ns* **ethnographer**; **ethnol'ogy**, the science that deals with races of people.—*adj* **ethnolog'ical.**—*adv* **ethnolog'ically.**

ethology [eth-ol'ōjė'] *n* a branch of knowledge dealing with human ethos and its formation and evolution; the scientific and objective study of animal behavior.—*n* **ethos**, the distinguishing character, sentiment, moral nature, or guiding beliefs of a person, group, or institution.

ethyl [eth'il] *n* the radical from which common alcohol and ether are derived; the abbreviation for gasoline additive.—**ethyl alcohol**, alcohol.

etiolate [ē'-ti-o-lāt] *vt* to cause to grow pale from want of light; to make pale and sickly.—*vi* to become pale.—*n* **etiolā'tion**.

etiology [ē-ti-ol'o-ji] *n* the study of causes.

etiquette [et'i-ket, or -ket'] *n* the forms of conduct or behavior prescribed by custom or authority to be observed in social, official or professional life.

etymology [et-i-mol'oj-i] *n* the science or investigation of the derivation and original meaning of words; the source and history (of a word).—*adj* **etymolog'ical** [-loj'-].—*adv* **etymolog'ically.**—*n* **etymol'ogist** [-jist].

eucalyptus [ū-kà-lip'tus] *n* any of a genus of mostly Australian evergreen trees wholly grown for useful products.—Also *gum tree*.—*n* **eucalyptus oil**, oil distilled from leaves of eucalyptus.

Eucharist [u'kä-rist] *n* the sacrament of communion; communion with God.—*adj* **eucharist'ic.**

eugenics [ū-jen'iks] *npl* science of improving the human race by selective breeding.

eulogy [ū'lo-ji] *n* a speech or writing in warm praise of (someone, occasionally something—*with* on).—*vt* **eu'logīze.**—*n* **eu'logist.**—*adj* **eulogist'ic.**—*adv* **eulogist'ically.**

eunuch [ū'nuk] *n* a castrated man, esp one in charge of a harem.

euphemism [ū'fem-izm] *n* a mild or inoffensive term employed to express what is disagreeable; the use of such a term.—*adj* **euphemist'ic.**

euphony [ū'fo-ni] *n* agreeableness of sound; pleasing to the ear.—*adjs* **euphon'ic**, **-al**, **euphō'nious.**—*adv* **euphō'niously.**

euphonium [u-fōn'ē-um] *n* a brass musical instrument with its oval bell pointed backwards.

euphoria [ū-fō'ri-à, -fō'] *n* a feeling of well-being.—*adj* **euphoric** [-for'].

euphuism [u'fū-izm] *n* any affected elegant style of writing; flowery, artificial language.—*n* **eu'phuist.**—*adj* **euphuist'ic.**

Eurasian [ūr-ā-zh(y)àn, -shàn] *adj* of Mongolian and Caucasian parents; of Europe and Asia (Eurasia) taken as one continent.—*Also n*.

eureka [ū-rēk'a] *interjection* used to express triumph on a discovery.

eurhyth'mics [ūr-rith'miks] *npl* the art of representing musical harmony by physical gestures.

European [ū-ro-pē'an] *adj* belonging to *Europe*.—*n* a native or inhabitant of Europe; a person of European descent; a white person.; **European Common Market**, popular name for the European Economic Community whose members aim to eliminate all obstacles to the free movement of goods, services, capital and labor between the member countries and to set up a common external commercial policy, agricultural policy, and transport policy.

euthanasia [ū-than-ā'zi-a] *n* the act or practice of putting to death painlessly, esp in order to release from incurable suffering.

euthenics [u-then'iks] *n* a science dealing with the improvement of human qualities by changes in the environment.

evacuate [e-vak'ū-āt] *vti* to make empty; to discharge wastes from the body; to leave empty, to vacate.—*n* **evacuā'tion**; **evac'uātor**; **evac'uēē**, a person removed in an evacuation.

evade [e-vād, ē-vād'] *vt* to manage to avoid, esp by dexterity or slyness.

evaluate [ē, or e-val'ū-āt] *vt* to fix the value of.—*n* **evaluā'tion**.

evanescent [ev-án-es'ént] *adj* fleeting; vanishing.—*n* **evan-es'cence**.—*adv* **evanes'cently**.

evangel [e-van'jèl] *n* gospel; evangelist.—*adjs* **evangelical**, **evangel'ic** [e-, ē-van-jel'ik-ál], of, according to, being in agreement with the Christian gospel esp as presented in the four Gospels; Protestant; emphasizing salvation by faith through personal conversion, the authority of Scripture, and the importance of preaching as contrasted with ritual; low church.—*adv* **evangel'ically**.—*n* **evangel'icalism**, evangelical principles.—*vt* **evan'gelize**, to make acquainted with the gospel.—*vi* to preach the gospel from place to place.—*n* **evan-'gelist**, one who evangelizes; one of the writers of the four gospels.—*adj* **evangelis'tic**.

evaporate [e-vap'ór-āt] *vti* to change into a vapor; to remove water from; to give off moisture; to vanish; to disappear.—*adj* **evap'orable**.—*n* **evaporā'tion**.

evasion [e-vā'zh(ó)n] *n* act of eluding; a means of evading, esp an equivocal statement used in evading.—*adj* **evā'sive**.—*adv* **evā'sively**.—*n* **evā'siveness**.

eve see **even²**.

even¹ [ēv'n] *adj* level, flat; smooth; regular, equal; balanced; fully revenged; exact; divisible by 2.—*vt* to make or become even.—*adv* exactly; precisely; fully, quite; at the very time; used as an intensive to emphasize the identity of something (*he looked content, even happy*), to indicate something unexpected (*she refused even to look at him*), or to stress the comparative degree (*she did even better*).—*adv* **ev'enly**.—*n* **ev'en-ness**.

even² [ēv'n] *n* (poet.) evening; (*obs* or *dial.*) eve.—*Also* **e'en** [ēn].—*ns* **eve** [ēv], the night, or the whole day, before a festival; the time just preceding an event; (*poet.*) evening; **evening** [ēv'ning], the close of the day and early part of the night.—*ns* **e'vensong** vespers; evening prayers; **ev'entide** the time of evening.

event [e-vent'] *n* something that happens; a social occasion; contingency; any occurrence; a contest in a program of sports.—*adjs* **event'ful**, full of events; momentous; **event'ual**, happening as a consequence; final.—*n* **event'ūal'ity**, a contingency.—*adv* **event'ūally**, finally, at length.—*vi* **event'ūate**, to turn out.

ever [ev'ér] *adv* always; at any time; in any case.—*adj* **ev'er-green**, having foliage that remains green.—*n .—adj* **everlast'ing**, enduring forever; eternal.—*n* eternity; a plant whose flowers may be dried without loss of form or color.—*adv* **everlast'ingly**.—*n* **everlast'ingness**.—*adv* **evermore'**, forever.

every [ev'ér-i, ev'ri] *adj* being one of the total.—*prons* **ev'ery-body**, **ev'eryone**, every person.—*adj* **ev'eryday**, daily; common, usual; pertaining to weekdays, not Sunday.—*pron* **ev'erything**, all things; all.—*adv* **ev'erywhere**, in every place.

evict [ē-, or e-vikt'] *vt* to expel from land or from a building by lawful methods; to expel.—*n* **evic'tion**.

evident [ev'i-dènt] *adj* easy to see or understand.—*adv* **ev'i-dently**.—*n* **ev'idence**, an outward sign; proof, testimony, esp matter submitted in court to determine the truth of alleged acts.—*vt* to indicate; to prove.—*adj* **eviden'tial** [-shàl].

evil [ē'vl, ē'vil] *adj* wicked; causing or threatening distress or harm.—*adv* **ē'villy**.

evince [e-vins'] *vt* to show (eg a quality).—*adj* **evinc'ible**.—*adv* **evinc'ibly**.—*adj* **evinc'ive**, showing, tending to show.

eviscerate [ē-, or e-vis'ér-āt] *vt* to tear out the entrails of.—*n* **viscerā'tion**.

evoke [e-vōk'] *vt* to call forth or up.—*adj* **evoc'ative** [-vok'], having power to evoke; serving to awaken.

evolution [ev-, ēv-ol-(y)ōō'sh(ó)n] *n* a process of change in a particular direction; one of a series of prescribed movements as in a dance or military exercise; the process by which something attains its distinctive characteristics; a theory that existent types of plants and animals have developed from previously existing kinds.—*adj* **evolu'tionary**.—*n* **evolu'tion-ist**.—*vi* **evolve** [ē-volv'] to develop by or as if by evolution.

ewe [ū] *n* a female sheep.

ewer [ū'ér] *n* a large water jug with a wide spout.

ex- [eks-] indicating that the following term is no longer applicable, eg.—**ex-pres'ident**, a former president.

exacerbate [eks-, or egz-as'ér-bāt] *vt* to make more violent, bitter, or severe.—*n* **exacerbā'tion**.

exact [egz-akt'] *vt* to compel to furnish; to extort, to require as

indispensable.—*adj* without any error; absolutely correct.—*adj* **exacting**, greatly demanding; requiring close attention and precision.—*ns* **exac'tion; exact'itūde**.—*adv* **exact'ly**.—*n* **exact'ness**.

exaggerate [egz-aj'er-āt] *vt* to enlarge beyond bounds.—*ns* **exaggerā'tion**, extravagant representation; a statement in excess of the truth; **exagg'erātor**.—*adjs* **exagg'erative**, **exag-g'eratory**.

exalt [egz-ölt'] *vt* to raise up, esp in rank, power, or dignity.—*n* **exaltā'tion**, elevation in rank or dignity; high estate; elation.—*adj* **exalt'ed**.

examine [egz-am'in] *vt* to look at closely and carefully, to investigate; to test, esp by questioning.—*ns* **examinā'tion**. Also **exam**.—*n* **examinee**, person who is examined; **examiner**.

example [egz-am'pl] *n* a representative sample; a model to be followed or avoided; a problem to be solved in order to show the application of some rule; a warning to others.

exasperate [egz-as'pèr-āt] *vt* to irritate in a high degree; to make worse.—*n* **exasperā'tion**.

excavate [eks'ka-vāt] *vt* to hollow out; to form by hollowing out; to dig out and remove (as earth); to reveal to view by digging away a covering.—*ns* **excavā'tion**, act of excavating; a hollow or cavity made by excavating; **ex'cavātor**.

exceed [ek-sēd'] *vt* to go beyond (the limit set or required); to be greater than; to surpass or excel.—*vi* to go beyond a given or proper limit.—*p adj* **exceed'ing**.—*adv* **exceed'ingly**.

excel [ek-sel'] *vt* to outdo, to surpass.—*vi* to do better than others (*with* **in, at**).—*n* **exc'ellence, exc'ellency**, great merit; any excellent quality; a title of honor given to persons high in rank or office.—*adj* **exc'ellent**, surpassing others, in some good quality; of great virtue, worth, etc.—*adv* **exc'ellently**.

except [ek-sept'] *vt* to leave out, to take out.—*vi* to object.—*prep* (also **except'ing**) not including; other than.—*n* **excep'tion**, the act of excepting; something excepted; an objection.—*adjs* **exceptionable**, liable to objection **excep'tional**, unusual, esp superior; **except'ive**, including, making, or being an exception.—**except for** but for.

excerpt [ek'sûrpt, or ek-sûrpt'] *n* a passage selected from a book, opera, etc.; an extract.

excess [ek-ses'] *n* a part that is too much, surplus; intemperance; that which exceeds; the degree or amount by which one thing exceeds another.—*adj* **excess'ive**.—*adv* **excessively**.

exchange [eks-chānj'] *vt* to give and take (one thing in return for another); to give and take mutually.—*n* the giving and taking of one thing for another; the thing exchanged; a place where things and services are exchanged, esp a marketplace for securities; a central office where telephone lines are connected for communication.—*adj* **exchange'able**.—*n* **exchangeabil'ity**.

Exchequer [eks-chek'ér] *n* the British governmental department in charge of finances.

excise¹ [ek-sīz'] *n* a tax on the manufacture, sale, or use of certain articles within a country.—*adj* **excīs'able**, liable to excise duty.

excise² [ek-sīz'] *vt* to remove by cutting out.—*n* **excision** [ek-sizh'(ó)n].

excite [ek-sīt'] *vt* to arouse strong emotion in, to agitate; to rouse to activity; to stimulate.—*adj* **excīt'able**.—*adj* **excīt'ed**, agitated; roused emotionally; in a state of great activity.—*n* **excīte'ment**, agitation; stimulation; that which excites.

exclaim [eks-klām'] *vi* to cry out.—*vt* to utter or speak vehemently.—*n* **exclāmā'tion**.—**exclamation point** the mark expressing this (!).—*adj* **exclamatory**, expressing exclamation.

exclude [eks-klōōd'] *vt* to shut out.—*n* to drive out; to keep out.—**exclu'sion**.—*adj* **exclus'ive**, reserved for particular persons; snobbishly aloof; sole, undivided.—*adv* **exclu'sively**.—*n* **exclu'siveness**.

excogitate [eks-koj'i-tāt] *vt* to think out; to devise.—*n* **excogi-tā'tion**.

excommunicate [eks-kom-ūn'i-kāt] *vt* to expel from communion with the church; to exclude from fellowship.—*n* **excommunicā'tion**.

excrement [eks'krē-mént] *n* waste matter discharged from the bowels.—*adj* **excrement'al**.

excrescence [eks-kres'éns] *n* an outgrowth or projection, esp abnormal, grotesque, or offensive.—*adj* **excres'cent**.

excrete [eks-krēt'] *vt* to separate and discharge wastes from the body, esp in urine.—*n* excrē'tion.—excrē'tory.

excruciate [eks-krōōshi-āt] *vt* to torture.—*adj* excru'ciating, intensely painful or distressful, agonizing.—*adv* excru'ciatingly.—*n* excructiā'tion.

exculpate [eks'kul-pāt, or -kul'-] *vt* to clear from alleged fault or guilt.—*n* exculpā'tion.—*adj* excul'patory, tending or serving to exculpate.

excursion [eks-kûr'sh(ó)n] *n* a pleasure trip; a digression; an outward movement or a cycle of movement.

excuse [eks-kūz'] *vt* to pardon; to forgive; to give a reason or apology for; to be a reason or explanation of; to let off.—*n* [eks-kūs'] the reason given.—*adj* excusable [eks-kūz'ábl]).—*adv* excus'ably.

execrate [eks'e-krāt] *vt* to curse; to detest utterly.—*adj* ex'ecrable.—*n* execrātion, act of execrating; a curse pronounced.

execute [ekse'e-kūt] *vt* to perform; to carry into effect; to put to death by law.—*adj* executable that can be performed.—*ns* exec'ūtant, one who executes or performs; ex'ecūter; execū'tion, act of executing or performing; carrying into effect the sentence of a court of law; the warrant for so doing; execū'tioner, one who executes, esp one who inflicts capital punishment.—*adj* exec'ūtive, designed or fitted to execute; concerned with performance, administration, or management; qualifying for or pertaining to the execution of the law.—*n* the power or authority in government that carries the laws into effect; the persons who administer the government or an organization; one concerned with administration or management.—*adv* exec'ūtively.—*n* exec'ūtor, one who executes or performs; the person appointed to see a will carried into effect.—*fem* exec'ūtrix.

exegesis [eks-e-jē'sis] *n* interpretation, esp Biblical.—*adjs* exegēt'ic, -al.—*adv* exegēt'ically.—*npl* exegēt'ics.

exemplar [eg-zem'plàr, -plär] *n* an ideal model; a typical instance or example.—*adj* exemplary.—*adv* exem'plarily.

exemplify [egz-em'pli-fī] *vt* to illustrate by example; to be an example of; to make an attested copy of; to prove by an attested copy.—*n* exemplificā'tion, act of exemplifying; that which exemplifies; a copy or transcript.

exempt [egz-emt'] *vt* to free, or grant immunity (*with* from).—*adj* not liable.—*n* exemp'tion.

exercise [eks'èr-sīz] *n* a putting in practice; exertion of the body for health or amusement or acquisition of skill; a similar exertion of the mind; a lesson or task; a written school task; military mock battle.—*vt* to train by use; to give exercise to; to trouble, worry; to put in practice, to use.

exert [egz-ûrt'] *vt* to bring into active operation.—*n* exer'tion, a bringing into active operation; striving; activity.

exhale [eks-hāl', egz-āl'] *vt* to breathe out; send out as vapor.—*vi* to emit breath; to rise as vapor.—*n* exhalation.

exhaust [egz-õst'] *vt* to draw out completely; to empty; to use the whole strength of; to wear or tire out; to treat of or develop completely (a subject).—*n* the escape of used gas or steam from an engine; the matter that escapes.—*adj* exhaust'ed, emptied; consumed; tired out.—*adj* exhaust'ible.—*n* exhaust'ion.—*adj* exhaust'ive.—*adv* exhaust'ively.

exhibit [egz-ib'it] *vt* to display, esp in public; to present to a court in legal form.—*n* an act or instance of exhibiting, something exhibited; something produced and identified in court for use as evidence.—*n* exhib'itor.—*adj* exhib'itory, exhibiting.—*ns* exhibi'tion, a showing, a display; a public show; exhibi'tionism, tendency to show what should not be shown; excessive tendency to show off one's abilities; exhibi'tionist.

exhilarate [egz-il'a-rāt] *vt* to make hilarious or merry; to enliven.—*adj* exhil'arant.—*n* exhilarā'tion.

exhort [eg-zört'] *vt* to urge strongly and earnestly; to warn.—*n* exhortā'tion.—*adjs* exhort'ative, exhort'atory.

exhume [eks-hūm'] *vt* to take (a dead person) out of the ground; to bring (a subject) back from neglect or obscurity.—*n* exhumā'tion.

exigent [eks'i-jènt] *adj* pressing, urgent; exacting.—*ns* ex'igence, ex'igency.

exiguous [egz-, eks-ig'ū-ùs] *adj* scanty in amount.

exile [eks'īl, or egz'īl] *n* a person driven from his native place; banishment.—*vt* to expel from one's country, often as punishment; to banish.

exist [egz-ist'] *vi* to have an actual being.—*n* exist'ence, state of existing or being; livelihood; life; anything that exists.—*adj* exist'ent, having being; at present existing.—*n* existen'tialism, a doctrine, popularly understood to be that life is purposeless and man petty and miserable.

exit [eks'it, egz'-] *n* a way out of an enclosed space; death; departure from a stage.

exodus [eks'o-dus] *n* the departure of many people; Exodus, the departure of the Israelites from Egypt led by Moses; 2nd book of the Old Testament.

exogamy [eks-og'a-mi] *n* the practice of marrying only outside of one's own group.

exonerate [egz-on'èr-āt] *vt* to free from blame; to acquit.—*n* exonerā'tion.—*adj* exon'erative.

exorbitant [egz-ör'bi-tànt] *adj* going beyond the usual limits; excessive.—*n* exor'bitance.

exorcise [eks'ör-sīz] *vt* to expel an evil spirit.—*ns* ex'orcism; ex'orcist (also exorcis'er).

exoteric [eks-o-ter'ik] *adj* suitable for communication to the public or multitude; not included among the initiated.

exotic [egz-ot'ik] *adj* foreign; strange; excitingly different or unusual; of or relating to striptease.—*n* a rare plant; stripteaser.

expand [eks-pand'] *vt* to spread out; to enlarge in bulk or surface; to develop in fuller detail, to express at length.—*vi* to become opened; to increase in size; (*fig*) to become communicative.—*n* expanse', a wide extent; amount of spread or stretch.—*ns* expansibil'ity, expan'sion, act of expanding, state of being expanded; enlargement; extension.—*adj* expans'ive, widely extended; having a capacity to expand; causing expansion; worked by expansion; comprehensive; talkative, communicative.—*adv* expans'ively.—*n* expansiveness.

expatiate [eks-pā'shi-āt] *vi* to talk or write at length.—*n* expatiā'tion.—*adj* expātiātory.

expatriate [eks-pā'tri-āt] *vti* to banish or exile .—Also *n*, *adj* (person) expatriated, exiled by self or other(s).—*n* expatriā'tion.

expect [eks-pekt'] *vt* to look forward to as likely to come or happen, or as due; to suppose.—*ns* expect'ance, expect'ancy.—*adj* expect'ant.—*n* expectā'tion, act or state expecting; that which is, or may fairly be, expected.

expectorate [eks-pek'to-rāt] *vti* to expel (mucus) from the respiratory tract by coughing; to spit.—*ns* expectorā'tion.

expedient [eks-pē'di-ènt] *adj* suitable or desirable under the circumstances.—*n* means suitable to an end; means devised or used for want of something better.—*ns* expē'dience, expē'diency, fitness, prudence, advisability; that which is opportune or politic; self-interest.—*adv* expē'diently.

expedite [eks'pe-dīt] *vt* to carry out promptly; to facilitate.—*n* expedī'tion, speed, promptness; an organized journey to attain some object, as exploration, etc.; the party undertaking such a journey.—*adj* expedi'tionary, expedi'tious, speedy.

expel [eks-pel'] *vt* to drive out, to eject; to banish.—*pr p* expell'ing; *pt p* expelled'.

expend [eks-pend'] *vt* to spend to employ or consume in some way.—*ns* expend'iture, act of expending; that which expended; money spent; **expense'**, outlay; cost; cause expenditure.—*adj* expens'ive, causing or requiring much expense, costly.—*n* expens'iveness.

experience [eks-pēri-èns] *n* observation or practice resulting in or tending toward knowledge; knowledge gained by seeing and doing; a state of being affected from without (as events).—*vt* to meet with, undergo; to prove or know by use.—*adj* expē'rienced, taught by experience—skillful, wise.—*adj* expērien'tial.

experiment [eks-per'i-mènt] *n* any test or trial to find out something; a controlled procedure carried out to discover, test, or demonstrate something.—*vi* to carry out experiments.—*adj* experiment'al.

expert [eks-pûrt'] *adj* thoroughly skilled; knowledgeable through training and experience.—*vti* to examine and give judgement on.—*ns* ex'pert, one who is specially skilled in any art or science; a scientific or professional witness; expertness.

expertise [eks-pûrt-ēz'] *n* expert knowledge; expertness, skill; expert appraisal, valuation.

piate [eks'pi-āt] *vt* to pay the penalty for; to make amends
r.—*ns* expiā'tion, ex'piātor.—*adj* ex'piātory.

pire [eks-pīr'] *vti* to breathe out; to die; to come to an end; to
apse or become void.—*n* expirā'tion.—*adj* expi'ratory.—*n*
xpi'ry.

plain [eks-plān'] *vt* to make plain or intelligible; to expound;
 account for.—*n* explānā'tion.—*adj* explan'atory.

pletive [eks'ple-tiv, eks-plē'tiv] *adj* filling out; added merely
 fill up.—*n* a word inserted to fill up a gap; a meaningless
ath.

plicate [eks'pli-kāt] *vt* to develop the implications of, to
xplain.—*n* explicā'tion.—*adjs* ex'plicātive, ex'plicatory,
rving to explicate or explain.

plicit [eks-plis'it] *adj* not implied merely, but distinctly
ated; plain in language; outspoken.

plode [eks-plōd'] *vt* to bring into disrepute, and reject; to
ause to blow up.—*vi* to burst with a loud report; to burst
ut.—*n* explō'sion.—*adj* explōs'ive; liable to or causing
xplosion; bursting out with violence and noise.—*n* some-
ing that will explode.

ploit [eks-ploit', or eks'ploit] *n* a deed or achievement, esp a
eroic one.—*vt* [eks-ploit'] to work, make available; to make
ain out of, or at the expense of.—*n* exploitā'tion.

plore [eks-plōr', -plōr'] *vti* to search or travel through for the
urpose of discovery; to examine thoroughly.—*n* explo-
a'tion.—*adjs* explor'ative, explor'atory.—*n* explor'er.

ponent [eks-pō'nént] *n* a symbol, usu. a number written
bove and to the right of a mathematical expression to indicate
ae operation of raising to a power; one who interprets, esp in
ae performance of music; one who champions, advocates, or
xemplifies.—*adj* exponen'tial.

port [eks-pōrt', -pōrt'] *vt* to send out (goods) of one country
or sale in another.—*n* ex'port, act of exporting; the article
xported.—*adj* export'able.—*ns* exportā'tion; export'er.

pose [eks-pōz'] *vt* to display; to lay bare; to deprive of
rotection or shelter; to subject to an influence (as light,
eather).—*adj* exposed, open to view; not shielded or pro-
cted.—*ns* exposé [eks-pō-zā], a showing up of crime, dis-
onesty, etc.; expō'sure [-zhùr], an exposing or state of being
xposed; time during which light reaches and acts on a photo-
aphic film, paper, plate or segment of a roll of film.

position [eks-po-zish'(ò)n] *n* a public show or exhibition; a
etailed explanation; a speech or writing explaining a process,
ing, or idea.

postulate [eks-post'ū-lāt] *vi* to remonstrate.—*n* expostū-
'tion.—*adj* expost'ūlatory.

pound [eks-pownd'] *vt* to present in detail (eg a doctrine); to
xplain, interpret (eg the Scriptures).

press [eks-pres'] *vt* to represent or make known by a like-
ess, signs, symbols, etc.; to put into words; (*reflex*) to put
ne's thought, feeling into words; to reveal (eg an emotion, a
uality).—*adj* exact; directly stated, explicit; traveling at high
eed with few or no stops along the way.—*adv* by express.—
 a system or company for sending articles, money, etc. at
tes higher than standard freight charges.—*adv*
xpress'ly.—*adjs* express'ible; express'ive.—*adv* express'-
ely.—*ns* express'iveness; expression, act of representing
giving utterance; representation or relevation by language,
t, the features, etc.; look; intonation; due indication of
eling in performance of music; word, phrase; express'ion-
m, a theory or practice that art seeks to depict the subjective
motions aroused in the artist by objects and events, not
jective reality.—*adj* express'ionless.

ropriate [eks-prō'pri-āt] *vt* to take (property) from its
wner.—*n* expropriā'tion.

ulsion [eks-pul'sh(ó)n] *n* the act of expelling or being
pelled.—*adj* expul'sive.

unge [eks-punj'] *vt* to obliterate, to erase.

urgate [eks'pûr-gāt] *vt* to purify (esp a book) from anything
oposed to be noxious or erroneous.—*ns* expurgā'tion;
purgātor.—*adj* expur'gātory.

uisite [eks'kwi-zit, also -kwiz'] *adj* of consummate excel-
nce (eg of workmanship); very beautiful; showing delicate
rception or close discrimination; fastidious; extreme, as
in or pleasure.—*n* one extremely fastidious in dress, a
p.—*adv* ex'quisitely.—*n* ex'quisiteness.

cind [eks-sind'] *vt* to cut off or out.

extant [eks'tánt'] *adj* still existing.

extempore [eks-tem'po-re] *adv* on the spur of the moment;
without preparation.—*adj* composed and delivered or performed impromptu—also extemporān'eous, extem'por-
ary.—*vi* extem'porize, to do something extemporaneously.—
n extemporizā'tion.

extend [eks-tend'] *vt* to stretch out; to prolong in any direction; to enlarge (eg power, meaning); to hold out (eg the
hand); to offer, accord (eg sympathy).—*vt* to stretch, reach.—
adjs extens'ible, extens'īle [or-il], that may be extended.—*ns*
extensibil'ity; exten'sion, act of extending; condition of
being extended; an added part; the property of occupying
space; an additional telephone using the same line as the main
one.—*adj* extens'ive, large; comprehensive.—*adv* exten-
s'ively.—*ns* extens'iveness; extent', the space or degree to
which a thing is extended; scope; degree or amount.

extenuate [eks-ten'ū-āt] *vt* to make (guilt, a fault, or offense)
seem less.—*adj* exten'ūāting.—*n* extenūā'tion.

exterior [eks-tē'ri-ór] *adj* outer; external; suitable for use on
the outside, as paint.—*n* the outside, outer surface; outward
manner or appearance.

exterminate [eks-tûr'mi-nāt] *vt* to destroy utterly.—*n* extermi-
nā'tion.—*n* exter'minātor.

external [eks-tûr'nál] *adj* outwardly perceivable; of, relating
to, or located on the outside or outer part.—*n* an external
feature.—*adv* exter'nally.

extinct [eks-tingkt'] *adj* put out, extinguished (as fire, life);
(of a volcano) no longer erupting; no longer existing.—*n*
extinc'tion.

extinguish [eks-ting'gwish] *vt* to quench; to destroy; to
obscure by superior splendour.—*adj* exting'uishable.—*n*
exting'uisher.

extirpate [eks'tér-pāt] *vt* to root out; to destroy totally.—*ns*
extirpā'tion; ex'tirpātor.

extol, extoll [eks-tol'] *vt* to praise highly.

extort [eks-tōrt'] *vt* to obtain (money, promises, etc.) by force
or improper pressure.—*n* extor'tion.—*adjs* extor'tionary,
extor'tionāte, exorbitant.—*n* extor'tioner.

extra [eks'tra] *adj* additional.—*adv* unusually.—*n* what is extra
or additional, esp a charge; a special edition of a newspaper.

extra- [eks'tra-] used to form adjectives, meaning beyond,
beyond the scope of, eg.—*adjs* ex'tracurric'ular, of a subject
or activity, outside, and additional to, the regular academic
course.

extract [eks-trakt'] *vt* to draw out by force; to withdraw by
chemical or physical means; to select, quote (passages from a
book, etc.).—*n* ex'tract, anything drawn from a substance; a
passage taken from a book or writing.—*adj* extract'able,
extract'ible.—*n* extrac'tion, act of extracting; lineage; that
which is extracted.—*adj* extract'ive.—*n* extract'or.

extradition [eks-tra-dish'(ò)n] *n* a surrendering of an alleged
criminal to a different jurisdiction for trial.—*vt* ex'tradīte.

extraneous [eks-trān'yùs] *adj* coming from without; foreign;
not belonging; not essential.—*adv* extrān'eously.

extraordinary [eks-trōr'di-nàr-i, or eks-tra-ōr'-] *adj* beyond
ordinary, not usual or regular; wonderful, surprising;
additional.—*adv* extraor'dinarily.

extrapolate [eks-trap'ō-lāt] *vti* to infer (unknown data) from
known data.—*n* extrapolā'tion.

extraterritorial [eks-trā-ter-i-tō'ri-ál, -tō'-] *adj* outside the territorial limits of a jurisdiction.—*n* extraterritorial'ity, exemp-
tion for the application or jurisdiction of local laws or tri-
bunals.

extravagant [eks-trav'a-gànt] *adj* (*obs*) wandering beyond
bounds; unrestrained, excessive (eg grief, praise); lavish in
spending; wasteful; exorbitant (price).—*n* extrav'agance.

extravaganza [eks-trav-a-gan'za] *n* an extravagant or eccentric
musical, dramatic, or literary production.

extravasate [eks-trav'a-sāt] *vt* to force out of vessels or arteries,
as blood.—*vi* to escape from its proper vessels.

extreme [eks-trēm'] *adj* outermost; most remote; last; highest
in degree, greatest (eg *extreme penalty*); very violent (eg pain);
stringent (eg measures); (of opinions) thoroughgoing, marked
by excess—opp to *moderate*.—*n* the utmost point or verge, the
end; utmost or highest limit or degree.—*adv* extrēme'ly.—*ns*
extrē'mist, one ready to use extreme measures; extremity

[-trem'i-ti], the utmost limit; the highest degree; greatest necessity or distress; (*pl*) extreme measures; (*pl*) hands or feet.
extricate [eks'tri-kāt] *vt* to set free, to disentangle.—*adj* **ex'tricable**.—*n* **extrica'tion**.
extrinsic [eks-trin'sik] *adj* not contained in or belonging to a body; operating from without; not essential.
extrovert [eks'tro-vert] *n* one whose interests are in matters and objects outside of himself.
extrude [eks-trōōd'] *vt* to force or thrust out.—*vi* to protrude.—*n* **extrusion** [-trōōzh(ó)n].—*adj* **extru'sive**.
exuberant [egz-, eks-(y)ōō'bér-ånt] *adj* luxuriant; lavish; effusive; in high spirits.—*ns* **exū'berance**.—*adv* **exū'berantly**.
exude [egz-, eks-ūd'] *vt* to discharge by sweating; to discharge through pores or incisions.—*vi* to ooze out of a body as through pores.—*n* **exudā'tion**.
exult [egz-ult'] *vi* to rejoice exceedingly (at); to triumph (over).—*adj* **exult'ant**.—*n* **exultā'tion**.
exuviae [egz-, eks-(y)ōō'vi-ē] *n pl* cast-off skins, shells, or other coverings of animals.—*vti* **exū'viāte**.
eye [I] *n* the one of two organs of sight; the power of seeing; sight; regard; keenness of perception; anything resembling an eye.—*vt* to look on; to observe narrowly.—*pr p* **eye'ing** or **ey'ing**; *pt p* **eyed** [īd].—*ns* **eye'ball**, the globe of the eye; **eye'bright**, any of the several herbs of the figwort family; **eye'brow**, the hairy arch above the eye.—*adj* **eye'cat'ching**, striking.—*n* **eye'lash**, hair, line of hairs that edges the eyelid.—*adj* **eyeless**; **eyelet**, [ī'let], a small eye or hole to receive a lace or cord, **eye'lid**, the lid of skin and muscle covering the eye; **eye'sight**, power of seeing; **eye'sore**, anything that is offensive to look at; **eye'tooth** canine tooth; **eye'wash**, a lotion for the eye; humbug, deception; **eye'wit'ness**, one who sees a thing done.
eyrie *see* aerie.

F

fable [fā'bl] *n* a short story, often with animal characters, intended to teach the moral lesson; any tale in literary form intended to instruct or amuse; a falsehood.—*vti* to invent (fables), tell (stories without basis in fact).—*adj* **fā'bled**.—*n* **fab'ulist** [fab'-], one who invents fables.—*adj* **fab'ulous**, feigned, related in fable; incredible, astonishing.
fabric [fab'rik] *n* framework, structure; manufactured cloth.
fabricate [fab'ri-kāt] *vt* to manufacture; to devise falsely (eg a lie).—*ns* **fabricā'tion**, construction; manufacture; a story; a falsehood; **fab'ricator**.
facade [fa-säd'] *n* the exterior front or face of a building.
face [fās] *n* the front of the head; the main or front surface of anything; outward show or appearance; cast of features; dignity, self respect; boldness, effrontery; a mine, drift, or excavation which is being worked.—*vt* to meet in the face or in front; to stand opposite to; to confront; to cover with a new surface.—*vi* to turn the face; to take or have a direction.—*adj* **face'less**, anonymous.—*n*, *adj* **face'-saving**, avoiding the appearance of climbing down or humiliation.
facet [fas'et] *n* a small plane surface (as on a cut gem).
facetious [fa-sē'shús] *adj* joking, esp in an inappropriate manner.—*n pl* **facetiae** [fasē'shi-ē], witty or humorous sayings or writings.
facial [fā'shàl] *adj* of or relating to the face.
facile [fas'īl, or -il] *adj* not hard to do; fluent; superficial.—*vt* **facil'itāte**, to make easy.—*n* **facil'ity**, ease; dexterity.
facsimile [fak-sim'i-le] *n* an exact copy.
fact [fakt] *n* a deed, esp a criminal deed; anything known to have happened or to be true; anything alleged to be true and used as a basis of argument; reality.—*adj* **fact'ual**, of, or containing, facts; actual.
faction[1] [fak'sh(ó)n] *n* a group of persons in an organization working together in a common cause against the main body; dissension.
faction[1] [fak'sh(ó)n] *n* a group of persons in an organization working together in a common cause against the main body; dissension.
faction[2] [fak'sh(ó)n] *n* a book based on facts but written in the form of a novel and published as fiction.

factitious [fak-tish'ús] *adj* produced or induced artificially.—*adv* **facti'tiously**.
factor [fak'tór] *n* a transactor of business for another; a circumstance that influences the course of events; (*math*) on of two or more quantities, which, when multiplied together produce a given quantity.—*n* **fac'tory**, a building or buildin where things are manufactured.
factotum [fak-tō'tum] *n* a person employed to do all kinds work.
faculty [fak'úl-ti] *n* any natural power of a living organisr special aptitude; all the teachers of a school or of one of departments.
fad [fad] *n* a whim, craze.—*adjs* **fadd'ish**, **fadd'y**.—*n* **fadd'ishness**; **fadd'ism**; **fadd'ist**.
fade [fād] *vi* to lose freshness or color gradually; to grow fair to die away.—*vt* to cause (an image or a sound) to becon gradually less distinct or loud.—*adj* **fade'less**, not liable fade.
faeces, faecal [fē'sēs, fē'kel] *see* feces.
fag [fag] *vti* to become or be tired by hard work.—*pr p* fag g'ing; *pt p* **fagged**.—*n* a homosexual; drudgery; a cigarette.
fagot, faggot [fag'ót] *n* a bundle of sticks for fuel; a bundle iron or steel rods.
Fahrenheit [fä'ren-hīt or far'en-īt] *adj* (of a thermometer thermometer scale) having the freezing-point of water marke at 32 degrees, and the boiling point at 212 degrees.
fail [fāl] *vi* to fall short; to be insufficient; to weaken, to d away; to stop operating; to be negligent on duty, expectatio etc.; to be unsuccessful; (*education*) to get a grade of failure; become bankrupt.—*vt* to disappoint (a person); to leave, abandon.—*ns* **fail**, the failure of a broker or brokerage firm deliver securities by a given time; **failing**, a fault, weakness foible.—*n* **fail'ure**.—*adj* **fail'-safe**, pertaining to a mechanis incorporated in a system to ensure that there will be a accident if the system does not operate properly.
fain [fān] *adj* (*arch*) glad or joyful; content for want of betw (to); compelled (to).—*adv* gladly.
fainéant [fen'ā-ä] *n* an irresponsible idler.—Also *adj.*
faint [fānt] *adj* lacking strength; dim; lacking distinctnes weak in spirit; done in a feeble way.—*vi* to lose strengt color, etc.; to swoon; to lose courage or spirit.—*n* syncope.—*adv* **faint'ly**.
fair[1] [fār] *adj* pleasing to the eye; clean, unblemished; blon clear and sunny; easy to read (*a fair hand*); just and hone according to the rules; moderately large; average (*in fair co dition*); that may be hunted (*fair game*); (*baseball*) that not foul.—*adv* in a fair manner; squarely.—*adv* **fair'ly**.—*n* **fair'ness**—**fair'ing**, adjustment or testing of curves in sh building; means of reducing head-resistance in an airplane.—*n* **fair'-way**, the channel by which vessels enter or leave harbor; any open path or space; the mowed part of a g course between the tee and the green.
fair[2] [fār] *n* a regular gathering for barter and sale of goods carnival or bazaar, esp for charity; a competitive exhibitior farm, household, and manufactured goods, with amusemen
fairy [fār'i] *n* an imaginary being, of diminutive and grace human form with magic powers; (*slang*) a male homosexual.—*adj* like a fairy, fanciful, delicate.—*ns* **fairy godmother**, fair **ring**, a ring of mushrooms, esp *Marasmius oreades*.—*n* **fai** **tale**.
faith [fāth] *n* trust or confidence; belief in the statement another; a belief in the truth of revealed religion; that which believed; any system of religious belief; fidelity to promis honesty of intention; word or honor pledged.—*adj* **faith'f** **faith'fully**.—*adj* **faith'less**, treacherous, disloyal; untruv worthy.
fake [fāk] *vt* to falsify or counterfeit.—*n* a swindle, dod sham; a faked article.—*n* **fak'er**.
fakir [fa-kēr' or fä'kir] *n* a (esp Muslim) religious mendicant India, etc.
falcate, -d [fal'kāt, -id] *adj* hooked or curved like a sickle.
falcon [föl'kón or fö'kn] *n* any of various hawks trained for in falconry, esp the peregrine; *ns* **fal'coner**, one who hu with, or who breeds and trains hawks for hunting.—**f** **conry**.
falderol *see* **fol'derol**.
fall[1] [föl] *vi* to descend by force of gravity; to drop prostrate,

ollapse; to be wounded or killed in battle; to take a down-ward direction; to become lower, weaker, less; to lose power, tatus, etc., to do wrong, to sin; to take place; to be directed y chance; to come by inheritance.—*pr p* **fall′ing**; *pt* fell; *pt p* **allen** [fô′l(è)n].—overthrow; descent from a better to a worse osition; slope or declivity; (*pl*) a descent of water; length of a all; decrease in value; a sinking; the time when the leaves fall, utumn; a long tress of hair added to a woman's hairdo.—*adj* f, relating to, or suitable for autumn.—**fall′ing star**, a eteor; **fall′-out**, a deposit of radioactive dust from a nuclear xplosion or comet; by-product, side benefit.

lacy [fal′à-si] *n* a false idea; a mistake in reasoning.—*adj* allacious [fa-lā′shùs], misleading.

lal [fal-al′] *n* a trifling ornament, esp in dress.—*adj* foppish.

lible [fal′i-bl] *adj* liable to error or mistake.—*n* fallibil′ity, ability to err.—*adv* **fall′ibly**.

low [fal′ō] *adj* (of land) plowed and left unseeded for a eason or more.—Also *n*—*vt* to plow land without seeding .—*n* **fall′owness**.

low deer [fal′ō dēr] *n* a yellowish-brown deer.

se [fôls] *adj* wrong, incorrect, untrue; untruthful; unfaith-al; misleading; artificial—*adv* **false′ly**.—*ns* **false′hood**, fals-y; a lie; **false′ness; fals′ity**.

setto [fôl-set′ō] *n* an artificial way of singing in which the oice is higher-pitched than normal.

sify [fôls′i-fī] *vt* to misrepresent; to alter (a document, etc.) audulently.

ter [fôl′tèr] *vi* to stumble; to fall or stammer in speech; to nch; to waver, hesitate in action.

ne [fām] *n* reputation, esp for good; state of being well nown.—*adj* famed.

iliar [fa-mil′yàr] *adj* well acquainted or intimate; showing e manner of an intimate, having a thorough knowledge f (*with* with); well known; common.—*n* one well or long quainted; a spirit or demon supposed to attend a person at all.—*vt* famil′iarize, *n* familiar′ity.—*adv* famil′iarly.

nily [fam′i-li] *n* a household; parents and their children; the scendants of one common progenitor; a group of related iants or animals forming a category ranking above a genus d below an order; a unit of a crime syndicate (as the Mafia).

ine [fam′in] *n* an acute general scarcity of food; extreme carcity of anything.

nish [fam′ish] *vti* to make or be very hungry.

nous [fā′mus] *adj* renowned, noted; (*inf*) excellent.—*adv* ′mously.

¹ [fan] *n* any device used to set up a current of air, esp a nd-waved triangular piece or a mechanism with blades; lding object of paper, feathers, etc. used for cooling the ce.—*vt* to cool, as with a fan; to ventilate; to stir up, to xcite.—*pr p* fann′ing; *pt p* fanned.—**fan′light**, a semicircu-r window with radiating bars like the ribs of a fan; fann′er, n′tail, a domestic pigeon having a broad rounded tail with) or 40 feathers.

² [fan] *n* an enthusiastic follower of some sport, or hobby, or blic favorite.—**fan club**, group united by devotion to a lebrity.

atic [fa-nat′ik] *adj* extravagantly or unreasonably zealous, cessively enthusiastic.—Also *n*—*adj* fanat′ical, fanatic.— *v* fanat′ically.—*n* fanat′icism, wild and excessive thusiasm.

cy [fan′si] *n* imagination when playful, light, etc.; a mental nage; caprice, a whim; fondness.—*adj* pleasing to, or guided , fancy or caprice; elegant or ornamental.—*vt* to portray in e mind; to imagine; to have a fancy or liking for; to be eased with.—*pr p* fan′cying; *pt p* fan′cied.—*n* fan′cier, a rson with a special interest in something, esp plant or imal breeding.—*adj* fan′ciful.—*adv* fan′cifully.—*n* n′cifulness.

dango [fan-dang′go] *n* Spanish dance, music for this dance; mfoolery.

e [fān] *n* temple; a church.

fare [fan′fär, fô′fär] *n* a flourish of trumpets.

g [fang] *n* a long sharp tooth as one by which an animal's ey is seized or the long hollow tooth through which venom-s snakes inject venom.—*adj* fanged.

tasia [fan-tā′zi-a] *n* a musical or prose composition not verned by the ordinary rules of form.

fantasy [fan′tà-si] *n* fancy; imagination; mental image; an imaginative poem, play or novel.—*adjs* fantas′tic, -al.—*adv* fantas′tically.

far [fär] *adj* distant in space or time.—*adv* very distant in space, time, or degree; to or from a distance in time or position, very much.—*adjs* far′away′, farfetched′, brought from a remote time or place; far′sight′ed, foreseeing what is likely to happen and preparing for it.

farad [far′ad] *n* SI derived unit of electrical capacitance.

farce [färs] *n* a style of comedy, marked by broad humor and extravagant wit; mockery.—*adj* far′cical, ludicrous.

fare [fär] *vi* to happen; to be in a specified condition (*to fare well*); to eat.—*n* money paid for transportation; a passenger in a public conveyance; food.—*interj* farewell′, goodbye.

farina [fa-rē′na] *n* flour or meal made from cereal grains, eaten as a cooked cereal.—*adj* farinā′ceous, mealy.

farm [färm] *n* a piece of land (with house, barns, etc.) on which crops and animals are raised.—*vt* to cultivate, as land.—*ns* farm′er, a person who manages or operates a farm; yokel; farmhouse, a house on a farm, farm′stead, a farm with the buildings belonging to it; farm′-yard, the yard or enclosure surrounded by the farm buildings.

faro [fär′o] *n* a gambling game in which players bet on cards drawn from a box.

farrago [fa-rä′gō, or -rä′] *n* a confused mixture.

farrier [far′i-èr] *n* one who shoes horses.

farrow [far′ō] *n* a litter of pigs.—*vti* to bring forth (pigs).

farther [fär᷆THèr] *adj* at or to a greater distance—Also *adv* to a greater degree.—*adj* far′thermost, far′thest.

farthing [fär′THing] *n* a former British monetary unit.

farthingale [fär′THing-gäl] *n* a support (as of hoops) worn, beneath a skirt to expand it at the hipline.

fascinate [fas′i-nāt] *vt* to hold spellbound; to charm, attract irresistibly.—*adj* fas′cinating.—*n* fascinā′tion.

fascism [fash′izm] *n* a system of government characterized by dictatorship, belligerent nationalism, racism, and militar-ism.—*n and adj* fasc′ist.

fashion [fash′(ó)n] *n* the form or shape of a thing; manner; the current style of dress, conduct, speech, etc.—*vt* to make; to suit or adapt.—*n* fash′ioner.—*adj* fash′ionable, according to prevailing fashion.—*adv* fash′ionably.

fast¹ [fäst] *adj* firm; fixed; loyal, devoted; non-fading; swift, quick; ahead of time; wild, promiscuous; (*inf*) glib.—*adv* firmly, thoroughly, rapidly, quickly; fastness, fixedness; swiftness; colorfast quality; a stronghold.

fast² [fäst] *vi* to abstain from all or certain foods.—*n* abstinence from food, a period of fasting.—*n* fast′ing.

fasten [fäs′n] *vti* to fix securely; to attach.

fastidious [fas-tid′i-us] *adj* difficult to please; daintily refined; oversensitive.—*adv* fastid′iously.

fat [fat] *adj* plump; corpulent; fruitful, profitable.—*n* an oily or greasy material found in animal tissue and plant seeds; the richest part of anything; superfluous part.—*vt* to make fat.— *vt* fatt′en, to make fat or fleshy; to make fertile.—*n* fatt′ening, the process of making fat; *adj* fatt′y.

fate [fāt] *n* inevitable destiny, appointed lot; ill-fortune; doom; ultimate lot.—*adj* fāt′al, belonging to, or appointed by, fate; causing ruin or death; mortal; disastrous (to); ill-advised.—*ns* fāt′alism, belief that all events happen by fate and are hence inevitable; acceptance of this doctrine; fāt′alist—*adj* fāt′al-istic.—*n* fatal′ity, an occurrence resulting in death; a death caused by a disaster or accident.—*adv* fāt′ally.—*adjs* fāt′ed, doomed; destined (to).

father [fä′THèr] *n* a male parent; fa′therhood, father-in-law, the father of one's husband or wife; fa′therland, one's native land—*adjs* fa′therless, fa′therly, like a father in affection and care.

fathom [faTH′óm] *n* a nautical measure = 6 feet.—*vt* to meas-ure the depth of; to comprehend.—*adjs* fath′omable; fath′omless.

fatigue [fa-tēg′] *n* weariness from labor of body or of mind; menial or manual work performed by military personnel; (*pl*) the clothing worn on fatigue or in the field.

fatuous [fat′ū-us] *adj* silly, idiotic.—*ns* fat′uousness, fatū′ity, silliness, inanity, an instance of this.

fauces [fô′sēz] *n pl* the upper part of the throat, from the root of the tongue to the entrance of the gullet.

faucet [fô'set] *n* a fixture for draining off liquid (as from a pipe or cask).

faugh [fô, fō] *interj* an exclamation of contempt or disgust.

fault [fôlt] *n* failing; blemish; a minor offence; an error in a racket game (as tennis); (*geol*) a fracture in the earth's crust causing displacement of strata.—*vt* to find fault with; to find flaw(s) in; (*geol*) to cause a fault in.—*adj* **fault'y**, imperfect.—*adv* **fault'ily**.—*adj* **fault'less**, without fault or defect.—*adv* **fault'lessly**.

fauna [fôn'a] *n* the animals or animal life of a region or a period.—*pl* **faun'as**, **faun'ae** [-ē].

faux pas [fō' pä'] *n* a false step; a social blunder.

favor [fā'vór] *n* goodwill; approval; a kind deed; partiality; a small gift given out at a party; (*usu. pl*) a privilege granted or conceded, esp sexual.—*vt* to regard with goodwill; to be on the side of; to treat indulgently; to afford advantage to; to oblige (with).—*adj* **fa'vorable**.—*adv* **fa'vorably**.—*ns* **fa'vorite**, a person or thing regarded with favor or preference; one unduly preferred; one expected to win.—*adj* esteemed, preferred; **fa'voritism**, the showing of undue favor.

fawn¹ [fôn] *n* a young deer, esp one still unweaned or retaining a distinctive baby coat.

fawn² [fôn] *vi* to make demonstrations of affection as a dog does; to flatter in a servile way (*with* (up) on).—*n* **fawn'er**.—*adv* **fawn'ingly**.

fay [fā] *n* a fairy.

faze [fāz] *vt* (*inf*) to disturb.

fealty [fē'al-ti or fēl'ti] *n* the vassal's obligation of fidelity to his feudal lord.

fear [fēr] *n* a painful emotion excited by danger, alarm; apprehension of danger or pain; the object of fear; risk; deep reverence.—*vt* to regard with fear; to expect with alarm; to be regretfully inclined to think.—*vi* to be afraid or apprehensive.—*adj* **fear'ful**.—*adv* **fear'fully**.—*n* **fear'fulness**.—*adj* **fear'less**, without fear; daring, brave.—*adv* **fear'lessly**.—*n* **fear'lessness**.—*adj* **fear'some**, causing fear, frightful.

feasible [fēz'i-bl] *adj* practicable, possible.—*ns* **feas'ibleness**, **feasibil'ity**.—*adv* **feas'ibly**.

feast [fēst] *n* an elaborate meal prepared for some special occasion; something that gives abundant pleasure; a periodic religious celebration.—*vi* to take part in a feast.—*vt* to entertain sumptuously.

feat [fēt] *n* a deed manifesting extraordinary strength, skill, or courage.

feather [feTH'ér] *n* one of the growths that form the covering of a bird; plumage.—(*pl*) plumage; attire.—*vt* to turn (an oar or propeller blade) so that the edge is foremost.—*ns* **feath'erweight**, a boxer weighing from 119 to 126 lbs; a wrestler weighing from 124 to 134 lbs.—*adj* **feath'ery**, pertaining to, resembling, or covered with, feathers.

feature [fē'tyùr, -chùr] *n* (*pl*) facial form or appearance; any of the parts of the face; a characteristic trait of something; a special attraction, sale item, newspaper article, etc.; a full-length motion picture.—*vti* to make or be a feature of (something).—*adj* **fea'tureless**, lacking distinct features.

febrifuge [feb'ri-fūj] *n* a medicine for reducing fever.

febrile [fēb'ril, or feb'ril] *adj* pertaining to fever.

February [feb'rōō-ár-i] *n* the second month of the year, having 28 days (or 29 days in leap years).

feces [fē'sēz] *n pl* excrement.—*adj* **fec'al**.

feckless [fek'les] *adj* shiftless, worthless, inefficient.

feculent [fek'ū-lent] *adj* foul with impurities.—*n* **fec'ulence**.

fecund [fek'und] *adj* fruitful, fertile, prolific.—*vt* **fec'undāte** [or fek-und'āt], to impregnate.—*ns* **fecundā'tion**, **fecund'ity**.

federal [fed'ér-ál] *adj* designating or of a union of states, etc., in which each member surrenders some of its power to a central authority; of a central government of this type, esp the government of the US.—*ns* **fed'eralism**, **fed'eralist**.—*vt* **fed'eralize**, to unite (states, etc.) in a federal union; to put under federal authority.—*vti* **fed'erate**.—*ns* **federa'tion**, a union of states, groups, etc., in which each subordinates its power to a central authority; a federated organization.

fee [fē] *n* price paid for professional services, licenses, etc.; (*law*) an inheritance in land.

feeble [fē'bl] *adj* weak, infirm; lacking force or effectiveness.—*adv* **fee'bly**.

feed [fēd] *vt* to give food to; to furnish with necessary material;

to gratify.—*vi* to take food.—*pr p* **feed'ing**; *pt, pt p* **fed**.—food for animals; material fed into a machine; the part of machine supplying this material.—*n* **feed'er**, one who feed or that which supplies.—*adj* secondary, subsidiary, tributary.—**feed'stock**, raw material supplied to a machine processing plant.

feel [fēl] *vt* to perceive by the touch, to try by touch; to grop (one's way); to be conscious of; to have an inward persuasi of; to experience.—*vi* to know by the touch, to have th emotions excited; to produce a certain sensation when to ched (*to feel hard or hot*).—*pr p* **feel'ing**; *pt, pt p* **felt**.—*n* th sense of touch; a quality as revealed to the touch.—*ns* **feel'e** a tactile process (as a tentacle or antenna) of an anim **feel'ing**, the sense of touch; perception of objects, by touc consciousness of pleasure or pain; tenderness; emotio emotional responsiveness; belief as resulting from emotio (*pl*) the affections or passions; (*pl*) sensibilities.

feign [fān] *vt* to invent; to dissemble.—*adj* **feigned**, pretende

feint [fānt] *n* a pretended attack, intended to take the oppone off his guard, as in boxing.—*vi* to make a feint.

feldspar [feld(')spär] *n* any member of the most importa group of rock-forming minerals.

felicity [fe-lis'i-ti] *n* happiness; a happy event; apt and pleasin expression in writing, etc.—*vt* **felic'itāte**, to express joy pleasure to; to congratulate.—*n* **felicitā'tion**, the act of co gratulating.—*adj* **felic'itous**—*adv* **felic'itously**.

feline [fē'līn] *adj* pertaining to the cat.

fell¹ [fel] *pt t* of **fall**.

fell² [fel] *vt* to cut, beat, or knock down; to kill, to sew (a sear by folding one raw edge under the other.—*n* **fell'er**.

fell³ [fel] *n* a skin, hide, pelt.

fell⁴ [fel] *adj* cruel, fierce, bloody, deadly.

fellah [fel'ä] *n* a peasant, esp in Egypt.—*pl* **fell'ahee fell'ahīn**.

fellow [fel'ō] *n* an associate; a comrade; one of a pair, a ma one holding a fellowship in a college; (*inf*) a man or boy; member of a learned society.—*adj* belonging to the sa group or class; **fell'owship**, companionship; a mutual sha ing; a group of people with the same interests.

felo-de-se [fel'ō di sē'] *n* one who kills himself; self-murder.

felon [fel'ón] *n* one guilty of felony; a convict; a whitlow.—*adj* **felō'nious**.—*adv* **felō'niously**.—*n* **fel'ony**, a grave crim declared to be a felony by the nature of the punishment.

felt¹ [felt] *pt, pt p* of **feel**.

felt² [felt] *n* a fabric of wool, often mixed with fur or ha worked together by pressure.—*vi* to become like felt.—*vt* make into felt.

female [fē'māl] *adj* of the sex that produces young; pertaini to females.

feminine [fem'i-nin] *adj* pertaining to women; womanl womanish; (*gram*) of that gender to which words denoti females belong.—*ns* **fem'inism**, the movement to win poli cal, economic and social equality for women; **fem'inist**, **fem ninity**.

femur [fē'múr] *n* the thighbone.—*adj* **fēm'oral**.

fen [fen] *n* an area of low marshy land; swamp; bog.

fence [fens] *n* a barrier for enclosing, bounding, or protectin land; a receiver of stolen goods.—*vt* to enclose with a fence; keep (out) as by a fence.—*vi* to practise the art of fencing; make evasive answers; to be a receiver of stolen goods.—*n* **fencing**.

fend [fend] *vi* to resist.

fender [fend'ér] *n* anything that protects or fends off som thing else, as the part of an automobile body over the wheel.

fenestrā'tion, the arrangement of windows in a building.

Fenian [fē'ni-án] *n* a member of an association of Irishm founded in 1857 for the overthrow of the English governme in Ireland.—*n* **Fē'nianism**.

fennel [fen'él] *n* a European herb of the carrot family grow its foliage and aromatic seeds; a herb grown for its edi bulbous stem tasting of licorice.

feral [fē'rál] *adj* wild; untamed; pertaining to or like a w beast.—Also **fēr'ine** [-rīn, -rin].

feria² [fē'ri-á] *n* a weekday of a church calendar of which feast falls.—*adj* **fer'ial**.

ferment [fûr'mènt] *n* a substance causing fermentation, yeast; excitement, agitation.—*vt* **ferment'**, to cause f mentation in; to excite, to agitate.—*vi* to be in the process of fermentation; to be stirred with anger.—*ns* **fermentā′tion**, the breakdown of complex molecules in organic components caused by the influence of a ferment; restless action of the mind or feelings.—*adjs* **ferment′ative**.

fern [fûrn] *n* any of a large class of nonflowering plants having roots, stems, and fronds, and reproducing by spores.—*adj* **fern′y**.

ferocious [fe-rō′shùs] *adj* savage, fierce; cruel; **feroc′ity**, savage cruelty of disposition.

ferret [fer′et] *n* a half-tamed albino variety of the polecat, employed in unearthing rabbits.—*vt* to drive out of a hiding-place; to search (out) cunningly and persistently.—*pr p* **fer′reting**; *pt p* **ferr′eted**.

ferri-, ferro-, (ferr-) of, containing iron [L *ferrum*, iron].—**ferrug′inous** [-ŏŏj- or -ûj-; L *ferrūgō, -inis*, iron rust], of, containing, or related to iron, resembling iron rust in color; **ferri′ferous** [-*ferous* from L *ferre*, to bear], of rocks, iron-yielding; **ferr′ocon′crete** reinforced concrete.

ferrule [fer′ùl, fer′(y)ŏŏl] *n* a metal ring or cap on a cane, umbrella, etc., to keep it from splitting.

ferry [fer′i] *vt* to carry or convey over water (or land), esp along a regular route, in a boat, ship, or aircraft; to deliver (an aircraft coming from a factory) under its own power.

fertile [fûr′til, -til] *adj* able to bear or produce (abundantly); rich in resources; inventive.—*adv* **fer′tilely**.—*vt* **fer′tilize**, to make fertile or fruitful.—*ns* **fertilizā′tion**; **fer′tilizer**; **fer′tility**.

ferule [fer′(y)ŏŏl] *n* a rod used for punishment.

fervent [fûr′vènt] *adj* hot; ardent, zealous, warm in feeling.—*n* **fer′vency**.—*adv* **fer′vently**.—*adj* **fer′vid** very hot; having burning desire or emotion; zealous.—*adv* **fer′vidly**.

festal [fes′tàl] *adj* pertaining to a feast or holiday; joyous; gay.—*adv* **fes′tally**.

fester [fes′tèr] *vi* to become corrupt; to suppurate; to rankle.—*vt* to cause to fester or rankle.

festive [fes′tiv] *adj* merry, joyous.—*n* **fes′tival**, a joyful celebration; a feast; a season of performances of music, plays, or the like.—*adv* **fes′tively**.—*n* **festiv′ity**, social mirth; a festive celebration; gaiety.

festoon [fes-tŏŏn′] *n* a garland suspended between two points; (*archit*) an ornament like a wreath of flowers, etc.—*vt* to adorn as with festoons.

fetal *see* **fetus**.

fetch[1] [fech] *vt* to go and bring back; to cause to come; to sell for.—*n* range, sweep (eg of imagination); a stratagem, trick.—*adj* **fetch′ing**, fascinating.

fetch[2] [fech] *n* the apparition of a living person.

fête [fet, fãt] *n* a festival; a holiday.—*vt* to entertain at a feast; to honor with festivities.

fetid [fē′tid or fet′id] *adj* stinking.

fetish [fet′ish] *n* an object believed to procure for its owner the services of a spirit lodged within it; something regarded with irrational reverence.

fetlock [fet′lok] *n* a tuft of hair that grows above a horse's hoof; the joint of the limb at the fetlock.

fetter [fet′èr] *n* (used chiefly in *pl*) a chain or shackle for the feet; anything that restrains.—*vt* to put fetters on; to restrain.—*adj* **fett′ered**.

fettle [fet′l] *n* condition, as in *fine fettle*.

fetus [fē′tus] *n* the unborn young of an animal, esp in its later stages; in man, the offspring in the womb from the fourth month until birth.—*adj* **fet′al**.

feud[1] [fūd] *n* a deadly quarrel, esp between families or clans.—*vi* to carry on a feud.

feud[2] [fūd] *n* a fief or land held on condition of service.—*adj* **feud′al**.—*n* **feud′alism**, the economic and social system in medieval Europe, in which land, worked by serfs, was held by vassals in exchange for military and other services to overlords.

fever [fē′vèr] *n* an abnormally increased body temperature; any disease marked by a high fever; a restless excitement.—*vt* to put into a fever.—*vi* to become fevered.—*adj* **fē′vered**.—*ns* **fē′verfew**, a perennial European composite herb (*Chrysanthemum parthenium*).—*adj* **fē′verish**.—*adv* **fē′verishly**.—*n* **fē′verishness**.

few [fū] *adj* small in number, not many.—*n* **few′ness**.

fey [fã] *adj* fated; strange and unusual.

fez [fez] *n* a red tapering cap usu. with black tassel worn esp by men in eastern Mediterranean countries.—*pl* **fezz′es**.

fiancé *fem* **fiancée** [fē-ä′sã] *n* a person engaged to be married.

fiasco [fi-as′kō] *n* an utter failure of any kind.—*pl* **fiascoes**.

fiat [fi′at] *n* a formal or solemn command; a decree.

fib [fib] *n* a lie about something unimportant.—*vi* to tell a fib or lie.—*pr p* **fibb′ing**; *pt p* **fibbed**.

fiber [fi′bèr] *n* any fine thread-like object of animal, vegetable or mineral origin, natural or synthetic; a structure of material composed of fibers; texture; short for dietary fiber.—*adj* **fibered**, having fibers.—*ns* **fiber′glass**, glass in fibrous form used in making various products (as glass wool, yarns, textiles, and structures); **fi′brin**, a threadlike elastic protein formed in blood clots; **fi′brinogen**, a protein in the blood from which fibrin is formed; **fibrōsi′tis**, inflammation of fibrous tissues.

fibula [fib′u-la] *n* the outer of the two bones from the knee to the ankle.—*pl* **fibulae**.

fichu [fē′shŭ] *n* a woman's three-cornered cape of lace or muslin for the neck and shoulders.

fickle [fik′l] *adj* inconstant; changeable.—*n* **fick′leness**.

fictile [fik′til -til], *adj* of pottery.

fiction [fik′sh(ó)n] *n* an invented story; any literary work with imaginary characters and events as a novel, play, etc.; such works collectively.—*adjs* **ficti′tious** [-tish′ús], imaginary, not real, feigned.—*adv* **ficti′tiously**.

fiddle [fid′l] *n* (among musicians) a violin; a device to keep dishes from sliding off a table aboard ship; a swindle.—*vt* to play on a violin.—*vi* to swindle; to falsify.—*vi* to be busy over trifles.—*interj* **fiddle-faddle, fidd′lesticks**, nonsense!—**fidd′ler**, one who fiddles.

fidelity [fi-del′i-ti] *n* faithful performance of duty; loyalty; faithfulness to a husband or wife.

fidget [fij′et] *vi* to be unable to rest; to move uneasily.—*adj* **fidg′ety**, restless; uneasy.—*n* **fidg′etiness**.

fiducial [fi-dū′shi-àl] *adj* showing confidence or reliance; of the nature of trust.—*adj* **fidū′ciary**.—*n* trustee.

fief [fēf] *n* in feudalism, heritable land held by a vassal.

field [fēld] *n* area of land free from trees and buildings; a piece of ground cleared for tillage, pasture, or sport; the locality of a battle; the battle itself; a tract yielding a natural product (eg gold, coal); the area visible through an optical lens; sphere of activity, knowledge, etc.; (*her*) the surface of a shield; the background on which figures are drawn; all entrants in a contest.—*vt* at baseball, to catch or stop and return to the fixed place; to put (eg a team) into the field to play.—*ns* **field′day**, a day when troops are drawn out for instruction in field exercises; a day of sports and athletic competition; any day of unusual bustle or success; **field′er**, one who fields; **field′glass(es)**, a small, portable binocular telescope for use outdoors.

fiend [fēnd] *n* an evil spirit; an inhumanly wicked person.—*adj* **fiend′ish**.—*n* **fiend′ishness**.

fierce [fērs] *adj* ferocious, angry; violent.—*adv* **fierce′ly**.—*n* **fierce′ness**.

fiery [fir′i] *adj* like, or consisting of, fire; ardent, impetuous; irritable.—*adv* **fier′ily**.—*ns* **fier′iness**.

fife [fif] *n* a small keyless variety of the flute.

fifteen [fif′tēn] (when used absolutely, [fif-tēn′] adj, n one more than fourteen; the symbol for this (15, XV, xv,); the first point scored by a side in a game of tennis.—*adj* **fifteenth**, the last of fifteen.

fifth [fifth] *adj* last of five; being one of five equal parts.

fifty [fif′ti] *adj n* five times ten; symbol for this (50, L, l.—**fif′ty-fif′ty**, half-and-half; (of chances) equal.

fig [fig] *n* any of a very large genus of trees of the mulberry family, yielding a pear-shaped fruit; a thing of little consequence.

fight [fit] *vi* to strive (for); to contend in war or in single combat.—*vt* to engage in conflict with; to win (one's way) by conflict.—*n* **fight′er**, one who fights; one who does not give in easily; an airplane designed to destroy enemy aircraft.

figment [fig′mènt] *n* a fabrication or invention.

figure [fig′ûr] *n* the form of anything in outline; a geometrical form; a representation in drawing, etc.; a design; a statue; appearance; a personage; a character denoting a number; a number; value or price; a deviation from the ordinary mode of expression, in which words are changed from their literal signification or usage; a set of steps in a dance or a series of movements in skating; a type or emblem; (*pl*) arithmetic. — *vt* to make an image of; to mark with figures or designs; (*inf*) to believe, to consider; to calculate with figures. — *vi* to play a part (in), be conspicuous (in); to do arithmetic. — *adj* figurative, metaphorical; using figures of speech. — *adv* figuratively. — **figurehead**, a carved figure on the bow of a ship; a nominal head or leader.

filament [fil'a-mènt] *n* a slender thread or threadlike part; a fiber; the fine wire in a light bulb or electron tube.

filbert [fil'bèrt] *n* the nut of the cultivated hazel.

filch [filch] *vt* to steal, to pilfer. — *n* **filch'er**, thief.

file¹ [fīl] *n* an container for keeping papers, etc., in order; an orderly arrangement of papers; a line of persons or things. — *vt* to dispatch or register; to put on public record. — *vi* to move in a line; to apply.

file² [fīl] *n* a steel instrument with sharp-edged furrows for smoothing or grinding. — *vt* to cut or smooth with, or as with, a file; to polish, improve. — *n* **fil'ing**, a particle rubbed off with a file.

filial [fil'yàl] *adj* pertaining to, or becoming in, a son or daughter; bearing the relation of a child. — *adv* **fil'ially**.

filibuster [fil'i-bus-tèr] *n* a member of a legislature who obstructs a bill by making long speeches. — *vti* to obstruct (a bill) by such methods.

filiform [fil'i-förm] *adj* having the form of a filament; long and slender.

filigree [fil'i-grē] *n* a kind of ornamental work in which threads of precious metal are interlaced; anything delicate and fragile like such metalwork.

fill [fil] *vt* to put as much as possible into; to occupy wholly; to put a person into (a position or job, etc.); to supply the things called for (in an order, etc.); to close or plug (holes, etc.). — *vi* to become full. — *n* enough to make full or to satisfy; anything that fills. — *ns* **filler**; **fill'ing**, anything that fills a hole, etc.; **filling station**, service station.

fillet [fil'et] *n* a thin strip or band; a thin boneless strip of meat or fish; (*archit*) a small space or band used along with mouldings. — *vt* to bone and slice (fish or meat). — *pr p* **fill'et-ing**; *pt p* **fill'eted**.

fillip [fil'ip] *vt* to strike with the nail of the finger, forced from the thumb with a sudden jerk.

filly [fil'i] *n* a young female horse.

film [film] *n* a fine, thin skin, coating, etc.; a flexible cellulose material covered with a light-sensitive substance used in photography; haze or blur; a motion picture. — *vi* to cover or be covered as with a film; to photograph or make a motion picture (of). — *adj* **filmy**, gauzy, sheer; blurred, hazy.

filter [fil'tér] *n* a device or substance straining out solid particles, impurities, etc., from a liquid or gas; a device or substance for screening out electric oscillations, light waves. — *vti* to pass through or as through a filter; to remove with a filter.

filth [filth] *n* foul matter; obscenity. — *adj* **filth'y**, foul, unclean; obscene. — *n* **filth'iness**. — *adv* **filth'ily**.

fin [fin] *n* an organ by which an aquatic animal balances itself and swims.

final [fi'nàl] *adj* of or coming at the end, last; decisive, conclusive. — *n* (*pl*) the last of a series of contests; a final examination. — *vt* **fi'nalize**, to make complete. **final'ity**. — *adv* **fi'nally**.

finale [fi-nä'lä] *n* the end; the last movement in a musical composition; the concluding piece in a concert.

finance [fi-nans', fī] *n* the art of managing money; (*pl*) money resources. — *vt* to supply or get money for. — *adj* **finan'cial** [-shàl]. — *adv* **finan'cially**. — *n* **finan'cier**, one skilled in finance.

finch [finch, -sh] *n* any of numerous songbirds.

find [fīnd] *vt* to discover by chance; to get by searching; to perceive; to recover (something lost); to reach, attain; to decide and declare to be. — *vi* to reach a decision (as by a jury). — *ns* **finder**, one that finds; a camera device for sighting the field of view; **finding**, a discovery.

fine [fīn] *adj* very good; with no impurities, refined; clear and bright (*fine weather*); not heavy or coarse (*fine sand*); very thin or small (*fine print*); sharp (*a fine edge*); subtle (*a fine distinc-*

tion); elegant. — *adv* in a fine manner; (*inf*) very well. — *adv* **finely**. — *ns* **fineness**.

fine [fīn] *n* a sum of money imposed as a punishment. — *vt* to impose a fine on. — **in fine**, in short.

finesse [fi-nes'] *n* subtlety of contrivance; a cunning strategy; (*bridge*) an attempt to take a trick with a card lower than a higher card held by an opponent. — *vi* to use artifice.

finger [fing'gér] *n* one of the five terminal parts of the hand, or of the four other than the thumb; anything shaped like a finger; the breadth of a finger. — *vt* to touch with the fingers; (*mus*) to use the fingers in a certain way when playing. — *adj* **fing'ered**, having fingers, or anything like fingers. — *n* **fing'ering**, act or manner of touching; the choice of fingers as in playing a musical instrument; the indication of this.

finial [fin'i-àl] *n* the decorative terminal part at the top of a spire, lamp, curtain rod, etc.

finicky [fin'i-kē] *adj* too particular, fussy. — Also **fin'ical**, **fin'icking**.

finis [fi'nis] *n* the end, conclusion.

finish [fin'ish] *vt* to bring to an end, to come to the end of; to consume all of; to perfect; to give a desired surface effect to. — *vi* to come to an end. — *n* the last part, the end; anything used to finish a surface; the finished effect; means or manner of completing or perfecting; polished manners, speech, etc. — *adj* **fin'ished**. — *n* **fin'isher**, one who completes or perfects.

finite [fi'nīt] *adj* having definable limits.

finnan-haddie [fin'àn-had'ē] *n* a kind of smoked haddock, originally prepared at Findon, Kincardineshire, Scotland.

fiord *see* **fjord**.

fir [fûr] *n* a genus of evergreen trees; its timber.

fire [fīr] *n* the flame, heat, and light of combustion; something burning; a destructive burning (*a forest fire*); a strong feeling; a discharge of firearms. — *vti* to ignite; to supply with fuel; to bake (bricks, etc.) in a kiln; to excite or become excited; to shoot (a gun, etc.); to hurl or direct with force; to dismiss from a position. — *ns* **fire'arm**, a hand weapon discharged by an explosion; **fire'ball**, a ball of fire; a meteor; the cloud created by a nuclear explosion; **fire'brand**, a brand or piece of wood on fire; one who foments strife; **fire'break**, a strip of land cleared to stop the spread of a fire; **fire' brigade'**, a brigade or company of men for extinguishing fires or conflagrations; **fire'damp**, a combustible mine gas; **fire'-eater**, a juggler who pretends to eat fire; one given to needless quarreling; **fire' escape'**, an iron stairway or other special means of exit from a building for use in case of fire; **fire'fly**, a winged nocturnal beetle whose abdomen glows with a soft intermittent light; **fire'man**, a man whose business it is to assist in extinguishing fires; **fire'place**, a place for a fire, esp an open place built in a wall; **fire'plug**, a street hydrant supplying water for fighting fires. — *adj* **fire'proof**, not easily destroyed by fire. — *vt* to make fireproof. — **fire'stone**, pyrite formerly used for striking fire; **fire'trap**, a building easily set afire or hard to get out of if on fire; **fire'water**, strong alcoholic beverage; **fireworks**, firecrackers, rockets, etc., for noisy effects or brilliant displays; such a display; **fir'ing**, application of fire or heat to; discharge of guns; fuel.

firkin [fûr'kin] *n* a small wooden vessel or cask.

firm¹ [fûrm] *adj* fixed; compact; strong; not easily moved or disturbed; unshaken; resolute; definite. — *adv* **firm'ly**. — *n* **firm'ness**.

firm² [fûrm] *n* a business company.

firmament [fûr'má-mènt] *n* the sky, viewed poetically as a solid arch or vault.

first [fûrst] *adj* before all others in a series; 1st; earliest; foremost, as in rank, quality, etc. — *adv* before anyone or anything else; for the first time; sooner. — *n* any person or thing that is first; the beginning; the winning place, as in a race; low gear. — *n* **first aid**, emergency treatment for an injury, etc., before regular medical aid is available. — **first'hand**, obtained directly. — *n* **first'ling**, the first produce or offspring. — *adv* **first'ly**, in the first place.

firth [fûrth] *n* an arm of the sea, esp a rivermouth. — Also **frith**.

fisc [fisk] *n* a state or royal treasury. — *adj* **fisc'al** of or relating to the public treasury and revenues; financial. — *n* revenue stamp; fiscal year.

fish¹ [fish] *n* any of a large group of coldblooded animals living in water having backbones, gills for breathing, and fins; the flesh of fish used as food.—*pl* **fish**, or **fish'es** when referring to different species.—*vi* to catch or try to catch fish; to seek to obtain by artifice (*with* for).—*vt* to grope for, find, and bring to view (*often with* out); **fish'erman**, a person who fishes for sport or for a living; a ship used in fishing; **fish farm**, a commercial facility for raising aquatic animals for human food; **fish'net**, netting fitted with floats and weights for catching fish; a coarse open-mesh fabric.—*adj* **fish-net**.—*n* **fish story**, an incredible and extravagant story.—*vi* **fishtail**, to swing the tail of an airplane from side to side to reduce speed, esp while landing; to have the rear end of a vehicle move from side to side out of control while moving forward.—*n* **fish'wife**, a coarse, scolding woman.—*adj* **fishy**, like a fish in odor, taste, etc.; creating doubt or suspicion.

fish² [fish] *n* (*naut*) a piece of wood placed alongside another to strengthen it.—*n* **fish'plate**, an iron plate, one of a pair used to join railway rails.

fissile [fis'il, -īl] *adj* that may be cleft or split in the direction of the grain; fissionable.—*n* **fission** [fish'ón], a split or cleavage.—*adj* **fiss'ionable**.

fissiparous [fi-sip'a-rus] *adj* propagated by fission or self-division.

fissure [fish'ùr] *n* a narrow opening or chasm.

fist [fist] *n* the closed or clenched hand.—*vt* to strike or grip with the fist.—*n pl* **fist'icuffs**, a fight with the fists.

fistula [fist'ū-la] *n* an abnormal passage as from an abscess to the skin.

fit¹ [fit] *adj* suited to some purpose, function, etc.; proper, right; healthy; (*slang*) inclined, ready.—*n* the manner of fitting.—*vt* to be suitable to; to be the proper size, shape, etc., for; to adjust so as to fit; to equip, to outfit.—*vi* to be suitable or proper; to have the proper size or shape.—*pr p* **fitt'ing**; *pt p* **fitt'ed**.—*adv* **fit'ly**.—*ns* **fitt'er**; **fit'ness**.—*adj* **fitting**, appropriate.—*n* an act of one that fits, esp a trying on of altered clothes; a small often standardized electrical part.—*adv* **fittingly**.

fit² [fit] *n* any sudden, uncontrollable attack, as of coughing; an outburst, as of anger; a seizure involving convulsions or loss of consciousness.—*adj* **fit'ful**, marked by intermittent activity; spasmodic.—*adv* **fitfully**.—*n* **fitfulness**.

fit³ [fit] *n* (*arch*) a division of a poem or song.

fitch [fich] *n* a polecat; the fur of the polecat.

five [fiv] *adj*, *n* one more than four; the symbol for this (5,V,v).—*adjs* **fifth**, see separate entry; **fivefold**, having five units or members; being five times as great as many.

fix [fiks] *vt* to fasten firmly; to set firmly in the mind; to direct (one's eyes) steadily at something; to make rigid; to make permanent; to establish (a date, etc.) definitely; to set in order; to repair; to prepare (food or meals); (*inf*) to influence the result or action of (a race, jury, etc.) by bribery; (*inf*) to punish.—*vi* to become fixed; (*inf*) to prepare or intend.—*n* the position of a ship, etc., determined from the bearings of two known positions; (*inf*) a predicament; (*inf*) a situation that has been fixed; (*inf*) something whose supply becomes continually necessary or greatly desired as a drug, entertainment, activity, etc.—*ns* **fixation**, a fixing or being fixed; an obsession; **fixative**.—*adj* **fixed**, settled; not apt to evaporate; steadily directed; fast, lasting.—*adv* **fix'edly** [-id-li].—*ns* **fix'edness**, **fix'ity**; **fix'er**; **fix'ture**, what is fixed to anything, as to land or to a house; a fixed article of furniture; a fixed or appointed time or event.

fizz [fiz] *vi* to make a hissing or spluttering sound.—*n* any effervescent drink.—*adj* **fizz'y**, effervescent.—*vi* **fizz'le**, to hiss or sputter.

flabbergast [flab'ér-gäst] *vt* to stun, confound.

flabby [flab'i] *adj* soft, yielding; weak and ineffective.—*n* **flabb'iness**.

flaccid [flak'sid] *adj* not firm or stiff; lacking vigor.

flag¹ [flag] *vi* to grow languid or spiritless.—*pr p* **flagg'ing**; *pt p* **flagged**.

flag² [flag] *n* a plant with sword-shaped leaves—an iris, or a reed.

flag³ [flag] *n* a piece of bunting, usu. with a design, used to show nationality, party, a particular branch of the armed forces, etc., or to mark a position, or to convey information.—*vt* to decorate with flags; to inform by flag-signals; **flag day**, a day on which charitable donations are solicited in exchange for small flags; **flag'ship**, the chief or leading item of a group or collection; **flag'staff**, a staff or pole on which a flag is displayed.

flag⁴ [flag] *n* a stone that separates in flakes or layers; a flat stone used for paving.—Also **flagstone**.

flagellate [flaj'él-āt] *vt* to whip.—*ns* **flagellā'tion**; **flagell'ant** [also flaj'-], one who scourges himself in religious discipline.

flageolet [flaj-o-let' or flaj'-] *n* a small flute resembling the treble recorder.

flagitious [fla-jish'ús] *adj* grossly wicked, guilty of enormous crimes.

flagon [flag'ón] *n* a pottery or metal container for liquids with handle and spout and often a lid.

flagrant [flā'grànt] *adj* glaring, notorious.—*n* **flā'grancy**.—*adv* **flā'grantly**.

flail [flāl] *n* a hand threshing implement.—Also *vt*.

flair [flār] *n* intuitive discernment; aptitude, bent.

flak [flak] *n pl* anti-aircraft guns; the missiles of such a gun; criticism, opposition.

flake [flāk] *n* a small layer or film; a very small loose mass, as of snow or wool; (*slang*) cocaine.—*vt* to form into flakes.—*adjs* **flak'y**.

flambeau [flam'bō] *n* a flaming torch.

flamboyant [flam-boi'ànt] *adj* flamelike or brilliant; ornate; strikingly elaborate.

flame [flām] *n* the burning gas of a fire, appearing as a tongue of light; the state of burning with a blaze; a thing like a flame; an intense emotion; (*inf*) a sweetheart.—*vi* to burst into flame.—*n* a strong reddish orange color.—*adj* **flammable**, easily set on fire; that will burn readily.—*n* **flammability**.—*ns* **flame'-thrower**, a weapon that shoots flaming gasoline, oil, etc.

flamingo [fla-ming'gō] *n* any of several aquatic birds with rosy-white plumage, long legs and neck.

flan [flan] *n* (Brit) an open case of pastry or sponge cake with custard, or fruit, or other filling.

flâneur [flä-nœr'] *n* a loafer.

flange [flanj] *n* a projecting or raised edge, as of a wheel or of a rail.—*adj* **flanged**.

flank [flangk] *n* the side of an animal from the ribs to the hip; the side or wing of anything.—*vt* to attack the side of; to pass round the side of; to be situated at the side of.

flannel [flan'él] *n* a cotton or woolen cloth of loose texture; (*pl*) trousers of such cloth.—*n* **flannelette'**, a soft, fleecy cotton fabric.

flap [flap] *n* the blow, or motion, of a broad loose object; anything broad and flexible hanging loose, as material covering an opening; (*inf*) fluster, panic.—*vi* to move, as wings; to hang like a flap; (*inf*) to get into a panic or fluster.—*ns* **flap'doodle**, nonsense.

flare [flār] *vi* to burn with a glaring, unsteady light, to flash suddenly; to blaze (*up—lit* or *fig*); to widen out bell-wise.—*n* an unsteady glare; a flash; a bright light used as a signal or illumination; a widening, or a part that widens like a bell.

flash [flash] *n* a sudden, brief light; a brief moment; a sudden brief display; a brief news item sent by radio, etc.; a gaudy display.—*vi* to send out a sudden, brief light; to sparkle; to come or pass suddenly.—*vt* to cause to flash; to send (news, etc.) swiftly.—*adj* **flashy**.—*n* **flash'back**, an interruption in the continuity of a story, etc., by telling or showing an earlier episode; **flash point**, the lowest temperature at which vapor, as of an oil, will ignite with a flash.

flask [flask] *n* a narrow-necked vessel for holding liquids; a bottle; a vessel for holding gunpowder.

flat [flat] *adj* having a smooth level surface; lying spread out; broad, even, and thin; not fluctuating; without gloss.—*adv* in a flat manner or position; exactly; (*mus*) below true pitch.—*n* anything flat, esp a surface, part, or expanse.—*adv* **flatly**.—*ns* **flatfish**, any of an order of marine fishes that as adults have both eyes on one side.

flatter [flat'ér] *vt* to treat with insincere praise and servile attentions; to represent over-favorably; to please (with false hopes).—*n* **flatt'erer**.—*adv* **flatt'eringly**.—*n* **flatt'ery**, false praise.

flatulent [flat'ū-lènt] *adj* affected with air in the stomach; apt to generate such; pretentious, vain.—*ns* **flat'ūlence**, **flat'ūlency**.

flaunt [flönt] *vi* to wave in the wind; to move or behave ostentatiously.—*vt* to display.—Also *n*.

flautist [flŏt'ist] *n* a flute player.

flavor [flā'vŏr] *n* that quality of anything which affects the smell or the taste; a relish; (*fig*) savor; characteristic quality.— *vt* to impart flavor to.—*adj* **flā'vorous**.—*n* **flā'voring**.

flaw² [flŏ] *n* a break, a crack; a defect; a fault in a legal paper that may nullify it.—*vt* to crack or break.—*adj* **flaw'less**.

flax [flaks] *n* any of a genus of herbs, esp a blue-flowered annual cultivated for its fiber and seed; the fiber of this plant.—*adj* **flax'en**, made of or resembling flax; light yellow.—*n* **flax seed**, linseed.

flay [flā] *vt* to strip off the skin.

flea [flē] *n* an order of parasitic insects of great agility.—**flea'-bane**, a genus of plants whose smell is said to drive away fleas; **flea'-bite**, the bite of a flea; (*fig*) a trifle.

fleck [flek] *n* a spot or speckle; a little bit of a thing.—*vs t* **fleck**, **fleck'er**, to spot; to streak.

fledge [flej] *vt* to bring up a bird until it is ready to fly; to furnish with feathers, as an arrow.—*vi* to acquire feathers for flying.—*n* **fledgling**, a little bird just fledged.

flee [flē] *vi* to run away, as from danger; to disappear.—*vt* to keep at a distance from.

fleece [flēs] *n* a sheep's coat of wool.—*vt* to clip wool from; to plunder; to cover, as with wool; **fleec'y**, woolly.

fleet¹ [flēt] *n* a number of warships under one command; any group of ships, trucks, etc., under one control.

fleet² [flēt] *adj* swift; nimble; transient.

fleet³ [flēt] *vi* to move, pass swiftly, hasten.—*vt* to while away.—*pr p* **fleet'ing**; *pt p* **fleet'ed**.

Flemish [flem'ish] *adj* people of Flanders, or their language.

flense [flenz, -sh] *vt* to cut out the blubber of, as a whale.

flesh [flesh] *n* the soft substance of the body, esp the muscular tissue; the pulpy part of fruits and vegetables; meat; the body as distinct from the soul; all mankind; yellowish pink.—*vt* to initiate or habituate by giving a foretaste; to give substance to (*usu. with* out); to free from flesh.—*vi* to become fleshy (*with* up *or* out).—*adj* **fleshed** [flesht], having flesh, esp of a specified kind (*pink-fleshed*).—*adjs* **fleshly**, corporeal; sensual; **fleshy**.—*ns* **fleshiness**, state of being fleshy; corpulence; **fleshpots**, luxury; place of lascivious entertainment.

fleur-de-lis [flĕr'-de-lē' *or* -lēs'] *n* the flower of the lily; an ornament and heraldic bearing borne by the kings of France.—*pl* **fleurs'-de-lis'**.

flex [fleks] *vti* to bend (arm, etc); to contract (a muscle).—*n* a bending.—*adjs* **flexible** [fleks'i-bl], **flexile** [fleks'il], easily bent, pliant; docile.—*n* **flexibil'ity.**—*adv* **flex'ibly.**—*ns* **flex'ion**.

flextime [fleks'tim] *n* the staggering of working hours to enable each employee to work the full quota of time but at periods most convenient for the individual.

flick [flik] *vt* to strike lightly.—*n* a flip.

flicker [flik'ĕr] *vi* to flutter and move the wings, as a bird; to burn unsteadily, as a flame.

flight¹ [flīt] *n* the act, manner, or power of flying; distance flown; a group of things flying together; an airplane scheduled to fly a certain trip; a trip by airplane; a set of stairs, as between landings; **flight'y**, fanciful; changeable; giddy.

flight² [flīt] *n* an act of fleeing.

flimsy [flim'zi] *adj* thin; without solidity, strength, or reason; weak.—*adv* **flim'sily.**—*n* **flim'siness**.

flinch [flinch, -sh] *vi* to shrink back; to wince.

fling [fling] *vt* to cast, toss, throw; to dart; to scatter.—*vi* to kick out; to dash or rush; to throw oneself impetuously.

flint [flint] *n* a very hard siliceous rock, usu. gray, that produces sparks when struck with steel; a material used for producing a spark used in lighters.—*adj* made of flint, hard; **flint'lock**, a gun having a flint fixed in the hammer for striking a spark to ignite the charge.

flip¹ [flip] *n* a hot drink of beer (or egg and milk) and spirits sweetened.

flip² [flip] *vt* to toss with a quick jerk; to snap (a coin) in the air with the thumb; to turn or turn over.—*vi* to move jerkily; **flipp'er**, a limb adapted for swimming; a rubber shoe expanded into a paddle, used in skin diving.

flippant [flip'ànt] *adj* quick and pert of speech; frivolous.—*ns* **flipp'ancy**.

flirt [flûrt] *vi* to trifle with love; to trifle or toy (to flirt with an

idea).—*vt* to move (a light article) jerkily.—*n* a sudden jerk; a trifler with the opposite sex.—*n* **flirta'tion**, the act of flirting.

flit [flit] *vi* to move lightly and rapidly.—*n* **flitt'ing**.

flitch [flich] *n* the side of a hog salted and cured.

flitter [flit'ĕr] *vi* to flutter.

float [flōt] *vi* to be supported or suspended in a liquid; to be buoyed up; to move lightly; to drift about aimlessly.—*vt* to cause to float; to put into circulation (*to float a bond issue*).—*n* anything that floats; a low flat vehicle decorated for exhibit in a parade; a tool for smoothing; **floatā'tion**.

flock¹ [flok] *n* a group of certain animals as birds, sheep, etc., living and feeding together; a group of people or things.—*vi* to assemble or travel in a flock or crowd.

flock² [flok] *n* tuft of wool or cotton fiber; woolen or cotton refuse used for stuffing furniture.

floe [flō] *n* a field of floating ice.

flog [flog] *vt* to beat with a rod or stick.

flood [flud] *n* an overflowing of water on an area normally dry; the rising of the tide; a great outpouring, as of words.—*vt* to cover or fill, as with a flood; to put too much water, fuel, etc. on or in.—*vi* to gush out in a flood; to become flooded.—*ns* **flood'gate**, a gate for allowing or stopping the flow of water, a sluice; **flood'-light**, **flood'lighting**, strong illumination from many points to eliminate shadows.—*vt* **flood'light**.—**the Flood**, Noah's deluge.

floor [flor] *n* the inside bottom surface of a room; the bottom surface of anything (*the ocean floor*); a story in a building; the right to speak in an assembly; the lower limit, the base.—*vt* to furnish with a floor; to knock down; (*inf*) to defeat; (*inf*) to shock, to confuse.

flop [flop] *vt* to swing or bounce loosely; to move in a heavy, clumsy or relaxed manner.—*n* a fall plump on the ground; a collapse; a complete failure.

flora [flō'ra, flō'] *n* the plants (collectively) of a region or of a period; a list of these.—*pl* **flōras**, **flōrae**, [*-ē*].—*adj* **flō'ral**, pertaining to the goddess Flora or to flowers.—*n* **flōres'cence**, a bursting into flower; (*bot*) the time when plants flower.—*adj* **flōres'cent**.—*n* **flō'ret** (*bot*), one of the small flowers forming the head of a composite plant.—*adj* **flō'riated**, decorated with floral ornaments; having a floral form.—*n* **flō'riculture**, the culture of flowers—*adj* **floricul'tural**.—*n* **flōricul'turist**.—*adj* **flor'id**, flowery; flushed with red; fully developed, esp of a disease.—*adv* **flor'idly**.—*n* **flor'idness**.—*n* **flōr'ist**, one who sells or grows flowers and ornamental plants.

floruit [flō'rŏŏ-it] *n* a period of flourishing, as of a person or movement. Abbrev **fl**.

floss [flos] *n* the rough outside of the silkworm's cocoon and other waste of silk manufacture; fine silk used in embroidery; any loose downy plant substance; dental floss.—*adj* **floss'y**, slick, stylish.

flotation [flo-tā'sh(ò)n] *n* the act of floating; the science of floating bodies; act of starting a business.

flotilla [flō-til'a] *n* a fleet of ships, esp two or more squadrons of small warships.

flotsam [flot'sàm] *n* floating debris.

flounce¹ [flowns] *vi* to move abruptly or impatiently.—*n* an impatient fling, flop, or movement.

flounce² [flowns] *n* a hanging strip sewed to the skirt of a dress.—*vt* to furnish with flounces.

flounder¹ [flown'dèr] *vi* to struggle with violent and awkward motion; to stumble helplessly in thinking or speaking.

flounder² [flown'dèr] *n* any of various flatfish.

flour [flowr] *n* the finely ground meal of wheat or other grain; the fine soft powder of any substance.—*vt* to sprinkle with flour.—*adjs* **flour'less flour'y**.

flourish [flur'ish] *vi* to grow luxuriantly; to thrive, be prosperous; to live and work (in, at, about, a specified time).—*vt* to adorn with flourishes or ornaments; to brandish in show or triumph.—*n* decoration; a figure made by a bold stroke of the pen; the waving of a weapon or other thing; a musical fanfare.—*adj* **flour'ishing**.

flout [flowt] *vt* to jeer at, to mock; to treat with contempt.—Also *vi*—*n* a scornful act or remark.

flow [flō] *vi* to run, as water; to rise, as the tide; to move in a stream; to glide smoothly; to be plentiful.—*n* a flowing; the rate of flow; anything that flows; the rising of the tide.—*adj* **flow'ing.**—*adv* **flow'ingly.**

flower [flow'ėr] *n* the seed-producing structure of a flowering plant, blossom; a plant cultivated for its blossoms; the best or finest part.—*vt* to cause to bear flowers; to decorate with floral designs.—*vi* to produce blossoms; to reach the best stage.—*n* **flow'eret,** a floret.—*adj* **flow'ery,** full of or adorned with flowers; full of ornate expressions and fine words.—*n* **flow'eriness.**

flown [flōn] *pt p* of **fly.**

flu [flōō] *n* short for influenza.

fluctuate [fluk'tū-āt] *vi* to be continually varying in an irregular way.—*n* **fluctua'tion.**

flue [flōō] *n* a shaft for the passage of smoke, hot air, etc., as in a chimney.

fluent [flōō'ėnt] *adj* flowing smoothly; ready in the use of words.—*n* **flu'ency.**—*adv* **flu'ently.**

fluff [fluf] *n* soft, light down; a loose, soft mass, as of hair.

fluid [flōō'id] *adj* that can flow as a liquid or gas does; that can change rapidly or easily.—*n* a liquid or gas.—*ns* **fluid'ity.**

fluke[1] [flōōk] *n* a flatfish; a flattened trematode worm.

fluke[2] [flōōk] *n* the part of an anchor which fastens in the ground; a lobe of a whale's tail.

fluke[3] [flōōk] *n* a stroke of luck.

flume [flōōm] *n* an inclined chute for carrying water; a gorge with a stream running through it.

flummery [flum'ėr-i] *n* a soft jelly made from flour or meal; mumbo-jumbo.

flunk [flunk] *vti* to fail, as in schoolwork.—Also *n.*

flunky [flung'ki] *n* a liveried manservant; a toady.

fluorite [flōō'rīt] *n* a mineral (CaF_2) of different colors used as a flux and for making opalescent and opaque glass.—*n* **fluores'cence,** the property of producing light when acted upon by radiant energy; light so produced.—*adj* **fluores'cent.**—*n* **flu'oride,** any of various compounds of fluorine.—*n* **flu'orine.**

flurry [flur'i] *n* a sudden gust of wind, rain, or snow; a sudden commotion.—*vti* to cause or become agitated and confused.

flush[1] [flush] *n* a rapid flow, as of water; sudden, vigorous growth; a sudden excitement; a blush; a sudden feeling of heat, as in a fever.—*vi* to flow rapidly; to blush or glow; to be washed out by a sudden flow of water.—*vt* to wash out with a sudden flow of water; to cause to blush; to excite.—*adj* abundant, well supplied, esp with money.

flush[2] [flush] *adj* having the surface in one plane with the adjacent surface.

flush[3] [flush] *vi* (of birds) to start up suddenly and fly away.

flush[4] [flush] *n* a run of cards all of the same suit.

fluster [flus'tėr] *vti* to make or become confused.—*n* being flustered.

flute [flōōt] *n* an orchestral woodwind instrument in the form of a straight pipe (with finger holes and keys) held horizontally and played through a hole located near one end; **flutist,** one who plays a flute.

flutter [flut'ėr] *vi* to flap the wings; to move about with bustle; to be in agitation or in uncertainty.—*vt* to throw into disorder.—*n* quick, irregular motion.

fluvial [flōō'vi-ål] *adj* of streams and rivers.

flux [fluks] *n* a flowing; a continual change; any abnormal discharge from the body; a substance used to help metals fuse together, as in soldering.

fly [flī] *vi* to move through the air, esp on wings or in aircraft; to move swiftly; to flee.—*vt* to avoid, flee from; to cause to fly, as a kite; to cross by flying.—*pr p* **fly'ing;** *pt p* **flew** [flōō]; *pt p* **flown** [flōn].—*n* a stout-bodied, two-winged insect; a fish-hook dressed with silk, etc., in imitation of a fly; a flap that conceals a fastening on a garment; a flap over the entrance to a tent.—*adj* **fly'blown,** tainted; covered with flyspecks.—**fly'ing bomb,** a robot bomb; **fly'ing butt'ress,** a buttress connected to a wall by an arch, serving to resist outward pressure; **fly'ing fish,** any of numerous fishes of warm seas with winglike fins used in gliding through the air; **fly'leaf,** a blank leaf at the beginning or end of a book; **fly'weight,** a boxer weighing not more than 112 pounds; **fly'wheel,** a wheel, usu. relatively massive, which stores energy by inertia, used eg to equalize effect of driving effort.

foal [fōl] *n* the young of the horse family.—*vti* to bring forth (a foal).

foam [fōm] *n* froth on the surface of liquid; something like foam, as frothy saliva; a rigid or springy cellular mass made from liquid rubber, plastic, etc.—*vi* to froth out.—**foam'y.**

fob [fob] *n* a small pocket for a watch; the watch chain or ribbon hanging from such a pocket.

fo'c'sle *see* forecastle.

focus [fō'kus] *n* a point where rays of light, heat, etc. meet after being bent by a lens, curved mirror, etc.; correct adjustment of the eye, lens, etc. to form a clear image; the central point.—*pl* **foci** [fō'sī].

fodder [fod'ėr] *n* food for cattle.—*vt* to supply with fodder.

foe [fō] *n* an enemy, an adversary.

foetid *see* fetid.

foetus *see* fetus.

fog [fog] *n* a large mass of water vapor condensed to fine particles just above the earth's surface; a state of mental confusion.—*vti* to make or become foggy.—**fogg'y,** misty; clouded in mind; confused, indistinct.—*ns* **fogg'iness;** **fog-horn,** a horn sounded as a warning signal in foggy weather.

fogy, fogey [fō'gi] *n* a dull old fellow; a person with antiquated notions.

foible [foi'bl] *n* a weakness; a failing; a penchant.

foil[1] [foil] *vt* to defeat; to baffle; to frustrate.

foil[2] [foil] *n* a very thin sheet of metal; anything that sets off or enhances another by contrast.

foist [foist] *vt* to bring in by stealth; to palm off (upon); to pass off as genuine.

fold[1] [fōld] *n* a doubling of anything upon itself; a crease; a part laid over on another.—*vt* to lay in folds; to wrap up, envelop; to interlace (one's arms); clasp (one's hands); to embrace.—*vi* to become folded; to fail completely; to collapse, esp to go out of business.—*n* **fold'er,** a person or thing that folds; a folded cover or large envelope for holding or filing papers.

fold[2] [fōld] *n* a pen for sheep; a flock of sheep; a group of people or institutions having a common belief, activity, etc.—*vt* to confine in a fold.

foliaceous [fō-li-ā'shus] *adj* pertaining to or consisting of leaves or laminae.

foliage [fō'li-ij] *n* leaves, as of a plant or tree; a representation of leaves, flowers, and branches in architectural ornamentation.

folio [fō'li-ō] *n* a large sheet of paper folded once; a book of such sheets; the number of a page in a book.—*vt* to put a serial number on each leaf or page of.

folk [fōk] *n* a people, a nation; the common people of a nation.—*pl* **folk, folks.** (*pl*) people, persons.—*adj* of or originating among the common people.—*ns* **folklore,** the traditional beliefs, legends, etc. of a people; **folk song,** a traditional or composed song marked by simplicity of melody, stanzaic form, and refrain.—*n* **folktale,** an anonymous, timeless, and placeless tale circulated orally among a people.

follicle [fol'i-kl] *n* any small sac, cavity, or gland.

follow [fol'ō] *vt* to go or come after or behind; to pursue; to proceed along (a road); to imitate; to obey; to adopt, as an opinion; to keep the eye or mind fixed on; to grasp or understand the whole course of; to come after in time; to result from.—*vi* to come after another; to result.—*ns* **foll'ower,** one who comes after; a disciple or adherent; **foll'owing,** the whole body of supporters; **follow through,** to continue a stroke or motion to the end of its arc; **follow up,** to pursue a question, inquiry, etc., that has been started.

folly [fol'i] *n* a lack of sense; a foolish thing; an extravagant and fanciful building.

foment [fo-ment'] *vt* to stir up (trouble); to apply a warm lotion to.—*ns* **fomenta'tion.**

fond [fond] *adj* tender and loving; weakly indulgent; prizing highly (*with of*).—*vt* **fond'le,** to treat with fondness; to caress.—*adv* **fond'ly.**—*n* **fond'ness.**

fondant [fon'dànt] *n* a soft sugar mixture for candies and icings; a candy made from this.

font[1] [font] *n* a receptacle for baptismal water; a receptacle for holy water.

food [fōōd] *n* any substance, esp a solid, taken in by a plant or animal to enable it to live and grow; anything that nourishes.

fool [fōōl] *n* a person showing lack of wisdom, or of common sense; a person of weak mind; a jester.—*vt* to deceive; to treat as a fool.—*vi* to play the fool; to joke.—*n* **fool'ery.**—*adj*

fool'hardy, foolishly bold; rash, incautious.—*n* **fool'-hard'i-ness.**—*adj* **fool'ish.**—*adv* **fool'ishly.**—*n* **fool'ishness.**—*adj* **fool'proof,** not liable to sustain or inflict injury as a result of wrong usage; **fool's paradise,** a state of delusory happiness; **fool's parsley,** a poisonous weed resembling parsley.

foolscap [fōōlz'kap] *n* a size of writing paper 13 by 16 inches, in the US, originally bearing the watermark of a fool's cap and bells.

foot [fŏŏt] *n* the end part of the leg, on which one stands; the lower part or base; a measure of length equal to 12 inches (symbol: '); a group of syllables serving as a unit of meter in verse.—*pl* **feet.**—*vi* to dance; to walk.—*vt* to put new feet to; to pay (a bill).—*pr p* **foot'ball,** a field game played with an inflated leather ball by two teams; the ball used; **foot'hill,** a hill at the foot of higher hills; **foot'ing,** place for the foot to rest on; placing of the feet; foundation; position, status, conditions; settlement; **foot'lights,** a row of lights in front of a stage floor; **foot'man,** a servant or attendant in livery; **foot'note,** a note of reference or comment, esp at foot of page.

footle [fŏŏt'l] *vi* to trifle, potter.—*adj* **foot'ling.**

foozle [fŏŏz'l] *n* a tedious fellow; a bungled stroke at golf, etc.—*vi* to fool away one's time.

fop [fop] *n* an affected dandy.—*n* **fopp'ery,** vanity in dress or manners.—*adj* **fop'pish.**—*adv* **fopp'ishly.**

for [fôr, fŏr] *prep.*—because of, in consequence of; in payment of, or recompense of; in order to be, to serve as; appropriate to, or adapted to; in quest of; in the direction of; on behalf of; in place of; in favor of; with respect to; notwithstanding, in spite of; to the extent of; through the space of; during.—*conj* because.

forage [for'ij] *n* food for domestic animals, esp when taken by browsing or grazing; a search for provisions.—*vi* to search for food.

foray [for'ā] *n* a raid.—*vti* to plunder.

forbade [for-bad'] *pt t* of **forbid.**

forbear [forbār'] *vi* to endure, to avoid.—*vt* to hold oneself back from.—*n* **forbear'ance.**

forbid [for-bid'] *vt* to prohibit; to prevent.—*pt* **forbade** [for-bad'], *pt p* **forbidd'en.**—*adjs* **forbidd'ing.**

force [fôrs, fŏrs] *n* strength, power, energy; efficacy; validity; significance; influence; vehemence; violence; coercion or compulsion; a body of people prepared for action.—*vt* to draw, push, by exertion of strength; to thrust; to compel, to constrain; to ravish; to take by violence; to achieve by force; to produce with effort.—*adj* **force'ful,** effective.—*adv* **force'-fully.**—*n* **force' pump,** a pump with a solid piston for drawing and forcing through valves a liquid (as water) to a great height above the pump.—*adj* **forc'ible.**—*n* **forc'ibleness.**—*adv* **forc'ibly.**

forcemeat [fôrs-mēt] *n* meat chopped fine and highly seasoned, used as a stuffing or alone.

forceps [fôr'seps] *n* an instrument for grasping and holding firmly, or exerting traction upon objects, esp by jewelers and surgeons.—*pl* **for'ceps.**

ford [fôrd, fŏrd] *n* a place where water may be crossed on foot.—*vt* to cross water on foot.—*adj* **ford'able.**

fore [fôr, fŏr] *adj* front.—*n* the front.—*adv* at or towards the front (of a ship).—*interj* (*golf*) a warning cry to anybody in the way of the ball.—*adj* **fore-and-aft,** from the bow to the stern; set lengthwise, as a rig.—**at the fore,** displayed on the foremast (of a flag); **to the fore,** prominent.

forearm[1] [fō'rärm] *n* the part of the arm between the elbow and the wrist.

forearm[2] [fôr-ärm'] *vt* to arm in advance.

forebear [fôr'bār] *n* an ancestor.

forebode [fôr-bōd'] *vt* to portend; to have a premonition (esp of evil).—*n* **forebod'ing.**

forecast [fôr'käst] *vt* to reckon beforehand; to predict; to foreshadow.—*vi* to estimate beforehand.

forecastle, fo'c'sle [fōk'sl, sometimes fôr'käs-l] *n* a short raised deck at the forward part of a ship; the ꞌforepart of the ship under the maindeck, the quarters of the crew.

foreclose [fôr-klōz'] *vt* to preclude; to prevent; to take away the right of redeeming (a mortgage).—*n* **foreclos'ure.**

forefather [fôr'fä-THėr] *n* an ancestor.

forefinger [fôr'fing-gėr] *n* the finger next to the thumb.

forefront [fôr'frunt] *n* the very front or foremost part.

forego [fôr-gō'] *vt* to go before, precede; chiefly used in *pr p* **foregoing** and *pt p* **foregone'.**

foreground [fôr'grownd] *n* the part of a picture or field of view nearest the observer's eye.

forehand [fôr'hand] *n* a stroke in a racket game; the part of a horse that is in front of its rider.

forehead [for'id, -ed, or -hed] *n* the part of the face above the eyes.

foreign [for'in] *adj* belonging to another country; from abroad; alien (to), not belonging (to), not appropriate; introduced from outside.—*n* **for'eigner.**

forejudge [fôr-juj'] *vt* to judge before hearing the facts and proof.

foreknow [fôr-nō'] *vt* to know beforehand.

foreland [fôr'länd] *n* a promontory, a headland.

forelock [fôr'lok] *n* the lock of hair on the forehead.

foreman [fôr'mån] *n* the first or chief man.

foremast [fôr'mäst, -mäst] *n* the mast nearest the bow.

foremost [fôr'mōst] *adj* first in place; most advanced; first in rank or dignity.

forenoon [fôr'nōōn, fôr-nōōn'] *n* morning.

forensic [fo-ren'sik] *adj* belonging to courts of law; used in law pleading.

foreordain [fôr-or-dān'] *vt* to predestine.

foresail [fôr's(ā)l] *n* the lowest square sail on the foremast; a triangular sail on the forestay.

foresee [fôr-sē'] *vt* to see or know beforehand.

foreshadow [fôr-shad'ō] *vt* to represent or indicate beforehand.—*n* **foreshad'owing.**

foreshore [fôr'shōr] *n* the space between the high and low water marks.

foreshorten [fôr-shört'n] *vt* in drawing, etc. to shorten some lines of (an object) to give the illusion of proper relative size.

foresight [fôr'sīt] *n* act of foreseeing; the power to foresee; prudent provison for the future.

forest [for'est] *n* a thick growth of trees, etc. covering a large tract of land; something resembling a forest.—*ns* **for'ester,** a person trained in forestry; an inhabitant of a forest; **for'estry,** the science of developing forests.

foretell [fôr-tel'] *vt* to tell beforehand, to predict.

foretop [fôr'top] *n* (*naut*) the platform at the head of the foremast.

forever [for-ev'ėr] *adv* for all time to come; continually.—*adv* **forev'ermore',** forever.

forewarn [fôr-wörn'] *vt* to warn beforehand.

foreword [fôr'wûrd] *n* a preface.

forfeit [fôr'fit] *vt* to lose the right to by some fault or crime; to penalise by forfeiture; *n* a penalty for a fault; something deposited and redeemable.—*adj* **for'feitable.**—*n* **for'feiture.**

forfend [fôr-fend'] *vt* to protect, to preserve.

forgather [fôr-gaTH'ėr] *vi* to assemble.

forge[1] [fôrj, fŏrj] *n* a furnace, esp one in which iron is heated; a smithy.—*vt* to shape (metal) by heating and hammering; to form; to counterfeit (eg a signature).—*vi* to commit forgery.—*ns* **forg'er, forg'ery,** fraudulently making or altering any writing.

forge[2] [fôrj, fŏrj] *vt* to move steadily on.

forget [fôr-get'] *vti* to be unable to remember; to overlook or neglect.—*adj* **forget'ful,** apt to forget, inattentive.—*adv* **forget'fully; forget'-me-not,** any of a genus of small herbs having bright-blue or white flowers.

forgive [fôr-giv'] *vt* to pardon, or cease to feel resentment against (a person); to pardon, overlook (a debt or trespass).—*vi* to be merciful or forgiving.—*n* **forgive'ness.**

forgo [fôr-gō', fôr-gō'] *vt* to give up.

fork [fôrk] *n* a pronged instrument; anything that divides into prongs or branches; the space or angle between two branches; one of the branches into which a road or river divides; the point of separation.—*vi* to divide into branches.—*vt* to form as a fork; to move with a fork.—*adjs* **forked.**

forlorn [fôr-lörn'] *adj* (*obs*) quite lost; forsaken; wretched.—*adv* **forlorn'ly.**

forlorn hope [fôr-lörn'-hōp] *n* a body of men selected for some service of uncommon danger; a desperate enterprise.

form [fôrm] *n* general structure; the figure of a person or animal; a mold; a particular mode, kind, type, etc. (*ice is a form of water, the forms of poetry*); arrangement; a way of doing something requiring skill; a conventional procedure; a printed document with blanks to be filled in; condition of mind or body; a chart giving information about racehorses; changed appearance of a word to show inflection; type locked in a frame for printing.—*vt* to shape; to train; to develop (habits); to constitute.—*vi* to be formed.—*adj* **form'al**, according to form or established mode; ceremonial; punctilious; stiff.—*n* a formal dance; a women's evening dress.—*ns* **form'alism, form'alist, formal'ity.**—*adv* **form'ally.**—*n* **formā'tion**, form of making or producing; that which is formed; structure; regular array or prearranged order helping development.—*adj* **form'ative.**

formaldehyde [för-mal'de-hīd] *n* a colorless pungent gas (CH₂O) used in solution as a disinfectant and preservative.

formalin [förm'alin] *n* an aqueous solution of formaldehyde used as an antiseptic, or preservative.

format [för'mat] *n* of books, etc., the size, form, shape in which they are issued.

former [förm'ér] *adj* before in time; past; first mentioned (of two).—*adv* **form'erly.**

formic [för'mik] *adj* of formic acid.—*n* **formic acid**, a colorless pungent liquid (CH₂O₂) found esp in ants and many plants, used chiefly in textile manufacture.—*n* **for'micary**, an ant nest.

formidable [för'mi-dà-bl] *adj* causing fear; redoubtable; difficult to deal with.—*adv* **for'midably.**

formula [förm'ū-la] *n* a prescribed form; a formal statement of doctrines; a list of ingredients, as for a prescription or recipe; a fixed method according to which something is to be done.—*pl* **form'ūlas, formulae** [form'ū-lē]—*ns* **formularizā'tion, formūlā'tion.**—*vst* **form'ūlāte**, to reduce to or express in a formula.

fornicate [för'ni-kāt] *vi* to commit fornication—*ns* **fornicā'tion**, sexual intercourse outside marriage.

forsake [för-sāk'] *vt* to desert; to give up.—*pr p* forsāking; *pt* **forsook'**; *pt p* **forsāk'en.**

forsooth [för-sōōth'] *adv* in truth, certainly, used ironically.

forswear [för-swār'] *vt* to renounce under oath.—*vi* to swear falsely.—*pt* **forswore'**; *pt p* **forswōrn'.**

fort [fört, fôrt] *n* a fortified place for military defense.

forte¹ [fört] *n* that in which one excels.

forte² [för'te] *adj, adv* (*mus*) loud.—*superl* **fortis'simo**, very loud.

forth [förth, fôrth,] *adv* forward; onward; out; into the open; progressively.—*adj* **forth'coming**, about to appear; readily available.—*adv* **forth'right**, straightforward.—*adv* **forth-with'**, immediately.

fortify [för'ti-fī] *vt* to strengthen physically, emotionally, etc.; to strengthen against attack, as with forts; to support.—*pt p* **for'ti-fied.**—*ns* **fortificā'tion.**

fortitude [för'ti-tūd] *n* courage in endurance.

fortnight [för'nīt] *n* (*Brit*) two weeks or fourteen days.—*adj, adv* **fort'nightly**, once a fortnight.

fortress [för'tres] *n* a fortified place.

fortuitous [för-tū'i-tus] *adj* happening by chance.—*adv* **fortū'itously.**—*ns* **fortū'itousness, fortū'ity.**

fortune [för'tūn, -chún] *n* whatever comes by chance or luck; the arbitrary ordering of events; prosperity, success; riches; wealth.—*adj* **for'tunāte**, having good luck.—*adv* **for'tunātely.**—*ns* **for'tunetell'er**, one who professes to foretell someone's fortune.

forty [för'ti] *adj n* four times ten, symbol for this (40, XL, xl).—Also *n* **for'ty-five**, a .45 caliber handgun, usu. written .45.

forum [fō'-, fö'rum] *n* the marketplace in Rome; an assembly, program or meeting to discuss topics of public concern.

forward [för'wárd] *adj* at, toward, or of the front; advanced; onward; prompt; bold; presumptuous; of or for the future.—*vt* to promote; to send on.—*adv* toward the front; ahead.—*adv* **for'wardly.**—*n* **for'wardness.**

fosse [fos] *n* (*fort*) a ditch or moat.

fossil [fos'il] *n* the petrified remains of an animal or vegetable found embedded in the strata of the earth's crust.—*adj* of or like a fossil; dug from the earth.—*vti* **foss'ilize**, to convert into or become changed to a fossil.

foster [fos'tèr] *vt* to bring up; to encourage.—*adj* having a specified standing in a family but not by birth (*a foster brother*).

foul [fowl] *adj* stinking, loathsome; extremely dirty; indecent; wicked; stormy; outside the limits set.—Also *adv.*—*vt* to make filthy; to dishonor; to obstruct (*grease fouls drains*); to entangle (a rope, etc.); to make a foul against, as in a game; (*baseball*) to bat (the ball) foul.—*vi* to be or become fouled.—*n* (*sports*) a hit, blow, move, etc. that is foul.—*ns* **foulness.**

foulard [fool'ard] *n* a lightweight silk, usu. decorated with a printed pattern.

found² [fownd] *vt* to set on something solid; to bring into being; to establish (as an institution) often with provision for future maintenance.—*ns* **foundation**, an endowment for an institution; such an institution; the base of a house, wall, etc.

founder, one that founds or establishes; **founding father**, an originator of an institution or movement.

found³ [fownd] *vt* to melt and pour (metal) into a mold.—*ns* **found'er**, one who founds metal, esp a typefounder; **found'ry.**

founder [fownd'ér] *vi* to subside, to collapse; (of a ship) to fill with water and sink; to go lame.—*vt* to cause to founder.

fount [fownt] *n* a spring of water; a source.

fountain [fownt'in, -ĕn] *n* a natural spring of water; a source; an artificial jet or flow of water; the basin where this flows; a reservoir, as for ink.

four [för, fôr] *adj, n* one more than three; the symbol for this (4, IV, iv); the fourth in a series or set; something having four units as members (as *a four-oared boat, a four-cylinder engine*).—*adj* **fourfold**, having four units or members; being four times as great or as many.—*n* **four-in-hand**, a necktie with long overlapping ends; a team of horses driven by one person; a vehicle drawn by such a team.

fourteen [för'tēn] (when used absolutely, förtēn') *adj, n* four and ten.—*adj* **fourteenth**, the last of fourteen.

fourth [förth] *adj* last of four; being one of four equal parts.

fowl [fowl] *n* a bird; any of the domestic birds used as food, as the chicken, duck, etc.; the flesh of these birds.—*ns* **fowl'er, fowl'ing-piece**, a light gun for small-shot.

fox [foks] *n* any of various small, alert mammals of the dog family; the fur of the fox; a sly, crafty person; **fox'hole**, a pit dug in the ground as a protection against enemy fire; **fox'-hound**, any of various large swift powerful hounds of great endurance used in hunting foxes; **fox'terr'ier**, any of a breed of small lively terriers formerly used to dig out foxes; **fox'trot**, a dance for couples in 4⁄4 time.—*adj* **foxy.**

foyer [foy'er, fwä'yā] *n* an anteroom; an entrance hallway, as in a hotel or theater.

fracas [frak'ä, frä-kä'] *n* uproar; a noisy quarrel.

fraction [frak'sh(ò)n] *n* a small part, amount, etc.; (*math*) a quantity less than a whole, expressed as a decimal or with a numerator and denominator.

fractious [frak'shús] *adj* ready to quarrel; peevish.

fracture [frak'tyúr, -chùr] *n* the breaking of any hard body; the breaking of a bone.—*vt* to break.

fragile [fraj'íl, fraj'il] *adj* easily broken; frail; delicate.—*n* **fragil'ity**, the state of being fragile.

fragment [frag'ment] *n* a piece broken off; an unfinished portion; an extant portion of something of which the rest has been destroyed or lost; **frag'mentary.**

fragrant [frāg'ránt] *adj* sweet-scented.—*ns* **frā'grance.**—*adv* **frā'grantly.**

frail [frāl] *adj* very easily shattered; of weak health or physique; morally weak.—*ns* **frail'ness, frail'ty.**

frame [frām] *vt* to form according to a pattern; to construct; to put into words; to enclose (a picture) in a border; to falsify evidence against (an innocent person).—*n* something composed of parts fitted together and united; physical makeup of an animal, esp a human body; the framework of a house; the structural case enclosing a window, door, etc.; an ornamental border, as around a picture; **frame-up**, an act in which someone is framed; **framework**, a structural frame; a basic structure (as of ideas); frame of reference.

franc [frangk] *n* a unit of money in France, Belgium, and Switzerland.

franchise [fran'chīz, -shīz, -chiz] *n* a privilege or right granted; the right of voting.

Franciscan [fran-sis'kán] *n* a member of the Order of Friars Minor founded by St Francis of Assisi in 1209.

frangible [fran'ji-bl] *adj* easily broken.

frank [frangk] *adj* free in expressing oneself; clinically evident.—*vt* to send (mail) free of postage.—*n* the right to send mail free; a mark indicating this right.—*n* **frank'ness.**

Frankenstein [frangk'en-stīn] *n* a work that ruins its originator.

frankincense [frangk'in-sens] *n* a fragrant gum resin.

frantic [fran'tik] *adj* mad; furious, wild.—*advs* **fran'tically, fran'ticly.**

frappé, frappe [fra'pā, frap] *n* a partly frozen drink.

fraternal [fra-tûr'nál] *adj* belonging to a brother or brethren; brotherly.—*adv* **frater'nally.**—*vi* **frat'ernize,** to associate as brothers; to seek brotherly fellowship. **frater'nity,** the state of being brethren; a society formed on a principle of brotherhood.

fratricide [frat'ri-sīd] *n* one who kills his brother; the murder of a brother.—*adj* **frat'-ricīdal.**

fraud [fröd] *n* deceit; (*law*) intentional deception; imposter.—*adj* **fraud'ulent.**—*n* **fraud'ulence.**

fraught [fröt] *adj* filled or loaded (with).

fray [frā] *n* a conflict; a brawl.

fray [frā] *vt* to wear off by rubbing; to ravel out the edge of.—*vi* to become frayed.

freak¹ [frēk] *n* a whim; an unusual happening; any abnormal animal, person, or plant.—*adj* **freak'ish.**

freckle [frek'l] *vti* to make or become spotted with freckles.—*n* a small, brownish spot on the skin.

free [fre] *adj* not under the control or power of another; having liberty; independent; able to move in any direction; not burdened by obligations; not confined to the usual rules (*free verse*); not exact (*a free translation*); generous (*a free spender*); frank; with no cost or charge; exempt from taxes, duties, etc.; clear of obstruction (*a free road*); not fastened (*a rope's free end*).—*adv* without cost; in a free manner.—*vt* to release from bondage or arbitrary power; to clear of obstruction, etc.—*pr p* **free'ing;** *pt p* **freed.**—*adv* **free'ly.**—**free'board,** the distance between the waterline and the freeboard deck of a ship; **free'dom,** being free, **free flight',** the flight of a rocket after the fuel supply has been used up or shut off.—*adj* **free'hand,** done without mechanical aids or devices (*a freehand drawing*).—Also *adv.*—*ns* **free hand',** freedom of action or decision; **free'lance,** a soldier available for hire; one who acts independently without regard to party lines; one who pursues a profession without long-term commitment to any employer.—*vi* **freeload',** to impose upon another's hospitality; **free'masonry, free' port,** a port where goods are received and shipped free of customs duty; **free'stone,** a peach etc in which the pit does not cling to the pulp; **free'think'er,** one who rejects authority in religion; a rationalist; **free trade',** trade based on the unrestricted international exchange of goods with tariffs used only as a source of revenue; **free will',** voluntary choice or decision; freedom of human beings to make choices that are not determined by prior causes or by divine intervention; **free world',** the part of the world where democracy and capitalism or moderate socialism rather than totalitarian systems prevail.

freebooter [frē'bōōt-êr] *n* a pirate; a plunderer.

freesia [fre'zhá] *n* any of a genus of the iris.

freeze [frēz] *vi* to be formed into, or become covered by ice; to become very cold; to be damaged or killed by cold; to become motionless; to be made speechless by strong emotion; to become formal and unfriendly.—*vt* to harden into ice; to convert from a liquid to a solid with cold; to make extremely cold; to act toward in a stiff and formal way; to act on (as. destructively by frost; to anesthetize by cold; to fix (prices, etc.) at a given level by authority; to make (funds, etc.) unavailable to the owners by authority.—*pr p* **freez'ing;** *pt* **froze;** *pt p* **frozen; freeze'-frame',** a frame of a motion-picture or television film that is repeated to give the illusion of a static picture; **freez'ing point,** the temperature at which a liquid solidifies.

freight [frāt] *n* the transportation of goods by water, land, or air; the cost for this; the goods transported.—*vt* to load with freight; to send by freight.—*ns* **freight'age; freight'er.**

French [french] *adj* of France, its people, culture, etc; **french curve',** a template used for drawing curved lines; **french fries,** strips of potato fried in deep fat; **French horn,** orches-

---

tral brass instrument with a narrow conical tube wound twice in a circle, funnel-shaped mouthpiece, and a flaring bell.

frenzy [fren'zi] *n* a violent excitement; paroxysm of madness.—*adj* **fren'zied.**

frequent [frē'kwènt] *adj* coming or occurring often.—*vi* [frē-kwent'] to visit often; to resort to.—*ns* **frē'quency.**—*adj* frequent'ative (*gram*), denoting the frequent repetition of an action.—*adv* **frē'quently.**

fresco [fres'kō] *n* a painting executed on walls covered with damp freshly-laid plaster.—*vt* to paint in fresco.

fresh [fresh] *adj* recently made, grown, etc. (*fresh coffee*); not salted, pickled, etc.; not spoiled; lively, not tired; not worn, soiled, faded, etc.; new, recent; inexperienced; cool and refreshing; (of wind) brisk; (of water) not salt.—Also *adv*—*n* an increased flow or rush (as of water); a stream of fresh water running into fresh water.—*vi* **freshen.**—*adv* **freshly;** freshness.—*adj.*

fret¹ [fret] *vti* to eat into; to wear away or roughen by rubbing; to irritate or be irritated.—*adj* **fret'ful,** peevish.

fret² [fret] *n* a running design of interlacing small bars.—*vt* to furnish with frets.—*n* **fret'saw,** a saw with a narrow blade and fine teeth held under tension in a frame.—*n* **fret'work,** ornamental carving or fancywork consisting of a combination of frets.

friable [frī'á-bl] *adj* easily crumbled.—*n* **friabil'ity.**

friar [frī'ár] *n* a member of a mendicant order.—*n* **frī'ary,** a monastery of friars.

fricassee [frik-a-sē'] *n* a dish made of fowl, rabbit, etc. cut into pieces and cooked in sauce.

friction [frik'sh(ò)n] *n* a rubbing of one object against another; conflict, as because of differing opinions; the resistance to motion of things that touch.—*adj* **frict'ional.**

Friday [frī'dā] *n* the sixth day of the week.

friend [frend] *n* a person whom one knows well and is fond of; an ally, supporter, or sympathizer.—*adj* **friend'less.**—*adj* **friend'ly.**—*ns* **friend'liness; friend'ship,** attachment from mutual esteem; friendly assistance.

frieze [frēz] *n* a decorative band along the top of the wall of a room.

frigate [frig'át] *n* a warship smaller than a destroyer used for escort, antisubmarine, and patrol duties.

fright [frīt] *n* sudden fear; alarm; something unsightly.—*vs* **fright, fright'en,** to make afraid.—*adj* **fright'ful.**—*n* **fright'fulness.**

frigid [frij'id] *adj* extremely cold; not warm or friendly; sexually unresponsive.—*n* **frigid'ity.**—*adv* **frig'idly.**

frill [fril] *vt* to furnish with a frill or frills.—*n* any superfluous ornament; a ruffle.

fringe [frinj] *n* a border of loose threads; an outer edge; marginal or minor part.—*vt* to be or make a fringe for.—*adj* at the outer edge; additional; minor.

frippery [frip'ėr-i] *n* cheap, gaudy clothes.

frisk [frisk] *vi* to gambol; to leap playfully. **frisk'y.**—*adv* **frisk'ily.**

frith [frith] *see* **firth.**

fritter¹ [frit'ėr] *n* a piece of fruit or meat fried in batter.

fritter² [frit'ėr] *vt;* to break into fragments.

frivolous [friv'ó-lús] *adj* trifling; silly.—*n* **frivol'ity.**

frizz [friz] *vti* to form into, or to be or become, small short crisp curls.—*n* hair that is frizzed.

frizzle² [friz'l] *vti* to sizzle, as in frying.

fro [frō] *adv* away; back; used in the phrase *to and fro.*

frock [frok] *n* a robe worn by friars, monks, etc.; a dress.—*n* **frock' coat,** a double-breasted full-skirted coat for men.

frog¹ [frog] *n* any of numerous tailless web-footed amphibians.

frog² [frog] *n* a V-shaped band of horn on the under-side of a horse's hoof.

frog³ [frog] *n* on a railway or a tramway, a structure in the rails allowing passage across, or to, another line.

frolic [frol'ik] *n* a lively party or game; merriment, fun.—*vi* to play wild pranks or merry tricks; to gambol.

from [from] *prep* beginning at, starting with (*from noon to midnight*); out of (*from her purse*); originating with (*a letter from me*); out of the possibility or use of (*kept from going*).

frond [frond] *n* (*bot*) a large leaf with many divisions, esp of a palm or fern.—*adj* **frond'ed.**

front [frunt] *n* outward behavior; (*inf*) an appearance of social standing, etc.; the part facing forward; the first part; a forward or leading position; the land bordering a lake, street, etc.; the advanced battle area in warfare; a person or group used to hide another's activity.—*adj* at, to, in, on, or of the front.—*vti* to face; to serve as a front (for).—*n* **front'age,** the front part of a building.—*adj* **front'al,** of or belonging to the forehead or a front.

frontier [frunt'-ēr'] *n* the border between two countries.

frontispiece [frunt'i-spēs] a picture in front of a book before the textual matter.

frost [frost] *n* the process of freezing; temperature at or below freezing point; frozen dew; coldness of manner.—*vt* to cover as if with frost, esp to put icing on (a cake); to give a frostlike opaque surface to (glass); **frost'bite,** injury to a part of the body by exposure to cold.—*adj* **frost'y.**—*adv* **frost'ily.**

froth [froth] *n* foam; foaming saliva; frivolity; chatter.—*vi* to foam.—*adj* **froth'y.**—*adv* **froth'ily.**—*n.*

froward [frō'wård] *adj* perverse.—*adv* **frō'wardly.**

frown [frown] *vi* to wrinkle the brow as in anger or concentration; to regard with displeasure or disapproval (*with* **upon**).

frowzy [frow'zi] *adj* dirty and untidy; unkempt.

fructify [fruk'ti-fī] *vti* to bear or cause to bear fruit.—*ns* **fructifica'tion.**

frugal [frōō'gål] *adj* economical in the use of resources; inexpensive, meager.—*n* **frugality.**—*adv* **fru'gally.**

frugiv'orous [frōō-jiv'ór-us] *adj* feeding on fruit.

fruit [frōōt] *n* a product of plant growth (as grain, vegetables, cotton, etc.); an edible plant structure containing the seeds inside a juicy pulp; (*bot*) the seed-bearing part of any plant; the result or product of any action.—*vt* to cause to bear fruit.—*vi* to bear fruit.—*adj* **fruit'ful.**—*n* **fruit'fulness.**—*adj* **fruit'less.**—*adj* **frui'ty.**

fruition [frōō-ish'(ó)n] *n* the bearing of fruit; a coming to fulfillment, realization.

frumenty [frōō'men-ti] *n* food made of hulled wheat boiled in milk.

frump [frump] *n* a plain and dowdy woman.

frustrate [frus-trāt'] *vt* to cause to have no effect; to prevent from achieving a goal or gratifying a desire.—*n* **frustrā'tion.**

frustum [frus'tum] *n* a slice of a solid body; the part of a cone or pyramid between the base and a plane parallel to it, or between two planes.

fry[1] [frī] *vti* to cook over direct heat usu. in hot fat.—*n* a social gathering at which food is fried and eaten.—*n pl* **fries,** fried potatoes.

fry[2] [frī] *n* recently hatched fishes.—**small fry,** persons of little importance.

fuchsia [fū'shi-a] *n* any of a genus of decorative shrubs.

fuddle [fud'l] *vt* to make drunk; to make confused.—*vi* to take part in a drinking bout.

fudge [fuj] *n* a soft candy made of butter, milk, sugar, flavoring, etc.—*vi* to refuse to commit oneself; to cheat.—*vt* to fake; to fail to come to grips with.—*interj* nonsense!

fuel [fū'ėl] *n* anything burned to supply heat and power; material from which atomic energy may be obtained.

fug [fug] *n* a hot, stuffy atmosphere.

fugacious [fū-gā'shùs] *adj* fugitive; fleeting.—*ns* **fugā'ciousness, fugac'ity** [-gas'i-ti].

fugitive [fūj'i-tiv] *adj* fleeing, as from danger or justice; apt to flee away; fleeting.—*one who flees.

fugue [fūg] *n* polyphonic musical composition with theme taken up successively by different voices.

fulcrum [ful'krum] *n* (*mech*) the fixed point on which a lever moves.—*pl* **ful'crums, ful'cra.**

fulfill, fulfil [fŏŏl-fil'] *vt* to carry out; to do; to satisfy; to bring to an end, complete.—*n* **fulfill'ment.**

fulgent [ful'jėnt] *adj* shining; bright.—*n* **ful'gency.**

fulgurant [ful'gū-rant] *adj* flashing like lightning.

fuliginous [fū-lij'i-nùs] *adj* sooty; dusky.

full[1] [fŏŏl] *adj* having all that can be contained; having eaten all one wants; having a great number (of); complete; having reached to greatest size, extent, etc.—*n* the greatest amount, extent, etc.—*adv* completely, directly, exactly.—*adv* **full'y,** thoroughly; at least. **full'-blown,** in full bloom; matured. **full'-ness, ful'ness,** the state of being full.—*adjs* **full'-out,** at full power; total.

full[2] [fŏŏl] *vt* to shrink and thicken (wool cloth).—*ns* **full'er,**

one that fulls cloth; **fuller's earth,** a soft earth or clay, used in fulling cloth.

fulmar [fŏŏl'mär, -mår] *n* an arctic seabird.

fulminate [ful'min-āt] *vi* to thunder or make a loud noise; to issue decrees with violence or threats; to inveigh (against).—*vt* to cause to explode; to send forth, as a denunciation.—*n* **fulminā'tion.**

fulsome [fŏŏl'sum, ful'sum] *adj* gross; offensive to smell or other sense; disgustingly fawning.

fulvous [ful'vus] *adj* deep or dull yellow, tawny.

fumble [fum'bl] *vi* to grope about awkwardly; to use the hands awkwardly.

fume [fūm] *n* smoke or vapor, esp if offensive or suffocating.—*vi* to give off fumes; to show anger.

fumigate [fūm'i-gāt] *vt* to expose to fumes, esp to destroy pests.—*ns* **fūmigā'tion.**

fun [fun] *n* what provides amusement and enjoyment.

funambulate [fū-nam'bū-lāt] *vi* to walk on a rope.

function [fungk'sh(ó)n] *n* activity proper to anything; duty peculiar to any office; a ceremony or formal entertainment; a thing so connected with another that any change in the one produces a corresponding change in the other.—*vi* to perform a function; to act, operate.—*adj* **func'tional,** regard to the purpose which it is to serve (as a building).—*ns* **func'tionary,** one who discharges a duty or holds an office.

fund [fund] *n* a supply that can be drawn upon; a sum of money set aside for a purpose; (*pl*) ready money.—*vt* to provide funds for; to put or convert into a long-term debt that bears interest.

fundamental [fun-då-ment'ål] *adj* basic; essential, primary.—*n* that which serves as a groundwork; an essential.—*ns* **funda'ment, fundament'alism,** belief in the literal truth of the Bible.

funeral [fū'nėr-ål] *n* the ceremony connected with burial or cremation.—*adj* pertaining to or used at a funeral.—*adj* **fūnēr'eal** [-ē-ål], pertaining to or suiting a funeral; dismal, mournful.

fungus [fung'gus] *n* any of a major group of lower plants, as molds, mildews, mushrooms, yeasts, etc. that lack chlorophyll, and reproduce by spores.—*pl* **fungi** [fun'jī].

funicular [fun-ik'yulår] *n* a cable railway ascending a mountain.

funk [fungk] *n* panic; one who funks.—*vti* to shrink through fear; to shirk.

funnel [fun'l] *n* a passage for the escape of smoke, etc.; a vessel, usually a cone ending in a tube, for pouring fluids into bottles, etc.

funny [fun'i] *adj* causing laughter; perplexing, odd.—*adv* **funn'ily.**

fur [fûr] *n* the thick, soft, fine hair of certain animals; their skins with the hair attached; a garment of fur; a fur-like coating on the tongue; the thick pile of a fabric (as chenille).—*vt* to line with fur; to coat.—*vi* to become coated.

furbelow [fûr'bē-lō] *n* a plaited border or flounce.

furbish [fûr'bish] *vt* to polish, to burnish, to renovate.

furcation [fûr-kā'shùn] *n* something that is branched, a fork; the act or process of branching.

furious [fū'ri-ùs] *adj* full of fury; violent.—*adv* **fū'riously.**—*n* **fū'riousness.**

furl [fûrl] *vt* to roll up (a sail, flag, etc.) tightly and make secure.

furlong [fûr'long] *n* 220 yards, one-eighth of a mile.

furlough [fûr'lō] *n* leave of absence, esp for military personnel.

furnace [fûr'nis] *n* an enclosed structure in which heat is produced, as by burning fuel.

furnish [fûr'nish] *vt* to fit up or supply completely, or with what is necessary; to supply (a person with).—*n* **fur'nisher.**

furniture [fûr'ni-tyûr, -chûr] *n* the things in a room, etc. which equip it for living, as chairs, beds, etc.

furor [fū'rör] *n* fury, frenzy; widespread enthusiasm.

furrow [fur'ō] *n* the trench made by a plow; a groove; a wrinkle.—*vti* to form furrows in; to wrinkle.

further[1] [fûr'THėr] *adv* at or to a greater distance or degree; in addition.—*adj* more distant; additional.—*adv* **fur'thermore,** moreover, besides.—*adj* **fur'thermost**—*adv* **fur'thest.**

further[2] [fûr'THėr] *vt* to help forward, promote.—*n* **fur'therance,** a helping forward.

furtive [fûr′tiv] *adj* stealthy; secret.—*adv* **fur′tively.**—*n* **fur′tiveness.**

fury [fû′ri] *n* rage; violent passion; madness.

furze [fûrz] *n* gorse.—*adj* **furz′y**, overgrown with furze.

fuscous [fus′kùs] *adj* of any color averaging brownish gray.

fuse [fûz] *vti* to melt or be melted; to join as if by melting together.—*n* a tube or wick filled with combustible material for setting off an explosive charge; a bit of fusible metal inserted as a safeguard in an electric circuit.—*adj* **fū′sible.**—*ns* **fūsibil′ity; fū′sion.**

fusee [fû-zē′] *n* the spindle in a watch or clock on which the chain is wound; a match with long, oval head for outdoor use; a red signal flare used esp for protecting stalled trains and trucks.

fuselage [fûz′èl-ij or -äzh] *n* the body of an airplane.

fusel oil [fû′zl-oil] *n* any oily liquid occurring in insufficiently distilled liquors used esp as a source of alcohol and as a solvent.

fusil [fû′zil] *n* a flint-lock musket.—*ns* **fusilier′, fusileer′**, formerly a British soldier armed with a fusil; **fusillade** [-äd′], simultaneous or continuous discharge of firearms.

fuss [fus] *n* excited activity, bustle; a nervous state; (*inf*) a quarrel; (*inf*) a showy display of approval.—*vi* to worry over trifles; to whine, as a baby.—*adj* **fuss′y.**—*n* **fuss′iness.**—*adv* **fuss′ily.**

fustian [fust′yàn] *n* kinds of twilled cotton fabric having a pile face; a pompous and unnatural style of writing or speaking, bombast.

fustic [fus′tik] *n* the wood of a tropical American tree, yielding a yellow dye (*old fustic*).

fustigate [fus′ti-gāt] *vt* to cudgel; to criticize severely.—*n* **fustigā′tion.**

futile [fû′til, fû′til] *adj* useless; frivolous.—*adv* **fū′tilely.**—*n* **fūtil′ity**, uselessness.

futon [fōō′ton] *n* a thick cotton mattress.

future [fût′yùr, -chùr] *adj* about to be; that is to come.—*ns* **fût′ûrism**, a movement in art, music, and literature begun in Italy about 1909 marked by an effort to give formal expression to the energy of mechanical processes; a point of view that finds meaning or fulfillment in the future; **fût′ûrist; futur′ity.**

fuzz [fuz] *n* fine light particles of fiber (as of down or fluff); a blurred effect; fluff; (*slang*) police.—*vi* to fly off in minute particles; to become blurred.—*adj* **fuzz′y.**

G

gab [gab] *n* idle talk.—*vi* to talk in a rapid or thoughtless manner, chatter.

gabble [gab′l] *vti* to talk or utter rapidly or incoherently; to utter inarticulate or animal sounds.

gabardine [gab′er-dēn] *n* a firm cloth of wool, rayon, or cotton.

gaberdine [gab′er-dēn] *n* a loose coat worn by Jews; a garment, esp a raincoat, of gabardine.

gable [gā′bl] *n* the triangular wall enclosed by the sloping ends of a ridged roof.

gad [gad] *vi* to rove restlessly or idly (*often with* **about**).—*n* **gad′about.**

gadfly [gad′flī] *n* any of various flies that bite or annoy livestock.

gadget [gaj′èt] *n* any small ingenious device.

Gael [gāl] *n* one whose language is Gadhelic, esp a Scottish Highlander.—*adj* **Gaelic** [gāl′ik, also gal′ik].—*n* the language of Ireland and that of the Scottish Highlands.

gaff [gaf] *n* a spear or spearhead for taking fish or turtles; a butcher's hook; the spar to which the head of a fore-and-aft sail is bent.

gaffe [gaf] *n* a social blunder.

gag [gag] *vt* to cause to retch; to keep from speaking, as by stopping the mouth of.—*vi* to retch.—*n* something put over or into the mouth to prevent talking; any restraint of free speech; a joke.

gaga [gä′ä] *adj* fatuous; marked by wild enthusiasm.

gage [gāj] *n* a pledge; something thrown down as a challenge, as a glove.—*vt* to bind by pledge or security; to stake.

gaggle [gag′l] *n* a flock of geese when not in flight.

gaiety, gaily *see* **gay.**

gain [gān] *vt* to earn; to win; to attract; to get as an addition (esp profit or advantage); to make an increase in; to reach.—*vi* to make progress; to increase in weight.—*n* an increase esp in profit or advantage; an acquisition.—*adj* **gainful.**—*adv* **gainfully.**

gainsay [gān-sā′ gān′sā′] *vt* to contradict; to deny.

gait [gāt] *n* way or manner of walking or running.

gaiter [gāt′ér] *n* a covering for the lower leg fitting down upon the shoe.

gala [gā′la, gäla] *n* a celebration.

galantine [gal′án-tēn, -tin] *n* a cold dish of poultry, veal, etc., covered in aspic.

galaxy [gal′ak-si] *n* (usu. **Galaxy**) the Milky Way, any similar system of stars; any splendid assemblage.—*adj* **galactic**, of a galaxy or galaxies; huge.

gale [gāl] *n* a wind from 32 to 63 miles per hour.

galena [ga-lē′na] *n* native lead sulphide; a lead-gray mineral with metallic luster.

gall¹ [göl] *n* bile; something bitter or distasteful; bitter feeling; brazen boldness marked by impudence and insolence.

gall² [göl] *n* an abnormal growth on plant tissue produced by fungi, insect parasites, etc.

gall³ [göl] *n* a sore due to chafing.—*vt* to hurt by rubbing: to irritate.

gallant [gal′ànt] *adj* stately, imposing; brave; noble; polite and attentive to women.—*Also n* [gal-ànt′].—*adv* **gall′antly.**—*n* **gall′antry.**

galleon [gal′i-òn] *n* a large Spanish ship of the 15th and 16th centuries.

gallery [gal′ér-i] *n* a covered walk or porch open at one side; a long narrow outside balcony; an upper floor of seats, esp (in a theater); the occupants of the gallery; a body of spectators; a room or building for the exhibition of works of art.

galley [gal′i] *n* a long, low-built ship of ancient times with one deck, propelled by oars; the kitchen of a ship or airplane; (*printing*) a shallow tray for holding composed type; proof printed from such type.—*n* **gall′ey proof**, a galley.

galliard [gal′yärd] *n* a spirited dance popular in the 16th century.

Gallic [gal′ik] *adj* of ancient Gaul or its people; French.—*n* **gall′icism** [-is-izm], the use in another language of a French expression or idiom or a French trait.

gallinaceous [gal-in-ā′shùs] *adj* of or relating to an order of heavy-bodied largely terrestrial birds including pheasants, and fowl.

gallipot [gal′i-pot] *n* a small glazed pot, esp for medicine.

gallivant [gal-i-vant′] *vi* to go about in search of amusement.

gallon [gal′òn] *n* a unit of liquid measure comprising four quarts or 231 cubic inches.

gallop [gal′óp] *vti* to go or cause to go at a gallop—*n* the fastest gait of a horse, etc.; a succession of leaping strides.—*pr p, adj* **gall′oping.**

gallows [gal′ōz] *n* a wooden frame on which criminals are hanged.

galop [ga-lop′, gal′óp] *n* a lively dance; music for such a dance.

galore [ga-lōr′, -lör′] *adv* in abundance.

galosh [gä-losh′] *n* a high overshoe worn esp in snow.

galvanism [gal′vàn-izm] *n* electricity produced by chemical action.—*adj* **galvanic** [-van′-].—*vt* **gal′vanīze**, to apply an electric current to; to startle; to excite; to plate (metal) with zinc.—*ns* **galvanom′eter**, an instrument for measuring electric current.

gambit [gam′bit] *n* (*chess*) an opening in which a sacrifice is offered for the sake of an advantage.

gamble [gam′bl] *vi* to play games of chance for money; to take a risk for some advantage.—*vt* to risk in gambling, to bet.—*n* **gam′bler.**

gambol [gam′bl, -ból] *vi* to jump and skip about in play; to frisk.

game¹ [gām] *n* any form of play, amusement; activity or sport involving competition under rules; a single contest in such a competition; a scheme, a plan; wild birds or animals hunted for sport or food, the flesh of such animals.—*vi* to play for a stake.—*ns* **game′cock**, a specially bred rooster trained for cockfighting; **game′keeper**, a person who takes care of game birds and animals, as on an estate. —*adj* **gam′y, gam′ey,** having the strong flavor of cooked game; risqué.

game² [gām] *adj* lame.

gamete [gam′ēt, gam-ēt′] *n* a reproductive cell that unites with another to form the cell that develops into a new individual.

gamin [gam′in] *n* a street Arab.

gamma [gam′a] *n* third letter of the Greek alphabet. —**gamma rays,** strong electromagnetic radiation from a radioactive substance.

gamut [gam′ut] *n* the whole compass of a voice or instrument; the full extent of anything.

gander [gan′dėr] *n* an adult goose; a look.

gang [gang] *n* a number of persons associating together.

ganglion [gang′gli-ón] *n* a mass of nerve cells from which nerve impulses are transmitted. —*pl* **gang′lia.**

gangrene [gang′grēn] *n* death of soft body tissue when the blood supply is obstructed. —*adj* **gang′rēnous.**

gangway [gang′wā] *n* a passageway, esp an opening in a ship's side for loading, etc.; a gangplank.

gannet [gan′et] *n* any of several large fish-eating seabirds (family Sulidae).

gantry [gan′tri] *n* a framework, often on wheels, for a traveling crane; a wheeled framework with a crane, platforms, etc. for readying a rocket to be launched; a stand for barrels.

gaol, gaoler British, esp English, spellings of **jail, jailer.**

gap [gap] *n* an opening or breach; a passage.

gape [gāp] *vi* to open the mouth wide; to yawn; to stare with the mouth open. —*n* act of gaping; a wide opening.

gar [gar] *n* any of various fishes having an elongated body and a beaklike snout.

garage [ga-räzh′] *n* an enclosed shelter for automotive vehicles. —*vt* to put or keep in a garage. —*n* **garage sale,** a sale of unwanted household goods, held in a garage or other part of the house.

garb [gärb] *n* clothing, style of dress.

garbage [gär′bij] *n* food waste; unwanted or useless material; trash.

garble [gär′bl] *vt* to distort (a message, story, etc.) so as to mislead.

garden [gär′dn] *n* a piece of ground for growing herbs, fruits, flowers, or vegetables; a fertile, well-cultivated region; a public parklike place, usu. ornamented with plants and trees. —*vi* to make, or work in, a garden.

gardenia [gär-dē′ni-a] *n* any of a genus of tropical shrubs, with beautiful fragrant white or yellow flowers.

garfish [gär′fish] *n* gar.

gargantuan [gär-gan′tū-ån] *adj* enormous, prodigious.

gargle [gär′gl] *vti* to wash (the throat), preventing the liquid from going down by expelling air against it. —*n* a liquid for washing the throat.

gargoyle [gär′goil] a grotesquely carved figure; a person with an ugly face.

garish [gär′ish] *adj* showy, gaudy; glaring.

garland [gär′lånd] *n* a wreath of flowers or leaves; a book of selections in prose or poetry. —*vt* to deck with a garland.

garlic [gär′lik] *n* a bulbous herb cultivated for its compound bulbs used in cookery; its bulb.

garment [gär′mėnt] *n* any article of clothing.

garner [gär′nėr] *n* a granary; *vt* to store.

garnet [gär′net] *n* a semiprecious stone.

garnish [gär′nish] *vt* to decorate; to decorate (food) with something that adds color or flavor. —*n* something used to garnish food; **garniture,** an embellishment; a decoration.

garret [gar′et] *n* a room just under the roof of a house.

garrison [gar′i-s(ó)n] *n* troops stationed at a fort; a fortified place with troops. —*vt* to station (troops) in (a fortified place) for its defense.

garrotte, garotte [ga-rot′] *n* a method of execution by strangling with an iron collar; the iron collar used. —*vt* to execute or attack by such strangling. —*n* **garroter.**

garrulous [gar′ū-lus, -oo-lus] *adj* talkative. —*ns* **garrulity** [gar-(y)ōō′li-ti].

garter [gär′tėr] *n* a band used to support a stocking.

gas [gas] *n* airlike substance with the capacity to expand indefinitely and not liquify or solidify at ordinary temperatures; any mixture of flammable gases used for lighting or heating; any gas used as an anesthetic; any poisonous subst-

ance dispersed in the air, as in war; gasoline. —*adj* **gaseous,** having the form of or being gas; of or being related to gases; lacking substance or solidity; **gasbag,** an idle talker; **gasoline, gasolene,** a volatile, flammable liquid distilled from petroleum and used chiefly as a fuel in internal-combustion engines.

gash [gash] *vt* to cut deeply into. —*n* a deep, open cut.

gasp [gäsp] *vi* to catch the breath with effort. —*vt* to utter with gasps. —*n* the act of gasping.

gastric [gas′trik] *adj* of, in, or near the stomach —also **gas′tral.**

gastronomy [gas-tron′o-mi] *n* the art or science of good eating.

gastropod [gas′trōpôd] *n* any of a large class (Gastropoda) of mollusks (as snails) with a univalve shell or none and usu. with a distinct head bearing sense organs.

gat [gat] *n* (*slang*) a handgun.

gate [gāt] *n* a movable structure controlling passage through an opening in a fence or wall; a gateway; a movable barrier; a structure controlling the flow of water, as in a canal; the total amount or number of paid admissions to a performance. —*vt* to supply with a gate. —*ns* **gate′-crasher,** one who attends an affair without being invited or a performance without paying.

gather [gaTH′er] *vt* to bring together in one place or group; to get gradually; to collect (as taxes); to harvest; to draw close to something (*gathering her skirts*); to pucker fabric by pulling a thread or stitching; to infer. —*vi* to come together in a body; to cluster around a focus of attention; to swell and fill with pus.

Gatling gun [gat′ling gun] *n* an early machine gun invented by R. J. *Gatling* about 1861.

gauche [gōsh] *adj* clumsy; tactless; not planar.

gaucho [gow′chō] *n* a cowboy of the pampas of South America.

gaud [göd] *n* an ornament, a piece of finery. —*adj* **gaud′y,** showy; vulgarly bright. —*adv* **gaud′ily.** —*n* **gaud′iness.**

gauge [gāj] *n* measurement according to some standard or system; any device for measuring; the distance between rails of a railway; the size of the bore of a shotgun; the thickness of sheet metal, wire, etc. —*vt* to measure the size, amount, etc. of.

gaunt [gönt] *adj* excessively thin as from hunger or age; looking grim or forbidding.

gauntlet¹ [gönt′let] *n* a knight's armored glove; a long glove, often with a flaring cuff.

gauntlet² [gönt′let] *see* **gantlet.**

gauze [göz] *n* a very thin, loosely woven fabric, as of cotton or silk; a firm woven material of metal or plastic filaments. —*adj* **gauz′y.**

gave [gāv] *pt* of **give.**

gavel [gav′l] *n* a mallet used by a chairman's hammer.

gavotte [ga-vot′] *n* a lively dance of French peasant origin marked by rising of the feet.

gawk [gök] *vi* to stare at stupidly. —*adj* **gawk′y,** awkward, ungainly. —Also *n.*

gay [gā] *adj* joyous and lively; brilliant (*gay colors*); homosexual. —*n* **gai′ety.** —*adv* **gai′ly.**

gaze [gāz] *vi* to look steadily. —*n* a steady look.

gazebo [ga-zē′bō] *n* a belvedere.

gazelle [ga-zel′] *n* any of numerous small swift antelopes noted for their large, lustrous eyes.

gazette [ga-zet′] *n* a newspaper, now mainly in newspaper titles; (*Brit*) an official publication listing government appointments; legal notices, etc. —*n* **gazatteer′** [gaz-], a geographical dictionary.

gear [gēr] *n* clothing; equipment, esp for some task or activity; a toothed wheel designed to mesh with another; (*often pl*) a system of such gears meshed together to pass motion along; a specific adjustment of such a system (*high gear*); a part of a mechanism with a specific function. —*vt* to connect by or furnish with gears; to adapt (one thing) to conform with another (*to gear supply to demand*). —*ns* **gear′wheel,** a cogwheel. —**in gear,** connected to the motor; **out of gear,** not connected to the motor.

gecko [gek′ō] *n* any of a family of small lizards.

Geiger (-Müller) counter [gī′gėr (mūl′ėr) kown′tėr] an instrument for detecting and counting ionizing particles, as from radioactive sources.

geisha [gā′sha] *n* a Japanese girl trained as an entertainer to serve as a hired companion to men.

gelatin, gelatine [jel'a-tin] *n* a tasteless, odorless substance extracted by boiling bones, hoofs, etc., or a similar vegetable substance.—*vt* gelat'inīze.—*adj* gelat'inous.

geld [geld] *vt* to castrate, esp a horse.—*n* geld'ing, a castrated horse.

gelid [jel'id] *adj* icy cold.—*adv* gel'idly.—*n* gelid'ity.

gelignite [jel'ig-nīt] *n* a powerful explosive.

gem [jem] *n* any precious stone, esp when cut for use as a jewel; anything extremely valuable.

gender [jen'dèr] *n* (*gram*) the classification by which words are grouped as feminine, masculine, or neuter.

gene [jēn] *n* any of the complex chemical units in the chromosomes by which hereditary characteristics are transmitted.

genealogy [jēn-i-al'o-ji, or jen-] *n* a recorded history of one's ancestry; the study of family descent; lineage.—*adj* genealog'ical.—*n* geneal'ogist.

general [jen'er-ǎl] *adj* not local, special, or specialized; of or for a whole genus, relating to or covering all instances or individuals of a class or group; widespread, common to many; not specific or precise (*in general terms*); holding superior rank (*attorney general*).—*n* something that involves or is applicable to the whole; a commissioned officer ranking next below a general of the army or a general of the air force, a commissioned officer of the highest rank in the marine corps; **general'ity**, the quality or state of being general; a vague or inadequate statement.—*vti* gen'eralize, to talk (about something) in general terms.—*adv* gen'erally, widely; popularly; usually; not specifically.

generate [jen'er-āt] *vt* to bring into existence; to produce.—*n* generation, a body of living beings constituting a single step in a line of descent from an ancestor; the average period between generations; production as of electric current.—*adj* gen'erative, gen'erator, one that generates, esp a machine which changes mechanical energy to electrical energy.

generic, -al, generically *see* genus.

generous [jen'ėr-us] *adj* magnanimous; of a noble nature; willing to give or share; large, ample.—*adv* gen'erously.—*ns* gen'erousness, generos'ity.

genesis [jen'es-is] *n* the beginning, origin; **Genesis**, (*Bible*) 1st book of the Old Testament.

genetic, -al [jen-et'ik, -ǎl] *adjs* of or relating to the origin, development or causes of something; of or relating to genetics; **gene'tics**, the branch of biology dealing with heredity and variation in plants and animals.—*adv* gene'tically.—*n* genet'icist.

genial [jē'ni-ǎl] *adj* cheering; kindly, sympathetic; healthful.—*ns* gēnial'ity.—*adv* gē'nially.

genital [jen'i-tǎl] *adj* of reproduction or the sexual organs.—*n* genital'ia, the external organs of the reproductive system.—*npl* genitals, genitalia.

genitive [jen'i-tiv] *adj* (*gram*) of or belonging to the case expressing origin, possession, or similar relation.—*n* the genitive case.

genius [jēn'yus] *n* the particular spirit of a nation, place, age, etc.; natural ability, strong inclination (*with* for); one having extraordinary intellectual power.

genre [zhän'rè] *n* a distinctive type of category, esp of literary composition; a style of painting in which everyday objects are treated realistically.

genteel [jen-tēl'] *adj* polite or well-bred; now esp affectedly refined.—*adv* genteel'ly.—*n* genteel'ness.

gentile [jen'tīl] *n* anyone not a Jew; a heathen.

gentle [jen'tl] *adj* belonging to a family of high social station; refined, courteous; generous; kind; kindly; patient; not harsh or rough; gentil'ity, the gentry or their status.

gentleman [jen'tl-màn] *n* a man of good family and social standing; a courteous, gracious, and honorable man; (*pl*) polite term of address; **gent'lewoman**, a woman of noble or gentle birth; a lady.

gentry [jen'tri] *n* people of high social standing; formerly, landed proprietors not belonging to the nobility; people of a particular class or group.

genuflect [jen-ū-flekt'] *vi* to bend the knee in worship or respect.—*n* genūflex'ion (also **genūflec'tion**).

genuine [jen'ū-in] *adj* not fake or artificial, real; sincere.—*adv* gen'uinely.—*n* gen'uineness.

genus [jē'nus] *n* (*biol*) a taxonomic division of plants and

animals below a family and above a species; a class of objects divided into several subordinate species.

geo- [jē'ō] earth, world, forming words.

geocentric [jē-ō-sen'trik] *adj* viewed as from the center of the earth; having the earth as a center.

geode [jē'ōd] *n* a nodule of stone having a cavity lined with crystals; the cavity in a geode.

geodesy [jē-od'e-si] *n* a branch of applied mathematics that determines the exact positions of points and the figures and areas of large portions of the earth's surface, the shape and size of the earth, and the variations of terrestrial gravity and magnetism.

geography [jē-og'ra-fi] *n* the science that describes the earth and its life; the physical features of a region.—*n* geog'rapher.—*adjs* geograph'ic [-graf'-], -al.—*adv* geograph'ically.

geology [jē-ol'o-ji] *n* the science relating to the history and development of the earth's crust, its rocks and fossils.—*n* geol'ogist.—*adjs* geolog'ic, -al.—*adv* geolog'ically.—*vi* geol'ogize, to study geology.

geometry [jē-om'e-tri] *n* the branch of mathematics dealing with the properties, measurement, and relationships of points, lines, planes, and solids; *ns* geom'eter, geometri'cian [-shán] a specialist in geometry.—*adjs* geomet'ric, -al.—*adv* geomet'rically.

georgette [jōr-jet'] *n* a thin strong fabric woven from hard-twisted yarns to produce a dull pebbly surface.

georgic [jōrj'ik] *n* a poem dealing with agriculture.—*adj* of or relating to agriculture.

geranium [je-rān'i-um] *n* a genus (*Geranium*) of plants with seed-vessels similar in shape to a crane's bill.

gerfalcon *see* gyrfalcon.

germ [jûrm] *n* a bit of living matter capable of growth and development into an organism; any microscopic, disease-causing organism; an origin (*the germ of an idea*).—*n* germ'icide, any antiseptic, etc. used to destroy germs.—*vti*, germ'inate, to start developing; to sprout, as from a seed.—*n* germina'tion.

german [jûr'màn], **germane** [-mān] *adj* having the same parents or same grandparents.

German [jûr'man] *n* a native or inhabitant of Germany; the language of Germany, Austria, etc.

gerrymander [ger-, jer-i-man'dèr] *vt* to rearrange (voting districts) in the interests of a particular party or candidate.—Also *n*.

gest, geste [jest] *n* an exploit; a romance.

gestapo [ge-stä'pō] *n* the secret police in Germany under the Nazis.

gestate [jes-tāt'] *vt* to carry in the womb during the period from conception to birth; to conceive and develop slowly in the mind.

gesticulate [jes-tik'ū-lāt] *vi* to make vigorous gestures, esp when speaking.—*n* gesticulā'tion, act of making gestures in speaking; a gesture.

gesture [jes'tyùr, -chúr] *n* movement of part of the body to express or emphasize ideas, emotions, etc.

get [get] *vt* to come into the state of having; to receive; to obtain; to acquire; to go and bring; to catch; to persuade; to cause to be; to prepare (*get dinner*); (*inf*) (*with* have *or* has) to be obliged to (*he's got to go*); to possess; (*inf*) to strike, kill, baffle, defeat, etc.—*vi* to come; to go; to arrive; to come to be (*to get caught*); to manage or contrive (*to get to do something*).—*pr p* gett'ing; *pt p* got, gott'en.—as an auxiliary verb for emphasis in passive construction (*to get praised*).

geum [jē'um] *n* a genus (*Geum*) of the rose family; the Latin name for arens.

gewgaw [gū'gö] *n* a showy trifle; a bauble.

geyser [gī'zèr] *n* a spring from which columns of boiling water and steam gush into the air at intervals.

ghastly [gäst'li] *adj* terrifying, horrible; intensely disagreeable; ghostlike.

ghat [göt] *n* in India, a flight of steps at a river landing.

ghee [gē] *n* clarified butter.

gherkin [gûr'kin] *n* a small cucumber used for pickling; the immature fruit of the cucumber.

ghetto [get'ō] *n* a section of some European cities to which Jews were restricted; any section of a city in which members

of a minority group live, esp because of social, legal or economic pressure.

ghost [gōst] *n* the supposed disembodied spirit of a dead person, appearing as a shadowy apparition; a faint trace or suggestion; a false image in a photographic negative.—*adj* **ghostly,** of or related to apparitions.

ghoul [gōōl] *n* in oriental folklore, an evil spirit that robs graves and feeds on the dead; an Eastern demon that preys on the dead; a human being whose tastes or pursuits are equally grim or revolting.—*adj* **ghoul'ish.**

giant [jī'ánt] *n* a huge legendary manlike being of great strength; a person or thing of great size, strength, intellect, etc.

gibber [jib'ér] *vi* to utter senseless or inarticulate sounds.—*n* **gibberish** [gib'ér-ish].

gibbet [jib'et] *n* a gallows; a structure from which bodies of executed criminals were hung and exposed to public scorn.—*vt* to hang on a gibbet.

gibbon [gib'ón] *n* any of several small tailless apes of southeastern Asia and the East Indies.

gibbous [gib'us] *adj* of the shape of the moon or a planet when between half full and full.

giblets [jib'lets] *n pl* the edible viscera of a fowl.

giddy [gid'i] *adj* dizzy; that causes giddiness; whirling; light-headed; flighty.—*adv* **gidd'ily.**—*n* **gidd'iness.**

gift [gift] *n* something given; the act of giving; a natural ability.—*vt* to present with or as a gift.—*adj* **gift'ed,** having great natural ability.

gig [gig] *n* a light two-wheeled carriage; a long, light boat.

gigantic [jī-gan'tik] *adj* exceeding the usual or expected (as in size, force or prominence).—*adv* **gigan'tically.**

giggle [gig'l] *vi* to laugh with short catches of the breath, or in a silly manner.—*n* a laugh of this kind.

gigolo [jib'ō-lō] *n* a man paid to be a woman's escort.

gild [gild] *vt* to coat with gold leaf ; to give money to; to give a deceptively attractive appearance to.

gill¹ [gil] *n* an organ for breathing in water; the flap below the beak of a fowl.

gill² [jil] *n* a liquid measure equal to ¼ pint.

gillyflower [jil'i-flow-(è)r] *n* a name for various flowers that smell like cloves, esp a carnation.

gilt [gilt] *pt, pt p* of **gild.**—*n* **gilding.**—*adjs* **gilt-edge, gilt'-edged,** of the highest quality.

gimbals [jim'bálz] *n pl* a pair of rings so pivoted that one swings freely within the other, used to keep a ship's compass level. Also called a **gim'bal ring.**

gimcrack [jim'krak] *adj* showy but cheap and useless.—*n* a gimcrack thing.—*n* **gimcrackery.**

gimlet [gim'let] *n* a small tool for boring holes, with a screw point and a wooden crosspiece as handle.

gimp [gimp] *n* an ornamental flat braid or round cord used as trimming.

gin¹ [jin] *n* an alcoholic liquor distilled from grain and flavored with juniper berries.

gin² [jin] *n* a snare or trap; a machine, esp one for hoisting; a cotton gin.

ginger [jin'jér] *n* a tropical plant with fleshy rhizomes used as a flavoring and in medicine; the spice prepared by drying and grinding; (*inf*) vigor; a strong brown.—*adv* **gin'gerly.**—*ns* **ginger ale,** a carbonated soft drink flavored with ginger; **gin'-gerbread,** a cake flavored with ginger.

gingerly [jin'jér-li] *adv* with care or caution.

gingham [ging'ám] *n* a kind of cotton cloth, woven from colored yarns with stripes or checks.

gipsy *see* **gypsy.**

giraffe [ji-räf'] *n* a large cud-chewing mammal (*Giraffa camelopardus*) of Africa, the tallest living quadruped, with very long legs and neck.

gird [gûrd] *vt* to encircle or fasten with a belt; to surround; to prepare (oneself) for action.—*pt, pt p* **gird'ed** or **girt.**—*n* **gird'er,** a large wooden or steel beam for supporting joists, the framework of a building, etc.

girdle [gûrd'l] *n* a belt for the waist.

girl [gûrl] *n* a female child; a young woman.—*n* **girl'hood,** the state or time of being a girl.—*adj* **girlish,** of or like a girl.

girth [gûrth] *n* a band put around the belly of a horse, etc. to hold a saddle or pack; the circumference.

gist [jist] *n* the ground of a legal action; the main point or pith of a matter.

give [giv] *vt* to hand over as a present; to hand over; to hand over in or for payment; to pass (regards etc.) along; to act as host or sponsor of; to supply; to yield; to offer (*give advice*); to inflict (punishment, etc.); to sacrifice.—*vi* to bend, move, etc. from force or pressure; *pr p* **giv'ing;** *pt p* **gave.**—*n* capacity or tendency to yield to force or strain; the quality or state of being springy.

gizzard [giz'árd] *n* the muscular second stomach of a bird.

glacé [glä'sā] *adj* glossy, as silk; candied, as fruit.

glacial [glā'shi-ál] *adj* extremely cold; of or relating to glaciers or a glacial epoch.

glacier [glas'i-ér, -yèr (also glāsh'-)] *n* a large mass of snow and ice moving slowly down a mountain.

glacis [glās'is] *n* a gentle slope; a buffer state.

glad [glad] *adj* happy; causing joy; very willing; bright.—*vti* **gladd'en,** *adv* **glad'ly.**—*n* **glad'ness.**—*adj* **glad'some.**

glade [glād] *n* an open space in a wood.

gladiator [glad'i-ā-tór] *n* in ancient Rome, a professional combatant with men or beasts in the arena.—*adjs* **gladiātō'rial, glad'iatory.**

gladiolus [glad-i-ō'lus] *n* any of a genus of the iris family with swordlike leaves and tall spikes of funnel-shaped flowers.—**gladiol'i.**

glair(-e) [glār] *n* egg white used as varnish.

glamour, glamor [glam'ór] *adj* seemingly mysterious allure; bewitching charm.—*adj* **glam'orous.**

glance [glâns] *vi* to strike obliquely and go off at an angle; to flash; to look quickly.—*n* a glancing off; a flash; a quick look.

gland [gland] *n* any organ for secreting substances to be used in, or eliminated from, the body.—*adj* **gland'ūlar.**

glanders [gland'érz] *n* a contagious bacterial disease esp of horses, often fatal.

glare [glār] *n* a harsh uncomfortably bright light, esp painfully bright sunlight; an angry or fierce stare.—*vi* to shine with a steady, dazzling light; to stare fiercely.

glass [glas] *n* a hard brittle substance, usu. transparent, made by fusing silicates with soda, lime, etc.; glassware; a glass article, as a drinking container; (*pl*) eyeglasses or binoculars; the amount held by a drinking glass.—*adj* of or made of glass.—*vt* to equip with glass panes.—*adj* **glass'y.**

glaucoma [glow-kō'má] *n* a disease of the eye.

glaucous [glô'kus] *adj* pale yellow-green.

gleam [glēm] *vi* to glow or shine, transiently or not very brightly.—*n* a faint or moderate glow (of light); a transient show of some emotion, esp hope.—*n* **gleam'ing.**]

glean [glēn] *vti* to collect (grain left by reapers); to collect (facts, etc.) gradually.

glee [glē] *n* mirth and gaiety; delight; (*mus*) a song in parts.—*adj* **glee'ful,** merry.

glen [glen] *n* a narrow secluded valley.

glib [glib] *adj* speaking or spoken smoothly, to the point of insincerity; lacking depth and substance.—*adv* **glib'ly.**—*n* **glib'ness.**

glide [glīd] *vi* to slide smoothly and easily; (*aeronautics*) to descend with little or no engine power.—*n* a gliding; a disk or ball, as of nylon, under a furniture leg to provide a smooth surface.—*n* **glider,** one that glides; an engineless aircraft carried along by air currents.

glimmer [glim'ér] *vi* to give a faint, flickering light; to appear faintly.—Also *n.*

glimpse [glimps] *n* a brief, quick view; appearance; a momentary view.—*vi* to look quickly.—*vt* to get a glimpse of.

glint [glint] *vi* to shine, gleam, sparkle.—*vt* to reflect.—*n* a gleam.

glissade [glēs-äd'] *vi* to slide down a snow-covered slope without the aid of skis.

glisten [glis'n] *vi* to shine as light reflected from a wet or oily surface.

glister [glis'tèr] *vi* to glitter.

glitter [glit'ér] *vi* to sparkle with light; to be splendid; to be showy.—*n* sparkle; showiness.

gloaming [glōm'ing] *n* twilight, dusk.

gloat [glōt] *vi* to gaze exultingly, esp with a wicked or a malicious joy.

globe [glōb] *n* anything spherical or almost spherical; the earth, or a model of the earth.—*adjs* **glob'al**, worldwide; **glob'ose** [-ōs], spherical; **globular** [glob'ū-lár], spherical; made up of globules.—*ns* **glob'alism**, a policy, outlook, etc. that is worldwide in scope.

gloom [glōōm] *n* partial darkness; deep sadness.—*vi* to be or look sullen or dejected; to be cloudy or obscure.—*adj* **gloom'y**, dim or obscure; depressed in spirits.—*adv* **gloom'ily**.—*n* **gloom'iness**.

glorify [glō'-, glō'ri-fī] *vt* to make glorious, invest with glory; to advance the glory of (God); to extol, to honor; to transform (an ordinary thing) into something more splendid—to regard it, or to speak of it, in such a way.—*pt p* **glo'rified**.—*n* **glorificā'tion**.

glory [glō'-, glō'ri] *n* great honor or fame, or its source; adoration; great splendor; heavenly bliss.—*vi* to exult (*with* in).—*adj* **glō'rious**, noble, splendid; conferring renown.

gloss¹ [glos] *n* the shine of a polished surface; external show.—*vt* to give a shiny surface to; to hide (an error, etc.) or make seem right or inconsequential.—*adj* **gloss'y**, smooth and shining; highly polished.—*n* **gloss'iness**.

gloss² [glos] *n* a marginal or interlinear explanation of an unusual word; an explanation; a collection of explanations of words.—*vt* to comment or make explanatory remarks; to read a different sense into.—*n* **gloss'ary**, a collection of glosses.

glottis [glot'is] *n* the opening between the vocal cords in the larynx.

glove [gluv] *n* a covering for the hand, a baseball player's mitt; a boxing glove.—*vt* to cover with, or as with, a glove.

glow [glō] *vi* to shine with an intense heat; to burn without flame; to emit a steady light; to flush; to tingle with bodily warmth or with emotion; to be ardent.—*n* shining due to heat; steady, even light; warmth of feeling.—*n* **glow'worm**, a larva that emits light from the abdomen.

glower [glow'èr] *vi* to stare frowningly; to scowl.

glue [glōō'] *n* a sticky, viscous liquid made from animal gelatin, used as an adhesive.

glum [glum] *adj* sullen; gloomy.—*adv* **glum'ly**.

glume [glōōm] *n* a chaff-like bract which encloses the spikelet in grasses.

glut [glut] *vt* to gorge; to overstock (the market).

gluten [glōō'tèn] *n* a tenacious elastic protein substance, esp of wheat flour that gives cohesiveness to dough.—*adj* **glu'tinous**.

glutton [glut'(ȯ)n] *n* one who eats and drinks to excess; one who has a great appetite (eg for work); a wolverine.—*adj*, **glutt'onous**.

glycerin, glycerine [glis'èr-in, ēn] *n* the popular and commercial name for glycerol.

glycerol [glis'er-ōl] *n* a colorless, syrupy liquid made from fats and oils, used in making skin lotions, explosives, etc.

gnarl [närl] *vt* to twist into a state of deformity.—*adj* **gnarled**, (of tree trunks) full of knots; crabby in disposition.

gnash [nash] *vti* to grind (the teeth) in rage or pain.

gnat [nat] *n* any of various small, two-winged insects that bite or sting.

gnaw [nö] *vti* to bite away bit by bit; to torment, as by constant pain.

gneiss [nīs] *n* a granitelike rock formed by layers of quartz, mica, etc.—*adj* **gneiss'oid**, like gneiss.

gnome [nōm] *n* in folklore, a dwarf who dwells in the earth and guards its treasure.

gnomon [nō'mon] *n* an object that by the position or length of its shadow serves as an indicator, esp of the hour of the day.

Gnostic [nos'tik] *n* (*theology*) one of a sect, esp in early Christian times, who maintained that knowledge, not faith, was the way of salvation, claiming themselves to have superior knowledge of spiritual things.

gnu [nōō, nū] *n* either of two large African antelopes with an oxlike head and a horselike tail.

go [gō] *vi* to move on a course; to proceed; to act, sounds, as specified (*the balloon went 'pop'*); to result (*the game went badly*); to become (*to go mad*); to be accepted, valid; to leave, to depart; to die; to be allotted or sold; to be able to pass (through); to fit (into); to be capable of being divided (into); to belong.—*vt* to travel along; (*inf*) to put up with; (*inf*) to provide (bail) for an arrested person.—*n* a success; (*inf*) a try; (*inf*) energy.—*pl* **goes**.

goad [gōd] *n* a sharp-pointed stick, often shod with iron, for

driving oxen; a stimulus.—*vt* to drive with a goad; to irritate, annoy excessively.

goal [gōl] *n* the place at which a race, trip, etc. is ended; an end that one strives to attain; in some games, the place over or into which the ball or puck must go to score; the score made.

goat [gōt] *n* a cud-chewing mammal related to the sheep that has backward curving horns, short tail, and usu. straight hair; a lecherous man; (*inf*) a scapegoat.

gobbet [gob'et] *n* a mouthful; a lump to be swallowed.

gobble [gob'l] *vt* to eat greedily; to take eagerly (*often with* up); to read rapidly (*often with* up).—*vi* to make a noise in the throat, as a turkey.

goblet [gob'let] *n* a large drinking cup without a handle.

goblin [gob'lin] *n* in folklore, an evil or mischievous sprite.

goby [gō'bi] *n* of small sea fishes.

god [god] *n* any of various beings conceived of as supernatural and immortal, esp a male deity; an idol; a person or thing deified; **God**, in monotheistic religions, the creator and ruler of the universe.—*ns* **goddess**, a female god; a woman of great beauty, charm, etc.; **godfather**, male godparent; man having analogous relationship to an enterprise, field of activity, etc.; **godhead**, the state of being a god; **godhood**, the state of being a god.—*adjs* **godless**, irreligious; wicked; **god'ly**, devout; devoted to God; **god'parent**, a person who sponsors a child, as at baptism or confirmation, taking responsibility for its faith; **god'send**, anything that comes unexpectedly and when needed or desired, as if sent by God.—**God's acre**, a churchyard.

godwit [god'wit] *n* any of a genus of wading birds with a long bill, related to the snipes but resembling curlews.

goffer [gof'èr] *vt* to plait or crimp with a heated iron.—Also *n*.

goggle [gog'l] *vi* to stare with bulging eyes.—*npl* large spectacles, sometimes fitting snugly against the face, to protect the eyes.

goiter [goi'tèr] *n* an enlargement of the thyroid gland.

gold [gōld] *n* a malleable yellow metallic element (symbol Au, at wt 197.0; at no 79) used esp for coins and jewelry; a precious metal; money, wealth; a yellow color.—*adj* of, or like gold.—*ns* **gold'digger**, (*inf*) a woman who uses feminine charms to extract money or gifts from men.—*adj* **golden**, bright yellow; **golden eagle**, a large eagle; **golden rule**, a guiding principle; **golden section**, a proportion in which the ratio of the whole to the larger part is the same as the ratio of the larger part to the small; **gold leaf**, gold beaten into very thin sheets, used for gilding; **gold standard**, a monetary standard in which the basic currency unit equals a specified quantity of gold.

golf [golf, galf] *n* an outdoor game in which the player attempts to propel a small resilient ball with clubs around a turfed course with widely spaced holes in regular progression with the smallest number of strokes.—*ns* **gol'fer**; **golf course**, a tract of land for playing golf.

gonad [gon'ad] *n* (*biol*) an animal organ that produces reproductive cells; ovary or testis.

gondola [gon'do-la] *n* a long, narrow, black boat used on the canals of Venice; a cabin suspended under an airship or balloon; an enclosed car suspended from a cable used to transport persons esp skiers up a mountain.—*n* **gondolier** [-lēr'].

gonfalon [gon'fa-lon] *n* an ensign of princes or states, as in medieval Italy; a flag that hangs from a crosspiece or frame.

gong [gong] *n* a disk-shaped percussion instrument struck with a usu. padded hammer.

gonorrhea [gon-o-rē'a] *n* a contagious infection of the mucous membrane of the genital tract.

good [gōōd] *adj* having the proper qualities; beneficial; valid; healthy or sound; honorable; enjoyable, pleasant, etc.; skilled; considerable.—*comparative* **better**; *superlative* **best**.—*n* something good; benefit; something that has economic utility; good persons (*with* the).—*pl* personal property; cloth; wares, commodities.—*adv* (*inf*) well; fully.—*n*, *interj.*—**good-bye, good-by**, a concluding remark at parting; farewell.—*n* **Good Friday**, the Friday before Easter, commemorating the Crucifixion of Christ.—*adjs* **good-looking**, handsome; **goodly**, of pleasing appearance; ample; **goodwill**, benevolence; willingness.

goon [gōōn] (*slang*) a ruffian or thug; a stupid person.

goop [gōōp] *n* (*slang*) any sticky, semiliquid substance.

goose [gōōs] *n* a large, long-necked, web-footed bird (family Anatidae) related to the swans and ducks; its flesh as food; a female goose as distinguished from a gander; a foolish person.—*pl* **geese**.—*pl* **gooses**, a tailor's smoothing iron; **goose-flesh**, a roughening of the skin caused usu. by cold or fear; **goose step**, a stiff-legged marching step used by some armies when passing in review.

gooseberry [gōōs′ber-i] *n* the acid berry of a shrub (genus *Ribes*) related to the currant and used esp in jams and pies.

gore[1] [gōr, gör] *n* blood from a wound, esp clotted blood.—*adj* **gor′y**.

gore[2] [gōr, gör] *n* a tapering piece let into a garment to widen it.—*vt* to shape with gores; to pierce as with a spear or horns.

gorge [görj] *n* the throat; a ravine.—*vt* to swallow greedily; to glut.—*vi* to feed gluttonously.—*n* **gorg′et**, a piece of armor for the throat.

gorgeous [gör′jus] *adj* brilliantly colored; magnificent.—*n* **gor′geousness**.

gorgon [gör′gón] *n* one of three fabled female monsters of horrible and petrifying aspect; any ugly or formidable woman.—*adjs* **gor′gon**, **gorgō′nian**.

gorgonzola [gör-gón-zō′la] *n* a semihard blue-veined cheese made from cow's milk, with a rich flavor.

gorilla [gor-il′a] *n* an anthropoid ape of western equatorial Africa related to the chimpanzee but much larger.

gormandise [gör′mánd-iz] *vti* to eat like a glutton.

gorse [görs] *n* a spiny yellow-flowered European shrub.

goshawk [gos′hawk] *n* any of several long-tailed hawks with short rounded wings, esp a hawk.

gosling [goz′ling] *n* a young goose.

gospel [gos′pèl] *n* the message concerning Christ, the Kingdom of God, and salvation; **Gospel**, any of the first four books of the New Testament; anything proclaimed or accepted as the absolute truth.

gossamer [gos′á-mér] *n* very fine spider-threads which float in the air or form webs on bushes in fine weather; any very thin material.

gossip [gos′ip] *n* one who chatters idly about others; such talk.—*vi* to be a gossip.—*adj* **goss′ipy**.

Goth [goth] *n* any member of a Germanic people that conquered most of the Roman Empire in the 3d, 4th, and 5th century, AD.—*adj* **Goth′ic**; of a style of architecture with pointed arches, steep roofs, elaborate stonework, etc.; barbarous.—*n* German black letter type; a bold type style without serifs.

gouge [gowj, also gōōj] *n* a chisel with a hollow blade, for cutting grooves, or holes.—*vt* to scoop out, as with a gouge; to force out.

goulash [gōō′lash] *n* a beef or veal stew seasoned with paprika.

gourd [görd or gōōrd] *n* any trailing or climbing plant of a family (Cucurbitaceae) that includes the squash, melon, pumpkin, etc.; the fruit of one species or its dried, hollowed out shell, used as a cup, vessel, etc. or ornament.

gourmand [gōōr′mánd, -mä] *n* one who likes good food and drink, often to excess.

gourmet [gōōr-mä] *n* one who likes and is an excellent judge of fine foods and drinks.

gout [gowt] *n* an acute inflammation of the joints, esp in the great toe.—*adj* **gout′y**.

govern [guv′érn] *vti* to exercise authority over; to rule, to control; to influence the action of; to determine; (*grammar*) to require (a word) to be in a certain case.—*adj* **governable**.—*ns* **governance**, the action, function, or power of government; **governess**, a woman employed in a private home to teach and train the children; **government**, the exercise of authority over a state, organization, etc.; a system of ruling, political administration, etc.; those who direct the affairs of a state, etc.; **government′al**, of government.—*ns* **governor**, the elected head of any State of the US; one appointed to govern a province, etc.; a mechanical device for automatically controlling the speed of an engine.

gown [gown] *n* a loose outer garment, specifically a woman's formal dress, a nightgown, a long, flowing robe worn by clergymen, judges, scholars, etc.; a coverall worn in the operating room.

grab [grab] *vt* to seize or grasp suddenly; to appropriate unscrupulously; *pr p* **grabb′ing**.

grace [grās] *n* beauty or charm of form, movement, or expression; good will; favor; a delay granted for payment of an obligation; a short prayer of thanks for a meal.—*vt* to decorate; to dignify.—*adj* **grace′ful**, having beauty of form, movement, or expression.—*n* **grace′fulness**.—*adj* **grace′less**, lacking sense of what is proper; clumsy.—*adj* **gracious** [grā′shus] having or showing kindness, courtesy, etc.; compassionate; polite to supposed inferiors; marked by luxury, ease, etc. (*gracious living*).—*adv* **graciously**.—*n* **graciousness**.

grade [grād] *n* a stage or step in a progression; a degree in a scale of quality, rank, etc.; a group of people of the same rank, merit, etc.; the degree of slope; a sloping part; a mark or rating in an examination, etc.—*vt* to arrange in grades; to give a grade to; to make level or evenly sloping.—*ns* **graduation**, an arranging in grades, or stages; a gradual change in stages; a step in a graded series; **grad′ient**, the degree of.—*adj* **grad′ual**, taking place by degrees.

graduate [grad′yū-āt] *n* one who has completed a course of study at a school, college, or university; a receptacle marked with figures for measuring contents.—*adj* holding an academic degree or diploma; of or relating to studies beyond the first or bachelor's degree.

graft [graft] *n* a shoot or bud of one plant inserted into another, where it grows permanently; the transplanting of skin, bone, etc.; the getting of money or advantage dishonestly.

grail [grāl] *n* in medieval legend the cup used by Jesus at the Last Supper.

grain [grān] *n* the seed of any cereal plant, as wheat, corn, etc.; cereal plants; a tiny, solid particle, as of salt or sand; a unit of weight, 0.002083 ounce, in avoirdupois, troy, or apothecaries' system; the arrangement of fibers, layers, etc. of wood, leather, etc.; the markings or texture due to this; natural disposition.—*vt* to form into grains; to paint in imitation of the grain of wood, etc.—*vi* to become granular.

gram, gramme [gram] *n* the basic unit of weight in the metric system, equal to about $\frac{1}{28}$ of an ounce.

graminiv′orous, grass-eating.

grammar [gram′ár] *n* language study dealing with the forms of words and with their arrangement in sentences; a system of rules for speaking and writing a language; a grammar textbook; the principles or rules of an art, science, or technique.—*ns* **grammarian**, **grammar school**, elementary school.—*adj* **grammatical**, conforming to the rules of grammar.—*adv* **grammatically**.

grampus [gram′pus] *n* a marine mammal, as the blackfish or killer whale; the giant whip scorpion.

granary [gran′ár-i] *n* a building for storing grain.

grand [grand] *adj* higher in rank than others; most important; imposing in size, beauty, extent, etc.; distinguished; illustrious; (*inf*) very good; delightful. A combining form meaning the generation older or younger than (eg **grand′mother**, the mother of one's father or mother; **grand′child**, the child of one's son or daughter); **grand′eur**, splendor; magnificence; nobility; dignity.—*adj* **grandil′oquent**, using pompous words.—*n* **grand mal**, severe epilepsy.—*adj* **grandiôse**', having grandeur; pompous and showy; **grand master**, an expert player (as of chess) who has scored consistently well in international competition.

grange [grānj] *n* a farm, esp a farmhouse with outbuildings attached.

granite [gran′it] *n* a hard, igneous rock consisting chiefly of feldspar and quartz; unyielding firmness of endurance.

grant [grant] *vt* to consent to; to give or transfer by legal procedure; to admit as true.—*n* the act of granting; something granted, esp a gift for a particular purpose; a transfer of property by deed; the instrument by which such transfer is made.

granule [gran′ūl] *n* a small grain or particle.—*adjs* **gran′ūlar**, consisting of granules; having a grainy texture.—*vt* **gran′ūlāte**, to form or crystallize into grains or granules.—*vi* to collect into grains or granules; to form granulations.—*n* **granūlā′tion**.

grape [grāp] *n* a small, round, juicy berry, growing in clusters on a vine; a grapevine; a dark purplish red.—*ns* **grape′fruit**, a large, round, sour citrus fruit with a yellow rind.

graph   110   grind

graph [graf] *n* a diagram representing the successive changes in the value of a variable quantity or quantities.—*adj* **graphic**, described in realistic detail; represented by a graph.—*ns* **graphite**, a soft, black form of carbon used in pencils, for lubricants, etc.; **graphology**, the study of handwriting, esp as a clue to character.

grapnel [grap'nèl] *n* a small anchor with several claws or arms; a grappling iron.

grapple [grap'l] *n* an instrument for hooking or holding.—*vt* to seize; to lay fast hold of; to grip.—*vi* to contend in close fight; to try to deal (with, eg a problem).—*n* **grapp'ling i'ron**.

grasp [gräsp] *vt* to grip, as with the hand; to seize; to comprehend.—*vi* try to seize; (*with* at) to accept eagerly.—*n* grip; power of seizing; mental power of comprehension—*adj* **grasp'ing**.

grass [gras] *n* any of a large family (Gramineae) of plants with jointed stems and long narrow leaves including cereals, bamboo, etc.; such plants grown as lawn; pasture.—*ns* **grass'hopper**, any of a group of plant-eating, winged insects with powerful hind legs for jumping; **grass widow**, (*inf*) a wife whose husband is absent.

grate[1] [grāt] *n* a framework of bars set in a window, door, etc.; a frame of metal bars for holding fuel in a fireplace; a fireplace.—*vt* to furnish with a grate.—*n* **grating**, a framework of bars.

grate[2] [grāt] *vt* to grind into particles by scraping; to rub against (an object) or grind (the teeth) together with a harsh sound; to irritate.—*vi* to rub or rasp noisily; to cause irritation.

grateful [grāt'fŏŏl, -fl] *adj* appreciative; welcome.—*adv* **grate'fully**.—*n* **grate'fulness**.—*vt* **grāt'ify**, to please; to indulge.—*pt p* **grat'ified**.—*adj* **grat'ifying**.—*n* **gratificā'tion**, a pleasing or indulging; that which gratifies; delight.

gratis [grā'tis, grä'-] *adj, adv* free of charge.

gratuity [gra-tū'i-ti] *n* a gift as of money, esp for a service, a tip.—*adj* **gratū'itous**, given free of charge; uncalled-for.—*adv* **gratū'itously**.

gravamen [grav-ā'men] *n* the essence or most important part of a complaint or accusation.

grave[1] [grāv] *vt* (*obs*) to dig; (*obs*) to carve, sculpture; to engrave.—*vi* to engrave.—*pt p* **graved** or **grav'en**.—*n* a pit or hole dug out, esp one to bury the dead in; any place of burial; (*fig*) death, destruction.

grave[2] [grāv] *vt* to clean (by burning, etc.) and smear with tar (a wooden ship's bottom).—*n* **graving dock**, a dry-dock.

grave[3] *adj* of importance, weighty; threatening, serious; not gay or showy, sober, solemn; low in pitch.—*adv* **grave'ly**.—*n* **grave'ness**.

gravel [grav'l] *n* an assemblage of small rounded stones; small collections of gravelly matter in the kidneys or bladder.—*vt* to cover with gravel.

gravity [grav'i-ti] *n* importance, esp seriousness; weight; the attraction of bodies toward the center of the earth, the moon, or a planet; specific gravity.—*vi* **grav'itate**, to move or tend to move under the force of gravitation; **gravita'tion**, a natural force of attraction that tends to draw bodies together.

gravy [grāv'i] *n* the juice given off by meat in cooking; the sauce made from this juice.

gray [grā] *n* any of a series of neutral colors ranging between black and white; something (as an animal, garment, cloth, or spot) of a gray color.

graze[1] [grāz] *vt* to eat or feed on (growing grass or pasture); to put to feed on growing grass; (of land) to supply food for (animals).—*ns* **grazier** [grā'-zi-èr, -zyèr, zhyèr], one who grazes or pastures cattle and rears them for the market; **graz'ing**, the act of feeding on grass; pasture.

graze[2] [grāz] *vt* to pass lightly along the surface of; to scrape.—*n* a passing touch; scratch, abrasion.

grease [grēs] *n* melted animal fat; any thick, oily substance or lubricant.—*vt* to smear with grease, to lubricate.—*adj* **greas'y**.—*ns* **greas'iness**.

great [grāt] *adj* of much more than ordinary size, extent, etc.; much above the average; intense (*great pain*); eminent (*a great writer*); most important; more distant in a family relationship by one generation (*great-grandparent*); (*inf*) skillful (*often with* at); (*inf*) excellent; fine.—*n* a distinguished person; great

divide, a watershed between major drainage systems, a significant point of division, esp death.

greave [grēv] *n* armor for the leg below the knee.

grebe [grēb] *n* any of a family of swimming and diving birds closely.

Grecian [grēsh'(y)àn] Greek.—*n* a Greek; one well versed in the Greek language and literature.

greedy [grēd'i] *adj* wanting more than one needs or deserves; having too strong a desire for food and drink.—*n* **greed**, *adv* **greed'ily**—*n* **greed'iness**.

Greek [grēk] *adj* of Greece, its people, or its language.

green [grēn] *adj* of the color green; covered with plants or foliage; having a sickly appearance; unripe; inexperienced, naive; not fully processed or treated (*green liquor, green hides*); (*inf*) jealous.—*n* a color between blue and yellow in the spectrum; the color of growing grass; something of a green color; (*pl*) green leafy vegetables, as spinach, etc.; a grassy plot, esp the end of a golf fairway.—*adj* **green'ish**.—*ns* **green'ness**; **green'back**, US paper money; **green'belt**, a belt of parkways or farms surrounding a community designed to prevent urban sprawl; **green'ery**, green vegetation; **green'horn**, an inexperienced person; a person easily duped; **green'house**, a heated building, mainly of glass, for growing plants.

greengage [grēn'gāj'] *n* a greenish yellow, very sweet variety of plum.

Greenwich time [grin'ij, gren'ich] the time of the meridian of Greenwich used as the basis of worldwide standard time.

greet [grēt] *vt* to address with friendliness; to meet (a person, event, etc.) in a specified way; to present itself to.—*pr p* **greet'ing**; *pt p* **greet'ed**.

gregarious [gre-gā'ri-us] *adj* associating in flocks and herds; fond of company.—*adv* **gregā'riously**.

Gregorian calendar [gre-gō', -gō', ri-an] the calendar as reformed by Pope Gregory XIII (1582); adopted in England and in the American colonies in 1752 in place of the Julian calendar.

gremlin [grem'lin] *n* an imaginary creature blamed for disruption of any procedure or of malfunction of equipment esp in an aircraft.

grenade [gre-nād'] *n* a small missile thrown by the hand or projected (as by a rifle or special launcher).

greyhound [grā'hownd] *n* any of a breed of tall and slender dogs with great speed and keen sight.

grid [grid] *n* a gridiron, a grating; a metallic plate in a storage battery; an electrode (as of wire mesh) for controlling the flow of electrons in an electron tube.

gridiron [grid'ī-èrn] *n* a frame of iron bars for broiling; anything resembling this, as a football field.

grief [grēf] *n* deep sorrow caused as by a loss; distress.—*adj* **grief-strick'en**, bowed down with sorrow.

grieve [grēv] *vti* to feel or cause to feel grief.—*n* **griev'ance**, a circumstance thought to be unjust and ground for complaint.—*adj* **griev'ous**, causing grief; full of grief; deplorable; severe.

griffin, griffon, gryphon [grif'in, -òn] *n* mythical animal, with lion's body and eagle's beak and wings.

grill [gril] *n* to broil; to question relentlessly.—*n* a gridiron; grilled food.

grille [gril] *n* an open grating forming a screen.

grilse [grils] *n* a young salmon on its first return from the sea.

grim [grim] *adj* hard and unyielding, stern; appearing harsh, forbidding; repellent, ghastly in character.—*adv* **grim'ly**.—*n* **grim'ness**.

grimace [gri-mās'] *n* a distortion of the face, in jest etc.; a smirk.—Also *vi*.

grimalkin [gri-mal'kin or -mawl'kin] *n* an old female cat.

grime [grīm] *n* sooty; dirt, rubbed into a surface, as of the skin.—*vt* to soil deeply.—*adj* **grim'y**

grin [grin] *vi* to smile broadly as in amusement; to show the teeth in pain, scorn, etc.

grind [grīnd] *vt* to reduce to powder by crushing; to wear down, sharpen, smooth, or roughen by friction; to rub (the teeth) together gratingly; to oppress; to work by a crank.—*vi* to be moved or rubbed together; to jar or grate; to drudge at any tedious task; to study hard; to rotate the hips in an erotic manner.—*pr p* **grind'ing**; *pt, pt p* **ground** [grownd].—*ns* **grind'er**; **grind'stone**, a circular revolving stone for grinding or sharpening tools.

gringo [gring′ō] *n* (*offensive*) among Hispanics, a foreigner, esp N Americans.—*pl* **gring′os.**

grip [grip] *n* a secure grasp; the manner of holding a bat, club, racket, etc.; the power of grasping firmly; mental grasp; mastery; a handle; a small traveling bag.—*vt* to take firmly and hold fast.

gripe [grīp] *vt* to cause sharp pain in the bowels of; (*slang*) to annoy.—*vi* (*slang*) to complain.

grippe [grēp] *n* earlier term for influenza.

grisly [griz′li] *adj* terrifying; ghastly; arousing horror.

grist [grist] *n* grain that is to be or has been ground; matter forming the basis of a story or analysis.

gristle [gris′l] *n* cartilage.—*adj* **grist′ly.**—*n* **grist′liness.**

grit [grit] *n* rough particles, as of sand; a coarse sandstone; firmness of character; stubborn courage.—*adj* **gritt′y.**—*n* **gritt′iness.**

grizzle [griz′l] *n* a gray or roan animal.—*adjs* **grizz′led,** gray or streaked with gray; having gray hair.

groan [grōn] *vi* to utter a deep sound as in distress or disapprobation; to make a harsh sound (as of creaking) under sudden or prolonged strain.

groat[1] [grōt] *n* an old English silver coin.

groat[2] [grōt] *n* hulled grain broken into fragments larger than grits.

grocer [grōs′ér] *n* a dealer in food and household supplies.

grog [grog] *n* originally, rum diluted with water, often spiced and served hot.—*adj* **grogg′y.**

grogram [grog′ràm] *n* a kind of coarse cloth of silk and mohair.

groin [groin] *n* the fold between the belly and the thigh; (*archit.* the angular curve formed by the crossing of two vaults.—*n* **groin′ing.**

groom [grōōm, grōōm] *n* one who has the charge of horses; a bridegroom.—*vt* to tend, esp a horse; to make tidy and neat; to train (a person) for a particular purpose.

groove [grōōv] *n* a long, narrow furrow, cut with a tool; any channel or rut; a settled routine.—*vt* to make a groove in.

grope [grōp] *vi* to search (for something) as if blind or in the dark.

grosbeak [grōs′bēk] *n* any finchlike bird of Europe or America with a large stout conical bill.

gross [grōs] *adj* fat and coarse-looking; flagrant, dense, thick; lacking in refinement; earthy; obscene; total, with no deductions; (*slang*) of anything objectionable.—*n* an overall total; twelve dozen.—*pl* **gross.**

grotesque [grō-tesk′] *adj* distorted or fantastic in appearance, shape, etc.; ridiculous; absurdly incongruous.—Also *n.*—*adv* **grotesque′ly.**

grotto [grot′ō] *n* a cave; an imitation cave, usu. fantastic.—*pl* **grott′oes.**

[Gr *kryptē*, a crypt, vault.]

grouch [growch] *vi* to grumble or complain.

ground [grownd] *n* the solid surface of the earth; soil; a basis for belief, action, or argument; the background, as in a design; the connection of an electrical conductor with the earth; (*pl*) the area about and relating to a building; a tract of land; sediment.—*vt* to set on the ground; to cause to run aground; to base, found, or establish; to instruct in the first principles of.—*vi* to run ashore; (*baseball*) to be put out on a grounder.—*ns* **ground cover,** low, dense-growing plants used for covering bare ground; **groundhog,** a woodchuck; **grounding,** basic general knowledge of a subject.—*adj* **groundless,** without reason; **groundswell,** a large rolling wave; a wave of popular feeling; **groundwork,** foundation, basis.

group [grōōp] *n* a number of persons or things considered as a collective unit; a small musical band of players or singers; two or more figures forming one artistic design.—*vti* to form into a group or groups.

grouse[1] [grows] *n* any of numerous birds that have a plump body, strong feathered legs and that include many important game birds.

grouse[2] [grows] *vi* (*inf*) to complain.

grout [growt] *n* a thin mortar used as between tiles.—*vt* to fill in with grout.

grove [grōv] *n* a small wood, generally without undergrowth.

grovel [gruv′el] *vi* to lie and crawl in a prostrate position, esp in token of subservience.—*n* **groveler.**

grow [grō] *vi* to come into being; to be produced naturally; to develop, as a living thing; to increase in size, quantity, etc.; *vt* to cause or let grow; to raise, to cultivate.—*pt* **grew** [grōō]; **growth,** a growing; gradual increase; development; that which has grown.

growl [growl] *vi* to utter a rumbling, menacing sound such as an angry dog makes.—*vt* to express by growling.—Also *n.*—*n* **growl′er,** one that growls.

grub [grub] *vi* to dig in the ground; to work hard.—*vt* to clear (ground) of roots; to uproot.—*n* the wormlike larva of a beetle; a drudge.—*adj* **grubb′y,** dirty.

grudge [gruj] *vt* to give or allow unwillingly; to be unwilling (to).—*n* a feeling of resentment (*with* **against**) due to some specific cause.

gruel [grōō′él] *n* a thin broth of meal cooked in water or milk.—*adj* **gru′eling, grue′lling,** exhausting.

gruesome [grōō′sùm] *adj* causing horror or loathing.

gruff [gruf] *adj* rough or surly; hoarse.—*adv* **gruff′ly.**—*n* **gruff′ness.**

grumble [grum′bl] *vi* to growl; to murmur with discontent; to rumble.—*n* the act of or an instance of grumbling.—*n* **grum′bler.**

grumpy [grum′pi] *adj* surly.—*adv* **grum′pily.**—*n* **grum′piness.**

grunt [grunt] *vi* to make a sound like a hog.—Also *n.*—*n* **grunt′er.**

Gruyère [grōō-yàr] *n* a cooked, hard, pale yellow cheese, made from whole cow's milk.

guanaco [gwä-nä′ko] *n* a S American mammal related to the camel but lacking a hump.

guano [gwä′no] *n* manure of sea birds.

guarantee [gar-àn-tē′] *n* a pledge or security for another's debt or obligation; a pledge to replace something if it is not as represented; assurance that something will be done as specified; a guarantor.—*vt* to give a guarantee for; to promise.—*ns* **guar′antor,** one who gives a guaranty or guarantee; **guar′anty,** an undertaking to answer for another's failure to pay a debt or perform a duty; an agreement that secures the existence or maintenance of something; guarantor.

guard [gärd] *vt* to watch over and protect; to defend; to keep from escape or trouble.—*vi* to keep watch (against); to act as a guard.—*n* defense; protection; a posture of readiness for defense; any device to protect against injury or loss; a person or group that guards; a defensive basketball player or offensive football lineman.—*adj* **guard′ed,** kept safe; cautious.—*ns* **guard′house,** (*military*) a building used by a guard when not walking a post; a jail for temporary confinement; **guard′ian,** custodian; a person legally in charge of a minor or someone incapable of taking care of his own affairs.—*adj* **protecting.**— *n* **guard′rail,** a protective railing, as along a highway.—**on one's guard,** vigilant.

guava [gwä′vä] *n* a tropical American shrubby tree widely cultivated for its sweet acid yellow fruit.

guelder rose [gel′dér rōz] *n* a cultivated variety of the cranberry bush with large globose heads of sterile flowers.

guerdon [gûr′dón] *n* a reward or recompense.

guerrilla, guerilla [gèr-il′a] *n* a member of a small force of irregular soldiers, making surprise raids.—Also *adj.*

guess [ges] *vt* to judge upon inadequate knowledge or none at all; to judge correctly by doing this; to think or suppose.— Also *vi, n.*—*n* **guess′work,** process or result of guessing.

guest [gest] *n* a person entertained at the home, club, etc. of another; any paying customer of a hotel, restaurant, etc.

guffaw [guf-ö′] *vi* to laugh loudly.—*n* a loud laugh.

guide [gīd] *vt* to point out the way for; to lead; to direct the course of; to control.—*n* one who leads or directs another in his way or course; one who exhibits and explains points of interest; something that provides a person with guiding information; a device for controlling the motion of something; a book of basic instruction.—*ns* **guid′ance,** leadership; advice or counsel; **guide′book,** a book containing directions and information for tourists; **guided missile,** a military missile whose course is controlled by radar, etc.

guild [gild] *n* an association for mutual aid and the promotion of common interests.

guile [gīl] *n* cunning, deceit.—*adj* **guile′ful,** crafty.—*adj* **guile′less,** without deceit; artless.

guillotine [gil′o-tēn, -tēn′] *n* an instrument for beheading by descent of a heavy oblique blade; a machine for cutting paper; a rule for limiting time for discussion in a legislature. Also *vt*.

guilt [gilt] *n* the fact of having done a wrong or committed an offense; a feeling of self-reproach from believing one has done a wrong. — *adj* **guilt′y**. — *adv* **guilt′ily**. — *n* **guilt′iness**. — *adj* **guilt′less**, innocent.

guinea [gin′i] *n* a former English gold coin equal to 21 shillings. — *ns* **guin′ea fowl**, an African bird of the pheasant family.

guise [gīz] *n* external appearance; assumed appearance (*in the guise of*).

guitar [gi-tär′] *n* a musical instrument with usu. six strings, a long, fretted neck, and a flat body.

gulch [gulch, gulsh] *n* a deep, narrow ravine.

gulf [gulf] *n* a large area of ocean reaching into land; a wide, deep chasm; a vast separation. — **Gulf Stream**, a warm ocean current flowing from the Gulf of Mexico northward toward Europe.

gull [gul] *n* any of numerous long-winged web-footed aquatic birds.

gull [gul] *n* a dupe; an easily tricked person. — *vt* to cheat, trick. — *adj* **gull′ible**, easily deceived. — *n* **gullibil′ity**.

gullet [gul′et] *n* the esophagus; the throat.

gully [gul′i] *n* a channel worn by running water after rain. — *vt* to wear a gully or channel in. — *vi* to undergo erosion.

gulp [gulp] *vt* to swallow hastily or greedily; to choke back as if swallowing. — *n* a gulping or swallowing.

gum[1] [gum] *n* the firm flesh that surrounds the teeth. — *n* **gum′boil**, an abscess on the gum.

gum[2] [gum] *n* a sticky substance found in certain trees and plants; an adhesive; chewing gum. — *vt* to coat or unite with gum. — *vi* to become sticky or clogged. — *adj* **gum′my**.

gumbo [gum′bō] *n* a rich soup thickened with okra.

gumption [gum(p)′sh(ó)n] *n* shrewd practical commonsense; initiative.

gun [gun] *n* a weapon with a metal tube from which a projectile is discharged by the force of an explosive; any similar device not discharged by an explosive (*an air gun*); the shooting of a gun as a signal or salute; anything like a gun; a throttle. — *vt* (*inf*) to shoot or hunt with a gun. — *vt* (*inf*) to shoot (a person); (*slang*) to advance the throttle of an engine. — *ns* **gun′boat**, a small armed ship; **gun′man**, an armed gangster; a hired killer; **gun′metal**, bronze with a dark tarnish; its dark-gray color; **gunn′er**, a soldier, etc. who helps fire artillery; a naval warrant officer in charge of a ship's guns; **gun′powder**, an explosive powder used in guns, for blasting, etc.; **gun′shy**, afraid of a loud noise; markedly distrustful.

gunny [gun′i] *n* a strong coarse fabric of jute or hemp esp for bagging.

gunwale [gun′l] *n* the upper edge of a ship's or boat's side. Also **gunnel**.

gurgle [gûr′gl] *vi* to make a bubbling sound.

gurnard [gûr′närd] *n* a sea robin.

guru [gōō′rōō] *n* a spiritual teacher; a venerable person.

gush [gush] *vi* to flow out plentifully; to have a sudden flow; to talk or write effusively. — *vt* to cause to gush. — *n* a gushing. — *n* **gush′er**, one who gushes; an oil well from which oil spouts forth. — *adj* **gush′ing**.

gusset [gus′et] *n* a triangular piece inserted in a garment to strengthen or enlarge some part of it.

gust[1] [gust] *n* a sudden brief rush of wind; a sudden outburst. — *vi* to blow in gusts.

gust[2] [gust] *n* inclination; keen delight. — *n* **gustā′tion**, the act of tasting; the sense of taste. — *n* **gust′o**, taste; zest — *pl* **gustoes**.

gut [gut] *n* (*pl*) the bowels or the stomach; the intestine; tough cord made from animal intestines; (*pl*) (*slang*) daring; courage. — *vt* to remove the intestines from; to destroy the interior of.

gutta-percha [gut′a-pûr′cha or -ka] *n* solidified juice of various Malayan trees (genera *Payena* and *Pala*-guium).

gutter[1] [gut′ér] *n* a channel for conveying away water, esp at a roadside or at the eaves of a roof; a channel or groove to direct something (as of a bowling alley); the lowest condition of human life. — *adj* marked by extreme vulgarity or indecency. — *vt* to provide with a gutter. — *vi* to flow in rivulets; (of a candle) to melt away or to incline downward in a draft.

guttural [gut′ùr-ál] *adj* pertaining to the throat; formed in the throat. — *n* velar. — *adv* **gutt′urally**.

guy[1] [gī] *n* a rope, rod, etc., to steady anything. — *vt* to keep in position by a guy.

guy[2] [gī] *n* (*slang*) a man or boy. — *vt* to tease.

guzzle [guz′l] *vti* to swallow greedily. — *n* **guzz′ler**.

gymkhana [jim-kä′na] *n* a meeting featuring sports contests or athletic skills.

gymnasium [jim-nā′zi-um] *n* a room or building equipped for physical training and sports. — *ns* **gym**; **gym′nast** [-nast], one skilled in gymnastics; **gymnas′tic**, a system of training by exercise; (*usu. in pl* **gymnas′tics**, *used as sing.*) exercises devised to strengthen the body; feats or tricks of agility. — *adjs* **gymnas′tic, -al**.

gynecology [gīn-, jin-ē-kol′o-ji] *n* that branch of medicine which treats of the diseases and hygiene of women. — *adj* **gynecolog′ical**. — *n* **gynecol′ogist**.

gypsum [jip′sum] *n* hydrous calcium sulphate (hydrated sulphate of lime).

Gypsy [jip′si] *n* a member of a wandering Caucasoid people of Indian origin; a Romany; **gypsy**, who looks or lives like a Gypsy.

gyre [jīr] *n* a circular or spiral motion. — *vi* **gyr′āte** [or -āt′], to spin, whirl. — *n* **gyra′tion**, whirling motion. — *adjs* **gy′ral, gyr′ātory**, spinning round. — *ns* **gyr′oscōpe**, a wheel mounted in a ring so that its axis is free to turn in any direction; when the wheel is spun rapidly, it will keep its original plane of rotation.

gyve [jīv] *vt* to fetter. — *n* shackle, fetter.

H

ha [ha, hä] *interj* used to express surprise.

habeas corpus [hā′be-as-kör′pus] *n* a writ requiring that a prisoner be brought before a court.

haberdasher [hab′ér-dash-ér] *n* a dealer in men's hats, shirts, neckties, etc. — *n* **habe′erdashery**.

habiliment [ha-bil′i-mènt] *n* clothing, attire.

habit [hab′it] *n* a distinctive costume, as of a nun, etc.; a thing done often and hence, easily; a usual way of doing things; an addiction, esp to narcotics. — *vt* to clothe; **habit′ual**, having the nature of a habit. — *vt* **habit′uate**, to accustom. — *ns* **habituation**; **hab′itūde**, characteristic condition; custom; **habitué** [hab-it′ū-ā], a habitual frequenter.

habitable [hab′it-a-bl] *adj* capable of being lived in. — *ns* **hab′itat**, the normal locality of an animal or plant.

habitā′tion, act of inhabiting; a dwelling or residence.

hacienda [(h)as-i-en′da] *n* (*Sp Amer*) an estate or ranch.

hack[1] [hak] *vt* to cut with rough blows; to chop or mangle. — *n* a gash or notch; a harsh, dry cough. — *adj* **hack′ly**.

hack[2] [hak] *n* a horse for hire; an old worn-out horse; a literary drudge; a coach for hire; (*inf*) a taxicab. — *adj* hired; hackneyed. — *vti* to use, let out, or act, as a hack.

hackle [hak′l] *n* a comb for hemp or flax; the neck features of a rooster, pigeon, etc. collectively.

hackney [hak′ni] *n* a horse for driving or riding; any of an English breed of high-stepping horses; a carriage or automobile for hire. — *adj* kept for public hire; hackneyed.

haddock [had′ók] *n* an important Atlantic food fish.

Hades [hā′dēz] *n* the home of the dead; (*inf*) hell.

haft [häft] *n* the handle of a weapon or tool.

hag [hag] *n* an ugly old woman; a witch. — *adj* **hag′ridd′en**, obsessed, tormented.

haggard [hag′ärd] *n* (*falconry*) an adult hawk caught wild. — *adj* (*of a hawk*) untamed; having a wild, wasted, worn look.

haggis [hag′is] *n* a Scottish dish made of the heart, lungs and liver of a sheep, calf, etc., chopped up with suet, onions, oatmeal, etc., seasoned and boiled in the animal's stomach.

haggle [hag′l] *vt* to cut unskilfully. — *vi* to bargain contentiously; to stick at trifles, to cavil. — *n* **hagg′ler**.

hagiology [hag-i-ol′o-ji or häj-] *n* history and legends of saints; a list of venerated persons.

ha-ha [hä′-hä] *n* a sunk fence.

hail[1] [hāl] *n* a calling to attract attention; a greeting; hearing distance.—*vt* to call to, from a distance; to greet, welcome (as).

hail[2] [hāl] *n* frozen raindrops.—*vti* to pour down in rapid succession.—*n* hail'stone, a pellet of hail.

hair [hār] *n* a filament growing from the skin of an animal; a mass of hairs, esp that covering the human head; a threadlike growth on a plant; a fiber; anything very small and fine; **hair'breadth, hairs'breadth**, a very small space or amount; **hair'splitting**, making petty distinctions; quibbling.—Also *n.*—*n* **hair'spring**, a slender, hairlike coil spring, as in a watch.—*adj* **hair'trigger**, immediately responsive.

hake [hāk] *n* a marine food fish allied to the cod.

halberd [hal'bèrd] *n* a weapon combining a spear and a battleax.—*n* halberdier' [-dēr'].

halcyon [hal'si-ón] *adj* calm, peaceful, happy.

hale[1] [hāl] *adj* healthy, robust.

hale[2] [hāl] *vt* to force (a person) to go.

half [haf, häf] *n* either of two equal parts of something.—*pl* **halves** [havz, hävz].—*adj* being a half; incomplete; partial.—*adv* to the extent of a half; (*inf*) partly (*half done*); (*inf*) at all (*with* not).—*ns* **half-and-half**, something half one thing and half another, as a mixture of milk and cream.—*adj* partly one thing and partly another.—*adv* in two equal parts.; **half-'breed**, one whose parents are of different races; **half brother**, a brother through one parent only; **half-caste**, half-breed; **half'hearted**, with little interest, enthusiasm, etc.—**half sister, halftone**, an illustration printed from a relief plate, showing light and shadow by means of minute dots.—*adj* **half'way'**, midway between two points, etc.

halibut [hal'i-but] *n* a marine food fish, the largest of the flatfishes.

halitosis [hal-i-tō'sis] *n* bad-smelling breath.

hall [höl] *n* the main dwelling on an estate; a public building with offices, etc.; a large room for exhibits, gatherings, etc.; a college building; a vestibule at the entrance of a building; a hallway.—*ns* **hall'mark**, a mark or symbol of high quality.

hallelujah [hal-ĕ-lōō'ya] *interj* and *n* the exclamation 'Praise Jehovah'; a song of praise to God.

hallo *see* hollo.

hallow [hal'ō] *vt* to make or regard as holy.—*ns* Hall'oween, the evening of October 31.

hallucination [hal-ōō-sin-ā'sh(ó)n] *n* the apparent perception of sights, sounds, etc. that are not actually present.—*vti* hallu'cinate, to have or cause to have hallucinations.

halo [hā'lō] *n* a ring of light, as around the sun; a symbolic ring of light around the head of a saint in pictures; the aura of glory surrounding an idealized person or thing.—*pl* halo(e)s [hā'lōz].

halt[1] [hölt] *vti* to stop.—Also *n*.

halt[2] [hölt] *vi* to hesitate.

halter [hölt'èr] *n* a rope or strap for tying or leading an animal; a hangman's noose.—*vt* to catch with or as if with a halter.

halve [häv] *vt* to divide into halves; in golf, to play one hole in the same number of strokes as one's opponent.

halyard [hal'yàrd] *n* (*naut*) a rope or tackle for hoisting or lowering a sail, yard, or flag.

ham [ham] *n* the back of the thigh; the upper part of a hog's hind leg, salted, smoked, etc.—*n* ham'string, any of three muscles at the back of the thigh that flex and rotate the leg.

hamadryad [ha-ma-drī'ad] *n* (*myth*) a wood-nymph who lived and died with the tree in which she dwelt; a king cobra.

hamburger [ham'bûrg-èr] *n* ground beef; a cooked patty of such meat, often in a sandwich.

hamlet [ham'let] *n* a very small village.

hammer [ham'èr] *n* a tool for pounding, having a heavy head and a handle; a thing like this in shape or use, as the part of the gun that strikes the firing pin; a bone of the middle ear.—*vti* to strike repeatedly, as with a hammer; to drive, force, or shape, as with hammer blows.—*ns* **hammerhead**, the head of a hammer; a blockhead; a shark with a mallet-shaped head having an eye at each end.

hammock [ham'ók] *n* a piece of strong cloth or netting suspended by the ends, and used as a bed.

hamper[1] [ham'pér] *vt* to hinder; to impede; to encumber.

hamper[2] [ham'pér] *n* a large basket, usu. with a lid.

hamster [ham'stèr] *n* a small short-tailed Old World rodent with cheek pouches.

hamstring *see* ham.

hand [hand] *n* the part of the arm below the wrist, used for grasping; a side or direction; possession or care; control; an active part; a promise to marry; skill; one having a special skill; handwriting; applause; help; a hired worker; a source ; anything like a hand, as a pointer on a clock; the breadth of a hand, 4 inches when measuring the height of a horse; the cards held by a player at one time; a round of card play.—*adj* of, for, or controlled by the hand.—*vt* to give as with the hand; to help or conduct with the hand; **hand'bill**, a small printed notice to be passed out by hand; **hand'cart**, a small cart pulled or pushed by hand; **hand'cuff**, either of a pair of connected rings for shackling the wrists of a prisoner (*usu. pl*).—*vt* to manacle.—*adj* **hand'ed**, having or involving (a specified kind or number of) hands.—*n* **handwriting**, a style of such writing.

handicap [hand'ikap] *n* a competition in which difficulties are imposed on, or advantages given to, the various contestants to equalize their chances; such a difficulty or advantage; any hindrance.—*vt* to give a handicap to; to hinder.—*ns* **hand'icapper**.

handicraft [hand'i-kräft] *n* skill with the hands.

handiwork [hand'i-wûrk] *n* handmade work; work done by a person himself.

handkerchief [hang'kèr-chif] *n* a small cloth for wiping the nose, etc.

handle [hand'l] *vt* to touch, hold, or feel with the hand; to wield, use; to manage (a person, affair); to deal with; to deal in (goods).—*n* that part of anything held in the hand.

handsome [han'sóm] *adj* good-looking; dignified; generous; ample.—*adv* hand'somely.

hang [hang] *vt* to support from above against gravity, to suspend; to decorate with pictures, etc., as a wall; to put to death by suspending by the neck; to exhibit (works of art); to prevent (a jury) from coming to a decision.—*vi* to be suspended, so as to allow of free lateral motion; to droop; to hover or impend; to be in suspense.—*pt t, pt p* hanged (by the neck) *or* hung.—*n* action of hanging; manner in which anything hangs or is disposed.—*adj* hang'dog, abject or ashamed.—*ns* hang'man, a public executioner.

hangar [hang'àr, hang'gär] *n* shelter for aircraft.

hank [hangk] *n* a coiled or looped bundle, usu. containing specified yardage.

hanker [hangk'èr] *vi* to yearn (*with* after, for).

Hannukkah *see* Chanukah.

hansom [han'sóm] *n* a light two-wheeled covered carriage, pulled by one horse, with driver's seat raised behind.

hap [hap] *n* luck.—*adj* hap'less, unlucky.—*adv* hap'lessly.—*n* hap'lessness.—*adv* hap'ly, by hap, chance, or accident; perhaps, it may be.

haphazard [hap-haz'àrd] *n* chance.—*adj* not planned; random.—*adv* by chance.

happen [hap'én] *vi* to take place; to be, occur, or come by chance.

happy [hap'i] *adj* lucky; possessing or enjoying pleasure or good; pleased; apt, felicitous (eg a phrase).—*adv* happ'ily.—*n* happ'iness.—*adj* happ'y-go-luck'y, easygoing; irresponsible.

hara-kiri [hä'ra-kē'rē] *n* ritual suicide by disembowelment.

harangue [ha-rang'] *n* a tirade; a pompous, wordy address.—*vti* to deliver a harangue.

harass [har'as] *vt* to annoy, to pester, to trouble by constant raid and attacks.—*pt, pt p* har'assed.

harbinger [här'bin-jèr] *n* a forerunner; a herald.

harbor [här'bór] *n* any refuge or shelter; a protected inlet for anchoring ships; a port.—*vt* to shelter or house.—*vi* to take shelter.

hard [härd] *adj* not easily penetrated, firm, solid; stiff; difficult to understand; difficult to do; difficult to bear, painful; severe, strenuous, rigorous; unfeeling; ungenerous; intractable; (of sound) harsh; (of color) brilliant and glaring; (of drug) habit-forming and seriously detrimental to health; (of news) definite, substantiated; (of drink) very alcoholic; (of water) that prevents lathering with soap.—*adj* hard'bitten, tough, seasoned.—*adj* hard-boiled, (of eggs) boiled until solid; (*inf*) unfeeling.—**hardcopy**, output (as from microfilm or computer storage) that can be read by eye.—*vti* **harden**, to make or become hard; **hardship**, something that causes suffering or privation; **hardware**, articles made of metal as tools, nails, etc.

hardy [härd'i] *adj* brave; resolute; audacious; robust; vigorous; able to bear cold, exposure or fatigue.—*ns* **hard'ihood**, **hard'iness**.—*adv* hard'ily.

hare [hār] *n* any of various timid and swift mammals, related to and resembling the rabbit.—**hare'bell**, a plant with blue bell-shaped flowers.—*adj* **hare'brained**, flighty; foolish.—*n* **hare'-lip**, a congenital deformity in the upper human lip.

harem [hā'rem, hä-rēm'] *n* the usu. secluded part of a Muslim's house where the women live; the women in a harem.

haricot [har'i-kō, -kot] *n* the ripe seed or the unripe pod of any of several beans.

hark [härk] *vi* to listen carefully (*usu with* to).

Harlequin [här'lê-kwin, or -kin] *n* a comic character in pantomime who wears a mask and colorful tights.—*n* **harlequin**.

harlot [här'lot] *n* a prostitute.—Also *adj*.

harm [härm] *n* hurt; damage; injury.—*vt* to injure.—*adj* **harm'ful**.—*adv* **harm'fully**.—*n* **harm'fulness**.—*adj* **harm'less**.

harmattan [här-mä-tan', här-mät'an] *n* a dust-laden wind on the Atlantic coast of Africa.

harmonic [här-mon'ik] *adj* (*music*) of or in harmony.—*n* an overtone; (*pl*) the science of musical sounds.—*adv* **harmonically**.—*ns* **harmonica**, a mouth organ; **harmonium**, a reed organ.—*adj* **harmō'nious**.—*vi* **har'monize**, to be in harmony; to sing in harmony.—*vt* to make harmonious.—*ns* **harmonization**; **harmony**, pleasing agreement of parts in color, size, etc.; agreement in action, ideas, etc.

harness [här'nes] *n* the leather straps and metal pieces by which a draft animal is fastened to a vehicle, plow, etc.; prefabricated wiring ready to be attached; the part of the loom controlling the heddles.—*vt* to put a harness on.—**in harness**, at work.

harp [härp] *n* a musical instrument with strings played by plucking.—*vi* to play on the harp; to persist in talking.—*n* **harp'ist**.

harpoon [här-pōōn'] *n* a barbed spear with an attached line, for spearing whales, etc.—*vt* to strike with the harpoon.—*n* **harpoon'er**.

harpsichord [härp'si-körd] *n* a musical instrument resembling a grand piano whose strings are plucked rather than struck.

harpy [här'pi] *n* (*myth*.) a malign monster, part woman and part bird; a shrewish woman.

harquebus [här'kui-bus] *see* **arquebus**.

harridan [har'i-dân] *n* a disreputable, shrewish old woman.

harrier [har'i-êr] *n* a small dog with a keen smell, for hunting hares; a cross-country runner.

harrow [har'ō] *n* a heavy frame with spikes, spring teeth, or disks for breaking up and leveling plowed ground.—*vt* to draw a harrow over (land); to cause mental distress to.—*adj* **harr'owing**.

harry [har'i] *vt* to raid and ravage or rob; to torment or worry.—*pr p* **harr'ying**; *pt p* **harr'ied**.—*n*

harsh [härsh] *adj* unpleasantly rough; jarring on the senses or feelings; rigorous; cruel.—*adv* **harsh'ly**.

harts'horn [härtz'horn] *n* a preparation of ammonia used as smelling salts.

harum-scarum [hā'rum-skā'rum] *n* a giddy, rash person.—Also *adj*.

harvest [här'vest] *n* the time of gathering in the ripened crops; a season's crop; the crops gathered in; the product of any labor or action.—*vti* to gather in (a crop).—*vt* to win by achievement.—*ns* **harvest fly**, cicada; **harvest home**, the time of harvest; a feast at the close of harvest; **harvest moon**, the full moon nearest the time of the September equinox; **har'vest time**, the time during which an annual crop (as wheat) is harvested.

hash [hash] *vt* to chop up (meat or vegetables) for cooking.—*n* a chopped mixture of cooked meat and vegetables.

Hasid [ha-sid'] *n* a sect of Jews holding fundamental, mystical views, identified by dress and customs.—*pl* **Hasid'im**.

hashish [hash'ish, -êsh] *n* the leaves, shoots, or resin of Indian hemp, smoked or swallowed in various forms as an intoxicant.

hasp [häsp] *n* a hinged fastening for a door, etc., esp a metal piece fitted over a staple and fastened as by a bolt or padlock.

hassock [has'ók] *n* a firm cushion used as a footstool or seat.

hastate, -d [hast'āt, -id] *adjs* (*bot*) spear-shaped.

haste [hāst] *n* quickness of motion.—*vt* **hasten** [hās'n], to accelerate; to hurry on.—*vi* to move with speed; to do without delay (eg *he hastened to add*).—*pr p* **hast'ening** [hās'ning]; *pt* **hastened** [hās'nd].—*adj* **hast'y**.—*adv* **hast'ily**.

hat [hat] *n* a covering for the head, generally with crown and brim.—*vti* to provide with a hat.—*ns* **hatt'er**, one who makes or sells hats.

hatch[1] [hach] *n* a small door or opening (as on an aircraft or spaceship); an opening in the deck of a ship or in the floor or roof of a building; a lid for such an opening; a hatchway, an opening in a ship's deck or in a floor or roof; passage giving access to an enclosed space (as a cellar).

hatch[2] [hach] *vt* to produce from the egg; to develop or concoct (eg a plot).—*vi* to produce young from the egg; to come from the egg.—*n* **hatch'ery**, a place for hatching eggs, esp of poultry or fish.

hatch[3] [hach] *vt* to shade by fine lines, incisions, etc., in drawing and engraving.

hatchet [hach'et] *n* a small ax with a short handle.

hate [hāt] *vt* to dislike intensely; to wish to avoid.—*vi* to feel hatred.—*n* a strong feeling of dislike or ill will; the person or thing hated.—*adj* **hate'ful**.—*adv* **hate'fully**.

hauberk [hö'bêrk] *n* a long coat of chain mail.

haughty [hö'ti] *adj* proud, arrogant.—*adv* **haught'ily**.—*n* **haught'iness**.

haul [höl] *vti* to move by pulling; to transport by wagon, truck, etc.—*n* the act of hauling; the amount gained, caught, etc. at one time; the distance over which something is transported.—*ns* **haul'age**, act of hauling; charge for hauling.

haulm [höm] *n* the stalk of beans, peas, etc., esp after the crop has been gathered.

haunch [hönch, -sh] *n* the part of the body around the hips; leg and loin of a deer, sheep.

haunt [hönt] *vt* to visit often or continually; to recur repeatedly to.—*vi* to linger; to appear habitually as a ghost.—*n* a place often visited.—*adj* **haunt'ed**, supposedly frequented by ghosts.

hauteur [ō-tûr', hō-tœr'] *n* haughtiness.

have [hav] *vt* to hold; to keep; to possess; to own; to entertain in the mind; to enjoy; to experience; to give birth to; to allow or to cause to be; to be obliged; (*inf*) to hold at a disadvantage; (*inf*) to deceive; as an auxiliary, used with the *pt p* to form the perfect tenses (eg *they have gone*).—*pr p* **hav'ing**; *pt t, pt p* **had**.

haven [hā'vn] *n* an inlet of the sea, or mouth of a river, where ships can get good and safe anchorage.

haversack [hav'êr-sak] *n* a bag similar to a knapsack but worn over one shoulder.

havoc [hav'ók] *n* great destruction and devastation.

haw[1] [hö] *n* the berry of the hawthorn; the hawthorn.—**haw'thorn**, any of a genus of spring-flowering spiny shrubs or trees.

hawk[1] [hök] *n* any of numerous diurnal birds of prey.—*vi* to hunt birds by using a trained hawk.—*vt* to hunt on the wing like a hawk.

hawk[2] [hök] *vti* to clear the throat (of) audibly.

hawker [hök'êr] *n* one who goes about offering goods for sale.—*vt* **hawk**, to convey about for sale.

hawse [höz] *n* part of a vessel's bow in which the hawseholes are cut.

hawser [hö'zèr] *n* a large rope for towing, etc.

hay [hā] *n* grass, clover, etc. cut down and dried for fodder.—*ns* **hay'cock**, a conical pile of hay in the field; **hay'rick**, **hay'stack**, a pile of stacked hay.—*adj, adv* **hay'wire**, (*slang*) out of order; disorganized.

hazard [haz'árd] *n* risk; danger; an obstacle on a golf course.—*vt* to risk.—*adj* **haz'ardous**, dangerous; risky.

haze[1] [hāz] *n* a thin vapor of fog, smoke, etc. in the air; slight vagueness of mind.—*vti* to make or become hazy.—*adj* **haz'y**.

haze[2] [hāz] *vt* to force to do ridiculous or painful things, as an initiation.

hazel [hā'zl] *n* a genus of small trees yielding an edible nut enclosed in a leafy cup.—*adj* pertaining to the hazel; of light-brown color.

he [hē] *nom masc pron of 3d pers* the male (or thing spoken of as male) named before.

head [hed] *n* the part of the animal body containing the brain, eyes, ears, nose and mouth; the top part of anything; the foremost part; the chief person; (*pl*) a unit of counting (*ten head of cattle*); the striking part of a tool; mind; understanding; the topic of a chapter, etc.; crisis, conclusion; pressure of water, steam, etc.; source of a river, etc.; froth, as on beer. — *adj* at the head, top, or front; coming from in front; chief, leading. — *vt* to command; to lead; to cause to go in a specified direction. — *vi* to set out; to travel (*head eastward*). — *adj* head'less. — *ns* head'ache, a continuous pain in the head; (*inf*) a cause of worry or trouble; head'board, a board that forms the head of a bed, etc.; head cold, a common cold with congestion of the nasal passages; head'dress, a decorative covering for the head; a hairdo. — *adj* head'first', with the head in front; recklessly. — *ns* head'gear, a hat, cap, etc; head'hunter, one who preserves the heads of enemies as trophies; one who recruits executive personnel; heading, something forming the head, top, or front; the title, topic, etc. of a chapter, etc.; the direction in which a vehicle is moving; head'land, a promontory; head'light, a light at the front of a vehicle; head'line', printed lines at the top of a newspaper article giving the topic. — *vt* to give featured billing or publicity to. — *adj, adv* head'long', with the head first; with uncontrolled speed or force; rash(ly); head'master, head'mis'tress, the principal of a private school. — *adj, adv* head'-on', with the head or front foremost. — *ns* head'phone, a radio receiver held to the head by a band; head'quarters, the center of operations of one in command, as in an army; the main office in any organization; head'rest, a support for the head; head'room, space overhead, as in a doorway or tunnel; head'shrinker, a headhunter who shrinks the heads of his victims; (*inf*) a psychotherapist, esp a psychoanalyst; head'start', an early start or any other competitive advantage; head'stone, a marker placed at the head of a grave. — *adj* head'strong', determined to do as one pleases. — *ns* head'waiter, the head of the dining-room staff in a restaurant; head'wa'ters, the small streams that are the source of a river; head'way, forward motion; progress; head'word, term placed at the beginning (as of an entry in a dictionary).

heal [hēl] *vt* to make whole and healthy; to cure; to remedy, repair. — *vi* to grow sound. — *pr p* heal'ing; *pt p* healed.

health [helth] *n* physical and mental well-being; freedom of disease, etc.; condition of body or mind (*poor health*); a wish for one's health and happiness, as in a toast; soundness, as of a society. — *adjs* healthful, wholesome; healthy, having good health.

heap [hēp] *n* a mass or pile of jumbled things; (*inf*) a large amount. — *vt* to throw in a heap; to pile high; to fill (a plate, etc.) full or to overflowing.

hear [hēr] *vt* to perceive by the ear; to listen to; to conduct a hearing of (a law case, etc.); to be informed of; to learn. — *vi* to be able to hear sounds; to be told (*with of or about*). — *pr p* hear'ing; *pt* and *pt p* heard [hûrd]. — *ns* hear'er; hear'say, rumor, gossip.

hearken [härk'n] *vi* to listen carefully; to pay heed.

hearse [hûrs] *n* a vehicle in which a corpse is conveyed to the grave.

heart [härt] *n* the hollow, muscular organ that circulates the blood; the central, vital, or main part; the human heart as the center of emotions, esp sympathy, spirit, etc.; a suit of playing cards marked with such a symbol in red. — *ns* heart'ache, sorrow or grief; heart'break, overwhelming sorrow or grief. — *adj* heart'broken. — *n* heart'burn, a burning sensation beneath the breastbone. — *vt* heart'en, to encourage. — *adj* heart'felt, sincere. — *adj* heart'less, unfeeling. — *adjs* heart'-rending, causing much mental anguish. — *adj* heart'y, warm and friendly; unrestrained, as laughter; strong and healthy; nourishing and plentiful.

hearth [härth] *n* the part of the floor on which the fire is made; the fireside; the house itself.

heat [hēt] *n* the quality of being hot; the perception of hotness; hot weather or climate; strong feeling, esp ardor, anger, etc.; a single bout, round, or trial in sports; the period of sexual excitement in female animals; (*slang*) coercion. — *vti* to make or become warm or hot; to make or become excited.

heath [hēth] *n* any of a family of shrubby evergreen plants that thrive on open barren usu acid soil.

heathen [hē'THn] *n* anyone not a Christian, Jew, or Muslim; a person regarded as irreligious, uncivilized, etc. — *pl* heathens, heathen.

heather [heTH'ér] *n* a common heath of northern and alpine regions with small sessile leaves and tiny usu purplish pink flowers.

heave [hēv] *vt* to lift, esp with great effort; to lift in this way and throw; to utter (a sigh, etc.) with effort; (*naut*) to raise, haul, etc. by pulling as with a rope. — *vi* to swell up; to rise and fall rhythmically; to vomit; to pant; to gasp; (*naut*) to haul. — *pr p* heav'ing; *pt p* heaved or hove. — *n* the act or effort of heaving.

heaven [hev'n] *n* (usu. *pl*) the visible sky; Heaven, the dwelling place of God and his angels where the blessed go after death; God. — *adj* heavenly, of or relating to heaven or heavens; beatific.

heavy [hev'i] *adj* hard to lift or carry; of more than the usual, expected, or defined weight; to an unusual extent; hard to do; hard to digest; cloudy; using massive machinery to produce basic materials, as chemicals and steel. — *ns* heavy water, deuterium oxide, water in which the normal hydrogen content has been replaced by deuterium.

hebdomadal [heb-dom'a-dàl] *adj* weekly.

Hebrew [hē'brōō] *n* a member of an ancient Semitic people; an Israelite; a Jew.

hecatomb [hek'a-tom] *n* a great public sacrifice.

heckle [hek'l] *vt* to harass (a speaker) with questions or taunts. — *n* heck'ler.

hectic, -al [hek'tik, -ál] *adj* pertaining to the constitution or habit of body; intense, feverish, rushed.

hectograph [hek'to-gräf] *n* a gelatine pad for printing copies of a writing or drawing.

hector [hek'tór] *n* a bully, a braggart. — *vt* to treat insolently; to annoy. — *vi* to play the bully.

hedge [hej] *n* a close row of bushes or small trees serving as a fence; a barrier. — *vt* to enclose with a hedge; to surround; to hem in; to guard; to place secondary bets as a precaution. — *vi* to avoid committing oneself, as in an argument. — *ns* hedge'hog, a small insectivorous Old World mammal with sharp spines on the back; hedge'row, a line of shrubs or trees separating or enclosing fields.

hedonism [hē'dón-izm] *n* the doctrine that pleasure is the highest good. — *n* hē'donist.

heed [hēd] *vt* to pay close attention (to). — *n* careful attention. — *adj* heed'ful. — *adj* heed'less, inattentive; careless.

heel [hēl] *n* the back part of the foot, under the ankle; the part covering or supporting the heel in stockings, etc. or shoes; a solid attachment forming the back of the sole of a shoe; (*inf*) a despicable person. — *vt* to furnish with a heel; to follow closely; (*inf*) to provide with money, etc. — *vi* to follow along at the heels of someone.

heel [hēl] *vi* to incline; to lean to one side, as a ship. — *vt* to tilt.

hefty [heft'i] *adj* (*inf*) heavy; large and strong; big.

hegemony [hē-, he-gem'ón-i, or -jem'-, or hē'-, he'-] *n* leadership; preponderant influence, esp of one nation over others.

hegira, hejira [hej'i-ra] *n* the flight of Mohammed from Mecca in 622 AD.

heifer [hef'ér] *n* a young cow that has not calved.

height [hīt] *n* the topmost point; the highest limit; the distance from the bottom to the top; altitude; a relatively great distance above a given level; an eminence; a hill. — *vti* heighten, to make or come to a higher position.

heinous [hā'nús] *adj* outrageously evil. — *adv* hei'nously. — *n* hei'nousness.

heir [ār] *n* one who inherits or is entitled to inherit another's property, title, etc. heir'ess, a woman or girl who is an heir, esp to great wealth; heir'loom, any possession handed down from generation to generation.

helicopter [hel'i-kop-tèr] *n* a kind of aircraft lifted and moved, or kept hovering, by large rotary blades mounted horizontally.

heliograph [hē'li-ō-gräf] *n* an apparatus for signalling by using the sun's rays reflected by a mirror.

heliolatry [hē-li-ol'a-tri] *n* sun worship.

heliometer [hē-li-om'e-tèr] *n* an instrument for measuring the angular distance between two celestial objects or between points on the moon.

heliport [hel′i-port] *n* a landing and takeoff place for a helicopter. Also **helipad**.

heliot′ropism the tendency of a plant to bend toward the light.

helium [hēl′i-um] *n* a gaseous element, in the sun's atmosphere.

helix [hē′liks] *n* a spiral; the rim of the ear.

hell [hel] *n* in Christian belief, the place or state of punishment of the wicked after death; the abode of evil spirits; any place of vice or misery; (a state of) supreme misery or discomfort; severe censure or chastisement.—*adj* **hell′ish**, pertaining to or like hell; very wicked.

hellebore [hel′é-bōr, -bōr] *n* any of a genus of plants of the buttercup family.

Hellenic [hel-en′ik] *adj* Greek; of the history, language, or culture of the ancient Greeks.

helm[1] [helm] *n* the apparatus by which a ship is steered.—*n* **helms′man**, one who steers.

helm[2] [helm], **helmet** [hel′met] *n* a covering of armor for the head.

helot [hel′ot] *n* a serf or slave.—*n* **hel′ot-ism**, a symbiotic relationship in which one member functions as the slave of the other.

help [help] *vt* to make things better or easier for; to aid; to assist; to remedy; to keep from; to serve or wait on.—*vi* to give aid; to be useful; *pt p* **helped**.—*n* a helping; aid; assistance; a remedy; one that helps, esp a hired person.—*n* **helper**.—*adj* **helpful**, giving help; useful.—*adv* **help′fully**.—*adj* **help′less**, unable to help oneself.—*adv* **help′lessly**.—**help′mate**, **help′meet**, a helpful companion, esp a wife or husband.

helter-skelter [hel′tèr-skel′tèr] *adv* in haste and confusion.—*adj* disorderly.

helve [helv] *n* the handle of an axe or similar tool.—*vt* to furnish with a helve.

hem [hem] *n* the border of a garment etc.—*vt* to form a hem on by preventing the fabric from fraying, usu. by folding and sewing down the edge; to edge; to sew with a stitch used in making a hem.—*pr p* **hemm′ing**; *pt p* **hemmed**.

hematite [hē′mä-tīt] *n* native ferric oxide, an important iron ore.

hemisphere [hem′i-sfēr] *n* half of a sphere or globe; any of the halves (northern, southern, eastern, or western) of the earth.

hemistich [hem′i-stik] *n* half a line, an incomplete line of poetry.

hemlock [hem′lok] *n* a poisonous plant ; a poison made from this plant; an evergreen tree; its wood.

hemoglobin [hēm′ō-glō-bin] *n* the red coloring matter of the red blood corpuscles.

hemophilia [hēm-ō-fil′ē-a] *n* a hereditary condition in which the blood fails to clot normally.—*adj*, *n* **he′mophiliac**.

hemorrhage [hem′er-ij, hem′rij] *n* the escape of blood from a blood vessel; heavy bleeding.

hemorrhoid [hem′e-roid, hem′roid] *n* a painful swelling of a vein near the anus, often with bleeding.—*n* **piles**.

hemp [hemp] *n* a widely cultivated Asian herb of the mulberry family; its fiber, used to make rope, sailcloth, etc.

hen [hen] *n* the female of many birds, esp the chicken.—*vt* **henpeck**, to nag and domineer over (one's husband).

hence [hens] *adv* from this place; from this time; from this cause or reason.—*interj* away! begone!—*advs* **hence′forth**, **hencefor′ward**.

henchman [hench′man, -sh′-] *n* a trusted helper or follower.

henna [hen′a] *n* a dye extracted from its leaves used to tint the hair or skin; reddish brown.

henry [hen′ri] *n* (*elect*) the unit of inductance

hepatic [hep-at′ik] *adj* belonging to the liver.—**heparin** [hep-ar′in], a substance produced by the liver that inhibits clotting of the blood.—*n* **hepati′tis**, inflammation of the liver.

heptagon [hep′ta-gon] *n* a polygon of seven angles and seven sides.—*adj* **heptag′onal**.

her [hûr] *pron* the objective case (*dat* or *acc*) of the *pron* **she**; also the possessive case (*gen*)—in this use described also as *possessive adjective*.

herald [her′àld] *n* in former times, an official who made public proclamations and arranged ceremonies; a proclaimer; a forerunner.—*vt* to usher in; to proclaim.—*adj* **heral′dic**.—*n* **her′-**

aldry, the science of dealing with genealogies and coats of arms; ceremony; pomp.

herb [ûrb, hûrb] *n* any seed plant whose stem withers away annually; any plant used as a medicine, seasoning, etc.—*adj* **herbā′ceous**, of the nature of, or containing, herbs.—*n* **herb′age**, pasturage; the succulent parts of herbs.—*adj* **herb′al**, pertaining to herbs.—*n* a book containing descriptions of plants with medicinal properties.—*ns* **herb′alist**, one who practices healing by using herbs; one who grows or deals in herbs; **herbā′rium**, a classified collection of dried plants.—*pl* **herbā′ria**; **herb′icide** [-i-sīd], a substance for killing plants; **herb′ivore** [-vōr, -vōr], a plant-eating animal.

Herculean [hûr-kū-lē′àn] *adj* extremely difficult or dangerous; of extraordinary strength and size.

herd [hûrd] *n* a number of animals of one kind, esp large animals, that habitually keep together.—*vi* to go in herds.—*vt* to tend, as a herdsman.—*n* **herds′man**.

here [hēr] *adv* at or in this place; to or into this place; now; on earth.

heredity [he-red′i-ti] *n* the transmission of physical characteristics from ancestors to their descendants.—*adj* **hered′itable**, that may be inherited.—*n* **heredit′ament**, any property that may pass to an heir.—*adj* **hered′itary**, descending by inheritance; transmitted to offspring.

heresy [her′i-si] *n* an opinion or belief (esp in theology) adopted in opposition to that accepted or usual in the community to which one belongs.—**her′etic**, a dissenter from an established belief or doctrine.—*adj* **heret′ical**.—*adv* **heret′ically**.

heritable [her′i-ta-bl] *adj* that may be inherited.

heritage [her′it-ij] *n* that which is inherited; tradition.

hermaphrodite [hûr-maf′rod-īt] *n* an animal or a plant with the organs of both sexes.—*adjs* **hermaphrodīt′ic**.

hermetic [hûr-met′ik] *adj* airtight.—*adv* **hermet′ically**.

hermit [hûr′mit] *n* a recluse.—*n* **her′mitage** [-ij]), the dwelling of a hermit.

hernia [hûr′ni-a] *n* the protrusion of an organ, esp part of the intestine, through an opening in the wall of the surrounding structure; a rupture.

hero [hē′rō] *n* a man of distinguished bravery; one admired for his exploits; the central male character in a novel, play, etc.—*pl* **hēroes**.—**heroine** [her′ō-in], a woman with the attributes of a hero.—*adj* **heroic** [hē-rō′ik].—*adv* **hero′ically**.—*ns* **heroism** [her′ō-izm], the qualities of a hero; high courage.

heroin [her′ō-in, her-ō′in] *n* a habit-forming derivative of morphine.

heron [her′ón] *n* wading bird.—*n* **her′onry**, a heron rookery.

herpes [hûr′pēz] *n* any of several virus diseases marked by small blisters on the skin or mucous membranes.

herring [her′ing] *n* a small food fish.—*adj* **herr′ingbone**, like the spine of a herring with the ribs extending in rows of parallel, slanting lines.

hertz [hûrts] *n* SI unit of frequency, equal to one cycle per second.

hesitate [hez′i-tāt] *vi* to pause irresolutely; to be in doubt; to be reluctant (to); no **hes′itancy**, **hesitā′tion**, wavering; doubt.—*adj* **hes′itant**, hesitating.

heterodox [het′èr-ō-doks] *adj* holding an opinion other than, different from, the one generally received, esp in theology; heretical.

heterodyne [het′èr-ó-dīn] in (radio) communication, applied to a method of imposing on a carrier wave another of different frequency to produce audible beats.

heterogeneous [het-èr-ō-jē′ni-ús] *adj* dissimilar; composed of parts or elements of different kinds.—*ns* **heterogenē′ity**.

hew [hū] *vt* to cut with blows; to shape; to cut (a path; eg *to hew one's way*).—*vi* to conform (to a rule, principle, etc.—*pt p* **hewed**, or **hewn**.

hexagon [heks′a-gon] *n* a figure with six sides and six angles.—*adj* **hexag′onal**.—*adv* **hexag′onally**.

hiatus [hī-ā′tus] *n* a break in continuity; (*gram*) a slight pause between two vowels coming together in successive words or syllables.

hibernate [hī′bèr-nāt] *vi*; to pass the winter in torpor; to remain in a state of inactivity.—*n* **hibernā′tion**.

Hibernian [hī-bŭr'ni-án] *adj* relating to *Hibernia* or Ireland. — *n* a native or inhabitant of Ireland.

hiccup [hik'up] *n* a sudden spasm of the diaphragm followed immediately by closure of the glottis; the sound caused by this. — *vi* to be affected with hiccup.

hick [hik] *n* (*inf*) an unsophisticated person, esp from a rural area.

hickory [hik'ŏr-i] *n* a genus of N American trees of the walnut family; its smooth-shelled edible nut.

hidalgo [hi-dal'gŏ] *n* a Spanish nobleman of the lowest class. — *pl* **hidalgōs**.

hide[1] [hīd] *vt* to conceal; to put out of sight; to keep secret; to screen. — *vi* to go into, or stay in, concealment. — *adj* **hidd'en**, concealed; unknown.

hide[2] [hīd] *n* the skin of an animal either raw or tanned. — *adj* **hide'bound** (of an animal), having the hide clinging too closely to the body; obstinately conservative and narrow-minded. — *n* **hid'ing**, a thrashing.

hideous [hid'i-ùs] *adj* frightful, horrible, ghastly; extremely ugly. — *adv* **hid'eously**.

hie [hī] *vti* to hasten.

hierarch [hī'er-ärk] *n* a religious leader, esp of high authority. — *adjs* **hī'erarchal, hierarch'ical**. — **hī'erarchy**. — *n* church government by clergy in graded ranks; the highest officials in such a system.

hieroglyph [hī'er-ŏ-glif] *n* a character used in a system of hieroglyphic writing. — *n* **hieroglyph'ic**, a picture or symbol representing a word, sound, etc. in a system used by ancient Egyptians and others. — *adjs* **hieroglyph'ic, -al**.

higgle [hig'l] *vi* to haggle. — *n* **higg'ler**.

higgledy-piggledy [hig'l-di-pig'l-di] *adv* and *adj* haphazard; in confusion.

high [hī] *adj* lofty, tall; extending upward a (specified) distance; situated at or done from a height; above others in rank, position, etc.; greater in size, amount, cost, etc. than usual; raised or acute in pitch; (of meat) slightly tainted. — *adv* in or to a high degree, rank, etc. — *n* a high level, place, etc.; that gear of a motor vehicle, etc. producing the greatest speed. — *adj* **high'born**, of noble birth.; **high'brow**, (*inf*) an intellectual. — *adj* **high'falut'in, hi'falut'in**, (*inf*) pretentious; pompous. — *adj* **high'-flown**, extravagantly ambitious; bombastic. — *adjs* **high'hand'ed**, overbearing; **highland**, a region with many hills or mountains; **the Highlands**, the mountainous region occupying most of northern Scotland. — *adv* **highly**, very much; favorably; at a high level, wage, rank, etc. — *adj* **high-mind'ed**, having high ideals, etc. — *n* **highness**, height; **Highness**, a title used in speaking to or of royalty; **high seas**, open ocean waters outside the territorial limits of any nation. — *adj* **high'-spirited**, courageous; lively; **high'-strung**, nervous and tense; excitable.; **high'way**, a public road; a main thoroughfare; **high'wayman**, one who robs travelers on a highway.

hijacker, highjacker [hī'jak-ér] *n* one who hijacks. — *vt* **hi'jack, high'jack**, to steal (goods in transit) by force; to force (an aircraft) to make an unscheduled flight.

hike [hīk] *vi* to take a long walk. — *vt* (*inf*) to pull up. — *n* a long walk; a tramp; . — *n* **hiker**.

hilarious [hi-lā'ri-ùs] *adj* gay, very merry. — *adv* **hilā'riously**. — *n* **hilarity** [hi-lar'-], gaiety.

hill [hil] *n* a high mass of land, less than a mountain; a mound; an incline on a road. — *n* **hill'ock**. — *adj* **hill'y**.

hilt [hilt] *n* the handle of a sword, dagger, tool, etc.

him [him] *pron* the objective case (*dat* or *acc*) of the *pron* **he**.

himself [him-self'] *pron* the emphatic form of **he, him**; in his real character; having command of his faculties; sane; in good form; the reflexive form of **him** (objective).

hind [hīnd] *adj* placed in the rear; of the part behind; back. — Also **hind'er**. — *adj*. — *n pl* **hind'quarters**, the rear parts of a quadruped. — *n* **hind'sight**, wisdom after the event.

hinder [hin'dér] *vt* to keep back, or prevent progress of. — *vi* to be an obstacle. — *n* **hin'drance**, an obstacle.

Hindu, Hindoo [hin'-dōō] *n* any of several peoples of India; a follower of Hinduism. — *n* **Hin'duism**.

hinge [hinj] *n* a movable joint on a door or lid; a natural joint, as of a clam. — *vti* to attach or hang by a hinge. — *pr p* **hing'ing**; *pt p* **hinged**.

hint [hint] *n* a distant or indirect indication or allusion; slight mention; a helpful suggestion. — *vt* to intimate or indicate indirectly. — *vi* to give hints.

hinterland [hint'ér-land] *n* the land behind that bordering a coast or river; a remote area.

hip[1] [hip] *n* either side of the body below the waist and above the thigh.

hip[2] [hip], **hep** [hep] *n* the fruit of the dog-rose or other rose. — *n* **hippie**, (*slang*) a person usu. young who has turned to mysticism, psychedelic drugs, communal living in his alienation from conventional society. — Also **hippy**.

hippocampus [hip-ō-kam'pus] *n* a genus of small fishes with horselike head and neck, the sea-horse.

hippodrome [hip'o-drōm] *n* a stadium for horses and chariots in ancient Greece.

hippogriff [hip'-ō-grif] *n* a fabulous animal, a winged horse with the head of a griffin.

hippopotamus [hip-ō-pot'a-mus] *n* any of several large African quadrupeds of aquatic habits, with very thick skin, short legs, and a large head and muzzle.

hire [hīr] *n* wages for service; the price paid for the use of anything. — *vt* to pay for the services of (a person) or the use of (a thing). — Also *adj*. — *ns* **hire'ling**, one who will follow anyone's order for pay.

hirsute [hér-sūt'] *adj* hairy; rough, shaggy.

his [hiz] *pron* possessive (*gen*) form of **he** — described also as a *possessive adjective*.

hiss [his] *vi* to make a sound like that of a prolonged *s*; to show disapproval by hissing. — *vt* to say or indicate by hissing. — *n* the act or sound of hissing. — *n* **hissing**.

hist [hist] *interj* be quiet!

histology [his-tol'o-ji], the study of the minute structure of the tissues of organisms.

history [hist'ŏr-i] *n* an account of the origin and progress of a nation, institution, etc.; all recorded past events; the branch of knowledge that deals with the recording, analysis, etc. of past events; a known past (*my coat has a history*.) — *pl* **-ies**. — *n* **historian**, [hist'-ŏr'i-án] a writer of history; one who is learned in history. — *adjs* **histôr'ical**, pertaining to history; containing history; derived from history; famous in history; **histôr'ic**, famous in history, memorable. — *adv* **histor'ically**. — *ns* **historic'ity** [-is'-], historical truth, actuality; **historiog'rapher**, historian; **historiog'raphy**, the principles of historical writing, esp that based on the use of primary sources and techniques of research.

histrionic [his-tri-on'ik, -ál] *adj* relating to the stage or actors; melodramatic. — *adv* **histrion'ically**.

hit [hit] *vti* to come against (something) with force; to give a blow (to), to strike; to strike with a missile; to affect strongly; to come (upon) by accident or after a search; to arrive at; (baseball) to get (a hit). — *n* a blow that strikes its mark; a collision; a successful and popular song, book, etc.

hitch [hich] *vi* to move jerkily; to become fastened or caught. — *vt* to move, pull, etc. with jerks; to fasten with a hook, knot, etc. — *n* a tug; a limp; a hindrance; a catching; a kind of knot. — *vi* **hitch'hike**, to travel by asking for rides from motorists along the way.

hither [hiŦH'ér] *adv* to this place. — *adj* toward the speaker; nearer. — *advs* **hith'erto**, up to this time.

Hitlerism [hit'lèr-izm] *n* the nationalistic and totalitarian principles and policies associated with Hitler. — *adj*, *n* **Hit'lerite**.

hive [hīv] *n* a shelter for a colony of bees; a beehive; the bees of a hive; a crowd of busy people; a place of great activity. — *vt* to gather (bees) into a hive. — *vi* to enter a hive.

hives [hīvs] *n pl* urticaria.

hoar'y white or grey with age; (*bot*) covered with short, dense, whitish hairs. — *n* **hoar'frost**, hoar.

hoard[1] [hŏrd, hôrd] *n* a store; a hidden stock. — *vti* to amass and deposit in secret. — *n* **hoard'er**.

hoard[2] [hŏrd, hôrd], **hoarding** [hŏrd'ing, hôrd-] *n* a screen of boards, esp for enclosing a place where construction is taking place.

hoarse [hŏrs, hôrs] *adj* having a rough, husky voice, as from a cold; harsh; discordant. — *adv* **hoarse'ly**. — *n* **hoarse'ness**.

hoax [hŏks] *n* a deceptive trick; a practical joke. — *vt* to deceive by a hoax. — *n* **hoax'er**.

hob [hob] *n* a surface beside a fireplace, on which anything may be laid to keep hot.—*n* **hob'nail**, a nail with a thick, strong head, used on the soles of heavy shoes.

hobble [hob'l] *vi* to walk with short unsteady steps; to limp.—*vt* to fasten the legs of (horses, etc.) loosely together.—*n* a limp; a rope etc. used to hobble a horse.

hobbledehoy [hob'l-di-hoi'] *n* an awkward youth.

hobby [hob'i]*n* a hobbyhorse; a spare-time activity.—*n* **hobb'yhorse**, a child's toy comprising a stick with a horse's head; a rocking horse.

hobnob [hob'nob] *vi* to associate familiarly.

hobo [hō'bō] *n* a vagrant workman; a tramp.

hock[1] [hok] *n*, *vt* (*slang*) to give something in security for a loan.

hock[2] [hok] *n* the joint bending backward on the hind leg of a horse, etc.

hockey [hok'i] *n* a team game played on ice skates, with curved sticks and a rubber disk, called a puck; a similar game played on foot in a field with a ball.

hocus-pocus [hō'kus-pō'kus] *n* meaningless words used by a conjurer; sleight of hand; deception.—*vt* **hō'cus**, to cheat; to drug.

hod [hod] *n* a tray or V-shaped stemmed trough for carrying bricks or mortar on the shoulder.

hoe [hō] *n* an instrument for scraping or digging up weeds and loosening the earth.—*vti* to cultivate with a hoe.—*pr p* **hoe'ing**; *pt p* **hoed**.

hog [hog] *n* a full-grown pig raised for its meat; (*inf*) a selfish, greedy, or filthy person; (*inf*) one that uses something to excess.

hogshead [hogz'hed] *n* a large cask or barrel holding from 63 to 140 gallons.

hoi polloi [hoi po-loi'] the common people.

hoist [hoist] *vt* to raise aloft, esp with a pulley, crane, etc.—*n* a hoisting; an apparatus for lifting.

hold[1] [hōld] *vt* to keep fast; to grasp; to maintain in position; to restrain or control; to retain; to contain; to own, to occupy; to remain firm; to carry on, as a meeting; to regard.—*vi* to go on being firm, loyal, etc.; to remain unbroken or unyielding; to be true or valid; to continue; *pr p* **holding**; *pt p* **held**.—*ns* **hold'all**, a container for miscellaneous articles; **holder**, **holdfast**, something that will hold something else securely; **holding** (often *pl*) property, esp land, stocks and bonds; **holdup**, an armed robbery.

hold[2] [hōld] *n* the interior of a ship or of an aircraft used for cargo.

hole [hōl] *n* a hollow place; a cavity; a pit; an animal's burrow; an aperture; a perforation; a small, squalid, dingy place.—*vti* to make a hole in (something); to drive into a hole.

holiday [hol'i-dā] *n* a religious festival; a day of freedom from work, etc., esp one set aside by law.

holland [hol'ånd] *n* a usu. heavily sized, plain-woven cotton or linen fabric.

hollow [hol'ō] *n* a hole; a cavity; a depression; a groove, channel.—*adj* having an empty space within or below; sunken; empty or worthless.—*vti* to make or become hollow.

holly [hol'i] *n* a genus (*Ilex*) of evergreen shrubs having prickly leaves and scarlet or yellow berries.

hollyhock [hol'i-hok] *n* a tall, widely cultivated perennial herb.

holm oak [hōm'ōk'] *n* the evergreen oak.

holocaust [hol'ō-köst] *n* a great destruction of life, esp by fire.

hologram [hol'ō-gram] *n* a photograph made without use of a lens by means of interference between two parts of a laser beam, the result appearing as a meaningless pattern until suitably illuminated, when it shows as a 3-D image (a number of pictures can be 'stored' on the same plate or film).

holograph [hol'ō-gräf] *n* a document wholly in the handwriting of the signer.

holster [hōl'stėr] *n* a pistol case attached to a belt.

holy [hō'li] *adj* dedicated to religious use; without sin; deserving reverence.—*ns* **hol'iness**, sanctity; **Holy Week**, the week before Easter.

homage [hom'ij] *n* anything done or given to show honor, reverence, etc.

home [hōm] *n* the place where one lives; the city, etc. where one was born or reared; a place thought of as home; a household and its affairs; an institution for the aged, orphans, etc.; **home plate**.—*adj* of one's home or country; domestic; central

(*home office*).—*adv* at, to, or in the direction of home; to the point aimed at.—*ns* **home economics**, the art and science of homemaking, nutrition, etc.; **home front**, civilian concerns during a war.—*adj* **home'grown'**, grown or produced at home or nearby; characteristic of a particular locale; **home'-like**, cozy; cheerful; wholesome; **homely**, everyday; crude; not good-looking; **home'made**, made, or as if made, at home.—*ns* **home'maker**, a housewife or one who manages a home; **home plate**, (*baseball*) the slab that the batter stands beside which is the last base touched in scoring a run; **home run**, (*baseball*) a hit that allows the batter to touch all bases and score a run.—Also **hom'er** (*inf*).—*adj* **home'sick'**, longing for home.—*n* **home'sick'ness**.—*adj* **home'spun**, cloth spun at home; made of homespun; plain.—*n* cloth made of yard spun at home; coarse cloth like this.—*ns* **home'stead**, a place for a family's home, including the land and buildings; a 160-acre tract of US public land, granted as a farm.—*n* **homesteader**.—*n* **home'stretch'**, the part of a race track between the last turn and the finish line; the final part.—*adj*, *adv* **homeward**, toward home.—*adv* **homewards**.—*n* **home'work'**, work, esp piecework, done at home; schoolwork to be done outside the classroom; preliminary study for a project.—*adj* **homey**, cozy, familiar, etc.

homeopathy [hōm-i-o'pathi] *n* the system of treating disease by small quantities of drugs that cause symptoms similar to those of the disease.—*ns* **home'eopath**; **homeo'pathist**.—*adj* **homeopath'ic**.—*adv* **homeopath'ically**.

Homeric [hō-mer'ik] *adj* pertaining to *Homer*, the great Greek epic poet of the 8th century B.C.; worthy of Homer; heroic.

homicide [hom'i-sīd] *n* the killing of a person by another; one who kills another.—*adj* **homici'dal**.

homily [hom'i-li] *n* a sermon; a solemn talk or writing.—*adjs* **homilet'ic**, **-al**.—*n* **homilet'ics**, the art of preaching.

hominy [hom'i-ni] *n* hulled and coarsely ground dry corn.

homogeneous [hom-ō-jēn'i-ùs] *adj* of the same kind or nature; having all the constituent parts or elements similar.—*ns* **homogene'ity**, homogeneousness; **homogē'neousness**, uniformity of nature or kind.—*vt* **homog'enize**, to make homogenousu

homologous [hom-ol'o-gùs] *adj* corresponding in relative position, general structure and descent.—*ns* **hom'ologue**, **homolog** [-log], somethingthat exhibits homology; **homology**, a similarity often attributed to a common origin.

homonym [hom'o-nim] *n* a word having the same sound as another, but a different meaning.

homosexual [hom-ō-seks'ū-ål] *adj* having sexual desire directed toward one of the same sex.—Also *n*.—*n* **homosexual'ity**.

hone [hōn] *n* a hard stone used to sharpen cutting tools.—*vt* to sharpen as on a hone.

honest [on'èst] *adj* truthful; trustworthy; sincere or genuine; gained by fair means; frank, open.—*adv* **hon'estly**.—*n* **hon'esty**.

honey [hun'i] *n* a sweet thick substance that bees make as food from the nectar of flowers; sweetness; a darling.—*adj* of, resembling honey; much loved.—**hon'eycomb**, the structure of six-sided wax cells made by bees to hold their honey, eggs, etc; anything like this.—*vt* to fill with holes like a honeycomb.—*ns* **hon'eydew**, a sugary deposit on leaves secreted by aphids, scale insects, or a fungus; **hon'eymoon**, the vacation spent together by a newly-married couple.—Also *vi*.—*n* **hon'eysuckle**, any of a genus of shrubs with small, fragrant flowers.

honk [hongk] *n* the cry of the wild goose; the noise of an automobile horn.—Also *vti*.

honorarium [hon-or-ā'ri-um, on-] *n* a voluntary fee paid, esp to a professional man for his services.

honorary [on'ór-år-i] *adj* given as an honor; holding a title or office without performing services, or without reward.

honorific [on-ór-if'ik] *see* **honor**.—Also *n*.

honor [on'or] *n* high regard or respect; glory; fame; good reputation; integrity; chastity; high rank; distinction.—*vt* to respect greatly; to do or give something in honor of; to accept and pay.—*adjs* **hon'orable**, worthy of being honored; honest; upright; bringing honor; **hon'orary**, given as an honor; designating or in an office held as an honor, without service or pay; **honorific** [on-or-if'ik], conferring honor.—Also *n*.

hooch [hōōch] *n* (*slang*) alcoholic liquor, esp when illicitly distilled or obtained.

hood [hŏŏd] *n* a flexible covering for the head and back of the neck; the metal cover over an automobile engine; any hood-like thing as the (adjustable) top of an automobile, baby carriage, canopy over stove, etc. — *vt* to cover with a hood.

hoodlum [hŏŏdl'ům] *n* a member of a lawless gang.

hoodoo [hŏŏd'dōō] *n* voodoo; a person or thing that brings bad luck; bad luck.

hoodwink [hŏŏd'wingk] *vt* to mislead by trickery.

hoof [hŏŏf] *n* horny substance on the feet of certain animals, as horses, etc., or the entire foot.

hook [hŏŏk] *n* an object of bent metal, such as would catch or hold anything; a fishhook; something shaped like a hook; a strike, blow, etc., in which a curving motion is involved. — *vt* to catch, fasten, hold, as with a hook. — *adj* **hooked** [hŏŏkt], addicted.

hookah [hŏŏk'a] *n* an Oriental tobacco-pipe, in which the smoke is passed through water.

hooligan [hŏŏl'i-gán] *n* a hoodlum.

hoop [hŏŏp] *n* a circular band for holding together the staves of casks, etc.; anything like this, as a ring in a hoop skirt. — *vt* to bind with hoops.

hoot [hŏŏt] *n* the sound that an owl makes; a shout of scorn. — *vi* to utter a hoot. — *vt* to express (scorn) of (someone) by hooting. — *n* hoot'er.

hop[1] [hop] *vi* to leap on one leg; to leap with all feet at once, as a frog, etc.; (*inf*) to go briskly. — *ns* **hopp'er**, one who hops; a hopping insect; **hop'scotch**, a game in which children hop over lines drawn on the ground.

hop[2] [hop] *n* a twining vine with small cone-shaped flowers; (*pl*) the dried ripe cones, used for flavoring beer.

hope [hōp] *n* a feeling that what is wanted will happen; the object of this; a person or thing on which one may base some hope. — *vt* to want and expect. — *vi* to have hope (for). — *adj* **hope'ful**, full of hope; having qualities that promise good or success. — *adv* **hope'fully**, in a hopeful manner. — *n* **hope'fulness**. — *adj* **hope'less**, without hope.

horary [hōr'ár-ē, hōr-, här-] *adj* pertaining to an hour; hourly.

horde [hōrd, hôrd] *n* a crowd or throng; a swarm.

horehound [hōr'-, hôr'hownd] *n* a bitter mint a medicine or candy made from its juice.

horizon [hor-ī'zón] *n* the circle in which earth and sky seem to meet; the boundary or limit of one's experience, interests, etc. — *adj* **horizontal** [hor-i-zont'ál], level; parallel to the plane of the horizon.

hormone [hôr'mōn] *n* a product of living cells formed in one part of the organism and carried to another part, where it takes effect. — *adjs* **hormonal**.

horn [hôrn] *n* a hard outgrowth on the head of an animal; the material of which this is made; any projection resembling a horn; a crescent tip; something made of, or curved like, a horn; a device to sound a warning. — *vt* to furnish with horns; to remove horns from. — *adj* **horn'y**, like horn; hard; callous. — *ns* **hornbeam**, any of a genus of the birch family; **horn'book**, formerly, a child's primer held in a frame with a thin pane of horn; **horn'pipe**, a lively dance formerly popular with sailors.

hornblende [hôrn'blend] *n* a mineral consisting of silica, with magnesia, lime or iron.

hornet [hôrn'et] *n* a large wasp with a severe sting.

horologe [hor'o-loj] *n* a device for keeping time. — *n* **horol'ogy**, the science of measuring time; the art of making timekeepers.

horoscope [hor'o-skōp] *n* a chart of the zodiacal signs and positions of planets, etc. by which astrologers profess to predict future events, esp in the life of an individual.

horrible [hor'i-bl] *adj* exciting horror; dreadful; (*inf*) very bad; ugly, unpleasant, etc. — *adv* **horr'ibly**.

horrid [hor'id] *adj* terrible; horrible. — *adv* **horr'idly**. — *n* **horr'idness**.

horrify [hor'i-fī] *vt* to strike with horror. — *pr p* **horr'ifying**; *pt p* **horr'ified**. — *adj* **horrif'ic**.

horror [hor'ór] *n* the strong feeling caused by something frightful or shocking; strong dislike; a source of such feeling; a disagreeable person or thing.

hors-d'œuvre [ör-dœ-vr'] *n* an appetizer served before a meal.

horse [hôrs] *n* four-legged, solid-hoofed herbivorous mammal

(*Equus caballus*) with flowing mane and tail, ranging in size from 24 to 68 inches at the shoulders, domesticated for drawing loads, carrying riders, etc.; (*pl*) cavalry; a vaulting horse; a frame with legs to support something. — *vt* to supply with a horse or horses; to put on horseback. — *vi* to engage in horseplay. — *ns* **horse'back**, the back of a horse; **horse chestnut**, a large tree with large palmate leaves and erect clusters of flowers; **horse'hair**, hair from the mane or the tail of a horse; **horse latitude**, either of two oceanic regions between 30° north and 30° south latitude marked by calms; **horse'laugh**, a boisterous, usu. derisive laugh; **horse'man**, a person skilled in the riding or care of horses; **horse'manship**, the art of being a horseman; **horse'play**, rough, boisterous fun; **horse'power**, a unit for measuring the power of engines, etc. equal to 746 watts or 33,000 foot-pounds per minute; **horse'radish**, a tall herb of the mustard family; a relish made up from its pungent root; **horse'shoe**, a flat, U-shaped, protective metal plate nailed to a horse's hoof; anything shaped like this. — **horse'trade**, a negotiation marked by shrewd bargaining and mutual concessions.

hortative [hôrt'a-tiv] *adj* inciting; encouraging; giving advice. — Also **hort'atory**.

horticulture [hôr'ti-kul-tyůr, -chůr] *n* the art or science of growing flowers, fruits, and vegetables. — *adj* **horticul'tural**. — *n* **horticul'turist**.

hosanna, hosannah [hō-zan'a] *n* an exclamation of praise to God.

hose [hōz] *n* stockings; socks; a flexible tube used to convey fluids. — *pl* **hoses, hose**. — *n* **hos'iery** [hō'zhėr-ē], stockings; socks.

hospice [hos'pis, -pēs] *n* a guesthouse for travelers; a homelike facility for the care of the dying.

hospitable [hos'pit-à-bl] *adj* kind to strangers; giving a generous welcome to guests. — *n* **hos'pital'ity**, the act, practice, or quality of being hospitable.

hospital [hos'pit-ál] *n* an institution for the treatment of the sick or injured; a building for any of these purposes. — *vt* **hos'pitalize**, to send to hospital.

host[1] [hōst] *n* one who lodges or entertains a stranger or guest at his house; an innkeeper; an animal or plant on or in which another lives. — *n* **hostess**.

host[2] [hōst] *n* an army, a large multitude.

host[3] [hōst] *n* the wafer or bread used in the Eucharist or Holy Communion.

hostage [hos'tij] *n* a person given or kept as a pledge until certain conditions are met.

hostel [hos'tél] *n* a lodging place. — Also **hos'telry**.

hostile [hos'tīl, -til] *adj* belonging to an enemy; showing enmity; warlike; adverse. — *n* **hostil'ity**, *pl* **hostil'ities**, acts of warfare.

hot [hot] *adj* of high temperature; very warm; giving or feeling heat; full of intense feeling; following closely; electrically charged; (*inf*) recent, new. — *adv* **hot'ly**. — *ns* **hot air'**, (*slang*) empty talk; **hot'bed**, a bed of heated earth enclosed by low walls and covered by glass for forcing plants. — *adj* **hot'blooded**, easily excited. — **hot'dog**, (*inf*) a wiener, esp one served in a long soft roll.

hotel [hō-tel'] *n* a commercial establishment providing lodging and meals for travelers, etc. — *n* **hotel keeper; hotel'ier**.

hound [hownd] *n* any of a class of purebred dogs with large drooping ears, which hunt by scent, and are used in the chase; any dog. — *vt* to hunt or chase as with hounds; to urge on by harassment.

hour [owr] *n* 60 min or the 24th part of a day; the time for a particular activity; the time of day. — *pl* the prescribed times for doing business. — *ns* **hour'-glass**, an instrument for measuring the hours by the running of sand from one part to another through a narrow neck; **hour'ly**, happening every hour; frequent.

houri [hŏŏ'ri, how'ri] *n* a beautiful woman of the Muslim paradise; a voluptuous young woman.

house [hows] *n* a building to live in esp by one person or family; a household; a family as including relatives, ancestors, and descendants; the audience in a theater; a business firm; a legislative assembly. — *pl* **houses** [howz'iz]. — *vt* **house** [howz], to shelter; to store; to provide houses for. — *vi* to take shelter. — **house'boat**, a barge furnished and used as a dwelling place or for cruising; **house′break′er**, one who breaks open and enters a house for a felonious purpose; **house′break′ing**.—**house′hold**, those living together in the same house.—*adj* pertaining to the house and family.—**house′keeper**, a woman who runs a home, esp one hired to do so; **house′maid**, a female servant employed to do housework.—*ns* **house′-warming**, a party given after moving into a new house; **housewife** [hows′wīf], the mistress of a house.

housing [howz′ing] *n* an ornamental covering for a horse.

hovel [hov′èl, huv′èl] *n* any small wretched dwelling; a shed.

hover [huv′èr, hov′èr] *vi* to remain aloft flapping the wings; to remain suspended; to linger.

how [how] *adv* in what manner; to what extent; by what means; in what condition.

howdah [how′da] *n* a pavilion or seat fixed on the back of an elephant or camel.

however [how-ev′èr] *adv* in whatever manner or degree; nevertheless.

howitzer [how′its-èr] *n* a short cannon used for shelling at a steep angle.

howl [howl] *vi* to utter the long, wailing cry of wolves, dogs, etc.; to utter a similar cry of anger, pain, etc.; to shout or laugh in mirth, etc.—*vt* to utter with a howl; to drive by howling.—*n* the wailing cry of a wolf, dog, etc.; any similar sound.—*n* **howler**.

hoy [hoi] *n* a large one-decked boat.

hoyden [hoi′dèn] *n* a bold, boisterous girl.

hub [hub] *n* the center part of a wheel; a center of activity.

hubbub [hub′ub] *n* a confused sound of many voices, riot, uproar.

huckaback [huk′a-bak] *n* an absorbent linen or cotton fabric with raised surface used for towels, etc.

huckleberry [huk′l-bèr-i] *n* a genus of N American shrubs with dark-blue to black berries.

huckster [huk′stèr] *n* a person using aggressive or questionable methods of selling.

huddle [hud′l] *vti* to crowd close together; to draw (oneself) up.—*n* a confused crowd or heap.

hue¹ [hū] *n* color; a particular shade or tint of a color.

hue² [hū] *n* a shouting; now only in **hue and cry**.

huff [huf] *n* state of smoldering resentment.—*vi* to blow; to puff.—*adj* **huff′y**.—*adv* **huff′ily**.

hug [hug] *vt* to clasp close with the arms; to cling to; to keep close to.—*vi* to embrace one another.

huge [hūj] *adj* enormous; gigantic.—*adv* **huge′ly**.

hugger-mugger [hug′èr-mug′èr] *n* secrecy; confusion.

Huguenot [hū′gè-not or -nō] *n* a French Protestant of the 16th and 17th centuries.

hulk [hulk] *n* the body of a ship, esp if old and dismantled; a large, clumsy person or thing.—*adjs* **hulk′ing**, **hulk′y**, clumsy.

hula, hula-hula [hōō′la, hōō′la-hōō′la] *n* a native Hawaiian dance.

hull [hul] *n* the outer covering of a fruit or seed; the frame or body of a ship.—*vt* to remove the hulls of; to pierce the hull of.

hullabaloo [hul′a-ba-lōō] *n* an uproar.

hum [hum] *vi* to make a sound like bees; to sing with closed lips; to pause in speaking and utter an inarticulate sound; to be busily active.—*vt* to render music by **humming**.—*pr p* **humm′ing**.—*n* the noise of bees; a murmur. **humm′ing bird**, a tiny brightly colored American bird with wings that vibrate rapidly, making a humming sound.

human [hū′màn] *adj* belonging or pertaining to man or mankind; having the qualities of a man.—*n* **hū′mankind**, people, mankind.—*adv* **hū′manly**.

humane [hū-mān′] *adj* having the feelings proper to man; kind, tender, merciful; benevolent.—*adv* **humane′ly**.

humanize [hū′man-īz] *vti* to make or become human.

humanist [hū′màn-ist] *n* advocate of humanism.—*adj* **human-ist′ic**.—*n* **hu′manism**, any system which puts human interests and the mind of man paramount, rejecting religion.

humanitarian [hū-man-i-tā′ri-àn] *n* a philanthropist.—*adj* of or belonging to humanity, benevolent.—*n* **humanitā′rianism**.

humanity [hū-man′it-i] *n* the nature peculiar to a human being; the kind feelings of man.

humble [hum′bl] *adj* lowly; unpretentious, modest.—*vt* to

bring down in condition or rank; to abase.—*n* **hum′bleness**.—*adv* **hum′bly**.

humble-bee [hum′bl-bē] *n* the bumble-bee.

humble pie [hum′bl pī] *n* apology, usu. under pressure.—**eat humble pie**, to undergo humiliation.

humbug [hum′bug] *n* fraud, sham, hoax.—*vt* to deceive; to hoax.

humdrum [hum′drum] *adj* dull, monotonous.—Also *n*.

humerus [hū′mèr-us] *n* the bone of the upper arm.

humid [hū′mid] *adj* moist, damp, rather wet.—*adv* **hū′midly**.—*vt* **humid′ify**, to make humid.

humiliate [hū-mil′i-āt] *vt* to humble; to wound the self-respect of, or mortify.—*n* **humiliā′tion**.

humility [hū-mil′i-ti] *n* the state of being humble.

hummock [hum′ók] *n* a small hillock; a ridge of ice.

humor [hū′mòr] *n* (*arch*) a fluid of the body, esp one of the four that were formerly believed to determine temperament; temperament, disposition; state of mind; inclination; caprice; the ability to appreciate or express what is funny, amusing, etc.; the expression of this.—*vt* to indulge; to gratify by compliance.—*ns* **humoresque′**, a musical caprice; **hū′morist**.—*adj* **hū′morous**, (*arch*) capricious; having a sense of the ludicrous and incongruous; funny, exciting laughter.—*adv* **hū′morously**.—*n* **hū′morousness**.

hump [hump] *n* a lump on the back of an animal (as a camel or whale).—*vt* to hunch; to arch.—*n* **hump′back**, a humped or crooked back; a hunchback.—*adj* **hump′backed**, having a humpback.

humus [hūm′us] *n* decomposed organic matter in the soil.

Hun [hun] *n* one of a savage nomad race of Asia, which overran Europe in 5th century AD; a ruthless savage.

hunch [hunch, -sh] *n* a hump.—*vt* to arch into a hump.—*vi* to move forward jerkily.—*n* **hunch′back**, a person with a humpback.

hundred [hun′dred] *adj, n* ten times ten.—*n* the symbol for this (100, c, C); the hundredth in a series or set; a subdivision of some American counties.—*adj* **hun′dredfold**.—*adj* **hun′dredth**, the last of a hundred.—*n* **hun′dred weight**, a unit of weight, equal to 100 pounds in the US and 112 pounds in Britain.

hunger [hung′gèr] *n* craving for food; need, or lack, of food; any strong desire.—*vi* to crave food; to long (for).—*adj* **hung′ry**, *adv* **hung′rily**.

hunk [hungk] *n* (*inf*) a large piece, lump, etc.—**hunker** [hungk′èr] *vi* to squat.—*n pl*, haunches or buttocks.

hunt [hunt] *vti* to seek out to kill or capture (game) for food or sport; to search (for); to chase.—*n* a chase; a search; a party organized for hunting.—*ns* **hunter**, **hunts′man**, a person who manages a hunt and looks after the hounds; **hunt′ress**.

hurdle [hûr′dle] *n* a portable frame of bars for temporary fences or for jumping over by horses or runners; an obstacle.—*pl* race over hurdles.—*n* **hurd′ler**.

hurdy-gurdy [hûr′di-gûr′di] *n* a barrel organ.

hurl [hûrl] *vt* to fling with violence; to cast down; to utter vehemently.—*n* **hurl′er**.

hurly-burly [hûr′li-bûr′li] *n* tumult; confusion.

hurrah [hur-ä′, hŏŏr-ä′] *interj* an exclamation of enthusiasm or joy.

hurricane [hur′i-kin, -kàn] *n* a violent tropical cyclone with winds of at least 74 miles per hour (12, the highest, on the Beaufort scale).

hurry [hur′i] *vt* to urge forward; to hasten.—*vi* to move or act with haste; etc.—*adv* **hurr′iedly**.

hurt [hûrt] *vt* to cause bodily pain to; to damage; to offend.—*vi* to give pain; to have pain.—*adj* **hurt′ful**, causing hurt or loss; injurious.

hurtle [hûrt′l] *vti* to move or throw with great speed and much force.

husband [huz′bànd] *n* a man to whom a woman is married.—*vt* to conserve; to manage thriftily.—*ns* **hus′bandman**, (*arch*) a farmer; **hus′bandry**, economical management; farming.

hush [hush] *interj* or *imper* silence! be still!—*vti* to quieten.—*n* a silence.

husk [husk] *n* the dry, thin covering of certain fruits and seeds; any dry, rough, or useless covering.—*vt* to remove the husk from.

usky[1] [husk'i] *adj* (of the voice) hoarse; rough in sound; sturdy, strong.

usky[2] [hus'ki] *n* a New World arctic sled dog.

ussar [hŏŏ-zär'] *n* a European soldier of a light cavalry regiment usu. with a brilliant dress uniform.

ussy [hus'i, huz'i] *n* a woman of low morals.

ustings [hus'tingz] *n sing* the process of, or a place for, political campaigning.

ustle [hus'l] *vt* to shake or push together; to push roughly or unceremoniously; to jostle. — *vi* to move hurriedly. — *n* a bustling.

ut [hut] *n* a very plain or crude little house or cabin.

utch [huch] *n* a pen or coop for small animals; a hut.

uzzah, huzza [huz-ä'] *interj, n* hurrah.

acinth [hī'a-sinth] *n* a bulbous genus of the lily family with spikes of bell-shaped flowers; the orange gemstone jacinth; a light violet to moderate purple.

aline [hȳ'a-lin] *adj* glassy; of or like glass.

brid [hī'brid] *n* the offspring of two plants or animals of different species; a mongrel. — *adj* crossbred. — *vti* (to cause) to produce hybrids.

dra [hī'dra] *n* a legendary many-headed water serpent; any of numerous freshwater polyps having a mouth surrounded by tentacles. — *adj* **hy'dra-head'ed**, difficult to root out.

drangea [hī-drān'j(y)a] *n* a genus of shrubby plants with large heads of showy flowers.

drant [hī'drànt] *n* a large pipe with a valve for drawing water from a water main.

draulic [hī-dröl'ik] *adj* relating to hydraulics: conveying water; worked by water or other liquid. — *adv* **hydraul'ically**. — *n pl* **hydraul'ics**, used as *sing*; the science dealing with the mechanical properties of liquids, as water, and their application in engineering.

drocarbon [hī-drō-kär'bòn] *n* a chemical compound containing only hydrogen and carbon.

drochloric acid [hī-drō-klor'ik] a strong, highly corrosive acid that is a solution of the gas hydrogen chloride in water.

drodynamics [hī-drō-di-nam'iks or -dī-] *n pl* used as *sing*, the science that treats of the motions and equilibrium of a material system partly or wholly fluid. — *adjs* **hydrodyna'ic, -al.**

droelectricity [hī-drō-el-ek-tris'i-ti] *n* electricity produced by water power. — *adj* **hydroelec'tric.**

drogen [hī'drō-jèn, -jen] *n* a flammable, colorless, odorless, gaseous chemical element, the lightest known substance.

drography [hī-drog'ra-fi] *n* the study of bodies of water (as seas, lakes, and rivers).

drokinetic [hī-drō-ki-net'ik] of the motion of fluids and forces affecting this motion.

drolysis [hī-drol'i-sis] *n* the decomposition of organic compounds by interaction with water.

drometer [hī-drom'èt-èr] *n* a device for measuring specific gravities of liquids, esp alcoholic beverages.

dropathy [hī-drop'a-thi] *n* the treatment of disease by water. — *adjs* **hydropathic** [hī-drō-path'ik].

drophobia [hī-drō-fō'bi-a] *n* a morbid fear of water; rabies. — *adj* **hydrophobic** [-fob'ik].

droponics [hī-drō-pon'iks] *n* the art or practice of growing plants in a chemical solution without soil.

drostatics [hī-drō-stat'iks] *n pl* used as *sing*, a branch of physics dealing with fluids at rest.

drous [hī'drûs] *adj* (*chem, min*) containing water.

na, hyaena [hī-ē'na] *n* a nocturnal, carnivorous, scavenging mammal.

giene [hī'ji-ēn, also -jen] *n* the principles and practice of health and cleanliness. — *adj* **hygienic** [hī-jēn'-ik]. — *adv* **hygien'ically.**

grometer [hī-grom'èt-èr] *n* an instrument for measuring the relative humidity of air.

menop'tera a large order of insects which have two pairs of membraneous wings.

mn [him] *n* a song of praise. — *vt* to celebrate in song; to worship in hymns. — *vi* to sing in adoration. — *ns* **hym'nal, m'nary**, hymn book. — *ns* **hymnol'ogy**, the study or composition of hymns.

per- [hī'pèr-] beyond; over, in excess [Gr *hyper*]. — *eg* **hyper-**

phys'ical, beyond physical laws, supernatural; **hypersen'sitive**, over-sensitive; **hypersen'sitiveness.**

hyperbola [hī-pûr'bo-la] *n* (*geom*) a curve, one of the conic sections, being the intersection of a double cone and a plane making a greater angle with the base than the side of the cone makes.

hyperbole [hī-pûr'bo-lē] *n* a figure of speech that produces a vivid impression by obvious exaggeration. — *adjs* **hyperbol'ic, al.** — *adv* **hyperbol'ically.**

hyperborean [hī-pêr-bō'ri-àn] *adj* belonging to the extreme north. — *n* an inhabitant of the extreme north.

hypercritic [hī-pêr-krit'ik] *n* one who is excessively critical. — *adjs* **hypercrit'ical.**

hypertrophy [hī-pûr'tro-fi] *n* abnormal enlargement of an organ or part. — *vi* to increase in size beyond the normal. — *adj* **hyper'trophied.**

hyphen [hī'fèn] *n* a short stroke (-) joining two syllables or words. — *vt* to join by a hyphen. — *vt* **hy'phenate**, to hyphen.

hypnosis [hip-nō'sis] *n* a sleeplike state in which the mind responds to external suggestion. — *adj* **hypnot'ic**, of or relating to hypnosis. — *n* any agent causing sleep. — *vt* **hyp'notize**, to put in a state of hypnosis; to fascinate. — *n* **hyp'notism**, the art or practice of inducing hypnosis.

hypochondria [hip-, hīp-ō-kon'dri-a] *n* morbid anxiety about health, often with imaginary illnesses. — *adj* **hypochon'driac.**

hypocrisy [hi-pok'ri-si] *n* pretending to be what one is not, as good or virtuous; simulating feeling one does not experience. — *n* **hyp'ocrite**. — *adj* **hypocrit'ical**. — *adv* **hypocrit'ically.**

hypodermic [hip-, or hīp-ō-dûr'mik] *adj* injected under the skin. — *n* a hypodermic needle, syringe or injection.

hypotenuse [hīp-, or hip-ot'ên-ūs, or -ūz] *n* the side of a right-angled triangle opposite to the right angle; the length of a hypotenuse.

hypoth'ecāte [hip-oth'é-kāt] *vt* to pledge without delivery of title or possession (of a property). — *n* **hypotheca'tion.**

hypothesis [hī-poth'e-sis] *n* an unproved theory, etc. tentatively accepted to explain certain facts. — *pl* **hypoth'eses** [-sēz]. — *adjs* **hypothet'ical**, assumed. — *adv* **hypothet'ically.**

hyssop [his'óp] *n* an aromatic plant of the mint family with blue flowers.

hysteria [his-tē'ri-a] *n* a mental disorder marked by excitability, anxiety, imaginary organic disorders, etc.; any outbreak of wild uncontrolled feeling. — *n pl* **hyster'ics**, fits of hysteria. — *adjs* **hysteric** [-ter'-ik], -al. — *adv* **hyster'ically.**

I

I [ī] *pron* the nominative case singular of the first personal pronoun.

iambus [ī-am'bus] *n* a metrical foot of two syllables, the first short and the second long. — Also **i'amb**. — *adj* **iam'bic.**

Iberian [ī-bē'ri-àn] *adj* of Spain and Portugal.

ibex [ī'beks] *n* any of several large-horned mountain wild goats.

ibis [ī'bis] *n* a genus of wading birds with curved bill.

ice [īs] *n* water frozen solid by cold; a frozen dessert of fruit juice, sugar, etc. — *vt* to freeze; to cool with ice; to cover with icing. — *vi* to freeze. — *ns* **ice age**, glacial epoch; **ice'berg**, a great mass of ice broken off a glacier and floating in the sea; **ice'cap**, a mass of slowly spreading glacial ice; **ice cream'**, a sweet, frozen food made from flavored cream or milk; **ice'field**, an extensive field of ice in the sea; **ice'floe**, a sheet of floating sea ice; **ic'ing**, a semisolid flavored sweet mixture used to coat cakes and cookies. — *adj* **icy** [ī'sē]. — *adv* **ic'ily**. — *n* **ic'iness.**

ichneumon [ik-nū'mòn] *n* a mongoose; an ichneumon fly. — *n* **ichneumon fly**, any of a large superfamily of insects whose larvae are parasitic.

ichthyology [ik-thi-ol'o-ji] *n* the branch of zoology dealing with fishes. — *n* **ichthyol'ogist.**

ichthyosaurus [ik'thi-ō-sör-us] *n* any of an order of extinct marine reptiles.

icicle [īs'i-kl] *n* a hanging piece of ice formed by the freezing of dripping water.

icon [ī'kon] *n* an image; in the Eastern Church, a sacred image usu on a wooden panel.

iconoclast [ī-kon'ō-klast] *n* one who attacks old cherished errors and superstitions. — *adj* **iconoclast'ic**.

id [id] *n* in psychoanalytic theory, that part of the psyche which is the source of psychic energy.

idea [ī-dē'a] *n* an image of an external object formed by the mind; a notion, thought, any product of intellectual action; an opinion or belief; a scheme; meaning or significance. — *adj* **idē'al**, existing in idea; existing in imagination only; highest and best conceivable; perfect. — *n* the highest conception of anything; a perfect model; a goal or principle. — *vti* **idē'alize**, to regard as, or to represent as, ideal. — *ns* **idealiza'tion**; **idē'alism**, behavior or thought based on a conception of things as one thinks they ought to be; a striving to achieve one's ideals; **idē'alist**

identify [ī-den'ti-fī] *vt* to ascertain or prove to be the same; to ascertain the identity of. — *ns* **identificā'tion**.

identity [ī-den'ti-ti] *n* state of being the same; sameness; individuality; personality; who or what a person is. — *adj* **iden't-ical**, the very same. — *adv* **iden'tically**.

ideology [id-, or īd-i-ol'o-ji] *n* the doctrines, beliefs, opinions, etc. of an individual, class, political party, etc. — *adjs* **ideolog'ic, -al**.

ides [īdz] *n pl* in ancient Rome, the 15th day of March, May, July, October, and the 13th of the other months.

idiom [id'i-ôm] *n* the dialect of a people, region, etc.; the usual way in which the words of a language are used to express thought; an accepted phrase or expression with a different meaning from the literal; a characteristic style, as in art or music. — *adjs* **idiomat'ic, -al**. — *adv* **idiomat'ically**.

idiosyncrasy [id-i-ō-sing'kra-si] *n* peculiarity of temperament or mental constitution; any characteristic of a person. — *adj* **idiosyncratic** [-krat'ik].

idiot [id'i-ôt, id'yôt] *n* an adult mentally inferior to a child of three; a foolish or unwise person. — *n* **id'iocy** [-si], state of being an idiot; imbecility; folly. — *adjs* **idiotic** [-ot'ik]. — *adv* **idiot'ically**.

idle [ī'dl] *adj* unemployed; averse to labor; not occupied or in use; useless, vain; baseless. — *vt* to spend in idleness. — *vi* to move slowly or aimlessly; to be unemployed or inactive. — *vt* to waste. — *ns* **i'dleness**. — *adv* **i'dly**.

idol [ī'dôl] *n* an image of some object of worship; a person or thing too much loved, admired, or honored. — *vt* **i'dolize**, to make an idol of, for worship; to love to excess.

idolater [ī-dol'à-tèr] *n* a worshipper of idols. — *fem* **idol'atress**. — *adj* **idol'atrous**. — *n* **idol'atry**, the worship of idols.

idyll [id'il, ī'd'il] *n* a short pictorial poem, chiefly on pastoral subjects; a story, episode, or scene of happy innocence or rusticity. — *adv* **idyll'ic**.

if [if] *conj* on condition that; in case that; supposing that; whether.

igloo [ig'lōō] *n* an Eskimo house built of soil, wood, or stone or of snow and ice.

igneous [ig'nē-us] *adj* of fire; (*geol*) produced by volcanic action or intense heat.

ignis fatuus [ig'nis-fat'ū-us] *n* the light of combustion of marsh gas, any delusive ideal. — *pl* **ignes-fatui** [ig'nēz-fat'ū-ī].

ignite [ig-nīt'] *vt* to set on fire; to heat to the point at which combustion occurs; to render luminous by heat. — *vi* to take fire. — *adj* **ignīt'able, ignīt'ible**. — *n* **igni'tion**, act of igniting; the firing of an explosive mixture of gases, vapors, or other substances, eg by an electric spark.

ignoble [ig-nō'bl] *adj* of low birth; mean or worthless; dishonorable. — *n* **ignō'bleness**. — *adv* **ignō'bly**.

ignominy [ig'nō-min-i] *n* the loss of one's good name, disgrace; infamy. — *adv* **ignomin'iously**.

ignoramus [ig-nō-ra-'mus] *n* an ignorant person.

ignorant [ig'nôr-ànt] *adj* without knowledge; uninformed; resulting from want of knowledge. — *n* **ig'norance**. — *adv* **ig'norantly**.

ignore [ig-nōr', -nōr'] *vt* to disregard.

iguana [i-gwä'na] *n* any of a family of large herbivorous arboreal lizards of tropical America.

il [il-] a form of **in-** used before *l*.

ilex [ī'leks] *n* the holm oak; the holly genus.

Iliad [il'i-ad] *n* a Greek epic, ascribed to Homer, about th Trojan War.

ill [il] *adj* not in good health; bad; evil; faulty; unfavorable. — *adv* badly, not well; with difficulty. — *n* mild disorder or di ease; evil; misfortune. — *adjs* **ill'-advised'**, imprudent. — **ill** ease, uncomfortable; embarrassed. — *adjs* **ill'-fāt'ed** unlucky; **ill'-favored**, ugly; unpleasant. — *n* **ill'ness**, sickness disease. — *adjs* **ill'-starred'**, unlucky. — *vt* **ill-treat**, to tre unkindly, unfairly, etc. — *n* **ill'-will'**, enmity.

illegal [il-ē-gàl] *adj* contrary to law. — *n* an illegal immigrant. *vt* **ille'galize**, to unlawful. — *n* **illegal'ity**, the quality or co dition of being illegal, or an instance of it. — *adv* **illē'gally**.

illegitimate [il-è-jit'i-māt] *adj* born of parents not married each other; contrary to law, rules, or logic. — *n* **illegit imacy**. — *adv* **illegit'imātely**.

illicit [il-is'it] *adj* improper; unlawful. — *adv* **illic'itly**. — **illic'itness**.

illimitable [il-im'it-à-bl] *adj* immeasurable; infinite. — **illim'itableness**. — *adv* **illim'itably**.

illiterate [il-it'ēr-àt] *adj* uneducated, esp not knowing how read or write; illiterate. — *n* **illit'eracy** [-si].

illuminate [il-(y)ōō'min-āt] *vt* to give light to; to light up; make clear; to inform; to decorate as with gold or lights. — **illuminant**, a substance or device that illuminates; illum **nation**. — *adj* **illu'minative**. — *n* **illu'minator**.

illusion [il-(y)ōō'zh(ó)n] *n* a false idea or conception; an unre or misleading image or appearance. — *n* **illu'sionist**, magician or sleight-of-hand performer. — *adjs* **illu'siv illu'sory**. — *adv* **illu'sively**. — *n* **illu'siveness**.

illustrate [il'us-trāt, il-us'trāt] *vt* to make clear as by example to furnish (books, etc.) with explanatory pictures, char etc. — *n* **illustrā'tion**, act of making clear, explaining; example; a picture or diagram accompanying a text. — *a* **ill'ustrated** [or -us'-], **illustrative** [il'us-trā-tiv or il-us'tiv], **illus'tratory**. — *adj* **illus'trious**, high distinguished; noble.

image [im'ij *n* a representation of a person or thing; the visu impression of something in a lens, mirror, etc.; a copy likeness; a mental picture; the concept of a person, produ etc. held by the public at large; a metaphor or simile. — *vt* make a representation of; to reflect; to imagine. — *ns* **image** [im'ij-ri or im'ij-èr-i], the work of the imagination; men pictures; figures of speech; images in general or collectively.

imagine [im-aj'in] *vt* to form an image of in the mind; conceive; to think vainly or falsely; to suppose, conjecture. *vi* to form mental images. — *adj* **imag'inable**. — *n* **imag'inab ness**. — *adv* **imag'inably**. — *adj* **imag'inary**, existing only the imagination. — *n* **imaginā'tion**, act of imagining; the f ulty of forming images in the mind; the artist's creat power; that which is imagined. — *adj* **imag'inātive**.

imago [i-mā'gō] *n* the last, adult, state of insect life; an ideal ized mental image of oneself or another.

imbecile [im'be-sil, -sēl] *adj* stupid or foolish. — *n* an adu with a mental age of a three- to eight-year-old child. — **imbecil'ity**.

imbibe [im-bīb'] *vti* to drink esp alcoholic liquor; to rece into the mind. — *n* **imbib'er**.

imbricate [im'bri-kāt] *vt* (*bot, zool*) to lay one over another, tiles on a roof. — *vi* to be so placed. — *adj*(-àt) overlapping l roof-tiles. — Also **im'bricāted**. — *n* **imbricā'tion**.

imbroglio [im-brōl'yō] *n* a complicated, confusing situatio confused misunderstanding.

imbrue [im-brōō'] *vt* to stain.

imbue [im-bū'] *vt* to dye; to permeate (with ideas, feelin etc.).

imitate [im'i-tāt] *vt* to strive to produce something like, o be like; to mimic. — *adj* **im'itable**. — *ns* **imitabil'ity**; im tā'tion.

immaculate [im-ak'ū-làt] *adj* spotless; unstained; pure. — **immac'ulately**.

immanent [im'a-nènt] *adj* inherent; pervading. — *n* **imm** **nence**.

immaterial [im-a-tē'ri-àl] *adj* spiritual; unimportant. — *vt* **immatē'rialize**, to separate from matter.

immediate [im-ē'di-àt] *adj* with nothing between; not act by second causes, direct; next, nearest; without delay. — *a* **immē'diately**. — *ns* **immē'diacy**.

immemorial [im-e-mōr′, mör′, i-ål] *adj* beyond the reach of memory; very old.

immense [i-mens′] *adj* vast in extent; very large.—*adv* **immense′ly.**—*ns* **immense′ness; immens′ity.**

immerse [im-(m)ûrs′] *vt* to dip under the surface of a liquid; to baptize by dipping the whole body; to engage or involve deeply.—*n* **immer′sion.**

immigrate [im′i-grāt] *vi* to come into a new country, esp to settle there.—*ns* **imm′igrant; immigrā′tion.**

imminent [im′i-nėnt] *adj* near at hand; impending; threatening.—*ns* **imm′inence.**—*adv* **imm′inently.**

immobile [im-(m)ō′bil, -bīl, bēl] *adj* immovable; not readily moved; motionless; stationary.—*n* **immobilizā′tion.**—*vt* **immob′ilize,** to render immobile; *n* **immobil′ity.**

immolate [im′ō-lāt] *vt* to kill as a sacrifice.—*ns* **immolā′tion.**

immortal [im-ör′tál] *adj* exempt from death; enduring; having lasting fame.—*n* an immortal being.—*vt* **immortalize** [im-ör′tál-iz].—*n* **immortality.**

immortelle [im-ör-tel′] *n* an everlasting flower.

immune [im-ūn′] *adj* exempt from or protected against something disagreeable or harmful; not susceptible to a specified disease.—*vt* **imm′unize.**—*ns* **immun′ity.**

immure [i-mūr′] *vt* to shut (oneself) up; to imprison.

imp [imp] *n* a teasing or mischievous child; a little devil or wicked spirit.—*adj* **imp′ish.**

impact [im-pakt′] *vt* to force tightly together.—*vi* to hit with force.—*n* **im′pact,** violent contact; a shocking effect.—*n* **im′pact,** the blow of a body in motion impinging on another body.

impair [im-pār′] *vt* to make worse, less, etc.

impale [im-pāl′] *vt* to fix on, or pierce through, with something pointed.—*n* **impale′ment.**

impart [im-pärt′] *vt* to give a share of; to make known.

impartial [im-pär′sh(ä)l] *adj* not favoring one more than another; just.—*n* **impartiality** [-shi-al′i-ti], quality of being impartial, freedom from bias.

impassable [im-päs′ä-bl] *adj* not capable of being passed or traversed.—*ns* **impassabil′ity, impass′ableness.**—*adj* **impass′ably.**—*n* **impasse** [ē-päs′, im-päs′], a place from which there is no outlet; a deadlock.

impassioned [im-pash′önd] *adj* passionate; ardent.

impassive [im-pas′iv] *adj* not feeling or showing emotion; imperturbable.—*adv* **impass′ively.**

impeach [im-pēch′] *vt* to discredit (a person's honor); to try (a public official) on a charge of wrongdoing.—*adj* **impeach′able, impeach′ment.**

impeccable [im-pek′ä-bl] *adj* without defect or error; faultless.—*n* **impeccabil′ity.**

impecunious [im-pi-kū′ni-us] *adj* habitually without money, poor.—*n* **impecunios′ity.**

impede [im-pēd′] *vt* to hinder to obstruct.—*n* **impēd′iment.**—*n pl* **impediment′a,** a military baggage, baggage generally.—*adj* **imped′itive.**

impel [im-pel′] *vt* to urge forward, to propel.

impend [im-pend′] *vi* to hang over; to threaten.

imperative [im-per′ä-tiv] *adj* expressive of command; authoritative; obligatory; urgently necessary; designating or of the mood of a verb that expresses a command, etc.—*adv* **imper′atively.**

imperfect [im-pûr′fekt] *adj* falling short of perfection; incomplete; defective; (*gram*) designating a verb tense that indicates a past action or state as incomplete or continuous.

imperial [im-pē′ri-ål] *adj* of the nature of an empire, emperor, or empress; majestic; august; or great size or superior quality; of the British system of weights and measures.—*n* a small pointed chin beard.—*adv* **impē′rially.**—*ns* **impē′rialism,** the policy of forming and maintaining an empire, as by subjugating territories, establishing colonies, etc.; **imperialist.**—Also *adj.*—*adj* **imperialistic.**

imperil [im-per′il] *vt* to put in peril, to endanger.

impersonate [im-pûr′sön-āt] *vt* to assume the role of another person for purposes of entertainment or fraud.—*ns* **impersonā′tion; imper′sonātor.**

impertinent [im-pûr′ti-nėnt] *adj* not pertinent; impudent; insolent.—*n* **imper′tinence.**—*adv* **imper′tinently.**

impervious [impėr′vi-ùs] *adj* incapable of being penetrated, as by water; not easily influenced by ideas, arguments, etc.

impetigo [im-pe-tīgo] *n* a contagious bacterial skin disease.

impetuous [im-pet′ū-us] *adj* acting or done suddenly with headlong energy; impulsive.—*adv* **impet′uously.**—*ns* **impet′uousness, impetuos′ity.**

impetus [im′pė-tus] *n* the force with which a body moves against resistance; driving force or motive.

impinge [im-pinj′] *vi* (*with* **on, upon**) to strike or fall; to encroach.

impious [im′pi-us] *adj* lack of reverence for God, profane.—*adj* **im′piously.**

implacable [im-plak′-ä-bl, or -plāk′-] *adj* not to be appeased, inexorable.—*n* **implācabil′ity.**—*adv* **implac′ably.**

implant [im-plänt′] *vt* to plant firmly.—*n* **implantā′tion,** the act of infixing.

implement [im′-ple-ment′] *n* something used in a given activity.—*vt* [im-ple-ment′] to fulfil or perform.

implicate [im′pli-kāt] *vt* to show to have a part or to be connected.—*n* **implicā′tion,** the act of implicating; entanglement; that which is implied.—*adj* **im′plicative,** tending to implicate; **implic′it** [plis′it], implied; unquestioning (eg trust).—*adv* **implic′itly.**—*n* **implic′itness.**

implore [im-plōr′, -plör′] *vt* to ask earnestly (for); to.—*adv* **implor′ingly,** beseechingly.

imply [im-plī′] *vt* to have as a necessary condition, part, etc.; to express indirectly; to hint, suggest.—*pr p* **imply′ing;** *pt p* **implied.**

imponderable [im-pon′dėr-ä-bl] *adj* that cannot be weighed or measured.—*ns* **imponderabil′ity; impon′derable.**

import [im-pört′, -pört′] *vt* to bring (goods) in from a foreign country for sale or use; to mean; to signify.—*vi* to be of importance, to matter.—*n* [im′pört] something imported; meaning; importance.—*adj* **import′able,** that may be brought into a country.—*adj* **import′ant** of great weight, significance, or consequence; having, or acting if having, power, authority etc.—*n* **import′ance.**—*adv* **import′antly.**—*ns* **importā′tion, import′er.**

importune [im-pör-tūn′] *vt* to ask urgently and repeatedly.—*adj* **import′unāte,** persistent in asking or demanding.—*adv* **import′unātely.**—*ns* **importun′er.**

impose [im-pōz′] *vt* to put (a burden, tax, punishment) on or upon; to force (oneself) on others.—*vi* (*with* **on** or **upon**) to take advantage of; to cheat or defraud. *adj* **impos′ing,** impressive because of size, appearance, dignity, etc.—*adv* **impos′ingly.**—*n* **imposition.**

impotent [im′po-tėnt] *adj* powerless; helpless; (of a man) unable to engage in sexual intercourse.

impound [im-pownd′] *vt* to confine (an animal) in a pound; to take legal possession of.

impoverish [im-pov′ėr-ish] *vt* to make poor; to deprive of strength.—*n* **impov′erishment.**

imprecate [im′pre-kāt] *vt* to invoke evil on; to curse.—*vi* to utter curses.—*n* **imprecā′tion.**—*adj* **im′precatory.**

impregnable [im-preg′nä-bl] *adj* that cannot be taken by force, unyielding.—*n* **impregnabil′ity.**—*adv* **impreg′nably.**

impregnate [im-preg′nāt] *vt* to make pregnant; to saturate (with); to imbue.—*n* **impregnā′tion.**

impresario [im-pre-zä′ri-ō, or -sä′-] *n* the manager of an opera, a concert series, etc.

impress [im-pres′] *vt* to stamp; to imprint; to affect strongly the mind or emotions of; to fix in the memory.—*n* [im′pres] an impressing; an imprint.—*adj* **impress′ible,** susceptible.—*n* **impression** [-presh′(ó)n], act or result of impressing; a single printing of a book; the idea or emotion left in the mind by any experience.—*adj* **impress′ionable,** easily impressed.

impress [im-pres′] *vt* to force into military service.—*n* **impress′ment.**

imprimatur [im-pri-mā′tùr] *n* permission or licence esp to publish.

imprimis [im-prī′mis] *adv* in the first place.

imprint [im-print′] *vt* to print; to stamp; to impress.—*n* **imprint** [im′print] a mark made by imprinting; a lasting effect; a note in a book giving the facts of publication.

imprison [im-priz′n] *vt* to put in or as prison.—*n* **impris′onment.**

impromptu [im-promp′tū] *adj* unprepared.—Also *adv.*—*n* an extempore speech.

improve [im-prōōv′] *vt* to use (time) well; to make better.—

vi to become better.—*adj* improv'able.—*n* improvabil'ity.—*adv* improv'ably.—*ns* improve'ment.

improvise [im-pro-vīz'] *vti* to compose and perform without preparation; to make or do with whatever is at hand.—*ns* improvisā'tion.

imprudent [im-prōōd'ėnt] *adj* lacking foresight or discretion; rash—*n* impru'dence.

impudent [im'pūdėnt] *adj* shamelessly bold; insolent.—*n* impudence.—*adv* im'pudently.

impugn [im-pūn'] *vt* to oppose or challenge as false.

impulse [im'puls] *n* the act of impelling; force suddenly and momentarily communicated; a stimulus traveling along a nerve or a muscle; a sudden inclination to act.—*n* impul'sion, impelling force; strong desire to perform an irrational act.—*adj* impuls'ive, acting or actuated by impulse.—*adv* impuls'ively.—*n* impuls'iveness.

impunity [im-pūn'i-ti] *n* freedom from punishment.

impute [im-pūt'] *vt* to attribute (esp a fault or misbehaviour) to another.—*n* imputabil'ity.—*n* imputā'tion.

in [in] *prep* expressing the relation of a thing to that which surrounds, encloses, or includes it, as contained by, during, at the end of, not beyond (*in sight*), affected by (*in trouble*); being a member of; using; because of; into.—*adv* to or at a certain place; so as to be contained by a certain space, condition, etc.—*adj* that is in power; inner; inside; gathered, counted, etc.; (*inf*) currently smart, fashionable, etc.—*n* (*pl*) the political party in office; (*inf*) special influence or favor.

in- [in-] *prefix* not [L].—eg insincere, insincerity. It appears also as i-, il-, im-, ir-; eg ignoble, illegal, immortal, irregular (see these words). It is allied to OE *un-* and is sometimes interchangeable with it.—eg *inexpressive, unexpressive*.

in- [in-] *prefix* in, into [L].—eg include, infuse, ingredient (see these words). It appears also as il-, im-, ir-;—eg illuminate, immerse, irrigate (see these words).

inadequate [in-ad'e-kwȧt] *adj* not adequate—*ns* inad'equacy, inad'equateness.—*adv* inad'e-quately.

inadvertent [in-ad-vûrt'ėnt] *adj* not attentive or observant; due to oversight.—*ns* inadvert'ence, inadvert'ency.—*adv* inadvert'ently.

inane [in-ān] *adj* empty, lacking sense, silly.—*ns* inanition [in-a-nish'(ȯ)n], exhaustion from lack of food; inan'ity, senselessness.

inanimate, -d [in-an'im-ȧt, -id] *adj* not animate; spiritless; dull.—*n* inanimā'tion.

inapplicable [in-ap'lik-ȧ-bl] *adj* not applicable.—*n* inapplicabil'ity.

inapposite [in-ap'oz-it] *adj* not apposite—*adv* inapp'ositely.

inappreciable [in-a-prē'sh(y)ȧ-bl] *adj* too small to be perceived.

inappropriate [in-a-prō'pri-ȧt] *adj* not suitable.—*adv* inappro-"priately.—*n*inapprō'priateness.

inapt [in-apt'] *adj* not apt; not suitable; unskilful.—*n* inapt'itude, inapt'ness, lack of aptitude.—*adv* inapt'ly.

inarticulate[1] [in-är-tik'ūl-ȧt] *adj* indistinctly uttered; incapable of clear and fluent expression.—*adv* inartic'ulately.—*ns* inartic'ulacy, inartic'ulateness, inarticulā'tion, indistinctness of sounds in speaking.

inarticulate[2] [in-är-tik'ūl-ȧt] *n* any of a class (Inarticulata) of brachiopods without a hinge between the shell valves.

inartistic [in-är-tis'tik] *adj* not artistic; not appreciative of art.—*adv* inartis'tically.

inasmuch as [in-az-much'] since; because; to the extent that.

inaugurate [in-ô'gūr-āt] *vt* to induct formally into an office; to cause to begin; to open formally to the public.—*n* inaugurā'tion.—*adj* inau'gural.—*n* a speech made at an inauguration.—*n* inau'gurātor.—*adj* inau'guratory.

inborn [in'bôrn] *adj* born in or with one; hereditary.

inbreed [in'brēd, in-brēd'] *vti* to breed by continual mating of individuals of the same or closely related stocks; to make or become too effete, refined, etc.—*adj* inbred' innate; produced by inbreeding.—*n* inbreed'ing.

incandescent [in-kan-des'ėnt] *adj* glowing or white with heat.—*n* incandescence [-es'ens], white heat.

incantation [in-kan-tā'sh(ȯ)n] *n* words chanted in magic spells or rites.

incapacitate [in-kap-as'it-āt] *vt* to make unable or unfit; (*law*) to disqualify.—*n* incapac'ity.

incarcerate [in-kär'sėr-āt] *vt* to imprison, to confine.—*n* incarcerā'tion, imprisonment.

incarnadine [in-kär'na-din, -dīn] *vt* to make red.—*adj* flesh-colored; bloodred.

incarnate [in-kär'nȧt] *adj* endowed with a human body; personified.—*vt* [-nāt] to give bodily form to; to be the type or embodiment of.—*n* incarnā'tion.

incendiary [in-sen'di-ȧr-i] *n* one that sets fire to a building, etc., maliciously; an incendiary agent (as a bomb); one who promotes strife.—*adj* relating to incendiarism; used for setting buildings, etc., on fire; tending to excite or inflame.—*n* incen'diarism.

incense[1] [in-sens'] *vt* to inflame with anger.

incense[2] [in-séns] *n* any material burned to give fragrant fumes, the fumes so obtained; any pleasant smell.

incentive [in-sent'iv] *n* a stimulus; a motive.

inception [in-sep'sh(ȯ)n] *n* a beginning.—*adj* incep'tive, beginning, or marking the beginning.

incessant [in-ses'ȧnt] *adj* never ceasing; continual, constant.—*adv* incess'antly.

incest [in'sest] *n* sexual intercourse between persons too closely related to marry legally.—*adj* incest'ūous, guilty of incest.

inch [inch] *n* a measure of length equal to 1/12 foot; symbol ''.—*vti* to move very slowly, or by degrees.

inchoate [in'kō-āt, in-kō'āt] *adj* only begun; rudimentary.

incident [in'si-dėnt] *adj* likely to happen as a result; falling upon or affecting.—*n* something that happens; an event, esp a minor one; a minor conflict.—*n* in'cidence, the degree or range of occurrence or effect.—*adj* incident'al, happening in connection with something more important—Also *n* (*pl*) miscellaneous items.

incinerate [in-sin'ėr-āt] *vt* to reduce to ashes.—*ns* incinerā'tion; incin'erător, a furnace for burning trash.

incipient [in-sip'i-ėnt] *adj* beginning; nascent.—*ns* incip'ience, incip'iency.—*adv* incip'iently.

incise [in-sīz'] *vt* to cut into with a sharp tool; to engrave.—*n* incision [in-sizh'(ȯ)n], the act of cutting into a substance; a cut, a gash.—*adj* incisive [-sīs'-], having the quality of cutting in; acute in mind; sharp; penetrating.—*adv* incisively.—*n* incisiveness; incisor [-sīz'ȯr], any of the front cutting teeth between the canines.

incite [in-sīt'] *vt* to urge to action; to rouse.—*ns* incitant [in-sīt'ȧnt], incitā'tion [-sit-, sīt-], incite'ment.

inclement [in-klem'ėnt] *adj* rough; stormy; lacking mercy; harsh.—*n* inclem'ency.

incline [in-klīn'] *vi* to lean; to slope; to be disposed; to have a preference or liking.—*vt* to cause to bend downwards; to cause to deviate; to dispose.—*n* [in'klīn, in-klīn'] a slope.—*adj* inclīn'able, capable of being tilted or sloped; somewhat disposed.—*n* inclīnā'tion, a bend or bow; a slope or tilt; angle with the horizon or with any plane or line; tendency; disposition of mind, natural aptness; favourable disposition, affection.—*adj* inclined', bent; sloping; disposed.

include [in-klōōd'] *vt* to enclose; to comprise as a part; to take in.—*n* inclusion [-klōō'zh(ȯ)n].—*adj* inclu'sive.—*adv* inclu'sively.

incognito [in-kog'ni-tō] *adj, adv* disguised under an assumed name.—*n* one appearing or living incognito.

incoherent [in-kō-hēr'ėnt] *adj* not coherent; loose, rambling.—*n* incoher'ence.—*adv* incoher'ently.

income [in'-kùm] *n* the money etc. received for labor or services, or from property, investments, etc.—*n* in'come tax, a tax levied on the net income of a person or a business.

incongruous [in-kong'grŏŏ-us] *adj* lacking harmony or agreement of parts; unsuitable; inappropriate.—*n* incongru'ity [-grŏŏ'-].—*adv* incong'ruously.

incorporate [in-kôr'pȯ-rāt] *vt* to combine; to include; to embody; to merge; to form into a corporation.—*vi* to unite into one group or substance; to form a corporation.—Also *adj*. incor'porated, united in one mass; formed into a legal corporation.—*n* incorporā'tion.

increase [in-krēs'] *vi* to become greater in size, numbers, amount, etc.—*vt* to make greater in size, numbers, etc.—*n* [in'krēs] an increasing or becoming increased; the result or amount of an increasing.—*adv* increas'ingly.

incriminate [in-krim'in-āt] *vt* to accuse of a crime; to implicate; to involve in a crime.—*adj* incrim'inatory [or-ā-].

incrust [in-krust′] *vt* to cover as with a crust.—*vi* to form a crust.—*n* **incrusta′tion**.—Also **encrust, encrustation**.

incubate [in′kū-bāt, or ing′-] *vti* to sit on and hatch (eggs); to keep (eggs, embryos, etc.) in a favorable environment for hatching or developing; to develop, as by planning.—*n* **incuba′tion**, **in′cubator**, an apparatus for hatching eggs by artificial heat.

incubus [in′kū-bus] *n* a nightmare; any oppressive burden.—*pl* **in′cubuses, incubi** [in′kū-bī].

inculcate [in′kul-kāt (or -kūl′-] *vt* to teach by frequent admonitions or repetitions.—*ns* **inculca′tion**; **in′culcator**.

incumbent [in-kum′bent] *adj* resting (on or upon) one as a duty or obligation; currently in office.—*n* the holder of an office, etc.—*n* **incum′bency**, a duty or obligation; a term of office.

incunabula [in-kū-nab′ū-la] *n pl* books printed before the year 1500; the origin, early stages of anything.

incur [in-kûr′] *vt* to bring upon oneself; *pt* (something undesirable); **incurr′ing**; *pt p* **incurred′**.

incursion [in-kûr′sh(ó)n] *n* an invasion or raid; an entering into as an activity.

indebted [in-det′id] *adj* in debt; obliged; owing gratitude.—*n* **indebt′edness**.

indeed [in-dēd′] *adv* in fact; in truth; in reality.—*interj* expresses surprise, disbelief, sarcasm, etc.

indefatigable [in-di-fat′i-gà-bl] *adj* tireless, unremitting in effort.—*n* **indefat′igableness**.—*adv* **indefat′igably**.

indefeasible [in-di-fēz′i-bl] *adj* not capable of being annulled.—*n* **indefeasibil′ity**.—*adv* **indefeas′ibly**.

indelible [in-del′i-bl] *adj* that cannot be blotted out or effaced; making a mark that cannot easily be removed.—*n* **indelibil′ity**.—*adv* **indel′ibly**.

indemnity [in-dem′ni-ti] *n* insurance against damage or loss, compensation for loss or injury.

indent [in-dent′] *vt* to notch; to begin farther in from the margin than the rest of a text.—*vi* to form an indentation.—*n* [in′dent, also in-dent′] a dent or notch.—*n* **indentā′tion**, being indented; a notch, cut, inlet, etc.; a dent; a spacing in from the margin, usu **inden′tion** in this sense; **inden′ture**, a written agreement, a contract binding one person to work for another.—*vt* to bind by indentures; to indent.

independent [in-di-pend′ént] *adj* freedom from the influence or control of others; self-governing; self-determined; not adhering to any political party; not connected with others; not depending on another for financial support.—*n* one who is independent in thinking, action etc.—*ns* **independ′ence; independ′ency**, a self-governing political unit.—*adv* **independ′ently**.—**Independence Day**, the anniversary of the adoption of the American Declaration of Independence on July 4, 1776.

index [in′deks] *n* the forefinger (also **in′dex fing′er**); a pointer or hand on a dial or scale, etc.; anything that gives an indication; an alphabetical list of subjects dealt with, usu at the end of a book; a figure showing ratio or relative change.

Indian [in′di-án] *n* a member of any of the aboriginal peoples of the Americas; a native of India or the East Indies.—Also *adj* **Indian corn**, maize; **Indian file**, single file; **Indian summer**, a period of unusually warm weather in the fall.

indicate [in′di-kāt] *vt* to point out; to show; to give some notion of; (*med*) suggest or point to (as suitable treatment); also (*pass*) used loosely of any desirable course of action.—*n* **indicā′tion**, act of indicating; mark; token; symptom.—*adj* **indic′ative**, showing the existence, presence, or nature (of), giving intimation (of); (*gram*) applied to the mood of the verb that affirms or denies.—*adv* **indic′atively**.—*n* **ind′icător**.

indict [in-dīt′] *vt* to charge with a fault or offense; to accuse; to charge with a crime through the due process of law as by a grand jury.—*adj* **indict′able**, subject to being indicted; making one liable to indictment.—*n* **indict′ment**; a formal written statement framed by a prosecuting authority charging a person of a crime.

indifferent [in-dif′èr-ent] *adj* neutral; without importance (to); unconcerned; fair; average.—*ns* **indiff′erence, indiff′erentism**, the belief that religious differences are of equal value.—*adv* **indiff′erently**, in an indifferent manner.

indigenous [in-dij′én-us] *adj* existing naturally in a country

region, or particular environment; native.—*n* **in′digène, in′digèn**.

indigent [in′di-jènt] *adj* poor, needy.—Also *n*.

indignant [in-dig′nánt] *adj* expressing anger, esp at mean or unjust action.—*adv* **indig′nantly**.—*ns* **indignā′tion**, righteous anger; **indig′nity**.

indigo [in′di-gō] *n* a violet-blue dye obtained from the leaves of plants of the indigo (genus *Indigofera*), or synthetically.

indite [in-dīt′] *vt* to compose or write.—*n* **indit′er**.

individual [in-di-vid′ū-ál] *adj* existing as a separate thing or being; of, by, for, or relating to a single person or thing.—*n* a single thing or being; a person.—*vt* **individ′ualize** to make individual; to treat as an individual.—*n* **individualīzā′tion**.—*ns* **individ′ualism**, individuality; the doctrine that the state exists for the individual; the leading of one's life in one's own way; **individ′ualist**, one who thinks and acts with great independence; one who advocates individualism; **individual′ity** [-al′i-ti], the sum of the characteristics that set one person or thing apart; existence as an individual.—*adv* **individ′ually**.—*vt* **individ′uāte**, to individualize; to give individuality to.—*n* **individuā′tion**.

indolent [in′dól-ént] *adj* idle; lazy.—*n* **in′dolence**.—*adv* **in′dolently**.

indomitable [in-dom′it-à-bl] *adj* not easily discouraged or defeated.—*adv* **indom′itably**.

indoor [in′dōr, -dôr] *adj* practised, used, or being, within a building.—*adv* **indoors′**, in or into a building.

indorse *See* endorse.

indubitable [in-dū′bit-à-bl] *adj* that cannot be doubted.—*n* **indū′bitableness**.—*adv* **indū′bitably**.

induce [in-dūs′] *vt* to persuade; to bring on; to draw (a conclusion) from particular facts; to bring about (an electric or magnetic effect) in a body by placing it within a field of force.—*n* **induce′ment**, that which induces; an incentive; a motive.

induct [in-dukt′] *vt* to place formally in an office, a society, etc.; to enroll (esp a draftee) in the armed forces.—*ns* **induct′ance**, the property of inducing an electromotive force by variation of current in a circuit; **induc′tion**, installation in office, etc.; reasoning from particular cases to general conclusions; the inducing of an electric or magnetic effect by a field of force.—*adj* **induc′tive**.—*adv* **induc′tively**.—*n* **induc′tor**.

indulge [in-dulj′] *vt* to satisfy (a desire); to gratify the wishes of; to humor.—*vi* to give way to one's desire.—*n* **indul′gence**, the act or practice of indulging; a thing indulged in; a favor or privilege; (*R C Church*) a remission of punishment still due for a sin after the guilt has been forgiven.—*adj* **indul′gent**, ready to gratify the wishes of others; compliant; lenient, often to excess.—*adv* **indul′gently**.

industry [in′dus-tri] *n* quality of being diligent; steady application to labor; any branch of productive, manufacturing enterprise or all of these collectively; any large-scale business activity; the owners and managers of industry.—*adj* **indus′trial**, relating to or consisting in industry.—*vt* **indus′trialīze**, to make industrial.—*vi* to become industrial.—*ns* **indus′trialism**, social and economic organization characterized by large industries, machine production, urban workers, etc. *adj* **indus′trious**.

inebriate [in-ē′bri-āte] *vt* to make drunk.—Also *n*.—*ns* **inebriā′tion, inebriety** [in-ē-brī-′iti].

ineffable [in-ef′à-bl] *adj* inexpressible; too sacred to be spoken.—*n* **ineff′ableness**.—*adv* **ineff′ably**.

ineluctable [in-e-luk′tà-bl] *adj* not to be escaped from.

inept [in-ept′] *adj* unsuitable; unfit; foolish; awkward; clumsy.—*n* **inept′itūde**.—*adv* **inept′ly**.

inert [in-ûrt′] *adj* without power to move or to resist; inactive; dull; slow; with few or no active properties.—Also *n.*—*ns* **inert′ness; inertia** [in-ûr′-shi-a], (physics) the tendency of matter to remain at rest (or continue in a fixed direction) unless acted on by an outside force; disinclination to act.—*adj* **iner′tial**, of, or pertaining to, inertia.—*adv* **inert′ly**.

inevitable [in-ev′it-à-bl] *adj* that must happen—*ns* **inev′itableness, inevitabil′ity**.—*adv* **inev′itably**.

inexorable [in-eks′ór-à-bl] *adj* not to be moved by entreaty, unrelenting.—*ns* **inex′orableness, inexorabil′ity**.—*adv* **inex′orably**.

infallible [in-fal'i-bl] *adj* incapable of error; dependable; reliable. — *n* infallibil'ity. — *adv* infall'ibly.

infamous [in'fa-mus] *adj* having a bad reputation; notorious; causing a bad reputation; scandalous. — *adv* in'famously. — *n* in'famy, very bad reputation; disgrace; great wickedness; an infamous act. — *pl* infamies.

infant [in'fant] *n* a very young child; a baby. — *adj* of or for infants; in a very early stage. — *n* in'fancy, the state or time of being an infant; the beginning of anything. — *adjs* infantile [in'fant-īl, also -til] of infants; like an infant, babyish.

infanticide [in-fant'i-sīd] *n* child murder; the murderer of an infant. — *adj* infant'icidal.

infantry [in'fant-ri] *n* that branch of an army consisting of soldiers trained to fight on foot.

infatuate [in'fat'ū-āt] *vt* to inspire with foolish passion. — *adj* infat'uated. — *n* infatua'tion.

infect [in-fekt'] *vt* to contaminate with microorganisms that cause disease; to imbue with one's feelings or beliefs, esp so as to harm. — *n* infection [in-fek'sh(ò)n]. — *adjs* infec'tious, denoting a disease caused in the body by the presence of germs.

infer [in-fûr'] *vt* to deduce; to conclude; to imply. — *pr p* infer'ring. — *pt p* inferred'. — *adjs* in'ferable, that may be inferred or deduced. — *n* in'ference. — *adj* inferential [-en'sh(à)l], based on or relating to inference.

inferior [in-fē'ri-òr] *adj* lower in space; subordinate; poor or poorer in quality. — *n* one lower in rank or station. — *n* inferior'ity. — inferior'ity complex (*psych*), an acute sense of inferiority expressed by a lack of confidence or in exaggerated aggression.

infernal [in-fûr'nàl] *adj* of hell or Hades; hellish; fiendish. — *adv* infer'nally.

infest [in-fest'] *vt* to overrun in large numbers, usu so as to be harmful; to be parasitic in or on.

infidel [in'fi-del] *n* one who does not believe in a certain religion; one who has no religion. — *n* infidel'ity, unfaithfulness, esp in marriage.

infiltrate [in'fil-trāt] *vti* to filter or pass gradually through or into; to penetrate (enemy lines, a region, etc.) gradually or stealthily, so as to attack or seize control from within. — *ns* infiltra'tion; infiltrator.

infinite [in'fin-it] *adj* without end or limit; very great; vast. — *n* something infinite (in extent, number, or duration. — *adv* in'finitely. — *ns* infin'itūde, infin'ity, immensity; a countless number; an infinite quantity. — *adj* infinites'imal, immeasurably small. — Also *n*. — *adv* infinites'imally. — infinite set (*math*), a set which can be put in a one-to-one correspondence with part of itself.

infinitive [in-fin'it-iv] *n* (*gram*) the form of a verb without reference to person, number or tense (*usu with* to, as in "I want to go.").

infirm [in-fûrm'] *adj* feeble; weak; not firm; unstable; frail; shaky. — *ns* infirm'ity; infirmary [in-fûrm'àr-i], a hospital or place for the treatment of the sick.

inflame [in-flām'] *vti* to arouse, excite, etc. or to become aroused, excited, etc.; to undergo or cause to undergo inflammation.

inflammable [in-flam'à-bl] *adj* flammable; easily excited. — *n* inflammabil'ity, inflamm'ableness. — *adv* inflamm'ably. — *n* inflammā'tion, an inflaming or being inflamed; redness, pain, heat, and swelling in the body, due to injury or disease. — *adj* inflamm'atory, rousing excitement, anger, etc.; of or caused by inflammation.

inflate [in-flāt'] *vt* to blow full with air or gas; to puff up with pride; to increase beyond what is normal, esp the supply of money and credit. — *adj* inflat'ed. — *n* inflation [in-flāsh(ò)n], the condition of being inflated; an increase in the currency in circulation or a marked expansion of credit, resulting in a fall in currency value, and a sharp rise in prices. — *adj* inflationary, pertaining to inflation.

inflect [in-flekt'] *vt* to turn from a direct line or course; to change the form (of a word) by inflection; to vary the tone of (the voice). — *n* inflec'tion, a bend; the change in the form of a word to indicate number, case, tense, etc.; a change in the tone of the voice. — *adjs* inflec'table, inflective.

inflexible [in-flek'si-bl] *adj* not flexible; stiff, rigid; fixed; unyielding. — *ns* inflexibil'ity, inflex'ibleness. — *adv* inflex'ibly.

inflict [in-flikt'] *vt* to cause (wounds, pain, etc.); to impose (as punishment) (*with on or upon*). — *n* inflic'tion, act of inflicting or imposing; that which is inflicted. — *adj* inflictive, tending or able to inflict.

inflorescence [in-flor-es'èns] *n* the producing of blossoms; the arrangement of flowers on a stem; a flower cluster; flowers collectively.

influence [in'flōō-èns] *n* the power to affect others; the power to produce effects by having wealth, position, ability, etc.; one with influence. — *vt* to have influence on. — *adj* influential [-en'shàl], having much influence; effectively active (in). — *adv* influen'tially.

influenza [in-flōō-en'zà] *n* a contagious feverish virus disease marked by muscular pain and inflammation of the respiratory system.

influx [in'fluks] *n* a flowing in.

inform [in-fôrm'] *vt* to give knowledge of something to. — *vi* to give information, esp in accusing another. — *ns* inform'ant, a person who gives information; informā'tion, something told or facts learned; news; knowledge; data stored in or retrieved from a computer. — *adjs* inform'ative, instructive; inform'atory, instructive. — *n* inform'er.

infraction [in-frak'sh(ò)n] *n* a violation of a law, pact, etc.

infra dig [in'frà dig] *adj* beneath one's dignity.

infringe [in-frinj'] *vt* to violate, esp a pact or a law. — *n* infringe'ment.

infuriate [in-fū'ri-āt] *vt* to enrage; to madden.

infuse [in-fūz'] *vt* to instill or impart (qualities, etc.); to inspire; to steep (tea leaves, etc.) to extract the essence. — *n* infusion [in-fū'zh(ò)n], something obtained by infusing.

infusorian [in-fūzō'ri-an] *n* any of a group of minute organisms found in semiliquid organic decomposition, esp a ciliiated protozoan. — *n* infusorial earth, kieselguhr.

ingenious [in-jē'ni-ùs] *adj* clever, resourceful, etc.; made or done in an original or clever way; skilfully contrived. — *adv* ingē'niously. — *n* ingē'niousness.

ingenuity [in-jen-ū'i-ti] *n* cleverness; ingenious quality.

ingenuous [in-jen'ū-ùs] *adj* frank, artless; simple; naive. — *adv* ingen'uously. — *ns* ingen'uousness; ingénue [ɛ̃-zhä-nü] (*theatre*), the role of a naive young woman, or an actress in this role.

ingle [ing'gl] *n* a fire, a fireplace. — *n* ing'lenook, a recess by a large open fireplace; a bench or settee in this recess; a fireside corner.

ingot [ing'got] *n* a mass of metal, esp gold or silver, cast into a bar.

ingratiate [in-grā'shi-āt] *vt* to bring (oneself) into another's favor.

ingredient [in-grē'di-ent] *n* that which enters into a mixture; a component.

ingress [in'gres] *n* entrance.

inguinal [ing'gwin-àl] *adj* relating to the groin.

inhabit [in-hab'it] *vt* to live in. — *adj* inhab'itable, that may be inhabited. — *ns* inhab'itant, a person or animal inhabiting a specified place. inhabitā'tion, the act of inhabiting; the state of being inhabited.

inhale [in-hāl'] *vti* to breathe in. — *ns* inhā'lant, a medicine, etc. to be inhaled; inhalātion [in-hā-lā'sh(ò)n], the act of drawing into the lungs; something to be inhaled.

inhere [in-hēr'] *vi* to be inherent. — *adj* inher'ent, existing in and inseparable from something else; innate. — *n* inher'ence — *adv* inher'ently.

inherit [in-her'it] *vt* to get as heir; to possess by transmission from past generations. — Also *vi* — *adj* inher'itable heritable. — *ns* inher'itance the action of inheriting; something inherited; inher'itor.

inhibit [in-hib'it] *vt* to hold in or back; to check. — *n* inhibi'tion, an inhibiting or being inhibited; a mental process that restrains an action, emotion, or thought — *adj* inhib'ited. — *n* inhib'itor, that which inhibits esp a substance that interferes with a chemical process.

inhume [in-hūm'] *vt* to inter — *n* inhumā'tion, burial.

inimical [in-im'i-kàl] *adj* unfriendly, hostile; unfavorable (to); opposed (to). — *adv* inim'ically.

inimitable [in-im′it-á-bl] *adj* that cannot be imitated; matchless. —*adv* inim′itably.

iniquity [in-ik′wi-ti] *n* wickedness; gross injustice. —*adj* iniq′uitous, marked by iniquity. —*adv* iniq′uitously.

initial [in-ish′ál] *adj* of or at the beginning. —*n* the first letter of each word in a name; a large letter at the beginning of a chapter, etc. —*vt* to put the initials of one's name to. —*pr p* ini′tialling; *pt p* ini′tialled. —*adv* ini′tially. —*vt* ini′tiate, to bring (something) into practice or use; to teach the fundamentals of a subject to; to admit as a member into a club, etc. esp with a secret ceremony. —*n* one who is initiated. —*adj* begun; initiated. —*ns* initiā′tion, act or process of initiating; act of admitting to a society; ini′tiative the action of taking the first step.

inject [in-jekt′] *vt* to force (a fluid) into a vein, tissue, etc. with a syringe or the like; to introduce (a remark, quality, etc.); to throw, drive, force into something. —*n* injec′tion, act of injecting.

injunction [in-jung(k)′sh(ó)n] *n* a command; an order; a court order prohibiting or ordering a given action.

injure [in′jùr] *vt* to wrong; to harm, damage, hurt. —*adj* injurious [in-jōō′ri-us]. —*adv* inju′riously. —*ns* inju′riousness; injury [in′jùr-i], that which injures; wrong; damage.

ink [ingk] *n* a colored liquid used for writing, printing, etc.; the dark protective secretion of a cephalopod. —*vt* to cover, mark, or color with ink. —*adj* ink′y, like very dark ink in color; black; covered with ink. —*ns* ink′iness; ink′stand, ink′well, a container for ink; ink′y cap.

inkling [ingk′ling] *n* a hint; a vague notion.

inland [in′land, in′lánd] *adj* of or in the interior of a country. —*n* [inland′] an inland region. —*adv* [inland′] into or toward this region. —*n* in′lander, one who lives inland.

in-law [in-lö′] *n* a relative by marriage. —*pl* in-laws′.

inlay [in-lā′] *vt* to insert; to ornament by inserting pieces of metal, ivory, etc. —*pt p* inlaid. —*n* [in′-] inlaying; inlaid work; material inlaid. —*ns* inlayer [in′lā-èr, in-lā′ér]; inlay′ing.

inlet [in′let] *n* a narrow strip of water extending into a body of land.

inly [in′li] *adv* inwardly; in the heart; thoroughly, entirely.

inmate [in′māt] *n* a person confined with others in a prison or institution.

inmost [in′mōst] *adj* farthest within; most secret.

inn [in] *n* a small hotel; a restaurant or tavern. —*n* inn′keeper, one who keeps an inn.

innate [in-āt′, or in′āt] *adj* inborn; inherent. —*adv* inn′ately. —*n* inn′āteness.

inner [in′èr] *adj* farther within; most secret. —*adj* in′nermost, inmost.

inning [in′ing] *n* (*baseball*) a team's turn at bat; a numbered round of play in which both teams have a turn at bat.

innocent [in′o-sènt] *adj* harmless; inoffensive; blameless; guileless; ignorant of evil; simple, not guilty of a specific crime. —*n* an innocent person, as a child. —*ns* inn′ocence, inn′ocency, the quality of being innocent. —*adv* inn′ocently.

innocuous [in-ok′ū-us] *adj* harmless. —*adv* innoc′uously. —*n* innoc′uousness.

innovate [in′o-vāt] *vi* to introduce new methods, devices, etc.; to make changes. —*n* innovā′tion; inn′ovātor.

innuendo [in-ū-en′dō] *n* a hint or sly remark usu derogatory; an insinuation. —*pl* innuen′do(e)s.

inoculate [in-ok′ū-lāt] *vt* to inject a serum or a vaccine into, esp in order to create immunity; to protect as if by inoculation. —*n* inoculā′tion, the process or instance of inoculating; substance used for inoculating, esp an antigen or pathogen to stimulate the production of antibodies.

inordinate [in-ör′di-nát] *adj* excessive, immoderate. —*n* inor′dinateness. —*adv* inor′dinately.

inorganic [in-ör-gan′ik] *adj* not having the structure or characteristics of living organisms. —*adv* inorgan′ically.

input [in′pŏŏt] *n* what is put in, as power into a machine, data in a computer, etc. —*vt* to enter into a computer.

inquest [in′kwest] *n* judicial inquiry before a jury esp any case of violent or sudden death.

inquire [in-kwīr′] *vi* to ask a question or questions; to investigate (*usu with* into). —*vt* to seek information about. —*n* inquir′er. —*adv* inquir′ingly. —*n* inquir′y, act of inquiring;

investigation; a question. —**inquire after**, to ask about the health of.

inquisition [in-kwi-zish′(ó)n] *n* a searching examination; investigation; **Inquisition** (*RC Church*) formerly, the tribunal for suppressing heresy; any relentless questioning or harsh suppression. —*adj* inquis′itive, inclined to ask many questions; unnecessarily curious; prying. —*adv* inquis′itively. —*ns* inquis′itiveness; inquis′itor.

inroad [in′rōd] *n* an incursion into an enemy's country, a raid; (*fig*) encroachment.

insane [in-sān′] *adj* not sane, mentally ill; of or for insane people; very foolish. —*adv* insane′ly. —*n* insanity [in-san′i-ti], lack of sanity; mental disorder.

inscribe [in-skrīb′] *vt* to mark or engrave (words, etc.) on (a surface); to add (a person's name) to a list; to dedicate (a book) to someone; to autograph; to fix in the mind. —*n* inscrib′er; inscription[in-skrip′sh(ó)n], something inscribed. —*adj* inscript′ive.

inscrutable [in-skrōōt′á-bl] *adj* that cannot be understood; inexplicable; enigmatic. —*ns* inscrutabil′ity, inscrut′ableness. —*adv* inscrut′ably.

insect [in′sekt] *n* any of a class (Insecta) of small arthropods with three pairs of legs, head, thorax, and abdomen and two or four wings. —*adj* like an insect. —*n* insec′ticide, a substance for killing insects.

inseminate [in-sem-′in-āt] *vt* to fertilize; to impregnate; to imbue (with ideas, etc.) —*n* inseminā′tion.

insensate [in-sen′sát] *adj* not feeling sensation; stupid; without regard or feeling; cold.

insert [in-sûrt′] *vt* to put or fit (something) into something else. —*n* [in′sèrt] something inserted. —*n* inser′tion.

inset [in′set] *n* something set in; an insertion or insert. —*vt* [in-set′] to set in; to insert.)

inshore [in′shōr′] *adj, adv* near or in toward the shore.

inside [in′sīd] *n* the inner side, surface, or part; (*pl*) (*inf*) the viscera. —*adj* internal; known only to insiders; secret. —*adv* [in-sīd′] on or in the inside; within; indoors. —*prep* [in-sīd′] in or within.

insidious [in-sid′i-us] *adj* marked by slyness or treachery; more dangerous than seems evident. —*adv* insid′iously. —*n* insid′iousness.

insight [in′sīt] *n* the ability to see and understand clearly the inner nature of things esp by intuition; an instance of such understanding.

insignia [in-sig′ni-a] *n pl* marks by which anything is known.

insinuate [in-sin′ū-āt] *vt* to introduce or work in slowly, indirectly, etc.; to hint. —*adj* insin′uating, gradually winning confidence and favor; causing doubt by subtle hints. —*adv* insin′uatingly. —*n* insinuā′tion. —*adj* insin′uative. —*n* insin′uātor.

insipid [in-sip′id] *adj* tasteless; without flavor; dull. —*adv* insip′idly. —*ns* insip′idness, insipid′ity.

insist [in-sist′] *vi* to take and maintain a stand (*often with* on *or* upon). —*vt* to demand strongly; to declare firmly. —*adj* insist′ent, insisting or demanding. —*n* insist′ence.

insolent [in′sol-ènt] *adj* boldly disrespectful; insulting; rude. —*n* in′solence. —*adv* in′solently.

insomnia [in-som′ni-a] *n* abnormal inability to sleep. —*n* insom′niac.

insouciant [in-sōō′si-ánt] *adj* calm and unbothered, carefree. —*n* insouciance [in-sōō′si-áns, ē-sōō-sē-äs]

inspect [in-spekt′] *vt* to look at carefully; to examine or review officially. —*ns* inspec′tion, inspec′tor, one who inspects; an examining officer; a police officer ranking below a superintendent; an examining officer at a polling place; inspec′torāte, a body of inspectors.

inspire [in-spīr′] *vt* to inhale; to impel, as to some creative effort; to motivate by divine influence; to arouse (a thought or feeling) in (someone); to cause. —*vt* to inhale; to give inspiration. —*n* inspirā′tion [in-spir-], an inhaling; a mental or emotional inspiring; any stimulus to creative thought; an inspired idea, action, etc.

inspirit [in-spir′it] *vt* to fill with spirit.

inspissate [in-spis′āt or in′-] *vti* to thicken. —*n* inspissā′tion.

install, instal [in-stöl′] *vt* to formally place in an office, rank, etc.; to establish in a place; to fix in position for use. —*ns* installā′tion; instal(l)′ment, to place in an office by seating in an official seat; **install'ment**, an installing or being installed; a sum of money to be paid at regular specified times; any of several parts, as of a serial.

instance [in'stàns] *n* an example; a step in proceeding; an occasion (in the first instance). —*vt* to give as an example.

instant [in'stànt] *adj* pressing, urgent; (*old fashioned*) as the current month; imminent; immediate; concentrated or precooked for quick preparation, as a food or beverage. —*n* a moment; a particular moment. —*adj* **instantān'eous**, occurring very quickly. —*advs* **instantān'eously**; **instanter** [in-stan'tèr] L, immediately; **in'stantly**, immediately.

instead [in-sted'] *adv* in place of the one mentioned.

instep [in'step] *n* the upper part of the arch of the foot, between the ankle and the toes.

instigate [in'sti-gāt] *vt* to urge on, incite; to foment rebellion. —*ns* **instigā'tion**, the act of inciting, esp to evil; **in'stigātor**, an inciter, generally in a bad sense.

instill, instil [in-stil'] *vt* to drop in; to infuse slowly; to put in drop by drop; to put (an idea, etc.) in or into gradually (into the mind). —*pr p* **instill'ing**; *pt p* **instilled'**. —*ns* **instillā'tion**; **instill'er**; **instil'ment**.

instinct [in'stingkt] *n* (an) inborn tendency to behave in a way characteristic of a species; a natural or acquired tendency; a knack. —*adj* [in-stingkt'] infused; imbued. —*adj* **instinc'tive**. —*adv* **instinctively**.

institute [in'sti-tūt] *vt* to set up, establish; to start, initiate. —*n* an organization for the promotion of science, art, etc.; a school, college, or department of a university specializing in some field. —*n* **institū'tion**, an established law, custom, etc.; an organization having a social, educational, or religious purpose; the building housing it; (*inf*) a long-established person or thing. —*adjs* **institut'ional**.

instruct [in-strukt'] *vt* to inform; to teach; to educate; to inform; to order or direct. —*n* **instruc'tion**. —*adjs* **instruc'tional**; **instruc'tive**. —*adv* **instruc'tively**. —*ns* **instruc'tiveness**; **instruc'tor**, a teacher, a college teacher of the lowest rank.

instrument [in'strōō-mènt] *n* a thing by means of which something is done; a tool or implement; any of various devices for indicating, measuring, controlling, etc.; any of various devices producing musical sound; a formal document. —*vt* [-ment'], to address a legal document; to score for musical performance; to equip with indicating, measuring, or controlling devices. —*adj* **instrumental** [-ment'àl]. —*ns* **instrument'alist**, one who plays on a musical instrument; **instrumentality** [-mènt-al'i-ti], agency—*adv* **instrument'ally**. —*n* **instrumentā'tion**, use or provision of instruments; the arrangement of a composition for performance by different instruments.

insubordinate [in-sub-ör'din-àt] *adj* not submitting to authority; rebellious. —*n* **insubordinā'tion**.

insular [in'sū-lár] *adj* of or like an island or islanders; narrow-minded; illiberal. —*n* **insularity** [-ar'i-ti]. —*adv* **in'sularly**. —*vt* **in'sulate**, to set apart; to isolate; to cover with a nonconducting material in order to prevent the escape of electricity, heat, sound, etc. —*ns* **insulā'tion**; **in'sulator**, one that insulates.

insulin [in'sè-lin] *n* a hormone vital to carbohydrate metabolism, secreted by islets of tissue in the pancreas; an extract from the pancreas of animals used in the treatment of diabetes.

insult [in-sult'] *vt* to treat with indignity or contempt; to affront. —*n* [in'sult] affront, a remark or act hurtful to the feelings or pride. —*adj* **insult'ing**. —*adv* **insult'ingly**.

insuperable [in-sū'pèr-á-bl] *adj* that cannot be overcome. —*n* **insuperabil'ity**. —*adv* **insu'perably**.

insure [in-shōōr'] *vt* to take out or issue insurance on; to ensure. —*vi* to contract to give or take insurance. —*adj* **insur'able**, that may be insured. —*ns* **insur'ance**, the act or system of insuring; a contract (or **insurance policy**) purchased to guarantee compensation for a specified loss by fire, death, etc.; the amount for which something is insured; the business of insuring against loss; **insur'er**.

insurgent [in-sûr'jènt] *adj* rising in revolt. —*n* one who rises in opposition to established authority, a rebel. —*ns* **insur'gence**, **insur'gency**.

intact [in-takt'] *adj* unimpaired; whole.

intaglio [in-tāl'yō] *n* a design carved or engraved below the surface; a printing process in which the ink-carrying areas of the printing surface are hollows below the surface.

intake [in'tāk] *n* that which is taken in; amount taken in; the place in a pipe, etc. where a fluid is taken in.

intangible [in-tan'ji-bl] *adj* that cannot be touched, incorporeal; representing value but without material being, as good will; that cannot be easily defined. —*n* something intangible. —*ns* **intan'gibleness, intangibil'ity**. —*adv* **intan'gibly**.

integer [in'tè-jèr] *n* any member of the set consisting of the positive and negative whole numbers and zero. Examples: –5, 0, 5. —*adj* **in'tegral** [-gràl], necessary for completeness; whole or complete; made up of parts forming a whole. —*n* the result of a mathematical integration. —*adv* **in'tegrally**. —*vti* **in'tegrāte** to make whole or become complete; to bring (parts) together into a whole; to remove barriers imposing segregation upon (racial groups); to abolish segregation. —*ns* **integrā'tion, integrity** [in-teg'ri-ti], completeness, wholeness; unimpaired condition; honesty, sincerity, etc.

integument [in-teg'ū-mènt] a natural covering as skin, a rind, a husk, etc. —*adj* **integumentary** [-ment'àr-i].

intellect [in'tè-lekt] *n* the ability to reason or understand; high intelligence; a very intelligent person. —*n* **intellec'tion**, reasoning; thought. —*adjs* **intellect'ive**, of, or related to the intellect; **intellectual** [-ek'tū-àl], of, involving, or appealing to the intellect; requiring intelligence.

intelligent [in-tel'i-jènt] *adj* having or showing intelligence; clever, wise, etc. —*n* **intell'igence**, the ability to learn or understand; the ability to cope with a new situation; news or information; those engaged in gathering secret, esp military, information. —*adj* **intelligential** [-jen'shàl]. —*adv* **intell'igently**. —*adj* **intell'igible**, that may be understood; clear. —*ns* **intell'igibleness, intelligibil'ity**. —*adv* **intell'igibly**.

intelligentsia [in-tel-i-jent'si-a] *n* intellectuals collectively.

intemperance [in-tem'pèr-àns] *n* excess of any kind; habitual over-indulgence in intoxicating liquor. —*adj* **intem'perate**, indulging to excess any appetite, esp intoxicating liquors. —*adv* **intem'perately**. —*n* **intem'perateness**.

intend [in-tend'] *vt* to design, to purpose; to mean something to be or be used (for); to mean, to signify.

intense [in-tens'] *adj* very strong, concentrated; strained to the utmost, strenuous; marked by much action, strong emotions, etc. —*adv* **intense'ly**. —*ns* **intense'ness, inten'sity**. —*vti* **inten'sify**, to make or become more intense. —*pr p* **intens'ifying**; *pt p* **intens'ified**. —*ns* **intensificā'tion; inten'sion**, intensity; (*logic*) the sum of the qualities implied by a general name. —*adj* **inten'sive**, of or characterized by intensity; thorough; denoting careful attention given to patients right after surgery, etc. (*gram*) giving force or emphasis. —*n* an intensive word. —*adv* **inten'sively**. —*n* **inten'siveness**.

intent [in-tent'] *adj* firmly directed; having one's attention or purpose firmly fixed. —*n* an intending; something intended; purpose or meaning. —*n* **intention** [in-ten'sh(ó)n], a determination to act in a specified way; anything intended. —*adjs* **inten'tional**, done purposely. —*advs* **inten'tionally, intent'ly**. —*n* **intent'ness**.

inter [in-tûr'] *vt* to bury. —*pr p* **interr'ing**; *pt p* **interred'**. —*n* **inter'ment**.

inter- [in'tèr] *prefix* [L] meaning: between, among, or involving the individual elements named in the base adjective or singular noun, as *intercultural, interdepartmental, interfaith, intergroup, interracial*; with or on each other.

intercalate [in-tèr'kàl-āt] *vt* to insert between others, as a day in a calendar; to interpolate. —*adj* **inter'calary**, inserted between others. —*n* **intercalā'tion**.

intercede [in-tèr-sēd'] *vi* to plead on behalf of another; to mediate. —*n* **interced'er**.

intercept [in-tèr-sept'] *vt* to stop or seize in its course; (*math*) to mark off between two points, lines, etc. —*n* [in'tèr-sept], a point of intersection of two geometric figures; interception by an interceptor. —*ns* **intercep'tor, intercep'ter**, one who or that which intercepts; a light, swift airplane for pursuit or missile designed for defense. **intercep'tion**.

intercourse [in'tèr-körs, -körs] *n* a connection by dealings; sexual union.

interdict [in-tèr-dikt'] *vt* to prohibit (an action); to restrain from doing or using something. —*n* an official prohibition. —

n interdic′tion. —*adjs* interdic′tive, interdic′tory, containing interdiction; prohibitory.

interest [int′(é-)rest, -rist] *n* a share in, or a right to, something; anything in which one has a share; (often *pl*) benefit; (usu *pl* those having a common concern or power in a cause, industry, etc.; a feeling of curiosity about something; the power of causing this feeling; money paid for the use of money; the rate of such payment. —*vt* to excite the attention of; to cause to have a share in; to regard as a personal concern. —*adj* in′terested, having an interest or concern; affected or biased by personal considerations, etc. —*adv* in′terestedly. —*adj* in′teresting, engaging or apt to engage the attention or regard; exciting emotion or passion. —*adv* in′terestingly.

interfere [in-tér-fēr′] *vi* to clash; to come between; to intervene; to meddle; (*sport*) to hinder an opponent in any of various illegal ways. —*ns* interfēr′ence, the act of interfering; (radio and television) the interruption of reception by atmospherics or by unwanted signals; interfēr′er.

interim [in′tér-im] *n* the period of time between; meantime. —*adj* temporary. —*adv* meanwhile.

interior [in-tē′ri-ór] *adj* situated within; inner; inland; private. —*n* the interior part, as of a room, country, etc.; the internal or domestic affairs of a country. —*adv* inte′riorly.

interject [in-tér-jekt′] *vt* to throw in between; to interrupt with. —*n* interjec′tion, (*gram*) an exclamation. —*adj* interjec′tional, parenthetical.

interlock [in-tér-lok′] *vt* to lock together; to join with one another. —*vi* to be locked together.

interlocution [in-tér-lo-kū′sh(ó)n] *n* conference. —*n* interloc′utor, one who speaks in dialogue. —*adj* interloc′utory.

interloper [in′tér-lōp-ér] *n* one who meddles. —*vi* interlope′, to encroach on the rights of others; to intrude.

interlude [in′tér-l(y)ōōd] *n* anything that fills time between two events, as music between acts of a play.

interlunar [in-tér-l(y)ōō′når] *adj* belonging to the moon's monthly period of invisibility. —Also **interlu′nary**.

intermediate [in-tér-mē′di-åt] *adj* in the middle; in between. —*n* (*chem*) a compound formed as a step between the starting material and the final product. —*adj* intermē′diary, acting between others; intermediate. —*n* an intermediate agent. —*adv* intermē′diately.

intermezzo [in-tér-med′zo′ or -met′sō] *n* a short dramatic or musical entertainment between parts of a play, etc.; a movement in a larger instrumental work; a similar independent work.

interminable [in-tûr′min-à-bl] *adj* lasting, or seeming to last forever; endless. —*n* inter′minableness. —*adv* inter′minably.

intermit [in-tér-mit′] *vti* to stop for a time. —*n* intermission [-mish′ón], act of intermitting; interval of time between parts of a performance. —*adj* intermitt′ent, stopping and starting again at intervals; periodic. —*n* intermitt′ence. *adv* intermitt′ently.

intern [in-tûrn′] *vt* to detain and confine within an area. —*n* [in′tûrn], a doctor serving in a hospital, usu just after graduation from medical school; an apprentice journalist, teacher, etc. —Also **interne**. —*ns* internēē′, one confined within fixed bounds; intern′ment, confinement of this kind.

internal [in-tûr′nål] *adj* of or on the inside; to be taken inside the body (*internal remedies*); intrinsic; domestic. —*adv* inter′nally. —inter′nal combust′ion en′gine, an engine as the automobile, powered by the explosion of a fuel-and-air mixture within the cylinders.

international [in-tér-nash′ón-ål] *adj* between or among nations; concerned with the relations between nations; for the use of all nations; of or for people in various nations. —*adv* internat′ionally. —**international date line**, date line.

internecine [in-tér-nē′sīn] *adj* extremely destructive to both sides. [L *internecīnus*, *-īvus*—*internecāre*—*inter*, between (used intensively), *necāre*, to kill, *nex*, *necis*, murder.]

interpellation [in-tér-pel-ā′sh(ó)n] *n* formal questioning of (a foreign minister) concerning an official policy or personal conduct. —*vt* interpell′ate.

interpolate [in-tér′po-lāt] *vt* to change (a text) by inserting new material; to insert between or among others; (*math*) to estimate a value between two known values. —*ns* interpolā′tion, inter′polātor.

interpose [in-tér-pōz′] *vti* to place or come between; to intervene (with); to interrupt (with). —*ns* interpos′er; interposition [in-tér-poz-ish′(ó)n], act of interposing; the action of a state when it places its sovereignty between its citizens and the federal government.

interpret [in-tûr′pret] *vt* to explain; to translate; to construe; to give one's own conception of, as in a play or musical composition. —*vi* to translate between speakers of different languages. —*n* interpretā′tion, act or result of interpreting; an instance of interpretation. —*n* inter′preter, one who translates orally for persons speaking in different languages; a computer program that translates an instruction into machine language.

interregnum [in-tér-reg′num] *n* the time between two reigns; the time between the cessation of one and the establishment of another government; a pause in a continuous series.

interrogate [in-tér′ó-gāt] *vti* to question esp formally. —*n* interrogā′tion. —*adj* interrogative [in-tér-og′á-tiv], asking a question. —*n* a word (as *who*, *what*, *which*) used in asking a question. —*adv* interrog′atively. —*ns* inter′rogātor, interrog′atory. —*adj* interrogative.

interrupt [in-tér-upt′] *vt* to break into (a discussion, etc.) or break in upon (a speaker, worker, etc.); to make a break in the continuity of. —*vi* to interrupt an action, talk, etc. —*adj* interrupt′ed, broken in continuity. —*adv* interrup′tedly. —*ns* interrup′ter, interrup′tion, act of interrupting.

intersect [in-tér-sekt′] *vti* to cut across; to cut or cross mutually; to divide by cutting or crossing. —*n* intersec′tion, an intersecting; the place where two lines, roads, etc. meet or cross.

intersperse [in-tér-spûrs′] *vt* to scatter or set here and there; to diversify with things scattered here and there. —*n* interspersion [-spér′sh(ó)n].

interstice [in-tûr′stis] *n* a crack; a crevice; a minute space. —*adj* interstitial [-stish′ål], occurring in interstices.

interval [in-tér-vål] *n* a space between things; the time between events; (*mus*) the difference of pitch between two tones.

intervene [in-tér-vēn′] *vi* to come or be between; to occur between two events, etc.; to come in to modify, settle, or hinder some action, etc. —*n* intervention [-ven′sh(ó)n], intervening; interference.

interview [in′tér-vū] *n* a personal meeting for conference; a meeting in which a person is asked about his views, etc. as by a reporter; a published account of this. —*vt* to have an interview with. —*ns* interviewee′; interviewer.

intestate [in-tes′tåt] *adj* having made no will. —*n* one who dies intestate. —*n* intes′tacy [-tà-si], the state of being or dying intestate.

intestine [in-tes′tin] *n* (usu *pl*) lower part of the alimentary canal between the stomach and the anus. —*adj* intes′tinal.

intimate [in′ti-måt] *adj* most private or personal; very close or familiar; deep and thorough. —*n* an intimate friend. —*vt* [-måt], to hint or imply. —*n* in′timacy [-må-si], state of being intimate. —*adv* in′timately. —*ns* intimā′tion, indication, hint.

intimidate [in-tim′i-dāt] *vt* to strike fear into esp by threats. —*n* intimidā′tion.

into [in′tōō, in′tōō] *prep* noting passage inwards (*lit*, *fig*); noting the passage of a thing from one state to another; noting parts made by dividing.

intonate [in′ton-āt] *vti* to intone, to utter. —*n* intonā′tion, an intoning; the manner of producing tones with regard to accurate pitch; variations in pitch within an utterance. *vti* intone [in-tōn′], to speak or recite in a singing tone; to chant. —*n* intōn′er.

intoxicate [in-toks′i-kāt] *vt* to poison; to excite greatly. —*ns* intox′icant, something that intoxicates esp a drug or an alcoholic drink; an intoxicating agent; intoxic′ātion, state of being poisoned; condition of being drunk; excitement to excess.

intra- [in′tra-] *prefix* within.

intransigent [in-tran′si-jént or -zi-] *adj* refusing to compromise, irreconcilable. —*n* intran′sigence.

intrepid [in-trep′id] *adj* bold; fearless; brave. —*n* intrepid′ity. —*adv* intrep′idly.

intricate [in′tri-kåt] *adj* involved; complicated. —*ns* in′tricacy [-å-si], in′tricateness. —*adv* in′tricately.

intrigue [in-trēg′] *n* a secret or underhanded plotting; a secret or underhanded plot or scheme; a secret love affair. —*vi* to engage in intrigue. —*vt* to excite the interest or curiosity of. —*n* intriguer [-trēg′ĕr]. —*adj* intrigu′ing. —*adv* intrigu′ingly.

intrinsic [in-trin′sik] *adj* belonging to the real nature of a thing; inherent. —*adv* intrin′sically.

intro- [in′trō-, in-trō′-] *prefix* within, into.

intro [in′trō] *n* (*inf*) introduction. Contraction of **introduction**.

introduce [in-trō-dūs′] *vt* to lead to bring in; to put (into a place); formally to make known or acquainted; to make acquainted with (*with* to); to bring into notice, or into practice; to preface. —*n* introduction [-duk′sh(ỏ)n]. —*adj* introduc′tory.

introspect [in-tro-spekt′] *vti* to (engage in) an inspection of one's own mind and feelings, etc. —*n* introspection [-spek′-sh(ỏ)n]. —*adj* introspec′tive.

introvert [in′-trō-vûrt] one who is more interested in his own thoughts, feelings, etc. than in external objects or events. —*vt* to turn inward. —*n* introver′sion.

intrude [in-trōōd′] *vti* to force (oneself) upon others unasked. *ns* intruder; intrusion [-trōōzh(o)n], act of intruding; the forcible entry of rock in a molten state among and through existing rocks. —*adj* intrusive.

intuition [in-tū-ish′(ỏ)n] *n* the capacity of the mind by which it immediately perceives the truth of things without reasoning or analysis; a truth so perceived. —*vt* intu′it, to apprehend by intuition. —*adj* intūit′ional.

inundate [in′un-dāt] *vt* to cover as with a flood; to deluge. —*n* inundā′tion.

inure [in-ūr′] *vt* to accustom to pain, hardship, etc.; to habituate. —Also enure′. —*n* inure′ment.

invade [in-vād′] *vt* to enter as an enemy; to encroach upon, to violate. —*ns* invad′er; invasion [vā′zh(ỏ)n]. —*adj* invasive [-vā′ziv], marked by military aggression; tending to spread; tending to infringe.

invalid [in-val′id] *adj* not valid —*adj* invalid, [in′val-id], sick, weak and sickly; of or for invalids. —*n* one who is ill or disabled. —*vt* inval′idāte, to render invalid; to deprive of legal force. —*ns* invalidā′tion; invalid′ity, want of cogency or force; state of illness or disability.

invaluable [in-val′ū-à-bl] *adj* too valuable to be measured in money. —*adv* inval′uably.

Invar [in′vär, in-vär′] *n* an alloy of iron and nickel that expands little on heating.

inveigh [in-vā′] *vi* to make an attack with words, to rail (against).

inveigle [in-vē′gl also in-vā′gl] *vt* to entice or trick into doing something. —*n* invei′glement.

invent [in-vent′] *vt* to think up; to think out or produce (a new device, process, etc.) to originate. —*n* inven′tion, that which is invented; the power of inventing. —*adj* inven′tive, of invention; skilled in inventing. —*adv* inven′tively. —*ns* inven′tiveness; inven′tor.

inventory [in′ven-tòr-i] *n* an itemized list of goods, property, etc. as of a business; the store of such goods for such listing; a list of the property of an individual or an estate. —*vt* to make an inventory of.

invert [in-vûrt′] *vt* to turn upside down; to reverse the customary order or position of. —*adj* inver′ted, turned upside down; reversed.

invertebrate [in-vûrt′e-bràt] *n* an animal without a backbone. —Also *adj*.

invest [in-vest′] *vt* to clothe; to install in office with ceremony; to furnish with power, authority, etc.; to put (money) into business, bonds, etc. for profit. —*vi* to invest money. —*ns* inves′titure, ceremony of investing; invest′ment, inves′tor, one who invests money.

investigate [in-vest′i-gāt] *vti* to search (into); to inquire. —*n* investigā′tion. —*adjs* invest′igative, invest′igatory. —*n* invest′igātor.

inveterate [in-vet′ĕr-àt] *adj* firmly established; habitual. —*adv* invet′erately. —*ns* invet′erateness, invet′eracy [-à-si] state of being obstinate.

invidious [in-vid′i-us] *adj* likely to provoke ill-will; offensively discriminating (eg *an invidious distinction*). —*adv* invid′iously. —*n* invid′iousness.

invigorate [in-vig′òr-āt] *vt* to give vigor to; to fill with energy. —*n* invigorā′tion.

invincible [in-vin′si-bl] *adj* that cannot be overcome;

unconquerable. —*ns* invin′cibleness, invincibil′ity. —*adv* invin′cibly.

invite [in-vīt′] *vt* to ask to come somewhere or do something; to ask for; to give occasion for (*his conduct invites gossip*); to tempt; to entice. —*n* (*inf*) an invitation. —*ns* invitation [in-vi-tā′sh(ỏ)n], the act of inviting; a message used in inviting; invītēe, an invited person; invīt′er. —*adj* invīt′ing, alluring, attractive. —*adv* invīt′ingly, in an inviting manner.

invoice [in′vois] *n* a letter of advice of the dispatch of goods, with particulars of their price and quantity. —*vt* to present an invoice for or to.

invoke [in-vōk′] *vt* to call on (God, the Muses, etc.) for help, blessing, etc.; to resort to (a law, etc.) as pertinent; to conjure; to beg for; to implore.

involuntary [in-vol′un-tàr-i] *adj* not done by choice; not consciously controlled. —*adv* invol′untarily. —*n* invol′untariness.

involve [in-volv′] *vt* to complicate; to implicate; to affect or include; to require; to occupy, to make busy. —*n* involve′-ment.

inward [in′wàrd] *adj* placed or being within, internal; mental or spiritual; directed toward the inside. —*adv* toward the inside; into the mind or soul. —*advs* in′wardly, within; in the mind or spirit; toward the inside or center; in′wards, inward.

ion [ī′ŏn] *n* an electrically charged atom or group of atoms formed through the gain or loss of one or more electrons. —*vt* i′onize, to dissociate into ions, as a salt dissolved in water, or become electrically charged, as a gas under radiation.

Ionic [ī-on′ik] *adj* denoting a Greek style of architecture distinguished by the ornamental scrolls on the capitals.

iota [ī-ō′ta] *n* the ninth letter of the Greek alphabet; a very small quantity; a jot.

ipecac [ip′e-kak] *n* an emetic made from the dried roots of a S American plant; any of several roots used in the same way.

ire [īr] *n* anger; wrath. —*adjs* irate [ī-rāt′ or īr′āt], enraged, angry; ire′ful, full of wrath; resentful. —*adv* ire′fully.

iris [ī′ris] *n* the round, pigmented membrane surrounding the pupil of the eye; any of a large genus of perennial herbaceous plants with sword-shaped leaves and a showy flower; the rainbow; an appearance resembling the rainbow. —*pl* i′rises. —*n* iridescence [ir-i-des′ĕns], play of rainbow colors, as on bubbles, mother-of-pearl. —*adjs* irides′cent.

irk [ûrk] *vt* to annoy, irritate, tire out, etc. —*adj* irk′some, tedious; burdensome. —*adv* irk′somely. —*n* irk′someness.

iron [ī′ĕrn] *n* a metallic element the most common of all metals; tool, etc. of this metal, esp one with a heated flat underface for pressing cloth; (*pl*) shackles of iron; firm strength; power; any of certain golf clubs with angled metal heads. —*adj* of iron; like iron, strong and firm. —*vti* to press with a hot iron. —i′ronclad, clad in iron; difficult to change or break (*an ironclad lease*)—*ns* i′ron gray′, a slightly greenish dark gray. **iron lung**, a large respirator that encloses all of the body but the head.

irony [ī′rŏni or ī-ĕr-ni] *n* expression in which the intended meaning of the words is the opposite of their usual sense; an event or result that is the opposite of what is expected. —*adjs* ironic [ī-ron′ik], iron′ical. —*adv* iron′ically.

irradiate [ir-ā′di-āt] *vt* to shine upon; to light up; to enlighten; to radiate; to expose to X-rays or other radiant energy. —*vi* to emit rays; to shine. —*n* irrā′diance. —*adj* irrā′diant. —*n* irradiā′tion, emission of radiant energy; exposure to radiation (as X-rays).

irrespective [ir-i-spek′tiv] *adj* regardless (*with* of). —*adv* irrespec′tively.

irrigate [ir′i-gāt] *vt* to supply (land) with water as by means of artificial ditches, pipes, etc.; (*med*) to wash out (a cavity, wound, etc.). —*ns* irrigā′tion, irrigāt′or.

irritate [ir′i-tāt] *vt* to provoke to anger; to annoy; to make inflamed or sore. —*adj* irr′itable, easily annoyed, irritated, or provoked; (*med*) excessively sensitive to a stimulus. —*ns* irr′itableness, irritabil′ity, the quality of being easily irritated; the susceptibility to stimuli possessed by living matter. —*adv* irr′itably. —*adj* irr′itant, irritating. —*n* that which causes irritation. —*n* irritā′tion, act of irritating or exciting; excitement; anger, annoyance; (*med*) a condition of irritability, soreness, inflammation of a part of the body. —*adj* irr′itātive, tending to irritate or excite; accompanied with or caused by irritation.

irruption [ir-up'sh(ò)n] *n* a breaking or bursting in; (*ecology*) an abrupt increase in size of population; a sudden invasion or incursion. —*adj* **irrup'tive**, rushing suddenly in. —*adv* **irrup'tively**.

is [iz] third pers sing pres indic of be.

-ish *adj suffix* meaning: of a specified people [Spanish], like (boyish), somewhat (tallish), and (*inf*) approximately (thirtyish).

isinglass [ī'zing-gläs] *n* a gelatin prepared from fish bladders; mica, esp in thin sheets.

Islam [is'läm or iz'-, or is-läm'] *n* the Muslim religion, a montheistic religion founded by Mohammed.

island [ī'land] *n* a land mass smaller than a continent and surrounded by water; anything like this in position or isolation. —**islander** [ī'land-èr], a native or inhabitant of an island.

isle [īl] *n* an island, esp a small one. **islet** [ī'let], a little isle.

-ism, -asm or [(with -ic) -icism], *suffix* forming abstract nouns signifying condition, system, as egoism, Calvinism, Anglicism.

ism [izm] *n* any distinctive doctrine, theory or practice.

iso- [ī-sō-] in composition, equal.

isobar [ī'sō-bär] *n* a line on a map passing through places of equal barometric pressure.

isolate [ī'sō-lāt] *vt* to set apart from others; to place alone. —*n* a person or thing that is isolated. —*ns* **isolā'tion; isolā'tionism,** the policy of avoiding political entanglements with other countries; **isolationist.**

isomer [ī'sō-mer] any of two or more chemical compounds whose molecules contain the same atoms but in different arrangements. —*adj* **isomer'ic.** —*n* **isom'erism.**

isosceles [ī-sos'e-lēz] *adj* denoting a triangle with two equal sides.

isotherm [ī'so-thèrm] *n* a line on a map connecting points of the same temperature, as **isotherm'ally.**

isotope [ī'sō-tōp] *n* any of two or more forms of an element having the same atomic number but different atomic weights. —*adj* **isotopic** [-top'ik]. —*n* **i'sotopy** [-tō-pē, ī-sät'é-pē].

issue [ish'(y)ōō, is'ū] *n* an outgoing; an outlet; a result; offspring; a point under dispute; a sending or giving out; all that is put forth at one time (an issue of bonds, a periodical, etc.). —*vi* to go or flow out; to result (from) or end (in); to be published. —*vt* to let out; to discharge; to give or deal out, as supplies; to publish.

-ist [-ist] a suffix meaning: one who does, makes, or practices (satirist), one skilled or occupied with (violinist, druggist), an adherent (anarchist).

isthmus [is(th)'mus] *n* a narrow strip of land having water at each side and connecting two larger bodies of land.

it [it] *pron* the thing spoken of; the subject of an impersonal verb (*it is raining*); a subject or object of indefinite sense in various constructions. —*n* the player, as in tag, who must catch another.

italic [i-tal'ik] *adj* denoting a type in which the letters slant upward to the right (*this is italic type*). —*n* (usu *pl*) italic type or handwriting.

itch [ich] *n* an uneasy irritating sensation in the skin; an eruptive disease in the skin, caused by a parasitic mite; a constant teasing desire. —*vi* to have an uneasy irritating sensation in the skin; to have a constant, teasing desire. —*adj* **itch'y**, pertaining to or affected with itch. —*n* **itch'iness.**

item [ī'tem] *n* an article; a unit; a separate thing; a bit of news or information. —*vt* i'temize, to specify the items of; to set down by items. —*n* **itemiza'tion.**

iterate [it'ér-āt] *vt* to do again; to say again, repeat. *n* **iterā'tion.** —*adj* **it'erātive.**

itinerant [īt-in'èr-ânt] *adj* traveling from place to place. —*n* a traveler. —*ns* **itin'eracy, itin'erancy.** —*n* **itin'erary,** a route; a record of a journey; a detailed plan of a journey. —*vi* **itin'erāte,** to travel, esp for the purpose of judging or preaching.

ivory [ī'vô-ri] *n* the hard, white substance composing the tusks of elephants, walruses, etc., any substance like ivory; creamy white. —*adj* of, or like ivory; creamy-white. —*ns* **i'vory black,** a black pigment made from burnt ivory.

ivy [ī'vi] *n* a climbing or creeping vine with a woody stem and evergreen leaves widely cultivated in many species as an ornamental.

J

jab [jab] *vti* to punch with short, straight blows. —*n* a sudden thrust or stab.

jabber [jab'èr] *vti* to talk rapidly, incoherently, or foolishly. —*n* **jabb'erer.** [Imit.]

jabot [zha'bō] *n* a frill, worn in front of a blouse or shirt.

jacinth [jas'inth] *n* a reddish-orange variety of zircon.

jack [jak] *n* a man or boy; any of various machines used to lift something heavy; a playing card with a page boy's picture on it, ranking below the queen; a small flag flown on a ship's bow as a signal or to show nationality. —*vt* to raise by means of a jack. —**jack'knife,** a dive in which the diver touches his feet with knees straight and then straightens out.

jackal [jak'öl] *n* any of several wild dogs.

jackanapes [jak'a-nāps] *n* an impudent fellow; a forward child.

jackass [jak'as] *n* a male donkey; a fool.

jackdaw [jak'dö] *n* black bird like the crow, but smaller.

jacket [jak'et] *n* a short coat; an outer covering, as the removable paper cover of a book.

Jacobean [jak-o-bē'an] *adj* of, or characteristic of, the period of James I of England (1603–1625).

Jacob's ladder [jā'kobz-lad'èr] *n* any of a genus of herbs with flat-topped blue or white flowers and leaves resembling a ladder; (naut) a ladder of ropes with wooden steps.

Jacussi [je-kōōz'ē] *n* trade name for a device which swirls water in a bath; a bath containing such a device.

jade[1] [jād] *n* a worthless nag; a disreputable woman. —*vt* to tire; to satiate.

jade[2] [jād] *n* a hard, ornamental semiprecious stone; its light green color.

jag[1] [jag] *n* a sharp, toothlike projection. —*adj* **jagged,** having sharp projecting points; notched or ragged.

jag[2] [jag] *n* a small load; (slang) intoxication from drugs or alcohol; a bout of drinking, crying, etc. a notch; a sharp or rugged point of rock, etc.; (*bot*) a cleft or division; (*Scot*) a prick; an inoculation, injection; a thrill; a bout of indulgence, eg in liquor or narcotics. —*vt* to cut into notches; to prick.

jaguar [jag'wär or jag'ū-ar] *n* a medium-sized, black-marked feline of tropical America.

jail [jāl] *n* a prison. —*vt* to send to or confine in prison. —*ns* **jail'-bird,** one who is or has been in jail; **jail'er.**

jalap [jal'ap] *n* the purgative root of a plant.

jalousie [zhal-ōō-zē' or zhal'-] *n* a shutter constructed with angled slats.

jam[1] [jam] *n* fruit boiled with sugar until thickened. —*adj* **jamm'y.** [Perh from jam (2).]

jam[2] [jam] *vt* to squeeze into a confined space; tight; to crowd full; to block by crowding; to wedge; to bring to a standstill by wedging; to interfere with a radio signal by sending out other signals on the same wavelength. —*vi* to become stuck. —*pr p* **jamm'ing;** *pt p* **jammed.** —*n* a crush; a block; a difficulty; (*inf*) a difficult or embarrassing situation.

jamb [jam] *n* the sidepost of a door, fireplace, etc.

jamboree [jam-bó-rē'] *n* (*slang*) a boisterous frolic, a spree.

jangle [jang'gl] *vi* to sound harshly or discordantly, as bells. —*vt* to cause to jangle; to irritate. —*n* **dissonant clanging.** —*ns* **jang'ler; jang'ling.**

janitor [jan'i-tòr] *n* one who takes care of a building.

January [jan'ū-âr-i] *n* the first month of the year.

japan [ja-pan'] *n* a hard, glossy varnish. —*vt* to lacquer with japan.

jar[1] [jär] *vi* to make a harsh sound; to have an irritating effect (on one); to vibrate from an impact; to clash. —*vt* to jolt. —*n* a grating sound; a vibration due to impact; a jolt. —*adv* **jar'ringly.**

jar[2] [jär] *n* an earthen or glass bottle with a wide mouth; the amount this will contain.

jargon [jär'gón] *n* confused talk, gibberish; the special or technical vocabulary of a science, etc.

jasmine [jaz'min] *n* any of a genus of climbing shrubs with fragrant white or yellow flowers.

jasper [jas'pèr] *n* a red, yellow, dark green or brown quartz used as a gemstone.

jaundice [jön'dis] *n* a disease, symptom characterized by a yellowing of the eyes, skin, etc., by bile; bitterness; ill-humor; prejudice.—*adj* **jaun′diced**, affected with jaundice; (of person, judgment) biassed by envy, disillusionment, etc.

jaunt [jönt] *vi* to go from place to place; to make an excursion.—*n* an excursion; a ramble.

jaunty [jönt′i or jänt′i] *adj* having an airy or sprightly manner.—*adv* **jaunt′ily**.—*n* **jaunt′iness**.

javelin [jav′(é-)lin] *n* a light spear esp one thrown for distance in a contest.

jaw [jö] *n* one of the bones in which teeth are set; either of two movable parts that grasp or crush something, as in a vise; the narrow opening of a gorge.

jay [jā] *n* any of several birds of the crow family with raucous voices, roving habits, and destructive behaviour to other birds.—*vi* **jay′walk**, to walk across a street carelessly without obeying traffic rules or signals.—*n* **jay′walker**.

jazz [jaz] *n* a general term for American popular music embracing ragtime, blues, swing, jive, and bebop.—*vt* to play as jazz; (*slang*) to enliven or embellish.

jealous [jel′us] *adj* suspicious of or incensed at rivalry: envious (of); anxiously heedful.—*adv* **jeal′ously**.—*n* **jeal′ousy**.

jean [jēn, jān] *n* a twilled cotton cloth; (*pl*) trousers or overalls or jean.

jeep [jēp] *n* a light military vehicle with heavy duty tyres and good ground clearance for use on rough terrain.

jeer [jēr] *vt* to treat with derision.—*vi* to scoff (at).—*n* a railing remark.—*adv* **jeer′ingly**.

Jehovah [ji-hō′vä] *n* God.

jejune [ji-jōōn′] *adj* lacking interest; naïve, immature.—*adv* **jejune′ly**.—*n* **jejune′ness**.

jelly [jel′i] *n* a soft, gelatinous food made from cooked fruit syrup or meat juice; any substance like this.—*vti* to jell.—*vti* **jell**, to become, or make into jelly; to crystallize, as a plan.— *adj* **jell′ied**; **jellyfish**, a coelenterate with a nearly transparent body and long tentacles.

jennet [jen′et] *n* a small Spanish horse.

jeopardy [jep′ärd-i] *n* great danger or risk.—*vt* **jeop′ardīze**, to put in jeopardy.

jerboa [jėr-bō′ä] *n* any of several desert rodents with long hind legs and a long tail.

jeremiad [jer-e-mī′ad] *n* a lamentation; a doleful story.

jerk[1] [jûrk] *n* a sudden sharp pull or twist; a sudden muscular contraction or reflex—*vti* to move with a jerk; to pull sharply; to twitch.—*adj* **jerk′y**.—*n* **jerki′ness**.

jerk[2] [jûrk] *vt* to preserve (meat) by cutting it into long strips and drying it in the sun.—*n* **jerk′y**.

jerkin [jûr′kin] *n* a close-fitting jacket, often sleeveless.

jerry-builder [jer′i-bild′ėr] *n* one who builds flimsy houses cheaply and hastily.—*adj* **jerr′y-built**.

jersey [jûr′zi] *n* any plain machine-knitted fabric of natural or man-made fibers; a circular-knitted sweater.

jessamine [jes′a-min] *see* **jasmine**.

jest [jest] *n* a mocking remark; a joke; a thing to be laughed at.—*vi* to jeer; to joke; **jest′er**, one who jests; esp one kept in a king's household.

Jesuit [jez′ū-it] *n* one of the Society of Jesus, founded in 1534 by Ignatius Loyola.

jet[1] [jet] *n* a black, very hard and compact coal that takes a high polish and is used in jewelry.

jet[2] [jet] *n* a stream of liquid or gas suddenly emitted; a spout for emitting a jet; a jet-propelled airplane (in full **jet** (**air**) **plane**).—*vti* to gush out in a stream; to travel or convey by jet airplane.—**jet′lag**, disruption of the daily body rhythms associated with crossing time zones at high speed; **jet propulsion**, propulsion of aircraft, boats, etc. by the discharge of gases from a rear vent.—**jet set**, moneyed social set who travel widely for pleasure.—*n* **jet′setter**.

jetsam [jet′säm] *n* goods thrown overboard and washed up on the shore.—*vt* **jett′ison**, to abandon, to throw overboard.

jetty [jet′i] *n* a wharf; a small pier.

jewel [jōō′él] *n* a precious stone; a gem; anything or anyone highly valued; a small gem used as a bearing in a watch.—*ns* **jeweler**, **jew′eller**, one who makes or deals in jewels.

jib [jib] *n* a triangular sail in front of the foremast in a ship.—*vi* (of a sail) to gybe or swing from one side to the other.—*vt* to cause to gybe.—*n* **jib′boom**, a boom or an extension to the bow-sprit.

jig [jig] *n* a lively dance; the music for this; a device used to guide a tool.—*vt* to dance (a jig).—**jigsaw puzzle**, a picture cut up into irregular pieces, to be fitted together.

jilt [jilt] *n* one who encourages and then rejects a lover.—*vt* to discard a lover after encouragement.

jingle [jing′gl] *n* a sound like that of small bells or of coins shaken together; a catchy verse or song with easy rhythm, simple rhymes, etc.—*vti* (to cause) to jingle like small bells.

jingoism [jing′gō-ism] *n* advocacy of an agressive foreign policy.—*n* **jing′oist**.—*adj* **jingoist′ic**.

jinx [jingks] *n* (*inf*) a bringer of bad luck.

jitter [jit′ėr] *vi* to be nervous, to show nervousness.—*adj* **jitt′ery**.—*ns* **jitt′ers** (*inf*), an uneasy nervous feeling; fidgets (*with* the); **jitt′erbug**, a fast acrobatic dance for couples, esp in the 1940s.

jive [jīv] *n* (*slang*) foolish, exaggerated, or insincere talk; formerly, improvised jazz played at a fast tempo.

job [job] *n* a piece of work done for pay; a task; a duty; the thing or material being worked on; work; employment; a criminal enterprise.—*adj* hired or done by the job.—*vti* to deal in (goods) as a jobber; to sublet (work, etc.).—*ns* **jobber**.

jockey [jok′i] *n* one whose job is riding horses in races—*vti* to cheat; to swindle.

jocose [jo-kōs′] *adj* full of jokes; facetious.—*adv* **jocose′ly**.—*n* **jocose′ness**.

jocular [jok′ū-lär] *adj* joking; full of jokes.—*n* **jocularity** [-ar′i-ti].—*adv* **joc′ularly**.

jocund [jōk′ùnd, jok′ùnd] *adj* genial, cheerful, pleasant.—*n* **jocundity** [-kund′i-ti].—*adv* **joc′undly**.

jodhpurs [jod′pûrz] *n pl* riding breeches fitting tightly from knee to ankle.

jog [jog] *vt* to shake with a push or a jerk; to stir up, as the memory.—*vi* to move up and down with a jerking motion; to move up and down with unsteady motion.—*n* a slight shake; a push; a slow walk or trot.—*ns* **jogg′ing**, exercising by running in a slow bouncing manner; **jog′-trot**, a slow jogging trot.

joggle [jog′l] *vti* to jog or shake slightly.—*n* a slight jolt.

join [join] *vti* to bring and come together (with); connect; unite; to become a part or member of (a club, etc.); to participate (in a conversation, etc.).—*n* a joining; a place of joining.—*ns* **join′er**, a carpenter who finishes interior woodwork; **join′ery**, the trade of a joiner.—*n* **joint**, a place where, or way in which, two things are joined; any of the parts of a jointed whole; in an animal, the parts where two bones move on one another.—*adj* common to two or more (*joint property*); sharing with another (a *joint owner*).—*vt* to connect by a joint or joints.—*adv* **joint′ly**, in common.

joist [joist] *n* a beam supporting the boards of a floor or the laths of a ceiling.

jojoba [hō-hō′ba] *n* a broadleaf evergreen shrub with edible seeds yielding a valuable oil.

joke [jōk] *n* anything said or done to excite a laugh; a thing done or said merely in fun; a person or thing to be laughed at.—*vi* to make jokes.—*n* **jok′er**.

jolly [jol′i] *adj* merry; full of fun; delightful; (*inf*) enjoyable.— *vti* (*inf*) to try to make (a person) feel good; to make fun of (someone).—*n* **jollifica′tion**, noisy festivity and merriment.— *ns* **joll′iness**, **joll′ity**.

jolt [jōlt] *vi* to shake; to proceed with sudden jerks.—*vt* to shake with a sudden shock.—*n* a sudden jerk. [Etymology obscure.]

jonquil [jon′kwil] *n* a species of narcissus.

jorum [jōr, jōr′ùm] *n* a large drinking vessel; its contents.

joss [jos] *n* a Chinese idol; fortune.—*n* **joss stick**, a stick of Chinese incense.

jostle [jos′l] *vti* to shake or jar by collision; to elbow.—Also *n*.

jot [jot] *n* a very small amount.—*vt* to set (down) briefly.—*pr p* **jott′ing**; *pt p* **jott′ed**.—*ns* **jott′er**, one who jots; **jott′ing**, a brief note.

joule [jōōl, jowl] *n* a unit of energy equal to work done when a force of one newton acts over a distance of one meter.

journal [jûr′n(à)l] *n* a daily record of happenings, as a diary; a newspaper or periodical; (*bookkeeping*), a book of original entry for recording transactions; that part of a shaft or axle that turns in a bearing.—*ns* **journalese′**, a facile style of writing found in many magazines, newspapers, etc.; **journal-**

ism, the work of gathering news for, or producing a newspaper or magazine; **journ′alist**. —*adj* **journalist′ic**.

journey [jûr′ni] *n* any travel; a tour. —*vi* to travel. —*pr p* **jour′neying**; *pt p* **jour′neyed** [-nid]. —*n* **jour′neyman**, one whose apprenticeship is completed; an average or mediocre performer.

joust [jowst, just] *n* the encounter of two knights on horseback at a tournament. —*vi* to tilt.

jovial [jō′vi-ăl] *adj* full of playful good humor.

jowl [jōl, jowl] *n* the lower jaw; the cheek esp of a hog.

joy [joi] *n* intense gladness; a cause of this. —*vi* to rejoice. —*adj* **joy′ful**, feeling, expressing, or giving joy. —*adv* **joy′fully**. —*n* **joy′fulness**. —*adj* **joy′less**, without joy; not giving joy. —*adv* **joy′lessly**. —*n* **joy′lessness**, joyful. —*adv* **joy′ously**. —*n* **joy′ousness**. —**joy ride** (*inf*), an automobile ride, often at reckless speed, just for pleasure; **joy′stick** (*inf*), the control lever of an airplane.

jubilant [jōō′bi-lănt] *adj* joyful and triumphant; elated; rejoicing. —*ns* **ju′bilance**. —*vi* **ju′bilate**.

jubilee [jōō′bi-lē] *n* a 50th or 25th anniversary; a time of rejoicing; jubilation.

Judaic, -al [jōō-dā′ik, -ăl] *adj* of the Jews or Judaism.

judge [juj] *n* a public official with authority to hear and decide cases in a court of law; a person chosen to settle a dispute or decide who wins; a person qualified to decide on the relative worth of anything. —*vti* to hear and pass judgment (on) in a court of law; to determine the winner of (a contest) or settle (a dispute); to form an opinion about; to criticize or censure; to suppose, think.

judicature [jōō′di-ka-tyûr] *n* the administering of justice; jurisdiction; judges or courts collectively.

judicial [jōō-dish′ăl] *adj* of judges, courts, or their functions; allowed, enforced, etc. by a court; befitting a judge; fair; impartial. —*adv* **judic′ially**.

judiciary [jōō-dish′(y)ar-i] *adj* of judges or courts. —*n* the part of government that administers justice; judges collectively.

judicious [jōō-dish′ús] *adj* according to sound judgment; possessing sound judgment; discreet. —*adv* **judic′iously**.

judo [jōō′dō] *n* ju-jitsu.

juggernaut [jug′ẽr-nöt] *n* a terrible, irresistible force.

juggle [jug′l] *vi* to toss up balls, etc. and keep them in the air. —*vt* to manipulate so as to deceive. —*n* a juggling. —*ns* **jug′ler; jugg′lery**.

jugular [jug′ū-lår] *adj* of the neck or throat. —*n* either of the large veins on each side of the neck carrying blood from the head. —Also **jugular vein**.

juice [jōōs] *n* the liquid part of fruit, vegetables, or of animal tissue; (*inf*) vitality; *vt* to extract juice from. —*adj* **juice′less**. —*n* **juic′er**, a device for extracting juice from fruit. —*adj* **juic′y**.

jujitsu [jōō-jit′sōō] *n* a Japanese system of wrestling.

ju-ju [jōō′jōō] *n* an object of superstitious worship in West Africa; a fetish or charm.

jujube [jōō′jōōb] *n* a gelatinous, fruit-flavored candy; the fruit of any of several small trees the trees themselves.

juke box [jōōk boks] coin-operated electric phonograph.

julep [jōō′lep] *n* a sweet drink of syrup, flavoring and water; tall drink of bourbon or brandy and sugar over crushed ice, garnished with mint.

Julian calendar [jōōl′yàn] *n* calendar introduced in 46 BC by Julius Caesar in which the year was made to consist of 365 days, 6 hours instead of 365 days by introducing a leap year.

July [jōō-lī] *n* the seventh month of the year having 31 days.

jumble [jum′bl] *vt* (*often with* **up**); to throw together without order. —*vi* to become mixed together confusedly. —*n* a hodge podge.

jump [jump] *vi* to spring or leap from the ground, a height, etc.; to jerk; to act swiftly and eagerly (*often with* **at**); to pass suddenly, as to a new topic; to rise suddenly, as prices; (*slang*) to be lively. —*vt* to leap or pass over (something); to leap upon; to cause (prices, etc.) to rise; (*inf*) to attack suddenly; (*inf*) to react to prematurely; (*slang*) to leave suddenly. —*n* a jumping; a distance jumped; sudden transition; a nervous start. —*adj* **jump′y**, moving in jumps, etc.; easily startled.

jumper [jump′er] *n* a loose jacket; a sleeveless dress for wearing over a blouse, etc.; rompers.

junco [junk′ō] *n* any of a genus of American finches.

junction [jungk′sh(ó)n] *n* a joining, a union or combination; place or point of joining.

juncture [jungk′tyúr, -chûr] *n* a junction; a point of time; a crisis.

June [jōōn] *n* the sixth month having 30 days.

jungle [jung′gl] *n* a dense tropical growth of thickets, brushwood, etc.; any wild tangled mass.

junior [jōon′yór] *adj* the younger, written 'Jr.' after the son's name if it is the same as his father's; of more recent or lower status; of juniors. —*n* one who is younger, of lower rank, etc.

juniper [jōō′ni-pẽr] *n* a genus of evergreen shrubs, one species of which yields berries used to flavour gin.

junk¹ [jungk] *n* a Chinese sailing vessel.

junk² [jungk] *n* discarded useless objects; (*inf*) trash. —*vt* (*inf*) to scrap. —**junk food**, snack food with little nutritional value.

junket [jung′ket] *n* curdled milk, sweetened and flavored; a picnic; an excursion, esp one by an official at public expense. —*vi* to go on a junket.

junta [jun′ta] *n* a government, esp military, formed by a group following a coup d'état.

Jupiter [jōō′pi-tẽr] *n* the chief god among the Romans.

juridical [jōō-rid′ik-ăl] *adj* of judicial proceedings or law. —*adv* **jurid′ically**.

jurisconsult [jōō-ris-kon-sult′] *n* a specialist in international and public law; a jurist.

jurisdiction [jōō-ris-dik′sh(ó)n] *n* the distribution of justice; legal authority; extent of power; district over which any authority extends.

jurisprudence [jōō-ris-prōō′dĕns] *n* the science or philosophy of law; a division of law.

jurist [jōō′rist] *n* an expert on law.

jury [jōō′ri] *n* a body of persons sworn to give a verdict on evidence before them; a committee that decides winners in a contest. —*n* **ju′ror**, one who serves on a jury.

just [just] *adj* fair, (*impartial*) righteous, deserved, due; in accordance with facts; exact. —*adv* exactly; nearly; only; barely; a very short time ago; immediately; (*inf*) really. —*adv* **just′ly**, equitably; by right.

justice [jus′tis] *n* quality of being just; integrity; impartiality; the use of authority to uphold what is just; the administration of law; the awarding of what is due; a judge.

justify [jus′ti-fī] *vt* to prove or show to be just or right, to vindicate; (of circumstances) to furnish adequate grounds for; to corroborate. —*pr p* **jus′tifying**; *pt p* **jus′tified**. —*adj* **just′ifiable** [or fī′-], that may be justified or defended. —*adv* **justifi′ably**. —*n* **justifica′tion**, vindication; sufficient grounds or reason (for); absolution.

jut [jut] *vti* to stick out; to project. —*n* a part that juts.

jute [jōōt] *n* the fiber of two Indian plants of the linden family, used for making coarse bags, mats, etc.

juvenile [jōō′vĕ-nīl] *adj* young; immature; of or for young persons. —*n* a young person; a book for children. —*n pl* **juvenilia** [-il′ya], writings or works of one's childhood or youth, artistic or literary works intended for children. —*ns* **juvenility** [-il′i-ti].

juxtaposition [juks-tă-poz-ish′(ó)n] *n* a placing or being placed side by side. —*vt* **juxtapose′**.

K

kaiser [kī′zẽr] *n* an emperor, esp a German Emperor.

kale [kāl] *n* a cabbage with open curled leaves.

kaleidoscope [ka-lī′dō-skōp] *n* a small tube containing bits of colored glass reflected by mirrors to form symmetrical patterns as the tube is rotated; anything that constantly changes. —*adj* **kaleidoscop′ic** [-skop′ik].

kangaroo [kang-går-ōō′] *n* a leaping, herbivorous marsupial mammal of Australia and nearby islands, with short forelegs and strong, large hind legs.

kaolin [kā′ō-lin] *n* a white clay used in porcelain, etc.

kapok [kāp′ok] *n* the silky fibers around the seeds of the ceiba tree, used for stuffing cushions.

karma [kär′mä] *n* the totality of one's acts in each state of one's existence; (*loosely*) fate.

katydid [kā'ti-did] *n* any of a number of American grasshoppers.

kayak [kī'ak] *n* an Eskimo canoe made of skins on a wooden frame.

kedge [kej] *n* a small anchor for kedging a ship.—*vt* to move (a ship) by dropping a kedge at the destination required.

kedgeree [kej'é-rē] *n* a dish made with fish, rice, etc.

keel [kēl] *n* the lowest part of a ship extending along the bottom from stem to stern, and supporting the whole frame.—*vti* (to cause) to turn over.

keen¹ [kēn] *adj* having a sharp point or a fine edge; affecting one as if by cutting; piercing; shrewd; perceptive; intense.—*adv* keen'ly.—*n* keen'ness.

keen² [kēn] *n* a lament for the dead.—*vi* to wail over the dead.—*n* keen'er, a professional mourner.

keep [kēp] *vt* to celebrate, observe; to fulfill; to protect, guard; to take care of; to preserve; to provide for; to make regular entries in; to maintain in a specified state; to hold for the future; to hold and not let go.—*vi* to stay in a specified condition; to continue, go on; to refrain or restrain oneself; to stay fresh, not spoil.—*pr p* keep'ing; *p t, pt p* kept.—*n* food and shelter; care and custody; the inner stronghold of a castle.—*ns* keep'er, keeping, care, charge; observance; agreement; keep'sake, something kept in memory of the giver.

keg [keg] *n* a small barrel.

kelp [kelp] *n* any large brown seaweed; the ashes used as a source of iodine.

kelpie [kel'pi] *n* (*Scot*) a water-sprite in the form of a horse.

ken [ken] *n* understanding; view; sight.

kennel [ken'él] *n* a doghouse; (often *pl*) a place where dogs are bred or kept.—*vt* to keep in a kennel.

keratin [ker'á-tin] *n* a tough, fibrous protein, the substance of hair, nails, feathers, etc.

kerchief [kûr'chif] *n* a square head cloth; a scarf.

kernel [kûr'nél] *n* a seed within a hard shell; the edible part of a nut; the important part of anything.

kerosene [ker'o-sēn] *n* a thin oil obtained by distillation of petroleum.—Also keg'osine.

kestrel [kes'trél] *n* a small European falcon.

ketch [kech] *n* a fore-and-aft rigged sailing vessel.

ketchup [kech'úp] *n* a sauce for meat, fish, etc.

kettle [ket'l] *n* a metal container for boiling or cooking things; a teakettle.—*n* kett'ledrum, a musical instrument consisting of a hollow metal hemisphere with a parchment head, tuned by screws.

key¹ [kē] *n* a device for locking and unlocking something; a thing that explains or solves, as the legend of a map, a code, etc.; a controlling position, person, or thing; one of a set of parts pressed in a keyboard.—*vt* to furnish with a key; to bring into harmony.—*adj* controlling; important.—*n* key'board, a set of keys in a piano, organ, typewriter, etc.—Also *adj*.—*ns* key'hole, an opening (in a lock) into which a key is inserted; key'note, the basic note of a musical scale; the basic idea or ruling principle.—*vt* to give the keynote to; to give the keynote speech at.—key'pad, a small usu hand-held keyboard of numbered buttons used to tap in a telephone number, to operate a television receiver, or to enter data in a computer; key'stone, the middle stone at the top of an arch, holding the stones or other pieces in place.

key² [kē] *n* a low island or reef.

khaki [kä'ki] *adj* dull yellowish-brown.—*n* strong, twilled cloth of this color; (often *pl*) a khaki uniform or trousers.

kibosh [kī'bosh] *n* (*slang*) end.

kick [kik] *vt* to strike with the foot; to drive, force, etc. as by kicking; to score (a goal, etc.) by kicking.—*vi* to strike out with the foot; to recoil, as a gun; (*inf*) to complain.—*n* an act or method of kicking; a sudden recoil; (*inf*) a complaint.

kickshaw [kik'shö] *n* a delicacy; a trinket.

kid [kid] *n* a young goat; anything of kidskin; (*inf*) a child.—*vti* (*inf*) to tease or fool playfully.—*vi* (of a goat or antelope) to bring forth young.

kidnap [kid'-nap] *vt* to seize and hold to ransom, as of a person; kid'napping.—*n* kid'napper.

kidney [kid'ni] *n* either of a pair of glandular organs excreting waste products from the blood as urine; an animal's kidney used as food; disposition; class; kind.

kill [kil] *vt* to cause the death of, to slay; to destroy; to neutral-ize (a color); to spend (time) on trivial matters; to turn off (an engine, etc.).—*n* the act of killing; an animal or animals killed.—*n* kill'er.

kiln [kil, kiln] *n* a furnace or oven.

kilo [kē'lō, kil'ō] *n* kilogram; kilometer.

kilogram [kil'ō-gram] *n* a unit of weight and mass, equal to 1000 grams or 2.2046 pounds.

kilometer [kil'é-mētér] *n* a unit of length equal to 1000 meters or 3,2808.8 feet.

kilowatt [kil'é-wät] *n* a unit of electrical power, equal to 1000 watts.

kilt [kilt] *n* a kind of short pleated skirt, forming part of the Scottish Highland dress; a similar skirt worn by women.—*vt* to tuck up (skirts).

kimono [ki-mō'nō] *n* a loose Japanese robe.

kin [kin] *n* relatives; family.—*adj* related as by blood.—*n* kin'ship, blood-relationship; close connection.

kind [kīnd] *n* sort; variety; class; a natural group or division; essential character.—*adj* sympathetic; friendly; gentle; benevolent.—kind'ly, kind; gracious; agreeable; pleasant.—*adv* in a kind gracious manner; favorably.—*ns* kind'liness'; kind'ness.

kindergarten [kin'dér-gär-t(è)n] *n* a class or school for children, usu four to six years old.

kindle [kin'dl] *vt* to set on fire; to excite (feelings, interest, etc.).—*vi* to catch fire; to become aroused or excited.—*n* kind'ling, material, such as bits of dry wood, for starting a fire.

kine [kīn] *n pl* (*arch*) cows; cattle.

kinematics [kin-é-mat'iks, or kīn-] *n* the branch of physics that deals with the characteristics of different kinds of pure motion, without reference to mass or the causes of the motion.—*adjs* kinemat'ic, -al.

kinesis [ki-nē'sis, kī] *n* a movement that depends on the force of the stimulus.

kinetics [ki-net'iks, or kī-] *n* the science of the action of force in producing or changing motion.

king [king] *n* the man who rules a country and its people; a man with the title of ruler, but with limited power to rule; man supreme in a certain sphere; something best in its class; the chief piece in chess; a playing card with a picture of a king on it; ranking above a queen; a checker that has been crowned; king'dom, a country headed by a king or queen; a realm, domain; any of the three divisions of the natural world; the animal kingdom, the vegetable kingdom, the mineral kingdom; king'fisher, a short-tailed diving bird that feeds chiefly on fish.—*adj* king'-size; king'-sized, larger than standard size.

kink [kingk] *n* a twisted loop in a string, rope, hair, etc.; a painful cramp in the neck, back, etc.; a mental twist; a whim.—*vti* to form or cause to form a kink or kinks.

kiosk [ki-osk'] *n* a small open structure used as a newsstand.

kipper [kip'ér] *vt* to cure (herring, salmon etc.) by salting and drying or smoking.—*n* a kippered herring, etc.

kismet [kis'met] *n* fate, destiny.

kiss [kis] *vti* to caress or salute with the lips; to touch gently or lightly.—*n* an act of kissing; a light, gentle touch; any of various candies.

kit [kit] *n* an outfit; equipment; a container and/or the tools, instructions, etc. assembled in it for some specific purpose.—*n* kitbag, a strong bag for holding one's kit or outfit.

kitchen [kich'én] *n* a place where food is prepared and cooked.—*ns* kitchenette'; a compact kitchen; kitchen gar'den, a garden where vegetables are cultivated for the kitchen.

kite [kīt] *n* any of several long-winged birds of the hawk family; a light frame covered with paper or cloth for flying in the wind.

kith [kith] *n* friends and relatives, now only in kith and kin.

kitten [kit'n] *n* a young cat; the young of other small mammals.—*vt* and *vi* (of a cat) to bring forth.

kittiwake [kit'i-wāk] *n* any of several gulls.

kiwi [kē'wi] *n* a flightless bird of New Zealand.

kleptomania [klep-to-mā'ni-a] *n* an uncontrollable impulse to steal.—*n* kleptomā'niac.

knack [nak] *n* ability to do something easily; a trick; a habit.

knapsack [nap'sak] *n* a bag for carrying equipment or supplies on the back.

knave [nāv] *n* a tricky or dishonest man; (*Brit*) a playing card: the jack.—*n* **knav'ery**, dishonesty.—*adj* **knav'ish**; rascally.—*adv* **knav'ishly**.

knead [nēd] *vt* to squeeze and press together into a mass, as flour into dough; to massage.

knee [nē] *n* the joint between the thigh and the lower leg; anything shaped like a bent knee.—*vt* to hit or touch with the knee.—*ns* **knee'cap**, the kneepan or patella.

kneel [nēl] *vi* to go down on one's knee or knees; to remain in this position.—*pt* and *pt p* **kneeled, knelt**.

knell [nel] *n* the sound of a bell at a death or funeral; a warning of death, failure, etc.—*vi* to sound slowly as a bell; to toll; to sound ominously.

knickerbockers [nik'ėr-bok-ėrz] *n pl* loose breeches gathered in at the knee.—Also **knick'ers**.

knickknack [nik'-nak] *n* a small ornamental article.

knife [nīf] *n* a flat piece of steel, silver, etc., with a sharp edge, set in a handle so that it can be used to cut; a sharp blade forming a part of a tool or machine.—*pl* **knives** [nīvz].—*vt* to cut or stab with a knife.

knight [nīt] *n* in the Middle Ages, a man raised to an honorable military rank and pledged to do good deeds; in modern times in Britain, a man who for some achievement is given honorary rank entitling him to use 'Sir' before his given name; a chessman shaped like a horse's head.—*vt* to make (a man) a knight. **knight'err'ant**, a knight who travelled in search of adventures; **knight'hood**, the rank, title, or status of knight; the order or fraternity of knights.—*adj, adv* **knight'ly**.

knit [nit] *vt* to form (material, or a garment) by interlooping yarn by means of knitting needles; to cause to grow together (eg broken bones); to draw close together; to contract, wrinkle (the brows).—*vi* to make material from yarn by means of needles; to grow together.

knob [nob] *n* a rounded lump or protruberance; a handle, usu round, of a door, drawer, etc.

knock [nok] *vi* to strike a blow; to rap on a door; to bump, collide.—*vt* to strike; to hit so as to cause to fall; *n* a knocking, a hit, a rap.—*n* **knock'er**, one that knocks, a device suspended to a door for making a knock.—*adj* **knock'kneed**, having knees that bend *inward at the knee*; **knock out**, to make unconscious or exhausted.

knoll [nōl] *n* a round hillock.

knot [not] *n* a lump in a thread, etc. formed by a tightened loop or tangling; a fastening made by tying lengths of rope, etc.; an ornamental bow; a small group, cluster; a hard mass of wood where a branch grows out from a tree, which shows as a roundish, cross-grained piece in a board; a unit of speed of one nautical mile (6,076.12 feet) per hour; something that ties closely, esp the bond of marriage.—*vti* to make or form a knot (in); to entangle or become entangled.

know [nō] *vt* to be well-informed about; to be aware of; to be acquainted with; to recognize or distinguish.—*adj* **know'ing**, having knowledge; shrewd; clever; implying a secret understanding.—*adv* **know'ingly**, in a knowing way; to one's own knowledge.

knowledge [nol'ij] *n* what one knows; the body of facts, etc. accumulated by mankind; fact of knowing; range of information or understanding; the act of knowing.—*adj* **knowl'edgeable**, having knowledge or intelligence.

knuckle [nuk'l] *n* a joint of the finger, esp at the roots of the fingers; the knee of an animal used as food.

knurl [nûrl] *n* a small knob or ridge; one of a series of knurls on a metal surface to prevent slippage.—*adj* **knurl'ed**.

koala [kō-ä'la] *n* an Australian tree-dwelling marsupial with thick, gray fur.

kohl [kōl] *n* a black powder used in Middle Eastern countries for staining the eyelids.

kola tree [kō'lä] *n* either of two tropical trees whose seeds (called ko'la-nuts) have stimulant properties.

kolinsky [ko-lin'ski] *n* any of several Asian minks; its fur.

kookaburra [kŏŏk'á-bur-a] *n* an Australian kingfisher with a harsh cry like loud laughter.

Koran [kō-rän', kō-rän'] *n* the sacred book of the Muslims.

kosher [kō'shėr] *adj* (*Judaism*) clean or fit to eat according to dietary laws.

kowtow [kow'tow'] *vi* to show great respect (to) by bowing.

koumiss [kōōmis] *n* fermented mare's milk.

kraal [kräl] *n* a S African native village; a corral; also, a native hut with bush stockade round it.

Kremlin [krem'lin] *n* the citadel of Moscow, formerly housing many Soviet government offices.

kudos [kū'dos] *n* (*inf*) fame, renown.

kudzu [kŏŏd'zōō] *n* a prostrate vine of the pea family used widely for erosion control and for forage.

kümmel [kim'ėl] *n* a German liqueur flavored with caraway seeds and cumin.

kymograph [kī'mō-graf] *n* a device for graphically recording motion or pressure (as of blood).—*n* **kym'ogram**, record produced by a kymograph.

Kyrie [kēr'i-e] *n* a short, liturgical prayer that begins with the words "Lord, have mercy"

L

laager [lä'gėr] *n* in South Africa, a camp made by a ring of oxwagons set close together for defence; an encampment.

label [lā'b(ė)l] *n* a small slip attached to anything to denote its nature, contents, ownership, etc.; term of generalized classification.—*vt* to affix a label to; to designate (as).

labial [lā'bi-ál] *adj* of the lips.—*n* a sound as *b, m,* and *p* formed by the lips.—*adv* **lā'bially**.—*adj* **lā'biate**, lipped; having a lipped corolla.

laboratory [lab'ō-rá-tō-ri] *n* a place where scientific work and research is carried out.

labor [lā'bôr] *n* work, physical or mental exertion; a specific task; all wage-earning workers; labor unions collectively; the process of childbirth.—*vi* to work; to work hard; to move with difficulty; to suffer (delusions, etc.); to be in childbirth.—*vt* to develop in unnecessary detail.—*adj* **laborious** requiring much work; industrious; labored.—*adv* **laboriously**.—*n* **laboriousness**.—*adj* **labored**, done with effort; strained; **laborer**, one who labors, esp one whose work requires strength rather than skill.—**Labor Day**, the first Monday in September in the US and Canada, a legal holiday honoring labor.

Labrador retriever [lab'rá-dör ri-trēv'ėr] *n* a breed of large, smooth-coated sporting dog.

laburnum [la-bûr'num] *n* a small genus of trees or shrubs with hanging yellow flowers.

labyrinth [lab'i-rinth] *n* a structure containing winding passages through which it is hard to find one's way; a maze.—*adjs* **labyrinth'ian, labyrinth'ine**.

lac¹ *See* **lakh**.

lac² [lak] *n* a resinous substance.

lace [lās] *n* a string, etc. used to draw together and fasten parts of a shoe, a corset, etc.; an ornamental fabric of delicately woven fine thread—*vt* to fasten with a lace; to intertwine, weave; to thrash, whip.

lacerate [las'ér-āt] *vt* to tear jaggedly.—*n* **lacerā'tion**.—*adj* **lac'erative**.

lachrymal, lacrimal [lak'ri-mál] *adj* of tears.—*adj* **lach'rymose**, shedding tears; given to weeping.

lack [lak] *n* the fact or state of not having any or not having enough; the thing that is needed.—*vti* to be deficient in or entirely without.

lackadaisical [lak-a-dā'zi-kál] *adj* showing lack of spirit or interest; listless.

lackey [lak'i] *n* a male servant of low rank; a servile, obsequious person; a toady.

laconic [la-kon'ik] *adj* using few words; concise.—*adv* **lacon'ically**.

lacquer [lak'ėr] *n* a varnish made of lac and alcohol.—*vt* to cover with lacquer; to make glossy.

lacrosse [la-kros'] *n* a game played by two teams, the ball being driven through the opponents' goal by a crosse.

lacteal [lak'ti-ál] *adj* of or like milk; milky.—*n* any of the lymphatic vessels of the intestines which convey the chyle to the thoracic duct.—*n* **lactā'tion**, the secretion of milk.—*adjs* **lac'tic** of or relating to milk; obtained from sour milk or whey; involving the production of lactic acid; **lactif'erous**, conveying or producing milk or milky juice.—*n* lac′tose, a sugar present in milk.—lactic acid, a hygroscopic organic acid normally present in animal tissue.

lacuna [la-kū′na] *n* a gap esp a missing portion in a text.—*pl* lacū′nae [-nē].

lad [lad] *n* a boy; a youth.

ladder [lad′ér] *n* a contrivance, with rungs between two supports, for going up and down; something that resembles a ladder in form or use, esp in ascending.

lade [lād] *vt* to load; to throw in or out, as a fluid, with a ladle or dipper.—*adj* lad′en, laded or loaded; burdened.—*n* lad′ing, the act of loading; that which is loaded; cargo; freight.

ladle [lād′l] *n* a long-handled, cuplike spoon; a device like a ladle in shape or use.

lady [lā′dē] *n* a woman of high social position; a woman who is polite, refined, etc.—*adj* la′dylike like or suitable for a lady.—*ns* la′dylove a sweetheart; lady-slipper a N American temperate-zone orchid with flowers somewhat like slippers.

lag¹ [lag] *n* a falling behind; the amount of this.—*vi* to move or walk slowly; to loiter; to become less intense; to roll a cue ball in billiards or a marble in a game of marbles to decide the order of play.—*vt* to lag behind; to shoot (as a marble) at a mark. —*adj* lagg′ard, lagging; slow.—*ns* lagg′ard, lagg′er, one who lags behind; a loiterer.

lager [lä′ger] *n* a beer that has been aged for several months.

lagoon [la-gōōn′] *n* a shallow lake or pond esp one connected with a larger body of water; the water enclosed by a circular coral reef.

lair [lār] *n* the den or retreat of a wild animal.

laissez-faire [les′ā-fer′] *n* noninterference with the free action of the individual.

laity *See* lay (4).

lake¹ [lāk] *n* a purplish-red; carmine.

lake² [lāk] *n* a large inland body of usu. fresh water.—*ns* lake′dwell′ing, a dwelling, esp prehistoric, built on piles in a lake.

lakh [lak] *n* one hundred thousand; a great number.—Also lac.

lam [lam] *vt* to beat.

lama [lä′mä] *n* a monk or priest in lamaism.—*ns* Lamaism [lä′mä-izm] a form of Buddhism in Tibet and Mongolia.

lamb [lam] *n* a young sheep; its flesh as food; a simple, innocent, or gentle person.—*vi* to bring forth (a lamb); to tend (ewes) at lambing time.

lambent [lam′bént] *adj* licking; moving about as if touching lightly; gliding over; flickering.

lame [lām] *adj* crippled, esp in the use of a leg; stiff and painful; poor; ineffectual.—*vt* to make lame.—*adv* lame′ly.—*n* lame′ness.

lamé [la-mā] *n* a fabric interwoven with flat metallic threads.

lament [la-ment′] *vti* to feel or express deep sorrow (for); mourn.—*n* a lamenting; an elegy, dirge, etc. mourning some loss or death.—*adj* lamentable [lam′éntábl or lê-mén′tàbl].—*ns* lamenta′tion.

lamina [lam′i-na] *n* a thin plate or layer; the expanded part of a foliage leaf.—*adj* lam′inar, consisting of, arranged in, or like laminae.—*vt* lam′inate, to cover with one or more thin layers; to make by building up in layers.—*vi* to divide into laminae.—*n* a product made by laminating.—*adj* built in thin sheets or layers.—*n* lamina′tion.

lamp [lamp] *n* a container with a wick for burning oil, etc. to produce light or heat; any device for producing light or therapeutic uses; a holder or base for such a device.

lampoon [lam-pōōn′] *n* a satirical writing attacking someone.—*vt* to ridicule maliciously in a lampoon.—*ns* lampoon′er, lampoon′ery.

lamprey [lam′pri] *n* vertebrates resembling an eel but having a jawless, round sucking mouth.

lance [läns] *n* a long wooden spear with a sharp iron or steel head; a soldier armed with a lance.—*vt* to pierce, as with a lance; to open with a lancet.—*n* lanc′er, a cavalry soldier armed with a lance.

lancet [län′set] *n* a small, usu. two-edged, pointed surgical knife.

land [land] *n* the solid portion of the earth's surface; ground, soil; a country and its people; real estate.—*vt* to set down on land or water; to put on shore from a ship; to bring to a particular place; to catch (a fish).—*vi* to go ashore from a ship;

(of a ship) to come to port; to arrive at a specified place; to come to rest.—*adj* land′ed.—*n* landing, the act of coming to shore or to the ground; the place where persons or goods are loaded or unloaded from a ship; a platform at the end of a flight of stairs.—*adj* land′locked, surrounded by land.—*ns* land′lord, a man who leases land, houses, etc. land′lubber, one who has had little experience on boats; land′mark, any prominent feature of the landscape distinguishing a locality; an important event or turning point; land mine, an explosive charge placed in the ground, usu. detonated by stepping or driving on it. landslide, the sliding of a mass of soil or rocks down a slope; lands′man, a fellow countryman; a landlubber.

landau [lan′dô] *n* a four-wheeled carriage with a top that may be opened centrally and thrown back.

landscape [land′skāp] *n* a picture of natural, inland scenery; an expanse of natural scenery seen in one view.—*vt* to make (a plot of ground) more attractive as by adding lawns, bushes, trees, etc.—*n* land′scaper.

lane [lān] *n* a narrow road, path, etc.; a path or strip designated, for safety reasons, for ships, aircraft, automobiles, etc.

language [lang′gwij] *n* human speech or the written symbols for speech; any means of communicating; a special set of symbols used in a computer; the speech of a particular nation, etc.; the particular style of verbal expression characteristic of a person, group, profession, etc.

languid [lang′gwid] *adj* feeble, flagging, exhausted, sluggish, spiritless.

languish [lang′gwish] *vi* to become languid; to lose strength and animation; to pine.—*adj* lang′uishing.

languor [lang′g(w)ôr] *n* state of being languid, faint; dullness, listlessness.—*adj* lang′uorous.

lank [langk] *adj* tall and lean; straight and limp.—*adj* lank′y, lean, tall, and ungainly.

lanolin [lan′ō-lin] *n* a fat extracted from wool.

lantern [lant′érn] *n* a transparent case for holding or carrying a light; an ornamental structure surmounting a building to give light and air.

lanthanum [lan′thàn-ùm] *n* a metallic element.

lanyard [lan′yàrd] *n* a short rope used for fastening or stretching; a cord for hanging a knife, whistle, or the like about the neck.

lap¹ [lap] *vti* to lick up with the tongue; (of waves) to wash or flow against.

lap² [lap] *n* the part from waist to knees of a person sitting; the part of the clothing covering this; that in which a person or thing is cared for; an overlapping; a part that overlaps; one complete circuit of a race track.—*vt* to fold (over or on); to wrap; —*vi* to overlap; to extend over something in space or time.

lapel [la-pel′] *n* part of a garment folded back, continuing the collar.—*adj* lapelled′.

lapidary [lap′i-dâr-i] *n* a cutter of gemstones.—*adj* cutting of stones; inscribed on stone.

lapis lazuli [lap′is laz′ûlī] *n* an azure, opaque, semiprecious stone.

lapse [laps] *vi* to fall away by cessation or relaxation of effort or cause; to fall from the faith; to fail in duty; to pass into disuse; to become void.—*n* a small error; a failure (in virtue, memory, etc.).

lapwing [lap′wing] *n* a crested plover.

larceny [lär′sén-i] *n* theft.

larch [lärch] *n* cone-bearing trees of the pine family.

lard [lärd] *n* the melted and clarified fat of the hog.—*vt* to insert strips of bacon or fat pork (in meat) before cooking; to embellish.

larder [lärd′èr] *n* a place where food supplies are kept; food supplies.

large [lärj] *adj* great in size, amount, or number; bulky; big; spacious; bigger than others of its kind; operating on a big scale.—*adv* large′ly.

largess, largesse [lärj′es] *n* a present or donation; money liberally bestowed.

largo [lär′gō] *adj* (*mus*) slow and dignified.—*n* a movement to be so performed.

lariat [lar′i-at] *n* a rope for tethering grazing horses; a lasso.

lark¹ [lärk] *n* a family of songbirds.

lark² [lärk] *n* a frolic; a piece of mischief.—*vi* to frolic.—*adj* **lark'y.**

larkspur [lärk'spûr] *n* an annual delphinium.

larva [lär'va] *n* an animal in an immature but active state, eg a caterpillar.—*pl* **larvae** [lär've].

larynx [lar'ingks] *n* the structure at the upper end of the windpipe, containing the vocal cords.

lascivious [la-siv'i-ùs] *adj* lustful.

laser [läz'er] *n* a device which amplifies an input of light, producing an extremely narrow and intense monochromatic beam.

lash [lash] *n* the flexible part of a whip; and eyelash; a stroke as with a whip; a stroke of satire.—*vt* to strike with or as if with a lash; to switch back and forth; to fasten or secure with a rope or cord; to scourge with censure or satire.—*vi* to make strokes as with a whip.—*n* **lash'ing.**

lass [las] *n* a young woman.

lassitude [las'i-tūd] *n* weariness.

lasso [las'ō, also la-sōō] *n* a long rope with a running noose for catching wild horses, etc.—*vt* to catch with the lasso.

last¹ [låst] *n* a shoemaker's model of the foot on which boots and shoes are made or repaired.—*vt* to shape with a last.

last² [last] *vi* to remain in existence, use, etc.; to endure.—*vt* to continue during; to be enough for.—*adj* **lasting.**

last³ [last] alternative superlative of **late.**—*adj* being or coming after all the others in time or place; only remaining; the most recent; least likely; conclusive.—*adv* after all the others; most recently; finally.—*n* the one coming last.

latakia [lat-a-kē'a] *n* a smoking tobacco.

latch [lach] *n* a fastening for a door, gate, or window, esp a bar, etc. that fits into a notch.—*vti* to fasten with a latch.—*n* **latch'key.**

late [lāt] *superlative:* **lāt'est** or **last.**—*adj* slow, tardy; behind-hand; coming after the expected time; long delayed; far advanced towards the close; last in any place or character; deceased; departed; out of office; not long past.—*advs* **late, late'ly,** recently.—*n* **late'ness.**

lateen [la-tēn'] *adj* of a triangular sail.—*n* a lateen-rigged ship; a lateen sail.

latent [lā'tènt] *adj* hidden; dormant; undeveloped, but capable of development.

lateral [lat'èr-ål] *adj* of, at, from, toward the side.—*adv* **lat'erally.** [L *laterālis—latus, latèris,* a side.]

latex [lā'teks] *n* the milky juice of plants. [L.]

lath [läth] *n* a thin slip of wood any framework for plaster.

lathe [lāTH] *n* a machine for turning and shaping articles of wood, metal, etc.

lather [läTH'èr] *n* a foam made with water and soap; froth from sweat.

Latin [lat'in] *adj* of ancient Rome, its people, their language, etc.; denoting or of the languages derived from Latin, the peoples who speak them, their countries, etc.—*n* a native or inhabitant of ancient Rome; the language of ancient Rome; a person, as a Spaniard or Italian, whose language is derived from Latin.—*ns* **Lat'inism,** a Latin idiom.

latitude [lat'i-tūd] *n* extent; scope; freedom from restrictions on actions of opinions; distance north or south of the equator, measured in degrees; a region with reference to this distance.—*adjs* **latitūd'inal; latitu+dinar'ian** broad and liberal in standards of religious belief and conduct.

latrine [la-trēn'] *n* a toilet for the use of many people.

latter [lat'èr] *adj* later; more recent; nearer the end; being the last mentioned of two.—*adv* **latt'erly.**

lattice [lat'is] *n* a network of crossed laths or bars.

laud [löd] *vt* to praise; to extol.—*adj* **laud'able.**

laudanum [löd'(a)-num] *n* formerly, any of various opium preparations; a solution of opium in alcohol.

laugh [läf] *vi* to emit explosive inarticulate sounds of the voice under the influence of amusement, joy, scorn, or other emotion.—*vt* to render, put, or drive with laughter.—*n* an act of laughing; a sound of laughing.—*adj* **laugh'able,** ludicrous.—*adv* **laugh'ingly.**—*ns* **laugh'ingstock,** an object of ridicule; **laugh'ter,** the act or sound of laughing.

launch¹ [lönch] *vt* to throw or hurl; to send forth; to start on a course; to cause to slide into the water or to take off from land.—*vi* to throw oneself into some activity.—*n* the act or occasion of launching.

launch² [lönch] *n* an open, or partly enclosed, motor boat.

launder [lön'dèr] *vti* to wash and iron, as clothes.—*vt* to legitimize (money) obtained from criminal activity.—*ns* **laun'derette,** a place equipped with laundry equipment that customers may use for a fee; **laun'dry,** a place where clothes are washed; clothes sent to be washed.

laureate [lö'ri-åt] *adj* crowned with laurel (as a mark of honor).

laurel [lö'rèl] *n* evergreen shrub with large, glossy leaves; the leaves used by the ancient Greeks to crown victors in games.

lava [lä'va] *n* molten rock discharged in a molten stream from a volcano.

lave [lāv] *vti* (*poetic*) to wash; to bathe; **làv'atory,** a washbowl with faucets and drain; a room with a washbowl and toilet.

lavender [lav'èn-dèr] *n* a Mediterranean mint dried and used in sachets; pale purple.

lavish [lav'ish] *vt* to give or spend freely or too freely.—*adj* bestowing profusely, prodigal; extravagant, unrestrained.

law [lö] *n* all the rules of conduct of a nation or smaller political authority; any one of such rules; obedience to such rules; the study of such rules, jurisprudence; the seeking of justice in courts under such rules; the profession of lawyers, judges, etc.; a sequence of events occurring with unvarying uniformity under the same conditions; any rule expected to be observed.—*adj* **law'ful,** in conformity with the law; recognized by law.—*n* **law'giver,** a lawmaker; a legislator.—*adj* **law'less,** not regulated by law; not in conformity with law, illegal.—*ns* **law'suit,** a suit between private parties in a law court; **law'yer,** one whose profession is advising others in matters of law or representing them in a court of law.

lawn¹ [lön] *n* a fine sheer cloth of linen or cotton.

lawn² [lön] *n* land covered with closely-cut grass, esp around a house.—*ns* **lawn mower,** a hand-propelled or power-driven machine to cut lawn grass; **lawn tennis,** tennis (see **tennis**).

lax [laks] *adj* slack, loose; not tight; not strict or exact.—*adj* **lax'ative,** having the power of loosening the bowels and relieving constipation.—*n* any laxative medicine.

lay¹ [lā] *pt* of **lie** (2).

lay² [lā] *vt* to beat or knock down; to put down; to allay or suppress; to place in a resting position; to place or set; to place in a correct position; to produce (an egg); to devise; to present or assert.—*n* **lay'er,** one that lays; a single thickness, fold, etc.—*vi* to separate into layers; to form by superimposing layers; (of a plant) to form roots when a stem is fixed to the earth.—*ns* **lay'off,** a putting out of work temporarily; the period of this; **lay'out,** the manner in which anything is laid out, the thing laid out.—*vt* **lay out,** to plan in detail; to arrange for display; to prepare (a corpse) for viewing.

lay³ [lā] *n* a short narrative poem; a lyric.

lay⁴ [lā] *adj* of a layman; not belonging to a profession.

layette [lā-yet'] *n* outfit for a newborn child.

lay figure [lā'-fig'úr] *n* a jointed figure used by painters in imitation of the human body.

lazy [lā'zi] *adj* disinclined to exertion, averse to labor; sluggish.—*vti* **laze,** to idle or loaf.—*adv* **lā'zily.**—*n* **lā'ziness.**

lea [lē] *n* (*poetic*) meadow.

leach [lēch] *vt* to wash with a filtering liquid; to extract from some material.—*vi* to lose soluble matter through a filtering liquid.

lead¹ [lēd] *vt* to show the way by going first; to precede; to guide; to direct by influence; to be head of; to be ahead of in a contest; to live, spend (*lead a full life*).—*vi* to show the way, as by going first; to tend in a certain direction (*with* to); to be or go first; *pt, pt p* **led.**—*n* the role of a leader; first place; the amount or distance ahead; anything that leads, as a clue; the leading role in a play; etc.; the right of playing first in cards or the card played.—*ns* **lead'er; lead'ership.**

lead² [led] *n* a heavy, soft, bluish-gray, metallic element; a weight for sounding depths at sea, etc.; bullets; a stick of graphite, used in pencils.—*adj* of or containing lead.—*vt* to cover or fit with lead.—*adj* **lead'en,** made of lead; heavy; dull; gloomy; gray.

leaf [lēf] *n* any of the flat, thin parts, usu. green growing from the stem of a plant; a sheet of paper; a very thin sheet of metal; a hinged or removable part of a table top.—*pl* **leaves** [lēvz].—*vi* to bear leaves; to turn the pages of (*with* **through**).—*adj* **leaf'less.**—*n* **leaf'let,** a small or young leaf; a separate sheet of printed matter, often folded.—*adj* **leaf'y**, having many or broad leaves.

league¹ [lēg] *n* a varying measure of distance, averaging about 3½miles.

league² [lēg] *n* an association of nations, groups, etc. for promoting common interests; (*sports*) groups of teams formed to play one another.—*vti* to form into a league.

leak [lēk] *n* a crack in a vessel through which liquid may pass; passage through such an opening; confidential information made public, deliberately or accidentally.—*vi* to have a leak; to pass through a leak; to give out information surreptitiously.—*n* **leak'age**.

lean [lēn] *vi* to bend or slant from an upright position; to rest (against); to bend (over); to rely (on).—*vt* to cause to lean.

lean [lēn] *adj* thin, with little flesh or fat; spare; meager.—*n* meat with little or no fat.

leap [lēp] *vi* to jump; to accept something offered eagerly (*with* at).—*vt* to pass over by a jump; to cause to leap.—*n* act of leaping; bound; space passed by leaping; an abrupt transition.

learn [lûrn] *vti* to be informed, to get to know; to gain knowledge, skill, or ability in; to commit to memory.—*adj* **learned** having learning; erudite; acquired by study, experience, etc.—*adv* **learn'edly**.—*ns* **learn'er**; **learning**.

lease [lēs] *n* a contract letting a house, farm, etc., the period of time for which the contract is made.—*vt* to grant or take under lease.

leash [lēsh] *n* a cord, strap, etc. by which a dog or animal is held in check.

least [lēst]. *adj* smallest in size, degree, etc.; slightest.—*adv* in the smallest degree.—*n* the smallest in amount.

leather [leᴛн'ér] *n* the skin of an animal prepared for use by removing the hair and tanning.—*adj* **leath'ery**, like leather; tough and flexible.

leave¹ [lēv] *n* permission; permission to be absent; period covered by this; formal parting; farewell.

leave² [lēv] *vt* to allow to remain; to depart from; to have remaining at death, to bequeath; to refer for decision (to); to abandon.—*vi* to depart.—*pr p* **leav'ing**; *pt, pt p* **left**.

leaven [lev'n] *n* a substance to make dough rise, esp yeast; anything that makes a general change.

leaves [lēvz] *pl* of leaf.

lecher [lech'ér] *n* a man addicted to lewdness.—*adj* **lech'erous**, lustful; provoking lust.

lectern [lek'térn] *n* a reading stand.

lection [lek'sh(ó)n] *n* a liturgical lesson for a specified day; a variant reading of a text.—*n* **lec'tionary**, a book of lections for the church year.

lecture [lek'chur] *n* an informative talk to a class, etc.; a lengthy scolding.—*vti* to give a lecture (to); to scold.—*n* **lecturer**.

led [led] *pt, pt p* of **lead**, to show the way.

ledge [lej] *n* a shelf; a ridge of rocks.

ledger [lej'ér] *n* a book in which a record of debits, credits, etc. is kept.—*n* **ledger line** a line above or below a musical staff to extend its range.

lee [lē] *n* shelter; (*naut*) the side or part away from the wind.—*adj* of or on the lee; the quarter toward which the wind blows.—*adj* **sheltered**.

leech [lēch] *n* any blood-sucking worms; one who clings to another

leek [lēk] *n* a vegetable that resembles a greatly enlarged green onion.

leer [lēr] *n* a sly, sidelong, or lecherous look.—*vi* to look with a leer.

lees [lēz] *n pl* dregs of liquor.

left¹ [left] *pt, pt p* of **leave**.

left² [left] *adj* of or on the side that is toward the west when one faces north; on, for, or belonging to the side which is less skilful in most people.—*n* the left side; left, in politics, a radical or liberal position, party, etc.—*adjs* **left-hand**; **left'-handed**.

leg [leg] *n* one of the limbs on which men and animals support themselves and walk; the part of a garment covering the leg; anything shaped or used like a leg; a stage, as of a trip.—*n* **legg'ing**.

legacy [leg'a-si] *n* that which is left to one by will; anything handed down by an ancestor.

legal [lē'gàl] *adj* of or based on law; permitted by law; of or for lawyers.—*vt* **lē'galize**, to make lawful.—*n* **lēgal'ity**.—*adv* **lē'gally**.

legate [leg'àt] *n* an envoy, esp from the Pope; an official emissary.—*n* **legā'tion**, a diplomatic minister and his staff and headquarters.

legend [lej'ènd] *n* a traditional story; a myth; a notable person or the stories of his exploits; an inscription on a coin, etc.—*adj* **leg'endary**.

legerdemain [lej-ér-dê-mān'] *n* trickery.

leghorn [leg'hörn, leg-örn'] *n* fine straw plait; a hat made of it; a breed of domestic fowl.

legible [lej'i-bl] *adj* clear enough to be read.—*ns* **leg'ibleness**, **legibil'ity**.—*adv* **leg'ibly**.

legion [lē'jón] *n* a large body of soldiers; a large number, a multitude.—*ns* **lē'gionary**, **legionnaire**.

legislate [lej'is-lāt] *vi* to make or pass laws—*vt* to cause to be, go, etc. by making laws.—*n* **legislā'tion**.—*adj* **leg'islative**.—*ns* **leg'islātor**, **leg'islāture**, the body of those in a state who have the power of making laws.

legitimate [le-jit'i-màt] *adj* born of parents married to each other; lawful; reasonable, justifiable; conforming to accepted rules, standards, etc.—*n* **legit'imacy**.—*adv* **legit'imately**.—*ns* **legitimā'tion**, act of rendering legitimate; **legit'imist**, one who believes in the right of royal succession.

legume [leg'ûm] *n* any of a large family of plants having seeds growing in pods.—*adj* **legū'minous**.

leisure [lēzh'úr, lezh'úr] *n* time free from employment and at one's own disposal; freedom from occupation.—*adj* free and unoccupied.—*adj* **lei'surely**.

leitmotiv, leitmotif [līt'mō-tēf] *n* a dominant theme.

lemming [lem'ing] *n* any of several small arctic rodents.

lemon [lem'ón] *n* a small oval fruit with an acid pulp; the tree that bears it.—*ns* **lemonade'**, a drink made with lemon juice.

lemur [lē'múr] *n* a superfamily of arboreal, primates related to monkeys.

lend [lend] *vt* to give the use of for a time; to let out (money) at interest; to give, impart.—*vi* to make loans.—*n* **lend'er**.

length [length] *n* extent from end to end; the longest measure of anything; long continuance; a piece of a certain length.—*vti* **length'en**.—*adj* **length'y**.—*adv* **length'ily**.—*n* **length'iness**.

lenient [lē'ni-ènt] *adj* not harsh or severe; merciful.—*ns* **lē'nience**, **lē'niency**.—*adv* **lē'niently**.—*adj* **lenitive** [len'-], soothing; mitigating.—*n* (*med*) an application for easing pain.

lens [lenz] *n* a curved piece of transparent glass, plastic, etc. for bringing together or passing rays of light through it, used in optical instruments to form an image; any device used to focus electromagnetic rays, sound waves, etc.; a similar transparent part of the eye which focuses light rays on the retina.—*pl* **lens'es**.

Lent [lent] *n* an annual fast of forty weekdays in commemoration of Christ's fast in the wilderness from Ash Wednesday to Easter.—*adj* **lent'en**.

lentil [len'til] *n* any of several leguminous plants used as fodder; their seed used for food.

Leo [lē'ō] *n* the 5th sign of the zodiac, in astrology operative July 22 to August 21; the Lion, a constellation.—*adj* **lē'onine** of or like a lion.

leopard [lep'àrd] *n* a large tawny feline with black spots.—Also **panther**.

leotard [lē'ō-tärd] *n* a skintight garment worn by dancers and acrobats.

leper [le'pèr] *n* one affected with leprosy.

lepidopteran [lep-i-dop'tèr-an] *adj* any of a large order of insects that as adults have four wings covered with fine, scales and that as larvae are caterpillars.—*adjs* **lepidop'teral**, **lepidop'terous**.

leprechaun [lep-rè-hön'] *n* in Irish folklore, a fairy.

leprosy [lep'ro-si] *n* a chronic infectious bacterial disease of the skin, Hansen's disease.—*adj* **lep'rous**.

lesbian [lez'bi-àn] *n* a homosexual woman.—*n* **les'bianism**.

lesion [lē'zh(ó)n] *n* an injury.

less [les] comparative of little. *adj* not so much, not so great, etc.; fewer; smaller.—*adv* to a smaller extent.—*n* a smaller amount.—*prep* minus.

lessen [les'n] *vti* to make or become less.

lesser [les'ẽr] *adj* less; smaller; less important.

lesson [les'(ό)n] *n* something to be learned or studied; something that has been learned or studied; a unit of learning or teaching; (*pl*) a course of instruction; a selection from the Bible, read as a part of a church service.

lest [lest] *conj* that not; for fear that.

let [let] *vt* to allow, permit; to rent; to assign (a contract); to cause to run out, as blood; as an auxiliary in giving suggestions or commands (eg *let us go*).—*vi* to be rented. **let down** to lower; to disappoint; **let off** to give forth; to deal leniently with; **let on** (*inf*) to pretend; (*inf*) to indicate one's awareness; **let out**, to release; to rent out; to make a garment larger.

lethal [lē'thäl] *adj* deadly.

lethargy [leth'är-ji] *n* an abnormal drowsiness; sluggishness; apathy.—*adj* **lethar'gic**.

letter [let'ẽr] *n* any character of the alphabet; a written or printed message; (*pl*) literature; learning; knowledge; literal meaning; a single piece of printing type; a style of type.—*vt* to mark with letters.—*vi* to win an athletic letter.—*adj* **lett'ered**, literate; highly educated; marked with letters.

lettuce [let'is] *n* a plant with succulent leaves.

leukocyte [lū'kō-sĭt] *n* a white corpuscle in the blood.

leukemia [lū-kē'mi-à] *n* a disease in which there is an abnormal increase in the number of leukocytes.

levee¹ [lev'ē, le-vē', lev'ā] *n* an assembly received by a sovereign or other great personage; a reception usu. in honor of a particular person.

levee² [lev'e, le-vē'] *n* an embankment.

level [lev'l] *n* an instrument for determining the horizontal; a horizontal line or plane; normal position with reference to height; position in a scale of values.—*vti* to make or become level; to demolish; to raise and aim.—*adj* **lev'el-head'ed**, having an even temper and sound judgment.

lever [le'vẽr or lē'vẽr] *n* a bar used as a pry; a means to an end; a device consisting of a bar turning about a fixed point, using force at a second point to lift a weight at a third.—*vt* to move, as with a lever—*n* **lē'verage**.

leveret [lev'ẽr-et] *n* a hare in its first year.

levitation [lev-i-tā'sh(ό)n] *n* the illusion of raising a body in the air without support.—*vt* **lev'itate**.

Levite [lē'vīt] *n* a member of the priestly Hebrew tribe of Levi.

levity [lev'iti] *n* frivolity; improper gaiety.

levy [lev'i] *vt* to raise, collect, esp by authority, as an army or a tax; to make (war).—*n* the act of collecting by authority; the troops or money so collected.

lewd [l(y)ōōd] *adj* indecent; lustful; obscene.

lexicon [leks'i-kon] *n* a dictionary; a special vocabulary.—*ns* **lexicog'raphy**, the editing or making of a dictionary; the principles and practices of dictionary making; **lexicog'rapher**, one skilled in lexicography.

liable [lī-à-bl] *adj* legally bound or responsible; subject to; likely (to).—*n* **liabil'ity**.

liaison [lē-ā-zō, li-āz'(ό)n] *n* intercommunication as between units of a military force; an illicit love affair.—*vi* **liaise**.

liana [li-än'a] *n* climbing plants in tropical forests.

liar [lī-àr] *n* one who utters lies.

libation [lī-bā'sh(ό)n] *n* the pouring of wine or other liquid in honor of a deity; an alcoholic drink.

libel [lī-bél] *n* any written or printed matter tending to injure a person's reputation unjustly.—*vt* to defame by a libel.—*adj* **libellous**.—*adv* **lī'bellously**.

liberal [lib'ẽr-ál] *adj* ample, abundant; not literal or strict; tolerant; favoring reform or progress.—*n* one who favors reform or progress.—*vti* **lib'eralize**.—*ns* **lib'eralism**, **liberal'ity**.—*adv* **lib'erally**.

liberate [lib'ẽr-āt] *vt* to release from occupation, etc.—*ns* **liberā'tion**; **lib'erator**.

liberty [lib'ẽr-ti] *n* freedom from slavery, captivity, etc.

libido [li-bē'do] *n* the sexual urge.—*adj* **libid'inous**, lustful, lascivious.—*n* **libid'inousness**.—*adv* **libid'inously**.

Libra [lī'bra, lē'-] *n* the 7th sign of the zodiac; in astrology operative September 24 to October 23; constellation represented as a pair of scales.

library [lī'brär-i] *n* a collection of books, etc.; a room or building for, or an institution in charge of, such a collection.—*ns* **librari'an**, one in charge of a library or trained in library science; **librar'ianship**.

libretto [li-bret'ō] *n* the words of an opera, oratorio, etc.—*pl* **librett'os**; **librett'i**.

license [lī'sėns] *n* a formal or legal permission to do something specified; a document granting such permission; freedom to deviate from rule, practice, etc. (*poetic license*); excessive freedom, an abuse of liberty.—*vt* to permit formally.—*ns* **licensee'**, a person to whom a license is granted; **licentiate**, a person having a professional license.—*adv* **licen'tious**, morally unrestrained; lascivious.

lichen [lī'kén] *n* a large group of plants consisting of an alga and a fungus in close association, growing on stones, trees, etc.

lich-gate [lich'-gāt] *See* **lych-gate**.

licit [lis'it] *adj* lawful.

lick [lik] *vt* to pass the tongue over; to lap; (*inf*) to whip; (*inf*) to vanquish.—*n* a licking with the tongue.

licorice [lik'or-is] *n* a black flavoring extract made from the root of a European plant.

lid [lid] *n* a removable cover as for a box, etc.; an eyelid.

lie¹ [lī] *n* a false statement made to deceive; anything that misleads.—*vi* to utter falsehood with an intention to deceive.—*pr p* **ly'ing**; *pt*, *pt p* **lied**.

lie² [lī] *vi* to be or put oneself in a reclining or horizontal position; to rest on a support in a horizontal position; to be in a specified condition; to be situated; to exist.—*n* the way in which something is situated; lay.

lied [lēt] *n* a German art song.

liege [lēj] *adj* loyal, faithful.—*n* in feudalism, a lord or sovereign; a subject or vassal.

lien [lē'én, lēn] *n* (*law*) a right to retain possession of another's property until the owner pays a debt due to the holder.

lieu [l(y)ōō] *n* place.—**in lieu of**, in place of, instead of.

lieutenant [lōōten'ánt] *n* a commissioned officer ranking below a captain.

life [līf] *n* that property of plants and animals (ending at death) that enables them to use food, grow, reproduce, etc.; the state of having this property; living things collectively; the time a person or thing exists; one's manner of living; one's animate existence; vigor, liveliness.—*pl* **lives**.—*adj* of animate being; lifelong; using a living model; of or relating to or provided by life insurance.—*ns* **life belt**, the life preserver in belt form; a safety belt; **life'boat**, a small rescue boat carried by a ship; **life buoy**, a ring-shaped life preserver; **life cycle**, a sequence of stages through which a living being passes during its lifetime; **life'guard**, an expert swimmer employed to prevent drownings; **life jacket**, a life preserver like a sleeveless jacket or vest.—*adjs* **life'less**, **life'like**.—*adj* **life'long**, lasting one's whole life.—*ns.*—*adj* **life'saving**, something (as drugs) designed to save lives.—*n* the skill or practice of saving lives, esp from drowning.

lift [lift] *vt* to bring to a higher position, raise; to raise in rank, condition, etc.; (*slang*) to steal.—*vi* to exert oneself in raising something; to rise; to go up.—*n* act or fact of lifting; distance through which a thing is lifted; elevation of mood, etc.; elevated position or carriage; a ride in the direction in which one is going; help of any kind; (*British*) an elevator.

ligament [lig'a-mént] *n* a band of tissue connecting bones; a unifying bond.—*adj* **ligament'ous**.—*n* **lig'ature** [lig'à-chur] a tying or binding together; a tie, bond, etc.; (*surgery*) a thread used to suture a blood vessel, etc.

light¹ [līt] *n* the radiant energy by which the eye sees; ultraviolet or infrared radiation; brightness, illumination; a source of light, as the sun, a lamp, etc.; daylight; thing used to ignite something; a window; knowledge, enlightenment; aspect.—*adj* having light; bright; pale in color.—*adv* palely.—*vt* to ignite; to cause to give off light; to furnish with light; to brighten, animate; *prp* **light'ing**; *pt* and *ptp* **light'ed** or **lit**.—*vti* **light'en**, to make or become light or lighter; to shine, flash.—*ns* **light'er**, **light'house**, a tower with a bright light to guide ships; **light'ing**, **light'ness**, the amount of light; brightness; paleness in color; **light'ning**, discharge or flash of electricity in the sky; **lightning rod**, a metal rod placed high on a building and grounded to divert lightning from the structure.

light² [līt] *adj* having little weight; not heavy; less than usual in weight, amount, force, etc.; of little importance; easy to bear; happy; dizzy, giddy; not serious; moderate; moving with ease; producing small products.—*adv* **lightly**.—*vi* to come to rest after traveling through the air; to come or happen on or upon; to strike suddenly, as a blow. —*prp* light'ing; *pt*, and *pt p* light'ed, or lit. —*vti* light'en, to make or become lighter in weight; to make or become more cheerful. —*adj* light'-fingered, thievish; light·'head'ed, dizzy; delirious; light·'heart'ed, carefree. —*adv* light'ly, lightness, not being heavy; being cheerful; lack of proper seriousness.

lighter [līt'er] *n* a large barge used in loading or unloading larger ships.

lignite [lig'nīt] *n* a soft, brownish-black coal with the texture of the original wood.

lignum vitae [lig'num vit'ē] *n* the very heavy hard wood of several tropical American trees.

like¹ [līk] *adj* having the same characteristics; similar; equal. —*prep* similar to; similarly to; characteristic of; in the mood for; indicative of; as for example. —*n* like'lihood, probability. —*adj* like'ly, credible; reasonably to be expected; suitable. —*adv* probably. —*vt* lik'en, to compare. —*n* like'ness, a being like; something that is like, as a copy, portrait, etc.; appearance, semblance. —*adv* like'wise, the same; also.

like² [līk] *vt* to be pleased with; to wish. —*vi* to be so inclined. —*adj* lik'able, like'able. —*n* lik'ing.

lilac [lī'lăc] *n* a shrub with large clusters of tiny, fragrant flowers. —*n, adj* a pale purple.

Lilliputian [lil-i-pū'sh(y)ăn] *adj* tiny; petty. —*n*.

lilt [lilt] *vi* to sing or play merrily. —*vt* to sing easily. —*n* a cheerful song or air.

lily [lil'i] *n* a bulbous plant having typically trumpet-shaped flowers; its flower. —lily of the valley, a small plant of the lily family with white bell-shaped flowers.

limb¹ [lim] *n* an arm, leg, or wing; a large branch of a tree.

limb² [lim] *n* an edge or border, as of the sun, etc.

limber [lim'bėr] *adj* flexible, able to bend the body easily. —*vti* to make or become limber.

limbo [lim'bō] *n* the abode after death assigned to the unbaptized; a place of oblivion.

lime¹ [līm] *n* any slimy or gluey material; the white caustic substance obtained by calcining limestone, etc., used for cement. —*vt* to cover with lime; to cement; to manure with lime; to ensnare. —*ns* lime'light, light produced by a blowpipeflame directed against a block of quicklime; the glare of publicity; lime'stone, a sedimentary rock composed essentially of calcium carbonate; lime'twig, a twig smeared with bird-lime; a snare.

lime² [līm] *n* a small yellowish-green fruit with a juicy, sour pulp; the tree that bears it. —*ns* limeade', a drink made with sweetened lime juice.

lime³ [līm] *n* the linden tree.

limerick [lim'er-ik] *n* a form of humorous verse in a five-line jingle.

limit [lim'it] *n* boundary; (*pl*) bounds; the greatest amount allowed. —*vt* to set a limit to; to restrict. —*adj*. —*n* lim'itā'tion.

limn [lim] *vt* to draw or paint; to outline in.

limousine [lim'ōō-zēn] *n* a large luxury automobile.

limp [limp] *vi* to walk with or as with a lame leg. —*n* a halt or lameness in walking.

limpet [lim'pet] *n* mollusks with a low conical shell that cling to rocks.

limpid [lim'pid] *adj* perfectly clear; transparent. —*ns* limpid'ity, lim'pidness. —*adv* lim'pidly.

linchpin [linch'pin] *n* pin to keep a wheel on its axle.

linden [lin'den] *n* any tree, having deciduous, heart-shaped, serrated leaves.

line¹ [līn] *vt* to put, or serve as, a lining in. —*n* lin'ing, the material covering an inner surface.

line² [līn] *n* a length of cord, rope, or wire; a cord for measuring, making level; system of conducting fluid, electricity, etc.; a thin threadlike mark; border, outline, contour; row of persons or things, a succession of persons, lineage; a connected series of things; the course a moving thing takes; a course of conduct, actions, etc.; whole system of transportation; a person's trade or occupation; field of experience or interest; the forward combat position in warfare; line, trenches or other defenses used in war; a stock of goods; a piece of information; a short letter, note; (*pl*) all the speeches of a character in a play. —*vt* to mark with lines; to form a line along; to cover with lines; to arrange in a line. —*vi* to hit a line drive in baseball; to align. —*ns* lineage [lin'ē-ij] direct descent from an ancestor; ancestry, family. —*adj* lineal [lin'i-ăl] hereditary; linear. —*n* lin'eament, (usu *pl*) feature. —*adj* lin'ear, of, made of, or using a line or lines.

linen [lin'ĕn] *n* thread or cloth made of flax. —*adj* made of flax; resembling linen cloth.

ling [ling] *n* heather.

linger [ling'gėr] *vi* to remain long; to loiter.

lingerie [lĕzh-(ė)rē] *n* women's underwear.

lingo [ling'gō] *n* a dialect, jargon, etc.

lingual [ling'gwăl] *adj* of, or pronounced with, the tongue. —*n* ling'uist, a specialist in linguistics. —*adjs* linguist'ic, -al.

liniment [lin'i-mėnt] *n* an embrocation.

link¹ [lingk] *n* a loop or ring of a chain; anything connecting a single part of a series. —*vti* to connect. —*ns* link'age, link'up, a linking together.

link² [lingk] *n* a torch.

links [lingks] *n pl* a golf course.

Linnaean, Linnean [lin-ē'ăn] *adj* of, or relating to, the system of binomial nomenclature.

linnet [lin'et] *n* a common small finch.

linoleum [lin-ō'li-um] *n* a floor covering of burlap with a smooth, hard decorative coating.

linocut [li'nō-kut] *n* a linoleum block cut in relief, or a print from it.

Linotype [līn'ō-tīp] *n* a typesetting machine for producing complete lines of words, etc.

linseed [lin'sēd] *n* flax seed.

linsey-woolsey [lin'zi, -wōōl'zi] *ns* a sturdy coarse fabric of linen or cotton and wool mixed.

lint [lint] *n* scraped and softened linen; bits of fluff, thread, etc. from cloth or yarn.

lintel [lint'(ė)l] *n* the horizontal crosspiece over a doorway or window.

lion [lī'ón] *n* a large, tawny feline with a shaggy mane in the adult male; a person of great courage or strength. —li'oness, a female lion. —*vt* lī'onize, to treat as a celebrity.

lip [lip] *n* either of the muscular flaps in front of the mouth; anything like a lip, as the rim of a pitcher; (*slang*) insolent talk. —*adj* spoken, but insincere (*lip service*). —*vt* to touch the edge of. —*adjs* lipped, having lips. —*n* lip'stick, a small stick of cosmetic for coloring the lips.

lip-, lipo- [lip-, līp-(ō-)] in composition, fat; fatty tissue.

liquate [lik'wăt] *vt* to cause to separate by applying heat. —*n* liquā'tion.

liquefy [lik'we-fī] *vti* to change to a liquid. —*pt, pt p* liq'uefied. —*n* liquefac'tion. —*adj* liques'cent, melting.

liqueur [li-kûr'] *n* a sweet, alcoholic liquor.

liquid [lik'wid] *adj* flowing; fluid; clear; limpid; flowing smoothly and musically, as verse; readily convertible into cash. —*n* a substance that, unlike a gas, does not expand indefinitely and unlike a solid, flows readily. —*n* a liquid substance; a flowing consonant sound, as *l, r*. —*ns* liquid'ity, liq'uidness. —*vt* liq'uidate, to settle the accounts of; to convert into cash. —*ns* liquidā'tion; liquidāt'or. —*vt* liq'uidize', to make liquid.

liquor [lik'ór] *n* any liquid; an alcoholic drink.

lisle [līl] *n* a fine hard-twisted cotton thread.

lisp [lisp] *vi* to substitute the sounds *th* for *s* or TH for *z*; to utter imperfectly. —*vt* to utter with a lisp. —*n* the act or habit of lisping.

lissome, lissom [lis'óm] *adj* lithe; supple; agile; etc.

list¹ [list] *n* a series of names, numbers, words, etc. —*vt* to make a list of; to enter in a directory, etc.

list² [list] *vti* to tilt to one side, as a ship. —*n* such a tilting. —*adj* list'less, having no desire or wish because of illness, dejection, etc.; languid.

listen [lis'n] *vi* to try to hear; to follow advice. —*n* list'ener.

litany [lit'ă-ni] *n* a prayer with responses.

literal [lit'er-ăl] *adj* following the exact words of the original in a basic or strict sense; real. —*adv* lit'erally. —*n* lit'eralness.

literary [lit'er-ar-i] *adj* of or dealing with literature; knowing much about literature. —*n* lit'eracy, ability to read and write. —*adj* lit'erate [-ăt] able to read and write; educated. — Also *n*. —*adj, adv* litera'tim [-rä or -rā] letter for letter. —*n*

lit′erature [-chùr], writings of a period or of a country; all the books and articles on a subject; (*inf*) any printed matter.

lithe [līTH] *adj* flexible, pliant.

lithium [lith′i-um] *n* the lightest metallic element.

lithograph [lith′ō-gräf] *n* a print made by lithography.—*vti* to make (prints or copies) by this method.—*n* **lithog′raphy**, printing from a flat stone or metal plate, parts of which have been treated to repel ink.—*n* **lithog′rapher.**—*adj* **lithograph′ic.**—*adv* **lithograph′ically.**—*n* **lithog′raphy**.

lithology [lith-ol′o-ji] *n* the study of rocks.—*adjs* **litholog′ic**, **litholog′ical**.

lithophyte [lith′ō-fīt] *n* a plant that grows on rocks.

lithosphere [lith′ō-sfēr] *n* the rocky crust of the earth.

lithotomy [lith-ot′o-mi] *n* surgical removal of a stone in the urinary bladder.

litigate [lit′i-gāt] *vti* to dispute by a lawsuit.—*n* **litigā′tion.**—*adj* **litigious** [li-tij′-us] inclined to engage in lawsuits.

litmus [lit′mus] *n* a substance obtained from certain lichens, turned red by acids, blue by bases.

litter [lit′ér] *n* things scattered about or left in disorder; young animals produced at one time; straw, hay, etc. used as bedding for animals; a stretcher for carrying a sick or wounded person.—*vt* to make untidy; to scatter about carelessly.

little [lit′l] *adj* not great or big, small in size, amount, degree, etc.; short in duration; small in importance or power; narrow-minded.—*n* small amount, degree, etc.—*adv* **less**, **least**, slightly; not much; not in the least.

littoral [lit′òr-ál] *adj* of or along the seashore.

liturgy [lit′ùr-ji] *n* the prescribed ritual of a church.

live [liv] *vi* to have life; to remain alive; to endure; to pass life in a specified manner; to enjoy a full life; to reside.—*vt* to carry out in one's life; to spend.—*adjs* **livable**; **live** [līv], having life; of the living state or living beings; of present interest; **live′stock**, domestic animals raised for use or sale.

livelihood [līv′li-hood] *n* means of living or of supporting life.

lively [līv′li] *adj* full of life; spirited; exciting; vivid; keen.—*adv* in a lively manner.—*n* **līve′liness**.

liver [liv′ér] *n* the largest glandular organ in vertebrate animals which secretes bile, etc. and is important in metabolism; the liver of an animal used as food.—*adjs* **liv′erish**, **liv′ery**, suffering from disordered liver; irritable.

livery [liv′ér-i] *n* an identifying uniform the care and feeding of horses for a fee; the keeping of horses or vehicles for hire.—*adj* **liv′eried**.

livid [liv′id] *adj* discolored; black and blue; of a lead color; pale with emotion.—*n* **liv′idness**.

living [liv′ing] *adj* having life; still in use; true to life, vivid; of life, for living in.—*n* a being alive; livelihood; manner of existence.

lizard [liz′árd] *n* reptiles with a slender body, four legs, and a tapering tail.

llama [lä′mä] *n* a ruminant related to the camel, used as a beast of burden and a source of wool.

llano [lyä′no or lä′no] *n* an open grassy plain in the southwestern US or Spanish America.

load [lōd] *n* an amount carried at one time; something borne with difficulty; burden; (often *pl*) (*inf*) a great amount.—*vt* to put into or upon; to burden; to oppress; to supply in large quantities; to alter, as by adding a weight to dice or an adulterant to alcoholic drink; to put a charge of ammunition into (a firearm).—*vi* to take on a load.

loaf [lōf] *n* a regularly shaped mass of bread.

loaf² [lōf] *vi* to loiter, pass time idly.—*n* **loaf′er**.

loam [lōm] *n* a fertile soil.

loan [lōn] *n* the act of lending; something lent, esp money at interest.—*vti* to lend.

loath, loathe [lōth] *adj* reluctant, unwilling (to).

loathe [lōTH] *vt* to dislike greatly, to feel disgust at.—*n* **loath′-ing**, *adjs* **loath′some** exciting loathing or abhorrence, detestable.

lobby [lob′i] *n* an entrance hall of a public building; a person or group that tries to influence legislators.

lobe [lōb] *n* a rounded projection, as the lower end of the ear; any of the divisions of the lungs or brains.

lobelia [lob-ē′li-a] *n* a genus of garden plants, usually with blue flowers.

lobster [lob′stèr] *n* any of a family of edible sea crustaceans with four pairs of legs and a pair of large pincers.

local [lō′kál] *adj* of or belonging to a place, confined to a spot or district; of or for a particular part of the body; making all stops along its run.—*n* **locale** [-käl′], the scene of some event.—*vt* **lōc′alize**.—*n* **local′ity**, existence in a place; position; a district.—*adv* **lō′cally**.—*vt* **locāte′**, to place, to set in a particular position; to find the place of, to show the position of.—*n* **locā′tion**, act of locating; position; place.

lock [lok] *n* a device to fasten doors, etc. part of a canal, dock, etc. in which the level of the water can be changed by the operation of gates; the part of a gun by which the charge is fired; a controlling hold.—*vt* to fasten with a lock; to shut; to fit, link; to jam together so as to make immovable.—*vi* to become locked; to interlock.—*ns* **lock′er**, a closet, chest, etc. that can be locked.—*n* **lock′et**, a little hinged ornamental case, hung from the neck; **lock′jaw**, tetanus; **lock′smith**, one whose work is making and repairing locks and keys; **lock′up**, a jail.

lock [lok] *n* a curl of hair; a tuft of wool, etc.

locomotive [lō-ko-mōt′iv] *adj* of locomotion.—*n* an electric, steam, or diesel engine on wheels, designed to move a railroad train.—*n* **locomō′tion**.

locum tenens [lō′kum (tēn′enz)] *n* a substitute, esp for a doctor or clergyman.

locus [lō′kus] *n* a place.

locust [lō′kust] *n* large grasshoppers often traveling in swarms and destroying crops; hard-wooded leguminous trees.—*n* **lō′cust-bean**, the sweet pod of the carob tree.

locution [lō-kū′sh(ò)n] *n* act or mode of speaking.

lode [lōd] *n* an ore deposit.

lodge [loj] *n* a small house for some special use; a resort hotel or motel; the local chapter or hall of a fraternal society.—*vt* to house temporarily; to shoot, thrust, etc. firmly (in); to bring before legal authorities; to confer upon—*vi* to live in a place for a time; to live as a paying guest; to come to rest and stick firmly (in).—*ns* **lod′ger**, lodg′ing, temporary habitation; **lodg′ment, lodge′ment**, act of lodging, or state of being lodged.

loft [loft] *n* a room or space immediately under a roof; a gallery in a hall or church.—*vt* to send into a high curve.—*adj* **loft′y**.—*adv* **loft′ily**.

log [log] *n* a section of a felled tree; a device for ascertaining the speed of a ship; a record of speed, progress, etc. esp one kept on a ship's voyage or aircraft's flight.—*vt* to record in a log; to sail or fly (a specified distance).—*ns* **log′book**, an official record of a ship's or aircraft's progress and proceedings on board; **log′wood**, a central American tree its very hard heartwood.

loganberry [lō′gàn-ber-i] *n* a hybrid developed from the blackberry and the red raspberry.

loggia [lōj′a, lōj′ya] *n* open gallery or balcony.

logic [loj′ik] *n* correct reasoning, or the science of this; way of reasoning; what is expected by the working of cause and effect.—*adj* **log′ical** according to the rules of logic.—*adv* **log′ically**.

loin [loin] *n* (usu. *pl*) the lower part of the back between the hipbones and the ribs; the front part of the hind-quarters of an animal used for food.

loiter [loi′tèr] *vi* to proceed slowly; to dawdle.

loll [lol] *vi* to lie lazily about, to lounge; to hang loosely (now mainly of the tongue).

lollipop [lôl′i-pop] *n* candy at the end of a stick.

lone [lōn] *adj* by oneself; isolated; solitary.—*adj* **lone′some**, *n* **lone′someness**.

lonely [lōn′li] *adj* isolated; unhappy about being alone.

long [long] *adj* measuring much in space or time; in length; having a greater than usual length, quantity, etc.; tedious, slow; far-reaching; well-supplied.—*adv* for a long time; from start to finish; at a remote time.—*vi* to desire earnestly esp for something not likely to be attained.—*n* a long time.—*n* **longevity** long life.

longitude [lon′ji-tūd] *n* distance east or west of the prime meridian, expressed in degrees or time.—*adj* **longitud′inal**, of or in length; of longitude.

loofah [lōō′fä] *n* gourds with white flowers and large fruits; its fruit; fibrous skeleton of the fruit used as a washcloth.

look [löök] *vi* to try to see; to see; to search; to appear, seem; to be facing in a specified direction. — *vt* to direct one's eyes on; to have an appearance befitting. — *n* a looking, glance; appearance; aspect. — *ns* **look-alike**, one that looks like another; **looking glass**, a mirror; **look'out'**, a place for keeping watch; a person assigned to watch. — **look after**, to take care of.

loom[1] [lööm] *n* a machine in which yarn or thread is woven. — *vt* to weave on a loom.

loom[2] [lööm] *vi* to appear indistinctly or as in a mirage; to take shape, as an impending event. — *n* a looming shadow or reflection.

loon [löön] *n* large fish-eating diving birds.

loop [lööp] *n* a figure made by a curved line crossing itself; a similar rounded shape in cord, rope, etc. crossed on itself; anything forming this figure. — *vt* to make a loop of; to fasten with a loop. — *vi* to form a loop or loops. — *n* **loophole** a slit in a wall for looking or shooting through; a means of evading an obligation, etc. — *vt* to make loopholes in; **loop'line**, a branch of a railroad that returns to the main line.

loose [löös] *adj* not confined; free; not firmly fastened; not tight or compact; not precise; inexact; (*inf*) relaxed. — *vt* to unfasten; to untie; to release; to relax. — *vi* to become loose. — *adv* **loose'ly**. — *vti* **loos'en**, to make loose. — *ns* **loose'ness**.

loot [lööt] *n* plunder; (*slang*) money.

lop[1] [lop] *vi* to hang down loosely. — *adjs* **lop'-eared**, having drooping ears; **lop'-sid'ed**, ill-balanced.

lop[2] [lop] *vt* to cut off the top or ends of, esp of a tree; to curtail by cutting away superfluous parts.

lope [löp] *vi* to run with a long stride.

loquacious [lo-kwā'shŭs] *adj* very talkative.

lord [lörd] *n* an owner, ruler, or master. — *adj* **lord'ly**. — *ns* **lord'ship**, the rank or authority of a lord; rule, dominion; a title used in speaking of or to a lord; **the Lord**, God; Jesus Christ.

lore [lör, lör] *n* knowledge; learning, esp of a traditional nature; a particular body of tradition.

lorgnette [lörn-yet'] *n* eye glasses with a handle.

lorn [lörn] *adj* (*arch*) lost; forsaken.

lory [löri] *n* parrots native to Australia, New Guinea, and adjacent islands etc.

lose [lööz] *vt* to have taken from one by death, accident, removal, etc.; to be unable to find; to fail to keep, as one's temper; to fail to see, hear, or understand; to fail to have, get, etc.; to fail to win; to cause the loss of; to wander from (one's way, etc.); to squander. — *vi* to suffer (a) loss. — *n* **los'er**, **loss**, a losing or being lost; the damage, trouble caused by losing; the person, thing, or amount lost.

lot [lot] *n* an object drawn from among a number to reach a decision by chance; one's share by lot; fortune; a plot of ground; a group of persons or things. — *n* **lottery**, a scheme for distributing prizes by lot or chance. — *vt* to allot; to separate into lots.

lotion [lö'sh(ö)n] *n* a liquid preparation for cosmetic or external medical use.

lotus [lö'tus] *n* in Greek legend, a plant whose fruit induced contented forgetfulness. — *ns*.

loud [lowd] *adj* making a great sound; noisy; emphatic; (*inf*) showy or flashy. — *advs* **loud**, **loud'ly**. — *n* **loud'ness**. — *n* **loud'speak'er** a device for converting electrical energy into sound.

lounge [lownj] *vi* to move, sit, lie, etc. in a relaxed way; to spend time idly. — *n* a room with comfortable furniture for lounging; a couch or sofa.

lour, louring [lowr, low'ring] *see* **lower**, **lowering**

louse [lows] *n* any of various wingless insects parasitic on men and animals; any similar small parasites on plants. — *pl* **lice** [lïs]. — *adj* **lousy** [low'zi], swarming with lice; (*slang*) disgusting, of poor quality, or inferior.

lout [lowt] *n* a clumsy, stupid fellow.

louver, louvre [löö'vėr] *n* one of a set of slats set parallel and slanted to admit air but not rain. — Also *adj* . — *n* a ventilatory structure of these.

love [luv] *n* a strong liking for someone or something; a passionate affection for another person; the object of such affection; (*tennis*), a score of zero. — *vti* to feel love (for). — *adj* **lov'able**, **lov'eable**. — *ns* **love apple**, a tomato; **love'bird**, any of various small parrots; **love-in-a-mist**, a garden plant; **love'-**

lorn, pining from love; **love'ly**, beautiful; (*inf*) highly enjoyable; **lov'er**, a sweetheart; **lov'ing** affectionate.

low[1] [lö] *vi* to moo. — *n* the sound a cow makes.

low[2] [lö] *adj* not high or tall; below the normal level; less in size, degree, amount, etc. than usual; deep in pitch; depressed in spirits; humble, of low rank; vulgar, coarse; not loud. — *adv* in or to a low degree, level, etc. — *n* a low level, degree, etc.; an arrangement of gears giving the lowest speed and greatest power; **low'down**, (*slang*) the true, pertinent facts (*with* **the**) — *adj* **lowdown'**, (*inf*) mean, contemptible. — *adj* **low'er**, below in place, rank, etc.; less in amount, degree, etc. — *vt* to let or put down; to reduce in height, amount, etc.; to bring down in respect, etc. — *vi* to become lower.

lower [low'er, lö'ėr] *vi* to look sullen; to become dark, gloomy, threatening. — *adj* **low'ery**, gloomy, lowering. — Also **lour** [low'ėr].

lower[1] [lö'ėr] *see* **low** (2).

loyal [loi'ăl] *adj* faithful; showing firm allegiance. — *n* **loy'alist**. — *adv* **loy'ally**. — *n* **loy'alty**.

lozenge [loz'enj] *n* a diamond-shaped figure; a cough drop, candy, etc. orig diamond-shaped.

lubber [lub'ėr] *n* an awkward, sturdy, clumsy fellow.

lubricate [l(y)öö'bri-kāt] *vt* to make smooth or slippery; to oil. — *ns* **lübricant**; **lubricā'tion**; **lubricity** slipperiness; smoothness; lewdness.

lucent [l(y)öö'sėnt] *adj* shining; clear.

lucid [l(y)öö'sid] *adj* shining; transparent; sane; easily understood.

Lucifer [l(y)öö'si-fėr] *n* Satan.

luck [luk] *n* chance; good fortune. — *adj* **luck'y**, having or bringing good luck.

lucre [l(y)öö'kėr] *n* (*derogatory*) riches, money. — *adj* **lu'crative**, producing wealth or profit; profitable.

ludicrous [l(y)öö'dik-rŭs] *adj* absurd, laughable.

luff [luf] *n* the windward side of a ship. — *vt* to turn a ship towards the wind.

lug [lug] *vt* to pull along, to drag with effort. — *pr p* **lugg'ing**; *pt*, *pt p* **lugged**. — *n* **lugg'age**, the trunks and other baggage of a traveller.

luge [lööj] *n* a small sled.

lugubrious [l(y)öö-gu'bri-us] *adj* mournful, dismal.

lukewarm [löök'wörm] *adj* barely warm, tepid; lacking enthusiasm. — *adv* **luke'warmly**.

lull [lul] *vt* to soothe, to quiet. — *vi* to become calm. — *n* a short period of calm. — *n* **lull'aby** [-bï] a song to lull children to sleep.

lumber[1] [lum'bėr] *n* timber, logs, beams, boards, etc., roughly cut and prepared for use — *vi* to cut down timber and saw it into lumber. — *vt* to clutter with lumber; to heap in disorder. — *n* **lum'berjack'**.

lumber[2] [lum'bėr] *vi* to move heavily and noisily.

luminary [l(y)öö'min-ăr-i] *n* a body that gives off light, such as the sun; a famous or notable person. — *n* **lumines'cence**.

lump [lump] *n* a small shapeless mass of something; a swelling. — *adj* in a lump or lumps. — *vt* to treat or deal with in a mass. — *vi* to become lumpy. — *ns*. — *adj* **lump'y**, full of lumps.

lunar [löö'nár] *adj* of or like the moon. — *adj* **lu'nāte** crescent-shaped.

lunatic [löö'nà-tik] *adj* insane; utterly foolish. — *n* an insane person. — *n* **lu'nacy**, insanity; utter folly.

lunch [lunch] *n* a light meal, esp between breakfast and dinner. — *vi* to eat lunch. — *ns* **lunch'eon** lunch, esp a formal lunch.

lung [lung] *n* either of the two spongelike breathing organs in the chest of vertebrates.

lunge [lunj] *n* a sudden thrust, as with a sword; a sudden plunge forward. — *vti* to move, or cause to move, with a lunge.

lupine, lupin [löö'pin] *n* plants of the pea family.

lupine [lū'pïn] *adj* wolfish.

lupus [löö'pus] *n* any of several diseases marked by lesions of the skin.

lurch [lûrch] *vi* to roll or pitch suddenly to one side. — *n* a sudden roll or pitch.

lurcher [lûr'chėr] *n* a crossbred dog trained to hunt.

lure [l(y)öör] *n* any enticement; fishing bait. — *vt* to entice, attract, or tempt.

lurid [lŏŏ'rid] adj lighted up with red or fiery glare; shocking; sensational. —adv **lū'ridly.**

lurk [lûrk] vi to lie in wait; to skulk.

luscious [lush'ùs] adj delicious, richly sweet; delighting any of the senses.

lush [lush] adj tender and juicy; of or showing abundant growth.

lust [lust] n longing desire (for), eagerness to possess; sensual appetite. —vi an intense desire. —adj **lust'ful.** —adj **lust'y,** vigorous; healthy; stout.

luster [lus'tẽr] n gloss; sheen; brightness; radiance; brilliant beauty or fame; glory. —adj **lus'trous.**

lute [lŏŏt, lūt] n an old stringed instrument.

Lutheran [lŏŏ'thẽr-àn] n a member of a Protestant Christian denomination. —adj of the Lutheran Church.

luxury [luk'shù-ri, lug'zhù-ri] n free indulgence in costly pleasures; something beyond what is essential or what one is accustomed to —adj relating to or providing luxury. —adj **luxū'riant,** exuberant in growth; overabundant. —adv **luxūriantly.** —vi **luxū'riate,** to live luxuriously; to revel (in). —adj **luxū'rious.**

Lyceum [lī-sē'um] n a lecture hall; an organization providing lectures, debates, etc.

lychgate [lich-gāt] n a roofed churchyard gate under which the bier rest before interment.

lyddite [lid'ĭt] n a powerful explosive.

lye [lī] n a strong alkaline solution obtained by leaching wood ashes.

lying [lī'ing] adj not truthful. —n the telling of a lie or lies.

lymph [limf] n a clear, yellowish body fluid, found in intercellular spaces and the lymphatic vessels. —adj **lymphat'ic,** of or containing lymph; sluggish. —n a vessel which conveys the lymph.

lynch [linch, -sh] vt to murder (an accused person) by mob action, without lawful trial, as by hanging. —n **lynch' law.**

lynx [lingks] n a wildcat. —adj **lynx'-eyed,** sharpsighted.

lyre [līr] n musical instrument like the harp. —adj **lyr'ic,** denoting or of poetry, expressing the writer's emotion; of, or having a high voice with a light, flexible quality. —adj **lyr'ical** lyric; expressing rapture or enthusiasm.

M

macabre [mà-kàb'rè, mà-kàb'] adj gruesome; grim.

macadam [mà-kad'àm] n small, broken stones, rolled until solid, often with tar and asphalt, to make roads.

macaroni [mak-a-rō'ni] n pasta in the form of tubes.

macaroon [mak-a-rōōn'] n a small, sweet cookie made of crushed almonds or coconut.

macaw [ma-kö'] n any of numerous large long-tailed showy tropical American parrots. [Port macao.]

mace[1] [mās] n a heavy, spiked war club used in the Middle Ages; a staff used as a symbol of authority by certain institutions.

mace[2] [mās] n an aromatic spice made from the husk of the nutmeg.

macerate [mas'ẽr-āt] vt to soften or separate the parts of by soaking in liquid.

machete [mà-shet'è, -chet'è] n a large knife used for cutting sugar cane, underbrush, etc.

Machiavellian [mak-i-a-vel'yàn] adj crafty; deceitful.

machinate [mak'i-nāt] vi to plot or scheme, esp for doing harm. —vt to plan or contrive to bring about. —ns **machinā'tion; mach'inator.**

machine [ma-shēn'] n a structure of fixed and moving parts, for doing some kind of work; an organization functioning like a machine; the controlling group in a political party; a device, as the lever, etc. that transmits, or changes the application of energy. —vt to shape or finish by machine-operated tools. — adj of machines; done by machinery. —ns **machine gun,** an automatic gun, firing a rapid stream of bullets. —ns **machinery,** machines collectively; the working parts of a machine; **machin'ist,** one who makes, repairs, or operates machinery.

machismo [mä-chēz'mō] n strong or assertive masculinity; virility. —adj **ma'chō.**

macho see **machismo.**

mackerel [mak'ẽr-él] n an important food fish, dark blue above and plain silvery below with about 30 dark wavy stripes across the back; **mackerel sky,** a sky full of cirrocumulus clouds, which resemble the stripes on a mackerel's back.

mackintosh, macintosh [mak'in-tósh] n a thin waterproof fabric, formerly of rubberized cotton.

macro- [mak-rō-] in composition, large, long. [Gr makros, large]. —eg **macrocosm** [mak'rōkozm] the universe; any large, complex entity.

macrobiotic [mak-rō-bī-ö'tik] adj of the art of prolonging life.

macroscopic [mak-rō-skop'ik] adj visible to the naked eye; considered in terms of large units.

macula [mak'ū-la] n a spot or blotch, as on the skin. —pl **maculae** [-lē]. —vt **mac'ulāte,** to mark with spots. —n **maculā'tion.**

mad [mad] adj insane; frantic; foolish and rash; infatuated; wildly gay; having rabies; angry. —n an angry mood. —n **mad'cap,** a reckless, impulsive person. —vti **madd'en,** to make or become insane, angry, or wildly excited. —adv **mad'ly.**

madam [mad'àm] n a courteous form of address to a woman; a woman in charge of a brothel.

madder [mad'ẽr] n any of various plants, esp a vine with yellow flowers and a red root; a red dye made from the root.

made [mād] pt, pt p of **make.**

Madeira [ma-dē'ra] n an amber-colored fortified dessert wine.

mademoiselle [mad-mwä-zel', mad-è-mô-zel'] n a form of address to a young lady; Miss.

Madonna [ma-don'a] n the Virgin Mary, esp as seen in works of art.

madrigal [mad'ri-gàl] n (mus) an unaccompanied song in several parts.

maelstrom [māl'strom] n a large and violent whirlpool; an agitated state of affairs, mind, etc.

maestro [mä-es'trō, mī'strö] n a master, esp an eminent musical composer or conductor.

Mafia [mä'fē-ä] n a secret society composed chiefly of criminal elements.

magazine [mag-à-zēn' also mag'-] n a place for military stores; a space where explosives are stored, as in a fort; a supply chamber as in a camera, a rifle, etc.; a periodical publication containing articles, stories, etc.

magenta [ma-jen'ta] n a purplish-red dye; purplish red. —Also adj.

maggot [mag'ót] n a wormlike larva, as of the housefly; a fantastic idea, a whim. —adj **magg'oty.**

magic [maj'ik] n the use of charms, spells, etc. in seeking or pretending to control events; any mysterious power; the art of producing illusions by sleight of hand, etc. —**mag'ical.** —adv **mag'ically.** —ns **magician; mag'ic lan'tern,** an early form of optical projector of still pictures.

magisterial [maj-is-tē'ri-àl] adj of, or suitable for a magistrate; authoritative. —adv **magistē'rially.** —ns **mag'istrate,** a civil officer empowered to administer the law.

magnanimity [mag-na-nim'i-ti] n that quality of mind which raises a person above all that is mean or unjust; generosity of spirit. —adj **magnan'imous.**

magnate [mag'nāt] n a very influential person.

magnet [mag'net] n any piece of iron, steel, or lodestone that has the property of attracting iron or steel; anything that attracts. —adj **magnet'ic.** —adv **magnet'ically.** —vt **mag'netize,** to give magnetic properties to. —ns **mag'netizer; mag'netism,** the property, quality, or condition of being magnetic; the force to which this is due; personal charm.

Magnificat [mag-nif'i-kat] n the song of the Virgin Mary, Luke i 46–55, beginning in the Vulgate with this word.

magnificence [mag-nif'i-sèns] n the quality of being magnificent. —adj **magnif'icent,** splendid, stately, sumptuous, as in form; exalted. —adv **magnif'icently.**

magnify [mag'ni-fī] vt to exaggerate; to increase the apparent size of —pt p **mag'nified.**

magniloquent [mag-nil'o-kwènt] adj speaking in a grand or pompous style. —n **magnil'oquence.**

magnitude [mag'ni-tūd] n greatness of size, extent, etc.; importance.

magnolia [mag-nōl′i-a or -ya] *n* a genus of shrubs and trees with evergreen or deciduous leaves and usu. showy flowers.

magnum [mag′nům] *n* a wine bottle holding about ⅖ of a gallon.

magpie [mag′pī] *n* any of a large number of black and white chattering birds of the crow family.

Magyar [mag′yär or mod′yor] *n* a member of the main ethnic group in Hungary.

Maharajah, Maharaja [mä-hä-rä′jä] *n* in India, a prince; formerly, the ruler of a native state.

mahatma [ma-hat′ma] *n* any of a class of wise and holy persons held in high regard.

mah-jongg [mä-jong′] *n* a game for four players.

mahlstick *see* **maulstick**.

mahogany [ma-hog′a-ni] *n* a tropical American tree; its wood; reddish-brown.

mahout [mä-howt′] *n* the keeper and driver of an elephant.

maid [mād] *n* a maiden; a girl or woman servant. [Shortened from **maiden**.]

maiden [mād′n] *n* a girl or young unmarried woman.—*adj* of or for a maiden; unmarried or virgin; untried; first.—*ns* **maid′enhair**, a fern with fine hairlike stalks; **maid′enhead**, virginity; **maid′enhood**.—*adj* **maid′enly**.

mail[1] [māl] *n* a body armor made of small metal rings or links; a hard enclosing cover of an animal.

mail[2] [māl] *n* letters, packages, etc. transported and delivered by the post office; a postal system.—*adj* of mail.—*vt* to send by mail.—*ns* **mail′box**, a box into which mail is delivered or a box for depositing outgoing mail; **mail′man**, a man who carries and delivers mail.

maim [mām] *vt* to cripple; to mutilate.

main [mān] *n* a principal pipe in a distribution system for water, gas, etc.; the essential point.—*adj* chief in size, importance, etc.; principal; **main′land**, the principal land mass of a continent, as distinguished from nearby islands.—*adv* **main′ly**, chiefly, principally.—*ns* **main′mast** [-mèst, -mast′], the principal mast of a sailing vessel; **main′sail** [-sl, säl′], the principal sail of a vessel, set from the mainmast; **main′spring**, the principal spring in a clock, watch, etc.; the chief incentive, motive, etc.; **main′stay**, the supporting line extending forward from the mainmast; a chief support.

maintain [mān-tān′, mèn-, men-] *vt* to keep in a particular condition; to preserve, continue in; to keep up; to support; to give support to.—*adj* **maintain′able**.—*n* **maintenance** [mān′-tèn-ȧns].

maize [māz] *n* corn; light yellow.

majesty [maj′es-ti] *n* grandeur; **Majesty**, a title used in speaking to or of a sovereign.—*adjs* **majes′tic**.

majolica [ma-jol′i-ka or -yol′-] *n* glazed earthenware esp an Italian decorated ware.

major [mā′jȯr] *adj* greater in size, importance, amount, etc.—*vi* (*education*) to specialize.—*n* an officer ranking just above a captain.—*ns* **major-dōmō**, a head steward; a butler; **majority**, the greater number; the excess of the larger number of votes cast for a candidate in an election; full legal age; the military rank of a major.

make [māk] *vt* to cause to exist, occur, or appear; to build, create, produce, etc.; to prepare for use; to amount to; to have the qualities of; to acquire, earn; to understand; to do, execute; to cause or force; to arrive at, reach.—*n* **make′er**.—*n* **make′shift**, a temporary substitute.—*adj* that will do as a temporary substitute.—*ns* **make′up′**, **make′-up′**, the way something is put together; composition; nature, disposition; the cosmetics, etc. used by an actor; cosmetics generally. **make′weight**, something that is thrown into a scale to make up the weight; something of little value added to supply a deficiency.

mal- [mal-] *prefix* meaning bad or badly, wrong, ill.

malacca [mal-ak′a] *n* a brown walking-cane.

malachite [mal′a-kīt] *n* a mineral that is a green.

malady [mal′a-di] *n* an illness, disease.

malaise [mal′āz, mälez′] *n* a feeling of discomfort or of uneasiness.

malapropism [mal′a-prop-izm] *n* a ludicrous misuse of words.

malaria [ma-lā′ri-a] *n* an infectious disease caused by parasites in the red blood cells.

male [māl] *adj* denoting or of the sex that fertilizes the ovum;

of, like, or suitable for men and boys; masculine.—*n* a male person, animal, or plant.

malice [mal′is] *n* active ill will, intention to harm another.—*adj* **malicious**.—*adv* **malic′iously**.

malign [ma-līn′] *adj* injurious; malignant.—*vt* to speak evil of; to slander.—*adv* **malign′ly**.

malignant [ma-lig′nȧnt] *adj* having an evil influence; wishing evil; causing or likely to cause death.—*ns* **malig′nance**; **malig′nancy**.—*adv* **malig′nantly**.

malinger [ma-ling′gèr] *vi* to feign sickness in order to avoid duty.—*n* **maling′erer**.

mall [möl] *n* a level shaded walk; a public walk; a shop-lined street for pedestrians only; an enclosed shopping center.

mallard [mal′ȧrd] *n* the common wild duck.

malleable [mal′é-abl] *adj* capable of being beaten, rolled, etc., into a new shape; malleabil′ity.

mallet [mal′et] *n* a small short-handled wooden hammer.

mallow [mal′ō] *n* a genus of plants including the hollyhock, cotton, and okra.

malmsey [mäm′zi] *n* the sweetest variety of Madiera wine.

malt [mölt] *n* barley or other grain soaked in water, allowed to sprout, and dried in a kiln.—*vt* to make into malt; to treat or combine with malt.—*vi* to become malt; to make grain into malt.

Malthusian [mal-thū+z′i-ȧn] *adj* of Malthus or his theory that as population increases faster than food production and unless checked by contraception, war, famine, disease, or other disaster, universal poverty is the inevitable result.

mamba [mam′ba] *n* any of several tropical and southern African snakes allied to the cobras.

mammal [mam′ȧl] *n* any member of a class of warm-blooded vertebrates that suckle their young with milk.

mammon [mam′ȯn] *n* riches regarded as an object of worship and greedy pursuit.—*ns* **mamm′onist**.

mammoth [mam′ȯth] *n* any of several extinct elephants.

man [man] *n* a human being esp an adult male; the human race; one having in high degree the qualities considered distinctive of manhood; a husband; an adult male servant or employee; one of the pieces used in chess, checkers. etc.—*vt* to furnish with men for work, defense, etc.; to brace (oneself for an ordeal).—*adj* **man′ful**.—*ns* **man′hole**, a hole through which one can enter a sewer, conduit, etc.; **man′hood**, the state or time of being a man; virility, courage, etc.; men collectively; **man jack**, individual man (*every man jack*); **man′kind′**, the human race; men as distinguished from women.—*adjs* **man′ly**, appropriate in character to a man; strong; virile; **man′-made**, manufactured or created by man, esp. synthetic fibers; **manned**; **man′power**, power furnished by human strength; the collective availability for work of people in a given area, nation, etc., **man′slaughter**, the killing of a human being by another, esp. when unlawful but without malice.

manacle [man′á-kl] *n* a handcuff (usu. *pl*)—*vt* to handcuff; to restrain.

manage [man′ij] *vt* to control the movement or behavior of; to have charge of; to direct; to succeed in accomplishing.—*vi* to carry on business; to contrive to get along.—*adj* **man′ageable**, that can be managed; submitting to control.—*n* **man′ageableness**.—*ns* **man′agement**, art or act of managing; manner of directing or of using anything; a body of managers; **man′ager**.—*adjs* **managerial**, of, pertaining to, management, a manager; **man′aging**, controlling; administering; domineering.

manana [man-yän′à] *n* tomorrow or an indefinite future time.

manatee [man-a-tē′] *n* a genus of large, plant-eating aquatic mammals of tropical waters.

mandarin [man′da-rin] *n* formerly, a high-ranking bureaucrat of the Chinese empire; the fruit of a small, spiny Chinese tree which has been developed in cultivation.—Also **tangerine**.

mandate [man′dāt] *n* an order or command; formerly, a League of Nations' commission to a country to administer some region; the will of constituents expressed to their representatives in legislatures.—*n* **man′datory**, the holder of a mandate.

mandible [man′di-bl] *n* the lower jaw of a vertebrate; either jaw of a beaked animal; *adj* **mandib′ular**.

mandolin, mandoline [man'do-lin] *n* a round backed instrument like a guitar.

mandragora *same as* **mandrake**.

mandrake [man'drāk] *n* a poisonous plant of the nightshade family.

mandrel, mandril [man'drěl] *n* blunted steel cone fitted to a lathe center by which articles are secured while they are being turned.

mandrill [man'dril] *n* a large fierce gregarious west African baboon.

mane [mān] *n* long hair on the back of the neck of the horse, lion etc.

maneuver [ma-nōō'vėr] *n* a planned and controlled movement of troops, warships, etc.; a skillful or shrewd move; a stratagem.—*vti* to perform or cause to perform maneuvers.—*adj* **maneu'vrable**.

mange *see* **mangy**.

mangel-wurzel [mang'gl-wûr'zl] *n* a variety of beet cultivated as cattle food.

manger [mānj'ėr] *n* a trough in which hay, etc. is laid for horses and cattle.

mangle[1] [mang'gl] *vt* to mutilate by roughly cutting, tearing, crushing, etc.; to spoil, botch, mar.

mangle[2] [mang'gl] *n* a machine for ironing sheets, etc. between rollers.—*vt* to smooth with a mangle.

mango [mang'gō] *n* the yellow-red fleshy fruit with a firm central stone.—*pl* **mang'oes**.

mangrove [mang'grōv] *n* a genus of trees that throw out root-forming branches.

mangy [mānj'i] *adj* affected with mange; shabby, seedy.—*ns*

mange [mānj], a skin disease of mammals, causing itching, hair loss, etc. transmitted by a minute parasite mite; **mang'iness**.

mania [mā'ni-a] *n* violent madness; excessive or unreasonable desire, excitement, or enthusiasm.—*adj* **ma'nic**.—*n* **mā'niac**, a person affected with mania; a madman.—*adj* **maniacal** [mā-nī'a-kl].

manicure [man'i-kūr] *n* trimming, polishing, etc. of fingernails and removing dead cuticle.—*vt* to do manicure work; to trim closely and evenly, as a lawn.—*n* **man'icurist**.

manifest [man'i-fest] *adj* that may be easily seen by the eye or perceived by the mind.—*vt* to show plainly; to reveal.—*n* an itemized list of a ships cargo; a list of passengers on an aircraft.—*n* **manifestā'tion**.

manifesto [man-i-fest'ō] *n* a public written declaration of intentions by an important person or group.

manifold [man'i-fōld] *adj* having many forms, parts, etc.; of many sorts.—*n* a pipe with many outlets.—*vti* to make copies of, as with carbon paper.—*adv* many times; a great deal.

manikin, mannikin [man'i-kin] *n* a mannequin.

manipulate [ma-nip'ū-lāt] *vt* to work or handle skillfully; to manage shrewdly or artfully, often in an unfair way.—*n* **manipulā'tion**.—*adjs* **manip'ulative**.—*n* **manip'ulator**.

manna [man'a] *n* the food of the Israelites in the wilderness; any help that comes unexpectedly.

mannequin [man'i-kin] *n* a dummy figure; a person employed to wear and display clothes.

manner [man'er] *n* the way in which anything is done; personal style of acting or deportment; distinguished deportment; style of writing, etc.; habit; (*pl*) morals, social customs; (*pl*) breeding, social conduct esp good.—*n* **mann'erism**, a peculiarity of style or manner in art, literature, etc., carried to excess.—*adj* **mann'erly**.

manor [man'ór] *n* in England, a landed estate; the main house on such an estate.—*adj* **manorial**.

mansion [man'sh(ó)n] *n* a large, imposing house.

mantel [man'tl] *n* the facing about a fireplace, including a projecting shelf; the ornamental shelf over a fireplace.—Also **man'telpiece, man'telshelf**.

mantilla [man-til'a] *n* a woman's scarf, as of lace covering the head and shoulders.

mantis [man'tis] *n* a genus of orthopterous insects, carrying their large spinous forelegs in the attitude of prayer.

mantle [man'tl] *n* a cloak or loose outer garment; anything that envelops or conceals; a small hood which when placed over a flame becomes white-hot and gives off light.—*vt* to cover as with a mantle.—*vi* to be or become covered; to blush or flush.

manual [man'ū-ál] *adj* of the hand; done, worked, or used by the hand; involving skill or hard work with the hands.—*n* a handy book for use as a guide, reference, etc.; prescribed drill in the handling of a weapon; a keyboard for the hands esp of an organ or harpsichord having several keyboards.

manufacture [man-ū-fak-chùr] *vt* to make, esp by machinery and on a large scale; to fabricate, concoct.—*n* the process of manufacturing; anything manufactured.—*n* **manufact'ory**, a place where goods are manufactured.—*n* **manufact'urer**, one who manufactures.

manumit [man-ū-mit'] *vt* to release from slavery; to set free.—*n* **manumission**.

manure [man-ūr'] *vt* to enrich with any fertilizing substance.—*n* any substance applied to land to make it more fruitful.

manuscript [man'ū-skript] *adj* written by hand or type written.—*n* book, etc. as submitted to a publisher.

Manx [mangks] *n* the language of the Isle of Man.

many [men'i] *adj* (comparative **more**, superlative **most**) numerous.—*n* a large number of persons or things.

Maori [mow'ri] *n* any of the Polynesians native to New Zealand; their language.—Also *adj*.

map [map] *n* a representation of all or part of the earth's surface, showing either natural features as continents and seas, etc. or manmade features as roads, railroad stations, parks, buildings, etc.; *vt* to make a map of.

maple [mā'pl] *n* any of a genus of trees with two-winged fruits, grown for shade, wood, or sap.

maquis [mä'kē] *n* a thicket formation of shrubs, esp along the Mediterranean coast.

mar [mär] *vt* to spoil, to impair, to injure.

marabou, marabout [mar'a-bōō] *n* a large African stork.

marathon [mar'a-thon] *n* a foot race of 26 miles, 385 yards; any endurance contest.

maraud [ma-röd'] *vi* to rove in quest of plunder.—*n* **maraud'er**.

marble [mär'bl] *n* any limestone taking a high polish; a slab, work of art, or other object made of marble; a little ball of stone, glass, etc; (*pl*) a children's game played with such balls.—*adj* of or like marble.

marc [märc] *n* remains of grapes etc. that have been pressed for wine-making; brandy distilled from these.

marcel [mär-sel'] *n* a deep soft wave in the hair made by using a heated curling iron. Also *vt*.

March[1] [märch] *n* the third month of the year having 31 days.

march[2] [märch] *n* a boundary; border; a frontier.

march[3] [märch] *vi* to walk with regular steps, as in military formation; to advance steadily.—*vt* to cause to march.—*n* a marching; a steady advance; a regular, steady step; the distance covered in marching; a piece of music for marching.

marchioness [mär'shòn-es] *n* the wife or widow of a marquess; a lady of the rank of a marquess.

mare [mār] *n* a mature female horse, mule, donkey.

margarine [mär'jàr-ēn] *n* a butter substitute made from vegetable oils and fats, etc.

margin [mär'jin] *n* a border, edge; the blank border of a printed or written page; an amount beyond what is needed; provision for increase, error, etc.—*adj* **mar'ginal**.—*adv* **mar'ginally**.

marigold [mar'i-gōld] *n* a yellow-flowered composite or its flower.

marimba [ma-rim'bá] *n* a kind of xylophone.

marina [mà-rēn'á] *n* a small harbor with docks, services, etc. for pleasure craft.

marinade [mar'i-nād] *n* a savory usu acidic solution in which meat, fish, etc. is soaked to enhance flavor or to tenderize it before cooking.—*vt* to marinate.

marine [ma-ren] *adj* of, in, near, or belonging to the sea; maritime; nautical; naval.—*n* a soldier trained for service at sea; naval or merchant ships.

Mariolatry [mä-ri-ol'a-tri] *n* excessive veneration of the Virgin Mary.

marionette [mar-i-o-net'] *n* a little jointed doll moved by strings or wires.

marital [mar'i-tàl] *adj* of marriage, matrimonial.

maritime [mar'i-tīm] *adj* on, near, or living near the sea; of navigation, shipping, etc.

marjoram [mär'jo-rȧm] *n* any of various fragrant mints used in cooking.

mark¹ [märk] *n* a spot, scratch, etc. on a surface; a printed or written symbol, as a punctuation mark; a brand or label on an article showing the maker, etc.; an indication of some quality, character, etc.; a standard of quality; impression, influence, etc.; *vt* to make a mark or marks on; to identify as by a mark; to show plainly; to set off, characterize; to grade, rate.— *adj* **marked** [märkt], having a mark or marks; noticeable; obvious.—*adv* **mark'edly.**—*ns* **mark'er,** one that marks; something used for marking; **marks'man,** one who shoots, esp one who shoots well.

mark² [märk] *n* a unit of money in Germany.

market [mär'ket] *n* a meeting of people for buying and selling; the people at such a meeting; space or building in which provisions, cattle, etc. are shown for sale; the chance to sell or buy; demand for; region where goods can be sold.—*vt* to offer for sale; to sell.—*vi* to buy provisions.—*adj* **marketable.**

marl [märl] *n* a limy clay often used as a soil conditioner; manure.—*vt* to dress (land) with marl.

marline, marlin [mär'lin] *n* a small rope for winding round a larger one to keep it from wearing.—*n* **mar'linespike,** a spike for separating the strands of a rope.

marmalade [mär'mȧ-lād] *n* a jamlike preserve made of oranges.

marmoreal [mär-mōr'e-ȧl, -môr'-] *adj* of, or like, marble or a marble statue.

marmoset [mär'mō-set, -zėt] *n* any of numerous small monkeys of South and Central America.

marmot [mär'mot] *n* a genus of stout burrowing rodents esp hoary marmot.

maroon¹ [ma-rōōn'] *n* a dark brownish red.

maroon² [ma-rōōn'] *n* a marooned person; **Maroon,** a fugitive Negro slave.

marquee [mär-kē'] *n* a rooflike projection over an entrance, as to a theater; a large tent.

marquetry, marqueterie [märk'et-ri] *n* decorative inlaid work, as in furniture.

marquess, marquis [mär'kwis] *n* a British title of nobility next below that of a duke.

marriage [mar'ij] *n* the ceremony, act, or contract by which a man and woman become husband and wife; a wedding; a close union.

marrow [mar'ō] *n* the soft tissue in the hollow parts of the bones; the essence or best part of anything; **marrowfat,** any of several wrinkle-seeded garden peas.—*adj* **marr'owy.**

marry [mar'i] *vt* to join as husband and wife; to take for husband or wife; to unite.—*vi* to get married.

Mars [märz] *n* the Roman god of war; the planet conspicuous for the redness of its light.

marsh [märsh] *n* a tract of soft wet land.—**marshmall'ow,** a pink flowered perennial used in confectionery and in medicine; **marsh marigold,** a swamp herb of the buttercup family.—*adj* **marsh'y.**

marshal, marshall [mär'shȧl] *n* an official in charge of ceremonies, parades, etc.—*vt* to arrange (ideas, troops, etc.) in order; to guide.

marsupial [mär-sū'pi-ȧl] *adj* of an order of mammals that carry their young in a pouch.—*n* an animal of this kind, as an opossum.

mart [märt] *n* a market.

marten [mär'tėn] *n* any of several mammals allied to the weasel, valued for their fur.

martial [mär'shȧl] *adj* of or belonging to war; warlike; bold; military.—*adv* **mar'tially.**

martin [mär'tin] *n* a small European swallow.

martinet [mär-ti-net' or mär'-] *n* a strict disciplinarian.

martingale [mär'tin-gȧl, -gal] *n* a strap fastened to a horse's girth, so as to keep his head down; a short spar under the bowsprit.

martyr [mär'tėr] *n* one who by his death bears witness to his belief; one who suffers for his belief; a chronic sufferer from a disease.—*vt* to put to death for his belief; to inflict suffering on.—*ns* **mar'tyrdom; martyrol'ogy,** a history of martyrs.

marvel [mär'vėl] *n* anything astonishing or wonderful.—*vti* to become full of wonder.—*adj* **mar'velous.**

Marxism [märks'izm] *n* the system of thought developed by Karl Marx and Friedrich Engels advocating public ownership of the means of production and the dictatorship of the proletariat until the establishment of a classless society.—*adj, n* **Marxist.**

marzipan [mär-zi-pan'] *n* a pastry confection of ground almonds, sugar, and egg white.

mascara [mas-kä'rä] *n* a cosmetic for coloring the eyelashes.

mascot [mas'kot] *n* a person, creature, or thing supposed to bring good luck.

masculine [mas'kū-lin] *adj* characteristic of, peculiar to, or appropriate to, a man or the male sex; (*gram*) of that gender to which belongs words denoting males.—*n* **masculin'ity.**

mash [mash] *n* in brewing, a mixture of crushed malt and hot water; a mixture, as of bran with meal beaten and stirred as food for animals; any soft mass.—*vt* to make into a mash; to crush or injure.

mask [mȧsk] *n* a covering to conceal or protect the face; anything that conceals or disguises.—*vt* to cover or conceal with a mask.

masochism [maz'o-kizm] *n* abnormal pleasure obtained from the suffering of physical or mental pain.

mason [mā'sn] *n* one who cuts, prepares, and lays stones; a builder in stone; a Freemason.—*adj* **Masonic** [ma-son'ik] relating to Freemasonry.—*n* **ma'sonry,** work executed by mason, stonework.

masque [mȧsk] *n* a masked ball.

masquerade [mȧsk-ėr-ād] *n* a ball or party at which fancy dress and masks are worn.

mass [mas] *n* a quantity of matter of indefinite shape and size; a large quantity or number; bulk; size; the main part.—*adj* **mass'ive** [-iv], forming or consisting of a large mass; big and solid; large and imposing.

Mass [mass] *n* the celebration of the Eucharist in RC churches.

massacre [mas'ak-ėr] *n* the indiscriminate cruel killing of many people or animals.—*vt* to kill in large numbers.

massage [ma-säzh] *n* a kneading and rubbing of the muscles to stimulate the circulation of the blood and make them work better.—*vt* to give a massage to.—*ns* **masseur** [-ėr'], **masseuse** [-œz'].

massif [ma-sēf', mas'if] *n* a principal mountain mass.

mast¹ [mȧst] *n* a tall vertical spar used to support the sails, yards, etc. on a ship; a vertical pole.

mast² [mȧst] *n* nuts (as acorns and beechnuts) accumulated on the forest floor.

master [mȧs'tėr] *n* a man who rules others or has control over something, esp the head of a household; an employer; an owner; the captain of a merchant ship; a male teacher in a private school; an expert craftsman; a writer or painter regarded as great; an original from which a copy can be made, esp a phonograph record or magnetic tape.—*adj* **mas'terful,** acting the part of a master; domineering; expert; skillful.—*adj* **mas'terly,** expert; skillful.—*adv* in a masterly manner.— **mas'termind,** a very clever person; **mas'terpiece',** a work done with extraordinary skill; the greatest work of a person or group; **mastery,** control as by a master; ascendancy or victory.

mastic [mas'tik] *n* an aromatic resin from mastic trees used chiefly in varnishes.

mastiff [mas'tif] *n* a thick-set and powerful breed of dog, used as watchdogs.

mastodon [mas'to-don] *n* a genus of extinct elephants.

mastoid [mas'toid] *n* the bony prominence behind the ear.

mat¹ [mat] *n* a piece of fabric of woven rushes, straw, coarse fiber, etc.; anything interwoven or tangled into a thick mass.—*vti* to cover as with a mat; to interweave or tangle in a thick mass.

mat² matt, matte [mat] *adj* having a dull surface.

matador [mat'a-dör] *n* the bullfighter who kills the bull with a sword.

match¹ [mach] *n* a short stick of wood or other material tipped with an easily ignited material.—**match'lock,** (*hist*) the lock of a musket containing a match for firing it; **match'wood,** splinters.

match² [mach] *n* any person or thing equal or similar to another; two persons or things that go well together; a contest or game; a mating or marriage.—*vt* to join in marriage; to put in opposition (with, against); to be equal or similar to; to suit one thing) to another.—*vi* to be equal, similar, suitable, etc.—*adj* **match'less**, having no equal.

ate¹ [māt] *n* a companion; a fellow worker; one of a matched pair; a husband or wife; the male or female of paired animals; an officer of a merchant ship, ranking below the captain.—*vti* to join as a pair; to couple in marriage or sexual union.

ate² [māt] *vt* to checkmate.

aterial [ma-tē'ri-ål] *adj* of matter; physical; of the body or bodily needs, comfort, etc.; not spiritual; important, essential, etc.—*n* what a thing is, or may be made of; elements or parts; cloth; fabric.—*ns* **materializa'tion; mate'rialism**, the doctrine that everything in the world, including thought, can be explained only in terms of matter; **mate'rialist**. *Also adj*. - *adj* **materialist'ic**.—*adv* **mate'rially**, physically; to a great extent; substantially.

ateria medica [må-tē'ri-a med'i-ka] (the science of) the substances used as remedies in medicine.

aternal [ma-tûr'nål] *adj* of, like, or from a mother; related through the mother's side of the family—*adv* **mater'nally**.—*n* **mater'nity**, the state, character, or relation of a mother.

athematical, mathematic [math-ê-mat'ik, -ål] *adj* of, like or concerned with mathematics; very accurate and precise.—*adv* **mathemat'ically**.—*ns* **mathematician** [-ish'ån]; **mathemat'ics**, the science dealing with quantities, forms, etc.

atinee, matinée [mat'i-nā], an afternoon performance of a play, etc.

atriarchy [mā'tri-är-ki] *n* form of social organization in which the mother is the ruler of the family or tribe and in which descent is traced through the mother.—*n* **mā'triarch**, a woman who is head and ruler of her family and descendants.—*adj* **matria'rchal**.

atricide [mat'ri-sīd] *n* one who murders his (her) own mother; the murder of one's own mother.

atriculate [ma-trik'ū-lāt] *vti* to enroll, esp as a student.—*n* **matricula'tion**.

atrimony [mat'ri-mòn-i] *n* the act or rite of marriage.—*adj* **matrimonial** [-mō'ni-ål].

atrix [mā'triks, or mat'riks] *n*; the cavity in which anything is formed; that in which anything is embedded; a mould.

atron [mā'tròn] *n* a wife or widow, esp one of mature appearance and manner; a woman in charge of nursing and domestic arrangements in a hospital, school, or other institution.

att *see* mat (2).

atter [mat'ér] *n* what a thing is made of; material; whatever occupies space and is perceptible to the senses; any specified substance; content of thought or expression; a quantity; a thing or affair; significance; trouble, difficulty; pus; mail.—*vi* to be of importance; to form pus.

attock [mat'ók] *n* a kind of pickax for loosening the soil, digging out roots, etc.

attress [mat'res] *n* a casing of strong cloth filled with cotton, foam rubber, coiled springs, etc., used on a bed.

ature [ma-tūr'] *adj* fully developed, ripe.—*vt* to bring ripeness, full development or perfection.—*vi* to become ripe; **matur'ity**.

atutinal [ma-tūt'i-nål] *adj* of, relating to, or occurring in the morning; early.

audlin [môd'lin] *adj* foolishly sentimental.

aul [môl] *n* a heavy hammer for driving stakes.—*vt* to bruise or lacerate; to handle roughly.

aulstick [môl'stik] *n* a long stick used by painters etc., as a support for the wrist.—*Also* **mahl'stick**.

aunder [mön'dèr] *vi* to talk or move in a confused or aimless way.

Maundy Thursday [mön'di thûrz'dā] the day before Good Friday.

ausoleum [mô-sô-lē'um] *n* a magnificent tomb.

auve [mōv, möv] *n* any of several shades of pale purple.—*adj* of this color.

aw [mö] *n* the throat, gullet, jaws or oral cavity of a voracious animal; something like a gaping maw.

awkish [mök'ish] *adj* insipid; sickly sentimental.

axilla [maks-il'a] *n* the upper jawbone in vertebrates.—*adj* **maxillary**.

axim [maks'im] *n* a concise rule of conduct; a precept.

aximum [maks'i-mum] *n* the greatest quantity, number, etc.—*adj* highest; greatest possible reached.—*pl* **max'ima.**—*adj* **maximal**.

may [mā] *verbal auxiliary expressing*: possibility; permission; wish or hope.

May [mā] *n* the fifth month of the year, having 31 days; may, the hawthorn or its blossom; spring-blooming spirea; **may'fly'**, any of an order (Ephemeroptera) of short-lived insects; ephemerid.

mayonnaise [mā'òn-āz'] *n* a salad dressing composed of the yolk of eggs, olive-oil, and vinegar or lemon-juice, seasoned.

mayor [mā'ór, mār] *n* the chief administrative officer of a municipality.—*ns* **may'oralty**, the office or term of office of a mayor.

maze [māz] *n* a confusing, intricate network of pathways; a confused state.—*vt* to bewilder.

mazurka [ma-zōōr'ka, or -zûr'-] *n* a lively Polish dance; a piece of music for it in triple time.

me [mē] *personal pron* the objective case of I.

mead¹ [mēd] *n* an alcoholic liquor made from fermented honey.

mead² [mēd] *n* (*poetic*) meadow.

meadow [med'ō] *n* a piece of land where grass is grown for hay; low, level, moist grassland.—*vt* to make a meadow of; **meadow saffron**, colchicum; **meadowsweet**, a tall shrub with purplish-red nearly smooth stems and flowers in.

meager, meagre [mē'gèr] *adj* lean; poor in quality; scanty, deficient in quantity.—*adv* **mea'gerly**.

meal¹ [mēl] *n* any of the times for eating, as lunch, dinner, etc.; the food served at such a time.

meal² [mēl] *n* any edible grain coarsely ground; any substance similarly ground.—*adj* **meal'y**.—*n* **meal'iness**.

mean¹ [mēn] *adj* low in quality or value; inferior; shabby; contemptibly selfish, bad-tempered, etc.; stingy.—*adv* **mean'ly**.—*n* **mean'ness**.

mean² [mēn] *adj* halfway between extremes; average.—*n* what is between extremes.—*advs* **mean'time, mean'while**, in or during the intervening time; at the same time.—*n* the intervening time.

mean³ [mēn] *vt* to have in mind; to intend; to intend to express; to signify.—*vi* to have a (specified) degree of importance, effect.—*n* **mean'ing**.

meander [mē-an'dèr] *n* a winding path esp a labyrinth; a winding of a stream or river.—*adjs* **mean'dering**.

measles [mē'zlz] *n* an acute, contagious virus disease, characterized by small red spots.

measure [mezh'úr] *n* the extent, dimension, capacity, etc. of anything; a determining of this, measurement; a unit of measurement; any standard of valuation; an instrument for measuring; a course of action; a statute, law; a rhythmical unit.—*vt* to find out the extent, dimensions, etc. of, esp by a standard; to mark off by measuring; to be a measure of.—*vi*; to be of specified measurements.—*adj* **meas'urable, meas'ured.**—*n* **meas'urement**.

meat [mēt] *n* anything eaten as food; the flesh of animals used as food.—*adj* **meat'y**, full of meat; substantial.

Mecca [mek'a] *n* the birthplace of Mohammed.

mechanic [me-kan'ik] *adj* of or relating to manual work or skill; of the nature of or resembling a machine.—*n* a manual worker; a machinist.—*adj* **mechan'ical**, having to do with machinery or tools; of the science of mechanics.—*adv* **mechan'ically**.—*ns* **mechanician, mechan'ics**, the science of motion and the action of forces on bodies.—*vt* **mech'anize**, *ns* **mech'anism**, the working parts of a machine.

Mechlin [mek'lin] *n* a delicate bobbin lace used for trimming clothing.

medal [med'ål] *n* a small, flat piece of inscribed metal, commemorating some event or awarded for some distinction; a disk bearing a religious symbol.—*adj* **medallic** [me-dal'ik], of or shown on a medal.—*ns* **medallion** [mè-dal'yòn], a large medal; **med'alist**, one awarded a medal.

meddle [med'l] *vi* to interfere in another's affairs.—*n* **medd'ler**.—*adj* **medd'lesome**.

medial [mē'di-ål] *adj* middle; ordinary.—*adj* **mē'dian**, middle; intermediate.

mediate [mē'di-àt] *adj* occupying a middle position; showing indirect causation or relation.—*vi* [-āt'] to be in an intermediate position.—*n* **mē'diator**.

medicament [med-ik′á-ment] *n* any substance used in curative treatment.

medicate [med′i-kāt] *vt* to treat with medicine.

medicine [med′sin, -sn] *n* any substance used for the treatment or prevention of disease.

medieval, mediaevel [med-i-ē′val] *adj* of the Middle Ages.—*ns* **medie′valist, mediae′valist,** a specialist in medieval history and culture.

mediocre [mē′di-ō′kèr] *adj* of middling goodness, ability, etc.; inferior.—*n* **mediocrity** [-ok′-].

meditate [med′i-tāt] *vi* to consider thoughtfully; to engage in contemplation, esp religious.—*vt* to consider deeply; to intend.—*n* **medita′tion.**

medium [mē′di-um] *n* the middle condition or degree; any intervening means, instrument, or agency; a substance through which any effect is transmitted; in spiritualism, the person through whom spirits are said to communicate with the material world.—*pl* **mē′dia,** or **mē′diums.**

medlar [med′lár] *n* a small tree akin to the apple; its fruit.

medley [med′li] *n* a miscellany; a musical piece made up of various tunes or passages.

medullary [me-dul′ár-i] *adj* consisting of, or resembling, marrow or pith.

medusa [me-dū′za] *n* a small hydrozoan jellyfish.

meek [mēk] *adj* mild and gentle of temper, submissive.—*adv* **meek′ly.**—*n* **meek′ness.**

meerschaum [mēr′shám] *n* a fine light whitish clay; a tobacco pipe made of it.

meet[1] [mēt] *adj* precisely suitable; proper.—*adv* **meet′ly.**

meet[2] [mēt] *vt* to come face to face with; to contend with, deal with; to experience.—*vi* to come together; to assemble; to be introduced; to have an encounter.—*ns* **meet′ing,** a coming together; an assembly.

mega- [mega′a-], **meg-,** [meg′-], in composition, great.

megalith [meg′a-lith] *n* a huge stone.

megalomania [meg-a-lō-mā′ni-a] *n* the delusion that one is great or powerful.

megaphone [meg′a-fōn] *n* a device for causing sounds to be heard better and at a greater distance.

megrim [mē′grim] *n* a migraine; vertigo.

meiosis [mī-ō′sis] *n* understatement, as a figure of speech.—*adj* **meiot′ic.**

melancholy [mel′án-kol-i, -kól-i] *n* depression of spirits, dejection; sadness.—*adj* depressed; depressing.—*n* **melanchō′lia,** a mental state characterized by dejection and often with delusions.—*adj* **melancholic** [-kol′ik].

mélange [mā-lāzh′] *n* a mixture; a medley.

melanin [mel′á-nin] *n* a dark brown pigment found in animals and plants.—*ns* **mel′anism,** an increased amount of melanin (as of skin, hair, feathers).

melee, mêlée [mel′ā] *n* a confused conflict between opposing parties.

meliorate [mē′li-ó-rāt] *vt* to make better.—*vi* to grow better.—*n* **meliorā′tion.**

mellifluous [mel-if′lōō-us] *adj* honey-producing; sweet as honey (eg of voice, words).

mellow [mel′ō] *adj* soft and ripe (of fruit); well matured.—*vt* to soften by ripeness or by age; to mature.—*vi* to become soft; to be matured.

melodrama [mel′ō-drä-ma] *n* a kind of sensational drama.—*adj* **melodramatic** [-at′ik].

melody [mel′o-di] *n* an air of tune; sweet music; tunefulness; the tune in harmonised music.—*n* **melō′dious,** **mel′odist.**

melon [mel′ón] *n* the large, juicy many-seeded fruit of trailing plants, as the watermelon, cantaloupe.

melt [melt] *vti* to become liquid; to dissolve; to dwindle or cause to dwindle away; to soften or to be softened emotionally.—*ns* **melt′down′,** the melting of the fuel core of a nuclear reactor; the drastic collapse of almost anything.

member [mem′bér] *n* a limb of an animal; one of a soceity; a representative in a legislative body.—*n* **mem′bership.**

membrane [mem′brān, -brin] *n* a thin flexible solid sheet or film, esp of animal or vegetable origin.

memento [me-men′tō] *n* a reminder esp a souvenir.

memoir [mem′wär, -wör] *n* (*pl*) record of events intended as material for history or biography; a biographical sketch.

memory [mem′ó-ri] *n* the power of retaining and reproducing

mental or sensory impressions; an impression so reproduce a having or keeping in the mind; time within which pa things can be remembered; commemoration; remembranc of computers, a store.—*adj* **mem′orable,** deserving to remembered; remarkable.—*adv* **mem′orably.**—*adj* **mem** ō′rial, serving or intended, to preserve the memory of an thing; pertaining to memory.—*n* that which serves to keep remembrance; a monument.—*vt* **memō′rialize,** to present memorial to; to petition by a memorial.—*n* **memō′rialist.**— **mem′orize,** to commit to memory.

menace [men′às] *n* a threat.—*vt* to threaten.

ménage [mā-näzh′] *n* a household; the management of a house

menagerie [men-aj′èr-i] *n* a place for keeping wild animals fe exhibition; a collection of such animals.

mend [mend] *vt* to repair; to correct, improve (one's way manners).—*vi* to grow better.

mendacious [men-dā′shùs] *adj* lying, untruthful.—*adv* **me** dā′ciously.—*n* **mendacity** [-das′i-ti].

mendicant [men′di-kánt] *adj* begging.—*n* a beggar.—*ns* **men** **dicancy, mendicity** [-dis′i-ti].

menial [mē′ni-ál] *adj* servile, humiliating.—*n* a domestic se vant; one performing servile work.

meningitis [men-in-jī′tis] *n* inflammation of the membran enveloping the brain or spinal cord.

meniscus [men-is′kus] *n* a crescent-shaped figure; a le convex on the one side and concave on the other.

menopause [men-ō-pöz] *n* permanent end of menstruation.

menses [men′sēz] *n pl* the monthly discharge from the uterus.

mensurable [men′sh(y)ùr-â-bl, or -sūr-, -shür-] *adj* measu able.—*n* **mensurā′tion,** the act or art of finding by measur ment and calculation the length, area, volume, etc., of bodies

mental [men′tàl] *adj* of, or relating to the kind; of, relating t or affected with a disorder of the mind.—*n* **mentality** [-tal′ ti].—*adv* **men′tally.**

menthol [men′thol] *n* an alcohol obtained from oil of peppe mint.

mention [men′sh(ó)n] *n* a brief notice; a casual introductic into speech or writing.—*vt* to notice briefly; to remark; name.—*adj* **men′tionable.**

mentor [men′tór] *n* a wise counsellor.

menu [men′ū, mè′nū] *n* the bill of fare.

mephitis [me-fī′tis] *n* a poisonous exhalation; a foul stink.-*adjs* **mephitic** [-fit′-], -al.

mercantile [mûr′kàn-tīl] *adj* of merchants or trade.

mercenary [mûr′sèn-âr-i] *adj* working or done for mone only.—*n* a soldier hired into foreign service.

mercerize [mûr′sèr-īz] *vt* to treat cotton.

merchant [mûr′chánt] *n* a trader; a shopkeeper.—*adj* comme cial.—*ns* **mer′chandise, merchandize** [-dīz], goods bough and sold for gain; **mer′chantman,** a trading-ship.

Mercury [mûr′kū-ri] *n* a Roman god who was the messenger the gods; the smallest planet in the solar system and neares the sun; **mercury,** a silvery, liquid metallic element; quicks ver.—*adj* **mercū′rial,** having the qualities of quicksilve active, volatile in temperament; etc.

mercy [mûr′si] *n* forbearance towards one who is in one power; a forgiving disposition; clemency; compassion for th unfortunate.—*adj* **mer′ciful.**—*adj* **mer′ciless,** withou mercy.

mere[1] [mēr] *n* a pool or lake.

mere[2] [mēr] *adj* only what the noun indicates and nothin else.—*adj* **mere′ly,** simply; solely.

meretricious [mer-è-trish′ús] *adj* flashy; gaudy or showi attractive (of dress, literary style, etc.).

merganser [mer-gan′sèr] *n* a large, fish-eating diving duck of America.

merge [mûrj] *vti* to cause to lose identity by being absorbed; unite.—*n* **mer′ger.**

meridian [me-rid′i-àn] *n* an imaginary circle on the earth surface passing through the poles and any given place.

meringue [mè-rang′] *n* a dessert topping made of a mixture o sugar and white of eggs.

merino [mè-rē′nō] *n* a breed of sheep with fine silky wool; th wool; yarn or cloth made from it.

merit [mer′it] *n* excellence that deserves honor or reward; th which one deserves; worth value; (*pl*) rights and wrongs (of case).—*vt* to deserve as reward or punishment.—*adj* **mer**

ŏ′rious, deserving (in a moderate degree) of reward, honor, or praise.

erle, merl [mûrl] n the blackbird.

erlin [mûr′lin] n a species of small falcon.

ermaid [mûr′mād] n in legend, a woman with a fish's tail.

erry [mer′i] adj pleasant; cheerful, noisily gay; causing laughter; lively. — adv merrily. — ns merr′iment.

esa [mā′sä] n a high plateau with steep sides.

esh [mesh] n an opening between the threads of a net, wires of a screen, etc. — vt to catch in a net, ensnare.

esmerize [mez′mèr-īz] vt to hypnotize; (loosely) to fascinate, dominate the will or fix the attention of. — adjs mesmeric. — nes′merist.

ess [mes] n a serving, as of porridge; a number of persons who take their meals together regularly; a dish of soft, pulpy or liquid stuff; disorder, confusion. — vt to supply with a mess; to make a mess of; to muddle. — vi to belong to a mess, eat one's meals; to potter. — adj mess′y, involving or causing dirt or mess; confused, disordered.

essage [mes′ij] n any communication, oral or written, from one person to another; the chief idea that the writer, artist, etc. seeks to communicate in a work messenger, one who carries messages or a message.

Messiah [me-sī′a] n the anointed one, the Christ—also Messī′as. — adj Messianic [mes-i-an′ik].

essieurs [mes-yø] pl of Monsieur

et(a)- [met(-ȧ)-] in composition, among with; after, later; often implies change; beyond.

etabolism [met-ab′ol-izm] n the process in organisms by which protoplasm is formed by food and broken down into waste matter, with release of energy. — adj metabol′ic.

etal [met′l] n any of a class of chemical elements having a peculiar luster and possessing fusibility, conductivity for heat and electricity, etc., such as gold, iron, copper, etc.; any alloy of such elements as brass, bronze et.;anything consisting of metal. — adjs met′alled; metallic [mè-tal′ik], consisting of a metal; like a metal.

etallurgy [met′a′l-ûr-ji] n the science of separating metals from their ores and preparing them for use by smelting, refining, etc.

etamorphosis [met-a-mör′fos-is] n transformation; change of form, structure, substance, appearance, character, etc., by natural development. — adj metamor′phic, showing or relating to, change of form.

etaphor [met′a-fôr] n a figure of speech by which a thing is spoken of as being that which it resembles, not fundamentally, but only in a certain marked characteristic, or marked characteristics.

etaphysics [met-a-fiz′iks] n the branch of philosophy that seeks to explain the nature of being and reality; speculative philosophy in general.

etathesis [met-ath′è-sis] n transposition or exchange of places, esp between the sounds or letters of a word.

ete [mēt] vt to allot; to portion (out).

etempsychosis [met-emp-si-kō′sis] n transmigration of the soul.

eteor [mĕtyòr] n a small particle of matter traveling through space, revealed to observation when it enters the earth's atmosphere, friction causing it to glow. — adj meteoric [mĕ-tè-or′ik]. — n mĕ′teorite, a meteor, that has reached the ground without being completely vaporized. — n mĕteor-ol′ogy, a study of weather and climate.

eter¹ [mĕ′ter] n rhythmic pattern in verse, the measured arrangement of syllables according to stress; rhythmic pattern in music. — adj met′ric, met′rical of, relating to, or composed in meter.

eter² [mĕ′ter] n the basic unit of length in the metric system, equal to 39.37 inches. met′ric, met′rical, based on the meter as a standard of measurement; of, relating to, or using the metric system.

eter³ [mĕ′tèr] n an apparatus for measuring and recording the quantity of gas, water, etc.

ethane [mĕth′ān] n a colorless, odorless flammable gas formed by the decomposition of vegetable matter, as in marshes.

ethod [meth′ód] n the mode or rule of accomplishing an end; orderly procedure; orderly arrangement; system; classifi-

cation. — adjs methodic [mĕ-thod′ik], -al. — ns Meth′odism, Meth′odist, one of a sect of Christians founded Protestant by John Wesley.

meticulous [me-tik′ū-lus] adj scrupulously careful about small details. — adv metic′ulously.

métier [mā-tyā] n one's calling or business.

metonymy [met-on′i-mi] n a figure of speech in which the name of one thing is put for that of another related to it as 'the bottle' for 'drink', etc.

metric [met′rik] See meter (1,2).

metronome [met′ro-nōm] n an instrument that sets a musical tempo. — adj metronom′ic.

metropolis [me-trop′o-lis] n the main city, often a capital of a country, state, etc.; adj metropol′itan. — n the primate of an ecclesiastical province.

mettle [met′l] n ardor spirit, courage. — adjs mett′led, mett′lesome.

mew¹ [mū] n the common European gull.

mew² [mū] vt to shut up; to confine (often with up). — n (pl) an enclosure for trained hawks;

mezzo-soprano [met′sō-, med′zō-si-prä′nō] n a range of voice between soprano and alto.

mezzotint [met′sō-tint or med′zō-tint] n a method of copper-plate engraving, producing an even gradation of tones.

miasma [mī-az′ma, mi-] n an unwholesome exhalation. — pl mias′mata, mias′mas. — adjs mias′mal.

mica [mīka] n a mineral that crystallizes in flexible layers, resistant to heat.

micro- [mīkrō] in composition, small.

microbe [mī′krōb] n an organism which can be seen by the aid of a microscope, esp a disease-causing bacterium.

microchip [mī′kro-chip] n a small wafer of silicon, etc. containing electronic circuits. — Also chip.

microcomputer [mī′kro-kom-pyōōt′er] n a computer in which the central processing unit is contained in one or more silicon chips.

microcosm [mīkrō-kozm] n a little universe or world. — adjs microcos′mic.

microfilm [mī′krō-film] n a roll of film on which documents are photographed in a reduced size for convenience. — vti to photograph on microfilm.

micrometer [mī-krom′è-tèr] n an instrument for measuring minute distances or angles.

microphone [mī′kro-fōn] n an instrument for transforming sound waves into electric signals.

microprocessor [mīk-rō-prō′ses-ór] n a computer processor contained on an integrated-circuit chip.

microscope [mīkrō-skōp] n an optical instrument for making magnified images of minute objects by means of a lens or lenses. — adjs microscop′ic.

microsurgery [mī′krō-sur′jer-e] n minute surgical dissection or manipulation of individual cells under a microscope.

mid [mid] adj middle. — prep amid. — n mid′day, the middle of the day. — adj mid′land, inland. — n the interior of a country. — n mid′night, twelve o'clock at night. — n mid′shipman, a student naval officer. — ns mid′summer, the middle of summer; the summer solstice about June 21; mid′way. — adj halfway. — n mid′winter, the middle of winter; the winter solstice (December 21 or 22).

midden [mid′èn] n a refuse heap.

middle [mid′l] adj halfway between two given points, times, etc.; intermediate; intervening. — n the middle point or part; something intermediate, waist. Middle Ages, the period of European history between about 500 to 1500 AD; midd′le-man, a dealer who intervenes between producer and consumer; an agent.

midge [mij] n any small gnat or fly. — n midg′et, a very small person; something very small of its kind.

midriff [mid′rif] n the middle part of the torso between the abdomen and the chest.

midst [midst] n middle. — prep amidst.

midwife [mid′wīf] n a woman who assists women in childbirth. — n mid′wifery [-wif-è-ri, -if-ri, -wīf-ri].

mien [mēn] n the air or look, expression of face.

might¹ [mīt] ptp of may (1).

might² [mīt] n power, strength; vigor — adj might′y. — adv might′ily.

mignonette [min-yo-net'] *n* a sweet-scented garden plant with spikes of greenish-yellow flowers.

migraine [mē-grān'] *n* an intense, periodic headache, usu. limited to one side of the head.

migrate [mī'grāt] *vi* to settle in another country or region; to move to another region with the change in season, as many birds. —*adj* **mī'gratory**.

mikado [mi-kä'dō] *n* (*obs*) an emperor of Japan.

mike [mīk] *n*(*inf*) microphone.

mil [mil] *n* a unit of length, .001 of an inch.

milch [milk, milch, milks] *adj* kept for milking.

mild [mīld] *adj* gentle in temper and disposition; not sharp or bitter; acting gently; gently and pleasantly affecting the senses. —*adv* **mild'ly**. —*n* **mild'ness**.

mildew [mil'dū] *n* a fungus that attacks some plants or appears on damp cloth, etc. as a whitish coating. —*vti* to affect or be affected with mildew.

mile [mīl] *n* a unit of linear measure equal to 5,280 feet; the nautical mile is 6,076.12 feet. —*ns* **mile'age**, total miles traveled; **mile'stone**, a stone set up to mark the distance of a mile.

miliary [mil'yàr-i] *adj* made up of many small projections or lesions.

milieu [mēl-yø] *n* environment, esp social setting.

militant [mil'i-tànt] *adj* fighting; ready to fight, esp for some cause; combative. —Also *n* **mil'itancy**. —*adv* **mil'itantly**. —*vt* **mil'itarize**, to equip and prepare for war. —*ns* **militarizā'tion**; **mil'itarism**, military spirit; a policy of aggressive military preparedness. —*adj* **mil'itary**, pertaining to soldiers or to warfare; warlike. —*n* soldiery; the army.

militia [milish'a] *n* an army composed of civilians called out in time of emergency. —*n* **milit'iaman**.

milk [milk] *vt* to squeeze or draw milk from: to extract juice, poison, money, etc., from; to exploit. —*n* a white liquid secreted by female mammals for the nourishment of their young. —*adj* **milk'y**, made of, full of, like or yielding milk; **milk'maid**, a girl or woman who milks cows or works in a dairy; **milk'sop**, an unmanly man; **milk'tooth**, one of the first, temporary teeth of a mammal.

mill [mil] *n* a machine for grinding by crushing between hard, rough surfaces; a building where grain is ground. —*vt* to grind; to press or stamp in a mill; **mill'er**, one who owns or works a mill; **mill'race**, the current of water that turns a millwheel, or the channel in which it runs; **mill'stone**, one of the two stones used in a mill for grinding corn; an oppressive burden.

millennium [mil-en'i-um] *n* a thousand years; the thousand years mentioned in *Revelation* xx between the second coming of Christ. —*adj* **millenn'ial**, of or relating to a millennium.

millesimal [mil-es'im-àl] *adj* thousandth.

millet [mil'et] *n* a food-grain. [Fr *millet*—L *milium*.]

milliard [mil'yàrd, mil'i-ärd] *n* in England, France and Germany, the term for one billion, the number one followed by nine zeros; 1,000,000,000.

milli- [mil'i-] in composition, in names of units a thousandth part.

milliner [mil'in-èr] *n* one who makes or sells women's headgear, trimmings, etc. —*n* **mill'inery**.

million [mill'yòn] *n* a thousand thousands (1,000,000); a very great number. —*n* **mill'ionaire** [-ār], a man worth a million of money or more or enormously rich.

millipede [mil'i-pēd] *n* a myriapod.

mime [mīm] *n* any dramatic representation consisting of action without words; a mimic or pantomimist. —*n* **mimic** [mim'ik], one who imitates, esp an actor skilled in mimicry. —*adj* imitative; mock or sham. —*vt* to imitate, esp in ridicule. —*n* **mim'icry** [-kri], practice, art, or way of mimicking.

mimosa [mim-ō'za] *n* a genus of trees or shrubs having fragrant spikes of yellow flowers.

minaret [mi'-nàr-et'] *n* a high, slender tower on a mosque.

minatory [min'a-tòr-i] *adj* menacing.

mince [mins] *vt* to cut up into small pieces, to diminish or suppress a part of in speaking. —*vi* to speak or act with affected daintiness. —*ns.* **mince'meat**, a mixture of chopped apples, raisins etc. used as a filling for pie.

mind [mīnd] *n* the faculty by which we think, etc.; the understanding; the whole spiritual nature; memory; intellect; reason; opinion; sanity. —*vt* to pay attention to; to obey; take care of; to be careful about; to care about; object to. —to pay attention; to be obedient; to be careful, object. —*ac* **mind'ed**, disposed; **mind'ful**, bearing in mind.

mine¹ [mīn] *pron* the possessive (*gen*) case of I (eg *the watch* *mine*). —Also *possessive adj*.

mine² [mīn] *n* a place from which metals, etc., are dug; a excavation dug under a fortification to blow it up; an explosi charge for this purpose; a rich source. —*vt* to excavate, mal passages in or under; to obtain by excavation; to beset with, destroy by, mines. —*vi* to dig or work a mine. **mine'laye** vessel for laying mines; **mine'sweeper**, a vessel for removing mines.

mineral [min'èr-àl] *n* an inorganic substance, found natural in the earth; any substance neither vegetable nor animal. —*a* of or containing minerals. —*adj* relating to, or having th nature of, minerals.

Ming [ming] *adj* of, pertaining to, the *Ming* dynasty in Chine history (1368–1643), famous for works of art.

mingle [ming'gl] *vti* to mix; to join in mutual intercourse.

mini- [min'i] in composition, small.

miniature [min'ē-a-chūr, min'i-chūr] *n* a painting on a ve small scale; a small or reduced copy of anything. —*adj* on small scale, minute.

minim [min'im] *n* (*mus*) a half note; (apothecaries' measur one-sixtieth of a fluid dram. —*adj.* —*vt* **min'imize**, to reduce or estimate at a minimum. —*n* **min'imum**, the least numbe quantity, or degree possible; the lowest degree or pri reached.

minion [min'yòn] *n* a favorite, esp term of contempt for servile dependent; a subordinate official.

minister [min'is-tèr] *n* a clergyman serving a church; pasto the responsible head of a department of government; th representative of a government at a foreign country. —*vi* serve as a minister in a church; to give help (to). —*adj* **mini** tē'rial. —*adj* **min'istrant**, administering; attendant. —*n* **mini** trā'tion, the act or process of ministering. —*n* **min'istry**, act ministering; office or duties of a pastor; the clergy.

miniver [min'i-vèr] *n* white fur worn by medieval nobles.

mink [mingk] *n* any of several carnivorous weasel like man mals valued for its durable, soft fur.

minnow [min'ō] *n* a very small freshwater fish.

minor [mī'nòr] *adj* lesser in size, importance, degree, bull etc. —*n* a person under full legal age. —*ns* **minor'ity**, the sta of being under age; the smaller number.

minotaur [min'ō-tör] *n* a fabulous bull-headed monster.

minstrel [min'strèl] *n* a traveling singer of the Middle Ages.

mint¹ [mint] *n* the place where money is coined by governmen

mint² [mint] *n* any of a large genus of aromatic plants produ ing highly odoriferous oil.

minuend [min'ū-end] *n* the number from which another is subtracted.

minuet [min-ū-et'] *n* a slow, graceful dance with short step the music for such a dance.

minus [mī'nus] *prep* less (*inf*) without. —*adj* involving subtra tion; negative. —*n* a sign (-).

minute¹ [mīn-ūt'] *adj* extremely small; attentive to sma things; exact. —*adv* **minute'ly**.

minute² [min'it] *n* the sixtieth part of an hour; the sixtieth pa of a degree; an indefinitely small space of time. —*vt* to make brief jotting or note of anything. —*ns* **minute hand**, the han that indicates the minutes on a clock or watch.

minx [mingks] *n* a pert young girl.

miracle [mir'á-kl] *n* a wonder; supernatural event. —*adj* **mi** ac'ulous [-ak'ū-lus]. —*adv* **mirac'ulously**.

mirage [mi-räzh'] *n* an optical illusion in which a distant obje seems to be nearby.

mire [mīr] *n* an area of wet, soggy ground; deep mud. —*v* plunge and fix in mire. —*adj* **mī'ry**.

mirror [mir'ör] *n* a smooth reflecting surface; a faithful rep resentation. —*vt* to reflect as in a mirror.

mirth [mûrth] *n* gaiety esp with laughter. —*adj* **mirth'ful**.

mis- prefix meaning; wrong(ly); bad(ly); no, not.

misadventure [mis-ad-vent'-chūr] *n* bad luck; mishap.

misalliance [mis-a-lī'áns] *n* an unsuitable alliance, esp mar riage.

misanthrope [mis'án-thrōp] n a hater of mankind.—adjs **misanthrop'ic**.—n **misan'thropy**.

misappropriate [mis-a-prō'pri-āt] vt to use (another's money or goods) wrongly or dishonestly.

misbegotten [mis-bi-got'n] adj illegitimate.

misbehave [mis-bi-hāv'] vi to behave wrongly or improperly.—n **misbehav'iour**.

miscall [mis-köl'] vt to call by a wrong name; to misname.

miscarriage [mis-kar'ij] n an act of miscarrying; the act of expelling a foetus prematurely and accidentally.—vi **miscarr'y**, to be unsuccessful; to fail of the intended effect; to bring forth prematurely.

miscegenation [mis-è-jèn-ā'sh(ô)n] n marriage or sexual relations between a man and woman of different races.

miscellaneous [mis-èl-ān'i-us] adj consisting of several kinds of qualities.

mischance [mis-chäns'] n bad luck; mishap.

mischief [mis'chif] n damage; source of harm of annoyance.—adj **mischievous** [mis'chi-vus], harmful, prankish.

miscible [mis'i-bl] adj that may be mixed.—n **miscibil'ity**.

misconceive [mis-kon-sēv'] vti to misunderstand.—n **misconcep'tion**, an erroneous idea.

misconduct [mis-kon'dukt] n dishonest management; improper behaviour.—vt **misconduct'**.

misconstrue [mis-kon-strōō' or -koň] vt to misinterpret.—n **misconstruc'tion**.

miscreant [mis'kri-ânt] adj villainous; evil.—n a villain.

misdeed [mis-dēd'] n a wrong or wicked act; crime; sin, etc.

misdemeanour [mis-di-mēn'er] n (law) any minor offense bringing a lesser punishment than a felony.

miser [mī'zèr] n a greedy, stingy person who hoards money for its own sake.—adj **mī'serly**, avaricious.

miserable [miz'ér-à-bl] adj wretched; causing misery; bad, inadequate; pitiable.—n **mis'erableness**.

miserere [miz-e-rā're] n Psalm 51.; a musical composition adapted to this psalm.

misfire [mis-fīr'] vi to fail to explode or ignite; to produce no effect.—n such a failure.

misfit [mis'fit] n a thing that fits badly; a maladjusted person.—Also vti.

misfortune [mis-för'tūn, -chùn] n ill fortune; trouble; a calamity.

misgive [mis-giv'] vti to give or cause fear or doubt.—n **misgiv'ing**.

mishap [mis'hap] n an unlucky accident.

mislay [mis-lā'] vt to lay in a place not remembered; to put down or install improperly.—pt p **mislaid'**.

mislead [mis-lēd'] vt to lead astray; to deceive; to lead into wrongdoing.—pt, pt p **misled'**.

misnomer [mis-nō'mèr] n a wrong or unsuitable name.

misogynist [mis-oj'i-nist] n a woman hater.—n **misog'yny**.

misprint [mis-print'] vt to print wrongly.

misquote [mis-kwōt'] vt to quote wrongly.—n **misquotā'tion**, an incorrect quotation.

misrepresent [mis-rep-rè-zent'] vt to represent falsely; to give an untrue idea of.—n **misrepresentā'tion**.

miss[1] [mis] n **Miss**, a title used before the name of an unmarried woman or girl.

miss[2] vt to fail to hit, reach, attain, find, observe, hear; to omit, fail to have; to discover the absence of; to feel the want of.—vi to fail to hit; to fail to be successful; to misfire, as an engine.—n a failure to hit, obtain, etc.

missal [mis'àl] n the book that contains the prayers used in celebrating Mass.

missile [mis'il, -īl] n an object, as a rock, spear, rocket, etc. to be thrown, fired.

missing [mis'ing] adj absent from the place where expected to be found.

mission [mish'(ô)n] n a sending of an agent, delegate, or messenger; a flight with a specific purpose, as a task assigned to an astronaut; the purpose for which one is sent; a vocation.—n **miss'ionary**, one sent on a mission.

missive [mis'iv] n a letter or written message.

mist [mist] n a large mass of water vapor, less dense than a fog; anything that dims or obscures.—adv **mist'ily**.

mistake [mis-tāk'] vt to understand or perceive wrongly.—vi to make a mistake.

mister [mis'tèr] n a title of address to a man.

mistletoe [miz'l-tō, or mis'-] n a parasitic evergreen plant, with white berries.

mistral [mis'träl] n a violent, cold, dry, north-west wind in the south of France.

mistress [mis'tres] n a woman who is head of a household; a country or state having supremacy; a woman with whom a man is having a prolonged affair.

mistrust [mis-trust'] n lack of trust.—vti to suspect; to doubt.

misunderstand [mis-un-dér-stand'] vt to misinterpret.—n **misunderstand'ing**.—adj **misunderstood'**.

mite [mīt] n any of a large number of very small parasitic on other insects or vertebrates or plants.

miter, mitre [mī'tèr] n a headdress worn by archbishops, bishops, and abbots; a joint between two pieces of wood to form a corner.

mitigate [mit'i-gāt] vt to alleviate (eg pain); to appease (eg anger); to lessen the severity of; to lessen the gravity of, partially excuse, an offence.—adj **mit'igable**.—n **mitigā'tion**.—adj

mitten [mit'n] n a glove with a thumb but no separate fingers.

mix [miks] vt to blend together in a single mass; to make by blending ingredients, as a cake; to combine.—vi to be mixed or blended; to get along together. **mix'ture** [-chùr], act of mixing or state of being mixed; a blend formed by mixing.

mizzen, mizen [miz'n] n a fore-and-aft sail on the mizzenmast.—adj belonging to the mizzen.—n **mizz'enmast**, the mast nearest the mainmast in a sloop.

mizzle [miz'l] vi to rain in very fine drops.

mnemonic [nē-mon'ik] adj assisting the memory.

moa [mō'a] n any of numerous extinct gigantic, flightless birds in New Zealand.

moan [mōn] n a low mournful sound as of sorrow or pain.—vti to utter a moan; to complain.

moat [mōt] n a deep trench round a castle or fortified place, sometimes filled with water.—vt to surround with a moat.

mob [mob] n a disorderly crowd; a large herd or flock; contemptuous term for the masses.—vt to attack in a disorderly crowd; to crowd around.

mobcap [mob'kàp] n a woman's indoor morning cap.

mobile [mō'bil, -bēl] adj able to move; easily moved; changing rapidly.—vt **mō'bilize**, to put in readiness for service; to call into active service, as troops.—ns **mobilizā'tion**.

moccasin [mok'a-sin] n a flat shoe based on Amerindian footwear; any soft, flexible shoe resembling this; water mocassin.

mocha [mō'ka] n a superior Arabian coffee.

mock [mok] vt to laugh at, to deride; to mimic in ridicule; to disappoint (hopes); to deceive; to defy.—n ridicule; an object of scorn.—adj sham, false.—ns **mock'er**; **mock'ery**, **mock'ingbird**, a common bird esp in southern US.—adv **mock'ingly**.

mode [mōd] n manner of acting, doing, or existing; fashion; form; a temporary or habitual manner or state of being of a thing.

model [mod'l] n something to be copied; something worthy to be imitated; an imitation, esp on a smaller scale; one who poses for an artist or photographer; one who displays clothes by wearing them.—vt to form after a model (with after, on); to display clothes by wearing.—vi to serve as a model for an artist, etc.

moderate [mod'èr-āt] vti to make or become moderate; to preside over (a meeting, etc.)—adj [-àt] kept within reasonable limits; avoiding extremes; mild, calm; of medium quality, amount, etc.—n one whose views are not extreme.—adv **mod'erately**.—ns **mod'erātor**, one who, or that which, moderates or restrains.

modern [mod'èrn] adj of the present or recent times; up-to-date.—n one living in modern times, whose views or tastes are modern.—vti **mod'ernize**, to make or become modern.—ns **modernizā'tion**; **mod'ernism**, modern practice or views.

modest [mod'est] adj restrained by a sense of propriety; decent; having a moderate estimate of one's own merits, not vain, boastful, or pushing.—n **mod'esty**.

modicum [mod'i-kum] n a small quantity.

modify [mod'i-fī] vt to change the form or quality of; to alter slightly.—ns **modificā'tion**

modulate [mod'ū-lāt] vt to regulate, to adjust; to vary the pitch, intensity, etc. of the voice.—*vi* to pass from one state to another.—*ns* **modulā'tion.**

mohair [mō'hār] *n* the long, white, fine silken hair of the Angora goat; cloth made of it.

Mohammedan [mō-ham'è-dàn] *See* **Muhammadan.**

moiety [moi'e-ti] *n* a half; an infinite part.

moire [mwär, mör], **moiré** [mwär'ā, moi'ri] *n* a fabric, esp silk, etc. having a wavy pattern.

moist [moist] *adj* damp; slightly wet.—*vti* **moisten, moist'ure.**

molar [mō'lär] *adj* used for grinding.—*n* a back tooth.

molasses [mo-las'ėz] *n* the thick brown sugar that is produced during the refining of sugar.

mold[1] [mōld] *n* a fungus producing a furry growth on the surface of organic matter.

mold[2] [mōld] *n* a hollow form in which anything is cast; a pattern; the form received from a mold.—*vt* to make in or on a mold; to form, shape.—*ns* **mold'er; mold'ing,** anything formed by or in a mold; a shaped strip of wood, as around the upper walls of a room.

mold[3] [mōld] *n* soft, loose soil rich in decayed vegetable matter.

mole[1] [mōl] *n* a small spot on the skin usu dark-colored and raised.

mole[2] *n* any of numerous small burrowing insectivores.

mole[3] [mōl] *n* a massive breakwater.

molecule [mol'ė-kūl] *n* the smallest particle of any substance that retains the properties of that substance; a small particle.—*adj* **molec'ular.**

molest [mō-lest', mó-lest'] *vt* to annoy; to make improper sexual advances.—*ns* **molesta'tion;**

mollify [mol'i-fī] *vt* to soften, to assuage; to make less severe or violent.—*ns* **mollificā'tion.**

mollusk, mollusc [mol'usk] *n* any of a large phylum of invertebrate animals, characterized by a soft body often enclosed in a shell.

molt, moult [mōlt] *vi* to shed hair, skin, horns, etc. prior to replacement of new growth.

molten [mōlt'n] *adj* melted by heat.

moment [mō'mėnt] *n* an indefinitely brief period of time; a definite point in time; a brief time of importance; importance.—*adv* **mo'mentar'ily.**—*adjs* **mo'mentary, momen'tous,** very important.—*n* **momen'tum,** the impetus of a moving object.

monad [mon'ad] *n* the number one; a unit; unit of being, material and psychical; a hypothetical primitive organism.—*adjs* **monad'ic, -al.**

monarch [mon'ärk] *n* a hereditary sovereign.—*adjs* **monarch'al; monarch'ic,** vested in a single ruler.—*ns* **mon'archy,** government by a monarch; **mon'archist,** an advocate of monarch.

monastery [mon'ás-tėr-i, -tri] *n* the residence of a group of monks, or nuns.—*adj* **monas'tic.**

Monday [mun'di, -dā] *n* the second day of the week.

monetary [mon'-, or mun'e-tar-i] *adj* of the coinage or currency of a country; of or relating to money.—*n* **mon'etarist.**

money [mun'i] *n* pieces of stamped metal, or any paper notes authorized by a government as a medium of exchange; property; wealth—*pl* **mon'eys, monies.**—*vt* **monetize** [mon'e-tīz], to make into or recognize as money.

monger [mung'gėr] *n* a trader; a dealer.

mongoose [mong'gōōs] *n* a common ichneumon of India, noted as a slayer of snakes.—*pl* **mong'ooses.**

mongrel [mung'grèl] *n* an animal or plant, esp a dog, of mixed breed.—Also *adj.*

mon'itor a student chosen to help the teacher; any device for regulating the performance of a machine, aircraft, etc.—*vti* to watch or check on (a person or thing).—*adj* **mon'itory.**

monk [mungk] *n* one of a religious community living in a monastery.—*adj* **monk'ish, monks'hood,** a woodland plant.

monkey [mungk'i] *n* any of the primates except man and the lemurs, esp the smaller, long-tailed primates.—*pl* **monk'eys.**—*vi* (*inf*) to play, trifle, or meddle; **monkey wrench,** a wrench with an adjustable jaw.

mono-, mon- *prefix* one, single.

monochromatic [mon-ō-krō-mat'ik] *adj* consisting of one color.—*n* **mon'ochrome,** a painting, drawing, picture, print, in a single color.

monocle [mon'o-kl] *n* a single eyeglass.

monogamy [mon-og'a-mi] *n* marriage to one wife or husband only.

monogram [mon'ō-gram] *n* a figure consisting of several letters interwoven or written into one.

monograph [mon'ō-gräf] *n* a treatise written on one particular subject or any branch of it.—Also *vt.*

monolith [mon'ō-lith] *n* a single large block of stone, as one made into an obelisk.

monologue, monolog [mol'ō-log] *n* a long speech; a soliloquy, a skit, etc. for one actor only.

monomania [mon-ō-mā'ni-a] *n* a craze confined to one subject.—*n* **monomā'niac.**

monoplane [mon'ō-plān] *n* an airplane with only one main supporting surface.

monopoly [mon-op'o-li] *n* the sole right of dealing in any commodity; exclusive command or possession; that which is thus controlled; such control granted by a government.—*vt* **monop'olize.**

monorail [mon'ō-rāl] *n* a single rail that is a track for cars suspended from it or balanced on it.

monosyllable [mon-ō-sil'à-bl] *n* a word of one syllable.—*adj* **monosyllab'ic.**

monotheism [mon'ō-thē-izm] *n* the belief in only one God.—*n* **mon'otheist.**—*adj* **monotheist'ic.**

monotone [mon'ō-tōn] *n* a single, unvaried tone; a succession of sounds having the same pitch.

monsoon [mon-sōōn'] *n* a seasonal wind of the Indian Ocean and southern Asia.

monster [mon'stèr] *n* any greatly malformed plant or animal; a fabulous animal; a very wicked person; an animal or thing very large of its kind.—*adj* unusually large, huge.—*adj* **mon'strous.**—*adv* **mon'strously.**—*n* **monstros'ity.**

montage [mō-täzh'] *n* a rapid sequence of movie scenes, often superimposed; a picture made partly by sticking objects on the canvas.

Montessori system [mon-tes-ōr'i sis'tem] a system of education, characterized by free discipline and informal, individual instruction.

month [munth] *n* the period from new moon to new moon; a *lunar* month (=29.5306 days); one of the twelve divisions of the year; a calendar month.—*adj* **month'ly,** continuing for a month; done, happening, payable, etc. every month.—*n* a monthly periodical.—*adv* once a month; every month.

monument [mon'ū-mėnt] *n* anything that preserves the memory of a person or an event; a notable or enduring example.—*adj* **monument'al.**

mooch [mōōch] *vti* (*slang*) to get (food, money, etc.) by begging, imposition, etc.—*n* **mooch'er.**

mood[1] [mōōd] *n* (*gram*) that aspect of verbs which indicates whether the action or state expressed is a fact (*indicative mood*), supposition (*subjunctive mood*) or command (*imperative mood*).

mood[2] [mōōd] *n* temporary state of the mind or emotions; a predominant feeling or spirit.—*adj* **mood'y,** subject to changing moods.

moon [mōōn] *n* the satellite which revolves round the earth and shines by reflected sunlight; a satellite of any other planet.—*vi* to behave in an idle or abstracted way.—*ns* **moon'light,** the light of the moon; **moon'shine, moonlight;** (*inf*) illegally-distilled whiskey; **moon'stone,** an opalescent feldspar, used as a gemstone.—*adj* **moon'struck,** lunatic, crazed.

moor[1] [mōōr] *n* in Great Britain, a tract of open wasteland, usu. covered with heather and often marshy.

moor[2] [mōōr] *vt* to fasten by cable or anchor.—*vi* to moor a ship.

moose [mōōs] *n* the largest member of the deer family.

moot [mōōt] *adj* debatable; hypothetical.

mop [mop] *n* a bunch of rags, a sponge, etc. fixed on a handle, for washing floors, windows, etc.; a thick or bushy head of hair.—*vt* to rub or wipe with a mop.

mope [mōp] *vi* to be gloomy and apathetic.—*n* **moper.**—*adj* **mopey.**

moquette [mō'kėt] *n* an upholstery fabric with a velvety pile.

moraine [mo-rān'] *n* a mass of rocks and gravel left by a glacier.

moral [mor'àl] *adj* of or relating to character or conduct; conformed to or directed towards right, virtuous; virtuous in matters of sex; capable of knowing right and wrong.—*n* a moral lesson taught by a fable, event, etc.—*vt* mor′alize, to explain or interpret morally; to give a moral direction to.—*vi* to make moral reflections.—*ns* mor′alizer; mor′alist, one who teaches or is a student of morals; moral′ity, that which renders an action right or wrong; virtue; moral principles.—*adv* mor′ally.

morale [mo-, mô-räl′] *n* moral or mental condition with respect to courage, discipline, confidence, etc.

morass [mo-ras′] *n* a bog, marsh.

moratorium [mor-a-tö′ri-um] *n* a legally authorized delay in the payment of money due; an authorized delay of any activity.

morbid [môr′bid] *adj* diseased, resulting as from a diseased state of mind; gruesome.—*n* morbid′ity.—*adv* mor′bidly.

mordacious [môr-dā′shùs] *adj* biting in style or manner; given to biting.

more [mör] *adj* (serves as comparative of **many** and **much**) in greater number or quantity; additional; other besides.—*adv* to a greater degree; again; further.—*superlative* most [möst].

moreover [mör-ö′vèr] *adv* in addition to what has been said before; besides.

morganatic [môr-gån-at′ik] *adj* denoting a marriage of a king or prince in which neither the wife nor her children enjoy the rank or inherit the possessions of her husband, though the children are legitimate.

morgue [môrg] *n* a place where the bodies of unknown dead or those dead of unknown causes are temporarily kept.

moribund [mor′i-bund] *adj* about to die.

Mormon [môr′mon] *n* member of the Church of Latter-Day Saints whose authority is the Bible and the Book of Mormon, revelations to Joseph Smith by the Angel Moroni in 1827 and certain pronouncements of the 1st Presidency.

morn [môrn] *n* dawn; morning.

morning [môrn′ing] *n* the first part of the day.

morocco [mo-rok′ö] *n* a fine leather of goatskins.

moron [mö′r-on] an adult mentally equal to a 8 to 12 year old child.

morose [mö-rös′] *adj* sullen, surly; gloomy.

morphia [môr′fi-a] *n* morphine.—*n* mor′phine [-fēn] an alkoloid derived from opium.

morphology [mö-fol′o-ji] *n* a branch of biology dealing with the form and structure of organisms.—*adj* morpholog′ical.—*n* morphol′ogist.

morrow [mor′ö] *n* (*arch* or *poetic*) morning; the following day.

Morse code [môrs] *n* either of two codes consisting of dots and dashes or long and short sounds used for transmitting messages by visual or audible signals.

morsel [môr′sèl] *n* a small piece of food; a small piece of anything.

mortal [môr′t(å)l] *adj* liable to death; causing death, deadly, fatal; implacably hostile.—*n* a human being.—*n* mortal′ity, condition of being mortal; death on a large scale, as from war.—*advs* mor′tally.—*n*.

mortar [môr′tàr] *n* a vessel in which substances are pounded with a pestle; a short piece of artillery for throwing a heavy shell; a cement of lime, sand, and water, used in building.

mortgage [môr′gij] *n* a transfer of rights to a piece of property usu. as security for the payment of a loan or debt that becomes void when the debit is paid.—*vt* to pledge as security for a debt; to put an advance claim on.—*ns* mortgagee′, mort′-gagor, -er.

mortify [môr′ti-fī] *vt* to subdue by severities and penance; to humiliate.—*vi* to practise mortification; to become gangrenous.—*n* mortificā′tion.

mortise, mortice [môr′tis] *n* a cavity cut into a piece of timber to receive a tenon.—*vt* to cut a mortise in; to join by a mortise and tenon.

mortuary [môrt′ū-àr-i] *adj* connected with death or burial.—*n* a funeral home.

mosaic [mö-zā′ik] *n* a surface decoration made by inlaying small pieces to form figures or patterns; a design made in mosaic.

Moslem [moz′lem] *n See* **Muslim**.

mosque [mosk] *n* a Muslim place of worship.

mosquito [mos-kē′tö] *n* a two-winged insect the females of which suck blood.

moss [mos] *n* a class of bryophytes, very small green plants that grow in clusters on rocks, moist ground, etc.—*vt* to cover with moss.—*ns* moss′ rose, an old-fashioned variety of rose having a mosslike growth on and below the calyx.—*adj* moss′y.

most [möst] *adj* (superlative of **many** or **much**, of which **more** is the comparative) greatest in number; greatest in amount or degree.—*adv* in or to the greatest degree or extent.—*n* the greatest amount or degree; (with *pl*) the greatest number (of).—*adv* most′ly.

mot [mö] *n* a pithy or witty saying.

mote [möt] *n* a particle of dust; a speck.

motet [mö-tet′] *n* a choral composition without instrumental accompaniment having a sacred text.

moth [moth] *n* a four-winged chiefly night-flying insect related to the butterfly.—*adj* moth′-eat′en.

mother [muTH′èr] *n* a female parent; an origin or source.—*adj* of or like a mother; native.—*vt* to be the mother of or a mother to. **moth′er-in-law**, the mother of one's husband or wife.—*adjs* moth′erless, without a mother; moth′erly.—*ns* moth′erliness; moth′er-of-pearl′, the internal layer of the shells of the pearl oyster.

motif [mö-tēf′] *n* a theme or subject for development in a dramatic, musical, or literary composition.

motion [mö′shòn] *n* act or state of moving, movement; a formal suggestion made in a meeting, law court, or legislative assembly.—*vt* to direct by a gesture.—*vi* to make a hand movement conveying a direction.—*adj* mö′tionless, without motion.

motive [mö′tiv] *adj* moving to action; of or relating to motion.—*n* something (as a need or desire) that causes a person to act; a recurrent theme in a musical composition.

motley [mot′li] *adj* of many colors; of many different or clashing elements.

motor [mö′tör] *n* anything that produces motion; a machine for converting electrical energy into mechanical energy. **mot′orboat**, a boat propelled by an internal-combustion engine or an electric motor; **mo′torcade**, a procession of motor vehicles; **mo′torist**, one who drives an automobile or travels by one.—*vt* mo′torize.

motto [mot′ö] *n* a short sentence or phrase adopted as a watchword or maxim.—*pl* mottoes [mot′öz].

moue [mŏŏ] *n* a little grimace.

moujik [mŏŏ-zhik′, mŏŏ′zhik] *See* **muzhik**.

mould [möld] *See* mold.

moult [mölt] *See* molt.

mound [mownd] *n* an artificial bank of earth or stones; a heap or bank of earth.

mount[1] [mownt] *n* a high hill.

mount[2] [mownt] *vi* to go up; to climb; to extend upward; to increase in amount.—*vt* to ascend; to get up on (a horse, platform, etc.); to provide with horses .—*n* an act of mounting; a riding animal that upon which a thing is placed for use or display.—*adj* mount′able.

mountain [mownt′in] *n* a landmass higher than a hill; a vast number or quantity.—*adj* of or in mountains. **mountaineer′**, an inhabitant of a mountain; a climber of mountains; **mountaineer′ing**, the technique of climbing the high places of the earth.—*adj* mount′ainous, full of mountains; **mount′ain sick′ness**, sickness brought on by breathing rarefied air.

mountebank [mown′ti-bangk] *n* a quack; a charlatan.

mourn [môrn, mörn] *vti* to grieve for (someone dead); to feel or express sorrow for (something regrettable).—*n* mourn′er.—*adj* mourn′ful.—*adv* mourn′fully.—*adj* mourn′ing.

mouse [mows] *n* any of numerous small rodents with pointed snout, long body, and slender tail; a timid person; *pl* mice [mīs].—*vi* [mowz] to hunt for mice; to prowl.—*vt* to toy with roughly.—*ns* mouser [mowz′èr] a cat that catches mice.

mousse [mŏŏs] *n* a chilled dessert containing eggs and whipped cream.

moustache *See* mustache.

mouth [mowth] *n* the opening in the head of an animal by which it eats and utters sound; opening or entrance, as of a bottle, river, etc.—*vt* [mowTH] to say, esp insincerely; to rub with the mouth.—*vi* to declaim, rant; to grimace. **mouth′ful**, as much as fills the mouth; *ns* mouth′ or′gan, a harmonica; **mouth′piece**, the part of a musical instrument, or tobacco pipe, held in the mouth; a person, periodical, etc. who speaks for others.

move [mōōv] *vt* to cause to change place; to set in motion; to persuade; to arouse.—*vi* to go from one place to another; to change place; to walk, to carry oneself; to change residence.—*n* the act of moving; a movement, esp at chess; one's turn to move.—*adj* **movable** [mōōv'a-bl].—*ns* **move'ment.**

mow [mō] *vti* to cut down (grass, etc.) from (a lawn, etc.) with a sickle or lawn mower.

much [much] *adj* (*comparative* more; *superlative* most) great in quantity.—*adv* to a great degree; by far; often.—*n* a great amount.

muck [muk] *n* moist manure; black earth with decaying matter, mud, dirt, filth.—*adj* **muck'y.**

mucus [mū'kus] *n* the slimy fluid secreted by the mucous membrane. **mucous,** mucous membrane, mucus-secreting lining of body cavities.

mud [mud] *n* wet soft sticky earth.—*vt* to treat or plaster with mud; to make turbid.—*adj* **mudd'y,** foul with mud; covered with mud; confused, stupid.—*vti* to make or become muddy.

muddle [mud'l] *vt* to render muddy or foul; as water; to bungle.—*vi* to blunder.—*n* confusion, mess; bewilderment.

muezzin [mōō-ez'in] *n* a Muslim crier who calls the hour of daily prayer.

muff[1] [muf] *n* a cylinder of fur or the like for keeping the hands warm.

muff[2] [muf] *n* a bungling performance; failure to hold a ball when trying a catch.—*vti* to bungle; muff a ball.

muffin [muf'in] *n* a quick bread baked in a muffin pan.

muffle [muf'l] *vt* to wrap up for warmth or concealment; to dull or deaden the sound of.—*n* **muff'ler,** a scarf for the throat; any means of muffling, esp the exhaust of a motor vehicle.

mufti [muf'ti] *n* civilian clothes.

mug [mug] *n* a cylindrical drinking cup, usu. of metal or earthenware; its contents.—*vt* to assault, usu. with intent to rob.

muggy [mug'i] *adj* hot, close, and damp.—*adj* **mugg'ish.**

mugwump [mug'wump] *n* an independent in politics.

Muhammadan [mō-ham'a-dan] *adj* of, or relating to Muhammad or Islam.

mulatto [mū-lat'ō] *n* the offspring of a Negro and a person of European stock.

mulberry [mul'ber-i] *n* a genus of trees on the leaves of some of which silkworms feed.

mulch [mulch, mulsh] *n* loose strawy dung, etc., laid down to protect the roots of plants.—*vt* to cover with mulch.

mulct [mulkt] *n* a fine, a penalty.—*vt* to fine.

mule[1] [mūl] *n* the offspring of a male donkey and a mare; an instrument for spinning cotton; an obstinate person.

mule[2] [mūl] *n* a heelless slipper.

mull[1] [mul] *n* a soft, fine, sheer fabric of cotton, silk, or rayon.

mull[2] [mul] *vti* (*inf*) to ponder (over).

mull[3] [mul] *vt* to warm, spice, and sweeten (wine, ale, etc.).—*adj* **mulled.**

mullet [mul'et] *n* any of a family of palatable fishes nearly cylindrical in form.

mulligatawny [mul-i-ga-tö'ni] *n* an East Indian curry-soup.

mullion [mul'yòn] *n* an upright division between the lights of windows, between panels, etc.

multi-, mult- in composition, much, many. [L *multus*].—eg **multiped,** [mul'ti-ped] an insect having many feet; **multilingual,** [mul-ti-ling'gwäl] in many languages; speaking many languages; **mul'ti-pur'pose.**

multifarious [mul-ti-fā'ri-us] *adj* having great diversity; manifold.

multiform [mul'ti-förm] *adj* having many forms.

multilateral [mul-ti-lat'èr-ál] *adj* many-sided; with several parties or participants.

multiply [mul'ti-plī] *vti* to increase in number, degree, etc.; to find the product (of) by multiplication.—*ns* **multiplic'ity,** a great number or variety (of).

multitude [mul'ti-tūd] *n* a large number of people.—*adj* **multitud'inous,** consisting of innumerable elements.

mum [mum] *adj* silent, not speaking—*n* silence.—*interj* not a word!—*vi* to act in dumb show.

mumble [mum'bl] *vti* to utter or speak indistinctly—*n* a mumbled utterance.—*n* **mum'bler.**

mumbo-jumbo [mum'bō-jum'bō] *n* an idol or fetish; meaningless ritual, talk, etc.

mummy [mum'i] *n* a carefully preserved dead body.—*n* **mummifica'tion.**—*vt* **mumm'ify.**

mumps [mumps] *npl* an acute contagious virus disease characterized by swelling of the salivary glands.

munch [munch, -sh] *vti* to chew steadily.

mundane [mun'dān] *adj* belonging to the world; ordinary, banal.—*adv* **mun'danely.**

municipal [mū-nis'i-pál] *adj* of or concerning a city, town, etc. or its local government.—*n* **municipal'ity,** a town or city having corporate status and powers of self-government; the governing body of a municipality.—*adv* **munic'ipally.**

munificence [mū-nif'i-sèns] *n* magnificent liberality in giving; bountifulness.—*adj* **munif'icent.**

munitions [mū-nish'óns] *npl* war supplies, esp weapons and ammunition.

mural [mū'rál] *adj* of, on, attached to, or of the nature of, a wall.—*n* a painting on a wall.

murder [mûr'dèr] *n* the act of putting a person to death, intentionally and unlawfully.—*vt* to kill unlawfully and with malice aforethought.—*n* **mur'derer;**—*adj* **mur'derous.**

murky [mûrk'i] *adj* dark, gloomy; darkly vague or obscure.—*adv* **murk'ily.**—*ns* **murk; murk'iness.**

murmur [mûr'mûr] *n* a low, indistinct sound, continuous sound; a mumbled complaint; *vi* to make a murmur.—*vt* to say in a murmur.

muscatel [mus-ka-tel'] *n* a sweet fortified white wine made from the muscat.—*n* **mus'cat,** a sweet European grape used in making wine and raisins.

muscle [mus'l] *n* an animal tissue by contraction of which bodily movement is effected; strength; brawn.—*adj* **muscular.**

muse [mūz] *vi* to meditate.—*vt* to say musingly.—*n* deep thought; contemplation.

muse [mūz] *n* one of the nine goddesses of poetry, music, and the other liberal arts.

museum [mū-zē'um] *n* a repository for the collection, exhibition, and study of objects or artistic, scientific or historic interest.—*pl* **museums.**

mush [mush] *n* a thick porridge of boiled meal; any thick, soft mass; (*inf*) maudlin sentimentality.

mushroom [mush'rōōm] *n* a fleshy fungus with a capped stalk, esp such as are edible.

music [mū'zik] *n* the art of combining tones into a composition having structure and continuity; vocal or instrumental sounds having rhythm, melody, or harmony; an agreeable sound.—*adj* **mū'sical.**—*adv* **mū'sically.**—*ns* **musi'cian,** [-shàn].

musk [musk] *n* an animal secretion with a strong odor, used in fixing perfumes; the odor of musk; the musk plant.—*ns* **musk' deer,** a small Asiatic deer that produces musk in the male; **musk-ox,** a shaggy-coated wild ox; **muskrat,** an aquatic rodent.—Also **musquash.**—*adj* **musky.**

muskeg [mus'keg] *n* a mossy bog.

musket [mus'kèt] *n* (*hist*) a smooth-bore military firearm.—*n.* **musketeer', mus'ketery.**

Muslim [mus'lim] *n, adj* (of) an adherent of Islam.

muslin [muz'lin] *n* a fine soft cotton fabric.

musquash [mus'kwosh] *n* the muskrat.

mussel [mus'l] *n* any of several marine bivalve shellfish, used for food.

Mussulman [mus'ul-man] *n* a Muslim.

must[1] [must] an auxiliary verb expressing necessity; probability; certainty.—*n* (*inf*) something that must be done, had, etc.

must[2] [must] *n* newly-pressed grape juice, unfermented or partially fermented wine.

mustache, moustache [mus-tash', mus'tash] *n* hair on the upper lip.

mustang [mus'tang] *n* the small wild horse of the western plains of N America.—Also **bronco.**

mustard [mus'tàrd] *n* any of several herbs with lobed leaves, yellow flowers, and long beaked pods; a pungent condiment made from the seeds of several common mustards; (*slang*) zest.—*n* mustard gas, the vapor from a poisonous blistering liquid.

muster [mus´tĕr] *vt* to assemble, as troops for duty or inspection; to gather.—*vi* to be gathered together, as troops.—*n* an assembling of troops for inspection, etc.; **mus´ter roll**.

musty [must´i] *adj* moldy, spoiled by damp; stale.

mutable [mū´ta-bl] *adj* that may be changed; inconstant.—*n* **mutā´tion**.

mute [mūt] *adj* dumb; silent.—*n* a deaf-mute; a device that softens the sound of a musical instrument.—*vt* to deaden the sound of a musical instrument.—*adv* **mute´ly.**—*n* **mute´ness.**

mutilate [mu´ti-lāt] *vt* to maim; to render defective; to remove a material part of.—*ns* **mutilā´tion; mūtilātor.**

mutiny [mūti-ni] *vi* to rise against authority in army, navy, or air force; to revolt against rightful authority.—*n* **mutineer´.**

mutter [mut´ĕr] *vi* to utter words in a low voice; to grumble.—*vt* to utter indistinctly.—*n* **mutt´erer.**

mutton [mut´n] *n* sheep's flesh as food.

mutual [mū´tū-ål] *adj* given and received in equal amount; having the same feelings one for the other; shared in common.—*adv* **mūtually.**

muzzle [muz´l] *n* the projecting jaws and nose of an animal; a fastening for the mouth to prevent biting; the extreme end of a gun, etc.—*vt* to put a muzzle on; to gag or silence.

my [mī] *poss adj* of or belonging to me.

mycology [mīkol´o-ji] *n* the study of fungi.

myopia [mī-ō´pi-a] *n* shortness of sight.—*adj* **myop´ic.**

myriad [mir´i-ad] *n* a great number of persons or things.—*adj* numberless.

myriapod [mir´i-a-pod] *n* a group of animals with many jointed legs.

myrmidon [mûr´mi-don] *n* an unquestioning follower.

myrrh [mûr] *n* a fragrant gum resin of Arabia and east Africa used in perfume, incense, etc.

myrtle [mûr´tl] *n* a genus of evergreen shrubs with beautiful and fragrant leaves.

mystery [mis´tĕr-i] *n* something unexplained and secret; a story about a secret crime, etc; secrecy.—*adj* **mystē´rious,**—*adv* **mystē´riously.**

mystic, -al [mis´tik, -ål] *adj* relating to, or containing, esoteric rites or doctrines; involving a sacred or a secret meaning revealed only to a spiritually enlightened mind.—*n* **mys´tic,** one who seeks for direct intercourse with God in elevated religious feeling or ecstasy.—*n* **mys´ticism** [-sizm].—*vt* **mys´tify.**

myth [mith] *n* an ancient traditional story of gods or heroes, offering an explanation of some fact or phenomenon; a fable; a fictitious person or thing; a commonly-held belief that is untrue or without foundation; myths collectively.—*adjs* **my´thical.**—*adv* **myth´ically.**—*n* **mythol´ogy,** a collection of myths; the study of myths.—*adjs* **mytholog´ical, mytholog´ic.**

myxomatosis [miks-ō-má-tō´sis] *n* a severe contagious virus disease of rabbits.

N

abob [nā´bob] *n* any man of great wealth or importance.

acre [nā´kĕr] *n* mother-of-pearl.

adir [nā´dēr, -dĕr] *n* the point opposite the zenith.

ag¹ [nag] *n* a horse, esp a small one.

ag² [nag] *vt* to find fault with constantly; to worry.

aiad [nī´ad] *n* a nymph, presiding over rivers.

ail [nāl] *n* a horny plate at the end of a finger or toe; a thin pointed piece of metal for fastening wood.—*vt* to fasten as with nails.

ainsook [nān-sŏŏk] *n* a soft lightweight muslin.

aive, naïve [nä-ēv´] *adj* with natural or unaffected simplicity in thought, speech, or manners.

aked [nāk´id] *adj* without clothes; without covering; without sheath or case; —*n* **nakedness.**

amby-pamby [nam´bi-pam´bi] *adj* insipid; weakly sentimental (of a person).

ame [nām] *n* that by which a person or a thing is known or called; a designation; reputed character; authority.—*vt* to give

a name to; to speak of by name; to nominate; to appoint to an office; **name´less,** without a name; anonymous;.—*adv* **name´ly,** videlicet, that is to say.—*n* **name´sake,** one bearing the same name as another.

nankeen, nankin [nan-kēn´] *n* a buff-colored cotton cloth; trousers made from this cloth.

nanny, nannie [nan´i] *n* (*Brit*) a child's nurse.

nanny goat [nan´i] *n* a female domestic goat.

nap¹ [nap] *vi* to take a short or casual sleep.

nap² [nap] *n* a hairy surface on cloth or leather; such a surface.—*adjs* **nap´less, napped.**

napalm [nā´päm, na´] *n* a substance added to gasoline to form a jellylike compound, used in fire bombs and flame-throwers.

nape [nāp] *n* the back of the neck.

napery [nā´pĕr-i] *n* household linen, esp for the table.

naphtha [naf´tha] *n* a flammable liquid distilled from coal tar, petroleum, etc.—*n* **naph´thalene.**

napkin [nap´kin] *n* a small square of linen, paper, etc. used while eating.

napoleon [na-pōl´yòn, or i-on] *n* an oblong, many-layered pastry filled with cream or custard; a former French gold coin.

narcissus [när-sis´us] *n* a spring-flowering bulb plant, esp one with a short trumpet and flowers borne separately.—*n* **narciss´ism,** excessive interest in one's own body or self.

narcotic [när-kot´ik] *adj* inducing sleep.—*n* any drug producing a narcotic effect.

nard [närd] *n* spikenard.

narrate [na-rāt´] *vt* to give a continuous account of.—*n* **narrā´tion.**—*adj* **narrative** [nar´a-tiv], narrating; giving an account of any occurrence; story-telling.—*n* **narrā´tor.**

narrow [nar´ō] *adj* of little breadth; of small extent; confining; with little to spare; careful bigoted or illiberal in views.—*n* (usu. in *pl*) a narrow passage, channel, or strait.—*vti* to make narrower; to contract.—*adj.*—*adv* **narr´owly.**—*adj* **narr´owmind´ed,** of a narrow or illiberal mind.—*ns* **narr´owness.**

narwhal, narwhale [när´wål] *n* an arctic whale with a long twisted projecting ivory tusk.

nasal [nā´zål] *adj* belonging to the nose; affected by, or sounded through, the nose.—*n* a sound uttered through the nose.—*vi* **nā´salize,** to render nasal, as a sound.

nascent [nās´ent] *adj* coming into being, beginning to form or develop.

nasturtium [nas-tûr´shùm] *n* a genus of plants with a pungent odor.

nasty [nas´ti] *adj* disgustingly foul, nauseous; morally offensive; disagreeable, unpalatable, or annoying.—*adv* **nas´tily.**—*n* **nas´tiness.**

natal [nā´tål] *adj* of or connected with birth; native.

natation [nat-, or nāt-ā´sh(ò)n] *n* swimming.—*adj* **nā´tatory.** [L *natāns, -antis,* pr p of *natāre,* freq of *nāre,* to swim.]

nation [nā´sh(ò)n] *n* a body of people marked off by common descent, language, culture, or historical tradition; people united under a single government.—*adj* **national** [na´shôn-ål], **na´tionalist,** one who favors the unity, independence, interests, or domination of a nation.—*adj* **nationalis´tic.**—*ns* **na´tionalism; nationality** [-al´iti], the status of belonging to a nation by birth or naturalization.

native [nā´tiv] *adj* natural to a person or thing, innate, inherent; of, pertaining to, or belonging to the place of one's birth (eg language); belonging to the people inhabiting a country originally or at the time of its discovery, indigenous; not exotic; occurring naturally.—*n* one born in the place indicated; an original inhabitant; an indigenous plant or animal.

natty [nat´i] *adj* dapper, spruce.—*adv* **natt´ily.**

natural [na´chùr-ål] *adj* produced by, or according to, nature; not artificial; innate, not acquired; true to nature; lifelike; at ease.—*n* one having a natural aptitude (for), or being an obvious choice (for).—*vt* **nat´uralize,** to confer citizenship upon (an alien).—*ns* **naturalīzā´tion; nat´uralist,** one who studies animals or plants esp in the field.—*n* **nat´urally** in a natural manner, by nature; of course.

nature [nā´chûr] *n* the power that regulates the world; the entire external world; the essential qualities of anything; constitution; a primitive undomesticated condition before society is organized; natural scenery.

naught [nöt] *n* nothing; a zero.—Also **nought.**

naughty [nöt'i] *adj* mischievous or disobedient; indelicate.— *adv* **naught'ily**.—*n* **naught'iness**.

nausea [nö'si-a, nö'shi-a] *n* a feeling of inclination to vomit; loathing.—*vi* **nau'seate**, to feel nausea or disgust.—*vt* to loathe; to strike with disgust.—*adjs* **nau'seating; nau'seous**.

nautical [nöt'ik-ål] *adj* of ships, sailors.

nautilus [nö'ti-lus] *n* any of a genus of cephalopod mollusks.

naval [nä'vål] *adj* pertaining to warships or to a navy.

nave¹ [näv] *n* the main part of a church.

nave² [näv] *n* the hub of a wheel.

navel [nä'vėl] *n* the small scar in the abdomen.

navigate [nav'i-gāt] *vti* to steer a ship, aircraft, motor vehicle, etc.; to travel through or over in a ship or aircraft.—*ns* **naviga-bil'ity**, **nav'igableness**.—*ns* **navigā'tion; nav'igator**, one skilled in the navigation of a ship or aircraft.

navy [nä'vi] *n* the whole of a nation's ships-of-war; (often **Navy**) a nation's entire sea force, including ships, men, stores, etc.; a very dark blue.

nay [nä] *adv* no; not only so but.

Nazi [nä'tsē] *n, adj* for *N*ational-so*z*ialist, National Socialist, Hitlerite.—*n* **Naz'ism**.—*vt* **Naz'ify**.

Neanderthal [ne-an'dèr-tal] *adj* of, or pertaining to, a Paleol-ithic species of man.

neap [nēp] *adj* either of the lowest high tides in the month.—*n* a neap tide.

near [nēr] *adv* to or at a little distance; almost.—*prep* close to.—*adj* not far away in place or time; narrow, barely missing or avoiding something.—*vti* to approach; to come nearer.— *adv* **near'ly**, almost.—*ns* **near'ness**.

neat¹ [nēt] *n* the common domestic bovine.—*n* **neat'herd**, herdsman.

neat² [nēt] *adj* clean and tidy; adroit or skilful; skilfully made or done; well and concisely put.—*adv* **neat'ly**.—*n* **neat'ness**.

nebula [neb'ū-la] *n* a faint, misty appearance in the heavens produced either by a group of stars too distant to be seen singly, or by diffused gaseous matter.—*adjs* **neb'ular**, **neb'ulous**.

necessary [nes'es-år-i] *adj* indispensable; required; inevit-able.—*n* something necessary.—*adv* **nec'essarily**.

necessity [nè-ses'i-ti] *n* compulsion exerted by the nature of things; the constraining power of circumstances; something that cannot be done without; imperative need; poverty.—*vt* **necess'itāte** to make necessary or unavoidable; *adj* **necess'i-tous**, urgent; pressing.

neck [nek] *n* the part connecting head and body; that part of a garment nearest the neck; a necklike part, esp a narrow strip of land;—*ns* **neck'erchief**, a kerchief for the neck; **neck'lace** [-lis], a chain, or string of beads or precious stones worn on the neck; **neck'tie**, a band tied round the neck under a collar and tied in front.

necro- [nek'rô-, -ro-] in composition, dead, dead body.— *ns* **necrol'ogy**, an obituary list; **nec'romancy**, divination by alleged communication with the dead; sorcery; **necrō'sis**, death of part of the living body.

nectar [nek'tår], *n* the beverage of the gods; a delicious bev-erage.

nectarine [nek-tàr-ēn] *n* a smooth-skinned peach.

née, *nee* [nä] *adj* born.

need [nēd] *n* necessity; a state that requires relief; want of the means of living.—*vt* to have need of; to require; to be obliged.—*vi* to be necessary; to be in want.—*adjs* **need'ful**, **need'less**.

needle [nē'dl] *n* a small, sharp piece of steel for sewing; any similar slender, pointed rod for knitting or crocheting; the pointer of a compass, gauge, etc.—*vt* (*inf*) to goad, prod, or tease.

nefarious [ni-fā'ri-us] *adj* extremely wicked.

negate [ni-gāt'] *vt* to deny; to nullify.—*n* **negation** [ne-gā'sh(ò)n], act of saying no; denial; the absence or opposite (of something that is actual, positive, or affirmative).—*adj* **negative** [neg'åtiv], expressing denial or refusal; lacking dis-tinguishing features, devoid of positive attributes.

neglect [ni-glekt'] *vt* to pay little or no respect or attention to; to ignore as of no consequence; to leave uncared for.—*n* disregard; slight; omission.—*adj* **neglect'ful**.

negligee [neg-li-jā'] *n* a woman's loosely fitting dressing gown.

negligence [neg'li-jèns] *n* carelessness or want of attention; an act of carelessness.—*adj* **neg'ligent**.—*adv* **neg'ligently**.

negotiate [ni-gō'shi-āt] *vi* to bargain (with), to confer (with) for the purpose of coming to an agreement or arrangement.—*vt* to settle by agreement to transfer or exchange for value.—*adj* **nego'tiable**; **negotiā'tion**; **negō'tiator**.

Negro [nē'grō] *n* a member of the dominant group of mankind in Africa.

neigh [nā] *vi* to utter the cry of a horse.—*n* the cry of a horse.

neighbor [nā'bór] *n* a person who lives near another; a fellow man.—*n* **neigh'borhood**, state of being neighbors; a particu-lar community, area, or district.—*adjs* **neigh'boring**, **neigh'borly**.

neither [nē'THėr or nī'THėr] *adj* and *pron* not one or the other (of two); not either.—*conj* not either.

nematode [nèm-å-tōd'] *n* any of a phylum of elongated cylin-drical worms

Nemesis [nem'e-sis] *n* (*myth*) the Greek goddess of retribution.

neo- [nē'ō] in composition, new, as in neoclassic.

neolithic [nē-ō-lith'ik] *adj* of the later Stone Age.

neon [nē'on] *n* an inert gaseous element found in the atmos-phere.

nepenthe [ni-pen'thē] *n* anything that causes forgetfulness of sorrow.

nephew [nev'ū or nef'ū] *n* the son of a brother or sister.

nepotism [nep'o-tizm] *n* favoritism shown to relatives, esp in securing jobs.—*n* **nep'otist**.

Neptune [nep'tūn] *n* the Roman god of the sea; the planet eighth in distance from the sun.—*adj*.

nereid [nē'rē-id] *n* any of the sea nymphs.

nerve [nûrv] *n* any of the fibers or bundles of fibers carrying impulses of sensation or of movement between the brain and spinal cord and all parts of the body; courage, coolness in danger; (*inf*) impudent boldness; (*pl*) nervousness, anxiety.— *vt* to give strength, courage, or vigor to.—*adjs* **nerve'less**, **ner'vous**, of the nerves or nervous system; excitable; easily agitated; timid; uneasy.—*adj* **nervy** (*inf*) bold and presump-tuous; cool and confident.

nescience [nesh'(y)èns] *n* ignorance; lack of knowledge.—*adj* **nes'cient**.

ness [nes] *n* a promontory.

nest [nest] *n* a structure prepared for egg-laying, brooding, and nursing, or as a shelter; a comfortable residence; the occu-pants of a nest, as a brood, a swarm, a gang; a set of things (as boxes) fitting one within another.—*vi* to build or occupy a nest; **nest'ling**, a young bird who has not abandoned the nest.

nestle [nes'l] *vi* to lie close or snug as in a nest; to settle comfortably; to lie sheltered.

net¹ [net] *n* an open fabric of twine, etc. knotted into meshes for catching birds, fishes, etc.; anything like a net; a snare; a difficulty.—*vt* to snare or enclose as with a net.—*ns* **nett'ing**, a netted material; **net'work**, an arrangement or pattern with intersecting lines.

net² [net] *adj* clear of all charges, allowances, or deductions.— a net amount, price, weight, profit.

nether [neTH'ėr] *adj* lower or under.

nettle [net'l] *n* a genus of plants with stinging hairs.—*vt* to irritate, annoy, or vex.

neur- [nūr-], **neuro-** [nū'rō-] in composition, nerve.—*ad* **neural** [nū'ral] of, or relating to, nerves.—*n* **neuralgia** pain, pain along a nerve.—*adj* **neural'gic**.—*n* **neurasthenia** ner-vous debility.—*adj* **neurasthen'ic**.—*n* one suffering fron neurasthenia.—*ns* **neuritis** [nū-rī'tis] inflammation of a nerve

neuter [nū'tėr] *adj* neither masculine nor feminine.

neutral [nū'trål] *adj* taking no part on either side; of no decide character; having no decided color.—*n* a neutral person nation; a neutral color.—*n* **neutrality**.—*vt* **neu'tralize**.

neutron [nū'tron] *n* an uncharged subatomic particle.

never [nev'èr] *adv* not ever, at no time; not at all; in no case.— *adv* **nevertheless'**.

new [nū] *adj* lately made, invented, discovered; recently hear of, or experienced for the first time; recently grown, fresh unused; starting as the repetition of a cycle, series, etc unaccustomed; recently commenced.—*adv* again; newl recently.—*adv* **newly**, recently; lately.

newel [nū'ėl] *n* the upright column about which the steps of a circular staircase wind; the post that supports the handrail of a flight of stairs.

newfangled [nū-fang'gld] *adj* (*contemptuous*) new.

news [nūz] *n* (*pl*) a report of a recent event; something one had not heard before. **news'deal'er**, a retailer of newspapers, magazines, etc.; **news'paper**, a paper published periodically for circulating news, etc.; —*adjs* **news'worthy**, timely and important or interesting.

newt [nūt] *n* any of various small amphibious salamanders.

next [nekst] *adj* (*superlative* of **nigh**) nearest; immediately preceding or following. —*adv* in the nearest time, place, rank, etc.; on the first subsequent occasion. —*prep* nearest.

nexus [nek'sus] *n* a link or connection.

nib [nib] *n* a bird's beak; a pen point.

nibble [nib'l] *vti* to eat food by small bites; to bite (at) lightly and intermittently. —*n* **nibb'ler**.

niblick [nib'lik] *n* a golf club with a heavy iron head with wide face, used for lofting.

nice [nīs] *adj* fastidious; able to make fine distinctions, minutely accurate (eg judgment, ear); displaying fine discrimination (eg a distinction); pleasant, attractive, kind, good, etc. —*adv* **nice'ly**. —*ns* **nicety** [nīs'i-ti] fastidiousness; fineness of perception.

Nicene [nī'sēn] *adj* of a church council.

niche [nich] *n* a recess in a wall for a statue, etc.

nick [nik] *n* a small cut, chip, etc. made on a surface. —*vt* to make a nick in; to wound superficially.

nickel [nik'él] *n* a US or Canadian coin, equal to five cents.

nickname [nik'nām] *n* a substitute name, often descriptive, given in fun; a familiar form of a proper name. —*vt* to give a nickname to.

nicotine [nik'ō-tēn] *n* a poisonous alkaloid got from tobacco leaves.

nidification [nid-i-fi-kā'sh(ó)n] *n* the act or process of building a nest.

niece [nēs] *n* the daughter of a brother or sister.

niggard [nig'árd] *n* one who grudges to spend or give away. —*adj* **nigg'ardly**, stingy.

nigh [nī] *adj* (*arch*) near. —*adv* nearly. —*prep* near to.

night [nīt] *n* the time from sunset to sunrise; nightfall; a specified or appointed evening. —*ns* **night blindness**, poor vision in near darkness; **night'club**, a place of entertainment for drinking, etc. at night; **night'fall**, the close of the day; **night'ly**, done or happening by night or every night; **night stick**, a short club carried by a policeman or policewoman.

nightingale [nīt'ing-gāl] *n* a small bird of the thrush family celebrated for its singing at night.

nightmare [nīt'mār] *n* a frightening dream; any horrible experience.

nightshade [nīt'shād] *n* any of a genus of flowering plants related to the potato and tomato, esp belladonna.

nihilism [nī'hil-izm] *n* belief in nothing, extreme scepticism; the rejection of customary beliefs in morality, religion, etc. —*n* **nī'hilist**.

nil [nil] *n* nothing.

nimble [nim'bl] *adj* light and quick in motion. —*adv* **nim'bly**.

nimbus [nim'bus] *n* a rain cloud; halo encircling the head of a saint as on a picture.

nincompoop [nin(g)'kom-pōōp] *n* a stupid, silly person.

nine [nīn] *adj*, *n* one more than eight. —*ns* the symbol for this; the ninth in a series or set.

ninny [nin'i] *n* a fool.

nip[1] [nip] *n* a small drink of liquor. —*vti* to drink in nips.

nip[2] [nip] *vt* to pinch; to press between two surfaces; to remove or sever shoots by pinching to check the growth of. —*n* a pinch; a bite; a check of growth of plants due to cold; biting coldness of air. —*n* **nipp'er**, one who, or that which, nips.

nipple [nip'l] *n* the small protuberance on a breast or udder through which the milk passes, a teat.

nirvana [nir-vä'nä] *n* the cessation of individual existence by the absorption of the soul into the supreme spirit, the state to which a Buddhist aspires as the best attainable; a state of supreme happiness.

nit [nit] *n* the egg of a louse or other parasitic insect.

niter *see under* **nitrogen**.

nitrogen [nī'trō-jén] *n* a gaseous element forming nearly 4/5 of air. —*adj* **nitrog'enous**, containing, having the nature of,

nitrogen. —*adjs* **nī'tric**, **nī'trous**, of, pertaining to, or containing nitrogen; of, pertaining to, or derived from niter; **nī'tro-glyc'erine**, a powerful explosive, the chief constituent of dynamite, used in medicine as a vasodilator.

nix[1] [niks] *n* in Germanic folklore, a male water spirit. —**nix'ie**, **nix'y**.

nix[2] [niks] *adv* (*slang*) no; not at all.

no[1] [nō] *adv* not so; (with *comp*) in no degree, as *no sooner than*, *no less than*. —*n* a denial; a refusal; a vote or voter for the negative.

no[2] [nō] *adj* not any; not one; by no means properly called (eg *no lady*).

nobility [nō-bil'i-ti] *n* being noble; high rank in society; the class of people of noble rank.

noble [nō'bl] *adj* famous or renowned; high in character or quality; of high birth. —*n* a person of exalted rank. —*ns* **nō'bleman**. —*adv* **nō'bly**.

nocturnal [nok-tûr'nål] *adj* belonging to night; happening, done, or active by night. —*adv* **noctur'nally**. —*n* **nocturne** [nok'tûrn, or -tûrn'] a dreamy or pensive piece for the piano.

nod [nod] *vi* to give a quick forward motion of the head, esp in assent, or salutation; to let the head drop in weariness. —*vt* to signify by a nod. —*n* a quick bending forward of the head.—

noddle [nod'l] *n* the crown of the head; the head.

node [nōd] *n* a knot; a knob; a swelling; a point or line of rest in a vibrating body. —*adjs* **nōd'al**. —**n** **nōd'üle**, a little rounded lump.

Noel, Noël [nō-el'] *n* Christmas.

noggin [nog'in] *n* a small quantity of alcoholic drink.

noise [noiz] *n* sound; an esp loud or disturbing sound, din. —*vt* to spread. —*vi* to sound loud. —*adj* **noise'less**, without noise; silent. —*adj* **nois'y**. —*adv* **nois'ily**.

noisome [noi'sùm] *adj* injurious to health; foul-smelling. —*n* **noi'someness**.

nomad [nōm'ad] *n* one of a wandering pastoral community; a rover. —*adj* **nomadic** [nōm-ad'ik].

no-man's-land [nō'manz-land] *n* a waste region to which no one has a recognized claim; land, esp between entrenched hostile forces.

nom de plume [nåm dè plōōm] *n* a pen name.

nomenclature [nō'men-klā-chür] *n* a system of names used in a science etc., or for parts of a device, etc.

nominal [nom'in-ål] *adj* of or like a name; existing only in name, not real or actual. —*adv* **nom'inally**.

nominate [nom'in-āt] *vt* to appoint to an office or position; to propose (a candidate) for election. —*n* **nom'ination**.

nominee [nom-in-ē'] *n* one who is nominated for an office, duty, or position.

non [non] *prefix* not.

nonage [non'ij] *n* the state of being under full legal age.

nonagenarian [non-a-jè-nā'ri-ån] *n* one who is ninety years old or between ninety and a hundred. —*adj* of that age.

nonagon [non'å-gon] *n* a polygon with nine angles.

nonce [nons] *n* the occasion; the moment, time being.

nonchalance [non'shá-låns] *n* unconcern, coolness, indifference. —*adj* **nonchalant** [non'shá-lånt].

nondescript [non'di-skript] *adj* not easily classified; not distinctive enough to be described.

none [nun] *pron* no one; not anyone; (*pl verb*) not any; no one. —*adj* (*arch*) no (before vowel or *h*). —*adv* not at all (eg *none too soon*). —*n* not any; no part.

nonentity [non-en'ti-ti] *n* a person or thing of no importance.

nonesuch [nun'such] *n* an unparalleled or extraordinary thing or person.

nonpareil [non-på-rel'] *n* a person or thing without equal; a small printing type. —*adj* without an equal.

nonplus [non'plus'] *vt* to cause to be so perplexed that one cannot go, speak, act further.

nonsense [non'séns] *n* language, actions, etc. that are absurd and without meaning. —*adj* **nonsensical**.

noodle[1] [nōōd'l] *n* a simpleton, a blockhead.

noodle[2] [nōōd'l] *n* pasta formed in ribbons.

nook [nōōk] *n* a corner; a recess; a secluded retreat.

noon [nōōn] *n* midday; twelve o'clock; highest point; **noon'-tide**, the time of noon; the culminating point.

noose [nōōs] *n* a loop with a running knot; a snare like a noose. —*vt* to tie in a noose; to make a noose in or of.

nor [nôr] *conj* and not; neither.

norm [nôrm] *n* a standard or model, esp the standard of achievement of a large group.—*adj* **nor´mal**, according to rule; ordinary, average in intelligence.—*n* anything normal; the usual state, amount, etc.—*ns* **nor´malcy, normal´ity, nor´malness.**—*vti* **nor´malize**, to make or become normal.—*adv* **nor´mally.**

Norman [nôr´màn] *n* any of the people of Normandy.

Norse [nôrs] *adj* Scandinavian.—*n* the Norwegian language.

north [nôrth] *n* the direction to the left of a person facing the rising sun; the region lying in that direction; (often **North**) the northern part of the earth.—*adj* in, of, or toward the north.—*adj* **nor´therly** [TH], in, from or toward the north.—*n* a northerly wind.—*adj* **northern** [TH] of or in the north.—*ns* **nor´therner** [TH] a native or inhabitant of the north.

Norwegian [nôr-wē´j(y)àn] *adj* of Norway.

nose [nōz] *n* the part of the face above the mouth, having two openings for breathing and smelling; the sense of smell; anything like a nose in shape or position.—*vt* to discover as by smell; to nuzzle; to push (away, etc.) with the front forward.—*vi* to sniff; to pry; to move nose first.

nosegay [nōz´gā] *n* a small bunch of flowers.

noso- [nos-o-] in composition, of, or relating to, disease.—eg *n* **nosology** [nos-ol´o-ji], a list of diseases; the branch of medicine that treats of the classification of diseases.

nostalgia [nos-tal´ji-a] *n* longing for past times or places.—*adj* **nostal´gic.**

nostril [nos´tril] *n* one of the openings of the nose.

nostrum [nos´trum] *n* a quack medicine; a panacea.

not [not] *adv* a word expressing denial, negation.

notable [nō´tà-bl] *adj* worthy of being known or noted; remarkable; distinguished.—*n* a person or thing worthy of note.—*ns* **notabil´ity.**—*adv* **not´ably.**

notary [nō´tà-ri] *n* an officer authorized to certify deeds or other formal writings.

notation [nō-tā´sh(ò)n] *n* a system of signs or symbols, esp in mathematics, music, etc.

notch [noch] *n* a V-shaped cut in an edge or surface; a narrow pass with steep sides.—*vt* to cut notches in.

note [nōt] *n* a brief record of topics for speech, sermon, article, etc. set down provisionally for use afterwards; a comment attached to a text; a mark representing a musical sound; the sound itself; a key of a piano or other instrument; the song, cry, or utterance of a bird or other animal; a short informal letter; a diplomatic paper; a memorandum; notice, attention.—*vt* to make a note of; to notice; to annotate.—*adjs* **not´ed**, well-known; renowned; **note´worthy**, worthy of notice; remarkable.

nothing [nuth´ing] *n* no thing; nothingness; a zero; a trifle.—*adv* in no degree, not at all.

notice [nōt´is] *n* intimation; information; warning; a writing, placard, etc., a short article about a book, play, etc.; attention, heed; a formal warning of intention to end an agreement at a certain time.—*vt* to observe; to mention.—*adj* **not´iceable.**

notify [nō´ti-fī] *vt* to inform; to give notice to.—*n* **notificā´tion.**

notion [nō´sh(ò)n] *n* a general idea; an opinion; a whim.

notorious [nō-tō´ri-us, -tō´] *adj* widely known, esp unfavorably.—*n* **notori´ety.**

notwithstanding [not-with-stand´ing] *prep* in spite of.—*conj* although.—*adv* nevertheless.

nougat [nōō´gät] *n* a confection of sugar paste with nuts.

noun [nown] *n* (*gram*) a word that names a person, living being, object, action, etc.

nourish [nur´ish] *vt* to feed; to help forward the growth of in any way; to bring up.—*adj* **nour´ishing.**—*n* **nour´ishment.**

novel [nov´l, nuv´l] *adj* new and unusual.—*n* a relatively long fictitious prose narrative.—*n* **novelette´**, a short novel; a long short story.—*ns* **nov´elist**, a writer of novels; **nov´elty**, newness; anything new or unusual.

November [nō-vem´bèr] *n* the eleventh month, having 30 days.

novice [nov´is] *n* a person on probation in a religious order before taking final vows; a beginner.—*n* **novi´tiate** [ish´i-àt].

now [now] *adv* at the present time; by this time; at once; at that time, **then**; with things as they are.—*conj* since; seeing that.—*n* the present time.—*adj* of the present time.

nowadays [now´a-dāz] *adv* in these days.

nowhere [nō´hwär, wèr] *adv* not in, at, or to any place.

noxious [nok´shùs] *adj* harmful, unwholesome.—*adv* **nox´iously.**—*n* **nox´iousness.**

nozzle [noz´l] *n* the spout at the end of a hose, pipe, etc.

nuance [nū-äs, nwäs] *n* a delicate degree or shade of difference.

nubile [nū´bil, -bīl] *adj* marriageable (of a girl).

nucleus [nū´klē-ùs] *n* that around which something may grow, or be collected, or be concentrated; something established that will receive additions; the centrally positively charged portion of an atom; the part of an animal or plant cell containing genetic material.—**nuclear energy**, energy released or absorbed during reactions taking place in atomic nuclei; **nuclear family**, father, mother, and children; **nuclear fission**, spontaneous or induced splitting of atomic nucleus; **nuclear physics**, the branch of physics dealing with forces and transformations within the nucleus of the atom; **nuclear reaction**, a reaction within the nucleus of an atom; **nucleic acid**, any of the complex acids which are important constituents of cell nuclei.

nude [nūd] *adj* naked; bare; **nū´dity**, the state of being nude.

nudge [nuj] *n* a gentle poke, as with the elbow.—*vt* to poke gently to urge into action.

nugatory [nū´ga-tòr-i] *adj* trifling, worthless.

nugget [nug´et] *n* a lump, esp of native gold.

nuisance [nū´sàns] *n* that which annoys or causes trouble; a person or thing that is troublesome or obtrusive.

null [nul] *adj* of no legal force; void, invalid.—*n* **null´ity.**

nullify [nul´i-fī] *vt* to make null, to cancel out.

numb [num] *adj* deadened; insensible.—*vt* to make numb.—*n* **numb´ness.**

number [num´bèr] *n* a symbol or word indicating how many; a numeral identifying a person or thing by its position in a series; a single issue of a magazine; a song or piece of music, esp as an item in a performance; (*inf*) an object singled out (*a smart number*); a total of persons or things; (*gram*) the form of a word indicating singular or plural; (*pl*) arithmetic; (*pl*) numerical superiority.—*adj* **numberless**, too many to count.—**num´eral**, a symbol or group of symbols used to express a number (eg two = 2, II, binary 10, beta, 4/2, etc.).—*adj* **num´erally**, expressing numbers; consisting of numbers.—*adj* **num´erate**, having the capacity for quantitive thought and expression.—*vt* [-rāt´] to count one by one.—*ns* **numera´tion; num´erator**, the number above the fraction line.—*adj* **numer´ical**, of or relating to numbers; expressed in numbers.—*adj* **num´erous**, many, consisting of many items.

numismatic [nū-miz-mat´ik] *adj* of paper money, coins, or medals.

numskull, numbskull [num´skul] *n* a dunce.

nun [nun] *n* a woman belonging to a religious order.—*n* **nun´ery**, a convent of nuns.

nuncio [nun´shi-ō] *n* an ambassador from the Pope to a foreign state.

nuptial [nup´shàl] *adj* pertaining to marriage.—*n* (usu. in *pl*) marriage; wedding ceremony.

nurse [nûrs] *n* one who tends a child; one who has the care of the sick, feeble, or injured.—*vt* to suckle; to tend, as an infant or a sick person; to foster.—*ns* **nurs´ery**, a room set aside for children; a place where young trees and plants are raised for transplanting; **nurs´eryman**, one who owns or works in a tree nursery; **nurs´ling**, that which is nursed; a nursing child.

nurture [nûr´chùr] *n* upbringing, rearing, training; food.—*vt* to nourish; to bring up, to educate

nut [nut] *n* any fruit with one seed in a hard shell; (*bot*) a hard dry fruit that does not open at maturity, formed from a gynoecium consisting of two or more united carpels, and usu. containing one seed; a small threaded block, usu. of metal for screwing on the end of a bolt.—*vi* to gather nuts.

nutmeg [nut´meg] *n* the aromatic seed produced by a tree, grated and used as a spice.

nutria [nū´tri-a] *n* the coypu, a S American aquatic rodent; its fur.

nutrient [nū´tri-ènt] *adj* nourishing.—*ns* **nū´triment**, that which nourishes; food; **nūtri´tion**, act or process of nourishing.—*adjs* **nūtri´tious; nū´tritive.**

nux vomica [nuks vom´ik-a] *n* a seed that yields strychnine; the Asian tree that produces it.

nuzzle [nuz′l] *vti* to push (against) or rub with the nose or snout; to nestle, snuggle.

nylon [nī′lón] *n* any of numerous strong, tough, elastic, synthetic materials used esp in plastics and textiles; (*pl*) stockings made of nylon.

nymph [nimf] *n* (*myth*) one of the divinities who inhabited mountains, rivers, trees, etc.; a young and beautiful maiden.

O

oaf [ōf] *n* a dolt; an awkward lout. — *adj* oaf′ish.

oak [ōk] *n* a genus of trees of the beech family; their timber valued in shipbuilding, etc. — *n* oak′ apple, a gall caused by a gall wasp on an oak leaf.

oakum [ōk′úm] *n* tarry ropes untwisted and teased into loose hemp for caulking seams of (as of wooden ships) and packing joints (as of pipes).

oar [ōr, ór] *n* a light pole with a flat blade for propelling a boat; an oarsman. — *vt* to impel as by rowing. — *vi* to row. — *n* oars′man.

oasis [ō-ā′sis, ō′ä-sis] *n* a fertile spot or tract in a desert. — *pl* oases [ō-ā′sēz].

oast [ōst] *n* a kiln to dry hops, malt or tobacco.

oat [ōt] *n* any of several grasses, esp a widely cultivated cereal grass whose seeds are much used as food; the seeds. — *n* oat′-cake′. — *adj* oat′en. — *n* oat′meal.

oath [ōth] *n* a solemn appeal to a god or to something holy or reverenced as witness of the truth of a statement or of the inviolability of a promise; an irreverent use of God's name.

obbligato [ob-li-gä′tō] *n* a musical accompaniment that is not to be omitted; a mere accompanying part.

obdurate [ob′dū-rāt] *adj* hardened in heart or in feelings; stubborn. — *n* ob′duracy.

obedience [ō-bē′-di-ēns] *n* state of being obedient; compliance with commands, instructions, etc.

obeisance [ō′bā′sàns] *n* a bow; homage; deference. — *n* ob′elisk, a tall, four-sided, tapering pillar, usu on one stone, finished at the top like a pyramid. [L *obelus*—Gr *obelos* (dim *obeliskos*), a spit.]

obese [ō-bēs′] *adj* very fat; stout. — *n* obes′ity, abnormal fatness.

obey [ō-bā′] *vi* to render obedience; to submit. — *vt* to do as told by; to comply with; to yield to.

obfuscate [ob-fus′kāt] *vt* to darken; to bewilder.

obi [ō′bē] *n* a broad sash worn with a Japanese kimono, esp by women and girls.

obit [ō′bit] *n* an obituary. — *n* obit′uary, a short biographical account of a deceased person, or a notice of his death. — Also *adj*.

object [ob′jekt] *n* a thing capable of being presented to the senses, a thing observed, a material thing; a sight, a person or thing to which action, feeling, etc. is directed; an end or aim. — *vt* object′, to form forward in opposition. — *vi* to be opposed (to); to feel or express disapproval; to refuse assent. — objec′tion. — *adjs* objec′tionable, object′ive. — *adv* object′ively. — *ns* object′iveness, objectiv′ity; objec′tor, one who objects.

objurgate [ob′júr-gāt] *vti* to upbraid severely; to rebuke. — *n* objurgā′tion. — *adj* objur′gatory.

oblate [ob-lāt′] *adj* flattened or depressed at opposite poles. — *n* oblate′ness.

oblation [ob-lā′sh(ò)n] *n* anything offered in worship; an offering.

oblige [ō-blīj′] *vt* to compel by moral, legal, or physical force; to bind by some favor rendered; to do a favor for. — *vt* ob′ligate. — *n* obligā′tion, act of obliging; a moral or legal bond; a debt; a favor. — *adj* oblig′atory. — *adv* oblig′atorily, (or ob′lig-]. — *adj* oblīg′ing, disposed to confer favors, ready to do a good turn.

oblique [ob-lēk′] *adj* slanting; not perpendicular; not parallel; not straightforward, indirect. — *adv* oblique′ly.

obliterate [ob-lit′ér-āt] *vt* to blot out, to efface, to destroy. — *n* obliterā′tion.

oblivion [ob-liv′i-ón] *n* forgetfulness; a state of being forgotten. — *adj* obliv′ious.

oblong [ob′long] *adj* deviating from a square, circle, or sphere by being long in one direction. — *n* any oblong figure.

obloquy [ob′lo-kwi] *n* widespread censure or abuse; disgrace or infamy resulting from this.

obnoxious [ob-nok′shùs] *adj* objectionable; highly offensive.

oboe [ō′bō] *n* an orchestral woodwind musical instrument, with a double reed and keys.

obscene [ob-sēn′] *adj* foul, disgusting, indecent, esp in a sexual sense; obscen′ity [-sen′i-ti].

obscure [ob-skūr′] *adj* dark, enveloped in darkness; not distinct; not clear or legible; not easily understood, doubtful; hidden; inconspicuous; lowly, unknown to fame. — *vt* to darken; to hide. — *n* obscū′rant, one who labors to prevent enlightenment or reform. — *ns* obscū′rantism, obscū′rantist, obscū′rity, state or quality of being obscure.

obsequies [ob′sē-kwiz] *n pl* funeral rites and solemnities.

obsequious [ob-sē′kwi-us] *adj* compliant to excess, fawning. — *adv* obsē′quiously.

observe [ob-zūrv′] *vt* to keep in view; to notice; to regard attentively; to remark; to comply with; to adhere to. — *vi* to take notice; to attend; to remark (on). — *adj* observ′able, *adv* observ′ably. — *adj* observ′ant, observing; taking notice. — *n* observā′tion, act of observing; habit, practice, or faculty of observing; the act of recognizing and noting phenomena as they occur, often involving measurement with instruments; that which is observed;. — *ns* observ′atory, a place for making astronomical observations; observ′er, one engaged in scientifically exact observation; a representative sent to listen to formal discussions but not to take part.

obsess [ob-ses′] *vt* to haunt; completely to engage the thoughts of. — *n* obsession [-sesh′-(ò)n].

obsidian [ob-sid′i-àn] *n* a hard, usu. black volcanic glass.

obsolescent [ob-so-les′ènt] *adj* going out of use. — *n* obsoles′cence. — *adj* ob′solete [-lēt], gone out of use, antiquated.

obstacle [ob′stà-kl] *n* anything that stands in the way of or hinders progress; an obstruction.

obstetric, -al [ob-stet′rik, -àl] *adj* pertaining to the care and treatment of women during pregnancy and childbirth. — *ns* obstetrician [-rish′àn], one skilled in obstetrics.

obstinate [ob′sti-nàt] *adj* blindly or excessively firm, stubborn; unyielding; not easily remedied. — *ns* ob′stinacy, ob′stinateness.

obstreperous [ob-strep′èr-us] *adj* noisy, clamorous, unruly. — *adv* obstrep′erously.

obstruct [ob-strukt′] *vt* to block up, make impassable; to hinder from passing; to hamper. — *n* obstruc′tion. — *adj* obstruct′ive, tending to obstruct; hindering. — *adv*.

obtain [ob′tān′] *vt* to get, to procure by effort, to gain. — *vi* to be established, prevalent; to hold good; to prevail. — *adj* obtain′able.

obtrude [ob-trōōd′] *vt* to thrust forward, or upon one, unduly or unwelcomely. — *vi* to thrust oneself forward. — *n* obtrud′ing, obtru′sion. — *adj* obtrusive [ob-trōō′siv]. — *adv* obtrus′ively.

obtuse [ob-tūs′] *adj* blunt; not pointed; (*geom*) greater than a right angle; stupid;. — *adv* obtuse′ly.

obverse [ob-vûrs′] *adj* turned toward one; complemental, constituting the opposite aspect of the same fact. — *n* ob′verse, the side of a coin containing the head or principal symbol.

obviate [ob′vi-āt] *vt* to prevent, get round, avert.

obvious [ob′vi-us] *adj* (*arch*) being in the way or in front; easily seen or understood; evident. — *adv* ob′viously. — *n* ob′viousness.

ocarina [ok-ä-rē′na] *n* a small wind instrument with finger holes and a mouthpiece.

occasion [o-kā′zh(ò)n] *n* a special time or season; an event; an opportunity; a reason or excuse. — *vt* to cause; to give occasion to. — *adj* occā′sional. — *adv* occā′sionally.

Occident [ok′si-dènt] *n* Europe and the Americas; occident (*poet*) the west. — *adj* occiden′tal.

occult [ok-ult′] *adj* hidden; beyond the range of sense; mysterious; magical; supernatural. — *ns*.

occult′ism, occult theory or practice; belief in the influence of supernatural or supernormal powers.

occupy [ok′ū-pī] *vt* to take or seize; to hold possession of; to take up, as room, etc.; to fill, as an office; to employ (oneself, one's mind, etc.); take up (time, space, etc.). — *ns* occ′u-

pancy, the act or fact of occupying; possession; **occ′upant**, one who takes or has possession; **occupā′tion**, **occ′upĭer**, an occupant.

occur [o-kûr′] *vi* to come into the mind of a person; to happen; to be, to be found. — *n* **occurr′ence**, act or fact of happening; an event.

ocean [ō′shán] *n* the vast expanse of salt water that covers the greater part of the surface of the globe; any one of its five great divisions; any immense expanse or vast quantity. — *adj* pertaining to the ocean. — *adj* **oceanic** [ō-shi-an′ik].

ocelot [os′ė-lot] *n* a medium-sized spotted wildcat of N and S America.

ocher, ochre [ō′kèr] *n* a fine clay, mostly pale yellow, used as a pigment.

octagon [ok′ta-gon] *n* a plane figure of eight sides and eight angles. — *adj* **octag′onal**.

octant [ok′tánt] *n* the eighth part of a circle; an instrument for observing altitudes of a celestial body from a moving ship or aircraft.

octave [oc′tiv, -tāv] *n* a set of eight; the last day of eight beginning with a church festival; (*mus*) the eighth full tone above or below a given tone.

octavo [ok-tā′vō] *adj* having eight leaves to the sheet.

October [ok-tō′bèr] *n* the tenth month of the year, having 31 days.

octogenarian [ok-tō-je-nā′ri-án] *n* one who is between the ages of eighty and ninety. — Also *adj*.

octopus [ok′tō-pus] *n* any of a genus of mollusks having a soft body and eight arms covered with suckers. — *pl* **oc′topusses**, **octopī′**.

octosyllabic [ok-tō-sil-ab′ik] *adj* consisting of eight syllables.

ocular [ok′ū-lár] *adj* pertaining to the eye; formed in, or known by the eye; eyepiece. — *adv* **oc′ularly**. — *n* **oc′ulist**.

odd [od] *adj* having a remainder of one when divided by two; with the other of the pair missing; unpaired; not one of a complete set; left over; extra; unusual, queer, eccentric; occasional. — *n pl* **odds** [odz] inequalities; difference in favor of one against another; chances; dispute, strife; scraps, miscellaneous pieces, as in the phrase **odd′ity**, the state of being odd or singular; strangeness. — *adv* **odd′ly**.

ode [ōd] *n* lyric poem generally addressed to some person or thing, marked by lofty feeling.

odium [ō′di-um] *n* a general hatred. — *adj* **o′dious**, hateful, offensive, repulsive, causing hatred. — *adv*.

odont- [od-ont′-, od′ont-], **odonto-** [-ō, -o] in composition, tooth. — *ns* **odontalgia** [-al′ji-a] toothache; **odontol′ogy**, the science of teeth.

odor [ō′dór] *n* smell; scent; aroma; a characteristic or predominant quality. — *adj* **odorif′erous**, emitting a (usu. pleasant) smell. — *adj* **o′dorous**. — *adv* **o′dorously**. — *adj* **o′dorless**, without odor.

of [ov, ov] *prep* now has many shades of meaning in idiomatic phrases, including. — from; belonging to; among; proceeding or derived from; concerning.

off [of] *adv* away; newly in motion; out of continuity; no longer available; in deterioration or diminution. — *adj* most distant; on the opposite or farther side; (*fig*) remote (eg *an off chance*); not devoted to usual business (eg *an off day*); not showing the usual activity; not up to the usual standard of quality or efficiency. — *prep* not on, away from. — *interj* away! depart! — *adj* **off′-color**, varying from the standard color; improper; risque. — *adv* **off′hand**, extempore; without hesitating. — *adj* unceremonious, free and easy; ungraciously lacking in ceremony. — *ns* **off′scouring**, matter scoured off, refuse, anything vile or despised; **off′set**, a thing or value set off against another as an equivalent or compensation. — *n* **off′shoot**, that which shoots off from the main stem; the shore. — **off′spring**, a child, or children; issue; production of any kind.

offal [of′ál] *n* the part of a carcase that is unfit for human food; entrails (eg heart, liver) eaten as food.

offend [of-end′] *vt* to displease, to make angry; to affront. — *vi* to sin; to transgress (against). — *ns* **offense′**, **offend′er**. — *adj* **offens′ive**.

offer [of′èr] *vt* to present, esp as an act of devotion; to hold out for acceptance or rejection; to declare a willingness (to do); to

at hand; to declare a willingness. — *n* act of offering; that which is offered; proposal made. — **off′ertory**, money collected at a church service.

office [of′is] *n* an act of kindness or attention, a service; a function or duty; a position of trust or authority, esp in the government; act of worship; a place where business is carried on; **off′icer**, a person holding a position of authority, in a government, business, club, etc.; a policeman; a person holding a commission in the armed forces. — *adj* **official** [of-ish′ál], pertaining to an office; holding a public position; done by, or issued by, authority; formal. — *n* one who holds an office. — *adv* **offic′ially**. — *vi* **offic′iāte**, to perform the duties of an office.

oft [oft], **often**, [of′n] *adv* frequently; many times.

ogee [ō′jē, ō-jē′] *n* a molding S-shaped in section.

ogive [ō′jiv, -jīv′] *n* (*archit*) a diagonal rib across a Gothic vault; a pointed arch.

ogle [ō′gl] *vt* to look at fondly or impertinently, with side glances. — *vi* to cast amorous glances.

ogre [ō′gèr] *n* a man-eating monster or giant of fairy tales

ohm [ōm] *n* unit of electric resistance.

oil [oil] *n* any of various greasy, combustible liquid substances obtained from animal, vegetable, and mineral matter; petroleum. — *vt* to smear, lubricate, or supply with oil. — *n* **oil′cake**, the solid residue after extracting the oil from seeds (as of cotton); **oil′cloth**, cloth made waterproof by being treated with oil or paint; **oil′skin**, cloth made waterproof by means of oil; a garment made of oilskin. — *adj* **oil′y**, consisting of, containing, or having the qualities of oil; greasy.

ointment [oint′ment] *n* a fatty substance used on the skin for healing or cosmetic purposes; a salve.

okapi [o-kä′pē] *n* an animal of Central Africa, related to the giraffe.

OK, O.K. [o-kä′] *adj* all correct; all right; satisfactory. — *adv* yes, certainly.

old [ōld] *adj* advanced in years; having been long in existence; worn or worn out; former; of long standing. — *adjs* **old′en**, relating to a bygone era; **old-fash′ioned**, of a fashion like that úsed long ago; out of date. — *n* **old′-timer**, one who has lived in a place or kept a position for a long time; something that is old-fashioned. — *adj* **old′-world**, belonging to earlier times, esp having the picturesque qualities of the old world. — **maid**, a woman, esp an older woman who has never married; a prim, prudish, fussy person.

oleaginous [ō-lė-aj′in-us] *adj* oily. — *n* **oleag′inousness**.

oleander [ō-lė-an′dèr] *n* an evergreen shrub with lance-shaped leaves and beautiful flowers.

oleaster [ō-lė-as′tèr] *n* any of several plants with bitter olive-shaped fruit.

oleograph [ō′lė-ō-gräf] *n* a lithograph printed on cloth to imitate an oil painting.

olfactory [ol-fak′tór-i] *adj* pertaining to, or used in, smelling.

oligarchy [ol′i-gärk-i] *n* government by a small exclusive class; a state governed by such.

olive [ol′iv] *n* an Old World evergreen tree cultivated for its oily fruit; its fruit. — *adj* of a brownish-green color like the olive.

-ology *see* **-logy**.

Olympus [ol-im′pus] *n* a mountain on border of Thessaly and Macedonia, home of the gods. — *n*. — **Olym′pic games**, games celebrated every four years at Olympia.

omega [ō-meg′a] *n* the last letter of the Greek alphabet (Ω, ω); (*B*) the end.

omelet, omelette [om′e-let] *n* eggs beaten and cooked flat in a pan.

omen [o′mèn] *n* a sign of some future event.

ominous [om′in-us] *adj* pertaining to, or containing, an omen; portending evil, inauspicious.

omit [ō-mit′] *vt* to leave out; to fail (to); to fail to use, perform. — *n* **omiss′ion**, act of omitting; a thing omitted.

omnibus [om′ni-bus] *n* a bus, a large public vehicle for passengers by road; a book containing reprints of a number of works.

omnipotent [om-nip′o-tènt] *adj* all powerful, possessing unlimited power.

omniscient [om-nish'ént] adj knowing all things.—adv **omnis'ciently.**—n **omnis'cience.**

omnivorous [om-niv'or-us] adj taking in everything indiscriminately.

on [on] prep in contràct with the upper or presented surface of; to and toward the surface of; at or near; acting by contact with; not off.—adv in or into a position on something; not off; in continuance; in progress; on the stage; not off.

once [wuns] adv a single time; at a former time; at some future time.

one [wun] adj a single; of unit number; undivided; the same; a certain.—n the first and lowest cardinal number; an individual person or thing.—pron a person (indefinitely), as in 'one may say'; any one; some one.—n **one'ness**, singleness, unity.—adj **one'-sid'ed**, unfair, partial.

onerous [on'ér-us] adj burdensome, oppressive.

onion [un'yón] n an edible bulb of the lily family.

only [ōn'li] adj single in number; without others of the kind.— adv not more than; exclusively; alone; merely; barely.—conj (inf) but; except that.

onomatopoeia [on-ō-mat-o-pē'ya] n the formation of a word in imitation of the sound of the thing meant.—adjs **onomatopoe'ic, onomatopoet'ic.**

onset [on'set] n violent attack, assault; beginning.

onslaught [on'slöt] n an attack, onset, assault.

ontology [on-tol'o-ji] n the science that treats of the principles of pure being, that part of metaphysics which treats of the nature of existence.—adjs **ontolog'ic, ontol'ogist.**

onus [ō'nus] n burden; responsibility.

onyx [on'iks] n a variety of chalcedony with parallel layers of different colors used for making cameos.

oolite [ō'o-līt] n (geol) a kind of limestone, composed of grains like the eggs or roe of a fish.—adj **oölit'ic.**

ooze [ōōz] n slimy mud; a fine-grained, soft, deposit, composed of shells and fragments of organisms on the bottom of a body of water.—vi to flow gently; to percolate, as a liquid through pores.

opacity See **opaque.**

opal [ō'pál] n a mineral consisting of silica with some water, usu. milky white with fine play of color, in some varieties semiprecious.

opaque [ō-pāk'] adj (obs) dark; impervious to light or other radiation; not transparent; obscure.

open [ō'pn] adj not shut; allowing passage; uncovered, unprotected; free from trees; not fenced; loose; widely spaced; not frozen up; not frosty; free to be used, etc.; public; without reserve; candid; undisguised; easily understood; liable (to); unrestricted.—vt to make open; to expose to view; to begin.— vi to become open; to have an opening; to begin to appear; to begin.—n a clear space.—n **o'pener.**—adjs **o'pen-hand'ed,** generous, liberal; **o'pen-heart'ed,** responsive to emotional appeal, frank.—n **o'pening,** an open place; a breach; an aperture.—adv **o'penly.**—adjs **o'pen-mind'ed,** free to receive and consider new ideas; **o'penmouthed,** gaping; expectant; clamorous.

opera [op'ér-a] n musical drama; a musical drama.—ns **op'era glass,** a small low-power binocular for use at operas, plays, etc.—adj **operat'ic,** pertaining to or resembling opera.

operate [op'ér-āt] vi to work; to exert power or influence; to produce any effect; to perform a surgical operation.—vt to effect; to work (eg a machine); to conduct, carry on.—n **oper-ā'tion,** act, process, or result of operating; agency; influence; method of working; surgical performance.—adjs **oper-ā'tional, op'erative,** having the power of operating or acting; acting; efficacious.—n a mechanic.—adv **op'eratively.**—n **op'erātor,** one who, or that which, operates or produces an effect.

ophidian [o-fid'i-án] adj pertaining to snakes; having the nature of a snake.

ophthalm- [of-thalm'-, of'-] in composition, eye.—n **ophthalm'ia,** inflammation of the conjunctiva or the eyeball.—adj **ophthal'mic.**—ns **ophthalmol'ogy,** the branch of medicine dealing with diseases of the eye; **ophthalmol'ogist.**

opiate [ō'pi-āt] n a drug containing opium; that which dulls sensation, physical or mental.

opinion [ō-pin'yón] n a belief based on what seems to one to be probably true; judgment; view; estimation, evaluation; a formal expert judgment.—adjs **opin'ionāted, opin'ionātive,** unduly attached to one's own opinions.

opium [ō'pi-um] n the bitter brownish addictive dried narcotic juice of the opium poppy.

opossum [o-pos'um] n any of various small American marsupial mammals.

opponent [o-pō'nènt] adj opposing; placed opposite or in front.—n an adversary; one who opposes a course of action, belief, person, etc.

opportune [op-ór-tūn', op'-] adj occurring at a fitting time, timely; convenient.—ns opportun'ist, one (eg a politician) who waits for events before declaring his opinions, or shapes his conduct or policy to circumstances of the moment; **opportun'ity,** an occasion offering a possibility or chance; a combination of favoring circumstances (eg *opportunity makes the thief*).

oppose [o-pōz'] vt to place in front of or in the way of; to set in contrast (to); to balance against; to place as an obstacle; to resist; to contend with.—n **oppos'er.**

opposite [op'o-zit] adj placed over against; face to face; opposed contrary.—n that which is opposed or contrary; an opponent.—prep across from.—adv **opp'ositely.**—n **opp'ositeness.**

opposition [op-o-zish'(ó)n] n state of being placed over against; position over against; contrast; contradistinction; act of setting opposite; act of opposing; resistance; that which opposes.

oppress [o-pres'] vt to press against or upon; to lie heavy upon; to overpower; to treat with tyrannical cruelty or injustice.—n **oppress'ion,** adj **oppress'ive,** adv **oppress'ively.**

opprobrium [o-prō'bri-um] n the disgrace or reproach of shameful conduct; infamy.—adj **oppro'brious.**

oppugn [o-pūn'] vt to assail, call in question; to attack or to resist.—n **oppugn'er.**

opt [opt] vi to choose.—**optative,** [op'ta-tiv] adj expressing desire or wish.

optic, -al [op'tik, -ál] adj relating to sight; (optical) constructed to help the sight; acting by means of light; visual.— adv **op'tically.**—ns **optician** [tish'án] one who makes or sells eyeglasses, etc.

optimism [op'ti-mizm] n the belief that everything is ordered for the best; a disposition to take a hopeful view of things; (loosely) hopefulness.—n **op'timist.**—adj **optimist'ic.**—adv **optimist'ically.**

option [op'sh(ó)n] n act of choosing; power of choosing; an alternative for choice.—adj **op'tional,** left to one's choice.

opulent [op'ū-lènt] adj wealthy.—n **op'ulence.**

opus [op'us or ō'pus] n a work, a musical composition, esp any of the numbered musical works of a composer.—pl **opera** (op'ér-a).

or [ōr] conj a coordinating conjunction introducing: an alternative; the last in a series of choices; a synonymous word or phrase.

oracle [or'a-kl] n a medium or agency, esp in ancient Greece, of divine revelation; a response by a god; a shrine where such responses are given; a person.

oral [ō'rál, ö'rál] adj relating to the mouth; uttered by the mouth; spoken, not written.—adv **o'rally.**

orange [or'inj] n the gold-colored fruit of certain trees; the trees themselves; a color between red and yellow.—adj pertaining to an orange; orange-colored.—**orange stick,** a thin pointed stick, esp one of wood from an orange tree, used for manicuring.

Orangeman [or'inj-man] n a member of a society instituted in Ireland in 1795 to uphold Protestantism, or the cause of William of Orange.

orangutan [ō-rang'ōō-tan'] n a largely herbivorous anthropoid ape.

oration [ō-rā'sh(ó)n] n a formal speech.

orator [or'a-tór] n a public speaker; a man of eloquence.—n **or'atory,** the art of speaking well, or so as to please and persuade, esp publicly; the exercise of eloquence; a place of prayer, esp a private or institutional chapel.

oratorio [or-a-tō'ri-ō] n a story, usually Biblical, set to music, without scenery, costumes, or acting.

orb [örb] n a sphere; a celestial body; the globe; a sphere

surmounted by a cross symbolizing regal power and justice.—
vt to form into a disk or circle.—*adj* **orbic'ular**,

orbit [ör'bit] *n* the path in which a heavenly body moves round
another, a path in space round a heavenly body; regular
course; sphere of action; the hollow in which the eyeball
rests.—*vt* to put into orbit; to circle round; to go round in
orbit.—*adj* **or'bital**.

orchard [ör'chård] *n* a planting of fruit trees.

orchestra [ör'kès-tra] *n* in the Greek theater, the place where
the chorus danced; now the part of a theater in which the
musicians are placed; the seats on the main floor of a theater; a
company of musicians playing together under a conductor;
their instruments.—*adj* **orches'tral**.—*vt* **or'chestrāte**, to
arrange (music) for an orchestra.

orchid [ör'kid] *n* any of a family of plants with rich, showy,
often fragrant flowers.

ordain [ör-dān'] *vt* (*obs*) to arrange in order; (*obs*) to appoint (to
a duty); to invest with the office of minister, priest, or rabbi;
to decree, destine; to order.—*vi* to enact, command.

ordeal [ör-dēl'] *n* an ancient form of referring a disputed
question to the judgment of God, by lot, fire, water, etc.; any
severe trial or examination.

order [ör'dèr] *n* arrangement; method; sequence; suitable,
normal, or fixed arrangement; regular government; an undisturbed condition; tidiness; a class of society; a body of persons
of the same profession, etc.; a religious fraternity; a dignity
conferred by a sovereign, etc.; an instruction or authorization;
a rule, regulation; a command; state or condition, esp with
regard to functioning; a request to supply something; the
goods supplied.—*vti* to put or keep (things) in order; to
arrange; to command; to request (something) to be supplied.—**or'derly**, in good order; methodical; *n* a soldier who
carries official messages for his superior officer; a hospital
attendant who does routine or heavy work.—*n* **or'derliness**.

ordinal [ör'din-ål] *adj* indicating order of sequence.—*n* an
ordinal numeral (as first, second, etc.).

ordinary [ör'di-nå-ri] *adj* usual; of common rank; plain, undis-
tinguished.—*n* something settled or customary; a judge of
probate in some states of the US.—*adv* **or'dinarily**.

ordnance [örd'náns] *n* military supplies; artillery.

ordure [ör'dūr] *n* excrement; dung.

ore [ör, ör] *n* a mineral aggregate from which one or more
valuable constituents may be obtained.

oregano [ö-reg-ä'nō, ö-reg'å-nō] *n* an aromatic culinary herb of
the mint family.

organ [ör'gån] *n* an instrument, or means by which anything is
done; a part of a plant or animal body fitted for carrying out a
natural or vital function; a means of communicating information or opinions, as a periodical; a subordinate group or
organization that performs specialized functions; a musical
instrument consisting of pipes made to sound by compressed
air or electronically, and played upon by means of keys; a
musical instrument in some way resembling the pipe organ, as
the barrel organ, etc.—*ns* **or'ganist**, one who plays an
organ.—*adjs* **organ'ic**, pertaining to, derived from, of the
nature of, a bodily organ or a living organism; systematically
arranged.—*adv* **organ'ically**.—*vt* **or'ganize**, to form into an
organized whole; to establish; to institute; to persuade to
join a cause, group, etc.; to arrange for.—*ns* **organizā'tion**,
or'ganism, any living thing.

organdy, organdie [ör'gan-di] *n* a fine transparent muslin with
a stiff finish.

orgasm [ör'gazm] *n* immoderate excitement or action, esp in
the culmination of sexual excitement; an instance of it. [Gr
orgasmos, swelling.]

orgy [ör'ji] *n* a riotous or drunken revel, esp with sexual
activity.

oriel [ö'ri-èl] *n* a recess with a window built out from a wall.—
Also *adj*.

Orient [ö'ri-ènt] *n* the East, or Asia, esp the Far East.—*adj*
(*arch*) of the east; lustrous, sparkling.—*vti* to adjust (oneself)
to a particular situation.—*vt* to arrange in a direction, esp in
relation to the points of the compass; to cause the axes of
molecules to assume the same direction. **orien'talist**.—*adv*
orien'tally.—*vt* **o'rientāte**, to orient; to face or turn to the
east.—*n* **orientā'tion**.

orifice [ör'i-fis] *n* a mouthlike opening.

oriflamme [or'i-flam] *n* a banner, symbol, or ideal inspiring
devotion or courage.

origin [or'i-jin] *n* the rising or first existence of anything; that
from which anything first proceeds, source; parentage.—*adj*
orig'inal, pertaining to the origin or beginning; existing from
or at the beginning; innate; not derived or imitated; being that
from which copies are made.—*n* a primary type that has given
rise to varieties; an original work, as of art or literature.—
original'ity.—*adv* **orig'inally**.—*vt* **orig'inate**.—*n* **orig-
inā'tion**.

oriole [öri'ōl] *n* any of a family of birds in which the males are
usu. bright yellow or orange and black and the females chiefly
greenish or yellowish.

Orion [ö-rī'on] *n* one of the constellations, containing seven
very bright stars, three of which form Orion's belt.

orison [or'i-zón] *n* a prayer.

orlop deck [ör'lop dek] *n* the lowest deck in a ship having four
or more decks.

ormolu [ör'mo-lōō] *n* an imitation gold made of a copper and
tin alloy.

ornament [ör'na-mènt] *n* anything that adds, or is meant to
add, grace or beauty; one whose character or talent adds luster
to his surroundings.—*vt* [or-na-ment'] to adorn, to furnish
with ornaments.—*adjs* **ornament'al**.—*n* **ornamentā'tion**.

ornate [ör-nāt'] *adj* decorated; much or elaborately ornamented.—*adv* **ornate'ly**.

ornithology [ör-ni-thöl'ó-jè] *n* the branch of zoology dealing
with birds; a treatise on ornithology.—*adj* **ornitholog'ical**.—
n **ornithol'ogist**.

orography [or-og'ra-fi] *n* a branch of physical geography dealing with mountains.

orphan [ör'fàn] *n* a child whose parents are dead.—*adj* being
an orphan;.—*vt* to cause to become an orphan.—*vt* **or'phan-
age**, an institution that is a home for orphans.

orpiment [ör'pi-mènt] *n* arsenic trisulfide, a yellow mineral
used as a pigment.

orrery [or'èr-i] *n* a clockwork model to illustrate the relative
positions, motions, etc., of the heavenly bodies.

orris [or'is] *n* a species of iris the dried root of which has the
smell of violets.

orthodontics, orthodontia [ör-thö-don'tiks, -don'shi-à] *ns* the
branch of dentistry dealing with rectification of abnormalities
of the teeth.

orthodox [ör'thö-doks] *adj* sound in doctrine; holding the
received or established opinions, esp in religion; according to
such opinions.—*n* **or'thodoxy**.

orthographer [ör-thog'ra-fèr] *n* one skilled in orthography.—
orthog'raphy (*gram*), the art or practice of spelling words
correctly.

orthopedic [ör-thö-pēd'ik] *adj* of, relating to, or used in
orthopedics; marked by deformities or crippling.

ortolan [ör'tō-làn] *n* a kind of bunting common in Europe, and
considered a great table delicacy.

oscillate [os'il-lāt] *vi* to swing to and fro like a pendulum; to
vary between certain limits (eg between extremes of opinion,
action, etc.); to vary above and below a mean value.—*n*
oscillā'tion;

osculate [os'kū-lāt] *vt* to kiss (someone).—*n* **osculā'tion**.—*adj*
os'culatory.

osier [özh'(y)èr, öz'i-èr, öz'yèr] *n* any willow.

osmium [os'mi-úm] *n* a metallic element.

osmosis [oz-mō'sis] *n* the passage of fluid through a semipermeable membrane from a low-to-high concentrate of sol-
utions.—*adj* **osmot'ic**.

osprey [os'prā] *n* a hawk that feeds on fish; an egret or other
plume used in millinery.

osseous [os'è-us] *adj* bony; composed of, or resembling,
bone.—*n* **oss'icle**, a small bone or bony structure.—*vt*.

ossifrage [os'i-frāj] *n* a large Eurasian vulture.

ostensible [os-tens'i-bl] *adj* that may be shown; pretended,
professed, apparent (eg of a reason).—*adv* **ostens'ibly**.—*adj*
ostens'ive, showing, exhibiting.—*n* **ostentā'tion**.—*adj*
ostentā'tious.

osteo- [os'tè-ō-], **oste-**, [os'tè-], in composition, bone.—
osteol'ogy, a branch of anatomy dealing with bones; the bony
structure of an organism. **osteop'athy**, a therapeutic system

which treats disease by manipulation and massage, often as an adjunct to medical and surgical measures

-ostomy *see* -stomy.

ostracize [os'tra-sīz] *vt* to exclude from society.—*n* os'tracism [-sizm].

ostrich [os'trich] *n* a genus of the largest living birds, remarkable for their speed in running.

other [uᴛʜ'ér] *adj* second; alternate; different from or not the same as; remaining.—*pron* the other one; some other one.—**oth'erwise**, in another way or manner.

otiose [ō'shi-ōs] *adj* unoccupied, idle; functionless.

otter [ot'ér] *n* any of several aquatic fish-eating carnivores of the weasel family; the fur or the pelt of an otter.

ottoman, an upholstered chair or couch usu without a back; an overstuffed footstool without a back.

oubliette [ōō-blē-et'] *n* a dungeon with an opening at the top.

ouch¹ [owch] *n* (*arch*) a brooch; the setting for a precious stone.

ouch² [owch] *interj* expressing sudden pain.

ought [öt] *pt* of owe; now an auxiliary *v* (with either present or past sense) to be under obligation.

Ouija [wē'ja] *n* (*trade name*) a board with an alphabet, used with a planchette.

ounce¹ [owns] *n*, a unit of weight, ¹/₁₆ pound avoirdupois or ¹/₁₂ pound troy.

ounce² [owns] *n* a snow leopard.

our [owr] *possessive adj* (or *possessive pron*) pertaining or belonging to us.

ousel *See* ouzel.

oust [owst] *vt* to eject, expel, dispossess..—*n* oust'er (*law*), ejection; a wrongful dispossession.

out [owt] *adv* not within; forth; abroad; in or into the open air; in, towards, or at the exterior; to the full stretch or extent; beyond bounds; in a state of exclusion; ruled out, not to be considered; no longer in concealment; no longer in office, in the game, in use, fashion, etc.; on strike; in error; loudly and clearly; (*slang*) into unconsciousness.—*adj* external; outlying; outward; exceeding the usual; in any condition expressed by the adverb *out*; (*inf*) having suffered a financial loss.—*prep* out of; along the way of.—*n* something that is out.—*vi* to become known.

out- [owt-] *pfx* (1) meaning in, or toward, a position external to a position understood (eg *outline, outbuilding, outlying, outdoor, outgoing, outlook*); also (*fig*) with suggestion of openness, frankness, completeness (eg *outcry, outspoken, outworn*); (2) prefixed to verbs to express the fact that, in some action, the subject goes beyond a standard indicated (eg to *outbid, outshine*), and to nouns and adjectives to express the fact of exceeding a standard (eg *outsize*).

outbreak [owt'brāk] *n* a breaking out (eg of anger, strife, contagious or infectious disease); a disturbance.

outcast [owt'käst] *n* one who is banished from society or home.

outclass [owt'kläs'] *vt* to surpass so far as to seem in a different class.

outcome [owt'kum] *n* the consequence, result.

outcrop [owt'krop] *n* the exposure of a stratum at the surface; the part of a stratum so exposed.—Also *vi*.

outer [owt'ér] *adj* further out or away.—*adjs* out'ermost, out'most, farthest out; most distant.

outing [owt'ing] *n* a pleasure trip; an outdoor excursion.

outlandish [owt-land'ish] *adj* foreign; strange; fantastic.

outlaw [owt'lö] *n* originally one deprived of the protection of the law; a habitual or notorious criminal.—*vt* originally, to place beyond the law, to deprive of the benefit of the law; to declare illegal.

outpost [owt'pōst] *n* (*mil*) a small group stationed at a distance from the main force, the station so occupied, or a foreign base; a frontier settlement.

outrage [owt'rāj'] *n* an extremely vicious or violent act; a grave insult or offense; great anger, etc. aroused by this.—*vt* to commit an outrage upon or against; to cause outrage in.—*adj* outrā'geous.

outré [ōōt'rā] *adj* eccentric, bizarre.

outrigger [owt'rig-ér] *n* a projecting spar for extending sails or any part of the rigging; a timber rigged out from the side of a canoe to prevent topping; a canoe of this type; a projecting frame to support the elevator or tail of an aircraft or the rotor of a helicopter.

outright [owt'rīt] *adj* out-and-out, downright, direct.—*adv* outright', unreservedly.

outside [owt'sīd] *n* the outer side; the surface, exterior; any area not inside.—*adj* on the outside; exterior; extreme; slight.—*adv* on or to the outside; not within.—*prep* outside of; beyond.

outskirt [owt'skûrt] *n* (*pl*) districts remote from the center, as of a city.

outstanding [owt-stand'ing] *adj* projecting; distinguished; prominent; unpaid; still to be attended to or done; (of stocks and bonds) issued and sold.

outstrip [owt-strip'] *vt* to outrun; to leave behind.

outward [owt'wàrd] *adj* toward the öutside; external; exterior; clearly apparent.—*adv* toward the exterior.

outwork [owt'wûrk] *n* a minor defensive position outside the principal wall or line of fortification.

ova [ō'va] *pl* of **ovum**.—*adj* o'val, having the shape of an egg.—*n* anything oval.—*adv* o'vally.

ovation [ō-vā'sh(ó)n] *n* an outburst of popular applause or public welcome.

oven [uv'n] *n* a chamber for baking, heating, or drying.

over [ō'vér] *prep* higher than—in place, rank, value, etc.; across; above; upon the whole surface of; concerning; on account of; in study of or occupation with; more than.—*adv* on the top; above; across; from beginning to end, up and down.—*adj* upper or superior; surplus; excessive; finished, at an end.

over- [ō-vér-] *prefix* meaning: (1) above in position across (eg *overleap, overlook*), across the surface, beyond, across the edge or boundary; (2) completely; (3) beyond the normal or desirable limit, excessively.

overawe [ō-vér-ö'] *vt* to restrain by fear or authority.

overbear [ō-vér-bār'] *vt* to bear down or overpower; to overwhelm.—*adj* **overbear'ing**, haughty and dogmatical; imperious.

overboard [ō-vér-bōrd'] *adv* over the board or side of a ship, etc.; (*inf*) to extremes of enthusiasm; into discord.

overcast [ō-vér-käst'] *vt* to cloud, cover with gloom; to sew over rough edges of (a piece of cloth).—*adj* clouded over.

overcome [ō-vér-kum'] *vt* to get the better of, to conquer or subdue.—*adj* helpless, overpowered by exhaustion or emotion.—*vi* to be victorious.

overdue [ō-vér-dū'] *adj* unpaid, unperformed, etc., though the time for payment, performance, etc., is past.

overflow [ō-vér-flō'] *vt* to flow over; to flood; (of eg people) to fill and then spread beyond (eg a room).—*vi* to run over; to abound.

overhaul [ō-vér-höl'] *vt* to turn over for examination; to examine; to catch up with.—*n* o'verhaul, examination; repair.

overhead [ō-vér-hed'] *adv* above the head; in the sky; on a higher level, with reference to related objects.—*n* the general, continuing costs of a business, as of rent, taxes, etc.—*adv* [o'vér-hed'] above the head; aloft.

overland [ō'vér-land'] *adj, adv* by, on, or across land.

overpass [ō'vér-päs] *n* a road crossing another highway, pedestrian path, or railroad crossing at a higher level; the upper level of such a crossing.

overreach [ō-vér-rēch'] *vt* to reach or extend beyond; to outwit or get the better of; (*refl*) to defeat by attempting too much or by being oversubtle.

oversee [ō-vér-sē'] *vt* to supervise; to superintend.—*n* o'verséer.

oversight [ō'vér-sīt] *n* superintendence; failure to notice; an omission.

overt [ō'vért, ō-vûrt'] *adj* open to view, public; (*law*) openly done with evident intent.—*adv* o'vertly.

overtake [ō-vér-tāk'] *vt* to come up with, to catch; to pass from behind; to come upon unexpectedly (eg *a storm overtook him*).

overthrow [ō-vér-thrō'] *vt* to throw over, overturn; to ruin, to subvert, to defeat utterly; to throw a baseball over or past (as a base).

overtime [ō'vér-tīm] *n* time employed in working beyond the regular hours; work done in such time; pay for such work.

overtone [ō'vér-tōn] *n* (*mus*) a harmonic, any of the components above the fundamental frequency of a tone; the color of light reflected (as by a paint).

overture [ō'vėr-chùr] *n* an opening of negotiations; a proposal; (*mus*) an instrumental prelude to an opera, oratorio, etc.

overweening [ō-vėr-wēn'ing] *adj* conceited, arrogant, presumptuous.

overwhelm [ō-vėr-hwelm'] *vt* to overspread and crush; to overpower.

ovine [ō'vīn] *adj*, *n* (of, or resembling) a sheep.

oviparous [ō-vip'á-rus] *adj* producing eggs that hatch after leaving the body.

owe [ō] *vt* to be indebted to for to be under an obligation to pay, restore, etc.; to have the need to give, do, etc. as because of gratitude.—*vi* to be in debt.

owing [ō'ing] *adj* due, to be paid; imputable, attributable (to).—**owing to**, in consequence of.

owl [owl] *n* any of an order (Strigiformes) of predacious nocturnal birds.—*n* **owl'et**, a little or young owl.—*adj* **owl'ish**, like an owl; solemn.

own[1] [ōn] *vt* to possess; to acknowledge as one's own; to admit.—*vi* to confess (to).—*n* that which belongs to oneself.—*ns* **own'er**, possessor; **own'ership**.

own[2] [ōn] *adj* belonging to oneself or itself, often used with reflexive force, *my own, his own*.

ox [oks] *n* any of various cud-chewing mammals of the cattle family, esp a domestic bovine mammal; a castrated bull.—*pl* **ox'en**, **ox.**—*ns* **ox'eye**, any of several composite plants having heads with both disk and ray flowers; **oxeye daisy**, a composite herb having a flowerhead with well-developed ray flowers.

oxalis [oks'a-lis] *n* wood sorrel.

oxide [oks'īd] *n* a compound of oxygen and another element or radical.—*vt* **ox'idize**, to combine with oxygen as in burning or rusting; to add an electropositive atom or group to, or remove an electronegative atom or group from, a molecule.—*vi* to become oxidized.—*n* **oxidā'tion**.

oxlip [oks'lip] *n* a Eurasian primula resembling the cowslip.

oxygen [oks'i-jèn] *n* a gaseous element without taste, color, or smell, forming part of the air, water, etc., and supporting life and combustion.

oxymoron [ok-si-mō', (-mō')ron] *n* a figure of speech in which contradictory terms are combined, as *falsely true*, etc.

oyez, oyes[ō-yes', ō'yes] *interj* the call of a public crier for attention.

oyster [ois'tèr] *n* any of various marine bivalve mollusks used as food.

ozone [ō'zōn] *n* an allotropic form of oxygen, with a peculiar smell, a powerful oxydizing agent.

P

pabulum [pab'ū-lum] *n* easily assimilated food; nourishment for the mind.

pace[1] [pās] *n* a stride, step; the space between the feet in walking; rate of motion (of a man or a beast).—*vt* to measure by steps.—*vt* to measure by steps; to train in walking or stepping; to set the pace for in a race by example.—**pace'-mak'er**, one who sets the pace, as in a race; an electronic device used to correct weak or irregular heart rhythms.

pachyderm [pak'i-dùrm] *n* one of an order of nonruminant, hoofed mammals, thick-skinned, as the elephant.—*adj* **pachyder'matous**.

pacify [pas'i-fī] *vt* to appease; to calm; to bring peace to.—*adj* **pacif'ic**, peacemaking; appeasing; peaceful.—*n* **pacifi-cā'tion**.—*ns* **pac'ifier**, a person or thing that pacifies; **pac'ifist**, **pac'ifism**, opposition to the use of force under any circumstances, specifically the refusal to participate in war.

pack[1] [pak] *n* a bundle (esp one for carrying on the back); a complete set of playing cards; a group or mass; a number of wild animals living together; act or method of packing; a compact package, esp of something for sale.—*vt* to make into a bundle or pack; to put into a bag or other article of luggage; to press together closely; to crowd, to cram; to press tightly, as for prevention of leaks; to carry in a pack; to send (off); (*slang*) to carry (a gun, etc.).—*vi* to form into a pack; to settle or be driven into a firm mass; to put one's belongings together in bags or boxes; to depart in haste .—*adj* used for carrying

packs, loads, etc.—*n* **pack'age**, a bundle, or parcel.—*vt* to make a parcel of.—*ns* **pack'er**, **pack'et**, a small package.—*n* **pack'horse**, a horse used to carry goods; **pack' sadd'le**, a saddle adapted for supporting the load on a pack animal; **pack'thread**, a coarse thread used to sew up packages.

pact [pakt] *n* an agreement or compact.

pad[1] [pad] *n* the dull sound of a footstep.—*vi* to walk esp with a soft step.

pad[2] [pad] *n* anything stuffed with a soft material to prevent friction or pressure or injury, or for filling out; a number of sheets of paper glued together at one edge; the cushioned thickening of an animal's sole; the floating leaf of a water lily; a piece of folded absorbent material used as a surgical dressing; to fill out to greater length with words or matter that add nothing to the meaning; to expand an expense account with fraudulent entries.—*n* **padd'ing**, stuffing; matter of less value introduced into a book or article to make it of the length desired.

paddle[1] [pad'l] *vi* to wade about or dabble in shallow water.

paddle[2] [pad'l] *n* a short oar with a wide blade at one or both ends, used without an oarlock.—*vti* to propel (a canoe etc.) by a paddle; to beat as with a paddle; to spank; **padd'le wheel**, a wheel with paddles, floats, or boards around its circumference used to propel a boat.

paddock [pad'ók] *n* an enclosed field under pasture.

paddy [pad'i] *n* threshed unmilled rice; a rice field.

padlock [pad'lok] *n* a detachable lock with a link to pass through a staple or other opening.—*vt* to fasten with a padlock.

padre [pa'drä] *n* father, a priest or chaplain.

paean [pē'án] *n* a song or hymn of triumph.

pagan [pā'gàn] *n* a heathen; one who has no religion.—Also *adj*.—*n* **pā'ganism**.

page[1] [pāj] *n* a boy attendant; at a formal function (as a wedding).

page[2] [pāj] *n* one side of a leaf of a book.—*vt* to number the pages of; to make up into pages.—*n* **pagination** [paj-i-nā'sh(ô)n] the act of paging a book; the arrangement and number of pages.

pageant [paj'ént] *n* a spectacle, esp one carried around in procession; a series of tableaux or dramatic scenes connected with local history or other topical matter held outdoors; a mere show.—*adj* of the nature of pageant.—*n* **page'antry**, splendid display; mere show.

pagoda [pa-gō'da] *n* in the Far East, a temple the form of a many-storied, tapering tower.

pail [pāl] *n* an open vessel with a hooped handle, usu. for holding or carrying liquids.

pain [pān] *n* bodily or mental suffering; anguish.—*vt* to cause suffering to; **pain'ful**.—*adv* **pain'fully.** *adj* **pain'less**.—*adv* **pains'taking**.

paint [pānt] *vt* to make (a picture) using oil pigments, etc.; to depict with paints; to cover or decorate with paint; to describe.—*vi* to practice painting.—*n* a coloring substance; a dried coat of paint.—*adj*.—*ns* **paint'er**.

painter [pānt'ėr] *n* a rope used to fasten a boat.

pair [pār] *n* two things equal, or suited to each other, or growing, grouped, or used together.—*vti* to form a pair (of); to mate.

pajamas [pá-jam'áz] *n pl* a loosely fitting sleeping or lounging suit consisting of jacket and trousers.

pal [pal] *n* a close friend.

palace [pal'ás] *n* the official residence of a sovereign; a large stately house or public building.

paladin [pal'a-din] *n* a champion of a medieval prince; an eminent champion of a cause.

palanquin [pal'-an-kēn'] *n* a covered litter, formerly used in the Orient, carried on the shoulders of four men. [Port *palanquim*; cf Hindustani *palang*, a bed—Sans *palyaṅka*, a bed.]

palate [pal'át] *n* the roof of the mouth; taste; mental relish.—*adj* **palatable** [pal'át-á-bl] acceptable.

palatial [pa-lā'sh(à)l] *adj* of or like a palace.

palaver [pa-läv'er] *n* a conference, usu. between persons of different levels of sophistication; idle talk.

pale[1] [pāl] *n* a stake of wood driven into the ground for fencing; anything that encloses; a broad stripe from top to bottom of a shield in heraldry.—*n* **pāl'ing**, wood or stakes for fencing.

pale² [pāl] *adj* (of a complexion) whitish; wan; dim. — *vt* to make pale.

pale-, paleo- prefix meaning; old.

paleobotany [pal-i-ō-bot'ȧn-i] *n* the study of fossil plants.

paleography [pāl-i-og'ra-fi] *n* ancient modes of writing; study of ancient modes of handwriting.

Paleolithic [pal-i-ō-lith'ik] *adj* of the earlier Stone Age.

paleontology [pāl-i-on-tol'o-ji] *n* the study of fossils. — *adj* **paleontolog'ical.** — *n* **paleontol'ogist.**

paleozoology [pāl-i-ō-zō-ol'o-ji] *n* the study of fossil animals.

palette [pal'ėt] *n* a little board on which a painter mixes his colors.

palfrey [pöl'fri] *n* (*arch*) a saddle horse, esp for a lady.

palimpsest [pal'imp-sest] *n* a parchment or other piece of writing material on which old writing has been rubbed out to make room for new.

palisade [pal-i-sād'] *n* a fence of stakes. — *vt* to surround or defend with a palisade.

pall¹ [pöl] *n* a rich cloth used as covering, esp for a coffin; a chalice cover; a mantle as of smoke.

pall² [pöl] *vi* to become insipid, or wearisome to appetite or interest; to become satiated.

pallet¹ [pal'ėt] *n* a portable platform for lifting and stacking goods.

pallet² [pal'ėt] *n* a mattress of straw, a small bed.

palliasse [pal-i-as', pal-yas'] *n* a thin straw mattress.

palliate [pal'i-āt] *vt* to extenuate, to soften by favorable representations; to alleviate without curing (a disease). — *n* **pallia'tion,** *adj* **pall'iative.**

pallid [pal'id] *adj* pale, wan.

pallor [pal'ör] *n* paleness, esp of the face.

palm¹ [päm] *n* the inner surface of the hand between wrist and fingers.

palm² [päm] *n* a tropical or subtropical tree, shrub or vine; a symbol or token of triumph or preeminence. **Palm' Sun'day,** the Sunday before Easter.

palpable [pal'pa-bl] *adj* that can be felt; readily perceived by any of the senses; readily perceived or detected by the mind (eg errors, lies. — *ns* **palpabil'ity, pal'pableness.** — *adv* **pal'pably.**

palpitate [pal'pi-tāt] *vi* to throb, beat rapidly and strongly; pulsate. — *n* **palpita'tion.**

palsy [pöl'zi] *n* paralysis; a condition marked by an uncontrollable tremor of a part of the body.

palter [pöl'tėr] *vi* to trifle; to haggle, bargain; to shuffle, equivocate, play false.

paltry [pöl'tri] *adj* almost worthless; trifling.

pamper [pam'pėr] *vt* to overindulge.

pamphlet [pam'flet] *n* a thin, unbound booklet, usu. on some subject of the day. — *n* **pamphleteer',** a writer of pamphlets.

pan¹ [pan] *n* a usu. broad, shallow container for domestic use a basin or depression in land. — *vt* to wash (gold-bearing gravel) in a pan; (*inf*) to criticize harshly. — *ns* **pan'cake,** a thin cake of eggs, flour, sugar, and milk cooked on a griddle; **pancake landing,** a landing of an airplane dropping from a relatively steep angle, with low forward speed.

panacea [pan-a-sē'a] *n* a universal medicine.

panache [pä-näsh'] *n* a plume, esp on a helmet; swagger, display, sense of style.

panada [pa-nä'dä] *n* a paste of flour or bread crumbs and water or stock.

panama [pan-a-mä'] *n* a hat made of plaited strips of the leaves of a S American plant.

pancreas [pan(g)'krė-as] *n* a large gland situated under and behind the stomach, secreting a digestive juice into the intestine and also producing insulin. — *adj* **pancreat'ic.**

panda [pan'dä] *n* a long-tailed Himalayan carnivore (*Ailurus fulgens*) related to the raccoon.

pandemic [pan-dem'ik] *adj* epidemic over a large region.

pandemonium [pan-dė-mō'ni-um] *n* tumultuous uproar.

pander [pan'dėr] *n* one who procures for another the means of gratifying his base passions; a pimp. — *vi* to act as a pander (to).

pane [pān] *n* a sheet of glass in a frame of a window, door, etc.

panegyric [pan-ė-jir'ik] *n* a eulogy, a formal speech or writing in praise of some person.

panel [pan'(ė)l] *n* a usu. rectangular section or division forming part of a wall, door, etc.; a board for instruments or controls; a lengthwise strip in a skirt, etc.; a list of names summoned for jury duty; a group of persons chosen for judging, discussing, etc. — *vt* to decorate or furnish with panels. — *n* **pan'elling,** panels collectively; sheets of wood, plastic, etc. used for panels.

pang [pang] *n* a sudden sharp pain or feeling.

panic [pan'ik] *n* frantic or sudden fright; contagious fear; general alarm. — Also *adj.*

pannier, panier [pan'yėr or pan'ē-ėr] *n* a large basket for carrying loads on the back of an animal or the shoulders of a person; one of a pair or packs of baskets slung over the rear wheel of a bicycle; a contrivance of whalebone, etc., for puffing out a woman's dress at the hips.

panoply [pan'ō-pli] *n* a full suit of armour; full or brilliant covering or array.

panorama [pan-ō-rä'ma] *n* a wide or complete view; a picture unrolled and made to pass before the spectator. — *adj* **panoramic** [-ram'ik].

pansy [pan'zi] *n* a garden plant derived chiefly from the wild pansy of Europe.

pant [pant] *vi* to gasp for breath; to wish ardently (for, after something). — *vt* to utter gaspingly.

Pantaloon [pan-ta-loon] *n* a character in Italian comedy, and afterwards in pantomime, a lean old man more or less a dotard; (*pl*) loose-fitting usu. shorter than ankle-length trousers.

pantheism [pan'thē-izm] *n* the doctrine that identifies God with the universe. — *n* **pan'theist.** — *adjs* **pantheist'ic, -al.** — *n* **pantheon** [pan'thē-on] *n* a temple of all the gods; a building in which the famous dead of a nation are entombed.

panther [pan'thėr] *n* a leopard, esp a black one; a cougar or jaguar.

pantile [pan'tīl] *n* a tile whose cross section is S-shaped.

pantograph [pan'tō-gräf] *n* a jointed framework of rods for copying drawings, plans, etc., on the same, or a different, scale. [Gr *pās*, neut *pān*, all, *graphein*, to write.]

pantomime [pan'tō-mīm] *n* a drama without words, using only actions and gestures; a British theatrical entertainment, usu. around Christmas, in which some nursery story is acted. — *vti* to express or act in pantomime. — *adjs* **pantomimic** [-mim'ik], -al.

pantry [pan'tri] *n* a small room or closet off the kitchen for storing cooking ingredients and utensils etc.

pants [pants] *n* trousers.

panzer [pant'zėr] *n* a tank. — *adj* armoured.

pap [pap] *n* soft food for infants or invalids; any oversimplified or insipid writing, ideas, etc.

papacy [pā'pa-si] *n* the office of pope; a pope's tenure of office; papal system of government.

papal [pā'pȧl] *adj* of the pope, the papacy.

paper [pā'pėr] *n* the material made from rags, wood, etc. on which we commonly write and print; similar material for wrapping and other purposes; a single sheet of this; an official document; (*pl*) documents proving identity, authorisation, etc. — *adj* consisting, or made, of paper. — *vt* to cover with wallpaper.

papier-mâché [pap'yä-mä'shä] *n* a material consisting of paper pulp mixed with size, glue, etc. and molded into various objects when moist.

papoose [pap-ōōs'] *n* an Amerindian baby.

paprika [pa-prē'kȧ, pap'ri-ka] *n* a mild red condiment ground from the fruit of certain peppers.

papyrus [pa-pī'rus] *n* a tall sedge; of the Nile Valley; its pith prepared as a writing material by the ancients; a manuscript on papyrus.

par [pär] *n* the established value of a currency in foreign-exchange rates; the face value of stocks, etc.; equality in value, condition, or circumstances.

parable [par'a-bl] *n* a fable or story told to illustrate some doctrine, or to make some duty clear.

parabola [par-ab'o-la] *n* a curve, one of the conic sections, being the intersection of a cone and a plane parallel to its side or slope. — *pl* **parab'olas.**

parachute [par'a-shōōt] *n* an apparatus like an umbrella for descending safely from a height. — *vti* to descend by parachute. — *n* **par'chutist.**

parade [pa-rād′] *n* display, ostentation; an assembling in order for exercise, inspection, etc.—*vt* to march or walk through, as for display; to show off.

paradigm [par′a-dīm] *n* an example, exemplar.

paradise [par′a-dīs] *n* a park or pleasure ground, esp in ancient Persia; **Paradise**, the garden of Eden.

paradox [par′a-doks] *n* that which is contrary to received opinion; a statement that is apparently absurd or self-contradictory, but is or may be really true.—*adv* **paradox′ically**.

paraffin [par′a-fin] *n* a white, crystalline substance obtained from shale, petroleum, etc.

paragon [par′a-gon] *n* a model of perfection or supreme excellence.

paragraph [par′a-gräf] *n* a distinct part of a discourse or writing, a short passage, or a collection of sentences with unity of purpose.—*vt* to write paragraphs about; to divide into paragraphs.

parakeet, parrakeet [par′a-kēt] *n* a small, parrot.

parallel [par′a-lel] *adj* extended in the same direction and equidistant in all parts; like in essential parts, analogous.—*n* a parallel line, surface, etc.; a line of latitude.—*vt* to place so as to be parallel; to represent as similar; to match.—*n* **par′allelism**.

parallelogram [par-a-lel′ō-gram] *n* a plane four-sided figure, the opposite sides of which are parallel and equal.

paralysis [pa-ral′i-sis] *n* a partial or complete loss of power of motion or sensation in any part of the body; a condition of helpless inactivity.—*vt* **paralyze** [par′a-līz].

paramount [par′a-mownt] *adj* superior to all others; supreme.—*n* **par′amountcy**.

paramour [par′a-mŏŏr] *n* an illicit lover.

paranoia [par-a-noi′ä] *n* a form of insanity characterised by fixed delusions.—*adj* **paranoi′ac**.

parapet [par′a-pet] *n* a bank or wall, to protect soldiers from the fire of an enemy in front; a low wall along the side of a bridge, etc.

paraphernalia [para-fēr-nāl′i-a] *n* personal belongings; equipment; miscellaneous accessories.

paraphrase [par′a-frāz] *n* expression of the same thing in other words; an exercise in such expression.—*vt* to express in other words.—*vi* to make a paraphrase.

parasite [par′a-sīt] *n* one who lives at the expense of society or of others and contributes nothing; an organism that lives in or on another organism without rendering it any service in return.—*adj* **parasitic** [-sit′ik].

parasol [par′a-sol] *n* a lightweight umbrella used as a sunshade.

paratroops [par′a-trŏŏps] *n pl* troops carried by an airplane to be dropped by parachute.

paravane [par′a-vān] *n* a fish-shaped rudder-steered device attached to a ship's bows for the purpose of cutting mines from their moorings.

parboil [pär′boil] *vt* to boil briefly as a preliminary cooking procedure.

parbuckle [pär′buk′l] *n* an arrangement for raising or lowering a heavy object that will roll (eg a barrel), the middle of a rope being made fast to a post and both ends being passed under and over the object; a double sling made of a single rope (as for slinging a cask).—*vt* to hoist or lower by means of a parbuckle.

parcel [pär′sl] *n* a tract or plot of land; a wrapped bundle; a package; a protective wrapping around rope.—*vt* to divide into portions; to make up into a parcel.

parch [pärch] *vt* to make hot and very dry; to roast slightly.—*vt* to be scorched; to become very dry.—*adj* **parched**.

parchment [pärch′mênt] *n* the skin of a sheep, goat, or other animal prepared for writing on; a document on parchment.

pard [pärd] *n* the leopard.

pardon [pär′d(ô)n] *vt* to forgive; to remit the penalty of; to make allowance for, excuse.—*n* forgiveness.—*adj* **par′donable**.—*adv* **par′donably**.

pare [pär] *vt* to cut or shave off the outer surface or edge of; to peel; to diminish by small quantities.

paregoric [par-ê-gor′ik] *n* a tincture of opium used to relieve pain and to treat diarrhea.

parent [pār′ênt] *n* a father or a mother; a plant or an animal from which others are derived (also *adj*); an author, cause, source.—*n* **par′entage**, descent from parents.—*adj* **parental** [pâ-rent′âl].

parenthesis [pä-ren′thê-sis] *n* a word or passage of comment or explanation inserted in a sentence that is grammatically complete without it; a figure of speech consisting of the use of such insertion; a digression; an interval, interlude; one or both of the curved marks () used to mark off a parenthesis or to group a symbolic unit in a logical or mathematical expression.—*adj* **parenthetic**.

pariah [pa-rī′ä] *n* in south India, one of low caste; a social outcast.

parietal [pä-rī′ê-tàl] *adj* of, relating to, or forming the walls of an anatomical structure; of or relating to college dormitory living and its regulations.

parish [par′ish] *n* an ecclesiastical area in the charge of one pastor; the congregation of a church.

parity [par′i-ti] *n* equality in status; equality in quantity and kind.

park [pärk] *n* a tract of land kept as a game preserve or recreation area; a piece of ground in a town or city kept for ornament and recreation, with playgrounds, etc.; an enclosed stadium, esp for ball games.—*vti* to leave (a vehicle in a certain place temporarily; to maneuver (a vehicle) into a parking space.

parlance [pär′làns] *n* mode of speech, phraseology (eg *legal parlance*).—*vi* **par′ley**, to confer; to treat with an enemy.—*n* a conference.

parliament [pär′li-mênt] *n* a meeting for deliberation; a legislative body; **Parliament**, the legislature of Great Britain, House of Commons, the House of Lords and the Sovereign, etc.—*n* **parliamentä′rian**.—*adj* **parliament′ary**.

parlor [pär′lôr] *n* a room in a house used primarily for conversation or for receiving guests; a room in a hotel or club for conversation or semiprivate use; any of certain business establishments.

parlous [pär′lus] *adj* full of danger or difficulty, very bad.

Parmesan [pär′mê-zăn, -zyä, -zän] *n* the hardest cheese, made from cow's milk, with mild flavor.

parochial [pär-ō′ki-âl] *adj* of or relating to a parish; restricted or confined within narrow limits—of sentiments, tastes, etc.—*n* **parō′chialism**, provincialism, narrowness of view.

parody [par′o-di] *n* a burlesque imitation of a literary or musical work or style.—*vt* to make a parody of.

parole [pàr-ōl′] *n* the release of a prisoner before his sentence has expired, on condition of future good behavior.—*vt* to release on parole.

paronomasia [par-on-o-mä′syä, -zyä, -zh(y)ä] *n* a play upon words, a pun.—*n* **paronym** [par′o-nim], a word formed from a word in another language; a word with a form similar to that of a cognate foreign word.

paroxysm [par′oks-izm] *n* a sudden attack of a disease; fit of acute pain; a fit of passion, laughter, coughing, etc.—*adj* **paroxys′mal**.

parquet [pär′kā] *n* the main floor of a theater, a flooring of parquetry.—*n* **par′quetry**, geometrically patterned inlaid work of wood.

parr [pär] *n* a young salmon.

parricide [par′i-sīd] *n* the murder of a parent or near relative.

parrot [par′ôt] *n* any of numerous widely distributed tropical and subtropical birds with brilliant plumage, hooked bill, good imitators of human speech; a person who repeats words mechanically and without understanding.

parry [par′i] *vt* to ward or keep off; to turn aside.

parse [pärz] *vt* (*gram*) to break (a sentence) down, giving the form and function of each part.

parsimony [pär′si-môn-i] *n* sparingness in the spending of money; economy in the use of means to an end.—*adj* **parsimonious**.

parsley [pärs′li] *n* a bright green umbelliferous annual or biennial herb used to flavor or garnish some foods.

parsnip [pärs′nip] *n* long tapered root used as a vegetable in some cultivated varieties.

parson [pär′s(ô)n] *n* a clergyman.—*n* **par′sonage**, the residence provided for a parson by his church.

part [pärt] *n* something less than the whole; portion (of a thing), some out of a larger number (of things); an essential, separable piece of a machine; words and actions of a character in a play; a copy of an actor's words. — *vt* to divide into parts or shares; to comb the hair so as to leave a part; to separate. — *vi* to become separated; to go different ways. — *adv* **part'ly**, in part; in some degree. — *adj* **part'time**, for part of working time only.

partake [pär-tāk′, pàr-tāk′] *vi* to take or have a part or share; to take some.

parterre [pär-ter′] *n* an arrangement of flowerbeds; the orchestra of a theater esp under the galleries.

partial [pär′shàl] *adj* not total or complete; inclined to favor one person or party, biased; having a preference or liking for (*with* to). — *n* **partiality**.

participate [pär-tis′i-pät] *vi* to take a share or part with others (in some activity). — *ns* **partic'ipant, participā'tion, partic'ipātor.**

particle [pär′ti-kl] *n* a minute piece of matter; a minute quantity of something immaterial; a short, invariable part of speech. — *adj* **particular** [pär-tik′ū-lár], indicating a single definite person or thing as distinguished from others; concerned with things single or distinct; minutely attentive and careful; fastidious in taste. — *n* a single point, a detail. — *vti* **partic'ularize**; to enumerate in detail. — *adv* **partic'ularly.**

partisan[1] partizan [pär-ti-zan′, pär′ti-zan] *n* a strong supporter of a person, party, or cause.

partite [pär′tīt] *adj* divided usu. in a specified number of parts; cleft nearly to the base. — *n* **partition** [-tish′(ó)n]; a wall between rooms. — *vt* to divide into shares; to divide into parts by walls.

partner [pärt′nèr] *n* one of two or more persons owning jointly a business who shares the risks and profits of the company or firm; one who plays on the same side with, and along with, another in a game; one who dances with another; a husband or wife. — *vt* to act as partner to; to join as partners. — *n* **part'nership;** a contract between persons engaged in any business.

partridge [pär′trij] *n* any of various medium-sized stout-bodied game birds of the grouse family.

parturient [pär-tū′ri-ènt] *adj* bringing, or about to bring, forth. — *n* **partūri'tion,** act of bringing forth.

party [pär′ti] *n* a side in a battle, game, lawsuit, etc.; a body of persons united for political or other action; a meeting or entertainment of guests; one concerned in a contract; a detachment. — *vi* to attend social parties. — *adj* **par'ticol'ored,** variegated.

parvenu [pär′ve-nū] *n* an upstart, one newly risen into wealth or power.

Pasch [päsk] *n* Passover; Easter.

pasha [pä′shä, pä-shä′] *n* a former Turkish title given to governors and high military and naval officers.

pass [päs] *vi* to proceed; to go from one place or state to another; to go by; to go unheeded or neglected; to elapse; to go away; to die; to happen. — *vt* to go by, over, beyond, through, etc.; to spend; to omit; to enact; to transfer; to excrete; to approve; to undergo (a test, course, etc.) successfully; to circulate. — *n* a way by which one may pass; a narrow passage or defile. — *adj* **pass'word,** a secret term by which a friend is recognized and allowed to pass.

passage [pas′ij] *n* act of passing; crossing; transition; lapse, course; a journey; means of passing to and fro; a corridor; a channel; occurrence, episode.

passé [pas′ā, pas-ā′] *adj* past one's best; out-of-date.

passe-partout [pas-pär-tōō′] *n* a method of framing, with glass front and pasteboard back.

passerine [pas′er-in] *adj* relating to the largest order of birds which includes more than half of all living birds and consists of songbirds of perching habits.

passion [pash′(ó)n] *n* the sufferings and death of Christ; a suffering or passive condition, as opposed to action; emotion or agitation of mind, esp rage; ardent love; eager desire. — *adj* **pass'ionate,** easily moved to anger, or other strong feeling; intense; sensual. — *adv* **pass'ionately.** — *n* **pass'ion flow'er,** any of a genus of chiefly tropical climbing vines; **passion fruit,** the edible fruit of a passion flower. — *ns* **Pass'ion play,** a religious drama representing the sufferings and death of Christ; **Pass'ion Week,** Holy Week.

passive [pas′iv] *adj* unresisting; lethargic; not reacting upon;

(*gram*) denoting the voice of a verb whose subject receives the action. — *adv* **pass'ively.**

Passover [päs′ō-vèr] *n* (*Judaism*) a spring holiday, celebrating the liberation of the Jews from slavery in Egypt. — Also **Pesach.**

past [päst] *pt p* of **pass.** — *adj* bygone; ended; in time already passed. — *prep* farther than; beyond; beyond the possibility of.

paste [pāst] *n* a soft plastic mass; dough for pies, etc. an adhesive made of flour, water, etc.; a fine kind of glass for making artificial gems. — *vt* to fasten with paste. — *n* **paste'board,** a stiff board made of sheets of paper pasted together, etc.

pastel [pas′tèl] *n* chalk mixed with other materials and colored for crayons; a drawing made with such.

pastern [pas′tèrn] *n* the part of a horse's foot from the fetlock to the hoof.

pastiche [pas-tēsh′] *n* a musical or literary composition made up of parts from other compositions.

pastille [pas-tēl′] *n* a small cone of charcoal and aromatic substances, burned to perfume; an aromatic or medicated lozenge.

pastime [päs′tīm] *n* that which serves to pass away the time; recreation.

pastor [päs′tôr] *n* a clergyman in charge of a congregation. — *adj* **pas'toral,** relating to shepherds or to shepherd life; rustic. — *adv* **pas'torally.** — *ns* **pas'torate,** the office of a pastor; the whole body of pastors.

pasture [päst′chùr] *n* growing grass for grazing; grazing land; the feeding of livestock. — *vt* to put (cattle, etc.) out to graze in a pasture. — *n* **past'ūrage.**

pat [pat] *n* a gentle tap, as with the palm of the hand; a small lump of butter molded by an instrument with flat surface; a light sound.

patch [pach] *n* a piece put on to mend or cover a defect; any similar scrap of material; a plot of ground; a bandage; an area or spot. — *vt* to mend with a patch; to mend or fashion clumsily or hastily. — *adj* **patch'y,** covered with, or consisting of, patches.

pate [pāt] *n* (*humorous*) the head.

pâté [pa-tā] *n* a paste made of blended meat, herbs, etc. — **pâté de fois gras** [dē fwa grä] paste of fat goose liver and truffles.

paten [pat′èn] *n* a plate for bread in the Eucharist. [Fr — L *patina,* a plate — Gr *patanē.*]

patent [pat′ént] *adj* [pā′tènt] lying open; obvious; [pat′ènt] open to public perusal; protected by patent. — *n* [pat′ènt] an official document, granting the exclusive right to produce and sell an invention, etc. for a certain time — *vt* to secure a patent for. — *adv* **pā'tently,** openly, obviously.

paternal [pa-tûr′nàl] *adj* fatherly; showing the disposition of a father; derived from a father. — *n* **pater'nity,** fatherhood; origin or descent from a father.

paternoster [pat-èr-nos′tèr or pā′tèr-nos-tèr] *n* the Lord's Prayer.

path [päth] *n* a way worn by footsteps; a way for people on foot; a track; course of action or con.

pathetic [pà-thet′ik] *adj* affecting the tender emotions, touching. — *adv* **pathet'ically.**

pathology [pa-thol′o-ji] *n* the branch of medicine that deals with the nature of disease, esp its functional and structural effects. — *adj* **patholog'ical.** — *adv* **patholog'ically.** — *n* **pathol'ogist.**

pathos [pā′thos] *n* the quality that excites pity.

patience [pā′shèns] *n* quality of being able calmly to wait or endure. — *adj* **pā'tient,** sustaining pain, etc., without repining; not easily provoked, long-suffering; waiting with calmness; persevering.

patina [pat′in-a] *n* a surface appearance of something grown beautiful by age or use.

patois [pat′wä] *n* a dialect, esp a local dialect of the lower social strata.

patriarch [pā′tri-ärk] *n* the father and head of a family in the Bible; a man of great age and dignity; a high-ranking bishop, as in the Orthodox Eastern Church. — *adj* **pātriarch'al.**

patrician [pä-trish′àn] *n* a member or descendant of one of the original families of citizens forming the Roman people; an aristocrat.

patricide [pat′ri-sīd] *n* the murder of one's own father; one who murders his father.

patrimony [pat′ri-mòn-i] *n* an inheritance from a father or from ancestors.

patriot [pā′tri-ot] *n* one who truly loves and serves his country.—*adj* devoted to one's country.—*adj* **patriotic** [pāt-ri-ot′ik]; actuated by a love of one's country.—*n* **pa′triotism**.

patristic, -al [pa-tris′tik, -àl] *adj* pertaining to the fathers of the Christian Church or their writings.

patrol [pa-trōl] *vti* to go the rounds of perambulate, in order to watch, protect, inspect.—a unit of persons or vehicles employed for reconnaissance, security, or combat.

patron [pā′trón] *n* a protector; one who countenances or encourages; customer; one who sponsors and supports some activity, person, etc.—*n* **pat′ronage**, the support given by a patron; clientele; business; trade.—*vt* **pat′ronize**, to treat condescendingly; to countenance, encourage; to give one's custom to, or to frequent habitually.

patronymic [pat-rō-nim′ik] *adj* derived from the name of a father or an ancestor.

patten [pat′n] *n* a clog, sandal, or overshoe with a wooden sole.

patter[1] [pat′ér] *vi* to strike against something with quick successive pats or taps; to run with light steps.—*n* the sound so produced.

patter[2] [pat′ér] *vi* to mumble; to talk rapidly.—*vt* to repeat hurriedly, to gabble.—*n* glib talk, chatter.

pattern [pat′èrn] *n* a person or thing to be copied; a model; a design or guide with the help of which something is to be made.

patty [pat′i] *n* a little pie; a small flat cake of ground meat, fish, etc. usu. fried.

paucity [pö′sit-i] *n* fewness; smallness of number or quantity; scarcity.

paunch [pön(ch)sh] *n* the belly and its contents.

pauper [pö′pér] *n* a destitute person, esp one supported by charity or by some public provision.—*n* **pau′perism**.—*vt* **pau′perize**.

pause [pöz] *n* a temporary ceasing, stop; cessation caused by doubt, hesitation.—*vi* to make a pause.

pave [pāv] *vt* to cover with concrete, etc., so as to form a level surface for travel.—*ns* **pave′ment**, a paved surface; that with which it is paved.

pavilion [pä-vil′yón] *n* a large and luxurious tent; an ornamental building often turreted or domed, as at a fair or park, for exhibitions.—*vt* to furnish with pavilions.

paw [pö] *n* a foot with claws; *vti* to touch, dig, hit, etc. with paws.

pawn[1] [pön] *n* something deposited as a pledge for repayment or performance; state of being pledged.—*vt* to give in pledge; to wager or risk.—*ns* **pawn′broker**, a person licensed to lend money at interest on personal property left with him as security; **pawn′er**, one who gives a pawn or pledge as security.

pawn[2] [pön] *n* a small piece in chess.

pay [pā] *vt* to discharge, as a debt, duty; to reward; to punish; to give, render; to be profitable to.—*vi* to hand over money or other equivalent; to yield a profit.— *n* money given for service; salary, wages.—*adj* **pay′able**, that may or should be paid on a specified date.—**pay′ment**, the act of paying; that which is paid; recompense, reward.

pea [pē] *n* the variable seed of a climbing leguminous annual plant.

peace [pēs] *n* a state of quiet; freedom from contention, disturbance, or war; a treaty that ends a war; silence.—*adj* **peace′able**, disposed to peace.—*adj* **peace′ful**.—*adv* **peace′fully**.

peach[1] [pēch] *vi* to give information against an accomplice. [ME *apeche*; cf **impeach**.]

peach[2] [pēch] *n* a sweet, juicy, velvety-skinned stone fruit; the tree bearing it.

peacock [pē′kok] *n* the male of a genus of large terrestial pheasants.

pea jacket [pē′-jak′èt] *n* a coarse thick jacket worn esp by seamen.

peak [pēk] *n* a point; the pointed end of anything; the top of a mountain, a summit; maximum value; the projecting front of a cap.—*vti* to reach or cause to reach the height of one's power, popularity, etc.

peal [pēl] *n* a loud sound as of thunder, laughter, etc.; a set of bells tuned to each other; the changes rung upon a set of bells.—*vti* to give forth in peals.

pear [pār] *n* a common fruit tapering towards the stalk and bulged at the end.

pearl [pûrl] *n* a concretion of nacre found in an oyster or other mollusks, prized as a gem; mother-of-pearl; anything resembling a pearl intrinsically or physically; one that is choice and precious; a bluish medium gray.—*adj* **pearl′y**.

peasant [pez′ánt] *n* a small farmer or farm laborer.—*n* **peas′antry**, the body of peasants.

pease [pēz] *n* (*obs*) a pea; peas collectively.

peat [pēt] *n* a shaped block dug from a bog and dried for fuel; the decayed vegetable matter from which such blocks are cut.

pebble [peb′l] *n* a small roundish stone; transparent and colorless quartz; rock crystal.

pecan [pi-kan′] *n* a large hickory; its wood; the smooth, oblong thin-shelled nut.

pecadillo [pek-ä-dil′ō] *n* a trifling fault.

peccary [pek′ár-i] *n* either of two gregarious largely nocturnal American mammals.

peck[1] [pek] *n* a measure of capacity for dry goods equal to 8 quarts or ¼ bushel; a large quantity.

peck[2] [pek] *vt* to strike or pick up with the beak; to eat sparingly; to strike with anything pointed; to strike with repeated blows.

pectin [pek′tin] *n* any of certain carbohydrates found in the cell walls of fruits and vegetables yielding a gel that is the basis of jellies.

pectoral [pek′to-rál] *adj* relating to the breast or chest.—*n* something worn on the breast.—*adv* **pec′torally**.

peculate [pek′ū-lāt] *vti* to appropriate dishonestly, to embezzle.—*ns* **pecula′tion; pec′ulātor**.

peculiar [pi-kūl′yàr] *adj* of one's own; belonging exclusively (to); characteristic; particular, special; strange.—*n* **peculiarity**, that which is found in one and in no other; a characteristic; oddity.

pecuniary [pi-kūn′i-àr-i] *adj* relating to money.

pedagogue, pedagog [ped′à-gog] *n* a teacher esp a pedantic one.

pedal [ped′ál] *adj* pertaining to the foot.—*n* a lever pressed by the foot.—*vi* to drive by pedals.

pedant [ped′ánt] *n* one who makes a vain and pretentious show of learning; one who attaches too much importance to minute details or to formal rules in scholarship.—*adjs* **pedant′ic**.

pedestal [ped′ès-tál] *n* the support of a column, statue, vase, etc.

pedestrian [pi-des′tri-án] *adj* on foot; of walking on foot; prosaic, commonplace.—*n* one who walks.

pedicel [ped′i-sel] *n* the stalk of a plant supporting a fruiting or spore-bearing organ.

pedicure [ped′i-kūr] *n* a chiropodist; cosmetic care of the feet, toes, and nails.

pedigree [ped′īgrē] *n* a line of ancestors; a scheme or record of ancestry, a genealogy; lineage.

pediment [ped′i-mènt] *n* (*archit*) a triangular structure crowning the front of a building.

pedlar [ped′lár] *n* (*Brit*) a peddler.

pedometer [pi-dom′èt-èr] *n* an instrument for counting paces and so measuring distance walked.

peduncle [pi-dung′kl] *n* a stalklike organ or process in some plants, animals, etc.—*adjs* **pedun′cular**.

peel [pēl] *vt* to strip off the skin or bark from; to bare.—*vi* to come off, as the skin.—*n* rind, esp that of oranges, lemons, etc.

peep[1] [pēp] *vi* to cheep as a young bird.—*n* a peeping sound.

peep[2] [pēp] *vi* to look through a narrow opening; to look stealthily or cautiously; (to begin) to appear; to be just showing.—*n* a sly look; a glimpse.—*ns* **peep′ show**, a show viewed through a small hole, usually fitted with a magnifying glass.

peer[1] [pēr] *n* an equal in rank, ability, etc.; a British nobleman.—*n* **peer′age**, the rank or dignity of a peer; the body of peers.—*adj* **peer′less**, unequalled, matchless.

peer[2] [pēr] *vi* to look narrowly or closely; to look with strain; to peep out, appear.

peevish [pēv′ish] *adj* fretful, querulous.—*adv* **peev′ishly**.—*n* **peev′ishness**.

peewit [pē'wit, pū'it] *n* the lapwing.

peg [peg] *n* a tapered piece (of wood) for hanging up or fastening things, or for marking a position. —*vt* to fasten, mark, score, etc. with a peg. —*vi* to work assiduously.

Pekingese, Pekinese [pē'kin-ez'] *n* a breed of small dog with long, silky hair, short legs, and a pug nose.

pekoe [pek'ō, pē'kō] *n* a tea made from the two youngest leaves and the end bud of the shoot.

pelargonium [pel-är-gō'ni-um] *n* a genus of southern African flowering plants of the geranium family.

pelf [pelf] *n* money or wealth regarded with contempt.

pelican [pel'i-kàn] *n* any of a genus of large waterbirds with an enormous pouched bill.

pelisse [pe-lēs'] *n* a long cloak or coat made of fur or trimmed or lined with fur.

pellagra [pel-ag'rä or -āg'-] *n* a deficiency disease marked by skin eruptions and nervous disorders.

pellet [pel'ét] *n* a little ball.

pell-mell [pel'-mel'] *adv* confusedly.

pellucid [pe-l(y)ōō'sid] *adj* perfectly clear; transparent—*adv* **pellū'cidly.**

pelota [pel-ō'tä] *n* a court game related to jai alai; the ball used in jai alai.

pelt[1] [pelt] *n* a usu. undressed skin with its hair, wool, or fur.

pelt[2] [pelt] *vt* to assail with blows, missiles, or words. —*vi* to fall heavily, as rain; to speed.

pelvis [pel'vis] *n* the bony cavity forming the lower part of the abdomen; the bones forming this.

pemmican, pemican [pem'i-kàn] *n* a preparation, consisting of lean meat, dried, pounded, and mixed with other ingredients.

pen[1] [pen] *n* a small enclosure, esp for animals; a small place of confinement; to confine within a small space.

pen[2] [pen] *n* an instrument used for writing or drawing with ink or a similar fluid. —*vt* to write; **pen'knife,** a small pocketknife usu. with only one blade; **pen'manship,** handwriting as an art or skill.

penal [pē'nàl] *adj* pertaining to, liable to, imposing, constituting, used for, punishment; constituting a penalty; very severe. —*vt* **pē'nalize,** to put under a disadvantage.

penalty [pen'ál-ti] *n* a punishment; suffering or loss imposed for a fault or breach of a law; a fine.

penance [pen'áns] *n* a penalty voluntarily undertaken.

pence [pens] *n* (*Brit*) plural of **penny.**

penchant [pä-shä] *n* inclination, decided taste (for).

pencil [pen'sl] *n* a pointed rod-shaped instrument with a core of graphite or crayon for writing, drawing, etc.; any small stick of similar shape. —*vt* to write, sketch, or mark with a pencil; to paint or draw.

pendant, pendent [pen'dànt] *n* anything hanging, esp for ornament; anything attached to another thing of the same kind. — *n* **pen'dency,** undecided state.

pending [pen'ding] *adj* impending; undecided.

pendulum [pen'dū-lum] *n* any weight so hung from a fixed point as to swing freely; anything that swings or is free to swing to and fro. —*adj* **pen'dulous,** hanging loosely; swinging freely.

penetrate [pen'ē-trāt] *vti* to thrust or force a way into the inside of; to pierce into or through; to reach the mind or feelings of; to see into, or through, understand. —*adj* **pen'etrable.** —*n* **penetrabil'ity.** —*n* **penetrā'tion,** acuteness; discernment. — *adj* **pen'etrātive.**

penguin [peng'gwin, or pen'-] *n* any of a family of seabirds, unable to fly.

penicillin [pen-i-sil'in] *n* an antibiotic produced synthetically or from molds.

peninsula [pen-in'sū-lä] *n* a piece of land that is almost an island.

penis [pē'nis] *n* the external male organ.

penitent [pen'i-tènt] *adj* sorry for sin, contrite, repentant. —*n* one who sorrows for sin. —*n* **pen'itence.** —*adj* **penitential** [-ten'shàl]. —*adj* **penitentiary** [-ten'shàr-i], relating to penance; penitential. —*n* a penitent.

pennant [pen'ànt] *n* a long narrow flag; such a flag symbolizing a championship.

pennon [pen'ón] *n* a medieval streamer attached to a lance; a long narrow flag; a wing; a pinion.

penny [pen'i] *n* a coin of the United Kingdom formerly 1/240 of £1, now (**new penny**) 1/100 of £1 (abbrev *p*); a small sum; (in *pl*) money in general. —. —*adj* **penn'iless,** without money; poor; **penn'yweight,** a unit of weight, equal to 1/20 ounce troy weight. —*adj* **penn'yworth,** a penny's worth; value for money.

pennyroyal [pen-i-roi'àl] *n* a European perennial mint.

pension [pen'shón] *n* a stated allowance to a person for past services; an allowance to one who has retired or has been disabled or reached old age, or who has been widowed, orphaned, etc. —*vt* to grant a pension to; to dismiss or retire from service with a pension. —*n* **pen'sioner.**

pensive [pen'siv] *adj* meditative; expressing thoughtfulness with sadness. —*adv* **pen'sively.**

pentagon [pen'tà-gon] *n* (*geom*) a rectilineal plane figure having five angles and five sides; **Pentagon,** the US military leadership.

pentameter [pen-tam'ē-tèr] *n* a verse of five measures or feet.

pentathlon [pen-tath'lon] *n* an athletic contest involving participation by each contestant in five different events.

Pentecost [pent'ē-kost] *n* shabuoth; a Christian festival on the seventh Sunday after Easter. Whit Sunday.

penthouse [pent'hows] *n* a shed or lean-to projecting from or adjoining a main building; a structure or dwelling on a roof.

penult [pē-nult', pē'nult], **penult'ima,** *ns* the syllable last but one. —*adj* **penult'imate,** last but one.

penumbra [pen-um'bra] *n* a partial shadow round the perfect shadow of an eclipse; the part of a picture where the light and shade blend.

penury [pen'ū-ri] *n* want, great poverty. —*adj* **penū'rious.**

peony [pē'o-ni] *n* a genus of plants with large showy flowers.

people [pē'pl] *n* the body of enfranchised citizens of a state; the persons of a certain place, group, or class.

pep [pep] *n* (*inf*) vigor.

pepper [pep'ér] *n* a pungent condiment made from the fruit of various plants; the fruit of the pepper plant which can be red, yellow, or green, sweet or hot, and is eaten as a vegetable.

pepsin [pep'sin] *n* a stomach enzyme, aiding in the digestion of proteins. —*adj* **pep'tic.**

peradventure [per-ad-vent'chur] *adv* by chance; perhaps.

perambulate [per-am'bū-lāt] *vt* to walk through, about, or over. —*ns* **perambulā'tion, peram'bulātor,** one who perambulates; (*Brit*) a baby carriage.

perceive [pèr-sēv'] *vt* to become or be aware of through the senses; to see. —*n* **perceiv'er.**

per cent [pèr sent'] *adv* in the hundred, for each hundred. —*n* **percent'age,** rate or amount per cent; a proportion.

perch[1] [pûrch] *n* a genus of spiny-finned chiefly freshwater fishes.

perch[2] [pûrch] *n* a rod on which birds alight, sit, or roost; any high seat or position. —*vti* to rest or place on or as on a perch.

perchance [pèr-chäns'] *adv* by chance; perhaps.

percipient [pèr-sip'i-ènt] *adj* perceiving; having the faculty of perception. —*n* one who perceives or can perceive.

percolate [pûr'kō-lāt] *vt* to pass (a liquid) through pores; to filter. —*vi* to ooze through a porous substance; to become percolated; to spread gradually. —*ns* **percolā'tion.**

percussion [pèr-kush'(ó)n] *n* impact; instruments played by striking—cymbals, etc.; **percussion instrument,** a musical instrument whose sounding agent is a stretched membrane or some solid material as steel or wood.

perdition [pèr-dish'(ó)n] *n* utter loss or ruin; the utter loss of happiness in a future state, hell.

peregrinate [per'ē-gri-nāt] *vi* to travel about, journey. —*n* **peregrinā'tion,** travel; pilgrimage.

peremptory [perèm(p)'tòr-i] *adj* admitting no refusal; dogmatic; imperious. —*adv* **peremp'torily.**

perennial [pèr-en'yàl] *adj* lasting through the year; perpetual; (*bot*) lasting more than two years.

perfect [pûr'fekt] *adj* done thoroughly or completely; complete; faultless; having every moral excellence; completely skilled or versed. —*n* a verb form in the perfect tense. —*vt* (or pèr-fekt') to make perfect; to finish; to make fully skilled in anything. —**perfec'tion, per'fectness,** state of being perfect; a perfect quality or acquirement.

perfervid [pèr-fûr'vid] *adj* excessively fervent.

perfidious [pèr-fid'i-us] *adj* treacherous, basely violating faith. —*adv* **perfid'iously.**

perforate [pûr′fō-rāt] *vt* to bore through or into, to pierce; to make a hole, or holes. —*ns* **perfora′tion**, act of boring through.

perforce [pér-fōrs′, -fôrs′] *adv* by force, of necessity.

perform [pér-fôrm′] *vt* to do; to carry out duly; to carry into effect; to act. —*vi* to execute an undertaking; to act a part. —*ns* **perform′ance**, act of performing; a piece of work; **perform′er**, one who performs, esp one who makes a public exhibition of his skill.

perfume [pûr′fūm or pér-fūm′] *n* a pleasing odor; fragrance; fluid containing fragrant essential oil and a fixative. —*vt* [pér-fūm′] to scent; to put perfume on. —*ns* **perfū′mer**, **perfū′mery**, perfume in general.

perfunctory [pér-fungk′tō-ri] *adj* done merely as a routine performed carelessly; hasty or superficial; acting without zeal or interest.

pergola, [pûr′go-la] *n* a latticework structure with climbing plants.

perhaps [pér-haps′] *adv* it may be, possibly.

peri [pē′ri] *n* a Persian fairy.

pericardium [per-i-kär′di-um] *n* the membrane round the heart. —*adjs* **pericar′diac, pericar′dial.**

pericarp [per′i-kärp] *n* (*bot*) the wall of a fruit if derived from that of the ovary. —*adj* **pericarp′ial.**

pericranium [per-i-krā′ni-um] *n* the membrane that surrounds the cranium.

perigee [per′i-jē] *n* the point nearest a heavenly body, as the earth, in the orbit of a satellite around it.

perihelion [per-i-hē′li-ôn] *n* the point of the orbit of a planet or a comet or of a man-made satellite at which it is nearest to the sun.

peril [per′il] *n* danger. —*vt* to expose to danger. —*adj* **per′ilous**, dangerous. —*adv* **per′ilously.**

perimeter [pér-im′é-tėr] *n* (*geom*) the circuit or boundary of any plane figure, or the sum of all its sides.

period [pē′ri-ôd] *n* the time in which anything runs its course; the time in which a heavenly body revolves through its orbit; a stated and recurring interval of time as in an academic day, playing time in a game, etc., an age, a stage or phase in history; conclusion; (*gram*) a mark (.) at the end of a sentence; a pause in speaking. —*adjs* **periodic** [pēr-i-od′ik]; occurring at regular intervals; **period′ical**, periodic; published in numbers at stated intervals. —*n* a magazine or other publication that appears at regular intervals. —*adv* **period′ically.**

peripatetic [per-i-pá-tet′ik] *adj* walking about; with **Peripatetic**, of or pertaining to the philosophy of Aristotle.

periphery [pér-if′ėr-i] *n* the bounding line or surface, esp of a rounded object the outside of anything. —*adj* **periph′eral.**

periphrasis [pér-if′rá-sis] *n* the use of more words than are necessary to express an idea. —*adj* **periphrastic** [per-i-fras′tik].

periscope [per′i-skōp] *n* a tube with mirrors by which an observer in a trench, submarine, etc., can see what is going on above or around an obstacle.

perish [per′ish] *vi* to be destroyed or ruined; to die, esp violently. —*adj* **per′ishable.**

peristyle [per′i-stīl] *n* a range of columns round a building or round a square; a court, square, etc.

peritoneum [per-i-tôn-ē′um] *n* a membrane that lines the abdomen. —*n* **peritonī′tis**, inflammation of the peritoneum.

periwig [per′i-wig] *n* a peruke.

periwinkle[1] [per′i-wingk-l] *n* a creeping evergreen plant, with blue, white, or pink flowers.

periwinkle[2] [per′i-wingk-l] *n* a genus of edible marine snails; any related marine mollusks.

perjure [pûr-jùr] *vt* to forswear (oneself). —*ns* **per′jurer; per′jury**, false swearing; (*law*) the crime of wilfully giving false evidence on oath.

perk [pûrk] *vi* to bear oneself with self-confidence. —*vt* to make smart or trim. —*adj* brisk. —*adj* **perk′y.**

perm [pûrm] *vt* to give (hair) a permanent wave.

permanent [pûr′má-nėnt] *adj* remaining, or intended to remain, indefinitely;. —*ns* **per′manence; per′manency.**

permeate [pûr′mē-āt] *vti* to pass through the pores, or interstices, of; to pervade. —*adj* **per′meable.**

permit [pėr-mit′] *vt* to allow to be done; to authorize. —*vi* to give opportunity. —*n* [pėr′mit] a license. —*adv* **per-**

miss′ibly. —*n* **permiss′ion**, act of permitting; leave. —*adj* **permiss′ive**, granting permission.

permute [pér-mūt′] *vt* to change the order or arrangement of, esp to arrange in all possible ways. —*adj* **permut′able.** —*n* **permuta′tion**, any radical alteration.

pernicious [pér-nish′ùs] *adj* destructive; highly injurious.

peroration [per-ō-rā′sh(ō)n] *n* the conclusion of a speech; a rhetorical performance.

peroxide [pėr-oks′īd] *n* an oxide whose molecules contain two atoms of oxygen linked together; hydrogen peroxide.

perpendicular [pér-pėn-dik′ū-lär] *adj* upright; erect; vertical; (*geom*) at right angles to a given line or surface. —*n* a perpendicular line or plane.

perpetrate [pûr′pė-trāt] *vt* to do (something evil, criminal, etc.). —*ns* **perpetrā′tion; per′petrātor.**

perpetual [pér-pet′ū-ál] *adj* never ceasing; everlasting; blooming continuously throughout the season. —*adv* **perpet′ually.**

perpetuate [pér-pet′ū-āt] *vt* to preserve from extinction or oblivion, give continued existence to.

perplex [pér-pleks′] *vt* to embarrass, puzzle, bewilder; to complicate. —*n* **perplex′ity.**

perquisite [pûr′kwi-zit] *n* an expected or promised privilege, gain, or profit incidental to regular wages or salary; a tip, gratuity.

perry [per′i] *n* fermented pear juice.

persecute [pûr′sė-kūt] *vt* to harass, afflict, hunt down, esp for reasons of race, religion, etc.; to worry continually, to importune. —*ns* **persecū′tion; per′secutor.**

persevere [pėr-sė-vēr′] *vi* to continue steadfastly, esp in face of discouragement. —*n* **persevē′rance.**

persiflage [per-si-fläzh] *n* banter, flippancy.

persimmon [pėr-sim′ôn] *n* any of a genus of trees of the ebony family or their fruit, esp the Virginian date-plum.

persist [pėr-sist′] *vi* to continue steadfastly or obstinately, in spite of opposition or warning; to persevere; to last, endure. —*ns* **persis′tence.** —*adj* **persis′tent**, persisting; constantly recurring or long-continued (eg efforts).

person [pûr′sôn] *n* an individual human being; an individual; a living soul; (*gram*) a form of inflexion or use of a word according as it or its subject represents the person(s) or thing(s) speaking (*first person*), spoken to (*second*), or spoken about (*third*); —*adj* **personable** [pėr′sôn-á-bl], of good appearance. —*n* **per′sonage**, an exalted or august person. —*adj* **per′sonal**, of the nature of a person as opposed to a thing or an abstraction; of, relating to, belonging to, or affecting the individual, the self; pertaining to or affecting the person or body. —*n* **personal′ity**, fact or state of being a person as opposed to a thing or an abstraction; distinctive or well-marked character. —*n* **per′sonalty**, personal property. —*vt* **per′sonate**, to assume the likeness or character of, esp for fraudulent purposes.

personify [pėr-son′i-fī] *vt* to represent as a person; to ascribe personality to; to be the embodiment of.

perspective [pėr-spek′tiv] *n* the art or science of drawing solid objects on a plane or curved surface as they appear to the eye; appearance, or representation of appearance, of objects in space with effect of distance, solidity, etc. —*adj* pertaining or according to perspective. —**in perspective**; in just relationship, with the important and the unimportant things in their proper places.

perspicacious [pėr-spi-kā′shùs] *adj* (*arch*) clear-sighted; having clear mental vision.

perspicuous [pér-spik′ū-us] *adj* clearly expressed, clear; (of a person) lucid, expressing himself clearly. —*adv* **perspic′uously.**

perspire [pėr-spīr′] *vi* to sweat. —*n* **perspiration.**

persuade [pėr-swād′] *vt* to induce by argument, advice, etc.; to convince. —*n* **persuad′er.** —*n* **persuasion.** —*adj* **persuasive.**

pert [pûrt] *adj* saucy, presumingly free in speech or conduct; sprightly. —*adv* **pert′ly.**

pertain [pėr-tān′] *vi* to belong as a characteristic quality, function, concern, etc.; to be appropriate; to relate. —*ns* **per′tinence, per′tinency**, *adj* **per′tinent**, pertaining or related to a subject.

pertinacious [pėr-ti-nā′shùs] *adj* holding obstinately to an opinion or a purpose; hard to get rid of. —**pertinā′ciousness, pertinacity.**

perturb [pėr-tûrb′] *vt* to disturb greatly; to agitate. —*n* per-turbā′tion.

peruke [pėr-ōōk′] *n* a wig.

peruse [pėr-ōōz′] *vt* to read attentively; to study; to read. —*ns* perus′al, a careful reading.

pervade [pėr-vād′] *vt* to diffuse or extend through the whole of. —*adj* perva′sive.

perverse [pėr-vûrs′] *adj* turned aside from right or truth; obstinate in the wrong; capricious and unreasonable in opposition. —*ns* perversion [-vėr′sh(ó)n], a turning from truth or propriety; a perverted or corrupted form of anything (eg of the truth); a misdirection of the sex instinct, which finds gratification in abnormal ways, eg in sadism; pervers′ity. —*vt* pervert′, to turn aside, derange to turn (a person) from truth or virtue. —*ns* per′vert. one suffering from derangement of the sex instinct.

pervious [pûr′vi-us] *adj* accessible; permeable, penetrable. —*adv* per′viously.

peseta [pe-sā′tä] *n* a Spanish silver coin.

pessimism [pes′i-mizm] *n* the doctrine that the world is bad rather than good; a temper of mind that always expects the worse things. —*n* pess′imist.

pest [pest] *n* (now *rare*) any deadly epidemic disease, esp plague; anything destructive like a pest, esp a plant or animal detrimental to man as rats, flies, weeds, etc.; one that pesters or annoys. —*ns* pest′icide [pes′ti-sīd], any chemical for killing pests. —*n* pest′ilence, any deadly epidemic disease. —*adjs* pest′ilent, hurtful to health and life; pestilential.

pester [pes′tėr] *vt* (*arch*) to crowd thickly; to annoy persistently. [App from OFr *empestrer* (Fr *empêtrer*).

pestle [pes′l also pest′l] *n* a usu. club-shaped tool for pounding or grinding substances in a mortar. —*vt* to beat, pound, or pulverize with a pestle.

pet[1] [pet] *n* a domesticated animal kept as a companion; a person treated as an indulged favorite. —*adj* kept as a pet; indulged; cherished. —*vt* to stroke or pat gently; to caress.

pet[2] [pet] *n* a sulky mood. —*adj* pett′ish.

petal [pet′ál] *n* a corolla leaf, any of the leaflike parts of a blossom.

petard [pe-tär(d)′] *n* a case containing an explosive, used for blowing in doors, etc.

petiole [pet′i-ōl] *n* (*bot*) a leaf stalk.

petit [pè-tē′] *adj* little, used chiefly in legal compounds.

petite [pè-tēt] *adj* of a woman, small and trim in figure.

petition [pe-tish′(ó)n] *n* a formal request to an authority; a written supplication signed by a number of persons. —*vt* to address a petition to; to ask someone. —*adj* petit′ionary. —*ns* petit′ioner.

petrel [pet′rėl] *n* any of a number of dark-colored.

petrify [pet′ri-fī] *vt* to turn into stone; to fix in amazement, horror, etc. —*vi* to become stone, or hard like stone. —*n* petrifac′tion.

petro-, in composition, stone.

petrochemical [pet-rō-kem′i-kål] *n* any chemical obtained from petroleum or natural gas.

petroleum [pe-trō′lé-um] *n* an oily liquid solution of hydrocarbons occurring naturally in certain rock strata which yields kerosene, gasoline, etc. —*n*.

petticoat [pet′i-kōt] *n* an underskirt.

pettifogger [pet′i-fog-ėr] *n* a lawyer who handles petty cash, esp unethically; one given to quibbling over trifles. —*n* pett′i-foggery.

petty [pet′i] *adj* of small importance, trivial; of inferior status, minor. —*adv* petty officer, a subordinate officer in the navy or coastguard.

petulant [pet′ū-lánt] *adj* showing peevish impatience, irritation, or caprice; forward, impudent in manner. —*ns* pet′ulance.

petunia [pe-tū′ni-à] *n* a tropical herbs of the nightshade family with funnel-shaped corollas.

pew [pū] *n* an enclosed compartment or fixed bench in a church.

pewit [pē′wit, pū′it] *See* peewit.

pewter [pū′tėr] *n* an alloy of tin and lead; sometimes tin with a little copper and antimony.

phaeton [fā′(i-)tn] *n* any of various light four-wheeled horse-drawn carriages.

phagocyte [fag′ō-sīt] *n* a white blood corpuscle that engulfs harmful bacteria and other particles.

phalanger [fal-an′jėr] *n* any one of a family of small arboreal Australian marsupials.

phalanx [fāl′angks] *n* a solid formation of ancient Greek heavily-armed infantry; a solid body of men, etc.

phantasm [fan′tazm] *n* a product of fantasy; a spectre; a supposed vision of an absent person, living or dead; an illusive likeness (of).

phantasmagoria [fan-taz-ma-gō′ri-a] *n* a fantastic series of images, produced by mechanical means, seen in a dream, or called up by the imagination.

phantasy, phantastic *See* fantasy, fantastic.

phantom [fan′tóm] *n* an apparition, a specter.

pharisee, a very self-righteous or hypocritical person. —*adjs* pharisā′ic, -al, pertaining to, or like, the Pharisees; hypocritical.

pharmaceutical [fär-ma-sū′tik-ál] *adj* pertaining to the knowledge of pharmacy or drugs. —*ns* pharmaceutical, a medicinal drug.

pharmacopoeia, pharmacopeia [fär-ma-kō-pē′-(y)a] *n* a book or list of drugs with directions for their preparation.

pharmacy [fä′má-si] *n* the art or profession of preparing drugs and medicines; a drug store. —*ns* phar′macist.

pharynx [far′ingks] *n* the cavity leading from the mouth and nasal passages to the larynx and esophagus.

phase [fāz] *n* the appearance of the moon or a planet at a given time according to the amount of illuminated surface exhibited; any transitory stage or stage in a regularly recurring cycle of changes; a stage in a development. —*vt* to do by phases or stages.

pheasant [fez′(á)nt] *n* a genus of richly colored, birds raised as ornamental or game birds.

phenomenon [fė-nom′é-nón] *n* anything directly apprehended by the senses or by one of them; any fact or event that can be scientifically described; a remarkable or unusual person, thing. —*pl* phenom′ena. —*adj* phenom′enal, very unusual or remarkable.

phial [fī′ál] *n* a small glass bottle; a vial.

phil-, philo- [fil-, -ō-] in composition, loving, friend. [Gr *philein*, to love, *philos*, loved, loving]. —*eg* philharmonic [fil-här-mon′ik], a society sponsoring a symphony orchestra.

philander [fil-an′dėr] *vi* of a man, to make love, esp in a trifling manner; to be in the habit of so doing.

philanthropy [fil-an′thrō-pi] *n* love of mankind, esp as shown in services to general welfare. —*n* philan′thropist.

philately [fil-at′é-li] *n* the study and collection of postage and imprinted stamps; stamp collecting.

philippic [fil-ip-′ik] *n* a bitter verbal attack.

philology [fil-ol′ó-ji] *n* the science of language which concerns itself with the sounds of speech, the history of sound changes, etymology, grammar, the history of inflections, etc;.

Philomel [fil′ō-mel] *n* the nightingale.

philosopher [fil-os′o-fėr] *n* a lover of wisdom; one who acts calmly and rationally in the affairs and changes of life. —*adjs* philosoph′ical, philosoph′ic. —*n* philos′ophy, the study of the principles underlying conduct, thought, and the nature of the universe; general principles of a field of knowledge.

philter, philtre [fil′tėr] *n* a magic potion, esp to excite love.

phlebitis [flé-bī′tis] *n* inflammation of a vein.

phlegm [flem] *n* thick mucus discharged from the throat, as during a cold; sluggishness; apathy. —*adjs* phlegmatic [fleg-mat′ik].

phlox [floks] *n* a genus of annual or perennial herbs having red, purple, white, or variegated flowers.

phobia [fō′bi-a] *n* an irrational, excessive, and persistent fear of some thing or situation.

phoenix [fē′niks] *n* a fabulous bird, the only one of its kind, that burned itself every 500 years or so and rose rejuvenated from its ashes; anything that rises from its own or its predecessor's ashes, the emblem of immortality.

phone [fōn] *n vti* (*inf*) telephone.

phonetic, -al [fō-net′ik, -ál] *adj* of, concerning, according to, or representing, the sounds of spoken language. —**phonet′ics,** the science that deals with pronunciation and the representation of the sounds of speech.

phonograph [fō'nō-gräf] *n* an instrument for reproducing sound recorded in a spiral groove on a revolving disk.

phonology [fō-nol'ō-ji] *n*; the study of the system of sounds in a language and of the history of their changes.

phony, phoney [fōn'i] *adj* (*int*) not genuine.

phosphorus [fos'fŏr-us] *n* a metalloid element; a phosphorescent substance or body, esp one that glows in the dark.—*ns* **phosphate** [fos'fāt] **phos'phide**, a compound of phosphorus *n* **phosphores'cence**, the property of giving off light without noticeable heat, as phosphorus does; such light.

photo- [fō'to-], **phot-**, *fŏt-*, in composition, light.

photo- [fō'to-] in composition, photographic; made by, or by the aid of, photographic means.

photography [fō-tog'ra-fi] *n* the art or process of producing permanent and visible images by the action of light on chemically prepared surfaces.—*ns* **phō'tograph** [-gräf], an image so produced.

photometer [fō-tom'é-tèr] *n* an instrument for measuring the intensity of light.

photosphere [fō'tō-sfēr] *n* a sphere of light or radiance.

Photostat [fō'tō-stat] *n* a photographic apparatus for making facsimiles of writings, drawings, etc.

photosynthesis [fō-tō-sin'the-sis] *n* (*bot*) the process by which a green plant manufactures sugar from carbon dioxide and water in the presence of light.

phrase [frāz] *n* a group of words, not a full sentence or clause, expressing a single idea by themselves; a pithy expression; an empty or high-sounding expression.—*vt* to express in words; **phraseol'ogy**, style or manner of expression or arrangements of phrases; peculiarities of diction; **phrā'sing**, the wording of a speech or passage.

phrenetic, frenetic [fren-et'ik] *adj* delirious; frenzied; proceeding from madness.—Also *n.*—*n* **phrenol'ogy**, a system, now rejected, of analyzing character from the shape of the skull.—*adjs* **phrenolog'ic, -al.**—*n* **phrenol'ogist.** [Gr *phrēn*, gen *phrenos*, midriff, supposed seat of passions, mind, will.]

phthisis [thī'sis, tī'-] *n* wasting disease, esp tuberculosis of the lungs.

physic [fiz'ik] *n* the science, art, or practice of medicine; a medicine, esp a cathartic.—*vt* to give medicine, esp a purgative, to; —*adj* **phys'ical**, pertaining to the world of matter and energy, or its study; material; bodily.—*adv* **phys'ically.**—*ns* **physician** [fi-zish'án] a doctor of medicine; (*arch*) a healer or healing influence; **phys'icist** [-sist], a specialist in physics; disease by physical and mechanical means (as massage, exercise, water, heat, etc.); **physical therapist.**

physiognomy [fiz-i-o(g)n'o-mē] *n* the art of judging character from appearance, esp from the face; the face as an index of the mind.

physiography [fiz-i-og'ra-fi] *n* physical geography.

physiology [fiz-i-ol'o-ji] *n* the science of the processes of life in animals and plants.

physique [fiz-ēk'] *n* bodily type, build.

phyto- [fī-tō-] in composition, plant.

pianoforte [pē-a'nō-fōrt or -ä or pē-an-e-fōrt'ē] *n* piano.—*n* **piano** (pē-a'nō, pya'nō), *n* a large stringed keyboard instrument in which each key operates a felt-covered hammer that strikes a corresponding steel wire or wires.—*n* **pianist** one who plays the pianoforte.

piazza [pē-ät'sä] *n* a walk under a roof supported by pillars; a veranda.

pibroch [pē'broH] *n* bagpipe music consisting of variations on a theme, often martial.

picador [pik'a-dōr] *n* a horseman in a bullfight with a lance who uses it to jab the bull.

picaresque [pik-a-resk'] *adj* resembling the characters or incidents of the *picaresque* novels.

piccolo [pik'ō-lō] *n* a small flute.

pick [pik] *n* a tool for breaking ground, rock, etc., with head pointed at one or both ends and handle fitted to the middle; an instrument of various kinds for picking as a toothpick or pectrum; an act, opportunity, or right of choice.—*vt* to break up, dress, or remove with a pick; to pull apart; to poke or pluck at; to pluck; to peck, bite, or nibble; to select.—*vi* to use a pick; to eat by morsels; to pilfer; **pickpocket**, one who picks or steals from other people's pockets.

pickaback [pik'a-bak] *adv* piggy back.

picket [pik'èt] *n* a pointed stake driven into the ground for fortification, tethering, surveying, etc.; a small outpost, patrol, or other body of men set apart for a special duty; a person posted for a demonstration or protest.—*vt* to tether to a stake; to post as a military picket.

pickle [pik'l] *n* a liquid, esp brine or vinegar, in which food is preserved; (*inf*) a plight.—*vt* to preserve with salt, vinegar, etc.

picnic [pik'nik] *n* a usu. informal meal taken on an excursion and eaten outdoors; an outdoor snack.—*vi* to have a picnic.

picric acid [pik'rik a'sid] an acid used as a yellow dyestuff in medicine, and as the basis of high explosives.

pictorial [pik-tō', tō', ri-ál] *adj* of or relating to painting or drawing; consisting of, expressed in, or of the nature of, pictures; graphic.—*adv* **picto'rially.**

picture [pik'tyùr, -chùr] *n* a representation on a surface, by painting, drawing, photography, etc., of an object or objects, or of a scene, esp when a work of art; an image formed in the mind.—*vt* to depict, represent in a picture; to form a likeness of in the mind.

picturesque [pik-tū-resk'] *adj* such as would make a striking picture, implying some beauty and much quaintness or immediate effectiveness.

pidgin [pij'in] *n* a jargon for trade purposes, using words and grammar from different languages.

pie[1] [pī] *n* a magpie; a chatterer.

pie[2] [pī] *n* a baked dish of fruit, meat, etc. with an under or upper crust, or both.

piebald [pī'bôld] *adj* covered with patches of two colors.—*n* a piebald horse, etc.

piece [pēs] *n* a part or portion of anything; a single article; a literary, dramatic, musical, or artistic composition.—*vt* to enlarge by adding a piece; to form from pieces.—*adv* **piece'-meal**, in pieces; to pieces; bit by bit.—*n* **piece'work**, work paid for by the piece.

pier [pēr] *n* a structure supporting the spans of a bridge; a structure built out over the water and supported by pillars, used as a landing place, pavilion, etc.—*ns* **pier glass**, a tall mirror.

pierce [pērs] *vt* to thrust or make a hole through; to enter, or force a way into.—*vi* to penetrate.

Pierrot [pē'ér-ō, pyer-ō'] *n* a figure in old Italian comedy and old French pantomime, usu. having a whitened face and wearing baggy white clothes.

piety [pī'é-ti] *n* the quality of being pious; devoutness; sense of duty towards parents, benefactors, etc.; dutiful conduct, **pi'etism.**

pig [pig] *n* a domesticated animal with a broad snout and a fat body raised for food; a swine; a greedy or filthy person; an oblong casting of metal poured from the smelting furnace.—*vi* to bring forth pigs; to live like pigs.—*adj*—**pigg'ery**, a place where pigs are kept.—*adjs* **pigg'ish, pig'head'ed**, stupidly obstinate, **pig'tail**, a tight braid of hair.

pigeon [pij'in] *n* any bird of the dove family; **pig'eonhole**, a compartment for storing papers, etc.

pigment [pig'mènt] *n* paint; any substance used for coloring.— *n* **pigmentā'tion.**

pigmy *See* **pygmy.**

pike[1] [pīk] *n* a pikestaff; a sharp point or spike; the top of a spear; a long-snouted fish, important as a food and game fish; **pike'staff**, a spiked staff for use on slippery ground.

pike[2] [pīk] *n* a turnpike; a railroad or a railroad line.

pilaster [pi-las'tèr] *n* a square column, partly built into, partly projecting from a wall.

pilchard [pil'chàrd] *n* a fish of the herring family.

pile[1] [pīl] *n* a heap of more or less regular shape; a heap of combustibles; a tall building, a form of battery.

pile[2] [pīl] *n* a large stake or cylinder driven into the earth to support foundations.

pile[3] [pīl] *n* a covering of hair, esp soft, fine or furry; a raised surface on cloth, as on a rug.

pile[4] [pīl] *n* a single haemorrhoid.

pilfer [pil'fèr] *vi* and *vt* to steal esp in small quantities.—*n* **pil'ferage**, petty theft.

pilgrim [pil'grim] *n* (*arch* and *poet*) a wanderer, wayfarer; one who travels a distance to visit a holy place.

pill [pil] *n* a little ball of medicine.

pillage [pil′ij] *n* act of plundering; plunder. —*vti* to plunder. —*n* **pill′ager.**

pillar [pil′ár] *n* a slender, vertical structure used as a support; a structure of like form erected as a monument, etc.

pillion [pil′yòn] *n* a pad or light saddle consisting chiefly of a cushion for a woman; a cushion behind a horseman for a second rider.

pillory [pil′ór-i] *n* a wooden frame, supported by an upright pillar or post, and having holes through which the head and hands of a criminal were put as a punishment. —*vt* to set in the pillory; to hold up to ridicule.

pillow [pil′ō] *n* a cushion for a sleeper's head; any object used for the purpose. —*vt* to lay for support (on). —*ns* **pill′owcase, pillowslip,** a cover for a pillow.

pilot [pī′lòt] *n* a steersman; esp one licensed to conduct ships in and out of a harbor, along a dangerous coast, etc.; one qualified to operate the flying controls of an aircraft; a guide. —*vt* to act as pilot to. —*ns* **pī′lotage,** piloting; pilot's fee; **pī′lot en′gine,** a locomotive sent before a train to clear its way, **pī′lot fish,** a fish that accompanies a shark.

pimento [pi-men′tō] *n* allspice or Jamaica pepper.

pimp [pimp] *n* a prostitute's agent. —Also *vi*

pimpernel [pim′pér-nel] *n* a genus of plants of the primrose family.

pimple [pim′pl] *n* a pustule; a small, elevated, inflamed swelling of the skin. —*adjs* **pim′pled.**

pin [pin] *n* a piece of wood or metal used for fastening things together; a peg for various purposes; a small piece of pointed wire with a head; an ornament or badge with a pin or clasp for fastening to clothing. —*vt* to fasten with a pin; to transfix with a pin or a sharp weapon; to hold firmly in one position; to fix or fasten (to); **pin mon′ey,** money allotted to a wife for private expenses; **pin′-point′,** anything very sharp and very minute (*vt* **pin′point,** to locate, place, very exactly; to define exactly).

pinafore [pin′a-fōr, -fôr] *n* a sleeveless garment worn over a dress, blouse, or sweater.

pince-nez [pēs′-nā] *n* pair of eyeglasses with a spring for catching the nose.

pincers [pin′sèrz] *n* a gripping tool, used for drawing out nails, etc; a grasping claw, as of a crab.

pinch [pinch] *vt* to nip; to squeeze or compress painfully. —*vi* to nip or squeeze; to be painfully tight. —*n* an act or experience of pinching; a quantity that can be taken up between the finger and thumb. —*adj* **pinched.**

pinchbeck [pinch′bek] *n* a yellow alloy of copper with much less zinc than ordinary brass, simulating gold; something counterfeit or spurious.

pine[1] [pīn] *n* any tree of the northern temperate coniferous genus with long needles growing two to five in a cluster and having large, well-formed cones; trees of the pine family—*ns* **pine′apple,** a tropical plant, and its fruit.

pine[2] [pīn] *vi* to waste away, esp under pain or mental distress.

ping [ping] *n* a whistling sound as of a bullet—*vti* to strike with a ping. —*n* **ping′ pong′,** a trade name for table tennis equipment.

pinion[1] [pin′yòn] *n* a wing. —*vt* to confine the wings of; to confine by binding the arms.

pinion[2] [pin′yòn] *n* a small toothed wheel.

pink[1] [pingk] *n* any plant or flower of the genus that includes carnation and Sweet William; pale-red; the most perfect condition; the highest point.

pink[2] [pingk] *vt* to stab, pierce; to cut a saw-toothed edge on (cloth, etc.); to perforate in an ornamental pattern.

pinnace [pin′ás] *n* a small vessel with oars and sails, esp one used as a ship's tender.

pinnacle [pin′à-kl] *n* a slender turret; a high pointed rock or mountain like a spire; the highest point.

pinnate [pin′āt] *adj* shaped like a feather, esp in having parts arranged in the opposite sides of an axis.

pint [pīnt] *n* measure of capacity equal to ½ quart.

pioneer [pī-ón-ēr′] *n* one who is among the first in new fields of enterprise, exploration, colonization, research, etc.; a plant or animal capable of establishing itself in a barren area and initiating an ecological cycle. —Also *vti*.

pious [pī′us] *adj* showing, having.

pip[1] [pip] *n* a disease of a bird.

pip[2] [pip] *n* a small hard body (seed or fruitlet) in fleshy fruit.

pip[3] [pip] *n* a spot on dice and dominoes to indicate numerical value.

pipe [pīp] *n* a tube of wood, metal, etc. for making musical sounds; any tube; a tube with a bowl at the end for smoking tobacco; a long tube or hollow body for conveying water, gas, etc. —*vi* to play upon a pipe; to whistle. —*vt* to play on a pipe; to utter shrilly in speech or song. —*ns* **pipe′ clay,** fine white clay used for making tobacco pipes and for whitening belts, etc.; **pip′er,** a player on a pipe, esp a bagpipe.

pipit [pip′it] *n* a larklike genus of birds.

pipkin [pip′kin] *n* a small earthenware or metal pot.

pippin [pip′in] *n* a kind of apple.

piquant [pē′kànt] *adj* stinging; pleasantly pungent; appetizing. —*n* **piq′uancy.** —*adv* **piq′uantly.**

pique [pēk] *n* animosity or ill-feeling; offense taken. —*vt* to wound the pride of; to nettle.

piqué [pē-kā] *n* a stiff corded cotton fabric.

piquet [pi-ket′] *n* a two-handed game played with a pack of 32 cards.

pirate [pī′rát] *n* one who practices piracy. —*vti* to take by piracy; to publish or reproduce in violation of a copyright.) —*n* **piracy.** —*adj* **piratical.** —*adv* **pirat′ically.**

pirouette [pir-ōō-et′] *n* a spinning about on tiptoe.

Pisces [pis′ēz] *n* the Fishes, the twelfth sign of the zodiac in astrology, operative from February 19 to March 20.

pismire [pis′mīr] *n* an ant or emmet.

pistil [pis′til, -tl] *n* properly the gynaeceum of a flower.

pistol [pis′tl] *n* a small handgun. —*vt* to shoot with a pistol.

piston [pis′tòn] *n* a solid piece moving to and fro in a close-fitting hollow container as in engines and pumps. —*n* **pis′ton rod,** the rod to which the piston is fixed, and which moves with it.

pit [pit] *n* a hole in the earth; a scooped-out place for burning something (as charcoal); a sunken or depressed area below the adjacent floor area; a space at the front of the stage for the orchestra; an area in a securities or commodities exchange in which members do the trading; a place beside the course where cars in a race can be refuelled and repaired; the indentation left by smallpox, etc.; an enclosure for cockfights or the like. —*vt* to mark with little hollows; to lay in a pit; to set to fight. —*vi* to become marked with pits; to make a pit stop. —*ns* **pit′fall,** a lightly covered hole as a trap for beasts; (*fig*) a hidden danger.

pit-a-pat [pit′a-pat] *adv* with palpitation or pattering.

pitch[1] [pich] *n* the black shining residue of distillation of tar, etc.; any of various bituminous substances; resin obtained from various conifers and often used medicinally. —*vt* to smear, cover, or caulk with pitch. —*adj* **pitch′-black,** black or extremely dark.

pitch[2] [pich] *vt* to thrust or fix in the ground; to fix in position by means of stakes, pegs, etc., driven into the ground, to erect; to arrange, to set in array; (*fig*) to give this or that emotional tone to; to throw or toss, esp in such a manner as to cause to fall flat or in a definite position; to let one's choice fall (upon). —*vi* to plunge or fall, esp forward; to slope down. —*n* a throw or cast; the place at which one (eg a street trader) is stationed; degree of slope; degree, esp of elevation or depression; the degree of acuteness of sounds. —*n* **pitch′fork,** a fork for pitching hay, etc. —*vt* to lift with a pitchfork; to throw suddenly into (*lit* and *fig*).

pitcher [pich′èr] *n* a vessel for holding or pouring liquids.

pith [pith] *n* the soft substance in the center of the stems of plants; similar material elsewhere, as the white inner skin of an orange; importance. —*adj* **pith′y,** full of pith; forcible; terse and full of meaning.

pithecanthropine [pith-i-kan(t)′thrō-pīn] *n* any of a group of pleistocene hominids having a smaller cranial capacity than modern man.

pittance [pit′àns] *n* a dole; a very small portion or quantity, or remuneration.

pity [pit′i] *n* a feeling for the sufferings and misfortunes of others; a cause or source of pity or grief; a regrettable fact. —*vt* to feel pity for. —*adj* **pit′iable.** —*adv* **pit′iably.** —*adj* **pit′iful.** —*adj* **pit′iless.**

pivot [piv′òt] *n* a pin on which anything turns; a key person upon whom, or position on which, a body wheels. —*vi* to turn on, or as if on, a pivot.

pixel [pik'sel] *n* one of the minute units which make up an image (as on a television screen).

pixy, pixie [pik'si] *n* a small fairy.

pizzicato [pit-si-kä'tō] *adj* (*mus*) played by plucking the string, not with the bow. — *adv* by plucking.

placable [plak'á-bl] *adj* that may be appeased, willing to forgive. — *vt* **plac'ate** [plāk-, plak'āte] to conciliate.

placard [plak'ärd] *n* a written or printed paper stuck upon a wall or otherwise displayed as an intimation. — *vt* [pla-kärd'] to display as a placard.

place [plās] *n* a court or short street in a city; space; room; a region; a particular point, part, position, etc.; a position in space or on the earth's surface, or in any system, order or arrangement. — *vt* to put in any place; to find a place for; to identify; to estimate; to rank. — *vi* to finish second or among the first three in a race.

placenta [pla-sen'ta] *n* the structure that unites the unborn mammal, to the womb of its mother; the part of a plant to which the seeds are attached.

placer [plas'ér, plas'ér] *n* a surface deposit, from which gold or other mineral can be washed.

placid [plas'id] *adj* calm, serene. — *ns* **placid'ity**.

plagiary [plā'ji-ár-i] *n* one who takes the writings of others and gives them out as his own. — *vt* **pla'giarize**, to steal from the writings of another. — *ns* **pla'giarism, pla'giarist**.

plague [plāg] *n* a deadly epidemic or pestilence; any troublesome thing or person. — *vt* to pester or annoy.

plaice [plās] *n* any of various flatfishes.

plaid [plad] *n* a long piece of woolen cloth worn over the shoulder, usu. in tartan (as part of Highland dress).

plain [plān] *adj* flat, level; unobstructed (eg view); open to the mind, manifest, obvious; readily understood; without ornament; not intricate or elaborate; not colored; not luxurious; without beauty. — *n* an extent of level land. — *adv* clearly, distinctly. — *adv* **plain'ly**. — *adj* **plain'spoken**, candid, frank.

plaint [plānt] *n* lamentation; complaint; a statement of grievance. — *n* **plaint'iff** (*law*) one who commences a suit against another.

plait [plat] *n* a flat fold; a pleat; straw, hair, etc., interlaced in a regular pattern; a pigtail, a braid. — Also *vt*. — *adj* **plait'ed**.

plan [plan] *n* a representation of anything projected on a plane or flat surface, a scheme or project; a way of proceeding; any outline or sketch. — *vt* to make a plan of; to design; to lay plans for; to intend. — *vi* to make plans.

plane¹ [plān] *n* any flat or level surface; one of the main supporting surfaces of an airplane; (short for) airplane. — *adj* perfectly level; pertaining to, lying in, or confined to a plane.

plane² [plān] *n* a carpenter's tool for producing a smooth surface. — *vt* to make (a surface, as of wood) level by means of a plane.

plane³ [plān] *n* any one of the genus of tall trees with large broad lobed leaves.

planet [plan'èt] *n* a body that revolves about the sun or other fixed star. — *adj* **plan'etary**, under the influence of a planet; wandering, erratic; terrestrial.

plank [plangk] *n* a long, broad, thick board; one of the principles or aims that form the platform of a political party.

plankton [plangk'tón] the drifting organisms in oceans, lakes, or rivers.

plant [plānt] *n* a living thing that cannot move voluntarily, a soft-stemmed organism of this kind, as distinguished from a tree or shrub; the machinery, buildings, etc. of a factory, etc. — *vt* to put into the ground for growth; to furnish with plants; to set firmly in position. — *vi* to plant something. — *ns* **plantā'tion**, a large cultivated planting of trees; an estate used for growing cotton, rubber, tea, or other product of warm countries, cultivated by resident laborers; **plant'er**, the owner of a plantation.

plantain¹ [plan'tän] *n* the roadside plant that presses its leaves flat on the ground.

plantain² [plan'tän] *n* a banana plant.

plaque [plāk] *n* a plate, tablet, or slab hung on, applied to, or inserted in a surface as an ornament; a brooch worn as a badge of honor.

plash¹ [plash] *n* a short plunge or pool.

plash² [plash] *vt* to splash.

plaster [plās'tér] *n* a fabric coated with a pasty substance for local application as a remedy, a pasty composition that sets hard, esp a mixture of lime, sand, and water, used for coating walls and ceilings, etc. — *vt* to cover as with plaster; to apply like a plaster; to make lie smooth and flat; to damage by a heavy attack. — *vi* to apply plaster. — **plas'terer**.

plastic [plas'tik] *adj* giving form to clay, wax, etc.; creative (eg of imagination); capable of being easily molded; made of plastic. — *n* any of various nonmetallic compounds synthetically produced, that can be molded, cast, extruded, drawn, or laminated into objects, films, or filaments. — *n* **plasticity** [-tis'i-ti], capacity for being molded or altered; the ability to retain a shape attained by pressure deformation.

plat¹ [plat] *n* a plait.

plat² [plat] *n* a plot of ground.

plate [plāt] *n* a flat sheet of metal, specifically one on which an engraving is cut; a broad piece of armor; an engraved sheet of metal for printing from; household utensils plated in gold or silver; plated ware; a shallow dish; contents of a plate; a helping (of food); a vessel used for church collection. — *vt* to overlay with metal; to cover with a thin film of another metal, mechanically, chemically, or electrically. — *adj* **plā'ted**, covered with metal; covered with a coating of another metal, esp gold or silver.

plateau [pla'tō, pla-tō'] *n* a tableland.

platen [plat'n] *n* the part of printing press that presses the paper against the type; the roller of a typewriter.

platform [plat'fôrm] *n* a raised level surface; a raised floor for speakers, musicians, etc.

platinum [plat'in-um] *n* a noble metal, grayish-white, very valuable, malleable and ductile, very heavy and hard to fuse.

platitude [plat'i-tūd] *n* commonplaceness; a dull commonplace or truism; an empty remark.

Platonic [pla-ton'ik] *adj* pertaining to *Plato* the Greek philosopher, or to his philosophy; **platonic**, of love, between soul and soul, without sensual desire.

platoon [pla'tōōn'] *n* a military unit consisting of two or more squads.

platter [plat'ér] *n* a large usu. oval flat plate.

plaudit [plôd'it] *n* (usu. *pl*) applause; praise bestowed emphatically. — *adj* **plaud'itory**.

plausible [plôz'i-bl] *adj* seemingly worthy of approval or praise; specious, apparently reasonable. — *ns* **plausibil'ity**.

play [plā] *vi* to gambol, to frisk; to engage in pleasureable activity; to behave without seriousness; to amuse onself; to take part in a game or sport; to move or function freely within prescribed limits; to act in a specified way. — *vt* to act a part on the stage or in life; to engage in (a game); to contend against in a game; to perform music on; to bet on. — *n* recreative activity; amusement; the playing of a game; manner of playing; gambling; a drama or dramatic performance; activity, operation; freedom of movement, scope for activity; **play'er**, one who plays a specified game or instrument; an actor. — *adj* **play'ful; play'fellow, play'mate**, a companion in play; **playhouse**, a theater; **play'thing**, a toy; **play'wright**, a dramatist.

plea [plē] *n* (*law*); defendant's answer to a charge or claim; an excuse; a request; urgent entreaty.

pleach [plēch] *vt* to intertwine the branches of, as a hedge; to plait, as hair.

please [plēz] *vi* to give pleasure to; to delight; to satisfy. — *vt* to give pleasure; to seem good. — *n* **pleasance** [plez'áns], (*arch*) enjoyment; a pleasure ground. — *adj* **pleas'ant**, pleasing; agreeable. — *adv* **pleas'antly**. — *ns* **pleas'antry**, jocularity. — *n* **pleasure** [plezh'ùr], agreeable emotions; gratification of the senses or of the mind; what the will prefers.

pleat [plēt] *n* a double fold of cloth, etc. pressed or stitched in place.

plebeian [plē-bē'án] *adj* of the common people; vulgar. — *n* a vulgar, coarse person.

plebiscite [pleb'i-sit, also -sīt] *n* a direct vote of the whole nation, on a political issue.

pledge [plej] *n* something given as a security; a token or assuring sign; a solemn promise. — *vt* to give as security; to pawn; to bind by solemn promise.

Pleistocene [plīs'tō-sēn] *adj* of the earlier epoch of the geological era.

plenary [plē'nàr-ē, or plen'á-rē] *adj* full, entire, unqualified; fully attended (eg of an assembly).

plenipotentiary [plen-i-pō-ten'shår-i] *adj* having full powers.—*n* a person invested with full powers.

plenitude [plen'i-tūd] *n* fullness, completeness.

plenty [plen'ti] *n* a full supply; abundance.—*adj* **plenteous.**—*adv* **plen'tiful,** copious; abundant.

pleonasm [plē'o-nazm] *n* redundancy, esp of words; a redundant expression.—*adj* **pleonas'tic.**

plethora [pleth'ôr-a] *n* a bodily condition marked by an excessive fullness of blood; over abundance of any kind.—*adj* **plethoric.**

pleura [plōō'rä] *n* a delicate membrane that covers the lung and lines the cavity of the chest.—*adj* **pleu'ral.**—*n* **pleurisy** [plōō'ri-si], inflammation of the pleura.

plexus [pleks'us] *n* a network of veins, nerves, etc.

pliable [plī'å-bl] *adj* easily bent or folded, flexible; easily persuaded.—*ns* **pliabil'ity, plī'ancy.**—*adj* **plī'ant.**

plied, pliers *See* ply.

plight[1] [plīt] *n* pledge; promise.—*vt* to pledge.

plight[1] [plīt] *n* condition, state, now usu. bad.

Plimsoll line or **mark** [plim'sôl, -sol] *n* a ship's load line, or set of load lines.

plinth [plinth] *n* the square block under the base of a column; any of various bases or lower parts.

plod [plod] *vi* to walk heavily and laboriously; to study or work steadily and laboriously.—*n* **plodd'er.**—*adj* and *n* **plodd'ing.**

plot [plot] *n* a small piece of ground; the story or scheme of connected events running through a play, novel, etc.; a conspiracy.—*vt* to make a plan of by means of a graph; to mark (points) on a graph; to conspire.—*n* **plott'er.**

plover [pluv'ér] *n* any of numerous shorebirds resembling the sandpiper.

plow [plow] *n* a farm implement for turning up the soil—*vt* **plow'man,** a man who guides a plow; a farm laborer.

plowshare [plow'shär] *n* the part of a plow that cuts the under surface of the sod from the ground.

pluck [pluk] *vt* to pull off, out, or away; to strip, as a fowl of its feathers.—*vi* to make a sharp pull or twitch.—*n* a single act of plucking; the heart, liver, and lungs of an animal; heart, courage.—*adj* **pluck'y.**—*adv* **pluck'ily.**

plug [plug] *n* a peg or any piece of wood, metal, or other substance stopping, or for stopping, a hole; a stopper; a compressed cake of tobacco; a kind of fishing lure.—*vt* to stop with a plug.

plum [plum] *n* the oval smooth-skinned stone fruit; any of various trees bearing similar edible fruit; **plum pudding,** a rich boiled or steamed dish made of flour and suet, with raisins, currants, and various species.

plumage [plōōm'ij] *n* a bird's feathers.

plumb [plum] *n* a lead weight attached to a line used to determine how deep the water is or whether a wall is vertical; any of various weights.—*adj* perfectly vertical.—*adv* vertically; in a direct manner; **plumb line,** a line directed to the center of gravity of the earth.

plumbago [plum-bā'gō] *n* graphite.

plume [plōōm] *n* a feather, esp a large showy one; a feather or tuft of feathers, or anything similar, used as an ornament.—*vt* to preen; to adorn with plumes.

plump[1] [plump] *vti* to fall, drop or sink, or come into contact suddenly and heavily; to favor or give support.—*adv* straight down; straight ahead.

plump[2] [plump] *adj* pleasantly fat and rounded, chubby.—Also *vti*—*n* **plump'ness.**

plunder [plun'dér] *vt* to carry off the goods by force; to pillage.—*n* pillage; booty.

plunge [plunj] *vt* to thrust suddenly to immerse to sink —*vi* to fling oneself or rush impetuously.—*n* **plung'er.**

pluperfect [plōō-pér'fèkt or plōō'-] *adj* (*gram*) the past perfect tense.

plural [plōōr'l] *adj* numbering or expressing more than one; consisting of or containing more than one kind or class.—*ns* **plur'alism,** the holding by one person of more than one office at a time, esp applied to ecclesiastical benefices.

plus [plus] *prep* added to; in addition to.—*adj* indicating addition; positive.—*n* the sign (+) prefixed to positive quantities.

plus fours [plus-förz'] *n pl* loose sports knickers.

plush [plush] *n* a fabric with an even and more open pile than velvet.

Pluto [plōō'tō] *n* the Greek god of the underworld; the planet furthest from the sun.—*adjs* **pluto'nian,** of Pluto; of the underworld; **plutonic,** [-ton'ik], of Pluto.

plutocracy [plōō-tok'ra-si] *n* government by the wealthy; a ruling body or class of rich men.—*n* **plutocrat.**

plutonium [plōō'tō'ni-üm] *n* a transuranic element.

pluvial [plōō'vi-ål] *adj* of or by rain; rainy.—*adj* rainy.

ply[1] [plī] *n* a layer or thickness, as of cloth, plywood, etc.; any of the twisted strands in a yarn, etc.

ply[2] [plī] *vt* to work at steadily and energetically; to use or wield diligently or vigorously; to assail persistently to sail back and forth across.—*vi* to keep busy.

pneumatic [nū-mat'ik] *adj* relating to wind, air, or gases; containing or inflated with air; filled with or worked by compressed air.

pneumonia [nū-mō'ni-a] *n* inflammation of the lung.

poach[1] [pōch] *vt* to cook (an egg without its shell, fish, etc.) in or over boiling water.

poach[2] [pōch] *vti* to take game or fish illegally.—*ns* **poach'er.**

pock [pok] *n* a small elevation of the skin containing pus, as in smallpox.

pocket [pok'et] *n* a little pouch or bag, esp one attached to a garment for carrying small articles; a pouchlike hollow, a cavity, or a place of lodgement; a deposit (as of gold, water, or gas); a portion of the atmosphere differing in pressure or in other condition from its surroundings.—*vt* to put in the pocket; to envelop; to enclose.—*ns* **pock'etbook,** a woman's purse; monetary resources.

pod [pod] *n* a dry fruit or seed vessel, as of peas, beans, etc..—*vi* to form pods.

poem [pō'ém] *n* an arrangement of words, esp in meter, often rhymed, in a style more imaginative than ordinary speech.

poesy [pō'e-si] *n* poetry.

poet [pō'ét, -it] *n* the author of a poem; one skilled in making poetry.—*ns* **pō'etess.**—*adj* **poetic, -al** the nature of, or pertaining to, poetry; expressed in poetry.—*adv* **poet'ically.**

pogrom [pog-rom'] *n* an organized massacre of helpless people.

poignant [poin'ánt] *adj* piercing; affecting one's feelings sharply or keenly.—*adv* **poign'antly.**

point [point] *n* a dot or other small mark used in writing or printing; a place or station considered in relation to position only; course, or cycle; a moment of time, without duration; one of thirty-two divisions of the compass; a detail taken into account in judging; the most important element in an argument, discourse, etc.; that without which a story, joke, etc., is meaningless; the tapering end of anything; the tip; a nib; a cape or headland.—*vt* to give point to; to sharpen; to aim (at); to direct attention to; to give point, force, or piquancy to.—*vi* to direct the finger, the eye, or the mind (at or to); to call attention (to).—*adj* **point'ed**—*adv* **point'edly.**—*ns* **point'er,** a rod for pointing to a blackboard, etc.; a breed of dogs that point on discovering game.—*adj* **point'less.**

point-blank [point'-blangk'] *adj* of a shot, fired horizontally; direct, unqualified, blunt.

poise[1] [poiz] *vt* to balance; to hold supported without motion.—*vi* to become drawn up into readiness; to hover.—*n* a balanced state; bearing, carriage.

poison [poi'zn] *n* a substance that usu. destroys life or impairs health; any malignant influence.—*vt* to injure or to kill with poison; to taint; to put poison into.—*ns* **poi'soner.**—*adj* **poi'sonous.**

poke[1] [pōk] *n* (*dial*) a sack, a bag.

poke[2] [pōk] *n* a projecting brim of front of a bonnet.

poke[3] [pōk] *vt* to thrust or push the end of anything against or into; to make by poking.—*vi* to jab (at); to pry or search.—*n* a jab; a thrust.—*n* **po'ker,** a rod for poking or stirring the fire.

poker [pō'kér] *n* one of several card games.

polar [pō'lár] *adj* of or near the North or South Pole; of a pole; having polarity.—*n* **polarity.**—*vt* **polarize** [pō'lár-īz] to cause (as light waves) to vibrate in a definite pattern; to give physical polarity to; to break up into opposing factions; to concentrate.—*vi* to become polarized.—*ns* **polarization; Polaroid,** trade name for a transparent material capable of polarizing light used esp in eyeglasses and lamps to prevent glare; a camera that produces a print in seconds.

pole¹ [pōl] *n* the end of an axis, esp of the earth, or any rotating sphere; either of two opposed forces, the terminals of a battery, etc. —*n* **pole′star**, a star near the north pole of the heavens.

pole² [pōl] *n* a long, slender piece of wood, metal, etc.; a measure of length, 5½ yards, or of area, 30¼ square yards.

poleax [pōl′aks] *n* a battle-ax; an ax used in slaughtering cattle.

polecat [pōl′kat] *n* a carnivorous mammal of which the ferret is considered a domesticated variety; a skunk.

polemic [po-lem′ik] *adj*; controversial. —*n* a controversialist; a controversy; (*pl*) practice or art of controversy. —*adj* **polem′ical**.

police [pol-ēs′] *n* the governmental department for keeping order, detecting crime, law enforcement, etc.; the members of such a department. —*vt* to control, protect, **police′ off′icer**, a policeman or policewoman.

policy¹ [pol′i-si] *n* a high-level overall plan embracing the general principles and aims of an organization, esp a government.

policy² [pol′i-si] *n* a writing containing a contract of insurance.

polio [pōl′i-ō] *n* short for *poliomyelitis*.

poliomyelitis [pōl-i-ō-mī-ē-lī′tis] *n* an acute infectious virus disease marked by inflammation of nerve cells in the spinal cord.

polish [pol′ish] *vt* to make smooth and glossy by rubbing; to make elegant. —*vi* to take a polish. —*n* an act of polishing; gloss; a substance used to produce a smooth surface; refinement.

polite [po-līt′] *adj* refined; of courteous manners. —*adv* **polite′ly**. —*n* **polite′ness**.

politic [pol′i-tik] *adj* in accordance with good policy, expedient, judicious; shrewdly tactful; political. —*vi* to campaign in politics. —*adj* **polit′ical**, pertaining to politics or government. —*adv* **polit′ically**. —*n* **politician** [-tish′ån] one engaged in political life, **pol′itics**, the art or science of government; the management of a political party.

polity [pol′i-ti] *n* the form or constitution of the government of a state, etc.; political organization.

polka [pōl′ka] *n* a Bohemian dance or its tune.

poll [pōl] *n* the head; a counting, listing, etc. of persons, esp of voters; the number of votes recorded. —*vt* to register, the votes of. —*vi* to cast one's vote at a poll. —**poll′ tax**, a tax of a fixed amount per person levied on adults.

pollack [pol′åk] *n* a common food fish of the north Atlantic of the cod family.

pollard [pol′ård] *n* a tree having the whole crown cut off to promote the growth of a dense head of foliage. —*vt* to make a pollard of (a tree).

pollen [pol′ēn] *n* the fertilizing powder formed in the anthers of flowers. —*n* **pollina′tion**, the transferring or supplying of pollen to the stigma of a flower, esp by aid of insects or other external agents.

pollute [pol-(y)ōōt] *vt* to contaminate, make filthy; to make unclean morally; to profane. —*ns* **pollu′tion**, act of polluting.

polo [pō′lō] *n* a game played on horseback by two teams, using a wooden ball and long-handled mallets.

polonaise [pol-o-nāz′] *n* a Polish national dance; music for such a dance.

polonium [po-lō′ni-ùm] *n* a transuranic element.

poltergeist [pol′tėr-gīst] *n* an alleged spirit said to move heavy furniture, etc., a noisy ghost.

poltroon [pol-trōōn′] *n* a thorough coward. —*n* **poltroon′ery**.

poly- [pol-i-] in composition, much, many.

polyandrous [po-li-an′drus] *adj* having several husbands or male mates at the same time.

polyanthus [pol-i-an′thus] *n* any of various hybrid primroses.

polychrome [pol′i-krōm] *adj* made with, or decorated in many colors.

polyethylene [pol-i-eth′i-lēn] *n* a plastic made by polymerizing ethylene.

polygamy [pol-ig′a-mi] *n* the practice of having more than one spouse at one time. —*n* **polyg′amist**.

polyglot [pol′i-glot] *adj* using many languages; composed of numerous linguistic groups.

polygon [pol′i-gon] *n* a plane figure bounded by straight lines, esp more than four.

polygyny [pol-ij′i-ni or -ig′-] *n* the social usage by which a man has more wives than one at the same time.

polyhedron [pol-i-hē′dron] *n* a solid figure with many (usu. more than six) faces.

polyp [pol′ip] *n* a small water animal with tentacles at the top of a tubelike body.

polysyllable [pol′i-sil-à-bl] *n* a word of many, or of more than four, syllables. —*adj* **polysyllab′ic**.

polytechnic [pol-i-tek′nik] *adj* of or providing instruction in many applied sciences and technical subjects. —*n* a school in which such subjects are taught.

polytheism [pol′i-thē-izm] *n* belief in more than one god.

pomade [po-mād′, -mäd′] *n* a perfumed ointment for the hair.

pomegranate [pom′gran-it] *n* a fruit with a thick rind and many seeds; a widely cultivated tropical tree.

Pomeranian [pom-e-rā′ni-ån] *adj*; a breed of very small compact dogs with a dense double coat.

pommel [pum′él] *n* the knob on the hilt of a sword; the rounded upward-projecting front part of a saddle. —*vt* to pummel.

pomp [pomp] *n* a splendid procession; ceremony. —*adj* **pomp′ous**, self-important. —*ns* **pompos′ity**.

pom-pom¹ [pom′-pom] *n* an automatic gun.

pom-pom² [pom′pom′] *n* an ornamental ball or tuft of fabric strands used on clothing as an ornament.

poncho [pon′chō] *n* a cloak like a blanket with a hole in the middle for the head.

pond [pond] *n* a body of standing water smaller than a lake.

ponder [pon′dėr] *vti* to think deeply; to consider carefully. —*adj* **pon′derable**, sufficiently significant to be worth considering; **pon′derous**, weighty; massive.

pongee [pon-jē] *n* soft unbleached washable silk woven from filaments of wild silkworms.

poniard [pon′yård] *n* a small dagger with a slender blade. —*vt* to stab with a poniard.

pontiff [pon′tif] *n* (*RC*) a bishop, esp the Pope. —*adj* **pontif′ical**, splendid; authoritative; pompously dogmatic. —*n* **pontif′icate**.

pontificis (partly through Fr *pontife*), perh from.

pontoon [pon-tōōn′] *n* a flat-bottomed boat; a float; such a boat or float used to support a bridge.

pony [pō′ni] *n* a small horse.

poodle [pōō′dl] *n* a breed of dog with a solid-colored curly coat of many colors and sizes.

pool¹ [pōōl] *n* a small pond; a puddle.

pool² [pōōl] *n* a game of billiards played on a table with six pockets; a combination of resources, funds, supplies, etc. for some common purpose.

poop [pōōp] *n* a high deck in the stern of a ship. —*vt* to break over the stern of.

poor [pōōr] *adj* possessing little, without means, needy; deficient; unproductive; inferior, paltry; —*adv* **poor′ly**. —*adj* not in good health. —*ns* **poor′ness**; **poor′house**, a house established at the public expense for sheltering the poor. —*adj* **poor′spir′ited**, lacking zest, confidence, or courage.

pop¹ [pop] *n* a sharp, quick sound, a shot; any carbonated, nonalcoholic beverage. —*vi* to make a pop; to shoot; to come or go suddenly or quickly. —*vt* to cause to pop, as corn by roasting; to put suddenly. —*ns* **pop′corn**, a kind of corn which when heated pops or bursts open.

pop² [pop] *adj* in a popular modern style. —*n* pop music; pop art; pop culture.

Pope [pōp] *n* the bishop of Rome, head of the Roman Catholic Church. —*ns* **pop′ery**. —*adv* **pop′ish**.

popinjay [pop′in-ja] *n* a strutting supericilious person.

poplar [pop′lår] *n* a genus of trees of the willow family.

poplin [pop′lin] *n* a corded fabric with a silk warp and worsted weft.

poppy [pop′i] *n* any of a genus of chiefly annual or perennial herbs that is the source of opium.

populace [pop′ū-lås] *n* the common people; the masses.

popular [pop′ū-lår] *adj* of the people; pleasing to, enjoying the favor of, prevailing among, the people. —*vt* **pop′ularize**, to make generally known or widely approved. —*n* **popular′ity**, quality or state of being popular. —*adv* **pop′ularly**. —*vt* **pop′ulāte**; to furnish with inhabitants. —*ns* **popula′tion**, the

habitants of any place or their number; *adj* **pop'ulous,**
ickly inhabited.

rcelain [pŏr'sĕ'lin] *n* a hard, white, translucent variety of
ramic ware. — Also *adj.*

rch [pŏrch] *n* a covered entrance to a building.

rcine [pŏr'sīn] *adj* of or like pigs or hogs.

rcupine [pŏr'kū-pīn] *n* a large rodent, bristling with quills.

re¹ [pōr, pŏr] *n* a tiny opening, as in plant leaves, stem,
c. — *n* **poros'ity.** — *adj* **por'ous,** having pores; permeable by
uids, etc.

re² [pōr] *vi* to study closely and attentively.

rk [pŏrk] *n* the flesh of a pig used as food; **pork'er,** a young
g; a pig fed for pork. — *adj* **pork'y,** of or like pork.

rnography [pŏr-nog'ra-fi] *n* writings, pictures, etc. intended
rimarily to arouse sexual desire.

rphyry [pŏr'fir-i] *n* any igneous rock with large, distinct
ystals. — *adj* **porphyritic** [-it'ik].

rpoise [pŏr'pùs] *n* any of several small whales.

rridge [pŏr'ij] *n* a food usu. made by slowly stirring oatmeal
boiling water.

rringer [por'in-jèr] *n* a small bowl for soup.

rt¹ [pŏrt] *n* the left side of a ship, or aircraft looking for-
ard. — Also larboard.

rt² [pŏrt] *n* bearing; the position in which a military weapon
carried at the command 'port arms'. — *adj* **port'able,** easily
conveniently carried or moved about.

rt³ [pŏrt] *n* a harbor; a city with a harbor where ships load
ad unload cargo; airport.

rt⁴ [pŏrt] *n* a porthole; an opening, as in a valve face, for the
assage of steam.

rt⁵ [pŏrt] *n* a fortified sweet dark-red.

rtal [pŏr'tăl] *n* a gate or doorway, esp a great or magnificent
ne.

rtcullis [pŏrt-kul'is] *n* a grating that can be let down to close
gateway.

rtend [pŏr-tend'] *vt* to betoken, presage. — *n* **portent** [pŏr'-
nt], that which portends or foreshows. — *adj* **portent'ous.**

rter¹ [port'er] *n* a doorman or gatekeeper.

rter² [port'ĕr] *n* a man who carries luggage, etc. for hire; a
ilroad attendant for passengers as on a sleeper; a dark-
rown beer.

rtfolio [pōrt-fōli-ō] *n* a portable case for loose papers, draw-
gs, etc.; a collection of such papers; the office of minister of
ate.

rthole [pōrt'hōl] *n* an opening (as a window) with a cover or
osure esp in the side of a ship or aircraft.

rtico [pōr'ti-kō] *n* (*archit*) a range of columns with a roof
rming a covered walk.

rtion [pōr'sh(ó)n] *n* a part, esp an alloted part of a dowry;
estiny. — *vt* to divide into portions; to allot as a share.
or'tionless.

rtmanteau [pōrt-man'tō] *n* a large traveling bag.

rtrait [pōr'trăt] *n* a painting, photograph, etc. of a person,
p of the face; the likeness of a real person. — *n* **por'trait-
re.** — *vt* **portray** [pōr-trā'], to paint or draw the likeness of; to
escribe in words.

rtuguese [pōr'tū-gēz'] *adj* of Portugal, its people.

se [pōz] *n* a position or attitude, an attitude óf body or of
ind assumed for effect. — *vt* to put in a suitable attitude. — *ns*
oser, one who poses; **poseur** [pōz-œr'; Fr] an affected
erson.

se [pōz] *vt* to puzzle, to perplex by questions. — *n* **pos'er,** a
fficult question.

sh [posh] *adj* (*inf*) elegant; fashionable.

sition [poz-ish'(ó)n] *n* situation; place occupied; state of
fairs; ground taken in argument or dispute; principle laid
own. — *vt* to set in place; to determine the position of.

sitive [poz'i-tiv] *adj* definitely, formally, or explicitly laid
own; express; downright; dealing with matters of fact,
quualified; expressed clearly, or in a confident or peremptory
anner. — *n* that which is positive; a positive quantity. — *adv*
os'itively. — *ns* **pos'itiveness.**

sse [pos'è] *n* a body of men summoned by a sheriff to assist
m in keeping the peace, etc.

ssess [poz-es'] *vt* to have or hold as owner; to occupy
ad dominate the mind of; *n* **possession.** — *adj* **possess'ive,**
ertaining to or denoting possession.

posset [pos'ĕt] *n* a drink, milk curdled, with wine, or ale.

possible [pos'i-bl] *adj* that may be or happen; that may be
done, practicable. — *n* **possibil'ity.** — *adv* **poss'ibly.**

post¹ [pōst] *n* a piece of wood, metal, etc. set upright to support
a building, sign, etc.*vt* to put up; to announce by posting
notices; to warn against trespassing on by posted notices. — *n*
post'er, a usu. decorative or ornamental bill or placard.

post² [pōst] *n* a fixed place or station, esp a place where a soldier
or body of soldiers is stationed; a trading post. — *vt* to station
in a given place. — *ns* **post'age,** money charged for mailing a
letter, etc. as represented by stamps; *adj* **pos'tal.** — *ns* **postal
card,** a card officially stamped and issued by the government
for use in the mail; a postcard; **post' chaise,** a carriage,
usually four-wheeled, for two or four passengers with a postilion. — *adv* **post'haste,** with all possible speed. — **post'-
horse,** a horse for use esp by couriers or mail carriers; **post'-
man,** a mailman; **post'mark,** the mark impressed upon a
letter at a post office cancelling the stamp or showing the date
and place of posting or of arrival; **post'master,** the manager
or superintendent of a post office; **post'master gen'eral,** an
official in charge of a national post office department or
agency; **post' office,** a government department or agency
handling the transmission of mail.

post- [pōst-] *prefix* after, behind — *vt* **postdate',** to date after
the real time; **post'grad'uate,** belonging to study pursued
after graduation. — Also *n.* — *n, adj.*

postern [pōst'ĕrn] *n* a back door or gate.

postilion, postillion [pŏs-til'yón] *n* one who rides as a guide on
the leading left-hand horse of a team drawing a carriage. —
Also postboy.

postpone [pōs(t)-pōn'] *vt* to put off to a future time.

postscript [pōs(t)'skript] *n* a part added to a letter after the
signature.

postulate [pos'tū-lāt] *vt* to claim; to take for granted,
assume. — *n* a position assumed as self-evident.

posture [pos'tūr] *n* the position and carriage of the body as a
whole; attitude of mind. — *vt* to place in a particular manner.

posy [pō'zi] *n* a motto, as on a ring; a bunch of flowers.

pot [pot] *n* a deep round vessel for various purposes, esp
cooking; an earthen vessel for plants. — *vt* to put in a pot or
pots, esp in order to preserve — *vi* to take a potshot; **potherb,**
an herb whose leaves or stems are cooked for use as greens;
pot'hook, a hook for hanging a pot over a fire; **pot'house,** a
tavern; **pot'luck',** what may happen to be in the pot.

potable [pō'ta-bl] *adj* fit to drink.

potash [pot'ash] *n* potassium carbonate, originally got in a
crude state by leaching woodash, an alkali. — *ns* **potass'ium,**
an alkali metal.

potato [pó-tā'tō] *n* a sweet potato; widely grown for food; its
tuber.

potent [pō'tènt] *adj* powerful, mighty, strongly influential. —
adv **pō'tently.** — *ns* **pō'tency; pō'tentate;** a ruler. — *adj* **pōten-
tial** [-ten'shl], (*rare*) powerful, efficacious; latent, existing in
possibility. — *n* anything that may be possible; possibility. — *n*
pōtentiality [pō-ten-shi-al'i-ti],. — *adv* **pōten'tially.**

pother [pоTH'ĕr] *n* a choking smoke or dust; turmoil; fuss,
commotion.

potion [pō'sh(ó)n] *n* a mixture of liquids (as liquor or
medicine).

potpourri [pō-pŏō-rē'] *n* a mixture of sweet-scented materials,
chiefly dried petals; a medley.

potsherd [pot'shèrd] *n* a piece of broken pottery.

pottage [pot'ij] *n* a thick soup of meat and vegetables.

potter¹ [pot'èr] *n* one who makes articles of baked clay, esp
earthenware vessels. — *n* **pott'ery,** earthenware vessels; a place
where such goods are manufactured.

potter² [pot'ĕr] *vi* to be fussily engaged about trifles.

pouch [powch] *n* a small bag or sack.

pouf, pouff, pouffe [pŏōf] *n* a soft loose roll of hair; a bouffant
part of a garment; an ottoman.

poult [pōlt] *n* a young fowl, esp a young turkey. — *ns* **poult'-
erer,** one that deals in poultry; **poult'ry,** domesticated birds.

poultice [pōl'tis] *n* a hot, soft mass applied to a sore part of the
body. — *vt* to put a poultice on.

pounce¹ [powns] *n* a sudden spring or swoop with intent to
seize. — *vi* to fix suddenly or eagerly.

pounce² [powns] n a fine powder formerly used to prevent ink from spreading.

pound¹ [pownd] n a unit of weight, equal to 16 ounces avoirdupois, or 12 ounces troy or apothecaries'; abbreviation lb; a unit of money in the United Kingdom and other countries, symbol £.—ns **pound'age**, a charge per pound of weight; weight in pounds.

pound² [pownd] n a municipal enclosure for stray animals.

pound³ [pownd] vt to beat into a powder or a pulp; to hit hard.—vi to deliver heavy blows repeatedly.

pour [pōr, pôr] vt to cause or allow to flow in a stream; to send forth or emit in a stream or like a stream.—vi to stream; to rain heavily.—n **pour'er.**

pourboire [pōō-bwär] n a tip.

pout [powt] vi to push out the lips, in sullen displeasure or otherwise.—Also vt—n a protrusion, of the lips expressive of displeasure.—n **pout'er**, a variety of pigeon, having a dilatable crop and an erect carriage.

poverty [pov'ėr-ti] n the state of being poor; necessity, want; lack, deficiency.

powder [pow'dėr] n any substance in fine particles; a specific kind of powder, esp for medicinal or cosmetic use.—vt to reduce to powder; to sprinkle, daub, or cover with powder.—adj **pow'dery.**

power [pow'ėr, powr] n ability to do anything: physical, mental, spiritual, legal, etc.; capacity for producing an effect; a wielder of authority, strong influence, or rule.—adj operated by electricity, a fuel engine, etc.—vt to supply with a source of power.—adj **pow'erful.**—ns **pow'erhouse.**—adj **pow'erless.**

powwow [pow'wow] n an American Indian medicine man; an American Indian ceremony.

pox [poks] n a virus disease (as *chicken pox*) marked by pustules.

practice [prak'tis] n actual doing; habitual action, custom; repeated performance to acquire skill.—adj **prac'ticable**, that may be practised, used, or is feasible.—ns **practicabil'ity.**—adj **prac'tical**, in, relating to, concerned with or well adapted to actual practice; practising; efficient in action; inclined to action; virtual.—vt **practice** [prak'tis] to put into practice; to perform; to do habitually; to exercise oneself in, or on, or in the performance of, in order to maintain or acquire skill.—vi to act habitually.—n **practitioner** [-tish'ön-ėr] one who is in practice.

praetor [prē'tŏr] n a magistrate of ancient Rome, next in rank to the consuls.—adj **praetorian.**

pragmatic [prag-mat'ik] adj practical; testing the validity of all concepts by their practical results.—adj **pragmat'ical.**—ns **prag'matism; prag'matist**, a pragmatic person.

prairie [prā'ri] n a land predominantly in grass; one of the dry treeless plateaus.

praise [prāz] vt to speak highly of, to commend, to extol.—vi to express praise.—n commendation; glorifying.—adj **praise'worthy.**

praline [prä'lēn] n any of various soft or crisp candies made of nuts and sugar.

prance [präns] vi to bound from the hind legs; to go with a capering or dancing movement; to swagger.

prank¹ [prangk] n a malicious or mischievous trick.

prank² [prangk] vt to dress or adorn showily.—vi to show oneself off.

prate [prāt] vi to talk foolishly; to be loquacious.—n trifling talk.—n **pra'ter.**—n, adj **pra'ting.**—adv **pra'tingly.**

prattle [prat'l] vt to say in a childish manner.—vi to talk much and idly; to utter child's talk.

prawn [prön] n any of numerous edible shrimplike crustaceans.

pray [prā] vi to ask earnestly; to speak and make known one's desires to God.——ns **pray'er**, the act of praying; entreaty; the words used.—adj **pray'erful**, devout; earnest; sincere.

pre- [prē-] (as living prefix), **prae-** prī-, prefix before, previous to.

preach [prēch] vi to pronounce a public discourse on sacred subjects.—vt to teach or publish in religious discourses—n **preach'er.**

preamble [prē-amb'bl] n preface; introduction.

prebend [preb'énd] n the share of the revenues of a cathedral

or collegiate church allowed to a clergyman.—n **preb'enda** a resident clergyman who enjoys a prebend, a canon.

precancerous [prē-kan'sėr-us] adj likely to become cancerou

precarious [pri-kā'ri-us] adj depending on the will of anoth depending on chance, uncertain; insecure.

precaution [pri-kö'sh(ó)n] n caution or care beforehand; preventive measure.

precede [prē-sēd'] vti to be, come or go before in time, rank, importance.—ns **precedence** the act of going before in tim the right of being before in rank; priority; the foremost pla in ceremony.—**precedent** [pres'éd-ént] a past instance, th may serve as an example or rule in the future.

precentor [pri-sen'tŏr] n the leader of the singing in a chur choir or congregation.

precept [prē'sept] n a rule of moral conduct; a maxim.—n **precep'tor**, a teacher.

precinct [prē'singkt] n (usu. pl) an enclosure between buil ings, walls, etc.; (pl) environs; a police district; a subdivisi of a voting ward; a limited area.

precious [presh'ús] adj of great price or worth; cherishe very fastidious; affected; thoroughgoing.—adv extremely.— **prec'iousness.**—adv **prec'iously.**

precipice [pres'i-pis] n a high vertical, or overhanging ro face.—vt **precip'itate**, to hurl headlong; to force; to bring suddenly or prematurely.—adv **precip'itately.**—n **preci** tā'tion.—ns **precip'itance, precip'itancy**, quality of be precipitate; headlong haste or rashness.

précis [prē'sē] n an abstract, a summary.

precise [pri-sīs'] adj definite, exact; very accurate; scrupulo formal.—adv **precise'ly, preci'sian**, a too precise perso **preci'sion**, quality of being precise; exactness.

preclude [pri-klōōd'] vt to rule out in advance; to ma impossible.

precocious [pri-kō'shús] adj early in reaching some stage development, eg. flowering, ripening, mental maturity.— **precoc'ity.**

precognition [prē-kog-nish'(ó)n] n the supposed extrasens perception of a future event.

preconceive [prē-kon-sēv'] vt to conceive or form a notion before having actual knowledge.—**preconcep'tion.**

preconcert [prē-kon-sûrt'] vt to settle, arrange beforehand.

precursor [prē-kûr'sŏr] n a forerunner.

predator [pred'á-tŏr] n one that preys, destroys or devours; animal that lives by predation.—adj **pred'atory.**

predecessor [prē-di-ses'ŏr] n one who has been before anoth in any office.

predestine [prē-des'tin] vt to destine or decree beforehand, foreordain.—vt **predes'tinate**, to preordain by an unchang able purpose.—n **predestinā'tion** (*theology*) God's decree fix unalterably from all eternity whatever is to happen, esp souls destined for salvation or damnation; destiny.

predicable [pred'i-kā-bl] adj that may be asserted.

predicament [pri-dik'á-mént] n an unfortunate or embarra ing position.

predicate [pred'i-kāt] vt to affirm as a quality or attribute.

predict [pri-dikt'] vt to foretell.—adj **predic'table.**—n p **dic'tion.**

predilection [prē-di-lek'sh(ó)n] n favorable prepossession mind; preference.

predominate [prē-dom'in-āt] vi to be dominant, to surp in strength or authority; to prevail.—adj **predom'inant.**— **predom'inance.**

preeminent [prē-em'in-ént] adj surpassing others in good bad qualities.

preemption [prē-em(p)'sh(ó)n] n action taken to check oth action beforehand.

preen [prēn] vt to arrange or trim as birds do their feathers; pride (oneself) for achievement.

prefabricate [prē-fab'ri-kāt] vt to build (a house, etc.) in sta dardized sections for shipment and quick assembly; to pr duce artificially.

preface [pref'is] n something said or written by way of intr duction or preliminary explanation.—vt to introduce by preface.—adj **pref'atory.**

prefect [prē'fekt] n one set in authority over others.—n p fecture, the office or district of a prefect.

prefer [pri-fûr'] vt (*arch*) to put forward, submit for acceptan or consideration; to promote, advance.—*adj* **pref′erable.**—*adv* **pref′erably.**—*n* **pref′erence.**—*adj* **preferential** [pref-ėr-en′shl] having, or giving, allowing, a preference.

prefix [prē-fiks′] *vt* to put before, or at the beginning.—*n* **prē′fix,** a syllable or group of syllables put before a word to affect its meaning.

pregnant [preg′nȧnt] *adj* having a child in the womb; mentally fertile; implying more than is actually expressed.

prehensile [pri-hen′sīl] *adj* capable of grasping.

prejudice [prej′ŏŏ-dis] *n* a judgment or opinion formed beforehand for or against due examination; prepossession for or against anything, bias; injury, or harm; intolerance or hatred of other races, etc.—*vt* to fill with prejudice, to bias the mind of; to injure, hurt, or to impair the validity of.—*adj* **prejudicial** [-dish′ål] causing prejudice or injury, detrimental.

prelate [prel′åt] *n* an ecclesiastic of high rank.—*n* **prel′acy.**

preliminary [pri-lim′in-ȧr-i] *adj* introductory; preparatory.—*n* that which precedes or prepares for.

prelude [prel′(y)ŏŏd] *n* a preliminary performance; an event preceding and leading up to another of greater importance—*vt* to precede as a prelude to play as a prelude.

premature [prē′mȧ-tūr or chūr or tyūr] *adj* unduly early; overhasty.—*adv* **prē′mature′ly.**

premeditate [prē-med′i-tāt] *vt* to meditate upon beforehand.

premier [pre′mi-ėr, pre′myėr] *adj* prime or first; chief.—*n* the first or chief; a prime minister.—*ns* **prem′iership; première,** [prè-myer′ or prē-mir′] first performance of a play, etc.

premise [prem′is] *n* (*logic*) one of the two propositions in a syllogism from which the conclusion is drawn; something assumed or taken for granted.—*vt* **premise,** [or pri-mīz′] to mention or state by way of introduction.

premium [prē′mi-um] *n* a reward, a prize, esp as an inducement to buy; payment made for insurance; excess over the original price.

preoccupy [prē-ol′ū-pī] *vt* to occupy or fill beforehand or before others.—*n* **prēoccupā′tion.**

prepare [pri-pār′] *vt* to make ready; to make; to put together.—*vi* to make things ready.—*n* **preparation.**—*adj* **preparative.**

prepense [pri-pens′] *adj* premeditated, intentional.

preponderate [pri-pon′dėr-āt] *vi* to weigh more, to turn the balance; to prevail or exceed in any respect, as number, quantity, importance, influence.—*n* **prepon′derance.**

preposition [prep-ō-zish′(ó)n] *n* a word placed before a noun or pronoun to show its relation to another word.

prepossess [prē-poz-es′] *vt* (*obs*) to take possession of beforehand; to bias or prejudice, esp favorably.—*adj* **prepossess′ing.**

preposterous [pri-pos′tėr-us] *adj* ridiculous; laughable; utterly absurd.

Pre-Raphaelite [prē-raf′ā-ėl-īt] *n* one of a school of English artists, formed about 1850, who sought inspiration in the works of painters before *Raphael.*

prerogative [pri-rog′ȧ-tiv] *n* a special right or privilege belonging to a particular rank or station.

presage [pres′ij] *n* an omen, an indication of the future; a presentiment.—*vt* **presage.**

presbyter [prez′bi-tėr] *n* in the Presbyterian Church, an elder; in the Episcopal Church, a priest or minister.—**presbytē′rian,** pres′bytery, a ruling body in presbyterian churches consisting of the ministers and representative elders from congregations within a district; (*RC*) a priest's house.

prescience [prē′shē-ėns] *n* knowledge of events beforehand; foresight.—*adj* **pre′scient.**

prescribe [pri-skrīb′] *vt* to lay down as a rule or direction; to order, advise, the use of; **prescrip′tion,** act of prescribing or directing; (*med*) a written direction for the preparation of a medicine; (*law*) custom continued until it becomes a right or has the force of law.—*adj* **prescrip′tive.**

presence [prez′ėns] *n* fact or state of being present; personal appearance and manner.

present¹ [prez′ėnt] *adj* being at the specified place; instant; immediate; now under consideration.—*n* the present time; *adv* **pres′ently,** now, without delay; soon.

present² [prez′ėnt′] *n* a gift.

present³ [pri-zent′] *vt* to set before, to introduce the presence of someone, esp socially; to bring before the public; to make a gift to.—*adj* **present′able;** fit to be seen.—*ns* **presentation; present′er; present′ment.**

presentiment [pri-zent′i-mėnt] *n* a vague foreboding.

preserve [pri-zûrv′] *vt* to keep safe from injury; to save from danger; to keep from decay; to can, pickle, or prepare (food) for future use.—*n* (usu. *pl*) fruit preserved by cooking in sugar; an area restricted for the preservation and protection of natural resources (as trees and game), esp one used for regulated hunting and fishing.—*ns* **preservā′tion,** preserved; safety; **preservāt′ionist,** a person who is interested in preservation (as of a biological species or a historic landmark).—*adjs* **preservative.**

preside [pri′zīd′] *vi* to sit in the chair or chief seat; to exercise authority or control.—*ns* **presidency; president,** the highest officer of a company, club, etc.—*adj* **presiden′tial.**

press¹ [pres] *vt* to act on with steady force or weight; to push against, squeeze, compress, etc.; to force, compel; to entreat; to emphasize.—*vi* to weigh down.—*n* pressure, urgency, etc.; a crowd; a machine for crushing, stamping, etc.; a printing press; a printing or publishing establishment; the gathering, publishing, and broadcasting of news; an upright closet for storing clothes, etc.—*adj* **pressing,** urgent; calling for immediate attention.

press² [pres] *vt* (*hist*) to carry off and force into service in the navy; to commandeer.—*n* **press′-gang** (*hist*), a gang or body of men under command of an officer empowered to force men into naval or military service.—Also *vt.*

pressure [presh′ùr] *n* act of pressing; the state of being pressed.—*vt* **press′urize.**

prestidigitation [pres-ti-dij-i-tā′sh(ó)n] *n* sleight of hand.—*n* **prestidig-itātor.**

prestige [pres-tēzh′] *n* standing in the eyes of people; commanding position in people's minds.

presto [pres′tō] *adv* quickly; at once.

presume [pri-zūm′] *vt* to take for granted.—*vi* take advantage of; to act without due regard to the claims of others.—*adj* **presūm′able.**—*adv* **presūm′ably.**—*n* **presumption**—*adj* **presump′tive,** grounded on probable evidence; that may be assumed as true, accurate, etc.; giving grounds for presuming.—*adj* **presumptuous.**—*adv* **presump′tuously.**

pretend [pri-tend′] *vt* to profess falsely that; to feign.—*vi* to put in a claim; to make-believe.—*ns* **pretense′; preten′der, preten′sion.**—*adj* **preten′tious** [-shùs], claiming more than is warranted; showy, ostentatious.

preterit(e) [pret′ėr-it] *adj* past.—*n* a verbal tense that indicates action in the past without reference to duration, continuance, or repetition.

preternatural [prē-tėr-na′chùr-ȧl] *adj* beyond what is natural; abnormal; supernatural.

pretext [prē′tekst] *n* an ostensible motive or reason put forward to conceal the real one, or as an excuse.

pretty [prit′i] *adj* artful; clever; apt; attractive in a dainty, graceful way but not strikingly beautiful.—*adv* in some degree; moderately.

prevail [pri-vāl′] *vi* to gain the mastery; to succeed; to be usual or customary; to predominate.—*adjs* **prev′alent,** prevailing.—*n* **prevalence.**

prevaricate [pri-var′i-kāt] *vi* to evade the truth, to quibble.—*ns* **prevaricā′tion.**

prevent [pri-vent′] *vt* to hinder; to keep from coming to pass, make impossible.—*adjs* **prevent′able.**—*n* **preven′tion.**—*adjs* **preven′tive.**

previous [prē′vi-ùs] *adj* going before in time; former; acting too soon.—*adv* previously.—*adv* **prē′viously.**

prey [prā] *n* an animal that is, or may be, killed and eaten by another; a victim.—*vi* to seize and devour prey; to commit violence or robbery or fraud.

price [prīs] *n* the amount, usu. in money, for which a thing is sold or offered; the cost, as in life, labor, etc. of obtaining some benefit; value or worth.—*vt* to fix the price of.—*adjs* **price′less,** beyond price, invaluable.

prick [prik] *n* a sharp point; the act or experience of piercing or puncturing with a small sharp point; the wound or mark so made; **prickle** [prik′l], a sharp point growing from the bark or epidermis of a plant.—*adj* **prick′ly,** full of prickles.

pride [prīd] *n* state or feeling of being proud; too great self-esteem; haughtiness; that of which one is proud; splendour, magnificence.—*vt* (*reflex*) to feel proud.

priest [prēst] *n* one with special rank who offers sacrifices or performs sacred rites;.—*ns* **priest′ess**; **priest′hood**, the office or character of a priest; the priestly order.—*adj* **priest′ly**.

prig [prig] *n* a person whose smug and scrupulous behavior offends others.—*adj* **prigg′ish**.

prim [prim] *adj* exact and precise in manner; demure.

prima donna [prē′mä don′(n)ä] *n* the leading lady in opera.

primary [prī′mår-i] *adj* first; original; fundamental; chief; primitive; elementary.—*n* that which is highest in rank or importance.—*adv* **prī′marily**.

primate [prī′māt, -måt] *n* an archbishop; or the highest ranking bishop in a province, etc; any of an order of mammals, including man.

prime¹ [prīm] *adj* first in order of time, rank, or importance; chief; of the highest quality.—*n* the beginning; the spring; the height of perfection; full health and strength; **prime minister**, in some countries, the chief executive of the government.

prime² [prīm] *vt* to charge, fill; to supply (a firearm) with powder; to prepare for painting by laying on a first coat of paint or oil.

primer [prī′mèr, prim′ér] *n* simple book for teaching.

primeval [prī-mē′vål] *adj* belonging to the first ages.

primitive [prim′i-tiv] *adj* belonging to the beginning, or to the first times; crude; simple; basic.—*n* that from which other things are derived.

primogenitor [prī-mō-jen′i-tôr] *n* an ancestor; a forefather.—*n* **primogen′iture**, the right of inheritance by the eldest son.

primordial [prī-môr′di-ål] *adj* existing from the beginning; original; rudimentary; primitive.

primrose [prim′rōz] *n* any of a genus of perennial herbs with tubelike, often yellow flowers.

primula [prim′ū-la] *n* primrose.

prince [prins] *n* a ruler ranking below a king; the son of a sovereign.—*ns* **prin′cess**, a daughter of a sovereign; **prince′ling**, a petty prince.—*adj* **prince′ly**.

principal [prin′si-pl] *adj* highest in rank, character, or importance; chief.—*n* a principal person; the head of a school; one who takes a leading part; money on which interest is paid.—*n* **principal′ity**, the position or responsibility of a principal (as of a school); territory of a prince.

principle [prin′si-pl] *n* a fundamental truth on which others are founded or from which they spring; a law or doctrine from which others are derived; a settled rule or action.

prink [pringk] *vti* to primp.

print [print] *n* a mark made on a surface by pressure; the impression of letters, designs, etc. made from inked type, a plate, or block; a photographic or motion-picture copy, esp from a negative.—*vti* to stamp on a surface; to produce the impressions of inked type, etc.; to produce; to write in letters resembling printed ones.—*ns* **printer**, a person engaged in printing; a device that produces printout.

prior [prī′ôr] *adj* previous.—*n* the superior ranking below an abbot in a monastery; the head of a house or group of houses in a religious community.—*ns* **pri′oress**, **prior′ity**, state of being prior or first in time, place, or rank, preference; **pri′ory**, a religious house under a prior or prioress.

prism [prizm] *n* (*geom*) a solid whose ends are similar, equal, and parallel polygons, and whose sides are parallelograms; a triangular prism of transparent glass.—*adjs* **prismat′ic**, resembling or pertaining to a prism; formed by a prism.—*adv* **prismat′ically**.

prison [priz′n] *n* a building for the confinement of persons while on trial for safe custody or after a trial for punishment.

pristine [pris′tīn] *adj* belonging to the earliest time; unspoiled.

privacy [priv′å-si] *n* seclusion.

private [prī′våt] *adj* of or concerning a particular person or group; not open to or controlled by the public; for an individual person.—*n* (*pl*) the genitals; an enlisted man of the lowest rank either in the US Army or the US Marine Corps.—*adv* **prī′vately**.

privateer [prī-vå-tēr′] *n* a private vessel commissioned in war to capture enemy ships.

privation [prī-vā′sh(ô)n] *n* state of being deprived of something, esp of what is necessary for comfort.—*adj* **privative**, expressing the absence of a quality.

privet [priv′et] *n* a half-evergreen shrub.

privilege [priv′i-lij] *n* an advantage granted to or enjoyed by an individual or a few; prerogative.—*vt* to grant a privilege to.—*adj* **priv′ileged**.

privy [priv′i] *adj* private; having knowledge of (something secret).—a small building with a bench having holes through which the user may urinate or defecate.—*adv* **priv′ily**.—**Privy Council**, a body of dignataries and officials chosen by the British monarch as an advisory council to the Crown usu. functioning through its committees.

prize¹ [prīz] *vt* to force (esp up or open) with a lever.

prize² [prīz] *n* anything taken from an enemy in war, esp a ship.

prize³ [prīz] *n* a reward or symbol of success offered or won in competition by; anything well worth striving for.—*ns* **prize′-fight**, a professional boxing match.

pro- [prō] *prefix* from Latin prep meaning before.

pro [prō] *adj*, *n* Abbrev for **professional**.

probable [prob′á-bl] *adj* that may be expected, likely.—*n* **probabil′ity**.—*adv* **prob′ably**.

probate [prō′bāt] *n* the judicial determination of the validating of a will; the official copy of a will, with the certificate of its having been proved.

probation [prō-bā′sh(ô)n] *n* testing; proof; suspension of prison sentence with liberty under the supervision of a probation officer.—*ns* **proba′tioner**; a convicted offender on probation.

probe [prōb] *n* an instrument for exploring a wound; an investigation.—*vt* to examine with, or as with, a probe.

probity [prōb′i-ti or prob′-] *n* uprightness, moral integrity.

problem [prob′lèm] *n* a person, thing, or matter difficult to deal with; a question propounded for solution.—*adjs* **problemat′ic, -al**.

proboscis [prō-bos′is] *n* the trunk of the elephant or any similar long, flexible snout.

proceed [prō-sēd′] *vi* to go on; to continue; to take legal action.—*n pl* **prō′ceeds**, the total amount of money brought in.—*ns* **procē′dure**, method of conducting business, esp in a law case or in a meeting; a step taken as part of an established order of steps.

process [pros′es] *n* state of being in progress or of being carried on; a series of actions or events; a sequence of operations, or of changes undergone.

procession [prō-sesh′(ô)n] *n* a large company advancing in order, as in a parade.—*adj* **process′ional**.

proclaim [prō-klām′] *vt* to publish abroad; to announce or declare officially.—*ns* **proclamation**.

proclivity [prō-kliv′i-ti] *n* inclination, tendency.

proconsul [prō-kon′sùl] *n* a governor or military commander of an ancient Roman province; an administrator in a modern colony.

procrastinate [prō-kras′ti-nāt] *vti* to put off action, to delay.—*ns* **procrastinā′tion**.

procreate [prō′krē-āt] *vt* to bring into being, to beget offspring.—*n* **procreā′tion**.

proctor [prok′tôr] *n* one appointed to supervise students.

procumbent [prō-kum′bènt] *adj* lying face down; lying along the ground without rooting.

procure [prō-kūr′] *vt* to obtain by effort; to bring about.—*adj* **procur′able**.—*ns* **procure′ment**, the act of procuring; management; agency; **procur′er**.

prod [prod] *vt* to poke; as with a pointed stick; to goad into activity.

prodigal [prod′i-g(å)l] *adj* wasteful; lavish.—*n* a waster; a spendthrift.—*n* **prodigal′ity**,—*adv* **prod′igally**.

prodigy [prod′i-ji] *n* an extraordinary person, thing, or act; a child of precocious genius or virtuosity.—*adj* **prodig′ious**.—*adv* **prodig′iously**.

produce [prō-dūs′] *vt* to bring forward or out; to bring into being, to yield; to bring about, cause; to extend.—*vi* to yield something.—*ns* **produce** [prod′ūs] that which is produced, esp fruit and vegetables; **produc′er**, one who produces; a farmer or a manufacturer.—*n* **product** [prod′ukt] a thing produced by nature, industry, or art; a result; an outgrowth; **produc′tion**, act or process of producing; that which is produced.—*adj* **produc′tive**.—*n* **productiv′ity**; **producer goods**, goods, such as tools and raw materials, used in the production of other goods.

proem [prō'em] *n* an introduction, preface.

profane [prō-fān'] *adj* not sacred, secular; heathen; showing contempt of sacred things, impious. — *vt* to violate, desecrate; **profan'ity**, irreverence; profane language or conduct.

profess [prō-fes'] *vt* to make open declaration of; to declare in strong terms; to claim to be expert in. — *n* **profession** [-fesh'(ŏ)n] the act of professing; open declaration; religious belief; avowal; pretence; an occupation requiring specialized knowledge and often long and intensive academic preparation. — *adj* **profess'ional**, pertaining to a profession. — *adv* **profess'ionally**. — *n* **profess'or**, one who professes, avows, or declares; a faculty member of the highest academic rank at a university; a teacher at a university, college.

proffer [prof'ėr] *vt* to tender, to offer.

proficient [prō-fish'ėnt] *adj* competent, skilled, thoroughly qualified (in, at). — *n* an adept, an expert. — *n* **profi'ciency**.

profile [prō'fīl] *n* a head or portrait in a side view.

profit [prof'it] *n* gain; advantage, benefit. — *vti* to benefit; to be of advantage (to). — *adj* **prof'itable**, yielding or bringing profit or gain; *adj*; **prof'itless**, without profit.

profligate [prof'li-gāt] *adj* abandoned to vice, dissolute; prodigal, extravagant. — *n* one leading a profligate life. — *n* **prof'ligacy**.

profound [prō-fownd'] *adj* deep; intense; penetrating deeply into knowledge. — *ns* **profund'ity**.

profuse [prō-fūs'] *adj* liberal to excess, lavish; excessively abundant; **profusion**.

progenitor [prō-jen'i-tôr] *n* a precursor, originator; an ancestor in a direct line. — *n* **prog'eny**; descendants.

prognosis [prog-nō'sis] *n* a forecast, esp of the course of a disease. — *n* **prognost'ic**, a foretelling. — *vt* **prognos'ticate**, to foretell. — *ns* **prognostica'tion**.

program, programme [prō'gram] *n* a sheet or booklet giving the details of proceedings arranged for any occasion or ceremony; the items of an entertainment, etc.; a curriculum or syllabus for a course of study. — *vt* to provide with, enter in, a program; to prepare a program for.

progress [prog'res] *n* forward movement; advance; passage from place to place. — *vi* **progress'**, to go forward; to go on, continue. — *n* **prŏgression**; prŏgress'ive.

prohibit [prō-hib'it] *vt* to forbid; to prevent. — *n* **prohibition** the act of prohibiting, forbidding, or interdicting; the forbidding by law of the manufacture and sale of alcoholic drinks. — *adj* **prohibitive**. — *adj* **prohib'itory**; forbidding.

project [proj'ekt] *n* a scheme, plan, proposal for an undertaking. — *vt* **project** to throw, impel, out or foward; to contrive or plan; to throw an image of; to externalize, make objective; — *vi* to jut out. — *adj* **projec'tile**, projecting or throwing forward. — *n* a body projected by force; a missile. — *ns* **projec'tion, projec'tor**, an apparatus for projecting, esp an image or a beam of light.

prolegomen [prō-le-gom'èn] *n* an introduction, esp to a treatise.

prolepsis [prō-lep'sis] *n* a figure of speech by which objections are anticipated and answered. — *adj* **prolep'tic**.

proletarian [prō-le-tā'ri-àn] *adj* of the proletariat. — *n* a member of the proletariat. — *n* **proletā'riat** [-àt] the laboring class, esp the industrial working class.

prolific [prō-lif'ik] *adj* bringing forth much offspring; fruitful, fertile. — *vi* **prolif'erate**, to grow by multiplication of parts (cells, buds, etc.); increase rapidly and abundantly. — *n* **proliferā'tion**.

prolix [prō'liks or -liks'] *adj* long and wordy; long-winded. — *n* **prolix'ity**.

prologue [prō'log] *n* in a Greek play, the part before the entry of the chorus; an introduction to a poem.

prolong [prō-long'] *vt* to lengthen in time or space. — *n* **prolongā'tion**.

promenade [prom-ė-näd' or -nād'] *n* a walk for pleasure; an esplanade. — *vti* to take a promenade.

prominent [prom'i-nėnt] *adj* projecting; conspicuous; distinguished. — *n* **prom'inence**.

promiscuous [prŏ-mis'kū-us] *adj* confusedly or indiscriminately mixed; indiscriminate, esp in sexual liaisons. — *ns* **promiscū'ity** [prom].

promise [prom'is] *n* an engagement to do or keep from doing something; indication, as of a successful future. — *vti* to afford

reason to expect. — *adv* **prom'isingly**. — *adj* **prom'issory**, containing or being a promise.

promontory [prom'ŏn-tōr-i] *n* a headland; a peak of high land that juts out into a body of water.

promote [prō-mōt'] *vt* to raise to a higher position; to advance from one grade to the next higher grade. — *ns* **promō'ter; promotion**, a being raised in position or rank.

prompt [prompt] *adj* ready in action; performed at once; immediate, unhesitating. — *vt* to incite; to inspire; to supply forgotten words, or elusive words, facts or ideas, to. — *adv* **prompt'ly**.

promulgate [prom'ul-gāt] *vt* to proclaim, publish abroad. — *ns* **promulgā'tion**.

prone [prōn] *adj* with the face, ventral surface, downward; disposed inclined (to).

prong [prong] *n* the spike of a fork or forked object.

pronoun [prō'nown] *n* a word used instead of a noun, to indicate without naming.

pronounce [prō-nowns'] *vt* to utter formally; to declare (eg a decision); to articulate. — *adjs* **pronounce'able, pronounced'**, marked, decided, noticeable. — *ns* **pronounce'ment**.

pronunciation [prō-nun-si-ā'sh(ŏ)n] *n* mode of pronouncing; articulation.

proof [prōōf] *n* that which proves; evidence that convinces the mind; the fact, act, or process of proving or showing to be true; test; demonstration. — *adj* impervious, invulnerable. **proof'read'er**, one who reads printed proofs to discover and correct errors.

prop [prop] *n* a rigid support. — *vt* to hold up by means of something placed under or against; to sustain.

propagate [prop'a-gāt] *vt* of a plant or animal, to reproduce (itself); to spread. — *vi* to reproduce, as plants or animals. — *ns* **propagan'da**, any concerted action for the spread of ideas, doctrines, etc.; the ideas, etc. so spread. **propagand'ist**. — Also *adj* — *ns* **propagā'tion, prop'agātor**.

propel [prō-pel'] *vt* to drive onward or forward. — **propell'er**, a device having two or more blades in a revolving hub for driving a ship or aircraft.

propensity [prō-pens'i-ti] *n* a natural inclination, tendency, disposition.

proper [prop'ėr] *adj* natural, characteristic, appropriate; fitting; correct; decorous. — *adv* **prop'erly**.

property [prop'ėr-ti] *n* a quality that is always present, a characteristic; any quality; that which is one's own; land or buildings.

prophecy, prophesy [prof'ė-si] *n* inspired utterance of divine will and purpose.

prophesy [prof'ė-si] *vi* to utter prophecies. — *vt* to foretell.

prophet [prof'èt] *n* a religious leader regarded as, or claims to be divinely inspired. — *n* **proph'etess**, a. — *adjs* **prophet'ic, -al**, pertaining to a prophet; containing prophecy.

prophylactic [prof-i-lak'tik] *adj* guarding against disease. — *n* a prophylactic medicine, device, etc.

propinquity [prō-ping'kwi-ti] *n* nearness.

propitiate [prō-pish'i-āt] *vt* to render favorable; to appease. — *ns* **propitiā'tion**, act of propitiating. — *adj* **propi'tiatory**. — *adj* **propi'tious**, favorable, of good omen.

proportion [prō-pōr'sh(ŏ)n] *n* the relation of one thing to another, or of a part to the whole, in regard to magnitude; ration; an equal or just share; (*pl*) dimensions. — *vt* to put in proper relation with something else; to adjust or fashion in due proportion (to) — *adjs* **propor'tionable**, having a due or definite relation (to); **propor'tional**. — *adv* **pro'tionally**.

propose [prō-pōz'] *vt* to put forward for consideration, to propound; to suggest; to put before one as an aim; to invite the company to drink; to purpose or intend. — *vi* to make an offer, esp of marriage. — *ns* **propō'sal**.

proposition [prop-o-zish'(ŏ)n] *n* an act of proposing; the thing propounded.

propound [prō-pownd'] *vt* to offer for consideration. — *n* **propound'er**.

proprietor [prō-prī'ė-tôr] *n* an owner. — *ns* **proprī'etress, proprī'etary**, a business secretly owned and run as a cover for an intelligence organization. — *adj* privately owned and managed and run as a profit-making organization.

propriety [prō-prī'ė-ti] *n* conformity with accepted standards of conduct; appropriateness.

propulsion [prō-pul'sh(ò)n] *n* act of propelling.
pro rata [prō rā'ta, rä'ta] in proportion.—*vti* **prōrate'**, to divide or assess proportionately.
prorogue [prō-rōg'] *vt* to terminate a session by royal prerogative.—*vi* to suspend or end a legislative session.—*n* **prorogā'tion**.
proscenium [prō-sē'ni-um] *n* the front part of the stage.
proscribe [prō-skrīb'] *vt* to outlaw; to refuse to tolerate, to prohibit the use of.—*ns* **proscrip'tion**.
prose [prōz] *n* ordinary spoken and written language with words in direct straightforward arrangement; all writings not in verse.—*adj* **prōs'y**, dull, tedious.
prosecute [pros'ė-kūt] *vt* to pursue until finished; to bring legal action against.—*ns* **prosecū'tion, pros'ecūtor.
proselyte [pros'e-līt] *n* one who has come over from one religion to another; a convert.—*vti* **pros'elytīze**.
prosody [pros'o-di] *n* the study of versification, **pros'odist**.
prosopopoeia [pros-ō-po-pē'a] *n* personification.
prospect [pros'pekt] *n* a wide view; outlook for the future.—*vti* **prospect'**, to explore or search (for).—*adj* **prospec'tive**, likely; expected.—*adv* **prospec'tively**.
prosper [pros'pėr] *vi* to thrive, to succeed; to turn out well.—*vt* to cause to thrive or succeed.—*n* **prosper'ity**, success, good fortune.—*adj* **pros'perous**.
prostitute [pros'ti-tūt] *vt* to offer indiscriminately for sexual intercourse, esp for money.—*n* a woman who offers herself to indiscriminate sexual intercourse for money.—*ns* **prostitū'tion**.
prostrate [pros'trāt'] *adj* lying with face on the ground; reduced to helplessness; completely exhausted.—*vt* [-āt] to lay flat; to overthrow.
protagonist [prō-tag'on-ist] *n* the main character in a drama, novel, etc.; a champion (of a cause).
protean [prō'tē-àn, prō-tē'àn] *adj* displaying great variety or diversity.
protect [prō-tekt'] *vt* to shield from danger, injury, capture, loss, change; to defend.—*ns* **protec'tion, protec'tionist**, one who favors the protection of trade by taxing imports.—Also *adj*.—*adj* **protec'tive**.—*n* **protec'tor**, one who protects from injury or oppression; a regent.—*ns* **protec'torate**, the rule of a protector; authority over a vassal state; relation assumed by a state over territory which it governs without annexing it.
protégé [prō'tā-zhā] *n* a person guided and helped in his career by another person.
protein [prō'tēn] *n* any one of a group of complex nitrogenous substances that play an important part in the bodies of plants and animals and are an essential food item.
protest [prō-test or prō-, prō-test'] *vi* to express or record dissent or objection.—*vt* to make a solemn declaration or affirmation of.—*ns* **pro'test**, a declaration of objection or dissent; **Prot'estant**, a Christian not of the Orthodox or Roman Catholic Church.—*ns* **protestation**.
protocol [prō'tō-kol] *n* an original note, minute, or draft of an instrument or transaction; the ceremonial forms accepted as correct in official dealings, as between heads of state or diplomatic officials.
proton [prō'ton] *n* an elementary particle in the nucleus of all atoms, carrying a unit positive charge of electricity.
protoplasm [prō'tō-plazm] *n* a semifluid viscous colloid, the essential living matter of all plant and animal cells.
prototype [prō'tō-tīp] *n* the first or original type or model from which anything is copied.
protozoan [prō-tō-zō'àn] *n* any of a phylum of mostly microscopic, single-celled animals.
protract [prō-trakt'] *vt* to draw out or lengthen in time or space; to extend forward and outward.—*n* **protrac'tion**.—*n* **protrac'tor**, an instrument for laying down angles on paper.
protrude [prō-trōōd'] *vt* to thrust or push on or forward; to obtrude.—*vi* to stick out, project.—*n* **protru'sion**.
protuberance [prō-tūb'ėr-àns] *n* a bulging out; a swelling.—*adj* **protū'berant**.
proud [prowd] *adj* having excessive self-esteem; haughty; ostentatious; having a proper sense of self-respect.—*adv* **proud'ly**.
prove [prōōv] *vt* to establish or ascertain as true or genuine; to demonstrate to show (oneself) to be worthy or capable.—*vi* to turn out.

provender [prov'èn-dėr] *n* dry food for domestic animals, esp livestock.
proverb [prov'èrb] *n* a short familiar sentence expressing a supposed truth or moral lesson.—*adj* **prover'bial**.
provide [prō-vīd'] *vt* to make ready beforehand; to supply.—*vi* to make provision.—*conj* **provi'ded**.
providence [prov'i-dèns] *n* foresight; timely preparation; prudent management and thrift.—*adj* **prov'ident**, seeing beforehand, and providing for the future; thrifty.
province [prov'ins] *n* an administrative district or division of a country.—*adj* **provincial**, [prō-vin'sh(à)l], relating to a province.—*n* an inhabitant of a province or country district.—*n* **provin'cialism**.
provision [prō-vizh'(ò)n] *n* act of providing; something provided for the future.
provoke [prō-vōk'] *vt* to call forth, give rise to, result in; to excite with anger; to annoy, exasperate.—*n* **prōvocā'tion**.—*adj* **provoc'ative**.
provost [prōv'òst] *n* a high executive official, as in some churches, colleges, or universities.
prow [prow] *n* the forward part of a ship.
prowess [prow'es,] *n* bravery, esp in war; skill.
prowl [prowl] *vi* to move about stealthily; to rove in search of prey or plunder.—*n* the act of prowling.
proximate [proks'i-màt] *adj* nearest or next; without anything between.—*adv* **prox'imately**.—*n* **proxim'ity**, immediate nearness in time, place, relationship, etc.—*adv* **prox'imo**, next month.
proxy [prok'si] *n* the agency of one who acts for another; one who acts or votes for another.
prude [prōōd] *n* one who is overly modest or proper in behavior, speech, etc.—*n* **pru'dery**.—*adj* **pru'dish**.
prudent [prōō'dènt] *adj* cautious and wise in conduct; discreet, dictated by forethought.—*n* **pru'dence**.—*adj* **pruden'tial**.
prune¹ [prōōn] *vt* to trim dead or living parts from to divest of anything superfluous.
prune² [prōōn] *n* a plum dried.
prurient [prōō'ri-ènt] *adj* tending to excite lust; having lascivious thoughts.—*ns* **pru'rience**.
Prussian [prush'àn] *adj* of or pertaining to Prussia.
pry¹ [prī] *n* a lever or crowbar.
pry² [prī] *vi* to try curiously or impertinently to find out about other people's affairs.
psalm [säm] *n* a devotional song or hymn.—*ns* **psalmist** a composer of psalms, **psalmody** the singing of psalms.
Psalter [sòl'tėr] *n* the Book of Psalms, esp when separately printed.
pseudo- [sū-dō-] in compositon, false or spurious.—*adj* **pseudo**, false, sham.
pseudomorph [sū'dō-mörf] *n* a deceptive of irregular form.
pseudonym [sū'dō-nim] *n* a fictitious name assumed, as by an author.
psyche [sī'kē] *n* the soul, spirit.—*adjs* **psych'ic, -al**, pertaining to the psyche; spiritual; sensitive to, or in touch with, that which cannot be explained physically.—*ns* **psychi'atrist**, one who practices psychiatry; **psychiatry**, the branch of medicine dealing with disorders of the mind, **psychoanalysis**, a method of treating neuroses, phobias, and some other mental disorders by analyzing emotional conflicts, repressions, etc. through the use of free association, dream analysis, etc.; **psych'o-an'alyst**.—*vt* **psych'o-an'alyze**.—*n* **psychol'ogy**, the science that investigates the phenomena of mental and emotional life.—*adjs* **psycholog'ical**,—*ns* **psychol'ogist**, one who studies psychology.—*adj* **psychosomat'ic**, of mind and body as a unit; concerned with physical diseases that have an emotional origin.—*n* **psychother'apy**, the treatment of disease by hypnosis, psychoanalysis and similar means.—*adj* **psychot'ic**, pertaining to a psychosis.
ptarmigan [tär'mi-gan] *n* any of various grouses.
pterodactyl [ter-ō-dak'til] *n* an order of fossil flying reptiles with a featherless wing membrane attached to an elongated finger.
ptomaine [tō-mān'] *n* substances, often poisonous, formed from putrefying tissues.
puberty [pū'bėr-ti] *n* the beginning of sexual maturity.—*n* **pūbescence, pubic**.
public [pub'lik] *adj* of, belonging to, or concerning, the

people; pertaining to a community or a nation; common to, or shared in by, all; generally known.—*n* the general body of mankind; the people, indefinitely.—*adv* **pub´licly.**—**publication,** the printing and distribution of books, magazines, etc.; **pub´licist,** a person whose business is publicity; **publicity,** any information or action that brings a person, cause to public notice.—*vt* **pub´licize,** to give publicity to.

publish [pub´lish] *vt* to make public, to divulge; to put forth and offer for sale (as a book).—*vi* to put out an edition; to have one's work accepted for publication.—*ns* **pub´lisher.**

puce [pūs] *n, adj* a dark red.

puck¹ [puk] *n* a goblin or mischievous sprite.

puck² [puk] *n* a vulcanized rubber disk used in ice hockey; the ball used in field hockey.

pucker [puk´ér] *vti* to wrinkle.

pudding [pŏŏd´ing] *n* a boiled or baked soft food usu. with a cereal base.

puddle [pud´l] *n* a small pool of water, a mixture of clay, sand, and water and gravel that becomes watertight when dry.—*vt* to make a puddle or puddles; to subject (iron) to puddling.

puerile [pū´ėr-īl] *adj* juvenile; childish.

puerperal [pū´ûr´pèr-ål] *adj* relating to childbirth.

puff [puf] *vt* to blow or issue in whiffs; to pant; to swell (up, out).—*vt* to blow, smoke, etc. in or with puffs; to inflate; to praise in exaggerated terms.—*n* a sudden, forcible breath; a gust or whiff; a light pastry.—**puff´ball,** a round, white-fleshed often edible fungus that discharges ripe spores in a smokelike cloud when touched; *adj* **puff´y.**

puffin [puf´in] *n* any of several seabirds having a short neck and a parti-colored laterally compressed bill.

pug¹ [pug] *n* a breed of small, short-haired dog with a snub nose; a pug nose.

pug² [pug] *vt* to work and mix (as clay) when wet.

pug³ [pug] *n* a footprint, esp of a wild animal.

pugilism [pū´jil-izm] *n* the sport of boxing.

pugnacious [pug-nā´shůs] *adj* fond of fighting, combative, quarrelsome.—*adv* **pugna´ciously.**

puke [pūk] *vti* (*inf*) to vomit.

pukka [puk´a] *adj* first-rate; genuine, real.

pulchritude [pul´kri-tūd] *n* beauty.

pule [pūl] *vi* to whimper or whine as a sick or fretful child.

pull [pŏŏl] *vt* to pluck, to cull; to move, or try or tend to move, towards oneself (or in a direction so thought of); to draw; to drag; to rip; to tear.—*vi* to perform the action of pulling anything; to be capable of being pulled.—*n* the act of pulling; a pulling force.

pullet [pŏŏl´et] *n* a young hen.

pulley [pŏŏl´i] *n* a wheel turning about on axis, and having a groove on its rim in which runs a rope.

pullman [pŏŏl´mán] *n* a railroad car with private compartments or berths for sleeping.

pulmonary [pul´món-ár-i] *adj* pertaining to, or affecting, the lungs.

pulp [pulp] *n* a soft, moist, sticky mass; the soft, juicy part of a fruit or soft pith of a plant stem; ground-up, moistened fibers of wood, rags, etc. used to make paper.—*vi* to become pulp or pulpy.—*vt* to reduce to pulp.

pulpit [pŏŏl´pit] *n* a raised structure, esp in a church, occupied by a preacher.

pulsate [pul´sāt] *vi* to beat or throb rhythmically; to vibrate, quiver.

pulse¹ [puls] *n* a measured beat or throb; the beating in the arteries.—*vi* to throb.

pulse² [puls] *n* the edible seed of beans, peas, and other leguminous plants; the plants bearing them.

pulverize [pul´vèr-īz] *vt* to reduce to dust or fine powder.—*ns* **pulveriza´tion.**

puma [pū´ma] *n* a cougar; the fur or pelt of a cougar.

pumice [pum´is] *n* a light, porous volcanic rock, used for removing stains, polishing, etc.

pummel [pum´l] *vt* to beat, pound, thump, esp repeatedly.

pump¹ [pump] *n* a machine that forces a liquid or gas into, or draws it out of, something.—*vt* to move with a pump; to remove water, etc.

pump² [pump] *n* a low-cut shoe without fastening.

pumpkin [pum(p)´kin] *n* a large, round, orange fruit of the gourd family widely cultivated as food.

pun [pun] *vi* to play humorously upon words.—*n* a play upon words.

punch¹ [punch] *n* a sweet drink made with fruit juices, sherbet, etc. often mixed with wine or liquor.

punch² [punch] *vt* to prod; to strike with a forward thrust; to stamp, pierce by a thrust of a tool.—*n* a vigorous thrust; striking power, vigor; a tool or machine for punching.

puncheon¹ [pun´-sh(ó)n] *n* a tool for piercing or working on stone.

puncheon² [pun´-sh(ó)n] *n* a large cask; any of various units of liquid capacity.

punctilio [pungk-til´i-ō, -yō] *n* a nice point in behavior or ceremony; nicety in forms.—**punctil´ious,** attentive to punctilios.

punctual [pungk´tū-ål] *adj* being on time; prompt.—*n* **punctual´ity.**—*adv* **punc´tually.**

punctuate [pungk´tū-āt] *vt* to use certain standardized marks in (written matter) to clarify meaning; to interrupt; to emphasize.—*vi* to use punctuation marks.—*n* **punctua´tion.**

puncture [pungk´-chùr] *n* a small hole made with a sharp point.—*vi* to become punctured.

pundit [pun´dit] *n* a learned man.

pungent [pun´jént] *adj* pricking or acrid to taste or smell; keen, sarcastic (eg of a comment).

Punic [pū´nik] *adj* of ancient Carthage; faithless, treacherous, deceitful.

punish [pun´ish] *vt* to cause to suffer for an offense; to chastise; to treat severely.—*adj* **pun´ishable,** (*inf*).—*n* **pun´ishment,** judical penalty imposed for an offense; severe treatment.—*adj* **punitive,** inflicting, or with the purpose of inflicting, punishment.

punk¹ [punk] *n* decayed wood used as tinder.

punk² [punk] *adj* (*slang*) worthless, of poor quality.—*n* (*slang*) a young hoodlum; a young person regarded as insignificant, inexperienced, etc. **punk rock.**

punt¹ [punt] *n* a flat-bottomed boat with square ends, usu propelled with a pole.—*vt* to propel by pushing a pole against the bottom of a river.

punt² [punt] *vi* to play at a gambling game against the banker.

punt³ [punt] *n* the act of kicking a dropped football before it touches the ground.—Also *vti*

puny [pū´ni] *adj* of inferior size.

pupa [pu´pa] *n* the stage that intervenes between the larva (eg caterpillar) and the imago (eg butterfly).

pupil¹ [pū´pil] *n* a child or young person taught under the supervision of a teacher or tutor.

pupil² [pū´pil] *n* the round opening, apparently black, in the middle of the eye.

puppet [pup´ét] *n* a doll or image moved by wires or hands in a show.—*adj* behaving like a puppet; actuated by others.—**puppet show,** a dramatic performance, usu grotesque or burlesque, carried on by means of puppets.

puppy [pup´i] *n* a young domestic dog less than a year old.

purblind [pûr´blind] *adj* partly blind.

purchase [pûr´chàs] *vt* to buy.—*n* any mechanical advantage in raising or moving bodies; means of exerting force advantageously.

purdah [pûr´dä] *n* the seclusion of women from public observation among Muslims and some Hindus.

pure [pūr] *adj* clean, unsoiled; unmixed; not adulterated; free from guilt or defilement; chaste, modest.—*adv* **pure´ly,** chastely; unmixedly; wholly, entirely; solely.

purée [pū-rā] *n* cooked food passed through a sieve, or reduced to pulp by a blending machine.

purge [pûrj] *vt* to purify; to cleanse of sin; to rid of undesirable persons; to clear from accusation.—*n* removing persons believed to be disloyal or treacherous to an organization, esp a political party.—*n* **purga´tion.**—*adj* **pur´gative.**—*n* **pur´gatory,** a place or state in which souls are after death purified from venial sins.

purify [pū´ri-fī] *vt* to make pure; to cleanse from foreign or hurtful matter.—*n* **purificā´tion.**

purism [pūr´izm] *n* fastidious insistence upon purity of language, style, etc.—*n* **pūr´ist.**

purity [pūr´i-ti] *n* condition of being pure.

purl¹ [pûrl] *vi* to flow with a murmuring sound.—*n* a soft murmuring sound, as of a stream.

purl² [pûrl] *vt* to fringe with a waved edging, as lace; to knit in purl stitch. — *n* an embroidered border; knitting in purl stitch — **purl stitch**, a knitting stitch.

purlieu [pûr´lū] *n* borders or outskirts.

purloin [pûr-loin´] *vt* to filch, steal.

purple [pûr´pl] *n* a dark, bluish red; crimson cloth or clothing, esp as a former emblem of royalty. — *adj*. — *vt* or *vi* to make or to become purple.

purport [pûr´pōrt] *n* meaning conveyed; substance, gist.

purpose [pûr´pus] *n* the end or object towards which effort is directed; intention; function. — *vt* to intend.

purr [pûr] *vti* to utter a low, murmuring sound, as a cat when pleased.

purse [pûrs] *n* a small bag for carrying money; finances, money; a woman's handbag. — *vt* to put into a purse; to pucker. — *ns* **purs´er**, an official on a passenger ship, in charge of accounts, tickets, etc.

purslane [pûrs´lin] *n* a fleshy-leaved trailing plant that is a common weed but sometimes eaten in salads.

pursue [pûr-sōō´] *vt* to follow in order to overtake and capture; to seek to attain; to be engaged in; to proceed with. — *vi* to go in pursuit. — *n* **pursu´ance**, act of following, or of carrying out.

pursuit [pûr-s(y)ōōt´] *n* the act of pursuing; endeavor to attain; occupation, employment.

pursy [pûrs´i] *adj* short-winded, esp because of corpulence; fat.

purulent [pûr´(y)ŏŏ-lėnt] *adj* discharging pus.

purvey [pûr-vā´] *vt* to provide or supply.

purview [pûr´vū] *n* scope or extent, as of control activity, etc.

pus [pus] *n* a thick yellowish fluid exuded from infected tissues.

push [pŏŏsh] *vt* to thrust or press against so as to move; to drive by pressure. — *vi* to make a thrust; to make an effort; to press forward. — *n* a thrust; an impulse; effort; enterprising or aggressive pertinacity. — *adjs* **push´ful**, energetically or aggressively enterprising.

pusillanimous [pū-si-lan´i-mus] *adj* lacking firmness of mind; cowardly. — *n* **pusillanim´ity**.

puss [pŏŏs] *n* a familiar name for a cat. — *n* **puss´y**.

pustule [pus´tūl] *n* a blister or pimple containing pus. — *adjs* **pus´tular**.

put [pŏŏt] *vt* to push or thrust; to cast, throw; to constrain, compel to go (to); to set, lay, or deposit; to add (to); to bring into any state or position; to express, state. — *vi* to start in motion; to go (in, out, etc.

putative [pū´ta-tiv] *adj* supposed, reputed.

putrefy [pū´tre-fī] *vti* to make or become putrid. — *vi* to rot. — *n* **putrefac´tion**. — *n* **putres´cence** rottenness. — *adj* **pū´trid**, rotten and foul-smelling.

putsch [pŏŏch] *n* a secretly plotted sudden revolutionary outbreak.

putt [put] *vti* to hit (a ball) with a putt. — *n* **putt´er** (*golf*) a straight-faced club used in putting.

puttee [put´i] *n* a cloth strip wound round the legs from ankle to knee, as a legging.

putter [put´ėr] *vi* to busy oneself in an aimless way.

putty [put´i] *n* a soft, plastic mixture of powdered chalk and linseed oil. — *vt* to fix or fill with putty.

puzzle [puz´l] *vt* to bewilder; to perplex. — *vi* to be perplexed. — *n* perplexity; a toy or problem for testing skill or ingenuity.

pye-dog [pī-dog] *n* an ownerless or pariah dog.

Pygmy, Pigmy [pig´mi] *n* any of a small people of equatorial Africa ranging under five feet in height.

pylon [pī´lon] *n* a gateway to an Egyptian temple; a towerlike structure supporting electric lines.

pyorrhoea [pī-ō-rē´a] *n* an infection of the gums and tooth suckers, with formation of pus.

pyramid [pir´a-mid] *n* a three-dimensional geometric figure having a polygon as base, and whose sides are triangles sharing a common vertex; a royal tomb of ancient Egypt. — *adjs* **pyram´idal**.

pyre [pīr] *n* a pile of wood, etc., for burning a dead body.

Pyrex [pī´reks] *n* a registered trademark applied to glassware resistant to heat.

pyrites [pīr-ī´tēz] *n* a yellow mineral compound of iron and sulphur.

pyro- [pīr-o-] in composition, fire.

pyrotechnics [pī-rō-tek´niks] *n* a display of fireworks; showy display in talk, music, etc. — *adjs*

Pyrrhic victory [pir´ik vik´tōr-i] a victory gained at too great a cost.

Pythagorean [pī-thag-ō-rē´an] *adj* pertaining to *Pythagoras* or to his philosophy.

Pythian [pith´i-an] *adj* pertaining to the *Pythia* or priestess of Apollo at Delphi.

python [pī´thon] *n* a large, nonpoisonous snake that kills by constriction. — *n* **py´thoness**, the priestess of the oracle of Apollo at Delphi; a witch.

pyx [piks] *n* a box; a box used in a mint containing sample coin for testing.

Q

quack¹ [kwak] *n* the cry of a duck. — *vi* to make such a sound.

quack² [kwak] *n* an untrained person who practices medicine fraudulently.

quad [kwod] *n* quadrangle; quadruplet.

quadrangle [kwod´rang-gl] *n* (*geom*) a plane figure with four angles (and therefore four sides); an object or space of that form.

quadrant [kwod´rant] *n* (*geom*) the fourth part of the circumference of a circle, an arc of 90°.

quadrate [kwod´rāt] *adj* square or nearly square; *adj* **quadrat´ic**, involving terms of the second degree at most.

quadri- [kwod-ri-] in composition, of or with four, as in **quadrisyllable**, a word of four syllables.

quadrilateral [kwod-ri-lat´ėr-ål] *adj* four-sided.

quadrille [kwŏ-dril´, or kā-] *n* a square dance for four couples; music for such a dance.

quadruped [kwod´rŏŏ-ped] *n* a four-footed animal.

quadruple [kwod´rŏŏ-pl] *adj* four times as much or as many; consisting of four. — *vti* to make or become four times as much or as many. — *n* **quad´ruplet**, a set of four things, usu of one kind; one of four born at a birth.

quadruplicate [kwod-rŏŏ-pli-kåt] *adj* fourfold; being the last of four identical copies. — *vt* to make four such copies of.

quaestor [kwēs´tôr] *n* a Roman magistrate.

quaff [kwäf, kwof] *vti* to drink (a beverage) deeply.

quag [kwag] *n* a marsh, a bog.

quagmire [kwag´mīr] *n* wet, muddy ground.

quail¹ [kwāl] *vi* to cower, to flinch.

quail² [kwāl] *n* any of various small game birds.

quaint [kwānt] *adj* odd, whimsical, esp because old fashioned. — *adv* **quaint´ly**. — *n* **quaint´ness**.

quake [kwāk] *vi* to tremble, esp with cold or fear; to quiver. — *n* a shaking or tremor; an earthquake.

Quaker [kwā´kėr] *n* a popular name for a member of the Society of Friends.

qualify [kwol´i-fī] *vt* to ascribe a quality to; to describe; to render capable or suitable; to limit by modifications — *vi* to reach an accepted standard of attainment, esp academic. — *n* **qualifica´tion**, that which qualifies; a quality or attainment that fits a person for a place, etc.; limitation.

quality [kwol´i-ti] *n* that which makes a thing what it is, nature; kind or degree of goodness or worth; attribute; degree of excellence; excellence. — *adj* of high quality. — *adj* **qual´itative**.

qualm [kwäm] *n* a sudden sensation of faintness or sickness; a doubt; a misgiving.

quandary [kwon´då-rē] *n* a state of perplexity; a predicament; a dilemma.

quantity [kwon´ti-ti] *n* an amount that can be counted or measured; an indefinite amount; a large amount; (*pl*) a great amount; that property by which a thing can be measured; a number or symbol expressing this property; *adj* **quan´titative** measurable in quantity; (*chem*) determining the exact proportions of components.

quantum [kwon´tum] *n* quantity; amount.

quarantine [kwor´ån-tēn] *n* a period of compulsory isolation to prevent infection. — *vt* to put in quarantine.

quarrel¹ [kwor´ėl] *n* arrow for a crossbow.

quarrel² [kwor´ėl] *n* a dispute; a breach of friendship; a ground of dispute.—*vi* to dispute violently; to disagree; to find fault (with).

quarry[1] [kwor′i] *n* an excavation from which stone is taken.—*vt* to excavate from a quarry.—*vi* to make, or dig in, a quarry.

quarry[2] [kwor′i] *n* (*obs*) a deer's entrails given to the dogs after the chase; a hunted animal.

quart [kwört] *n* a liquid measure, equal to ¼ gallon; a dry measure, equal to 1/8 peck.

quartan [kwör′tån] *adj* occurring every third day or recurring at 72-hour intervals.

quarter [kwör′ter] *n* a fourth of something; one fourth of a year; one fourth of an hour; one fourth of a dollar; 25 cents, or a coin of this value; (*pl*) lodgings.—*vt* to divide into four equal parts; to divide (a human body) into four parts; *vi* to lodge, dwell; to crisscross a district.—*adj* constituting a quarter.—*adj* **quar′terly**, recurring, issued, or spaced at 3-month intervals.—*adv* once a quarter.—*n* a periodical published four times a year.

quartern [kwör′tèrn] *n* a fourth part.

quartet, quartette [kwör-tet′] *n* a set of four; a composition for four voices or instruments; a set of performers for such compositions.

quarto [kwör′tö] *n* the page size of a book made up of sheets each of which is folded twice to form four leaves.

quartz [kwörts] *n* a crystalline mineral, a form of silica, usu. colorless and transparent.

quasar [kwä′sar] *n* a distant, starlike, celestial object that emits much light and powerful radio waves.

quash [kwosh] *vt* to crush; to annul.

quasi [kwä′sī, kwä′sē] *adv* as if; in composition, **quasi-**, in a certain manner or sense; in appearance only, as *quasi-historical*, etc.

quassia [kwosh′(y)a] *n* a drug from the heartwood of various tropical trees used as a bitter tonic, a remedy for roundworms.

quatrain [kwot′rān] *n* a stanza or poem of four lines.

quaver [kwā′vèr] *vi* to speak or sing with tremulous modulations.—*n* a trembling, esp of the voice.

quay [kē] *n* a wharf for the loading or unloading of vessels.

queasy, quezy [kwē′zi] *adj* sick, squeamish; over-fastidious; causing nausea.—*adv* **quea′sily**.

queen [kwēn] *n* the wife of a king; a female monarch; a woman, or anything, of surpassing beauty, excellence, etc.; the sexually functional (egg-laying) female of bees and other social insects; a playing card with a picture of a queen.—*vi* to act like a queen, esp to put on airs.

queer [kwēr] *adj* odd, strange; (*inf*) eccentric; arousing suspicion; sick or faint.

quell [kwel] *vt* to subdue; to quiet; to allay.

quench [kwench] *vt* to put out, extinguish, as a flame; to cool; to slake (thirst); to subdue, suppress.

quern [kwûrn] *n* a handmill for grinding grain.

querulous [kwer′ū-lùs, -ôô-lùs] *adj* complaining, peevish.—*adv* **quer′ulously**.—*n* **quer′ulousness**.

query [kwē′ri] *n* a question; a question mark; doubt.—*vti* to question.—*pt, pt p* **quē′ried**.

quest [kwest] *n* the act of seeking; a journey for adventure.—*vt* to search for; to ask for.

question [kwes′ch(ô)n] *n* an enquiry; an interrogative sentence; a problem; a subject of doubt or controversy.—*vt* to ask questions of; to interrogate intensively; to dispute; to subject to analysis.—*vi* to ask questions.—*adj* **quest′ionable**, doubtful.

queue [kū] *n* a pendent braid of hair at the back of the head, a pigtail.

quibble [kwib′l] *n* an evasive turning away from the point in question; a minor objection or criticism.—*vi* to evade a question by caviling about words.—*n* **quibb′ler**.

quick [kwik] *adj* speedy; nimble; readily responsive; prompt in perception, learning, or repartee; hasty.—*adv* in a quick manner; the sensitive area of flesh lying under a fingernail or toenail; the inmost sensibilities.—*adv* **quick′ly**.—*vt* **quick′en**, to make alive; to invigorate, reinvigorate; to sharpen; to accelerate.—*vi* to come to life, esp to enter into a phase of active growth and development (as the stage when fetal motion is felt); **quick′lime**, calcium oxide; **quickness**; **quick′sand**, loose wet sand easily yielding to pressure and engulfing persons, animals, etc.; something that entraps or frustrates;

quick′silver, mercury; **quick′step**, a march, step, dance, or tune in quick time.

quid [kwid] *n* a piece of something chewable.

quiddity [kwid′i-ti] *n* the essence of anything; a trifling point; a quibble; an eccentricity; a crotchet.

quidnunc [kwid′nungk] *n* a gossiping busybody.

quiet [kwī′èt] *adj* at rest, calm; peaceable; gentle, unobtrusive, inoffensive; silent; undisturbed.—*n* rest, repose, calm, stillness, peace.—*vti* to make or become quiet.—*adv* **quī′etly**.—*ns* **quī′etness, quī′etude**.

quietus [kwī-ē′tùs] *n* a discharge from debt, etc.; death.

quill [kwil] *n* the hollow basal part of a feather; anything made from this, as a pen; a spine, of a porcupine or hedgehog.

quilt [kwilt] *n* a decorative, bedcover of two thicknesses of material, any material so treated.—*vt* to stitch like a quilt.—*vt* to make a quilt.

quince [kwins] *n* the fruit of an Asian tree that resembles a hard-fleshed yellow apple.

quinine [kwī′nīn, kwin′īn, kwin-īn, kwe′n-ēn′] *n* a bitter alkaloid used in medicine.

Quinquagesima [kwin-kwä-jes′i-ma] the Sunday before Lent, being the fiftieth day before Easter.

quinquennial [kwin-kwen′yàl] *adj* occurring once in five years; consisting of, lasting five years.

quinsy [kwin′zi] *n* a severe infection of the throat or adjacent parts.

quintain [kwin′tin, -tàn] *n* a post for tilting at.

quintessence [kwin-tes′èns] *n* the purest concentrated essence of anything; the most typical example of anything.—*adj* **quintessen′tial** [-shàl].

quintet, quintette [kwin′tet′] *n* a musical composition for five voices or instruments; a set of performers or instruments for such compositions.

quintuple [kwin′tū-pl] *adj* fivefold; having five parts or divisions.—*vti* to increase fivefold.

quip [kwip] *n* a short, clever remark; a repartee.

quipu [kē′pôô] *n* a device consisting of cord with attached strings of various colors used by ancient Peruvians for recording events and for calculating.

quire [kwīr] *n* a set of 24 or 25 sheets of paper of the same size and quality; one twentieth of a ream.

quirk [kwûrk] *n* a quick turn or twist; an oddity of character, or behavior.—*vt* to curl, twist.

quisling [kwiz′ling] *n* a traitor who takes office under a government formed by an enemy who has occupied his country.—Also *adj*.

quit [kwit] *vt* to pay, requite; to release from obligation; to acquit; to depart from.—*vi* to cease; to desert one's job or task; to admit defeat.—*adj* quit, set free; acquitted; rid (of); **quits**, even; neither debtor nor creditor.

quite [kwīt] *adv* completely; really; positively.

quiver[1] [kwiv′èr] *n* a case for arrows.

quiver[2] [kwiv′èr] *vi* to shake with slight and tremulous motion; to tremble, to shiver.—*n* **quiv′er**.

quixotic [kwiks-ot′ik] *adj*, extravagantly chivalrous; idealistic but impracticable (eg a project).

quiz [kwiz] *n* an eccentric person; a practical joke; a short written or oral test.—*vt* to make fun of; to tease; to eye with mockery; to interrogate.—*adj* **quizz′ical**.

quoin [koin] *n* the external corner of a building; any of the large stones at such a corner; a wedge-shaped block.

quoit [koit] *n* a heavy flat ring thrown in quoits.—*vt* to throw like a quoit.

quondam [kwon′dam] *adj* former.

quorum [kwō′rum, kwö′-] *n* the fixed minimum attendance necessary for the transaction of business at an assembly.

quota [kwō′ta] *n* a proportional share.

quote [kwōt] *vt* to refer to; to cite; to give the actual words of; to adduce for authority or illustration.—*n* (*inf*) something quoted; a quotation mark.—*ns* **quōtā′tion, quōtā′tion mark**, marks used to note the beginning and the end of a quotation.

quoth [kwōth] *vt* said.

quotidian [kwō-tid′i-àn] *adj* occurring every day; belonging to each day; commonplace.

quotient [kwō′shènt] *n* (*math*) the number of times one quantity is contained in another.

R

rabbet [rab'ét] *n* a groove cut in the edge of a board so that another piece may be fitted into it. —*vti* to cut, or be joined by, a rabbet.

rabbi [rab'ī] an ordained Jewish clergyman, spiritual leader of a congregation.

rabbit [rab'it] *n* a small burrowing animal of the hare family their flesh (as food); their fur.

rabble[1] [rab'l] *n* a disorderly, noisy crowd, a mob.

rabid [rab'id] *adj* violent; fanatical; affected with rabies. —*adv* **rab'idly.** —*ns* **rab'idness; rabies** [rā'-bez] a disease, transmitted by the bite of an infected animal.

raccoon [ra-kōōn'] *n* a small nocturnal carnivore of N America that lives in trees; its fur.

race[1] [rās] *n* any of the divisions of mankind distinguished esp by color of skin; any geographical, national, or tribal ethnic grouping; any distinct group of plants or animals having the potential to interbreed. —*adj* **racial** [rā'sh(i-á)l]. —*n* **ra'cialism,** hatred, rivalry or prejudice accompanying difference of race; belief in inherent superiority of some races over others, usu. with implication of right to rule; **ra'cialist; rac'ism, rac'ist.**

race[2] [rās] *n* a strong and rapid current of water or its channel; a competitive trial of speed, as in running; any contest like a race; the course of life. —*vi* to run at top speed or out of control; to compete in a trial of speed; to revolve too fast under a diminished load. —*vt* to cause to race; to oppose in a race; to rush.

raceme [rā-sēm'] *n* a cluster of flowers attached by stalks to a central stem.

rack[1] [rak] *n* an instrument for racking or stretching, esp an instrument of torture; extreme pain, anxiety, or doubt; a framework on which articles are arranged; a bar with teeth to work into those of a wheel pinion, or worm gear. —*vt* to stretch forcibly; to arrange in or on a rack; to torture, torment. —*ns* **rack' rent,** an excessively high rent.

rack[2] [rak] *n* destruction.

rack[3] [rak] *n* a wind-driven mass of clouds.

racket[1] [rak'ét] *n* a bat strung with catgut or nylon, for playing tennis, etc. —*pl* a game for two or four players played in a 4-walled court

racket[2] [rak'ét] *n* din, clamor; an obtaining money illegally; (*inf*) any fraudulent activity. —*n* **racketeer',** one who extorts money by threats or makes profit by illegal action.

radar [rā'där] *n* a system or device for using reflection of radio waves for locating objects.

radiant [rā'di-ânt] *adj* emitting rays; issuing in rays; glowing; shining; beaming with joy.

radiate [rā'di-āt] *vt* to emit rays; to shine; to issue in rays. —*adj* [-āt] having ray flowers; spreading like a ray or rays. —*vt* to send out in or by rays; to spread around as if from a center; to give forth. —*ns* **rādiā'tion,** the emission and diffusion of rays; that which is radiated; **rādiātor,** an apparatus for emitting heat, as for warming a room, or from an automobile engine.

radical [rad'ik(á)l] *adj* pertaining to the root or origin; fundamental; relating to, or constituting a linguistic root; *n* **rad'icalism,** the principles or spirit of a radical.

radio- [rā'di-ō, -o] *n*, the transmission of sounds or signals by electromagnetic waves through space, without wires, to a receiving set; such a set; broadcasting by radio as an industry, entertainment, etc. —*adj* of, using, used in, or sent by radio. —*vti* to transmit, or communicate with, by radio. —*n* **radioactiv'ity,** a giving off of radiant energy in the form of particles or rays by the disintegration of atomic nuclei. —*adj* **radioact'ive.** —*ns* **radio astron'omy,** astronomy dealing with radio waves in space in order to obtain information about the universe; **radio frequency,** a frequency intermediate between audio frequencies and infrared frequencies used esp in radio and television transmission. **rā'diograph,** an X-ray or gamma ray photograph. —*vt* to make a radiograph of; to send a radiogram to. —*ns* **rādiog'raphy,** the technique, or practice, of making radiographs; **rādiol'ogy,** a branch of medicine concerned with the use of radiant energy (as X-rays and radium) in the diagnosis and treatment of disease; **radiol'ogist, radiosonde,** a miniature radio transmitter carried aloft to broadcast

information on humidity, temperature, and pressure; **radiotelephone,** wireless telegraph, telephone; **radio telescope,** a radio-antenna combination used for observation in radio astronomy; **rādiother'apy,** treatment of disease by X-rays or by radioactive substances.

radish [rad'ish] *n* pungent root eaten as a salad.

radium [rā'di-um] *n* a radioactive metallic element.

radius [rā'di-us] *n* (*geom*) a straight line from the center to the circumference of a circle and a straight line extending from the center to a point on the surface of a sphere.

radix [rā'diks] *n* the base of a number system or of logarithms; the primary source.

raffia [raf'i-a] *n* strips of the pliant fiber of the leaves of the raffia palm of Madagascar.

raffle [raf'l] *n* a lottery to decide which of the subscribers shall receive a certain article. —*vt* to offer as a prize in a raffle; *vi* to engage in a raffle.

raft [raft] *n* a flat structure of logs or planks for support or conveyance on water; an inflatable boat.

rafter [räft'èr] *n* the beams supporting the roof of a house.

rag [rag] *n* worn, torn, or waste scrap of cloth; a tatter or shred; a worthless piece of any material. —*adj* **ragg'ed,** shaggy; jagged; uneven; irregular; torn into rags. —*n* **rag'time,** music having more or less continuous syncopation.

ragamuffin [rag'a-muf-in] *n* an ill-clad dirty person, esp a boy.

rage [rāj] *n* overmastering passion of any kind, as desire or (esp) anger; frenzy; vogue. —*vi* to behave with passion, esp with furious anger; to storm; to be prevalent and violent.

raglan [rag'làn] *n* an overcoat, with the sleeve in one piece with the shoulder.

ragout [ra-gōō'] *n* a highly seasoned stew of meat and vegetables.

ragwort [rag'wûrt] *n* any of several composite herbs with a yellow flower.

raid [rād] *n* a sudden swift inroad, for assault or seizure. —*vt* to make a raid on. —*vi* to go on a raid. —*n* **raid'er.**

rail[1] [rāl] *n* a bar extending from one support to another, as in fences, staircases, etc.; one of the steel bars used to form a track for wheeled vehicles; the railway as a means of travel or transport. —*vt* to enclose or separate by rails.

rail[2] [rāl] *vi* to utter angry taunts or reproaches. —*n* **raillery** [rāl'èr-i], good-natured banter.

rail[3] [rāl] *n* any of numerous wading birds related to the cranes.

raiment [rā'mènt] *n* (*arch*) clothing.

rain [rān] *n* water from the clouds in drops; a shower; a fall of anything in the manner of rain. —*vi* to fall like rain. —*vt* to pour down (rain, etc.); to give in large quantities. —*ns* **rain'bow,** the arc containing the colors of the spectrum formed in the sky; **rain' check,** a ticket stub, allowing future admission if the event is rained out; a promise to accept an invitation at a later date; **rain'coat,** a light waterproof overcoat; **rain'fall,** a fall of rain; the amount of rain that falls in a given time; **rain' gauge,** an instrument for measuring rainfall.

raise [rāz] *vt* to cause to rise; to lift up; to set up or upright; to increase in size, amount, degree, intensity, etc; to rear, grow or breed; to get, collect, or levy. —*n* a rising road.

raisin [rā'z(i)n] *n* a sweet dried grape.

raj [räj] *n* rule, sovereignty. —*n* **ra'ja(h),** an Indian or Malay prince or chief.

rake[1] [rāk] *n* a toothed bar on a handle for scraping, gathering together, smoothing, etc. —*vt* to draw a rake over; to gather as with a rake; to sweep with gunfire from stem to stern; to scrape, gather (together).

rake[2] [rāk] *n* a dissolute, debauched man.

rake[3] [rāk] *n* (*naut*) the projection of the stem and stern of a ship beyond the extremities of the keel; the slope or slant (of a mast); the slope of a stage, auditorium, etc.

rally[1] [ral'i] *vti* to reassemble; to gather for renewed and united effort; to muster by an effort; to recover to some degree of health or vigor. —*n* act of rallying.

rally[2] [ral'i] *vti* to tease or banter.

ram [ram] *n* a male sheep; a battering ram; a hydraulic ram or water-ram. —*vt* to push or press hard, to cram; to drive by hard blows; to strike, batter, pierce, with a ram.

Ramadan [ram'-a-dän] *n* the ninth month of the Islamic year throughout which Muslims are required to fast from dawn to sunset.

ramble [ram'bl] *vi* to wander at will for pleasure; to straggle; to wander in mind or discourse; to be incoherent.—*n* a leisurely walk with no fixed goal.—*n* **ram'bler**, one who rambles; a climbing rose.—*adj* **ram'bling**.

ramify [ram'i-fī] *vt* to divide into branches.—*n* **ramification** [ram-i-fi-kā'sh(ó)n], division into branches.

ramp [ramp] *vi* to stand or advance menacingly with forelegs or arms raised.—*n* a sloping walk or runway joining different levels; a wheeled staircase for boarding a plane; a sloping runway for launching boats, as from trailers.—*n* **rampage'**.—*vi* to rush about wildly. **ramp'ant**, unrestrained; prevalent.

rampart [ram'pärt] *n* a flat topped defensive mound; a protective barrier.

ramshackle [ram'shak'l] *adj* tumbledown; rickety.

ranch [ränch] *n* a large farm, for raising cattle, horses, or sheep; a style of house with all the rooms on one floor.

rancid [ran'sid] *adj* rank in smell and taste, as stale fats or oil.—*ns* **rancid'ity**, **rancidness**.

rancor [rang'kūr] *n* bitter deep-seated enmity.

random [ran'dóm] *n* a haphazard course.—*adj* haphazard; chance.

range [rānj] *vt* to place in proper order; to determine the range of; to graze (livestock) on a range.—*vi* to lie in a certain direction; to extend; to move freely.—*n* a system of points in a straight line; variety; area within which movement takes place; position in relation to a person taking aim; ground on which shooting is practiced; a cooking stove.—*ns* **range' find'er**, an instrument for finding the range of a target; **rang'er**.

rani, ranee [rän'ē] *n* a Hindu queen; a rajah's wife.

rank[1] [rangk] *n* a row or line; a line of soldiers standing side by side; order, grade, or degree; high standing.—*vt* to place in a line; to assign to a definite class or grade; to outrank.—*vi* to have a specified place in a scale, or a place in a specified class.

rank[2] [rangk] *adj* growing high and luxuriantly; coarsely overgrown; offensive in odor or flavor.

rankle [rangk'l] *vi* to fester; to cause persistent pain, vexation, or bitterness.

ransack [ran'sak] *vt* to search thoroughly; to plunder.

ransom [ran'sóm] *n* redemption from captivity; price of redemption; a huge sum.—*vt* to pay ransom.

rant [rant] *vti* to use vehement or extravagant language.—*n* loud, wild declamation, bombast.

rap[1] [rap] *n* a sharp blow; a sound made by knocking.—*vt* to hit sharply.—*vi* to knock or tap.

rap[2] [rap] *n* (*inf*) talk, conversation.

rapacious [ra-pā'shùs] *adj* given to plunder; ravenous; greedy of gain.—*adv* **rapā'ciously**.

rape [rāp] *n* the plundering (of a city, etc.) as in warfare; sexual intercourse with a woman without her consent.—*vt* to commit rape upon.

rapid [rap'id] *adj* swift; quickly accomplished.—*ns* **rapid'ity**, **rap'idness**.—*adv* **rap'idly**.

rapier [rā'pi-ér] *n* a sword with a pointed blade.

rapine [rap'in] *n* plunder, robbery.

rapparee [rap-a-rē'] *n* an Irish irregular soldier.

rapport [rä-pōr'] *n* relation, connection, sympathy.

rapprochement [rä-prosh'mä] *n* a drawing together; establishment or state of cordial relations.

rapscallion [rap-skal'yón] *n* a rascal.

rapt [rapt] *adj* carried away; transported, enraptured; wholly engrossed.

rapture [rap'chùr] *n* extreme delight, ecstasy.—*adj* **rap'tūrous**.—*adv* **rap'tūrously**.

rare[1] [rar] *adj* thin, not dense; uncommon; excellent.—*adv* **rāre'ly**, **rarity** [rar'i-ti], state of being rare; thinness; uncommonness.—*vt* **rarefy**, **rarify** [rar'i-fī], to make or become less dense.

rare[2] [rar] *adj* not completely cooked, partly raw.

rascal [ras'kál] *n* a knave, rogue, scamp.

rase [rāz] *vt* to erase; to demolish.

rash[1] [rash] *adj* overhasty, wanting in caution.—*adv* **rash'ly**.—*n* **rash'ness**.

rash[2] [rash] *n* a slight eruption on the skin.

rasher [rash'ér] *n* a thin slice of bacon or ham.

rasp [räsp] *n* a coarse file.—*vt* to grate as with a rasp; *vi* to scrape; to produce a grating sound.

raspberry [räz'bèr-i] *n* any of various edible usu. black or red berries that are aggregate fruits consisting of small drupes.

rat [rat] *n* any of numerous rodents closely allied to mice but larger; (*slang*) a sneaky, contemptible person.—*vi* to hunt or catch rats; to betray, desert, or inform on one's associates.

ratafia [rat-à-fē'a] *n* a flavoring essence made with the essential oil of almonds.

ratch [rach] *n* a ratchet.—*n* **ratch'et wheel**, a wheel with inclined teeth with which a pawl engages.

rate[1] [rāt] *n* the amount, degree, etc. of something in relation to units of something else; price, esp per unit; a class or rank.—*vt* to estimate the value of; to settle the relative rank, scale, or position of; to regard as.—*vi* to have value or status.

rate[2] [rāt] *vt* to scold, to chide, to reprove.

rather [rä'тнèr] *adv* more willingly; in preference; somewhat, in some degree; more accurately.

ratify [rat'i-fī] *vt* to approve, esp by official sanction; to confirm.—*n* **ratificā'tion**.

ratio [rā'shi-ō] *n* the measurable relation of one thing to another; proportion.

ratiocination [rash-i-os-i-nā'sh(ó)n] *n* the process of reasoning; deduction from premises.

ration [ra'sh(ó)n or rā'-] *n* a fixed allowance or portion of food.—*vt* to supply with rations.

rational [ra'shón-ål] *adj* of or based on reason; endowed with reason.—*vt* **ra'tionalize**, to make rational, to conform to reason; **ra'tionalism**, (*phil*) a system which regards reasoning as the source of knowledge; **ra'tionalist**.—*adj* **rationalist'ic**.—*adv* **rationalist'ically**.—*n* **rationality** [ra-shòn-al'i-ti].

ratline [rat'lin] *n* one of the small lines or ropes forming steps of the rigging of ships.

rattan [ra-tan'] *n* any of a number of climbing palms with very long thin stem.

rattle [rat'l] *vi* to clatter; to move along rapidly with a clatter; to chatter briskly and emptily.—*vt* to cause to rattle; to utter glibly, as by rote; to disturb the equanimity of.—*n* the sound of rattling; an instrument or toy for rattling; **ratt'lesnake**, venomous snakes with rattling bony rings on the tail.

raucous [rö'kus] *adj* hoarse, harsh.

ravage [rav'ij] *vt* to lay waste, to pillage; to despoil (of).—*n* devastation; ruin.—*n* **rav'ager**.

rave [rāv] *vi* to rage; to talk as if mad, delirious, or enraptured.—*adj* **rā'ving**.

ravel [rav'l] *vti* to separate into its parts, esp thread; fray; untwist.

raven[1] [rav'vèn] *n* a large glossy black crow.

raven[2] [rav'en] *vt* to devour hungrily or greedily.—*vi* to prey rapaciously.—*adj* **rav'enous**, intensely hungry.

ravine [ra-vēn'] *n* a deep, narrow gorge.

ravish [rav'ish] *vt* to seize or carry away by violence; to rape; to enrapture.—*adj* **rav'ishing**, charming, enrapturing.

raw [rö] *adj* not altered from its natural state; not cooked; having the skin abraded or removed; unrefined; untrained; immature, inexperienced; chilly and damp.

ray[1] [rā] *n* a line along which light comes from a bright source; a moral or intellectual light; any of several lines radiating from a center.

ray[2] [rā] *n* any of various fishes with a flattened body and the eyes on the upper surface.

rayon [rā'on] *n* a textile fiber made from a cellulose solution; a fabric of such fibers.

raze [rāz] *vt* to graze; scrape off; to erase; to lay level with the ground.

razor [rā'zòr] *n* a sharp-edged implement for shaving.—*n* **rā'zorbill**, a N Atlantic auk.

re [rā or rē] *prep* in the matter of, concerning.

rē- [rē-] prefix meaning: again or anew; back. *re-* is sometimes hyphenated.

reach [rēch] *vt* to stretch forth; to hand, pass; to succeed in touching or getting; to arrive at.—*vi* to stretch out the hand; to extend in influence, space, etc.—*n* act or power of reaching; extent of stretch; range, scope; a continuous extent, esp of water.

react [rē-akt'] *vi* to act reciprocally or in return to respond to a stimulus; to have a reciprocatory effect.—*adj* **reac'tionary**, of, or favoring, reaction.—*n* one who attempts to revert to past political conditions.

read [rĕd] *vt* to utter aloud, or go over with silent understanding; to observe and interpret; to study.—*vi* to perform the act of reading.—*adjs* **read** [red], versed in books, learned; **read'able** [rĕd'-], legible; interesting and attractively written.

ready [red'i] *adj* prepared; willing; inclined; liable; dexterous; prompt.—*vt* to make ready.—*n* the state of being ready, esp the position of a firearm ready to be fired.—*adv* **read'ily**.—*n* **read'iness**.

real[1] [rē'ăl] *adj* actually existing; not counterfeit or assumed; true, genuine, sincere.—*vt* **rē'alize**, to make real; to convert into money; *ns* **realīzā'tion**, **rē'alism**, the doctrine that general terms, or universals, have an equal or superior reality to actual physical particulars; the tendency to look at, to accept, or to represent, things as they really are and be practical; **realist**.—*adj* **rēalis'tic**.—*n* **reality** [rē-al'i-ti], the state or fact of being real; truth.—*adv* **rē'ally**.

realm [relm] *n* a kingdom; province; sphere.

ream[1] [rēm] *n* a quantity of paper varying from 480 to 516 sheets; (*pl*) (*inf*) a great amount.—*ns* **reap'er**.

reap [rēp] *vti* to cut down, as grain; to clear by cutting a crop.—*ns* **reap'er**.

rear[1] [rēr] *n* the back or hindmost part or position; a position behind.—*adj* of, at, or in the rear; **rear' guard**, the rear of an army; troops protecting it.

rear[2] [rēr] *vt* to raise; to bring up, breed and foster; to set up; to educate, nourish, etc.—*vi* to rise on the hind legs.

reason [rē'zn] *n* ground, support, or justification (of an act or belief); a cause; a motive or inducement; conformity to what is fairly to be expected or called for; moderation; sanity.—*vti* to think logically (about); analyze; to argue or infer.—*adj* **rea'sonable**.—*adv* **rea'sonably**.

reassure [rē-a-shōōr'] *vt* to assure anew; to reinsure; to give confidence to.—*n* **reassur'ance**.

reave [rēv] *vt* to plunder; to rob.—*pt, n* **reav'er**.

rebate [ri-bāt'] *vt* to reduce, abate; to dull, to blunt.—*vi* to give rebates.—*n* abatement.

rebec [rē'bek] *n* a medieval instrument of the viol class.

rebel [reb'(ê)l] *n* one who rebels.—*adj* rebellious.—*vi* [ri-bel'] to renounce the authority of the laws and government, or to take up arms and openly oppose them.—*n* **rebell'ion** [-yón], act of rebelling; revolt.—*adj* **rebell'ious** [-yùs].

rebound [ri-bownd'] *vi* to bound or start back from collision; to spring back.—*n* recoil.

rebuke [ri-būk'] *vt* check; put to shame; reprove.—*n* a reproach; stern reproof, reprimand.

rebus [rē'bus] *n* an enigmatical representation of a name, etc., by pictures or signs punningly representing parts of a word or phrase.

rebut [ri-but'] *vt* to drive back; to repel; to refute in a formal manner by argument, proof, etc.—*ns* **rebutt'al**.

recal'citrant refusing to obey authority, etc.; refractory; obstinate in opposition.

recant [ri-kant'] *vti* to revoke a former declaration; to declare one's renunciation of one's former religious or political belief or adherence.

recapitulate [rē-ka-pit'ū-lāt] *vt* to go over again the chief points of.—*n* **recapitūlā'tion**.

recast [rē-kást'] *vt* to cast again; to reconstruct.

recede [ri-sēd'] *vi* to go, draw, or fall back; to withdraw (from).—*adj* **reced'ing**.

receipt [ri-sēt'] *n* receiving; place of receiving; a written acknowledgement of anything received; that which is received.—*vt* to mark (a bill) as paid; to write a receipt for.

receive [ri-sēv'] *vt* to take, get, or catch, usu. more or less passively; to admit, take in, or serve as receptacle of.—*adj* **receiv'able**.—*adj* **received'**.

recent [rē'sènt] *adj* of late origin or occurrence; relatively near in past time; modern.—*adv* **rē'cently**.

receptacle [ri-sep'tà-kl] *n* that in which anything is or may be received or stored.

reception [ri-sep'sh(ò)n] *n* the act, fact, or manner of receiving; social gathering often for the purpose of extending a formal welcome.—*n* **recep'tionist**.—*adj* **recept'ive**.

recess [ri-ses'] *n* temporary halting of work, a session, school, etc.; a hidden or inner place; a niche or alcove; **recessional** [ri-sesh'òn-àl], a hymn sung during recession or retirement of clergy and choir.—*adj* **recess'ive**, tending to recede.

recherché [rè-sher'shā] *adj* choice, select, refined.

recidivism [ri-sid'i-vizm] *n* the habit of relapsing into crime.—*n* **recid'ivist**.

recipe [res'i-pi] *n* directions for making something, esp a food or drink; a method laid down for achieving a desired end.—*pl* **rec'ipes**.

recipient [ri-sip'i-ênt] *adj* receiving.—*n* one who or that which receives.

reciprocal [ri-sip'ro-k(à)l] *adj* acting in return; mutual.—*adv* **recip'rocally**.—*vt* **recip'rocāte**, to give and receive mutually; to return, repay in kind. **reciprocā'tion**. **reciprocity**.

recite [ri-sīt'] *vt* to repeat from memory; to read aloud publicly.—*vi* to give a recitation.—*n* a public performance given by an individual musician or dancer or by a dance troupe; **recitation**.

reck [rek] *vt* (*arch*) to care for, heed; to matter.—*vi* to care; to worry.—*adj* **reck'less**, careless, rash.

reckon [rek'òn] *vt* to count; to regard as being; to estimate.—*vi* to calculate.—*ns* **reck'oner**.

reclaim [ri-klām'] *vt* to win back; to make (wasteland) fit for cultivation.—*vi*, *adj* **reclaim'able**.

recline [ri-klīn'] *vt* to cause or permit to incline or bend backwards.—*vi* to lean in a recumbent position, on back or side.

recluse [ri-klōōs'] *adj* secluded, retired, solitary.—*n* a religious devotee who lives shut up in a cell.

recognize [rek'og-nīz] *vt* to know again; to show signs of knowing; to acknowledge, admit, realize.—*adj* **rec'ognizable**.

recoil [ri-koil'] *vti* to rebound; to kick back, as a gun.—*n* [rē'koil'] a starting or springing back, rebound; the kick of a gun.

recollect [rek-òl-ekt'] *vt* to remember; to remind (oneself) of something temporarily forgotten.—*vi* to call something to mind.—*n* **recollec'tion**.

recommend [rek-o-mend'] *vt* to commend, commit; to introduce as worthy of confidence or favor; to make acceptable.—*n* **recommendā'tion**.

recompense [rek'òm-pens] *vt* to return an equivalent for; to repay.—*n* that returned; repayment.

reconcile [rek'on-sīl] *vt* to restore to friendship or union.—*adj* **rec'oncil'-able**.—*ns* **rec'oncilement**; **reconciliā'tion** [-sil-].

recondite [rek'on-dīt, ri-kon'dīt] *adj* obscure, abstruse, profound (of subject, style, author).

recondition [rē-con-dish'(ò)n] *vt* to repair and refit; to restore to sound condition.

reconnaissance [ri-kon'i-sàns] *n* the survey of a region, esp for obtaining military information about an enemy.

reconnoiter [rek-ò-noi'tèr] *vti* to make a reconnaisance (of).

reconstruct [rē-kon-strukt'] *vt* to rebuild.—*n* **reconstruc'tion**, a reconstructing.

record [ri-körd'] *vt* to set down in writing; to state as if for a record.—*n* **record** a register; a performance or event that surpasses all others previously noted; a grooved disc for playing on a phonograph; the sounds so recorded.—*ns* **record'er**, an official who keeps records; a machine or device that records; a flute of the earlier style **record'ing**, what is recorded, as on a disc or tape; the record.

recount [ri-kownt'] *vt* to narrate the particulars of; to detail.

recoup [ri-kōōp'] *vt* to make good (losses); to recover expenses or losses; to regain.

recourse [rē'kòrs or ri-kors'] *n* a turning for aid or protection; that to which one turns seeking aid.

recover [ri-kuv'èr] *vt* to get back or find again; to reclaim *vi* to regain health or any former position.—*adj* **recov'erable**.—*n* **recov'ery**.

recreant [rek'ri-ànt] *adj* surrendering, craven; false, apostate.—*n* a craven; a deserter; a renegade.

recreate [rek'rē-āt] *vt* to reinvigorate, to refresh, *vi* to take recreation, amuse oneself.—*n* **recreā'tion**, any refreshment of the body or mind after toil, sorrow, etc.; **re-c'rēātive** [rē-].

recriminate [ri-krim'in-āt] *vi* to charge an accuser.—*n* **recriminā'tion**.

recrudesce [rē-krōō-des'] *vi* to break out afresh after a period of inactivity.—*n* **recrudes'cence**.

recruit [ri-krōōt'] *n* a newly enlisted soldier, etc. or member.—*vti* to enlist (personnel) into an army or navy; to enlist (new members) for an organization.—*n* **recruit'ment**, a recruiting.

rectangle [rek′tang-gl] *n* a four-sided plane figure with all its angles right angles. — *adj* **rectang′ular**.

rectify [rek′ti-fī] *vt* to set right, to correct, to adjust. — *ns* **rectifica′tion; rec′tifier**.

rectilin′ear [rek-ti-lin′ē-ár] *adj* moving in or forming a straight line; characterized by straight lines.

rectitude [rek′ti-tūd] *n* straightness; uprightness; integrity; being correct in judgement or procedure.

rector [rek′tór] *n* in some churches, a clergyman in charge of a parish; the head of certain schools, colleges, etc *adj* **rectorial**. — *n* **rec′tory**, the house of a minister or priest.

rectum [rek′tum] *n* the terminal part of the large intestine.

recumbent [ri-kum′bènt] *adj* leaning; lying down.

recuperate [ri-kū′pér-āt] *vti* to get well again; to recover (losses, etc.). — *n* **recupera′tion**.

recur [ri-kûr′] *vi* to come back in thought, talk, etc.; to occur again or at intervals. — *n* **recurr′ence**. — *adjs* **recurr′ent**.

recycle [rē-sī′kl] *vt* to pass through a cycle again.

red [red] *adj* (*comparative* **redd′er**; *superlative* **redd′est**) of a color like blood. — *n* the color of blood; any red pigment. — *vt* **redd′en**, to make red. — *vi* to grow red; to blush. — *ns* **red′ ad′miral**, a common butterfly; **red′breast**, a bird (as a robin) with a reddish breast; **red-hot**, one who shows intense partisanship or emotion. — *adj* glowing with heat; extremely hot; very excited, angry, etc.; very new. — *adj* **red-letter**, of special significance. — *ns* **red light**, a warning signal, a cautionary sign; a deterrent; **red tape**, rigid adherence to routine and regulations, causing delay.

redact [ri-dakt′] *vt* to edit, work into shape.

redeem [ri-dēm′] *vt* to buy back, recover by payment, etc.; to deliver from sin; to ransom; to atone for; to fulfil Redeemer, Jesus.

redemption [ri-dem(p)′sh(ó)n] *n* act of redeeming.

redolent [red′ō-lènt] *adj* fragrant; smelling (of); suggestive (of). — *ns* **red′olence, red′olency**.

redouble [ri-dub′l] *vti* to double again; to make or become twice as much.

redoubt [ri-dowt′] *n* a fieldwork enclosed on all sides, its ditch not flanked from the parapet.

redoubt′able [ri-dowt′á-bl] *adj* formidable; valiant.

redound [ri-downd′] *vi* to flow back, or to become swollen; to have an effect for good or ill.

redress [ri-dres′] *vt* to set right to; readjust (the balance). — *n* relief; reparation.

reduce [ri-dūs′] *vt* to degrade; to impoverish; to subdue; to lessen; to diminish in size; to weaken. — *adj* **reduced′**, in a state of reduction; weakened; impoverished; diminished; simplified. — *n* **reduction**, [-duk′sh(ó)n].

redundant [ri-dun′dànt] *adj* superfluous, excessive, wordy. — *n* **redun′dancy**.

reduplicate [ri-dū′pli-kāt] *vt* to double; to repeat. — *n* **reduplica′tion**. — *adj* **redu′plicative**.

reed [rēd] *n* a tall stiff hard-culmed grass, esp the ditch reed, found in marshes; a musical instrument made from a hollow stem. — *adj* **reed′y**, abounding with reeds; having the tone quality of a reed instrument.

reef¹ [rēf] *n* a chain of rocks at or near the surface of water; a hazardous obstruction.

reef² [rēf] *n* a portion of a sail that may be rolled or folded up. — *vti* to reduce the exposed surface to lower or bring inboard.

reek [rēk] *n* smoke; vapor; fume. — *vi* emit smoke, fumes, or strong or offensive smell. — *adj* **reek′y**, smoky.

reel [rēl] *n* a cylinder, drum, or spool on which wire, cables, films, etc., may be wound; a lively dance, a tune for it; a length of material wound on a reel. — *vt* to wind on a reel. — *vi* to dance the reel; to stagger; to waver.

reeve [rēv] *vt* to pass the end of a rope through any hole, as the channel of a block.

refection [ri-fek′sh(ó)n] *n* refreshment of mind, spirit, or body; a meal or repast. — *n* **refectory** [ri-fek′tór-i], a dining hall, esp monastic.

refer [ri-fûr′] *vt* to assign; to hand over for consideration; to direct for information. — *vi* to have recourse for information; to make mention or allusion. — *ns* **referee** [ref-è-rē′] an arbitrator, or judge; **ref′erence, referen′dum**, the principle or practice of submitting a law directly to the vote of entire electorate.

refine [ri-fīn′] *vt* to purify; to clarify; to free from coarseness, vulgarity, crudity. — *vi* to become more fine, pure, subtle, or cultured. — *adj* **refined′**. — *ns* **refine′ment, refin′er; refin′ery**, a place for refining eg sugar.

reflect [ri-flekt′] *vt* to bend back or aside; to throw back after striking; to give an image of in the manner of a mirror. — *vi* to bend or turn back or aside; to mirror; to meditate. — *adj* **reflect′ing**. — *n* **reflection**. — *adj* **reflect′ive**. — *ns* **reflect′iveness; reflect′or**, a reflecting surface, instrument, or body. — *adj* **reflex** bent or turned back; reflected; reactive; involuntary response from a nerve center to a stimulus from without.

re-form [rē-fórm′] *vti* to form again. — *vt* **reform′** to remove defects from. — *vi* to abandon evil ways. — *n* amendment or transformation, esp of a system or institution; removal of political or social abuses. **reformation** *adjs* **rē-formed′**, formed again, anew; **reformed** amended, improved.

refract [ri-frakt′] *vt* to cause (a ray of light, etc.) to undergo refraction. — *ns* **refrac′tion**, the bending of a ray or wave of light, heat, or sound as it passes from one medium to another; **refractor**.

refractory [ri-frak′tór-i] *adj* unruly, unmanageable, obstinate, perverse; not yielding to treatment.

refrain¹ [ri-frān′] *n* a line or phrase recurring.

refrain² [ri-frān′] *vt* restrain. — *vi* to abstain (from).

refrangible [ri-fran′ji-bl] *adj* that may be refracted. — *n* **refrangibil′ity**.

refresh [ri-fresh′] *vt* to make fresh again; to give new vigor, spirit, brightness, etc., to. — *n* **refresh′er**. — *n* **refresh′ment**, that which refreshes, as food or rest; (*pl*) food or drink, or both.

refrigerate [ri-frij′ér-āt] *vt* to make cold; to expose to great cold, as (food) for preservation. — *n* **refrig′erator** [-ér-ā-tór], a cabinet, room or appliance for keeping food and other items cool.

refuge [ref′ūj] *n* a shelter or protection from danger or trouble; an asylum or retreat. — *n* **refugee′**, one who flees for refuge to another country.

refulgent [ri-ful′jènt] *adj* casting a flood of light, radiant, beaming. — *n* **reful′gence**.

refund [rē-fund′] *vti* to repay; to restore what was taken. — *n*.

refuse¹ [ri-fūz′] *vt* to decline. — *vi* to make refusal. — *n* **refū′sal**.

refuse² [ref′ūs] *adj* rejected as worthless. — *n* waste.

refute [ri-fūt′] *vt* to disprove. — *adj* **refutable**.

regal [rē′gál] *adj* royal; kingly. — *n* **regality**. — *adv* **rē′gally**.

regale [ri-gāl′] *vt* to entertain, as with a feast.

regard [ri-gärd′] *vt* to look at, to observe; to esteem highly, to respect. — *n* look; attention with interest; concern; esteem, respect.

regatta [ri-gat′a] *n* a boat race; a series of boat races.

regenerate [ri-jen′ér-āt] *vt* to produce anew; to renew spiritually; to reform completely; to reproduce; **regenerā′tion**. — *adj* **regen′erative**.

regent [rē′jènt] *adj* invested with interim or vicarious sovereign authority. — *n* one invested with interim authority on behalf of another.

regicide [rej′i-sīd] *n* the killing or killer of a king.

regime, régime [rā-zhēm′] *n* regimen; a political or ruling system.

regimen [rej′i-men] *n* government; rule; a system of diet, exercise, etc. for improving the health;

regiment [rej′i-mènt] *n* a military unit, smaller than a division, consisting usu. of a number of battalions. — *adj* **regimental**.

region [rē′jón] *n* a large, indefinite part of the earth's surface; one of the zones in which the atmosphere is divided; a part of the body.

register [rej′is-tèr] *n* a written record, the book containing such a record; a variety of language that is appropriate to a subject or occasion; the compass of a voice or instrument. — *vt* to enter in a register; to indicate by bodily expression. — *vi* to enter one's name in a list, as of voters; to enroll formally as a student; to be in correct alignment; to make or convey an impression; correspond. — *ns* **reg′istrar** one who keeps records, esp the officer of an educational institution in charge of student records; **registrā′tion, reg′istry**, registration; a place of registration.

regnant [reg′nánt] *adj* reigning; having the chief power; prevalent.

regress [rē′gres] *n* passage back; return; right or power of returning.—*vi* [ri-gres′], to go back; to return to a former place or state.—*n* regression.—*adj* regressive.

regret [ri-gret′] *vt* to remember with sense of loss or of having done amiss; to feel sorrow or dissatisfaction because, or because of.—*n* sorrowful wish that something had been otherwise; compunction; an intimation of regret or refusal.—*adjs* regret′ful, feeling regret; regrett′able.

regular [reg′ū-lár] *adj* belonging to a religious order; governed by or according to rule, law, order, habit, custom, established practice, mode prescribed, or the ordinary course of things; uniform; periodical.—*n* a regular soldier or player.—*n* regularity [-ar′i-ti].—*n* regulā′tion, act of regulating; state of being regulated.—*adj* reg′ulative.

regurgitate [rē-gûr′ji-tāt] *vt* to cast out again, to pour back; to bring back into the mouth after swallowing.—*n* regurgitā′tion.

rehabilitate [rē-(h)a-bil′i-tāt] *vt* to reinstate, restore to former privileges, rights, etc.; to put back in good condition.—*n* rehabilitā′tion.

rehearse [ri-hûrs′] *vt* to repeat, to recount, narrate in detail; to practice.—*ns* rehears′al.

reign [rān] *n* rule of a monarch; predominating influence; time of reigning.—*vi* to be a monarch; to be predominant.

reimburse [rē-im-bûrs′] *vt* to repay; to pay an equivalent to (for loss or expense).—*n* reimburse′ment.

rein [rān] *n* the strap of a bridle.—*vt* to govern with the rein; to restrain or control.

reindeer [rān′dēr] *n* any of several large deer.

reinforce [rē-in-fōrs′] *vt* to enforce again; to strengthen with new force or support.—*n* reinforce′ment.—**reinforced concrete**, concrete strengthened by embedded steel bars.

reinstate [rē-in-stāt′] *vt* to restore or re-establish in a former station, condition.—*n* reinstate′ment.

reiterate [rē-it′é-rāt] *vt* to repeat; to repeat again and again.—*n* reiterā′tion.—*adj* reit′erative.

reject [ri-jekt′] *vt* to throw out; to refuse to adopt, to have, to believe, etc.—*n* rejec′tion.

rejoice [ri-jois′] *vt* to make joyful, to gladden.—*vi* to feel joy, to exult; to make merry.

rejoin [ri-join′].—*vt* to say in answer; to join again.—*n* rejoin′der.

rejuvenate [ri-jōō′vé-nāt] *vt* to make, feel or seem young again.—*n* rejuvenā′tion.—*vi* rejuvenesce′.

relapse [ri-laps′] *vi* to slide, sink or fall back; to return to a former state or practice, to backslide.

relate [ri-lāt′] *vt* to recount, narrate, tell; to ally by connection or kindred.—*vi* to have reference or relation (to).—*n* relā′tion, act of relating; recital; a narrative; state or mode of being related; way in which one thing is connected with another; connection by blood or marriage; a relative; relā′tionship.—*adj* relative in or having relation; corresponding; relevant.—*adv* rel′atively.—*n* relativ′ity, state or fact of being relative; (*physics*) the theory of the relative, rather than absolute, character of motion, velocity, mass, etc. and the interdependence of time, matter, and space.

relax [ri-laks′] *vt* i to loosen; to make or become less, rigid, *n* rēlaxā′tion.

relay [rē′lā] a fresh set of dogs, horses, etc., to relieve others; a relieving shift of men; a race between teams, each member of which goes a part of the distance.

release [ri-lēs′] *vt* to let loose; to set free; to give up to another.—*n* a setting free; a book, news item, etc. released to the public.

relegate [rel′é-gāt] *vt* to banish; to consign.—*n* relegā′tion.

relent [ri-lent′] *vi* to soften or grow less severe.—*adj* relent′less.—*adv* relent′lessly.—*n*.

relevant [rel′é-vánt] *adj* bearing upon, or applying to, the matter in question, pertinent.—*ns* rel′evance.

reliable, etc. *See* rely.

relic [rel′ik] *n* that which is left after loss or decay of the rest; (usu. in *pl*) a corpse.

relict [rel′ikt] *n* a survivor or surviving trace; widow.

relief [ri-lēf] *n* the lightening or removal of any discomfort, stress, or evil; release from a post or duty; one who relieves another by taking his place; that which relieves or mitigates; aid; assistance to the poor.—*adj* providing relief in cases of distress, danger, or difficulty.

relieve [ri-lēv′] *vt* to bring, give, or afford relief to; to release; to ease, to mitigate.

religion [ri-lij′ón] *n* belief in, acceptance of God or gods, with the emotion and morality connected therewith; rites or worship.

relinquish [ri-ling′kwish] *vt* to give up; to renounce or surrender).—*n* relin′quishment.

relish [rel′ish] *n* an appetizing flavor; zest-giving quality; zestful enjoyment.—*vt* to like the taste of; to be pleased with; to appreciate discriminatingly.

reluctance [ri-lukt′áns] *n* unwillingness.—*adj* reluct′ant.

rely [ri-lī] *vi* to depend confidently.—*adj* reli′able, trustworthy.—*ns* reliabil′ity.—*adv* reli′ably.—*n* reli′ance, trust.

remain [ri-mān′] *vi* to stay or be left behind; to continue in the same place.—*n* remain′der, that which remains after the removal of a part.

remand [ri-mand′] *vt* to send back (esp a prisoner into custody to await further evidence).

remark [ri-märk′] *vt* to notice; to observe; to comment.—*n* a brief comment.—*adj* remark′able, noteworthy; unusual.—*adv* remark′ably.

remedy [rem′é-di] *n* any means of curing a disease, redressing, counteracting or repairing any evil or loss.—*vt* to put right, repair, counteract—*adjs* remē′diable, remē′dial.

remember [ri-mem′bèr] *vt* to keep in, or recall to, memory or mind.—*vi* to exercise or have the power of memory.—*ns* remem′brance, memory; that which serves to bring to or keep in mind.

remind [ri-mīnd′] *vt* to put in mind (of), to cause to remember.—*n* remind′er.

reminiscence [rem-i-nis′éns] *n* the recurrence to the mind of the past; a recollection; reminis′cent.

remiss [ri-mis′] *adj* negligent, slack.—*adj* remiss′ible, that may be remitted.

remit [ri-mit′] *vt* to relax; to refrain from exacting or inflicting; to transmit, as money, etc., in payment.—*vi* to abate, to relax.—*ns* remitt′ance, the sending of money, etc.

remnant [rem′nánt] *n* a fragment or a small number remaining after destruction, removal, sale, etc.

remonstrance [ri-mon′stráns] *n* a strong or formal protest; expostulation.—*adj* remon′strant, remonstrating.—*n* one who remonstrates.

remorse [ri-mörs′] *n* the gnawing pain of conscience; compunction.—*adj* remorse′ful.—*adv* remorse′fully.—*adj* remorse′less.

remote [ri-mōt′] *adj* far removed in place, or time; widely separated (fròm); out-of-the-way, not quickly reached.—*adv* remote′ly.

remove [ri-mōōv′] *vt* to put or take away; to dismiss.—*vi* to go away; to change abode.—*adj* remov′able; remov′al, the act or process of removing; the fact of being removed.

remunerate [ri-mū′né-rāt] *vt* to recompense; to pay.—*adj* remū′nerable.—*n* remunerā′tion.

renaissance [ren′i-sáns′] *n* a new birth or revival; **Renaissance**, revival of arts and letters, under classical influence, period of this revival beginning in the 14th century in Italy, and lasting into the 17th century.

renal [rē′n(à)l] *adj* of or near the kidneys.

renascent [ri-nas′ént, also -nās′-] *adj* coming into.

rend [rend] *vt* to tear asunder with force; to split.

render [ren′dèr] *vt* to submit, as for approval, payment, etc.; to give back; to give in return; to pay; to represent as by drawing; to translate; to cause to be; rendi′tion, surrender; translation.

rendezvous [rändä-vōō] *n* an appointed meeting place; a meeting by appointment; such a meeting.—*vi* to assemble at any appointed place.

renegade [ren′é-gād] *n* one faithless to principle or party, apostate, a turncoat.

rennet [ren′it] *n* an extract from the stomach of calves, etc., used to curdle milk.

renounce [ri-nowns′] *vt* to disclaim, repudiate; to reject.—*ns* renounce′ment; renounc′er.

renovate [ren′ō-vāt] *vt* to make new again; to make as if new. — *ns* renovā′tion; ren′ovātor.

renown [ri-nown′] *n* fame. — *adj* renowned′, famous.

rent[1] [rent] *n* an opening or hole made by rending.

rent[2] [rent] periodical payment for use of another's property, esp houses and lands; revenue. — *vt* to hold or occupy by paying rent; to let or hire out for a rent. — *ns* ren′tal, an amount paid or received as rent.

renunciation [ri-nun-si-ā′sh(ō)n] *n* act of renouncing; ascetic self-denial.

rep[1], **repp** [rep] *n* a corded cloth.

repair[1] [ri-pār′] *vi* to betake oneself, to go, to resort. — *n* a resort, haunt.

repair[2] [ri-pār′] *vt* to mend; to remedy; to make amends for. — reparable. — *n* reparā′tion.

repartee [rep-ár-tē′] *n* a ready and witty retort; skill in making such retorts.

repast [ri-päst′] *n* a meal; food and drink.

repatriate [rē-pāt′ri-āt, or -pat′-] *vt* to restore or send back to one's country of origin, allegiance.

repay [rē-pā′] *vt* to pay back; to make return for; to recompense. — *adj* repay′able. — *n* repay′ment.

repeal [ri-pēl′] *vt* to revoke, to annul. — *n* abrogation, annulment.

repeat [ri-pēt′] *vt* to say, do, perform, again; to say or do after another. — *vi* to say, do, or accomplish something again, repeat′ed, repeat′edly, repeat′er

repel [ri-pel′] *vt* to drive back; to repulse; to hold off. — *adj* repell′ent.

repent [ri-pent′] *vi* to regret, sorrow for, or wish to have been otherwise, what one has done or left undone (*with* of); to change from past evil; to feel contrition. — *vt* to regret. — *n* repent′ance . — *adj* repent′ant.

repercussion [rē-pėr-kush′(ō)n] *n* driving back; reverberation; echo; a far-reaching, often indirect reaction to some event.

repertory [rep′ėr-tōr-i] *n* a repertoire. — *n* repertoire [rep′ėr-twär], the stock of plays, songs, etc., that a company, singer, etc., is prepared to perform.

repine [ri-pīn′] *vi* to express or feel discontent.

replace [ri- or rē-plās′] *vt* to put back; to provide a substitute for; to take the place of. — *n* replace′ment.

replenish [ri-plen′ish] *vt* to fill again; to fill completely; to stock abundantly. — *n* replen′ishment.

replete [ri-plēt′] *adj* full, well stored; completely filled; filled to satiety. — *n* replē′tion.

replica [rep′li-ka] *n* a duplicate, esp one by the original artist; a facsimile.

reply [ri-plī′] *vi* to say or write in answer. — *vt* to give as an answer. — *n* an answer. — *n* replī′er.

report [ri-pōrt′, -pört′] *vt* to bring back, as an answer, news, or account of anything; to give a formal statement of; to make a complaint about, against. — *vi* to make a formal statement; to write an account of occurrences; to present oneself (for duty). — *n* a statement; a newspaper account of an event; rumor, repute; explosive noise. — report′er, one who reports.

repose [ri-pōz′] *vt* to lay at rest; to place at rest; to place (trust, etc.) in someone. — *vi* to rest; to lie at rest; to lie dead. — *n* rest; stillness.

repoussé [rĕ-pōō′sā′] *adj* raised in relief by hammering from behind or within. — *n* repoussé work.

reprehend [rep-rē-hend′] *vt* to find fault with, to reprove. — *adj* reprehen′sible, blameworthy. — *n* reprehen′sion.

represent [rep-rē-zent′] *vt* to present to, bring before, the mind; to point out; to make to appear (as), to allege (to be); to depict; to act the rôle of on the stage; to serve as a symbol for; to correspond to. — *adj* represent′able. — *n* representation. — *adj* representative [rep-rē-zent′a-tiv].

repress [ri-pres′] *vt* to restrain; to keep under. — *n* repression.

reprieve [ri-prēv′] *vt* to delay or commute the execution of; to give a respite to; to rescue, redeem.

reprimand [rep′ri-mänd′] *n* a severe or formal reproof. — *vt* to reprove severely.

reprint [rē-print′] *vt* to print again. — *n* rē′print, a later impression.

reproach [ri-prōch′] *vt* to accuse of a fault; to censure, upbraid. — *n* upbraiding, reproof, censure; a source or matter of disgrace or shame. — *adjs* reproach′ful.

reprobate [rep′rō-bāt] *adj* given over to sin, depraved, unprincipled; condemnatory. — *n* an abandoned or profligate person. — *vt* to reject; to disapprove, of. — *n* reprobā′tion.

reproduce [rē-prō-dūs′] *vt* to produce a copy of; to form anew; to propagate. — *vi* to produce offspring; to undergo reproduction. — *n* reproduction.

reproof [ri-prōōf′] *n* a reproving; rebuke, censure, reprehension. — *n* reproval.

reptile [rep′tīl] *adj* creeping; like a reptile in nature. — *n* any of a class of cold-blooded, air-breathing vertebrates with horny scales or plates, as turtles, alligators and crocodiles, lizards, snakes, etc.

republic [ri-pub′lik] *n* a form of government headed by a president, in which the supreme power is vested in the people and their elected representatives; a state or country so governed. — *adj* repub′lican, of or favoring a republic.

repudiate [ri-pū′di-āt] *vt* to disown; to refuse to recognize, acknowledge or pay to deny as unfounded.

repugnance [ri-pug′nâns] *n* inconsistency; aversion. — *adj* repug′nant, inconsistent; incompatible.

repulse [ri-puls′] *vt* to drive back, to beat off; to rebuff. — *n* a driving back, a beating off; a check; a refusal. — *n* repulsion. — *adj* repul′sive.

repute [ri-pūt′] *vt* to consider, deem. — *n* general opinion or impression; attributed character; widespread or high estimation. — *adj* reputable, respectable. — *adv* rep′ūtably. — *n* repūtā′tion; estimation, character generally ascribed; good report, fame; good name.

request [ri-kwest′] *n* an asking for something; a petition; a favor asked for.

requiem [rek′wi-em] *n* a mass for the rest of the soul of the dead; music for it.

require [ri-kwīr′] *vt* to demand, to exact; to direct. — *n* require′ment.

requisite [rek′wi-zit] *adj* required, needful, indispensable. — *n* that which is required, necessary, or indispensable. — *n* requisi′tion, the act of requiring; a formal demand, request, or order, as for the supply of anything for military purposes.

requite [ri-kwīt′] *vt* to repay; to avenge. — *n* requī′tal.

reredos [rēr′dos] *n* an ornamental wood screen, a stone screen, or partition wall behind an altar.

rescind [ri-sind′] *vt* to annul, abrogate. — *n* rescission.

rescue [res′kū] *vt* to free from danger, captivity, or evil plight; to deliver forcibly from legal custody. — *n* the act of rescuing. — *n* res′cuer.

research [ri-sėrch′] *n* a careful search or investigation. — *vi* to make researches. — *n* research′er.

resemble [ri-zem′bl] *vt* to be like; to represent as like. — *n* resem′blance.

resent [ri-zent′] *vt* to take badly, to consider as an injury or affront. — *adj* resent′ful.

reserve [ri-zûrv′] *vt* to hold back, to save up for future use or emergency; to have set aside to save one's energies (for). — *n* that which is reserved; a reservation; (*pl*) a military force not usually serving but liable to be called up when required; restrained manner; reticence; a mental reservation. — *n* reservā′tion, the act of reserving or keeping back or keeping for oneself; an expressed, or tacit, proviso, limiting condition, or exception; something withheld. — *adj* reserved.

reservoir [rez′ėr-vwär] *n* a receptacle for fluids, esp an artificial lake or tank for storing water.

reset [rē-set′] *vt* to set again; to change the reading of.

reside [ri-zīd′] *vi* to dwell permanently; to be vested (in); to inhere (in). — *ns* residence, act of dwelling in a place; period of dwelling; a house where one lives permanently; res′idency, a usu. official place of residence. — *adj* res′ident, dwelling in a place; residing at the place of one's duties; not migratory. — *n* one who resides. — *adj* residential.

residue [rez′i-dū] *n* that which is left, remainder. — *adjs* resid′ual, remaining as residue; resid′uary.

resign [ri-zīn′] *vt* to yield up, to relinquish; to submit calmly; to entrust (to). — *vi* to give up office, employment, etc. — *n* resignation. — *adj* resigned.

resile [ri-zīl′] *vi* to recoil, to rebound, to spring back into shape or position. — *ns* resilience [ri-zil′i-ėns], recoil; elasticity, physical or mental.

resin [rez'in] *n*, products obtained from the sap of certain plants and trees. — *adj* **res'inous.**

resist [ri-zist'] *vt* to strive against; to oppose with success; to be little affected by. — *vi* to oppose or withstand something. — *n* **resis'tance.** — *adj* **resis'tant, resistible.**

resoluble [rez'ol-ū-bl] *adj* capable of being resolved. — *adj* **res'olute,** having a fixed purpose, constant in pursuing a purpose, determined. — *adv* **res'olutely.** — *ns* **res'oluteness; resolution,** act of resolving; analysis; solution; state of being resolved; fixed determination; that which is resolved. — *vt* **resolve,** to separate, to analyze; to solve, to free from doubt or difficulty, to explain. — *vi* to undergo resolution; to melt. — *n* anything resolved or determined; resolution, fixed purpose.

resonance [rez'on-ăns] *n* resounding; sympathetic vibration; sonority. — *adj* **res'onant.**

resort [ri-zört'] *vi* to have recourse; to turn (to) for help, etc. — *n* a source of help, support, etc.; recourse.

resound [ri-zownd'] *vt* to echo; to sound with reverberation; to sound or spread (the praises of).

resource [ri-sōrs', -sörs'] *n* source or possibility of help; an expedient; (*pl*) wealth; assets; resourcefulness. — *adj* **resource'ful.** — *n* **resource'fulness.**

respect [ri-spekt'] *vt* to feel or show esteem, deference or honor to. — *n* honor or esteem; consideration; regard; (*pl*) a greeting or message of esteem; reference; relation. — *adj* **respec'table.** — *n* **respectabil'ity.** — *adj* **respect'ful.**

respire [ri-spīr'] *vti* to breathe. — *ns* **respiration .** — **res'pirător,** an apparatus to maintain breathing by artificial means. — *adj* **respiratory.**

respite [res'pit] *n* temporary cessation of something that is tiring or painful; postponement requested or granted. — *vt* to grant a respite to; to relieve by a pause; to delay.

resplendent [ri-splen'dĕnt] *adj* very splendid, gorgeous, shining brilliantly. — *ns* **resplen'dence.**

respond [ri-spond'] *vi* to answer; to show a favorable reaction; to be answerable. — *vt* to reply. — *adj* **respon'dent,** answering; corresponding; responsive. — *n* one who answers. — *adj* **respon'sible,** liable to be called upon to answer; answerable; deserving the blame or credit of; trustworthy; involving responsibility. — *n* **responsibil'ity.**

rest[1] [rest] *n* repose, refreshing inactivity; intermission of, or freedom from, motion; tranquillity; a place for resting; a pause in speaking or reading. — *vi* to repose; to be at ease; to be still; to remain. — *vt* to give rest to; to place or hold in support; to lean; to base. — *adj* **rest'ful,** at rest. — *adj* **rest'less,** without rest.

rest[2] [rest] *n* remainder; the others. — *vi* to remain.

restaurant [res'tă-rănt] *n* a place where meals can be bought and eaten. — *n* **restaurateur,** the keeper of a restaurant.

restitution [res-ti-tū'sh(ȯ)n] *n* act of restoring what was lost or taken away; a reimbursement.

restive [res'tiv] *adj* unwilling to go forward; obstinate, refractory, uneasy, as if ready to break from control. — *n* **res'tiveness.**

restore [ri-stōr'] *vt* to bring, put, or give back; to reestablish; to repair; to bring back to a known or conjectured former state. — *n* **restoration** [res-tō-rā'sh(ȯ)n]. — *adj* **restorative.**

restrain [ri-strān'] *vt* to hold back; to control; to subject to forcible repression. — *n* **restraint,** act of restraining; state of being restrained.

restrict [ri-strikt'] *vt* to keep within limits. — *adj* **restrict'ed.** — *n* **restric'tion,** act of restricting; limitation; confinement; a limiting or restraining regulation. — *adj* **restric'tive.**

result [ri-zult'] *vi* to issue as an effect); to follow as a consequence. — *n* consequence; effect; quantity obtained by calculation. — *adj* **resul'tant.**

resume [ri-zŏŏm'] *vt*; to take up again. — *vi* to proceed after interruption. — *ns* **résumé,** a summary, resumption.

resurge [ri-sûrj'] *vi* to rise again into life, activity, or prominence. — *n* **resur'gence.** — *adj* **resur'gent.**

resurrect [rez-ŭr-ekt'] *vt* to restore to life.

resuscitate [ri-sus'i-tāt] *vti* to revive when apparently dead or in a faint, etc. — *n* **resuscitā'tion.** —

retail [rē'tāl] *n* sale to consumer in small quantities. — *adj* pertaining to such sale. — *adv* at a retail price. — *vti* to sell or be sold by retail. — *ns* **retail'er; retailing.**

retain [ri-tān'] *vt* to keep; to hold back; to continue to keep, to

hold secure. — *ns* **retain'er,** one who or that which retains; a person attached to, and owing service to, a family; a fee paid to retain a lawyer's services.

retaliate [ri-tal'i-āt] *vt* to repay in kind. — *vi* to return like for like. — *n* **retaliā'tion.** — *adjs* **retal'iatory.**

retard [ri-tärd'] *vt* to slow, to delay. — Also *vi.* — *n* **retardā'tion.**

retch [rech] *vi* to strain as if to vomit. — *vt* to vomit.

reticent [ret'i-sĕnt] *adj* reserved or sparing in communication. — *n* **ret'icence, ret'icency.**

reticle [ret'i-kl] *n* a system of lines, dots, cross hairs, or wires in the focus of the eyepiece of an optical instrument. — *vt* **retic'ulate,** to form into, or mark with, a network. — *n* **reticulā'tion, reticule;** a drawstring bag.

retina [ret'i-na] *n* the innermost coat of the back part of the eye, on which the image is formed.

retinue [ret'i-nū] *n* a body of retainers or attendants.

retire [ri-tīr'] *vi* to withdraw; to retreat; to recede; to withdraw from office, business, profession, etc. to go to bed. — *vt* to cause to retire from a position, office, etc.; to withdraw from use. — *adj* **retired'.** — *n* **retire'ment.**

retort [ri-tört'] *vt* to throw back; to return upon an assailant or opponent; to answer in retaliation, sharply, or wittily. — *vi* to make a sharp reply. — *n* retaliation; a ready and sharp or witty answer.

retract [ri-trakt'] *vt* to draw back or in; to withdraw, to revoke, to unsay. — *vi* to take back, or draw back from, what has been said or granted. — *adj* **retrac'table.** — *n* **retractā'tion** [rē-], revoking, recantation.

retreat [ri-trēt'] *n*; an orderly withdrawal before an enemy, or from a position of danger or difficulty; a signal for withdrawal or retirement; seclusion; place of privacy, seclusion, refuge or quiet. — *vi* to draw back; to retire.

retrench [rē-trench'] *vti* to cut down (esp expenses); to economize. — *n* **retrench'ment.**

retribution [ret-ri-bū'sh(ȯ)n] *n* deserved reward; something given or exacted in compensation, esp punishment. — *adj* **retrib'ŭtive** [ri-], involving retribution, punishing suitably.

retrieve [ri-trēv'] *vt* to recover, repossess; to restore; to make good, of dogs, to find and bring back. — *vi* to retrieve game. — *adj* **retriev'able.** — *ns* **retriev'al,** retrieving.

retro- [ret'ro-] *pfx* backwards; behind.

retrograde [ret'rō-grād] *adj* going backward; falling from better to worse. — *vi* to go back or backwards; to become worse.

retrospect [ret'rō-spekt] *n* a looking back; a contemplation of the past.

return [ri-tûrn'] *vi* to come or go back; to recur; to reply. — *vt* to give, put, cast, bring or send back; to answer, to retort. — *n* the act of returning; something returned; a recurrence; that which comes in exchange. — *adj* **retur'nable.**

rev [rev] *vt* (*inf*) to increase the speed of an engine (*with* up). — *vi* to operate at an increase in speed of revolution (*with* up).

reveal [ri-vēl'] *vt* to make known (something hidden or secret); to disclose; to make visible. — *adj* **reveal'ing.**

reveille [rev'ė-lē] *n* the sound of the drum or bugle at daybreak to awaken soldiers.

revel [rev'l] *vi* to feast or make merry in a riotous or noisy manner; to take intense delight (*with* in). — *n* a riotous feast. — *ns* **rev'eller; rev'elry.**

revelation [rev-ė-lā'sh(ȯ)n] *n* the act or experience of revealing; that which is revealed.

revenant [rèv'nǎ, rev'é-nǎnt] *n* one who returns from the dead, or a long absence.

revenge [ri-venj'] *vt* to inflict injury in retribution for; to avenge by retaliating. — *n* (act of inflicting) a malicious injury in return for an injury received; the desire for retaliation; its satisfaction. — *adj* **revenge'ful.**

revenue [rev'ėn-ū] *n* the total income produced by a given source; the income from taxes, licenses, etc., as of a city, state, or nation.

reverberate [ri-vûr'bėr-āt] *vt* to send back, to reflect. — *vi* to recoil, rebound, be reflected; to reecho, resound. — *adj* **rever'-berant.** — *n* **reverberā'tion.**

revere [ri-vēr'] *vt* to regard with high respect, to venerate. — *n* **reverence,** high respect; respectful awe; state of being held in high respect; a gesture or observance of respect. — *adjs* rev′erend, worthy of reverence; of or relating to the clergy; rev′erent, feeling or showing reverence.

everie, revery [rev′ė-ri] n an undirected train of thoughts or fancies in meditation.

evers [ri-vēr′] n a lapel, esp on a woman's garment.

everse [ri-vûrs′] vt to turn the other way about, as upside down, outside in, etc.; to invert; to set moving backwards. — vi to move in the opposite direction. — n the contrary, opposite; the back, a mechanism for reversing. — adj contrary, opposite; turned about. — n revers′al. — adj rever′sible. — n a reversible cloth or article of clothing. — n rever′sion, the act or fact of reverting or returning; that which reverts or returns; the return, or the future possession (of any property) after some particular event; a throwback. — adj rever′sionary.

evert [ri-vûrt′] vi to fall back (to a former state); to recur (to a former subject).

eview [ri-vū′] n a viewing again, a reconsideration; a descriptive and critical account, a critique; a periodical with critiques of books, etc.; a display and inspection of troops or ships. — vt to reexamine; to examine critically; to write a critique on. — n review′er.

evile [ri-vīl′] vti to use abusive language.

evise [ri-vīz′] vt to examine and correct; to make a new, improved version of; to study anew. — n a revision; a later printing proof embodying previous corrections. — ns reviš′al, revision; revi′ser, revisor; revision, act, or product, of revising.

evive [ri-vīv′] vti to return to life, vigor, memory, notice, use, the stage, etc. — ns revi′val, renewed performance of, renewed interest or attention; revi′valist.

evoke [ri-vōk′] vt to annul; to retract. — adj revocable. — n revocā′tion.

evolt [ri-vōlt′] vi to renounce allegiance, to rise in opposition; to experience disgust or shock. — vt to cause to turn away or shrink with disgust. — n rebellion; insurrection; secession.

evolution [rev-ol-ōō′sh(ò)n] n act or condition of revolving; motion round a center; a complete turn by an object or figure, about an axis; overthrow of a government, social system, etc. — adj revolu′tionary. — vt revolu′tionize.

evolve [ri-volv′] vt to ponder; to travel or cause to travel in a circle or orbit; to rotate or cause to rotate. — n revol′ver, a handgun with a rotating magazine.

vue [ri-vū′] n a musical show with skits, dances, etc., often parodying recent events.

evulsion [ri-vul′sh(ò)n] n disgust; a sudden change or reversal, esp of withdrawal with a sense of utter distaste or repugnance. — adj revul′sive.

eward [ri-wôrd′] n that which is given in return for something done; money offered, as for the capture of a criminal. — vt to give a reward to (someone) for (service, etc.).

abdomancy [rab′dō-man-si] n divination by rod or wands.

adamanthine [rad-a-man′thīn] adj rigorously just.

apsody [raps′o-di] n a portion of an epic poem adapted for recitation; any ecstatic or enthusiastic speech or writing; adjs rhapsodic [-od′ik] rhap′sodist.

esus monkey [rē′sùs] n a pale brown Indian monkey often used in medical research. — Rh factor, a genetically determined substance present in the red blood cells.

etoric [ret′ôr-ik] n the theory and practice of effective speaking and writing; skill in using speech; false, showy, or declamatory expression. — adj rhetor′ical, n rhetorician [ret-ôr-ish′(â)n].

eum [rōōm] n mucous discharge. — adj rheumat′ic. — n rheu′atism, diseases causing inflammation and pain in muscles, joints.

inoceros [rī-nos′ėr-os] n a family of large animals, having a very thick skin, and one or two horns on the nose.

ododendron [rō-dō-den′dron] n a genus of trees and shrubs of the heath family.

omb [rom(b)] n a rhombus; a rhombohedron. — pl rhomuses, rhombi; rhomboid, like a rhombus or rhomboid. — n a arallelogram whose adjacent sides are unequal and whose angles are not right angles.

ubarb [rōō′bärb] n a genus of plants, the leafstalks of which re used as food, and the root in medicine.

umb [rum] n a line or course on a single bearing; any point of he compass.

rhyme, rime [rīm] n the repetition of sounds usu at the ends of lines in verse; such poetry or verse or such correspondence of sound; a word corresponding with another in end sound. — vi to make (rhyming) verse; to form a rhyme. — vi to put into rhyme; to use as a rhyme. — ns rhy′mer, a versifier, a poetaster; a minstrel.

rhythm [riTHm] n regular recurrence of beat, accent or silence, in the flow of sound; pattern of recurring stresses in music. — adjs rhyth′mic, -al. — adv rhyth′mically.

rib¹ [rib] n one of the bones attached to the spine that curve around and forward enclosing the chest cavity; a curved member of the side of a ship running from keel to deck.

rib² vt (inf) to tease, ridicule, make fun of.

ribald [rib′áld] n a loose, low character. — adj low, licentious, foul-mouthed. — n rib′aldry, obscenity.

riband [rib′ánd] n a ribbon used esp as a decoration.

ribbon [rib′òn] n material woven in narrow bands or strips; (pl) torn shreds.

rice [rīs] n an annual cereal grass grown in warm climates; its grain, a valuable food. — ns rice′ pā′per, sliced and flattened pith of a small Asian tree or shrub.

rich [rich] adj abounding in possessions, wealthy; abounding (in, with); costly, splendid, elaborately decorated; fertile; deep in color; full-toned; full-flavored; abounding in oily ingredients. — adv rich′ly.

riches [rich′iz] n pl wealth.

rick [rik] n a stack of hay in the open.

rickets [rik′ėts] n sing a disease of children, characterized by softness of the bones. — adj rick′ety, rick′etty, affected with rickets; feeble; tottery, unsteady.

ricksha, rickshaw [rik′shô] n a small, two-wheeled, hooded vehicle drawn by a man, orig used in Japan.

ricochet [rik′ō-shā′] n a glancing rebound or skip, as an object striking a surface at an angle. — vi to make a ricochet

rid [rid] vt to free from, clear of, disencumber (of). — n rid-d′ance, clearance; deliverance.

riddle¹ [rid′l] n a puzzling question; anything puzzling. — vt to solve as a riddle; to set a riddle for.

riddle² [rid′l] n a coarse sieve. — vt to separate with a riddle; to make full of holes like a riddle.

ride [rīd] vi to travel or be borne on the back of an animal, on a bicycle, or in a vehicle; to float or move on the water; to lie at anchor. — vt to traverse on horseback, on bicycle, etc.; to control at will or oppressively. — n a journey on horseback, on bicycle, or in a vehicle; a thing to ride at an amusement park. — n rī′der, one who rides or can ride.

ridge [rij] n the back of an animal; the earth thrown up by the plough between the furrows; a long narrow top or crest; a narrow elevation; a hill range. — vti to form into ridges.

ridicule [rid′i-kūl] n derision, mockery. — vt to laugh at, to expose to merriment, to mock. — adj ridic′ulous, deserving or exciting ridicule.

rife [rīf] adj prevalent; abounding. — adv rife′ly.

riffraff [rif′raf] n disreputable persons; refuse, rubbish.

rifle¹ [rī′fl] vt to plunder thoroughly; to steal, carry away. — vi to engage in ransacking and stealing. — n rī′fler.

rifle² [rī′fl] vt to groove spirally within. — n a shoulder gun with spirally grooved barrel.

rift [rift] n a cleft; a fissure. — vti to cleave, split. — n rift′ valley, valley formed by subsidence of a portion of the earth's crust between two faults.

rig [rig] vt (naut) to fit with sails and tackle; to fit up or fit out; to set in working order. — n the way sails, etc., are rigged; equipment, gear; a tractor-trailer. — ns rigg′ing, tackle.

right [rīt] adj straight, direct; perpendicular; forming one-fourth of a revolution; (arch) true, genuine; truly judged or judging; in accordance, or identical, with what is true and fitting; not mistaken; just, normal, sane; conservative; designating the side meant to be seen. — adv straight; directly; exactly; in a right manner; to or on the right side. — n that which is right or correct; equity; truth; justice; just or legal claim; to set in order; to do justice to. — vi to recover an erect position. — adj right′ful. — adv right′ly.

righteous [rī′chùs] adj just, upright. — adv right′eously. — n right′eousness.

rigid [rij′id] adj stiff, unbending; rigorous, strict. — adv rig′idly. — ns rig′idness, rigid′ity.

rigmarole [rig'ma-rōl] *n* nonsense; a foolishly involved procedure.

rigor [ri'gòr] *n* harsh inflexibility; severity; strict precision; a tremor caused by a chill. — *adj* **rigorous.**

rile [rīl] *vt* (*inf*) to irritate, make angry.

rill [ril] *n* a very small brook. — *vi* to flow like a rill.

rim [rim] *n* a border, brim, edge, or margin, esp of something circular; the outer part of a wheel. — *adj* **rim'less.**

rime[1] [rīm] *n* a hoarfrost or frozen dew. — *adj* **rī'my.**

rime[2] *See* **rhyme.**

rind [rīnd] *n* bark; peel; crust; skin.

rinderpest [rin'dėr-pest] *n* a contagious virus disease of cattle.

ring[1] [ring] *n* a circlet or small hoop, esp one of metal, worn on the finger, in the ear, nose, or elsewhere; any object, mark, group, etc., circular but hollow in form. — *vt* to encircle; to put a ring on or in. — *vi* to move in rings; to gather or be in a ring. — *n* **ring'dove,** a common European pigeon; **ring'leader,** one who takes the lead in mischief; **ring'let,** a long curl of hair; **ring'worm,** a contagious skin disease.

ring[2] [ring] *vi* to give a metallic or bell-like sound; to sound aloud and clearly; to resound. — *vt* to cause to give a metallic or bell-like sound; to summon or announce by a bell or bells; to resound, proclaim; to call on the telephone.

rink [ringk] *n* an expanse of ice for skating; a smooth floor for roller-skating; an alley for lawn bowling.

rinse [rins] *vt* to wash lightly by pouring, shaking, or dipping; to wash in clean water to remove soap traces. — *n* an act of rinsing.

riot [rī'òt] *n* tumult; a disturbance of the peace by a crowd; an exuberance. — *vi* to take part in a riot. — *adj* **rī'otous.** — *adv* **rī'otously.**

rip [rip] *vt* to cut or tear apart roughly; to remove in this way; to sever the threads of. — *vi* to become ripped. — *n* a tear; a rent.

riparian [rī-pā'ri-àn] *adj* of, or inhabiting, a river bank, sometimes of a lake or tidewater.

ripe [rīp] *adj* ready for harvest; fully developed; mature; arrived at perfection, consummate; mature.

riposte [ri-pōst'] *n* a quick return thrust after a parry; a repartee; a retaliatory maneuver.

ripple [rip'l] *n* light fretting of the surface of a liquid; a little wave; a sound as of rippling water. — *vti* to have or form little waves on the surface (of).

rise [rīz] *vi* to get up; to stand up; to revolt; to move upward; to come up to the surface; to come above the horizon; to grow upward; to attain (to); to swell; to take origin; to tower; to slope up. — *n* rising; ascent; origin; an increase of salary, price, etc.; a sharpening of pitch.

risible [riz'i-bl] *adj* able or inclined to laugh; of laughter; ludicrous. — *n* **risibil'ity.**

risk [risk] *n* hazard; chance of loss or injury; person, thing, or factor likely to cause loss or danger. — *vt* to venture. — *adj* **risk'y.**

risotto [ri-sot'to] *n* dish of rice cooked in meat stock, mixed with savory ingredients, as chicken, onions.

rite [rīt] *n* a ceremonial form or observance, esp religious; a liturgy.

ritual [rit'ū-àl] *adj* relating to, or of the nature of, rites. — *n* manner of performing divine service, or a book containing it. — *ns* **rit'fialism** and **rit'fialist.**

rival [rī'vàl] *n* one pursuing an object in competition with another, one who strives to equal or excel another; one for whom, or that for which, a claim to equality might be made. — *adj* standing in competition. — *vt* to try to gain the same object as; to try to equal or excel. — *n* **rī'valry,** competition, emulation.

rive [rīv] *vt* to tear asunder; to split. — *vi* to tug, tear.

river [riv'ėr] *n* a natural stream of water flowing into an ocean, lake, etc.; something resembling a river; large quantities. — *ns* **river basin,** the area drained by a river and its tributaries; **riv'er horse,** a hippopotamus.

rivet [riv'et] *n* a bolt fastened by hammering the end. — *vt* to fasten with rivets; to fix immovably.

rivulet [riv'ū-let] *n* a little stream.

roach[1] [rōch] *n* cockroach.

roach[2] [rōch] *n* a silvery freshwater fish.

road [rōd] *n* a way made for traveling; a highway; a road-stead. — *ns* **road'house,** a tavern usu. outside the city limi providing meals; **road metal,** broken stones and cinders use in making and repairing roads; **road'stead,** a place near shore where ships may ride at anchor; **road'ster,** a horse fo riding or driving on roads; an automobile with an open bod that seats two; **road'way,** the strip of land over which a roa passes; a roadbed.

roam [rōm] *vi* to rove about; to ramble. — *vt* to wander over. — *n* **roam'er.**

roan [rōn] *adj* having a base color (as red, black, or brown thickly sprinkled with white or gray. — *n* an animal (as a horse with a roan coat.

roar [rōr, rör] *vi* to make a full, loud, hoarse, low-pitche sound, as a lion, fire, wind, the sea. — *vt* to utter, say, ve loudly. — *n* a sound of roaring.

roast [rōst] *vt* to cook (meat, etc.) with little or no moisture, a before an open fire or in an oven; to process (coffee, etc.) b exposure to heat; to expose to great heat; (*inf*) to criticiz harshly. — *adj* **roast.** — *vi* to undergo roasting. — *n* roaste meat; cut of meat for roasting; a picnic at which food roasted.

rob [rob] *vt* to deprive (of), esp wrongfully and forcibly; steal from; to plunder; to take as plunder. — *vi* to comm robbery. — *ns* **robb'er, robb'ery.**

robe [rōb] *n* a long loose outer garment; a dress of offic dignity, or state. — *vti,* to dress in a robe.

robin [rob'in] *n* a large N American thrush with a dull-re breast.

robot [rō'bot] *n* a mechanical device acting in a seemingl human way; a mechanism guided by automatic controls; a efficient, insensitive often brutalized person.

robust [rō-bust'] *adj* stout, strong, and sturdy.

roc [rok] *n* a fabulous bird of great size and strength believed inhabit the Indian Ocean area.

rock[1] [rok] *n* a large outstanding natural mass of stone; flavored stick candy with color running through; a sure foun dation or support. — *ns* Also **rock pigeon; rock garden,** garden among rocks for alpine plants. — *adj* **rock'y,** full rocks; like rock.

rock[2] [rok] *vti* to move to and fro, tilt from side to side; to sw strongly; to shake. — *ns* **rock'er,** either of the curved pieces which a cradle, etc., rocks; a chair mounted on such pieces. **rock and roll,** popular music usu. played on electronical amplified instruments with a heavily accented beat and cou try, folk, and blues elements.

rocket [rok'ėt] *n* any device driven forward by gases escapin through a rear vent as a firework, projectile, or the propulsi mechanism of a spacecraft. — *vi* to move in or like a rocke soar. — *n* **rock'etry.**

rococo [rō-ko'kō, rō-kō-kō'] *n* a style of architecture, deco ation, and furniture-making, any art in this style. — Also *adj.*

rod [rod] *n* a long straight shoot; a slender stick; a slender b of metal or other matter; a wand for magic, divination.

rodent [rō'dėnt] *n* any of an order of relatively small gnawi mammals (as a mouse, rat, squirrel, or a beaver).

rodeo [rō-dā'ō] *n* a round-up of cattle; an exhibition of cowb skill; a contest suggestive of a rodeo.

rodomontade [rod-ō-mon-tād'] *n* extravagant boasting; va bluster. — Also *adj.*

roe [rō] *n* the eggs or spawn of fishes.

roe deer [rō] *n* a species of small deer.

rogation [rō-gā'sh(ó)n] *n* an asking; supplication. — **Rogati days,** the three days before Ascension Day.

rogue [rōg] *n* a vagrant; a rascal; a wag, a mischievous person sport, or variation from type. — *vt* to cheat; to eliminate rogu from. — *n* **roguery** [rōg'ér-i]. — *adj* **roguish** [rōg'ish].

roister [rois'tėr] *vi* to bluster, swagger, revel noisily. — *n* rois terer.

role, rôle [rōl] *n* a part played by an actor or other; a functi assumed by someone else.

roll [rōl] *n* a scroll; a sheet of paper or other material wou upon itself into cylindrical form; a revolving cylinder; a sm cake of bread; act of rolling; a trill of some birds, esp canary. — *vi* to move like a ball, a wheel, a wheeled vehicle, a passenger in one; to turn on an axis; to turn over or fr side to side; to sound with a roll; to undulate; to curl. — *v cause to roll; to turn on an axis; to wrap round on itself;

press or smooth with a roller or between rollers; to beat rapidly, as a drum. —ns **roll' call**, the calling of a list of names to ascertain attendance; **roll'er**, a revolving or rolling cylinder used for grinding, rolling, etc.; a long heavy wave; **roll'er skate**, **roll'ing stock**, all the vehicles of a railroad or trucking company.

rollicking [rol'ik-ing] adj careless, swaggering, exuberantly gay or jovial.

roly-poly [rōl'i-pōl'i] n a dessert made of a sheet of paste, covered with jam or fruit, and rolled up; a round podgy person.

Roman [rō'mân] adj pertaining to Rome, esp ancient Rome, its people, or the empire founded by them; **roman** (of type) of the ordinary upright kind. —n a native or citizen of Rome; a Roman Catholic. —adj **Roman'ic**, **Romance**. —vt **Ro'manize**, to make Roman or Roman Catholic; **Roman numerals**, the letters I, V, X, L, C, D, and M used to represent numbers in the manner of the Romans.

Romance [rō-mans'] adj of the languages that developed out of popular Latin: French, Provençal, Italian, Spanish, Portuguese, Rumanian, Romansch and Catalan, with their various dialects. —Also —n **romance**, a tale of chivalry, orig one in verse, written in one of the Romance tongues; any fictitious and wonderful tale; a fictitious narrative in prose or verse which passes beyond the limits of ordinary life; a love story, romantic fiction as a branch of literature. —vi to write or tell romances; to talk extravagantly; to lie. —n **roman'cer**.

romantic [rō-man'tik] adj pertaining to, inclining toward, or suggesting, romance; fictitious; extravagant, fantastic. —ns **roman'ticism** [-sizm].

Romany [rom'â-ni] n a gypsy; the language of the gypsies. —adj gypsy.

romp [romp] vi to frolic actively. —n a child or girl who romps; a vigorous frolic; a swift, easy run.

rondeau [ron'dō] n a French verse form freely adapted by many English poets, the traditional rondeau consisting of 15 tetrameter lines divided into three stanzas; (mus) an instrumental form of the 17th century. —ns **ron'del**, a similar form of French verse, consisting of thirteen or fourteen lines in iambic pentameter, **ron'do**, a musical form often used for the final movement of classical sonatas, string quartets, symphonies, and concertos.

rood [rōōd] n Christ's cross, esp a cross or crucifix, esp at the entrance to the chancel of a medieval church.

roof [rōōf] n the top covering of a building or vehicle; a ceiling; an upper limit. —vt to cover with a roof; to be the roof of.

rook¹ [rōōk] n a gregarious species of crow —n **rook'ery**, a breeding place of rooks in a group of trees; a breeding ground.

rook² [rōōk] n (chess) a piece with the power to move horizontally or vertically. —Also **castle**.

rookie [rōōk'i] n (slang) an inexperienced army recruit; any novice. —Also **rooky**.

room [rōōm] n space; necessary or available space; space unoccupied; stead; a compartment of a house, a chamber. —adj **room'y**, having ample room, wide, spacious.

roost [rōōst] n a perch or place for a sleeping bird; a sleeping place. —vi to settle or sleep on a roost or perch. —n **roost'er**, an adult male domestic fowl.

root¹ [rōōt] n the part of a plant, usu. underground, that anchors the plant, draws water from the soil, etc.; the embedded part of a tooth, a hair, etc.; a supporting or essential part; something that is an origin or source. —vi to take root; to be firmly established. —vt to fix the roots of in the earth; to implant deeply.

root² [rōōt] vt to turn up with the snout. —vi to grub; to search about.

rope [rōp] n a thick twisted cord of fibers or wires. —vt to fasten, enclose, or mark off, with a rope. —ns **ropedanc'er**, a tightrope performer; **rope'walk**, a long narrow shed or alley where ropes are manufactured; **rope'walker**, an acrobat that walks on a rope high in the air. —adj **rō'py**, stringy; glutinous.

rorqual [rōr'kwàl] n any of several large whalebone wales esp the blue whale.

rosary [rō'zàr-i] n a string of beads used in counting prayers.

rose [rōz] n the flower of a plant of many species; emblem of the US; a rosette; a perforated nozzle; pinkish red or purplish red; (pl) a comfortable situation or an easy task. —adjs **roseàte**

[rō'zė-āt], rosy; overly optimistic. —ns **rō'sery**, a place where roses are grown; **rose'wood**, heavy dark-colored wood streaked with black of various tropical trees. —adj **rō'sy**, of the color of roses; blooming; blushing; bright, hopeful.

rosemary [rōz'má-ri] n a fragrant shrubby mint.

rosin [roz'in] n a resin obtained eg when turpentine is prepared from dead pine wood.

roster [rōs'tèr, ros'-] n a list or roll, as of military personnel.

rostrum [ros'trum] n a beak; pl rostrums, rostra, a platform for public speaking.

rot [rot] vti to putrefy; to decay. —n decay; putrefaction; corruption; (slang) nonsense.

Rota [rō'ta] .—adj **rotary** [rō'tàr-i], turning like a wheel; having parts that rotate; resembling the motion of a wheel. — vti **rōtāte'**, to turn like a wheel; to put, take, go, or succeed in rotation. —n **rotā'tion**.

rote [rōt] n a fixed, mechanical way of doing something. —**by rote**, by memory alone, without regard to the meaning.

rotor [rō'tôr] n a rotating part, esp of a dynamo, motor, or turbine.

rotund [rō-tund'] adj round; rounded; nearly spherical. —ns **rotund'a**, a round (esp domed) room, **rotund'ity**.

rouge [rōōzh] n a powder used to color the cheeks or lips; a red polishing powder for jewelry, etc.

rough [ruf] adj uneven; rugged; unshorn; unpolished; harsh; crude; unfinished; coarse in texture; unrefined; ungentle; turbulent; approximate; (inf) difficult. —n untended ground; (golf) any part of the course with grass, etc. left uncut; a preliminary sketch. —vt to make rough; to shape or depict roughly. —n **rough'age**, rough or coarse food or fodder, as bran, straw, etc. —vt **rough'cast**, to shape roughly; to cover with roughcast. —n plaster mixed with small stones, used to coat buildings. —n **roughhouse**, (slang) a disturbance, a brawl; boisterous play. —adv **rough'ly**. —ns **roughneck**, (slang) an unmannerly lout; a hooligan.

rouleau [rōō-lō] n a little roll, esp a roll of coins put up in paper.

roulette [rōōl-et'] n a game of chance.

round [rownd] adj having a curved outline or surface; circular, globular, or cylindrical in form; plump; full; considerable. — adv about; on all sides; in a ring; from one to another successively; Also **around**. —prep on every side of; so as to encircle; in the vicinity of; in a circuit through. —vt to make round; to make plump; to express as a round number; to complete; to go or pass around. —vi to make a circuit; to turn; to reverse direction; to become plump. —adj **round'about**, circuitous; indirect. —n (Brit) a merry-go-round; a circuitous route. —adv **round'ly**. —n **round trip**, a trip to a place and back again. —n **roundup**, a driving together, as all the cattle in a ranch, a set of persons wanted for the police, etc.

roundel [rown'dl] n a round figure or object; a rondeau, a rondel.

rouse¹ [rowz] vt to start; to stir up; to awaken; to excite, to anger; to put in action. —vi to awake; **rous'ing**, stirring.

rouse² [rowz] n a carousal.

rout¹ [rowt] n a tumultuous crowd, a rabble; a pack, herd, flock; a defeated body; an utter defeat; disorderly flight. —vt to defeat utterly; to put to disorderly flight.

route [rōōt, rowt] n a course to be traversed. —vt to fix the route of; to send (by a particular route).

routine [rōō-tēn'] n regular, unvarying, or mechanical course of action or round.

rove [rōv] vti to roam. —n **rō'ver**, a wanderer; (usu pl) a random or long-distance target in archery.

row¹ [rō] n a line or rank of persons or things a series in line, or in ordered succession.

row² [rō] vti to impel with an oar; to transport by rowing. —n an act or instance of rowing.

row³ [row] n a noisy squabble, a brawl; a din, hubbub.

rowan [row'ân, also rō'ân] n an American mountain ash.

rowdy [row'di] n a noisy turbulent person. —Also adj. —ns **rowd'iness; rowd'yism**.

rowel [row'èl] n a little spiked wheel on a spur.

royal [roi'âl] adj of a king or queen; like, or fit for, a king or queen; magnificent; founded, chartered, or patronized by a king or queen. —adv **roy'ally**. —n **roy'alty**, the rank or power of a king or queen; a royal person or persons; royal quality; a share of the proceeds from a patent, book, song, etc. paid to the owner, author, composer, etc.

rub [rub] *vt* to move something with pressure along the surface of; to clean, polish, or smooth, by friction; to remove, erase, or obliterate by friction. — *vi* to move with friction, to chafe, to grate. — *n* **rubb′er**, one who, or that which, rubs or massages; an eraser; an elastic substance made from the milky sap of various tropical plants or synthetically; a rubber overshoe. — *n* **rubb′er stamp**, an instrument for stamping by hand with ink.

rubber[1] *See* **rub**.

rubber[2] [rub′ér] *n* a contest consisting of an odd number of games won by the side that takes a majority (as two out of three).

rubbish [rub′ish] *n* waste matter; litter; trash; nonsense. — *adj* **rubb′ishy**, worthless.

rubble [rub′l] *n* loose fragments of rock of ruined buildings; undressed irregular stones used in rough masonry; masonry of such a kind.

rubicund [rŏŏ′bi-kund] *adj* ruddy. — *n* **rubicun′dity**.

rubric [rŏŏ′brik] *n* a heading, entry, or liturgical direction often in red; any rule, explanatory comment, etc. — *adj* in red; ruddy. — *adj* **ru′brical**.

ruby [rŏŏ′bi] *n* a highly-prized precious stone of a deep red color. — *adj* red as a ruby.

ruche [rŏŏsh] *n* a pleated, gathered, or fluted piece of fabric used as trimming. — *adj* **ruched**.

ruck[1] [ruk] *n* a wrinkle, fold, or crease. — *vti* to wrinkle.

ruck[2] [ruk] *n* the usual run of persons or things; the persons or things following the vanguard.

rucksack [ruk′-sak] *n* a bag carried on the back by hikers.

rudder [rud′ér] *n* a steering apparatus; a flat structure hinged to the stern of a ship or boat for steering.

ruddy [rud′i] *adj* red; reddish; of the color of the skin in health. — *adv* **rudd′ily**. — *n* **rudd′iness**.

rude [rŏŏd] *adj* uncultured; unskilled; ungentle, harsh; crude, coarse. — *adv* **rude′ly**. — *n* **rude′ness**.

rudiment [rŏŏd′i-mént] *n* a first principle or element; a first slight beginning of something. **rudiment′ary**, of rudiments; elementary.

rue[1] [rŏŏ] *n* a strong-smelling Mediterranean shrub.

rue[2] [rŏŏ] *n* (*arch*) sorrow. — *vti* feel remorse for; to regret. — *adj* **rue′ful**. — *adv* **rue′fully**.

ruff[1] [ruf] *n* a frill, worn round the neck, a frilled appearance on the neck of a bird or animal.

ruff[2] [ruf] *n* the act of trumping. — *vti* to trump.

ruffian [ruf′i-án, -yán] *n* a brutal, violent person; a bully. — *adj* brutal; violent. — *n* **ruff′ianism**.

ruffle [ruf′l] *vt* to make uneven, disturb the smoothness of; to wrinkle; to disorder; to agitate, to disturb the equanimity of.

rufous [rŏŏ′fus] *adj* reddish.

rug [rug] *n* a thick heavy fabric used as a floor covering.

rugged [rug′id] *adj* rough; uneven, massively irregular; unpolished; strong, robust. — *adv* **rugg′edly**. — *n* **rugg′edness**.

rugose [rŏŏ′gōs′] *adj* wrinkled.

ruin [rŏŏ′in] *n* (*pl*) the remains of something destroyed, decayed, etc.; downfall; cause of ruin. — *vt* to reduce or bring to ruin; destroy; spoil; bankrupt. — *vi* to come to ruin. — *n* **ruinā′tion**. — *adj* **ru′inous**.

rule [rŏŏl] *n* an instrument used in drawing straight lines; a ruler; government; a straight line; a regulation, an order. — *vt* as with a ruler; to govern, to manage. — *n* **ru′ler**, one who governs; a strip of wood, etc. with a straight edge, used in drawing lines, measuring, etc.

rum [rum] *n* a spirit distilled from fermented sugarcane juice, molasses, etc.

rumba [rum′ba] *n* a dance of Cuban Negro origin.

rumble [rum′bl] *vti* to make or cause to make a low heavy grumbling or rolling noise; to move with such a sound. — *n* a sound of rumbling.

ruminant [rŏŏ′mi-nánt] *n* an animal, as cattle, deer, camels, etc., that chews the cud. — *vi* **ru′mināte**, to chew the cud; to meditate. — *n* **ruminā′tion**.

rummage [rum′ij] *n* odds and ends; a thorough search. — *vti*.

rummer [rum′ér] *n* a large footed drinking glass.

rummy [rum′i] *n* any of certain card games.

rumor [rŏŏ′môr] *n* hearsay, general talk not based on definite knowledge; an unconfirmed report, story. — *vt* to put about by rumor.

rump [rump] *n* the hind part of an animal's body, the root of the tail with parts adjoining; the buttocks.

rumple [rum′pl] *n* a fold or wrinkle. — *vti* to crush.

rumpus [rum′pus] *n* an uproar, a disturbance.

run [run] *vi* to go swiftly; to flee; to go by moving the legs faster than in walking; to hurry; to ply (from, to, between); to proceed through a sequence of operations, or go, as a machine; to follow a course; to be current; to be valid; to compete in a race, election, etc. — *vt* to cause to run; to drive into a specified condition, place, etc.; in a newspaper. — *n* an act, spell, or manner of running; a trip; distance or time of running; a continuous stretch or series; a brook; ravel, as in a stocking; course; prevalence; the usual kind; a spell of being in general demand; an enclosure for chickens, etc.; freedom of access to all parts. **runn′er-up**, the competitor next after the winner or winners. — *n* **run′way**, track or channel along which something moves, esp a strip of leveled ground used by airplanes in taking off and landing.

runagate [run′á-gāt] *n* a vagabond.

rune [rŏŏn] *n* a letter of the ancient Germanic alphabet.

rung[1] [rung] *n* a spoke; a crossbar or rail; a ladder round or step.

runnel [run′l] *n* a little stream; a brook.

runt [runt] *n* an unusually small animal, esp the smallest of a litter of pigs; a person of small stature.

rupee [rŏŏ-pē′] *n* the unit of money in India.

rupture [rup′-chûr] *n* a breach, breaking, or bursting; the state of being broken; hernia. — *vti* to cause or suffer a rupture.

rural [rŏŏ′rál] *adj* of the country. — *adv* **ru′rally**.

ruse [rŏŏz] *n* a trick, stratagem, artifice.

rush[1] [rush] *vti* to move, push, drive, etc. swiftly or impetuously; to make a sudden attack (on); to pass, go, send, do, act, etc. with unusual haste; to hurry. — *adj* requiring or marked by special speed or urgency; haste suggesting this; a hurry.

rush[2] [rush] *n* a grasslike marsh-growing plant; a stalk of such a plant. — *ns* **rush′ cand′le**, **rush′light**, a candle consisting of the pith of a rush dipped in grease.

rusk [rusk] *n* a sweet or plain bread baked, sliced, and baked again until dry and crisp.

russet [rus′ét] *n* a coarse homespun usu. reddish brown cloth; a reddish-brown color; a winter apple having a russet rough skin.

rust [rust] *n* the reddish-brown coating on iron or steel exposed to moisture; any stain resembling this; any plant disease characterized by rusty blotches caused by fungi; the color of rust. — *vti* to form rust (on); to deteriorate, as through disuse. — *adj* **rust′y**, *adjs* **rust′less**; **rust′proof**.

rustic [rus′tik] *adj* of, or characteristic of, the country; simple or artless; rough or uncouth. — *n* a country person. — *adv* **rust′ically**. — *vti* **rust′icate**. — *ns* **rusticā′tion**.

rustle[1] [rus′l] *vti* to make a soft, whispering sound, as of dry leaves. — *n* a quick succession of small sounds.

rustle[2] [rus′l] *vi* to act energetically. — *vt* to steal, esp cattle. — *n* **rust′ler**, a hustler; a cattle thief.

rut[1] [rut] *n* a furrow made by wheels; a fixed course difficult to depart from. — *vt* to furrow with ruts.

rut[2] [rut] *n* sexual excitement in male deer; also in other animals. — *vi* to be in heat.

ruth [rŏŏth] *n* pity, sorrow, remorse. — *adj* **ruth′less**, pitiless. — *adv* **ruth′lessly**.

rye [rī] *n* a hardy annual grass; its grain, used for making bread, ect.; rye whiskey. — *ns* **rye′grass**, any of several grasses used widely as pasture and as cover crops.

S

Sabbath [sab′ath] *n* among the Jews, Saturday, set apart for rest from work; among most Christians, Sunday; a time of rest. — *adj* of, or appropriate to, the Sabbath. — *n* **Sabbatā′rian**, a very strict observer of the Sabbath on Saturday.

saber, sabre [sā′bér] *n* a heavy one-edged sword, slightly curved towards the point, used by cavalry.

sable [sā'bl] *n* a carnivorous mammal of arctic regions valued for its glossy fur; its fur; black.

sabot [sab'ō] *n* a wooden shoe, worn in various European countries.—*n* **sabotage** deliberate destruction of machinery, etc.—*n* **saboteur**.

sac [sak] *n* (*biol*) a pouch within a plant or animal.

saccharine [sak'a-rin, -rēn] *adj* pertaining to, or having the qualities of, sugar; yielding or containing sugar.

sacerdotal [sas-èr-dō'tál] *adj* priestly.

sachet [sa'shā] *n* a small bag or packet; a small perfumed packet used to scent clothes.

sack¹ [sak] *n* a large bag of coarse cloth material for holding grain, flour, etc.; (*slang*) to dismiss (a person).—**get the sack**, to be dismissed from a post, esp summarily; **give the sack**, to dismiss.

sack² [sak] *n* the plunder or devastation of a town.—*vt* to plunder; to strip of valuables.—*n* **sack'ing**, the storming and pillaging of a town.

sack³ [sak] *n* a dry white Spanish wine.

sackbut [sak'but] *n* medieval trombone.

sacrament [sak'rá-mènt] *n* any of certain Christian rites, as baptism, the Eucharist, marriage, etc.—*adj* **sacramen'tal**.

sacred [sā'krid] *adj* holy; dedicated to a god or God; having to do with religion; worthy of religious veneration; not to be violated; **sā'credness**.—*n* **sā'credness**.

sacrifice [sak'ri-fīs] *n* the act of sacrificing or offering to a deity, that which is sacrificed or offered; destruction or surrender of anything to gain an important end; that which is surrendered or destroyed for such an end.—*adj* **sacrifi'cial**.—*adv* **sacrifi'cially**.

sacrilege [sak'ri-lèj] *n* profanation of anything holy.—*adj* **sacrilegious**.

sacristan [sak'ris-tàn] *n* an officer in a church who has charge of the sacred vessels and other movables.—**sãc'risty**, a room in a church where the sacred utensils, vestments, etc., are kept.

sacrosanct [sak'rō-sang(k)t] *adj* inviolable, that must not be profaned; holy and worthy of reverence.

sad [sad] *adj* expressing grief or unhappiness; sorrowful, dejected; regrettable, calamitous; deplorable; of a dull somber color.—*vt* **sadd'en**.—*adv* **sad'ly**.

saddle [sad'l] *n* a seat for a rider on a horse, bicycle, etc. a ridge connecting two higher elevations; a cut of lamb.—*vt* to put a saddle on, to load; to encumber; to fix the responsibility for.—*ns* **sadd'lebag**, a bag carried at or attached to the saddle; **sadd'lebow** the arched front of a saddle or the pieces forming it; **sadd'le horse**, a horse suitable for riding; **sadd'ler**, a maker or seller of saddles; **sadd'lery**, occupation of a saddler; **sadd'letree**, the frame of a saddle.

Sadducee [sad'ū-sē] *n* ancient Jewish priesthood that accepted only the doctrines in the written Law.

sadism [sad'- or säd'izm] *n* a perversion in which pleasure is obtained by mistreating others; pleasure in inflicting or watching cruelty.—*n* **sad'ist**.—*adj* **sadis'tic**.

safari [sa-fä'ri] *n* the caravan and equipment of a hunting expedition, esp in eastern Africa.

safe [sāf] *adj* unharmed; free from danger; secure; not involving risk; trustworthy; giving protection; cautious.—*n* a locking metal container for valuables.—*ns* **safe'-con'duct**, a writing, passport, or guard granted to a person to enable him to travel with safety, **safe'guard**, anything that increases security or averts danger; a guard, passport, or warrant to protect a traveler.—*vt* to protect.—*n* **safe'keep'ing**, protection; custody.—*adv* **safe'ly**.—*ns* **safe'ness**; **safety**.

saffron [saf'rón] *n* a crocus with purple flowers; a coloring and flavoring substance prepared from its yellow stigmas; orange yellow.

sag [sag] *vi* to bend, sink or droop, esp in the middle; to hang down unevenly; to yield or give way as from weight or pressure.

saga [sä'ga] *n* a medieval Scandinavian story of battles, legends, etc.; any long story of heroic deeds.

sagacious [sa-gā'shùs] *adj* keen in perception or thought, shrewd, having practical wisdom.

sage¹ [sāj] *n* a plant of the mint family with leaves used for seasoning meats, etc.

sage² [sāj] *adj* wise through reflection and experience.—*n* a man of great wisdom.—*adv* **sage'ly**.

Sagittarius [saj-i-tār'i-us] *n* the Archer, the 9th sign of the zodiac; in astrology, operative November 22 to December 20.

sago [sā'gō] *n* a starch produced from sago palm used in foods and as textile stiffening.

sahib [sä'ib] *n* a term of respect given in colonial India to Europeans of rank.

said [sed] *pt, pt p* of **say**.—*adj* aforesaid.

sail [sāl] *n* a sheet of canvas, etc., spread to catch the wind, by which a ship is driven forward; sails collectively; anything like a sail; a trip in a vessel.—*vt* to move upon in a vessel; to manage (a vessel).—*ns* **sail'boat**, a boat that is propelled by means of a sail or sails; **sail'cloth**, a strong cloth for sails, tents, etc.; **sail'er**, a boat or ship with respect to its mode of sailing, or its speed; **sail'ing**, act of sailing; motion of a vessel on water; **sail'or**, one who sails in a ship.

sainfoin [sān'foin] *n* a leguminous forage plant.

saint [sānt] *n* a holy person; a person who is exceptionally patient, charitable, etc.; one canonized by the RC Church.

sake¹ [sāk] *n* purpose, motive (eg *for the sake of peace, argument*); behalf, advantage (eg *for my, pity's, sake*).

sake² [sä'ki] *n* an alcoholic beverage made by the Japanese from fermented rice.

salacious [sal-ā'shùs] *adj* lustful, lecherous; obscene.

salad [sal'àd] *n* a dish, usu. cold, of fruits, vegetables, meat, eggs, etc. usu. mixed with salad dressing.

salamander [sal'a-man-dèr or -man'-] *n* any of numerous scaleless, tailed amphibians.

salami [sa-lä'mi] *n* a highly seasoned sausage of dried or fresh pork or beef.

salary [sal'á-ri] *n* periodical payment at a fixed rate for services.—*adj* **sal'aried**, receiving a salary.

sale [sāl] *n* act of selling; the exchange of anything for money; power or opportunity of selling; an auction; a public offer of goods to be sold, esp at reduced prices.—*n* **saleable**, fit to be sold; easy to sell; in good demand.—*n* **salabil'ity**.—*ns* **sales'man**, one who sells either in a given territory or in a store; **sales'manship**, the art of selling.

Salic law [säl'ik lô] a rule limiting succession to males.

salient [sä'li-ènt] *adj* leaping or springing; (*fort*) projecting outwards, as an angle; outstanding, prominent, striking.—*adv* **sä'liently**.

saline [sä'lēn or sä'līn] *adj* consisting of, or containing, salt; partaking of the qualities of salt.—*n* a metallic salt; a saline solution.

saliva [sa-lī'va] *n* the watery fluid secreted by glands in the mouth which aids in digestion.—*adj* **sa'livary**.

sallow¹ [sal'ō] *n* a willow (as *Salix caprea*) esp of the broad-leaved kind with comparatively brittle twigs.

sallow² [sal'ō] *adj* of a grayish, greenish, yellow color.—*n* **sall'owness**.

sally [sal'i] *n* a leap; a sudden rush forth to attack besiegers; excursion; outburst (of fancy, wit, etc.)—*vi* to rush out suddenly; to set forth, issue.

salmon [sam'ón] *n* a large game and food fish with silvery sides and delicate flesh, that lives in salt water and spawns in fresh water.

salon [sal'õ] *n* a large reception hall or drawing room; a fashionable reception, esp a periodic gathering of notable persons, in the house of an eminent hostess.

saloon [sa-lōōn'] *n* a large public room for holding salons, receptions, etc.; a large cabin for the social use of a ship's passengers; a room or establishment where alcoholic drinks are sold and consumed.

salsify [sal'si-fi] *n* a biennial plant whose long and tapering root has a flavor resembling oysters.

salt [sôlt] *n* a white crystalline substance, sodium chloride, or common salt, used for seasoning, either found in natural beds or obtained by evaporation from brine, etc.; seasoning; piquancy, esp pungent wit; that which preserves from corruption.—*adv* **salt'ly**.

saltcellar [sôlt'sel-är] *n* a small vessel for holding salt at the table; a saltshaker.

saltire [sal'tīr, sôl'-] *n* a diagonal cross, also called a St Andrew's Cross.

saltpeter [sôlt-pē'tèr] *n* potassium nitrate, niter.

saltshaker [sŏlt′shā′kèr] *n* a small container for salt, with a perforated top.

salubrious [sa-lōō′bri-ús] *adj* healthful; wholesome. — *adv* **sal-u′briously.**

salutary [sal′ū-tàr-i] *adj* promoting health; beneficial. — *adv* **sal′ūtarily.** — *n* **sal′ūtariness.**

salute [sal-ūt′] *vt* to greet with words or a gesture to honor by performing a prescribed act, such as raising the hand to the head, in military and naval practice; to commend. — *n* **salūtā′tion.**

salvage [sal′vij] *n* reward paid for saving or rescuing a ship or cargo from danger or loss; the act of saving a ship or cargo, or of saving goods from fire, etc.; goods so saved.

salvation [sal-vā′sh(ó)n] *n* the act of saving; means of preservation from evil; (*theol*) the saving of man from the power and penalty of sin. — *n* **Salvā′tionist,** a soldier or officer of the Salvation Army; **salvationist,** an evangelist.

salve[1] [salv] *vt* to salvage.

salve[2] [säv, also salv] *n* an ointment; a remedy; anything to soothe the feelings or conscience. — *vt* to anoint; to heal; to soothe.

salver [sal′vèr] *n* a tray, esp for serving food or drink.

salvo [sal′vō] *n* a simultaneous discharge of artillery, or of bombs; a sudden burst.

same [säm] *adj* identical; not different; unchanged; mentioned before. — *pron* the same person or thing. — *adv* in like manner. — *n* **same′ness,** the being the same; tedious monotony.

samite [sam′īt] *n* a heavy medieval silk fabric.

samovar [sam′ō-vär, -vär′] *n* an urn with a spigot at its base and an internal tube for heating water used esp in Russia to boil water for tea.

sampan [sam′pan] *n* a flat-bottomed Chinese skiff propelled by two short oars.

sample [säm′pl] *n* a specimen; a small portion to show the quality of the whole; an example. — *vt* to make up samples of; to test or estimate by taking a sample. — *n* **sam′pler.**

sampler [säm′plèr] *n* a piece of ornamental embroidery, containing names, figures, texts, etc. in different stitches as an example of skill.

sanative [san′á-tiv] *adj* tending, or able, to heal, healing. — *n* **sanator′ium.**

sanctify [sang(k)′ti-fī] *vt* to make sacred or holy, to set apart to sacred use; to free from sin or evil; to make efficient as the means of holiness. — *pt, pt p* **sanc′tified.** — *ns* **sanctificā′tion,** act of sanctifying; state of being sanctified; **sanc′tifier.** — *adj* **sanctimō′nious,** simulating or pretending holiness. — *adv* **sanctimō′niously.** — *ns* **sanctimō′niousness, sanc′timony,** affected devoutness, show of sanctity; **sanctity** quality of being sacred or holy, purity, godliness.

sanction sang(k)′sh(ó)n] *n* a law, decree; act of ratifying, or giving authority to; permission, countenance (eg of social custom).

sand [sand] *n* a mass of fine particles of crushed or worn rocks; (*pl*) land covered with sand; a sandy beach; moments of a lifetime. — *vt* to sprinkle or fill with sand; to smooth or polish, as with sandpaper. — *n* **sand′bag,** a bag filled with sand used for ballast, to protect levees, etc. — *ns* **sand′bank,** a sand bar; a large deposit of sand forming a hill or mound; **sand′paper,** a paper coated on one side with sand or another abrasive, used for smoothing and polishing. — *vt* to rub with sandpaper. **sand′storm** a windstorm driving clouds of sand before it. — *adj* **sand′y,** of, like, or sprinkled with sand; yellowish-gray.

sandal [san′d(á)l] *n* a sole bound to the foot by straps; any of various low slippers or shoes. — *adj* **san′daled,** wearing sandals.

sandalwood [san′d(á)l-wŏŏd] *n* the compact, close-grained, fragrant heart-wood of a parasitic tree.

sandwich [san(d)′-wich] *n* two slices of bread with any sort of food between; anything in like arrangement.

sane [sān] *adj* sound in mind; rational, sensible. — *adv* **sane′ly.**

sangfroid [sä-frwä′] *n* coolness, composure, absence of excitement.

sanguinary [sang′gwin-àr-i] *adj* attended with much bloodshed; bloodthirsty.

sanguine [sang′gwin] *adj* bloodred; ruddy; ardent, hopeful,

cheerfully confident. — *adv* **san′guinely,** hopefully, confidently. — *n* **san′guineness.** — *adj* **sanguin′eous.**

sanitary [san′i-tàr-i] *adj* pertaining to the promotion of health; of drainage and sewage disposal; characterized by or readily kept in cleanliness.

sanity [san′i-ti] *n* state of being sane; soundness of judgment.

sank [sangk] *pt* of **sink.**

Sanskrit [sans′krit] *n* an ancient Indo-European language which was the literary language also used by educated persons about the 4th century BC;.

Santa Claus [san′ta klōz] *n* a fat white-bearded old fellow who brings good children Christmas presents.

sap[1] [sap] *n* juice, esp the vital juice of plants. — *vt* to drain or withdraw the sap from; to knock out with a sap. — *adj* **sap′less.** — *n* **sap′ling.**

sap[2] [sap] *n* the extension of a trench from within the trench itself to a point within the enemy's fortifications.

sapid [sap′id] *adj* perceptible by taste; having a strong agreeable flavor.

sapience [sā′pi-èns] *n* discernment, judgment, wisdom. — *adj* **sā′pient,** wise, sagacious. — *adv* **sā′piently.**

saponaceous [sap-o-nā′shús] *adj* soapy; resembling soap.

Sapphic [saf′ik] *adj* pertaining to *Sappho,* a Greek lyric poet (*c* 600 BC), or to her poetry.

sapphire [saf′īr] *n* a brilliant precious stone, a variety of corundum, of deep clear blue.

saprophagous [sap-rof′á-gús] *adj* feeding on decaying organic matter.

saprophyte [sap′rō-fīt] *n* any plant that feeds upon decaying organic matter. — *adj* **saprophytic.**

sarcasm [sär′kazm] *n* a satirical remark in scorn or contempt, esp one worded ironically; the tone or language of such sayings; the use of such. — *adj* **sarcas′tic,** containing sarcasm; given to sarcasm. — *adv* **sarcas′tically.**

sarcenet, sarsenet [sär′snèt] *n* a soft thin silk in plain or twill weaves.

sarcophagus [sär-kof′a-gus] *n* a stone coffin; a tomb. — *pl* **sarcoph′agi, sarcoph′aguses.**

sard [särd] *n* a deep-red chalcedony, sometimes classed as carnelian.

sardine [sär-dēn′] *n* a young pilchard.

sardonic [sär-don′ik] *adj* forced, heartless, or bitter (said of a laugh, smile, etc.). — *adv* **sardon′ically.**

sardonyx [sär′do-niks] *n* an onyx with layers of cornelian or sard.

sargasso [sär-gas′ō] *n* a mass of floating vegetation and esp sargassum. — *n* **sargassum.**

sari, saree [sär′ē] *n* a Hindu woman's chief garment, wrapped round the waist and passed over the shoulder.

sarong [sä-rong′] *n* a loose skirt made of a long strip of cloth wrapped around the body.

sartorial [sär-tō′ ri-ál] *adj* pertaining to a tailor or tailoring; of men's dress.

sash[1] [sash] *n* a band or scarf worn round the waist or over the shoulder.

sash[2] [sash] *n* a frame, esp a sliding frame, for panes of glass.

sat [sat] *pt, pt p* of **sit.**

Satan [sā′tän] *n* the adversary of God and lord of evil in Judaism and Christianity. — *adj* **sătan′ic.**

satchel [sach′él] *n* a small bag for carrying clothes, books, etc.

sate [sāt] *vt* to satisfy fully; to glut.

sateen [sa-tēn′] *n* a glossy fabric of cotton made to imitate satin.

satellite [sat′èl-īt] *n* an attendant of some important person; a small planet revolving round one of the larger planets; a man-made object put into orbit around the earth, moon, etc.; a small state economically dependent on a larger one.

satiate [sā′shi-āt] *vt* to provide with more than enough, so as to weary or disgust; to glut. — *adj* **sā′tiable.**

satin [sat′in] *n* a closely woven silk with a lustrous and unbroken surface on one side. — *adj* made of satin; resembling satin.

satire [sat′ir] *n* a literary composition, orig in verse, essentially a criticism of folly or vice, which it holds up to ridicule or scorn; cutting comment; ridicule. — *adjs* **satir′ic, -al.**

satisfy [sat′is-fī] *vt* to give enough to; to supply fully and hence appease; to pay in full; to meet in full. — *vi* to give content, leave nothing to be desired.—*pt, pt p* **sat'isfied.**—*n* **satisfac'-tion.**—*adj* **satisfactory.**—*adv* **satisfac'torily.**—*n* **satisfac'toriness.**

satsuma [sat-sōō'ma, sat'sōō-ma] *n* a thin-skinned seedless type of mandarin orange or its tree.

saturate [sat'ū-rāt] *vt* to impregnate (with); to unite with till no more can be absorbed; to soak; to fill completely; to pervade; to surfeit.—*adjs* **sat'urable**, that may be saturated; **sat'urate**, **sat'urated**, charged to the fullest extent; pure in color.—*n* **satūrā'tion.**

Saturday [sat'ūr-dā] *n* the seventh and last day of the week.

Saturn [sat'ūrn] *n* the ancient Roman god of agriculture; the second largest planet in the solar system, with three rings revolving about it.

satyr [sat'ėr] *n* a sylvan deity, represented as part man and part goat, a lecherous man.

sauce [sös] *n* a liquid or soft dressing poured over food; anything that gives relish; stewed or preserved fruit eaten with other food or as a dessert.

saucer [sö'sėr] *n* a shallow dish, esp one placed under a tea or coffee cup; anything of like shape.

saucy [sö'si] *adj* pert, bold, forward; rude, impudent.—*adv* **sau'cily.**

sauna [sow'na, sö'na] *n* a Finnish bath with exposure to hot, dry air.

saunter [sön'tėr] *vi* to wander about idly, to loiter, to stroll.—*n* a leisurely stroll.—*n* **saun'terer.**

sausage [sos'ij] *n* chopped meat, esp pork, seasoned and stuffed in a tube of gut or other casing.

sauté [sö'tā] *adj* fried lightly and quickly.—*vt* to fry in a small amount of fat.—*n* a sautéed dish.

savage [sav'ij] *adj* in a state of nature; wild; uncivilized; ferocious; primitive.—*n* a member of a primitive society; a brutal, fierce, or cruel person.—*adv* **sav'agely.**—*ns* **sav'ageness; sav'agery.**

savanna, savannah [sa-van'a] *n* a treeless plain, esp in Florida.

savant [sa'vä] *n* a learned man.

save [sāv] *vt* to bring safe out of evil or danger; to rescue; to protect, prevent the loss of; to keep, preserve (from); (*theol*) to deliver from sin; to prevent waste of; to use thriftily with a view to future need; to set aside for future use; to obviate the necessity of.—*n* **sā'ver**, one who saves.—*adj* **sā'ving**, thrifty; making a reservation; redeeming; **savings bank**, a bank organized to hold funds of depositors in interest bearing accounts and to make long-term investments.

savior, saviour [sā'vyor] *n* one who saves from destruction or danger; **Savior, Saviour**, Jesus Christ.

savor, savour [sā'vór] *n* taste or smell of something; characteristic flavor; distinctive quality.—*vi* to have a specified taste, smell, or quality.—*adj* **sā'vory, sā'voury**, having savor, of good savor or relish.—*n* **sā'voriness.**

savvy [sav'ē] *n* (*slang*) shrewdness or understanding.

saw [sö] *pa t* of **see.**

saw [sö] *n* an instrument for cutting, formed of a blade, band, or disk of thin steel, with a toothed edge.—*vt* to cut with a saw.—*vi* to use a saw.—*pt* sawed; *pt p* sawed or sawn.—*n* **saw'dust**, dust or fine particles of wood, etc., made in sawing.—*adj* **sawed' off'**, short or shortened.

saw [sö] *n* a saying; a proverb.

Saxon [saks'ón] *n* one of a North German people that conquered part of Britain in the 5th and 6th centuries.—*adj* pertaining to the Saxons.

saxophone [sak'sö-fōn] *n* a metal woodwind instrument with a conical bore, using a single reed, available in six sizes, played in bands.

say [sā] *vt* to utter; to state in words; to assert, affirm, declare; to go through in recitation or repetition; to estimate; to assume.—*vi* to make a statement; to affirm.—*pt, pt p* said.—*n* **say'ing**, an expression; a maxim, proverb, or adage.

scab [skab] *n* a crust formed over a sore; any of various diseases of plants characterized by crustaceous spots; a worker who refuses to join a union or who replaces a striking worker.

scabbard [skab'árd] *n* the case in which the blade of a sword is kept; a sheath.

scabies [skā'bi-ēz] *n* a contagious, itching skin disease.

scabrous [skab'rûs] *adj* bristly, rough; indecent; shocking.

scaffold [skaf'old] *n* a temporary erection for men at work on a building; a raised platform.

scald [sköld] *vt* to injure with hot liquid; to heat almost to boiling point; to heat short of boiling.—*n* a burn caused by hot liquid.

scale [skāl] *n* (*obs*) a ladder; a graduated measure; any instrument so marked; (*mus*) a sequence of tones, rising or falling in pitch, according to a system of intervals; the proportion that a map, etc bears to the thing it represents; a series of degrees classified by size, amount, etc.; relative scope of an activity or size, grandeur, of a production.

scale [skāl] *n* a small, thin plate on a fish or reptile; a thin layer.—*vt* to clear of scales; to peel off in thin layers.—*vi* to come off in thin layers or flakes.—*adjs* **scaled**, having scales, covered with scales; **scale'less**, without scales; **scal'y**, covered with scales; like scales; formed of scales.

scale [skāl] *n* either pan or tray of a balance; (*pl*) a beam supported freely in the center having two pans of equal weight suspended at each end.

scalene [skālēn', skā'lēn] *adj* (*geom*) having three unequal sides.—*n* a scalene triangle.

scall [sköl] *n* a scabby disorder of the scalp.

scallop [skal'óp, skol'óp] *n* a marine bivalve mollusk.

scalp [skalp] *n* the outer covering of the skull, usu covered with hair.

scalpel [skalp'él] *n* a small straight, thin knife used esp for surgery.

scaly *See* scale (2).

scamp [skamp] *n* a rascal; a playful young person.—*vi* **scam'per**, to run in alarm or haste; to run gaily.—*n* a hurried or playful run or movement.

scamp [skamp] *vt* to do, execute, perfunctorily, without thoroughness.

scampi [skam'pē] *n* a large shrimp or prawn.

scan [skan] *vt* to analyze the structure of (verse) by marking the metrical feet; to examine carefully, to scrutinize; to cast an eye quickly over.—*pr p* **scann'ing**; *pt, pt p* **scanned.**—*n* **scann'er.**

scandal [skan'd(á)l] *n* anything that brings discredit on the agent or agents by offending the moral feelings of the community; a feeling of moral outrage, or the talk it gives rise to; ignominy, disgrace; malicious gossip, slander.—*vt* **scan'dalize**, to give scandal or offense to, to shock; to disgrace.

scant [skant] *adj* not full or plentiful, scarcely sufficient, deficient.—*adj* **scan'ty**, scant; meager, deficient.—*adv* **scant'ily.**—*n* **scant'iness.**

scape [skāp] *vti* to escape.

scape [skāp] *n* a peduncle, quite or nearly leafless, arising from the middle of a rosette of leaves, and bearing a flower, several flowers, or a crowded inflorescence.

scapegoat [skāp'gōt] *n* one who is made to bear the misdeeds of another.

scapegrace [skāp'grās] *n* an incorrigible scamp.

scapula [skap'ū-la] *n* the shoulder blade.—*adj* **scap'ūlar**, pertaining to the shoulder.

scar [skär] *n* the mark left by a wound, sore or injury; any mark or blemish resulting from damage or wear.—*vt* to mark with a scar.—*vi* to become scarred.—*pr p* **scarr'ing**; *pt, pt p* **scarred.**

scar [skär] *n* a protruding or isolated rock; a steep rocky eminence.

scarce [skärs] *adj* not plentiful; hard to get; rare, not common.—*adv* **scarce'ly**, hardly, only just; probably not or certainly not.—*ns* **scarce'ness; scarc'ity.**

scare [skär] *vt* to startle, to affright; to drive or keep (off) by frightening.—*vi* to become frightened.—*n* a sudden fear.

scarf [skärf] *n* a light piece of material worn loosely on the shoulders or about the neck or head.

scarf [skärf] *vt* to join two pieces of timber endwise, so that they may appear to be used as one.

scarfskin [skärf'skin] *n* skin, esp that forming the cuticle of a nail.

scarify [skar'i-fī] *vt* to make a number of scratches or slight cuts in. *pt, pt p* **scar'ified.**—*n* **scarificā'tion**, act of scarifying.

scarlatina [skär-lā-tē'na] *n* scarlet fever.

scarlet [skär'lėt] *n* a brilliant red; a brilliant red cloth or garb.—*adj* of the color called scarlet; glaringly offensive; whorish.

scarp [skärp] *n* the inner side of a ditch below a fortification; a line of cliffs produced by faulting or erosion.

scathe [skāᴛʜ] *n* damage, injury.—*vt* to scorch, sear; to denounce witheringly.—*adj* **scā'thing**, damaging; vehement, bitter.

scatter [skat'ér] *vt* to disperse widely; to throw loosely about, to strew, to sprinkle.—*adj.* **scatt'ered.**—*ns* **scattering**, dispersion.

scavenger [skav'en-jèr] *n* one who gathers things discarded by others.

scenario [sè-ner'ē-ō] *n* the working script of a motion picture, television play, etc.

scene [sēn] *n* the place of action in a play, or a story, or that of an actual occurrence; a division of a play; a dramatic or stagy incident; a landscape, picture or a place of action; a view, spectacle; (*inf*) the locale for a specified activity.—*ns* **scē'nery.**

scent [sent] *vt* to discern by the sense of smell; to have some suspicion of; to perfume.—*n* a perfume; an odor; the sense of smell.—*adjs* **scent'ed**, perfumed; having or exhaling an odor.

scepter [sep'tèr] *n* the staff or baton borne by kings as an emblem of authority; royal power.—*adj* **scep'tered**, bearing a scepter; regal.

schedule [sked'ūl] *n* (*obs*) a slip or scroll with writing; a list, inventory, or table; (*obs*) a supplementary, explanatory, or appended document; a timetable.

scheme [skēm] *n* a diagram; a system; a plan of proposed action, a project; a plan pursued secretly, insidiously or by intrigue.—*vti* to devise or plot.—*adj* **schēmat'ic.**—*n* **schē'mer.**

schism [sizm skizm] *n* division, separation; discord, disharmony.

schist [shist] *n* a metamorphic crystalline rock easily split into layers.—*adj* **schist'ose**, like schist.

schizoid [skit'soid] *adj* showing qualities of a schizophrenic personality.

schizophrenia [skit-zō-frē'ni-a] *n* a mental disorder marked by introversion, loss of connection between thoughts, feelings and actions, and by delusions; the presence of mutually contradictory parts or qualities.—*adj, n* **schizophrenic** [-fren'ik].

scholar [skol'àr] *n* a pupil, a disciple, a student; an educated person; one whose learning is extensive and exact; the holder of a scholarship.—*adj* **schol'arly.**—*n* **schol'arship.**

scholastic [skol-as'tik] *adj* pertaining to schools or scholars, esp to high school or secondary school.

school[1] [skōōl] *n* a place or institution, with its buildings, for instruction and learning; all of its teachers and students; a regular session of teaching; formal education, schooling; a particular division of a university; a group following the same beliefs, methods, etc.—*vt* to train; to teach; to discipline or control.—*ns* **school'board**, a group of people in charge of local public schools; **school'boy**, a boy attending a school; **school'ing**, instruction in school; the teaching and exercise of horse and rider in the formal techniques of equitation.

school[2] [skōōl] *n* a shoal of fish, whales, or other aquatic animals of one kind swimming together.

schooner [skōōn'èr] *n* a sailing vessel, generally two-masted, rigged with fore-and-aft sails on both masts; a large beer glass; a large sherry glass.

schuss [shōōs] *vi* to ski directly down a slope at high speed.

sciatic [sī-at'ik] *adj* of, or in the region of, the hip.—*n* **sciat'ica**, pain along the sciatic nerve, esp in the back of the thigh.

science [sī'ens] *n* knowledge ascertained by observation and experiment, critically tested, systematized, and brought under general principles; a branch of such knowledge; skill or technique.—*adj* **scientif'ic**, of or dealing with science; based on, or using the principles and methods of science; systematic and exact.—*adv* **scientif'ically.**—*n* **scī'entist, science fiction**, fiction involving scientific phenomena.

sci-fi [sī'fī] science fiction.

scimitar [sim'i-tàr] *n* a short, single-edged curved sword, broadset at the point end.

scintilla [sin-til'a] *n* a spark, a trace.—*vi* **scin'tillate**, to spark; to sparkle, twinkle; to talk wittily.

sciolism [sī'ō-lizm] *n* superficial pretentious knowledge.—*n* **sci'olist.**

scion [sī'ón] *n* a cutting or twig for grafting; a young member of a family; a descendant.

scissors [siz'órz] *n pl* a cutting instrument with two blades, whose cutting edges slide past each other.

sclerosis [sklèr-ō'sis] *n* pathological hardening of body tissue; a disease marked by sclerosis.

scoff[1] [skof] *vti* to mock or jeer (at).—*n* an expression of scorn; mockery; an object of derision.

scoff[2] [skof] *vt* (*dial and slang*) to devour; to plunder.

scold [skōld] *n* one who scolds habitually; a woman who disturbs the public peace by noisy, quarrelsome, abusive behavior.—*vi* to find fault with.—*vt* to censure angrily.—*ns* **scold'er; scold'ing**, a harsh reprimand.

sconce[1] [skons] *n* a detached defensive work.

sconce[2] [skons] *n* a candlestick with a handle or on a bracket fixed to a wall.

scone [skōn] *n* a rich quick bread cut int usu. triangular shapes and cooked on a griddle or baked on a sheet.

scoop [skōōp] *n* any of various small, shovellike utensils, as for taking up flour, ice cream, etc.; (*inf*) to publish news before (a rival).

scoot [skōōt] *vti* (*inf*) to hurry (off).—*n* **scoot'er**, a child's two-wheeled vehicle with steering handle.

scope [skōp] *n* extent of the mind's grasp; range, field of activity, extent of field covered.

scopolamine [sko-pol'à-mēn (also -min)] *n* a poisonous alkaloid, used as a truth serum and with morphine as a sedative.

scorbutic [skòr-bū'tik] *adj* pertaining to, resembling, or affected by, scurvy.

scorch [skòrch] *vt* to burn slightly; to parch; to singe; to wither with scorn, censure, etc.

score [skōr, skòr] *n* a notch; an incised line; a line drawn to indicate deletion or to define a position; a copy of a musical composition, showing all the parts for the instruments or voices; a grievance come wishes to settle; a reason or motive; (*mus*) to arrange in a score.—*vi* to make points, as in a game; to keep the score of a game; to gain an advantage, a success, etc.—*n* **scōr'er.**

scorn [skòrn] *n* extreme contempt; object of contempt.—*vt* to feel or express scorn for; to refuse with scorn.—*n* **scorn'er.**— *adj* **scorn'ful.**—*adv* **scorn'fully.**

scorpion [skòr'pi-ón] *n* animals with head and thorax united, pincers, four pairs of legs, and a segmented abdomen including a tail with a sting.

Scotch [skoch] *adj* a form of **Scottish**, or **Scots.**

scotch [skoch] *vt* to maim; stamp out (eg a rumor).

Scots [skots] *adj* Scottish (almost always used of money, manners, and law; preferably also of language and persons).

Scottish [skot'ish] *adj* of Scotland, its people, or its English dialect.

scoundrel [skown'drèl] *n* a low mean blackguard, an utter rascal.—Also *adj.*—*adj* **scoun'drelly**, fit for or like a scoundrel.

scour[1] [skowr] *vt* to clean by hard rubbing, as with abrasives; to clear out by a current of water.

scour[2] [skowr] *vt* to move quickly, esp in search.—*vt* to pass over quickly, or range over, as in search.

scourge [skûrj] *n* a whip made of leather thongs; an instrument of punishment; a cause of widespread and great affliction.

scout[1] [skowt] *n* a person, plane, etc. sent to spy out the enemy's strength, actions, etc.; a person sent out to find new talent, survey a competitor, etc.; a Boy Scout or Girl Scout.

scout[2] [skowt] *vt* to mock; to scorn.—*vi* to scoff.

scowl [skowl] *vi* to contract the brows in displeasure; to look gloomy.—*n* the contraction of the brows in displeasure.

scrabble [skrab'l] *vt* to scramble; to scribble.—*vi* to scrape, scratch, etc.

scrag [skrag] *n* a scrawny person or animal; the lean end of a neck of mutton or veal.—*vt* to put to death by hanging; to throttle.—*adjs* **scragg'ed, scragg'y**, lean and gaunt.

scram [skram] *vi* (*slang*) to get out, to go away at once.

scramble [skram'bl] *vi* to move or climb hastily on all fours; to scuffle or struggle for something; to move with urgency or panic.

scrap[1] [skrap] *n* a small piece; a fragment of discarded material;

(*pl*) bits of food.—*adj* in the form of pieces, leftovers, etc.; used and discarded.—*vt* to consign to the scrapheap; to make into scraps.

scrap² [skrap] *n* (*inf*) a fight or quarrel.—Also *vi*.

scrape [skrāp] *vt* to rub with something sharp; to remove by drawing a sharp edge over; to gain or collect by laborious effort.—*ns* **scrap'er**, an instrument used for scraping, esp the soles of shoes; **scrap'ing**, a piece scraped off.

scratch [skrach] *vt* to draw a sharp point over the surface of; to leave a mark on by so doing; to tear or dig with the claws; to write hurriedly; to withdraw from a competition.

scrawl [skröl] *vti* to mark or write irregularly or hastily, to scribble.—*n* irregular, often illegible handwriting.—*n* **scrawl'er**.

scrawny [skrö'ni] *adj* gaunt and lean.

scream [skrēm] *vti* to cry out in a loud shrill voice, as in fear, pain, or immoderate mirth, to shriek.—*n* a shrill, sudden cry.

scree [skrē] *n* loose debris on a rocky slope.

screech [skrēch] *vti* to utter (with) a harsh, shrill, and sudden cry.—*n* a harsh, shrill, and sudden cry.

screed [skrēd] *n* a long and tedious discourse; an informal piece of writing; a leveling device drawn over freshly poured concrete.

screen [skrēn] *n* that which shelters from danger or observation; that which protects from heat, cold, or the sun; a surface on which motion pictures, etc. are projected; a coarse mesh of wire used as a sieve.

screw [skrōō] *n* a cylindrical or conical metal piece threaded in an advancing spiral, for fastening things by being turned; any spiral thing like this; a turn of a screw; a twist.—*adj* **screw'y** (*slang*), eccentric, slightly mad. **screw up** (*slang*), to bungle.

scribble [skrib'l] *vt* to scrawl, to write badly or carelessly (as regards handwriting or substance); to fill with worthless writing.—*n* **scribb'ler**.

scribe [skrīb] *n* a public or official writer; (*Bible*) an expounder, jurist and teacher of the Mosaic and traditional law; a journalist.

scrim [skrim] *n* a light, sheer, loosely woven cotton or linen cloth; such a cloth used as a stage backdrop.

scrimmage [skrim'ij] *n* (*football*) the play that follows the pass from center or a practice game.

scrimp [skrimp] *vti* to be sparing or frugal (with).

scrip¹ [skrip] *n* a short writing; a certificate of a right to receive something, as money.

scrip² [skrip] *n* (*arch*) a small bag, a satchel, a pilgrim's pouch.

script [skript] *n* an original document; a manuscript; the text of a stage play, screenplay or broadcast.

scripture [skrip'chúr] *n* any sacred writing; something written; Scripture, (often *pl*) the Jewish Bible or Old Testament; the Christian Bible or Old and New Testaments.

scrod [skröd] *n* a young codfish or haddock, filleted for cooking.

scroll [skröl] *n* a roll of paper or parchment; a writing in the form of a roll; a list; a riband partly coiled or curved, often bearing a motto; anything shaped more or less like a scroll.

scrotum [skrōt'úm] *n* the pouch of skin containing the testicles.—*pl* **scrot'a**, **scrotums**.

scrub¹ [skrub] *vt* to rub hard in order to clean; to rub hard.—*pr p* **scrubb'ing**; *pt*, *pt p* **scrubbed**.

scrub² [skrub] *n* a stunted tree; stunted trees and shrubs collectively; country covered with bushes or low trees.—*adj* small, stunted, inferior, etc.

scruff [skruf] *n* the nape of the neck.—*adj* **scruff'y**, shabby, unkempt.

scruple [skrōō'pl] *n* a small weight—in apothecaries' weight, 20 grains; a very small quantity; a doubt or hesitation, usu. moral, restraining one from action, esp a difficulty turning on a fine point of right or wrong.—*vti* to hesitate (at) from doubt.—*adj* **scru'pulous**.

scrutiny [skrōō'ti-ni] *n* close, careful, or minute investigation; a searching look.—*vt* **scru'tinize**.

scud [skud] *vi* to move or run swiftly; to be driven before the wind.

scuffle [skuf'l] *vi* to struggle closely; to fight confusedly; to drag the feet.—*n* a confused fight; a shuffling of feet.

scull [skul] *n* an oar worked from side to side over the stern of a boat; a light rowboat for racing.

scullery [skul'èr-i] *n* a room for rough kitchen work, as cleansing of utensils.

scullion [skul'yón] *n* (*arch*) a servant for drudgery.

sculpt *vt* to sculpture; to carve.

sculptor [skulp'tòr] *n* an artist in carving.

scum [skum] *n* a thin layer of impurities on top of a liquid; refuse.

scupper [skup'èr] *n* a hole in a ship's side to drain the deck.

scurf [skûrf] *n* small flakes or scales of dead skin; any scaly coating.—*adj* **scurf'y**.

scurrilous [skur'il-ús] *adj* vulgarly evil; grossly abusive.—*adjs* **scurr'il**, **scurr'ile**, scurrilous.

scurry [skur'i] *vi* to hurry along, to scamper.—*n* a flurry, bustle.

scurvy [skûr'vi] *adj* vile, contemptible.—*n* a disease marked by general debility, due to a lack of Vitamin C.

scuttle¹ [skut'l] *n* a shallow basket; a bucket with a lip for holding coal.

scuttle² [skut'l] *n* an opening in a ship's deck or side; its lid.—*vt* to make a hole in the lower hull of a ship, esp in order to sink; to destroy, ruin.—*n* **scutt'lebutt**, a drinking fountain on shipboard.

scuttle³ [skut'l] *vi* to scamper, to withdraw in haste.—*n* a short swift run; a quick shuffling pace.

scythe [sīṬH] *n* an instrument with a large curved blade for mowing grass, etc.—*vti* to mow with a scythe.

sea [sē] *n* the ocean; any great expanse of salt water less than an ocean; a large body of fresh water; the state of the surface of the ocean; a heavy wave or swell; something like the sea in vastness; the seafaring life.—*adj* of the sea, marine.—*ns* **sea' breeze**, a breeze blowing from the sea toward the land, **sea' coast**, the land adjacent to the sea; *ns* **sea' level**, the mean level of the surface of the sea; **sea'man**, a sailor; one of the three ranks below petty officer in the navy or coast guard.—*adj* **sea'sick'**, affected with sickness through the rolling of a vessel at sea.—*ns* **sea'sickness**; **sea'side**, seashore.—*adj* **sea'ward**, toward the sea.—*adv* (also **sea'wards**) toward or in the direction of the sea.

seal¹ *n* a piece of wax, lead, or other material, stamped with a device and attached as a means of authentication or attestation; an engraved stone or other stamp for impressing a device; a closure that must be broken to be opened and thus reveal tampering; a tight or perfect closure to prevent the passage or return; an ornamental paper stamp; anything that pledges.

seal² [sēl] *n* numerous carnivorous aquatic mammals with a torpedo-shaped body and limbs modified into webbed flippers; the fur of some seals.

seam [sēm] *n* the line formed by the sewing together of two pieces; a line of union; a wrinkle, furrow; (*geol*) a stratum of ore, coal, etc.

séance [sā'äs] *n* a meeting at which spiritualists try to communicate with the dead.

search [sûrch] *vt* to survey inquiringly, to examine or inspect closely; to probe.—*vi* to make a search.—*n* inquisition; investigation; quest.—*n* **search'er**, one who searches.—*adj* **search'ing**, penetrating; examining thoroughly.—*adv* **search'ingly**.

season [sē'z(ò)n] *n* one of the four divisions of the year: spring, summer, fall or winter; the usual or appropriate time; any particular time; any brief period of time; seasoning, relish.—*vt* to make (food) more tasty by adding salt, spices, etc.—*adj* **sea'sonable**, happening in due season; timely, opportune.—*n* **sea'sonableness**.—*adv* **sea'sonably**.—*adj* **sea'sonal**, belonging to a particular season.—*n* **sea'soning**.

seat [sēt] *n* a chair, bench, etc.; the part of a chair on which the body rests; that part of the body or of a garment on which one sits; the manner in which one sits on a horse; a place where anything is settled or established.

sebaceous [se-bā'shús] *adj* secreting sebum; pertaining to, producing, or containing fatty material.

secant [sē'kant, ànt] *n* (*geom*) a straight line that intersects a curve in two or more points.

secede [si-sēd'] *vi* to withdraw formally from a society, federation or organization, esp a religious communion or political party.—*ns* **secē'der**, one who secedes; **secess'ion**, the act of seceding; withdrawal into privacy or solitude.

seclude [si-klōōd'] *vi* to shut off, esp from association or influence (*with* from).—*adj* **seclud'ed**, withdrawn from observation or society.—*adv* **seclud'edly**.—*n* **seclusion**.

second [sek'ónd] *adj* next after the first in time, place, power, quality, etc.; other, alternate; another of the same kind; next below the first in rank, value, etc.—*n* one who, or that which, is second; an article of merchandise not of first quality; an aid or assistant, as to a boxer; the gear after low gear; (*mus*) an interval embracing two diatonic degrees; 1/60th of a minute of time or of angular measure.—*adj* **sec'ondary**, subordinate; of a second stage.—*n* **sec'ond class**, the class next to the first in a classification; a class of mail comprising periodicals sent to regular subscribers.—*adj* **second-class**, relating to a second class; inferior, mediocre.—*adv* **sec'ondly**, in the second place.—*adj* **sec'ond-rate**, inferior, mediocre.

secret [sē'kret] *adj* concealed from others, guarded against discovery or observation.—*n* **sē'crecy**, the state of being secret; concealment; privacy; the power or habit of keeping secrets.—*adj* **secretive**.—*adv* **sē'cretly**.

secretary [sek'rē-tà-ri] *n* one employed to conduct correspondence and transact business for an individual, society, etc.—*adj* **secretā'rial**, pertaining to a secretary or his duties.

secrete [si-krēt'] *vt* to appropriate secretly; to hide; to form and release (a substance) as a gland, etc., does.—*n* **secrē'tion**, the act, or process, of secreting; a substance secreted by an animal or plant.—*adj* **secrē'tive**, tending to, or causing, secretion.—*adv* **secrē'tively**.—*adj* **secrē'tory**, having the function of secreting, as a gland.

sect [sekt] *n* a religious denomination; a body of persons who unite in holding some particular views, esp those who dissent from an established religion.—*adj* **sectā'rian**, of a sect; *ns* **sectā'rianism**, excessive devotion to a sect; **sec'tary**, a member of a sect.

section [sek'sh(ò)n] *n* act of cutting; a division; a portion; one of the parts into which anything may be considered as divided, or of which it may be built up.—*adjs* **sec'tile**, capable of being cut with a knife; **sec'tional**, of a section; in section; built up by sections; local or regional rather than general in character.

sector [sek'tòr] *n* a plane figure bounded by two radii and an arc; a length or section of a fortified line or army front; a distinctive part.

secular [sek'ū-làr] *adj* pertaining to an age or generation; occurring or observed only once in a century.—*vt* **sec'ularize**, to change from religious to civil use or control.—*ns* **seculariz-ā'tion**.

secure [si-kūr'] *adj* (*arch*) without care or anxiety; confident in expectation, assured; free from danger, safe; affording safety; firmly fixed or held.—*adj* **secūr'able**, that may be secured.—*adv* **secūre'ly**.—*ns* **secūre'ness**; **secūr'ity**.

sedan [si-dan'] *n* a covered chair for one, carried on two poles by two men; an enclosed automobile with front and rear seats and two or four doors.

sedate [si-dāt'] *adj* quiet; composed; serious and unemotional.—*adv* **sedāte'ly**.—*ns* **sedāte'ness**; **sedā'tion**, act of calming, or state of being calmed, by means of sedatives; use of sedatives to calm a patient.—*adj* **sed'ative**.

sedentary [sed'(è)n-tà-ri] *adj* not migratory; passed chiefly in sitting, requiring much sitting.

sederunt [si-dē'runt] *n* a prolonged sitting.

sediment [sed'i-mènt] *n* matter that settles at the bottom of a liquid; (*geol*) matter disposited by water or wind.—*adj* **sedi-men'tary**, pertaining to, consisting of, or formed by sediment.

sedition [si-dish'(ò)n] *n* stirring up of rebellion against the government.—*adj* **sedi'tious**.

seduce [si-dūs'] *vt* to draw aside from right conduct or belief; to entice into unlawful sexual intercourse, esp for the first time.—*ns* **sedū'cer**; **sedūc'tion**, act of enticing from virtue by promises; allurement, attraction.—*adj* **sedūc'tive**.

sedulous [sed'ū-lùs] *adj* diligent, assiduous.—*n* **sed'ulous-ness**.—*adv* **sed'ulously**.

sedum [sē'dum] *n* a large genus of plants, often with tufted stems; the stonecrop.

see[1] [sē] *n* the seat or jurisdiction of a bishop or archbishop.

see[2] [sē] *vt* to perceive by the eye; to observe, to discern;

to perceive with the understanding.—*pt* **saw**; *pt p* **seen**.—*n* **see'ing**, sight, vision.—*adj* having sight or insight; observant.

seed [sēd] *n* a cellular structure containing the embryo of a flowering plant together with stored food, the whole protected by a seed coat; a seeded tournament player.—*vi* **seed'y**, abounding in seed; shabby; rundown.—*adv* **seed'ily**.—*ns* **seed'iness**, the state of being seedy.

seek [sēk] *vt* to look for; to try to find, get, or achieve.

seem [sēm] *vi* to appear to be; to have the impression *adj* **seem'ing**, that seems real, true; apparent; ostensible.—*n* appearance; semblance.—*adv* **seem'ingly**.—*adj* **seem'ly** proper; suitable; decent.

seep [sēp] *vi* to ooze gently, to percolate.—*n* **seep'age**, act or process of seeping.

seer [sē'er] *n* one who sees.

seesaw [sē'sö or -sö'] *n* alternate up-and-down or back-and-forth motion; repeated alternation in a contest or struggle.

seethe [sēTH] *vt* (*arch*) to boil; to soak or saturate in liquid.—*vi* (*arch*) to boil; to be violently agitated.

segment [seg'mènt] *n* a part cut off; a portion; of a line, that portion bound by two points; of a circle.—*n* **segmentā'tion**, the act or process of dividing into segments.

segregate [seg'rē-gāt] *vt* to separate from others, to group apart.—*vi* to separate, withdraw; to practice or enforce a policy of segregation; to undergo genetic segregation.—*n* **seg-regā'tion**.

seismograph [sīs'mō-gräf] *n* an instrument for registering the direction, intensity, and time of earthquakes.—*adj* **seis'mic**, belonging to an earthquake.—*n* **seismol'ogy**.

seize [sēz] *vt* to take legal possession of; to take possession of suddenly, eagerly, or forcibly; to snatch, to grasp; to attack or afflict suddenly.—*vi* to jam, become stuck.—*adj* **seiz'able**.—*ns* **seiz'er**; **seiz'ure**.

seldom [sel'dòm] *adv* rarely, not often.

select [si-lekt'] *vti* to choose or pick out.—*adj* picked out; choice; careful in choosing; exclusive.—*n* **selec'tion**, act of selecting; thing, or a collection of things, selected.—*adj* **selec-'tive**, exercising power of selection.

selenography [se-lēn-og'raf-i] *n* study of the moon's physical features; the physical geography of the moon.

self [self] *n* the identity, character, etc. of any person or thing; one's own person as distinct from all others; what one is; personal advantage.—*pl* **selves**.—*adj* (*obs*) very same; having one color only; of the same kind as something with which it is used.—*adj* **self'ish**, chiefly or wholly regarding oneself, heedless of others.—*adv* **self'ishly**.—*n* **self'ishness**.—*adj* **self'less**, regardless of self, utterly unselfish.

self- [self-] in composition, indicating that the agent is also the object of the action; by, of, for, in, in relation to, oneself or itself; automatic.—eg **self'-pleas'ing**, pleasing oneself etc.

sell [sel] *vt* to exchange for money, etc.; to offer for sale; to promote the sale of; to make seem desirable.—*vi* to make sales; to attract buyers.—*pt, pt p* **sold**.—*n* an act or instance of selling; a fraud.—*ns* **sell'er**; **sellout**, a show for which all seats are sold.

seltzer [selt'zèr] *n* an artificially prepared carbonated mineral water.

selvage, selvedge [sel'vij] *n* the firm edge of a woven piece of cloth; a border.

selves [selvz] *pl* of **self**.

semantic [si-man'tik] *adj* pertaining to meaning, esp of words.—*n* (*pl*) the study of the development of the meaning of words.

semaphore [sem'á-fōr, -för] *n* a signaling apparatus, consisting of an upright with arms that can be turned up and down.

semblance [sem'blàns] *n* likeness, image, guise; a deceptive appearance; a faint indication.

semen [sē'men] *n* the fluid that carries spermatozoa.

semester [si-mes'tèr] *n* either of the two terms usu. making up a school year.

semi- [sem'i-] *prefix* half; not fully; twice in a (specified period).—*adj* **sem'iann'ual**, half-yearly; lasting half a year.—*n* **sem'icircle**, half a circle.

semiconductor [sem-i-kon-dukt'òr] *n* a substance, as germanium or silicon, used in transistors to control current flow.

seminal [sem'in-àl] *adj* pertaining to, or of the nature of, seed or of semen; that is a source; generative, originative.

seminar [sem'in-àr] *n* a group of advanced students working under a teacher in some specific branch of study; a course for such a group.

Semite [sem'- or sēm'īt] *n* a member of any of the peoples now inhabiting the Middle East including Arabs and Jews.—*adj* **Semit'ic.**

sempiternal [sem-pi-tûr'nàl] *adj* everlasting.

senary [sēn'-, sen'àr-i] *adj* of, involving, based on, six.

senate [sen'àt] *n* a legislative or deliberative body; **Senate**, the upper branch of the US Congress or of most of the State legislatures; a governing body of some universities charged with maintaining academic standards.—*n* **sen'ator**, a member of a senate.—*adj* **senatō'rial.**

send [send] *vt* to cause or direct to go; to cause to be conveyed, to dispatch, to forward; to propel; to commission (to do); to cause to happen, come, etc.; *pt, pt p* **sent.**—*ns* **sen'der**, one who sends.

senescent [sen-es'ènt] *adj* growing old.—*n* **senes'cence.**

seneschal [sen'é-shàl] *n* (*hist*) a steward of a lord's estate.

senile [sē'nīl] *adj* pertaining to, old age; showing the feebleness of old age.—*n* **senility.**

senior [sēn'yòr] *adj* older, written *Sr* after a father's name if his son's name is the same; older in office or higher in standing; of or for seniors.

senor, señor [se-nyōr'] *n* a gentleman; prefixed to a name.

sensation [sen-sā'sh(ó)n] *n* awareness of a physical experience; awareness by the senses generally; an effect on the senses; a thrill; a state, or matter, of general and excited interest; melodramatic quality or method.—*adj* **sensā'tional**, pertaining to sensation; tending to excite violent emotions; melodramatic.—*ns* **sensā'tionalism, sensā'tionalist**, a believer in sensationalism.

sense [sens] *n* a faculty by which objects are perceived (sight, hearing, smell, taste, or touch); immediate consciousness; impressions.—*adj* **sense'less**, deficient in good sense, foolish; meaningless, purposeless.—*adv* **sense'lessly.**—*n* **sense'lessness.**—*adj* **sen'sible**, perceptible by sense; easily perceived; appreciable; cognisant, aware (of); prudent, judicious; having power of sensation.—*adv* **sen'sibly**, prudently, appreciably.—*vt* **sen'sitize**, to render sensitive.—*ns* **sensitizā'tion**, the action or process of sensitizing; quality or state of being sensitized; **sen'sitizer.**—*adj* **sen'sitive**, having power of sensation.—*adv* **sen'sitively**—*ns* **sen'sitiveness; sensitiv'ity; sen'sor** [-sór] a device to detect, measure, or record physical phenomena, as heat, pulse, etc.; sense organ.—*adj* **sensō'rial**, sensory.—*adj* **sen'sory** of the sensorium; of sensation.—*adj* **sensual** of the senses as distinct from the mind.

sent [sent] *pt, pt p* of **send.**

sentence [sen'tèns] *n* (*obs*) opinion; a judgment; determination of punishment pronounced by a court or judge; the punishment; (*arch*) a maxim; (*gram*) a number of words making a complete grammatical structure.—*adj* **senten'tious**, ponderously trite; fond of moralizing.

sentient [sen'sh(y)ènt] *adj* conscious; capable of sensation, responsive to stimulus.

sentiment [sen'ti-mènt] *n* a thought, or body of thought, tinged with emotion; an opinion.—*adj* **sentimen'tal; sentimen'talism, sentimental'ity**, quality of being sentimental; affectation of fine feeling.

sentinel [sen'ti-nèl] *n* one posted on guard, a sentry.

sentry [sen'tri] *n* a sentinel, a soldier on guard to prevent or announce the approach of an enemy.

separate [sep'á-ràt] *vt* to divide, part; to sever; to disconnect; to set apart; to keep apart; to sort into different sizes, divide into different constituents, etc.—*vi* to part, go different ways; to cease to live together as man and wife; to become isolated from a mixture.—*adj* divided; apart from another; distinct; not shared.—*n* an article of clothing designed to be worn interchangeably with others to form various outfits.—*adj* **sep'arable**, that may be separated or disjointed.—*n* **separabil'ity.**—*advs* **sep'arably; sep'arately.**—*ns* **separā'tion.**—*adj* **sep'arative**, tending to separate.—*n* **sep'arātor**, one who, or that which, separates.

sepia [sē'pi-a] *n* a cuttlefish; the ink of a cuttlefish; a pigment made from it; a dark reddish brown.

sepsis [sep'sis] *n* septicemia.

September [sep-tem'bèr] *n* the ninth month of the year, having 30 days.

septennial [sep-ten'i-àl] *adj* lasting seven years; happening every seven years.—*adv* **septenn'ially.**

septic [sep'tik] *adj* putrefactive; suppurating.—**septic tank**, an underground tank in which sewage is partially purified by the action of certain bacteria.

septicemia [sep-ti-sē'mi-a] *n* presence of poisonous bacteria in the blood.

septum [sep'tum] *n* (*biol*) partition separating two cells or cavities as in the nose, fruit, etc.

sepulcher, sepulchre [sep'ul-kèr] *n* a place of burial, tomb.—*adj* **sepul'chral**, pertaining to a sepulcher.

sequel [sē'kwèl] *n* that which follows, the succeeding part; result, consequence; a resumption of a story begun in an earlier literary work.

sequence [sē'kwèns] *n* state of being sequent or following; order of succession; a series of things following in order; (*mus*) a succession of repetitions of a harmonic pattern or melodic phrase each in a new position; a single, uninterrupted episode, as in a movie.—*adjs* **sē'quent**, following; successive; **sequen'tial.**

sequester [si-kwes'tèr] *vt* to set aside; to seclude; (*law*) to remove from one's possession until a dispute be settled, creditors satisfied, or the like.—*adj* **seques'tered**, retired, secluded.—*vt* **seques'trate**, to sequester.—*ns* **sequestrā'tion.**

sequin [sē'kwin] *n* an old Italian or Turkish gold coin; a spangle.

seraph [ser'àf] *n* an angel of the highest rank; one of the 6-winged angels standing in the presence of God.

sere, sear [sēr] *adj* (*poetical*) dried up, withered; (*arch*) threadbare.

serenade [ser-è-nād'] *n* evening music in the open air; music played or sung by a lover under his lady's window at night; a piece of music suitable for such an occasion.

serendipity [ser-èn-dip'i-ti] *n* the faculty of making happy chance finds.

serene [si-rēn'] *adj* calm; unclouded; tranquil; august, used as an adjunct to a title.—*adv* **serēne'ly**, calmly, tranquilly.

serf [sûrf] *n* a person in feudal service attached to his master's land and transferred with it to a new owner.—*pl* **serfs.**—*n* **serf'dom**, condition of a serf.

serge [sûrj] *n* a strong twilled fabric.

sergeant [sär'jànt] *n* a noncommissioned officer next above a corporal in the army and marine corps; a police officer ranking next below a captain or a lieutenant.

series [sē'rēz] *n sing* and *pl* a set of things of the same class coming one after another in spatial or temporal succession; a set of things having something in common; a set of things differing progressively; a succession of quantities each derivable from its predecessor by a law.—*adj* **sē'rial**, forming a series; in series; in a row; of publications, films, or broadcasts, in installments at regular intervals.

serious [sē'ri-ús] *adj* solemn, grave; in earnest; demanding close attention; important; dangerous.—*advs* **sēriously.**—*n* **sē'riousness.**

sermon [sûr'mòn] *n* a speech on religion or morals, esp by a clergyman; any serious admonition or reproof, esp a tedious one.

serpent [sûr'pènt] *n* (*arch*) any reptile or creeping thing, esp if venomous; a snake; the Devil; a treacherous person.—*adj* **ser'pentine.**

serrate [ser'āt] *adj* notched like a saw.—*vt* to notch.

serried [ser'id] *adj* crowded, dense, set close together; marked by ridges.

serum [sē'rum] *n* any watery fluid from an animal; blood serum used as an antitoxin, taken from an animal inoculated for a specific disease.—*adj* **sē'rous.**

servant [sûr'vànt] *n* one hired to work for another.

serve [sûrv] *vt* to be a servant to, to work for; to do military or naval service for; to provide (customers) with (goods or services); to be of use to or for; to suffice for; to help to food, etc.—*n* **ser'ver**, one who serves.

service [sûr'vis] *n* occupation of a servant; public employment; a branch of this, specifically the armed forces; work done for others; any religious ceremony; benefit, advantage; (*pl*) friendly help or professional aid; a system of providing people with some utility, as water, gas, etc.; a facility providing some public demand.—*adj* **ser'viceable**, durable; useful; durable or useful.

servile [sûr'vīl] *adj* pertaining to slaves; suitable to a slave; meanly submissive, cringing.—*adv* **ser'vilely**.—*n* **servil'ity**.

servitor [sûr'vi-tôr] *n* a male servant.

servitude [sûr'vi-tūd] *n* bondage or slavery; work imposed as punishment for crime.

servomechanism [sûr'vō-mek'ån-izm] *n* an automatic control system of low power.

sesame [ses'å-me] *n* annual herb, whose seed yields valuable oil.

sesquipedalian [ses-kwi-pĕ-dā'li-ån] *adj* having many syllables; given to the use of long words.

session [sesh'(ò)n] *n* the meeting of a court, legislature, etc.; a series of such meetings; a period of these; a period of study, classes, etc.

sestet, sestette [ses-tet'] *n* a stanza or poem of six lines, specifically, the last six lines of an Italian sonnet.

set [set] *vt* to seat; to put in a specified place, condition, etc.; to fix (a trap for animals), adjust (a clock or dial), arrange (a table for a meal), fix (hair) in a desired style, put (a broken bone, etc.) into normal position, etc.; to make settled, rigid, or fixed; to mount (gems); to direct; to furnish (an example) for others; to fit (words to music or music to words); to arrange (type) for printing.—*pr p* **sett'ing**; *pt*, *pt p* **set**.—*adj* fixed, established; intentional; rigid, firm; obstinate; ready.—*n* a setting or being set; the way in which a thing is set; direction; the scenery for a play, etc.; a group of persons or things classed or belonging together; assembled equipment for radio or television reception, etc.

settee [se-tē'] *n* a long seat with a back esp a sofa for two.

settle [set'l] *n* a long high-backed bench.—*vt* to place at rest or in comfort; to establish, install; to colonize; to restore to order; to quiet, compose; to determine, decide; to put beyond doubt or dispute; to cause to sink and become more compact.

seven [sev'n] *adj*, *n* one more than six.—*n* the symbol for this (7, VII, vii); the seventh in a series or set; something having seven units as members.—*adj* **sevenfold**, having seven units as members; being seven times as great or as many.—*n* **seventh** (*mus*) an interval of seven diatonic degrees; the leading note.

seventeen [sev'n-tēn] *adj*, *n* one more than sixteen; the symbol for this (17, XVII, xvii).

seventy [sev'n-ti] *adj*, *n* seven times ten; the symbol for this.—*pl* **seventies** (70s) the numbers from 70 to 79; the same numbers in a life or a century.—*adj* **seventieth**.

sever [sev'ėr] *vti* to separate, to divide; to cut or break, or be broken, off, away from.

several [sev'ėr-ål] *adj* particular, distinct; respective; various; more than two but not very many.—*n* (with *pl v*) a small number (of).—*pron* (with *pl v*) a few.—*adv* **sev'erally**, separately.

severe [sė-vēr'] *adj* rigorous, very strict; unsparing; inclement; hard to endure.

sew [sō] *vti* to join or fasten together with a needle and thread; to make, mend, etc. by sewing.

sewer [sū'ėr] *n* a pipe or drain, used to carry off liquid waste matter and sometimes surface water.

sex [seks] *n* the total characteristics, structural and functional, which distinguish male and female organisms; either of the divisions of organisms according to this distinction, or its members collectively; the attraction between the sexes; sexual intercourse.—*ns* **sex'ism**, exploitation and domination of one sex by the other, **sex'ist**.—*adjs* **sex'ūal**, pertaining to sex; distinguished by, founded on, sex; relating to the distinct organs of the sexes.—*n* **sexual'ity**, sexual activity; expression of sexual interest, esp when excessive.—*adv* **sex'ūally**.—*ns* **sex' appeal'**, power of attracting the other sex.

sex- [seks-], **sexi-** [seks-i-] in composition, six.

sextant [seks'tånt] *n* an instrument for measuring the angular distance of the sun, a star, etc. from the horizon, as to determine position at sea.

sextet [seks-tet'] *n* (*mus*) a work for six voices or instruments; the performers of a sextet.

sexton [seks'tòn] *n* a church officer or employee in charge of the maintenance of church property.

sextuple [seks'tū-pl] *adj* sixfold.

shabby [shab'i] *adj* threadbare or worn, as clothes; run down, dilapidated; mean, shameful.—*adv* **shabb'ily**.—*n* **shabb'iness**.

shack [shak] *n* a small, crudely built house or cabin; a shanty.

shackle [shak'l] *n* a metal fastening, usu. in pairs, for the wrists or ankles of a prisoner; anything that restrains freedom, as of expression.

shade [shād] *n* a partial or relative darkness; interception of light; obscurity; a shady place; shelter from light or heat; a screen; degree of darkness of a color.—*n* **shā'ding**, a shielding against light; the effect of light and shade; fine gradations, nuances; toning down, modification.—*adj* **shā'dy**, having, or in, shade; sheltered from light or heat; (*inf*) disreputable.—*adv* **shā'dily**.—*n* **shā'diness**.

shadow [shad'ō] *n* shade due to interception of light by an object; the dark shape of that object so projected on a surface; protective shade; the dark part, eg of a picture; gloom, affliction.

shaft [shäft] *n* an arrow or spear, or its stem; anything hurled like a missile; a stem; a narrow beam (of light); an arrow, esp for a longbow; a bar, usu. cylindrical, used to support rotating parts of machinery; a pole; the part of a column between the base and capital.

shag [shag] *n* a ragged mass of hair, or the like; a long coarse nap; a kind of tobacco cut into shreds; the green cormorant.—*adj* **shagg'y**.

shagreen [sha-grēn'] *n* an untanned leather covered with small round granulations and usu. dyed green; the skin of shark, ray, etc., covered with small nodules.—*adj* of, or covered with, shagreen.

shake [shāk] *vti* to move with quick, short motions, to agitate; to tremble or cause to tremble; to become or cause to become unsteady; to unnerve or become unnerved; to clasp (another's hand) as in greeting.—*p t* **shook**; *pt p* **shāk'en**. **shake-'up**, an extensive reorganization.—*adj* **shāk'y**, shaking or inclined to shake; loose; tremulous; precarious; unreliable.—*adv* **shāk'ily**.—*n* **shak'iness**.

Shakespearean [shāk-spē'ri-ån] *adj* of or relating to, or in the style of, *Shakespeare*, or his works.

shale [shāl] *n* a rock formed by the consolidation of clay, mud, or silt, splitting readily into thin laminae.

shall [sh(a)l] *vt* an auxiliary verb used in formal speech to express futurity in the 1st person, and determination, obligation or necessity in the 2d and 3d persons.

shallot [shå-lot'] *n* a perennial herb having small clustered bulbs used in seasoning; a green onion.

shallow [shal'ō] *adj* not deep; not profound; not wise; superficial.—*n* a place where the water is not deep; a shoal.—*n* **shall'owness**.

sham [sham] *n* a pretense; a person or thing that is a fraud.—*adj* not real, pretended, false.—*vti* to pretend, to feign.

shamble [sham'bl] *vi* to walk with an awkward, unsteady gait.—*n* a shambling gait.

shambles [sham'blz] *n pl* a slaughterhouse; a scene of great slaughter, destruction, or disorder.

shame [shām] *n* the sense of humiliation due to fault or failure; modesty; dishonor, disgrace; a cause or source of disgrace; a thing to be ashamed of.

shampoo [sham-pōō'] *vt* (*arch*) to massage; to wash (the hair); to clean (carpet, etc.) by rubbing with a special preparation.

shamrock [sham'rok] *n* a cloverlike plant with leaflets in groups of three, the national emblem of Ireland.

shamus [shäm'us] *n* the sexton of a synagogue; (*slang*) a detective or private eye; an unimportant menial.

shandy [shan'di] *n* shandygaff; a mixture of beer with lemonade.

shank [shangk] *n* the leg from knee to foot in man, or a corresponding part in animals.

shan't [shänt] a contraction of **shall not**.

shantung [shan-tung'] *n* a plain rough cloth of wild silk.

shanty[1] [shan'ti] *n* a roughly built hut; a ramshackle dwelling.—*n* **shant'ytown**, a town, or an area of one, where housing is makeshift and ramshackle.

shanty[2] [shant'i] a song sung by sailors in rhythm with their work.

shape [shāp] *vt* to form, to fashion, to frame; to model, to mold; to regulate, direct, to determine; to adapt. —*vi* to take shape, to develop; to happen; to befall. —*pt p* **shāped.**

shard [shärd] *n* a fragment, as of an earthen vessel.

share¹ [shār] *n* a part shorn or cut off; a division, section, portion; a fixed and indivisible section of the capital of a company. —*vt* to divide into shares; to apportion; to give or take a share of; to have in common. —*vi* to have a share. —*n* **share′holder.**

share² [shār] *n* a plowshare.

shark [shärk] *n* large voracious fishes of warm seas, some of which are dangerous to man; an extortioner, a swindler, a sponging parasite.

sharp [shärp] *adj* cutting, piercing; having a thin edge or fine point; not rounded; not gradual; severe; harsh; pungent; high in pitch; raised a semitone; sarcastic; of keen or quick perception; alert; abrupt; clear-cut; well-defined; crafty; underhanded; intense, as a pain; nippy, as a wind. —*vti* **shar′pen,** to make or become sharp. —*n* **sharp′er,** a trickster, a swindler. —*adv* **sharp′ly.** —*n* **sharp′ness.**

shatter [shat′ẽr] *vti* to break into fragments suddenly; to damage or be damaged severely.

shave [shāv] *vt* to scrape or pare off a superficial slice, hair (esp of the face), or other surface material from; to graze the surface of. —*vi* to remove hair by a razor. —*pt p* **shāved** or (*arch*) **shā′ven; shā′ving,** the act of scraping or using a razor.

shawl [shöl] *n* an oblong or square cloth worn as a covering for the head or shoulders.

shawm [shöwm] *n* an early woodwind instrument.

shay [shā] *n* (*dial*) a chaise.

she [shē] *pron fem* the female (or thing spoken of as a female) named before, indicated or understood.

sheaf [shēf] *n* a bundle of things bound side by side, esp stalks of grain, etc.; a collection of papers, etc. bound in a bundle. —*pl* **sheaves.**

shear [shēr] *vt* to cut, esp to clip with shears; to divest. —*vi* to separate. —*pt* **sheared;** *pt p* **sheared** or **shorn.**

sheath [shēth] *n* a case for a blade; a covering; a woman's closefitting dress. —*vt* **sheathe** to put into, or cover with, a sheath or case; to withdraw (a claw) into a sheath.

sheave [shēv] *n* a grooved wheel or pulley.

shed¹ [shed] *vt* (*dial*) to set apart, segregate; to pour out; to cause to flow; to radiate; to cause to flow off; to cast off (a natural growth, as hair, etc.)

shed² [shed] *n* a structure, often with one or more sides not enclosed, for storing or shelter; (*arch*) a hut.

sheen [shēn] *n* a shine, luster; brightness.

sheep [shēp] *n* a genus (*Ovis*) of beardless, woolly, wild or domesticated, cud-chewing animals closely allied to goats, with edible flesh called mutton; a silly, helpless submissive person. —*pl* **sheep.**

sheer¹ [shēr] *adj* absolute, utter (eg *sheer folly*); extremely steep; (of fabric) very thin, diaphanous. —*adv* vertically; outright.

sheer² [shēr] *vti* to deviate or cause to deviate from a course; to swerve. —*n* the fore-and-aft upward curve of a ship's deck as shown in a side elevation.

sheet¹ [shēt] *n* a broad thin piece of any material, as glass, plywood, metal, etc.; a large piece of cloth for a bed; a single piece of paper; (*inf*) a newspaper; a wide expanse; a suspended or moving expanse (as of fire or rain). —*vt* to cover with, or as with, a sheet; to furnish with sheets; to form into sheets.

sheet² [shēt] *n* a rope for controlling the set of a sail.

sheikh, sheik [shāk, shēk] *n* an Arab chief.

sheldrake [shel′drāk] *n* a merganser; a shelduck.

shelf [shelf] *n* a board fixed in a cupboard, on a wall, etc., for laying things on; a flat layer of rock, a ledge; a shoal, a sandbank.

shell [shel] *n* a hard outer covering, esp of a shellfish, a tortoise, an egg, or a nut; something like a shell in being hollow, empty, a covering, etc.

shelter [shel′tẽr] *n* a structure that shields or protects, esp against weather; a place of refuge, retreat, or temporary lodging in distress; protection. —*vt* to take shelter.

shelve [shelv] *vt* to furnish with shelves; to place on a shelf; to put aside. —*vi* to slope, incline. —*n pl* **shelves,** *pl of* **shelf.** —*n* **shelv′ing,** material for shelves; shelves collectively.

shepherd [shep′ẽrd] *n* one who tends sheep; a clergyman. —*n*

shep′herdess a woman or girl who tends sheep; a rural girl or woman. —*vt* to tend, or to guide, as a shepherd.

sheriff [sher′if] *n* (*hist*) the king's representative in a shire, with wide judicial and executive powers; the chief law-enforcement officer of a county. —*n* **sher′iffdom.**

sherlock [shûr′lok] *n* a detective.

sherry [sher′i] *n* a fortified wine made in Spain; a similar wine produced elsewhere.

shield [shēld] *n* a piece of armor carried for defense against weapons and missiles; anything that protects; a person who protects; defense; the escutcheon used for displaying arms; a trophy shaped like a shield.

shift [shift] *vi* to manage, get on, do as one can; to change position. —*vt* to move from one person or place to another; to replace by another or others; to change the arrangement of (gears).

shill [shill *n* (*slang*) a confederate, as of a gambler, who acts as a decoy.

shilly-shally [shil′i-shal′i] *n* a vacillation, indecision. —*vi* to hesitate feebly.

shim [shim] *n* a thin wedge of wood, metal, etc. as for filling space.

shimmer [shim′ẽr] *vi* to gleam tremulously, to glisten. —*n* **shimm′er,** a tremulous gleam.

shimmy [shim′i] *n* a marked vibration or wobble, as in a car's front wheels. —*vi* to vibrate or wobble.

shin [shin] *n* the forepart of the leg below the knee. —*vti* to climb (a pole, etc.) by gripping with hands and legs. —*n* **shin′bone,** tibia.

shindig [shin′dig] *n* (*inf*) a dance, party or other lively celebration.

shine [shīn] *vi* to give or reflect light; to beam with steady radiance, to glow, to be bright; to excel, or to appear preeminent. —*vt* to cause to shine by polishing; to direct the light of.

shingle¹ [shing′gl] *n* a thin, wedge-shaped piece of wood, slate, etc. laid in overlapping rows to cover the sides or roof of a building.

shingle² [shing′gl] *n* coarse waterworn gravel as on a beach; an area covered with this. —*adj* **shing′ly.**

shingles [shing′glz] *n pl* a virus disease marked by a painful eruption of clusters of firm vesicles along the course of a nerve.

ship [ship] *n* any large vessel navigating deep water; a ship's officers and crew; an aircraft. —*vt* to put, receive, or take on board; to send or convey by any carrier; to take in (water) over the side in a heavy sea. —*vi* to embark; to go or travel by ship. —*pr p* **shipp′ing;** *pt, pt p* **shipped.**

shirk [shûrk] *vti* to evade or neglect duties or obligations. —*n* **shir′ker.**

shirr [shûr] *vt* to make shirrings in cloth; to bake (eggs) in buttered dishes. —*n* **shirring,** a gathering made in cloth by drawing the material up on parallel rows of short stitches.

shirt [shûrt] *n* a man's loose sleeved garment for the upper body; typically with fitted collar and cuffs; an undershirt.

shit [shit] (*vulgar*) —*vi* to defecate. —*vt* to defecate in. —*n* excrement; an act of defecation; something worthless; nonsense.

shiver¹ [shiv′ẽr] *n* a splinter, a chip, a small fragment. —*vti* to break into splinters. —*adj* **shiv′ery,** brittle.

shiver² [shiv′ẽr] *vi* to quiver or tremble, to make an involuntary movement as with cold or fear. —*vt* to cause to quiver. —*n* a shivering movement.

shmalz [shmölts, shmälts] *n* (*inf*) excessive sentimentality; rendered chicken fat. —*vi* to express inappropriate emotion.

shoal¹ [shōl] *n* a large crowd; a multitude of fishes swimming together. —*vi* to crowd.

shoal² [shōl] *adj* shallow. —*n* a shallow; a sandbar. —*vi* to become shallow. —*vt* to come to a shallow or less deep part.

shock¹ [shok] *n* a violent impact, a collision; a sudden jarring or shaking as if by a blow; an alarming and disconcerting experience; the cause of this; a convulsive excitation of nerves, as by electricity; a disorder of the blood circulation, produced by hemorrhage, disturbance of heart function, etc.

shock² [shok] *n* bundles of grain stacked together.

shock³ [shok] *n* a shaggy mass (of hair).

shod [shod] *pt, pt p* of **shoe.**

shoddy [shod′i] *n* wool from shredded rags; cloth made of it, alone or mixed; any inferior article seeking to pass for better than it is.

shoe [shōō] *n* a stiff outer covering for the foot, not coming above the ankle; a horseshoe; the part of a brake that presses against a wheel.—*pl* **shoes**.

shoot [shoot] *vt* to move swiftly over, by, etc.; to thrust or put forth; to discharge or fire; to send forth swiftly, esp with force; to wound with a bullet, arrow, etc.—*pt, pt p* **shot**.—*n* a contest, shooting trip, etc.; a new growth or sprout.—*ns* **shoot'er**, one who, or that which, shoots; a marble shot from the hand; **shoot'ing**, act of discharging firearms or an arrow.

shop [shop] *n* a place in which goods are sold, esp a small store; a place where mechanics work, or where any kind of industry is carried on; details of one's own work, business, or profession, or talk about these; a school laboratory equipped for manual training.—*pr p* **shopp'ing**; *pt p* **shopped**.—*n* **shop'keeper**, one who owns or operates a small store.

shore¹ [shōr, shör] *n* land bordering on the sea or an expanse of water.

shore² [shōr, shör] *n* a prop or beam used for support.—*vt* to prop (up).

shorn [shörn, shörn] *pt p* of **shear**.

short [shört] *adj* not measuring much from end to end in space or time; not great in range or scope; not tall; brief; concise; not retentive; curt; abrupt; less than a correct amount; crisp or flaky, as rich pastry; denoting a sale of securities, etc.—*adv* **short'ly**, in a short time, soon; briefly; curtly.—*ns* **short'ness; short'age**, deficiency.—*vti* **short-circuit**.—*ns* **short'coming**, a defect or deficiency; **short'cut**, a shorter route; any way of saving time, effort, etc.—*vt* **short'en**, to make or become shorter.

shot¹ *pt, pt p* of **shoot**.—*adj* hit or killed by shooting; (*inf*) ruined or worn out.

shot² [shot] *n* the act of shooting; range, scope; an attempt; a pointed, critical remark; the path of a thrown object, etc.; a projectile for a gun; projectiles collectively; small pellets of lead for a shotgun; the heavy metal ball used in the shot put; a marksman; a photograph or a continuous film sequence; a hypodermic injection, as of vaccine; a drink of liquor.

should [shŏŏd] *pt* of **shall**, an auxiliary used to express obligation, duty, expectation or probability, or a future condition.

shoulder [shōl'dèr] *n* the part of the trunk between the neck and the forelimb in mammals; the joint making this connection; a cut of meat including this joint; (*pl*) the capacity to bear a task or blame; a bulge, a prominence; either edge of a road.—*vti* to thrust with the shoulder; to take upon the shoulder, to sustain; to undertake; to take responsibility for.

shout [showt] *n* a loud cry; a call.—*vti* to utter or cry out in a shout.

shove [shuv] *vti* to thrust; to push along; to jostle.—*n* act of shoving; a push.

shovel [shuv'l] *n* a broad tool, like a scoop with a long handle for moving loose material.—*vt* to move with, or as if with, a shovel.—*vi* to use a shovel.

show [shō] *vt* to exhibit, to display; to cause or allow to be seen or known; to prove; to manifest; to usher or conduct; to bestow.—*vi* to appear; to come into sight; to finish third in a horse race.—*pt p* **shōwn** or **shōwed**.—*n* act of showing; display; a spectacle, an entertainment; a theatrical performance; a radio or television program; **show off**, to display or behave ostentatiously.

shower [show'èr] *n* a short fall, as of rain or hail; a fall, flight of many things together, as of meteors, arrows, etc.; a copious supply; a shower bath; a party at which gifts are presented to the guest of honor, esp a prospective bride or mother.

shrapnel [shrap'n(è)l] *n* an artillery shell filled with small metal balls and a bursting charge.

shred [shred] *n* a strip cut or torn off; a scrap, fragment.—*vt* to cut or tear into shreds.

shrew [shrōō] *n* small nocturnal mouse-like animals with a long snout, very small eyes, and velvety fur; a brawling, troublesome woman, a scold.—*adj* **shrewd**, (*obs*) ill-natured; having, or showing, an acute judgment; biting, keen (eg pain, cold).

shriek [shrēk] *vti* to utter with or make a loud, piercing cry; to screech.

shrift [shrift] *n* (*arch*) a confession made to a priest; (*obs*) time

granted to a condemned criminal to make such a confession before execution.

shrill [shril] *adj* high pitched and piercing; strident.—*vti* to sound or cry shrilly.

shrimp [shrimp] *n* small edible marine crustaceans.

shrine [shrīn] *n* a case for sacred relics; a saint's tomb; a place of worship.

shrink [shringk] *vi* to contract as from cold, wetting, etc.; to give way, to draw back, to recoil (from).

shrive [shrīv] *vt* (*arch*) to hear a confession and give absolution to.—*vi* (*arch*) to receive, or make, confession.—*pt* **shrōve** or **shrīved**; *pt p* **shriv'en**.

shrivel [shriv'l] *vti* to contract into wrinkles.

shroud [shrowd] *n* the dress of the dead; that which clothes or covers; any of the ropes from the masthead to a ship's sides.

shrub¹ [shrub] *n* a low woody plant with several stems; a bush.

shrub² [shrub] *n* a drink prepared from the juice of lemons, or other acid fruit, with spirits.

shrug [shrug] *vti* to draw up (the shoulders) as an expression of doubt, indifference, etc.

shuck [shuk] *n* a shell, pod, or husk.—*vt* to remove the shucks of; to lay aside (*with off*).

shudder [shud'èr] *vi* to shiver from cold or horror; to vibrate.—*n* a tremor as from cold or horror; a vibration.

shuffle [shuf'l] *vti* to mix at random, as playing cards; to shove (the feet) along without lifting them.

shun [shun] *vt* to avoid; to keep clear of.

shunt [shunt] *vti* to turn or move to one side; to switch, as a train, from one track to another.

shut [shut] *vt* to close the opening of; to lock, bar, fasten; to forbid entrance into; to confine; to catch or pinch (in a fastening).—*ns* **shutdown**, a stoppage of work or activity, as in a factory.—*n* **shutout**, (*sports*) a preventing of the opposing side from scoring.—**shut up**, to confine; (*inf*) to silence.

shuttle [shut'l] *n* an instrument used for shooting the thread of the woof between the threads of the warp in weaving, or through the loop of thread in a sewing machine; a bus, etc. making back-and-forth trips over a short route.

shy¹ [shī] *adj* timid, shrinking from notice or approach; bashful; doubtful, suspicious (of).

shy² [shī] *vti* to fling, toss, esp sideways.—*n* a throw; a verbal fling; a thing to shy at.

sib [sib] *adj* related by blood.—*n* a blood relation; *n* **sib'ling**, one who has a parent, or parents, in common with another.

sibilate [sib'i-lāt] *vti* to hiss.—*adj* **sib'ilant**, hissing.—*n* hissing consonant sound, as of *s* or *z*.

sic¹ [sik] *adv* so, thus; printed within brackets [sic] in quoted matter to show that the original is being faithfully reproduced, even though incorrect or seemingly so.

sic² [sik] *vt* to incite (a dog) to attack.—Also **sick**.

siccative [sik'à-tiv] *adj* drying.—*n* a drying agent.

sick [sik] *adj* unwell, ill; having nausea; out of condition; suffering the effects (of); thoroughly wearied (of); disgusted by an excess; (*inf*) of humor, comedy, macabre, gruesome.—*n* **sick'ness**.—*adj* **sick'ly**.—*ns* **sick'liness; sick' bay**, a compartment in a ship used as a dispensary and hospital.

sickle [sik'l] *n* a tool with a crescent-shaped blade for cutting tall grasses and weeds.

side [sīd] *n* a line or surface forming part of a boundary; the part near such a boundary; the margin; a surface or part turned in a certain direction, espone more or less upright, or one regarded as right or left (not front or back, top or bottom); side' effect, a secondary and usu. adverse effect; **side'-glance**, a sidelong glance; a passing allusion; **side'kick** (*slang*), a confederate; a partner; a close friend; **side'line**, either of two lines marking the side limits of a playing area, as in football; a subsidiary activity.—*adj* **side'splitting**, provoking uncontrollable laughter.—*n* **side' step**, a step taken to one side.—*vti* to avoid as by a step aside.—*n* **side'track**, a siding.—*vt* to divert into a siding; to prevent action on by diversionary tactics.—*n* **side'walk**, a path for pedestrians, usu. paved, at the side of a street.

sidle [sī'dl] *vi* to move sideways, esp to edge along.

siege [sēj] *n* (*obs*) a seat, throne; an attempt to take a fortified place by keeping it surrounded by an armed force; a persistent attempt to gain possession or control (of).

sienna [sē-en'a] *n* an earthy substance that is brownish yellow when raw and orange red or reddish brown when burnt and is used as a pigment.

sierra [si-er'a] *n* a jagged ridge of mountain peaks.

siesta [si-es'ta] *n* a short sleep or rest usu taken in the afternoon.

sieve [siv] *n* a vessel with many small holes to separate the fine part of anything from the coarse or for straining liquids.

sift [sift] *vt* to separate as by passing through a sieve; to examine closely; to separate.—*vi* to pass as through a sieve.— *n* sift'er.

sigh [sī] *vi* to inhale and respire with a sigh; to yearn (for); to grieve; to sound like a sigh.

sight [sīt] *n* act of seeing; faculty of seeing; an opportunity of seeing, view; that which is seen; a spectacle; space within vision; a small opening for observing objects; a device in a gun, or optical or other instrument, to guide the eye.—*adjs* sight'ed, having sight of a specified character (eg *short'-sighted*); sight'less, blind.—*adj* sight'ly, pleasing to the sight or eye, comely.—*ns* sight'liness; sight'read'ing; sight'see'ing, visiting scenes or objects of interest; sight'se'er.—at sight, as soon as seen; out of sight, not in sight; far off; (*inf*) beyond reach; (*slang*) excellent, wonderful.

sigma [sig'mä] *n* the 18th letter of the Greek alphabet; (*math*) the symbol Σ, indicating summation.

sign [sīn] *n* a gesture expressing a meaning, a signal; a mark with a meaning; a symbol, an emblem; a token, proof, outward evidence; a portent; a miracle; a device marking an inn, etc.; a board or panel giving a shopkeeper's name or trade, etc.; a placard, etc. bearing information, etc.

signal [sig'n(à)l] *n* a, usu visible or audible, intimation, eg of warning, conveyed to a distance; in radio, etc. the electrical impulses transmitted or received; a sign or event that initiates action.—*vti* to make a signal or signals (to); to communicate by signals.—*pr p* sig'naling; *pt, pt p* sig'naled.—*vt* sig'nalize, to mark or distinguish; to make known or draw attention to.

signature [sig'na-chŭr] *n* a person's name written by himself; a signing of one's own name; a signed name; an indication of key, also of time, at the beginning of a line of music; a letter or numeral at the foot of a page to indicate sequence of sheets; a folded sheet that is one unit of a book.

signify [sig'ni-fī] *vt* to be a sign of; to mean; to indicate or declare.—*vi* to have importance.—*adj* signif'icant, having, or conveying, meaning, esp a special or hidden one; expressive of much; important; indicative (of).—*adv* signif'icantly.—*n* significa'tion, act of signifying; accepted meaning.

silage [sī'lij] *n* green fodder preserved in a silo.

silence [sī'lens] *n* absence of sound; forbearance from sounding, or from speech; abstention from mentioning or divulging something; a time characterized by absence of sound.—*vt* to cause to be silent.—*interj* be silent!.—*n* sī'lencer, a device to muffle the sound of a gun.—*adj* sī'lent, noiseless.

silhouette [sil-õõ-et'] *n* a solid outline drawing, usu. filled in with black, esp of a profile; an outline showing an object against a contrasting background.

silica [sil'i-ka] *n* a compound of silicon and oxygen, the most abundant solid constituent of our globe, existing both in the crystalline amorphous and impure forms and present in animal and plant tissue.

silk [silk] *n* a fiber produced by various insect larvae, usu. for cocoons, esp a lustrous tough elastic fiber produced by silkworms and used for textiles; a thread, yarn, cloth, or garment, or attire, made from silk.

sill [sil] *n* a heavy, horizontal timber or line of masonry supporting a house wall, etc.; the timber, stone, etc., at the foot of an opening, as for a door or window.

silly [sil'i] *adj* simple; witless; foolish; lacking in sense or judgment; being stunned or dazed.—*n* a silly person.—*adv* silly; sill'ily.—*n* sill'iness.

silo [sī'lõ] *n* an airtight pit or tower in which green fodder is preserved; a deep bin for storing material (as cement or coal); an underground structure for housing a guided missile.

silt [silt] *n* a fine-grained sandy sediment carried or deposited by water.—*vti* to fill or choke up with silt.

silver [sil'vèr] *n* a metallic element, capable of a high polish; money made of silver; silverware; anything having the appearance of silver; a lustrous, grayish white.—*adj* made of silver; plated with, or containing silver; silvery; clear and ringing

in tone.—*vt* to cover with silver; to coat with a substance resembling silver; to make silvery.—*adj* sil'very, covered with silver; resembling silver in color; clear and musical in tone.—*n* sil'veriness.

similar [sim'i-lár] *adj* somewhat like, resembling; having resemblance (to).

simile [sim'i-le] *n* a figure of speech likening one thing to another by the use of *like, as*, etc.

simmer [sim'ér] *vi* to remain at or just below boiling point; to be about to break out, as in anger.—*vt* to cause to simmer.—*n* a simmering.

simper [sim'pér] *vi* to smile in a silly, affected manner.—*n* a silly or affected smile.

simple [sim'pl] *adj* consisting of one thing or element; not complex or compound; easy; plain, unornate; unpretentious.—*n* a simple person; a vegetable drug of one constituent.—*ns* sim'pleness; simplic'ity; simplifica'tion, the act, or result, of making simple.—*vt* sim'plify, to make simple, simpler, less difficult.

simulate [sim'ū-lāt] *vt* to feign; to have or assume a false appearance of.—*n* simula'tion, the act of simulating or putting on a character or appearance which is not true.

simultaneous [sim-ul-tā'nyùs] *adj* being, or happening, at the same time.

sin [sin] *n* moral offense or shortcoming, esp from the point of view of religion; condition of so offending; an offense generally; transgression of the law of God.—*vi* to commit a sin.— *adj* sin'ful, tainted with sin; wicked.—*n* sinn'er.

since [sins] *adv* from then until now; at some time between then and now; before now, ago.

sincere [sin-sēr'] *adj* pure, unadulterated, unmixed; unfeigned, genuine, the same in reality as in appearance.— *adv* sincēre'ly.—*n* sincer'ity [ser'-].

sine [sīn] *n* (*math*) one of the six trigonometrical functions of an angle, the ratio of the perpendicular to the hypotenuse.

sinecure [sī'nè-kūr (or sin'-)] *n* any position that provides an income without involving much work.

sinew [sin'ū] *n* a tendon, esp one dressed for use as a thread or cord.

sing [sing] *vi* to utter melodious sounds in successive musical notes; to emit songlike sounds; to compose poetry; to give a cantabile or lyrical effect; to ring.

singe [sinj] *vt* to burn on the surface, to scorch, esp to remove feathers, etc.

single [sing'gl] *adj* consisting of one only, individual, unique; uncombined; unmarried; for one person or family; consisting of one part, undivided; between two persons only; whole, unbroken.—*adv* sing'ly, one by one; alone.

singsong [sing'song] *n* monotonous up-and-down intonation; verse with regular, marked rhythm and rhyme.—*adj* of the nature of singsong.

singular [sing'gū-lár] *adj* (*gram*) denoting one person or thing; unique; preeminent, exceptional; unusual, extraordinary, strange, odd.—*n* singular'ity, the state of being singular; peculiarity; anything curious or remarkable.—*adv* sing'ularly, unusually; strangely.

sinister [sin'is-tèr] *adj* left; on the left side (eg of the bearer of a shield); unlucky, inauspicious, threatening harm, disaster; wicked, evil.—*adj* sin'istral.

sink [singk] *vi* to become submerged, wholly or partly; to subside; to fall slowly; to pass to a lower level or state; to slope away, dip; to subside, as wind or sound; to become hollow, as the cheeks; to approach death.—*p t* sank (now rarely) sunk; *p* sunk, sunk'en.

sinter [sin'tèr] *n* a deposit formed by the evaporation of spring or lake water.—*vt* to cause to coalesce into a single mass under heat without actually liquefying.—*vi* to undergo sintering.

sinus [sī'nus] *n* an indentation, a notch; a cavity, specifically, any of the air cavities in the skull which open in the nasal cavities.

sip [sip] *vti* to drink in small quantities.—*pr p* sipp'ing; *pt, pt p* sipped.—*n* an act of sipping; the quantity sipped at once.

siphon [sī'fòn] *n* a bent tube full of water, connecting two reservoirs so that flow can take place over an intervening barrier under atmospheric pressure.

sir [sûr] *n* a word of respect used in addressing a man; a word of address to a man in a formal letter.

sire [sīr] *n* a term of address to a king; (*poetical*) a father or forefather; the male parent of a four-legged animal. —*vt* to beget.

siren [sī'ren] *n* a charming temptress; a warning device, etc., producing a loud wailing sound.

sirloin [sûr'loin] *n* a choice cut of beef from the loin end in front of the rump.

sirrah, sirra [sir'a] *n* sir, used in anger or contempt.

sister [sis'tèr] *n* the name applied to a female by other children of the same parents; a friend who is like a sister; a female fellow member of the same race, creed, etc.; a nun; one of the same kind, model, etc. —*adj* closely related, akin. —*ns* **sis'terhood**, fact or state of being a sister; the relationship of sister; a society, esp a religious community, of women; **sis'-ter-in-law**, a husband's or wife's sister, or a brother's wife. — *adj* **sis'terly**, like or befitting a sister, kind, affectionate.

sit [sit] *vi* to rest oneself upon the buttocks, as on a chair; to rest on the haunches with the forelegs braced, as a dog; to perch, as a bird; to cover eggs for hatching, as a hen; to occupy a seat as a judge, legislator, etc.; to be in session, as a court; to pose, as for a portrait; to be located; to rest or lie; to take an examination; to take care of a child, pet, or house while the parents or owners are away. —*vt* to cause to sit; to provide seats or seating room for. —*pr p* **sitt'ing**; *pt, pt p* **sat.**

site [sīt] *n* situation, esp of a building; ground occupied by, or set apart for, a building, etc.; the place or scene of something. —*vt* to locate.

situate [sit'ū-āt] *vt* to place in a site, situation, or category. — *adj* having a site; located. —*adj* **sit'uated**, situate; provided with money or possessions.

six [siks] *adj*, *n* one more than five. —*n* the symbol for this; the sixth in a series or set; something having six units as members as an ice hockey team or a 6-cylinder engine.

sixteen [siks'tēn] *adj*, *n* one more than fifteen; the symbol for this. —*adj*, *n* **sixteenth.**

sixty [siks'tē] *adj*, *n* six times ten; the symbol for this.

size¹ [sīz] *n* magnitude; (*obs*) a portion of food and drink; an allotted portion; one, or belonging to one, of a series of classes according to standard dimensions, esp of merchandise. —*vt* to arrange according to size; to measure. —*adjs* **sī'zable**, **size'-able.**

size² [sīz], **sizing** [sī'zing] *n* a pasty substance used as a glaze or filler on paper, cloth, etc. —*vt* to cover with size.

sizzle [siz'l] *vi* to make a hissing sound of frying; to be extremely hot. —*vt* to fry, scorch, sear with a sizzling sound. —*n* a hissing sound.

skate¹ [skāt] *n* a metal runner in a frame, fastened to a shoe for gliding on ice; a boot with such a runner attached. —*ns* **skā'ter; skā'ting.**

skate² [skāt] *n* a fish with a broad, flat body and short, spineless tail.

skeleton [skel'e-tòn] *n* the bony framework of an animal; the framework or outline of anything.

skeptic [skep'tik] *n* an adherent of skepticism; one who habitually questions matters generally accepted; one who doubts religious doctrines. —*adj* **skeptical**, doubting; questioning.

sketch [skech] *n* a drawing, slight, rough, or without detail, esp as a study towards a more finished work. —*vti* to make a sketch. —*adj* **sketch'y**, like a sketch; incomplete, slight; imperfect, inadequate.

skew [skū] *adj* oblique. —*adv* awry. —*vti* to slang or set at a slant. —*adj* **skewed**, distorted.

skewer [skū'ėr] *n* a long pin of wood or metal, used for keeping meat together while roasting.

ski [skē, shē] *n* a long narrow runner orig of wood, now also of metal, etc., fastened to the foot to enable the wearer to slide across snow, etc.. —*pl* **ski**, or **skis.** —*vi* to travel on skis. —*pt* **skied, ski'd.** —*ns* **ski'er; ski'ing.**

skid [skid] *n* a support on which something rests, is brought to the desired level, or slides; (*pl*) (*slang*) a route to defeat or downfall. —*vti* to slide or slip, as a vehicle on ice.

skiff [skif] *n* a small light rowboat, often with sails or a motor.

skill [skil] *n* expertness; expert knowledge; a complex movement or action carried out with facility as a result of practice; a developed aptitude or ability. —*adj* **skilled**, expert.

skillet [skil'et] *n* a shallow metal vessel with a long handle, used in cooking, etc.

skim [skim] *vti* to remove (floating matter) from the surface of; to glide lightly over; to read superficially, skipping portions. —*pr p* **skimm'ing**; *pt, pt p* **skimmed.** —*ns* **skimm'er.**

skimp [skimp] *vti* (*inf*) to be sparing or frugal. —*adj* (*inf*) scanty, spare. —*adj* **skim'py.**

skin [skin]*n* the natural outer covering of an animal; a hide; an integument; a thin outer layer or covering; a vessel for containing wine or water made of an animal's skin; a casing forming the outside surface of a structure.

skip [skip] *vti* to spring or hop lightly over; to pass from one point to another, omitting or ignoring; to leave hurriedly. —*pr p* **skipp'ing**; *pt, pt p* **skipped.** —*n* an act of skipping.

skipper [skip'ér] *n* the master of a fishing, small trading, or pleasure boat; the captain or first pilot of an airplane.

skirmish [skûr'mish] *n* a brief fight between small parties. —*vi* to take part in a skirmish.

skirt [skûrt] *n* a garment, generally a woman's, that hangs from the waist; the lower part of a dress, coat or other garment.

skit [skit] *n* a short humorous sketch, as in the theater.

skittish [skit'ish] *adj* shy, nervous, easily frightened; frivolous, frisky; lively; coquettish, coy.

skittle [skit'l] *n* (*Brit*) a pin, or wooden object set on end, for the game of **skittles** (English ninepins).

skulk [skulk] *vi* to move in a stealthy manner; to conceal (oneself) out of cowardice, fear, or with sinister intent. —*n* **skulk'er.**

skull [skul] *n* the bony case that encloses the brain; the head.

skunk [skungk] *n* a small bushy-tailed N American mammal.

sky [skī] *n* the upper atmosphere that constitutes an apparent vault over the earth; heaven; the weather in the upper atmosphere; the climate. —*adj, adv* **sky'ward**, toward the sky. —*adv* **sky'wards.**

slab [slab] *n* a flat, broad, and fairly thick piece (as of stone, wood, or bread, etc.).

slabber [slab'er] *vti* to slaver, to drool; to slobber.

slack¹ [slak] *adj* loose, not tight; slow, sluggish; not busy; dull; careless; lacking in completeness, finish, or perfection. —*vti* to slacken. —*n* a part that hangs loose; a lack of tension; a dull period; a lull; (*pl*) trousers for men or women. —*adv* **slack'ly.** —*vti* **slack'en**, to make or become less active, brisk, etc.; to loosen or relax, as a rope. —*n* **slack'er**, an idler, shirker. —*adv* **slack'ly.** —*n* **slack'ness.** —*n, adj* **slack'ening.**

slack² [slak] *n* coal dross.

slag [slag] *n* vitrified cinders from smelting; scoriae from a volcano.

slake [slāk] *vti* to quench, satisfy.

slam¹ [slam] *vti* to shut with violence and noise, to bang; to put forcibly, noisily, hurriedly; (*inf*) to criticize severely. —*pr p* **slamm'ing**; *pt, pt p* **slammed.**

slam² [slam] *n* grand slam; little slam.

slander [slän'dèr] *n* the utterance of a falsehood that damages another's reputation; such a statement. —*vt* to utter such a statement about. —*adj* **slan'derous.**

slang [slang] *n* cant, jargon peculiar to a social class, or age group; words or phrases common in colloquial speech.

slant [slänt] *vti* to slope; to tell so as to express a particular bias. —*n* a slope; obliquity; a sloping surface, line, ray, or movement. —*adj* **sloping**, oblique, inclined from a direct line. —*adj* **slanted**, sloping; biased, prejudiced.

slap [slap] *n* a blow with the hand or anything flat; an insult; a rebuff. —*vt* to strike with something flat; to put, hit, etc. with force.

slash [slash] *vt* to cut by striking with sweeping strokes, as of a knife; to make long cuts in.

slat [slat] *n* a thin strip of wood, etc. —*adj* **slatt'ed**, having slats.

slate¹ [slāt] *n* a piece of construction material prepared as a shingle for roofing or siding; a tablet of material (as slate) for writing on; a list of proposed candidates. —*adj* of slate. —*ns* **slā'ter**, one who covers roofs with slates; a wood louse; any of various marine isopods.

slate² [slāt] *vt* to thrash severely.

slaughter [slö'tèr] *n* the killing of animals for food; killing of great numbers, carnage. —*vt* to slay in large numbers; to butcher; to kill in a violent manner. —*ns* **slaugh'terer.**

slave [slāv] *n* a person owned by another; one who is submissive under domination; one who works like a slave, a

dge.—*adj* slā′vish, befitting a slave, servile, abject; serly following guidance or conforming to pattern or rule.

r [slav′ěr] *n* saliva running from the mouth.—*vi* to let the
va run out of the mouth; to drivel; to fawn.—*vt* (*arch*) to
ear with saliva.

[slā] *vt* to kill violently, wantonly, or in great numbers;
ng) to overwhelm.—*vi* to kill, murder.—*pt* slew; *pt p*
n.—*n* slay′er.

[sled] *n* a vehicle with runners made for sliding upon
w; a rocket sled.—*vti* to carry or travel in a sled.

ge¹ [slej] *n* a sled or sleigh.

ge² [slej] *n* a large heavy hammer.—Also sledgehammer.

. [slēk] *adj* smooth, glossy, and soft; having a well-fed or
l-groomed appearance; insinuating, plausible.—*vt* to make
k.

[slēp] *n* a natural, regularly recurring rest for the body,
ing which there is little or no conscious thought; any state
this; death; a trance; a coma; a period spent sleeping;
ate of numbness followed by tingling.—*adj* sleep′less,
out sleep; unable to sleep.—*adv* sleep′lessly.—*ns*
p′lessness; sleepwalk′er, one who walks in sleep, a som-
ambulist; sleepwalk′ing.—*adj* sleep′y.

. [slēt] *n* partly frozen rain.

ve [slēv] *n* the part of a garment which covers the arm; a
elike part fitting around another.

h [slā] *n* a light vehicle on runners, as for travel on snow.—
drive or travel in a sleigh.

ht [slīt] *n* cunning, dexterity; an artful trick.—*n* sleight
hand′, legerdemain; expert manipulation; skill in tricks
ending on such.

ler [slen′dĕr] *adj* thin or narrow; slim; slight.—*adv* slen′-
ly.—*n* slen′derness.—*vti* slen′derize, to make or become
der.

h [slooth] *n* (*inf*) a detective.

[slīs] *n* a thin flat piece cut from something; a wedge-
ped piece; a spatula for spreading paint or ink; a serving
a wedge-shaped blade; a portion, a share.—*n*
cer.—*n*, *adj* slīc′ing.

[slik] *adj* sleek, smooth, trim; adroit, dexterous; wily;
) smooth but superficial, tricky, etc.

[slīd] *vi* to move along in constant contact with a smooth
face, as on ice; to coast over snow and ice; (*baseball*) to
roach a base by gliding along the ground; to slip; to glide.

t [slīt] *adj* frail, flimsy—lacking solidity, massiveness,
ght; slim; trifling, insignificant.—*vt* to ignore or overlook
respectfully.—*n* discourteous disregard; an affront by
wing neglect or want of neglect.—*adv* slight′ly.

[slim] *adj* small in girth, slender; small in amount, degree,
—*vti* to make or become slim.—*ns* slim′ness; slimm′ing.

e [slīm] *n* ooze, very fine, thin, slippery, or gluey mud;
viscous organic secretion, as mucus secreted by various
mals (as slugs and catfishes); (*inf*) one that is odious.—*adj*
n′y.—*n* slim′iness.

¹ [sling] *n* a strap or pocket with a string attached to each
for hurling a stone; a loop for hoisting, lowering, or
rying, a weight; a hanging support for an injured arm.—*vt*
hrow (as) with a sling.—*pt*, *pt p* slung.

² [sling] *n* a hot or cold alcoholic drink consisting of liquor,
ar, lemon juice and plain or carbonated water.

[slingk] *vi* to move stealthily, to sneak.—*pt*, *pt p* slunk.—
slink′y, slinking.

[slip] *vi* to slide or glide along; to move out of position; to
foothold; to escape; to slink; to move unobserved; to
ke a slight mistake; to lapse morally; to lose one's grip on
ngs, one's control of the situation; to become worse.—*pt*, *pt*
pped.

[slip] *vt* to take cuttings from (a plant); to divide into
s.—*n* a stem, root, etc., of a plant, used for planting or
fting; a descendant, offspring; a small piece of paper; a
ng, slim person; a long seat or narrow pew.

slit] *vt* to cut open lengthwise; to cut into strips.—*pr p*
t′ing; *pt*, *pt p* slit.—*n* a long cut; a narrow opening.

er [slīTH′ěr] *vi* to slide, as on mud or scree; to slip or slide
a snake.—*vt* to cause to slide.

r [sliv′ěr] *vti* to split or cut into slivers.—*n* a long thin
ce cut or rent off; a splinter.

[slob] *n* (*inf*) a coarse or sloppy person.

slobber [slob′ěr] *vt* to smear with dribbling saliva or food.—*vi*
to drool; to speak in a maudlin way.—*n* saliva drooled; drivel-
ling or incoherent utterance.

sloe [slō] *n* a small sour plum, the fruit of the blackthorn; the
blackthorn.

slog [slog] *vti* to hit hard; to make (one's way) laboriously; to
toil (at).—*n* a strenuous spell of work; a hard dogged march or
tramp.—*n* slogg′er.

slogan [slō′gän] *n* a catchword or motto associated with a
political party, etc.;

sloop [sloop] *n* a small sailing vessel with a single mast and a
jib.

slop¹ [slop] *n* slush; spilled liquid; a puddle; unappetizing
liquid or semiliquid food; (*pl*) liquid refuse; gush; effusive
sentiment in speech or writing.—*vti* to spill or splash.—*adj*
slopp′y.

slop² [slop] *n* a loose smock or overall.

slope [slōp] *n* rising or falling ground; an inclined surface; the
amount or degree of this.

slot¹ [slot] *n* the track of an animal (as a deer).

slot² [slot] *n* a long narrow depression or opening to receive a
coin, or part of a mechanism, etc.; a slit.

slouch [slowch] *n* a loose, ungainly, stooping posture; a lazy or
incompetent person; a lout.

slough¹ [slow] *n* a hollow filled with mud: deep, hopeless
dejection.—*vt* to engulf in a slough.

slough² [sluf] *n* castoff skin of a snake; dead tissue in a sore;
something that may be shed or cast off.—*vi* to come away as a
slough (*with* off); to cast the skin.—*vt* to cast off, as a slough.

sloven [sluv′n] *n* a person carelessly or dirtily dressed.

slow [slō] *adj* not quick in understanding; not swift; not hasty;
not progressive; dull; behind in time.—*adv* slowly.

sludge [sluj] *n* soft mud or mire; any heavy, slimy deposit,
sediment, etc.; partly melted snow.

slug¹ [slug] *n* a habitually lazy fellow; a mollusk resembling a
snail but having no outer shell; a smooth soft larvae of a moth
that creeps like a mollusk.

slug² [slug] *n* a lump of metal, esp one for firing from a gun; a
disk for insertion in a slot machine, esp one used illegally
instead of a coin; (*inf*) a hard blow, with the fist or a bat.—*vt*
(*inf*) to hit hard with the fist or a bat.

sluice [sloos] *n* a structure with a gate for stopping or regulating the flow of water; a drain, channel.

slum [slum] *n* an overcrowded area characterized by poverty,
etc.

slumber [slum′bĕr] *vi* to sleep; to be inactive.—*n* sleep; a light
sleep; lethargy; torpor.

slump [slump] *vi* to fall or sink suddenly; to drop or slide
suddenly; to collapse; to have a drooping posture; to go into a
slump.

slur [slûr] *vt* to disparage, asperse; to sound indistinctly; to
glide (over) quickly and carelessly; (*mus*) to produce by gliding without a break.—*pr p* slurr′ing; *pt*, *pt p* slurred.

slush [slush] *n* liquid mud; melting snow; worthless sentimental drivel.

slut [slut] *n* a dirty, untidy woman; a lewd woman; a prostitute.—*adj* slutt′ish.

sly [slī] *adj* skillful in doing anything so as to be unobserved;
cunning, wily, secretive; done with artful dexterity; with
hidden meaning.

smack¹ [smak] *n* taste; a distinctive or distinguishable flavor;
small quantity, a trace, tinge.—*vi* to have a taste (of).

smack² [smak] *n* a fishing vessel fitted with a well to keep fish
alive.

smack³ [smak] *vt* to strike smartly, to slap loudly; to kiss
roughly and noisily; to make a sharp noise with, as the lips by
separation.

small [smöl] *adj* little in size, extent, quantity, or degree; fine
in grain, texture, gauge, etc.

smarmy [smärm′-ē] *adj* fawning, ingratiatingly and fulsomely.

smart [smärt] *n* a quick, stinging pain; *intelli-*
gence.—*vi* to cause sharp, stinging pain (as by a slap); to
feel such pain; to feel distress or irritation.—*adj* sharp and
stinging; vigorous, brisk; acute, witty; vivacious; keen,
quick, and efficient in business; trim, spruce, fine; fashionable, stylish.—*vti* smart′en, to make or become smart.—*adv*
smart′ly.—*n* smart′ness.

smash [smash] *vti* to break into pieces with noise or violence; to hit, collide, or move with force; to destroy or be destroyed.—*n* a hard, heavy hit; a violent, noisy breaking; a violent collision; total failure, esp in business; a popular success.

smattering [smat'ẻr'ing] *n* a scrappy superficial knowledge; a small number.

smear [smẻr] *vt* to cover with anything sticky or oily, as grease; to rub in such a way as to make a smear; to defame, slander.

smell [smel] *n* the sense by which odors are perceived; the specific sensation excited by an odor; the property of exciting it; a perfume, scent, odor, or stench; an act of instance of smelling; a pervading, characteristic quality; a very small amount.

smelt¹ [smelt] *n* a small, silvery food fish shaped like a salmon.

smelt² [smelt] *vt* to melt (ore) in order to separate metal; to refine (metal) in this way.

smile [smīl] *vi* to express amusement, slight contempt, favor, pleasure, etc., by a slight drawing up of the corners of the lips.

smirch [smûrch] *vt* to dishonor; to soil, stain, or sully.—*n* a stain on reputation; a smudge, smear.

smirk [smûrk] *vi* to put on a complacent, conceited, or foolish smile.—*n* an affected or foolish smile.

smite [smīt] *vt* to strike, to beat; to kill or injure; to strike, affect suddenly and powerfully.

smith [smith] *n* a worker in metals; one who makes anything; a blacksmith.

smithereens [smiTH-ẻr-ēnz'] *n pl* (*inf*) fragments.

smitten [smit'n] *pt p* of smite.

smock [smok] *n* (*arch*) a chemise; a loose shirtlike outer garment to protect the clothes.

smog [smog] *n* a mixture of fog and smoke.

smoke [smōk] *n* the gases, vapors, and small particles that come off from a burning substance; any similar vapor; a cigar or cigarette; an act of smoking tobacco, etc.—*vi* to give off smoke; to draw in and puff out the smoke of tobacco, etc.—*adj* smo'ky.—*adv* smo'kily.—*n* smo'kiness.—**smoke out**, to destroy or expel by diffusion of smoke.

smolder, smoulder [smōl'dẻr] *vi* to burn slowly or without flame; to persist, linger on.

smolt [smōlt] *n* a young salmon or sea trout.

smooth [smōōTH] *adj* having an even surface; not rough; evenly spread; glossy; slippery; hairless; of even consistency; gently flowing in rhythm or sound; easy; bland, agreeable.—*adv* smooth'ly.

smote [smōt] *pt* of smite.

smother [smuTH'ẻr] *vt* to suffocate by excluding the air, esp by means of a thick covering; to cover over thickly; to stifle (a yawn).

smudge [smuj] *n* a dirty spot; a fire made to produce dense smoke.

smug [smug] *adj* neat, spruce; complacent, self-satisfied.—*adv* smug'ly.—*n* smug'ness.

smuggle [smug'l] *vt* to import or export illegally or without paying duties imposed by law; to convey secretly.—*adj* smug'gled.—*ns* smugg'ler.

smut [smut] *n* soot; a flake or spot of dirt, soot, etc; indecent talk or writing; *adj* smutt'y.

smutch [smuch] *n* a dirty mark.

snack [snak] *n* a light meal between regular meals.

snaffle [snaf'l] *n* a jointed bit for a horse's mouth having no curb.—*vt* to get possession of.

snag [snag] *n* a sharp point or projection; an underwater tree stump or branch; a tear, as in cloth, made by a snag, etc.; an unexpected or hidden difficulty.

snail [snāl] *n* a mollusk having a wormlike body and a spiral protective shell; a slow-moving or sluggish person or thing.

snake [snāk] *n* limbless, scaly reptiles with a long, tapering body and with salivary glands often modified to produce venom.

snap [snap] *vti* to bite or grasp suddenly (*with* at); to speak or utter sharply (*with* at); to break suddenly; to make or cause to make a sudden, cracking sound; to close, fasten, etc. with this sound; to move or cause to move suddenly and sharply; to take a snapshot (of).—*adj* snappish, given to curt irritable speech; arising from annoyance; inclined to bite.—*adv* snapp'ily.

snare [snār] *n* a running noose of string or wire, etc catching an animal; a trap; an allurement.

snarl¹ [snärl] *vi* to make a surly resentful noise with sh teeth; to speak in a surly manner.—*vt* to utter snarlingl an unnatural growl; a surly malicious utterance.—*n* snar

snarl² [snärl] *vti* to twist, entangle.—*n* a tangle; disorder.

snatch [snach] *vt* to seize suddenly; to pluck away quick take as opportunity occurs.

snazzy [snaz'i] *adj* (*slang*) very attractive or fashionable; fl

sneak [snēk] *vti* to move, act, give, put, take, etc., secre stealthily.—*n* one who sneaks; an act of sneaking.—*adj* out warning.—*n* sneak'er, one who sneaks; a shoe w cloth upper and a soft rubber sole.—*adj* sneak'ing, underhand.

sneer [snēr] *vi* to show cynical contempt by the express the face, as by drawing up the lip.—*n* sneer'er.—*n* sneer'ing.—*adv* sneer'ingly.

sneeze [snēz] *vi* to eject air violently through the nose wi explosive sound.—*n* an act of sneezing.

snick [snik] *vt* to cut, snip, nick.—*n* a small cut or nic snick'ersnee, a large knife.

snicker [snik'ẻr] *vti* to laugh or utter with a sly, partly s manner.—*n* a snickering.

snide [snīd] *adj* base, mean, cheap; sham, insincere; su in attitude; sneering.

sniff [snif] *vti* to draw in by the nose with the breath; to by sniffing.

snigger [snig'ẻr] *vti* to snicker.—*n* a snicker.

snip [snip] *vti* to sever instantaneously, esp by a single cu scissors.

snipe [snīp] *n* birds with long straight flexible bills.—*vi* to snipe; to shoot at individuals from a hidden positio snip'er.

snivel [sniv'l] *vi* to whimper and sniffle; *n* sniv'eller sniv'elling.

snob [snob] *n* one animated by obsequious admiration for of higher social rank or by a desire to dissociate himself those whom he regards as inferior.—*n* snobb'ery, the q of being snobbish.—*adj* snobb'ish.—*n* snobb'ishness.

snood [snōōd] *n* a conspicuous net supporting the back ha

snooker [snōōk'ẻr] *n* a variation of pool played with l balls and 6 variously colored balls.

snoop [snōōp] *vi* (*inf*) to pry about in a sneaking wa snoop'er, (*inf*) one who snoops.

snooze [snōōz] *vi* (*inf*) to doze.—*n* (*inf*) a nap.

snore [snōr] *vi* to breathe roughly and hoarsely in sleep vibration of uvula and soft palate.

snorkel [snôr'kẻl] *n* a breathing tube extending abov water, used in swimming just below the surface.

snort [snôrt] *vi* to force the air with violence and noise th the nostrils.

snot [snot] *n* mucus of the nose.—*adj* snott'y, like, o with, snot; irritatingly unpleasant.

snout [snowt] *n* the projecting nose of an animal as of a sw

snow [snō] *n* the frozen atmospheric vapor, in crystalline which falls as light, white flakes; a snowfall; a mass or ex of snow; (*slang*) cocaine or heroin.—*vi* to fall in snowflak *vt* to pour abundantly, as if snow; to whiten like sno snow'ball, a ball made of snow pressed hard togethe snow'drift, a bank of drifted snow; snow'fall, a fall of the amount falling in a given time; snow'plow, a machi clearing away snow; snow'-white, as white as snow; sn abounding or covered with snow; white, like snow; pure snub [snub] *vt* to check, curb (a rope, etc.); to humiliate intentional rebuff or crushing retort.—*pr p* snubb'ing; snubbed.—*n* an act of snubbing.—*adjs* short and turne as a nose.

snuff¹ [snuf] *vti* to sniff or smell.—*n* a powdered preparat tobacco; the amount taken at one time.—*ns* snuff'box, box for snuff.

snuff² [snuf] *n* the charred portion of a wick.—*vt* to c pinch the snuff from, as a burning candle.

snuffle [snuf'l] *vi* to breathe hard or in an obstructed m through the nose; to sniff; to speak through the nose.

snug [snug] *adj* lying close and warm; neat; trim; sheltere exposed to view or notice; tight in fit; offering safe conceal-ment. —vi **snug′gle**, to cuddle, nestle.

[sō] adv in this way; as shown; as stated; to such an extent; ery; (inf) very much; therefore; more or less; also, likewise; hen.

ak [sōk] vt to steep in a fluid; to take in. —vi to be steeped in a quid; to penetrate.

ap [sōp] n a substance used with water to produce suds for washing, made by the action of an alkali on a fat; soap. —ns oap′box, a street orator's improvised platform; **soap opera**, nf) a daytime radio or television serial melodrama; **soap′**-tone, steatite. —adj **soap′y**.

ar [sōr] vi to mount high in the air; to glide along high in the ir; to rise high.

b [sob] vi to catch the breath convulsively in distress or other motion; to make a similar sound. —vt to utter with sobs.

ber [sō′bėr] adj not drunk; temperate, esp in use of intoxi-ants; moderate; without excess or extravagance; serious; edate; quiet in color.

briquet [sō′brē-kā] n a nickname; an assumed name.

occer [sok′ėr] n a football game played on a field by two teams f 11 players with a round inflated ball.

ciable [sō′shà-bl] adj inclined to society; companionable; avorable to social intercourse. —n an informal party. —n ociabil′ity, quality of being sociable. —adv sō′ciably. —adv ō′cial, pertaining to society or companionship. —adv sō′ci-ally. —vt sō′cialize, to train or adapt to fit social environ-ment. —ns sō′cialism, a theory, principle, or scheme of social rganization which places the means of production and distri-ution in the hands of the community; sō′cialist, an adherent f socialism. —adj sōcialis′tic. —ns sō′cialite, a person who as a place in fashionable society.

ociology [sō-shi-ol′o-ji] n the science that treats of the evelopment and structure of society and social relation-ships. —n sociol′ogist.

ck¹ [sok] n a light shoe worn by Greek and Roman actors of omedy; a kind of short stocking.

ck² [sok] vt (slang) to strike hard. —n (slang) a violent blow.

cket [sok′et] n a cavity into which something is inserted, as he receptacle of the eye, of a bone, a tooth, an electric light ulb, etc.

d [sod] n any surface of earth grown with grass turf; a piece f this; one's native land.

da [sō′da] n sodium bicarbonate; sodium carbonate; soda vater; a confection of soda water, syrup, and ice cream.

dality [sō-dal′i-ti] n a fellowship or sorority.

dden [sod′n] adj soaked thoroughly; boggy; doughy, not well baked; dull or stupefied, as from liquor.

dium [sō′di-um] n a metallic element.

domy [sod′om-i] n any sexual intercourse considered abnor-mal, as copulation between males or with an animal, etc.

fa [sō′fa] n long upholstered seat with fixed back and arms.

ft [soft] adj easily yielding to pressure; easily cut, shaped, etc.; not as hard as normal, desirable, etc.; smooth to the touch; of drinks, nonalcoholic; mild, as a breeze; weak, not vigorous; easy; of color or light, not bright; of sound, gentle, low; of a drug, considered less detrimental than other mood-altering substances. —n a soft object, material, or part. —advs soft, softly, in a soft or gentle manner. —vti soften [sof′n] to make or become soft or softer. —n soft′ener.

ggy [sog′i] adj soaked with water; moist and heavy.

i-disant [swä-dē-zä] adj self-styled; so-called; pretended.

igné, soignée [swä-nyā] adj very well groomed; elegantly designed or maintained.

il¹ [soil] n the surface layer of the earth in which plants grow; country.

il² [soil] n dirt; dung; sewage; a spot or stain. —vt to make dirty; to stain. —vi to become dirty. —n soil′ pipe, a pipe for carrying off wastes from toilets.

irée, soirée [swär-ā, swor′ā] n an evening social meeting.

journ [sō′jûrn, sō-jûrn′] vi to stay for a short time. —n a emporary stay. —n so′journer.

ol [sōl] n (mus) the fifth tone of the diatonic scale.

lace [sol′ás] n consolation, comfort in distress; a source of comfort or pleasure.

lar [sō′lär] adj of, from, like, or pertaining to, the sun; nfluenced by the progress of the sun; measured by the progress of the sun; influenced by the sun;

powered by energy for the sun's rays. —n sōlä′rium, a glass-enclosed room or porch; a place, in a hospital, for sunning or sunbathing. —**solar system**, the sun and the attendant bodies moving about it under the attraction of gravity.

solatium [sō-lā′shi-um] n compensation for disappointment, inconvenience, or wounded feelings.

sold [sōld] pt, pt p of sell.

solder [sod′ėr] something that unites; a metal alloy used when melted to join or patch metal parts, etc.

soldier [sōl′jėr] n a man engaged in military service; an enlisted man, as distinguished from an officer; one who works for a specified cause. —vi to serve as a soldier. —n sol′diering. —adj sol′dierly.

sole¹ [sōl] n the underside of the foot; the bottom of a boot or shoe; the bottom, understructure, floor, or undersurface of various things. —vt to put a sole on (a shoe).

sole² [sōl] adj not married, esp of a woman; (arch) alone; only (eg the sole heir); acting without another. —adv sole′ly, alone; only; exclusively.

solecism [sol′é-sizm] n a flagrant grammatical error; any con-spicuous breach of the rules of usage of language.

solemn [sol′em] adj attended with, or marked by, special (esp religious) ceremonies, pomp, or gravity; attended with an appeal to God, as an oath. —adv sol′emnly. —n sol′emness.

solenoid [sōle-noid] n a coil of wire that acts like a bar magnet when carrying a current.

solicit [sō-lis′it] vti to petition, importune (a person for some-thing); to entice or lure. —ns sol- ic′itant, one who solicits; solicitā′tion, act of soliciting; earnest request; invitation; sol-ic′itor, an agent that solicits (as contributions to charity); solic′itor gen′eral; a law officer appointed to assist an attorney general; solic′itorship. —adj solic′itous.

solid [sol′id] adj resisting change of shape, having the parts firmly cohering; distinguished from liquid and gaseous; hard; compact; full of matter, not hollow; strong, strongly con-structed; having three dimensions; of uniform undivided sub-stance, color, etc. —n solidar′ity, firm union in sentiment and action. —vti solid′ify, to make or become solid, compact, hard, etc. —pt p solid′ified. —ns solidificā′tion, act of making, becoming, solid; solid′ity, the state of being solid; fullness of matter; strength or firmness, moral or physical; soundness; volume. —adv sol′idly. —n sol′idness.

soliloquy [sō-lil′ó-kwi] n talking to oneself when no one else is present; a discourse uttered with none to hear; a speech of this nature made by a character in a play, etc.

solitaire [sol-i-tār′] n a card game for one; a gem, esp a dia-mond, set by itself.

solitary [sol′i-tàr-i] adj alone; without company; only; single; living alone, not social or gregarious.

solo [sō′lō] n a piece or passage for one voice or instrument; a piece by two or more performers if one is featured. —n sō′loist.

solstice [sol′stis] n either of the two points in the ecliptic at which the sun is farthest from the equator and consequently appears to pause and turn in its course.

soluble [sol′ū-bl] adj capable of being dissolved in a fluid; capable of being solved. —n solubil′ity.

solution [sol-ūsh(ó)n] n the act or process of discovering the answer to a problem; the answer discovered; the dispersion of one substance in another, usu. a liquid, so as to form a homogenous mixture; the mixture so produced. —n sol′ute.

solve [solv] vt to discover the answer to; to clear up, explain; to pay (as a debt) in full. —vi to solve something. —adj sol′vable, capable of being solved or explained. —n sol′vency, state of being solvent, or able to pay all debts. —adj sol′vent, able to solve or to dissolve; able to pay all debts. —n anything that dissolves another substance.

somber, sombre [som′bėr] adj dark and gloomy or dull; dismal; sad.

some [sum] adj certain but not specified or known; of a certain unspecified quantity, degree, etc.; about; (inf) remarkable, striking, etc. —pron a certain unspecified quantity, number, etc. —advs some′day, at some future day or time; some′how, in a way or by a method not known or stated. —n some′one′, somebody; some′thing, a thing not definitely known, under-stood, etc. —adj having been formerly; being so occasionally or in only some respects. —adv some′times′, at times; now and then.—*adj* **sometime**.—*advs* **some'way**; **some'ways**, somehow.—**some'what'**, some degree, amount, part, etc.—*adv* to some extent, degree, etc.; a little.—*adv* **some'where**, in, to or at some place not known or specified.

somersault [sum'ėr-sölt] *n* a leap in which a person turns with his heels over his head.

somnambulate [som-nam'bū-lāt] *vi* to walk while asleep.

somniferous [som-nif'ėr-us] *adj* bringing or causing sleep.

somnolence [som'nō-lens] *n* sleepiness.

son [sun] *n* a male child or offspring, or a descendant, or one so treated; a disciple; a native or inhabitant.—*pl* **sons'-in-law**, a daughter's husband.—*pl* **sons'-in-law; sonn'y**, a little son; a familiar mode of address to a boy.

sonata [sò-, sō-nä'ta] *n* (*mus*) a composition for a solo instrument in contrasting forms and keys.

sonde [sond] *n* any device for obtaining information about atmospheric and weather conditions at high altitudes.

song [song] *n* that which is sung; a short poem or ballad for singing, or set to music; the melody to which it is sung; an instrumental composition of like form and character; singing; the melodious outburst of a bird; any sound; a fuss.

sonic [son'ik] *adj* pertaining to sound or the speed of sound.

sonnet [son'et] *n* a poem in which one thought is developed in a single stanza of fourteen lines.—*ns* **sonneteer'**, a composer of sonnets.

sonorous [sò-nö'rus] *adj* sounding or ringing when struck (eg *sonorous metal*); full, rich, or deep in sound; imposing in style or effect.

soon [sōōn] *adv* immediately or in a short time; without delay; early.

soot [sŏŏt] *n* a black deposit from imperfect combustion of carbonaceous matter; a smut.

sooth [sōōth] *n* (*arch*) truth, reality.—*adj* (*arch*) true; (*poet*) pleasant.—*ns* **sooth'-sayer**, one who divines or foretells events.

soothe [sōōTH] *vt* to calm, comfort, compose, tranquillize; to relieve (pain, etc.).—*adj* **sooth'ing**.

sop [sop] *n* (*dial*) bread or other food dipped or soaked in liquid; something given to appease.

sophism [sof'izm] *n* a clever and plausible but fallacious argument. **sophist**, a captious or fallacious reasoner.—*adjs* **sophis'tic, -al**, pertaining to a sophist or to sophistry; fallaciously subtle.—*adv* **sophis'tically**.—*adj* **sophis'ticāted**, adulterated, falsified; not simple or natural; worldly-wise and disillusioned.—*ns* **sophisticā'tion**, act of sophisticating; state of being sophisticated.

sophomore [sof'ò-mör] *n* a second-year student at college or secondary school.

soporific [sop-, sŏp-or-if'ik] *adj* inducing sleep.—*n* anything that causes sleep.

sorcery [sör'ser-i] *n* divination by the assistance of evil spirits; enchantment; magic.—*n* **sor'cerer**, one who practices sorcery.

sordid [sör'did] *adj* dirty, squalid; meanly avaricious, mercenary; of low or unworthy ideals, ignoble.

sore [sör, sōr] *n* a painful or tender injured or diseased spot; an ulcer or boil; grief; an affliction.—*adv* **sore'ly**, painfully; grievously; urgently.

sorority [sò-rör'i-tē] *n* a group of women or girls joined together for fellowship, as in some colleges.

sorrel¹ [sor'èl] *n* any of several plants with sour juice.

sorrel² [sor'èl] *n* a reddish-brown color.

sorrow [sor'ō] *n* pain of mind, grief; an affliction, misfortune; an expression of grief.—*vi* to feel sorrow or pain of mind, grieve.—*adj* **sorr'owful**.—*adv* **sorr'owfully**.

sorry [sor'i] *adj* regretful; regretful in sympathy with another (eg *sorry for her, for her disappointment*); poor, worthless, contemptible.—*adv* **sorr'ily**.—*n* **sorr'iness**.

sort [sört] *n* (*arch*) a company, group; a class, kind, or species; quality or type; an instance of a kind; (*arch*) way, fashion.—*n* **sort'er**, one who separates and arranges, as letters.

sortie [sör'tē] *n* a sally of besieged to attack the besiegers; one mission by a single military plane.

SOS [es-ō-es'] *n* a radio code signal (in Morse . . . — — — . . .) calling for help; an urgent summons for help or rescue.

sot [sot] *n* a habitual drunkard.

soufflé [sōō'flā] *n* a baked dish made light and puffy by addin[g] beaten egg whites before baking.

sough [sow, suf] *vi* to sigh, as the wind in trees.—*n* a moanin[g] or sighing sound.

sought [söt] *pt, pt p* of **seek**.

soul [sōl] *n* that which thinks, feels, desires, etc.; a spiri[t] embodied or disembodied; innermost being or nature; noble[ness] ness of spirit or its sincere expression; embodiment or exemp[]lification; essence; the moving spirit, inspirer, leader, a pe[r]son, a human being.—*adjs* **souled**; **soul'ful**, having o[r] expressive of elevated feeling or yearning, sentiment; **soul music**, music derived from Afro-American gospel singin[g] marked by intensity of feeling and closely related to rhythm and blues.

sound¹ [sownd] *adj* healthy; uninjured, unimpaired, in goo[d] condition; deep (as sleep); solid; thorough.—*adv* **sound'ly**, deeply; thoroughly; in a manner accordant with logic o[r] common sense.

sound² [sownd] *n* a narrow passage of water connecting, eg tw[o] seas or separating a mainland from an island.

sound³ [sownd] *n* sensation of hearing; a transmitted disturb[]ance perceived by, or perceptible by, the ear; a noise, repor[t] range of audibility; mental impression produced by wording.

sound⁴ [sownd] *vt* to measure the depth of; to probe; to try t[o] discover the thoughts and intentions of.

soup [sōōp] *n* the nutritious liquid obtained by boiling mea[t] vegetables, etc., in water, milk, etc.

sour [sowr] *adj* having an acid taste or smell; spoiled by fer[]mentation; cross; bad-tempered; distasteful or unpleasant; o[f] soil, acid in reaction.—*vti* to make or become sour.—*ad[v]* **sour'ly**.

source [sörs, sōrs] *n* a spring; the head of a stream; that fro[m] which anything rises or originates; a person, book, etc., tha[t] provides information.

souse [sows] *n* pickled meat, esp pig's feet or ears; picklin[g] liquid; a plunge in pickling or other liquid; a ducking; (*slang*[)] a drunkard; a heavy blow or fall.

south [sowth] *n* the direction in which the sun appears at noo[n] to people north of the Tropic of Cancer; the region lying i[n] that direction; a part of a country, continent, etc., lyin[g] relatively in that direction.

souvenir [sōō-vè-nēr'] *n* a memento, a keepsake.

sovereign [sov'(è)rin] *adj* supreme, possessing absolute auth[]ority within a given sphere; superior to all rivals; invariabl[y] efficacious.

Soviet [sō'vi-et or sō'-] *n* a council, esp one of those formin[g] (since 1917) the machinery of local and national governmen[t] in Russia.

sow¹ [sow] *n* an adult female pig; a female bear, etc.; a channe[l] for molten iron, leading to pig beds.

sow² [sō] *vt* to scatter or put in the ground, as seed; to plant b[y] strewing; to scatter seed over; to spread, disseminate.—*vi* t[o] scatter seed for growth.—*pt* **sowed**; *pt p* **sown** or **sowed**.—*[n]* **sow'er**.

soy, soya [sō'yä, soi'a] *n* a dark, salty sauce made from fer[]mented soybeans; the soybean.—*n* **soybean, soya bean**.

spa [spä] *n* a mineral spring; a resort where there is a minera[l] spring; a fashionable resort or hotel.

space [späs] *n* that in which material bodies have extension[;] extension in one, two, or three dimensions; room; an inter[]vening distance; an open or empty place; regions remote fro[m] the earth; an interval between lines or words.—*adjs* **spä'cial** same as **spatial**; **spä'cious** [spä'shùs], large in extent; roomy[,] wide.—*adv* **spä'ciously**.—*n* **spä'ciousness**.

spade¹ [späd] *n* a broad-bladed tool with a handle, used fo[r] digging.

spade² [späd] *n* a black figure resembling a stylized spearhead[,] marking one of the four suits of playing cards; a card of thi[s] suit.

spaghetti [spa-get'i] *n* pasta made in thin, solid strings.

span¹ [span] *n* the space from the end of the thumb to the end of the little finger when the fingers are extended (about nin[e] inches); the full extent between any two limits; the full dur[]ation of; the distance between abutments, piers, supports etc.

span² [span] *n* a pair of horses or a team of oxen.

spandrel, spandril [span'drèl] *n* the space between the curve of an arch and an enclosing right angle; the irregular space beneath the string of a stair.

pangle [spang'gl] *n* a thin glittering plate of metal; a sparkling speck, flake, or spot.—*vt* to glitter.

panish [span'ish] *adj* of or pertaining to Spain.—*n* the Romance language of Spain and Spanish Americans.

pank[1] [spangk] *vi* and *vt* to move, or drive, with speed or spirit.

pank[2] [spangk] *vt* to strike with the flat of the hand, to smack.—*n* a loud slap, esp on the buttocks.

panking [spangk'ing] *adj* remarkable of its kind; being fresh and strong, brisk.

panner [span'ér] *n* a wrench with a hole, projection, or hook that corresponds to a device on the object to be turned.

par[1] [spär] *n* a pole, as a mast or yard supporting the rigging of a ship; one of the main longitudinal members of the wing of an airplane.

par[2] [spär] *n* any of various nonmetallic minerals, usu. cleavable and lustrous.

par[3] [spär] *vi* to fight with spurs, as cocks; to box, or make the motions of boxing; to exchange provocative remarks.

pare [spär] *vt* to use frugally; to refrain from using; to do without or afford; to forbear to hurt, injure, kill, etc.; to treat mercifully.—*adv* **spare'ly.**—*n* **spare'ness.**—*adj* **spä'ring,** scanty; frugal, economical.

park [spärk] *n* a glittering or glowing particle of matter thrown off by an incandescent substance; anything of like appearance or character, as anything easily extinguished, ready to cause explosion, burning hot; a flash; an electric discharge across a gap.

parkle [spärk'l] *n* a little spark; emission of sparks; bright effervescence, as in wines; vivacity; coruscation of wit.

parse [spärs] *adj* thinly scattered; scanty.

partan [spär'tán] *adj* of or pertaining to Sparta in ancient Greece; rigorously severe.

pasm [spazm] *n* a sudden, involuntary contraction of muscles; any sudden strong short burst (of feeling or activity).—*adj* **spasmod'ic;** intermittent.—*adv* **spasmod'ically.**—*adj* **spastic** [spas'-], of the nature of, characterized by muscle spasm.

pat[1] [spat] *pt* of spit (2).

pat[2] [spat] *n* a young bivalve (as an oyster).

pat[3] [spat] *n* a short gaiter covering the ankle and instep.

pat[4] [spat] *n* (*inf*) a brief, petty quarrel.

pate [spät] *n* a freshet; a large amount; a sudden outburst (as of words).

patial [spä'sh(à)l] *adj* relating to space.

patter [spat'ér] *vti* to scatter or spurt out in drops; to splash.

patula [spat'ū-la] *n* an implement with a broad, flexible blade for spreading or blending foods, paints, scooping, lifting, etc.

pawn [spön] *n* a mass of eggs, as of fishes, mollusks, or other aquatic animals; something produced, esp in great quantity, as offspring.

peak [spēk] *vi* to utter words; to talk; to hold a conversation (with—*or with* to); to make a speech; to sound; to convey an impression (of), be evidence (of).—*pt* **spöke,** (*arch*) **späke;** *pt p* **spöken.**—*adj* **speak'ing,** seeming to speak; expressive, or lifelike; used to assist the voice.

pear [spēr] *n* a weapon used in war and hunting, having a long shaft pointed with iron; a lance with barbed prongs used for catching fish.

pec [spek] *vt* to write specifications for.

pecial [spesh'(à)l] *adj* exceptional, uncommon, marked; peculiar to one person or thing; limited (to one person or thing); designed, appointed, arranged, run, etc., for a particular purpose.—*adv* **specially** [spesh'ál-i].—*vt* **spec'ialize,** to narrow and intensify.—*adj* **spec'ialized,** adapted to a particular function, or limited purpose; restricted and made more exact.—*ns* **specializā'tion,** the act or process of specializing; **spec'ialist; specialty** a special activity or object of attention; a special product.

pecie [spē'shi] *n* money in coin.

pecies [spē'shēz] *n* a group of individuals having common characteristics, a kind or sort of human beings; a category of biological classification immediately below the genus potentially capable of inter-breeding.

pecify [spes'i-fī] *vt* to mention particularly; to mention in detail; to set down as a requisite.—*pt, pt p* **spec'ified.**—*n*

specif'ic.—*adj* **specif'ic,** distinctive, peculiar.—*n* **specificā'tion,** the act of specifying; any point or particular specified.

specimen [spes'i-mèn] *n* an object or portion serving as a sample, esp for purposes of study or collection.

specious [spē'shùs] *adj* that looks well at first sight; deceptively attractive; plausible.

speck [spek] *n* a small spot.

speckle [spek'l] *n* a little speck.—*vt* to mark with speckles.—*adj* **speck'led.**—*adv* **speck'lessly.**

spectacle [spek'tà-kl] *n* a sight; a large public show; (*pl*) an old-fashioned term for eyeglasses.—*adjs* **spec'tacled,** having markings suggesting a pair of spectacles; **spectacular,** of the nature of, or marked by, unusual display.

spectator [spek-tā'tór] *n* one who looks on.

specter, spectre [spek'tér] *n* a ghost.—*adj* **spec'tral,** relating to, or like, a specter.—*adv* **spec'trally.**

spectrum [spek'trum] *n* the range of color produced by passing a white light through a prism, etc.; violet, indigo, blue, green, yellow, orange, red.—*pl* **spec'tra, spectrums.**

speculate [spek'ū-lāt] *vi* to reflect (on); to theorize, make conjectures or guesses (about).—*n* **speculā'tion.**—*adj* **spec'ulātive,** of the nature of, based on, speculation; given to speculation or theory; engaging in speculation in business, etc.—*adv* **spec'ulātively.**—*n* **spec'ulātor.**

speculum [spek'ū-lum] *n* a reflector in an optical instrument.

speech [spēch] *n* that which is spoken; language; the power of speaking; manner of speaking; oration, discourse.—*vi* **speech'ify,** to make speeches, harangue.—*adj* **speech'less,** unable to speak; silent, as from shock.—*adv* **speech'lessly.**

speed [spēd] *n* quickness, velocity; rate of motion; good progress—*pr p* **speed'ing;** *pt, pt p* **sped.**—*adj* **speed'y,** swift; prompt; soon achieved.—*adv* **speed'ily.**

spell[1] [spel] *n* any form of words supposed to possess magical power; fascination.—*adj* **spell'bound,** entranced, fascinated.

spell[2] [spel] *vt* to name or set down in order the letters of; to represent in letters (eg *c-a-t* spells 'cat'); to read laboriously, letter by letter; to make out, decipher, laboriously; to mean.—*vi* to spell words.—*pr p* **spell'ing;** *pt, pt p* **spelled.**

spell[3] [spel] *vt* (*inf*) to take the place of (another) for an interval; to relieve.

spelter [spel'tér] *n* zinc cast in slabs for commercial use.

spend [spend] *vt* to expend, pay out (money); to give, bestow, employ (eg one's energies) for any purpose; to exhaust; to pass, as time.—*vi* to expend money.—*pr p* **spend'ing;** *pt, pt p* **spent.**—*n* **spen'der.**—*adj* **spent,** physically exhausted.

spendthrift [spend'thrift] *n* one who wastes money; a prodigal.—*adj* excessively lavish.

spent [spent] *pt, pt p* of **spend.**

sperm [spûrm] *n* semen; a spermatozoon; a product of the sperm whale.—*adj* **spermat'ic,** pertaining to, consisting of, conveying, sperm; relating to sperm or a spermary.

spermaceti [spér-ma-sēt'i, or -sē'ti] *n* a waxy matter obtained mixed with oil from the head of the sperm whale and other cetaceans, used for candles and ointment.—Also *adj.*

spew [spū] *vti* to vomit; to flow or gush forth.—*n* something spewed.

sphenoid, sphenoidal [sfē'noid, -noid'ál] *adj* wedge-shaped, esp a set of bones at base of the skull.

sphere [sfēr] *n* a solid body bounded by a surface of which all points are equidistant from a center; its bounding surface; a ball or other spherical object.—*adjs* **spher'al; spheric** [sfer'ik], **-al,** of a sphere or spheres; having the form of a sphere or one of its segments.—*adv* **spher'ically.**

sphincter [sfingk'tér] *n* (*anat*) a ring-shaped muscle whose contraction narrows or shuts an orifice.

spice [spīs] *n* an aromatic and pungent vegetable substance used as a condiment and for seasoning food.

spick'-and-span, spic-and-span [spik and span] *adj* perfectly new, spotlessly clean.

spicy [spī'si] *adj* producing or abounding with spices; fragrant; pungent; piquant, pointed, racy, sometimes with a touch of indecency.—*adv* **spī'cily.**—*n* **spī'ciness.**

spider [spī'der] *n* arachnids with a body of two main divisions, four pairs of walking legs, and abdominal spinnerets for spinning silk threads to make cocoons, nests, or webs.

spigot [spig'ót] *n* a small pointed peg or bung; a faucet.

spike¹ [spīk] *n* an ear of grain; an inflorescence in which sessile flowers, or spikelets are arranged on a long axis.

spike² [spīk] *n* long heavy nail; a sharp-pointed projection, as on a shoe to prevent slipping.

spikenard [spik'närd] *n* (*hist*) a fragrant ointment.

spill¹ [spil] *vt* to allow, esp unintentionally, to run out of a container; to shed (blood).—*vi* to be shed; to be allowed to fall, be lost, or wasted.—*pt, pt p* **spilled, spilt**.—*n* a fall, a tumble; something spilled; a spillway.

spill² [spil] *n* a small peg or pin to stop a hole; a thin strip of wood or twisted paper for lighting a pipe, etc.

spin [spin] *vt* to draw out and twist into threads; to shape into threadlike form; to draw out (a story) to a great length.—*vi* dizziness; to go swiftly, esp on wheels; *pr p* **spinn'ing**; *pt, pt p* **spun**.

spinach [spin'ij] *n* a plant whose young leaves are eaten as a vegetable.

spinal [spīn'ál] *adj See* **spine**.

spindle [spin'dl] *n* the pin by which thread is twisted in spinning; a pin on which anything turns; a spindlelike thing; the part of an axle on which a vehicle wheel turns.

spindrift [spin'drift] *n* the spray blown from the crests of waves; spoondrift.

spine [spīn] *n* a sharp, stiff projection, as a thorn of the cactus; anything like this; a spinal column; the backbone of a book; a sharp process on an animal.—*adj* **spīn'al**, of the spine or spinal column.—*adjs*, **spine'less**, having no spine or spines; unable to make a firm stand; irresolute; **spī'ny**, full of spines; thorny; troublesome, perplexed.

spinnaker [spin'à-kèr] *n* a jib-shaped sail sometimes carried by racing yachts.

spinster [spin'stèr] *n* an unmarried woman, esp an old maid.

spiracle [spīr'á-kl] *n* a breathing hole, a vent, (*zool*) a breathing aperture, ranging from the minute orifices of insects to the blowhole of whales, etc.

spire¹ [spīr] *n* a tapering or conical body, esp a tree-top; a tall, slender architectural structure tapering to a point.—*vi* to sprout; to shoot up.

spire² [spīr] *n* a coil; a spiral; the spiral part of a shell, excluding the whorl in contact with the body.—*vi* to wind, mount, or proceed, in spirals.

spirit [spir'it] *n* an entity without material reality; life, will, thought, etc., regarded as separate from matter; a supernatural being, as a ghost, angel, etc.; an individual; (*pl*) disposition; mood; vivacity, courage, etc.; enthusiastic loyalty; real meaning; a pervading animating principal; essential quality; (*usu. pl*) distilled alcoholic liquor; an alcoholic solution of a volatile substance.—*vt* to carry (away, off, etc.) secretly and swiftly.—*adj* **spir'ited**, full of spirit, life, or fire; animated.—*adv.* **spir'itedly**.—*ns.* **spir'itedness**—*adj.* **spir'itless**.—*adv* **spir'itually**.—the Spirit, in Christian Science, God.

spit¹ [spit] *n* a prong, usu. iron, on which meat is roasted; a long narrow strip of land extending into the water.—*vt* to fix as on a spit.—*pr p* **spitt'ing**; *pt, pt p* **spitt'ed**.

spit² [spit] *vt* to throw out from the mouth; to eject with violence; to utter with scorn.—*vi* to throw out saliva from the mouth; to rain in scattered drops.—*pr p* **spitt'ing**; *pt, pt p* **spit**, **spat**.—*n* saliva; a light fall of rain or snow; an exact replica.

spite [spīt] *n* a grudge; ill will; malice.—*vt* to annoy spitefully, to thwart out of hatred.—*adj* **spite'ful**, showing spite, desirous to vex or injure; arising from spite, malignant.—*adv* **spite'fully**.—*n* **spite'fulness**.

splash [splash] *vt* to spatter with liquid or mud; to throw (about), as liquid; to dash liquid on or over; to variegate as if by splashing.

splatter [splat'ėr] *vti* to splatter, splash.

splay [splā] *vt* (*archit*) to slope, slant or bevel; to turn out at an angle; to spread out.

spleen [splēn] *n* a large lymphatic organ in the upper left part of the abdomen which modifies the blood structure.

splendid [splen'did] *adj* brilliant; magnificent; (*inf*) excellent.—*adj* **splen'dent**, brightly shining.—*adv* **splen'didly**.—*ns* **splen'didness, splen'dor**, brilliance; magnificence.

splice [splīs] *vt* to unite (two ends of a rope) by separating and interweaving the strands; to join together (two pieces of timber) by overlapping.

splint [splint] *n* a thin strip of wood, etc. woven with others make baskets, etc.; a thin piece of padded wood, etc., f keeping a fractured limb in its proper position.—*vt* to put splints.—*n* **splint'er**, a thin, sharp piece of wood, split off.— *vti* to split into splinters.

split [split] *vti* to cleave lengthwise; to break in pieces, asunde to divide into shares; to disunite.

splurge [splûrj] *n* (*inf*) any very showy display or effort.

splutter [splut'ėr] *vi* to eject drops of liquid with spittin noises; to articulate confusedly and hurriedly.

spoil [spoil] *vt* to damage as to make useless, etc.; to impa the enjoyment, etc., of; to cause to expect too much b overindulgence; (*arch*) to rob; to plunder.—*vi* to become sp iled; to decay, etc., as food.—*pt, pt p* **spoiled, spoilt**.

spoke¹ [spōk] *pt* of **speak**.

spoke² [spōk] *n* any of the braces extending from the hub to th rim of a wheel.

spoken [spōk'n] *pt p* of **speak**.

spokeshave [spōk'shāv] *n* a small transverse plane with er handles for planing convex or concave surfaces.

spokesman [spōks'mán] *n* one who speaks for another, or fo others.

spoliate [spō'li-āt] *vti* to despoil, to plunder.

sponge [spunj] *n* a plantlike marine animal with an intern skeleton of elastic interlacing horny fibers.

sponsor [spon'sôr] *n* one who promises solemnly for another, surety; a godfather or godmother; a business firm etc. th pays for a radio or TV program advertising its product.—*vt* t act as sponsor for.—*n* **spon'sorship**.

spontaneous [spon-tā'nē-ús] *adj* uttered, offered, done, etc of one's free will; natural; unforced; involuntary; acting by i own impulse or natural law; produced of itself or withou interference.—*ns* **spontane'ity, spontā'neousness**.—*ad* **spontā'neously**.

spoof [spōōf] *n* (*slang*) a hoax or joke; a light satire.

spook [spōōk] *n* a ghost; (*inf*) an undercover agent.

spool [spōōl] *n* a cylinder, bobbin, or reel, for winding threac photographic film, etc., upon; the material wound.—*vt* t wind on a spool; to wind.

spoon [spōōn] *n* utensil with a shallow bowl and a handle, fo eating, stirring, etc.

spoonerism [spōōn'ėr-izm] *n* transposition of the initial sound of spoken words—eg 'shoving leopard' for 'loving shepherd'.

spoor [spōōr] *n* a track, trail, scent, or droppings of a wil animal.—*vti* to track (something) by a spoor.

sporadic [spo-rad'ik] *adj* occurring here and there and nov and then; occurring casually.—*adv* **sporad'ically**.

spore {spōr, spôr] *n* a unicellular asexual reproductive bod produced by mosses, ferns, and some invertebrates and cap able of giving rise to new individuals.

sporran [spor'án] *n* an ornamental pouch worn in front of th kilt by the Highlanders of Scotland.

sport [spôrt] *vi* to play, to frolic; to trifle; (of a plant bud) to deviate from the normal.—*vt* (*inf*) to display, flaunt.—*n* pastime, amusement; a game, esp one involving bodily exe cise; a field diversion (eg hunting, fishing, athletics); a thin joked about; (*inf*) a sportsmanlike person; (*inf*) a showy, flash fellow.—*adj* **sport'ing**.

spot [spot] *n* a small area differing in color, etc., from th surrounding area; a stain, speck, etc.; a taint on character o reputation; a small quantity or amount; a locality; a place on an entertainment program.—*pr p* **spott'ing**; *pt, pt p* **spot** t'ed.—*adj* **spot'less**, without a spot; untainted, pure.—*ad* **spot'lessly**.—*n* **spot'lessness**.—*adjs* **spott'ed, spott'y**.

spouse [spowz] *n* (one's) husband or wife.—*adj* **spous'al**, nup tial; matrimonial.

spout [spowt] *vti* to throw out as from a spout; to declaim.—*n* projecting lip or tube for discharging liquid from a vessel, roof, etc.

sprain [sprān] *n* a wrenching of a joint with tearing or stretchin of ligaments.

sprawl [sprôl] *vi* to stretch the body carelessly when lying; t spread ungracefully, as handwriting.—*n* sprawling posture.— *n* **sprawl'er**.

spray¹ [sprā] *n* a cloud of many flying drops; such a clou applied as a disinfectant, insecticide, etc.; an atomizer o other apparatus for dispersing it.

' [sprā] n a shoot or twig, esp one spreading out in branches or flowers; an ornament, casting, etc.,

read [spred] vt to cause to extend more widely or more thinly; to scatter abroad or in all directions; to extend; to overlay; to shoot out (branches); to circulate (news); to convey to others, as a disease; to set with provisions, as a table.—n

spread' ea'gle, a heraldic eagle with wings and legs stretched out.

ree [sprē] n a merry frolic; a drunken bout; a period of uninhibited activity.

rig [sprig] n a small shoot or twig; a scion, a young person; a small nail with little or no head.

rightful [sprīt'fúl] n full of life or spirit; sprightly.—adjs **spright'less, spright'ly,** vivacious, animated; lively; brisk.

ring [spring] vi to move suddenly, as by elastic force; to bound, to leap; to start up suddenly, to break forth; to appear, to issue; to take origin; to sprout; to become warped, split, etc.—vt to cause to spring up, to start; to release the elastic force of; to let off, allow to spring.—pt sprang (now rarely sprung); pt p sprung.—n a leap; a sudden movement; a recoil or rebound; elasticity; an elastic device or appliance used eg for setting in motion, or for reducing shocks.

ringe [sprinj] n a noose fastened to an elastic body to catch small game; a snare, trap.

rinkle [spring'kl] vt to scatter in small drops or particles (on something).

rint [sprint] n a short run, row, or race, at full speed.—vi to run at full speed.—n **sprin'ter.**

rit [sprit] n (naut) a spar set diagonally to extend a fore-and-aft sail.

rite [sprīt] n (arch) a soul; a goblin, elf, imp, impish or implike person.

rocket [sprok'ét] n a tooth on the rim of a wheel or capstan for engaging the chain.

rout [sprowt] n a new growth; a young shoot; a side bud; a scion, descendant; a sprouting condition.

ruce¹ [sprōōs] adj smart, neat, dapper; over-fastidious, finical.—vt to smarten.

ruce² [sprōōs] n evergreen trees of the pine family with a conical head and soft light wood.

ry [sprī] adj nimble, agile, esp though elderly.

pud [spud] n a small narrow digging tool; (inf) a potato.

pume [spūm] n foam; scum.

pun pt, pt p of **spin.**

punk [spungk] n touchwood, tinder; any fungi used to make tinder; (inf) spirit, mettle, courage.—adj **spunk'y.**

pur [spûr] n an instrument on a rider's heel, with sharp point for goading the horse; incitement, stimulus; a hard sharp projection.

purious [spūr'i-ùs] adj bastard, illegitimate; not genuine, sham; forged; (bot) simulating but essentially different.

purn [spûrn] vt to reject with contempt.—n disdainful rejection.

purt, spirt [spûrt] vt to spout, or send out in a sudden stream or jet.

putter [sput'ér] vi to spit or throw out moisture in scattered drops; to speak rapidly and indistinctly.

putum [spū'tum] n matter composed of secretions from the nose, throat, bronchi, lungs, which is spat out.

py [spī] n agent employed to watch others secretly or to collect information, esp of a military nature.—pt, pt p spied [spīd].

quab [skwob] adj fat, clumsy; newly hatched.

quabble [skwob'l] vi to dispute noisily, to wrangle.—n a noisy, petty quarrel.—n **squabb'ler.**

quad [skwod] n a small group of soldiers drilled or working together; any working party; a set or group.

quadron [skwod'rón] n a unit of warships, cavalry, military aircraft, etc.

qualid [skwol'id] adj filthy, foul; neglected, sordid and dingy.—adv **squal'idly.**—ns **squal'idness; squal'or,** state of being squalid; dirtiness.

quall [skwöl] vi to cry out violently; to sing loudly and unmusically.—n a loud cry or scream; a violent gust of wind.

quander [skwon'dèr] vt to spend lavishly or wastefully.—n **squan'derer.**

quare [skwär] n an equilateral rectangle; an object, piece, space, figure of approximately that shape; an open space.—

adv **square'ly.**—n **square'ness.**—adj **square'-rigged,** rigged chiefly with square sails.

squash¹ [skwosh] vt to press into pulp; to crush flat; to put down, suppress; to snub.—vi to form a soft mass as from a fall; to become crushed or pulpy; to squelch; to crowd.—n something squashed; the act or sound of squashing; a game played in a walled court with rackets and rubber ball.—adj **squash'y,** like a squash; muddy.

squash² [skwosh] n any of several species of gourd eaten as a vegetable.

squat [skwot] vi to sit down upon the heels; to sit close, as an animal; to settle on land or in occupied property, without permission or title; to settle on public land in order to get title to it.

squaw [skwö] n an American Indian woman; a woman, wife, usu. disparaging.

squawk [skwök] n a croaky call or cry; (inf) a raucous complaint.

squeak [skwēk] vi to utter, or to give forth, a high-pitched cry, or note.—n a squeaky sound; or bare chance.—n **squeak'er.**—adj **squeak'y.**

squeal [skwēl] vi to utter a shrill and prolonged sound; (slang) to be an informer.

squeamish [skwēm'ish] adj inclined to nausea; easily shocked or disgusted; fastidious; reluctant from scruples or compunction.—adv **squeam'ishly.**

squeeze [skwēz] vt to crush, press hard, compress; to grasp tightly; to embrace; to force (through, into) by pressing; to force liquid, juice, from by pressure; to force to discard winning cards; to fleece, extort from.

squib [skwib] n a paper tube filled with combustibles, used as firework; a petty lampoon.

squid [skwid] n ten-armed cephalopods often confined to those in which the internal shell, the pen, is not calcified and is hence flexible; also called calamary.

squint [skwint] adj looking obliquely; squinting; oblique.

squire [skwīr] n an esquire, an aspirant to knighthood attending a knight; an attendant, esp a man escorting a woman.

squirm [skwûrm] vi to writhe; to go writhing; to feel or show distress.

squirrel [skwir'él] n any of a family of rodents, of arboreal habit, which have a bushy tail and strong hind legs; the pelt of such an animal.

squirt [skwûrt] vt to throw out liquid in a jet.—vi to spurt.—n an instrument for squirting; a jet; (inf) an insignificant person.

stab [stab] vt to wound or pierce with a pointed weapon; to pain suddenly and deeply; to injure secretly, or by slander; to aim (at).—Also vi.

stable¹ [stā'bl] adj standing firm; firmly established; durable; firm in purpose or character, constant; not decomposing readily.—ns **stabil'ity,** steadiness; **stā'bleness.**—vt **stab'ilize,** to render stable or steady; to limit the fluctuations of.

stable² [stā'bl] n a building for housing horses or cattle; a group of racehorses under one ownership; a group of athletes (as boxers) or performers under one management.

stack [stak] n a large neatly arranged pile of hay, straw, etc.

stadium [stā'di-úm] n a Greek measure of length; a large structure for football, baseball, etc. surrounded by tiers of seats.—pl **stā'dia.**

staff [stäf] n a stick carried in the hand as a symbol of authority; (pl **stāves**); a prop; a pole; a flagstaff; the long handle of an instrument; a stick or ensign of authority; lines and spaces on which music is written or printed; (pl **stāves**); a body of officers who help a commanding officer, or perform special duties; a body of persons employed in an establishment—business, professional, or domestic.

stag [stag] n a full-grown male deer.—adj for men only.—adv unaccompanied by a woman.

stage [stāj] n an elevated platform, esp for acting on; the theater, theatrical representation, the theatrical calling (with the); any field of action, scene; a place of rest on a journey or road; the portion of a journey between two such places; a point reached in, or a section of, life, development, or any process; a subdivision of a geological series or formation; a stagecoach.—adj **stagy, stagey,** [stā'ji] theatrical, artificial, melodramatic.—n **stā'giness.**

stagger [stag'ér] vi to reel; to go reeling or tottering; to waver. — *vt* to cause to reel; to give a shock to; to nonplus, confound; to cause to waver; to arrange on each side of a line, at equal distances and symmetrically, or otherwise. — *adj* **stagg′ering,** disconcerting, overwhelming. — *adv* **stagg′eringly.**

stagnant [stag′nànt] *adj* not flowing, motionless; impure through lack of inflow and outflow; inactive, dull. — *ns* **stag′nancy, stagnā′tion.** — *adv* **stag′nantly.** — *vi* **stag′nate,** to be, or become, stagnant.

staid [stād] *adj* steady, sober, grave; sedate.

stain [stān] *vt* to impart a new color to with a dye; to tinge, to discolor, spot, sully.

stair [stār] *n* a series of steps from landing to landing; one of such steps. — *ns* **stair′case,** the structure enclosing a stair; stairs with banisters, etc.

stake[1] [stāk] *n* a strong stick pointed at one end; one of the upright pieces of a fence; a post to which one condemned to be burned was tied, hence, death or martyrdom by burning.

stake[2] [stāk] *vt* to bet, hazard; (*inf*) to furnish with money or resources. — *n* anything pledged as a wager; anything to gain or lose.

stalactite [sta-lak′tīt] *n* an icicle-like pendant, formed by evaporation of water percolating through limestone, as on a cave roof.

stalagmite [sta-lag′mīt] *n* a deposit on the floor of a cavern, usually cylindrical or conical in form, caused by the dripping from the roof, or from a stalactite, of water holding calcium carbonate in solution. — *adj* **stalagmit′ic.**

stale[1] [stāl] *adj* altered for the worse by age; tainted; vapid or tasteless from age.

stale[2] [stāl] *n* urine of a domestic animal. — *vi* to urinate, used chiefly of camels and horses.

stalemate [stāl′māt] *n* (*chess*) a situation in which the person to play, while not actually in check, cannot move without getting into check; a deadlock. — Also *vt*.

stalk[1] [stök] *n* the stem of a plant; the stem on which a flower or fruit grows; anything resembling the stem of a plant. — *adj* **stalk′less,** having no stalk.

stalk[2] [stök] *vi* to stride stiffly or haughtily; to go after game, keeping under cover.

stall[1] [stöl] *n* a compartment for one animal in a stable; a bench, table, booth, or stand, for display or sale of goods; a space marked off for parking a motor vehicle; a pew in a church; a small compartment; a stop, esp due to malfunction.

stall[2] [stöl] *vti* to play for time, avoid a decision or decisive action. — *n* (*inf*) any action used in stalling.

stallion [stal′yòn] *n* a male horse, esp one kept for breeding.

stalwart [stöl′wàrt] *adj* stout, sturdy; staunch, resolute. — *n* a resolute person. — *n* **stal′wartness.**

stamen [stā′mèn] *n* the pollen-producing part of a flower, consisting of anther and filament; **stam′ina,** constitutional strength; staying power.

stammer [stam′ér] *vi* to falter in speaking; to stutter. — *vt* to utter falteringly or with a stutter. — *n* hesitation in speech; a stammering mode of utterance. — *n* **stamm′erer.** — *adv* **stamm′eringly.**

stamp [stamp] *vt* to trample; to bring (the foot) forcibly down; to impress, imprint, or cut with a downward blow, as with a die or cutter; to mint, make, shape, by such a blow; to fix or mark deeply; to affix an adhesive stamp to; to characterize.

stampede [stam-pēd′] *n* a sudden rush of a panic-stricken herd; any impulsive action of a large number of people.

stance [stans] *n* manner of standing; the attitude taken in a given situation.

stanch [stän(t)sh], **staunch** [stön(t)sh] *vt* to stop the flow of, as blood; to allay. — *vi* to cease to flow.

stanchion [stan′sh(ô)n] *n* an upright iron bar of a window or screen; a device to confine a cow.

stand [stand] *vi* to be, become, or remain, upright, erect, rigid, or still; to be on, or rise to one's feet; to be supported on a base, pedestal, etc.; to have a (specified) height when standing; to gather and remain, as water; to make resistance; to halt or be stationary; to have or take a position; to be or remain; to be set or situated; to come from a specified direction; to endure, continue; to hold good. — *vt* to set upright; to endure, bear, tolerate; to endure the presence of (a person); to withstand; to undergo. — *pt, pt p* **stood.** — *n* an act, manner, or

place, of standing; a taking up of a position for resistan resistance; a standing position; a standstill; a post, statior place for vehicles awaiting hire; (*pl*) an erection for spectato the place taken by a witness for testifying in court; a base structure for setting things on; a piece of furniture for hang things from; a stop on tour to give one or more theatri performances, or the place where it is made; a small of open-air structure for a small retail business; a group plants, esp trees, growing in a continuous area.

standard [stand′àrd] *n* a flag, banner, etc., as an emblem military unit, etc., formerly used to mark a rallying poin flag generally; the uppermost petal of a papilionaceous flow that which stands or is fixed; an upright post, pillar; a sta ing shrub or tree not trained on an espalier or a wall; a basis measurement, esp a specimen weight or measure preserv for reference; the legally fixed fineness of coinage metal, weight of a new coin; a criterion; an established or accep model; a definite level of excellence or adequacy require aimed at, or possible. — *adj* serving as, or conforming to standard; growing as a standard.

stanza [stan′za] *n* a group of lines which form a division poem.

staple[1] [stā′pl] *n* a leading commodity of trade or industr main element (eg of diet, reading, conversation); wool other raw material.

staple[2] [stā′pl] *n* a bent rod or wire, both ends of which driven into a wall, post, etc., to form a fastening or throu papers as a binding. — *vt* to fasten with a staple.

star [stär] *n* any one of the heavenly bodies, esp of those visib by night whose places in the firmament are relatively fixe sometimes (*loosely*) including planets, comets, meteors, e commonly the sun and moon, or even the earth; a preemine or exceptionally brilliant person; a leading performer.

starboard [stär′bô(r)d, -bôrd] *n* the right side of a ship aircraft looking forward, when one is looking towards bow.

starch [stärch] *n* a white, tasteless, odorless food substar found in potatoes, cereal, etc.

stare [stär] *vi* to look with a fixed gaze, as in horror, astonis ment, etc.; to glare; to be insistently or obtrusively conspic ous, or obvious to (eg *to stare one in the face*). — *vt* to lo fixedly at. — *n* a fixed look. — *n* **stā′rer.**

stark [stärk] *adj* stiff, as a corpse; sharply outlined; ble downright. — *adv* utterly.

start [stärt] *vi* to shoot, dart, move, suddenly forth or out; spring up or forward; to break away, become displaced; make a sudden involuntary movement, as of surprise becoming aware; to begin; to set forth on a journey, ra career.

startle [stärt′l] *vi* to start, to feel sudden alarm. — *vt* to cause person) surprise mingled with alarm, outrage to sense propriety or fitness, or similar emotion; to cause (a person) start with surprise and alarm.

starve [stärv] *vi* to die of hunger; to suffer extreme hunger; be in want; to feel a great longing (for). — *vt* to cause to starv to force (into) by want of food; to deprive (of) anythi needful. — *n* **starvā′tion.**

state [stāt] *n* condition; circumstances at any time; a phase stage; station in life; high station; pomp, display, ceremon dignity; an estate, order, or class in society or the body politi the civil power; **State,** a body of people politically organiz and independent; **State,** any of the members of a federation in the US; the territory of such. — *adj* of, belonging to, rela ing to, the state or State; public; ceremonial. — *adjs* **stāt′e** settled, fixed, regular; **stāte′ly,** showing state or dignity. — **State′house,** the building in which the legislature of a Sta meets. — *ns* **states′manship; states′ rights,** all rights re vested by the Constitution of the US in the Federal goverr ment nor forbidden by it to the separate States; **the State** the United States.

static [stat′ik] *adj* pertaining to statics; pertaining to bodie forces, charges, etc., in equilibrium; stationary; stable; activ by mere weight. — *n* statics; atmospheric disturbances causir noise on radio or TV.

station [stā′sh(ô)n] *n* the place or building where one stands is located; a standing place, fixed stopping place as on a b line or railroad; a local office, headquarters, or depôt. — *adj* a station.—*vt* to assign a station to; to appoint to a post, place, of office.—*adj* **stā'tionary**, standing, not moving; fixed; permanently located.—*ns* **sta'tioner**, a dealer in stationery, office supplies, etc.; **stā'tionery**, writing materials, esp paper and envelopes.

statue [stat'ū] *n* a representation of a human or animal form in the round.—*adj* **stat'uary**, of, or suitable for, sculpture; sculptured.—*n* statues collectively.—*adj* **statuesque**; like a statue.—*adv* **statuesquely**.—*n* **statuette'**, a small statue, figurine.

stature [stat'yùr] *n* the standing height of the body; level of attainment.

status [stā'tus] *n* social position; standing in profession, in society, or in any organization of persons; condition, description from the point of view of the law, determining capacity to sue, etc.; position of affairs, existing before a certain event, date.—**status quo**, the state, condition of affairs, existing before a certain event, date.

statute [stat'ūt] *n* a law enacted by a legislature; an established rule or law; the act of a corporation or its founder, intended as a permanent rule or law.

staunch [stönch, stanch] *adj* seaworthy; firm in principle; trusty, constant, zealous.

stave [stāv] *n* one of the shaped side pieces of a cask or barrel; a staff, rod, bar, shaft; (*mus*) a staff; a stanza, verse of a song.

stay [stā] *n* a rope supporting a mast; a guy; a prop, support; a brace, connecting piece to resist tension; a strip of stiffening material used in a corset, shirt collar, etc.; a stopping, bringing or coming to a standstill; a suspension of legal proceedings; delay; a sojourn; staying power.

stead [sted] *n* the place which another had, or might have; service, advantage.

steadfast [sted'fast] *adj* firmly fixed or established; firm, constant, resolute.—*adv* **stead'fastly**.

steady [sted'i] *adj* firm in standing or in place; stable; unshaking, unfaltering; constant, consistent.—*adv* **stead'ily**.—*n* **stead'iness**.

steak [stāk] *n* a slice of meat, esp beef or fish, for broiling or frying; ground meat prepared for cooking in the manner of a steak.

steal [stēl] *vt* to take by theft, esp secretly; to take, gain, or win, by address, by contrivance, unexpectedly, insidiously, or gradually; to take (a look, etc.) slyly; to move, put, etc., stealthily (in, from, etc.).—*pt* **stōle**; *pt p* **stōl'en**.—*n inf* an extraordinary bargain.

stealth [stelth] *n* secret procedure or manner, furtiveness.—*adj* **stealth'y**, acting, or acted, with stealth, furtive.—*n* **stealth'iness**.—*adv* **stealth'ily**.

steam [stēm] *n* the vapor into which water is converted by boiling; the condensation of this vapor; the power of steam under pressure; (*inf*) energy, force, spirit.—*vi* to rise or pass off in steam or vapor; to become covered with condensed vapor; to move by steam power.—*adj* **steam'y**, of, like, full of, covered with, as if covered with, emitting steam.

steed [stēd] *n* a horse, esp a spirited horse.

steel [stēl] *n* iron containing a little carbon, with or without other substances; a cutting tool or weapon; an instrument, object, or part, made of steel, eg a steel knife sharpener, a skate; a piece of steel as for stiffening a corset, striking fire from a flint; extreme hardness, staying power, trustworthiness; (*pl*) shares of stock in steel companies.—*adj* of, or like, steel.—*vt* to cover or edge with steel; to harden, make obdurate; to nerve (oneself).

steep¹ [stēp] *adj* rising or descending with great inclination, precipitous, headlong; (*inf*) excessive, exorbitant.—*n* a precipitous place.—*vti* **steep'en**.—*n* **steep'ness**.—*adv* **steep'ly**.

steep² [stēp] *vt* to dip or soak in a liquid; to wet thoroughly; to saturate; to imbue.—*vi* to undergo soaking or thorough wetting.—*n* a soaking process; a liquid, for steeping anything in.

steeple [stēp'l] *n* a tower of a church or other building, with or without, including or excluding, a spire; the spire alone.

steer¹ [stēr] *n* a castrated male of the cattle family; (*loosely*) any male of beef cattle.

steer² [stēr] *vt* to direct with, or as with, the helm; to guide; to direct (one's course).—*vi* to direct a ship, cycle, etc., in its course; to be directed or guided; to move (for, toward).

stellar [stel'àr] *adj* of the stars; of the nature of a star; composed of stars; relating to a theatrical or film star; chief; excellent.—*adj* **stell'āte**.

stem¹ [stem] *n* the leaf-bearing axis of a plant, a stalk, anything like a stalk, as the upright slender part of a note, of a wineglass, etc.—*pr p* **stemm'ing**; *pt*, *pt p* **stemmed**.—*adj* **stem'less**.

stem² [stem] *vt* to stop, check, to dam, to staunch; to tamp; to turn (skis) in stemming.—*pr p* **stemm'ing**; *pt*, *pt p* **stemmed**.

stench [stench] *n* stink.

stencil [sten's(i)l] *vti* to paint by brushing over a perforated plate or sheet; to make a stencil for producing copies of typewriting, etc.

stenography [sten-og'rå-fi] *n* the art, or any method, of writing very quickly, shorthand.—*n* **stenog'rapher**.—*adj* **stenographic**.

stentorian [sten-tö'ri-àn] *adj* very loud or powerful.

step [step] *n* a pace; a movement of the leg in walking, running, or dancing; the distance so covered; a footstep; a footfall, a footprint; gait; a small space; a short journey; a degree; a degree of a scale; a stage upward or downward; one tread of a stair, rung of a ladder; a rest for the foot; a move towards an end or in the course of proceeding; coincidence in speed or phase; a support for the end of a mast, pivot, or the like.

step- [step-] in composition denotes the mutual relationship between children who, in consequence of a subsequent marriage, have only one parent in common (as **step'sister**) or between such children and the later husband or wife of the mother or father (as **step'mother**, **step'son**).

stereograph [ster'i-ō-gräf] *n* a pair of photographs for viewing in a stereoscope or special eyeglasses.—*n* **ste'reogram**, a stereograph; a diagram or picture giving an impression of solidity or relief.

stereophonic [ster-i-ō-fon'ik] *adj* giving the effect of sound coming from different directions.—*n* **ster'eo**, a stereophonic record player, radio, system, etc.; a stereoscopic system, effect, picture, etc.

stereoscope [ster'i-ō-skōp] *n* an instrument by which the images of two pictures differing slightly in point of view are seen one by each eye and so give an effect of solidity.—*adv* **stereoscop'ically**.—*n* **stereos'copy**.

stereotype [ster'i-ō-tīp] *vt* a solid metallic plate for printing, cast from a mold from movable types.—*adj* **ste'reotyped**, fixed, unchangeable (eg patterns, opinions); conventionalized.

sterile [ster'il] *adj* unfruitful, barren; not producing, or unable to produce, offspring, fruit, seeds, or spores; (of a flower) without pistils; sterilized; destitute of ideas or results; free from living microorganisms.—*vt* **ster'ilize**, to cause to be fruitless.

sterling [stûr'ling] *n* sterling silver; British money of standard value.

stern¹ [stûrn] *adj* severe of countenance, manner, or feeling—austere, harsh, unrelenting; rigorous.—*adv* **stern'ly**.—*n* **stern'ness**.

stern² [stûrn] *n* the hind part of a vessel; the rump or tail.—*adj* **stern'most**, farthest astern.

sternum [stûr'num] *n* the breastbone.—*adj* **ster'nal**.

sternutation [stûr-nū-tā'sh(ò)n] *n* sneezing.

stertorous [stûr'tó-rus] *adj* with a snoring sound.

stet [stet] *vt* to restore after marking for deletion.

stethoscope [steth'ō-skōp] *n* an instrument used in auscultation.—*adj* **stethoscop'ic** [-skop'ik].

stevadore [stēv'e-dör] *n* one who loads and unloads vessels.

stew [stū] *n* (*obs*) a utensil used for boiling; a hot bath; mental agitation; (*pl*) a brothel, or a prostitutes' quarter; a dish of stewed food, esp meat with vegetables.—*vt* to simmer or boil slowly.

steward [stū'àrd] *n* one who manages the domestic concerns of a family or institution; one who superintends another's affairs, esp on an estate or farm.

stick¹ [stik] *vt* to pierce, transfix; to stab; to spear; to thrust; to fasten by piercing; to insert; to set in position; to set or cover (with things fastened on); to cause to adhere; to bring to a standstill; (*inf*) to put, set, etc.; (*inf*) to puzzle, baffle.—*vi* to be fixed by means of something inserted; to adhere; to become or remain fixed; to remain; to be detained by an impediment; to jam; to fail to proceed or advance; to hold fast, keep resolutely (to); to hesitate, scruple; to protrude or project (out, up, etc.).—*pt, pt p* **stuck.**

stick[2] [stik] *n* a small shoot or branch of a tree, broken or cut off; a walking stick; a piece of firewood; an instrument for beating a percussion instrument; an instrument for playing hockey or other game; a control rod of an airplane; anything in the form of a stick or rod.

stickle [stik'l] *vi* to be scrupulous or obstinately punctilious.

stiff [stif] *adj* not easily bent; rigid; wanting in suppleness; moved or moving with difficulty or friction; approaching solidity of joints and muscles, sore or limited in movement.—*adv* **stiff'ly.**—*adj* **stiff'-necked**, obstinate, hard to move; haughty; formal and unnatural.—*n* **stiff'ness.**

stifle [stī'fl] *vt* to suffocate; to make breathing difficult for; to smother or extinguish; to suppress, hold back; to stop.—*vi* to suffocate.—*adj* **stī'fling.**

stigma [stig'ma] *n* a brand, a mark of infamy; any special mark; a place on the skin which bleeds periodically; the part of a carpel that receives pollen.—*pl* **stig'mas**, or **stig'mata.**—*adv* **stigmat'ically.**—*vt* **stig'matize**, to mark with a stigma or with stigmata; to describe abusively (as).

stile[1] [stīl] *n* a step, or set of steps, for climbing over a wall or fence.

stile[2] [stīl] *n* an upright member in framing or panelling.

stiletto [sti-let'ō] *n* a dagger with a narrow blade; a pointed instrument for making holes for eyelets or embroidery.—*pl* **stilett'os.**

still[1] [stil] *adj* motionless; silent; calm; not carbonated; designating or of a single photograph taken from a motion-picture film.

still[2] [stil] *vt* to distill.—*n* an apparatus for distilling liquids.

stilt [stilt] *n* one of a pair of poles with a rest for the foot, mounted on which one can walk, as in play.

stimulant [stim'ū-lànt] *adj* stimulating; increasing or exciting vital action.—*n* anything that stimulates or excites; a stimulating drug; alcoholic liquor, not in a technical sense.—*adj* **stim'ulätive.**

sting [sting] *n* in some plants and animals a weapon (hair, tooth, etc.) that pierces and injects poison; the act of inserting a sting; the pain or the wound caused; any sharp tingling or irritating pain or its cause; an elaborate confidence game, esp one worked by undercover police in order to trap criminals.—*pt, pt p* **stung.**—*n* **sting'er**, one who, or that which, stings, specifically, a sharp blow or remark.

stingy [stin'ji] *adj* niggardly, parsimonious.—*adv* **stin'gily.**—*n* **stin'giness.**

stink [stingk] *vi* to give out a strong smell; to be of bad repute; (*inf*) to possess something to an offensive degree; (*inf*) to be extremely bad in quality.—*pt, pt p* **stunk.**—*n* disagreeable smell.

stipend [stī'pènd] *n* a salary paid for services, settled pay.—*n* **stipend'iary**, one who performs services for a salary.

stipple [stip'l] *vt* to engrave, paint, draw, etc., in small dots.

stipulate [stip'ū-lāt] *vt* to specify or require as a condition or essential part of an agreement; to give a guarantee of.—*vi* to make an agreement or covenant to do or forbear something (*with* for).—*ns* **stipulā'tion, stip'ulātor.**

stir[1] [stûr] *vt* to change the position of; to set in motion; to move around; to rouse, to move to activity, to excite.—*vi* to move oneself; to be active.—*pr p* **stirr'ing**; *pt, pt p* **stirred.**—*n* tumult; bustle; sensation.—*n* **stirr'er.**—*adj* **stirr'ing.**

stir[2] [stûr] *n* (*slang*) prison.

stirrup [stir'ùp] *n* a flat-bottomed ring suspended by a strap from the saddle, for a rider's foot.

stitch [stich] *n* a single in-and-out movement of a threaded needle in sewing, embroidery, or suturing; a portion of thread left in the material or tissue after one stitch; a single loop of a yarn in knitting or crocheting; a sudden, sharp pain, esp in the side; a least part, esp of clothing; a stitch formed in a specified way.

stock [stok] *n* (*arch*) a log, a block of wood; a stupid person; the trunk or main stem of a plant; raw material; shares of corporate capital, or the certificates showing such ownership; of herbs or subshrubs with racemes of sweet-scented flowers; a part into which another is fixed, as the handle of a whip, family, race; a store, the cattle, horses, etc., kept on a farm;

the liquor obtained by boiling meat or bones, a foundation for soup, etc.

stockade [stok-ād'] *n* a palisade formed of stakes fixed in the ground.—*vt* to fortify with such.

stockfish [stok'fish] *n* fish (as cod, haddock, or hake) dried hard in the open air without salt.

stocking [stok'ing] *n* a close covering for the foot and lower leg.—*n* **stockinette, stockinet,** a soft elastic knitted fabric for bandages and infant's wear.

stocky [stok'i] *adj* short and stout, thickset; having a strong stem.—*adv* **stock'ily.**

stodgy [stoj'i] *adj* heavy and indigestible; heavy and uninteresting.—*vt* **stodge,** to stuff full, esp with food.—*n* a thick filling food (as oatmeal or stew).

stoic [stō'ik] *n* a disciple of the school founded by the philosopher Zeno, who taught in Athens; one indifferent to pleasure or pain.—*adjs* **stō'ic, -al.**—*adv* **stō'ically.**

stoke [stōk] *vt* to feed (a fire) with fuel.—*ns* **stoke'hold,** the hold containing the boilers of a ship; one of the spaces in front of a ship's boilers from which the furnaces are fed.

stole[1] [stōl] *pt* and *obs pt p* of **steal.**

stole[2] [stōl] *n* a long robe; a narrow vestment worn on the shoulders, hanging down in front; a woman's outer garment, of similar form.

stolen [stōl'èn] *pt p* of **steal.**

stolid [stol'id] *adj* dull, heavy, impassive; unemotional.—*ns* **stolid'ity.**—*adv* **stol'idly.**

stomach [stum'àk] *n* the strong muscular bag into which the food passes when swallowed, and where it is principally digested; (in ruminants, etc.) one of several digestive cavities; the belly; appetite, or inclination generally; (*arch*) courage, pride.—*vt* to brook or put up with.

stomp [stomp] *vti* (*inf*) to stamp; to dance.—*n* an early jazz dance with foot stamping.

-stomy [stōm-i] in composition, indicating a new surgical opening into an organ.

stone [stōn] *n* a detached piece of rock; a piece of such material fashioned for a particular purpose, as a *grindstone*; a precious stone or gem; a tombstone; a concretion formed in the kidney or gallbladder; a round playing piece used in various games (as backgammon or go).—*n* **Stone Age,** the first known period of prehistoric human culture identified by the use of stone tools.

stood [stööd] *pt, pt p* of **stand.**

stooge [stööj] *n* (*inf*) a comedian's assistant and foil; anyone who plays a subordinate or compliant role to a principal; *n* **stool pigeon.**—*vi* to act as a stooge.

stool [stööl] *n* a seat without a back; a low support for the feet when sitting, or the knees when kneeling; the seat used in evacuating the bowels; the act of evacuating the bowels.

stoop[1] [stööp] *vi* to bend the body forward; to lean forward; to submit; to descend from rank or dignity (to do something); to degrade oneself; (*arch*) to swoop down on the wing, as a bird of prey.—*vt* to debase, degrade; to bend (a part of the body downward and forward.—*n* the act of stooping; inclination forward; a swoop.—*adj* stooped.

stoop[2] [stööp] *n* a small porch at the door of a house.

stop [stop] *vt* to stuff up and so close or partially close; to obstruct, to render impassable, to close; to bring to a stand still, prevent the motion of; to prevent (from); to put an end to; to discontinue; to keep back (eg *to stop payment of a check*); (*mus*) of woodwind and stringed instruments, to alter the pitch of by means of a stop.—*vi* to cease going forward, halt, to cease from any motion; to leave off, desist; to come to an end; to stay.—*pr p* **stopp'ing**; *pt, pt p* **stopped.**

store [stōr, stôr] *n* a hoard or quantity gathered; (in *pl*) supplies of food, clothing, etc.; abundance; a storehouse; a retail establishment where goods are offered for sale.—*vt* to accumulate and put in a place for keeping; to put in a storehouse, warehouse, etc.; to furnish (with supplies); to put (data) into a computer memory.—*ns* **stō'rage,** the act of placing in a store.

stork [störk] *n* any of various long-necked and long-legged wading birds allied to the herons.

storm [störm] *n* a violent commotion of the atmosphere producing wind, rain, etc., a tempest; a violent commotion outbreak of any kind; a paroxysm; wind having a speed of 64 to 72 miles an hour; (*mil*) an assault on a fortified place.

story[1] [stō'ri] *n* a narrative of consecutive events; an anecdote; an account, allegation; a fictitious narrative; the plot of a novel, etc.; (*inf*) an untruth; a news article.

story[2] [stō'ri] *n* a horizontal division of a building, from a floor to the ceiling above it; a set of rooms in such a space; a unit of measure equal to the number of stories in a building.

stoup [stōōp] *n* a flagon, or its contents; a small measure for liquids; a basin for holy water.

stout [stowt] *adj* strong, robust; corpulent; of strong material; resolute; staunch; forceful; (*Bible*) stubborn.—*n* type of strong dark beer.—*adj* **stoutheart'ed**, having a brave heart; courageous; stubborn.—*adv* **stout'ly**.—*n* **stout'ness**.

stove[1] [stōv] *n* a closed heating or cooking apparatus; a kiln.

stove[2] [stōv] *pt, pt p* of **stave**.

stow [stō] *vt* to place, arrange, pack, in an orderly way; to put away in a convenient place; (*slang*) to put aside; to cease.

straddle [strad'l] *vi* to part the legs wide; to stand or walk with the legs far apart; (of legs) to spread apart.

straggle [strag'l] *vi* to stray from the course or line of march; to wander beyond, or to escape from, proper limits; to move in an irregular way, not as a compact body; to grow irregularly and untidily.—*n* **stragg'ler**.

straight [strāt] *adj* (of a line) invariable in direction, determined by the position of two points; not curved or bent; direct.—*vt* **straight'en**, to make straight.—*ns* **straight face**, a sober, unsmiling face.—*adj* **straightfor'ward**, going forward in a straight course; honest, open, downright.—*advs* **straightfor'wardly; straight'ly**, evenly; tightly, closely.

strain[1] [strān] *vt* to stretch tight; to make tight; to stretch beyond due limits, make cover too much (eg *to strain credulity, the meaning, the law*); to exert to the utmost (eg *to strain every nerve*); to injure by overtaxing; to constrain, make uneasy or unnatural; to separate the solid from the liquid part of by a filter.—*adj* **strained**.—*n* **strain'er**.

strain[2] [strān] *n* race, stock, generation; (in domestic animals) individuals of common descent; hereditary character; natural tendency, element in character.

strait [strāt] *adj* difficult; distressful; (*arch*) strict, rigorous; (*arch*) narrow.—*n* a narrow pass in a mountain (*arch*), or in the ocean (often in *pl*) between two portions of land; (usu. *pl*) difficulty, distress.

strand[1] [strand] *n* the margin or beach of the sea.—*vt* to run aground.—*vi* to drift or be driven ashore.—*adj* **strand'ed**, driven on shore; friendless and helpless.

strand[2] [strand] *n* one of the strings or parts that compose a rope; a tress of hair.—*vt* to break a strand; to form by uniting strands, compose of strands.

strange [strānj] *adj* foreign, alien; from elsewhere; not of one's own place, family, or circle; not one's own; not formerly known or experienced; unfamiliar; interestingly unusual; odd; estranged; distant or reserved; unacquainted, unversed.—*adv* **strange'ly**.—*ns* **strange'ness; strän'ger**, a foreigner.

strangle [strang'gl] *vt* to kill by compressing the throat, to choke; to suppress, stifle.

strangulate [strang'gū-lāt] *vt* to strangle; to compress so as to suppress or suspend the function of.

strap [strap] *n* a narrow strip of leather or cloth, esp one with a buckle or other fastening; a razor-strop; an iron plate secured by screw-bolts, for connecting two or more timbers.—*vt* to beat with a strap; to bind with a strap; to strop, as a razor.—*pr p* **strapp'ing**; *pt, pt p* **strapped**.

stratagem [strat'ȧ-jem] *n* action planned to outwit an enemy; an artifice.—*adjs* **strategic**.—*n* **strat'egy**, generalship, the act of managing armed forces in a campaign (cf **tactics**); artifice or finesse generally.—*adv* **stratēg'ically**.

stratify [strat'i-fī] *vt* to form or lay in strata or layers.—*n* **stratificā'tion**.

stratosphere [strät'- or strat'ō-sfēr] *n* a layer of the earth's atmosphere, beginning about 4½ to 10 miles up, in which temperature does not fall as height increases.

stratum [strä'tum] *n* a bed of sedimentary rock, consisting usually of a series of layers; level (of society).—*pl* **strä'ta**.

stratus [strä'tus] *n* a long, low, gray cloud layer.—*pl* **strä'tī**.

straw [strö] *n* the stalk on which grain grows, and from which it is thrashed; a quantity of dried stalks of corn, etc.; a tube for sucking up a beverage; a straw hat; a trifle, a whit.

stray [strā] *vi* to wander; to wander (from eg the proper place, the company to which one belongs); to deviate from duty or rectitude.

streak [strēk] *n* a line or long mark different in color from the surface on which it is traced; a stripe; a flash; a slight characteristic, a trace.—*adj* **streak'y**.

stream [strēm] *n* a current (of water, air, light, etc.); running water; a river, brook, etc.; anything flowing out from a source; anything flowing and continuous; a large quantity coming continuously.

street [strēt] *n* a public road in a town or city lined with houses; such a road with its buildings and sidewalks; the people living, working, etc., along a given street.—*ns* **street'car**, a car on rails for public transportation along the street; **street'walker**, a prostitute.—*adj* **street'wise**', (*inf*) experienced in dealing with people in urban poverty areas where crime is common.

strength [strength] *n* quality of being strong; power of any kind, active or passive—force, vigor, solidity or toughness, power to resist; degree in which a person or thing is strong.—*vt* **strength'en**, to make strong or stronger; to confirm; to encourage; to increase the power or security of.

strenuous [stren'ū-ùs] *adj* vigorous, urgent, zealous; necessitating exertion.—*adv* **stren'uously**.—*n* **stren'uousness**.

stress [stres] *n* pressure, urgency, strain, violence (eg *stress of circumstance, weather*), emphasis; (*mech*) a system of forces operating over an area, esp a combination producing or sustaining a strain.—*vt* to put pressure on; to emphasise.

stretch [strech] *vt* to extend, to draw out; to lay at full length; to reach out; to exaggerate, strain, or carry further than is right.—*adj* capable of being stretched.—*n* **stretch'er**, anything for stretching; a frame on which anything is stretched; a frame for carrying the sick or wounded.

strew [strōō] *vt* to scatter loosely; to cover by scattering (with).—*pt p* **strewed** or **strewn**.

stricken [strik'n] *pt p* of **strike**.—*adj* struck or wounded; afflicted, as by something painful.

strict [strikt] *adj* exact; allowing of no exception, irregularity, laxity.—*adv* **strict'ly**, narrowly, closely, rigorously, exclusively.

stride [strīd] *vi* to walk with long steps; to take a long step.—*vt* to stride over; to bestride.—*pt* **strōde**.

strident [strī'dént] *adj* loud and grating.—*adv* **strīdently**.—*ns* **strī'dence, -cy**.

stridulate [strid'ū-lāt] *vi* (of insects) to make a chirping or scraping sound.

strife [strīf] *n* contention; fight, quarrel; struggle.

strike [strīk] *vt* to hit with force, to smite; to stab, pierce; to move in a specified direction by hitting; to cause to pierce; to collide with, knock against; to attack, punish; to give (a blow); to ignite (a match) by friction; to produce by friction (eg a light, sparks); to cause to sound; to mint; to lower, let down (a flag, sail, or tent); (*theat*) to dismantle a stage set, etc. (also *n*); to impress, or to affect in a specified way, with force or suddenness like that of a blow; to light upon, to come upon, esp unexpectedly; to make (a compact or agreement); to assume (an attitude); to cancel, erase (*with* off, out, from).—*pt* **struck**; *pt p* **struck** [*arch* **strick'en**].—*n* act of striking for higher wages, etc.—*n* **strik'er**.—*adj* **strik'ing**, that strikes; for hitting, smiting, attacking; surprising; impressive.—*adv* **strik'ingly**.—*n* **strikebreak'er**, one hired to replace a striking worker; **strike'breaking**, action designed to break up a strike.—**on strike**, taking part in a strike.

string [string] *n* coarse material in very narrow and relatively long pieces, made by twisting threads, used for tying, fastening, etc.; a portion of this; a piece of anything for tying; anything of like character as a nerve, tendon, fiber; a stretched piece of catgut, silk, wire, or other material in a musical instrument; (*pl*) the stringed instruments played by a bow in an orchestra; their players; a cord on which things are filed (eg a string of beads); a line or series of things.—*vt* to supply with strings; to put on a string; to remove the strings from, as beans; to stretch out in a long line; *pt, pt p* **strung**.—*adjs* **stringed**, having strings; **string'less**, having no strings.

stringent [strin'jént] *adj* binding strongly, exact and strictly enforced (eg *stringent regulations*).—*n* **strin'gency**, state or quality of being stringent; severe pressure.—*adv* **stri'gently**.

strip [strip] *vt* to pull off in strips; to tear off; to deprive of a covering.

stripe [strīp] *n* a line, or long narrow division of a different color from the ground; a chevron on a sleeve, indicating noncommissioned rank, years served, etc.

stripling [strip'ling] *n* a lad who has not reached full growth.

strive [strīv] *vi* to endeavor earnestly, labor hard; to struggle, contend.—*pt* **strôve**.

strode [strōd] *pt* of **stride**.

stroke [strōk] *n* an act of striking; a blow; an attempt to hit; a sudden attack of apoplexy; the sound of a clock; a dash in writing; the sweep of an oar in rowing; a movement in one direction of a pen, pencil, or paintbrush; a method of striking in games, etc.

stroke [strōk] *vt* to rub gently in one direction; to do so as a sign of affection.

stroll [strōl] *vi* to ramble idly, to saunter; to wander on foot.—*n* a leisurely walk; a ramble on foot.

strong [strong] *adj* able to endure—eg firm, solid, well fortified, having wealth or resources; hale, healthy; having great physical power; having great vigor, as the mind; forcible; energetic; convincing; powerfully affecting the sense of smell or taste, pungent; having a quality in a great degree.—*adv* **strong'ly**.

structure [struk'chúr] *n* manner of building or putting together, construction; arrangement of parts or of particles in a substance, or of atoms in a molecule; manner of organization; an erection; a building, esp one of large size; an organic form.—*vt* to organize, build up; to construct a framework for.—*adj* **struc'tûral**.—*adv* **struc'tûrally**.

strudel [s(h)trōōdl] *n* very thin pastry rolled up enclosing fruit and baked.

struggle [strug'l] *vi* to make great efforts with contortions of the body; to make great exertions (to); to contend (with, for, against); to make one's way (along, through, up, etc.) with difficulty.

strum [strum] *vt* to play on (a guitar, etc.), in an inexpert manner.

strut[1] [strut] *vi* to walk in a pompous manner, with affected dignity.

strut[2] [strut] *n* any light structural part or long column that resists pressure in the direction of its length; a prop.—*vt* to brace.

stub [stub] *n* a short piece left after the larger part has been used.—*pr p* **stubb'ing**; *pt, pt p* **stubbed**.—*adjs* **stubbed**, short and thick like a stump, blunt, obtuse; **stubb'y**, abounding with stubs or stubble; short and dense; short and thickset.—*n* **stubb'iness**.

stubble [stub'l] *n* the stubs or stumps of corn left in the ground when the stalks are cut; any short, bristly growth, as of beard.—*adj* **stubb'ly**.

stubborn [stub'órn] *adj* immovably fixed in opinion, obstinate; persevering; stiff, inflexible.—*adv* **stubb'ornly**.—*n* **stubb'ornness**.

stuck [stuk] *pt, pt p* of **stick**.—*adj* **stuck'-up'**, (*inf*) self-importantly aloof.

stud[1] [stud] *n* a male animal, esp a horse; a collection of breeding horses and mares.

stud[2] [stud] *n* a nail with a large head; a headless bolt; a double-headed button worn eg in a shirt; an ornamental knob or boss.

student [stū'dènt] *n* one who studies or investigates; one who is enrolled for study at a school, college, etc.

studio [stū'di-ō] *n* the workshop of a painter, sculptor, or of a photographer; a place where dancing lessons are given; a building or (also in *pl*) place where motion pictures are made.

studious [stū'di-ús] *adj* fond of study; careful.

study [stud'i] *vt* to observe (eg phenomena) closely; to examine (information) thoroughly so as to understand, interpret, select data from, etc.—*pt, pt p* **stud'ied**.—*n* application of the mind to a subject, to books; a room devoted to study; an artist's preliminary sketch from nature, a student's exercise in painting or sculpture.—*adv* **stud'ied**, deliberate, premeditated (eg *a studied insult*); prepared by careful study.

stuff [stuf] *n* material of which anything is made; essence, elemental part; textile fabrics; cloth, esp when woolen; some-

thing consumed or taken into the body by humans, as food or drugs; worthless matter; possessions generally, esp household furniture, etc.; *ns* **stuff'ing**, material used to stuff or fill anything.

stuffy [stuf'i] *adj* badly ventilated, musty; causing difficulty in breathing; (*inf*) obstinate, ungracious, sulky.—*n* **stuff'iness**.

stultify [stul'ti-fī] *vt* to cause to appear foolish, or absurd; hence, to make of no effect, value, or weight.

stumble [stum'bl] *vi* to strike the feet against something and trip or lose balance; to falter; to light (on) by chance; to slide into crime or error.—*vt* to cause to trip or stop; to puzzle.—*n* a trip in walking or running; a faltering; a blunder, a failure.

stump [stump] *n* the part of a tree left in the ground after the trunk is cut down; the part of a limb, tooth, remaining after a part is cut off or destroyed; a similar remnant, eg of a pencil.

stun [stun] *vt* to stupefy with a loud noise, or with a blow; to surprise completely, to amaze.—*pr p* **stunn'ing**; *pt, pt p* **stunned**.

stunt[1] [stunt] *vt* to check the growth of, to dwarf, check.—*adj* **stunt'ed**, dwarfed, checked in development.

stunt[2] [stunt] *n* a spectacular feat; a project designed to attract attention.—*vi* to perform stunts.

stupefy [stū'pe-fī] *vt* to make stupid or insensible (with drink, drugs, misery, etc.).

stupendous [stū-pen'dús] *adj* wonderful, amazing.

stupid [stū'pid] *adj* struck senseless; deficient or dull in understanding; formed or done without reason or judgement, foolish.—*ns* **stūpid'ity**, **stū'pidness**.—*adv* **stū'pidly**.

stupor [stū'pór] *n* suspension of sense either complete or partial, dazed condition.

sturdy [stûr'di] *adj* resolute, firm, forcible; strong, robust.—*adv* **stur'dily**.—*n* **stur'diness**.

stutter [stut'ér] *vi* to hesitate in utterance, repeating initial consonants, to stammer.—*n* **stutt'erer**, one who stutters.

sty[1] [stī] *n* a small inflamed swelling on rim of an eyelid.

sty[2] [stī] *n* a pen for swine; any extremely filthy place.—*pl* **sties**.

style [stīl] *n* a stylus; anything long and pointed; mode of expressing thought in language ideas in the visual arts, etc.; manner of performing an action or of playing a game; the distinctive manner peculiar to an author, painter, etc. or to a period; manner, method; form (*good style, bad style*); fashion; air of fashion, elegance, consequence; title, mode of address.—*adjs* **sty'lar**, pertaining to the style of a plant ovary; **sty'lish**, conforming to current style, as in dress; fashionable.—*adv* **sty'lishly**.—*adj* **stylis'tic**.—*adv* **stylist'ically**.

styptic [stip'tik] *adj* astringent; that stops bleeding.—*n.* an astringent agent for application to bleeding.

suasion [swā'zh(ó)n] *n* the act of persuading, persuasion.—*adj* **suā'sive**, tending to persuade.

suave [swäv] *adj* pleasant, agreeable, polite; bland, mollifying.

sub- [sub'] *pfx* (by assimilation before *c, f, g, m, p, r, s,* **suc-**, as **succeed**, **suf-**, as **suffuse**, **sug-**, as **suggest**, **sum-**, as **summon**, **sup-**, as **support**, **sur-**, as **surreptitious**, **sus-**, as **suspend**—also as **s-**, in *sombre* and **so-**, in *sojourn*) denotes.—

    (1) under, below, as **subterranean**, *substratum, substructure, subway*;

    (2) below the level of, less than, as **subconscious**, *subhuman, subnormal*;

    (3) slightly less than, almost, as **subacute**, *subarctic, subtemperate, subtorrid, subtropical*;

    (4) formed by subdivision, as **subtype**, *subphylum, subclass, sub order, subfamily, subgenus, subspecies, subgrade, subgroup, subsection, subvariety*;

    (5) under the control of, subordinate, as **subagent**, *subcontract, suboffice, substation*;

    (6) next in rank to, under (*fig*) as **subdeacon**, *subdean, subinspector, sublibrarian*.

sub [sub] *n* a submarine; a substitute.

subacute [sub-a-kūt'] *adj* having a tapered but not sharply pointed form.

subaqueous [sub-ā'kwe-ús] *adj* lying under water.

subatomic [sub-â-tom'ik] *adj* smaller than an atom; occurring within an atom.

subclinical [sub-klin'i-kal] *adj* of a slightness not detectable by usual clinical means.

subconscious [sub-kon'shús] *adj* of, pertaining to, mental operations just below the level of consciousness; active beneath consciousness.

subcontinent [sub-con'tinent] *n* a land mass having great size (as Greenland) but smaller than any of the usu. recognized continents.

subcontract [sub-kon'träkt] *n* a secondary contract.

subcutaneous [sub-kū-tā'ne-ùs] *adj* under the skin.

subdivide [sub-di-vīd'] *vt* to divide into smaller divisions, esp to divide (a tract of land) into building lots; to divide again. — *vi* to be subdivided; to separate into smaller divisions. — *n* **subdivi'sion**, the act of subdividing; a part made by subdividing.

subdue [sub-dū'] *vt* to conquer; to render submissive, to tame; to overcome (eg a desire, impulse), discipline (eg the flesh); to soften, tone down (often in *pt p* —eg color, light, mood or manner, emotion or feeling). — *adj* **subdū'able**. — *n* **subdū'er**.

subjacent [sub-jā'sènt] *adj* lying under or below, being in a lower situation.

subject [sub'jekt] *adj* under the power of, owing allegiance to, another; not independent; liable. — *n* one under the power of another; one under allegiance to a sovereign; the person or thing on which any operation or experiment is performed; (*anat*) a dead body for dissection; that which the artist is trying to express, the scheme or idea of a work of art, as a painting, poem, etc. — *n* **subjec'tion**, the act of subjecting; the state of being subjected. — *adj* **subjec'tive**, relating to the subject. — *adv* **subject'ively**. — *ns* **subject'iveness**; **subjectiv'ity**.

subjoin [sub-join'] *vt* to add at the end or afterwards.

subjugate [sub'jŏŏ-gāt] *vt* to bring under the yoke, under power or dominion; to conquer.

subjunctive [sub-jungk'tiv] *adv* denoting that mood of a verb which expresses condition, hypothesis, or contingency. — *n* the subjunctive mood.

sublease [sub-lēs'] *n* a lease by a tenant to another, the subtenant. — Also *vt*.

sublet [sub-let'] *vt* to let to another.

sublimate [sub'lim-āt] *vt* to refine and exalt; to sublime; (*psych*) to use the energy of (a primitive impulse) for purposes of a high nature such as artistic creation.

sublime [sub-līm'] *adj* lofty, majestic, awakening feelings of awe or veneration. — *adv* **sublime'ly**. — *n* **sublim'ity**.

subliminal [sub-lim'i-nàl] *adj* beneath the level of consciousness.

sublunar [sub-lū'när] *adj* earthly, belonging to this world; *also* **sub'lunary, sublunary**.

submarine [sub-mà-rēn'] *adj* underwater, esp under the sea. — *n* [sub'-] a submersible boat, capable of being propelled under water, esp for firing torpedoes.

submerge [sub-merj'], **submerse** [sub-mèrs'] *vt* to plunge under water; to flood with water.

submit [sub-mit'] *vt* to surrender (oneself) to another; to offer to another for consideration or criticism; to offer as an opinion. — *vi* to yield, to surrender; to yield one's opinion; to be resigned; to consent. — *pr p* **submitt'ing**; *pt, pt p* **submitt'ed**.

subnormal [sub-nör'mål] *adj* lower or smaller than normal; less than normal, esp of a person with less intelligence.

subordinate [sub-ör'di-nàt] *adj* lower in order, rank, nature, power, etc.; of less authority, weight, or importance than (*with* to).

suborn [sub-örn'] *vt* to procure, persuade (a person) eg by bribery, to commit a perjury or other unlawful act. — *ns* **subornā'tion**; **suborn'er**.

subpoena [sub-pē'na] *n* a written legal order commanding the attendance of a person in court under a penalty. — *vt* to summon by a subpoena.

subscribe [sub-skrīb'] *vt* to write (usu. one's name) underneath, eg a document; to give consent to (something written) by writing one's name underneath; to authenticate (a document) officially in this way; to sign; to promise to give or pay by attaching one's name to a list; to assent to; to support.

subsequent [sub'sè-kwènt] *adj* following or coming after. — *adv* **sub'sequently**.

subserve [sub-sûrv'] *vt* to promote the welfare or purposes of; to serve subordinately or instrumentally, to help forward (eg a purpose, plan).

subside [sub-sīd'] *vi* to sink or fall to the bottom; to flatten out so as to form a depression; to let oneself settle down; to fall into a state of quiet. — *n* **subsi'dence**.

subsidy [sub'si-di] *n* (*hist*) a sum of money formerly granted by the British parliament to the sovereign raised by special taxes; a sum of money paid by one state to another; money granted by the government to a private person or company to assist an enterprise considered to be of public benefit. — *adv* **subsid'iarily**.

subsist [sub-sist'] *vi* to have existence; to remain, continue; to keep oneself alive (on). — *vt* to provide food for. — *n* **subsist'ence**, state of being subsistent.

subsoil [sub'soil] *n* the under soil, the bed or stratum of earth lying immediately beneath the surface soil.

subsonic [sub-son'ik] *adj* of speed, less than that of sound.

substance [sub'stàns] *n* that which underlies outward manifestation, the essential nature; the essential part, purport, meaning.

substantial [sub-stan'sh(à)l] *adj* consisting of, of the nature of, substance; real, not merely seeming; virtual, in total effect though not in all details. — *n* **substantial'ity**. — *adv* **substan'tially**, in essence, in total effect, to all intents and purposes. — *vt* **substantiate** [-stan'shi-āt], to make substantial; to prove, to show the validity of, grounds for. — *n* **substantiā'tion**.

substitute [sub'sti-tūt] *vt* to put in place of another person or thing (*with* for); to replace (by). — *n* one who, or that which, is put in place of, or used instead of, for want of, another. — *adj* put instead of another.

subtenant [sub-ten'ánt] *n* a tenant who leases from one who is also a tenant.

subtend [sub-tend'] *vt* to extend under or be opposite to, as a hypotenuse a right angle.

subterfuge [sub'tèr-fūj] *n* an artifice to escape censure or the force of an argument, evasion.

subterranean [sub-te-rā'nè-àn] *adj* under the earth or ground; hidden, secret. — *also* **subterrā'neous**.

subtile [sut'il *or* sub'til] *adj* subtle, elusive; cunning, crafty; sagacious, discerning. — *adv* **sub'tilely**.

subtitle [sub'tī-tl] *n* an explanatory, usu. secondary, title to a book; a line or lines as of dialogue shown on a TV or movie screen.

subtle [sut'l] *adj* pervasive but difficult to describe; difficult to define, put into words.

subtract [sub-trakt'] *vti* to take away or deduct, as one quantity from another.

subtropical [sub-trop'ik-ál] *adj* of, characteristic of, the regions bordering on the tropics.

suburb [sub'ûrb] *n* a district, town, etc., on the outskirts of a large city.

subvention [sub-ven'sh(ó)n] *n* a subsidy.

subvert [sub-vûrt'] *vt* to overthrow, to ruin utterly (something established); to corrupt, as in morals. — *n* **subver'sion**, act of subverting; entire overthrow, ruin. — *adj* **subver'sive**. — *n* **subvert'er**.

subway [sub'wā] *n* a passage under a street; an underground metropolitan electric railway.

succeed [suk-sēd'] *vt* to come after, to follow in order; to follow, take the place of. — *n* **success'**, the gaining of wealth, fame, etc.; the prosperous termination (of anything attempted); a successful person or affair. — *adj* **success'ful**, having, achieving, the desired end or effect, gaining the prize aimed at; prosperous. — *adv* **success'fully**. — *n* **success'ion**. — *adj* **success'ive**, following in succession or in order. — *adv* **success'ively**. — *n* **success'or**, one who succeeds another, as to an office.

succinct [suk-singkt'] *adj* short, concise.

succor [suk'ór] *vt* to assist, to relieve. — *n* aid, relief.

succulent [suk'ū-lènt] *adj* full of juice, juicy; moist and tasty; of a plant, having fleshy tissue designed to conserve moisture; rich in interest. — *n* a succulent plant (as a cactus). — *n* **succ'ūlence**.

succumb [su-kum'] *vi* to yield to superior strength or overpowering desire; to die.

such [such] *adj* of this or that kind (eg *such people, such a man*); of the quality or character mentioned or implied; used to give emphasis.

suck [suk] *vt* to draw into the mouth; to draw milk or other liquid from with the mouth; to lick, squeeze, and roll about in the mouth; to draw in as if by sucking (*with in, up,* etc.).—*n* **suck'er,** one who, or that which, sucks; (*slang*) a gullible person.

suckle [suk'll] *vt* to feed at the breast or udder.—*n* **suck'ling,** a young child or animal still being fed on its mother's milk.—*adj* sucking.

sucrose [sū'krōs] *n* the form of sugar obtained from sugarcane and sugar beet.

suction [suk'sh(ô)n] *n* act, or power, of sucking; act or process of exhausting the air and creating a vacuum into which fluids are pushed by atmospheric pressure or, more generally, of exerting a force on a body (solid, liquid, or gas) by reducing the air pressure on part of its surface.

sudden [sud'ĕn] *adj* unexpected hasty, abrupt.—*adv* **sud'd'enly.**

sudorific [sū-dor-if'ik] *adj* causing sweat.—*n* a medicine producing sweat, a diaphoretic.—*n* sū'dor, sweat.

sue [sōō] *vt* to entreat, make petition to; to prosecute at law.

suffer [suf'ĕr] *vt* to undergo; to endure; to permit (to do); to tolerate.—*vi* to feel pain; to undergo punishment (for); to sustain loss or injury.—*adj* **suff'erable,** that may be suffered; endurable; allowable.

suffice [su-fīs'] *vi* to be enough; to be equal (to do), adequate (for the end in view).—*vt* to satisfy.—*adj* **suffi'cient** [-fi'shĕnt], enough; equal to any end or purpose.—*adv* **suffi'ciently.**—*n* **sufficiency.**

suffix [suf'iks] *n* a letter, syllable, or syllables added to the end of a word to modify its meaning or to form a new derivative.

suffocate [suf'ō-kāt] *vt* to kill by stopping the breath, to stifle; to cause to feel unable to breathe freely; to deprive of conditions necessary for growth or expression, to destroy (eg aspirations).—*adj* **suff'ocating,** choking, hindering respiration; hindering self-expression.—*adv* **suff'ocatingly.**—*n* **suffoca'tion.**

suffrage [suf'rij] *n* a vote; a vote in approbation or assent; the right to vote.—*n* **suffragette',** a woman who advocates female suffrage.

suffuse [su-fūz'] *vt* to overspread or cover, as with a fluid, or with color or light.

sugar [shŏŏg'ár] *n* a sweet substance obtained chiefly from sugarcane and the sugar beet, and also from maple and palm trees, etc.

suggest [sug-jest'] *vt* to put into one's mind; to bring to one's mind; to bring to one's mind by association of ideas; to imply or seem to imply; to propose; to hint (to).—*adj* **suggest'ible.**—*n* **suggestion.**—*adj* **suggestive,** containing a hint; fitted to bring to one's mind the idea (of); of, pertaining to, suggestion; rather indecent.—*adv* **sugges'tively.**

suicide [sū'i-sīd, or sōō'-] *n* one who dies by his own hand; the act of killing oneself intentionally; ruin of one's own interests.—*adj* **suici'dal,** of, pertaining to, suicide; directed towards, or with an impulse towards, suicide; destructive of one's own interests.—*adv* **suici'dally.**

suit [sūt, sōōt] *n* act of suing; an action at law; petition; a courtship; a set of playing cards of one kind (eg of hearts); all the dominoes bearing the same number; a number of things made to be worn together, esp a jacket and skirt (or trousers).—*pt p* **suit'ed,** fitted (to, for).—*adj* **suit'able,** fitting, agreeable (to), convenient (to, for).—*ns* **suitabil'ity, suit'ableness.**—*adv* **suit'ably.**

suite [swēt] *n* a train of followers or attendants; a regular set, esp of rooms, furniture, pieces of music.

sulcate [sul'kāt] *adj* furrowed, grooved.

sulfur [sul'fûr] *n* a yellow nonmetallic element (symbol S; at wt 32.1; no 16), very brittle, fusible, and inflammable.—*ns* **sul'fate,** a salt of sulfuric acid; **sul'fide,** a compound of sulfur with another element or radical; **sul'fite,** a salt of sulfurous acid.—*adj* **sulfu'reous,** consisting of, containing, or having the qualities of, sulfur.

sulk [sulk] *vi* to be sulky.—*n pl* **sulks,** a fit of sulkiness.—*adj* **sulk'y,** silently sullen, withdrawn and unresponsive because of (usu. petty) resentment.

sullen [sul'ĕn] *adj* gloomily angry and silent; dark, dull (eg *a sullen sky).—adv* **sull'enly.**—*n* **sull'enness.**

sully [sul'i] *vt* to soil, to spot, to tarnish.—*vi* to be soiled.—*pt t* and *pt p* **sull'ied.**

sultan [sul'tan] *n* a sovereign, esp of a Muslim state.—**sultana** [sul-tä'na], the mother, a wife, or a daughter of a sultan; a pale yellow seedless grape grown for raisins and wine; the raisin of a sultana.

sultry [sul'tri] *adj* sweltering, very hot and oppressive, close; hot with rage; passionate.—*adv* **sul'trily.**—*n* **sul'triness.**

sum [sum] *n* the amount of two or more things taken together; the whole amount, aggregate; a quantity of money; a problem in arithmetic; the substance or result of reasoning; summary, gist (also **sum and substance).**

summary [sum'á-ri] *adj* short, brief, compendious; quick, without waste of time or words, without formalities.—*n* an abstract, abridgment, or compendium.—*adv* **summ'arily.**

summation [sum-ā'sh(ô)n] *n* act of forming a total or sum; cumulative action or effect; a final part of an argument expressing conclusions, as in a trial.

summer [sum'ĕr] *n* the second and warmest season of the year, following the spring.

summit [sumit] *n* the highest point, the top.—*n* **summ'itry,** the practice or technique of holding summit conferences.

summon [sum'ón] *vt* to call with authority; to command to appear, esp in court; (also **summon up**) to rouse to activity (eg *to summon energy, courage to do this).—ns* **summ'oner; summ'ons.**

sump [sump] *n* a small pit at the lowest point of a mine or excavation into which water can drain and out of which it can be pumped.

sumpter [sump'tĕr] *n* a pack animal.

sumptuary [sumpt'ū-ár-i] *adj* pertaining to or regulating personal expenditures and esp preventing extravagance, usu. by imposing taxes on luxuries.

sumptuous [sumpch'ū-ùs] *adj* costly; magnificent.—*n* **sumpt'úousness.**—*adv* **sumpt'úously.**

sun [sun] *n* the star which gives light and heat to the solar system; a body which, like the earth's sun, forms the center of a planetary system; that which resembles the sun in position of importance or in brightness; the sunshine.

sundae [sun'dā] *n* a serving of ice cream covered with a topping (as of crushed fruit, syrup, nuts, etc.)

Sunday [sun'dā] *n* the first day of the week, now regarded as the Sabbath by most Christians.

sunder [sun'dĕr] *vti* to separate, to divide.

sundry [sun'dri] *adj* miscellaneous, various.—*pron* (plural in construction) an indeterminate number.—*n pl* **sun'dries,** various small things.

super- [sōō'pĕr-] *pfx* [L *super,* prep and pfx, above, etc.] conveys meanings such as the following.—(1) above, on the top of, eg **superstructure, superimpose.**

super [sōō'pĕr] *n* a supernumerary actor; superintendant, supervisor, esp the superintendent of an apartment building; a superfine grade or large size; a fabric used for reinforcing books.

superable [sōō'pĕr-â-bl] *adj* able to be surmounted.

superabundant [sōō-pĕr-ab-und'ánt] *adj* abundant to excess, more than enough.

superannuate [sōō-pĕr-an'ū-āt] *vt* to make, declare or prove obsolete or out-of-date; to pension on account of old age or infirmity.—*n* **superannua'tion,** state of being superannuated.

superb [sōō-pûrb'] *adj* proud, magnificent, stately; of the highest, most impressive, quality.—*adv* **superb'ly.**

supercalender [sōō-pĕr-kal'ĕn-dĕr] *vt* to give (paper) an extra smooth surface by means of supercalenders.

supercharger [sōō'pĕr-chär'jĕr] *n* a compressor used to supply air or combustible mixture to an internal-combustion engine at a pressure greater than atmospheric.

supercilious [sōō'pĕr-sil'i-us] *adj* prone to despise others; haughty, disdainful.

superdominant [sōō'pĕr-dom'i-nánt] *adj* the tone next above the dominant; submediant.

superficies [sōō'pĕr-fish-i-ēz] *n* the upper surface, outer face; the external area; external features, appearance.—*adj* **superficial,** of, or near, the surface; not going deeper than the surface; slight, not thorough; (of a person) shallow in nature or knowledge.—*adv* **superfi'cially.**

superfine [sōō'pĕr-fīn] *adj* finer than ordinary.

superfluous [sōō'pĕr'flōō-ùs] *adj* beyond what is enough; unnecessary.—*n* **superflu'ity,** a superfluous quantity or more than enough, superabundance; state of being superfluous; something unnecessary. —*adv* super'fluously.

superhighway [sōō′per-hī′wā] *n* an expressway or turnpike.

superimpose [sōō′per-im-pōz′] *vt* to put or lay upon something else.

superincumbent [sōō′per-in-kum′bént] *adj* resting or lying, esp heavily (on a person or thing).

superinduce [sōō′per-in-dūs′] *vt* to bring in over and above, in addition to, something else.

superintend [sōō′per-in-tend′] *vt* to have the oversight or charge of, to control, manage.

superior [sōō′pē′ri-òr] *adj* upper; higher in place; higher in rank; higher in excellence; greater in number, power. —*n* superior'ity, quality or state of being superior. —superiority complex, overvaluation of one's worth.

superlative [sōō′per′là-tiv] *adj* of the highest degree or quality (eg *a superlative example, superlative insolence, skill*); (*gram*) denoting the extreme degree of comparison of adjectives and adverbs. —*adv* super'latively.

supermarket [sōō′per-mär-ket] *n* a large, usu. self-service, retail store selling food and other domestic goods.

supernal [sù-pûr′nál] *adj* (*poet*) that is above or in a higher place or region; celestial.

supernatural [sōō-per-nach′ū-rál] *adj* not according to the usual course of nature; miraculous; involving God or ghosts, spirits, etc. —*adv* supernat'urally.

supernumerary [sōō-per-nūm′er-àr-i] *adj* over and above the number stated, or which is usual or necessary. —*n* a person or thing beyond the usual, necessary, or stated number; one who appears on stage or screen without a speaking part.

supersede [sōō-per-sēd′] *vt* to take the place of by reason of superior right, power, etc.

supersensitive [sōō-per-sen′si-tiv] *adj* extremely, or unduly, sensitive; specially treated to increase sensitivity.

supersonic [sōō-per-son′ik] *adj* faster than the speed of sound; ultrasonic.

superstition [sōō-per-sti′sh(ò)n] *n* excessive reverence or fear, based on ignorance; false worship or religion; an ignorant and irrational belief in supernatural agency.

superstructure [sōō′per-struk′-chùr] *n* a structure above or on something else, as above the main deck of a ship; that part of a building above a foundation.

supervene [sōō-per-vēn′] *vi* to come or happen as something additional or unexpected. —*n* superven'tion.

supervise [sōō-per-vīz] *vti* to oversee, to superintend.

supine [sōō-pīn′] *adj* lying on the back; negligent, indolent, lacking in energy and initiative.

supper [sup′er] *n* a meal taken at the close of the day, esp when dinner is eaten at midday; an evening social, esp for raising funds; the food served at a supper; a light meal served late in the evening.

supplant [su-plänt′] *vt* to displace by guile; to remove in order to replace with something else.

supple [sup′l] *adj* pliant; lithe; yielding to others; of the mind, adaptable.

supplement [sup′lè-mént] *n* that which completes or brings closer to completion; a special part of a periodical publication accompanying an ordinary part; the quantity by which an angle or an arc falls short of 180° or a semi-circle. —*vt* supp'lement, to add to. —*adjs* supplemen'tal, supplement'ary.

suppliant [sup′li-ánt] *adj* supplicating, asking earnestly, entreating. —*n* a humble petitioner. —*adv* supp'liantly.

supplicate [sup′li-kāt] *vt* to entreat earnestly; to address in prayer.

supply [su-plī′] *vt* to fill up, meet (a deficiency, a need); to furnish; to fill (a vacant place). —*pt, pt p* supplied′.

support [su-pört′] *vt* to hold up, bear part of the weight of; to give power of resistance, enable to endure; to supply with means of living; to subscribe to; to uphold by advocacy (a cause, policy). —*adj* support'ive.

suppose [su-pōz′] *vt* to assume, state as true, for the sake of argument; to presume, think probable; to believe without sufficient proof; to consider as a possibility; to expect. —*vi* to conjecture. —*adjs* suppos'able; supposed′. —*adv* suppō's-edly, according to supposition. —*n* supposi'tion, act of supposing; that which is supposed, assumption.

suppository [su-poz′i-tòr-i] *n* a conical or cylindrical plug of medicated soluble material for insertion into the rectum or vagina.

suppress [su-pres′] *vt* to crush, put down (eg a rebellion, rebels, freedom of speech); to restrain (a person); to keep in (eg a sigh, an angry retort). —*ns* suppress'or, one that suppresses, esp a gene that suppresses the expression of another gene when both are present; suppress'ion, act of suppressing; stoppage; concealment. —*adj* suppress'ive, tending to suppress.

suppurate [sup′ū-rāt] *vi* to form or discharge pus. —*n* suppurā'tion. —*adj* supp'urātive.

supra- [s(y)ōō′pra-] *prefix* above, situated above; over; beyond. —eg supramundane.

supreme [s(y)ōō-prēm′] *adj* highest; greatest; final; ultimate. —*n* suprēm'acy.

surcease [sûr-sēs′] *vti* to cease, or cause to cease. —*n* cessation, esp a temporary respite or end.

surcharge [sûr-chärj′] *vt* to overcharge (a person); to charge in addition; to overload; to fill excessively (with); to mark (a postage stamp) with a surcharge. —*n* sur'charge, an additional or abnormal tax or charge; an excessive load.

sure [shōōr] *adj* secure, safe; firm, strong; reliable, to be depended on, certain; certain (to do); certain, having apparently adequate grounds for belief, or for expectation; convinced (of, that).

surety [shōōr′ti] *n* sureness, certainty; security against loss or for payment; a guarantee; one who undertakes responsibility for the default of another.

surf [sûrf] *n* the waves of the sea breaking on the shore or a reef.

surface [sûr′fis] *n* the exterior part of anything; any of the faces of a solid; superficial features. —*adj* of, on, or near a surface.

surfeit [sûr′fit] *v* to fill to satiety and disgust.

surge [sûrj] *n* the rising or swelling of a large wave; a sudden, strong increase, as of power.

surgeon [sûr′jòn] *n* a medical specialist who practices surgery. —*n* sur'gery, act and art of treating diseases or injuries by manual or instrumental operations; the operating room of a surgeon or hospital; alterations made as if by surgery.

surly [sûr′li] *adj* ill-natured, growling, morose, uncivil; gloomy, angry. —*adv* sur'lily.

surmise [sûr-mīz′] *n* a conjecture. —*vt* to infer the existence of from slight evidence.

surmount [sûr-mownt′] *vt* to mount above, surpass; to top, be the top of; to climb over.

surname [sûr′nãm] *n* the family name. —*vt* to give a surname to.

surpass [sûr-pas′] *vt* to exceed, to excel, outdo.

surplus [sûr-plùs] *n* the excess above what is required.

surprise [sûr-prīz′] *n* act of taking unawares; the emotion caused by anything sudden and/or unexpected; something that surprises.

surrealism [su-rē′àl-izm] *n* a form of art claiming to express activities of the unconscious mind.

surrender [su-ren′dér] *vt* to deliver over, yield (to another); to give up, relinquish (eg a right a claim); to abandon (oneself to, eg grief).

surreptitious [sûr-ep-ti′shùs] *adj* done by stealth or fraud; enjoyed secretly. —*adv* surrepti'tiously.

surrogate [sûr′ō-gāt] *n* a substitute, deputy; a person or thing standing for another person or thing.

surround [su-rownd′] *vt* to encircle on all or nearly all sides; to form or be the member of the entourage of; to constitute part of the environment.

surtax [sûr′taks] *n* an additional tax on top of the regular tax.

surveillance [sûr-vāl′áns] *n* watch kept over a person, esp a suspect.

survey [sûr-vā′] *vt* to see or look over; to take a general view of; to inspect, examine; to measure and estimate the position, extent, contours of (eg a piece of land). —*ns* sur'vey, a detailed study, as by gathering information and analyzing it, a general view; the process of surveying an area; a written description of the area; survey'ing, the science or work of making land surveys; survey'or, a measurer of land surfaces, etc.

survive [sûr-vīv′] *vt* to live longer than, to out-live; to come through alive. —*vi* to remain alive. —*n* survī'val, the state of surviving; anything that survives; a relic.—*adj* designed to help one to survive exposure or other dangerous condition.

susceptible [su-sep'ti-bl] *adj* liable to be affected by (*with to*; eg *susceptible to colds, flattery, feminine charm*); easily affected, impressionable; capable (of), admitting (of—eg *susceptible of proof, of a specified interpretation*).—*n* **susceptibil'ity**, quality of being susceptible; sensibility; (in *pl*) feelings.—*adv* **suscep'tibly**.—*adj* **suscep'tive**, receptive, susceptible.

suspect [sus-pekt'] *vt* to mistrust (eg *to suspect one's motives*); to imagine to be guilty; to conjecture, be inclined to think (that).

suspend [sus-pend'] *vt* to hang; to hold floating in a fluid, hold in suspension; to discontinue, or discontinue the operation of, for a time (eg *to suspend publication, a law*); to debar for a time from a privilege, etc.

suspicion [sus-pi'sh(ò)n] *n* act of suspecting; an opinion formed or entertained on slender evidence; mistrust; a very slight amount.—*adj* **suspi'cious**.

sustain [sus-tān'] *vt* to hold up, bear the weight of, support; to maintain; to prolong (eg a musical note).—*adjs* **sustain'able**; **sustained'**.

suture [s(y)ōō'chùr] *n* a line of junction of two structures; an immovable articulation between bones as between the various bones of the cranium and face; (*bot*) a line of union between two adjacent edges, or of dehiscence; (*surg*) the sewing up of a wound and the thread, etc.

swab [swob] *n* a mop for cleaning or drying floors or decks, or for cleaning out the bore of a cannon; a wad of absorbent material usu. wound around the end of a small stick used to medicate or clean the throat, mouth, etc.—*pr p* **swabb'ing**; *pt, pt p* **swabbed**.—*n* **swabb'er**, one who, or that which, swabs.

swaddle [swod'l] *vt* formerly, to swathe or bind tight with clothes, as an infant.

swag [swag] *vt* to hang in a swag.—*n* a valance, garland, etc. hanging decoratively in a curve; (*slang*) loot.

swagger [swag'ér] *vi* to swing the body proudly or defiantly; to brag noisily, to bully.—*n* boastfulness; insolence of manner; a self-confident, swinging gait.—*adj* very fashionable.—*n* **swagg'erer**.

swain [swān] *n* a shepherd; an admirer, suitor.

swallow¹ [swol'ō] *n* migratory birds with long wings and a forked tail, which seize their insect food on the wing.

swallow² [swol'ō] *vt* to receive through the gullet into the stomach.

swamp [swomp] *n* wet, spongy land, low ground saturated with water.

swan [swon] *n* a group of large, usu. white, birds constituting a distinct section of the duck family (Anatidae), having a very long neck and noted for grace and stateliness of movement on the water.

swap [swäp, swop] *vti* (*inf*) trade, barter.—*n* (*inf*) the act of exchanging one thing for another.

sward [swörd] *n* the grassy surface of land; turf.—*adj* **sward'ed**, covered with sward.

swarm¹ [swörm] *n* a number of bees migrating under the guidance of a queen to establish a new colony; a colony of bees in a hive; a moving mass, crowd, or throng.

swarm² [swörm] *vti* to climb by scrambling up by means of arms and legs (*often with up*).

swarthy [swörTH'i] *adj* dark-skinned—also **swart**.—*n* **swarth'iness**.

swash [swosh] *vt* to dash or splash.

swastika [swas'ti-ka] *n* a widespread symbol of the form of a cross with equal arms and a limb of the same length projecting at right angles from the end of each arm.

swat [swot] *vt* (*inf*) to hit smartly.—*n* (*inf*) a quick sharp blow.—*n* **swatt'er**.

swath [swöth] *n* the width cut by a scythe or other mowing device; a strip, row, etc., mowed.

swathe [swäTH] *vt* to bind, wrap round, with a band or with loose material as if with a bandage; to envelop, enclose.

sway [swä] *vi* to swing or move from one side to the other or to and fro; to lean to one side; to incline in judgment or opinion.

swear [swär] *vi* to make a solemn declaration, promise, etc., calling God to witness; to give evidence on oath.

sweat [swet] *n* the moisture from the skin, perspiration; moisture in drops on any surface; the state of one who sweats; a state of eagerness, anxiety.

Swede [swēd] *n* a native or inhabitant of Sweden; a person of Swedish descent; **swede**, a yellow turnip (*Brassica napobrassica*), rutabaga.—*adj* **Swed'ish**, pertaining to Sweden.—*n* the Scandinavian language of Sweden.

sweep [swēp] *vt* to brush dirt, etc., from with a broom; to carry (away, down, off, along) by a long brushing stroke; to strike with a long, esp light, stroke.—*adj* **sweep'ing**, that sweeps; comprehensive, complete (eg changes, victory); marked by wholesale and indiscriminate inclusion; having a curving line or form.—*n* **sweep'er**.—*adv* **sweep'ingly**, in a sweeping manner.

sweet [swet] *adj* pleasing to the taste; tasting like sugar; pleasing to other senses, fragrant, melodious, beautiful; not rancid or sour; not salty or salted; amiable, kindly, gracious.

swell [swel] *vi* to expand, to be inflated; to rise into waves; to heave; to bulge out; to become elated, arrogant, or angry; to grow louder.

swelter [swelt'ér] *vi* to be oppressed by great heat.—*n* a condition of oppressive heat; an overwrought state of mind.—*adj* **swelt'ering**, oppressively hot.—*adv* **swelt'eringly**.

swept [swept] *pt, pt p* of **sweep**.

swerve [swûrv] *v* to turn aside from a line or course, etc.—*n* an act of swerving.

swift [swift] *adj* moving, or able to move, quickly—fleet or fast; rapid, taking only a short time; not long delayed; speedy; quick in action.

swill [swil] *vti* to drink greedily or copiously; to feed swill to (pigs, etc.)—*n* liquid garbage fed to pigs; garbage.—*n* **swill'er**.

swim [swim] *vi* to move on or in water by using limbs or fins; to move with a gliding motion; to be dizzy; to be drenched, overflow, abound (with).

swindle [swin'dl] *vti* to cheat (another) of money or property.—*n* the act of swindling or defrauding; a fraud.—*n* **swin'dler**.

swine [swīn] *n sing* and *pl* a quadruped with bristly skin and long snout, reared for its flesh.

swing [swing] *vi* to sway or wave to and fro, as a body hanging in air; to oscillate; to hang (from); to move forward with swaying rhythmical gait; to turn round on some fixed center, as a ship at anchor, a door on its hinges; to turn quickly; to move to and fro on a swinging seat; to be hanged.—*n* **swing'ing**, the act of moving back and forth, esp the pastime of moving in a swing.—*adj* (*inf*) fully alive to, and appreciative of, the most recent trends and fashions in living; (*inf*) up-to-date.

swinish [swī'nish] *adj* like or befitting swine; gross, sensual, bestial.—*adv* **swin'ishly**.

swipe [swīp] *n* (*inf*) a hard, sweeping blow.—*vt* (*inf*) to hit with a swipe; (*slang*) to steal.

swirl [swûrl] *vti* to sweep along with a whirling motion.—*n* a whirl, an eddy; a twist; a curl.

swish¹ [swish] *vt* to brandish, or to strike, with a whistling sound; to flog.—*vi* to move with a hissing sound.—*n* a swishing sound.

swish² [swish] *adj* (*inf*) smart, fashionable.

Swiss [swis] *adj* of or belonging to Switzerland.—*n* a native of Switzerland; one that is of Swiss descent; **swiss**, any of various fine sheer fabrics of cotton.

switch [swich] *n* a small flexible twig; a whip; a separate tail of hair attached to supplement the wearer's own hair; a device which, by means of movable sections of rails, transfers rolling stock from one track to another; a mechanical device for opening or closing an electric circuit; an act of switching, a changing, change(-over).

swivel [swiv'l] *n* something fixed in another body so as to turn round it; a ring or link that turns round on a pin or neck.—*vi* to turn on a pin or pivot.

swoon [swōōn] *vt* to faint, fall into a faint.—*n* the act of swooning; a faint.

swoop [swōōp] *vt* to carry off abruptly.—*vi* to make a sudden attack (*usu. with* down) as a bird in hunting.

swop [swop] *vt* to exchange, to barter.—*pr p* **swopp'ing**; *pt, pt p* **swopped**.—*n* an exchange.

sword [sörd] *n* a hand weapon with a long blade, sharp on one or both edges, set in a hilt for cutting or thrusting; destruction by the sword or by war; military force; coercive power; something that resembles a sword.

sycophant [sik'ō-fânt] *n* a servile flatterer. — *n* **syc'ophancy**, the behavior of a sycophant; obsequious flattery. — Also **syco-phant'ism**. — *adjs* **sycophant'ic, sycophant'ish**, like a sycophant.

syllable [sil'á-bl] *n* word or part of a word uttered by a single effort of the voice; one or more letters written to represent a spoken syllable. — *vt* to give a number or arrangement of syllables to (a word or verse); to pronounce syllable by syllable; to utter. — *adj* **syllab'ic**, consisting of, constituting, a syllable; articulated in syllables. — *adv* **syllab'ically**. — *vs t* **syllab'icate, syllab'ify** (*pt, pt p* **syllab'ified**), to form into syllables. — *ns* **syllabica'tion, syllabifica'tion**.

syllabus [sil'á-bus] *n* a summary or outline of a course of study or of examination requirements. — *pl* **syll'abuses, syll'abī**.

syllogism [sil'ō-jizm] *n* a logical form of argument, consisting of three propositions, of which the first two are called the premises (major and minor), and the last, which follows from them, the conclusion.

sylvan [sil'vàn] *adj* of, characteristic of, or living in the woods or forests; wooded.

symbiosis [sim-bī-ō'sis] *n* the living together in close association or union of two organisms of different kinds to their mutual advantage.

symbol [sim'bòl] *n* an authoritative summary of faith or doctrine; an object used to represent something abstract; an arbitrary or conventional sign standing for a quality, process, relation, etc. as in music, chemistry, mathematics, etc.

symmetry [sim'e-tri] *n* the state in which one part exactly corresponds to another in size, shape, and position; balance or beauty of form resulting from this. — *adjs* **symmet'rical, symmet'ric**, having symmetry or due proportion in its parts.

sympathy [sim'pa-thi] *n* a state of conformity of tastes and inclinations, or of understanding of one another's tastes and inclinations, or the goodwill based on such conformity or understanding. — *adj* **sympathet'ic**, showing, or inclined to, sympathy; compassionate. — *adv* **sympathet'ically**. — *vi* **sym'-pathīze**, to feel with or for another.

symphony [sim'fò-ni] *n* (*mus*) a composition for a full orchestra in several movements; a large orchestra for playing symphonic works.

symposium [sim-pō'zi-um] *n* in ancient Greece, a banquet with philosophic conversation; a conference at which several specialists deliver short addresses on a topic.

symptom [sim(p)'tòm] *n* that which attends and indicates the existence of a disease or disorder, not as a cause, but as a constant effect.

synagogue, synagog [sin'a-gog] *n* an assembly of Jews for worship and religious study.

synchromesh [sing'krō-mesh] *adj* designed for effecting synchronized shifting of gears. — Also *n*.

synchronous [sing'krò-nus] *adj* happening or being at the same time, simultaneous; having the same period, or period and phase. — *adj* **synchronis'tic**, showing synchronism. — *adv* **synchronis'tically**.

syncopate [sing'kō-pāt] *vt* to contract a word by taking away letters from the middle; (*mus*) to alter rhythm by transferring the accent to a normally unaccented beat. — *ns* **syncopā'tion**, act of syncopating; state of being syncopated.

syndic [sin'dik] *n* a municipal magistrate in some countries; an agent of a university or corporation. — *adj* **syn'dical**, relating to a syndic or a committee that assumes the power of a syndic; of or relating to syndicalism. — *n* **syn'dicāte**, an association of individuals or corporations formed for a project requiring much capital; any group, as of criminals, organized for some undertaking; an organization selling articles or features to many newspapers, etc. — *vt* to manage as or form into a syndicate; to sell (an article, etc.) through a syndicate. — *vi* to form a syndicate.

syndrome [sin'drōm] *n* a characteristic pattern or group of symptoms of a disease.

synecdoche [sin-ek'dó-kē] *n* a figure of speech in which a part represents the whole object or idea.

synod [sin'od] *n* an ecclesiastical council; the governing assembly of an Episcopal province; a Presbyterian governing

body ranking between the presbytery and the general assembly.

synonym [sin'o-nim] *n* a word having the same, or very nearly the same, meaning as another or others in the same language. — *adj* **synon'ymous**, pertaining to synonyms; expressing the same thing; having the same implications, connotations, or reference.

synopsis [si-nop'sis] *n* a collective or general view of any subject, a summary. — *pl* **synop'sēs**. — *adjs* **synop'tic, -al**, affording a general view of the whole. — *ad* **synop'tically**.

synovial [sin-ō'vi-ál] *adj* of, pertaining to, **synō'via**, a lubricating fluid occurring typically within tendon sheaths surrounding moveable joints.

syntax [sin'taks] *n* (*gram*) the arrangement of words in a sentence; the rules governing this. — *adjs* **syntac'tic, -al**, pertaining to syntax; according to the rules of syntax. — *adv* **syntac'tically**.

synthesis [sin'the-sis] *n* the process of making a whole by putting together its separate component parts; the combination of separate elements of thought into a whole, as opposed to analysis; reasoning from principles to a conclusion; the dialectical combination of thesis and antithesis into a higher stage of truth; (*chem*) the uniting of elements, groups, or simpler compounds or the degradation of a complex compound to form a compound.

syphilis [sif'i-lis] *n* a contagious, infectious venereal disease. — *adj* **syphilit'ic**.

syringe [sir-inj'] *n* a tube with a piston or a rubber bulb, by which liquids are sucked up and ejected, used to inject or withdraw fluids, esp in medicine and surgery. — *vt* to inject, or to clean, with a syringe.

syrup [sir'up] *n* a solution made by boiling sugar with water, often flavored or medicated; the concentrated juice of a fruit or plant; cloying sweetness. — Also **sir'up**. — *adjs* **syr'upy, sirupy**.

system [sis'tèm] *n* anything formed of parts placed together to make a regular and connected whole working as if one machine (eg *a system of pulleys, the solar system*); the body regarded as functioning as one whole; a set of organs that together perform a particular function (eg *digestive system*). — *adj* **systemat'ic**, constituting or based on a system; according to a system. — *adv* **systemat'ically**. — *vt* **sys'tematize**, to reduce to a system. — *adj* **system'ic**, of or affecting the body as a whole; acting through the bodily systems after ingestion to make the organism toxic to a pest. — *n* a systemic pesticide.

T

tab [tab] *n* a small tag, flap, or strap; (*inf*) a bill, as for expenses. — *vt* to fix a tab on; to tabulate.

tabard [tab'árd] *n* a coat worn by heralds; a sleeveless tunic.

tabby [tab'i] *n* (*arch*) a coarse kind of waved or watered silk; a domestic cat, esp a female.

tabernacle [tab'ėr-na-kl] *n* (*Bible*) **Tabernacle**, the movable tent carried by the Jews through the desert, and used as a temple.

table [tā'bl] *n* a smooth, flat slab or board, with legs, used as an article of furniture; supply of food, entertainment; the company at a table; a surface on which something is written or inscribed; that which is cut or written on a flat surface.

tablet [tab'let] *n* a small flat surface; something flat on which to write, paint, etc.

tabloid [tab'loid] *n* a digest, summary; a newspaper of halfsize sheets, consisting mostly of pictures, and news in condensed form.

taboo, tabu [tá-bōō'] *n* an institution among the Polynesians, whose penal system is based on religious sanctions, any prohibition, interdict, restraint, ban, exclusion, ostracism.

tabour, tabor [tā'bôr] *n* a small drum, *ns* **tab'oret, tab'ouret**, a low stool; a portable stand.

tabular [tab'ū-làr] *adj* of the form of a table; having the form of laminae or plates.

tacit [tas'it] *adj* implied, but not expressed by words; silent. — *adv* **tac'itly**. — *adj* **tac'iturn**.

tack¹ [tak] *n* a short, sharp nail with a broad head; the course of a ship in reference to the position of her sails; a course of policy; a strategical move; adhesiveness, sticky condition.

tack² [tak] *n* stuff, substance; food, fare, as *hard-tack*.

tackle [tak'l] [*naut* tāk'l] *n* ropes, rigging, etc., of a ship; tools, gear, weapons, equipment; ropes, etc.

tact [takt] *n* adroitness in managing the feelings of persons dealt with; *adjs* tact'ful; tact'less.

tactics [tak'tiks] *n sing* the science or art of maneuvering fighting forces in the presence of the enemy.

tactile [tak'til] *adj* capable of being touched or felt.

tag¹ [tag] *n* a tack or point of metal at the end of a string or lace; any small thing tacked or attached to another—eg a luggage label; a trite quotation.—*vt* to tack, fasten, or hang (to).—*vi* to string words or ideas together.

tag² [tag] *n* a children's game in which one player chases the rest till he touches one, who then takes his place—also **tig**.

tail¹ [tāl] *n* the prolonged hindmost extremity of an animal, generally hanging loose; the back, lower, or hinder part of anything.

tail² [tāl] *n* entail.—*adj* limited as to tenure; entailed.

tailor [tāl'ór] *n* one whose business is to cut out and make outer garments, as coats, suits.—*vi* to work as a tailor.

taint [tānt] *vt* to tinge, moisten, or impregnate with anything noxious, to infect.—*vi* to be affected with something corrupting.—*n* a stain or tincture; infection or corruption.

take [tāk] *vt* to lay hold of; to get into one's possession; to capture; to choose; to accept; to captivate; to lead or carry with one; to travel by; to deprive one of, steal from one; to choose and range oneself on (a side); to experience, enjoy; to have room for; to swallow; to allow, agree to, accept; to infer (*with* it); to become infected with; to endure calmly.

tale [tāl] *n* a narrative or story; an invented account, a lie; idle or malicious gossip.

talent [tal'ént] *n* an ancient weight for money and commodities; any natural or special gift or aptitude; eminent ability.

talisman [tal'iz-man, or -is-] *n* a species of charm, supposed to exert some protective influence over the wearer; an amulet.

talk [tök] *vi* to speak; to converse; to speak to little purpose; to gossip; to divulge information.—*vt* to utter, express.—*n* familiar conversation; a discussion; a lecture; subject of discourse.—*adj* talk'ative, given to much talking, prating.—*adv* talk'atively.

tall [töl] *adj* high, esp in stature; lofty; (*arch*) sturdy; hardly to be believed (*a tall story*).—*ns* tall'ness.

tallow [tal'ō] *n* the hard fat of animals melted, used to make soap, candles, etc.

tally [tal'i] *n* a stick cut or notched to match another stick, used to mark numbers or keep accounts by; anything made to correspond with, duplicate another; a label.

talon [tal'ón] *n* the claw of a bird of prey.

tambour [tam'bōōr] *n* a small, shallow drum; a frame on which muslin or other material is stretched for embroidering; a rich kind of gold and silver embroidery.

tambourine [tam-bōō-rēn'] *n* a shallow drum (with one skin and jingles) played with the hand.

tame [tām] *adj* having lost native wildness and shyness; domesticated; gentle; spiritless, without vigor; dull.

tamper [tam'pèr] *vi* to meddle (with); to make changes in without necessity or authority; to practice upon, influence secretly and unfairly.

tan [tan] *n* bark of the oak, etc., bruised and broken for tanning hides; a yellowish-brown color; suntan.

tandem [tan'dem] *adv* applied to the position of horses harnessed singly one before the other instead of abreast; in single file.

tang [tang] *n* a prong or tapering part of a knife or tool that goes into the haft; a strong or offensive taste.

tangent [tan'jént] *n* a line which touches a curve; one of the six trigonometrical functions of an angle, the ratio of the perpendicular to the base.

tangerine [tan-je-rēn] *n* a mandarin orange, a small, flattish, loose-skinned variety.

tangible [tan'ji-bl] *adj* perceptible by the touch; capable of being realized by the mind (eg a distinction); real, substantial.—*n* tangibil'ity.

tangle [tang'gl] *n* a knot of things united confusedly; a large seaweed; a complication; conflict.

tango [tang'gō] *n* a dance of Argentine origin.

tank [tangk] *n* a large basin or cistern; a reservoir of water, oil, etc.; an armored motor vehicle, with caterpillar wheels, mounted with guns.

tankard [tangk'árd] *n* a tall, one-handled drinking vessel, often with a hinged lid.

tannin [tan'in] *n* an astringent substance found in plant material used in tanning.—*adj* tann'ic, of or from tannin.

tantalize [tan'ta-līz] *vt* to torment by presenting something to excite desire, but keeping it out of reach.

tantamount [tan'ta-mownt] *adj* amounting (to), equivalent (to), in effect or meaning.

tantrum [tan'trùm] *n* a capricious fit of ill temper.

tap¹ [tap] *n* a gentle blow or touch, esp with something small.—*vt* to strike lightly, touch gently.—*vi* to give a gentle knock.

tap² [tap] *n* a hole or short pipe through which fluid is drawn; a faucet or spigot; a tool used to cut threads in a female screw; a place in an electrical circuit where a connection can be made.

tape [tāp] *n* a strong, narrow strip of cloth, paper, etc., used for tying, binding, etc.; tape measure; magnetic tape.—*vt* to furnish, or tie up, with tape; to record on magnetic tape.

taper [tā'pèr] *n* a long, thin candle.—*adj* narrowed towards the point, like a taper; long and slender.—*vi* to become gradually smaller towards one end.—*vt* to make to taper.

tapestry [tap'es-tri] *n* a woven fabric with wrought figures, used for the covering of walls and furniture, and for curtains and hangings.

tapeworm [tāp'wùrm] *n* tape-like parasitic worms, found in the intestines of men and animals.

tapir [tā'pèr] *n* a family of thick-skinned, short-necked quadrupeds with a short flexible proboscis.

tar [tär] *n* a dark, viscous, resinous mixture obtained from wood, coal, peat, etc.

tarantula [tar-an'tū-la] *n* any of several large, hairy spiders that are somewhat poisonous.

tardy [tär'di] *adj* slow, late, sluggish; out of season.—*adv* tar'dily.—*n* tar'diness.

tare¹ [tār] *n* any of several vetches (esp *Vicia hirsuta* and *V sativa*); (*pl*) an undesirable element.

tare² [tār] *n* the weight of the vessel or package in which goods are contained; an allowance made for it, the remainder being the *net* weight.

target [tär'gét] *n* a mark to aim at; any object of desire or ambition; a standard of quantity set for output, etc.

tariff [tar'if] *n* a list of the taxes, etc.

tarmacadam [tär-mak-ad'âm] *n* a road surfacing formed of broken stone which has been covered with tar and rolled.

tarn [tärn] *n* a small lake among mountains.

tarnish [tär'nish] *vt* to diminish the luster or purity of (a metal) by exposure to the air, etc.

tarpaulin [tär-pö'lin] *n* canvas cloth coated with tar, pitch, etc. to render it waterproof; a sailor.

tarry¹ [tär'i] *adj* consisting of, covered with, or like tar.

tarry² [tar'i] *vi* to be tardy or slow; to stay, lodge; to wait (for); to delay.

tart¹ [tärt] *adj* sharp or sour to the taste; sharp, severe.—*adv* tart'ly.—*n* tart'ness.

tart² [tärt] *n* a fruit pie; a small, uncovered pastry cup, containing fruit or jelly; a prostitute.

tartan [tär'tán] *n* a woolen or worsted stuff checked with various colors, once the distinctive dress of the Scottish Highlanders.

tartar [tär'tàr] *n* a salt formed on the sides of wine casks; a concretion which forms on the teeth.—*adj* tartar'ic, pertaining to, or obtained from, tartar.

task [täsk] *n* a set amount of work, esp of study, given by another; work; drudgery.—*vt* to impose a task on; to burden with severe work, to tax, strain.

tassel [tas'l] *n* a hanging ornament consisting of a bunch of silk or other material.

taste [tāst] *vt* to perceive (a flavor) by the touch of the tongue or palate; to try by eating or drinking a little; to experience.—*vi* to try or perceive by the mouth; to have a flavor (of).—*n* the act or sense of tasting; the particular sensation caused by a substance on the tongue; a small portion.—*adj* taste'ful, having a high relish; showing good taste.—*adv* taste'fully.—*n*

taste′fulness.—*adj* **taste′less**, without taste, insipid; unsuitable; ugly.—*adv* **taste′lessly.**—*ns* **taste′lessness.**

tatter [tat′ėr] *n* a torn piece; a loose hanging rag.—*adj* **tat′t′ered**, in tatters or rags; torn.

tattle [tat′l] *n* trifling talk or chat.—*vi* to talk idly or triflingly; to tell tales or secrets.—*n* **tatt′ler.**

tattoo¹ [ta-tōō′] *n* a beat of drum and a bugle call to call soldiers to quarters; a drumming, rapping, etc.

tattoo² [ta-tōō′] *vt* to mark permanently (as the skin) with figures, by pricking in coloring matter, or by making symmetrical scars.—*n* marks or figures made on the skin in these ways.

taunt [tönt] *vt* to reproach or upbraid jeeringly or contemptuously.—*n* upbraiding, sarcastic.

Taurus [tö′rus] *n* the Bull, the 2d sign of the zodiac.

taut [töt] *adj* tightly drawn; trim, tidy; tense.

tautology [tö-tol′o-ji] *n* needless repetition of the same thing in different words.

tavern [tav′ėrn] *n* a saloon, bar; an inn.

taw¹ [tö] *n* a special marble chosen to be aimed with; a game at marbles; the line from which to play.

taw² [tö] *vt* to prepare and dress, as skins into white leather.

tawdry [tö′dri] *adj* showy, cheap, and tasteless; gaudily dressed.—*adv* **taw′drily.**—*n* **taw′driness.**

tawny [tö′ni] *adj* of the color of things tanned, a yellowish brown.—*n* **taw′niness.**

tax [taks] *n* a rate imposed on property or persons for the benefit of the state; a strain.

taxi [tak′si] *n* **tax′icab**, an automobile usu. fitted with a taximeter, licensed to ply for hire.

taxidermy [taks′i-dėr-mi] *n* the art of preparing and stuffing the skins of animals.—*n* **tax′idermist.**

taxis [tak′sis] *n* arrangement; (*biol*) movement of a whole organism in response to a stimulus.

tea [tē] *n* a shrub (*Camellia sinensis*, family Theaceae) growing in China, India, Ceylon, etc.

teach [tēch] *vt* to impart knowledge to; to impart knowledge of; to explain; train in.—*vi* to give instruction, esp as a profession.—*pt, pt p* **taught** [tawt].—*adj* **teach′able**, capable of being taught; apt or willing to learn.

teal [tēl] *n* any of several river duck (genus *Anas*) of Europe and America.

team [tēm] *n* a number of animals moving together or in order; two or more oxen or other animals harnessed to the same vehicle; a number of persons associated for doing anything conjointly, playing a game, etc.—*vi* to join in cooperative activity (*with* **up**).

tear¹ [tēr] *n* a drop of the fluid secreted by the lachrymal gland, appearing in the eyes; anything like a tear.—*adj* **tear′ful**, shedding tears; mournful.—*adv* **tear′fully.**

tear² [tär] *vt* to to lacerate; to pull violently (away from) or separate violently (from).—*vi* to move or act with speed or impetuosity; to rage.

tease [tēz] *vt* to separate into single fibers; to vex with importunity, jests, etc., esp playfully; to torment, irritate.—*n* one who teases or torments.

teasel [tēz′l] *n* a plant with large burs used attached to revolving cylinder, in raising a nap on cloth.

teat [tēt] *n* the nipple on a breast or udder.

technical [tek′nik-ál] *adj* pertaining to skill in the arts; concerned with the mechanical or applied arts; belonging to, peculiar to, a particular art or profession.—*n* **technical′ity.**—*adv* **tech′nically.**—*n* **technician**, one skilled in the practice of any art.—*ns* **technique**, method of performance, manipulation, or execution; individualized execution; formal construction (eg of poetry); **technol′ogy**, the practice of any or all of the applied sciences that have practical value and/or industrial use.—*adjs* **technolog′ic, -al.**—*n* **technol′ogist.**

tedious [tē′di-ús] *adj* wearisome, tiresome.

tee [tē] *n* (*golf*) the place from which the ball is first played at each hole; a small peg from which the ball is driven.

teem [tēm] *vi* to be full or prolific of (*with* **with**).

teens [tēnz] *n pl* the years of one's age from thir**teen** to nine**teen**.—*n* teen′ager.

teething [tēTH′ing] *n* the first growth of teeth.—*vi* **teethe**, to grow or cut the teeth.

teetotaler, teetotaller [tē-tō′tal-ėr] *n* one pledged to entire abstinence from intoxicating drinks.—*adj* **teetō′tal.**—*n* **teetō′talism.**

teetotum [tē-tō′tùm] *n* a small top, for use in a game of chance.

tegument [teg′ū-mént] *n* an integument, skin.

tele- [tel′i-] in composition, distant; television.

telecommunication [tel′i-kó-mū-ni-kā′shón] *n* communication of information, by telephone, cable, radio, television.

telegram [tel′i-gram] *n* a message sent by telegraph.—*n* **tel′egraph**, an apparatus for transmitting, messages to a distance, using electricity, wires, and a code.—*adj* **telegraphic.**—*n* **teleg′raphy.**

telepathy [te-lep′a-thi] *n* a communication between mind and mind otherwise than through the senses.—*adj* **telepath′ic.**—*adv* **telepath′ically.**

telephone [tel′e-fōn] *n* an instrument for reproducing sound, esp speech, at a distance, esp by means of electricity.—*vt* to communicate by telephone.

telescope [tel′e-skōp] *n* an optical instrument for viewing objects at a distance.—*adj* **telescop′ic.**

television [tel-e-vizh′(ó)n] *n* the wireless transmission and reproduction on a screen of a view of objects, etc. at a place distant from the beholder; a television receiving **set.**

tell [tel] *vt* to number, count; to utter; to narrate; to disclose; to inform; to discern; to distinguish.—*vi* to produce or have a marked effect; to tell tales, play the informer.—*n* **tell′er**, one who tells; a bank clerk whose duty it is to receive and pay money.—*adj* **tell′ing.**

temerity [te-mer′i-ti] *n* rashness.

temper [tem′pėr] *vt* to bring to a proper degree of hardness; to moderate; to moderate by blending.—*n* due mixture or balance of different or contrary qualities; state of a metal as to hardness, etc.; constitutional state of mind, esp with regard to feelings, disposition, mood; passion, irritation; a disposition, proneness, to anger.

temperament [tem′pėr-a-mént] *n* disposition, characteristic mental and emotional reactions as a whole; passionate disposition.—*adj* **temperamen′tal.**—*adv* **temperamen′tally.**

temperance [tem′pėr-áns] *n* moderation.

temperate [tem′pėr-at] *adj* moderate in degree of any quality; cool, mild, moderate in temperature.—*adv* **tem′perately.**—*n* **tem′perature**, degree of any quality, esp of hotness or coldness.

tempest [tem′pest] *n* a violent storm; any violent commotion.—*adj* **tempes′tuous.**

temple¹ [tem′pl] *n* an edifice erected to a deity; a place of worship.

temple² [tem′pl] *n* the flat portion of either side of the head above the cheekbone.—*adj* **tem′poral.**

tempo [tem′pō] *n* (*mus*) time, rhythmic speed; rate of any activity.

temporal [tem′por-ál] *adj* pertaining to time.—*n* **tempo′rality.**—*adj* **tem′porary**, lasting, used, for a time only.—*adv* **tem′porarily.**—*vi* **tem′porize**, to play for time.

tempt [temt] *vt* (*obs*) to test; to try to persuade, esp to evil; to entice, induce.—*ns* **tempta′tion, temp′ter.**—*adj* **temp′ting.**

ten [ten] *adj* and *n* the cardinal number next above nine.—*adj* **tenth** (see below).

tenable [ten′a-bl] *adj* capable of being retained, held, or defended against attack.

tenacious [ten-ā′shús] *adj* retaining or holding fast.—*n* **tenac′ity.**

tenant [ten′ánt] *n* one who holds or possesses land or property under another.—*n* **ten′ancy.**—*n* **ten′antry**, a body of tenants.

tench [tench, -sh] *n* a freshwater fish.

tend¹ [tend] *vt* to take care of, look after.—*n* **ten′der**, a small craft that attends a larger with stores, etc.; a vehicle attached to locomotives to carry fuel and water.

tend² [tend] *vi* to be directed, move, or incline, in a specified direction.—*n* **ten′dency.**

tender¹ [ten′dėr] *vt* to offer for acceptance; to offer as payment.—*vi* to make an offer.—*n* an offer or proposal.

tender² [ten′dėr] *adj* soft, delicate; succulent; not hardy, fragile; easily moved to pity, love, etc.; apt to feel pain, sensitive.—*n* **ten′derfoot**, an inexperienced beginner.—*adv* **ten′derly.**—*n* **ten′derness.**

tendon [ten′dón] *n* a cord, band, or sheet of fibrous tissue by which a muscle is attached to a bone.

tendril [ten'dril] *n* a slender, spiral shoot of a plant by which it attaches itself for support.

tenebrous [ten'e-brus] *adj* dark, gloomy.

tenement [ten'e-ment] *n* a dwelling or habitation, or part of it; a building divided into apartments, each occupied by a separate tenant.

tenet [ten'et, tēn'-] *n* any opinion, or doctrine.

tennis [ten'is] *n* a game for two to four persons, played with ball and rackets within a building; lawn tennis.

tenon [ten'on] *n* a projection at the end of a piece of wood.

tenor [ten'ór] *n* a general run or course, prevailing direction; purport; the highest regular adult male voice.

tense¹ [tens] *n* (*gram*) the form of a verb which indicates the time of the action.

tense² [tens] *adj* tightly strained, hence rigid; critical, exciting; nervous and highly strained.—*adj* ten'sile.—*ns* ten'sion, act of stretching; state of being stretched or strained; strain, effort; mental strain.

tent [tent] *n* a portable shelter, of canvas stretched on poles.

tentacle [ten'ta-tiv] *n* a long, slender flexible growth of certain animals for feeling or motion, etc.

tentative [ten'ta-kl] *adj* of the nature of an attempt; experimental.—*adv* ten'tatively.

tenter [ten'tèr] *n* a machine on which cloth is extended or stretched by hooks.

tenth [tenth] *adj* the last of ten; being one of ten equal parts.—*n* one of ten equal parts.

tenuity [te-nū'i-ti] *n* thinness; rarity; meagerness.—*adj* ten'ŭous.

tenure [ten'ūr] *n* conditions of holding property; the period during which office or property is held.

tepee [tē'pē, tep'ē] *n* an American Indian tent formed of skins.

tepid [tep'id] *adj* moderately warm, lukewarm.

teredo [tè-rē'dō] *n* shipworms, that burrow into wood and are very destructive of it.

tergiversation [ter-ji-ver-sā'sh(ó)n] *n* shuffling flight, desertion.

term [tûrm] *n* a limit; any limited period; the time for which anything lasts; that by which a thought is expressed, a word or expression; (*pl*) mutual relationship between persons; (*pl*) conditions of a contract, etc.; (*pl*) words, speech.—*vt* name.—*n* terminol'ogy, the terms used in any art, science, etc.—*adj* terminolog'ical.—*adv* terminolog'ically.

termagant [tûr'ma-gànt] *n* a boisterous, bold woman.

terminate [tûr'min-āt] *vt* to put an end to, to finish.—*vi* to be limited; to come to end either in space or in time.—*adjs* ter'minable, ter'minal, pertaining to, or growing at, the end or extremity; ending a series or part; .—*n* an end.—*n* termin-ā'tion, act of terminating or ending; end; the ending of words as varied by their signification.

terminus [tûr'mi-nus] *n* the end or extreme point; a limit; end of a transportation line.

termite [tûr'mīt] *n* insects resembling the ants.

tern [tûrn] *n* a seabird allied to the gulls.

ternary [tûr'nà-ri] *adj* proceeding by, or consisting of, threes.

terrace [ter'às] *n* a raised level bank of earth; an unroofed paved area between a house and a lawn; a row of houses.—*vt* to form into a terrace.

terra cotta [ter'a-cot'a] *n* clay and sand used for statues, hardened like bricks by fire; brown-red color.

terrain [ter'ān] *n* a tract of land; field of activity.

terrapin [ter'a-pin] *n* any of several edible tortoises.

terrestrial [te-res'tri-àl] *adj* pertaining to, or existing on, the earth; earthly.

terrible [ter'i-bl] *adj* fitted to excite terror or awe, awful, dreadful; (*inf*) very unpleasant.—*n* terr'ibleness.—*adv* terr'ibly.

terrify [ter'i-fī] *vt* to cause terror in, to frighten greatly, to alarm.—*pt, pt p* terr'ified.

territory [ter'i-tó-ri] *n* land under the jurisdiction of a city or state; domain.—*adj* territō'rial, pertaining to te_ritory.

terror [ter'ór] *n* extreme fear; an object of fear or dread.—*vt* terr'orize, to terrify; to govern by terror.—*ns* terroriza'tion; terr'orism.

terse [tûrs] *adj* compact or concise, with smoothness or elegance.

tertiary [tûr'shi-âr-i] *adj* third.

tessera [tes'e-ra] *n* one of the small square tiles or cut stones used in forming tessellated pavements.

test [test] *n* any critical trial; means of trial.—*vt* to put to proof; to examine critically. **test pilot**, one whose job it is to take up new types of aircraft to test their quality; **test' tube**, a cylinder of thin glass closed at one end, used in testing substances chemically.

testament [tes'ta-mènt] *n* a will; a covenant made by God with men; **Testament**, one of the two great divisions of the Bible.—*adjs* testamen'tal, testamen'tary, tes'tāte, having made and left a will.—*n* testā'tor.

testicle [tes'ti-kl] *n* a gland that secretes spermatozoa in males.

testify [tes'ti-fī] *vi* to give evidence; to bear witness (to).—*vt* to be evidence of.

testimony [tes'ti-mò-ni] *n* evidence; declaration to prove some fact.—*adj* testimō'nial, containing testimony.—*n* a testimony to one's character or abilities.

testy [tes'ti] *adj* touchy, easily irritated.

tetanus [tet'a-nus] *n* an intense and painful spasm of muscles, usu. introduced through a wound; lockjaw.

tête-à-tête [tet'-a-tet'] *n* a private conversation.—*adj* confidential, secret.

tether [teTH'èr] *n* a rope or chain for tying an animal.—*vt* to restrain within certain limits.

tetragon [tet'ra-gon] *n* a figure of four angles.

tetrahedron [tet-ra-hē'dron] *n* a solid figure enclosed by four triangles.

Teuton [tū'ton] *n* one of ancient probably Germanic or Celtic people.

text [tekst] *n* the original words of an author; any concise phrase or statement on which a written or spoken discourse is based; a theme; the main printed part of a book.—*n* text'-book, a book containing the leading principles of a subject.—*adj* tex'tūal, pertaining to, or contained in, the text.

textile [teks'tīl, -tl] *adj* woven, or capable of being woven.—*n* a knitted or woven fabric.

texture [teks'-chūr] *n* the manner in which threads, etc., in a material, etc., are interwoven or combined; the manner of arrangement of particles in a substance; the quality conveyed to the touch by woven fabrics, etc.

than [THan] *conj* a word placed after the comparative of an adjective or adverb to introduce the second part of a comparison.

thank [thangk] *vt* to express gratitude to; to acknowledge indebtedness to.—*n* (usually in *pl*) expression of gratitude.—*adj* thank'ful.—*adj* thank'less, unthankful; not expressing thanks for favors; **Thanksgiving Day**, a US legal holiday observed on the fourth Thursday of November.

that [THat] as a *demons pron* or *adj* (*pl* those), points out a person or thing—the former or more distant thing, not this but the other.—*rel pron* who or which.—*conj* used to introduce a noun clause, and various types of adverbial clauses.

thatch [thach] *vt* to cover, as a roof, with straw, reeds, etc.—*n* straw, etc., used to cover the roofs of buildings and stacks.

thaumaturgy [thö'ma-tûr-ji] *n* the art of working wonders or miracles, esp magic.

thaw [thö] *vi* to melt or grow liquid, as ice.—*vt* to cause to melt.—*n* the melting of ice or snow by heat.

the¹ [THe or (when emphatic) THē], *demons adj* usu. called the definite article, used to denote a particular person or thing; also to denote a species.

the² [THè] *adv* used before comparatives, as, 'the more the better'.

theater, theatre [thē-a-tèr] *n* a place where public representations as plays, motion pictures, etc. are seen; dramatic literature; the stage; dramatic effect.—*adjs* theat'ric, -al, pompous, melodramatic, affected.—*adv* theat'rically.

theft [theft] *n* act of thieving.

their [THâr, THer] *possessive adj* (also called *possessive pron*) of or belonging to them.

theism [thē'izm] *n* belief in the existence of a god or gods; monotheism.—*n* thē'ist, one who believes in a god or gods.

them [THem] *pron* the objective case (*accusative* or *dative*) of they.

theme [thēm] *n* a subject set or proposed for discussion, or on which a person speaks or writes.—*adj* themat'ic.

then [THen] *adv* at that time; afterwards; immediately; at another time.—*conj* for that reason.

thence [THens] *adv* from that time or place; for that reason.—*advs* thence'forth.

theodolite [thē-od'ō-līt] *n* an instrument used in surveying for the measurement of angles horizontal and vertical.

theology [thē-ol'o-ji] *n* the study of God and of religious doctrine and matters of divinity.—*n* theolō'gian.—*adjs* theolog'ic, -al.

theorem [thē'o-rem] *n* a proposition that can be proved from accepted principles; law or principle.—*adjs* theoret'ic, -al.—*adv* theoret'ically.—*vi* the'orize; to form opinions solely by theories; to speculate. the'ory, an explanation or system of anything; an exposition of the abstract principles of a science or art; a hypothesis.

theosophy [thē-os'o-fi] *n* immediate divine illumination or inspiration claimed to be possessed by specially gifted persons, who are also held to possess abnormal control over natural forces; the doctrines of various sects, which profess to attain knowledge of God by inspiration.

therapeutic [ther-a-pū'tik] *adj* pertaining to healing, curative. ther'apy, the curative and preventive treatment of disease or an abnormal condition.

there [THār, THèr] *adv* in that place; at that point; to that place or point; in that respect; in that matter.

therm [thûrm] *n* any of several units of energy; 100,000 British thermal units (105.5 megajoules), that unit being the amount of heat necessary to raise the temperature of 1 lb of water at maximum density 1° Fahrenheit.—*adjs* ther'mal, having to do with heat; ther'mic, pertaining to heat; *ns* ther'modynam'ics, the branch of physics concerned with energy utilization and transfer.—*n* ther'mostat, an automatic device for regulating temperatures.

thermionics [thûr-mi-on'iks] *n sing* the science dealing with the emission of electrons from hot bodies.

thermometer [thûr-mom'e-tèr] *n* an instrument for measuring temperature.—*adjs* thermomet'ric, -al.

thermostat *See* therm.

thesaurus [thē-sö'rus] *n* a treasury or repository, esp of knowledge, words, quotations, etc., a lexicon or cyclopaedia.

thesis [thē'sis] *n* a position, or that which is set down or advanced for argument; an essay on a theme.

Thespian [thes'pi-àn] *adj* pertaining to tragedy; tragic.

thew [thū] *n* (used chiefly in *pl*) muscle or sinews; strength; resolution.

they [THā] *pers pron*, *pl* of he, she, or it.

thick [thik] *adj* dense; firm; crowded; closely set, abundant; frequent, in quick succession; not transparent or clear; misty.—*vt* thick'en, thick'et, a collection of trees or shrubs thickly or closely set, a close wood or copse.—*adjs* thickset, closely planted; having a short, thick body.

thief [thēf] *n* one who steals or takes unlawfully what is not his own.—*pl* thieves.

thieve [thēv] *vi* to practice theft, to steal.

thigh [thī] *n* the thick fleshy part of the leg from the knee to the trunk.

thimble [thim'bl] *n* a cap or cover to protect the finger and push the needle in sewing.

thin [thin] *adj* having little thickness; slim; lean; rarefied; not dense; not close or crowded.—*adv* not thickly, not closely, in a scattered state.—*vt* to make thin; to make less close or crowded.—*adv* thin'ly.—*ns* thinn'er, a substance added to paint, shellac, etc., to thin it; thin'ness.

thine [THīn] *pron*, (arch) possessive (*gen*) case of thy.

thing [thing] *n* an inanimate object; a living being an event; an action.

think [thingk] *vi* to exercise the mind; to revolve ideas in the mind; to consider; to purpose or design.—*vt* to imagine; to judge, to believe or consider.—*n* think'er.

third [thûrd] *adj* the last of three; being one of three equal parts.—*n* one of three equal parts.—*adv* third'ly.—**third degree**, (*inf*) cruel treatment and questioning to force confession.

thirst [thûrst] *n* the uneasiness caused by lack of drink; vehement desire for drink.—*vi* to feel thirst.—*adj* thirst'y.

thirteen [thûr'tēn] *adj*, *n* three and ten.

thirty [thûr'ti] *adj* and *n* three times ten.

this [THis] *demons pron* or *adj* denoting a person or thing near, just mentioned, or about to be mentioned.—*pl* these.

thistle [this'l] *n* any of various composite prickly plants.

thither [THiTH'èr] *adv* to that place; to that end or result.

thole [thōl] *n* a pin in the side of a boat to keep the oar in place.

thong [thong] *n* a piece or strap of leather to fasten anything; the lash of a whip.

thorax [thō'raks] *n* the part of the body between the neck and belly, the chest.

thorn [thörn] *n* a sharp, woody projection on the stem of a plant; a shrub or small tree having thorns, esp hawthorn.

thorough [thûr'ō] *adj* complete, consummate; very exact and painstaking—whole-hearted, or exhaustive.—*adj* thor'oughbred, bred from a dam and sire of the best blood, as a horse; aristocratic—well-bred, spirited, having distinction.—*n* an animal, esp a horse, of pure blood.—*n* thor'oughfare, a place or passage for going through; a public way or street.

those [THōz] *adj* and *pron*, *pl* of that.

thou [THow] *pron* of the second person sing.

though [THō] *conj* admitting, allowing, even if; (used absolutely) however.

thought [thöt] *n* the act of thinking; power of reasoning; conception; deliberation; consideration; meditation.—*adj* thought'ful, employed in meditation; marked by or showing thought.—*adj* thought'less, without thought or care.

thousand [thow'zànd] *adj* ten hundred; denoting any great number.—*n* the number ten hundred.

thrall [thröl] *n* a slave, serf; slavery, servitude.—*vt* to enslave.—*n* thrall'dom, thral'dom.

thrash [thrash] *vt* to beat out grain from the straw by means of eg a flail or machinery; to beat soundly.—*vi* to thresh grain.

thread [thred] *n* a very thin line of any substance twisted and drawn out; a filament of any fibrous substance; a fine line of yarn.—*vt* to pass a thread through the eye of (as a needle); to pass or pierce through, as a narrow way.

threat [thret] *n* a declaration of an intention to inflict punishment or other evil upon another.—*vti* threat'en, to declare an intention; to declare the intention of inflicting; to terrify by menaces.

three [thrē] *adj* and *n* the cardinal number next above two.—*n* the symbol 3, III, iii denoting this.

threnody [thren'ó-dē] *n* an ode or song of lamentation.

threshold [thresh'ōld, -hōld] *n* the piece of timber or stone under the door of a building; doorway, entrance.

thrice [thrīs] *adv* three times.

thrift [thrift] *n* careful management, frugality.—*adj* thrift'y.

thrill [thril] *vt*, *vi* to tingle with excitement; to throb or pulse.—*n* a thrilling sensation; vibration.—*n* thrill'er, an exciting novel or play.

thrive [thrīv] *vi* to prosper, to increase in goods; to be successful; to grow vigorously, to flourish.

throat [thrōt] *n* the forepart of the neck; an entrance; a narrow part of anything.—*adj* throat'y.

throb [throb] *vi* to beat, as the heart or pulse, with more than usual force; to vibrate.

throe [thrō] *n* (usu *pl*) suffering, pain; the pains of childbirth; distressing effort or struggle.

thrombosis [throm-bō'sis] *n* a coagulation of blood, forming a clot in a blood-vessel.

throne [thrōn] *n* a chair of state richly ornamented and raised; sovereign power.—*vt* to place on a royal seat.

throng [throng] *n* a crowd.—*vt* to press or crowd upon.

throstle [thros'l] *n* the song thrush.

throttle [throt'l] *n* a valve controlling the flow of steam or other gas to an engine.

through [thrōō] *prep* from end to end, or from side to side, of; into and then out of; over the whole extent of; from beginning to end of.—*prep* throughout', in every part of.

throw [thrō] *vt* to hurl, to fling; to shed, cast off.—*vi* to cast or hurl; to cast dice.—*ns* throw'back, a reversion to an ancestral or more primitive type.

thrum[1] [thrum] *n* the end of a weaver's thread; any loose thread or fringe; coarse yarn.—*vt* to tuft; to fringe.

thrum[2] [thrum] *vt* to strum.

thrush[1] [thrush] *n* a genus of passerine birds, including the robin.

thrush[2] [thrush] *n* a disease of the mouth and throat, characterized by white patches and caused by a yeast, usu. affecting infants.

thrust [thrust] *vt* to push or drive with force; to press (in); to stab, pierce; to force. — *vi* to make a push, to intrude. — *n* a stab; pressure; the driving force of a propeller.

thud [thud] *n* a dull, hollow sound, caused by a blow or a heavy body falling. — *vi* to make such a sound.

thug [thug] *n* one of a class of professional robbers and assassins in India. — *n* **thugg'ery**, organized robbery and violence.

thumb [thum] *n* the short, thick finger of the human hand. — *vt* to handle awkwardly; to turn over, or to soil, **thumb'-screw**, an old instrument of torture for compressing the thumb by means of a screw; **thumb'tack**, a tack with a wide, flat head that can be pressed into a board, etc. with the thumb.

thump [thump] *n* a heavy blow. — *vt* to beat with something heavy. — *vi* to strike or fall with a dull heavy blow.

thunder [thun'dèr] *n* the deep rumbling sound after a flash of lightning; any similar sound. — *vi* to sound as thunder. — *vt* to utter loudly and emphatically. — *ns* **thun'derbolt**, a bolt or shaft of lightning and a peal of thunder; anything sudden and shocking. — *adjs* **thun'dering**, **thun'derous**, angry-looking.

Thursday [thûrz'dā] *n* the fifth day of the week.

thus [THus] *adv* in this or that manner; to this degree or extent; so; therefore.

thwack [thwak] *vt* to strike with something blunt and heavy, to thrash. — *n* a heavy blow.

thwart [thwört] *adj* cross, lying crosswise. — *vt* to baffle, to frustrate.

thy [THī] *possessive adj* (*arch, pretic*) your. of or pertaining to thee.

thyme [tīm] *n* a genus of aromatic herbs.

thyroid [thī'roid] *adj* denoting a ductless gland located near the trachea.

tiara [ti-ä'ra] (*inf*) *n* the lofty ornamental headdress of the ancient Persians; a circular or semicircular head ornament, often of jewels.

tibia [tib'i-a] *n* the larger of the two bones between the knee and the ankle.

tic [tik] *n* any involuntary, regularly repeated, spasmodic contraction of a muscle. — *n* **tic doul'oureux**

tick¹ [tik] *n* any of numerous bloodsucking arachnids that infest men and animals.

tick² [tik] *n* the cover in which feathers, etc., are put for bedding.

tick³ [tik] *vi* to make a small, quick noise; to beat, as a watch. — *n* the sound of a watch; a moment.

tick⁴ [tik] *n* credit, trust.

tick⁵ [tik] *vt* (*often with* off) to mark off lightly, as items in a list. — *n* a light mark.

ticket [tik'et] *n* a printed card, etc., that gives one a right, a label on merchandise giving size, price, etc.

tickle [tik'l] *vt* to touch lightly and provoke to laughter; to please or amuse. — *adj* **tick'lish**, easily tickled; easily affected; nice, critical, difficult to handle.

tide [tīd] *n* time, season; the regular ebb and flow of the seas, oceans, etc. usu. twice a day. — *vt* to help along temporarily. — *vi* to work in or out of a river or harbor with the tide. — *adj* **ti'dal**, pertaining to, or having, tides; **tide'wa'ter**, the water overflowing land at flood tide; water that is affected by the tide.

tidings [tī'dingz] *n pl* news, intelligence.

tidy [tī'di] *adj* neat; in good order. — *vt* to make neat; to put in good order.

tie [tī] *vt* to bind; to fasten with a cord; to make a bow or knot in; to constrain. — *vi* to score the same number of points. — *n* a knot, bow, etc.; a bond; something for tying; necktie; an equality in numbers, as of votes, or of points in a game.

tier [tēr] *n* a row or rank, especially when several rows are placed one above another.

tiff [tif] *n* a slight quarrel or disagreement.

tiger [tī'gèr] *n* a large, fierce Asiatic quadruped of the cat genus.

tight [tīt] *adj* close; compact; rigid; taut; not loose; fitting closely; snug, trim; not leaky; concise. — *vt* **tight'en**. — *vi*.

tile [tīl] *n* a piece of baked clay used for covering roofs, floors, etc. — *vt* to cover with tiles.

till¹ [til] *n* a drawer for keeping money.

till² [til] *prep* until. — *conj* until.

till³ [til] *vt* to cultivate (land) for raising crops, as by plowing; **till'er.**

till⁴ [til] *n* an unstratified mixture of glacial drift consisting of sand, clay, gravel, and boulders.

tiller [til'èr] *n* the handle or lever for turning a rudder.

tilt¹ [tilt] *n* the canvas covering of a stall or wagon; an awning in a boat. — *vt* to cover with an awning.

tilt² [tilt] *vi* to ride against another and thrust with a lance; to attack; to fall into a sloping posture, to heel over. — *n* in the Middle Ages, an exercise in which combatants rode against each other with lances.

timber [tim'bèr] *n* wood for construction purposes. — *vt* to furnish with timber or beams. — *adj* **tim'bered**, built of wood.

timbre, timber [tēbr' or tim'bèr] *n* character or quality of a musical sound.

timbrel [tim'brèl] *n* a small hand drum or tambourine.

time [tīm] *n* a point at which, or period during which, things happen; hour of the day; an appropriate season or moment; an opportunity; duration; an interval; a period in the past; occasion. — *vt* to do at the proper season; to regulate as to time; to measure or record the duration of; to measure rate of movement. — *adj* **time'hon'ored**, venerable on account of antiquity. — *adj* **time'ly**, in good time; opportune. **time'-serv'er**, one who suits his opinions to the occasion or circumstances; **time'tā'ble**, a table or list showing the times of certain things, as arrival or departure of trains, steamers, etc.

timid [tim'id] *adj* timorous, shy; wanting courage, faint-hearted. — *n* **timid'ity**, *adv* **tim'idly.**

timorous [tim'òr-ús] *adj* timid, easily frightened.

timpani, tympani [tim'pán-ē] *n pl* kettledrums; the set of kettledrums used in an orchestra.

tin [tin] *n* a metallic element; a vessel of tin or tinplate, etc. — *adj* made of tin or tinplate. — *ns* **tin'plate**, thin sheets of iron or steel plated with tin.

tincture [tingk'-chùr] *n* a tinge, shade; a slight taste added to anything. — *vt* to tinge; to imbue.

tinder [tin'dèr] *n* anything used for kindling fire from a spark.

tine [tīn] *n* a slender projecting point, as a spike of a fork or harrow, or of a deer's antler.

tinge [tinj] *vt* to tint or color. — *n* a slight tint or flavor.

tingle [ting'gl] *vi* to feel a thrilling sensation, as in hearing a shrill sound; to feel a prickling or stinging sensation.

tinker [tingk'èr] *n* a mender of brazen or tin kettles, pans, etc; a bungler. — *vi* to work ineffectively.

tinkle [tingk'l] *vi* to make small, sharp sounds, to clink, to jingle. — *vt* to cause to make quick, sharp sounds. — *n* a sharp, clinking sound.

tinsel [tin'sel] *n* a stuff for ornamental dresses; anything showy, *adj* like tinsel; gaudy; superficial.

tint [tint] *n* a variety of any color, esp diluted; a tinge; a hair dye. — *vt* to give a slight coloring to.

tintinnabulation [tin-tin-ab-ū-lā'sh(ò)n] *n* the tinkling sound of bells.

tiny [tī'ni] *adj* very small.

tip¹ [tip] *n* the small top or point of anything; the end, as of a billiard cue, etc. — *vt* to form a point to; to cover the tip or end of.

tip² [tip] *vt* to strike lightly; to cause to slant; to overturn; to give a small gift of money to, as a waiter, etc. — *vi* to slant; to give tips. — *n* a tap or light stroke; private information about horse-racing, stock speculations, etc.; *ns* **tip'-cat**, a game in which a pointed piece of wood called a cat is made to spring up from the ground by being struck on the tip with a stick, and is then driven as far as possible.

tippet [tip'et] *n* the cape of a coat; a cape of fur, etc.

tipple [tip'l] *vi* to drink in small quantities; to drink strong liquors often or habitually. — *vt* to drink.

tipsy [tip'si] *adj* partially intoxicated.

tirade [ti-rād'] *n* a long vehement speech of censure or reproof.

tire¹ [tīr] *n* (*arch*) attire, apparel; (*arch*) a head-dress. — *vt* to dress, as the head.

tire² [tīr] *n* the hoop of iron, rubber band, cushion or tube round a wheel rim.

tire³ [tīr] *vt* to exhaust the strength of, to weary. — *vi* to become weary. — *adj* **tire'some**, fatiguing.

tissue [tish′ū] *n* cloth interwoven with gold or silver, a very finely woven fabric; the substance of which the organic body is composed.

tit¹ [tit] *n* a titmouse; any of various plump, long-tailed birds.

tit² [tit] *n* in phrase tit for tat, properly *tip for tap*, blow for blow.

tit³ [tit] *n* (*vulgar*) female breast.

titanic *adj* enormous in size and strength.

tithe [tīTH] *n* the tenth of the produce of land and stock, allotted for the maintenance of the clergy and other church purposes. — *vi* to pay a tithe.

titillate [tit′il-lāt] *vt* to tickle; to excite pleasurably. — *n* titil-lā′tion.

title [tī′tl] *n* an inscription placed over, or at the beginning of a thing, by which that thing is known; an epithet; a name denoting nobility or rank, (*law*) that which gives a just right (to possession); *adj* tī′tled, having a title. — *ns* tī′tle deed, a deed or document that proves a title or right to exclusive possession; tī′tle page, the page of a book containing its title and usually the author's and publisher's names.

titmouse [tit′mous] *n* a genus of little birds.

titter [tit′ér] *vi* to giggle, laugh restrainedly. — *n* a restrained laugh.

tittle [tit′l] *n* a small mark, point or sign, as the dot over *i* or *j*.

tittle-tattle [tit′l-tat′l] *n* idle, empty gossip.

titular [tit′ū-lår] *adj* held by virtue of a title; existing in name of title only.

to [tōō, tŏŏ, tŏ] (according to word or sentence stress), *prep* in the direction of; as far as; expressing the end or purpose of an action; the sign of the infinitive mood; introducing the indirect object of a verb; in comparison with, with reference to, etc.

toad [tōd] *n* a family of amphibious reptiles, like the frogs. — *ns* toad′eater, (*arch*) a fawning sycophant; toad′stool, any of various umbrella-shaped mushrooms, esp a poisonous or inedible one.

toast [tōst] *vt* to brown by means of the heat of fire; to warm; to name when a health is drunk; to drink to the health of. — *vi* to drink toasts. — *n* bread toasted; toast′master, the announcer of toasts at public dinners.

tobacco [to-bak′ō] *n* any plant of the genus native to America, the dried leaves of which are used for smoking, chewing, or as snuff.

toboggan [tŏ-bog′ån] *n* a kind of sled without runners turned up at the front for sliding down snow-covered slopes.

toccata [to-kä′tå] *n* (*mus*) a work for keyboard instrument in a free style.

tocsin [tok′sin] *n* an alarm bell, or the ringing of it.

today [tŏ-dā′] *n* this day; the present time. — *adv* on the present day; nowadays.

toddle [tod′l] *vi* to walk with short feeble steps, as a child. — *n* todd′ler, a young child.

toddy [tod′i] *n* drink of whiskey, sugar, and hot water.

toe [tō] *n* one of the five small members at the point of the foot; the forepart of the foot. — *vt* to touch or strike with the toe(s).

toffee, toffy [tof′i] *n* a candy of brittle but tender texture made by boiling sugar and butter together.

tog [tog] *n* (*slang*) a garment—generally in *pl*.

toga [tō′ga] *n* the mantle or outer garment of a Roman citizen.

together [tŏ-geTH′ér] *adv* gathered to one place; in the same place, time, or company.

toil¹ [toil] *n* a net or snare (esp in *pl*; *fig*).

toil² [toil] *vi* to labor; to work with fatigue; to move with great effort. — *n* labor, esp of a fatiguing kind. — *adj* toil′some. — *adj* toil′worn.

toilet [toil′et] *n* mode or process of dressing; any particular costume; a room with a bowl-shaped fixture for defecation or urination; such a fixture. — *ns* toil′etry.

token [tō′kén] *n* something representing another thing or event; a symbol, sign, a memorial. — *adj* serving as a symbol, hence being a mere show or semblance, not effective reality.

tolerable [tol′ér-å-bl] *adj* that may be endured; moderately good or agreeable. — *n* tol′erance, endurance of, or permitting liberty to, uncongenial persons, or opinions differing from one's own. — *adj* tol′erant. — *adv* tol′erantly. — *vt* tol′erāte, to endure; to allow by not hindering.

toll¹ [tōl] *n* a tax for the liberty of passing over a bridge or road.

toll² [tōl] *vi* to sound, as a large bell, esp with a measured sound, as a funeral bell. — *n* the sound of a bell when tolling.

tomahawk [tom′a-hŏk] *n* a light ax used by N American Indians. — *vt* to cut or kill with.

tomato [tŏ-mä′tō] *n* a plant with red (or yellow) pulpy edible fruit; used as a vegetable.

tomb [tōōm] *n* a pit or vault in the earth, in which a dead body is placed; a memorial sarcophagus.

tomboy [tom′boi] *n* a girl who prefers boyish games.

tomcat [tom′kat] a male cat.

tome [tōm] *n* a book, a volume, esp a large heavy one; a book, esp a learned one.

tomfool [tom′fŏŏl′] *n* a great fool; a blockhead. — *adj* foolish.

tommy gun [tom′i gun] a submachine gun invented by US General John Thompson.

tomorrow [tŏ-mor′ō] *n* and *adv* the day after today.

ton [tun] *n* a unit of weight equivalent to 2,000 pounds.

tone [tōn] *n* the character of a sound; quality of the voice. — *vt* to give tone to; to alter or modify the color of. — *vi* to harmonize (with).

tongs [tongz] *n pl* a domestic instrument, consisting of two shafts of metal jointed, pivoted, or sprung, used for grasping and lifting.

tongue [tung] *n* the fleshy organ in the mouth, used in tasting, swallowing, and speech; power of speech; a language.

tonight [tŏ-nīt′] *n, adv* this night; the night after the present day.

tonne [tòn] *n* metric ton.

tonneau [ton′ō] *n* the rear seating compartment of an automobile; the entire seating compartment.

tonsil [ton′sil] *n* either of two bodies consisting of lymphoid tissue and situated one on each side of the throat. — *n* tonsil-lī′tis, inflammation of the tonsils.

tonsure [ton′shùr] *n* the shaving of the head as a sign of dedication to the special service of God; the part of the head so shaven.

tontine [ton-tēn′] *n* a financial arrangement in which a number of participants usu. contribute equally to a prize that is eventually awarded to the last survivor.

too [tōō] *adv* over, extremely; also, likewise.

tool [tōōl] *n* an implement for manual work; an instrument for achieving any purpose. — *vi* to install tools, equipment, etc. needed.

toot [tōōt] *vi* to sound a horn, whistle, etc. in short blasts. — Also *vt*. — *n* a sound, as of a horn.

tooth [tōōth] *n* one of the hard bodies in the mouth, attached to the skeleton but not forming part of it, used in biting and chewing; anything toothlike, as one of the projections on a comb, saw, or wheel. — *adj* tooth′some, pleasant to the taste.

top¹ [top] *n* the highest part of anything; the upper end or surface; (*naut*) a small platform at the head of the lower mast. — *vt* to cover on the top; to rise above; to surpass; to reach the top of; to take off the top of; top′most, next to the top, highest.

top² [top] *n* a child's toy, with a point on which to spin.

topaz [tō′paz] *n* any of various yellow gems.

tope¹ [tōp] *n* a Buddhist tumulus for the preservation of relics.

tope² [tōp] *vi* to drink hard.

topiary [tō′pi-a-ri] *n* the art and practice of clipping trees and shrubs into ornamental shapes.

topic [top′ik] *n* a subject of discourse or argument. — *adj* top′-ical, relating to a topic or subject; of current interest.

topographer [to-pog′raf-ér] *n* one who describes a place, etc.; one skilled in topography. — *n* topog′raphy, the description of a place.

topple [top′l] *vi* to fall forward, to tumble.

topsy-turvy [top′si-tûr′vi] *adv* bottom upwards. — *adj* turned upside down; disordered, in confusion.

toque [tōk] *n* a close-fitting brimless hat for women.

torch [tôrch] *n* a light formed of twisted tow dipped in pitch or other inflammable material; a large candle or a small flambeau.

torment [tôr′ment] *n* torture, anguish; that which causes pain. — *vt* torment′, to torture, to put to extreme pain, physical or mental. — *n* tormen′tor, -er.

tornado [tôr-nā′dō] *n* a violently whirling column of air seen as a funnel-shaped cloud that usu. destroys everything in its narrow path.

torpedo [tŏr-pē'dō] *n* a family of fishes related to skates and rays, with organs on the head that give an electric shock; self-propelled submarine offensive weapon, carrying explosive charge.—*vt* to attack, hit or destroy, with torpedo(es).

torpid [tŏr'pid] *adj* stiff, numb, having lost the power of motion and feeling; sluggish.—*ns* **torpid'ity**.

torque [tŏrk] *n* a necklace of metal rings interlaced.

torrent [tor'ĕnt] *n* a rushing stream.—*adj* **torren'tial**.

torrid [tor'id] *adj* burning hot; dried with heat.—*ns* **torrid'ity**, **torr'idness**.

torsion [tŏr'sh(ŏ)n] *n* act of twisting or turning a body.

tortoise [tŏr'tŭs, or -toiz] *n* an order of reptiles, distinguished esp by the dorsal and ventral shields which protect the body.

torture [tŏr'-chùr] *n* subjection to the rack or severe pain to extort a confession, or as a punishment.—*vt* to put to torture; etc.—*n* **tor'turer**.

Tory [tō'ri, tō'ri] *n* a Conservative in English politics.

toss [tos] *vt* to throw up, esp suddenly or violently; to throw back; to throw; to pass.—*vi* to be tossed, to be agitated violently; to tumble about.—*n* act of throwing upward.—*ns* **toss'er**.

tot¹ [tot] *n* anything little, esp a child; a small dram.

tot² [tot] *vt* to add or sum up (usu. **tot up**).

total [tō'tål] *adj* whole, complete; ute.—*n* the sum; the entire amount.—*vt* to bring to a total, add up.—*n* **tōt'alīzāt'or**, a machine for registering bets and computing the odds and payoffs, as at a horse race.—*adj* **totalitā'rian**, belonging to a system of government in which one political group maintains complete control, esp under a dictator.—*n* **tōtal'ity**.

totem [tō'tem] *vt* (*inf*) a type of animal, plant, or object chosen as the badge of a primitive clan or group.

totter [tot'ĕr] *vi* to walk unsteadily; to shake as if about to fall.

toucan [tōō-kan', or tōō'-] *n* a family of South American birds, with an immense beak.

touch [tuch] *vt* to be, or to come, in contact with; to strike, handle, gently or slightly; to reach; **touch'stone**, a compact silicious or other stone for testing gold or silver by the streak of the touchneedle.—*n* **touch'wood**, soft combustible material, used as tinder.

tough [tuf] *adj* not easily broken; stiff, viscous, tenacious; difficult; strong; brutal or rough; stubborn.

toupee [tōō-pā'] *n* a wig or section of hair to cover a bald spot, esp worn by men.

tour [tōōr'] *n* a turn, period, etc. as of military duty; a long trip, as for sightseeing.—*vti* to go on a tour (through). **tour'-ist**, one who makes a tour, a sightseeing traveler.

tournament [tûr'na-mènt] *n* any contest in skill involving a number of competitors and a series of games.

tourniquet [tûr'ni-ket] *n* a device for compressing a blood vessel to stop bleeding, as a bandage.

tousle [tow'zl] *vt* to make untidy, disarrange, make tangled (esp hair).

tout [towt] *vti* (*inf*) to praise highly; (*inf*) to sell betting tips on (race horses).—*n* (*inf*) one who does so.

tow¹ [tō] *n* the coarse part of flax or hemp.

tow² [tō] *vt* to pull (a vessel) through the water with a rope; to pull along with a rope.—*n* a rope for towing with.—*ns* **tow'age**.

toward [tōrd or tô-wàrd] *prep* in the direction of; facing; along a likely course to; concerning; just before; for.—Also **towards**.

towel [tow'ėl] *n* a cloth for wiping the skin after it is washed, and for other purposes.—*n* **tow'eling**, cloth for towels.

tower [tow'ĕr] *n* a lofty building, standing alone or forming part of another; a fortress.—*vi* to rise into the air, to be lofty.

town [town] *n* a place larger than a village; a city; the inhabitants of a town.—*ns* **town'ship**, a division of a county, constituting a unit of local government.

toxicology [tok-si-kol'o-ji] *n* the science of poisons.—*n* **tox-ē'mia**, a type of blood poisoning.—*adjs* **tox'ic**, caused by acting as, or affected by, a poison; **tox'in**, a poison produced by microorganisms and causing certain diseases.

toy [toi] *n* a child's plaything; a trifle; a thing only for amusement.—*vi* to trifle; to dally amorously.

trace¹ [trās] *n* a mark etc. left by a person, animal or thing; a

barely perceptible footprint; a small quantity.—*vt* to follow by tracks; to sketch; to copy (a map or drawing) by the following lines on transparent paper; **trā'cery**, ornamentation traced in flowing outline.

trace² [trās] *n* either of two straps, etc. connecting a draft animal's harness to the vehicle.

trachea [trā'ke-a] *n* the windpipe.—*pl* **trachē'ae**.

track [trak] *vt* to follow by marks or footsteps; to find by so doing; to tread.—*n* a mark left; footprint; a beaten path.

tract [trakt] *n* a region, area; a part of a bodily system or organ.—*adj* **trac'table**, easily worked or managed; easily taught; docile.—*ns* **trac'tion**, act of drawing or state of being drawn.

trade [trād] *n* buying and selling; commerce; occupation, craft; men engaged in the same occupation.—*vi* to buy and sell.—*vt* to barter.—*ns* **trade'mark**, name or distinctive device warranting goods for sale as the production of any individual or firm; **trā'der; trade' un'ion (trades')**, an organized association of workmen of any trade or industry for the protection of their common interests; **trade' wind**, a wind blowing steadily toward the equator at either side of it.

tradition [tra-dish'(ŏ)n] *n* the handing down in unwritten form of opinions or practices to posterity; a convention established by habitual practice.—*adjs* **tradi'tional**.—*adv* **tradi'tionally**.

traduce [tra-dūs'] *vt* to calumniate, to defame.—*n* **tradū'cer**.

traffic [traf'ik] *n* trade; the movement or number of automobiles, pedestrians, etc. along a street, etc.—*vi* to have dealings.

tragedy [traj'e-di] *n* a species of drama in which the action and language are elevated, and the climax a catastrophe; one such drama.—*ns* **tragē'dian**, a writer of tragedy; an actor in tragedy.—*adjs* **trag'ic, -al**, pertaining to tragedy; sorrowful; calamitous.—*adv* **trag'ically**.—*n* **trag'icom'edy**, a dramatic piece in which grave and comic scenes are blended.

trail [trāl] *vt* to draw along the ground; to have in one's, its, wake; to follow behind.—*vi* to hang or drag loosely behind.—*n* anything drawn out in length.—*ns* **trail'er**; a wagon, van, etc. designed to be pulled by an automobile, truck, etc.; such a vehicle designed to be lived in.

train [trān] *vt* to educate, to discipline; to tame for use, as animals; to cause to grow properly; to aim, a gun, etc.—*vi* to undergo systematic exercise or preparation.—*n* that which is drawn along after something else; any connected order; a sequence; a line of connected railroad cars pulled by a locomotive.—*adj* **trained**, disciplined by training; skilled.—*ns* **trainee'**, one who is being trained.

trait [trāt] *n* a feature, lineament; a distinguishing feature of character or mind; a touch (of a quality).

traitor [trā'tór] *n* one who, being trusted, betrays his country, friends, etc.; one guilty of treason.

trajectory [tra-jek'tó-ri] *n* the curve described by a body under the action of given forces.

tram [tram] *n* an open railway car used in mines; a streetcar.—*n* **tramway**, a way for trams.

trammel [tram'l] *n* a net used in fowling and fishing; anything that hampers movement.—*vt* to shackle, hamper.

tramp [tramp] *vt* to travel over on foot; to tread on heavily.—*vi* to walk, to go on foot; to wander about as a vagrant; to tread heavily.—*n* a journey on foot; a vagrant.

trample [tramp'l] *vt* to tread under foot.

trampoline [tram'pō-lēn] *n* a sheet of strong canvas stretched tightly on a frame, used in acrobatic tumbling.

trance [trans] *n* a state of unconsciousness, as under hypnosis, in which some of the powers of the waking body may be retained.

tranquil [trang'kwil] *adj* quiet, serene, peaceful.—*vt* **tran'quillize**.—*ns* **tran'quillizer**, a sedative drug; **tranquill'ity**.

trans- [tranz-, trans-] *prefix* meaning across, through, on the other side of.

transact [trans-akt', tranz-akt'] *vt* to carry through, perform.—*n* **transac'tion**.

transcend [tran-send'] *vt* to rise above, to surpass; to be outside the range of.—*adj* **transcen'dent**.—*ns* **transcen'dence**.—*adj* **transcenden'tal**.

transcribe [tran'skrīb'] *vt* to write over from one book into another, to copy.—*ns* **trans'cript**, that which is transcribed, a copy.

transept [tran'sept] *n* one of the wings or cross-aisles of a church, at right angles to the nave.

transfer [trans-fûr'] *vt* to carry, convey, to another place; to give, hand over, to another person, esp legally.—*n* trans'fer, the act of transferring.—*adj* trans'ferable [or -fer'-]; trans'-ference.

transfiguration [trans-fig-ūr-ā'sh(ó)n] *n* a change of form or appearance; glorifying; idealization.—*vt* transfig'ure [-fig'ėr].

transfix [trans-fiks'] *vt* to pierce through; to paralyze with emotion.

transform [trans-förm'] *vt* to change the shape, appearance, character, or disposition of.—*ns* transformā'tion, change of form or substance.

transfuse [trans-fūz'] *vt* to pour out into another vessel; to transfer blood from one to another.

transgress [trans-gres'] *vt* to pass beyond; to break.—Also *vi.*—*ns* transgress'ion; transgress'or.

transient [tran'shėnt] etc., *adj* passing, not lasting; of short duration, momentary.—*n* transience.

transit [tran'zit or -sit] *n* a passing over; act or duration of conveyance; transi'tion, passage from one place or state to another; change.—*adjs* transi'tional, trans'itiveness.—*adj* trans'itory.

translate [trans-lāt'] *vt* to remove to another place or office; to render into another language; to express in a different artistic medium from that in which it was originally expressed; to explain, interpret.—*ns* translā'tion, translā'tor.

transliterate [trans-lit'e-rāt] *vt* to express the words of one language in the alphabetic characters of another.—*ns* translit-erā'tion; translit'erātor.

translucent [trans-lū'sėnt] *adj* allowing light to pass, but not transparent; clear.

transmarine [trans-ma-rēn'] *adj* across or beyond the sea.

transmigrate [trans'mī'grāt] *vi* to migrate across, esp to another country; (of a soul) to pass into another body.—*ns* transmigrā'tion.

transmit [trans-mit'] *vt* to pass on to another person or place; to cause to pass through; to convey; to send out (radio or television signals).—transmiss'ion, transmitt'al; transmit't'er, one who transmits; an apparatus for converting sound waves into electrical waves.

transmute [trans-mūt'] *vt* to change to another form or substance.—*n* transmutā'tion.

transom [tran'sóm] *n* a horizontal beam or lintel across a window or the top of a door; a small window just above a door or window.

transparency [trans-par'en-si] *n* quality of being transparent; a picture on seen by means of light shining through.—*adj* transpar'ent.

transpierce [trans-pērs'] *vt* to breathe out or pass through the pores of the skin.—*vi* to exhale; to come to light; to occur.—*n* transpirā'tion.

transplant [trans-plänt'] *vt* to remove and plant in another place; to remove and resettle.

transport [trans-pört'] *vt* to carry from one place to another; to banish oversea, esp to a penal colony; to carry away.—*n* trans'port, carriage from one place to another; the convey-ance of troops and their necessaries by sea or land; a ship, truck, etc., for this purpose; the system organized for trans-porting goods or passengers; ecstasy.—*adj* transport'able.—*n* transportā'tion.

transpose [tranz-poz'] *vt* to put each in the place of the other; (*mus*) to change the key of.—*ns* transpō'sal, a change of place or order; transposi'tion.

transubstantiation [tran-sub-stan-shi-ā'sh(ó)n] *n* a change into another substance.

transverse [tranz-vûrs'] *adj* turned or lying, or acting, cross-wise.—*vt* to cross; to thwart; to reverse; to transform.—*n* transver'sal.—*adv* transverse'ly.

transvest [tranz-vest'] *vti* to dress oneself in the clothes of another, esp of the opposite sex.—*n* and *adj* transvestite.

trap[1] [trap] *n* an instrument for snaring animals; an ambush; a trick to catch someone out; a carriage, a gig.—*vt* to catch in a trap.—*pr p* trapp'ing; *pt, pt p* trapped.—*ns* trap'door, a hinged or sliding door in a roof, ceiling, or floor; trapp'er.

trap[2] [trap] *vt* to drape or adorn with trappings; trapp'ings, colorful clothes; ornaments.

trapezium [tra-pē'zi-um] *n* a quadrilateral with no sides paral-lel.—*n* trapēze', a gymnastic apparatus consisting of a hori-zontal bar suspended by two parallel ropes.—*n* trapē'zoid, a quadrilateral with two sides parallel.

trash [trash] *vt* to vandalize, to destroy; to attack, assault.—*n* refuse; rubbish.

trauma [trö'ma] *n* bodily condition arising from physical injury; disturbing experience that may be the origin of a neurosis.—*adj* traumat'ic.

travail [trav'āl] *n* excessive labor, toil; labor in childbirth.—*vi* to labor; to suffer the pains of childbirth.

trave [trāv] *n* a traverse beam.

travel [trav'ėl] *vi* to journey; to move.—*vt* to journey along, through.—*pr p* trav'eling; *pt, pt p* trav'eled.—*n* act of passing from place to place; journey.—*ns* trav'eler; travelogue, tra-velog, a talk, lecture, or article about travels.

traverse [trav'ėrs] *adj* lying across; denoting drapes drawn by pulling a cord across.—*n* anything laid or built across; side-ways course in rock climbing, skiing, etc.; the place where this is done.—*vt* to cross.

travesty [trav'es-ti] *n* burlesque in which the original charac-ters are preserved, the situations parodied; any grotesque or misrepresentative imitation.

trawl [tröl] *vi* to fish by dragging a trawl along.—*vt* to catch with a trawl.—*n* traw'ler.

tray [trā] *n* a flat board, or sheet of metal, etc., surrounded by a rim, used for carrying or containing sundry articles; a salver.

treachery [trech'ėr-i] *n* faithlessness, betrayal of trust.—*adj* treach'erous, faithless; liable to deceive, betray confidence.

tread [tred] *vi* to set the foot down; to walk or go.—*vt* to walk on; to press with the foot.—*pr p* trod or trodd'en.—*n* press-ure with the foot; a step, way of stepping; the part of a shoe, wheel, or tire that touches the ground.

treason [trē'zn] *n* betraying of the government or an attempt to overthrow it; disloyalty.—*adj* trea'sonable.

treasure [trezh'ûr] *n* wealth stored up; riches; anything much valued.—*vt* to hoard up; to value greatly.—*ns* treas'urer, one who has the care of a treasure or treasury; treas'ury, a place where treasure is deposited.

treat [trēt] *vt* to handle, use, deal with, act towards; to subject to the action of a chemical; to discourse on.—*vi* to negotiate; to entertain, act as host.—*n* an entertainment; turn at being host; a pleasure seldom indulged; an unusual cause of enjoy-ment.—*ns* treat'ise [-is], a written composition in which a subject is treated systematically; treat'ment; treat'y, a formal agreement between states.

treble [treb'l] *adj* triple, threefold; (*mus*) denoting the treble; that plays or sings the treble.—*n* the highest of the four principal parts in singing, soprano.—*vt* to make three times as much.—*vi* to become threefold.

tree [trē] *n* a perennial plant having a single trunk, woody, branched, and of a large size.

trefoil [trē'foil, tre'-] *n* plant whose leaves are divided into three leaflets.

trek [trek] *vi* to travel slowly or laboriously.—*n* a journey; a migration; a long or wearisome journey.

trellis [trel'is] *n* a structure of lattice work, for supporting plants, etc.

tremble [trem'bl] *vi* to shake, shiver.

tremendous [trė-men'dús] *adj* such as astonishes or terrifies by its force or greatness; very large or great.

tremolo [trem'o-lō] *n* (*mus*) a tremulous effect; the device in an organ by which this is produced.

tremor [trem'ór] *n* a quivering; a vibration; an involuntary shaking.

trench [trench] *vt* to dig a ditch in; to dig deeply with the spade or plow; to cut a groove in.—*vi* to make a trench; to encroach (on).—*n* a long narrow cut in the earth; such an excavation made for military purposes.

trenchant [tren'chánt] *adj* sharp, cutting; incisive.

trencher [tren'chėr] *n* a wooden plate.

trend [trend] *vi* to tend, to go in a particular direction; to show a drift or tendency.—*n* tendency; a current style.—*n* trend'sett'er, one who helps to give a new direction to follow.—*adj* trend'y, (*inf*) in the forefront of fashion.

trepan [tri-pan'] *n* (*surg*) an early form of the trephine.—*vt* to use a trephine on (the skull); to remove a disk or cylindrical core.

trepidation [trep-i-dā'sh(ó)n] *n* a state of confused hurry or alarm; an involuntary trembling.

trespass [tres'pàs] *vi* to enter unlawfully upon another's land; to encroach upon another's rights; to sin.—*n* act of trespassing.

tress [tres] *n* a lock, braid, or ringlet of hair.

trestle [tres'l] *n* a movable support.

trews [trōōz] *n pl* trousers, esp of tartan cloth.

trial [trī'ál] *n* the act of trying; the state of being tried; examination by a test; experimental use; judicial examination; an attempt; a preliminary race, game, etc.; suffering, hardship; a source of suffering or of annoyance.

triangle [trī'ang-gl] *n (math)* a plane figure with three angles and three sides; a musical instrument of percussion.

tribe [trīb] *n* a race or family descended from the same ancestor.—*adj* trib'al.

tribulation [trib-ū-lāsh(ó)n] *n* severe affliction, distress, trial, hardship.

tribunal [trī-bū'nál] *n* a court of justice; something that decides or determines.

tribune¹ [trib'ūn] *n* a champion of the people.

tribune² [trib'ūn] *n* the raised platform from which speeches are delivered.

tribute [trib'ūt] *n* a fixed amount paid at certain intervals by one nation to another; an expression of respect or gratitude.—*adj* trib'ūtary, paying tribute; making additions; flowing into a larger one.—*n* one who pays tribute; a tributary river.

trice [trīs] *vt (naut)* to haul or lift up by means of a rope.—*n* a haul or tug *(obs)*.

trick¹ [trik] *vt* to dress, to decorate *(with out, up)*.

trick² [trik] *n* any fraud or stratagem to deceive; an illusion; a clever contrivance to puzzle, amuse, or annoy.—*adj* using fraud or clever contrivance to deceive.—*vt* to deceive, to cheat.—*ns* trick'er; trick'ery.—*adj* trick'y.

trickle [trik'l] *vi* to flow gently or in a small stream.

tricolor, tricolore [trī'kûl-ôr or trī'-] *n* a flag of three colors, esp the flag of France; having three colors.

tricycle [trī'si-kl] *n* a child's vehicle with three wheels.

trident [trī'dént] *n* three-pronged spear.

tried *see* try.

trifle [trī'fl] *vi* to act, or to talk, lightly, without seriousness.—*n* anything of little value; a dessert of whipped cream or white of egg, sponge cake, wine, etc.—*n* trī'fler.—*adj* trī'fling, of small value or importance.

trigger [trig'èr] *n* a catch which when pulled looses the hammer of a gun in firing.—*vt* to initiate.

trigonometry [trig-o-nom'è-tri] *n* the branch of mathematics which treats of the relations between the sides and angles of triangles.—*adjs* trigonomet'ric, -al.

trill [tril] *vti* to utter with a tremulous vibration; to pronounce with a quick vibration of one speech organ against another.

trilogy [tril'o-ji] *n* any series of three related dramatic or literary works.

trim [trim] *adj* in good order, tidy, neat.—*vt* to make trim; to put in due order; to decorate; to clip.

trinitrotoluene [trī-nī-trō-tol'û-ēn] *n* a highly explosive agent, commonly known as TNT.

trinity [trin'i-ti] *n* a group of three; **Trinity,** the union of three in one Godhead; the persons of the Godhead.

trinket [tring'kèt] *n* a small ornament for the person; anything of little value.

trio [trē'o, trī'o] *n* a set of three.

trip [trip] *vi* to move with short, light steps; to stumble and fall; to err.—*vt* to cause (a person) to stumble by impeding his feet *(often with up)*.—*n* a light, short step; a catch by which an antagonist is thrown; a false step, a mistake; a short voyage or journey, an excursion; *(slang)* a hallucinatory experience under the influence of a drug.

tripe [trīp] *n (pl)* parts of compound stomach of a ruminant; *(inf)* rubbish, poor stuff.

triple [trip'l] *adj* consisting of three united; three times repeated.—*vti* to treble.—*n* trip'let, three of a kind.—*adjs* trip'licate [-át], threefold; made thrice as much.—*n* triplicā'tion.

tripod [trī'pod] *n* anything on three feet or legs, as a stool, etc.

triptych [trip'tik] *n* a set of three hinged writing tablets.

trireme [trī'rēm] *n* an ancient galley having three banks of oars.

trisect [trī-sekt'] *vt* to cut or divide into three, usu. equal parts.—*n* trisec'tion.

trite [trīt] *adj* worn by use; hackneyed.

triturate [trit'ū-rāt] *vt* to rub or grind to a fine powder.—*n* triturā'tion.

triumph [trī'ûmf] *n* victory; success; a great achievement; joy for success.—*vi* to obtain victory or success; to rejoice for victory; to boast.—*adjs* trium'phal, trium'phant.

triumvir [trī-um'vêr] *n* one of three men in the same office or with the same authority.—*n* trium'virate.

triune [trī'ūn] *adj* being three in one.

trivet [triv'èt] *n* a movable iron frame for hooking to a grate for supporting kettles, etc.

trivia [triv'i-à] *n pl* trifles, unimportant details.—*adj* tri'vial, of little importance; trifling; commonplace.—*n* trivial'ity.

trochee [trō'kē] *n* a metrical foot of two syllables, consisting of a long and a short, as *dûlcĕ.*—*adj* trochā'ic.

trod [trod] *pt* of tread.

trodden [trod'n] *pt p* of tread.

troglodyte [trog'lō-dīt] *n* a cave dweller.

troll¹ [trōl] *n* a supernatural being, sometimes a giant, sometimes a dwarf, dwelling in a cave, hill, etc.

troll² [trōl] *vt* to sing loudly and light-heartedly; to fish for in a certain way.—*vi* to move, stroll, ramble; to sing a catch; to fish.—*n* a moving round, repetition; a round song.—*ns* troll'er; trolley [trol'i], troll'y, an overhead current collector for trolley cars, having a small grooved wheel running under the contact wire; troll'eybus (or car), an electric bus (or streetcar) powered from an overhead wire by means of a trolley.

trollop [trol'op] a prostitute.

trombone [trom-bōn' or trom'bōn] *n* brass musical wind instrument, consisting of a tube whose length is varied with a U-shaped sliding section.

troop [trōōp] *n* a crowd or collection of people; *(pl)* soldiers taken collectively; a subdivision of a cavalry regiment.—*vi* to go in a crowd.—*ns* troop'er, a cavalryman; a mounted policeman.

trope [trōp] *n* a figurative use of a word or expression.

trophy [trō'fi] *n (Gr hist)* a memorial of a victory; a possession that is evidence of achievement in any sphere.

tropic [trop'ik] *n* one of the two imaginary circles on each side of the celestial equator, where the sun turns, as it were, after reaching its greatest declination north or south; *(pl)* the regions lying between these circles.—*adjs* trop'ic, -al.

troposphere [trop'ō-sfēr] *n* the lowest layer of the atmosphere.

trot [trot] *vi* (of a horse) to go, lifting the feet quicker and higher than in walking; to walk or move fast; to run.—*vt* to ride at a trot.

troth [troth or trōth] *n* faith, fidelity.

troubadour [trōō'ba-dōōr] *n* poet-musicians who appeared in Provence from the 11th to the 13th century.

trouble [trub'l] *vt* to agitate; to disturb; to worry; to pain, afflict; to put to inconvenience.—*vi* to take pains (to).—*n* disturbance; uneasiness; affliction; that which disturbs or afflicts.—*adj* troub'lesome.

trough [trof, or trôf] *n* a long, hollow vessel for water or other liquid.

trounce [trowns] *vt* to punish or beat severely.

troupe [trōōp] *n* a company, esp of actors, dancers or acrobats.

trousers [trow'zèrs] *n pl* a two-legged garment worn on the lower limbs and trussed or fastened up at the waist by suspenders or belt.

trousseau [trōō'sō] *n* a bride's outfit.

trout [trowt] *n* fish of the salmon family living practically exclusively in fresh water.

trowel [trow'el] *n* a tool used in spreading mortar, paint, etc., and in gardening.

troy weight [troi'-wāt] *n* a system of weights for gold, silver, gems, etc.,

truant [trōō'ànt] *n* pupil who, without excuse, absents himself from school; anyone who absents himself from his work without reason.

truce [trōōs] *n* a suspension of hostilities between two armies.

truck¹ [truk] *vti* to exchange or barter.—*n* small articles of little value; (*inf*) dealings; payment in goods instead of cash wages.—**truck farm**, a farm where vegetables are grown to be marketed.

truck[2] [truk] *n* a two-wheeled barrow or a low, wheeled frame, for carrying heavy articles; an automotive vehicle for hauling goods.

truckle [truk'l] *vi* to submit slavishly.—*n* **truckle bed**, a low bed on wheels that could be pushed under another.

truculent [truk'ū-lent] *adj* very fierce; threatening and over-bearing in manner.

trudge [truj] *vti* to travel on foot, esp with labor or weariness.—*n* a weary walk.

true [trōō] *adj* agreeing with fact; correct, accurate, placed, fitted accurately; perfectly in tune; (*arch*) honest; (of persons—*rare*) in the habit of telling the truth, truthful; sincere; faithful, loyal.—*adv* **tru'ly**.

truffle [truf'l, trōōf'l] *n* a round underground fungus used in cookery.

truism [trōō'izm] *n* a plain or self-evident truth.

trumpery [trump'è-ri] *n* something showy but worthless.

trump[1] [trump] *n* a trumpet; a sound of trumpeting.

trump[2] [trump] *n* a card of the suit which takes precedence of any card of any other suit.—*vt* to play a trump card on.

trumpet [trum'pet] *n* a brass wind instrument with a clear ringing tone.—*vt* to proclaim.—*vi* to sound a trumpet, or to make a sound suggestive of one.

truncate [trungk-āt'] *vt* to cut the top or end off, to lop, to maim.—*n* **trunca'tion**.

truncheon [trun'ch(ò)n] *n* a cudgel; a baton or staff of authority.

trundle [trun'dl]—*vt* to roll.

trunk [trungk] *n* the stem of a tree; the body of a man or an animal apart from the limbs; the main body of anything; the proboscis of an elephant; a portable box or chest for clothes, etc., esp on a journey; a compartment in an automobile usu. in the rear, for a spare tire, luggage, etc.—*ns* **trunk' line**, a transportation system handling through traffic; a communications system.

truss [trus] *n* a bundle; timbers fastened together for supporting a roof.—*vt* to bind (up).

trust [trust] *n* confidence in the truth of anything, faith; confident expectation; an arrangement by which property is transferred to a person, in the trust or confidence that he will use and dispose of it for a specified purpose; in modern commerce, an arrangement for the control of several companies under one direction.—*adj* held in trust.—*vt* to place confidence in; to believe.—*ns* **trustēē'**, one to whom anything is entrusted; one to whom the management of a property is committed in trust for the benefit of others; **trustee'ship.**—*adj* **trust'ful**, trusting.—*adj* **trust'worthy**.—*adj* **trust'y**.

truth [trōōth] *n* that which is true or according to the facts of the case; agreement with reality.—*adj* **truth'ful**.

try [trī] *vt* to put to the test or proof, to test by experiment; to examine judicially; to examine carefully; to put to severe trial, cause suffering to.—*vi* to endeavor, attempt; to make an effort.—*adjs* **tried, try'ing**.

trysail [trī'sāl or trī'sl] *n* a small fore-and-aft sail set with a boom and gaff.

tryst [trist] *n* an appointment to meet.

tsar *see* **czar**.

tsetse fly [tset'si] *n* insect whose bite conveys protozoan parasites.

tub [tub] *n* a vessel, made of staves and hoops, to hold water; a bathtub.—*vt* to give or take a bath or store in a tub.—*adj* **tubb'y**.

tube [tūb] *n* a pipe, a long hollow cylinder for the conveyance of fluids, etc.—*adj* **tū'bular**.

tuber [tū'bèr] *n* a swelling in the root of a plant where reserves of food are stored up, as a potato.

tubercle [tū'bèr-kl] *n* a small swelling; a small tuber; a small mass or nodule of cells resulting from infection with the bacillus of tuberculosis.—*adj* **tuber'cular, tuber'culous**, affected with, or caused by, tuberculosis.

tuberose [tū'be-rōs, tūb'rōz] *n* a bulbous plant with creamy white, fragrant flowers.

tuck [tuk] *vt* to draw or press; to fold; to gather (up).

Tuesday [tūz'dā] *n* the third day of the week.

tuft [tuft] *n* a crest of hair or feathers; a small bunch or knot of fragments, wool, etc.

tug [tug] *vt* to pull with effort; to drag along.—*vi* to pull with great effort.

tuition [tū-ish'(ò)n] *n* teaching, private coaching.

tulip [tū'lip] *n* bulbous plants with highly-colored cup-shaped flowers.

tulle [tūl, or tōōl] *n* a delicate kind of thin silk, rayon, nylon, etc. net used for scarves and veils.

tumble [tumb'l] *vi* to fall, to twist the body, as an acrobat.—*vt* to throw headlong; to turn over.—*n* a fall; a somersault.—*n* **tum'bler**, acrobat or contortionist; a large drinking glass.

tumbril, tumbrel [tum'bril, tum'brèl] *n* a cart with two wheels that can be tilted for emptying; the name given to the carts which conveyed victims to the guillotine during the French Revolution.

tumid [tū'mid] *adj* swollen or enlarged, inflated.

tumour [tū'mór] *n* a swelling of the body, of independent growth.

tumult [tōō'mult] *n* uproar of a multitude, violent agitation with confused sounds; high excitement.—*adjs* **tumult'uous, tumulus** [tū'mū-lus] *n* a mound of earth over a grave, a barrow.—*pl* **tū'mūli**.

tun [tun] *n* a large cask.

tuna [tōō'na] *n* a large ocean fish of the mackerel group.

tundra [tundra] *n* a level treeless plain of arctic or subarctic regions.

tune [tūn] *n* a melody; state of giving a sound or sounds of the correct pitch harmony.—*vt* to adjust the tones of, as a musical instrument.—*adj* **tune'ful**.—*adv* **tune'fully**.

tungsten [tung'sten] *n* a metallic element.

tunic [tū'nik] *n* a short, loose, usu. belted blouselike garment; a close-fitting jacket worn by soldiers and policeman, etc.;

tunnel [tun'èl] *n* an underground passage, esp one by which a road or railway is carried under an obstacle.—*vt* to make a passage through.—*vi* to make a tunnel.

tunny [tun'i] *n* tuna.

turban [tûrbán] *n* a headdress consisting of cloth wound in folds around the head worn by men.—*adj* **tur'banned**.

turbid [tûr'bid] *adj* muddy, thick.—*adv* **tur'bidly**.

turbine [tûr'bin, or tûrbīn] *n* a machine in which the forced passage of steam causes the rotor to rotate.

turbot [tûr'bot] *n* a large, flat, round fish.

turbulent [tûr'bûlènt] *adj* tumultuous, disturbed, in violent commotion.

tureen [tū-rēn'] *n* a large dish for holding soup, etc.

turf [tûrf] *n* the surface of land matted with the roots of grass, etc.; horse racing (*with* the); a racetrack.

turgid [tûr'jid] *adj* swollen; extended beyond the natural size; pompous, bombastic.—*ns* **turgid'ity**.

Turk [tûrk] *n* a native of Turkey, an Ottoman.

turkey [tûrk'i] *n* a large gallinaceous bird, a native of America; its flesh, used as food.

turmoil [tûr'moil] *n* physical or mental agitation; disturbance, confusion.

turn [tûrn] *vi* to revolve; to go in the opposite direction; to turn one's head; to hinge (on), or to depend on; to be shaped on the lathe.—*vt* to cause to revolve; to reverse; to change the position or direction of; to reach and go round; to direct, apply; to transfer.—*n* act of turning; new direction or tendency; a walk to and fro; a turning point, crisis; a spell of work; performer's act, or performer.—*ns* **turn'coat**, one who abandons his principles or party; **turn'ing point**, the point at which a significant change occurs; **turn'key**, a jailer; **turn'-over**, act of turning over, upset, overthrow; a fruit or meat pasty; the rate of replacement of workers; **turn'pike**, a toll road, esp one that is an expressway; **turn'stile**, a revolving frame across a footpath or entrance which admits only one person at a time; **turn'tā'ble**, a circular revolving platform for turning wheeled vehicles.

turnip [tûr'nip] *n* a plant with swollen and fleshy root—cultivated as a vegetable.

turpentine [tûr'pen-tīn] *n* a semi-solid resinous substance secreted by coniferous trees; the oil or spirit of turpentine.

turpitude [tûr'pi-tūd] *n* baseness.

turquoise [tûr'koiz, or tûr'kwoiz] *n* an opaque greenish-blue mineral, valued as a gem.

turret [tŭr'et] *n* a small tower on a building or structure, rising above it; a dome or revolving structure for guns as on a warship, tank, or airplane.

turtle [tûr'tl] *n* any of an order of land, freshwater, or marine reptiles having a soft body encased in a hard shell. — *ns* **tur'- tleneck**, a high close-fitting neckline; **turn turtle**, to turn upside down.

tusk [tusk] *n* a long, protruding tooth on either side of the mouth, as of the elephant.

tussle [tus'l] *n* a struggle. — *vi* to struggle.

tussock [tus'ók] *n* a tuft of grass or sedge.

tutelage [tū'te-lij] *n* guardianship; tū'telary.

tutor [tū'tór] *n* one who has charge of the education of another, esp a private teacher; one who directs the studies of students in a British university. — *vt* to instruct; to direct the studies of. — *n* **tutō'rial**.

tuxedo [tuk-sē'dō] *n* a man's semiformal suit with a tailless jacket.

twaddle [twod'l] *vi* to talk in a silly manner. — *n* silly talk. — *n* **twadd'ler.**

twain [twān] *n* two, a couple, pair.

twang [twang] *n* a sharp, quick sound, as of a tight string when pulled and let go; a nasal tone of voice. — *vt* to make to sound with a twang.

tweak [twēk] *vt* to twitch, to pull to pull with sudden jerks. — *n* a sharp pinch or twitch.

tweed [twēd] *n* a kind of woolen twilled cloth of various patterns. — *adj* made of tweed.

tweezers [twēz'érz] *n sing* nippers; small pincers.

twelfth [twelfth] *adj* the last of twelve; being one of twelve equal parts.

twelve [twelv] *adj*, *n* the cardinal number next after eleven.

twenty [twen'ti] *adj*, *n* two times ten. — *adj* **twen'tieth**.

twice [twīs] *adv* two times, once and again; doubly.

twiddle [twid'l] *vt* to twirl idly, to play with.

twig¹ [twig] *n* a small shoot or branch of a tree.

twig² [twig] *vti* (*inf*) to notice; to understand, grasp the meaning.

twilight [twī'līt] *n* the faint light after sunset and before sunrise; partial darkness.

twill [twil] *ns* woven fabric, in which the warp is raised one thread, and depressed two or more threads for the passage of the weft.

twin [twin] *n* one of a pair; one of two born at a birth; one very like another. — *adj* twofold, double.

twine [twīn] *n* a cord composed of two or more threads twisted together. — *vt* to twist together. — *vi* to unite closely.

twinge [twinj] *vt* to affect with a sharp, sudden pain. — *n* a sudden, sharp pain.

twinkle [twing'kl] *vi* to shine with a trembling, sparkling light, to sparkle. — *ns* **twink'le, twink'ling**, an instant.

twirl [twûrl] *vt* to turn round rapidly, esp with the fingers. — *vi* to turn round rapidly.

twist [twist] *vt* to twine; to unite or form by winding together; to encircle (with); to wreathe. — *n* that which is twisted; a cord; a single thread.

twitch [twich] *vt* to pull with a sudden jerk, to pluck, to snatch. — *vi* to be suddenly jerked. — *n* a spasmodic contraction of the muscles.

twitter [twit'ér] *n* a chirp, as of a bird. — *vi* to make a succession of small tremulous noises, to chirp.

two [tōō] *adj and n* the cardinal number next above one. — *n* the symbols 2, II, ii denoting this; **two'-faced**, having two faces; deceitful, hypocritical; **two'fold**, multiplied by two; double. — *adv* doubly.

tycoon [tī-kōōn'] *n* a powerful industrialist, etc.

tympanic [tim'pan-ik] *adj* of, relating to, or being a tympanum. — *n* **tympanum**, (*anat*) the membrane that separates the external from the internal ear; the drum of the ear.

type [tīp] *n* the characteristic form, plan, style, etc. of a class or group; an examplar, pattern; the general effect of printing in one set of types or of the types chosen. — *vt* to reproduce by means of a typewriter; to classify. — *vt* **type'script**, a copy of a book, document, etc., produced by means of a typewriter. — *ns* **type'writer**, a machine for producing characters resembling printed ones on paper by mechanical means. — *adj* **typ'i-**

cal [tip'-] pertaining to, or constituting, a type; emblematic; characteristic. — *adv* **typ'ically**. — *vt* **typ'ify** [tip'-].

typhoid [tý'foid] *adj* pertaining to typhus or typhoid. — *n* an acute infectious disease acquired by ingesting contaminated food or water.

typhoon [tī-fōōn'] *n* a violent tropical cyclone originating in the western Pacific. — *adj* **typhon'ic**.

tyrant [tī'rànt] *n* one who uses his power arbitrarily and oppressively; an absolute ruler. — *adjs* **tyrann'ic, -al, tyr'annous** [tir'-]. — *n* **tyr'anny** [tir'-], the government or authority of a tyrant; oppression, harshness.

U

U: **U-boat** [ū'bōt], a German submarine.

ubiquity [ū-bi'kwi-ti] *n* existence everywhere at the same time. — *adj* **ubi'quitous.**

udder [ud'ér] *n* a milk-secreting organ containing two or more mammary glands, as in cows.

ugly [ug'li] *adj* offensive to the eye; (*inf*) ill-natured; very discreditable; dangerous. — *n* **ug'liness**.

uhlan [u'làn] *n* a mounted lancer in the Polish army.

ukelele [ū-ku-lā'lé] *n* a small, four-stringed musical instrument.

ulcer [ul'sèr] *n* an open sore usu. a result of infection. — *vti* **ul'cerate**, to make or become ulcerous. — *n* **ulcerā'tion.** — *adj* **ul'cerous**.

ulster [ul'stèr] *n* a long and loose kind of overcoat.

ulterior [ul-tē'ri-òr] *adj* situated on the further side; remoter, beyond what is seen or avowed.

ultimate [ul'ti-màt] *adj* furthest; final. — *adv* **ul'timately**. — *n* **ultimā'tum**, the final proposition or terms whose rejection will end a negotiation. — *adj* **ul'timo**, in the last (month).

ultra- [ul'trä-] *prefix* meaning beyond.

ultramarine [ul-trä-ma-rēn'] *adj* deep blue. — *n* a blue pigment.

ultramontane [ul-trä-mon'tān] *adj* being beyond the mountains (ie the Alps); favoring the absolute supremacy of papal over national or diocesan authority in the Roman Catholic church.

ultrasonic [ul-trä-son'ik] *adj* of waves and vibrations, having a frequency above the human ear's audibility limit.

ultraviolet [ul'trä-vī'o-let] *adj* of light waves shorter than the wavelengths of visible light and longer than X-rays, beyond the violet end of the visible spectrum.

umbel [um'bèl, um'bl] *n* an inflorescence in which a number of stalks, each bearing a flower, radiate from one center.

umber [um'bèr] *n* a kind of earth used as a reddish-brown pigment.

umbilical [um-bil'i-kál] *adj* pertaining to the navel.

umbrage [um'brij] *n* suspicion of injury, sense of injury, offense. — *adj* **umbrā'geous**, shady.

umbrella [um-brel'a] *n* a covered collapsible frame carried in the hand, as a screen from rain or sun.

umpire [um'pīr] *n* a third person called in to decide a matter on which arbitrators disagree; an impartial person chosen to enforce the rules.

un- [un-] *pfx* attached to verbs to denote reversal of an action implied by the simple verb, as **unfasten**.

un- [un-] *negative pfx* denoting the opposite of the word to which it is attached, as **unbleached**.

unanimity [ū-nà-nim'i-ti] *n* state of being unanimous. — *adj* **unan'imous**, agreeing, one and all, in opinion or will.

unassuming [un-à-sōōm'ing] *adj* not forward or arrogant, modest.

uncanny [un-kan'i] *adj* weird, unearthly;' suggestive of supernatural powers, inexplicable on rational grounds.

unciform [un'si-förm] *adj* hook-shaped. — *adj* **un'cinate**, hooked at the end.

uncle [ung'kl] *n* the brother of one's father or mother; an aunt's husband.

unconscious [un-kon'shùs] *adj* not aware (of); deprived of perception by the senses, insensible; not present to, or a part of, the conscious mind. — *n* the deepest level of mind, frequently providing motives for conscious action otherwise inexplicable. — *adv* **uncon'sciously**.

uncouth [un-kōōth'] *adj* awkward, ungraceful, esp in manners or language, grotesque, odd.—*n* **uncouth'ness**.

unction [ungk'sh(ó)n] *n* an anointing as for medical or religious purposes; that which is used for anointing; ointment; anything that soothes or comforts.—*adj* **unctuous** [ungk'tū-ùs], oily, greasy.

under [un'dèr] *prep* in a lower position than; beneath the surface of; below and to the other side of; covered by; below; less than, falling short of.—*adv* in, or to, a lower place or condition; below, lower down, in subjection.—*adj* lower in position, rank, or degree.

under- [un'dèr-] *prefix* meaning beneath, below.

underbred [un-dèr-bred'] *adj* of inferior breeding or manners.

undercarriage [un'dèr-kar-ij] *n* the landing gear of an airplane.

underclothes [un'dèr-klōтнz] *n pl* underwear.

undercut [un-dèr-kut'] *vt* to cut below or under; to sell at a price lower than (a competitor); to accept (wages) lower than the standard.

underestimate [un-dèr-es'ti-māt] *vti* to set too low an estimate on or for.—*n* an estimate that is too low.

underfoot [un-dèr-fŏŏt'] *adv* under the foot or feet; in the way.

undergraduate [un-dèr-grad'ū-āt] *n* a student at a college or university who does not have a first degree.

underground [un'dèr-grownd] *adj* under the surface of the ground; secret; of noncommercial newspapers, movies, etc. that are unconventional, radical, etc.—*n* a secret movement working for the overthrow of the government or the expulsion of a foreign power in control of the country.

underhand [un'dèr-hand'].—*adv* with an underhand motion; underhandedly.—*adj* **un'derhand'ed**, sly, deceitful, etc.

underling [un'dèr-ling] *n* an agent of inferior rank; a subordinate, esp one of servile character.

underneath [un-dèr-nēth'] *adv* beneath, below, in a lower place.—*prep* under, beneath.

underpass [un'dèr-päs] *n* a road passing under another road, a railway, etc.

underrate [un-dèr-rāt'] *vt* to rate at less than the real value.

undershoot [un-dèr-shŏŏt'] *vt* to shoot below or short of a target; to fall short of (a runway) in landing an airplane.—*adj* **un'dershot**, having the lower teeth protruding beyond the upper when the mouth is closed; driven by water flowing along the lower part.

understand [un-dèr-stand'] *vt* to comprehend, to have just ideas of; to grasp without explanation; to know thoroughly; to take for granted as part of an agreement; to take as meant though not expressed; to be sympathetic with.—*vi* to have the use of the intellectual faculties; to be informed; to believe.—*n* **understan'ding**.

understate [un-dèr-stāt'] *vt* to state too weakly.

understrapper [un'dèr-strap-èr] *n* an inferior agent, an underling, a petty fellow.

understudy [un'dèr-stud-i] *vti* to study a dramatic part so as to be able to take the place of (the actor playing it); to prepare to act as a substitute for.

undertake [un-dèr-tāk'] *vt* to attempt, enter upon, engage in; to take upon onself; to promise; to guarantee.—*vi* (*arch*) to take upon onself.

undertow [un'dèr-tō] *n* a current of water moving beneath the surface in a different direction from that at the surface.

underworld [un'dèr-wûrld *n* Hades; criminals as an organized group.

underwrite [un-dèr-rīt'] *vt* to agree to finance (an undertaking, etc.); to sign one's name to (an insurance policy), thus assuming liability.—*vi* to work as an underwriter.—*n* **un'derwriter**.

undulate [un'dū-lāt] *vti* to move or cause to move like waves; to have or cause to have a wavy form or surface.—*adjs* **un'dulant**.—*n* **undulā'tion**, a waving motion.

unduly [un-dū'li] *adv* in undue measure, too, excessively; improperly.

unequal [un-ē'kwàl] *adj* not equal or alike in quality, extent, duration, etc.; unfair, unjust, varying.

unequivocal [un-ė-kwiv'o-kàl] *adj* unambiguous; explicit; clear and emphatic.

unfilial [un-fil'yàl] *adj* not observing the obligations of a child, undutiful.

unfrock [un-frok'] *vt* to deprive of the rank of priest or minister.

ungainly [un-gān'li] *adj* awkward; clumsy.—*n* **ungain'liness**.

ungual [ung'gwàl] *adj* relating to, like, or resembling a nail, claw, or hoof.

unguent [ung'gwènt] *n* a salve or ointment.

ungulate [ung'gū-lāt] *adj* having hoofs; of or relating to the ungulates.

unhinge [un-hinj'] *vt* to take from the hinges; to render unstable, to upset; to derange (the mind).

unicameral [ūni-kam'èr-àl] *adj* of a legislature, consisting of one chamber.

unicorn [ū'ni-körn] *n* a fabulous animal with a body like that of a horse and one straight horn on the forehead.

uniform [ū'ni-förm] *adj* having one or the same form; not varying, always of the same quality, character, degree, etc.; undiversified in appearance; consistent.—*n* the distinctive clothes of the same kind for persons (eg soldiers) who belong to the same organization.—*vt* to supply with a uniform.—*n* **uniform'ity**, u'niformly.

unify [ū'ni-fī] *vt* to make into one; to make consistent.—*n* **unificā'tion**.

unilateral [ū-ni-lat'è-ràl] *adj* one-sided; on one side only; involving one only of several parties; not reciprocal.—*adv* **unilat'erally**.

union [ūn'yòn] *n* act of uniting or state of being united; a whole formed by the combination of individual parts or persons; concord, agreement; marriage; an association between those in the same or kindred employment to safeguard wages and conditions; a device for uniting parts.—*ns* **un'ionist**, an advocate or supporter of union or unionism; **un'ionism**.

unique [ū-nēk] *adj* without a like or equal.

unison [ū'ni-sòn] *n* identity of musical pitch; agreement.

unit [ū'nit] *n* the smallest whole number, one; a single thing or person; a known determinate quantity by which other quantities of the same kind are measured.—*adj* u'nitary, pertaining to unity or to a unit.

unite [ū-nīt'] *vti* to join into one; to make to agree, feel as one, or act in concert.—**United Nations**, an international organization of nations for world peace and security formed in 1945.

unity [ū'ni-ti] *n* oneness, state of being one or at one; the arrangement of all the parts to one purpose or effect; harmony; continuity of purpose, action, etc.

universal [ū-ni-vûr'sàl] *adj* comprehending, affecting, or extending to the whole; comprising all the particulars; applied to a great variety of uses; affecting, including, or applicable to all mankind.—*ns* **univer'salism**, something that is universal in scope; the state of being universal.

universe [ū'ni-vûrs] *n* the whole system of existing things; all existing things viewed as one whole; the world.

university [ū-ni-vûr'si-ti] *n* an educational institution with an undergraduate college which confers bachelor's degrees and graduate and professional schools each of which may confer master's degrees and doctorates; the physical plant of a university.

unkempt [un-kemt'] *adj* uncombed; untidy, slovenly.

unknown [un-nōn] *adj* not known or well-known; having an unknown value.

unleaded [un-led'èd] *adj* of gasoline, not mixed with tetraethyl lead.

unless [un-les'] *conj* if not, supposing that not.—*prep* save; except.

unmitigated [un-mit'i-gā-tid] *adj* not mitigated; unqualified; out-and-out.

unnatural [un-na'chùr-àl] *adj* not following the course of nature; artificial; strange; cruel, wicked, without natural affection.

unpleasant [un-plez'ànt] *adj* not pleasant, disagreeable.—*adv* **unpleas'antly**.—*n* **unpleas'antness**.

unpopular [un-pop'ū-làr] *adj* disliked; not winning general approval.—*n* **unpopular'ity**.

unprecedented [un-pres'i-den-tid] *adj* having no precedent; novel.

unquiet [un-kwī'èt] *adj* not at rest, disturbed; restless; anxious.

unreasonable [un-rēz'òn-à-bl] *adj* not agreeable to reason;

exceeding the bounds of reason; immoderate; not influenced by reason.

unregenerate [un-ri-jen′é-rát] *adj* not spiritually reborn; stubbornly defiant.

unrequited [un-rē-kwīt-éd] *adj* not repaid, not returned.

unruly [un-rōō′li] *adj* hard to control, restrain, or keep in order; disobedient.

unseen [un-sēn′] *adj* not seen; invisible.

unsettle [un-set′l] *vti* to move from being settled; to disturb, displace, or disorder.—*adj* **unsett′led**, changeable; undecided; unpaid; having no settlers.

unsightly [un-sīt′li] *adj* not pleasing to the eye, ugly.

unthinkable [un-thingk′á-bl] *adj* inconceivable.

until [un-til′] *prep* up to the time of; before.—*conj* up to the time when or that; to the point, degree, etc. that; before.

unto [un′tōō] *prep* (*arch*) to or until; used as a function word to indicate reference or concern.

untouchable [un-tuch′á-bl] *adj* not to be touched or handled; exempt from criticism or control; lying beyond reach; disagreeable to the touch.

untoward [un-tō′árd, un-tōrd′] *adj* not easily guided, perverse; unseemly; not favorable; adverse.

untrue [un-trōō′] *adj* not true, false; not faithful, disloyal; not in accordance with a standard; not level, not straight.—*n* **untruth′**, falsehood; falsity.

unwieldy [un-wēl′di] *adj* not easily moved or handled, as because of large size.—*adv* **unwield′ily**.

unwritten [un-rit′n] *adj* not written; not committed to writing or record, traditional; oral.—**unwritten law**, law based on custom or mores rather than legislative enactment.

up [up] *adv* towards a higher place; aloft, on high; from a lower to a higher position, to a later period; so as to be even with in time, degree, etc.; so as to be tightly bound, closed, etc.—*prep* from a lower to a higher place on or along.—*adj* inclining up, upward.—*vt* to raise; to lift or haul up; to move up.—*vi* to set up; to move up; to intervene boldly.

upbraid [up-brād′] *vt* to rebuke severely; to reproach.

upbringing [up′bring-ing] *n* the process of nourishing and training (a child).

upholster [up-hōl′stèr] *vt* to furnish (furniture) with stuffing, springs, etc.—*ns* **uphōl′sterer**, one who does this; **uphōl′stery**, materials used to make a soft covering esp for a seat.

upon [úp-on′] *prep* on, on the top of.

upper [up′ér] *adj* (*comparative* of **up**) farther up; higher in position, dignity, etc.; superior.—*superl* **upp′ermost**, **up′most**.—*ns* **upp′er**, the part of a boot or shoe above the sole and welt; *adj* **upp′ish** (*inf*) haughty, arrogant, affecting superiority.

upright [up′rīt] *adj* straight up, in an erect position; possessing moral integrity—honest, just.—*n* a vertical post or support.—*adv* vertically.

uproar [up′rōr] *n* noise and tumult, bustle and clamor.—*adj* **uproar′ious**.—*adv* **uproar′iously**.

upset [up-set′] *vt* to turn upside down; to overthrow; to put out of order; to distress.—*n* **up′set**, an overturning; an unexpected defeat; distress or its cause.—*adj* relating to what is set up for sale, in phrase **upset price**, the minimum sum fixed for a bid at a sale by auction.

upshot [up′shot] *n* the conclusion; the result.

upstart [up′stärt] *n* one who has suddenly risen from poverty or obscurity to wealth or power but who does not appear to have the appropriate dignity or ability.

upthrust [up′thrust] *n* a thrust upward, esp an upheaval of a mass of rock.

uptight [up′tīt] *adj* (*slang*) very tense, nervous, etc.

upward [up′wård] *adj* directed up or to a higher place.—*advs* **up′ward**.

uranium [ū-rā′ni-úm] *n* a metallic element.

Uranus [ū-rā′nus] *n* a Greek god, grandfather of Zeus; one of the most distant of the major planets.

urban [ûr′bán] *adj* of or belonging to a city.—*adj* **urbāne**, pertaining to, or influenced by, city life, civilized, polished, suave.—*n* **urbān′ity** the quality of being urbane.

urchin [ûr′chin] *n* a hedgehog; a pert or mischievous child; a sea urchin.

Urdu [ōōr′dōō] *n* the official language of Pakistan.

urge [ûrj] *vt* to drive forward, make to move faster; to press, entreat earnestly.—*vi* to insist; to press.—*n* an impulse, inner prompting.—*n* **ur′gency**.—*adj* **ur′gent**, impelling; pressing with importunity; calling for immediate attention.—*adv* **ur′gently**.

urine [ū′rin] *n* the yellowish fluid which is secreted or separated by the kidneys from the blood and conveyed to the bladder.—*n* **u′rinal**, accommodation provided for discharging urine.

urn [ûrn] *n* a vase with a pedestal; such a vessel used for preserving the ashes of the dead.

ursine [ûr′sīn, ûr′sin] *adj* of or resembling a bear.

us [us] *pron* the objective (accusative or dative) case of **we**.

usage [ū′zij] *n* act of using; mode of using, treatment; customary use; practice, custom.

use¹ [ūz] *vt* to put to some purpose; to avail oneself of; to employ as an instrument; make use of (a person); to exercise; to deal with; treat; to consume; *úst.*—*adj* **used**, not new; second-hand.

use² [ūs] *n* act of using or putting to a purpose; usage; employment; need (for), opportunity of employing; advantage, suitability, effectiveness; practice, custom.—*adj* **use′ful**.—*adv* **use′fully**.—*n* **use′fulness**.—*adj* **use′less**, having no use.—*adv* **use′lessly**.—*n* **use′lessness**.

usher [ush′ér] one who shows people to their seats in a theater, church, etc.; a bridegroom's attendant.—*vt* to escort (others) to seats, etc.

usurp [ū-zûrp′] *vt* to take possession of by force without right; to assume (eg a right) that properly belongs to another.

usury [ū′zhû-ri] *n* the taking of excessive interest on a loan; an excessive interest rate.—*n* **u′surer**, one who practices usury.

utensil [ū-ten′sil] *n* an implement or container, esp one for use in a kitchen.

uterine [ū′tė-rin, -rīn] *adj* pertaining to the womb; born of the same mother by a different father.—*n* **ū′terus**, a womb.

utilize [ū′ti-līz] *vt* to make use of.

utility [ū-til′i-ti] *n* usefulness, profit; something useful, as the service to the public of gas, water, etc.—*adj* of a serviceable type of article, capable of serving as a substitute; kept for production rather than show (as of animals); of a company providing utilities; utilitarian.—*adj* **ūtilitā′rian**.—*n* **utilitā′rianism**, the ethical theory which finds the basis of moral distinctions in the utility of actions, ie their fitness to produce happiness of the greatest number.

utmost [ut′mōst] *adj* most extreme; farthest.—*n* the most possible.

Utopian [ū-tō′pi-án] *adj* ideally perfect.—*n* one that believes in the perfectibility of human society; one proposing or advocating utopian schemes.—*n* **Utopia**, any idealized place; any visionary scheme for a perfect society.

utter¹ [ut′ér] *adj* extreme; complete.—*adv* **utt′erly**, completely.

utter² [ut′ér] *vt* to emit; to put into circulation; to speak, give voice to.—*ns* **utt′erance**, manner of speaking; expression in speech, or in other sound, of a thought or emotion; words spoken, a saying.

uvula [ū′vū-la] *n* the fleshy conical body suspended from the palate over the back part of the tongue.

uxorious [uk-sō′ri-ús] *adj* excessively or submissively fond of a wife.—*adv* **uxō′riously**.

V

vacant [vā′kánt] *adj* empty; free, unoccupied; unreflecting; inane.—*n* **vā′cancy**, emptiness; empty space.—*adv* **vā′cantly**.—*vt* **vā-cāte′**, to leave empty; to quit possession of.—*n* **vācā′tion**, (time of) freedom from regular duties and engagements; a holiday, esp from academic or legal duties.

vaccinate [vak′si-nāt] *vt* to inoculate with *vaccine* as a preventive against certain diseases.—*n* **vaccinā′tion**.—*adj* **vaccine** [vak′sēn], pertaining to, derived from, cows; of, relating to, vaccination.

vacillate [vas′i-lāt] *vi* to sway to and fro; to waver, show indecision.—*n* **vacillā′tion**.

vacuous [vak′ū-us] *adj* empty, void; lacking intelligence, inane.—*ns* **vacū′ity**, **vac′ūum**, a space empty or devoid of all matter; (in practice) a region in which the gas pressure is considerably lower than atmospheric; a vacuum cleaner; **vac′uum clean′er**, an apparatus for removing dust from carpets, etc., by suction.

vade-mecum [vā′di-mē′kùm] n a handbook carried for reference.

vagabond [vag′à-bond] adj wandering; having no settled home. — n a vagrant; a rascal. — n **vag′abondage**.

vagary [vā′gà-ri, và-gā′ri] n a wandering of the thoughts; a whim. — pl **vagaries**.

vagrant [vā′grànt] adj without a settled abode; wandering, erratic. — n one who has no settled home. — n **va′grancy**.

vague [vāg] adj indefinite; indistinct, lacking precision; (of a person) lacking character and purpose. — adv **vague′ly**. — n **vague′ness**.

vain [vān] adj unsatisfying; fruitless, unavailing, ineffectual; empty, worthless; conceited; showy. — adv **vain′ly**. — ns **van′ity**.

vainglory [vān-glō′ri, -glō′-] n boastful pride.

valance [val′àns] n hanging drapery for a bed; a short curtain forming a border.

vale [vāl] n a tract of low ground, esp between hills, a valley.

valediction [val-e-dik′sh(ò)n] n a farewell. — adj **valedic′tory**, saying farewell.

valence [vā′len-si] n (chem) the combining power of an atom.

valentine [val′en-tīn] n a lover or sweetheart chosen on St Valentine's Day, February 14; a love letter or other token sent on that day.

valerian [va-lē′ri-àn] n a genus of dicotyledons, with medicinal properties.

valet [val′et, or val′ā] n a manservant, esp one who attends on a gentleman's person.

valetudinarian [val-e-tū-di-nā′ri-àn] adj pertaining to ill health; sickly, weak. — Also **valetū′dinary**.

valiant [val′yànt] adj strong; brave, heroic.

valid [val′id] adj strong; having sufficient strength or force, founded in truth, sound; fulfilling all the necessary conditions.

valise [va′lēs′] n a traveling bag, generally of leather.

valley [val′i] n low land between hills or mountains.

valor [val′ór] n stoutness of heart, intrepidity; prowess. — adj **val′orous**, intrepid, valiant.

value [val′ū] n worth, that which renders anything useful or estimable; efficacy, importance, excellence; relative worth. — vt to estimate the worth of; to rate; to esteem; to prize. — adj **val′uable**, having considerable value or worth. — n a thing of value. — ns **valuā′tion**, **val′uātor**.

valve [valv] n a lid that opens in one direction and not in the other for controlling the flow of liquid or gas in a pipe.

vamp [vamp] n front upper part of a boot or shoe; a patch; (mus) an improvised accompaniment. — vt to patch old with new; (mus) to improvise.

vampire [vam′pīr] n a corpse which by night leaves its grave to suck the blood of sleeping men; an extortioner.

van¹ [van] n the front; the front of an army or a fleet; the pioneers of any movement.

van² [van] n covered wagon for conveying goods, etc.

vandal one who wantonly damages property; one who destroys what is beautiful. — n **van′dalism**, behavior of a vandal.

vane [vān] n a thin slip of wood or metal at the top of a spire, etc., a weathercock.

vanilla [va-nil′a] n the dried aromatic sheathlike pod or fruit of climbing orchid used in confectionery, etc.

vanish [van′ish] vi to pass suddenly out of sight, to disappear; to become gradually less, to fade away.

vanquish [vangk′wish] vt to conquer.

vantage [vän′tij] n a favorable position; a position allowing a clear view or understanding.

vapid [vap′id] adj flat, insipid, without zest. — adv **vap′idly**. — ns **vapid′ity**.

vapor [vā′pór] n the gaseous state of a substance normally liquid or solid; water or other matter (eg smoke) suspended in the atmosphere; an exhalation. — vi to pass off in vapor; to emit vapors. — vt **vā′porize**.

variable [vā′ri-à-bl] adj that may be varied; liable to change, unsteady. — ns **vāriabil′ity**. — adv **vā′riably**. — ns **vāriā′tion**,

act or process of varying or being varied; an instance of it; extent to which a thing varies.

varicose [var′i-kōs] adj abnormally swollen and dilated.

variety [va-rī′e-ti] n the quality of being various; absence of uniformity or monotony; many-sidedness.

various [vā′ri-ùs] adj varied, different.

varlet [vär′let] n a footman; a low fellow, a scoundrel.

varnish [vär′nish] vt to cover with a liquid so as to give a glossy surface to. — n a sticky liquid which dries and forms a hard, lustrous coating.

vary [vā′ri] vt to make different, to diversify, modify. — vi to alter, to be or become different.

vase [väz or vāz] n a vessel of greater height than width, anciently used for domestic purposes and in sacrifices; an ornamental vessel.

Vaseline [vas′i-lēn] n trade name for petrolatum.

vassal [vas′àl] n one who holds land from, and renders homage to, a superior.

vast [väst] adj of great extent; very great in amount or degree. — adv **vast′ly**. — n **vast′ness**.

vat [vat] n a large vessel or tank.

Vatican [vat′i-kan] n the part of Rome, built on the Vatican hill, in which the Pope resides and which is an independent city under his temporal jurisdiction; the papal authority.

vaudeville [vōd′vil] n a stage show consisting of various acts.

vault [völt] n an arched roof; a chamber with an arched roof, esp one underground; a cellar; the bound of a horse. — vt to arch; to roof with an arch. — vi to curvet or leap, as a horse.

vaunt [vönt or vänt] vti to make a vain display, or display of; to boast. — n vain display; a boast.

veal [vēl] n the flesh of a calf.

Veda [vā′dä, vē′dä] n one or all of the four holy books, collections of hymns, prayers, etc., of the Hindus — written in ancient Sanskrit.

vedette [ve-det′] n a mounted sentry.

veer¹ [vēr] vi (of the wind) to change direction clockwise; to pass from one mood or opinion to another.

veer² [vēr] vt to slacken, let out (as a rope).

vegetable [vej′e-tà-bl] n an organized body without sensation and voluntary motion, usu. nourished by roots fixed in the ground; a plant grown for food. — adj belonging to plants. — n **vegan** [veg-an′ or vē′gan] a strict vegetarian who consumes no animal or dairy products; **vegetā′rian**, consisting of vegetables; pertaining to a diet confined to vegetables. — n **vegetā′rianism**. — vi **veg′etāte**, to grow by roots and leaves; to sprout; to lead an idle, aimless life. — n **vegetā′tion**, process of growing, as a plant; vegetable growth; plants in general.

vehement [vē′e-mént] adj passionate; very eager or urgent; violent, furious. — n **vē′hemence**.

vehicle [vē′i-kl] n any kind of carriage or conveyance; that which is used to convey; (med) a substance in which a medicine is taken. — adj **vehicular**.

veil [vāl] n a curtain; anything that hides an object; a piece of fabric worn by ladies to shade or hide the face; the headdress of a nun. — vt to cover with a veil; to cover; to conceal.

vein [vān] n one of the vessels or tubes that convey the blood back to the heart; one of the horny tubes forming the framework of an insect's wings; (bot) one of the small branching ribs in a leaf; a seam of mineral through a rock of different formation; a streak of different quality. — vt to form veins or the appearance of veins in.

veld [velt, felt] n in S Africa, open, unforested, or thinly forested grassland.

vellum [vel′úm] n a superior kind of parchment prepared from the skins of calves, kids, or lambs.

velocipede [ve-los′i-pēd] n a vehicle propelled by the feet of the rider.

velocity [ve-los′i-ti] n quickness of motion.

velour, velours [ve-lōōr′] n any of several materials with a velvety nap; a hat of such material.

velvet [vel′vét] n a cloth made from silk, rayon, etc. with a soft, thick pile; anything like velvet in texture. — n **velveteen′**, a cotton cloth with a pile like velvet. — adj **vel′vety**, soft in taste or touch.

venal [vē′nàl] adj (of a person or his services) that may be sold or got for a price; mercenary, corrupt. — n **vēnal′ity**.

vend [vend] *vt* to give for sale, to sell; to make an object of trade. —*n* ven′dor, -der. —*adj* vend′ible.

vendetta [ven-det′a] *n* a sanguinary feud in pursuit of private vengeance for the death of a kinsman.

veneer [ve-nēr′] *vt* to overlay or face with another and superior wood, or with a thin coating of another substance. —*n* a thin coating, as of wood.

venerate [ven′e-rāt] *vt* to honor or reverence with religious awe; to reverence, to regard with the greatest respect. —*n* venerā′tion.

venereal [ve-nē′re-ål] *adj* pertaining to, or arising from, sexual intercourse; exciting desire for sexual intercourse.

Venetian [ve-nē′sh(å)n] *adj* of or belonging to Venice.

venge [venj] *vt* (*arch*) to avenge. —*n* **vengeance** [venj′åns] the infliction of punishment upon another in return for an injury or offense, retribution. —*adj* venge′ful.

venial [vē′ni-ål] *adj* pardonable, excusable. —*adv* vē′nially.

venison [ven′i-sn, or ven′i-zn] *n* the flesh of animals taken in hunting, esp the deer.

venom [ven′óm] *n* any liquid injurious or fatal to life, poison; spite, malice. —*adj* ven′omous.

vent[1] [vent] *n* a small opening, slit, or outlet; outlet, expression. —*vt* to provide with vent or opening.

vent[2] [vent] *n* a vertical slit in a garment.

ventilate [ven′ti-lāt] *vt* to admit fresh air to; to oxygenate, aerate; to expose to examination and discussion. —*n* ventilā′tion. —*n* **ventricle** [ven′tri-kl] a small cavity as in the heart or brain.

ventriloquism [ven-tril′o-kwizm] *n* the act or art of speaking in such a way that the hearer imagines the voice to come from a source other than the actual speaker.

venture [ven′chùr] *n* chance, luck, hazard; that which is put to hazard; an undertaking whose issue is uncertain or dangerous. —*vt* to risk. —*vi* to run a risk; to dare. —*adjs* ven′turous, ven′turesome.

venue [ven′ū] *n* the scene of an action or event.

veracious [ve-rā′shùs] *adj* truthful; true. —*n* **veracity**.

veranda, verandah [ve-ran′da] *n* a kind of covered balcony or open portico, supported by light pillars.

verb [vûrb] *n* (*gram*) the part of speech which expresses an action, a process, state or condition or mode of being. —*adj* ver′bal, relating to or consisting in words; spoken; verbā′tim, word for word. —*n* ver′biāge, abundance of words, wordiness, verbosity. —*adj* verbōse′, containing more words than are necessary, wordy.

verbena [vèr-bē′na] *n* vervain, esp garden plants of hybrid origin.

verdant [vûr′dånt] *adj* green; fresh (as grass or foliage); flourishing; inexperienced. —*adv* ver′dantly.

verdict [vûr′dikt] *n* the finding of a jury on a trial; decision, opinion pronounced.

verdigris [vûr′di-grēs] *n* the greenish or bluish deposit formed on copper, brass, or bronze surfaces.

verge[1] [vûrj] *n* a rod, staff, or mace, or the like, used as an emblem of authority; extent of jurisdiction; the brink, extreme edge or margin. —*vi* to be on the verge. —*n* ver′ger, a church official.

verge[2] [vûrj] *vi* (of the sun) to incline toward the horizon.

verify [ver′i-fī] *vt* to establish as true by evidence; to confirm as true by research. —*adj* ver′ifiable, that may be verified, proved, or confirmed. —*n* verificā′tion.

verisimilar [ver-i-sim′i-lår] *adj* having the appearance of truth, likely, probable.

verity [ver′i-ti] *n* the quality of being true or real.

verjuice [vûr′jōōs] *n* the sour juice of unripe fruit.

vermicelli [ver-mi-sel′i, or -chel′i] *n* a pasta like spaghetti, but in thinner strings.

vermicide [vûr′mi-sīd] *n* an agent that destroys worms. —*adj* ver′miform, having the form of a worm.

vermilion [vèr-mil′yón] *n* a bright red pigment; any beautiful red color.

vermin [vûr′min] *n* (*collectively*) loathsome parasites; any contemptible and obnoxious person or persons. —*adj* ver′minous.

vermouth [vûr′-mōōth] *n* a fortified white wine flavored with herbs, used in cocktails and as an aperitif.

vernacular [vèr-nak′ū-lår] *adj* native, belonging to the country of one's birth.

vernal [vûr′nål] *adj* belonging to the spring.

vernier [vèr′ni-èr] *n* a contrivance consisting of a short scale made to slide along a graduated instrument and measure very small intervals.

versatile [vûr′sa-til] *adj* capable of moving or turning freely; changeable. —*n* versatil′ity.

verse [vûrs] *n* a line of poetry; metrical arrangement and language; poetry; versificā′tion, the act, art or practice of composing metrical verses. —*vi* ver′sify, to make verses. —*vt* to relate in verse; to turn into verse.

versed [vûrst] *adj* skilled or learned on a subject.

verso [vûr′sō] *n* a left-hand page.

versus [vûr′sùs] *prep* against; in contrast to.

vertebra [vûr′te-bra] *n* one of the segmented portions of the spinal column. —*n* ver′tebrāte, an animal with a backbone.

vertex [vûr′teks] *n* the top or summit; the point of a cone, pyramid, or angle. —*pl* **vertices**. —*adj* ver′tical, perpendicular to the plane of the horizon; straight up and down. —*n* a vertical line.

vertigo [vûr′ti-gō] *n* a sensation of giddiness, dizziness. —*adj* vertig′inous.

vervain [vûr′vān] *n* any of several plants of the genus *Verbena*, esp one with small spicate flowers.

verve [vûrv] *n* the enthusiasm that animates a poet or artist; animation, energy.

very [ver′i] *adj* complete; absolute; same. —*adv* extremely; truly; really.

Very light [ver′i līt] *n* a small colored flare fired from a pistol—used for signaling.

vesical [ve-sī′kal] *adj* of or relating to a bladder and esp the urinary bladder. —*n* vesicā′tion, a blister. —*adjs* vesic′ular.

vessel [ves′èl] *n* a vase or utensil for holding something, a ship or boat.

vest [vest] *n* a short, sleeveless garment, esp one worn under a suit coat by men. —*vt* to clothe; to invest. —*vi* to become vested as property.

Vesta [ves′ta] *n* the Roman goddess of the hearth. —*n* ves′ta, a short wooden match.

vestibule [ves′ti-būl] *n* formerly an open court before a house; a hall next to the entrance to a building.

vestige [ves′tij] *n* a track or footprint; a trace.

vetch [vech] *n* a genus of plants, mostly climbing, some cultivated for fodder, esp a tare.

veteran [vet′é-rån] *adj* old, experienced, long exercised, esp in military life; pertaining to a veteran.

veterinary [vet′e-ri-nå-rij] *adj* pertaining to the art of treating the diseases of animals; a veterinarian.

veto [vē′tō] *n* any authoritative prohibition; the power of rejecting or forbidding, specif, the right of one branch of a government to reject bills passed by another.

vex [veks] *vt* to annoy; to pain, grieve. —*n* vexā′tion.

viable [vī′å-bl] *adj* capable of living; capable of growing or developing.

viaduct [vī′a-dukt] *n* a road or railroad carried by a structure over a valley, river, etc.

vial [vī′al] *n* a small vessel or bottle for liquids.

viand [vī′ånd] *n* an article of food.

vibrate [vi′brāt] *vi* to shake; to move, swing, backwards and forwards, to oscillate. —*vt* to cause to shake; to move to and fro. —*adj* vī′brant. —*ns* vibrā′tion. —*adj* vī′bratory.

vicar [vik′år] *n* a parish priest; a bishop's assistant. —*ns* vic′arage, the benefice, or residence, of a vicar. —*adjs* vicā′rial. —*adj* vicā′rious, filling the place of another.

vice [vīs] *n* an evil action or habit, a blemish or fault. —*adj* vicious. —*adv* vic′iously.

vice- [vīs-] *prefix* forming compounds denoting one who acts in place of, or ranks second to, another.

vicinage [vis′i-nij] *n* neighborhood; the places near. —*n* **vicin′ity**, a nearby area; proximity; nearness.

vicissitudes [vi-sisi-tūds] *n pl* ups and downs; successive changes of fortune.

victim [vik′tim] *n* a living creature offered as a sacrifice; anyone who incurs loss or harm; a dupe. —*vt* vic′timize, to make a victim. —*n* victimīzā′tion.

victor [vik′tὸr] *n* one who conquers in battle or other contest, a winner. —*adjs* vic′tor, victō′rious. —*adv* victō′riously.

victual [vit′l] *n* food usable by man. —*vt* to supply with food. —*vi* to eat; to lay in provisions.

video [vid′i-ō] *adj* pertaining to television; of the picture portion of a television broadcast. —*n* television; videocassette; videotape or other clipped forms. —**vid′eotape′**, a magnetic tape on which images and sounds can be recorded for reproduction on TV.

vie [vī] *vi* to strive for superiority.

view [vū] *n* sight; reach of the sight; whole extent seen; direction in which a thing is seen; scene, natural prospect. —*vt* to see; examine intellectually. —*adj* view′less, invisible; having no view.

vigil [vij′il] *n* watching; keeping awake for religious exercises. —*n* vig′ilance. —*adj* vig′ilant.

vignette [vin-yet′] *n* any small ornamental engraving, design, or photograph, not enclosed by a definite border; an ornamental flourish of vine leaves and tendrils on manuscripts and books.

vigor [vig′ὸr] *n* active strength, physical force; vital strength in animals or plants; energy. —*adj* vig′orous. —*adv* vig′orously.

Viking [vī′king, also vik′ing], *n* one of the Norse invaders in the 8th, 9th, and 10th centuries.

vile [vīl] *adj* worthless, mean; morally impure, very bad. —*vt* vil′ify [vil′-], to make vile; to slander.

villa [vil′a] *n* a country residence or retreat. —*ns* vill′age [-ij], any small assemblage of houses, less than a town; vill′ager, an inhabitant of a village.

villein [vil′ån] *n* an English serf in the late Middle Ages.

vim [vim] *n* energy, force.

vinaigrette [vin-ā-gret′] *n* a mixture of oil, vinegar and seasoning used as a salad dressing.

vindicate [vin′di-kāt] *vt* to justify, to defend with success; to clear from blame. —*n* vindicā′tion, defence; justification. —*adj* vin′dicative. —*n* vin′dicātor.

vine [vīn] *n* any climbing or trailing plant, or its stem; a grape. —*ns* vī′nery, an area or building in which vines are grown; vineyard, a plantation of grapevines.

vinegar [vin′e-gàr] *n* a liquor containing acetic acid, made by fermentation from malt, or from fruit juices.

vintage [vin′tij] *n* the produce of grapes, or of wine, for one season; wine, esp of good quality; a wine of a particular season or region.

vintner [vint′nèr] *n* a wine merchant.

viol [vī′ol] *n* a musical instrument which was the immediate precursor of the violin.

viola[1] [vē-ō′la, vi′ō-la] *n* a stringed instrument of the violin family, and tuned a fifth below it.

viola[2] [vī′ō-la] *n* the genus of plants of which the pansy is a species.

violate [vī′ō-lāt] *vt* to profane, treat with disrespect; to break, to transgress; to abuse; to rape, ravish. —*n* violā′tion.

violent [vī′ō-lènt] *adj* acting with, or characterized by, physical force or strength; moved by strong feeling; passionate; intense. —*n* vī′olence. —*adv* vī′olently.

violet [vī′ō-let] *n* any plant of genus, of many species, with a flower, generally blue.

violin [vī-ō-lin′ or vī′-] *n* any instrument of the modern family of four-stringed instruments.

violoncello [vē-ō-lon-chel′ō] *n* a large four-stringed instrument of the violin family.

viper [vī′pèr] *n* common European venomous snake.

virago [vi-rā′gō] *n* a masculine woman.

virgin [vûr′jin] *n* a maiden, a woman who has had no sexual intercourse; Virgo [vûr′gō] the Virgin, the 6th sign of the zodiac.

virginal [vûr′jin-ål] *n* one of the three forms of harpsichord.

viridity [vi-rid′i-ti] *n* greenness; freshness.

virile [vir′īl] *adj* having the qualities of, or belonging to, a man or to the male sex; of a man, sexually potent. —*n* viril′ity.

virtu [vûr′tōō] *n* a love of the fine arts; taste for curiosities; objects of art of antiquity.

virtue [vûr′tū] *n* worth; moral excellence; the practice of duty; inherent power, efficacy. —*adj* vir′tual, in effect, though not in fact or strict definition. —*adv* vir′tually. —*adj* vir′tuous. —*adv* vir′tuously.

virulent [vir′ū-lent] *adj* full of poison; very active in injury; deadly. —*ns* vir′ulency. —*adv* vir′ulently.

virus [vī′rus] *n* a transmissible disorder of computer function; a harmful influence.

visa [vēz′a] *n* an endorsement on a passport denoting that it has been officially examined.

visage [viz′ij] *n* the face or look. —*adj* vis′aged.

viscera [vis′e-ra] *n pl* the inner parts of the animal body, the entrails.

viscount [vī′kownt] *n* an officer who formerly acted as deputy to an earl; a title of nobility next below an earl.

viscous [vis′kūs] *adj* sticky, tenacious. —*n* viscos′ity. —*adj* viscid.

visible [viz′i-bl] *adj* that may be seen; obvious. —*ns* visibil′ity, clearness of the atmosphere.

vision [vizh′(ὸ)n] *n* the act or sense of seeing, sight; anything seen; a supernatural appearance, an apparition. —*adj* vis′ionary, affected by visions; imaginative; unpractical; existing in imagination only, not real.

visit [viz′it] *vt* to go to see or inspect; to pay a call upon. —*n* act of going to see. —*adj* vis′itant. —*n* a visitor. —*ns* visitā′tion, a formal visit by a superior; vis′itor, one who visits, calls on.

visor [vīz′ὸr] *n* a part of a helmet covering the face, movable.

vista [vis′ta] *n* a view or prospect through trees.

vital [vī′tàl] *adj* contributing to, or necessary to, life; manifesting or containing life. —*vt* vī′talīze, to make alive, to give life to. —*adv* vī′tally.

vitamin [vīt′a-min] *n* organic substance, present in minute quantities in nutritive foods, which is essential for the health of the animal organism.

vitiate [vish′i-āt] *vt* to render faulty or defective; to make less pure, to deprave, to taint. —*n* vitiā′tion.

vitreous [vit′ri-ūs] *adj* glassy. —*vt* vit′rify, to make into glass. —*vi* to become glass. —*n* vitrificā′tion.

vitriol [vit′ri-ōl] *n* sulfuric acid. —*adj* vitriol′ic.

vituperate [vī-tū′pè-rāt or vi-] *vt* to assail with abusive reproaches, revile. —*vi* to use abusive language. —*n* vitūperā′tion. —*adj* vitū′perātive.

vivacious [vi-vā′shùs (or vī-)] *adj* lively or full of vitality, sportive. —*ns* vivacity.

vivarium [vī-vā′ri-úm] *n* an artificial enclosure for keeping or raising living animals indoors.

vivid [viv′id] *adj* lively or lifelike, forming brilliant images; striking; intense. —*adv* viv′idly.

viviparous [vī-vip′a-rus] *adj* producing young alive.

vivisection [viv-i-sek′sh(ὸ)n] *n* the practice of performing surgical operations on living animals.

vixen [vik′sn] *n* a female fox; an ill-tempered woman.

vizier [vi-zēr′, viz′i-èr] *n* an oriental minister or councillor of state.

vocal [vō′kàl] *adj* having a voice; talkative; having a vowel function. —*vt* vō′calize, to give utterance to. —*ns* vō′calist, a vocal musician, a singer. —*adv* vō′cally.

vocation [vō-kā′sh(ὸ)n] *n* call or act of calling; talent; calling, occupation.

vociferate [vō-sif′e-rāt] *vi* to cry with a loud voice. —*adj* vocif′erous. —*adv* vocif′erously.

vodka [vod′ka] *n* a Russian spirit distilled from rye.

vogue [vōg] *n* the prevalent mode or fashion.

voice [vois] *n* sound from the mouth; sound given out by anything; medium of expression; expressed opinion, vote. —*vt* to give utterance to; to regulate the tone of (organ pipes); voice′less.

void [void] *adj* unoccupied, empty. —*n* an empty space. —*vt* to make vacant.

voile [voil] *n* a thin semi-transparent dress material.

volant [vō′lànt] *adj* flying, able to fly; nimble. —*adj* vōl′atile, evaporating very quickly.

volcano [vol-kā′no] *n* a hill or mountain formed by ejection of lava, ashes, etc. through an opening in the earth's crust. —*adj* volcan′ic.

vole [vōl] *n* any of various small rodents.

volition [vō-li′sh(ὸ)n] *n* act of willing or choosing, the exercise of the will; the power of determining.

volley [vol′i] *n* the discharge of many missiles or small arms at once; a vehement outburst; in tennis and volleyball, the flight of the ball before it reaches the ground. —*vt* to return (a ball) before it bounces.—*n* **volleyball**, a team game played by volleying a large inflated ball over a net; the ball used.

volt[1] [vōlt] *n* (*fencing*) a sudden movement or leap to avoid a thrust.

volt[2] [vōlt] *n* the unit of electromotive force.—*n* **vōl'tage**, potential difference reckoned in volts.

voluble [vol'ū-bl] *adj* overwhelmingly fluent in speech.—*n* **volubil'ity**.—*adv* **vol'ubly**.

volume [vol'ūm] *n* a roll or scroll of papyrus or the like, on which ancient books were written; any book; cubical content; dimensions.

voluntary [vol'un-tà-ri] *adj* acting by choice; proceeding from the will; brought about by, free action.—*n* a piece of music to be played at will on a church organ.—*adv* **vol'untarily**.

volunteer [vol-un-tēr'] *n* one who enters any service, or undertakes any task, esp military, voluntarily.

voluptuary [vo-lup'tū-à-ri] *n* a person excessively given to bodily enjoyments or luxury, a sensualist.—*adj* **volup'tuous**.

volute [vo-lūt'] *n* in Greek architecture, a spiral scroll in capitals; a kind of spiral shell, chiefly tropical; whorl of a spiral shell.—*adj* **volū'ted, volū'tion**.

vomit [vom'it] *vi* to throw up the contents of the stomach by the mouth, to spew.—*vt* to throw out with violence.—*n* matter ejected from the stomach.

voodoo [vōō'dōō] *n* a primitive religion in the West Indies, based on a belief in sorcery, etc.

voracious [vo-rā'shus] *adj* eager to devour; very greedy.—*adv* **vorā'ciously**.—*n* **vorac'ity** [-as'].

vortex [vor'teks] *n* a whirlpool; a whirlwind.—*pl* **vor'tices**.

votary [vō'tà-ri] *adj* bound or consecrated by a vow.—*n* one devoted as by a vow to some service.

vote [vōt] *n* expression of a wish or opinion as to a matter on which one has a right to be consulted; decision by a majority; something granted by the will of the majority.—*vi* to express choice by a vote.—*vt* to grant by a vote.

vouch [vowch] *vt* to maintain by repeated affirmations, to warrant.—*vi* to bear witness (for), answer (for).—*n* **vouch'er**, a paper that vouches or confirms the truth of anything, as of accounts.

vouchsafe [vowch-sāf'] *vt* to condescend (to).

vow [vow] *n* a voluntary promise solemnly made to God; a solemn or formal promise.—*vt* to give by solemn promise.

vowel [vow'èl] *n* a simple vocal sound produced by continuous passage of the breath; a letter representing such a sound, as *a, e, i, o, u.*

voyage [voi'ij] *n* a journey, esp a passage by water or by air.—*vi* to make a voyage.—*n* **voy'ager**.

vulcanize [vul'kan-īz] *vt* to convert latex to rubber by heating with sulfur.—*n* **vul'canite**.

vulgar [vul'gàr] *adj* pertaining to the common people; public; common, usual; coarse.—*vt* **vul'garize**, to make vulgar.—*ns* **vul'garism**, a vulgar phrase; coarseness; **vulgar'ity**.—*adv* **vul'garly**.

vulnerable [vul'nè-ra-bl] *adj* capable of being wounded, liable to injury or hurt; exposed to attack.—*ns* **vulnerabil'ity**.

vulpine [vul'pīn] *adj* relating to or like the fox; cunning.

vulture [vul'-chùr] *n* any of a number of large birds of prey, temperate and tropical, allied to the hawks and eagles.

W

wad [wod] *n* a small, soft mass, as of cotton or paper; a disk of felt or paper, to keep the charge in a gun; a bundle of paper money.—*vt* to pad, stuff out; to stuff a wad into.—*n* **wadd'ing**, any soft material for use in padding, packing, etc.

waddle [wod'l] *vi* to take short steps and move from side to side in walking.

wade [wād] *vi* to walk through any substance that yields to the feet, as water; to pass (through) with difficulty or labor.—*n* **wa'der**, a bird that wades, eg the heron.

wadi [wod'i] *n* the dry bed of a torrent.

wafer [wā'fèr] *n* a thin crisp cracker or cookie; any small, thin, flat disklike thing.

waffle [wof'l] *n* a kind of batter cake cooked in a **waff'le iron**.

waft [wäft] *vt* to bear lightly through a fluid medium, as air or

water.—*n* a breath, puff, slight odor or sound carried through the air.

wag[1] [wag] *vti* to move from side to side, to shake to and fro up and down.

wag[2] [wag] *n* a droll, mischievous fellow, a habitual joker, a wit.—*n* **wagg'ery**.

wage [wāj] *vt* (*arch*) to pledge; to carry on.—*n* payment for work, wages.—*n* **wā'ger**, (*arch*) a pledge; a bet.

waggle [wag'l] *vti* to wag.

wagon [wag'òn] *n* a four-wheeled vehicle for carrying heavy goods.—*ns* **wag'oner, wagonette'**, a kind of open carriage.

waif [wāf] *n* anything found astray without an owner; a homeless wanderer, esp a child.

wail [wāl] *vi* to lament or sorrow audibly.

wain [wān] *n* a wagon esp a heavy one for farm use.

wainscot [wān'skòt] *n* a wooden lining, usu. paneled, applied to the walls of rooms.—*vt* to line with, or as if with, boards or panels.

waist [wāst] *n* the smallest part of the human trunk, between the ribs and the hips; the narrow part of anything that is widest at the ends.—*ns* **waist'coat**, a short coat, usu. sleeveless worn immediately under the coat.

wait [wāt] *vi* to stay, or to be, in expectation; to tarry remain.—*vt* to stay for, to await.—*n* act or period of wait ing.—*ns* **wait'er**, one who waits, esp a man who serves a table.

waive [wāv] *vt* to give up, not insist upon; to relinquish voluntarily.

wake[1] [wāk] *vi* to cease from sleep; to be awake.—*vt* to rouse from sleep; to revive.—*n* act of waking; a watch or vigi beside a corpse, sometimes with revelry.—*adj* **wake'ful**.—*vt* **wā'ken**.

wake[2] [wāk] *n* the streak of smooth or foamy water left in the track of a ship.

wale [wāl] *n* a welt raised by a whip, etc.; a ridge on the surface of cloth.—*vt* to mark with welts.

walk [wök] *vi* to move along on foot with alternate steps; to travel on foot; to follow a certain course.—*vt* to pass through or upon.—*n* act of walking; gait; distance walked over.—*n* **walk'er; walk'way**, road, path, etc., constructed for pedestrians only.

wall [wöl] *n* an erection of brick, stone, etc. for enclosing dividing or protecting.—*vt* to enclose with, or as with, a wall to close up with a wall.—*ns* **wall'flower**, a plant with fragran flowers, yellow when wild, found on old walls.

wallaby [wol'ab-i] *n* any of various small kangaroos.

wallah [wol'a] *n* one who occupies an eminent position in an organization, etc.

wallet [wol'èt] *n* a flat pocketbook for paper money, cards etc.]

walleye [wöl'-ī].—*adj* **wall'-eyed**, very light grey in the eyes esp of horses; having a blank or staring appearance or glaring eyes.

wallop [wol'op] *vt* (*inf*) to beat or defeat soundly.

wallow [wol'ō] *vi* to roll about in mud, etc., as an animal; to indulge oneself fully.—*n* a wallowing.

walnut [wöl'nut] *n* a genus of beautiful trees, its nut or fruit.

walrus [wöl'rus or wol'-] *n* a large aquatic animal, allied to the seals, having long canine teeth.

waltz [wöl(t)s] *n* a whirling or slowly circling dance.—*vi* to dance a waltz.

wampum [wom'pum] *n* the American Indian name for shel beads used as money.

wan [won] *adj* lacking color, pale and sickly; feeble or weak.—*adv* **wan'ly**.—*n* **wan'ness**.

wand [wond] *n* a rod of authority, or of conjurers.

wander [won'dèr] *vi* to ramble with no definite object; to depart from the subject; to be delirious; to lose one's way.

wanderlust [vän'der-lōōst, won'dèr-lust] *n* a craving for change of place, thirst for travel.

wane [wān] *vi* to decrease, esp of the moon; to decline, to fail.—*n* decline, decrease.

wangle [wang'gl] (*inf*) *vti* to achieve (something) by trickery.

want [wont] *n* state of privation; lack of what is needful o desired; poverty; scarcity.

wanton [won'tòn] *adj* sportive; licentious; wilful; running to excess, or unrestrained (eg of vegetation).—*n* a wanton or lewd person.

wapiti [wop′i-ti] *n* the N American elk.

war [wör] *n* a state of opposition or contest; a contest between states carried on by arms.—*vi* to make war.—*ns* war′fare, armed contest, hostilities.—*adj* war′like, fond of war.—*ns* warmonger [wör′-mung-gèr], one who encourages war, esp for personal gain; warr′ior, a veteran soldier.

warble [wör′bl] *vi* to sing in a quavering way, or with variations; to sing sweetly as birds do.—*n* war′bler.

ward [wörd] *vt* to guard or take care of.—*n* act of warding; state of being guarded; one who is under a guardian; a division of a city, town, jail or hospital, etc.—*ns* ward′en, the chief official of a prison; ward′robe, a cupboard or piece of furniture for clothes; ward′ship.

ware[1] [wār] *n* (*pl*) merchandise, commodities, goods for sale; pottery.—*n* ware′house, a building for wares or goods.

ware[2] [wār] *adj* aware.

warlock [wör′lok] *n* a sorcerer, a wizard.

warm [wörm] *adj* having moderate heat, hot; excited; angry.—*vt* to make warm.—*vi* to become warm or ardent.—*adv* warm′ly.—*ns* warmth.

warn [wörn] *vt* to give notice of danger to; to caution (against).—*ns* war′ning.

warp [wörp] *vt* to twist out of shape; to pervert.—*vi* to be twisted out of the straight.—*n* the threads stretched out lengthwise in a loom to be crossed by a weft or woof.

warrant [wor′ânt] *vt* to guarantee; to justify.—*n* that which warrants or authorizes, esp a document; warr′anty, a pledge to replace something if it is not as represented.

warren [wor′èn] *n* an area in which rabbits breed.

wart [wört] *n* a small, hard excrescence on the skin; a small protuberance.—*adj* wart′y

wary [wā′ri] *adj* warding or guarding against deception, etc.; cautious.—*adv* wā′rily.—*n* wā′riness.

wash [wosh] *vt* to cleanse with water or other liquid; to cover with a thin coat of metal or paint; in mining, to separate from earth by means of water.—*vi* to be engaged in cleansing with water.—*n* a washing; the break of waves on the shore; the rough water left behind by a boat; wash′er, a flat ring of metal, rubber, etc., to keep joints or nuts secure.

wasp [wosp] *n* any of a large number of winged insects.—*adj* was′pish, like a wasp; spiteful.

wassail [wos′(ā)l] *n* festive occasion; a drunken bout.—*vi* to hold a wassail or merry drinking meeting.

waste [wāst] *adj* empty, desert, desolate; uncultivated or uninhabited.—*vt* to lay waste or make desolate; to squander; to impair.—*vi* to lose strength, etc. as by disease.—*n* act of wasting.—*n* was′tage.—*adj* waste′ful.—*adv* waste′fully.—*ns* waste′fulness.

watch [woch] *n* act of looking out; close observation; guard; a small timepiece for carrying in a pocket, wearing on the wrist, etc.—*vi* to look with attention; to be awake, to keep vigil.—*vt* to keep one's eyes fixed on; to observe closely.—*n* watch′er.—*adj* watch′ful.—*adv* watch′fully.—*ns* watch′fulness; watch′māk′er, one who makes and repairs watches.

water [wö′tèr] *n* the substance H₂O, a clear transparent liquid, devoid of taste or smell; any body of it, as the ocean, a lake, river, etc.—*vt* to wet, overflow, or supply with water; to dilute with water.—*vi* to shed water; to take in water.—*ns* wa′tercress, a plant growing in watery places, esteemed as a salad; wa′terfall, a fall or perpendicular descent of a stream of water; wa′ter glass, a silicate of sodium or potassium, dissolved in water to form a syrupy liquid used as a preservative for eggs, etc.—*adj* wa′terlogged, soaked or filled with water so as to be heavy and sluggish.—*ns* wa′termark, a mark showing the height to which water has risen; a mark in paper produced by the impression of a design, as in the mold.—*adj* wa′tertight, so tight as not to let water pass through; completely separate.

watt [wot] *n* a unit of electrical power.

wattle [wot′l] *n* a twig or flexible rod; a hurdle.—*vt* to bind with wattles or twigs.

wave [wāv] *n* a surge traveling on the surface of water; a line or streak like a wave; an undulation.—*vi* to move like a wave; to move backward and forward; to flutter, as a signal; to undu-late; to move the raised hand in greeting, farewell, etc.—*vt* to move backward and forward, to brandish, to flourish.

wax[1] [waks] *n* beeswax; this substance used to make candles, etc.—*vt* to rub, polish, cover or treat with wax.—*ns* wax′-work, work made of wax, esp figures or models formed of wax.

wax[2] [waks] *vi* to increase in strength, size, etc.

way[1] [wā] *n* passage; road; length of space, distance; room to advance; direction; means; manner of living; way′farer, a traveler or passenger, esp on foot.—*vt* way′lay, to watch or lie in ambush for.—*adj* way′ward, wilful, capricious; perverse.—*n* way′wardness.

we [wē] *pron pl* of I; I and others.

weak [wēk] *adj* wanting strength; not able to sustain a great weight; easily overcome or subdued.—*vt* weak′en, to make weak; to reduce in strength or spirit.—*vi* to grow weak or weaker.—*adv* weak′ly.—*n* weak′ness.

weal[1] [wēl] *n* (*arch*) state of being well.

weal[2] [wēl] *n* a raised streak left by a blow with a lash, etc; welt.

weald [wēld] *n* a heavily wooded area; a wild or uncultivated, usu. upland, region.

wealth [welth] *n* possessions of any kind; riches; an abundance (of).—*adj* wealth′y.

wean [wēn] *vt* to accustom to nourishment other than the mother's milk; to estrange the affections of.

weapon [wep′ón] *n* any instrument or means of offense or defense.

wear [wār] *vt* to carry on the body; to exhaust, tire.—*vi* to be wasted by use or time; to be spent tediously.—*n* act of wearing; lessening or injury by use or friction; articles worn.

weary [wē′ri] *adj* tired, tedious.—*vt* to wear out or make weary.—*vi* to become weary or impatient.—*n* wea′riness.—*adj* wea′risome.

weasel [wē′zl] *n* a genus of small carnivores with long slender body.

weather [weTH′èr] *n* atmospheric conditions as to heat or cold, wetness, cloudiness, etc.—*vt* to affect by exposing to the air; to sail to the windward of; to come safely through.—*ns* weather′cock, a weather vane in the form of a cock to show the direction of the wind.

weave[1] [wēv] *vt* twine threads together; to interlace threads in a loom to form cloth.—*vi* to practice weaving.—*ns* weav′er.

weave[2] [wēv] *vi* to move to and fro, or in and out.

web [web] *n* that which is woven; the fine texture spun by the spider; the membrane joining the digits of various water birds, animals, etc.

wed [wed] *vt* to marry; to unite closely.—*vi* to marry.—*ns* wedd′ing, marriage.

wedge [wej] *n* a piece of wood or metal, thick at one end and sloping to a thin edge at the other.—*vt* to fasten, or to fix, with a wedge or wedges; to press, thrust (in), tightly.

wedlock [wed′lok] *n* matrimony; married state.

Wednesday [wenz′dā] *n* fourth day of the week.

wee [wē] *adj* small, tiny, very early.

weed[1] [wēd] *n* any undesired plant, esp one that crowds out desired plants.—*vt* to remove anything troublesome or useless.—*vi* to remove weeds.—*adj* weed′y.

weed[2] [wēd] *n* (used in *pl*) a widow's mourning apparel.

week [wēk] *n* the space of seven days, esp from Sunday to Sunday.—*adj* week′ly, coming, happening, or done once a week.

weep [wēp] *vi* to express grief by shedding tears.—*vt* to lament.—*adj* weep′ing.

weevil [wēv′il] *n* one of a group of beetles having an elongated snout.

weft [weft] *n* the threads woven into and crossing the warp.—Also woof.

weigh [wā] *vt* to find the heaviness of.—*vi* to have weight; to be considered of importance.—*n* weight, the heaviness of a thing when weighed, or the amount which anything weighs.—*vt* to attach or add a weight or weights to.—*n* weight′lessness, the condition where little or no reaction to the force due to gravity is experienced.—*adj* weigh′ty, heavy; important.—*adv* weigh′tily.

weir [wēr] *n* a dam across a river.

weird [wērd] *n* fate; that which comes to pass.—*adj* skilled in witchcraft; unearthly, mysterious.

welcome [wel′kóm] *adj* received with gladness. —*n* (kindly) reception. —*vt* to receive with kindness.

weld [weld] *vt* to join together, as metal by heating until fused or soft enough to hammer together; to join closely. —*n* a welded joint.

welfare [wel′fãr] *n* state of faring or doing well; those government agencies which grant aid to the poor, the unemployed, etc.

welkin [wel′kin] *n* (*arch*) the sky or region of clouds.

well[1] [wel] *n* a spring; a source; a lined shaft made in the earth whence a supply of water, oil, etc., is obtained. —*vi* to issue forth.

well[2] [wel] *adj comparative* **bett′er**, *superlative* **best**; fortunate; comfortable; in health. —*adv* in a proper, satisfactory, or excellent manner; thoroughly; prosperously; with good reason; to a considerable degree; definitely; familiarly. —*interj* expressing surprise, etc. —*n* **well′-bē′ing**, state of being well, welfare, **well′-bred**, of polished manners; of good stock; **well′-fāv′ored**, good-looking; handsome. —*adv* **well′-nigh**, nearly, almost. —*adjs* **well′-off**, in good circumstances; prosperous; **well′-to-do**, prosperous.

Welsh [welsh] *adj* pertaining to *Wales*, or its inhabitants.

welsh [welsh] *vi* (*slang*) to fail to pay a debt, fulfill an obligation, etc. (*often with on*). —*n* **welsh′er**.

welt [welt] *n* a band or strip fastened to an edge to give strength or for ornament; a narrow strip of leather used in one method of sewing the upper to the sole of a shoe.

welter [wel′tér] *vi* to roll or wallow, esp in dirt. —*n* a turmoil.

wen [wen] *n* a benign skin tumor, most commonly on the scalp.

wench [wench] *n* a derogatory term for a girl.

wend [wend] *vi* to go, to wind or turn.

went [went] *pt* of **go**.

werewolf [wēr′wŏŏlf] *n* a person supposed to be able to change himself for a time into a wolf.

west [west] *n* the quarter where the sun sets; one of the four chief points of the compass; the region in the west of any country. —*adj* situated toward, or coming from, the west. —*adv* in or toward the west. —*adj, adv* **wes′terly**. —*adj* **wes′t-ern**. —*adj, adv* **west′ward**.

wet [wet] *adj* covered or saturated with water or other liquid; rainy; misty; not yet dry. —*n* water or other liquid; rain or rainy weather. —*vti* to make or become wet; **wet nurse**, a nurse who suckles a child for its mother.

wether [weTH′ér] *n* a male sheep castrated.

whack [hwak] *vti* (*inf*) to strike smartly, esp making a sound. —*n* (*inf*) a blow; a stroke.

whale [hwāl] *n* any of numerous cetaceous mammals, esp the larger kinds. —*ns* **whale′-bone**, a light flexible substance from the upper jaw of certain whales; **whaler**, a ship or a person employed in whaling.

wharf [hwórf] *n* a landing stage, for loading and unloading ships. —*ns* **wharf′age**, the dues paid for using a wharf; accommodation at a wharf.

what [hwot] *interrog pron* neuter of **who**—also used elliptically and as an interjection of astonishment. —*interrog adj* of what sort, how much, how great. —*rel pron* that which.

wheat [hwēt] *n* a cereal grass, the grain furnishing a nutritious flour for bread.

wheatear [hwēt′ēr] *n* a small white-rumped northern bird.

wheedle [hwēd′l] *vt* to entice by soft words, flatter, cajole (into); to coax.

wheel [hwēl] *n* a circular frame turning on an axle; *vt* to cause to whirl; to convey on wheels. —*vi* to turn round or on an axis; to be provided with wheels on which to be propelled; to change direction. —*ns* **wheelbarrow**, a barrow with one wheel in front and two handles and legs behind; **wheel′wright**, one who makes and repairs wheels and wheeled vehicles.

wheeze [hwēz] *vi* to breathe with a hissing sound; to breathe audibly or with difficulty.

whelk [hwelk] *n* any of numerous edible mollusks.

whelm [hwelm] *vt* to cover completely, to submerge; to overpower.

whelp [hwelp] *n* the young of the dog and of lions, etc. —a puppy, a cub.

when [hwen] *adv, conj* at what time? at which time? at or after the time that; while; even though.

where [hwār] *adv, conj* at which place; at what place? to which

place; to what place?—**whereof′**, of which; of what; of whom; **whereon′**, on which; **wheresoev′er**, in or to what place soever; **wherewithal′**, with which; with what?

wherry [hwer′i] *n* a racing scull for one person; a light rowboat.

whet [hwet] *vt* to sharpen by rubbing; to make keen.

whether [hweTH′ér] *conj* introducing the first of two alternative words, phrases, clauses, the second being introduced by *or*.

whey [hwā] *n* the watery part of milk, separated from the curd, esp in making cheese.

which [hwich] *interrog pron* what one of a number?—also used adjectivally.

whiff [hwif] *n* a sudden puff of air or smoke from the mouth; a slight blast.

while [hwīl] *n* space of time. —*conj* during the time that; at the same time that; although. —*vt* to cause to pass without irksomeness.

whim [hwim] *n* a caprice, a fancy. —*adj* **whim′sical**, full of whims, odd, fantastical. —*ns* **whimsical′ity**.

whimper [hwim′pér] *vi* to cry with a low, whining voice. —*n* a peevish cry.

whin [hwin] *n* gorse, furze. —*adj* **whinn′y**.

whine [hwīn] *vi* to utter a plaintive cry; to complain in an unmanly way. —*n* a plaintive cry.

whinny [hwin′i] *vi* to neigh.

whip [hwip] *n* a flexible lash with a handle for punishing or driving. —*vt* to move, pull, throw, etc. suddenly; to strike, as with a lash. —*vi* to move nimbly; to flap about. —*ns* **whip′cord**, cord for making whips; a strong worsted material with ribs; **whip′ hand**, control or advantage; **whipp′ersnapp′er**, a pretentious but insignificant person.

whippet [hwip′et] *n* a small dog like a greyhound.

whir, whirr [hwûr] *n* a sound from rapid whirling. —*vti* to whirl round with a noise.

whirl [hwûrl] *n* a turning with rapidity; anything that turns with velocity. —*vi* to revolve rapidly. —*vt* to turn (round) rapidly. —*ns* **whirl′igig**, a child's toy which is spun or whirled rapidly round; **whirl′pool**, a circular current in a river or sea; **whirl′wind**, a violent aerial current, with a whirling, rotary, or spiral motion.

whisk [hwisk] *vt* to move with a quick motion; to sweep, or stir, rapidly. —*vi* to move nimbly and rapidly. —*n* a rapid sweeping motion; a brushing with such a motion. —*n* **whis′ker**, (*pl*) the hair growing on a man's face, esp the cheeks.

whiskey [hwis′ki] *n* a strong alcoholic beverage distilled from grain.

whisper [hwis′pér] *vi* to speak with a low sound. —*vt* to utter in a low voice or under the breath, or covertly, or by way of gossip. —*n* a low hissing voice or sound.

whist [hwist] *n* a card game.

whistle [hwis′l] *vi* to make a sound by forcing the breath through the lips or teeth. —*vt* to form or utter by whistling; to call by a whistle. —*n* the sound made in whistling.

whit [hwit] *n* the smallest particle imaginable; a bit.

white [hwīt] *adj* of the color of milk or pure salt; stainless; pure; bright; light-colored. —*n* the color of anything white. —*vt* to make white. —*vti* **whit′en**. —*adj* **whit′ish**, somewhat white. —*ns* **white ant**, a termite; **white′bait**, the fry of the herring and sprat. —*ns* **white elephant**, an albino elephant, held as sacred in southeast Asia; a thing of little use; **White House**, official residence of the President of the US in Washington, DC. —*adj* **white′-livered**, cowardly. —*ns* **white slave**, a woman forced into prostitution for others' profit; **white′-wash**, a mixture of whiting or lime and water, used for whitening walls and as a disinfectant.

whither [hwiTH′ér] *adv* to what place? to which place; to what. —*adv* **whithersoev′er**, to whatever place.

whitlow [hwit′lō] *n* a painful inflammation of a finger or toe, esp near the nail, tending to suppurate.

whittle [hwit′l] *vt* to pare or cut thin shavings from (wood) with a knife; to shape with a knife.

whiz, whizz [hwiz] *vi* to make a hissing sound, like an arrow or ball flying through the air.

who [hŏŏ] *pron* (both *rel* and *interrog*) what person? which person. —*pron* **whoev′er**, every one who.

whole [hōl] *adj* not broken, unimpaired; containing the total amount, number, etc.; all complete; *n* the entire amount; a thing complete in itself. —*ns* **whole′ness, whole′sāle**, selling of goods, usu. at lower prices and in quantity, to a retailer.—*adj* **whole'some**, healthy; sound; salutary.—*adv* **whole'-somely**.—*adv* **wholly**.

whoop [hwōōp] *n* a loud eager cry; the long noisy inspiration heard in whooping cough; **whoop'ing cough**, an infectious and epidemic disease, esp of children, causing a convulsive cough.

whore [hōr] *n* a prostitute; any unchaste woman.

whorl [hwôrl, hwûrl] *n* a number of leaves in a circle round the stem; a turn in a spiral shell.

whortleberry [hwûr'tl-ber-i] *n* a European heath plant with a dark blue edible berry, called also the **bilberry**.

whose [hōōz] *pron* the possessive case of **who** or **which**.—*pron* **whosesoev'er**.

why [hwī] *adv*, *conj* for what cause or reason (?).

wick [wik] *n* the twisted threads of cotton or other substance in a candle, lamp, etc.

wicked [wik'id] *adj* evil in principle or practice, deviating from morality, sinful, ungodly.—*n* **wick'edness**.

wicker [wik'èr] *n* a long, thin, flexible twig; such twigs or long, woody strips woven together, as in making baskets.

wicket [wik'et] *n* a small door or gate, (croquet) any of the small wire arches through which the balls must be hit.

wide [wīd] *adj* extending far; having a considerable distance between the sides; open fully.—*adv* **wide'ly**.—*vti* **wi'den**, to make or grow wide or wider.—*n* **width**, wideness, breadth.

widgeon [wij'ón] *n* a genus of freshwater duck.

widow [wid'ō] *n* a woman who has lost her husband by death and has not remarried.—*vt* to cause to become a widow.—*ns* **wid'ower**, a man whose wife is dead and has not remarried.

wield [wēld] *vt* to use with full command; to manage, to use.—*adj* **wiel'dy**, manageable.

wife [wīf] *n* a married woman; the woman to whom one is married; a woman.—*pl* **wives**.

wig [wig] *n* an artificial covering of real or synthetic hair for the head.

wigwam [wig'wom, -wam] *n* a N American Indian shelter.

wild [wīld] *adj* being in a state of nature; not tamed or cultivated; uncivilized; lawless; violent; distracted.—*n* (usu. *pl*) wilderness or wasteland.—*ns* **wil'derness**, a wild or waste place; **wild'fire**, a fire that spreads fast and is hard to put out.—*adv* **wild'ly**.—*n* **wild'ness**.

wile [wīl] *n* a trick, a sly artifice.—*vt* to beguile, inveigle.

will [wil] *n* power of choosing or determining; act of using this power, volition; choice or determination; pleasure; a legal document directing the disposal of one's property after death.—*vi* to be accustomed, ready, or sure to.—*vt* to desire; to be resolved; to command.—*adj* **will'ing**, not reluctant (to), disposed (to); eager.—*adv* **will'ingly**.—*n* **will'ingness**.

will-o'-the-wisp [wil'-o-the-wisp'] *n* a luminous marsh gas, the ignis fatuus; an elusive person or thing.

willow [wil'ō] *n* a genus of trees or shrubs with slender, pliant branches; the wood of the willow.

willy-nilly [wil'i-nil'i] *adv* whether one wishes it or not.

wilt [wilt] *vi* to become limp, as from heat; of a plant, to droop; to become weak or faint.—*vt* to cause to wilt.

wimple [wim'pl] *n* (*hist*) a wrapping folded round neck and face (still part of a nun's dress).

win [win] *vt* to get to with effort; to gain in contest; to gain eg by luck; to gain influence over.—*vi* to gain a victory.—*n* a victory, success.—*ns* **winn'er**.

wince [wins] *vi* to shrink or start back; to make an involuntary movement (as in pain).

winch [winch] *n* a crank with a handle for transmitting motion; a kind of hoisting machine.

wind¹ [wind] *n* air in motion; a current of air; breath.—*vt* to put out of breath; to perceive by scent.—*ns* **wind'fall**, fruit blown off a tree; any unexpected gain or advantage; **wind'-jammer**, large sailing vessel; **wind'mill**, a machine driven by the force of the wind acting on a set of sails; **wind'pipe**, the passage for the breath between the mouth and lungs, the trachea.—*adv*, *adj* **wind'ward**, toward where the wind blows from.—*adj* **wind'y**, consisting of or resembling wind; exposed to the winds.

wind² [wīnd] *vt* to turn (a crank); to coil into a ball around something else; to encircle; to make by turning and twist-ing.—*vi* to turn completely or often; to turn round something, to twist, to move spirally.

windlass [wind'las] *n* a winch, esp one worked by winding a rope round a revolving cylinder.

window [win'dō] *n* an opening in a wall of a building, etc., for air and light.

wine [wīn] *n* the fermented juice of grapes used as an alcoholic beverage; the fermented juice of other fruits or plants.—*ns* **winepress**, a vat in which grapes are pressed in the manufacture of wine.

wing [wing] *n* the organ of a bird, bat or insect, by which it flies; a flying, or manner of flying.—*vt* to furnish or transport with wings; to lend speed to; to traverse by flying.—*vi* to soar.

wink [wingk] *vi* to move the eyelids quickly; to give a hint by winking.—*n* act of winking.

winkle [wing'kl] *n* any of various whelks.

winnow [win'ō] *vt* to separate the chaff from (the grain) by wind; to fan; to sift.

winsome [win'sóm] *adj* cheerful; pleasant, attractive.—*adv* **win'somely**.

winter [win'ter] *n* the cold season of the year—in northern temperate regions, from November or December to January or February.—*vi* to pass the winter.—*vt* to feed, or to maintain, during winter.—*n* **win'tergreen**, a low evergreen herb with white bell-shaped flowers and spicy red berries.—*n pl* **win'ter quar'ters**, a winter residence or station.

wipe [wīp] *vt* to clean or dry by rubbing with a cloth, etc.—*n* a wiping.

wire [wīr] *n* a thread of metal; a length of this; the finish line of a race; telegraph; a telegram.—*adj* formed of wire.—*vt* to fasten, furnish, connect, etc. with wire; to telegraph.—*vi* to telegraph.—*adjs* **wire'drawn**, spun out into needless fine distinctions; **wire'less**, wireless telegraphy; radio telephony; **wi'ry**, made of, or like, wire.

wise¹ [wīz] *adj* having knowledge; learned; able to use knowledge well, discreet.—*adv* **wise'ly**.

wise² [wīz] *n* way, manner.

wiseacre [wīz'â-kèr] *n* one who unduly assumes an air of superior wisdom.

wish [wish] *vi* to have a desire; to express a desire.—*vt* to desire or long for.—*n* desire, longing; thing desired.—*adj* **wish'ful**, having a wish or desire.

wisp [wisp] *n* a small tuft or thin strand.

wistful [wist'fōōl -fl] *adj* pensive; yearning with little hope.—*adv* **wist'fully**.

wit² [wit] *n* understanding; a mental faculty (chiefly in *pl*); common sense; facility in combining ideas with a pointed verbal effect.—*n* **witticism** [wit'i-sizm], a witty remark.—*adv* **witt'ingly**, knowingly, by design.

witch [wich] *n* a woman regarded as having supernatural or magical power and knowledge through compact with the devil.—*ns* **witch'craft**, **witch'ery**.

witch' ha'zel [wich'hā'zèl] *n* a N American shrub or tree with yellow flowers.

with [wiтн, with] *prep* denoting nearness, agreement, or connection.

withdraw [wiтн-drö' or -th] *vt* to draw back or away; to take back or away.

withe [wiтн, with or wīтн], **withy** [wiтн'i] *n* a flexible twig, esp of willow; a band of twisted twigs.

wither [wiтн'èr] *vi* to fade or become dry.—*vt* to cause to dry up, fade, or decay.

withers [wiтн'èrz] *n pl* the part of a horse's back between the shoulder blades.

withhold [wiтн-hōld' or with-] *vt* to restrain; refuse to give.

within [wiтн-in'] *prep* in the inner part of, inside.

without [wiтн-owt'] *prep* outside or out of, beyond.

withstand [wiтн-stand' or with-] *vt* to stand against, to oppose or resist, esp successfully.

witness [wit'nes] *n* knowledge brought in proof; testimony (of a fact); that which furnishes proof.—*vt* to have direct knowledge of; to see; to be the scene of; to testify to, or (that); to show.—*vi* to give evidence; to attest.

wizard [wiz'ärd] *n* one (usu. a man) who practices witchcraft or magic; one who works wonders.

wizen [wiz'n], **wizened** [wiz'nd] *adj* dried up, thin, shriveled.—*vti* to become or make dry.

woad [wōd] *n* a genus of plants yielding a blue dye.

wobble [wob'l] *vi* to rock unsteadily from side to side; to waver, to vacillate. — *adj* wobb'ly.

woe [wō] *n* grief, misery; a heavy calamity. — *adjs* woe'begone, beset with woe; woe'ful.

wolf [wŏŏlf] *n* a gregarious beast of prey of the dog genus. — *pl* wolves.

wolfram [wŏŏl'fràm] *n* an ore containing iron, manganese, and tungsten.

wolverine [wŏŏl-ve-rēn'] *n* a carnivorous quadruped of N America; a glutton.

woman [wŏŏm'àn] *n* the female of man, an adult female of the human race; the female sex. — *pl* women [wim'èn]. — *n* wom'anhood. — *adj* wom'anish.

womb [wŏŏm] *n* the organ in which the young of mammals are developed and kept till birth.

wombat [wom'bat] *n* any of several Australian marsupial mammals resembling small bears.

wonder [wun'der] *n* the state of mind produced by something new, unexpected, or extraordinary; a strange thing; a prodigy. — *vi* to feel wonder. — *adj* won'derful. — *adv* won'derfully. — *adj* won'drous. — *adv* won'drously.

wont [wunt, wŏnt] *adj* accustomed. — *n* habit. — *vi* to be accustomed. — *adj* won'ted, accustomed.

woo [wŏŏ] *vt* to ask in marriage; to court, to solicit eagerly; to seek to gain. — Also *vi*. — *n* woo'er.

wood [wŏŏd] *n* the hard part of trees; trees cut or sawn, timber; a kind of timber. — *vt* to cover with trees. — *ns* wind flower; wood'bine, wood'bind, the honeysuckle; wood'cock, a genus of bird allied to the snipes; wood'craft, skill in the chase and everything pertaining to life in the forests; wood'cut, an engraving cut on wood; an impression from it; wood'-land, land covered with trees; wood'man, a man who cuts down trees; wood'pecker, any of a family of birds that peck holes in the wood or bark of trees and extract the insects on which they feed; woodwind, section of an orchestra in which wind instruments, originally made of wood are played.

woof [wŏŏf] *n* the horizontal threads crossing the warp in a woven fabric.

wool [wŏŏl] *n* the soft hair of sheep and other animals; thread or yarn made of wool. — *adj* woolen, wooll'y.

word [wûrd] *n* an oral or written sign denoting a thing or an idea; talk, discourse; a message; a promise; information. — *adj* wor'dy. — *adv* wor'dily.

work [wûrk] *n* effort directed to an end; employment; that on which one works; the product of work, anything made or done; needlework; deed; doings; a literary composition; a book; (*pl*) a manufactory; workshop. — *vi* to make efforts; to be in action; to be occupied in business or labor; to produce effects; to strain or labor; to ferment, to seethe. — *vt* to make by labor; to bring by action; to effect. — *adjs* work'able; work-'force, the number of workers who are engaged in particular industry; the total number of workers who are potentially available; work'house, a house of correction for petty offenders; work'ing, the act of one that works; wor'king man, one who works for wages, usu. at manual labor. — *adj* work'man-like, befitting a skillful workman; well performed. — *ns* work'shop, a room or building where work is done; a seminar for specified intensive study, work, etc.

world [wûrld] *n* the earth and its inhabitants; the universe; present state of existence. — *n* world'ling, one who is devoted to worldly pursuits and temporal possessions. — *adj* world'ly; devoted to this life and its enjoyments.

worm [wûrm] *n* an earthworm, loosely applied to invertebrate animals which more or less resemble the earthworm; anything helical; the thread of a screw. — *vi* to make one's way like a worm. — *vt* to work (oneself into a position) slowly or secretly; to elicit by slow and indirect means.

wormwood [wûrm'wood] *n* a plant with a bitter taste, bitterness.

worry [wur'i] *vt* to tear with the teeth; to harass; to tease. — *vi* to be unduly anxious; to fret. — *n* trouble, perplexity, vexation.

worse [wûrs] *adj* bad or evil in a greater degree; not so well as before. — *adv* badly in a higher degree. — *vti* wor'sen.

worship [wûr'ship] *n* a religious service; fervent esteem; ador-

ation paid to God. — *vt* to adore or idolize. — *vi* to perform acts of adoration. — *n* wor'shipper.

worst [wûrst] *adj* (used as *superl* of bad; see also worse) bad or evil in the highest degree.

worsted [wŏŏst'id, or wûrst'id] *n* twisted thread or yarn spun out of long, combed wool.

wort [wûrt] *n* an herbaceous plant.

worth [wûrth] *n* value; that quality which renders a thing valuable; price; moral excellence; importance. — *adj* equal in value to; deserving of. — *adj* worth'less. — *adv* worth'lessly. — *n* worth'lessness. — *adjs* worthwhile' worthy.

would [wŏŏd] *pt p* of will.

wound [wŏŏnd] *n* any cut, bruise, hurt, or injury caused by external force. — *vt* to injure.

wrack [rak] *n* seaweed; destruction.

wraith [rāth] *n* a specter, an apparition, esp of a living person; a thin, pale person.

wrangle [ran'gl] *vi* (*arch*) to dispute; to dispute noisily or peevishly. — Also *vt*. — *n* a noisy dispute.

wrap [rap] *vt* to roll or fold together; to enfold; to cover by folding or winding something round. — *n* wrapp'er.

wrath [rath] *n* intense anger; rage. — *adj* wrath'ful.

wreak [rēk] *vt* inflict or execute (eg vengeance).

wreath [rēth] *n* a twisted ring of leaves, flowers, etc.; something like this in shape. — *vt* wreathe [rēth], to form into a wreath; to encircle.

wreck [rek] *n* destruction of a ship; a badly damaged ship; remains of anything ruined; a run-down person. — *vt* to destroy or disable; to ruin. — *vi* to suffer wreck or ruin. — *n* wreck'age.

wren [ren] small brownish songbirds, with a short erect tail.

wrench [rench] *vt* to wring or pull with a jerk; to injure with a twist; to distort. — *n* a violent twist; a sprain; an instrument for turning nuts, etc.

wrest [rest] *vt* to twist by force (from); to get by toil.

wrestle [res'l] *vti* to contend with another by grappling and trying to throw down; to struggle. — *n* wrest'ler.

wretch [rech] *n* a most miserable person; a despised and scorned person. — *adj* wretch'ed, very miserable. — *adv* wretch'edly. — *n* wretch'edness.

wriggle [rig'l] *vi* to twist to and fro; to move with a twisting or sinuous motion; to use evasive tricks. — *vt* to cause to wriggle. — *n* the motion of wriggling. — *n* wrigg'ler.

wright [rīt] *n* a maker.

wring [ring] *vt* to twist; to force by twisting; to pain; to extort.

wrinkle [ring'kl] *n* a small crease or furrow on a surface. — *vti* to contract into wrinkles.

wrist [rist] *n* the joint by which the hand is united to the arm.

write [rīt] *vt* to form letters as with a pen or pencil; to express in writing; to compose; to record; to communicate by letter. — *vi* to perform the act of writing. — *ns* wrī'ter, one who writes; a professional scribe or clerk; an author; wrī'ting, the act of forming letters as with a pen; that which is written; literary production. — *adj* writt'en.

writhe [rīth] *vt* to twist violently. — *vt* to twist this way and that; to squirm (under, at).

wrong [rong] *adj* not according to rule, incorrect; mistaken, misinformed. — *n* whatever is not right or just; wrong'ful.

wroth [roth, rōth] *adj* highly incensed; wrathful.

wrought [rōt] *pt, pt p* of work. — *adj* formed; made; of metals, shaped by hammering, etc.

wrung [rung] *pt, pt p* of wring.

wry [rī] *adj* twisted or turned to one side; distorted. — *n* wry'-neck, woodpeckers, which twist round their heads strangely.

X

Xmas written abbreviation for Christmas. x-ray, X-ray [eks-rā] radiation of very short wavelengths, capable of penetrating solid bodies, and printing on a photographic plate a shadow picture of objects not permeable by light rays. — *vt* to photograph by x-rays.

xenon [zen'on] *n* a gaseous element present in the atmosphere.

xenophobia [zen-ō-fō'bi-à] *n* fear or hatred of strangers or things foreign.

xylography [zī-log'rȧ-fi] *n* the art of engraving on wood.—*ns* **xy'lograph**, a wood engraving.

xylophone [zī'lo-fōn] *n* an orchestral musical instrument consisting of a series of bars.

Y

yacht [yot] *n* a sailing or mechanically driven vessel—generally of light tonnage, fitted for pleasure trips or racing.—*vi* to race or cruise in a yacht.

yahoo [ya-hōō'] *n* a name given by Swift in *Gulliver's Travels* to a class of animals which have the forms of men but the understanding and passions of the lowest brutes; a boorish or stupid person.

yak [yak] *n* a species of ox found in Tibet.

yam [yam] *n* the edible, starchy tuberous root of a tropical climbing plant, sweet potato.

Yankee [yang'ki] *n* a New Englander; a native of a Northern State; a citizen of the US.

yap [yap] *vi* to yelp, bark sharply; (*slang*) to speak constantly, esp in a noisy or foolish manner.

yard¹ [yärd] *n* a unit of measure of 3 feet or 36 inches, and equivalent to 0.9144 meters; a great length or quantity; a long beam on a mast for spreading sails.—*ns* **yard'arm**, either end of a yard of a square-rigged ship.

yard² [yärd] *n* an enclosed place, esp near a building; an enclosure for a special purpose.

yarn [yärn] *n* fibers of wool, cotton, etc. spun into strands for weaving, knitting, etc.; (*inf*) a tale or story.—*vi* to tell a yarn.

yashmak, yasmak [yash'mak'] *n* the veil worn by Muslim women, covering the face so that only the eyes are exposed to public view.

yaw [yö] *vi* to deviate from a set course as a ship, spacecraft, etc.—Also *n*.

yawl [yöl] *n* a small two-masted sailboat rigged fore-and-aft.

yawn [yön] *vi* to open the jaws involuntarily from drowsiness; to gape.—*n* the opening of the mouth from drowsiness.—*adj* **yawn'ing**.

yea [yā] *adv* yes; verily.

year [yēr] *n* a period of time determined by the revolution of the earth around the sun (365 days, 5 hours, 48 minutes, 46 seconds); the period beginning with January 1 and ending with December 31, a space of twelve calendar months reckoned from any date; **year'ling**, an animal a year old or in its second year.—*adj* **year'ly**, happening every year; lasting a year; of a year, or each year.—*adv* once a year; from year to year.

yearn [yûrn] *vi* to feel earnest desire (for); to feel uneasiness, from longing or pity.

yeast [yēst] *n* a substance, consisting of certain minute fungi, which causes alcoholic fermentation, used in brewing and baking; yeast dried in flakes or granules or compressed into cakes.—*adj* **yeast'y**, frothy, foamy.

yell [yel] *vti* to howl or cry out with a sharp noise; to scream.— *n* a sharp outcry.

yellow [yel'ō] *adj* of the color of ripe lemons; having a somewhat yellow skin; (*inf*) cowardly; sensational, as a newspaper.—*n* the color of the rainbow between orange and green; an egg yolk.—*vi* to become or turn yellow.—*vt* to make yellow or give a yellow tinge or color to.—*ns* **yellow fever**, a pestilential tropical fever caused by a virus transmitted by certain mosquitoes; **yell'ow hamm'er**, a common European finch.

yelp [yelp] *vti* to utter a sharp bark.—*n* a sharp, quick cry or bark.

yeoman [yō'màn] *n* a naval petty officer assigned to clerical duties; after the fifteenth century, one of a class of small farmers, the next grade below gentlemen.—*n* **yeo'manry**, the collective body of yeomen.

yes [yes] *adv* ay; a word of affirmation or consent.—*n* **yes' man**, (*slang*) one who agrees with everything that is said to him, an obedient follower with no initiative.

yester [yes'tèr] *adj* relating to yesterday last.—*n* **yes'terday**, the day last past; a recent day of time.—*adv* on the day last past; recently.

yet [yet] *adv* in addition, besides; still; up to the present time; even.—*conj* nevertheless; however.

yew [ū] *n* an evergreen tree or shrub.

Yiddish [yid'ish] *n* a language derived from medieval High German, written in the Hebrew alphabet, and spoken esp by eastern European Jews.

yield [yēld] *vt* to resign; to grant; to give out, to produce, as a crop, result, profit, etc.—*vi* to submit; to give way to physical force; to produce.—*n* amount yielded; the return on a financial investment.

yodel [yō'dl] *vti* to sing, changing frequently from the ordinary voice to falsetto and back again.

yoga [yō'ga] *n* a system of exercises for attaining bodily or mental control and well-being; **Yoga**, a Hindu theistic philosophy.—*n* **yō'gi**, a person who practices yoga.

yogurt, yoghurt [yog'ėrt] *n* a semi-liquid food made from fermented milk.

yoke [yōk] *n* that which joins together; the frame of wood joining oxen for drawing together; such a harnessed pair; any similar frame, part of a garment which fits the shoulders.—*vt* to put a yoke on; to join together.

yokel [yō'kl] *n* (*offensive*) a country bumpkin.

yolk [yōk] *n* the yellow part of an egg.

yon [yon], **yonder** [yon'dėr] *advs* in that place (referring to somewhere specified or relatively distant).

yore [yōr, yòr] *n* old time, time long past.

you [ū] *pron* (*gram*) 2d person singular or plural; the person or persons spoken to.

young [yung] *adj* not long born; in early life; in the first part of growth; inexperienced.—*n* young people; offspring, esp young offspring.

your [ūr] *possessive adj* of or belonging to or done by you.

yourself [ūr-self'] *pron* the intensive form of **you**; the reflexive form of **you**; your true self.

youth [yōōth] *n* state of being young; early life; young persons collectively.—*adj* **youth'ful**.

yule [yōōl] *n* the season or feast of Christmas.—*n* **yule'tide**, the Christmas season.

yuppie [yup'ē] *n* (*inf*) any of those young professionals regarded as affluent, ambitious, materialistic, etc.

Z

zany [zā'ni] *n* a clown, a buffoon; a fool.

zeal [zēl] *n* intense or passionate ardor, enthusiasm.—*n* **zealot** [zel'ot].—*adj* **zealous**, full of zeal, warmly engaged or ardent in anything.—*adv* **zealously**.

zebra [zē'bra] *n* any of several beautifully striped animals related to the horse.

zebu [zē'bū] *n* the humped domestic ox found in many parts of India, China.

Zen [zen] *n* a Japanese Buddhist sect which holds that the truth is not in scriptures but in man's own heart if he will but strive to find it by meditation and introspection.

zenana [ze-nä'na] *n* the apartments in which women are secluded in upper crust families in India.

zenith [zen'ith] *n* that point of the heavens which is exactly overhead; greatest height, summit of ambition, etc.

zephyr [zef'ir] *n* a soft, gentle breeze, esp from the west.

zeppelin [zep'el-in] *n* a rigid, dirigible, cigar-shaped airship.

zero [zē'ro] *n* the symbol 0; cipher; nothing; the point from which the reckoning begins in scales, such as those of the barometer, etc.; the lowest point.

zest [zest] *n* the outer part of the skin of an orange or lemon used to give flavor; relish.

zigzag [zig'zag] *n* a series of short, sharp angles in alternate directions; a design path, etc. in this form.—*adj* having sharp turns.—*vti* to move or form in a zigzag.

zinc [zingk] *n* a bluish-white metallic element.

zinnia [zin'i-a] *n* a tropical American plant having colorful, composite flowers.

Zion [zī'on] *n* a hill in Jerusalem; the site of Solomon's temple; Jerusalem; Israel; heaven.

zip [zip] *n* a whizzing sound; (*inf*) energy, vigor.—*vi* to make or move with, a zip—*vt* to fasten with a zipper.

zip code [zip kōd] *n* a system combining a two-letter abbreviation for a State and a five-figure number identifying each postal delivery area in the US.

zircon [zir'kon] *n* a tetragonal mineral, zirconium silicate, sometimes used as a gem.

zither [zith'ér] *n* a flat many-stringed musical instrument of ancient origin.

zodiac [zō'di-ak] *n* an imaginary belt in the heavens along which the sun, moon, and chief planets appear to move, divided crosswise into twelve equal areas, called 'signs of the zodiac', each named after a constellation; a diagram representing this.

zombie, zombi [zombi] *n* orig in Africa, the deity of the python; a supernatural power by which a corpse may be reanimated.

zone [zōn] *n* a girdle, a belt; one of the five great belts in which the surface of the earth is divided.—*vt* to encircle as with a zone; to divide into zones.

zoo [zōō] *n* a place where a collection of wild animals is kept for public showing.

zoology [zō-ol'o-ji] *n* the science that deals with animals and animal life and is a branch of biology.—*adj* **zoolog'ical.**—*n* **zool'ogist.**

zoophyte [zō'o-fīt] *n* any animal, as a sponge, that looks and grows somewhat like a plant.

Zoroastrianism [zor-ō-as'tri-án-izm] *n* the ancient Persian religion founded or reformed by *Zoroaster.*

Zouave [zōō'äv] *n* a member of a former French military unit with colorful uniforms.

Zulu [zōō'lōō] *n* a member of a people of South Africa; their language.

zygote [zī'gót] *n* the cell formed by the union of two gametes; the developing individual from such a cell.

zymurgy [zī'mur-jē] *n* the chemistry of fermentation processes.